CASES, PROBLEMS AND MATERIALS

The Law of Sales and Secured Financing

SEVENTH EDITION

by

JOHN O. HONNOLD
William A. Schnader Professor Emeritus
University of Pennsylvania Law School

STEVEN L. HARRIS
Norman & Edna Freehling Scholar and Professor of Law
Chicago–Kent College of Law

CHARLES W. MOONEY, JR.
Professor of Law
University of Pennsylvania Law School

CURTIS R. REITZ
Algernon Sydney Biddle Professor of Law
University of Pennsylvania Law School

NEW YORK, NEW YORK
FOUNDATION PRESS
2002

COPYRIGHT © 1954, 1962, 1968, 1976, 1984, 1993 FOUNDATION PRESS
COPYRIGHT © 2002 By FOUNDATION PRESS
                    395 Hudson Street
                    New York, NY 10014
                    Phone Toll Free 1–877–888–1330
                    Fax (212) 367–6799
                    fdpress.com
All Rights Reserved
Printed in the United States of America

ISBN 1–56662–948–9

TEXT IS PRINTED ON 10% POST CONSUMER RECYCLED PAPER

To our students who for five decades
have shared the exploration that led to this book
J.O.H. & C.R.R.

To Barbara, with love.
S.L.H.

To Carla, Mia, and Tasha, and in remembrance
of Peter F. Coogan and Fairfax Leary, Jr.
C.W.M.

PREFACE

In the years since the Sixth Edition, burgeoning case law and scholarly commentary have given rise to new problems and issues and have illuminated the breadth and depth of others. In addition, during these years Article 9 of the Uniform Commercial Code (UCC) has been substantially rewritten. The Seventh Edition reflects these developments.

The General Introduction provides an overview of commercial law, both in the United States and internationally. Chapter 1 examines the rights of unsecured creditors and the state-law collection process. It considers the in rem rights of a seller of goods to withhold delivery, stop goods in transit, and reclaim delivered goods as against the buyer and as against third parties. Chapter 1 covers basic conveyancing principles for goods, including voidable title and good faith purchase, reclamation, and entrustment. It also introduces good faith purchase of negotiable instruments, other rights to payment, and documents of title. Chapters 2 through 5 deal primarily with domestic and international sales transactions. Chapters 6 through 12 address secured transactions in personal property.

The principal role of a course based on sales transactions is to build upon the first-year course in contracts.[1] A course in contracts typically introduces students to the matters of contract formation, validity, breach, and remedies. Contracts casebooks now commonly incorporate some provisions of UCC Article 2. Contracts courses, however, remain broadly eclectic in the types of transactions covered.

The authors envision a course covering sales as a sequel to the course in contracts. The materials center on the performance of agreements for the sale of goods. The cases and problems, focused on one generic type of transaction, permit sustained examination of the significance of context to give meaning to contract obligations and rights.[2] Chapters 1 through 5 also are intended to permit broad and deep consideration of both United States com-

---

1. A course in Sales also might be an extension of the first-year course in property. Property courses, however, tend to give dominant consideration to the law of real property and may treat personal property or personalty only in passing. Thus, students in a course in sales may be meeting the law of personal property for the first time. Chapter 1 explores several important areas of doctrine relating to personal property.

2. This tends to offset one of the drawbacks of typical first-year contracts courses. A hallmark of the basic course in contracts is the relentlessly doctrinal structure of the traditional syllabus.

mercial statutes and an important and widely-adopted international convention providing uniform law for international sale of goods.

Study of Article 2, a fundamental article of the UCC, with the overlay of federal laws, is an excellent way to develop understanding of the nature and sources of domestic United States law in this sphere. In this course, we hope that students will get a sense of Article 2 as a whole and begin to understand how codes are used, and should be used, in shaping commercial transactions and in resolving commercial disputes.[3] The materials are concerned with techniques of statutory construction for this special kind of uniform legislation. This involves intelligent attention to statutory text, in light of legislatively defined terms. It involves appreciation of the value and limitations of the "official comments" to the UCC. Beyond these textual concerns, these materials inquire into the legislative purposes and the intended social benefits of this kind of statute.

Commercial transactions in the modern world are increasingly international in character. The United States is a huge consumer of products produced abroad and a huge producer of products for export. Nearly half (by value) of all goods bought and sold by persons in this country involve imports or exports, and the percentage is rising steeply. For transactions of this nature, the world community is establishing a growing body of international private law, notably for our purposes the Convention on Contracts for the International Sale of Goods. This Convention, now part of the law of the United States and 60 nations in all, must be considered in comparison with and in contrast to the UCC, which governs in domestic or intra-national sales. The Convention is vitally important for its own substance and the methods of its construction and implementation. Further, however, the Convention represents an emerging body of international private laws that will be fundamental to tomorrow's professional work of today's law students. In every chapter, and in almost every section, Chapters 2 through 5 of these materials address the commercial issues under the Convention as well as under the domestic law of the United States.

Chapter 6 provides an introduction to secured financing that describes the differing treatment afforded unsecured and secured debt, canvasses prevailing consumer and business financing patterns and explains the diverse roles of lawyers in secured financings. In addition, Chapter 6 contains an overview of Revised UCC Article 9, to which the student and the instructor can refer throughout the course.

Chapters 7 through 12 address the details of secured financing. They focus on the scope and fundamental concepts of UCC Article 9, the rights of the parties to a secured transaction between themselves, the rights of Article 9 secured parties against the holders of competing claims, and the treat-

---

3. The introduction to the UCC that students receive in the contracts course may lead them to see Article 2 as a repository of discrete provisions on offer and acceptance, remedies for breach, and so forth—more like a restatement of the common law than a code with an overall style and philosophy.

ment of Article 9 security interests in bankruptcy. These Chapters contain many explanatory Notes, designed to draw the student's attention to the applicable legal principles and the policies that underlie them. The Notes also encourage the student to probe the background that led to the extensive revision of Article 9. In addition, these Chapters explain and define dozens of important business, financial, and legal terms, which are printed in bold-face type.

As in the previous editions, the problems throughout the book are tailored to focus the student's attention on both the language of the relevant statutes and its application to common patterns of secured financing. Some new problems have been added, and some old problems have been revised, to increase the emphasis on counseling, planning, drafting, and litigation skills. In addition to more traditional problems, which ask the student to predict the outcome, the Seventh Edition contains problems that ask the student to give advice to clients, to structure transactions, and to draft certain provisions of documents.

Also as with previous editions, the principal cases have been chosen on the ground that they are worthy of classroom discussion. In Chapters 2 through 5, the cases tend to be recent for the good reason that they arise from current commercial practices and reflect the types of legal issues that are being adjudicated or arbitrated today. The treatment of cases in Chapters 6 through 12 differs somewhat. On reason for revising Article 9 was to resolve ambiguities in, and unanswered questions under, Former Article 9. Many of these ambiguities arose from reported cases, whose relevance is reduced, if not altogether eliminated, by the revision. Accordingly, these Chapters contain fewer cases than did earlier editions. For obvious reasons, none of the cases was decided under Revised Article 9.

We wish to thank our colleagues and the many law librarians, secretaries, and students whose encouragement and support have made the Seventh Edition and earlier editions possible. Special thanks are due to those law teachers, users of the prior edition, who suggested revisions for this work. In addition, Ms. Huang Chi-Wei (LL.M. 2000, University of Pennsylvania Law School), provided valuable research and editorial assistance. Thanks also are owed to Professor Allan Farnsworth for the use of cases and notes developed in connection with materials on which he and Professor Honnold collaborated.

Although this edition is a collaborative effort of the authors, Professor Reitz took primary responsibility for producing Chapters 2 through 5 of this edition and Professors Harris and Mooney took primary responsibility for producing Chapter 1 and Chapters 6 through 12.

We owe a great debt to John Honnold. Although he was not directly involved in the preparation of the Seventh Edition, these materials still bear the stamp of his creativity and thoughtfulness. We hope that we have succeeded in maintaining the high standard he set.

The study of law can be interesting and challenging. We hope this book to be both.

JOHN O. HONNOLD
Philadelphia
October, 2001

STEVEN L. HARRIS
Chicago
October, 2001

CHARLES W. MOONEY, JR.
Philadelphia
October, 2001

CURTIS R. REITZ
Philadelphia
October, 2001

NOTE ON SOURCES AND CITATION CONVENTIONS

We appreciate the kindness of the authors and publishers who have permitted us to reproduce portions of the following copyrighted works:

- Baird & Jackson, Possession and Ownership: An Examination of the Scope of Article 9, 35 Stanford Law Review 175 (1983).

- Braucher, The Repo Code: A Study of Adjustment to Uncertainty in Commercial Law, 74 Washington University Law Quarterly 549 (1997).

- Carlson, Bulk Sales Under Article 9: Some Easy Cases Made Difficult, 41 Alabama Law Review 729 (1990).

- Clark, The Law of Secured Transactions under the Uniform Commercial Code (rev. ed. 2000).

- Cohen & Gerber, The After-Acquired Property Clause, 87 University of Pennsylvania Law Review 635 (1939).

- Frisch, Buyer Status Under the U.C.C.: A Suggested Temporal Definition, 72 Iowa Law Review 531 (1987).

- Gilmore, The Commercial Doctrine of Good Faith Purchase, 63 Yale Law Journal 1057 (1954).

- Gilmore, Security Interests in Personal Property (1965).

- Harris, The Interaction of Articles 6 and 9 of the Uniform Commercial Code: A Study in Conveyancing, Priorities, and Code Interpretation, 39 Vanderbilt Law Review 179 (1986).

- Harris, The Interface Between Articles 2A and 9 Under the Official Text and the California Amendments, 22 Uniform Commercial Code Law Journal 99 (1989).

- Harris, A Reply to Theodore Eisenberg's Bankruptcy Law in Perspective, 30 UCLA Law Review 327 (1982).

- Harris & Mooney, How Successful Was the Revision of UCC Article 9?: Reflections of the Reporters, 74 Chicago-Kent Law Review 1357 (1999).

- Harris & Mooney, A Property-Based Theory of Security Interests: Taking Debtors' Choices Seriously, 80 Virginia Law Review 2021 (1994).

- Hillman, McDonnell & Nickles, Common Law and Equity Under the Uniform Commercial Code (1985). Reprinted with the permission of Warren Gorham Lamont, a division of Research Institute of America, 210 South Street, Boston, MA 02111. All rights reserved.

- Jackson & Kronman, A Plea for the Financing Buyer, 85 Yale Law Journal 1 (1975).
- Kripke, Should Section 9-307(l) of the Uniform Commercial Code Apply Against a Secured Party in Possession?, 35 The Business Lawyer 153 (1977).
- Kupfer, Accounts Receivable Financing—A Legal and Practical Look–See, The Practicing Lawyer, November 1956.
- Mooney, Beyond Negotiability: A New Model for Transfer and Pledge of Interests in Securities Controlled by Intermediaries, 12 Cardozo Law Review 305 (1990).
- The Philadelphia Inquirer, "They're the Night Stalkers" (November 20, 1988).
- Plumb, Legislative Revision of the Federal Tax Lien, 22 The Business Lawyer 271 (1967).
- Recovery and Return of Stolen Cultural Property, 16 International Enforcement Law Reporter 709 (2000).
- Report of the American Bar Association Stock Certificate Committee (1975).
- Revised Uniform Commercial Code Article 9 (draft of March, 1998).
- Restatement (Third) Suretyship and Guaranty (1996).
- Schill, An Economic Analysis of Mortgagor Protection Laws, 77 Virginia Law Review 489 (1991).
- Schwarcz, Structured Finance (2d ed.). Copyright 1993, Practising Law Institute (New York City).
- Schwartz, A Theory of Loan Priorities, 18 Journal of Legal Studies 209(1989).
- Scott, The Truth About Secured Financing, 82 Cornell Law Review 1436 (1997).
- A Second Look at the Amendments to Article 9 of the UCC, 29 The Business Lawyer 973 (1974).
- Shupack, Solving the Puzzle of Secured Transactions, 41 Rutgers Law Review 1067 (1989).
- Turner, Barnes, Kershen, Noble & Shumm, Agricultural Liens and the U.C.C.: A Report on Present Status and Proposals for Change, 44 Oklahoma Law Review 9 (1991).
- Uniform Commercial Code, 2000 Official Text. Copyright 2000 by The American Law Institute and the National Conference of Commissioners on Uniform State Laws. Reprinted with the permission of the Permanent Editorial Board for the Uniform Commercial Code.
- Wittie, Review of Recent Developments in U.C.C. Article 8 and Investment Securities, 52 The Business Lawyer 1575 (1997).

In editing the foregoing works and the principal cases, we have taken the liberty of making minor adjustments to style and deleting footnotes and authorities without indication. We have retained the original footnote numbers for footnotes that remain. Editorial interpolations, including additional footnotes, have been bracketed.

The citations in principal cases generally are to the 1990 Official Text of the Uniform Commercial Code ("UCC"). In principal cases that involve a pre–1972 version of the UCC, we have added footnotes to indicate that fact. Citations to Revised UCC Article 9 and accompanying amendments to other Articles are to the 2000 Official Text of the UCC. They are preceded by the letter "R" (e.g., R9–320(a), R2–502). Earlier Official Texts of Article 9 are referred to as "Former Article 9"; citations to Former Article 9 are preceded by the letter "F" (e.g., F9–307(1)). Citations to the United States Code are current through August 1, 2000. Citations to the Bankruptcy Code ("BC") are to Title 11, U.S.C.

The Notes and Problems contain many business, financial, and legal terms that lawyers often use. When these terms first appear, they are printed in bold-face type and are explained briefly. A useful source for those who wish more detailed explanations is J. Dolan, Commercial Law: Essential Terms and Transactions (2d ed. 1997).

*

SUMMARY OF CONTENTS

DETAILED TABLE OF CONTENTS

*

TABLE OF CASES

Principal cases are in bold type. Non-principal cases are in roman type. References are to Pages.

THE LAW OF SALES AND SECURED FINANCING

*

GENERAL INTRODUCTION

(A) SCOPE

Chapter 1 of this book covers the fundamentals of the legal rights of owners of personal property and of creditors. It also addresses the resolution of a variety of conflicting claims to personal property—tangible and intangible—among owners, buyers, sellers, and creditors. For example, goods are delivered to the buyer on credit. To protect against the risk that the buyer may fail to pay, can the seller who is financing the sale obtain a claim to the goods that will permit the seller to recapture them from the buyer or from the buyer's other creditors?

Chapters 2 through 5 focus chiefly on sales of goods. They emphasize primarily the two dominant sources of statutory law—Article 2 of the Uniform Commercial Code ("UCC") and the United Nations Convention on Contracts for the International Sale of Goods ("CISG"). However, these Chapters also deal with related fields such as the laws governing documents of title and letters of credit. Chapter 2 begins with the basics (scope, relationship between the codifications and other law, and the regulation of private conduct). Chapter 3 focuses on sellers' responsibilities and buyers' rights concerning title to the goods being sold as well as their quality, with emphasis on warranties of quality. Chapter 4 then addresses the performance of sales contracts by buyers and sellers. Finally, Chapter 5 explores the resolution of controversies that arise in the performance stage of sales contracts.

The dominant theme of Chapters 6 through 12 is the extension of credit. The fascination of the subject results in part from its astonishing variety: complex financings in corporate merger and acquisition settings, involving millions (even billions) of dollars; short-term credit extended in business settings by sellers of goods and providers of services; credit given to consumers who wish to buy automobiles, furniture, and many other kinds of goods. This enormous variety places heavy strain on both the rules of law and the ingenuity of counselors and lawmakers. These Chapters center on legal arrangements that give a creditor powers over personal property of the debtor. It embraces an enormous variety of financing transactions, some of which have little or nothing to do with the distribution of goods. For example, a business needs more cash in order to operate profitably. Can a loan at an acceptable interest rate be arranged if the borrower agrees that the lender will have a claim on the borrower's equipment, inventory of goods held for sale, accounts receivable, and other personal property that will survive attack by other creditors? What is the impact of this arrangement on the borrower's suppliers and other creditors? Will courts permit the lender to enforce against the borrower the full range of rights that lenders write into credit agreements? If the debtor defaults, may the creditor seize and resell the borrower's personal property and, if the loan is not satisfied, recover any shortfall?

(B) Nature and Significance of Commercial Law

To understand commercial law, one must first consider commercial transactions and transactors. A free market economy is an economy in which independent actors exchange things of value. Each side makes its own determination of the value of what is to be received compared to the value of what is to be given up. Agreement occurs when both sides perceive that the exchange will make them better off, the paradigmatic win-win situation.[1] Basic exchange transactions involve a transfer of a thing of value for a price. The things exchanged include goods, services, investment securities, intellectual property, other intangible property, or real property in exchange for a price. The price side of exchange transactions, usually expressed in terms of money, may involve transfer of currency ("legal tender") or of bank credits.

Some exchange transactions occur in "spot" markets. Transactors meet, negotiate their deal, and promptly complete the exchange. This simple type of transaction can occur only if both parties have the thing of value they propose to exchange at the time of contracting. Frequently, however, one or both parties to a contract for an exchange transaction cannot perform instantaneously. Thus, a transferor may obligate itself to produce or acquire the thing of value to be exchanged. Familiar examples include contracts for goods to be manufactured, crops to be raised, and real estate improvements to be constructed. Most contracts for services necessarily contemplate a time period, after contract formation, during which the service providers give performance.

On the payment side, the purchaser may not have enough ready money to pay the full price, but may expect to be able to pay over a period of time. The number of, and the sizes of economic exchanges that may occur in any economy are largely determined by the availability of credit. The extent to which potential purchasers can obtain credit, that is, can defer payment of the full price, determines the level of exchange activity that can occur. Extension of credit is, itself, an exchange transaction, a transaction in which a credit provider gives up present value in exchange for the credit recipient's later payment of larger amount.

Another important type of exchange transaction involves transfer of risk. Property owners may contract to transfer risk of property loss or

---

1. Transactions of exchange can and do occur within a single firm or enterprise, between actors that are elements of the firm rather than independent economic entities. Intra-firm activities are, of course, not market transactions. Managers of the firm determine whether such exchanges occur and the terms of them. Prices, for example, are set administratively and are often described as "administered prices."

In management theories of the business firm, one of the most basic determinations is the "make or buy" decision. A "make" choice is to provide the thing needed from sources inside the firm. "Make" choices may lead to vertical integration of activities within a single firm. A "buy" choice is to go into the market and enter into an exchange transaction with one of the providers of the thing desired.

The distinction between intra-firm transactions and market transactions blurs when strong commercial relationships are established. Independent entities may become interdependent as a result of a pattern of transactions with each other.

damage to insurers in exchange for payment of money, the insurance premium. Persons whose activities may expose them to potential legal liability may contract to transfer that risk to insurers. Other common forms of insurance involve transfer of the risk of individuals' death, illness or incapacity.

Most legal systems treat real estate transactions, including construction contracts, and real estate finance as separate from commercial transactions generally. Insurance transactions are also governed by a special body of law. These materials touch on real estate and insurance transactions only tangentially.

Commercial law provides the essential legal infrastructure that makes exchange transactions feasible. The law functions in several ways. Commercial law is, in part, *facilitative*. In the broadest sense, it assists diverse transactors to achieve their respective objectives and thereby advances the societal value of private ordering. Commercial law is also facilitative in that it simplifies the task of bargaining by providing, for recurring transaction-types, reasonable terms that the parties to a particular transaction can adopt without significant *ex ante* negotiation costs. Commercial law is in part *evaluative and remedial*. Although most exchange transactions are carried out without significant controversy, not all transactions conclude satisfactorily to both sides. When friction occurs and disputes arise as to the nature or performance of the obligations of the parties, commercial law determines what are the respective rights and duties and, in the cases of breach, what are the remedies available to the aggrieved parties. Commercial law is also in part *regulative*. Thus it may forbid use of certain terms or it may shape transactions to deny the effectiveness of terms that are unjust or unfair or otherwise violative of public policy. Commercial law provisions of a regulatory nature are exceptions to the general norm of private ordering. They are invoked, typically, as part of the controversies over disputed performance.

(C) DEVELOPMENT OF COMMERCIAL LAW

The history of commercial law is important not only for insight into the past but also for understanding of the present. In spite of recent reformulations of commercial law, it would be crippling to know nothing of the roots from which this branch of the law has grown. As we shall see, old issues keep coming back. The following outline highlights the origins of commercial law.

(1) Mercantile Custom and Nationalization. Until the seventeenth century a large share of commercial law was merchants' law—a body of customs made and administered by the merchants themselves. Some of the rules were international in scope: maritime insurance policies still bear the marks of customs from Genoa and Antwerp. These *pie poudre* (dusty foot) courts also decided controversies that developed at the fairs that were the centers for much of early trade; important staple commodities (such as wool) were governed by specialized courts with a jury of merchants presided over by a "mayor of the staple," skilled in mercantile practice.

In the seventeenth century the merchants' courts were shouldered to one side by the King's judges, who in 1666 proclaimed that "the law of merchants is the law of the land"[2]—a hollow claim, but one that later was in part fulfilled by the work of a renowned Scotsman, William Murray. In 1756 Murray was made Chief Justice of the King's Bench and was given the title of Lord Mansfield. In controversies between merchants, Mansfield made it a point to ascertain and apply the customs of the trade. One of his tools for this work was a special group of merchants who acted as a jury in commercial cases and gave him advice on commercial practice.[3]

(2) Nineteenth Century Codification. In the nineteenth century codification was in the air. In 1804, in the aftermath of revolution and under Napoleon's firm hand, conflicting local rules and customs in France were supplanted by the Civil Code. Napoleon carried the Code to much of Europe. Even after his armies were driven out, the Code remained. It also was followed in most of Latin America and in substantial parts of Africa and Asia.

Jeremy Bentham argued the case for codification in England. In 1811 he wrote to President Madison volunteering personally to write a code of law for use in the United States. In New York, the constitution of 1846 called for the codification of the entire body of law of the state. Under the leadership of David Dudley Field, New York adopted the first Code of Civil Procedure and prepared a code of substantive law which, although rejected in New York, was adopted in 1872 in California, and in the Dakotas, Idaho, and Montana. For the most part, proposals for general codification were rejected.

(3) Federal Courts and the "General Commercial Law." In the early nineteenth century United States, the law "received" from England after the Revolution prevailed among the settled states along the Eastern seaboard. Maintaining uniformity of commercial law among those states was difficult enough. The problem became wholly unmanageable as new states were carved out of the wilderness. Frontier law was rough and ready, marked by a shortage of law books and legal education, and a cheerful willingness to improvise. The rapidly developing commerce lacked uniform, or even ascertainable, rules of law.

In 1821 Joseph Story, speaking in his home state of Massachusetts, called for codification of some aspects of commercial law. This call went unanswered. In 1842 Story wrote the opinion in Swift v. Tyson, holding that federal courts, unhampered by divergent state court decisions, could declare uniform rules for "general commercial law." Indeed, the opinion opened up wider vistas: Lord Mansfield and Cicero were cited for the proposition that commercial law was "in a great measure, not the law of a

2. Woodward v. Rowe, 2 Keb. 132, 84 Eng. Rep. 84 (1666).

3. Mansfield's Scottish background is not irrelevant, for it may explain his recep- tiveness to civil law doctrines prevalent in Scotland. (Like the Civil Code, described be- low, Scottish law derived from Roman law.)

single country only, but of the commercial world."[4] The federal courts continued to declare rules of "general commercial law," in a sporadic manner and with decreasing effectiveness, until 1938. In that year such federal law-making was held unconstitutional in Erie Railroad Co. v. Tompkins.[5]

(4) Specialized Statutes in Britain and America. A development like Swift v. Tyson was not needed in England. Royal judges already had established a common law.[6] But towards the end of the century pressure for certainty led to statutory enactments in specific fields of commercial law. In 1882 Parliament enacted the Bills of Exchange Act and in 1893 enacted the Sale of Goods Act—laws that still are in force in various parts of the world as part of the British legacy of empire.

Enactment of these two important laws in Britain was soon followed by similar legislation in the United States. The National Conference of Commissioners on Uniform State Laws ("NCCUSL")[7] in 1895 requested John J. Crawford to draft a Uniform Negotiable Instruments Law ("NIL"). Within one year the NIL was completed; by 1924 it had been enacted by every state. By 1906 the Uniform Sales Act ("USA") had been drafted by Professor Samuel Williston and approved by the Commissioners. The USA was eventually adopted in over thirty states; the principal exceptions were in the South.

The NIL and the USA were patterned closely after the British Bills of Exchange Act and Sale of Goods Act. Those Acts had been based on case-law doctrine developed in the nineteenth century. The legislative goals were stability, clarity, and uniformity, rather than reform. The NIL and the USA were followed by more specialized uniform laws on warehouse receipts (1906), bills of lading (1909), conditional sales (1918), and trust receipts (1933).

(D) THE UNIFORM COMMERCIAL CODE

(1) Commercial Law in the United States. Commercial law in the United States is primarily state law. The UCC is a major part of that body

4. Swift v. Tyson, 41 U.S. (16 Pet.) 1, 10 L.Ed. 865 (1842).

5. 304 U.S. 64, 58 S.Ct. 817, 82 L.Ed. 1188 (1938).

6. Scotland held to Roman law. In 1855, a Royal Commission brought in an important and fascinating report on ways in which "the Mercantile Laws in the different parts of the United Kingdom of Great Britain and Ireland may be advantageously assimilated." Second Report of the Commissioners on Mercantile Laws of the United Kingdom, 354 Parliamentary Papers (1855). In 1856 Parliament enacted legislation to deal with some of these divergences. Mercantile Law Amendment Act, Scotland, 1856, 19 & 20 Vict. c. 60;

Mercantile Law Amendment Act, 1856, 19 & 20 Vict. c. 97.

7. NCCUSL was formed through enactment of legislation, by each state, to create a uniform state law commission for that state. The number of Commissioners and the method of their selection is provided by each state's law. The Commissioners of all the states meet annually in a Conference of Commissioners, a meeting that typically lasts eight working days. Between annual meetings, drafting committees made up of Commissioners and aided by Reporters prepare drafts for submission at an annual meeting. Under NCCUSL procedures, no act can be approved unless it has been "read" and debated at two annual meetings.

of commercial law. The UCC has been adopted, in whole or in part, by every state legislature (and by Congress for the District of Columbia).

As explained below, the UCC is only part of the commercial law of the states of the United States. Many kinds of commercial transactions are still governed entirely by state common law. None of the transactions to which the UCC applies are completely governed by it. Commercial law, at the state level, is a blend of statutory provisions and common law doctrines.

(2) Development of the UCC. In 1936 the New York Merchants' Association launched a movement to modernize sales law; it proposed that Congress adopt a Federal Sales Act to govern foreign and interstate trade. In part to avoid the problems that could be posed by separate federal law, NCCUSL in 1940 started work on a Revised Sales Act to supplant the Uniform Sales Act. The scope of revision was expanded to the other areas of commercial law that had been addressed in uniform acts, and beyond. The American Law Institute ("ALI")[8] joined with NCCUSL to sponsor this ambitious project. The Chief Reporter and overall architect of the project was Professor Karl Llewellyn. The result of this enormous effort was the UCC.

The original UCC contained nine substantive Articles. Articles 2 and 3 supplanted the Uniform Sales Act and the Negotiable Instruments Law. In other respects, the UCC created positive commercial laws for which there were no historic statutory counterparts. Article 9 on secured transactions was the most innovative of these creations.

The story of subsequent modification and enactment of the UCC is complex. For now it is sufficient to note the highlights. The first version of the UCC's Official Text was released in 1952 and promptly enacted in Pennsylvania. Further enactments were deferred pending action by New York. Studies by the New York Law Revision Commission led to substantial revisions that were embodied in the 1957 and 1958 Official Texts. Thereafter, for over a decade, the UCC's sponsors held the line against proposals for change; only a few serious errors were corrected in the Official Texts of 1962 and 1966.

By 1968 the UCC had been adopted by all states except Louisiana, where integration with the Civil Code presented difficulties. (Since then, Louisiana has enacted Articles 1, 3, 4, 4A, 5, 8, and 9.) The UCC has been enacted by Congress for the District of Columbia and also by Guam, Puerto Rico (in part), and the Virgin Islands.

The perceived need for further revision eventually eclipsed the extraordinary success of the original UCC as supplemented by the New York-inspired revision. Article 9 (Secured Transactions), in which the original drafters had gone well beyond existing law, was modified substantially in 1972. Responding to the perceived need for certificateless securities, the

---

8. The ALI is a membership organiza-   ing Restatements of the Law.
tion that probably is best known for produc-

UCC's sponsors made important changes centering on Article 8 (Investment Securities) in 1977.

(3) Continued Revision. In the 1980's the UCC's sponsors, NCCUSL and the ALI, launched a program of major additions and revisions that continues to the present day.

Two new Articles were added in the late 1980's—Article 2A (Leases) (1987 with 1990 amendments) and Article 4A (Funds Transfers) (1989). In 1988, the sponsors of the UCC recommended that states repeal Article 6 (Bulk Sales). For those states reluctant to repeal, the sponsors prepared a substantially revised Article 6. A major revision of Article 3 (Negotiable Instruments), with related changes in Article 4 (Bank Deposits and Collections), was concluded in 1990. A revised Article 8 (Investment Securities) was completed in 1994, and a revised Article 5 (Letters of Credit) was completed the following year. These revisions have been enacted in most, but not all, states.

As this book was going to press, the UCC's sponsors completed revision of Article 1, which contains definitions and general principles applicable to the entire UCC. As of this date it is unclear when NCCUSL will present this revision to state legislatures for adoption. Other than in this General Introduction, citations to Article 1 refer to the pre-revised version of that article.[9]

Of particular importance to this course is the complete revision of Article 9 that was promulgated in 1998. To minimize the problems that will attend the transition from Former Article 9 to the revised Article, the sponsors recommended a uniform effective date of July 1, 2001. By that date all 50 states and the District of Columbia had enacted Revised Article 9, and it had become effective in the District and in all states but four. By January 1, 2002, Revised Article 9 will be effective in all states.

Of the original UCC Articles, only Articles 1, 2, and 7 have not been revised during the past two decades. Each of these Articles is currently under consideration by the UCC's sponsors. Inasmuch as this book discusses Article 2 at length, a few words are in order concerning the ongoing process of revising or amending that Article. In 1991 a drafting committee was appointed to revise Article 2. That step followed the completion of a major report by a study committee of the Permanent Editorial Board for the Uniform Commercial Code ("PEB") on that Article. See PEB Article 2 Study Group Report (1990) (hereinafter cited as "PEB Article 2 Report"). The draft revisions of Article 2 proved to be controversial. In 1999 NCCUSL reconstituted the drafting committee, the Reporter and Associate Reporter (i.e., the principal drafters) resigned, and the scope of the project was limited. A more modest draft—denoted as a set of amendments instead of a revised Article—was approved by the ALI in May 2001. This ALI-approved draft Article 2 was presented to NCCUSL for consideration at its

---

9. Citations to sections of Revised Article 1 in this General Introduction are preced- ed by an "R" (e.g., R103).

2001 Annual Meeting. Amendments to UCC Article 2—Sales (August 2001) (hereinafter cited as "Proposed Revised Article 2"). However, following several amendments to the draft, a motion to approve the draft failed. At this writing it remains unclear whether the project will proceed—in some form—or will be abandoned. If the project eventually succeeds, the revision would be accompanied by corresponding revisions to Article 2A (Leases). Notwithstanding this uncertain situation, this book discusses the proposed revisions in several contexts, both as a useful pedagogical exercise and as a basis for considering policy choices.

Two other drafting committees currently are at work. One is addressing a narrow set of issues arising under Articles 3 (Negotiable Instruments), 4 (Bank Deposits and Collections), and 4A (Funds Transfers). This committee is scheduled to complete its work in 2001 or possibly 2002. The drafting committee for the revision of Article 7 (Documents of Title) began its work in 2001.

Students studying commercial law while these important changes are in progress have an obvious problem and a significant opportunity. Because uniform enactment of revisions and additions takes several years to complete, both the new and old versions of various articles of the UCC will be in force in different states. Inevitably, the UCC will not be "uniform" for some years.[10] We shall see as well that the revision of Article 9 presents special problems: Certain aspects of Former Article 9 remain relevant to transactions entered into before and after the effective date of the revised Article.

For other parts of the UCC, students can know that changes are forthcoming but cannot know what the new texts and Comments will be. This may be unsettling to someone looking merely to learn what the law "is." But considering a major body of statutory law in flux is a unique opportunity to gain the deeper understanding that comes from evaluating the perceived weaknesses in older texts and considering whether the new or proposed changes will be better.[11]

A practicing lawyer must, of course, work from the version enacted in the state whose law governs a particular aspect of a particular transaction. Judicial decisions, including cases in this book, are governed by the version of the UCC in effect in the jurisdiction whose law governs the transaction in question. (As we shall see in Chapter 7, determining the applicable law sometimes can be a daunting exercise.)

---

10. Over the years the UCC as proposed has not been adopted uniformly by state legislatures. Hundreds of changes (usually minor) were made by various states in enacting the UCC. Current statutory supplements of the UCC published for student use may contain recently superseded versions of the text and Comments in appendices to the most recent Official Text promulgated by NCCUSL and the ALI.

11. Current students may find that their up-to-date knowledge of the recently emerged and emerging UCC is an asset that prospective employers will value, as happened nearly five decades ago when very few practicing lawyers had studied the UCC as initially promulgated.

(4) Consumer Transactions. In many countries the "Commercial Code" is applicable only when one (or both) of the parties is a merchant. Lawyers schooled in such a legal setting are startled to learn that the "Uniform Commercial Code" extends to transactions among ordinary consumers and that (with a few exceptions) the rules are the same for both commercial and consumer transactions.

It must quickly be added that these general rules may lead to different results in commercial and in consumer settings. One example is the rule of UCC 2–315 that gives special protection to a buyer who relies "on the seller's skill or judgment"; similar flexibility is inherent in the UCC's rules on "good faith" and "unconscionability." The point is that the applicability of these rules does not depend on placing the parties or the transaction in a "commercial" or "consumer" category, although the results may differ.

(5) Reference Materials. A most useful tool for intensive research on the UCC is the Uniform Commercial Code Reporting Service and Case Digest. This service includes the UCC and Comments, including local variations. It also reproduces all the cases that cite the UCC and provides a digest that arranges the cases according to the UCC sections they cite. Another helpful research guide is the Uniform Laws Annotated. Useful insights into the drafting history of the UCC are provided by the twenty-three volumes of Uniform Commercial Code Drafts (E. Kelly ed. 1984) (hereinafter cited as "Kelly, Drafts") and the ten volumes of Uniform Commercial Code: Confidential Drafts (E. Kelly & A. Puckett ed. 1995).

On the UCC as a whole, see J. White & R. Summers, Uniform Commercial Code (5th ed. 2000) (hereinafter cited as "White & Summers"). For good descriptions of many patterns and structures of commercial transactions, including many illuminating charts and forms, see J. Dolan, Commercial Law: Essential Terms and Transactions (2d ed. 1997). The myriad intersections between the UCC and other law are thoroughly developed in R. Hillman, J. McDonnell & S. Nickles, Common Law and Equity Under the UCC (1984 & Supp.) (hereinafter cited as "Hillman, McDonnell, & Nickles, Common Law"). In view of the rapid evolution of laws regarding consumer protection, loose-leaf services are useful. See, e.g., Consumer Credit Guide (CCH).

There are many resources for further study of the law of sales under UCC Article 2. Among these are: Chapters 1 through 12 of White & Summers; C. Gillette & S. Walt, Sales Law: Domestic and International (1999); J. Brook, Sales and Leases: Examples and Explanations (2d ed. 1999); Part I of J. Dolan, Commercial Law: Essential Terms and Transactions (2d ed. 1997); A. Meyer & R. Speidel, Sales and Leases of Goods (1993).

Comprehensive and frequently updated treatment of Article 9 is B. Clark, The Law of Secured Transactions under the Uniform Commercial Code (rev. ed.) (hereinafter cited as "Clark, Secured Transactions"). In addition, chapters 21–25 of White & Summers deal incisively with the essential issues raised by Article 9. A clear and thorough explanation of many of the transactional patterns in secured financing, with numerous examples of documentation, is found in Part II of J. Dolan, Commercial Law: Essential Terms and Transactions (2d ed. 1997).

The field of secured transactions has been blessed by a book that belongs on the short list of classics in legal literature: G. Gilmore, Security Interests in Personal Property (1965) (cited herein as "Gilmore, Security"). Those of you who wish to probe deeply should consult this work for perspective and for intensive examination of the history of personal property security law as well as the policies and provisions of Article 9 (and when you are in the mood for the refreshment offered by writing that combines charm with insight). Although portions are quite dated (the book deals with the 1962 Official Text of the UCC), Professor Gilmore's treatise remains an important resource.

Counsel for banks and finance companies that operate on a multi-state basis need current and readily accessible material on developments in each state. The CCH Secured Transactions Guide can be helpful in this regard. In addition, the Uniform Commercial Code Reporting Service (U.C.C. Rep. Serv.), mentioned above, tracks adoptions of both the official text of, and nonuniform amendments to, the UCC on a state-by-state basis. For many of the difficult issues posed by secured financing under Article 9, the most thorough treatment will be found in legal periodicals.

(E) United States Commercial Law Outside the UCC

(1) Other Recent Uniform Laws. For a number of years, the sponsors of the UCC worked on developing a new Article governing licenses of software and information. The Article was designated tentatively as UCC Article 2B. In April, 1999, the sponsors decided that this law should not be incorporated into the UCC. The project was renamed the Uniform Computer Information Transactions Act ("UCITA") and was approved by NCCUSL later that year. The ALI had no role in UCITA's promulgation. UCITA's prospects seem dim; it has been enacted by only two states.

UCITA contemplates that many transactions in information will be electronic. Likewise, each of the recently revised Articles of the UCC has made appropriate provision for electronic commerce. For other fields of law, NCCUSL promulgated the Uniform Electronic Transactions Act ("UETA") in 1999. We shall have occasion to consider select provisions of UETA as well as of the federal legislation that derives from it, the Electronic Signatures in Global and National Commerce Act (hereinafter cited as "E-SIGN"); Pub. L. No. 106–229, 114 Stat. 464 (2000) (codified at 15 U.S.C. § 7001 et seq.).

(2) Consumer Law. One of the striking legal developments of the past four decades has been the enactment of legislation designed to give special protection to ordinary consumers, individuals who engage in transactions for personal, family, or household purposes. Consumer-protection legislation has been enacted at both the state and federal levels.

The federal government created a substantial body of consumer-protection law. In 1960 Senator Paul Douglas introduced his first legislative proposal for "Truth in Lending." In 1968 Congress passed the Consumer Credit Protection Act, 15 U.S.C. §§ 1601–1693r, which includes the Truth in Lending Act (Title I), the Fair Credit Reporting Act (Title VI), the Equal Credit Opportunity Act (Title VII), and the Fair Debt Collection Practices Act (Title VIII). Sweeping regulation of some seller's warranties in the interests of consumers first became effective on July 4, 1975, under the federal Magnuson–Moss Warranty Act, 15 U.S.C. §§ 2301–2312. In addition, the Federal Trade Commission has issued important regulations for the protection of consumers. See, e.g., 16 C.F.R. part 433 (preserving consumers' claims and defenses); 16 C.F.R. part 444 (regulating unfair credit practices).

Senator Douglas's proposal stimulated countermeasures for state enactment, including the preparation by NCCUSL of a Uniform Consumer Credit Code ("U3C"). The U3C, as promulgated in 1968, provided the basis for legislation in a number of states; a revised version was issued in 1974.

(3) Bankruptcy Law. In all commercial transactions, the possibility exists that one (or both) of the parties to the transaction will become insolvent. The consequences for the parties to exchange transactions are likely to be significant, particularly for those parts of transactions that are executory (unperformed). Credit transactions are especially vulnerable when debtors cannot pay.

Some insolvent persons file a petition for bankruptcy under the federal Bankruptcy Code ("BC"), 11 U.S.C. §§ 101–1330. A person's entry into bankruptcy gives rise to important and potentially adverse consequences for the person's secured creditors. The effects of bankruptcy on secured creditors is discussed in Chapter 10, infra.

(F) COMMERCIAL LAW FOR INTERNATIONAL TRANSACTIONS

Economic activity of all kinds is increasingly becoming globalized. In the absence of international commercial law, the law governing an international transaction will be the domestic law of one nation. Important steps have been and are being taken to unify the law applicable to international commercial transactions.

(1) International Conventions. Most efforts to develop international commercial law have been in the form of international conventions, multilateral agreements comparable to treaties. Nations that ratify an international convention incorporate the content of the convention into their national laws. The object of efforts of this kind is to create uniform bodies of national law that supersede the various domestic laws of ratifying nations that would otherwise be applicable.

Transnational Sales of Goods. One field for unification is the law applicable to the international sale of goods. Because earlier unification efforts had met with only limited success, in 1966 the General Assembly of the United Nations provided for the creation of the United Nations Commission on International Trade Law ("UNCITRAL"). UNCITRAL's membership, limited to 36 States, is allocated among the regions of the world:

Africa, 9; Asia, 7; Eastern Europe, 5; Latin America, 6; Western Europe and Others, 9. This last region (the industrial West) extends to Australia, Canada, and the United States. The United States has been a member from the outset and has played an active role in UNCITRAL's work.

After several years of effort, in 1980 a diplomatic conference of 62 States, at the end of five weeks of intensive work, approved the CISG. The Convention went into force on January 1, 1988, following ratification (or similar implementation) by eleven nations. The United States was one of those nations. By 2001 the Convention had been ratified by 60 nations, including nations on each continent and with diverse legal and economic systems. The United Nations Convention on the Limitation Period of the International Sale of Goods specifies the limitations period applicable to actions under CISG.

Negotiable Instruments and Letters of Credit. Another field for unification involves the rules governing the principal instruments used in international payments—bills of exchange, promissory notes, checks, and letters of credit. In this field, UNCITRAL developed uniform rules that led in 1988 to the United Nations Convention on International Bills of Exchange and International Promissory Notes. An unusual feature of this convention, which has yet to enter into force, is that its rules apply only to a special international instrument that states it is issued under the Convention. In 1995 it promulgated the UNCITRAL Convention on Independent Guarantees and Stand-by Letters of Credit, which entered into force in five nations in 2000.

Financing Transactions. Two international conventions sponsored by the International Institute for the Unification of Private Law ("UNIDROIT") that cover important areas of international financing were adopted in 1988 at a diplomatic conference in Ottawa. They are the UNIDROIT Convention on International Financial Leasing and the UNIDROIT Convention on International Factoring.

Another UNCITRAL project addresses uniform rules on the assignment of receivables. In 2001 UNCITRAL completed its work on the Convention on the Assignment of Receivables in International Trade. Following the anticipated approval of the United Nations General Assembly, the convention will be presented to states for signature and ratification.

A draft convention on Uniform Rules on International Interests in Mobile Equipment is being prepared under the auspices of UNIDROIT. Secured financing of large civil aircraft is one of the matters within the scope of this project; the scope also includes the secured financing of railroad rolling stock and space stations and satellites. The draft convention will be considered by a diplomatic conference scheduled to meet in October and November 2001 in Capetown, South Africa.

Sea Transport. Because of the vital part that sea transport plays in international trade, UNCITRAL developed new rules that govern the responsibility of ocean carriers for cargo. Despite the active opposition of the carriers, the United Nations Convention on Carriage of Goods by Sea (hereinafter cited as the "Hamburg Rules") came into force in 1991. Ratifications came primarily from developing countries.

Enforcement of Awards of Commercial Arbitrators. International commercial law is well developed with regard to judicial enforcement of arbitration awards. The United Nations Convention on the Recognition and Enforcement of Foreign Arbitral Awards, commonly known as the "New York Convention," commits signatory nations to enforcement of arbitration awards. The United States, a party to the New York Convention, fulfilled its obligation by adding chapter 2 to the Federal Arbitration Act, 9 U.S.C. §§ 201–208, in 1970. The New York Convention is reprinted in the notes of 9 U.S.C.A. § 201.[12]

(2) Projects for Harmonization of Domestic Law. International projects aimed at improvement of domestic laws are an alternative to creation of uniform bodies of international commercial law that, when ratified, supersede otherwise applicable domestic laws. International projects of this kind create models that national lawmakers can use in revising their domestic laws. The object of this process is commonly referred to as seeking to harmonize national laws, i.e., to reduce or eliminate differences that may exist. Several notable examples of harmonization projects are found in the work of UNCITRAL and UNIDROIT.

Principles of International Commercial Contracts. UNIDROIT promulgated a set of contract principles in 1994. The UNIDROIT Principles of International Commercial Contracts (hereinafter cited as the "UNIDROIT Principles") are intended to enunciate rules that are common to most existing domestic legal systems, but that are best adapted to the special requirements of international trade. The Principles deal with a number of matters that are either completely excluded from CISG or not sufficiently covered in that Convention. The UNIDROIT Principles can be applied when contracting parties have agreed to be governed by them, but are also

---

12. Arbitration is a longstanding type of dispute resolution. Several systems are available to transactors who agree to submit their disputes to arbitration rather than to take those disputes to a court of a nation or state. One of these systems exists pursuant to rules and procedures of the International Chamber of Commerce (ICC), which established in 1923 what is now called the International Court of Arbitration. Since its founding, the ICC Court has handled more than 6,700 cases. Most of those decisions are unreported. However, since 1974, selected arbitral awards have been published. The initial collection spanned eleven years. Since 1976, the International Council for Commercial Arbitration has been publishing Yearbooks of Commercial Arbitration which contain a selection of arbitral awards and other materials.

Another arbitration system devoted substantially to arbitration of international commercial disputes is the London Court of International Arbitration (LCIA). The LCIA, which has been in existence for more than a century, is a corporation under the control of its constituent bodies, the Corporation of the City of London, the London Chamber of Commerce, and the Chartered Institute of Arbitrators. Under LCIA rules, arbitral tribunals are required to make their awards in writing; an award must include the reasons on which the award is based unless the parties agree otherwise. The LCIA Rules are annexed to the Report of the ILEX Delegation to International Arbitration Centers: An Update on Commercial Dispute Resolution Developments in London and Paris (ABA Section of International Law and Practice, (1995)).

offered as guides to solving issues when tribunals cannot ascertain the relevant rule of the applicable law.

The complete version of the UNIDROIT Principles contains black-letter rules, comments, and illustrations. The format resembles that used by the American Law Institute in its Restatements of the Law.

Commercial Arbitration. There are other examples of the rapidly growing body of uniform law for international arbitration. These include the 1976 UNCITRAL Arbitration Rules, which become effective by a reference in a contractual arbitration clause, and the 1985 UNCITRAL Model Law on International Commercial Arbitration.

International Credit Transfers. In 1992 UNCITRAL promulgated a Model Law on International Credit Transfers (i.e., funds transfers). An objective of this project is to provide a body of legal rules that can be applied to commercial payment transactions in which the parties communicate with each other electronically.

(G) INTERPRETING AND WORKING WITH COMMERCIAL CODES

Much of this book deals with the examination and interpretation of the texts of statutory law and international conventions, primarily the UCC and the CISG. The objective is to find the meaning of the text as applied to factual circumstances found in reported decisions or posed in problem situations, many of which are set out in these materials. Given the central importance of this task, it is useful at the outset to consider how to go about it.

(1) The UCC.

Two Polar Approaches to Statutory Interpretation. Four hundred years ago, during the reign of Elizabeth I, one of the greatest common-law judges, Lord Coke, proposed a maxim for statutory interpretation: Identify the "mischief . . . for which the common law did not provide [a remedy]," and then identify precisely the "remedy the Parliament hath resolved."[13] Lord Coke's maxim posits that statutes are corrective measures, enacted from time to time to overcome particular deficiencies in the common law. On this view, each statute is only a patch on the broad cloth of common law and its meaning can be ascertained by examining the nature of the hole the legislature sought to mend.

When the statute to be construed is a large, integrated work, such as a code, a quite different approach is to seek the meaning of its various provisions in light of the overarching purposes and policies that animate the whole work. A piecemeal, mischief-correction reading would not take adequate account of the greater set of principles envisioned by the legislature. Gaps in the text of a code can be filled by interpolating provisions that serve the code's general policies.

---

13. Heydon's Case, 3 Co. Rep. 7a, 7b, 76 Eng. Rep. 637, 638 (1584).

General Provisions. Like most codes, the UCC contains a number of important provisions that are applicable generally. These include a statement of the purposes and policies of the UCC, see UCC 1–102, as well as a provision linking the UCC to other bodies of law. See UCC 1–103. These provisions will be combined in R1–103 without any change in substance.

The text of the UCC is a product of its two sponsoring organizations and the source of legislation in all states of the United States. While many legislatures have chosen not to adopt that text exactly as promulgated by the NCCUSL and the ALI, the statutory law in place is substantially the text proposed for uniform enactment. Interpretation of a uniform statute is a process of applying its provisions of general applicability to the facts of particular situations, regardless of otherwise applicable state law. That process is in some respects the same as the process of interpretation of other statutes, but in other respects it differs.

We focus first on the differences. Unlike most domestic statutes, the UCC has within itself statements on its proper interpretation. The very first substantive provision states: "This Act shall be liberally construed and applied to promote its underlying purposes and policies." UCC 1–102(1).[14] Subsection (2) describes the "underlying purposes and policies" in three branches:

(a) to simplify, clarify and modernize the law governing commercial transactions;

(b) to permit the continued expansion of commercial practices through custom, usage and agreement of the parties;

(c) to make uniform the law among the various jurisdictions

Section 1–102 reveals the UCC's basic attitude toward the arrangements made by transactional parties in the private sector. It declares that the law's primary purpose is to facilitate market transactions. Simplicity and clarity of rules enable actors to act expeditiously with an understanding of the background legal environment. Uniformity of law facilitates interstate commerce by eliminating concerns for conflicts of law in transborder transactions. Modernization involves casting off anachronistic rules that no longer fit current market practices.[15] Flexibility assures that the

---

14. The provisions found in Article 1 are "general provisions" that apply to all of the other Articles.

15. At the time of drafting the original UCC, the 1906 Sales Act was seen as an anachronism:

> In nineteenth-century commerce, the prototypical sales transaction was the face-to-face sale in which the buyer paid cash and took her goods home. [The picture of a commercial transaction in the Sales Act ... is typified "by the horseman who stops at the saddler's door to buy a new saddle."] ... In the modern

world of sales, ... most commercial sellers and buyers ... contract for a sale in the future; their agreement is usually on the buyer's or seller's printed form; their sale is on credit; and their relationship has just begun. In addition, there may be one or more middlemen between the seller-manufacturer and the buyer, who may be buying for resale or use. Both the commercial structure of a sale and the needs of the parties to it will vary markedly depending on whether it is a sale to a business buyer for resale or use, or to a consumer.

law, without amendment, will adapt to evolving commercial practices in a way that leads to economic growth.

Section 1–102 says nothing about regulation of the marketplace. There is no suggestion that the UCC is intended to address market failures or intervene to change the balance of the market power of private actors.[16] A

By the late 1930s, Llewellyn was not alone in seeing problems of obsolescence in the Uniform Sales Act. Indeed, the merchants were the first to complain, followed by the academic community and the commercial bar.

Z. Wiseman, The Limits of Vision: Karl Llewellyn and the Merchant Rules, 100 Harv. L. Rev. 465, 475–477 (1987).

16. Some commentators have criticized the drafters of the UCC as lacking the willingness to make moral or ideological judgments about the nature of a just society and to shape the UCC toward such objectives. Thus, Richard Danzig concluded that the UCC was premised on what he termed a triad of dubious assumptions:

> [1] that self-evident ideal resolutions of situational problems exist [and need not be declared by the legislature], [2] that they can be discovered by careful scrutiny of actual situations [in case-by-case litigation], and [3] that once articulated they will be widely accepted.

R. Danzig, A Comment on the Jurisprudence of the Uniform Commercial Code, 27 Stan. L. Rev. 621, 635 (1975).

John Murray took a different view. He posited that Article 2 requires courts to give particular meaning to very broad legislative norms and that the UCC permits and requires courts to support and regulate the marketplace, and he concluded that the drafters had done their work well:

> One critic characterizes Article 2 as a direction to discover the law—the standards and morality of commercial law—in the practices of the market place. But what if those practices—at least as pursued by the majority of traders in a given industry—are unfair, inequitable or unjust? . . . The overriding standards of commercial reasonableness, honesty-in-fact, conscionability and, yes, decency, are the ultimate principles which may not be overcome in any application of Article 2. . . . In this effort, Article 2 not only enables but directs courts to impose

> their understanding of commercial morality on the market place.

J. Murray, The Article 2 Prism: The Underlying Philosophy of Article 2 of the Uniform Commercial Code, 21 Washburn L.J. 1, 19–20 (1981).

Zippora Wiseman offered a more sympathetic view of Llewellyn's legislative vision:

> Llewellyn . . . was not entirely uncritical in his acceptance of mercantile reality. His vision also encompassed a normative belief that the law should encourage the better practices and control the worst abuses of the market. . . . [H]e recognized the potential unfairness of applying merchant standards to individuals who lacked knowledge of these standards and experience with them. . . .
>
> Llewellyn's vision of the possibility of Grand Style judging in sales litigation was . . . based on his assessment of the . . . institutional organization of those groups affected by the Sales Act. He frequently asserted that sales law was "nonpolitical." Llewellyn's idiosyncratic use of the term meant that sales law was noncontroversial in the sense that no organized constituency of those affected would see itself as having a vested interest in outcomes tilted in a particular direction. An organized consumer movement did not yet exist. Merchants were both sellers and buyers; and for that reason a consensus existed among the "better" merchants that fair and balanced rules as between merchant sellers and buyers were desirable.

Z. Wiseman, The Limits of Vision: Karl Llewellyn and the Merchant Rules, 100 Harv. L. Rev. 465, 492, 540 (1987).

Professor Wiseman concluded, however, that a large part of Llewellyn's personal vision, encapsulated in his proposals for a considerable number of "merchant rules," was lost as the these proposals were dropped from the UCC or their content was diluted in the lengthy drafting process.

substantial body of trade regulation law exists in the United States. One might infer from UCC 1–102 that the UCC is not, in any respect a regulatory statute, but that would be a mistake. Although the UCC is not primarily a part of the law of trade regulation, we shall see that the UCC does contain some regulatory provisions.[17] One should be aware that regulatory provisions may be found throughout the UCC.

An interesting provision in Article 1 declares a general obligation that all parties to UCC transactions must act in "good faith" in the performance or enforcement of any contract or duty. UCC 1–203; R1–304. This statutorily created good faith obligation has overtones of a regulatory kind. It is important, therefore, to consider what the content of good faith may be and how the obligation could be given effect. The current UCC Article 1 defines "good faith" to mean "honesty in fact in the conduct or transaction concerned." UCC 1–201(19). Revised Article 1 expands that definition by adding an additional term so that "good faith" will mean "honesty in fact in the conduct or transaction concerned and observance of reasonable commercial standards of fair dealing." This expanded definition is in accord with the definition of "good faith" that has been used for merchants in Article 2 since the Code was first promulgated[18] and the definition that was adopted in revisions of other Articles other than Article 5 on letters of credit.[19]

The declaration that parties to transactions within the scope of the UCC must observe *reasonable* commercial standards of *fair dealing in the trade* reaches significantly beyond the provision that usages of trade in a vocation or trade "give particular meaning to and supplement or qualify terms of an agreement." UCC 1–205(3). (R1–303(d) is to the same effect.) The UCC's provision on usage of trade does not inject a normative requirement of reasonableness.[20]

If the good faith obligation is only to be honest, it would have little effect. However, good faith is defined more broadly in some other articles. Thus, in sales transactions, parties who are "merchants," a defined term, not only must behave honestly but also must act in accordance with "reasonable commercial standards of fair dealing in the trade." UCC 2–

---

17. The most well known of these may be the provision, in Article 2, that empowers courts to deny legal force to unconscionable contracts. UCC 2–302.

18. UCC 2–103(1)(b).

19. See UCC 4A–105(a)(6); UCC 8–102(a)(10); R9–102(a)(43); but see UCC 5–102(a)(7). The new R1–304 definition explicitly excepts Article 5.

20. "A usage of trade is any practice or method of dealing having such regularity of observance in a place, vocation or trade as to justify an expectation that it will be observed with respect to the transaction in question." UCC 1–205(2); R1–303(c). Literally, this language would incorporate practices of chicane that regularly are observed in a thieves' market. On the other hand, the Comment states that UCC 1–205(2) provides for full recognition "for new usages and usages currently observed by the great majority of *decent* dealers, even though dissidents *ready to cut corners* do not agree." The Comment, with a little effort, can be squared with the statutory language that usage of trade gives "particular meaning" to an agreement; in most settings a contracting party will assume that the other party is one of the "great majority of decent dealers" and not one of the few "dissidents ready to cut corners."

103(1)(b). In recently completed additions and revisions of UCC articles, "good faith" is sometimes defined to incorporate a fair dealing standard.

A signal that a UCC provision may have a regulatory function is the ability of parties, by contract, to depart from the provision. A provision that cannot be abrogated by agreement of the parties is likely to have its roots in some public policy. Section 1–102 is again instructive. Subsection (3) provides:

> (3) The effect of provisions of this Act may be varied by agreement, except as otherwise provided in this Act and except that the obligations of good faith, diligence, reasonableness and care prescribed by this Act may not be disclaimed by agreement but the parties may by agreement determine the standards by which the performance of such obligations is to be measured if such standards are not manifestly unreasonable.

This provision is found in R1–302. Subsection (4) of UCC 1–102 notes that, while some provisions may explicitly defer to agreements of the parties, absence of such explicit language should not be construed to narrow the freedom of private ordering.

Definitions. The UCC has a large number of definitions and contains ingenious devices to aid in finding them. Some of the Articles provide a fast and easy way to find many of these definitions: "Definitional Cross References" are found at the end of the Official Comments to each section. However, a careful lawyer will not rely on the completeness of these cross-references. For a thorough job, one will check Article 1, which contains important provisions applicable to the UCC as a whole; UCC 1–201 and R1–201 contain the definitions of terms used throughout the UCC. In addition, one should check the definitions contained in, and specially applicable to, a particular Article. See, e.g., UCC 2–103 (which contains definitions, an index of definitions inserted in the text of the Article, and an index of applicable definitions in other Articles).

It would be useful for you to skim through the sections of Article 1 at this time. You should pay particular attention to UCC 1–102, UCC 1–103, and UCC 1–203 (and, in Revised Article 1, R1–103, R1–302, R1–303, and R1–304).

Official Comments to the UCC: Uses and Hazards. A hazard for the lazy mind, and a help for the responsible lawyer, are the Official Comments that follow each section of the UCC. We should note some of the troublesome problems concerning the role of the Comments in the UCC scheme.

The most obvious point about the Comments is the one that, curiously enough, is most often overlooked: The text to the UCC was enacted by the legislature; the Comments were not. One is tempted to ignore this point because the Comments, written in an explanatory and non-statutory style, are easier to read. *Facilis est descensus Averno.*

But the tempter will whisper: The drafters wrote these Comments, didn't they? If they say what the UCC does, that's bound to be right, isn't it? Why bother then with this prickly statutory language? (You may find it easier to resist these temptations if you put yourself, in your mind's eye, in the role of a judge to whom this argument has been made and then imagine your response to that hapless attorney.)

The problem of the force of the Comments is sufficiently important to justify some background. Versions of the UCC prior to 1957 included a significant provision about the Comments in the general provisions of Article 1. Section 1–102, Purposes; Rules of Construction, stated in subsection (3)(f):

> The Comments of the National Conference of Commissioners on Uniform State Laws and the American Law Institute may be consulted in the construction and application of this Act but if text and Comment conflict, text controls.

In 1956 the sponsoring organizations released the 1956 Recommendations of the Editorial Board for the Uniform Commercial Code, recommending widespread revisions (many of which were adopted by the sponsors). These recommendations called for the deletion of the above-quoted UCC 1–102(3)(f) and did not substitute any new provision on the status of the Comments.[21] The question immediately arises: Does this deletion imply the rejection of the idea behind the deleted provision so that reference to the Comments has become illegitimate?

An answer appears in the Comments to the 1956 Recommendations. The reasons for this and other changes were only briefly stated; the explanation for this change was as follows: "paragraph (3)(f) was deleted because the old Comments were clearly out of date and it was not known when new ones could be prepared."[22] Revised Comments accompanied the 1957 and subsequent versions of the UCC, but without any statutory provision referring to them.

Embarrassing questions arise if one subjects the Comments to the standards often imposed for recourse to legislative history. In some states the revised Comments had not yet been drafted at the time of the UCC's adoption. In others it is highly doubtful that the Comments were laid before the legislators in the form of a committee report explaining the legislation that the legislators were asked to adopt. Moreover, some of the Comments were not even written by those who drafted the Official Text. Nor are the Comments approved by the sponsors of the UCC. The practice for some Articles has been for the Reporter to draft Official Comments in consultation with the Chair of the drafting committee after the sponsors have approved the text. In recent years draft Comments to other Articles were available to aid the sponsors in their consideration of the text (as well as to the public on the Internet). The final versions were approved by a

---

21. 1956 Recommendations of the Editorial Board for the Uniform Commercial Code (hereinafter cited as 1956 Recommendations), 18 Kelly, Drafts 27.

22. Id. Perhaps we face here an engineering problem: How high can the Comments lift themselves by their own bootstraps? Are the authors violating their own principles in quoting this Comment?

relatively small number of persons entrusted with this task by the sponsors.

It would be very wrong, however, to conclude that the Comments are without value to lawyers and to courts. Professor Williston's treatise on Sales was given heavy weight by courts in construing the Uniform Sales Act on the ground that it reflected the intent of the drafter although it was written subsequent to the drafting of the Act; as you will see, courts repeatedly have quoted the Comments in construing the UCC and often have given the Comments substantial weight in their reasoning.

Surely the Comments may be given at least as much weight as an able article or treatise construing the UCC. It is equally clear that the Comments do not approach the weight of legislation. If the statutory provisions adopted by the legislature contradict or fail to support the Comments, then the Comments must be rejected.

The point is significant, for we shall see instances, easily understood in the light of the Comments' bulk and the many successive revisions of the UCC, where the Comments have been less than faithful to the statute. More frequent are instances of enthusiastic discussion of significant problems on which the statute is silent.

A thorough job of construing the UCC calls for using the Comments to make sure one has found the pertinent language of the statute, as a double-check on a tentative construction, and as a secondary aid where the language of the statute is ambiguous. However, we warn you that we sternly reject any reference to Comments until after the pertinent statutory language has been carefully examined in the light of the statutory definitions and the statutory structure.

One relatively recent development necessitates yet another warning. Pursuant to its resolution of March 14, 1987, the PEB has issued (and continues to issue) PEB Commentaries. The PEB Commentaries (and the cited resolution) are set out in full in most statutory supplements published for student use. The PEB Commentaries have necessitated supplemental changes to the Comments. Although the Comments refer to the relevant PEB Commentaries, in some cases portions of the Comments have been deleted and replaced by entirely new language. Because the Comments have been relied upon by legislators, courts, and counsel alike, one hopes that the UCC's sponsors will find a way to preserve the Comments intact as supplemented by the PEB Commentaries.

(2) International Conventions. Unlike the UCC, which is part of the jurisprudence of a single nation, international commercial conventions are legally stateless. Lawyers and judges can approach the UCC from within a recognized tradition of the construction and application of statutes generally. The special aspects of giving meaning to the UCC, discussed above, are not fundamental departures from the general jurisprudence of statutory interpretation in the United States. International conventions have no similar context.

Interpretation of International Conventions on Commercial Law. Many nations are parties to CISG. The jurisprudence of statutory construction within the nations' domestic legal systems may be quite diverse. If a body of international law were viewed through different prisms of domestic legal systems, the meaning of the international law would vary with the background of the observer. That result is, of course, inconsistent with the fundamental idea of law as international law.

Drafters of CISG included a one-sentence provision on interpretation of the Convention. "In the interpretation of this Convention, regard is to be had to its international character and the need to promote uniformity in its application and the observance of good faith in international trade." CISG 7(1). Reference to the Convention's *international character* and appeal for *uniformity* constitute a rhetorical effort that tries to remind judges and arbitrators not to use parochial approaches to statutory construction in the interpretation of this body of law. Professor Honnold writes: "To read the words of the Convention with regard for their 'international character' requires that they be projected against an international background. With time, a body of international experience will develop through international case law and scholarly writing." J. Honnold, Uniform Law for International Sales Under the 1980 United Nations Convention § 88 (3d ed. 1999) (hereinafter cited as "Honnold, International Sales").

A body of international law on the interpretation of all treaties helps the project of interpreting international economic law. The Vienna Convention on the Law of Treaties, which entered into force in 1980, contains standards for interpretation. 1155 U.N.T.S. 331, 8 I.L.M. 679. Articles 31 and 32 of that Convention are most salient in this regard.[23]

23. These articles provide:

Article 31 General rule of interpretation

1. A treaty shall be interpreted in good faith in accordance with the ordinary meaning to be given to the terms of the treaty in their context and in the light of its object and purpose.

2. The context for the purpose of the interpretation of a treaty shall comprise, in addition to the text, including its preamble and annexes:

(a) any agreement relating to the treaty which was made between all the parties in connexion with the conclusion of the treaty;

(b) any instrument which was made by one or more parties in connexion with the conclusion of the treaty and accepted by the other parties as an instrument related to the treaty.

3. There shall be taken into account, together with the context:

(a) any subsequent agreement between the parties regarding the interpretation of the treaty or the application of its provisions;

(b) any subsequent practice in the application of the treaty which establishes the agreement of the parties regarding its interpretation;

(c) any relevant rules of international law applicable in the relations between the parties.

4. A special meaning shall be given to a term if it is established that the parties so intended.

Article 32 Supplementary means of interpretation

Recourse may be had to supplementary means of interpretation, including the preparatory work of the treaty and the circumstances of its conclusion, in order to confirm the meaning resulting from the application of article 31, or to

Negotiating History. Preparatory work in the drafting and negotiation of international treaties may be used as a guide to interpretation. This is evident in Article 32, and in Article 31(2)(b), of the Vienna Convention on the Law of Treaties. A very useful compilation of the preparation of CISG through many drafts and negotiating rounds is J. Honnold, Documentary History of the Uniform Law for International Sales (1989).

Commentaries. Commentaries written by respected scholars are a traditional source of international law. Uniform interpretation of international commercial law conventions may be achieved through the work of such scholars whose works are known and respected generally. A number of highly regarded commentaries on CISG have been published. Among these are Honnold, International Sales; P. Schlectriem, ed., Commentary on the UN Convention on the International Sale of Goods (1995, English translation 1998); H. Bronstein & J. Lookosky, Understanding CISG in Europe (1997); C. Bianca & M. Bonnell, Commentary on the International Sales Law (1987). For a broader bibliography, see Honnold, International Sales at xxiii–xxvi. See also C. Gillette & S. Walt, Sales Law: Domestic and International (1999).

For cross references between the Convention and the UCC, see A. Kritzer, Guide to Practical Applications of the United Nations Convention on Contracts for the International Sale of Goods (1989). See also R. Speidel, The Revision of UCC Article 2, Sales in Light of the United Nations Convention on Contracts for the International Sale of Goods, 16 Nw. J. of Int'l L. & Bus. 165 (1995). Legislative history of the Convention is compiled in J. Honnold, Documentary History of the Uniform Law for International Sales (1989).

Multiple Languages. When international conventions are negotiated, the product is usually stated in multiple languages and each version is declared to be equally official. International agreements prepared under the auspices of the United Nations are drafted in six official languages. The interpretation problems generated by this common form of international law making are a potentially severe impediment to finding a single proper reading of the provisions of the law.[24]

(3) Commercial Lawyers' Roles and Tasks. Lawyers play several roles in bringing commercial law to bear on commercial transactions. Lawyers in private practice, commonly organized into law firms, are

---

determine the meaning when the interpretation according to article 31:

(a) leaves the meaning ambiguous or obscure; or

(b) leads to a result which is manifestly absurd or unreasonable.

24. The United States–Canada Free Trade Agreement, predecessor of the North American Free Trade Agreement (NAFTA), was promulgated in English and French versions. When a dispute arose in a NAFTA tribunal as to the meaning of a term in the chapter on agriculture, it appeared that the term expressed in English had a different meaning from the term expressed in French. Ironically, counsel for the United States, not a French-speaking country, argued that the term had the meaning expressed in French. The tribunal did not agree. U.S. Regulation of U.H.T. Milk from Quebec, 16 ITRD 1769 (1993).

retained by clients to provide professional services. Similar services may be provided to organizations by salaried lawyers such as the lawyers on a corporation's legal staff. Clients retain or employ lawyers to handle commercial legal matters in different ways. Some lawyers serve primarily as advocates, often in litigation after a contract has been breached or a transaction has failed. Others serve primarily as advisors and counselors. In the period when transactions are being negotiated, these lawyers may serve as negotiators or drafters of documents, or may provide assistance in countless ways to "close the deal." If transactions later threaten to break down, lawyers may be called on to give counsel on how to deal with the turbulence.

From clients' standpoint, lawyer-counselors or lawyer-litigators earn their fees or their salaries by using sound judgment to achieve cost-effective results. Lawyer-counselors can add significant value by enabling the clients to obtain many or all of the benefits the clients had anticipated when deals were made. Clients appreciate lawyers who can keep them out of controversy or, when controversy arises, can extricate them from the trouble without becoming embroiled in lawsuits. Clients also appreciate lawyer-advocates who help them assess their options with respect to a dispute, including whether to pursue mediation or litigation and whether and when to settle the matter. Litigants are usually seeking to avoid or limit loss. The transaction costs, delays, and uncounted other negative aspects of being a party to a legal dispute often mean that neither side is likely to come out ahead. However, a lawyer who effectively and efficiently maximizes the client's return (or limits the client's loss) serves the client well.

Commercial law is one of the tools that is used by lawyer-counselors and by lawyer-advocates. In studying and evaluating the content of commercial law, one can get considerable insight by considering how a tool works for counselors and how it works for litigators. For example, consider how important it may be whether a statutory provision states a "bright line" rule that has clear meaning and sharp edges or broadly states a general principle that must be construed in light of the unique facts and circumstances of particular transactions. Deal makers, it is said, have a greater need for legal certainty, a need that expands when more than two parties are or may become involved. Dispute resolvers have a greater need for rules that achieve just and fair results. The tension between law as a planning device and law as an instrument of justice, while not unique to commercial law, is nonetheless pervasive in that domain. It is a tension that can never be resolved perfectly.

A major part of the grist for study of commercial law consists of reported decisions of courts or arbitrators. Underlying every such opinion is a failed contract or transaction. One sees in these decisions an application of commercial law to resolve disputes. When evaluating decisions in such cases, one's understanding can be deepened by rolling the narratives back to the earlier stages when the deals were set up and when the deals began to break down. Very important lessons can be learned by considering when lawyers were first brought into the matter, what the lawyers did, and whether some different professional conduct, at earlier stages, might have produced better outcomes.

Another way of putting the point is this: the professional work of the most valued commercial lawyers is unlikely ever to be seen in the reported judicial opinions. To learn how to be a successful lawyer-counselor in commercial matters, one can be a legal pathologist, searching the remains of failed transactions for ways to avoid such failures in the future.

CHAPTER 1

RIGHTS OF CREDITORS, OWNERS, AND PURCHASERS

This Chapter introduces the duality of property and contract in a variety of transactional settings. A property interest may consist of full "title" or "ownership" or a more limited property interest such as a leasehold interest. Before turning to property interests in personal property, Section 1 introduces the rights of unsecured creditors by examining the rights of a person (a creditor) who has only a contract claim against another (a debtor). The remainder of the Chapter deals with purchasers of three types of property: goods, rights to payment, and documents of title. Sections 2 and 3 address purchasers of goods. Section 2 considers the bilateral powers of a seller as against a buyer. Section 3 then examines the powers of a seller over goods as against various third parties. Section 4 turns to rights to payment, commonly called "receivables," some of which are evidenced by negotiable instruments (e.g., promissory notes) or security certificates (e.g., bonds). It addresses the rights of various purchasers of these right to payment. Section 5 considers goods covered by documents of title.

SECTION 1.   THE RIGHTS OF UNSECURED CREDITORS

Much of law school is devoted to determining whether one person is legally obligated to another and, if so, the amount of damages recoverable or other appropriate remedy. The part of this course that is addressed to secured transactions is unusual for a law school course in that it generally assumes the defendant's liability and explores how the aggrieved party can turn its claim into cash. We begin, however, with a preliminary consideration of the legal platform for the enforcement of the duty to pay in an unsecured credit transaction.

Consider a simple case of an unsecured loan: Bank lends Dana $1,000, which Dana agrees to repay, together with stated interest, in one year. At the end of the year, Dana fails to pay. What can Bank do to recover its claim?

Above all, and particularly when the claim is very small, Bank wishes to avoid incurring the expense and delay inherent in legal proceedings. Accordingly, it strongly prefers to encourage Dana to pay voluntarily. Bank's first approach is likely to be informal. It may write one or more **dunning letters** to Dana, in which it demands payment and threatens suit if payment is not forthcoming immediately. The letter may suggest that failure to pay will adversely affect Dana's ability to obtain credit in the future. It may suggest also that, if Dana cannot make full payment, Bank would be willing to enter into an arrangement for Dana to pay in installments.[1]

It is worth stressing what may not be obvious to everyone: Bank has a right to be paid; however, it has no interest whatsoever in any property that Dana may own. Bank may not send its agents to Dana's house or place of business to take whatever they can find. To collect a claim in this way would be to engage in conduct that is both tortious and criminal. If Dana does not pay voluntarily, Bank is relegated to the judicial process.

Judicial process is commenced commonly by the preparation and filing of a complaint. Bank's lawyers will file a complaint and summons with the clerk of an appropriate court and cause them to be served upon Dana. Dana will have a period of time in which to respond. In many cases of this kind, where the facts are simple and the defenses are likely to be few, the debtor may fail to respond at all. If so, Bank will be able to obtain the entry of a **default judgment** upon an ex parte showing that the debt is owed. If Dana does respond, then the case will proceed through pretrial stages and, if settlement is not forthcoming, to trial and the entry of judgment. The time required to reach entry of judgment depends upon the nature of the process and the amount of "docket delay" in the court's calendar.

Assume that, whether by default or after trial, Bank obtains judgment in the amount of $1,000 plus interest and costs. Dana is now a **judgment debtor**, that is, the court has declared formally that Dana owes the amount of the judgment to Bank. Dana ignores the entry of the judgment and continues to fail to pay. What can Bank do?

A judgment is an adjudication that the judgment debtor owes a particular amount to the **judgment creditor**. It is not a court order requiring the judgment debtor actually to pay. Dana's failure to pay does not constitute an act of contempt of court. Even so, a judgment is not without practical value. Without a judgment, a creditor must rely on persuasion and other informal techniques to induce a debtor to pay. A judgment entitles the judgment creditor in addition to invoke the "long arm of the law" to dispossess the debtor from property (other than

---

1. Rather than attempt to collect the claim itself, Bank may refer the claim to a **collection agency**, which, for a fee, will attempt collection. The collection agency's first approach also is likely to be informal.

Employees of Bank or its collection agency may be tempted to induce Dana to pay by "making an offer you can't refuse." The criminal law, the common law of tort, and federal and state statutes regulating debt collection provide some check against the over-exuberance of those who wish to collect what is due and owing, particularly when the debtor is a consumer. For example, the Fair Debt Collection Practices Act, 15 U.S.C. §§ 1692–1692o, affords remedies to persons who are subjected to harassment, misrepresentations, and certain other unfair practices by collection agencies. Some states have extended similar protection against abuses by creditors themselves, as well as by collection agencies. See, e.g., Wis. Stat. Ann. §§ 427.104, 427.105.

property that is exempt from the reach of creditors[2]) and cause the property to be sold and the proceeds applied toward the satisfaction of the claim.

Courses on creditors' rights provide a detailed examination of the legal process for collection of judgments. For our purposes, the following, highly simplified overview should suffice. Collecting a judgment through the judicial process typically involves two steps. The first is to obtain a **judicial lien** on particular property of the judgment debtor. The second is to turn the lien into cash.[3]

A lien is a property interest of a particular kind. The holder of the lien (the **lienor**) may use the property subject to the lien for only one purpose, to apply toward satisfaction of the debt it secures. Although state laws and procedures governing postjudgment liens vary, generally speaking a judgment creditor acquires a lien in one of two ways. The creditor may obtain from the clerk of the court a **writ of execution**, instructing the sheriff to **levy** upon or attach (seize) goods or other personal property of the judgment debtor located within the sheriff's bailiwick (usually a county). Normally, a judgment creditor's attorneys will have to search for a judgment debtor's property and, when they find some property, inform the sheriff of its whereabouts.[4]

While levy is a suitable means for acquiring a lien upon **tangible** personal property, a different method is necessary when the creditor seeks to acquire a lien on a debtor's **intangible** personal property, which, by its very nature, cannot be seized. A common example of intangible property is a claim against a third party. Suppose, for example, that Bank has reason

2. All states have laws providing that certain property of individuals (as opposed to partnerships or corporations) is **exempt** from the reach of creditors. These laws vary widely: some award liberal **exemptions** and other afford only meager protection. Exempt property typically includes the home, household and personal effects, and tools of the trade. Often, the extent to which property is exempt is limited to a specified dollar amount (e.g., up to $750 in jewelry; up to $10,000 of the value of one's home).

3. Although the following discussion focuses on postjudgment liens, most states make some provision for prejudgment liens under limited circumstances, e.g., upon a showing that the defendant is about to abscond from the jurisdiction or hide property otherwise available to creditors. Many of the restrictions on the availability of prejudgment remedies, including those affording the debtor notice of the exercise of the remedy and an opportunity to be heard, reflect cases decided under the due process clause of the fourteenth amendment. See, e.g., North

Georgia Finishing, Inc. v. Di–Chem, Inc., 419 U.S. 601, 95 S.Ct. 719, 42 L.Ed.2d 751 (1975) (discussing constitutional requirements surrounding prejudgment garnishment of corporate debtor's bank account). See also Note (3) on Wrongful Repossession, Chapter 12, Section 1, infra. Prejudgment liens are similar in many ways to the postjudgment liens discussed below. The principal difference is that the creditor ordinarily cannot cause the former to be turned into cash until judgment is entered against the defendant-debtor.

4. In the majority of states, the creditor acquires an **execution lien** on whatever property the sheriff levies upon before the writ expires. In a minority of states, an **inchoate** execution lien arises on all property of the judgment debtor that is located and that can be found within the bailiwick when the writ is delivered to the sheriff; however, the inchoate lien cannot be enforced against specific property until the sheriff levies upon the property and the lien becomes **consummate**. If the sheriff fails to levy before the writ expires, the inchoate lien is discharged.

to know that Kerry owes Dana $100. Bank could cause the clerk of the court to issue a **writ of garnishment** instructing Kerry to inform the court whether Kerry is indebted to Dana and, if so, for how much. In most jurisdictions, a **garnishment lien** on Kerry's debt to Dana arises when the writ is served upon Kerry.

In most states, a judgment creditor may obtain a **judgment lien** on a debtor's real property by recording a memorandum or abstract of the judgment in the real estate records or (depending on local law) having the court clerk enter the judgment in the docket book. Upon the recordation or docketing, a judgment lien arises on all of the debtor's interests in real property in the county. In only a few states does the judgment lien extend to personal property. See, e.g., Cal. Code Civ. Proc. § 697.530 (judgment lien arises on most nonexempt personal property upon filing a notice with the Secretary of State). Because this book is concerned almost exclusively with personal property, we shall have no more to say about judgment liens.

An execution lien on personal property affords two important advantages to the judgment creditor. First, it provides a means for applying the judgment debtor's property to satisfaction of the judgment. To turn the lien into cash, the judgment creditor usually looks to the sheriff, who sells the property at a **sheriff's sale**.[5] Because the sale usually is poorly advertised (often in a legal newspaper), because a buyer must pay the sales price promptly, because the sheriff makes no warranty of title, and because the judgment debtor is an unwilling seller, the price agreed to be paid at a sheriff's sale rarely, if ever, approaches the price that the property would command in a private sale in the marketplace. The first three reasons also explain why few, if any, buyers appear at the sale other than the judgment creditor. Inasmuch as the judgment creditor is entitled to the proceeds of the sale (less the costs of sale), the judgment creditor need not pay cash. Rather, the creditor may **bid in the judgment**, i.e., reduce the amount of the judgment debt by the amount it agrees to pay for the property. If the judgment creditor is the successful bidder, it becomes the owner of the property and must thereafter retain the property or resell it in a private sale to obtain cash.

An execution lien enables the judgment creditor not only to apply particular property toward the satisfaction of its claim against the debtor but also to reach the property to the exclusion of other, competing creditors who have not obtained liens. Although more than one execution lien may attach to particular property, liens generally rank in temporal order; that is, the holder of the debt secured by the earliest lien (*not* the earliest debt) is entitled to be paid first from the proceeds of the sale of the property. Thus, by winning the "race of diligence" and obtaining a lien on specific assets, Bank generally acquires not only a property interest in those assets but also **priority** over other, subsequently arising liens.

---

5. To turn a garnishment lien into cash, the court will order the **garnishee** (Kerry, in the example above) to pay the debt to Bank, either directly or through a judicial officer.

Any consideration of the judicial collection system should take into account its costs. These include Bank's out-of-pocket expenses as well as the cost of delay. How much would it cost to obtain and collect a judgment against Dana? How long would it take? What risks attend the delay?

All things being equal, Bank would be in a better position if it could acquire a lien without first having to obtain a judgment and invoke the power of the sheriff. At the time Bank extended credit, or at any time thereafter, Bank and Dana could have *agreed* that Bank would have a limited interest in particular property. The nature of this interest could be such that if Dana failed to pay, Bank could cause the property to be sold and apply the proceeds to the satisfaction of its claim without the need to incur the costs and delay attendant to obtaining a judgment and collecting it through the judicial process. When the property concerned is personal property, this kind of **consensual lien**, which arises by the agreement of the parties, is called a **security interest**. (A consensual security interest must be distinguished from a **judicial lien**, which arises through the exercise of judicial process, and a **statutory lien**, which arises by operation of law in favor of certain suppliers of goods and services.) A security interest affords yet another benefit to the holder that a judicial lien does not. Whereas the law governing judicial liens differs from state to state, the law governing security interests, including the rights and duties of the immediate parties (debtor and creditor) and the rights of third parties, is found largely in UCC Article 9. Security interests under UCC Article 9 are the principal focus of Part II Chapters 6 through 12.

SECTION 2.   SELLER'S POWER OVER THE GOODS AS AGAINST BUYER

As described in Section 1, an unsecured lender must resort to the judicial process if the borrower does not repay the loan voluntarily. A seller of goods becomes an unsecured creditor if the seller delivers goods to a buyer in exchange for buyer's promise to pay the price at a later date. Is an unsecured credit seller of goods in any better position with respect collection of the debt that an unsecured lender?

Generally, the answer is "no." Under the UCC, "a 'sale' consists in the passing of title [i.e., a "property" interest] from the seller to the buyer for a price." UCC 2–106(1).[1] For present purposes, the legal significance of having, or not having, title to goods is largely a matter of excluding

---

1. The Uniform Sales Act used the passing of title ("property") as the fulcrum for resolving a number of legal issues that may arise during the performance of sales contracts. The Article 2 rules on performance and remedies are not based on title passing. However, passing of title continues to be of importance to the parties to sales contracts because legal rights and duties not governed by the UCC may turn upon the question of ownership. For example, tax obligations may fall upon the owner of property. In this Section, however, we are concerned primarily with the role of title in resolving conflicting ownership claims to the goods.

ownership claims of other persons to those goods. In general the person with title to goods is entitled to possess, use, or dispose of them.

Title to goods passes under contracts for sale. A "present sale" is a sale "which is accomplished by the making of the contract." Id. Title passes when the contract is made. A contract for sale may also be "a contract to sell goods at a future time." Id. When title passes in a contract to sell goods at a future time is largely within the control of the contracting parties. However, if the parties do not expressly agree otherwise, "title passes to the buyer at the time and place at which the seller completes his performance with respect to the physical delivery of the goods." UCC 2–401(2).

If the seller delivers goods on credit to the buyer and the buyer, having received a conforming tender, fails to pay, the law affords the seller exactly what the seller bargained for: the right to recover the price from the buyer. See UCC 2–709. The seller ordinarily has no right to recover the goods themselves. See generally UCC 2–703.

Suppose that the seller advances the following argument: Buyer promised to pay for the goods and broke that promise. For such a serious (indeed, fundamental) breach I should have a right to **rescind** (undo) the transaction and recover the goods by a possessory remedy, such as **replevin.**[2]

This argument echoes a common misunderstanding. Many people believe that if they don't pay for a good, the seller can "take it back." This argument may be sound in some civil-law legal systems, but it is not supported by the common law. Any attempt by a seller to replevy goods sold on credit would have failed under the English common law, which was codified in the (British) Sale of Goods Act, which in turn was followed in the Uniform Sales Act. The drafters of the UCC did not dream of overturning the basic common-law approach. The catalogue of the seller's remedies in UCC 2–703 does not mention recovery of the goods, and the seller's limited rights to recover goods under UCC 2–507 and UCC 2–702 (discussed below in Section 2(C)) do not extend to the buyer's failure to pay for goods delivered on credit.

Although a credit seller ordinarily may not recover goods delivered to the buyer and must instead enforce the buyer's promise to pay, the following materials suggest that the law does afford to a seller of goods certain rights that a lender does not enjoy.

(A) THE RIGHT TO WITHHOLD DELIVERY

Problem 1.2.1. On January 3, Seller and Buyer entered into a contract for the sale of a garden tractor, which Buyer agreed to pay for and take away by January 30. The agreement specified that "title" passed to

---

2. Replevin, like sequestration and claim and delivery, is a judicial remedy to recover possession of personal property. Replevin statutes are procedural: They do not create the right to possession but rather aid those who are entitled to possession under other law.

Buyer on January 3. On January 30, Buyer demands the tractor but declines to pay. Is Seller justified in denying Buyer possession of "Buyer's" goods? May Seller close out the transaction by reselling "Buyer's" tractor to another customer? See UCC 2–401; UCC 2–511(1); UCC 2–703; UCC 2–706.

Problem 1.2.2. On January 3, Seller and Buyer entered into a contract for the sale of a power lathe. Seller agreed to deliver the lathe on January 30, and Buyer agreed to pay for the lathe within 30 days thereafter. On January 15, Seller received an updated credit report, showing that Buyer recently had become extremely slow in paying its debts. Seller is concerned that Buyer will take delivery and will not pay. What can Seller do? See UCC 2–609; UCC 2–702(1); UCC 1–201(23).

(B) THE RIGHT TO STOP DELIVERY

In many transactions, the seller ships the goods to the buyer on a truck, railroad, or other common carrier. A seller who wishes to prevent the buyer from obtaining the goods from the carrier without first paying for them can structure the transaction accordingly. (One of these structures is discussed briefly in the Introductory Note to Section 5, infra.) Often, however, a seller ships goods to the buyer on **open account**, with the expectation that the buyer will pay for them at a specified time after delivery. What happens under these circumstances if, while the goods are in transit, the seller becomes concerned about the buyer's ability to pay? Who has the better claim to goods in transit, the seller or the buyer? Even if the seller has the better claim, what, if anything, can the seller do to stop the carrier from delivering the goods to the buyer? The following Problem explores these issues.

Problem 1.2.3. A contract for sale between Seller in San Francisco and Buyer in New York called for shipment of a carload of oranges at $12,000, f.o.b. San Francisco. (See UCC 2–319(1)(a).) Terms: Cash 30 days after delivery. Seller shipped oranges in conformity with the contract on a **straight (non-negotiable) bill of lading** (see UCC 1–201(6)) naming Buyer as **consignee** (i.e., as the person to whom delivery is to be made, see UCC 7–403(1), (4)).[3]

After the carload arrives in the New York freight yards but before the oranges are unloaded, Seller learns that Buyer's creditors have begun to obtain judgments against Buyer and judicial liens against Buyer's property.

(a) Has Seller a chance to keep the oranges for itself? See UCC 2–705; UCC 1–201(23); UCC 2–609. (Note the UCC's extension of the grounds for stoppage beyond insolvency, for carload and similarly large shipments.) See also In re National Sugar Refining Co., 27 B.R. 565 (S.D.N.Y.1983) (rejecting, in buyer's bankruptcy, several challenges to seller's rights of stoppage

---

3. "Documents of title," including both negotiable and non-negotiable bills of lading issued by carriers such as railroads and ocean freight companies (see UCC 1–201(15)), are discussed in greater detail in Section 5, infra. For now, try to work your way through the cited UCC provisions as they apply to this Problem.

under UCC 2–702(1) and UCC 2–705(1), but not discussing the significance of the fact that seller held the negotiable bill of lading).

(b) Assume Seller instructs the railroad not to deliver the oranges to Buyer but rather to transport them to Philadelphia.

(i) If the railroad refuses to release the oranges to Buyer, would it be liable for failing to honor the terms of its bill of lading? See UCC 7–403; UCC 7–303.

(ii) Under what circumstances, if any, may the railroad ignore Seller's instructions with impunity? See UCC 2–705; UCC 7–403(1); UCC 7–303. See also Butts v. Glendale Plywood Co., 710 F.2d 504 (9th Cir.1983) (carrier's rerouting of shipment to buyer's buyer, made at buyer's direction while goods still in transit, held to be "reshipment" under UCC 2–705(2)(c)).

Would you advise a seller to ship on credit to a shaky buyer in view of the seller's stoppage rights? Would sellers often hear of insolvency during the time required for shipment? On the other hand, an attorney would probably be liable for malpractice if a client presented the facts in the preceding Problem, and the attorney could think of no course of action other than taking a day or so to research the point.

(C) THE RIGHT TO RECOVER DELIVERED GOODS

Problem 1.2.4. Boris Bilk, who only recently entered business and has no credit history, went to Seller's place of business with a forged letter of introduction. Relying upon the letter, which showed Bilk to be Sterling Worth, a merchant with well-established credit, Seller delivered cotton valued at $100,000 to Bilk on credit. Before payment became due, Seller discovered the fraud and consults you to determine the remedies that might be available. In particular, Seller would prefer not to wait for the outcome of a lawsuit and instead recover the goods immediately (assuming Bilk can be found). What is your advice? See UCC 2–703; UCC 1–103; Note on the Defrauded Seller's Right to Reclaim, infra.

NOTE ON THE DEFRAUDED SELLER'S RIGHT TO RECLAIM

In this area, the drafting style of Article 2 is especially incomplete and allusive. We need to be aware of this approach; one who assumes that the UCC lays down the basic rules on the seller's right to reclaim goods will come to odd and unintended consequences. Indeed, one who searches the UCC for Seller's remedies against Bilk will be disappointed. True, one could not expect a statute on the sale of goods to repeat the general rule of torts allowing Seller to recover damages for deceit. In any event, such an *in personam* claim for damages would be scarcely more useful than Seller's action against Bilk for the price (UCC 2–709). Neither action would be of practical use, since, after the delay involved in obtaining judgment, a sheriff trying to execute on the judgment is not likely to find any substantial assets of someone like Bilk (i.e., Bilk is likely to be or become **judgment proof**).

On the other hand, one might expect that a "Code" on "Sales" would say something about Seller's possessory or *in rem* rights to the goods. May Seller **replevy** the goods from Bilk? If Bilk is hiding the goods, may Seller obtain an equity decree ordering Bilk to return the goods? In more conventional terms, how do we know whether Seller has a *property* remedy to recover the goods?

The drafters of the 1906 Uniform Sales Act and the UCC may well have assumed that "everyone knows" that one who is induced by fraud to enter into a contract may rescind the contract. The drafters may have assumed, as well, that "everyone knows" that one who rescinds for fraud has effective remedies to recover the assets obtained by fraud-by seizure through replevin and, in case of need, by the coercive command of an equity decree. In the dim past, advanced law-school courses (and codifying statutes) could build safely on the students' knowledge of these principles. But today's curriculum seems to pass these principles by.

Moreover, sustained exposure to detailed statutory regimes may foster the impression that if an idea is not set forth in the UCC, then it doesn't exist. This assumption is not only contrary to the UCC (see UCC 1–103) but also dangerous. Important parts of the UCC (especially Article 2) are characterized by provisions addressed to specific problems that had proved troublesome at common law. What one misses is a statement of the basic principles for which the narrow rules provide a fringe or border.

Prior to the UCC, the sharpest controversy over reclamation of goods by the seller grew out of attempts to base reclamation not on overt fraud by the buyer but on an implied false representation of an intent to pay. See Keeton, Fraud—Statements of Intention, 15 Tex. L.Rev. 185 (1937) (decisions in Illinois, Missouri, Indiana, Pennsylvania and Vermont refused to base fraud remedies on such an "implied" misrepresentation). As the following Problem suggests, the drafters of the UCC addressed this controversy directly. (One wonders whether the drafters were so bemused by this vexing question that they failed to set their solution to this narrow question in a wider context. Perhaps that approach to drafting statutes is in the "common-law tradition.")

Problem 1.2.5. Buyer induced Seller to deliver goods on credit by fraudulently promising to pay for them in 30 days. (What is a "fraudulent promise"?) Shortly after delivering the goods, Seller discovered that, when Buyer promised to pay, Buyer was hopelessly insolvent. Seller seeks to recover the goods. May Seller do so? See UCC 2–702(2). What difference, if any, would it make if:

(a) Two months prior to delivery Seller had received Buyer's **financial statement** showing Buyer to be solvent? Would your answer depend on when the sales contract was formed?

(b) Seller had been delivering goods to Buyer for several months; most of Buyer's checks were good, but one or two were dishonored (i.e., "bounced")? See Theo. Hamm Brewing Co. v. First Trust & Savings Bank, 103 Ill.App.2d 190, 242 N.E.2d 911 (1968) (check may constitute representation of solvency if seller relied upon it as such).

(c) Two months prior to delivery Seller had received a report from a credit reporting agency erroneously showing Buyer to be solvent?

Problem 1.2.6. Seller and Buyer made a contract for the sale of a quantity of mink pelts. The contract required Seller to send the pelts to Buyer immediately by air freight and required Buyer to transfer the agreed price of $250,000 to Seller's account in Firstbank before obtaining the pelts from the air carrier. Relying on Buyer's honesty, Seller consigned the goods to Buyer by a straight (non-negotiable) bill of lading, which permitted the air carrier to deliver the goods to Buyer. The shipment arrived in Buyer's city on June 1; on the same day, without paying the price, Buyer took the pelts from the air carrier and placed them in its warehouse. May Seller recover the pelts? See UCC 2–507(2); UCC 2–702(2). Are both provisions applicable to this case? What risks does Seller increase by delay? See Note on the Cash Seller's Right to Reclaim, infra.

Problem 1.2.7. On June 1 Seller and Buyer tentatively agreed on a sale to Buyer of a load of cotton; the price was $4,000. Buyer then said, "I hope you can give me a week to pay." Seller replied, "I'm afraid I'll have to ask for cash." Buyer said, "I'll arrange for my driver to bring my check for the price tomorrow." The next day (June 2) Buyer's driver gave Seller a $4,000 check drawn by Buyer to Seller's order on Firstbank, and removed the cotton. Seller deposited the check in an account with Secondbank. Five days later (June 7) Secondbank notified Seller that Buyer's check had been returned because of insufficient funds. Seller immediately brings a replevin action for the cotton.

(a) What result? See UCC 2–507; UCC 2–511; Problem 1.2.6, supra; Note on the Cash Seller's Right to Reclaim, infra.

(b) Would the result in part (a) change if Seller waits until June 15 to take any action? See UCC 2–507, Comment 3; PEB Commentary No. 1.

NOTE ON THE CASH SELLER'S RIGHT TO RECLAIM

UCC 2–507(2) deals with transactions in which sellers have not agreed to extend credit. By custom, these transactions are called "cash sales," and the sellers are called "cash sellers." In these transactions, "tender of payment is a condition to the seller's duty to tender and complete any delivery." UCC 2–511(1). What relief, if any, is available to a cash seller who has delivered the goods but has not received the price?

In stark contrast to UCC 2–702(2), which expressly grants a credit seller the right to reclaim goods under certain circumstances, UCC 2–507(2) refers cryptically to the buyer's "right as against the [cash] seller to retain or dispose of" the goods as being "conditional upon his making the payment due."[4] Nevertheless, courts routinely have concluded that the unpaid cash seller enjoys a right to reclaim goods from the buyer. One court has referred to the cash seller's reclamation right as "judicially-confected." In re Samuels & Co., 526 F.2d 1238 (5th Cir.) (en banc), cert. denied 429 U.S. 834, 97 S.Ct. 98, 50 L.Ed.2d 99 (1976). Is this a fair characterization? Can you articulate a statutory basis for the cash seller's reclamation right? Does it help to characterize reclamation as a remedy for enforcing a statutory right to possession of the goods? Is the fact that the seller enjoyed such a right under pre-UCC law relevant?

Assuming that the UCC affords a reclamation right to cash sellers, does it also impose a time limit on the exercise of that right? From the 1951 Official Text of the UCC until 1990, Comment 3 to UCC 2–507 provided that "[t]he provision of this Article for a ten-day limit within which the seller may reclaim goods delivered on credit to an insolvent buyer is also applicable here." The UCC itself, however, imposed no such limitation.

The time limit, if any, for reclamation under UCC 2–507 has been litigated most often under facts like the following: Buyer and Seller agree for payment on delivery. Buyer tenders its check (see UCC 2–511(2)), which Seller deposits and Buyer's bank dishonors ("bounces"). Having not received payment (see UCC 2–511(3)), Seller seeks to reclaim the goods. Seller fails to demand their return within ten days after their delivery to Buyer, perhaps because Seller did not learn of the dishonor within that time.

Some courts followed Comment 3 and permitted a seller to reclaim only when demand was made within the ten-day period. See, e.g., Szabo v. Vinton Motors, 630 F.2d 1 (1st Cir.1980) ("Comment 3 does not contradict, but merely complements and explains the Code."). Others, observing that the text of the UCC itself contains no time limit, refused to apply the limit contained in the Comment. See, e.g., Burk v. Emmick, 637 F.2d 1172 (8th Cir.1980) ("the only limitation imposed upon the seller's [reclamation] right is a reasonableness requirement").

All probably would agree that even a seller who exchanges goods for an **NSF check** (drawn on insufficient funds) or who is the victim of active fraud should not have an unlimited time for reclamation. One way to fill gaps in the UCC is to extend other UCC provisions by analogy. If rules of limited scope (e.g., the time limits in UCC 2–702(2)) are to be extended by analogy, surely one should use the provision that is most analogous to the problem posed by the gap in the UCC. Dealing with the gap in UCC 2–507 by analogical extension of the time limits in UCC 2–702 leads to these questions: (a) Under UCC 2–702(2) is the ten-day rule applicable to all reclamations? (Suppose the buyer gave the seller a written misrepresentation of solvency.) (b) Is a seller who agrees to deliver only for cash and

---

4. Originally drafted in the 1940's and 1950's, the UCC follows then-prevailing English usage and utilizes the masculine pronoun to signify antecedents of indefinite gender. See UCC 1–102(5)(b). Recent revisions to articles of the UCC have taken account of changes in English usage and no longer follow this practice (although the style persists in Articles 1, 2, and 7).

exchanges the goods for a worthless check more comparable to (i) a seller who delivers to a buyer who proves to be insolvent or (ii) a seller who delivers to a buyer who has made a written misrepresentation of solvency?

Another approach to gap-filling, suggested by UCC 1–103, is to turn to the common-law rule. At common law an attempt to reclaim after excessive delay would be defeated by doctrines such as waiver, estoppel, or ratification of the buyer's property interest. See, e.g., Frech v. Lewis, 218 Pa. 141, 67 A. 45 (1907). The PEB adopted this approach in PEB Commentary No. 1 and it revised Comment 3 to UCC 2–507 accordingly. Is the revised comment any more or less binding on a court than the original Comment?

Problem 1.2.8. Buyer acquired goods under circumstances giving Seller a right to reclaim. Before Seller could exercise its rights, Buyer resold the goods to Purchaser, who took delivery in good faith and without notice of Seller's rights. Buyer extended credit to Purchaser, who has not yet paid Buyer. Assume for now that Purchaser cuts off Seller's property right in the goods. (Purchaser's rights are discussed in Section 3, which follows.) Does Seller's property (reclamation) right against the goods shift to the property received by Buyer upon resale of the goods—Buyer's claim against Purchaser for the price? (Although it is intangible, a right to payment is property and can be transferred.)

Neither UCC 2–507 nor UCC 2–702 refers to a seller's claim against what the buyer receives upon disposition of the goods (the **proceeds** of the goods). Does the absence of a statutory reference to proceeds necessarily mean that Seller has no claim to them? Or, should a court validate such a claim by reference to the common law or by analogy? The cases are divided, but the majority do not permit sellers with reclamation rights to reach proceeds. Compare, e.g., United States v. Westside Bank, 732 F.2d 1258 (5th Cir.1984) (credit seller who complies with all the requirements of UCC 2–702 retains claim against traceable proceeds from the sale of the goods) with, e.g., In re Coast Trading Co., Inc., 744 F.2d 686 (9th Cir.1984) (UCC 2–702 does not in and of itself create a right to reclaim proceeds). The Article 2 Study Group's "tentative conclusion is that a reclaiming seller should not have a right to proceeds." PEB Article 2 Report 200. Do you agree?

SECTION 3.   SELLER'S POWER OVER THE GOODS AS AGAINST THIRD PARTIES

The Problems in Section 2, supra, deal with the seller's power over goods when only two parties (Seller and Buyer) are involved. Often, however, a third party claims an interest in the goods. This third party may claim an interest through Seller (e.g., one of Seller's creditors may levy upon the goods while they are in transit) or through Buyer (e.g., Buyer may contract to resell the goods, as in Problem 1.2.8, supra). The rights of secured creditors of Seller are discussed below in Chapter 7, Section 6(B). This Section discusses the rights of those who claim through Buyer.

(A) Transfer of Interests in Goods: The Basic Rules

Introductory Note. A paradigmatic sequence of events, which we shall see recur in various settings, is as follows: A is the owner of goods. B acquires the goods under circumstances that give A the right to recover the goods from B. B, voluntarily (e.g., by sale or by grant of a security interest) or involuntarily (e.g., by sheriff's levy), purports to transfer an interest in the goods to C. A seeks to recover the goods from C, or to hold C liable for **conversion**.[1]

For such cases, the traditional rule is this: B can convey to C, and C can acquire from B, whatever rights B had in the goods.[2] Two different, but interrelated, ideas are packed into this rule. First, the rule enables B to dispose of any and all rights that B has. Thus, if B acquires goods free and clear of all third-party claims, B will be able to convey the goods to C free and clear. Were the rule otherwise, the value of the goods to B would be substantially reduced in many cases. When the rule is applied to enable C to defeat a third party's claim on the ground that B could have done so, it sometimes is referred to as a "shelter" or "umbrella" rule.

The second idea is that B cannot transfer any greater rights than B has; that is, B may convey whatever rights B has and no more. This aspect of the rule, which sometimes is referred to by the Latin phrase *nemo dat quod non habet* (one cannot give what one does not have), appears to flow from the broader principle that, in a regime of private property, the law should keep property rights secure.[3] Security of property means that a person may not be deprived of property rights without the person's consent. It means, for example, that a thief cannot transfer the real owner's property interest to a third party. A rule of law contrary to *nemo dat*, one that would enable a person to convey rights that the person did not have, would enable the person to deprive another person of the other's rights and would violate the security of property principle.

The security of property principle is far from ironclad; in fact, the law often enables a person to convey greater rights to personal property than the person has. Because those to whom the law affords greater rights than their transferors had often are good faith purchasers for value, the exceptions to *nemo dat* often are termed "good-faith-purchase" rules. As you

1. The Restatement (Second) of Torts defines conversion of personal property as "an intentional exercise of dominion or control over a chattel which so seriously interferes with the right of another to control it that the actor may justly be required to pay the other the full value of the chattel." Restatement (Second) of Torts § 222–A(1) (1965). As with A's replevin suit to recover the cotton, C will be liable to A in conversion only if A's right to control the cotton is paramount to C's right.

2. The principle that the transferee of property acquires all rights that the transferor had applies not only to goods (see UCC 2–403(1) (1st sentence)) but also to negotiable instruments (see UCC 3–203(b)), documents of title (see UCC 7–504(1)), and investment securities (see UCC 8–302(a)). The conveyancing rules governing negotiable instruments and securities are discussed in Section 4, infra; those governing documents of title, in Section 5.

3. For this reason, sometimes the principle is referred to as "security of property."

work through the following materials, try to articulate the reasons underlying the various good-faith-purchase rules and to assess the validity of those reasons. You may also wish to consider whether *nemo dat* no longer is the baseline rule but rather has become the exception.

Before turning to the primary focus of this Section—the rights of a reclaiming seller (*A*) against a person (*C*) who claims through the buyer (*B*)—we examine the application of the basic rules in another setting.

Problem 1.3.1. *A*'s bales of cotton worth $5,000 were stored in *A*'s warehouse. *B* broke into the warehouse and stole the cotton. *B* resold the cotton to *C*, who paid B $5,000, not suspecting the cotton was stolen.

(a) *C* is in possession of the cotton. *A* brings a replevin action against *C*. What result? See UCC 2–403; Note (2) on the Basic Conveyancing Rules, infra.

(b) Assume that *C*, before learning of *A*'s interest resold the cotton to *D*. Does *A* have a cause of action against *C*? On what theory?

(c) Does *A* have any rights against *D*?

(d) If *A* recovers from *D*, does *D* have a right of recourse against *C*? See UCC 2–312; Note (6) on the Basic Conveyancing Rules, infra.

(e) Might *A* prejudice its rights against *C* or *D* by obtaining a judgment against *B* that (as normally would be the case) turns out to be uncollectible? See Linwood Harvestore, Inc. v. Cannon, 427 Pa. 434, 235 A.2d 377 (1967) (owner's (*A*'s) obtaining judgment against converter (*B*) changes balance of equities between *A* and purchaser *C*; balance never swings to *C* if *C* does not act in good faith; case remanded for determination of *C*'s knowledge of *A*'s claim to goods).

Problem 1.3.2. *B*, who only recently entered business and has no credit history, went to *A*'s place of business with a forged letter of introduction. Relying upon the letter, which showed *B* to be Sterling Worth, a merchant with well-established credit, *A* delivered cotton valued at $100,000 to *B* on credit. (These are the facts of Problem 1.2.4, supra.) *B* resold the cotton to *C*, who paid $100,000 for it and took delivery, not suspecting the fraud. *A* sues *C* to replevy the cotton.

(a) What result? See UCC 2–403; Note (2) on the Basic Conveyancing Rules, infra. What result if *A* sues *C* in conversion?

(b) Would any of the following make any difference?

(i) *C* is in business.

(ii) *C* is in the cotton business.

(iii) *C* is a cotton dealer who never dealt with *B* previously and took no measures to check on *B*'s background. (It is customary for cotton dealers in the area to purchase only from growers or from other dealers whom they know.)

See UCC 1–201(19); UCC 2–103(1)(b); UCC 2–104(1).

(c) What result if C had paid B only $60,000? Cf., e.g., Funding Consultants, Inc. v. Aetna Casualty and Surety Co., 187 Conn. 637, 447 A.2d 1163 (1982) (trier of fact may reasonably consider whether an instrument was purchased in good faith if a party pays an amount considerably less than face value).

(d) Would it make any difference if C had promised to pay $100,000 but has not yet paid anything? See UCC 1–201(44). Under these circumstances, should the law award the goods to a person who has not paid for them? Does this transaction pose the same risks to C as does C's payment of cash to B? Does this transaction jeopardize A's interests as much as C's payment of cash? Consider the possibility of an equity action by A against B and C, invoking the doctrine that A can follow its property interest in the cotton into its proceeds. Recall Problem 1.2.8, supra. (Do not confuse this *in rem* action with A's garnishment of C's debt to B to satisfy an *in personam* claim or judgment. In garnishment, A may need first to obtain a judgment against B; in any event, A's garnishment may be subordinate to earlier garnishments by B's other creditors, who, in this setting, are likely to be numerous and hungry.)

(e) Would it make any difference if C paid B $100,000 but had not yet taken delivery when A notified C of the fraud? See Note (7) on the Basic Conveyancing Rules, infra.

NOTES ON THE BASIC CONVEYANCING RULES

(1) Crimes and Torts. Owners of property may be deprived of possession by theft or fraud. This violates the basic principle that owners should be secure in control and use of their property. This principle of security of property overlaps sales law only partially. Thieves are not buyers. In criminal law, they commit larceny, robbery, and burglary. Sales law is not germane to the legal relationship between thief and victim. Sales law has more overlap with the law of fraudulent transactions. Fraudulent misstatements can induce owners to enter into sales contracts whereby the owners surrender possession of their goods to "buyers" who do not pay the contract price and have no intention to pay it.

The most practical form of relief for victims of these crimes or fraud is to recover their property. The law permits rightful owners specific relief, usually in the form of an action for replevin, that will result in restoration of the goods to the rightful owners if the goods are found in the possession of the wrongdoers. Theoretically, tort victims have claims for damages under the tort theory of conversion; moreover, defrauded owners could "ratify" the fraud-tainted transactions and sue the cheats for the agreed price. Collecting money judgments in these circumstances is highly unlikely.[4]

---

4. Criminal law has been reformed in recent years to increase victims' rights. One aspect of this reform has been to order restitution and reparation as a part of offenders' sentences.

(2) Void Title and Voidable Title. The first sentence of UCC 2–403(1), which embodies the *nemo dat* principle, takes one only so far. To determine what the purchaser *(C)* acquires, one needs to know what rights the transferor *(B)* has or has power to convey. What rights does a thief have? The traditional rule, which still is dominant in Anglo–American law, is that a thief has no rights or "void title."

The "void title" of a thief is to be distinguished from the "voidable title" referred to in the second sentence of UCC 2–403(1). The seminal case in the voidable title area is the English case of Parker v. Patrick, 101 Eng. Rep. 99 (1793), which was followed in Mowrey v. Walsh, 8 Cow. 238 (N.Y.Sup.Ct.1828). The latter posed the question: "where the goods are obtained by fraud from the true owner [A], and fairly purchased of, and the price paid to the fraudulent vendee [B], without notice, by a stranger [C], which is to sustain the loss, the owner or the stranger?" The court's answer: "the innocent purchaser for valuable consideration must be protected." The only reason mentioned by the New York court for distinguishing fraud from theft was the one given by the English court in its one sentence, per curiam opinion-the existence of a statute as to theft. By the time of White v. Garden, 10 Common Bench, 919, 138 Eng. Rep. 364 (Q.B. 1851), however, doctrine had developed to the point that the court could write that where fraud was involved, "the transaction is not absolutely void, except at the option of the seller; that he may elect to treat it as a contract, and he must do the contrary before the buyer has acted as if it were such, and re-sold the goods to a third party."

Professor Gilmore's summary of the historical development deserves an extended quotation:

> The initial common law position was that equities of ownership are to be protected at all costs: an owner may never be deprived of his property rights without his consent. That worked well enough against a background of local distribution where seller and buyer met face to face and exchanged goods for cash. But as the marketplace became first regional and then national, a recurrent situation came to be the misappropriation of goods by a faithless agent in fraud of his principal. Classical theory required that the principal be protected and that the risks of agency distribution be cast on the purchaser. The market demanded otherwise.

> The first significant breach in common law property theory was the protection of purchasers from such commercial agents. The reform was carried out through so-called Factor's Acts, which were widely enacted in the early part of the 19th century. Under these Acts any person who entrusted goods to a factor—or agent—for sale took the risk of the factor's selling them beyond his authority; anyone buying from a factor in good faith, relying on his possession of the goods, and without notice of the limitations on his authority, took good title against the true owner. In time the Acts were expanded to protect people, i.e., banks, who took goods from a factor as security for loans made to the factor to be used in operating the factor's own business. The Factor's Acts, as

much in derogation of the common law as it is possible for a statute to be, were restrictively construed and consequently turned out to be considerably less than the full grant of mercantile liberty which they had first appeared to be. Other developments in the law gradually took the pressure off the Factor's Acts, which came to be confined to the narrow area of sales through commission merchants, mostly in agricultural produce markets.

Even while they were cutting the heart out of the Factor's Acts, the courts were finding new ways to shift distribution risks. Their happiest discovery was the concept of "voidable title"—a vague idea, never defined and perhaps incapable of definition, whose greatest virtue, as a principle of growth, may well have been its shapeless imprecision of outline. The polar extremes of theory were these: if B buys goods from A, he gets A's title and can transfer it to any subsequent purchaser; if B steals goods from A, he gets no title and can transfer none to any subsequent purchaser, no matter how clear the purchaser's good faith. "Voidable title" in B came in as an intermediate term between the two extremes: if B gets possession of A's goods by fraud, even though he has no right to retain them against A, he does have the power to transfer title to a good faith purchaser.

The ingenious distinction between "no title" in B (therefore true owner prevails over good faith purchaser) and "voidable title" in B (therefore true owner loses to good faith purchaser) made it possible to throw the risk on the true owner in the typical commercial situation while protecting him in the noncommercial one. Since the law purported to be a deduction from basic premises, logic prevailed in some details to the detriment of mercantile need, but on the whole voidable title proved a useful touchstone.

The contrasting treatment given to sales on credit and sales for cash shows the inarticulate development of the commercial principle. When goods are delivered on credit, the seller becomes merely a creditor for the price: on default he has no right against the goods. But when the delivery is induced by buyer's fraud—buyer being unable to pay or having no intention of paying—the seller, if he acts promptly after discovering the facts, may replevy from the buyer or reclaim from buyer's trustee in bankruptcy. The seller may not, however, move against purchasers from the buyer, and the term "purchaser" includes lenders who have made advances on the security of the goods. By his fraudulent acquisition the buyer has obtained voidable title and purchasers from him are protected.

Gilmore, The Commercial Doctrine of Good Faith Purchase, 63 Yale L.J. 1057, 1057–60 (1954).

Why do you suppose the UCC neither explains that a thief has void title nor sets forth a definition of voidable title? Perhaps the drafters thought that their project—codifying the law of sales—did not require codification of all the basic common-law rules of personal property conveyancing. Even if so, it remains puzzling that Article 2 contains some of the "building block" rules (e.g., the "shelter" principle in the first sentence of UCC 2–403(1)) but not others. Should Article 2 be revised to set forth basic conveyancing rules?

(3) Conflicting Rules on Good Faith Purchase: Unification. Consider the observations of the Ontario Law Reform Commission:

> It is necessary in every legal system to reconcile the conflict that arises when a seller purports to transfer title of goods that he does not own, or that are subject to an undisclosed security interest, to a person who buys them in good faith and without notice of the defect in title. The alternative means of resolving this conflict are usually stated in terms of a policy favouring security of ownership, as opposed to a policy that favours the safety of commercial transactions. Few, if indeed any, legal systems have committed themselves fully to the adoption of one or the other solution. Between these extremes there lies a, range of compromise solutions that depend on the nature of the goods, the persons involved, and the type of transaction.

2 Ontario Law Reform Commission, Report on Sale of Goods 283 (1979).

As we have seen, the common law begins with the principle that a buyer acquires no better title to goods than the seller had. To this principle the common law admits a number of exceptions, the most significant of which has been the doctrine of voidable title for cases of fraud. English law makes another exception to the principle of *nemo dat* by protecting the good faith purchaser of stolen goods where the goods "are sold in market overt according to the usage of the market." (British) Sale of Goods Act § 22(1). The doctrine of market overt was not "received" in the United States as a part of the common law, see 2 Williston, Sales § 347 (1948), but UCC 2–403(2) and (3) represent a modest step in this direction. See Section 3(C), infra.

The civil law (including the law of France and Germany) begins with a very different principle under which the good faith purchaser of goods generally is protected against the original owner, a principle expressed in the phrase *possession vaut titre* (possession is the equivalent of title). Civil law systems therefore have no need for a doctrine of voidable title for cases of fraud. But many such systems make an exception for cases of theft, allowing the original owner of stolen goods to reclaim them from a good faith purchaser within a statutory period. Some of these systems, however, require the good faith purchaser who has acquired stolen goods at a fair or a market or from a merchant who deals in similar goods to return the goods to the original owner only on reimbursement of the purchase price. This rule has particular significance when the goods have special value to the true owner or when the purchaser has "snapped up" the goods at a cheap price but the true owner has difficulty proving that the purchaser did not act in good faith. Cf. Brown & Root, Inc. v. Ring Power Corp., 450 So.2d 1245 (Fla.App.1984) (the court refused to follow usual choice-of-law rules that called for applying the Louisiana civil law rule requiring the reclaiming owner to reimburse the price paid by the buyer of stolen goods;

the court concluded that the civil law rule "contravenes a positive policy of the law of Florida").

What accounts for the variety of approaches to the universal problem raised by good faith purchasers of stolen property? One author links the variety to "the difficulty of discerning the best solution to a hard question. Societies may share the goal of minimizing the costs associated with the theft of property but may disagree over the way to achieve this goal." Levmore, Variety and Uniformity in the Treatment of the Good–Faith Purchaser, 16 J. Legal Stud. 43, 45 (1987). In this regard, consider Problem 1.3.1, supra. As between the two innocent parties, A and C, the more efficient rule would allocate the loss to the party who could have avoided the loss at lower cost. Who is that party? Is it less costly for A to protect the goods from theft (e.g., by hiring more guards or building a stronger fence) than for C to protect itself from acquiring stolen goods (e.g., by investigating the circumstances under which B acquired the goods)?

Although the lower-cost loss avoidance analysis projects an aura of simplicity, its application can be enormously difficult. A complete analysis would take into account not only the costs of preventing the loss but also a variety of other costs, including the costs to A (the owner) and C (the good faith purchaser) of insuring against the loss and the litigation costs attendant to determining the foregoing costs. And even when efficiency analysis can be applied with some degree of assurance, other normative concerns may override it. Judge Posner, for example, assumes that A would be the lower-cost loss avoider, but he explains that A is the winner under current law (in the U.S.) because allowing C to win would encourage theft and "[w]e do not want an efficient market in stolen goods." R. Posner, Economic Analysis of Law 91 (5th ed. 1998). See also Weinberg, Sales Law, Economics, and the Negotiability of Goods, 9 J. Legal Stud. 569, 592 (1980) (concluding that the "efficiency criterion has proved useful in explaining the pattern of protection for legally innocent purchasers of goods that exists under American law," but recognizing that other issues, such as "costs of a rule change" and "public and private costs of alternative regimes," should be considered before deciding to change the legal rules).

International traffic in ill-gotten goods, like other types of international trade, seems to be accelerating; even the newspapers report on international traffic in stolen paintings and other art objects. A 1986 article contained an estimate that "around $1 billion a year in cultural property is stolen from around the world." N.Y. Times, October 19, 1986, at C25. More recently, heightened concerns have been expressed about stolen goods that are important cultural property.

> You will recall that in my acceptance speech before this august body on 14 September, I stated that the horrors of slavery and destruction wrought upon Africa and its peoples could not be forgotten. ... I also pointed out that ... mutual affirmation would, however, never be complete unless Africa's sacred relics, icons, artworks and other priceless cultural objects were returned—lock, stock and barrel—to the rightful owners. Moreover, I expressed Africa's collective sadness and

anguish in seeing that these stolen African treasures adorn public museums, libraries, art galleries and private homes in foreign lands, and insisted that they must come home to assuage the pain and anger in the hearts of the succeeding generations of Africans. It is a moral problem of heart and soul and of conscience. What I stated then about the return of priceless African art and icons is equally applicable to the cultural treasures illegally exported from other countries throughout the centuries. It is time to return them.

Remarks of Theo–Ben Gurirab, President of the United Nations General Assembly, during a debate on the return of cultural property on December 7, 1999. M2 Presswire (Dec. 8, 2000). And recent years have seen increased attention given to artwork that may have been looted in Europe immediately prior to and during World War II.

On February 29, 2000, Britain's art museums and galleries released a list of more than 350 works of art that have ambiguous provenances for the period around World War II and may have been seized by the Nazis. The list comes from 10 major institutions across Britain....

According to Sir Nicholas Serota, the chairman of the National Museum Directors' Conference, which prepared the report, no factual evidence exists that any of the works had been stolen by the Nazis before they came to Britain after the war. However, Serota said the institutions were eager to solve the mystery of where the pieces had been and who had owned them from 1933 to 1945, when the Nazis seized the leading art in Europe.

Serota announced that the British institutions want to share the information with their colleagues, nationally and internationally. ...

16 Int'l Enforcement L. Rep. 709 (2000).

The variations in national rules, and the difficulty of determining which law governs, have led to efforts at international unification of the law governing the rights of owners of stolen goods. See International Institute for the Unification of Private Law (UNIDROIT), Draft Uniform Law on the Protection of the Bona Fide Purchaser of Corporeal Movables with Explanatory Report (1968). The Report contains (pp. 5–11) a helpful review of the varying national rules in the field. Article 10(2) of the Draft adopted the principle of *possession vaut titre* in the case of stolen goods that were bought in good faith "under normal conditions from a dealer who usually sells goods of the same kind." A committee of governmental experts studied this draft and prepared a 1974 revision, which receded from this extreme position because a majority feared that it might encourage trafficking in stolen goods, particularly works of art. The revised text therefore provides that the "transferee of stolen moveables cannot invoke his good faith." Uniform Law on the Acquisition in Good Faith of Corporeal Moveables art. 11, in Uniform Law Review (UNIDROIT), No. I, p. 79 (1975). The draft Uniform International Law was prepared on the assumption that it would be submitted to a diplomatic conference and the final text submitted to governments for ratification, but the diplomatic conference never was held.

UNIDROIT has prepared another convention relating to stolen goods. See UNIDROIT Convention on Stolen or Illegally Exported Cultural Objects (1995). Article 2 of the convention defines "cultural objects" as "those which, on religious or secular grounds, are of importance for archaeology, prehistory, history, literature, art or science" and which fall within one of 12 categories, including products of archaeological excavations, antiquities more than one hundred years old, property of artistic interest, and rare specimens of fauna, flora, minerals, and anatomy. Although more limited in scope, the new effort has been somewhat better received than the earlier draft uniform law. As of April 20, 2000, it had entered into force among 12 nations. See http://www.unidroit.org/english/implement/i-95.htm (visited August 30, 2000).

Even within a given legal system, efforts have been made to adjust the tension between *nemo dat* and *possession vaut titre*. See, e.g., (English) Law Reform Committee, Twelfth Report (Transfer of Title to Chattels) Cmnd. 2958 (1966); Ontario Law Reform Commission, Report on Sale of Goods (1979). The major recommendations of each of these reports have yet to be enacted. The PEB Article 2 Report did not address these issues.

CISG Article 4(b) declares that the Convention "is not concerned with the effect which the contract may have on the property in the goods sold." Given CISG 4(b)'s disclaimer of concern with property rights in the goods even between sellers and buyers, not surprisingly the CISG has no provision on the property or ownership rights of third parties. When these issues arise in relation to sales transactions otherwise governed by CISG, what law would apply to resolve conflicting claims to the goods?

(4) Adverse Possession; Statute of Limitations. Under adverse possession doctrine, a possessor who has actual, exclusive, open, notorious, continuous, and hostile possession of land under a claim of right for a statutory period can take good title and defeat the original owner's claim. After 1870, a number of courts applied the doctrine to cases involving stolen horses and farm animals. Later cases applied the doctrine to manufactured goods, such as a piano, violin or typewriter. See P. Gerstenblith, The Adverse Possession of Personal Property, 37 Buff. L. Rev. 119 (1988).

Understandably, it generally is very difficult to locate stolen goods. Even when they are found, a considerable time may have elapsed since the theft occurred. For this reason, other courts have sought to resolve the timeliness of property claims of aggrieved owners against innocent possessors by using conventional statutes of limitations principles. The owners' claims are cut off after the passage of a statutory period. When is the original owner of stolen goods barred by the statute of limitations from reclaiming them? The few reported cases reflect a variety of views.

Rejecting the view of the Appellate Division, based on New Jersey precedents, "that an action might have accrued more than six years before the date of suit if possession by the defendant or his predecessors satisfied the elements of adverse possession," the New Jersey Supreme Court applied a discovery rule, under which a cause of action accrues when the owner "first knew, or reasonably should have known through the exercise of due diligence, of the cause of action, including the identity of the possessor of the paintings." O'Keeffe v. Snyder, 83 N.J. 478, 416 A.2d 862 (1980) (concerning an action brought in 1976 by the noted artist Georgia O'Keeffe to replevy from a Princeton art gallery three of her pictures that allegedly had been stolen in 1946 from a New York art gallery). The court also concluded that subsequent transfer of the stolen property did not constitute "separate acts of conversion that would start the statute of limitations running anew." The court recognized, however, that "subsequent transfers ... may affect the degree of difficulty encountered by a diligent owner seeking to recover his goods. To that extent, subsequent transfers and their potential for frustrating diligence are relevant in applying the discovery rule."

A vigorous dissent argued that the majority opinion placed too heavy a burden on the original owner and that "by making it relatively more easy for the receiver or possessor of an artwork with a 'checkered background' to gain security and title than for the artist or true owner to reacquire it, it seems as though the Court surely will stimulate and legitimize art thievery." After remand by the Supreme Court but before trial, the case was settled.

For a fascinating case involving an international controversy over the ownership of two paintings by Albrecht Dürer that had disappeared from Germany after the Second World War (the "discovery of the century," according to an official of the Metropolitan Museum of Art), see Kunstsammlungen Zu Weimar v. Elicofon, 678 F.2d 1150 (2d Cir.1982). The court applied New York law, under which "an innocent purchaser of stolen goods becomes a wrongdoer only after refusing the owner's demand for their return." Where, as under New York law, "the demand requirement is *substantive,* that is, where a demand and refusal are requisite elements of the cause of action, it accrues and the statute of limitation begins to run only after such demand and refusal."

The court rejected the contention that the rule treats good faith purchasers as worse than thieves "since for a thief the statute of limitations begins to run immediately upon the theft while a *bona fide* purchaser must wait, possibly indefinitely, for a demand from the owner." The court thought that "familiar principles of equitable estoppel will prevent a wrongdoer from asserting the statute of limitations defense" and, in any case, "we are charged only with applying New York law, not with remaking or improving it."

The New York Court of Appeals confirmed this aspect of New York law in Solomon R. Guggenheim Foundation v. Lubell, 77 N.Y.2d 311, 567 N.Y.S.2d 623, 569 N.E.2d 426 (1991). This case can be understood as adopting a third approach—resolving property claims by examining the relative blameworthiness of the two contesting parties. The court rejected the argument that a true owner's failure to exercise due diligence should cause the statute of limitations to begin running before the owner makes a demand for return of stolen goods from a good faith purchaser. However, the court acknowledged that the issue of diligence could be considered in connection with the defense of laches raised by the good faith purchaser.

A recent law review note challenged the conventional wisdom with respect to fine art, one kind of personal property that is likely to be the subject of litigation many years after thefts. Observing the advent of computer networks and high-quality digitized color imaging that have made possible the recent creation of an international theft registry, the author concludes that adverse possession and multi-factor balancing tests are no longer suited to the realm of such movable and concealable personal property and that these tests hurt diligent owners who have reported thefts but have been unable to find their property. The author advanced this thesis: Victims of art thefts who promptly report the thefts to the police and to an international theft database should never be legally barred from recovering their property, inasmuch as buyers, for a small fee, can search the registry. S. Bibas, The Case Against Statutes of Limitations for Stolen Art, 103 Yale L.J. 2437 (1994).

(5) Good Faith Purchase and Notice or Knowledge of Conflicting Claims. UCC 1–201(19) defines "good faith" as "honesty in fact." UCC 2–103(1)(b) provides a narrower definition in the case of a merchant: "honesty in fact and the observance of reasonable commercial standards of fair dealing in the trade." See also UCC 3–103(a)(4); UCC 4–104(c); UCC 4A–105(a)(6); R9–102(a)(43) (good faith definitions similar to UCC 2–103(1)(b)). Both formulations of good faith are silent concerning the effect of *C*'s (a putative good faith purchaser from *B)* knowledge or notice of *A*'s claim to the goods (e.g., that *B* had only voidable title). Despite this silence, no one would doubt that *C* would not have acted in good faith if it purchased goods with actual knowledge of *B's* fraud. Aside from the relatively easy case of actual knowledge, however, there is a wide range of possible application of the "good faith" requirement, depending on the facts. Of what relevance is the fact that purchasers under other UCC articles must act not only in good faith but also without notice of claims in order to benefit from good-faith purchase rules? See UCC 3–302(a)(2)(ii) and (v); UCC 7–501(4); UCC 8–303(a)(2); F9–206(1); R9–403(b)(3). Of what relevance is the pre-UCC law? "Both case law and commentators agree that subjective knowledge of the original seller's claim was not necessary to disqualify a purchaser from the protection of the voidable-title or estoppel concepts. Reason to know or circumstances that would put a reasonable man on inquiry were, sufficient." McDonnell, The Floating Lienor as Good Faith Purchaser, 50 S.Cal.L.Rev. 429, 442 (1977).

For a case applying the UCC 2–103(1)(b) "merchant" standard of good faith in this context, see Johnson & Johnson Products, Inc. v. Dal International Trading Co., 798 F.2d 100 (3d Cir.1986). In that case the court "predict[ed] that the New Jersey Supreme Court would not impose [on a buyer] a duty to inquire ... into the chain of title of gray market goods." (Gray market goods are goods legitimately manufactured and sold abroad under a trademark and imported for sale in competition with goods sold by the American owner of an identical trademark.) The court apparently ignored the possibility that "reasonable commercial standards of fair dealing in the trade" may have required an inquiry by the buyer. See UCC 2–103(1)(b).

(6) Warranty of Title. Assume that *C* must return the goods to *A* either because *C*'s seller, the wrongdoing *B*, stole the goods from *A* or because *B* defrauded *A* and *C* fails to qualify as a good faith purchaser for value. Does *C* have a claim against *B*? UCC 2–312(1) provides an affirmative answer in most cases: "there is in a contract for sale a warranty by the seller that ... the title conveyed shall be good, and its transfer rightful." An exception in UCC 2–312(2) provides that the warranty of title can be "excluded or modified only by specific language or by circumstances which give the buyer reason to know that the person selling does not claim title in himself or that he is purporting to sell only such right or title as he or a third person may have." One easily can imagine a case in which *C*'s actual knowledge of *B's* theft or fraud would constitute "circumstances" that would exclude *B's* warranty of title; however, in many other cases in which *B* has void or voidable title, *C* would have a valid warranty claim. Whether *B* can be found and the warranty claim turned into cash is, of course, another (not insignificant) matter. Chapter 3, Section 1, infra, addresses warranty of title in detail.

(7) Delivery and Bona Fide Purchase. The role of delivery in good faith purchase presents an awkward, unsolved problem under Article 2 of the UCC. As we shall see in Section 6(B), similar problems arise under Article 9. In contrast, Articles 3, 7, and 8 face the issue. Articles 3 and 7 confer protection on the "holder" of instruments and documents, which UCC 1–201(20) defines as a person "in possession." See UCC 3–305 (defenses); UCC 3–306 (claims); UCC 7–502.[5] Article 8 makes clear when possession of an investment security (by the transferee itself or by a third party acting on its behalf) is a necessary condition to becoming a "protected purchaser" and when it is not. See UCC 8–303(a).

In analyzing the solicitude the law should pay to a buyer (*C*) who pays before delivery, consider whether it is usual and necessary for a buyer to pay before receiving the goods. In most cases of payment before delivery, is it difficult for the buyer (*C*) to take precautions against misconduct by the seller (*B*)? Would it be easier for the original owner (*A*) to take precautions?

Should it make any difference whether *C* has a right to possession as against its seller, *B*? If *C* has no right to recover the goods from *B*, the malefactor, it would be surprising if *C* could recover them from *A*, who also is a victim of *B's* wrongdoing. Article 2 provides pre-delivery possessory rights to a buyer only under very limited circumstances. See R2–502(1)(b) (reclamation right with respect to consumer goods if at least part of the

---

5. A transfer of a negotiable instrument from a holder to a non-holder can vest the non-holder transferee with the right to enforce the instrument. See UCC 3–203(b).

price is paid and the seller repudiates or fails to deliver; reclamation right with respect to all goods "if the seller becomes insolvent within ten days after receipt of the first installment on their price"); UCC 2–716(1) (right to specific performance of the sale contract "where the goods are unique or in other proper circumstances"); R2–716(3) (right to replevin of goods identified to the contract in two limited circumstances). This approach would answer Problem 1.3.2(e) in favor of A in all but a few cases.

The problem extends beyond "buyers" to a wider category—called "purchasers"—that, as we shall see, includes financers who extend credit on the security of goods. When (in our model sequence) B gives C a security interest in goods to secure a loan, B usually needs to keep the goods for B's personal or business use. Accordingly, B usually will not deliver the goods to C. In this setting, the public filing of a "financing statement," indicating that C may have a security interest in the goods, is a substitute for delivery. But this public filing has been conceived with concern for the creditors of B and other "purchasers" from B—not prior owners of the goods.

Should Article 2 be revised to answer clearly the question whether delivery, or some equivalent, objective step is necessary for protection as a good-faith purchaser?

(B) RIGHTS OF RECLAIMING SELLER AS AGAINST THIRD PERSONS

Problem 1.3.3. Assume that instead of buying the cotton in Problem 1.3.2, supra, C acquired a judgment against B and caused the sheriff to levy on the cotton pursuant to a writ of execution. Before the sheriff sells the goods, A discovers the fraud.

(a) Who has the better claim to the goods? See UCC 2–403; Oswego Starch Factory v. Lendrum, infra; R1–201(32); UCC 1–201(33), (44); Notes on Reliance and Nonreliance Parties, infra.

(b) What result if the sheriff sells the cotton to D before A discovers the fraud? See Mazer v. Williams Bros., 461 Pa. 587, 337 A.2d 559 (1975) (buyer at sheriff's sale not "bona fide purchaser" under UCC 1–201(32), (33), F8–302).

Problem 1.3.4. What result in Problem 1.3.2 if, instead of buying the cotton, C took it as security for a loan that C had extended to B six months earlier? See R1–201(32), UCC 1–201(33), (44); Notes on Reliance and Nonreliance Parties, infra.

Problem 1.3.5. On June 1 Seller and Buyer tentatively agreed on a sale to Buyer of a load of cotton; the price was $4,000. Buyer then said, "I hope you can give me a week to pay." Seller replied, "I'm afraid I'll have to ask for cash." Buyer said, "I'll arrange for my driver to bring my check for the price tomorrow." The next day (June 2) Buyer's driver gave Seller a $4,000 check drawn by Buyer to Seller's order on Firstbank, and removed the cotton. Seller deposited the check in an account with Secondbank. Five days later (June 7) Secondbank notified Seller that Buyer's check had been returned because of insufficient funds. Seller immediately brings a replevin action for the cotton. (These are the facts of Problem 1.2.7, supra.)

(a) Would the result in Problem 1.2.7(a) change if, in the meantime, Buyer had sold and delivered the goods to C, who did not suspect Buyer's wrongdoing? See UCC 2–511; UCC 2–403.

(b) Would the result in Problem 1.2.7(a) change if, in the meantime, a judgment creditor of Buyer had levied on the cotton? See UCC 2–511; UCC 2–403.

(c) Would the result in Problem 1.2.7(a) change if, in the meantime, Buyer had granted a security interest in the cotton to secure an antecedent debt to C, who did not suspect Buyer's wrongdoing? See UCC 2–511; UCC 2–403.

Problem 1.3.6. Suppose, in Problem 1.3.5, when Buyer asked for a week to pay for the cotton, Seller had replied, "I'm afraid I'll have to have your check within three days after delivery, with the understanding that you won't dispose of the cotton until the check clears." Buyer agreed. Buyer took delivery on June 2 and sent Seller the check on June 5. On June 10, Seller received word that the check had "bounced." On June 12, Seller brings a replevin action to recover the cotton.

(a) What result? What, if any, additional facts are needed? See Problems 1.2.5 and 1.2.6, supra; Note on the Cash Seller's Right to Reclaim, Section 2, supra; UCC 2–702; UCC 1–201(23); UCC 2401(1).

(b) Would the result in part (a) change if Seller waits until June 15 to take any action? See UCC 2–702.

(c) Would the result in part (a) change if, in the meantime, Buyer had sold and delivered the goods to C, who did not suspect Buyer's wrongdoing? Does Buyer have the "right" to sell the goods? The "power"?

(d) Would the result in part (a) change if, in the meantime, a judgment creditor of Buyer had levied on the cotton?

(e) Would the result in part (a) change if, in the meantime, Buyer had granted a security interest in the cotton to secure an antecedent debt to C, who did not suspect Buyer's wrongdoing?

(f) Compare the results in Problem 1.3.5 with those in this Problem. What, if anything, remains of the common-law distinction between the cash seller and the credit seller? Should any distinction be preserved?

Oswego Starch Factory v. Lendrum

Supreme Court of Iowa, 1881.
57 Iowa 573, 10 N.W. 900.

Action of replevin by Oswego Starch against sheriff Lendrum. Plaintiff's petition alleged that plaintiff had sold and shipped goods to Thompson & Reeves, and that this firm prior to the purchase was knowingly insolvent and intended to defraud plaintiff of the purchase price. Defendant Lendrum levied on the goods for creditors of Thompson & Reeves and thereafter plaintiff elected to rescind the sale because of fraud.

Lendrum demurred on the ground, inter alia, that he and the attaching creditors had no knowledge of the alleged fraud and that therefore the contract could not be rescinded after the levy. From a decision for Lendrum, plaintiff appealed.

■ BECK, J. ... [T]he point of contest involves the rights of an attaching creditor without notice.

The title of the property was not divested by the attachment, but remained in the vendees. The seizure conferred upon the creditors no right to the property as against plaintiff other or different from those held by the vendee. The sole effect of the seizure was to place the property in the custody of the law, to be held until the creditors' execution. They parted with no consideration in making the attachment, and their condition as to their claims were in no respect changed. Their acts were induced by no representation or procurement originating with plaintiff which would in law or equity give them rights to the property as against plaintiff. Plaintiff's right to rescind the sale inhered in the contract and attached to the property. It could not be defeated except by a purchaser for value without notice of the fraud....

Our position is simply this, that as an attaching creditor parts with no consideration, and does not change his position as to his claim, to his prejudice, he stands in the shoes of the vendee. ... The innocent purchaser for value occupies a different position, and his rights are, therefore, different. [Reversed.]

NOTES ON RELIANCE AND NONRELIANCE PARTIES

(1) The Position of a Creditor Who Levies. The *Oswego Starch* decision represents the preponderant view of the pre-UCC case law. See *3 Williston, Sales § 620 (1948).* Is it persuasive? What is the basis of the distinction the court draws between a judicial lien creditor, against whom the right to rescind may be exercised, and a "purchaser for value," who would defeat this right? Is the court correct that "an attaching creditor parts with no consideration"? If so, then how can the creditors in *Oswego Starch* obtain judgment against Thompson & Reeves, the debtor?

Does UCC 2–403(1) change the pre-UCC result? *B's* rights to the goods are subject to *A's* right to rescind the transaction and recover the goods. See Problem 1.2.4, supra. But does *B* have *power* to convey greater rights? Even if *B* has "voidable title" (see Note (2) on the Basic Conveyancing Rules, supra), the answer is "no," unless the lien creditor is a "good faith purchaser for value."

A lien creditor is likely to meet the good faith and value requirements. See UCC 1–201(19); UCC 1–201(44). Is the lien creditor a "purchaser"? The UCC defines "purchase" (R1–201(32)) to include "taking by sale, discount, negotiation, mortgage, pledge, lien, security interest, issue or re-issue, gift or any other voluntary transaction creating an interest in property." One will note that the list of transactions includes "taking by . . . lien," and a judgment creditor who levies execution on property often is called a *"lien* creditor." See R9–102(a)(52). But the word "lien" is a chameleon; prior to the UCC voluntary transactions creating mortgages and similar security interests were often said to create a "lien." In the setting of the types of transactions listed in the definition of "purchase" and the concluding characterization that the list applies to "any other *voluntary* transaction," it seems fairly clear that the drafters did not mean to say that the seizure of a debtor's property by a sheriff acting for a creditor makes the creditor a "purchaser." This conclusion becomes inescapable in the light of UCC sections that distinguish between, on the one hand, lien creditors and, on the other, transferees or purchasers. See, e.g., R9–317(a), (b).

Does any policy justify distinguishing between a judicial lien creditor and a buyer? Consider some of the ways in which the two are different. Unlike a buyer, who contracts to purchase all of the rights to the goods, a lien creditor acquires only a limited interest in (i.e., a **lien** on) the goods. And unlike a buyer, whose rights arise by virtue of its contract, a judicial lien creditor acquires its rights through the judicial process (a overview of which appears in Section 1, supra). Finally, whereas a buyer typically acquires its rights in exchange for new consideration (current payment or a promise to pay), a lien creditor's extension of credit is divorced from the property on which it subsequently obtains a lien. Is any of these distinctions relevant?

(2) The Position of an Article 9 Secured Party. Like the lien creditor, an Article 9 secured party can be expected ordinarily to meet the good faith and value requirements.[6] Is a secured party a "purchaser"? Interestingly, until it was revised in conjunction with the recent revision of Article 9, the definition of "purchase" did not specifically include taking by "security interest." However, there was general agreement that the creation of an Article 9 security interest was an "other voluntary transaction creating an interest in property," if not a "lien."

Together with Note (1), supra, the foregoing paragraph suggests that one might read the UCC to provide that a judicial lien creditor is not a "purchaser," and thus takes subject to A's right to rescind the transaction and recover the goods, whereas an Article 9 secured party (like a buyer) is a "purchaser," and thus may cut off A's rights. Can one justify this distinction?

One can draw several comparisons with buyers and judicial lien creditors. An Article 9 secured party is like a buyer, in that its rights in the goods (a security interest, defined in R1–201(37)) arise by contract. See R9–109(a)(1). It is like a judicial lien creditor in that it acquires only a limited

---

6. The most serious challenge to a secured party's good faith is likely to arise from its knowledge or notice of competing claims. See Note (5) on the Basic Conveyancing Rules, supra.

interest in the goods. This limited interest entitles the secured party, upon its debtor's (*B*'s) default, to repossess the goods, sell them, and apply the proceeds to its claim against the debtor.

Sometimes, an Article 9 secured party takes a security interest in specific goods owned by the debtor at the time the loan is made or acquired by the debtor in conjunction with the extension of credit.[7] In this respect a secured party is like a buyer, exchanging new consideration for an interest in goods. Other times, as in Problem 1.3.4, supra, an Article 9 secured party takes a security interest to secure an antecedent debt, i.e., a debt owed before the security interest is taken. This secured party seems to be analogous to a judicial lien creditor—it has extended credit on an unsecured basis, and its acquisition of rights in particular property is not a *quid pro quo* for the loan (although it may have taken the security interest in exchange for its forbearance in exercising its remedies).

Sometimes a secured party takes a security interest in both property existing at the time credit is extended as well as **after-acquired property,** i.e., property the debtor may acquire after the loan is made. See R9–204. A security interest covering both existing and after-acquired property (often referred to as a **"floating lien"**) is particularly common when the collateral is inventory (goods held for sale) or accounts receivable (rights to payment, often for goods sold or services rendered). The rights of a reclaiming seller as against a buyer's secured creditor who claims a "floating lien" are considered in Chapter 11, Section 3, infra.

(3) The Position of a Lessee and Purchasers from a Lessee. The preceding Note suggests that the good faith purchase doctrine protects not only buyers but also other "purchasers" for "value." There are many exchange transactions in which value is given for an interest in property other than full title. Section 2–403(1) refers to purchase of a "limited interest" in property. This leads to the question of the power of a purchaser other than a buyer to transfer "good title" to a "good faith purchaser" who is not a buyer.

Because a lessee is a "purchaser," it seems to follow that one who leases goods from a person with voidable title would be protected under UCC 2–403(2) in the right to possess and use the goods for the term of the lease. One would have to infer that the power to create "good title" includes the lesser power to transfer a protected limited interest, but the protection would not extend beyond the limited leasehold interest and the rightful owner would retain the reversion. In other words, the owner of

---

7. Two variations of this paradigm are common. In one, the seller of goods retains a security interest to secure the purchase price. In the other, a lender takes a security interest in goods acquired with the borrowed funds. A security interest arising under either of these circumstances is called a "purchase-money security interest" ("PMSI") and receives special treatment under both the UCC and the Bankruptcy Code. See, e.g., R9–103 (explanation of "purchase-money security interest"); R9–324 (priority rules for PMSI's); BC 547(c)(3) (protecting certain PMSI's that otherwise would be avoidable as preferences). PMSI's are discussed in Chapter 7, Section 6(A)(II), infra.

goods with voidable title would have the power to transfer to a good faith lessee "good title" to a leasehold interest.

Suppose, however, that a good faith lessee acquires its interest from a prior *lessee* rather than from a transferor with full (albeit voidable) title. The second and third sentences of UCC 2–403(1) might be construed to fit this circumstance, but the matter is more clearly addressed in the UCC article on leases, Article 2A. See UCC 2A–305(1). Under that provision it is clear that a lessee with a "voidable leasehold interest" could transfer a "good leasehold interest" to a buyer or sublessee, but only to the extent of the "voidable leasehold interest." Lease agreements commonly contain provisions that restrict alienability by the lessee, one effect of which may be to terminate the lease if a transfer is made. For the central provisions dealing with this matter, see R2A–303 and 9–407.

(4) The Role of Reliance in Resolving Competing Claims. Personal property law often distinguishes among third-party claimants on the basis of whether they gave value in reliance upon the transferor's (in our case, *B*'s) apparent ownership of particular property. This distinction is reflected in *Oswego Starch,* supra, as well as in Mowrey v. Walsh, 8 Cow. 238, 245 (N.Y.Sup.Ct.1828) ("The judgment creditor had not advanced money upon these goods, and his loss placed him in no worse situation than he was in before the fraud.") It also underlies the delivery requirement in the third sentence of UCC 2–403(1).

We shall have occasion later to consider how the UCC resolves competing claims. In that connection, you may wish to think about the following questions:

(i) Is a third party's reliance at all relevant to whether that party's claim to goods should prevail?

(ii) If reliance is relevant, should the strength of a person's claim to goods turn on whether the person actually relied, or should it turn on (i) whether the person belongs to a class that generally relies and on (ii) whether, had the person investigated, it would have uncovered facts that would have formed the basis for reasonable reliance upon the debtor's ownership (e.g., the goods in question were located in the debtor's warehouse in boxes addressed to the debtor)?

(iii) As an empirical matter, do buyers generally give value in reliance upon their seller's ownership of particular property? Do judicial lien creditors? Do Article 9 secured parties?

(C) THE BASIC CONVEYANCING RULES IN OTHER SETTINGS

Problem 1.3.7. On January 3, Seller (*A*) and Buyer *(B)* entered into a contract for the sale of a garden tractor, which *B* agreed to pay for and take away by January 30. The agreement specified that "title" passed to *B* on January 3. (These are the facts of Problem 1.2.1, supra.) On January 15, *B* contracted to sell the tractor to *C*. *B* told *C* that the tractor was in storage with A and was ready for immediate delivery. *C* had no reason to doubt *B's* honesty and paid $5,000 to *B*.

That afternoon C went to A's place of business to take delivery of the tractor. A said that the tractor would be released to C only on payment of the \$5,000 that B had agreed to pay. May C replevy the tractor from A? May C recover from A for conversion of the tractor?

(a) Which sentence of UCC 2–403(1) applies to these facts? Did the transaction of January 3 give B a property interest in the tractor? See UCC 2–401(1).[8] If so, was B's interest most analogous to (1) the "void" title of a thief, (2) a "voidable title" of one who acquires goods through fraud, or (3) the "good title" of an owner?

Consider in this regard the relevance, if any, of the fact that A retained possession of the goods. This fact necessarily implies that neither B nor C took delivery of the goods.

With respect to B's failure to take delivery:

(i) does the reference in the third sentence of UCC 2–403(1) to goods that "have been delivered under a transaction of purchase" suggest that delivery generally is a condition to obtaining voidable title? Paragraphs (a)-(d) of UCC 2–403(1) describe situations in which transfers from A to B, according to some pre-UCC cases, had given B only a "void" title. Is the sentence in which these paragraphs appear designed only to settle the "void-voidable" question for "a number of specific situations that have been troublesome under prior law," or does it have broader application? See Comment 1 to UCC 2–403.

(ii) is there any reason to construe the concept of "voidable title" in UCC 2–403(1) so broadly as to eliminate the requirement of possession, which the common law imposed? See Dolan, The Uniform Commercial Code and the Concept of Possession in the Marketing and Financing of Goods, 56 Tex.L.Rev. 1147, 1172–73 (1978) ("The doctrine of voidable title manifests the law's concern that possession not mislead").

With respect to C's failure to take delivery, is C disqualified from being a "good faith purchaser for value" by the fact that C had not taken delivery when it learned of A's claim to the tractor? Does the definition of "purchase" in R1–201(32) require delivery? Is it implicit in UCC 2–403? If so, then what are the implications for a secured party who seeks to qualify as a good faith purchaser for value of collateral that its debtor acquired by fraud? See Problem 1.3.2(e), supra; Note (7) on the Basic Conveyancing Rules, supra; Problem 1.3.4, supra; Note (2) on Reliance and Nonreliance Parties, supra.

(b) Is it conceivable that the drafters of UCC 2–403 failed to face the question whether delivery is necessary for protection as a good faith purchaser of goods? Do the Comments give any indication of attention to

---

8. B also received a "special property and an insurable interest" upon identification of the tractor to the contract. UCC 2–501(1). But only in limited circumstances do those interests give a buyer a possessory right to goods or protection against claims to the goods by the seller's creditors. See UCC 2–402(1); R2–502; R2–716.

this question? Is it appropriate to resolve the problem by applying the basic conveyancing principle, *nemo dat*? If so, who prevails?

(c) A buyer in ordinary course of business ("BIOCOB") is one type of good faith purchaser. In construing UCC 2–403(1), is it relevant that, in conjunction with the revision of Article 9, the definition of "buyer in ordinary course of business" was revised to make clear that a person does not qualify as a BIOCOB unless the person "takes possession of the goods or has a right to recover the goods from the seller under Article 2"? R1–201(9).

(d) If the law protects C in this Problem, how would this rule affect the way transactions between A and B would be conducted? What could A have done to avoid the loss of both the tractor and its value? Would the precautions necessary to protect A be consistent with the efficient conduct of business?[9]

Problem 1.3.8. A owned cotton worth $100,000. A placed it in storage with B, who not only stores cotton but also regularly buys and sells it. B wrongfully sold and delivered the cotton to C, who did not suspect B's wrongdoing, for $100,000. A sues C to replevy the cotton.

(a) What result? See UCC 2–403; UCC 1–201(9); Notes on Entrustment, infra.

(b) What result in part (a) if C had promised to pay $100,000 but has not yet paid it when A claims the cotton?

(c) What result in part (a) if C, instead of buying the cotton from B, had taken it as security for a loan that C had extended to B six months earlier. Compare Problem 1.3.4, supra.

(d) What result if B had wrongfully delivered the cotton to C who is in the cotton business, as security for a loan that C had extended to B six months earlier, and C had sold the cotton to D, who suspected nothing, for $100,000? Cf. Canterra Petroleum, Inc. v. Western Drilling & Mining

---

9. Delivery of the goods may affect the rights of good faith purchasers in another context, that of the seller's right to stop delivery under UCC 2–705. (This right is discussed in Problem 1.2.3, supra.). Unlike UCC 2–702, and like UCC 2–507, UCC 2–705 does not address the circumstances, if any, in which a good faith purchaser from the buyer takes free of the seller's right to stop delivery. The few reported cases have refused to afford good faith purchase rights to persons who have not taken delivery. In In re Murdock Machine & Engineering Co., 620 F.2d 767 (10th Cir.1980), the court observed that the "old equitable right of stoppage *in transitu* has been repeatedly held to defeat rights of good faith purchasers for value," and that "if the drafters of the Code had intended to give third party purchasers greater rights than under previous law, we believe that the official comments to the Code provisions on stoppage in transit would reflect that intention. Instead, the official comments do not indicate a change from prior law. *See* U.C.C. § 1–103." (The case also suggests that delivery of the goods to the "subpurchaser" (i.e., the purchaser from the buyer) does not cut off the seller's right to stop delivery unless the seller acquiesced in the transfer from its buyer to the subpurchaser). See also Ceres Inc. v. ACLI Metal & Ore Co., 451 F.Supp. 921 (N.D.Ill.1978) (holding that under UCC 2–403, a good faith purchaser prevails over a seller seeking to stop delivery but that "without delivery, the buyer did not obtain power under § 2–403 to confer good title upon the bona fide purchaser").

Supply, 418 N.W.2d 267 (N.D.1987) (buyer in ordinary course of business can cut off rights of true owner who entrusts goods to merchant-dealer when employees of merchant-dealer transfer goods to "dummy corporation," which then sells to the buyer). See also PEB Article 2 Report 130 ("[I]t should be made clear that if the goods are entrusted to Merchant #1, who sells to non-BIOCB [non-buyer in ordinary course of business] Merchant #2, who sells to BIOCB, the BIOCB takes 'all rights' or takes 'free' of a security interest."). Would the result be different if *B* had wrongfully delivered the cotton to *C* for temporary storage purposes and not as security?

NOTES ON ENTRUSTMENT

(1) The Historical Development of the Law of "Entrusting." UCC 2–403(2) represents a sharp break with the traditional law of good faith purchase. Under facts similar to those in Problem 1.3.8, the common law usually favored the original owner. Merely entrusting possession to a dealer was not sufficient to clothe the dealer with the authority to sell. "If it were otherwise people would not be secure in sending their watches or articles of jewelry to a jeweller's [sic] establishment to be repaired, or cloth to a clothing establishment to be made into garments." Levi v. Booth, 58 Md. 305 (1882).

During the nineteenth century, however, many states enacted "Factor's Acts" under which an owner of goods who entrusted them to an agent (or "factor") for sale took the risk that the agent might sell them beyond the agent's authority. A good faith purchaser from the agent, relying on the agent's possession of the goods and having no notice that the agent's sale was unauthorized, took good title against the original owner. (See the discussion by Professor Gilmore in Note (2) on the Basic Conveyancing Principles, supra.) But the Factor's Acts did not protect the good faith purchaser where, as in Problem 1.3.8, the owner entrusted the goods to another for some purpose other than that of sale. A mere **bailee** could not pass good title, even to a good faith purchaser for value.

In this regard UCC 2–403(2) goes well beyond the Factor's Acts, since it applies to "[a]ny entrusting," i.e., "any delivery" under UCC 2403(3), regardless of the purpose. The section gives protection, however, only to a "buyer," not to all those who give value and take in good faith from the person to whom the goods are entrusted. Contrast the narrow scope of "buyer in ordinary course" under R1–201(9) with the definitions of "purchase" and "purchaser" in R1–201(32) and UCC 1–201(33). See Comment 3 to UCC 2–403.[10]

---

10. According to Professor Gilmore: "For some reason, the security transferees who were protected in the voidable title subsection by the use of the term 'purchaser' do not qualify for protection under the entrusting section. I have no idea why the draftsmen chose thus to narrow the protected class." Gilmore, The Good Faith Purchase Idea and the Uniform Commercial Code: Confessions of a Repentant Draftsman, 15 Ga. L. Rev. 605, 618 (1981). The Ontario Law Reform

(2) Testing the Limits of UCC 2–403(2): Porter v. Wertz. Despite its apparent simplicity, UCC 2–403(2) contains a number of wrinkles, several of which came to light in Porter v. Wertz, 68 A.D.2d 141, 416 N.Y.S.2d 254 (1979), affirmed mem., 53 N.Y.2d 696, 439 N.Y.S.2d 105, 421 N.E.2d 500 (1981), a case with particularly interesting facts:

Samuel Porter, an art collector, owned Utrillo's painting "Chateau de Lion-sur-Mer," but lost the painting through the machinations of one Harold "Von" Maker—sometimes operating under the name of Peter Wertz, a junior collaborator over whom, the trial judge observed, Von Maker "cast his hypnotic spell . . . and usurped his name, his signature and his sacred honor."

Von Maker had engaged in several transactions as an art dealer. (Other activities had led to arrests for possession of obscene literature and theft of checks, and to conviction for transmitting a forged cable in connection with a scheme to defraud the Chase Manhattan Bank.) Von Maker (alias "Wertz"), in his capacity as art dealer, approached Porter and expressed an interest in the Utrillo. Porter, unaware of Von Maker's illegal activities, permitted Von Maker to hang the Utrillo temporarily in Von Maker's home pending a decision as to purchase.

Without Porter's knowledge, Von Maker's junior collaborator, the true Peter Wertz, sold the Utrillo to an art dealer, Feigen Galleries. Feigen sold the painting to Brenner, who resold it to a third party, who took the painting to South America.

Porter brought actions for conversion against Wertz and Von Maker and also against the purchasers, Feigen and Brenner. Defendant Feigen argued that Porter "entrusted" the painting to Von Maker and as a consequence: (1) Feigen was protected under UCC 2–403(2) as a "buyer in ordinary course of business," and (2) Porter's claim as owner was barred by equitable estoppel.

The trial court rejected Feigen's defense based on UCC 2–403(2) but concluded that Porter was barred by equitable estoppel and dismissed his action. The Appellate Division reversed the trial court and held that neither statutory estoppel (UCC 2–403(2)) nor equitable estoppel barred recovery. It found that Feigen was not a buyer in ordinary course because Wertz, from whom Feigen bought the Utrillo, was not an art dealer ("[i]f

---

Commission was "attracted to the distinction":

    The supporting theory is, presumably, grounded on either of the following premises: namely, that commerce will not be impeded if lenders are required to assume the risk of a merchant-borrower exceeding his actual authority; or, that lenders are in as good a position as are entrusters, or perhaps even better, to protect themselves against a dishonest merchant.

2 Ontario Law Reform Commission, Report on Sale of Goods 314–15 (1979).

    It also has been suggested that transfers for security are transfers "in which the price or consideration received for the goods . . . is likely to be considerably less than the amount normally received in a sale of the same goods in other transactions." Leary & Sperling, The Outer Limits of Entrusting, 35 Ark.L.Rev. 50, 65 (1981).

anything, he was a delicatessen employee'') and because Feigen did not act in good faith (good faith, as defined in UCC 2–103(1)(b) ''should not—and cannot—be interpreted to permit, countenance, or condone commercial standards of sharp trade practice or indifference as to the 'provenance', *i.e.*, history of ownership or the right to possess or sell an object d'art, such as is present in the case before us.'').

Feigen appealed to the Court of Appeals, which affirmed the Appellate Division. The court wrote (421 N.E.2d at 501):

> Because Peter Wertz was not an art dealer and the Appellate Division has found that Feigen was not duped by Von Maker into believing that Peter Wertz was such a dealer, subdivision (2) of section 2–403 of the Uniform Commercial Code is inapplicable for three distinct reasons: (1) even if Peter Wertz were an art merchant rather than a delicatessen employee, he is not the same merchant to whom Porter entrusted the Utrillo painting; (2) Wertz was not an art merchant; and (3) the sale was not in the ordinary course of Wertz' business because he did not deal in goods of that kind [UCC 1–201(9)].[11]

Would it have made any difference if Feigen had bought the Utrillo from Von Maker rather than from Wertz? Why?

What is the relevance, if any, of the knowledge of either the entruster or the buyer? Does it make a difference under UCC 2–403(2) if the original owner of the goods does not know that the person to whom the owner entrusts them is a merchant who deals in goods of that kind? See Atlas Auto Rental Corp. v. Weisberg, 54 Misc.2d 168, 281 N.Y.S.2d 400 (Civ.Ct. 1967) (knowledge of dealer-merchant status is necessary element of entrusting). Accord, Leary & Sperling, The Outer Limits of Entrusting, 35 Ark. L. Rev. 50, 83–85 (1981) (relying on *Atlas Auto*). But cf. Antigo Co-op. Credit Union v. Miller, 86 Wis.2d 90, 271 N.W.2d 642 (1978) (knowledge by secured party that debtor was a dealer-merchant not necessary for applicability of analogous provision in F9–307(1)).

Suppose Feigen had been duped by Von Maker into believing that Wertz was an art dealer. Suppose that Feigen had been duped by Wertz, who held himself out as an art dealer. Compare UCC 2–104(1) with UCC 2–403(2). In Sea Harvest, Inc. v. Rig & Crane Equipment Corp., 181 N.J.Super. 41, 436 A.2d 553 (Ch.Div.1981), the court said: "A buyer's misunderstanding that the seller was in the business of selling does not improve the former's position." Do you agree with this reading of the UCC?

(3) Leases: "Entrusting" and "Lessee[s] In Ordinary Course of Business." Consider a sale of a power shovel by M, a merchant who deals in goods of that kind, to B who pays for the equipment. With M's consent,

---

11. Although it received amicus briefs on the ''good faith'' question from both the New York State Attorney General (arguing that good faith among art merchants requires inquiry as to ownership) and the Art Dealers Association of America, Inc. (arguing that a duty of inquiry would cripple the art business), the court found no need to reach the question.

B leaves the power shovel with M pending B's need for it on a construction project that B expects to begin shortly. Before B returns to take possession of the power shovel, M leases it to L. B discovers that L has the power shovel and demands that L surrender it to B.

Is L's right to possession protected under UCC 2–403(2)? Apparently not; see the definition of "buyer" in UCC 2–103(1)(a). Is L's right to possession protected under UCC 2A–304(2)? Is L a "subsequent lessee"? Comment 3 to this section provides:

> Section 2A–307(2) resolves the potential dispute between B, M and L. By virtue of B's entrustment of the goods to M and M's lease of the goods to L, B has a cause of action against M under the common law. … Thus, B is a creditor of M. … Section 2A–307(2) provides that B, as M's creditor, takes subject to M's lease to L. Thus, if L does not default under the lease, L's enjoyment and possession of the goods should be undisturbed.

Is there legal slight of hand in characterizing B as merely a creditor of M? Although UCC 2A–304(2) would have protected L as a "lessee in ordinary course of business" (defined in UCC2A–103(1)(*o*)) had B *leased* the power shovel from M, it does not apply because B *bought* it. Was this a drafting oversight?

SECTION 4.   GOOD FAITH PURCHASE OF RIGHTS TO PAYMENT

As the previous Section explains, a purchaser of goods ordinarily acquires no better rights than its transferor has. In a few, narrowly circumscribed situations, however, a purchaser who qualifies as a "good faith purchaser for value" or a "buyer in ordinary course of business" takes free of otherwise valid third-party claims and thereby acquires greater rights than its transferor had. As we shall see in this Section and the one following, the two primary conveyancing principles discussed in Section 3—security of property and good faith purchase—apply not only to goods but also to other kinds of personal property.

Problem 1.4.1. The Atlas Co. was the owner of a negotiable promissory note, made by Merchant, who promised "to pay on demand to the order of The Atlas Co. $100,000." In preparation for a proposed sale of the note to Hometown Bank, Atlas's president indorsed the company's name on the back of the note. That night, Atlas's bookkeeper (Bates) arranged to work late and took the note from the vault. The following day Bates delivered the note to Crispy Bank to secure a loan for $80,000 and promptly disappeared.

(a) Who has the better claim to the note? See UCC 3–306; UCC 3–302; UCC 1–201(20); UCC 3–201; UCC 3–109; UCC 3–205; UCC 3–303; UCC 3–103(a)(4); UCC 1–201(25); Note (1) on Competing Claims to Negotiable Instruments and Certificated Securities, infra.

(b) What result if the note had not been indorsed? See UCC 3–306; UCC 3–201; UCC 3–203(c).

Problem 1.4.2. What result in the preceding Problem if the property at issue is not a note but rather one of a series of 500 Class A Bonds (debt obligations) issued by the I Corporation? (You may assume that The Atlas Co. was the registered owner.) See UCC 8–102(a)(4); R8–302; R8–301; UCC 8–303; UCC 8–106(b); Note (2) on Competing Claims to Negotiable Instruments and Certificated Securities, infra.

NOTES ON COMPETING CLAIMS TO NEGOTIABLE INSTRUMENTS, CERTIFICATED SECURITIES, AND OTHER RIGHTS TO PAYMENT

(1) Negotiable Instruments. Negotiable instruments (most commonly, checks and promissory notes) have a long history—one that is best left to courses in Commercial Paper or Payment Systems. For our purposes, it is sufficient to recognize that rights to payment that are embodied in a writing in a particular form constitute a different kind of property from rights to payment that are not so embodied.

UCC Article 3 applies to "negotiable instruments." UCC 3–104(a), which defines the term, preserves the tradition that form triumphs over substance in negotiable instruments law. The term includes only a "promise" (defined in UCC 3–103(a)(9)) or an "order" (defined in UCC 3–103(a)(6)) to pay a fixed sum of "money" (defined in UCC 1–201(24)).[1] Succeeding sections explain the requirements that the promise or order be "unconditional" (UCC 3–106); that it be for a fixed amount of money, with or without "interest" (UCC 3–112(b)); that it be "payable to bearer or to order" (UCC 3–109); and that it be "payable on demand" or "at a definite time" (UCC 3–108). Other sections in Part 1 of the Article are devoted to other aspects of the form of negotiable instruments.

The "formal requisites" of negotiability now found in UCC 3–104 were based initially on commercial practice and case law. They were embodied in the pre–1990 version of UCC Article 3 and its predecessors, the Negotiable Instruments Law of 1896 (which was adopted in each of the United States) and the (British) Bills of Exchange Act of 1882. The continued emphasis on form may seem an anachronism, but perhaps it serves a purpose. As we shall see, one who becomes a party to a negotiable instrument assumes special risks. The formal requisites, like the fence and warnings around high voltage equipment, arguably confine and identify the danger areas. Of course, the formalities afford no warning to one who is unfamiliar with this specialized branch of the law.

In the commercial setting, negotiable notes rarely are used to evidence an obligation to pay for goods sold on credit.[2] When negotiable notes are

---

1. An instrument is a "note" if it is a promise and a "draft" if it is an order. UCC 3–104(e).

2. This has been true for some time. Writing nearly sixty years ago, Karl Llewellyn observed:

I shall not undertake to explain how or why the commercial system of a century ago lost the use of notes to evidence the credit-price of freshly delivered goods. It is enough here that the practice went into decline, and that between merchants goods are now delivered typically

used, it is typically in connection with a loan of money. Nevertheless, in either case, the person to whom the note is payable (The Atlas Co., in Problem 1.4.1) may sell the note or use it to secure a loan. Like Articles 2 and 9, Article 3 contains both security of property and good-faith-purchase rules governing the extent to which a purchaser (buyer or secured party) takes a negotiable instrument free from competing claims. Unless a person has the rights of a holder in due course ("HDC"), the person takes the instrument subject to any existing claim of a property or possessory right in the instrument or its proceeds. A person having rights of a holder in due course takes free of the claim to the instrument. UCC 3–306. The freedom from "claims" is analogous to the protection from outstanding ownership interests that Article 2 affords to the good faith purchaser of goods. See UCC 2–403 and Section 3, supra.

The typical commercial note is payable to the order of an identified person (the payee). Although a note may be transferred or negotiated many times, most negotiable notes are transferred or negotiated once (if at all), from the payee to a purchaser. The risk that the transferor acquired the note through theft or fraud and that the true owner will claim it from the purchaser, as in Problem 1.4.1., is negligible. A greater risk, but one that is still rather small, is that the note is encumbered with a security interest. As we shall see in Chapter 9, Section 2, infra, a purchaser who takes possession of a note is likely to prevail over competing secured parties. See R9–330(d). But even when the purchaser would be junior under the normal Article 9 priority rules, the purchaser will take free of competing claims to the note if it can establish that it is an HDC. See R9–331(a); UCC 3–306.

The Holder in Due Course. "Holder in due course" is the name given to good faith purchasers for value of negotiable instruments under Article 3. UCC 3–302(a) defines the term. Observe that not every person who takes an instrument in good faith[3] and for value[4] qualifies as an HDC. One also must be without notice of any of a variety of claims, defenses, and irregularities. (You may recall that notice of competing claims may be relevant to a putative good faith purchaser's "good faith" under Article 2.)

Two other requirements for becoming a holder in due course are less obvious. First, one must be the holder of an "instrument," which UCC 3–104(b) defines as a "negotiable instrument." Second, the person must be a "holder." When the instrument is payable to an identified person and the

---

on purely "open" credit (resulting in a "book account," and "account receivable"), often with the buyer, if he is financially strong, paying within ten days against a large "cash discount." The giving of a commercial note between dealers has come to be the gesture with which a stale account, long overdue, is promised *really* to be met next time. Such a note smells.

Llewellyn, Meet Negotiable Instruments, 44 Colum.L.Rev. 299, 321–22 (1944).

3. In Article 3, " 'Good faith' means honesty in fact and the observance of reasonable commercial standards of fair dealing." UCC 3–103(a)(4).

4. UCC 3–303(a)(2) expressly provides that an instrument is transferred for value if the transferee acquires a security interest in it. This is consistent with the definition of "value" in UCC 1–201(44).

identified person is in possession of the instrument, the person is the holder. Alternatively, when the instrument is payable to bearer, the person in possession is the holder. See UCC 1–201(20).

Merchant's note in Problem 1.4.1, like the overwhelming majority of negotiable promissory notes, is payable to the order of an identified person (Atlas) and not payable to bearer. To become a holder, Crispy Bank not only must take possession but also must obtain the indorsement (signature) of The Atlas Co., the payee. Custom dictates that Atlas will indorse the note on the back. Atlas's indorsement may identify Crispy Bank as a person to whom the instrument is payable (e.g., Atlas's signature may be accompanied by the words "Pay to Crispy Bank") or it may identify no such person (e.g., it may consist only of Atlas's signature), thereby making the note payable to bearer. See UCC 3–205(a), (b). In either case, Crispy Bank will become a holder upon taking possession of the note. If it meets the other requirements of UCC 3–302(a), then Crispy Bank will become a holder in due course and take free of all claims, including Atlas's ownership claim.

(2) Certificated Securities. Some rights to payment, such as the corporate **bonds** in Problem 1.4.2, are traded on securities exchanges or securities markets. These rights to payment often are used as collateral. The UCC distinguishes between securities, which by definition are, or are of a type, dealt in or traded on securities markets or exchanges, and negotiable instruments. Compare UCC 8–102(a)(15) (defining "security") with UCC 3–104(a) (defining "negotiable instrument"). The transfer of interests in securities—i.e., the mechanisms by which a person becomes the owner of a security—is governed by Article 8 and not by Article 3. See UCC 8–103(d); UCC 3–102(a). (The federal securities laws, which are discussed in courses on Business Organizations, Corporations, and Securities, are regulatory and anti–fraud statutes.)

Bonds, stocks, and other securities frequently are represented by a piece of paper, which Article 8 calls a "security certificate." UCC 8–102(a)(16) (defining "security certificate").

To fall within the scope of Article 8, a "certificated security" (i.e., a security represented by a security certificate) must be in bearer or registered form. See UCC 8–102(a)(15) (defining "security"), (a)(2) (defining "bearer form"), (a)(13) (defining "registered form"). This requirement is somewhat analogous to the requirement that a negotiable instrument be payable to bearer or order. See UCC 3–104(a)(1); UCC 3–109.

Like the purchaser of a negotiable instrument, a purchaser (buyer or secured party) of a certificated security may acquire greater rights than the transferor. Qualifying good faith purchasers for value of a security, whether or not the security is represented by a certificate, are called "protected purchasers." UCC 8–303(a). A protected purchaser takes free of any adverse claim to the security. UCC 8–303(b). The requirements for becoming a protected purchaser of a security are similar to those for becoming an HDC of a negotiable instrument. Compare UCC 8–303(a) with UCC 3–302(a). The differences are attributable largely to the fact that, unlike negotiable instruments, securities are traded in markets, where the parties to a transaction are unknown to each other. Buyers under these circumstances are unable to investigate the title of their sellers; they need comfort that they will be able to enjoy what they paid for without having to defend against the claims of third parties.[5]

(3) Other Rights to Payment. Many rights to payment are not evidenced by a negotiable instrument or a certificated security. The Restatement (Second) of Contracts § 342 contains a good faith purchase rule for assignments of contracts generally.[6] However, much of the law relating to competing claims to these rights to payment now is found in Article 9. We shall consider the relevant Article 9 provisions in Chapter 9, Section 1.

———

When property that is purchased consists of a right to payment of some kind (e.g., the assignor's right to payment for goods sold or the payee's right to payment of a negotiable instrument), the purchaser is concerned not only with taking the collateral free from the *claims* of third parties but also, and usually more so, with its ability to enforce the obligation free of the obligor's *defenses*.

Problem 1.4.3. *B* manufactures and sells auto parts on credit to wholesale dealers. To secure a **line of credit** from *C* finance company, *B* granted to *C* a security interest in "all *B*'s existing and after-acquired rights to payment for goods sold ('accounts') and all notes and other instruments representing such rights to payment." *B* defaults on its obligations to *C*, and *C* demands payment from each of *B*'s customers. One customer, *A*, contracted to pay $60,000 for a shipment of goods but now is willing to pay only $40,000 because the goods were seriously nonconforming. See UCC 2–714; UCC 2–717. *C* brings suit against *A*.

(a) What result? See R9–404(a); Note (1) on Defenses to Payment Obligations, infra.

(b) What result if *A* refused to pay for the goods because *B* had failed to repay a $20,000 loan from *A*? Does it matter when *B*'s default occurred? See R9–404(a). Cf. Restatement (Second) of Contracts § 336(2).[7]

---

5. Investment property other than certificated securities, such as uncertificated securities and security entitlements, is considered in Chapter 9, Section 3, infra.

6. § 342 Successive Assignees From the Same Assignor

Except as otherwise provided by statute, the right of an assignee is superior to that of a subsequent assignee of the same right from the same assignor, unless

(a) the first assignment is ineffective or revocable or is voidable by the assignor or by the subsequent assignee; or

(b) the subsequent assignee in good faith and without knowledge or reason to know of the prior assignment gives value and obtains

(i) payment or satisfaction of the obligation,

(ii) judgment against the obligor,

(iii) a new contract with the obligor by novation, or

(iv) possession of a writing of a type customarily accepted as a symbol or as evidence of the right assigned.

7. Restatement (Second) of Contracts § 336(2) provides: "The right of an assignee

(c) Assume the contract of sale contained the following provision: "Buyer [A] understands and acknowledges that Seller [B] may assign Seller's rights under this Agreement for collateral purposes or otherwise. Buyer agrees that, in the event of any such assignment, Buyer will not assert against any assignee any claims or defenses that Buyer may have against Seller arising under this Agreement or otherwise." What result in parts (a) and (b)? See R9–403(a)–(c); UCC 3–305.

(d) Why would anyone sign a contract that contains the provision set forth in part (c)?

Problem 1.4.4. *B* manufactures and sells auto parts on credit to wholesale dealers. To secure a line of credit from *C* finance company, *B* granted to *C* a security interest in "all *B*'s existing and after-acquired rights to payment for goods sold ('accounts') and all notes and other instruments representing such rights to payment." *B* undertakes to deliver, and does deliver, each such instrument to *C* immediately upon its receipt by *B*. *B* defaults on its obligations to *C*, and *C* demands payment from each of *B*'s customers. One customer, *A*, signed a negotiable promissory note, in which *A* agreed to pay $60,000 "to the order of *B*" for a shipment of goods. *A* now is willing to pay only $40,000 because the goods were seriously nonconforming. *C* brings suit against *A*.

(a) What result if *B* had indorsed the note, "pay to *C*, [signed] *B*" before delivering it? See UCC 3–412; UCC 3–104; UCC 3–301; UCC 3–305(a), (b); UCC 3–302; UCC 1–201(20); UCC 3–205; UCC 3–303; UCC 3–103(a)(4); UCC 1–201(25); Note (2) on Defenses to Payment Obligations, infra.

(b) What result if *B* delivered the note without having indorsed it? Can *C* even bring suit against *A*? See UCC 3–412; UCC 3–301; UCC 3–203; UCC 3–305. Would *C* improve its position by obtaining *B*'s indorsement before bringing suit?

(c) Assume that *B* delivered the note without having indorsed it. What result if *A* refused to pay for the goods because *B* had failed to repay a loan from *A*? Does it matter when *B*'s default occurred? See UCC 3–203(c); UCC 3–305(a) and Comment 3 (last paragraph).

NOTES ON DEFENSES TO PAYMENT OBLIGATIONS

(1) Rights to Payment. Problem 1.4.3 represents a typical commercial transaction with which you will become increasingly familiar. Seller (B) sells goods to Buyer (A) on **open account**, i.e., Buyer's unsecured obligation is not represented by a negotiable promissory note but simply by a purchase order or other writing that, perhaps taken together with other writings, creates a contract. Finance Company (C) finances Seller's rights to payment (accounts) by advancing funds against the accounts as they

is subject to any defense or claim of the obligor which accrues before the obligor receives notification of the assignment but not to defenses or claims which accrue thereafter except as stated in this Section or as provided by statute."

arise. In this way, Seller obtains cash immediately, without having to wait for the credit period to expire. (Accounts receivable financing is quite complicated; it is discussed in detail in Chapter 9, Section 1, infra.)

Upon Seller's default on its obligation to Finance Company, and even before if Seller agrees, Finance Company may collect from Buyer on Buyer's obligation. See R9–607(a)(1) (in Article 9 terminology, Finance Company is the "secured party" and Buyer is an "account debtor"). Whether Finance Company will succeed in collecting from Buyer depends in large part on whether Buyer is able to pay and whether it is legally obligated to do so. Finance Company may be concerned about the credit risk, i.e., the risk that, when the obligation is enforced, Buyer will be unable or unwilling to pay. Finance Company may choose to investigate the creditworthiness of Buyer. Or, if Finance Company is receiving an assignment of a large number of receivables, then it may elect to investigate the creditworthiness of Seller's customers *generally* before it agrees to take Seller's accounts as collateral. In addition, Finance Company can take steps to minimize the risk that Buyer can assert valid defenses to its obligation. These steps may include determining Seller's reputation for performing its contracts before Finance Company extends credit.

When Finance Company calls upon Buyer to pay, Buyer may raise a defense to its obligation to pay for the goods. For example, if the goods never were delivered, Buyer would have a defense of failure of consideration. If the goods were delivered and accepted but were nonconforming, as in Problem 1.4.3, Buyer would have the right to deduct from its obligation for the price (UCC 2–709) its damages for breach of warranty (UCC 2–714). See UCC 2–717. The right to deduct sometimes is called **recoupment**. See Note (2), infra. Under some circumstances, Buyer may be able to revoke its acceptance of the goods. See UCC 2–608. Are these defenses (or claims in recoupment) available to defeat Finance Company?

R9–404(a) contains a provision that protects parties to contracts, like Buyer, from unexpected inroads on their contractual relationships—another example of the "security of property" principle discussed in Section (3)(A), supra. Under this provision, the assignee of a right to payment, like the purchaser of goods, ordinarily acquires no better rights than the assignor had.[8] Thus, the assignment of Seller's right to payment does not ipso facto deprive Buyer of its right to defend against the claim.[9] On the other hand, R9–403(b) contains a good-faith-purchase rule: A **waiver-of-defense clause**, whereby Buyer agrees not to assert against an assignee any claim or defense that Buyer may have against Seller, is enforceable by

---

8. With respect to transactions not covered by Article 9, see Restatement (Second) of Contracts §§ 336(1), (2), which contain rules that are similar to R9–404(a).

9. R9–404(a) subjects the assignee to a buyer's claims as well as its defenses. A buyer who pays the contract price for defective goods has a claim against the seller for damages. See UCC 2–714. A buyer may assert this claim against the seller's assignee (here, Finance Company) only to reduce the amount the buyer owes; the buyer may not recover from Finance Company any payments already made. R9–404(b).

an assignee (i.e., a secured party) who takes the assignment for value, in good faith, and without notice of any claim or defense.[10]

The implications of the preceding sentence may not be readily apparent. Buyer buys goods on credit from Seller pursuant to an agreement containing a waiver-of-defense clause. Seller borrows from Finance Company and uses Buyer's obligation (and the obligations of Seller's other customers) as collateral. The goods prove to be defective. If *Seller* were to demand payment from Buyer, Buyer would have a defense. But *Finance Company* may enforce the agreement and take free of that defense if it acquired its security interest for value, in good faith, and without notice of any claims or defenses. In short, Buyer is legally obligated to pay Finance Company for the defective goods.

Of course, even if Buyer must pay the price to Finance Company, Buyer still has a claim against Seller. The following considerations, which are particularly striking in consumer transactions (discussed below in Note (4)), suggest that Buyer is in a stronger position if it can assert a defense against Finance Company: (1) *The inertia of litigation.* Setting up a defense as a defendant is easier than starting an action, even though the "burden of proof" with regard to Seller's breach may fall on Buyer in either case. In practice, this consideration has its greatest impact on the settlement value of Buyer's claim, since a reduction in price is much easier to negotiate than a cash refund. (2) *The strain of current cash outlay.* Buyer may not have the resources to pay the full amount for defective goods and wait (perhaps for years) until a legal action against Seller can reach trial and finally be converted into a judgment. (3) *The risk of Seller's insolvency.* Seller may be insolvent or **judgment proof**. Seller may have been a fly-by-night operator, or driven into sharp practice by financial pressure, or forced to the wall by keen competition, poor management, or a business recession.

Conversely, these advantages to Buyer in preserving defenses against an action for the price suggest the importance to Finance Company of freeing itself from these defenses. Finance Company's interest is magnified to the extent that buyers interpose spurious defenses in an attempt to scale down or avoid their obligation to pay for what they buy.

(2) Negotiable Instruments. Like accounts, negotiable instruments are used as collateral. If the payee-debtor defaults on its obligation to the secured party, the secured party has a right (as against the debtor) to collect on the note from the maker (here, Buyer). See R9–607(a). However, the secured party normally must have possession of the instrument as a condition to enforcing it. See UCC 3–412; UCC 3–301.

As is the case with claims, Article 3 contains both a security of property rule and a good-faith-purchase rule with respect to defenses. The former is found in UCC 3–203(b): "Transfer of an instrument . . . vests in the transferee any right of the transferor to enforce the instrument. . . ." The right to enforce the obligation of a party to an instrument ordinarily is

---

10. The agreement is not enforceable with respect to defenses that may be asserted against a holder in due course unless other law would give it effect. R9–403(c), (f). These few defenses are set forth in UCC 3–305(a)(1). See UCC 3–305(b).

subject to the claims and defenses set forth in UCC 3–305(a). These include "a defense of the obligor that would be available if the person entitled to enforce the instrument were enforcing a right to payment under a simple contract," UCC 3–305(a)(2), as well as certain "claim[s] in recoupment." UCC 3–305(a)(3). A holder in due course (UCC 3–302(a)) takes free of most defenses and claims in recoupment. See UCC 3–305(b). A person having the rights of an HDC can transfer those rights, even to a person who does not itself qualify as an HDC (e.g., because it is not a holder or did not give value for the instrument). Under those circumstances, the transferee acquires the rights of the HDC and takes free of most defenses and claims in recoupment. See UCC 3–203(b).

The UCC does not define "recoupment." Generally speaking, it means the right of a defendant to reduce its liability for damages by deducting damages caused by the plaintiff's failure to comply with its obligations under the *same contract*. Consider the facts of Problems 1.4.4(a) and (b). By accepting nonconforming goods, Buyer becomes liable for their price under UCC 2–709; however, the nonconformity gives rise to a claim for damages against Seller under UCC 2–714. UCC 2–717 affords Buyer a right of recoupment: "The buyer on notifying the seller of his intention to do so may deduct all or any part of the damages resulting from any breach of the contract from any part of the price still due under the contract." Ordinarily, Finance Company will take subject to this right of recoupment.[11]

Not uncommonly, as in Problem 1.4.4(c), Buyers seek to **set off** against their obligation to pay for goods, a claim against the Seller arising from an *unrelated* transaction.[12] In some jurisdictions, Buyer's right to set off would be a good defense against Seller's action for the price. Regardless of whether Buyer enjoys setoff rights against Seller, the drafters of Article 3 apparently intended that Buyer not be permitted to set off against Seller's transferees, such as Finance Company. They accomplished this result through the negative implicit in UCC 3–305(a)(3): The right to enforce *is* subject to "a claim in recoupment . . . if the claim arose from the transaction that gave rise to the instrument." The right to enforce *is not* subject to claims in recoupment that arise from other transactions. See UCC 3–305, Comment 3 (last paragraph).

Enabling the transferee of a note to take free of the maker's rights of setoff may result in the anomaly that a transferee who gives no value for

---

11. Buyer may use its claim for breach of warranty "only to reduce the amount owing on the instrument at the time the action is brought." UCC 3–305(a)(3). Buyer may not use this claim to recover from Finance Company amounts previously paid. Article 9 takes the same approach to rights to payment that have not been embodied in a negotiable instrument. See note 7, supra.

12. Setoff is not restricted to merchants and other commercial parties. Suppose Jack and Jill go out to dinner and a movie. Jack pays $9 for Jill's dinner and Jill pays $6 for Jack's movie ticket. Rather than give Jack $9 for dinner and then collect $6 from Jack for the movie, Jill will set off her $6 claim against her $9 obligation and pay Jack the difference, $3.

In many jurisdictions, setoff differs from recoupment: the former relates to claims unrelated to the contract upon which the defendant is being sued, whereas the latter relates to claims based upon the same contract. Often, however, the term setoff is used to encompass both concepts.

the note (e.g., Buyer's donee) acquires better rights than a person who gives value for an assignment of an obligation that is not represented by a note (e.g., *C* in Problem 1.4.3(b)), supra. See R9–404(a). Can this anomaly be justified, especially given that R9–403 analogizes good-faith purchasers of rights to payment with holders in due course of negotiable instruments?

Other Consequences. Although waiver-of-defense clauses and negotiable notes may accomplish the same primary objective—insulation of the secured party from the buyer's defenses—the negotiable note can have legal consequences that reach beyond a contractual "cut-off" clause. For example, a person who has executed a negotiable note cannot safely make payment without obtaining the instrument and seeing that the payment is noted on it. The reason is that the instrument might be negotiated thereafter to a holder in due course, who, under the basic rules of UCC 3–305, takes free of the maker's defenses, including payment. See also UCC 3–601(b) (discharge is not effective against a person acquiring rights of an HDC without notice of the discharge). (A railroad or warehouse that has issued a negotiable document of title—bill of lading or warehouse receipt—runs a similar risk if it delivers the goods without surrender of, or notation on, the document. See Section 5, infra.)

(3) "Transferable Records." To qualify as a negotiable instrument under UCC Article 3, a note must be written. See UCC 3–104(a); UCC 3–103(a)(9). In the 1990's business transactions increasingly became evidenced by electronic rather than paper records. We have seen that one of the major benefits of negotiability—the ability to acquire a right to payment free of the claims and defenses of the person obligated to pay—can be acquired by obtaining the obligated person's agreement to that effect. See R9–403(b). Other benefits, including the ability to acquire the right to payment free of third-party claims, cannot be achieved readily (if at all) by contract. To enable businesses to acquire the benefits of negotiability in an electronic environment, in 1999 NCCUSL promulgated section 16 of UETA. As of this writing (September 2001), UETA has been enacted in 36 states and the District of Columbia.

UETA 16(a) provides for the creation of a "transferable record"—an electronic record that would be a note under UCC Article 3 if it were in writing.[13] An electronic record can qualify as a transferable record only if the issuer agrees that it is a transferable record. UETA 16(a)(2). A person can become the holder of a transferable record and acquire the same rights as a holder of a negotiable note under Article 3 by having "control" of the electronic record. UETA 16(d). As Comment 3 to UETA 16 explains, "Under Section 16 acquisition of 'control' over an electronic record serves as a substitute for 'possession' in the paper analog. More precisely, 'control' under Section 16 serves as the substitute for delivery, indorsement and possession of a negotiable promissory note." A person who has control and also satisfies the requirements of UCC 3–302(a) acquires the rights of a holder in due course. UETA 16(d).

---

13. The term "transferable record" also encompasses an electronic record that would be a document under UCC Article 7 if it were in writing. See Section 5, infra.

UETA 16 establishes a general standard for control: "A person has control of a transferable record if a system employed for evidencing the transfer of interests in the transferable record reliably establishes that person as the person to which the transferable record was issued or transferred." UETA 16(b). It also provides, in UETA 16(c), "a safe harbor list of very strict requirements for such a system." UETA 16, Comment 3. Neither the general standard nor the safe harbor mandates the use of particular technology; rather, any system that accomplishes the purpose of "control"—to reliably establish the identity of the person entitled to payment—is sufficient. For the most part, systems for control are still under development. However, at least one system has begun to be used for the creation and transfer of home mortgage notes. See http://www.eoriginal.com/news/press/pr072400.htm (visited 7/31/00).

Federal law also contemplates the creation of negotiable, "transferable records." See E–SIGN § 201. Section 201 of E–SIGN generally tracks UETA 16, but the federal rule applies only to an electronic record that "relates to a loan secured by real property." Id. § 201(a)(1)(C). The transfer of mortgage notes is discussed in more detail in Chapter 11, Section 4(B), infra.

(4) Good Faith Purchase in Consumer Transactions. Permitting *commercial* buyers to waive their right to assert defenses against third parties, whether by a waiver-of-defense clause or a negotiable note, for the most part has been uncontroversial. Application of the rule to consumer buyers has presented a special problem. For several decades, opposing interests struggled over whether a financing agency should be permitted to insulate itself from defenses that a consumer buyer would have had against the seller. The result was a substantial revision of the traditional concept of good faith purchase as applied in consumer transactions.

The first victories for the consumer-protection view came in the courts, which began to hold by the early 1950's that a financing agency that was closely connected with a retailer could not be an HDC and was not protected by a waiver-of-defense clause. (The Article 9 provision that generally validated waiver-of-defense clauses was expressly "[s]ubject to any statute or decision which establishes a different rule for buyers or lessees of consumer goods." F9–206(1)). R9–403(f) is similar in effect. In the teeth of statutory language designed to protect the negotiability of notes, a substantial number of courts found legal grounds to place the burden of adjustment for the sellers' defaults upon secured parties.

Inasmuch as buyers had to show a sufficiently close connection between the seller and the financing agency in each case, judicial decisions fell short of giving buyers optimum protection. By the early 1970's, however, most state legislatures had enacted statutes applicable to consumer transactions prohibiting negotiable instruments and waiver-of-defense clauses, limiting their effectiveness, or depriving them of effect altogether. Under these statutes, some of which derive from 1974 version of the Uniform Consumer Credit Code ("U3C") 3.307, 3.404, it is no longer necessary to show that the financing agency and the seller were closely connected.

The 1974 U3C also dealt with a developing practice, known as "dragging the body," whereby a seller refers the buyer to a financing agency that makes a direct loan to the buyer. The loan is secured by an interest in the goods purchased by the buyer, and the financing agency makes sure that the loan proceeds are applied to purchase the goods by making its check payable jointly to the buyer and the seller. Should the buyer refuse payment of the loan on the ground of a defense against the seller, the financing agency responds that its contract with the buyer is entirely separate from the seller's contract with the buyer and was fully performed when it gave the buyer the money. Statutes protecting consumers in the case of direct loans include a requirement that there be a sufficient connection between the seller and the lender; for this reason they tend to be complex.

In 1976, Federal Trade Commission Rule 433 took effect, making it an "unfair and deceptive trade practice" for a seller to fail to incorporate in a contract of sale to a consumer a legend that preserves the buyer's defenses against the financing agency. In addition, if a seller receives the proceeds from a direct loan made to the buyer by a financing agency to which the seller "refers consumers" or with whom the seller "is affiliated . . . by common control, contract, or business arrangement," the loan contract must include a similar legend. 16 C.F.R. 433.1(d); 433.2. Placing the required legend on a note does not of itself destroy the note's negotiability; however, there cannot be an HDC of the note, even if the note otherwise is negotiable. UCC 3–106(d).

Staggering numbers of sellers and lenders, large and small, fall within the terms of the FTC Regulation. Suppose that sellers and lenders are not inclined to obey the Regulation and fail to use the prescribed provision. How effective are the FTC's tools to compel compliance? The FTC is authorized to bring civil actions against persons who violate FTC cease and desist orders and (more importantly) against persons who violate FTC rules respecting "unfair or deceptive acts or practices." See 15 U.S.C. § 57b.

Suppose a seller or lender nevertheless fails to include the prescribed formula in a contract and that, under state law, negotiable notes and waiver-of-defense clauses are effective to bar buyers from asserting defenses against transferees. Will the FTC Regulation override state law and allow the buyer to assert a defense or claim a refund? A substantial body of case law holds that FTC regulations do not ipso facto modify private rights or confer private rights of action. However, Revised Article 9 provides that the rights of an assignee of a contract that fails to include the required formula are the same as if the contract had included the formula. See R9–403(d); R9–404(d).

SECTION 5.   GOOD FAITH PURCHASE OF DOCUMENTS OF TITLE

Introductory Note. A "document of title" is another type of personal property that may be purchased. As the definition of the term suggests

(UCC 1–201(15)), documents of title purport to cover goods in the possession of a **bailee**. The two major types of documents of title are the "bill of lading" (UCC 1–201(6)), as to which the bailee is in the business of transporting or forwarding goods (e.g., a railroad), and the "warehouse receipt" (UCC 1–201(45)), as to which the bailee is engaged in the business of storing goods for hire (e.g., a warehouse).

A description of the common uses for the bill of lading and the warehouse receipt will aid in understanding the rights of secured parties whose collateral consists of documents of title and the rights of transferees of documents generally.

Bills of Lading. A bill of lading (originally, "bill of loading") is a document of title that a railroad or other **carrier** issues when goods are delivered to it for shipment. See UCC 1–201(6), (15). The UCC's rules governing bills of lading are collected in Article 7.[1] However, bills of lading in interstate shipments and exports are governed by the federal law, 49 U.S.C. §§ 80101–16, and not by the UCC. For present purposes, however, the differences are not crucial.

The bill of lading, in part, embodies a contract between the carrier and the shipper (often termed the "consignor," see UCC 7–102(1)(c)). This contract sets forth, inter alia, the consignor's obligations to pay freight and other charges and the carrier's obligations with respect to the transportation and delivery of the goods. It also addresses the carrier's liability in the event of casualty to the goods or failure to deliver.

Control of the bill of lading can be used to control delivery of the goods. In this regard, one must distinguish between the non-negotiable (or **straight**) bill of lading and the negotiable one. As is true with instruments, see supra Section 4, the form of the paper is determinative. See UCC 7–104. Under the *non-negotiable* bill of lading, the carrier undertakes to deliver the goods to a stated person (the "consignee"). See UCC 7–102(1)(b); UCC 7–104(2). For example, if the bill of lading runs "to Buyer & Co.," then the carrier discharges its delivery obligation by delivering the goods to Buyer & Co. Because the carrier can perform its contract by delivering to the named person (Buyer & Co.), Buyer need not present the bill of lading or even have taken possession of it. See UCC 7–403; UCC 7–404. Cf. Section 2(B), supra.

Buyer may have bought the goods for resale (to, say, *C*). If *C* contracts to buy the goods before Buyer takes delivery, Buyer will give written instructions to the carrier to deliver the goods to *C*, thereby entitling *C* to enforce the carrier's delivery obligation. See UCC 7–403. In this way, Buyer can transfer control over the goods without taking possession of them. Note, however, that although notification of the carrier entitles *C* to obtain delivery, the carrier nevertheless may honor Seller's instruction to stop

---

1. Not all of Article 7 applies to bills of lading; Part 2 contains special provisions applicable only to warehouse receipts.

delivery if it wishes to do so. See UCC 7–403(1)(d); UCC 2–705; Problem 1.2.3, supra.

Under the *negotiable* bill of lading, the carrier agrees to deliver the goods to the order of a stated person, e.g., "to the order of Seller & Co.," or occasionally to "bearer." The carrier's delivery obligation runs to the holder of the document. See UCC 7–403; UCC 1–201(20). If the document runs to the order of Seller but the person to receive the goods is someone other than Seller (say, Buyer or *C*), then Seller must indorse and deliver the bill of lading to that person so that the person becomes a holder.

One of the important practical consequences of shipping under a negotiable bill of lading is that the carrier will deliver the goods only to one who surrenders the bill of lading. See UCC 7–403(3). If Seller wants to be sure of being paid before Buyer gets the goods, Seller may use a negotiable bill of lading, consign the shipment to the order of Seller, and thereby maintain control over the goods until Buyer pays. When Seller (or, more often, its local agent) receives payment, the agent will deliver the indorsed bill of lading to Buyer. At that point Buyer can take the bill of lading to the carrier and receive the goods.

Warehouse Receipts. Warehouse receipts (receipts issued by a person in the business of storing goods for hire, see UCC 1–201(45)) function much like bills of lading: They serve as a receipt for goods delivered to a bailee, set forth the terms of the contract between the bailor and bailee (warehouse), and enable parties to transfer control over goods without the need to take possession of them. Like bills of lading, warehouse receipts may be negotiable or non-negotiable, depending upon their form. See UCC 7–104.

Nature delivers great crops at annual harvests, while consumption is gradual throughout the year. Consequently, commodities of enormous value must be kept in storage pending processing, distribution, and use. Other commodities—like fuel oil—are stored in large quantities because their use is seasonal. In other instances, storage is a significant part of preparation for use. Seasoning for years in charred oak barrels is of the essence in making good whiskey. Warehouse receipts may be employed as a means for traders to deal in these goods without the inconvenience of physical delivery. A slightly different use arises when a concern, such as a brewer or a mill, needs to hold commodities that tie up more capital than it can spare. Using warehouse receipts as collateral may facilitate a low-interest loan that otherwise would not be available.

Both a negotiable warehouse receipt and a non-negotiable warehouse receipt are reproduced in the following pages:

AMERICAN WAREHOUSE COMPANY
A PUBLIC WAREHOUSE
2121 AMERICAN AVENUE   •   AMERICA

Date of Issue   January 20, 1976   Consecutive No. 432

THIS IS TO CERTIFY that we have received in Storage Warehouse _____

situated at ____2121 American Avenue____

for the account of ____O Company, Inc.____

in apparent good order, except as noted hereon (contents, condition and quality unknown) the following described property, subject to all the terms and conditions contained herein and on the reverse hereof, such property to be delivered to (His) (Their) (Its) order, upon payment of all storage, handling and other charges and the surrender of this Warehouse Receipt properly endorsed.

LOT NO.	QUANTITY	SAID TO BE OR CONTAIN	STORAGE PER MONTH		HANDLING IN AND OUT	
			RATE	PER	RATE	PER
3628	250 bales	Cotton	¢	bale	¢	bale

NEGOTIABLE
Quantities subject to deliveries noted below.

Advances have been made and liability incurred on such goods, as follows:

_____

_____

    The property covered by this receipt has NOT been insured by this company for the benefit of the depositor against fire or any other casualty.

(This clause to be omitted from forms used in those states where warehousemen are required by law to insure goods.)

American Warehouse Company claims a lien for all lawful charges for storage and preservation of the goods; also for all lawful claims for money advanced, interest, insurance, transportation, labor, weighing, coopering and other charges and expenses in relation to such goods.

AMERICAN WAREHOUSE COMPANY

By   *John Jones*

        John Jones, Vice President

THE GOODS MENTIONED BELOW ARE HEREBY RELEASED FROM THIS RECEIPT FOR DELIVERY FROM WAREHOUSE. ANY UNRELEASED BALANCE OF THE GOODS IS SUBJECT TO A LIEN FOR UNPAID CHARGES AND ADVANCES ON THE RELEASED PORTION.

DELIVERIES

DATE	LOT NUMBER	QUANTITY RELEASED		SIGNATURE	QUANTITY DUE ON RECEIPT
2/25/76	3628	50	bales	*Henry Smith*	200 bales

This Receipt Is Valid Only When Signed by an Officer of the Company.

[B2873]

NEGOTIABLE WAREHOUSE RECEIPT

[Front—Printed on Green Paper—Reduced in Size]

AMERICAN WAREHOUSE COMPANY
STREET ADDRESS • CITY & AMERICA 00000
TELEPHONE: (312) – 123-4567

ORIGINAL
NON-NEGOTIABLE WAREHOUSE RECEIPT

AMERICAN WAREHOUSE COMPANY claims a lien for all lawful charges for storage and preservation of the goods; also for all lawful claims for money advanced, interest, insurance, transportation, labor, weighing, coopering and other charges and expenses in relation to such goods, and for the balance on any other accounts that may be due. The property covered by this receipt has NOT been insured by this Company for the benefit of the depositor against fire or any other casualty.

DOCUMENT NUMBER
1046

DATE
Jan. 20, 1976

CUSTOMER NUMBER
8919

CUSTOMER ORDER NO

O Company, Inc.
200 State Street
Statesville, New York

THIS IS TO CERTIFY THAT WE HAVE RECEIVED the goods listed hereon in apparent good order, except as noted herein (contents, condition and quality unknown), SUBJECT TO ALL TERMS AND CONDITIONS INCLUDING LIMITATION OF LIABILITY HEREIN AND ON THE REVERSE HEREOF. Such property to be delivered to THE DEPOSITOR upon the payment of all storage, handling and other charges. Advances have been made and liability incurred on these goods as follows.

O Company, Inc.
200 State Street
Statesville, New York

WAREHOUSE NO
1046

DELIVERING CARRIER	CARRIER NUMBER	PREPAID/COLLECT	SH PRESS NUMBER
PC	PC 458632	Prepaid	

QUANTITY	SAID TO BE OR CONTAIN (CUSTOMER ITEM NO. WAREHOUSE ITEM NO. LOT NUMBER DESCRIPTION ETC.)		WEIGHT	REC'D	STORAGE RATE / HANDLING RATE	DAMAGE & EXCEPTIONS
250	bales cotton	500 lbs.	125,000		¢cs / ¢cs	None
	TOTALS					

NO DELIVERY WILL BE MADE ON THIS RECEIPT EXCEPT ON WRITTEN ORDER.

AMERICAN WAREHOUSE COMPANY

BY _John James_
AUTHORIZED SIGNATURE

[B2875]

NON–NEGOTIABLE WAREHOUSE RECEIPT

[Front—Printed on White Paper—Reduced in Size]

The property described on this receipt is stored and handled in accordance with the terms and conditions of the Contract and Rate Quotation approved by the American Warehousemen's Association. These Contract and Rate Quotation terms and conditions are repeated below for the convenience of the storer and others having an interest in the property.

STANDARD CONTRACT TERMS AND CONDITIONS FOR MERCHANDISE WAREHOUSEMEN

(APPROVED AND PROMULGATED BY THE AMERICAN WAREHOUSEMEN'S ASSOCIATION, OCTOBER 1968)

ACCEPTANCE — Sec. 1

(a) This contract and rate quotation including accessorial charges endorsed on or attached hereto must be accepted within 30 days from the proposal date by signature of depositor on the reverse side of the contract. In the absence of written acceptance, the act of tendering goods described herein for storage or other services by warehouseman within 30 days from the proposal date shall constitute such acceptance by depositor.

(b) In the event that goods tendered for storage or other services do not conform to the description contained herein, or conforming goods are tendered after 30 days from the proposal date without prior written acceptance by depositor as provided in paragraph (a) of this section, warehouseman may refuse to accept such goods. If warehouseman accepts such goods, depositor agrees to rates and charges as may be assigned and invoiced by warehouseman and to all terms of this contract.

(c) This contract may be cancelled by either party upon 30 days written notice and is cancelled if no storage or other services are performed under this contract for a period of 180 days.

SHIPPING — Sec. 2

Depositor agrees not to ship goods to warehouseman as the named consignee. If, in violation of this agreement, goods are shipped to warehouseman as named consignee, depositor agrees to notify carrier in writing prior to such shipment, with copy of such notice to the warehouseman, that warehouseman named as consignee is a warehouseman and has no beneficial title or interest in such property and depositor further agrees to indemnify and hold harmless warehouseman from any and all claims for unpaid transportation charges, including undercharges, demurrage, detention or charges of any nature in connection with goods so shipped. Depositor further agrees that, if it fails to notify carrier as required by the next preceding sentence, warehouseman shall have the right to refuse such goods and shall not be liable or responsible for any loss, injury or damage of any nature to, or related to, such goods. Depositor agrees that all promises contained in this section will be binding on depositor's heirs, successors and assigns.

TENDER FOR STORAGE — Sec. 3

All goods for storage shall be delivered at the warehouse properly marked and packaged for handling. The depositor shall furnish at or prior to such delivery, a manifest showing marks, brands, or sizes to be kept and accounted for separately, and the class of storage and other services desired.

STORAGE PERIOD AND CHARGES — Sec. 4

(a) All charges for storage are per package or other agreed unit per month.

(b) Storage charges become applicable upon the date that warehouseman accepts care, custody and control of the goods, regardless of unloading date or date of issue of warehouse receipt.

(c) Except as provided in paragraph (d) of this section, a full month's storage charge will apply on all goods received between the first and the 15th, inclusive, of a calendar month; one-half month's storage charge will apply on all goods received between the 16th and last day, inclusive, of a calendar month, and a full month's storage charge will apply to all goods in storage on the first day of the next succeeding calendar months. All storage charges are due and payable on the first day of storage for the initial month and thereafter on the first day of the calendar month.

(d) When mutually agreed by the warehouseman and the depositor, a storage month shall extend from a date in one calendar month to, but not including, the same date of the next and all succeeding months. All storage charges are due and payable on the first day of the storage month.

TRANSFER, TERMINATION OF STORAGE, REMOVAL OF GOODS — Sec. 5

(a) Instructions to transfer goods on the books of the warehouseman are not effective until delivered to and accepted by warehouseman, and all charges up to the time transfer is made are chargeable to the depositor of record. If a transfer involves rehandling the goods, such will be subject to a charge. When goods in storage are transferred from one party to another through issuance of a new warehouse receipt, a new storage date is established on the date of transfer.

(b) The warehouseman reserves the right to move, at his expense, 14 days after notice is sent by certified or registered mail to the depositor of record or to the last known holder of the negotiable warehouse receipt, any goods in storage from the warehouse in which they may be stored to any other of his warehouses; but if such depositor or holder takes delivery of his goods in lieu of transfer, no storage charge shall be made for the current storage month. The warehouseman may, without notice move goods within the warehouse in which they are stored.

(c) The warehouseman may, upon written notice to the depositor of record and any other person known by the warehouseman to claim an interest in the goods, require the removal of any goods by the end of the next succeeding storage month. Such notice shall be given to the last known place of business or abode of the person to be notified. If goods are not removed before the end of the next succeeding storage month, the warehouseman may sell them in accordance with applicable law.

(d) If warehouseman in good faith believes that the goods are about to deteriorate or decline in value to less than the amount of warehouseman's lien before the end of the next succeeding storage month, the warehouseman may specify in the notification any reasonable shorter time for removal of the goods and in case the goods are not removed, may sell them at public sale held one week after a single advertisement or posting as provided by law.

NEGOTIABLE OR NON–NEGOTIABLE WAREHOUSE RECEIPT

[*Back—Printed on Same Color Paper as Front*]

(e) If as a result of a quality or condition of the goods of which the warehouseman had no notice at the time of deposit the goods are a hazard to other property or to the warehouse or to other persons, the warehouseman may sell the goods at public or private sale without advertisement on reasonable notification to all persons known to claim an interest in the goods. If the warehouseman after a reasonable effort is unable to sell the goods he may dispose of them in any lawful manner and shall incur no liability by reason of such disposition. Pending such disposition, sale or return of the goods, the warehouseman may remove the goods from the warehouse and shall incur no liability by reason of such removal.

HANDLING — Sec. 6

(a) The handling charge covers the ordinary labor involved in receiving goods at warehouse door, placing goods in storage, and returning goods to warehouse door. Handling charges are due and payable on receipt of goods.

(b) Unless otherwise agreed, labor for unloading and loading goods will be subject to a charge. Additional expenses incurred by the warehouseman in receiving and handling damaged goods, and additional expense in unloading from or loading into cars or other vehicles not at warehouse door will be charged to the depositor.

(c) Labor and materials used in loading rail cars or other vehicles are chargeable to the depositor.

(d) When goods are ordered out in quantities less than in which received, the warehouseman may make an additional charge for each order or each item of an order.

(e) The warehouseman shall not be liable for demurrage, delays in unloading inbound cars, or delays in obtaining and loading cars for outbound shipment unless warehouseman has failed to exercise reasonable care.

DELIVERY REQUIREMENTS — Sec. 7

(a) No goods shall be delivered or transferred except upon receipt by the warehouseman of complete instructions properly signed by the depositor. However, when no negotiable receipt is outstanding, goods may be delivered upon instructions by telephone in accordance with a prior written authorization, but the warehouseman shall not be responsible for loss or error occasioned thereby.

(b) When a negotiable receipt has been issued no goods covered by that receipt shall be delivered, or transferred on the books of the warehouseman, unless the receipt, properly endorsed, is surrendered for cancellation, or for endorsement of partial delivery thereon. If a negotiable receipt is lost or destroyed, delivery of goods may be made only upon order of a court of competent jurisdiction and the posting of security approved by the court as provided by law.

(c) When goods are ordered out a reasonable time shall be given the warehouseman to carry out instructions, and if he is unable because of acts of God, war, public enemies, seizure under legal process, strikes, lockouts, riots and civil commotions, or any reason beyond the warehouseman's control, or because of loss or destruction of goods for which warehouseman is not liable, or because of any other excuse provided by law, the warehouseman shall not be liable for failure to carry out such instructions and goods remaining in storage will continue to be subject to regular storage charges.

EXTRA SERVICES (SPECIAL SERVICES) — Sec. 8

(a) Warehouse labor required for services other than ordinary handling and storage will be charged to the depositor.

(b) Special services requested by depositor including but not limited to compiling of special stock statements; reporting marked weights, serial numbers or other data from packages; physical check of goods; and handling transit billing will be subject to a charge.

(c) Dunnage, bracing, packing materials or other special supplies, may be provided for the depositor at a charge in addition to the warehouseman's cost.

(d) By prior arrangement, goods may be received or delivered during other than usual business hours, subject to a charge.

(e) Communication expense including postage, teletype, telegram, or telephone will be charged to the depositor if such concern more than normal inventory reporting or if, at the request of the depositor, communications are made by other than regular United States Mail.

BONDED STORAGE — Sec. 9

(a) A charge in addition to regular rates will be made for merchandise in bond.

(b) Where a warehouse receipt covers goods in U. S. Customs bond, such receipt shall be void upon the termination of the storage period fixed by law.

MINIMUM CHARGES — Sec. 10

(a) A minimum handling charge per lot and a minimum storage charge per lot per month will be made. When a warehouse receipt covers more than one lot or when a lot is in assortment, a minimum charge per mark, brand, or variety will be made.

(b) A minimum monthly charge to one account for storage and/or handling will be made. This charge will apply also to each account when one customer has several accounts, each requiring separate records and billing.

LIABILITY AND LIMITATION OF DAMAGES — Sec. 11

(A) THE WAREHOUSEMAN SHALL NOT BE LIABLE FOR ANY LOSS OR INJURY TO GOODS STORED HOWEVER CAUSED UNLESS SUCH LOSS OR INJURY RESULTED FROM THE FAILURE BY THE WAREHOUSEMAN TO EXERCISE SUCH CARE IN REGARD TO THEM AS A REASONABLY CAREFUL MAN WOULD EXERCISE UNDER LIKE CIRCUMSTANCES AND WAREHOUSEMAN IS NOT LIABLE FOR DAMAGES WHICH COULD NOT HAVE BEEN AVOIDED BY THE EXERCISE OF SUCH CARE.

(B) GOODS ARE NOT INSURED BY WAREHOUSEMAN AGAINST LOSS OR INJURY HOWEVER CAUSED.

(C) THE DEPOSITOR DECLARES THAT DAMAGES ARE LIMITED TO _____ PROVIDED, HOWEVER, THAT SUCH LIABILITY MAY AT THE TIME OF ACCEPTANCE OF THIS CONTRACT AS PROVIDED IN SECTION 1 BE INCREASED ON PART OR ALL OF THE GOODS HEREUNDER IN WHICH EVENT A MONTHLY STORAGE CHARGE OF _____ WILL BE MADE IN ADDITION TO THE REGULAR MONTHLY STORAGE CHARGE.

NOTICE OF CLAIM AND FILING OF SUIT — Sec. 12

(a) Claims by the depositor and all other persons must be presented in writing to the warehouseman within a reasonable time, and in no event longer than either 60 days after delivery of the goods by the warehouseman or 60 days after depositor of record or the last known holder of a negotiable warehouse receipt is notified that loss or injury to part or all of the goods has occurred, whichever time is shorter.

(b) No action may be maintained by the depositor or others against the warehouseman for loss or injury to the goods stored unless timely written claim has been given as provided in paragraph (a) of this section and unless such action is commenced either within nine months after date of delivery by warehouseman or within nine months after depositor of record or the last known holder of a negotiable warehouse receipt is notified that loss or injury to part or all of the goods has occurred, whichever time is shorter.

(c) When goods have not been delivered, notice may be given of known loss or injury to the goods by mailing of a registered or certified letter to the depositor of record or to the last known holder of a negotiable warehouse receipt. Time limitations for presentation of claim in writing and maintaining of action after notice begun on the date of mailing of such notice by warehouseman.

(B2874)

NEGOTIABLE OR NON–NEGOTIABLE WARE-HOUSE RECEIPT

[Back—Printed on Same Color Paper as Front]

Purchasers of Documents of Title. A purchaser who takes a warehouse receipt or bill of lading wishes to be sure that it takes both the document and the goods free from the claims of third parties, including secured parties. The first three Problems below address some of the risks that the purchaser runs in this regard. A purchaser also wishes to take free of any defenses the issuer (warehouse or carrier) may raise to its delivery obligation. Problem 1.5.4 addresses three of these potential defenses as they apply to warehouse receipts: non-receipt (the warehouse never received the goods); misdescription (the goods actually received were not as described in the receipt); and disappearance (the goods disappeared). As for misdelivery (delivery of goods by the issuer to the wrong person), the UCC generally imposes absolute liability on a bailee who delivers goods to one other than a "person entitled under the document." See UCC 7–403(1).

Electronic Documents of Title. Although UCC Article 7 contemplates only written documents of title, the storage and transportation industries have begun to use electronic documents. The first statutory basis for electronic documents appeared in the United States Warehouse Act, which authorizes the use of electronic warehouse receipts covering cotton and contains provisions specifically addressing security interests in cotton covered by an electronic receipt. See 7 U.S.C. § 259(c). Efforts currently are underway to amend the Act to authorize the use of electronic documents covering all agricultural products.

We saw in Section 4, supra, that the Uniform Electronic Transactions Act provides a statutory framework for the transfer of an electronic record that would be a note under UCC Article 3 if it were in writing. The same framework applies to an electronic record that would be a document under Article 7 if it were in writing. As with electronic notes, an electronic document (warehouse receipt or bill of lading) is a "transferable record" under UETA only if the issuer of the electronic record expressly agrees that the record is to be considered a "transferable record." See UETA 16(a). A person can become the holder of a transferable record and acquire the same rights as a holder of an equivalent document under Article 7 by having "control" of the electronic record. Id. A person who has control and also satisfies the requirements of UCC 7–501 acquires the rights of a holder to whom a negotiable document of title has been duly negotiated ("HTWAN-DOTHBDN"). UETA 16(d).

———

A warehouse receipt embodying the obligation of the bailee to deliver goods has some similarity to a promissory note embodying the obligation of the maker to pay money. After you have worked through the following three Problems, consider the following: To what extent are the rules applicable to the transfer of warehouse receipts similar to those applicable to the transfer of negotiable instruments calling for the payment of money? To what extent are they similar to those applicable to the transfer of the goods themselves? To what extent must a person acquire the status of

HTWANDOTHBDN in order to take free of claims to the goods and defenses of the warehouse? To what extent does such a holder enjoy the same freedom from claims and defenses as a holder in due course?

Problem 1.5.1. A warehouse receipt covering 600 barrels of whiskey was issued to "Old Soak Beverage Company or order." In preparation for a proposed sale of the whiskey to another company, the president of Old Soak (A) indorsed the Company's name on the receipt. That night, Sal Sly (B), an ambitious bookkeeper, arranged to work late and took the receipt from the vault. Sly delivered the receipt to a friend in the liquor business (C), who sold and delivered the receipt to DT Beverage Company (D) for $120,000 cash (the fair market value). Both Sly and the friend disappeared.

(a) Who has the better claim to the whiskey? See UCC 7–104; UCC 7–502; UCC 7–501.

(b) Suppose D is Downtown Bank, which took the receipt to secure a new $25,000 loan. Is A's claim of ownership of the whiskey superior to D's security interest in it? Would the answer change if D took the warehouse receipt to secure a preexisting, unsecured loan?

(c) What result if B, rather than C, sold and delivered the warehouse receipt to DT Beverage Company? See UCC 7–501(4) and Comment 1; UCC 7–504. Does the statutory text adequately support the Comment?

(d) Suppose that A's president had not endorsed the document, but that B supplied a clever imitation of the president's signature. Is A or D entitled to the whiskey? See UCC 7–502(1) ("negotiated"); UCC 7–501(1) ("*his* indorsement"); UCC 7–504.

(e) Suppose that the warehouse receipt ran "for the account of Old Soak Beverage Company." Is A or D entitled to the whiskey? See UCC 7–504.

Problem 1.5.2. Old Soak Beverage Company (A) instructed Dale Driver (B), one of its truck drivers, to haul 100 barrels of whiskey from Old Soak's warehouse to the bottling works. Instead, Driver hauled the whiskey to Waiting Warehouse Company, stored the whiskey, and took a warehouse receipt deliverable to "Dale Driver or order." Driver then indorsed and delivered the warehouse receipt to Creative Finance Company (C) to secure a previously unsecured note. Driver is unable to pay the note, and both Creative Finance and Old Soak claim the whiskey.

(a) Who prevails? See UCC 7–502; UCC 7–503; UCC 7–504; Note on Authority and Power of Disposition, infra.

(b) What result if Driver had negotiated the receipt to a friend in the liquor business, who had negotiated it to Creative Finance?

Problem 1.5.3. While its own warehouse was being refurbished, Old Soak Beverage Company (A) temporarily stored several hundred barrels of whiskey with B, a competitor. Without Old Soak's consent, B delivered the goods to Waiting Warehouse Company, which issued a negotiable warehouse receipt to "B or order."

(a) *B* indorsed and delivered the receipt to DT Beverage Company (*C*), which promised to pay fair value for the whiskey in 30 days and did not suspect *B*'s wrongdoing. Who has the better claim to the whiskey, *A* or *C*? Would the answer change if the warehouse receipt were non-negotiable?

(b) What result if *B* indorsed and delivered the negotiable warehouse receipt to Downtown Bank, which took the receipt to secure a new loan and did not suspect *B*'s wrongdoing? Would the answer change if the warehouse receipt were non-negotiable?

(c) Compare your answers to this Problem with your answers to Problem 1.3.8, supra. Can you account for the differences in result?

NOTE ON AUTHORITY AND POWER OF DISPOSITION

Problem 1.5.2 invites you to consider, inter alia, whether Driver had "actual or apparent authority to ship, store or sell" the whiskey. UCC 7–503(1)(a). The Restatement (Second) of Agency (1958) does not use the term "actual authority," preferring instead the term "authority," which section 7 defines as "the power of the agent to affect the legal relations of the principal by acts done in accordance with the principal's manifestations of consent to him." What is the least authority that would empower Driver to pass good title under UCC 7–502 and 7–503? Consider: (i) authority to transport the whiskey to Old Soak's warehouse; (ii) authority to transport the whiskey to Waiting Warehouse; (iii) authority to deliver the whiskey to a named purchaser; (iv) authority to complete a sale to a named purchaser at a named price.

The near demise of law school courses in Agency makes it desirable to underline the limited applicability of the term "apparent authority" in UCC 7–503(1)(a). According to comment *a* to section 8 of the Restatement (Second) of Agency, "[a]pparent authority results from a manifestation by a person that another is his agent, the manifestation being made to a third person and not, as when authority is created, to the agent." The illustrations to that section give this example:

> P writes to A directing him to act as his agent for the sale of Blackacre. P sends a copy of this letter to T, a prospective purchaser. . . . [I]n the letter to A, P adds a postscript, not included in the copy to T, telling A to make no sale until after communication with P. A has no authority to sell Blackacre but, as to T, he has apparent authority.

Does the notion of "apparent authority" extend to the situations covered by the "entrusting" provision of UCC 2–403(2), discussed in Section 3(C), supra? Even if it does not, "power of disposition" under UCC 2–403 affords an alternative ground for depriving a person of its ownership interest or security interest in the goods when that interest comes in conflict with a claim of a HTWANDOTHBDN. UCC 2–403(2) affords a merchant to whom goods have been entrusted and who deals in goods of that kind the "power to transfer all rights of the entruster to a buyer in ordinary course of business." As the Notes on Entrustment, Section 3(C), supra, suggest, the merchant does not enjoy the power to transfer the entruster's rights to other (non-buyer) purchasers. Does UCC 7–503(1)(a) expand this "power of disposition"? Should it?

Note that even if *B* (in Problems 1.5.2 and 1.5.3) has "actual or apparent authority" or "power of disposition," Old Soak is not necessarily out of luck. See UCC 7–501(4).

Problem 1.5.4. Boris Bilk (*B*) fraudulently induced Acme Warehouse (*A*) to issue a negotiable warehouse receipt for 100 barrels of whiskey that was not delivered to the warehouse. Bilk duly negotiated the receipt to Creative Finance Company (*C*) to secure a loan. Creative Finance did not suspect the fraud.

(a) What are *C*'s rights against *A*? See UCC 7–203. (As to *C*'s recourse against *B*, see UCC 7–507.) Would it make a difference if the warehouse receipt had not been indorsed? If it had not been negotiable?

(b) What result if *A* had taken delivery of the barrels but they had contained water instead of whiskey? (Is the answer affected by any of the language of the warehouse receipt forms, supra?)

(c) What result if *A* had received the barrels from *B* but had lost them in some way? See UCC 7–204; Notes on the Scope of the Warehouse's Responsibility When Goods Disappear, infra. (Is the answer affected by any of the language of the warehouse receipt forms, supra?)

NOTES ON THE SCOPE OF THE WAREHOUSE'S RESPONSIBILITY WHEN GOODS DISAPPEAR

(1) I.C.C. Metals v. Municipal Warehouse. Under UCC 7–204, a warehouse is liable for loss of (or injury to) the goods caused by its failure to exercise reasonable care but is not liable for damages that could not have been avoided by the exercise of such care. Observe that this section does not limit the universe of potential plaintiffs to holders to whom negotiable warehouse receipts have been duly negotiated or even to holders of negotiable warehouse receipts.

Although the burden of going forward with evidence normally rests on the plaintiff (here, the bailor), a number of cases applying UCC 7–204 have imposed this burden on the defendant warehouse. Of particular interest is I.C.C. Metals, Inc. v. Municipal Warehouse Co., 50 N.Y.2d 657, 431 N.Y.S.2d 372, 409 N.E.2d 849 (1980), in which a commercial warehouse informed the bailor, an international metals trader, that it was unable to locate three lots (845 pounds) of an industrial metal called indium that it had taken for storage. The bailor commenced an action in conversion, seeking to recover the value of the indium, $100,000. The warehouse contended that the metal had been stolen through no fault of its own and that, in any event, the terms of the warehouse receipt limited the bailor's potential recovery to a maximum of $50 per lot, or $150. (The limitation complied with UCC 7–204(2).)

The trial court granted summary judgment for the bailor for the full value of the metal. It found that the bailor had made out a prima facie case of conversion by proffering undisputed proof that the indium had been delivered to the warehouse and that the warehouse had failed to return it upon a proper demand. The court concluded that the warehouse's contention that the metal had been stolen was completely speculative and that the warehouse had failed to raise any question of fact sufficient to warrant a trial on the issue. Finally, the trial court held that the contractual limitation upon liability was inapplicable to a conversion action. The Appellate Division affirmed, as did the Court of Appeals.

The Court of Appeals observed that UCC 7–204 contemplates that "a warehouse which fails to redeliver goods to the person entitled to their return upon a proper demand, may be liable for either negligence or conversion, depending upon the circumstances." Moreover, "although the merely careless bailee remains a bailee and is entitled to whatever limitations of liability the bailor has agreed to, the converter forsakes his status as bailee completely and accordingly forfeits the protections of such limitations." See UCC 7–204(2).

In negligence cases, the established rule in New York is that once the plaintiff proffers proof of delivery to the defendant warehouse, of a proper demand for its return, and of the warehouse's failure to honor the demand, then "the warehouse must come forward and explain the circumstances of the loss of or damage to the bailed goods upon pain of being held liable for negligence." For the first time, the court unambiguously applied the same burden-shifting rule to conversion cases. Thus, unless the warehouse comes forward with "an explanation supported by evidentiary proof in admissible form," the plaintiff will not be required to prove that the warehouse converted the goods.

Applying this rule to the explanation presented by the warehouse, the court stated the following in a footnote:

> Viewed most favorably to defendant, this evidence would indicate at most that theft by a third party was one possible explanation for the defendant's failure to redeliver the indium to plaintiff. This is simply insufficient, since the warehouse is required to show not merely what might conceivably have happened to the goods, but rather what actually happened to the goods. Defendant proved only that theft was possible, and presented no proof of an actual theft. Hence, the proffered explanation was inadequate as a matter of law.

409 N.E.2d at 853 n.3. The bailor having made a prima facie case of conversion and the warehouse having failed to present an adequate explanation, the bailor was entitled to summary judgment. Inasmuch as judgment was entered for conversion, rather than for negligence, the contractual limitation of damages became ineffective, see UCC 7–204(2) (2d sentence), and the bailor became entitled to recover the actual value of the missing indium.

A dissenting opinion accused the majority of "eras[ing] the critical distinction between negligence and conversion" and "doing violence to the law, without rhyme or reason." What policy considerations support imposing on the warehouse the burden of going forward with an explanation of what happened to the goods when *negligence* is alleged? Do these considerations support the two principal rulings in *I.C.C. Metals*: (i) permitting a plaintiff to sustain a *conversion* action without proving any intentional wrongdoing by the defendant and (ii) rendering ineffective a contractual limitation on liability entered into between two commercial parties? In practical effect, how far removed is the approach in *I.C.C. Metals* from the imposition of absolute liability on the warehouse? Is the result consistent with the standard of "care" in UCC 7–204(1)? Judicial response to *I.C.C. Metals* has been mixed.

(2) The Great "Salad Oil Swindle." Questions of warehouse responsibility *in excelsis* arose in connection with the 1963 disappearance from **field warehouse** tanks in Bayonne, New Jersey, of over a billion pounds of vegetable oils—one of the great commercial frauds of modern times. Leading banks in the United States and Britain had made loans totaling $150 million "secured" by warehouse receipts for oil for which the bailee was unable to account. See Procter & Gamble Distrib. Co. v. Lawrence American Field Warehousing Corp., 16 N.Y.2d 344, 266 N.Y.S.2d 785, 213 N.E.2d 873 (1965); N. Miller, The Great Salad Oil Swindle (1965); Brooks, Annals of Finance: Making the Customer Whole, The New Yorker, Nov. 14, 1964, at 160.

(3) Warehouses, Carriers, and Statutory Interpretation. An interesting (and puzzling) contrast is presented by the UCC's language on the responsibility of warehouses (UCC 7–204) and the provision on the responsibility of carriers (UCC 7–309). Subsection 4 of UCC 7–204 states: "This section does not impair or repeal ..." and leaves a blank for the preservation of *named* statutes that may impose a higher responsibility on the warehouse. On the other hand, UCC 7–309(1) on the responsibility of carriers, after articulating the "reasonably careful man" test, adds: "This subsection does not repeal or change any law *or rule of law* which imposes liability upon a common carrier for damages not caused by its negligence" (emphasis added). The phrase "rule of law" (as contrasted with the reference to specific statutes in UCC 7–204) provides access to (and possibly development of) the broad common-law liability of carriers as insurers of goods.[2] Do the reasons that led to the absolute liability of carriers apply to warehouses? Does the difference between the approaches of these two sections of the UCC bar the extension by analogy of absolute liability to warehouses? Would the failure of a warehouse to carry insurance protecting both itself and the owner constitute a default in the "reasonable care"

---

2. Federal law codifies the common-law liability of certain carriers for loss or injury to goods in interstate shipments, imports, and exports. See 49 U.S.C. §§ 11706, 14706 (imposing liability for "actual loss or injury to the property caused by" certain carriers). For certain carriers, the remedies provided "are in addition to remedies existing under another law or common law." 49 U.S.C. § 13103.

standard? If so, should the net result be simplified by a change in the language of the UCC?

In the drafting of statutory provisions like those of Article 7, who are likely to be more vocal—warehouses or those who may store goods with warehouses? In construing statutes that are reasonably susceptible to two interpretations, should courts give voice to those who are less vocal during the legislative process? Cf. Restatement (Second) of Contracts § 206 (1981) ("In choosing among the reasonable meanings of a promise or agreement or a term thereof, that meaning is generally preferred which operates against the party who supplies the words or from whom a writing otherwise proceeds."). Or should courts assume that the squeaky wheel got the grease and construe the statute to favor the "prevailing" interests?

CHAPTER 2

BASIC PRINCIPLES OF SALES LAW

DOMESTIC UNITED STATES LAW

Principles of law are basic if they are broad and deep in their application. In the United States law of sales, one of the most fundamental problems is the relationship between codified law and common law. Another set of fundamental problems in the law of sales centers on the relationship between the law and the marketplace. In this Chapter we consider both sets of basic legal problems.

A number of principles address the problem of the scope of application of Article 2 of the UCC. The first of these to be considered is the extent to which Article 2 has displaced common law, and the nature of that displacement. The initial question can be framed this way: What transactions (or parts of transactions) are governed by the Code and what transactions are governed by other law, usually the common law of contracts and other matters? As we will see, however, the relationship is codified and common law is not bipolar. Even when transactions are governed by Article 2, the common law is never completely displaced. The common law, in all transactions, undergirds and supplements the law found in the statute.

Article 2 is both facilitative and regulatory in nature. Overwhelmingly, the Code is intended to assist parties to exchange transactions, but broad regulatory provisions overlay the Code. Two of the most important of these are the transcendent obligation that all parties act in good faith in the performance and enforcement of sales contracts and the power of courts to strike down contracts or contract terms that are unconscionable.

SECTION 1. SCOPE OF UNIFORM COMMERCIAL CODE ARTICLE 2

UCC 2–102 declares that it "applies to transactions in goods." The principal transaction, reflected in the title of Article 2, is "sales." The principal actors are "buyers," defined somewhat tautologically in UCC 2–103(1)(a), and "sellers," similarly defined in (1)(d). The core meaning of "sale" is "the passing of title [to goods] from the seller to the buyer for a price." UCC 2–106(1). "Sales" result from "contracts for sale," defined in the same section and divided into "present sales" and "future sales." For the most part, these elementary concepts have clear meanings that do not often blur at the edges.[1]

The same cannot be said of "goods," the object of "sales." The Code defines "goods" as "all things (including specially manufactured goods) which are movable at the time of identification to the contract for sale other than the money in which the price is to be paid, investment securities (Article 8) and things in action." UCC 2–105(1). "Goods" has a clear core of meaning but bristles with difficulties in many settings.[2]

Are contracts for supply of electricity contracts for the sale of goods? Compare Singer Co. v. Baltimore Gas & Electric Co., 79 Md.App. 461, 558 A.2d 419 (1989), with Helvey v. Wabash County REMC, 151 Ind.App. 176, 278 N.E.2d 608 (1972). Is a contract for telephone service an Article 2 transaction? See Whitmer v. Bell Telephone Co., 361 Pa.Super. 282, 522 A.2d 584 (1987). Why would any advocate contend that Article 2 applied to transactions of this kind? What might be the practical consequences?

(A) GOODS AND SERVICES

Article 2 applies to transactions in goods but does not govern transactions in services, which remain essentially common-law contracts. Obviously, many familiar transactions require one party to deliver goods and render services for a single price. Would UCC Article 2 or common law govern? Should the contracts be divided, with different law governing its parts, or should transactions treated by the parties as indivisible be placed entirely under or outside Article 2? The Code gives no guidance to the parties or the courts[3] Not surprisingly, the result has been much unsatisfactory litigation.

1. The draft of Proposed Revised Article 2 that was presented to the ALI in May 2001 and to NCCUSL for its annual meeting in August 2001 did not change these basic provisions.

Late in the NCCUSL meeting, the drafting committee, by a 6–3 vote, presented a new draft of the scope provision to NCCUSL. The new draft would carve out of Article 2 transactions in information, such as transactions to license software, but to leave transactions in "smart goods," i.e., products in which computers and computer programs are integrated into the products. A familiar example is the modern automobile, in which many functions are controlled by computers and computer programs. The draft would address the common transaction of sales of personal computers with seller-installed operating systems and applications by placing the hardware within UCC Article 2 and the software outside of Article 2. The drafting committee decided explicitly not to provide a definition of "computer." The draft made no reference to the UCITA as a possible law governing the software.

A motion was made to strike the new scope provision from the draft, and the motion failed. A motion was then made to approve the entire draft of Article 2, and that motion failed.

The future of the amended scope provision as well as the future of the entire package of amendments to Article 2 are in doubt. The subject remains on the agendas of the ALI and NCCUSL, which meet again in May 2002 and July 2002 respectively.

2. See Annot., What constitutes "goods" within the scope of UCC Article 2, 4 ALR 4th 912; Annot., Applicability of UCC Article 2 to mixed contracts for sale of goods and services, 5 ALR 4th 501.

3. The Code does address transactions in which sellers perform services in contracts to manufacture goods to buyers' specifications. The definition of goods in UCC 2–105(1) expressly includes specially manufac-

BMC Industries, Inc. v. Barth Industries, Inc.

United States Court of Appeals, Eleventh Circuit, 1998.
160 F.3d 1322.

■ TJOFLAT, CIRCUIT JUDGE:

This appeal arises from a contract entered into between BMC Industries, Inc., and Barth Industries, Inc., for the design, manufacture, and installation of equipment to automate BMC's production line for unfinished eyeglass lenses. Eighteen months after the delivery date set out in the contract had passed, BMC filed suit against Barth for breach of contract. Barth, in turn, counterclaimed for breach of contract. . . .

A jury resolved the breach of contract and promissory estoppel issues in favor of BMC, and returned a verdict of $3 million against Barth. . . . Barth . . . appealed. We affirm the district court's decision denying Barth judgment as a matter of law. We conclude, however, that the court erroneously instructed the jury on the contract issues, and therefore vacate the judgment against Barth and remand the case for a new trial on these issues. . . .

I.

A.

BMC, through its Vision–Ease division, manufactures semi-finished polymer ophthalmic lenses that are used in the production of eyeglasses. These lenses are created by an assembly-line process. First, an employee fills a mold assembly with a monomer fluid, and places the mold assembly on a conveyor. Next, the assembly is inspected and then heated and cured until the monomer solidifies into a plastic lens. Finally, the lens is removed from the mold assembly through a process called "de-clipping and de-gasketing"; an employee removes the spring clip holding the mold assembly together and slices open the rubber gasket that holds the lens. The lens is then packaged and sold to a finished eyeglass retailer.

In order to decrease labor costs, and thereby remain competitive with other lens manufacturers who were utilizing cheaper foreign labor, BMC decided to become the first company to automate portions of its lens manufacturing process. Consequently, in early 1986, BMC commissioned Barth to complete a preliminary design and feasibility study. Barth's subcontractor, Komech, finished the study in June 1986. Based on this study, Barth and BMC entered into a contract (the "Contract") which provided that Barth would "design, fabricate, debug/test and supervise field installation and start up of equipment to automate the operations of mold assembly declipping, clip transport, mold assembly clipping, and mold filling." The Contract, which stated that it was governed by Florida law, listed a price of $515,200 and provided for delivery of four automated

tured goods. In special-order contracts, typically the services would be performed at seller's place of business before the goods were tendered to buyer. See, e.g., California & Hawaiian Sugar Co. v. Sun Ship, Inc., 794 F.2d 1433 (9th Cir.1986) (construction of ocean-going barge).

production lines by June 1987. The Contract also stated that time was of the essence.

On November 4, 1986, Barth and BMC executed a written amendment to the Contract, extending the delivery date by one month. In February 1987, Barth terminated Komech as design subcontractor, and hired another engineering company, Belcan, in its place. Belcan subsequently redesigned the automation equipment, which delayed Barth's progress and led the parties to execute the second (and last) written amendment, which extended the delivery date to "October 1987."

After this second amendment, Barth continued to experience technical problems and design difficulties that caused repeated delays. The parties did not extend the delivery date beyond October 1987 to accommodate these delays, however. Instead, Barth and BMC each demonstrated a willingness to continue performance under the Contract.

One such delay, for example, occurred in June 1987, when Belcan decided that the equipment design posed a risk of explosion because of the proximity of certain chemicals to electrical components. Although BMC perceived no such risk, it told Barth and Belcan to "go ahead" and redesign the equipment. Barth revised its estimated delivery schedule to account for the resulting delay, listing December 1987 as the new delivery deadline. It sent this schedule to BMC with a cover letter that stated: "Please look over the attached & let me know what you think." BMC's response, if any, is not contained in the record.

This design problem was only one of many technical difficulties that developed; other problems arose with the filling nozzles and mold assembly springs, among other components. Consequently, by October 1987, the amended Contract's delivery deadline, Barth estimated that it could not deliver the equipment until April 1988. BMC executives were still anxious, however, to continue the automation project. Thus, during the spring of 1988, although they protested Barth's failure to deliver the equipment on time, these executives encouraged Barth to continue working on the project.

In June 1988, Barth completed the four automated de-clip/de-gasket machines and delivered them to BMC. Without the entire automated system, however, BMC could not fully test these machines; the whole production line had to be in place.

By August 1988, BMC's mounting apprehension about Barth's ability to perform led it to seek assurance that Barth would be able to complete performance under the Contract. In an effort to obtain such assurance, BMC executives met with Robert Tomsich, a Barth officer (and director).... According to these executives, Tomsich ensured them that Barth would perform the Contract....

Although BMC had considered terminating the Contract and suing Barth for breach, BMC took neither step. Instead, it continued to lead Barth ... to believe that it was determined to finish the project; BMC collaborated with Barth's engineers to overcome difficulties, suggested design changes, and asked Barth whether more money (presumably provided by BMC) would help it complete the equipment in less time.

By January 1989, Barth still had not produced a functioning automation system. Due to time and cost overruns, Barth had invested over $1 million of its own money in the project. BMC previously had agreed to compensate Barth for these additional expenses; consequently, during that month, Tomsich asked BMC for $250,000 to cover some of Barth's cost overruns. One month later, BMC responded with a $100,000 payment, along with a letter stating that BMC was "insisting on Barth's adherence to the projected schedule," and was "not waiving any rights or remedies" for any breach, including "Barth's failure to meet the delivery dates specified in the contract." Barth's latest schedule called for delivery in June 1989.

Barth's delays and setbacks continued throughout the spring of 1989; but while BMC encouraged Barth to carry on, and continued to cooperate with Barth's engineers to solve problems, BMC also became increasingly impatient. In March, and again in April 1989, BMC pointed out Barth's unacceptable failure to meet deadlines.

Near the end of May 1989, Barth notified BMC that it had finally completed the mold assembly filling machine and that it would deliver the equipment F.O.B. Barth's dock in accordance with the Contract. BMC refused delivery of the mold assembly filler, and instead filed this lawsuit on June 5, 1989.

B.

BMC's breach of contract count alleged that the second written amendment to the Contract established October 1987 as the deadline for Barth's performance. Because Barth failed to deliver the automated equipment by that date, Barth was in default of its contractual obligations. BMC sought damages for Barth's breach in the sum of $6.4 million. Two separate injuries suffered by BMC comprised this measure of damages. First, BMC sought to recover the labor costs that it would have saved had it been able to use the automated equipment rather than pay employees to produce the lenses manually. Because BMC executives predicted that the automated equipment would have a useful life of ten years, BMC sought these lost labor savings for the ten year period from October 1987 until October 1997. Second, BMC sought compensation for what it termed the "working capital effect." This effect is an estimate of the money BMC lost because its capital was tied up paying higher labor costs rather than being used for investment or being used to pay off the company's debt (and thus reducing the interest BMC paid to its creditors).

As an affirmative defense to BMC's breach of contract claim, Barth asserted that BMC's conduct after the October 1987 delivery date had passed amounted to a waiver of the delivery date under Article 2 of the UCC ("UCC"). Although Barth failed to deliver the machines by October 1987, Barth argued, BMC executives urged Barth to keep working, BMC engineers continued to assist Barth in overcoming technical problems, and

BMC executives agreed to increase the purchase price. Therefore, Barth claimed, BMC waived its entitlement to delivery of the machines in October 1987.

Additionally, Barth counterclaimed against BMC for breach of contract. Barth repeated its argument that BMC's conduct amounted to a waiver of the October 1987 delivery date, and asserted that the delivery deadline therefore became indefinite. Because Barth tendered the machines within a reasonable amount of time, Barth substantially performed its contractual obligations. Consequently, Barth claimed, BMC's refusal to accept delivery of the machines in May 1989 constituted breach of the Contract. Barth sought damages totaling $1.13 million, which consisted of the original purchase price of $515,200 specified in the Contract, plus Barth's cost overruns that BMC had agreed to reimburse.

* * *

As an affirmative defense, Barth responded that BMC fraudulently failed to inform Barth of problems BMC was unable to solve in its manual lens production process, and that BMC misrepresented that problems experienced by the automated equipment did not occur when BMC produced lenses manually. Barth claimed that it would not have entered into the Contract had BMC not made these misrepresentations; BMC's own fraud, therefore, barred BMC from recovery on its claims against Barth. Barth also counterclaimed against BMC for fraud, and sought both compensatory and punitive damages.

* * *

At the pretrial conference, the district court concluded that the Contract was predominantly a transaction in services rather than goods, and therefore held that Article 2 of the UCC did not apply. Instead, Florida common law would govern the Contract. That law does not recognize a waiver of a contract term unless the waiver is supported by detrimental reliance or consideration. Consequently, in order to establish a waiver of the October 1987 delivery date, Barth would have to show that it detrimentally relied on, or gave consideration for, BMC's waiver of the delivery date.

... The court submitted the ... issues to the jury using a special verdict form that contained eight interrogatories. In response to the first interrogatory, which asked, "Did Barth breach its contract with BMC?" the jury answered affirmatively, and awarded BMC $3,001,879 in damages. ... The jury responded "No" to the remaining interrogatories, which asked whether BMC was liable on Barth's counterclaims.

C.

On appeal, Barth contends that the district court erred when it concluded that the UCC did not apply to the Contract, and thus did not govern the waiver issue. Had the court applied the UCC, Barth argues, it would have concluded that BMC waived the October 1987 delivery date, and therefore breached the Contract by refusing to accept delivery in May

1989. Having reached that conclusion, the court would have granted Barth's motion for judgment as a matter of law on the breach of contract issues, and awarded Barth damages in the sum of $1.13 million. Assuming a dispute of material fact on the waiver issue, Barth contends alternatively that BMC's judgment on the breach of contract count should be vacated, and the case remanded for a new trial on that count and its breach of contract counterclaim.

* * *

II.

A.

The district court held that the Contract was predominantly for services rather than goods, and that the UCC was therefore inapplicable. We disagree.

The UCC's Article 2 only applies to "transactions in goods." Fla. Stat. ch. 672–102 (1997). Goods are defined as "all things (including specially manufactured goods) which are movable at the time of identification to the contract for sale other than the money in which the price is to be paid, investment securities ... and things in action." Fla. Stat. ch. 672.105(1) (1997). A contract that is exclusively for services, therefore, is not governed by Article 2. Courts are frequently faced, however, with contracts involving both goods and services—so-called "hybrid" contracts. Most courts follow the "predominant factor" test to determine whether such hybrid contracts are transactions in goods, and therefore covered by the UCC, or transactions in services, and therefore excluded. See Bonebrake v. Cox, 499 F.2d 951, 960 (8th Cir.1974). Under this test, the court determines "whether their predominant factor, their thrust, their purpose, reasonably stated, is the rendition of service, with goods incidentally involved (e.g., contract with artist for painting) or is a transaction of sale, with labor incidentally involved (e.g., installation of a water heater in a bathroom)." Id. (footnotes omitted). At least one Florida court has implicitly adopted the predominant factor test. See United States Fidelity & Guar. Co. v. North Am. Steel Corp., 335 So. 2d 18, 21 (Fla. 2d DCA 1976) ("Since the predominate nature of the transaction was the furnishing of a product rather than services, we believe that the fabricated pipe could properly be characterized as goods.").

Although courts generally have not found any single factor determinative in classifying a hybrid contract as one for goods or services, courts find several aspects of a contract particularly significant. First, the language of the contract itself provides insight into whether the parties believed the goods or services were the more important element of their agreement. Contractual language that refers to the transaction as a "purchase," for example, or identifies the parties as the "buyer" and "seller," indicates that the transaction is for goods rather than services. See Bonebrake, 499 F.2d at 958 (stating that language referring to "equipment" is peculiar to goods rather than services); Bailey v. Montgomery Ward & Co., 690 P.2d

1280, 1282 (Colo.Ct.App.1984) (holding that a contract that identifies the transaction as a "purchase" and one of the parties as the "customer" signals a transaction in goods); Meeker v. Hamilton Grain Elevator Co., 442 N.E.2d 921, 923 (Ill. App. Ct. 1982) (stating that a contract that calls the parties "seller" and "purchaser" indicates a contract for goods).

Courts also examine the manner in which the transaction was billed; when the contract price does not include the cost of services, or the charge for goods exceeds that for services, the contract is more likely to be for goods. See Triangle Underwriters, Inc. v. Honeywell, Inc., 604 F.2d 737, 743 (2d Cir.1979) (stating that a bill that does not include services indicates a contract for goods); Lincoln Pulp & Paper Co. v. Dravo Corp., 436 F. Supp. 262, 275 & n. 15 (D.Me.1977) (holding that the contract at issue was for services after noting that the bill did not allocate costs between services and goods, and the evidence showed that the cost of the goods was less than half of the contract price).

Movable goods is another hallmark of a contract for goods rather than services. The UCC's definition of goods makes clear the importance of mobility in determining whether a contract is for goods; the UCC states that goods are "all things (including specially manufactured goods) which are movable at the time of identification to the contract for sale." Fla. Stat. ch. 672.105(1) (1997). Noting the importance of mobility, one Florida court held that a contract to edit and publish printed materials was a contract for goods after stating that "the items allegedly furnished by the appellant were specially produced or manufactured and were movable." Lake Wales Publ'g Co. v. Florida Visitor, Inc., 335 So. 2d 335, 336 (Fla. 2d DCA 1976); see also Smith v. Union Supply Co., 675 P.2d 333, 334 (Colo.Ct.App.1983) (holding that a contract to provide the materials and labor for installation of a new roof was a contract for goods because "[t]he materials to be installed . . . were 'movable at the time of identification to the contract for sale' " (quoting Colorado's version of the UCC)).

In this case, the district court relied primarily on Lincoln Pulp & Paper for its conclusion that the contract was for services rather than goods. The contract at issue in Lincoln Pulp & Paper involved the design and construction of a heat and chemical recovery unit in a pulp mill. The district court noted that, similar to Lincoln Pulp & Paper, the Contract obligated Barth to design, manufacture, test, and construct equipment, and also that the Contract's price did not allocate expenses between services and materials. The district court concluded that this case was sufficiently analogous to Lincoln Pulp & Paper to warrant the same result: a determination that the Contract was for services rather than goods.

The question whether a contract is predominantly for goods or services is generally one of fact. See Allmand Assocs., Inc. v. Hercules Inc., 960 F. Supp. 1216, 1223 (E.D.Mich.1997). When there is no genuine issue of material fact concerning the contract's provisions, however, a court may determine the issue as a matter of law. See id. Concluding that there are no material issues of fact as to the terms of the contract, the district court decided as a matter of law that the contract was for services. We review questions of law de novo. See Preserve Endangered Areas of Cobb's History, Inc. v. United States Army Corps of Eng'rs, 87 F.3d 1242, 1246 (11th Cir.1996).

Applying the "predominant factor" test to the Contract, we conclude that it was predominantly a transaction in goods. We reach this conclusion based on the contractual language, the circumstances surrounding the Contract, and the nature of the goods at issue.

Our starting point is the language of the Contract itself, which provides a number of indicia that the parties intended a contract for goods rather than services. First, the Contract is titled "PURCHASE ORDER," a reference that is used repeatedly throughout the document. This title is most instructive, as the parties have chosen to identify their agreement with a name that is almost exclusively used for transactions in goods. Second, the parties refer to themselves in the Contract as the "Buyer" and "Seller." Third, the Contract states that it is a purchase order "for the fabrication and installation of automated equipment." (emphasis added). All of this contractual language is "peculiar to goods, not services," Bonebrake, 499 F.2d at 958, and indicates that the parties had a contract for goods in mind.

Additionally, the Contract involves movable goods. Barth designed and fabricated the automated equipment in its own facilities, and planned to move the equipment to BMC's plant only once it was completed. Barth's original offer, which was incorporated into the Contract, included the term "F.O.B. Barth dock," meaning that the equipment was tendered to BMC once it was delivered to Barth's loading dock. Consequently, although Barth was still obligated to install and debug the equipment, it was clearly movable at the time it was identified to the Contract.

Lincoln Pulp & Paper is distinguishable from this case. The district court stated that the Contract price, similar to Lincoln Pulp & Paper, does not allocate costs between services and goods. The district court failed to note, however, that the Contract allocates payments according to delivery of automated equipment; the Contract's payment schedule calls for the delivery and acceptance of each automated equipment line to be met by a $70,050 payment from BMC. If the Contract price were being paid predominantly for Barth's design and engineering services as BMC claims, then the parties would have pegged payments to completion of the engineering and design services, not to the delivery of equipment. Furthermore, while the cost of services made up over half of the contract price in Lincoln Pulp & Paper, the opposite appears to be true in this case. A total of $280,200, which is over half of the contract price, is pegged to the delivery of equipment.

Finally, we note that the court in Lincoln Pulp & Paper stated that "[a] sale of equipment is not removed from the scope of Article 2 merely because the equipment was specially designed and manufactured before delivery or installed by the supplier." 436 F. Supp. at 276 n. 16. In fact, it is not surprising that the Barth–BMC Contract included such a significant services element (i.e., design and manufacturing). Because no other company had successfully automated its eyeglass lens production, Barth had to spend considerable time designing this first-of-its-kind machinery. This necessary services element, however, does not remove the Contract from the category of agreements for specially designed and manufactured equipment to which Article 2 applies.

The other two cases on which BMC relies are also inapposite. Both cases involved parties that clearly contemplated a contract for services. The first case, Wells v. 10–X Mfg. Co., 609 F.2d 248 (6th Cir.1979), involved the production of cloth hunting shirts. In that case, however, the buyer provided all of the materials (except thread) that the manufacturer used to produce the clothing. Id. at 252. Consequently, the manufacturer did not sell goods, only the service of turning the materials into a finished product.

The other case BMC cites, Inhabitants of the City of Saco v. General Elec. Co., 779 F. Supp. 186 (D.Me.1991), involved a contract for the design and construction of a solid waste disposal facility. That case is also distinguishable because it involved a typical construction contract for a non-movable product—the disposal facility. The only movable goods were the materials that were used to construct the immobile structure. Even more significantly, the contractual language in that case clearly identified the contract as a transaction in services. The contract stated that its purpose was "for the furnishing of services in Phase I of the project, and 'to establish the conditions on which Contractor [GE] will propose to furnish services under Phase II'." Id. at 197 (first and second emphases added). Not only did the language state that the contract was for services, it also referred to one of the parties as the "Contractor," a term typically used in services transactions.

B.

Having determined that the UCC governs this case, we must next apply Article 2's waiver provision to the Contract. The UCC waiver provision states in relevant part:

(2) A signed agreement which excludes modification or recession except by a signed writing cannot be otherwise modified or rescinded. . . .

(4) Although an attempt at modification or recission does not satisfy the requirements of subsection (2) or (3) [regarding the statute of frauds] it can operate as a *waiver*.

(5) A party who has made a waiver affecting an executory portion of the contract may retract the waiver by reasonable notification received by the other party that strict performance will be required of any term waived, unless the retraction would be unjust in view of a material change of position in reliance on the waiver.

Fla. Stat. ch. 672.209 (1997) (emphasis added).

1.

Although the UCC does not specifically lay out the elements of waiver, we have stated that waiver requires "(1) the existence at the time of the waiver a right, privilege, advantage, or benefit which may be waived; (2) the actual constructive knowledge thereof; and (3) an intention to relinquish such right, privilege, advantage, or benefit." Dooley v. Weil (In re Garfinkle), 672 F.2d 1340, 1347 (11th Cir. 1982). Conduct may constitute waiver of a contract term, but such an implied waiver must be demonstrated by clear evidence. See American Somax Ventures v. Touma, 547 So. 2d 1266, 1268 (Fla. 4th DCA 1989). Waiver may be implied when a party's actions are inconsistent with continued retention of the right. See First Pa. Bank, N.A. v. Oreck, 357 So. 2d 743, 744 (Fla. 4th DCA 1978).

As an initial matter, we must determine whether, under the UCC, waiver must be accompanied by detrimental reliance. Although it is settled that waiver under Florida common law must be supported by valid consideration or detrimental reliance, see Masser v. London Operating Co., 106 Fla. 474, 145 So. 72 (1932), courts disagree on whether the UCC retains this requirement. We conclude, however, that the UCC does not require consideration or detrimental reliance for waiver of a contract term.

Our conclusion follows from the plain language of subsections 672.209(4) and (5). While subsection (4) states that an attempted modification that fails may still constitute a waiver, subsection (5) provides that the waiver may be retracted unless the non-waiving party relies on the waiver. Consequently, the statute recognizes that waivers may exist in the absence of detrimental reliance—these are the retractable waivers referred to in subsection (5). Only this interpretation renders meaning to subsection (5), because reading subsection (4) to require detrimental reliance for all waivers means that waivers would never be retractable. See Wisconsin Knife Works v. National Metal Crafters, 781 F.2d 1280, 1291 (7th Cir.1986) (Easterbrook, J., dissenting) (noting that reading a detrimental reliance requirement into the UCC would eliminate the distinction between subsections (4) and (5)). Subsection (5) would therefore be meaningless.

At least one Florida court implicitly agrees with this conclusion; in Linear Corp. v. Standard Hardware Co., 423 So.2d 966 (Fla. 1st DCA 1982), the court held that a contract term had been waived despite the absence of any facts showing detrimental reliance. The court in Linear addressed a contract between a manufacturer and a retailer for the sale of electronic security devices. The contract included a provision stating that the manufacturer would not repurchase any devices the retailer was unable to sell, and another term providing that contract modifications must be in writing. Despite this contractual language, the retailer filed suit claiming that the manufacturer subsequently made an oral agreement to repurchase unsold devices, but failed to adhere to this oral agreement.

Citing chapter 672.209(4), the court concluded that the parties' conduct demonstrated that they had waived the requirement that modifications be in writing, and therefore gave effect to the oral modification. See id. at 968. The court recognized this waiver despite the apparent absence of any detrimental reliance by the retailer—in fact the court never even mentioned any reliance requirement for waiver under the UCC. Consequently, the court implicitly held that a contract term could be waived without the existence of detrimental reliance by the non-waiving party.

Although other courts have held that waiver requires reliance under the UCC, those courts have ignored the UCC's plain language. The leading case espousing this view of waiver is Wisconsin Knife Works v. National Metal Crafters, 781 F.2d 1280 (7th Cir.1986) (addressing section 2–209 of the model version of the UCC, from which Florida adopted section 672.209 verbatim), in which a panel of the Seventh Circuit addressed a contract that included a term prohibiting oral modifications, and considered whether an attempted oral modification could instead constitute a waiver. Writing for the majority, Judge Posner concluded that the UCC's subsection (2), which gives effect to "no oral modification" provisions, would become superfluous if contract terms could be waived without detrimental reliance. Judge Posner reasoned that if attempted oral modifications that were unenforceable because of subsection (2) were nevertheless enforced as waivers under subsection (4), then subsection (2) is "very nearly a dead letter." Id. at 1286. According to Judge Posner, there must be some difference between modification and waiver in order for both subsections (2) and (4) to have meaning. This difference is waiver's detrimental reliance requirement.[19]

Judge Posner, however, ignores a fundamental difference between modifications and waivers: while a party that has agreed to a contract modification cannot cancel the modification without giving consideration for the cancellation, a party may unilaterally retract its waiver of a contract term provided it gives reasonable notice. The fact that waivers may unilaterally be retracted provides the difference between subsections (2) and (4) that allows both to have meaning. We therefore conclude that waiver under the UCC does not require detrimental reliance. Consequently, without reaching the issue of detrimental reliance, we consider whether BMC waived the Contract's October 1987 delivery date.

2.

Applying the elements of waiver to the facts before us, we hold as a matter of law that BMC waived the October 1987 delivery date. The October 1987 delivery date was a waivable contract right, of which BMC

19. Contrary to our reasoning above, Judge Posner claims that reading a reliance requirement into waiver under subsection (4) is not inconsistent with subsection (5). According to Judge Posner, subsection (5) is broader than subsection (4), covering waivers other than mere attempts at oral modification. Judge Posner argues as an example that subsection (5) covers express waivers that are written and signed. See id. at 1287. In dissent, however, Judge Easterbrook convincingly dissects this argument. As Judge Easterbrook explains, subsection (5) is narrower than subsection (4)—limiting the effect of waivers that are not detrimentally relied upon, not the reverse as Judge Posner claims. Furthermore, Judge Easterbrook demonstrates that subsection (5) cannot cover express written and signed waivers because such writings are not waivers, but rather effective written modifications under subsection (2). See id. at 1291 (Easterbrook, J., dissenting).

had actual knowledge. We also conclude that BMC's conduct impliedly demonstrated an intent to relinquish that right.

* * *

BMC argues, however, that while it agreed to delay enforcing its rights against Barth ..., it did not waive those rights. BMC's argument defies logic. ...

BMC's own complaint buttresses our conclusion that BMC waived the October 1987 delivery date. According to BMC's complaint, [Barth's parent company] promised "that Barth would meet dates, performance and reliability criteria under the agreement, as amended," and that [the parent] "ensured that the equipment was timely completed and delivered to BMC in Florida." (emphasis added). Because the October 1987 delivery date had already passed, however, Barth could not "meet dates" or "timely" complete the equipment unless the delivery date had been extended.

Furthermore, BMC's course of dealing with Barth evidenced BMC's waiver of the October 1987 delivery date, because BMC failed timely to demand compliance with that contract term or terminate the Contract and file suit. When a delivery date passes without the seller's delivery, the buyer must object within a reasonable time and warn the seller that it is in breach. See KLT Indus., Inc. v. Eaton Corp., 505 F. Supp. 1072, 1079 (E.D.Mich.1981); see also Harrison v. City of Tampa, 247 F. 569, 572 (S.D.Fla.1918) ("I do not recognize any principle by which one party to a contract, after a breach by the other party, may continue acting under such contract to some future time, and then abrogate the contract by reason of such former breach.").

Although BMC maintained at trial that Barth breached the contract as of October 1987, BMC did not tell Barth it intended to terminate the contract and hold Barth liable for the breach until May 1989. In fact, the earliest indication from BMC that it was considering termination was August 1988, when BMC executives met with Tomsich to seek assurance that Barth would perform. As we have already stated, however, the result of that meeting was a waiver of the October 1987 delivery date, not a timely exercise of BMC's right to terminate the Contract. BMC did not warn Barth in earnest of its intent to terminate until February 1989, when BMC sent Barth a letter along with $100,000 of the $250,000 payment Tomsich had requested at the August 1988 meeting. This letter warned Barth that BMC was not waiving its rights and remedies for Barth's failure to meet contractual delivery dates. BMC warned Barth again in March when it sent a letter advising of its intent to "hold [Barth] responsible, both for the initial breach and for all failures to meet subsequently promised dates."

Until 1989, however, BMC continued to act as though both parties were bound by the Contract and that Barth was not in default of its obligations: the October 1987 delivery date passed without comment from BMC; engineers from BMC frequently provided advice or assistance to help Barth personnel overcome technical problems; BMC executives frequently visited Barth's production facilities and encouraged Barth to continue working to complete the equipment; BMC even continued to spend money on the project—in December 1987, over one month after the October 1987 delivery date had passed, BMC purchased an additional $71,075 worth of springs and tooling for the machines. In sum, rather than terminating the Contract, or at least warning Barth that it was in breach after the October 1987 delivery date had passed, BMC continued to act as though the Contract remained in effect.

This is not to say that BMC never complained that Barth had missed deadlines; BMC executives frequently expressed their concern and disappointment that the project was so far behind schedule. On April 5, 1988, for example, the Chairman, President, and CEO of BMC sent a letter to Barth in which he stated: "The project is well behind schedule, and each day of delay represents lost savings for Vision–Ease. I hope that Barth will exert every effort to ensure the speedy completion and installation of the equipment and avoid any further delay." But while BMC complained of delays, it never declared Barth in default or terminated the contract—instead, BMC told Barth to keep working. After Barth had spent an additional eighteen months of time and money and, according to Barth, was prepared to deliver the machines, however, BMC suddenly decided to terminate the Contract. This BMC could not do.

The UCC states that when a contractual delivery date is waived, delivery must be made within a reasonable time. See Fla. Stat. ch. 672.309(1) (1997); KLT Indus., Inc. v. Eaton Corp., 505 F. Supp. 1072, 1079 (E.D.Mich.1981). Consequently, because BMC waived the October 1987 delivery date, Barth was only obligated to deliver the machines within a reasonable time period. We remand this case to the district court for a new trial on the question of whether Barth tendered the machines within a reasonable time period.[23]

* * *

IV.

For the foregoing reasons, we hold that the district court erred in concluding that the UCC did not apply to the Contract. Furthermore, we conclude that BMC waived the October 1987 delivery date. We therefore VACATE the district court's judgment against Barth and REMAND the case to the district court for retrial of BMC's claims against Barth as well as Barth's counterclaims in accordance with the UCC. . . .

NOTES

(1) Equipment Purchases. Transactions for acquisition of equipment, particularly industrial equipment, are difficult to characterize under

---

23. On remand, if the jury concludes that Barth did not deliver the machines within a reasonable time period, then BMC will prevail on its breach of contract claim against Barth. BMC's damages should then be calculated according to Fla. Stat. ch. 672.713 (1997). If instead, however, the jury finds that BMC terminated the contract before a reasonable time had passed, then Barth will prevail on its counterclaim. BMC has stipulated that Barth is entitled to recover $1.13 million if it prevails.

Article 2. Frequently these transactions obligate the provider of the equipment to do more than simply deliver the machinery to the buyer. A very common add-on is a requirement that the equipment provider deliver the equipment to the buyer's facility and install it there, to which may be added other post-delivery obligations such as testing the equipment, training buyer's employees on use of the equipment, providing support and technical service, and so forth. All of this may be bundled into a single contract price. In addition to undertaking the wide array of possible delivery and post-delivery obligations, equipment providers may commit to designing new equipment, sometimes requiring development of new and untried technological applications. At what point on a continuum of obligations of this kind does a contract become a contract other than for the sale of goods?

Article 2 provides little guidance. The definition of "goods" includes "specially manufactured goods," UCC 2–105(1). This term was clearly intended, at the time of drafting, to extend the scope of the statute to transactions other than sales from inventory. A similar term appeared in § 5 of the Sale of Goods Act and in § 5 of the Uniform Sales Act, 19th century laws drafted in the early stage of the Industrial Revolution, when commercial practices may have differed substantially from those found today. The Article 2 Comments are silent on characterization of contracts that combine design, manufacture, installation, and other services.

The problem was passed to courts, with the results indicated by the opinion of the Eleventh Circuit in *BMC Industries*. How well have the courts handled the problem?

(2) Construction Contracts. Improvement of real estate takes many forms. The most common are construction and repair of buildings. Another kind of improvement is the construction of roads and bridges, railroads, airports, etc. Contractors engaged to do this kind of work will need a lot of materials, as well as labor. Construction contracts are not within the scope of Article 2 if the obligation of the contractors is to provide a completed improvement. Thus, contracts to build a house or a "turn key" facility are not deemed to involve transactions in goods. Even though the materials to be incorporated into the improvement were originally goods and, in the completed project, may retain their identity as goods that have been affixed to the real estate, contractors do not "sell" goods; what the contractors commit to provide is not movable. See UCC 2–105(1).

A construction project is likely to have a congeries of lesser contracts, some of which are indisputably contracts for sales of goods. A contract by a lumber yard to supply lumber or bricks to a builder is an Article 2 contract between those parties. Sometimes, however, materials suppliers also engage to do work with the materials at the site of an improvement. As with equipment acquisition transactions, the value of the additional work may begin to eclipse the value of the materials. A case of this kind arose in New York, early after Article 2 had been adopted there. The contract was to supply and install the structural steel necessary for a bridge. Three levels of the New York courts struggled inconclusively with the question of characterization. In the end, the Court of Appeals (the highest court of that state) bypassed the issue on the view that the questions presented in that case would be decided the same way whether Article 2 or the common law applied. Schenectady Steel Co. v. Bruno Trimpoli General Construction Co., 34 N.Y.2d 939, 316 N.E.2d 875, 359 N.Y.S.2d 560 (1974). Not all difficult cases can be so finessed.

The scope issue in *BMC Industries* juxtaposed the Florida version of the UCC with Florida common law of contracts. On the critical issue of waiver, the Eleventh Circuit found that UCC Article 2 and Florida common law were quite different, a difference that was determinative of the outcome in the case.

(3) Service Contracts. Most service contracts do not involve "sale" of tangible products, but many service providers do "deliver" products in performance of their service functions. Sometimes, the buyer of services seeks to recover under UCC Article 2.

At common law, service of food in a restaurant was considered an "uttering" and not a sale. Article 2 declared, nonetheless, that the warranty of quality under UCC 2–314 was a part of these transactions.

(4) The Uniform Commercial Code: Which Version? The NCCUSL and the ALI, sponsors of the UCC, are not legislatures empowered to create law. An Article of the UCC takes effect only when duly enacted as a state or federal statute. In that process, legislatures may—and sometimes do—modify the proposed Official Text in a non-uniform way. A practicing lawyer or judge, applying the Code, must use a version enacted into law and in force when the disputed transaction occurred. In *BMC Industries*, note that the courts cited and applied the Florida version of the Code. (The contract specified that it was governed by Florida law.) Throughout the course, you will see citations to state-enacted versions of the Code.

Because variations in the state-enacted versions of the Code exist, it is often a necessary step in litigation to identify which state's version governs the issue arising in a dispute. The UCC's general choice of law provision is found in UCC 1–105.

(5) Litigation: Which Court? Unless the contract has a clause that requires submission of disputes to arbitration or some other alternative form of dispute resolution, the aggrieved party may initiate judicial proceedings. Absent a contract term specifying the forum, the moving party in a sales dispute can select the court anywhere so long as that court is authorized to hear the submitted dispute (commonly referred to as jurisdiction over the subject matter) and is able to compel the defendant to respond to the complaint (jurisdiction over the person of the defendant). Subject-matter jurisdiction is determined by the domestic law of the place of the forum. Personal jurisdiction is a more complex matter, only partly determined by domestic law. In the United States, the extent of personal jurisdiction is restricted by the standard of due process of law in the Fourteenth Amendment of the U.S. Constitution.[4]

In BMC Industries the plaintiff sued in a U.S. federal district court. Whether that was the result of a contractual choice of forum term in the agreement or of the plaintiff's lawyer's decision is unknown. Federal courts have subject-matter jurisdiction to entertain cases in which the parties are from different jurisdictions, including a foreign litigant suing a United States party. In these so-called "diversity cases," federal district courts are required to apply the law of the state in which they sit. Erie Railroad Co. v. Tompkins, 304 U.S. 64, 58 S.Ct. 817, 82 L.Ed. 1188 (1938). As will be seen in the cases to be read in this Part, the federal courts are frequently the forum for resolution of major disputes under Article 2 of the UCC, but a federal court is obliged to follow the state court's interpretation of the Article.

(B) GOODS AND INFORMATION

We live today in what is often called the Age of Information.[5] Much of what people buy and sell is information, knowledge, know-how, and the like. Education and entertainment (there is a difference) involve transfers

---

4. See Vermeulen v. Renault, U.S.A., Inc., 965 F.2d 1014 (11th Cir.1992). A Georgia resident sued Regie Nationale Des Usines Renault (RNUR), the French automobile manufacturer of LeCar, and other defendants, for serious injuries sustained as a result of negligent manufacture and design of the LeCar passenger restraint system. Defendants removed the case to federal district court, which granted the French corporation's motion to dismiss for lack of personal jurisdiction. The Court of Appeals for the Eleventh Circuit reversed.

At that time, RNUR sold its automobiles to American Motors Corporation (AMC), which resold them in the United States through one of its subsidiaries. The RNUR–AMC master agreement stated that title to the vehicles passed to AMC in France and that AMC would take full responsibility for marketing and distributing RNUR vehicles in the United States. The agreement also contemplated that RNUR would be involved in decisions affecting marketing and could advise on suggested retail prices for RNUR vehicles, that RNUR would provide assistance in training AMC personnel on servicing and repair of RNUR vehicles, and that RNUR retained the full and exclusive ownership of the "Renault" trademark. The AMC subsidiary provided retail warranties to U.S. buyers of RNUR vehicles, but RNUR agreed to reim-

burse AMC for warranty work performed by AMC or authorized dealers.

The Eleventh Circuit held that RNUR had purposefully availed itself of the privilege of conducting business in Georgia because (1) it had designed its vehicles to accommodate the American market, and (2) RNUR had taken some part with AMC's conducting of a nationwide advertising campaign in the U.S., and (3) that RNUR had played a role in AMC's establishment of Renault dealerships in the U.S., including six dealerships in Georgia, and (4) RNUR retained ultimate control of the U.S. distribution network through various provisions in the master agreement with AMC.

Compare Asahi Metal Industry Co., Ltd. v. Superior Court of California, 480 U.S. 102, 107 S.Ct. 1026, 94 L.Ed.2d 92 (1987) (indemnity suit by Taiwanese tire manufacturer, which had sold tires in California, against Japanese manufacturer of valve incorporated into the tire for which tire manufacturer had incurred liability in California: Court held that exercise of jurisdiction did not comport with traditional notions of fair play and substantial justice and therefore violated the Due Process Clause); cf. World–Wide Volkswagen Corp. v. Woodson, 444 U.S. 286, 100 S.Ct. 559, 62 L.Ed.2d 490 (1980).

5. See M. Castells, The Information Age: Economy, Society and Culture (1996).

of information. Technology is the heart of the process of economic growth and development. Currently, rapid advances in information technology are reshaping the economy in fundamental ways. One application of information technology is the input of amounts of information into products. A set of legal principles fashioned in the 19th century is hard pressed to deal with transactions in which the core value in an exchange is information.

Information tends to become a commodity when it is packaged and delivered. With the advent of computers and of digitalization of information, vast amounts of data can be installed into tiny chips and diskettes and other devices. One set of such information-in-a-package is "software," which usually refers to the informational content of a computer program. Computers, one type of electronic device that uses "software," are called "hardware."

As transactions in information proliferated, with a certain portion of inevitable transaction failures, lawyers and judges had to characterize the transactions in order to identify the governing law. They characterized some of these transactions to be governed by Article 2 of the UCC. The following case is illustrative.

Advent Systems Limited v. Unisys Corp.

United States Court of Appeals, Third Circuit, 1991.
925 F.2d 670.

■ WEIS, C.J.

In this diversity case we conclude that computer software is a good within the Uniform Commercial Code; in the circumstances here a non-exclusive requirements contract complies with the statute of frauds; and expert testimony on future lost profits based on prior projections is suspect when actual market performance data are available. Because the district court ruled that the Code did not apply, we will grant a new trial on a breach of contract claim. . . .

Plaintiff, Advent Systems Limited, is engaged primarily in the production of software for computers. As a result of its research and development efforts, by 1986 the company had developed an electronic document management system (EDMS), a process for transforming engineering drawings and similar documents into a computer data base.

Unisys Corporation manufactures a variety of computers. As a result of information gained by its wholly-owned United Kingdom subsidiary during 1986, Unisys decided to market the document management system in the United States. In June 1987 Advent and Unisys signed two documents, one labeled "Heads of Agreement" (in British parlance "an outline of agreement") and, the other, "Distribution Agreement."

In these documents, Advent agreed to provide the software and hardware making up the document systems to be sold by Unisys in the United States. Advent was obligated to provide sales and marketing material and manpower as well as technical personnel to work with Unisys employees in building and installing the document systems. The agreement was to continue for two years, subject to automatic renewal or termination on notice.

During the summer of 1987, Unisys attempted to sell the document system to Arco, a large oil company, but was unsuccessful. Nevertheless, progress on the sales and training programs in the United States was satisfactory, and negotiations for a contract between Unisys (UK) and Advent were underway.

The relationship, however, soon came to an end. Unisys, in the throes of restructuring, decided it would be better served by developing its own document system and in December 1987 told Advent their arrangement had ended. Unisys also advised its UK subsidiary of those developments and, as a result, negotiations there were terminated.

Advent filed a complaint in the district court alleging ... breach of contract.... The district court ruled at pretrial that the Uniform Commercial Code did not apply because although goods were to be sold, the services aspect of the contract predominated.

A jury ... awarded damages to Advent in the sum of $4,550,000 on the breach of contract claim....

On appeal ... Unisys contends that the relationship between it and Advent was one for the sale of goods and hence subject to the terms of the statute of frauds in the Uniform Commercial Code. Because the agreements lacked an express provision on quantity, Unisys insists that the statute of frauds bans enforcement. In addition, Unisys contends that the evidence did not support the damage verdict.

* * *

II.   SOFTWARE AND THE UNIFORM COMMERCIAL CODE

The district court ruled that as a matter of law the arrangement between the two parties was not within the Uniform Commercial Code and, consequently, the statute of frauds was not applicable. As the district court appraised the transaction, provisions for services outweighed those for products and, consequently, the arrangement was not predominantly one for the sale of goods.

In the "Heads of Agreement" Advent and Unisys purported to enter into a "joint business collaboration." Advent was to modify its software and hardware interfaces to run initially on equipment not manufactured by Unisys but eventually on Unisys hardware. It was Advent's responsibility to purchase the necessary hardware. "In so far as Advent has successfully completed [some of the processing] of software and hardware interfaces," Unisys promised to reimburse Advent to the extent of $150,000 derived from a "surcharge" on products purchased.

Advent agreed to provide twelve man-weeks of marketing manpower, but with Unisys bearing certain expenses. Advent also undertook to furnish an experienced systems builder to work with Unisys personnel at Advent's prevailing rates, and to provide sales and support training for Unisys staff as well as its customers.

The Distribution Agreement begins with the statement, "Unisys desires to purchase, and Advent desires to sell, on a non-exclusive basis, certain of Advent hardware products and software licenses for resale worldwide." Following a heading "Subject Matter of Sales," appears this sentence, "(a) Advent agrees to sell hardware and license software to Unisys, and Unisys agrees to buy from Advent the products listed in Schedule A." Schedule A lists twenty products, such as computer cards, plotters, imagers, scanners and designer systems.

Advent was to invoice Unisys for each product purchased upon shipment, but to issue separate invoices for maintenance fees. The cost of the support services "was set at 3% per annum of the prevailing Advent user list price of each software module for which Unisys is receiving revenue from a customer." Services included field technical bulletins, enhancement and maintenance releases, telephone consultation, and software patches, among others. At no charge to Unisys, Advent was to provide publications such as installation manuals, servicing and adjustment manuals, diagnostic operation and test procedures, sales materials, product brochures and similar items. In turn, Unisys was to "employ resources in performing marketing efforts" and develop "the technical ability to be thoroughly familiar" with the products.

In support of the district court's ruling that the U.C.C. did not apply, Advent contends that the agreement's requirement of furnishing services did not come within the Code. Moreover, the argument continues, the "software" referred to in the agreement as a "product" was not a "good" but intellectual property outside the ambit of the Uniform Commercial Code.

Because software was a major portion of the "products" described in the agreement, this matter requires some discussion. Computer systems consist of "hardware" and "software." Hardware is the computer machinery, its electronic circuitry and peripheral items such as keyboards, readers, scanners and printers. Software is a more elusive concept. Generally speaking, "software" refers to the medium that stores input and output data as well as computer programs. The medium includes hard disks, floppy disks, and magnetic tapes.

In simplistic terms, programs are codes prepared by a programmer that instruct the computer to perform certain functions. When the program is transposed onto a medium compatible with the computer's needs, it becomes software. . . .

The increasing frequency of computer products as subjects of commercial litigation has led to controversy over whether software is a "good" or intellectual property. The Code does not specifically mention software.

In the absence of express legislative guidance, courts interpret the Code in light of commercial and technological developments. The Code is designed "to simplify, clarify and modernize the law governing commercial transactions" and "to permit the continued expansion of commercial practices." 13 Pa. Cons. Stat. Ann. § 1102 (Purdon 1984). As the Official Commentary makes clear:

> This Act is drawn to provide flexibility so that, since it is intended to be a semi-permanent piece of legislation, it will provide its own machinery for expansion of commercial practices. It is intended to make it possible for the law embodied in this Act to be developed by the courts in the light of unforeseen and new circumstances and practices.

Id. comment 1.

The Code "applies to transactions in goods." 13 Pa. Cons. Stat. Ann. § 2102 (Purdon 1984). Goods are defined as "all things (including specially manufactured goods) which are movable at the time of the identification for sale." Id. at § 2105. The Pennsylvania courts have recognized that " 'goods' has a very extensive meaning" under the U.C.C. Duffee v. Judson, 251 Pa. Super. 406, 380 A.2d 843, 846 (1977); see also Lobianco v. Property Protection, Inc., 292 Pa. Super. 346, 437 A.2d 417 (1981) ("goods" under U.C.C. embraces every species of property other than real estate, choses in action, or investment securities.).

Our Court has addressed computer package sales in other cases, but has not been required to consider whether the U.C.C. applied to software per se. See Chatlos Systems, Inc. v. National Cash Register Corp., 635 F.2d 1081 (3d Cir.1980) (parties conceded that furnishing the plaintiff with hardware, software and associated services was governed by the U.C.C.); see also Carl Beasley Ford, Inc. v. Burroughs Corporation, 361 F.Supp. 325 (E.D.Pa.1973) (U.C.C. applied without discussion), aff'd, 493 F.2d 1400 (3d Cir.1974). Other Courts of Appeals have also discussed transactions of this nature. RRX Industries, Inc. v. Lab–Con, Inc., 772 F.2d 543 (9th Cir.1985) (goods aspects of transaction predominated in a sale of a software system); Triangle Underwriters, Inc. v. Honeywell, Inc., 604 F.2d 737, 742–43 (2d Cir.1979) (in sale of computer hardware, software, and customized software goods aspects predominated; services were incidental).

Computer programs are the product of an intellectual process, but once implanted in a medium are widely distributed to computer owners. An analogy can be drawn to a compact disc recording of an orchestral rendition. The music is produced by the artistry of musicians and in itself is not a "good," but when transferred to a laser-readable disc becomes a readily merchantable commodity. Similarly, when a professor delivers a lecture, it is not a good, but, when transcribed as a book, it becomes a good.

That a computer program may be copyrightable as intellectual property does not alter the fact that once in the form of a floppy disc or other medium, the program is tangible, movable and available in the marketplace. The fact that some programs may be tailored for specific purposes need not alter their status as "goods" because the Code definition includes "specially manufactured goods."

The topic has stimulated academic commentary[2] with the majority espousing the view that software fits within the definition of a "good" in the U.C.C.

Applying the U.C.C. to computer software transactions offers substantial benefits to litigants and the courts. The Code offers a uniform body of law on a wide range of questions likely to arise in computer software disputes: implied warranties, consequential damages, disclaimers of liability, the statute of limitations, to name a few.

The importance of software to the commercial world and the advantages to be gained by the uniformity inherent in the U.C.C. are strong policy arguments favoring inclusion. The contrary arguments are not persuasive, and we hold that software is a "good" within the definition in the Code.

The relationship at issue here is a typical mixed goods and services arrangement. The services are not substantially different from those generally accompanying package sales of computer systems consisting of hardware and software. See Chatlos Systems, Inc. v. National Cash Register Corp., 479 F. Supp. 738, 741 (D.N.J.1979); Beasley Ford, 361 F. Supp. at 328.

Although determining the applicability of the U.C.C. to a contract by examining the predominance of goods or services has been criticized, we see no reason to depart from that practice here. As we pointed out in De Filippo v. Ford Motor Co., 516 F.2d 1313, 1323 (3d Cir.), cert. denied, 423 U.S. 912 (1975), segregating goods from non-goods and insisting "that the Statute of Frauds apply only to a portion of the contract, would be to make the contract divisible and impossible of performance within the intention of the parties."

We consider the purpose or essence of the contract. Comparing the relative costs of the materials supplied with the costs of the labor may be helpful in this analysis, but not dispositive. Compare RRX, 772 F.2d at 546 ("essence" of the agreement) with Triangle, 604 F.2d at 743 ("compensation" structure of the contract).

In this case the contract's main objective was to transfer "products." The specific provisions for training of Unisys personnel by Advent were but a small part of the parties' contemplated relationship.

The compensation structure of the agreement also focuses on "goods." The projected sales figures introduced during the trial demonstrate that in

---

2. Among the articles and notes that have reviewed extant case law are: Boss & Woodward, Scope of the Uniform Commercial Code; Survey of Computer Contracting Cases, 43 Bus. Law. 1513 (1988); Owen, The Application of Article 2 of the Uniform Commercial Code To Computer Contracts, 14 N. Kentucky L. Rev. 277 (1987); Rodau, Computer Software: Does Article 2 of the Uniform Commercial Code Apply, 35 Emory L.J. 853 (1986); Holmes, Application of Article Two of the Uniform Commercial Code to Computer System Acquisitions, 9 Rutgers Computer & Technology L.J. 1 (1982); Note, Computer Software As A Good Under the Uniform Commercial Code: Taking a Byte Out of the Intangibility Myth, 65 B.U.L. Rev. 129 (1985); Note, Computer Programs as Goods Under the U.C.C., 77 Mich. L. Rev. 1149 (1979).

the contemplation of the parties the sale of goods clearly predominated. The payment provision of $150,000 for developmental work which Advent had previously completed, was to be made through individual purchases of software and hardware rather than through the fees for services and is further evidence that the intellectual work was to be subsumed into tangible items for sale.

We are persuaded that the transaction at issue here was within the scope of the Uniform Commercial Code and, therefore, the judgment in favor of the plaintiff must be reversed.

III.   THE STATUTE OF FRAUDS

This brings us to the Unisys contention that the U.C.C. statute of frauds bars enforcement of the agreement because the writings do not contain a quantity term.

Section 2–201(a) provides that a contract for the sale of goods of $500 or more is not enforceable unless in writing. "[A] contract ... is not enforceable ... unless there is some writing sufficient to indicate that a contract for sale has been made.... A writing is not insufficient because it omits ... a term agreed upon but the contract is not enforceable ... beyond the quantity of goods shown in such writing." 13 Pa. Cons. Stat. Ann. § 2201(a) (Purdon 1984). The comment to this section states that although the required writing need not contain all the material terms "there are three definite and invariable requirements as to the memorandum," one of which is that "it must specify a quantity." Id. comment 1.

* * *

The circumstances here do not require us to adopt an open-ended reading of the statute but permit us to apply a narrower holding. Nothing in the Code commands us to ignore the practicality of commercial arrangements in construing the statute of frauds. Indeed, the Code's rule of construction states that the language "shall be liberally construed and applied to promote its underlying purposes and policies." 13 Pa. Cons. Stat. Ann. § 1102(a). As noted earlier, Comment 1 to that section observes that the Code promotes flexibility in providing "machinery for expansion of commercial practices." Following this guidance, we look to the realities of the arrangement between the parties.

In the distribution agreement, Unisys agreed to engage in the business of selling identified document systems during the two-year term of the contract and to buy from Advent on stated terms the specified products necessary to engage in that venture. The detailed nature of the document, including as it does, such provisions as those for notice of breach, opportunity for cure, and termination leaves no doubt that the parties intended to create a contract.

The parties were obviously aware that they were entering a new, speculative market and some uncertainty was inevitable in the amount of sales Unisys could make and the orders it would place with Advent. Consequently, quantity was not stated in absolute terms. In effect, the parties arrived at a non-exclusive requirements contract, a commercially useful device. We do not consider that in the circumstances here the arrangement raises the statute of frauds bar.

The Code recognizes exclusive requirements contracts in section 2–306, and imposes on the parties to such agreements a duty of good faith. For present purposes, the salient factor is that exclusive requirements contracts satisfy the quantity requirements of the statute of frauds, albeit no specific amount is stated. . . .

The reasons for excepting exclusive requirements contracts from the strictures of the statute of frauds are strong. The purchasing party, perhaps unable to anticipate its precise needs, nevertheless wishes to have assurances of supply and fixed price. The seller, on the other hand, finds an advantage in having a steady customer. Such arrangements have commercial value. To deny enforceability through a rigid reading of the quantity term in the statute of frauds would run contrary to the basic thrust of the Code—to conform the law to business reality and practices.

By holding that exclusive requirements contracts comply with the statute of frauds, courts have decided that indefiniteness in the quantity term is acceptable. If the agreement here does not satisfy the statute of frauds because of indefiniteness of a quantity term, then neither does an exclusive requirements contract. We find no reason in logic or policy to differentiate in the statute of frauds construction between the contract here and an exclusive requirements arrangement.

The same reasons that led courts to dispense with a specific and certain quantity term in the exclusive requirements context apply equally when a continuing relationship is non-exclusive. The same regulating factor—good faith performance by the parties—applies and prevents the contracts from being illusory. The writings here demonstrate that the parties did not articulate a series of distinct, unrelated, simple buy and sell arrangements, . . . but contemplated what resembles in some respects a joint venture or a distributorship.

A construction of the statute of frauds which does not recognize the quite substantial difference between a simple buy and sell agreement and what occurred here is unduly restrictive. Section 2–306 in recognizing exclusive requirements and output contracts does not purport to treat them as the only permissible types of open quantity agreements. We do not read section 2–306 as an exclusionary measure, but rather as one capable of enlargement so as to serve the purposes of the Code.

* * *

In sum, we hold that the writings here satisfy the statute of frauds.

IV.   ENFORCEABILITY

Having concluded that the statute of frauds is not a bar, we now confront the issue of enforceability.

Section 2–204 provides that a contract does not fail for indefiniteness even though one or more terms have been left open if the parties intended to make a contract and there is a reasonably certain basis for giving an appropriate remedy. 13 Pa. Cons. Stat. Ann. § 2204(c) (Purdon 1984). As Professor Murray has explained:

> Rather than focusing upon what parties failed to say, the Code and RESTATEMENT 2d focus upon the overriding question of whether the parties manifestly intended to make a binding arrangement. If that manifestation is present, the only remaining concern is whether the terms are definite enough to permit courts to afford an appropriate remedy. The second requirement assists courts to determine the degree of permissible indefiniteness.

J. Murray, Murray On Contracts § 38, at 85 (3d ed. 1990).

Unlike the statute of frauds issue discussed earlier, the definiteness required to provide a remedy rests on a very solid foundation of practicality. A remedy may not be based on speculation and an award cannot be made if there is no basis for determining if a breach has occurred.

Unisys argues that since there are specific non-exclusive stipulations in the agreement, they negate the implication found in most exclusive requirements contracts that a "best efforts clause" is included. That may be so, but that does not nullify the obligation of the parties to deal in good faith.

Section 1–203 of the Code provides that contracts require a "good faith performance." This requires the parties to observe "reasonable commercial standards of fair dealing in the trade."

The Pennsylvania Superior Court has concluded that in the absence of any express language, the law will imply an agreement by the parties to do those things that "according to reason and justice they should do in order to carry out the purposes for which the contract was made and to refrain from doing anything that would destroy or injure the other party's right to receive the fruits of the contract." Slater v. Pearle Vision Center, Inc., 376 Pa. Super. 580, 546 A.2d 676, 679 (1988). See Restatement (Second) of Contracts § 205 (1979). . . .

The terms of the agreement between Unisys and Advent lend themselves to imply a good faith obligation on the parties of at least some minimal effort: "A fundamental assumption of both parties is that throughout the term of this agreement, Unisys will employ resources in performing marketing efforts involving Advent Products and will develop the technical capability to be thoroughly familiar with these products."

On remand, Advent may be able to show that it was inconsistent with good faith for a party that has committed itself to engage in particular business for a specified period of time to cease devoting any resources to that venture prior to the end of the stated period. . . . We leave open the possibility that the performance of the parties following signing of the documents and perhaps pre-contractual expectations will provide evidence to satisfy the requirements of section 2–204. See §§ 2–208, 1–205 (course of performance, usage of trade).

On the other hand, it may be that the reason Unisys decided to devote no resources to the project of selling document systems is relevant to whether the standard of fair dealing in the trade was breached. Simply because no resources were devoted, does not mean in and of itself that there was a breach of the covenant of good faith. See, e.g., Angelica Uniform Group, Inc. v. Ponderosa Systems, Inc., 636 F.2d 232, 232 (8th Cir.1980); R.A. Weaver & Assoc., Inc. v. Asphalt Construction, Inc., 587 F.2d 1315, 1321–22 (D.C.Cir.1978); Southwest Natural Gas Co. v. Oklahoma Portland Cement Co., 102 F.2d 630, 632–33 (10th cir. 1939); 1 J. White & R. Summers, Uniform Commercial Code § 3–8, at 169 (3d ed. 1988).

Whether Advent can establish the definiteness required to sustain a remedy is a serious question. The record before us consists of evidence submitted on the basis of the pretrial ruling denying application of the U.C.C. Our contrary holding will require the parties to reassess the proofs necessary to meet the Code. We are in no position to anticipate the evidence that may appear in further proceedings and, thus, at this juncture cannot rule whether the agreement between Unisys and Advent is enforceable.

* * *

The judgment in favor of the defendant on the tortious interference claim will be affirmed. The judgment in favor of the plaintiff on the breach of contract claim will be reversed and the case will be remanded for further proceedings.

NOTES

(1) Information as Goods. The scope issue was contested by the parties in this case. Which party argued for the application of Article 2 and which opposed? Can you reconstruct the reasoning that might lie behind the choices of the litigation position to be taken? Was the outcome in the long term interest of Unisys?

With regard to the applicability of Article 2 to this transaction, is the rationale of the Court of Appeals persuasive? What "substantial benefits" may result from applying the Article to computer software transactions? Who are the potential beneficiaries? Was the seller in *Advent Systems* a beneficiary?

Should the scope of a statute's coverage be determined on the basis of "policy arguments" weighed by courts?

The UCC was drafted and enacted before advances in physics and engineering produced the marvels of data processing by computer. No draft of Article 2 was ever done on a word processor. Would the standards of Article 2 be likely to fit a "product" like computer software with its unique combination of intellectual property, design and performance services, and relatively inexpensive tangible components?

Commonly, owners of software copyright or patent the program and, when they market their intellectual property, they only "license" others to use it; license agreement typically provide that licensees may not sell or transfer the program, and may not decompile or reverse engineer it or modify it without permission of the licensor. To this extent, the transaction does not fit the "passing of title" element in the UCC 2–106(1) definition of "sale." Should that have been given more weight in the court's decision on the applicability of Article 2? Note that the title of Article 2 is "Sales," but the scope provision in UCC 2–102 refers to "transactions in goods," not merely to "sales of goods." What might explain the use of the broader term, "transactions," instead of the more specific term?

(2) Contract Formation: Statute of Frauds; Definiteness. Having succeeded in persuading the court to apply Article 2, counsel for Unisys chose to defend on the alternative grounds that, under the Article 2 version of the Statute of Frauds, the alleged contract was not enforceable, or that the contract failed of formation because the agreement lacked sufficient specificity. We will consider the merit of these defenses later.

(3) Domestic Law: Which Nation's? The seller in *Advent Systems*, a United Kingdom company, contracted with a United States company, whose headquarters is in Pennsylvania. The courts applied Pennsylvania law to the contract dispute. The probable explanation is that the contract had a specific choice of law clause to that effect. In bargaining for contracts, how important are the terms of a choice-of-law clause likely to be to the representatives of the parties? Would a party be likely to use much of its bargaining leverage, e.g., give up something of economic value, to prevail on this clause? Absent a choice-of-law clause in the contract, the court or tribunal in which the dispute is pending would have to choose the governing law. The principles used for this purpose are referred to as private international law.

(4) Uniform Computer Information Transactions Act (UCITA). The Uniform State Laws Conference approved UCITA in July 1999. The scope of UCITA extends to computer information (basically software) and, further, to computer equipment (hardware) that is sold together with the information. UCITA has been adopted by two states, Maryland and Virginia. If, and when UCITA is enacted by a state, the scope provision of UCC Article 2 might be amended to complement the scope provision of UCITA so that only one of the statutes would govern a transaction like that in *Advent Systems*.

(C) GOODS AND REAL PROPERTY

The line between real property and goods is necessarily somewhat artificial. Movability, the essential characteristic of things defined to be goods, is not uncharacteristic of land. Rocks and soil can be moved; top soil, gravel and "fill" are regularly bought and sold. The Code brings into Article 2 some things that are, by the terms of a contract, to be severed by the seller, including specifically minerals, growing crops, and timber. UCC

2–107(1). See, e.g., Manchester Pipeline Corp. v. Peoples Natural Gas Co., 862 F.2d 1439 (10th Cir.1988).

The Code is also helpful in characterizing transactions that go the other way, goods that are, by terms of a contract, to be affixed to realty. So long as the things are movable at the time of identification to a contract for sale, they are "goods" under UCC 2–105(1). The time of "identification" is set forth in UCC 2–501(1). Under this provision, a thing to be affixed to real estate is almost certain to be identified to the goods contract while still movable. The two Pennsylvania cases relied upon by the court in concluding that Article 2 applied in Advent Systems arose out of transactions of this kind.

Contracts may involve transfer of both real estate and goods for a single price, the analogue of transactions in goods and services. Consider, for example, the sale of a new house in which the builder-developer has installed a stove, a refrigerator, other appliances and fixtures. Real estate sales are governed by common law.[6] Should Article 2 apply to any part of the contract?

(D) SALE OF THE ASSETS OF A BUSINESS

Suppose the owner of a business, such as an automobile tire store, contracts to sell all of the assets of the business, including the inventory, the display cases, the accounts receivable, the trade name under which the store has operated and other "goodwill," and the balance of a lease on the building. Should the contract be governed by Article 2? See Knoxville Rod & Bearing, Inc. v. Bettis Corp., 672 S.W.2d 203 (Tenn.App.1983); Melms v. Mitchell, 266 Or. 208, 512 P.2d 1336 (1973).

SECTION 2.   THE RELATIONSHIP OF THE COMMERCIAL CODE AND COMMON LAW

One of the manifest purposes of the drafters of Article 2 was to create body of law for sales that was better than the common law. At the same time the drafters also accepted much of the common law of contracts, in part by their explicit codification of some common-law doctrines and in part by their acceptance of the base of common law that supplements the provisions in the statute. Section 1–103 declares:

Unless displaced by the particular provisions of this Act, the principles of law and equity, including the law merchant and the law relative to the capacity to contract, principal and agent, estoppel, fraud, misrepresentation, duress, coercion, mistake, bankruptcy, or other validating or invalidating cause shall supplement its provisions.

6. The Commissioners on Uniform State Laws promulgated a Uniform Land Transactions Act in 1977. No state has adopted this act.

The fundamental importance of UCC 1–103 cannot be overstated. The application of this section to disputes that arise, in part, under Article 2 is virtually universal. For discussion of the interaction of common law and the Code, see R. Hillman, J. McDonnell and S. Nickles, Common Law and Equity Under the UCC (1984 and Supp.)

This Section considers a number of issues on which the Code has deliberately superseded common law.

(A) THE "NO CONTRACT" AND "NO ENFORCEABLE CONTRACT" DEFENSES

Drafters of Article 2 of the UCC, notably Chief Reporter Karl Llewellyn, were critical of the extent to which some courts, as a matter of common law, had adopted a formalistic approach in the analysis of legal issues arising in sales transactions. One manifestation of this formalism was evident in the success of the defense, in actions for breach of sales contracts, that no contract had been formed even though both parties had taken action to perform their parts of the bargain. A number of the provisions in Part 2 of Article 2 were designed to override decisions of this kind when the "no contract" contention was not commercially reasonable. Another manifestation was evident in the success of the defense that enforcement was barred because the defendant had not signed a contract writing that stated the terms of the contract. Technically, successful invocation of the Statute of Frauds does not establish that no contract was formed, but only that the claimant is not entitled to enforcement.[1] (If the defense fails, the claimant must still prove the existence of the contract.) The Article 2 version of the Statute of Frauds retained this defense, but narrowed it significantly.

Offer and Acceptance. One reform was to jettison the notion that contracts could be formed only by the dialectic process of a communication by one party that constituted an "offer" and response by the other party that constituted an "acceptance." In the informal, messy real world of commercial transactions, it was often impossible to identify an offer and an acceptance, but the parties' conduct was indicative that both believed that a contract existed. If the "no contract" defense is upheld when a contract had been substantially performed before a dispute arose, the parties' reasonable expectations would be disappointed. Indeed, the possibility of a successful "no contract" defense invited strategic behavior by transactors looking to escape from deals no longer seen as desirable, perhaps based on advice of counsel that an escape door was available. UCC 2–204(1) and (2) dispensed with the need to find an offer and acceptance in contracts for the sale of goods. A related provision, addressed to transactions in which an

---

1. The distinction between "no contract" and "no enforceable contract" may have resulted from the way the Statute of Frauds was drafted. In its original 1677 incarnation, the law was known as the Statute for the Prevention of Frauds and Perjuries. Its manifest purpose was to counter spurious claims of contracts in a period when the actual parties to an alleged contract were not allowed to testify.

offer could be identified, relaxed the requirements of a verbal acceptance that was communicated in a particular manner or medium. UCC 2–206, among other things, validates seller's performance conduct as an acceptance

Statute of Frauds. The Article 2 version of the Statute of Frauds, in UCC 2–201, narrowed the defense considerably. UCC 2–201(1) minimized the required content of a sufficient writing. UCC 2–201(2) dispensed with the requirement of the defendant's signature if a sufficient writing had the plaintiff's signature, in transaction where both parties were merchants (a defined term). More fundamentally, UCC 2–201(3)(c) eliminated the defense after contracts had been performed. UCC 2–201(3)(a) eliminated the defense of buyers in executory contracts for goods to be specially manufactured after the sellers had commenced performance, if the circumstances indicate that the goods were for the buyers and were not suitable for sale to others in the ordinary course of business.

While all parts of the Statute of Frauds have been tested in litigation, the text of UCC 2–201 created special uncertainty about the quantity term of contracts. Counsel for Unisys argued in Advent Systems that the Statute of Frauds was not satisfied because there was no quantity term in the writings. The premise of the argument was that a contract that lacks a quantity term cannot satisfy UCC 2–201(1). An alternative reading of the same sentence of the statute is that a quantity term in the writing is not essential, but—if a quantity term is present—it forecloses proof that the contract was for a larger quantity. Which is the better reading of the text? Comment 1 declares that a quantity term "must appear." What weight should that have if the alternative reading of the text is more sound?

Which interpretation did the Court of Appeals adopt?[2]

(B) ESTABLISHING THE TERMS OF THE CONTRACTS

The legislative move that allows courts to find contracts from conduct had the consequence of giving rise to disputes about the content of contracts. When contract formation follows from exchange of offers and acceptances that are "mirror images" of each other, the terms would be a matter of expressed agreement. If the expressed terms did not include a term that a court thought to be essential, the court would tend to hold that there was no contract.[3] If the expressed terms of the parties differed, usually because they used different standard forms, courts would find that no contract had been formed.

2. The Commercial Code has a Statute of Frauds, found in Article 1, that applies to contracts for the sale of "personal property" other than goods. UCC 1–206. Counsel for Unisys might have argued that the subject matter of the contract was non-goods personal property and sought shelter under UCC 1–206. Would this litigation strategy have been successful?

3. A highpoint of cases of this kind was the decision of the then highly respected New York Court of Appeals, in an opinion by then Judge Cardozo, that the parties' failure to fix the price term was fatal to the process of contract formation. Sun Printing & Publishing Ass'n v. Remington Paper & Power Co., 235 N.Y. 338, 139 N.E. 470 (1923).

Gap Fillers. Article 2 overruled these common law requirements. One approach was to provide by statute terms that would be incorporated into contracts where there were gaps in the express agreements. Many of the "gap fillers" are found in Part 3 of Article 2. Thus, UCC 2–305 deals with absence of an agreed price term, and UCC 2–308 and 2–309 with the absence of terms for place and time of delivery. "Gap fillers," in many guises, are found throughout Article 2. The difference between "agreement" and "contract," as defined by the Code, is largely the terms that are supplied by Article 2. See UCC 1–201(3) and (11).

Indefiniteness. Another approach was to enact a general principle on the required degree of specificity of agreements. This principle declares that "even though one or more terms are left open a contract does not fail for indefiniteness if the parties intended to have a contract and there is a reasonably certain basis for giving an appropriate remedy." UCC 2–204(3).

The second substantive defense argued by counsel for Unisys in Advent Systems was the defense of indefiniteness. The contract term claimed to be missing was a term defining the obligation of Unisys! The anomaly of Unisys' counsel's argument that the contract was unenforceable because Unisys had no definite contractual obligation went unremarked by the court. Rather, the Court of Appeals inferred a general "gap filler" from Unisys' statutory obligation of good faith in performance of the contract. Having thus found an implied obligation, the court was unwilling to conclude that the obligation had been breached. The case was remanded to the trial court for a hearing on this point.[4]

Battle of the Forms. Another problem, known as the battle of the forms, was, in a sense, exacerbated by Article 2. Unlike transactions in which the parties were insufficiently expressive, transactions with battling forms contained too much expressive content, albeit expressions that do not coincide. The chief purpose of UCC 2–207 was to recognize that contracts may be formed despite the parties' use of non-matching forms. Its success in that regard has stimulated the use of standard forms by parties who engage in frequent, repetitive transactions. Typically these transactions involve the sale of supplies or equipment by one business entity to another. Not enough is at stake in any one of these transactions to justify using lawyers and negotiators, but it is feasible for the entities to use lawyers to draft "standard" terms that can be deployed, over and over, by employees unaware of and unconcerned with the "boilerplate" legal provisions. This scenario is a recipe for contractual disaster.

The difficulty is to find the terms of the contracts formed by exchange of forms. The kindest thing to say is that, on this matter, Article 2 is muddled. Several very different approaches emerged in a welter of litigated cases, but two became dominant. One is called the "knock out" rule and other is called the "last shot" rule. The "knock out" rule, based on UCC 2–

---

4. On remand, the case was tried to a jury which awarded plaintiff $1,020,000. 1992 WL 185606 (July 23, 1992). The verdict was considerably smaller in amount than the original verdict. There is no reported opinion for the last phase of the case.

207(3), is premised on the finding that a contract was formed by the parties' conduct and finds the terms of that contract in the expressed terms, to the extent they agree, and for the rest turns to the "gap fillers" of Article 2. The "last shot" rule, based in part on UCC 2–206(1), is premised on the finding that no contract was formed until the party receiving the last of the battling forms had "accepted" it; the terms are those in the last form, plus any needed "gap fillers." A "first shot" rule, of sorts, can be discerned in UCC 2–207(1) and (2).

Lawyers drafting these forms found a way to escalate the difficulty by including provisions declaring that there could be no contract formed except on the terms in the form. "My way or the highway" clauses, ignored of course by the people transacting business, began to show up in litigation. In due course, all standard forms will have such clauses, but for a time the original users of such forms may extract some legal advantage, the equivalent to the last shot rule. The resulting confusion, affecting lawyers and judges, was demonstrated dramatically in two recent First Circuit decisions. Ionics, Inc. v. Elmwood Sensors, Inc., 110 F.3d 184 (1st Cir.1997); JOM, Inc. v. Adell Plastics, Inc., 151 F.3d 15 (1st Cir.1998). It is safe to conclude that the mess is not likely to be cleaned up satisfactorily under the current version of Article 2. Most of these deformed agreements will be recognized as enforceable contracts, but dispute as to their terms will continue. Legislative reform is essential.

Written Agreements and Parol Evidence. The negotiated terms of agreements in commercial transactions are often set down in writings. The circumstances for this vary from carefully crafted writings created for that purpose by the parties to standard forms in which most of the terms were not negotiated. However created, both parties to a contract frequently sign the writing as the final expression of their agreement. Later, one of the parties may declare that the writing did not contain all of the agreed terms or that some term is not accurately stated in the record. If the other party stands on the writing as both correct and complete, the dispute that results is a matter for the parol evidence rule.

The parol evidence rule is a major piece of the common law of contracts and reflects an important societal value that respects the integrity of writings as the best evidence of what the parties to commercial transactions agreed to. Some people even refer to the sanctity of writings in this respect. The drafters of Article 2 were not content to leave the sales contracts to the common law parol evidence rule, perhaps because there was no consensus as to the rule at common law. Among the several differences was a fundamental disagreement over the way to determine whether a writing was complete. Some espoused the view that a writing's completeness could be inferred from looking at it, the so-called "four corners" rule. This approach gave the greatest weight to a clause in the writing that declared the writings completeness, often called a "merger clause." Others contended that completeness of a writing could be found only after considering all proffered evidence, including testimony of witnesses. Even "merger clauses" could be overridden by other evidence.[5]

UCC 2–202 displaced the common law on parol evidence, but did not choose clearly between the competing views. The text provides that additional terms are admissible unless the court finds the writing to have been intended as a complete and exclusive statement of the terms of the agreement, but is silent on how that critical finding is to be made. Comment 3 suggests that a decision can be made on the face of the writing, but the decision must allow the additional evidence unless the terms, if agreed upon, "would certainly have been included in the document." A criterion phrased in certainty would have little exclusionary effect. To see the effect, substitute "probably" for "certainly." Neither the text nor the Comment refers to merger clauses.

(C) MODIFICATION AND WAIVER; ADEQUATE ASSURANCE OF PERFORMANCE

In the performance stage of many contracts of sale, the parties individually or jointly change the deal. Common-law contract doctrines were not well suited to this commercial flexibility. Article 2 therefore includes provisions that permit parties to accomplish their commercial purposes.

UCC 2–209(1) declares that an agreement to modify a contract needs no consideration to be binding. One important effect is to enforce agreements that modify the obligation of one party without any change in the obligation of the other.

Waiver is another method by which flexibility can be introduced into the performance of contracts of sale. Under common-law contract doctrine, if a promise is subject to a condition, the promisor can waive the condition with the result that the promise can be enforced even if the condition is not fulfilled.[6] Article 2 deals with the law of waiver, but only with respect to the effect of retractions of waivers. UCC 2–209(5).

In *BMC Industries*, the Court of Appeals for the Eleventh Circuit held that the law of waiver under Article 2 differed from Florida's common-law waiver doctrine. The court found that, under Florida common law, a waiver must be supported by consideration or detrimental reliance. The court concluded that the common-law requirement did not apply to waiver in a sales contract. Although the issue in the case was whether an effective waiver had been made, not whether the waiver had been retracted, the court's conclusion was based on UCC 2–209(5). Was the court's analysis sound?

---

5. The "four corners" rule was attributed to Samuel Williston; the consider-all-the-evidence rule was attributed to Arthur Linton Corbin. Both were renowned contracts teachers and scholars in the early part of the 20th century.

6. See, e.g., Restatement (Second) of Contracts § 84 (1981).

SECTION 3.   REGULATION OF PRIVATE CONDUCT

Most of the provisions in Article 2 are subject to contrary agreement by the parties to sales contracts. In that sense, most of Article 2 is not regulatory in nature. But there are some provisions in Article 2 that do have broad regulatory effect. Key provisions of this kind apply to different phases of sales contracts. One applies to the contract formation stage and the other to the stages of performance and enforcement. If a contract, as formed, is unconscionable in whole or in part, the aggrieved party may persuade a court to refuse to enforce the unconscionable agreement. The relevant time frame is the period of contract formation. Another regulatory provision has no application to the formation of sales contracts, but applies at a later stage. An obligation of good faith applies to the performance and enforcement of these contracts.

(A) UNCONSCIONABLE CONTRACTS OR TERMS

A striking provision of UCC 2–302 authorizes courts to deny enforcement to "unconscionable" agreements. The section provides:

> (1) If the court as a matter of law finds the contract or any clause of the contract to have been unconscionable at the time it was made the court may refuse to enforce the contract, or it may enforce the remainder of the contract without the unconscionable clause, or it may so limit the application of any unconscionable clause as to avoid any unconscionable result.

> (2) When it is claimed or appears to the court that the contract or any clause thereof may be unconscionable the parties shall be afforded a reasonable opportunity to present evidence as to its commercial setting, purpose and effect to aid the court in making the determination.

The most difficult (and intriguing) problem is the lack of any textual definition of the key concept of "unconscionability." By implication, subsection (2) indicates that the meaning of the word is derived from "commercial setting, purpose and effect," but these references do not specify what is to be found in setting, purpose and effect.

Comment 1 to UCC 2–302 seeks to meet the gap in the text. At one point the Comment refers to the "basic test" of whether the clause is "one-sided," at another the Comment states that "the principle is one of the prevention of oppression and unfair surprise (cf. Campbell Soup Co. v. Wentz, 172 F.2d 80 (3d Cir.1948), and not of disturbance of allocation of risks because of superior bargaining power." Can these two comments be reconciled? Are "oppression" and "surprise" commensurate concepts? The former seems concerned with substantive fairness, the latter with procedural regularity.

The Comment states that "the underlying basis of the section is illustrated by the results in cases such as the following. . . ." The Comment then summarizes the holdings of ten cases. Five of these involved narrow construction of clauses disclaiming implied warranties of quality; the Code deals with this problem specifically in UCC 2–316. The remaining five cases limited the impact of clauses restricting remedies for breach, a problem covered in UCC 2–719. Cf. 2–718 (agreements for unreasonably large liquidated damage are void as a penalty). Thus, even if these Comments are influential in construing the Code, the possible scope of UCC 2–302, in areas not duplicated by UCC 2–316, 2–718 and 2–719, is left for case-law development.[1]

Although the precise meaning of unconscionability may be obscure, the UCC is quite clear on the process of wielding the power to refuse enforcement. The issue is not one for determination by a jury. Redundantly, UCC 2–302 refers to "the court" and "as a matter of law" to eliminate any doubt that the issue cannot be given to a jury for determination.[2]

(B) The Obligation of Good Faith

A good faith obligation, stated in Article 1, spans the entire UCC. UCC 1–203 provides that: "Every contract or duty within this Act imposes an obligation of good faith in its performance or enforcement." Supplementing this provision in Article 1 is the definition of "good faith" that is provided, in Article 2, for persons who are merchants. UCC 2–103(1)(b) provides that: " 'Good faith' in the case of a merchant means honesty in fact and the observance of reasonable commercial standards of fair dealing in the trade.[3] 'Merchant' is defined in UCC 2–104.

The potential power of this obligation is enormous, but the broad principle does not easily convert into specific commands or proscriptions. Parties make many decisions during the performance stage of sales contracts. At the time, they have no way to obtain definitive guidance as to whether or not the specific decisions will be found, in hindsight, to have

---

1. Professor Karl Llewellyn's understanding of the provision is found in 1 N.Y. Law Rev. Comm. Report 177–178 (1954). The unconscionability provision has been much discussed by academic scholars. See, e.g., A. Leff, Unconscionability and the Code—The Emperor's New Clause, 115 U. Pa. L. Rev. 485 (1967); M. Eisenberg, The Bargain Principle and Its Limits, 95 Harv. L. Rev. 741 (1982); A. Schwartz, Unconscionability and Imperfect Information: A Research Agenda, 19 Can. Bus. L.J. 437 (1991). It is a staple of texts on the law of sales. See, e.g., C. Gillette & S. Walt, Sales Law: Domestic and International 154 (1999); White & Summers 137; J. Brook, Sales and Leases 129 (2d ed. 1999).

Many standard Contracts casebooks contain Williams v. Walker-Thomas Furniture Co., 350 F.2d 445 (D.C.Cir.1965), perhaps the most well-known case involving the doctrine of unconscionability. *Williams* involved an abusive credit practice. In a transactional context of a buyer's repeated purchases of goods on secured credit, the seller structured the contracts so that no property would ever become free of the seller's security interest so long as any debt was unpaid.

2. Application of UCC 2–302 in commercial arbitration, where there is no judge, is not clear.

3. A lesser obligation, defined in Article 1, would apply to non-merchants. See UCC 1–201(19).

been made in good faith. If counsel is consulted for advice at this stage, the advice must be shaped in light of the risk of potential later challenge in court. Moreover, unlike litigation involving the provision on unconscionability, discussed next, the issue of compliance with the good faith obligation can be a jury decision.

As we have seen already, good faith was used by the Court of Appeals in Advent Systems, first in analysis of the issue under the Statute of Frauds, and then in analysis of the issue of sufficient definiteness of the contract in that case.

The following case applies the good faith requirement in another context. The case also illustrates the relationship between the good faith obligation and unconscionability.

El Paso Natural Gas Co. v. Minco Oil & Gas Co.

Court of Appeals of Texas, 1997.
964 S.W.2d 54.

■ BOYD, C.J., and QUINN and REAVIS, JJ.

■ BRIAN QUINN.

El Paso Natural Gas Company (El Paso) appeals from a final judgment awarding Minco Oil & Gas Company (Minco) and Charles F. Doornbos, as trustee for the Charles F. Doornbos Revocable Trust, (Doornbos) damages against it. Through three points of error, El Paso raises questions regarding unconscionability, breached duty of good faith, and the sufficiency of the evidence. By cross-point, Doornbos decries the trial court's refusal to find that the life of a particular contract was extended past its original term. We reverse in part and affirm in part.

Background

The dispute revolves around take-or-pay gas purchase agreements executed in 1979 (1979 Agreements) by El Paso, and the predecessors of Doornbos, and Minco. Under these agreements, Doornbos and Minco dedicated to El Paso all the natural gas which could be produced from their properties located in Hemphill County, Texas. In turn, El Paso agreed to purchase a specified minimum quantity (80% "of the aggregate maximum delivery capacity of the Seller's wells") per day. If it failed to purchase same or if it bought an amount less than the minimum quantity, then El Paso was obligated to pay Doornbos and Minco the difference between the amount actually taken and the minimum quantity it was required to take; thus, arose the concept of take-or-pay.

For several years after the 1979 Agreements were executed, all parties performed as expected. Then, the natural gas market began to experience change in the mid–1980's. To put it mildly, gas prices fell substantially. Soon El Paso realized that to continue acquiring the gas as required under the 1979 Agreements would be unprofitable and, in time, it obtained from Minco and Doornbos various amendments to the Agreement. Those amendments (referred to as the Amendatory Agreements) retroactively altered El

Paso's take-or-pay obligation from 80% to 50% of the sellers' "aggregate daily producing ability" for the period of January 1, 1982, through December 1984, and from 80% to 60% for the period "from and after January 1, 1985," through the end of the contract term. So too was the buyer granted the right to unilaterally reduce the price it paid for the gas. Finally, if the buyer decided to reduce the price to a level unacceptable to Minco and Doornbos, the two producers had the chance to end "this Agreement" but only after all obligations due El Paso were satisfied.

In addition to the foregoing amendments, approximately 80 other contracts were executed between the parties over the remaining terms of the 1979 Agreements. These other contracts (referred to herein as the Monthly Releases) 1) released El Paso from its monthly obligation to take-or-pay, 2) extended to Minco and Doornbos the opportunity to sell their gas on the spot market during the pertinent period often at a lesser price, and 3) gave El Paso the option to reduce its annual take-or-pay obligation by the amount of gas they sold on the spot market or to simply ignore its obligation for the month covered by the contract.

In time, Minco grew dissatisfied with its relationship with El Paso and requested that it be ended. Consequently, in November of 1988 the two entities signed a letter (the November Termination Letter) terminating the 1979 Agreement and releasing each other of any and all claims or causes of action which they may have had against each other. Several more years passed before El Paso obtained, in February of 1991, two termination letters (February Termination Letters) from Doornbos and his predecessors in interest. They, like the November Termination Letter, also purported to waive "all past liabilities that might exist between the parties."

More time passed before Minco and Doornbos learned that others had begun asserting take-or-pay claims against El Paso. Thus, they too joined the fray and sued the company to recover sums equal to the take-or-pay obligations thought due them under the unamended 1979 Agreements. Though the causes of action averred were numerous, only three concern us for they were the claims upon which the court awarded damages. The first is breach of contract. As to this allegation, it was determined that El Paso failed to perform its take-or-pay obligations as per the original 1979 gas purchase agreements. However, before recovery could be had upon that claim, the court had to set-aside the Amendatory Agreements, Monthly Releases, and the November and February Termination Letters. It did so by first holding all of them unconscionable. Then, it concluded that all but the February Termination Letters were obtained by El Paso in violation of its duty of good faith. As a result, El Paso was ordered to pay Minco and Doornbos damages equal to the amount of gas which it agreed to take-or-pay for under the unamended 1979 Agreement.

On appeal, the true issue is not whether El Paso breached the 1979 Agreements. Rather, it concerns whether the other contracts and releases were properly voided so that the claim of breached contract could be pursued. And, of paramount importance is whether the November and February Termination Letters were properly negated. Again, they released

El Paso from all claims and liability. So, if they remained binding, it mattered not whether any of the other Agreements were avoidable.

Point of Error One—Unconscionability

In its first point of error, El Paso attacks the trial court's decision to avoid the release agreements on the basis of unconscionability. It posits that same were not unconscionable as a matter of law. So too does it argue that the court's "Findings of Fact/Conclusions of Law Nos. 5–16," which purportedly involved unconscionability, were legally or factually insufficient. We sustain the point.

A.   Controlling Law

As per the Texas Business and Commerce Code, a court may refuse to enforce a contract which it holds unconscionable. TEX. BUS. & COM. CODE ANN. § 2.302(a) (Vernon 1994). Yet, a problem arises in determining what is encompassed within the theory. Those who codified the concept into section 2.302 did not deign to define it; nevertheless, we are not without guidance. Both the commentary following the provision and the writings of our judicial brethren provide assistance. . . .

1.   Standard of Review

We are told that the ultimate question as to whether an agreement is unconscionable is one of law. . . . This suggests that our review of the matter is de novo. Yet, it cannot be forgotten that the decision of whether some agreement is or is not unconscionable is dependent upon the existence of facts which allegedly illustrate unconscionability. And, as to the existence of those facts, our review is not de novo. In other words, we cannot review the record, divine our own inferences from the evidence contained therein, resolve conflicts in same, or decide what evidence to believe and what not to believe. The power to do those things, that is, to find facts, lies with the trial court. Once it has exercised that power, we must then defer to the findings made. And, as long as the findings enjoy sufficient evidentiary support, they cannot be disturbed, even though we may have construed the evidence differently. Nevertheless, this does not prevent us from assessing whether the findings made illustrate unconscionability for, again, that is a question of law. Nor does it prevent us from deciding whether the evidence of record, when viewed in a light most favorable to the court's findings and regardless of its potential inferences, illustrates unconscionability, for that too is a question of law. . . .

2.   The Scope of Unconscionability

According to those who incorporated it into chapter two of the Texas Business and Commerce Code, unconscionability serves the purpose of negating an advantage gained through oppression and unfair surprise. TEX. BUS. & COM. CODE ANN. § 2.302, cmt. 1. At one time, it was perceived as a way of protecting the downtrodden against the overpowering. Though the concept has changed somewhat, it nevertheless retains many of its historic characteristics. For instance, it must be shown that the agreement in question arose through procedural and substantive abuse. . . . The former means that oppression and unfairness must taint the negotiation process leading to the agreement's formation. . . . And, this is illustrated through such things as 1) the presence of deception, overreaching, and sharp business practices, . . . 2) the absence of a viable alternative, . . . and 3) the relative acumen, knowledge, education, and financial ability of the parties involved. . . . Furthermore, no one indicia is determinative; rather, the totality of the circumstances must be assessed before it can be said that someone fell prey to procedural abuse. . . . Moreover, the situation must be assessed as of the time it occurred, not via hindsight. . . .

As to the latter prong, that concerning substantive abuse, the fairness, or oppressiveness of the contract itself is considered. . . . Admittedly, this prong is not easily quantified for the notions of fairness and oppressiveness themselves elude ready grasp. What may be fair in one scenario may not be in another. Thus, the totality of the situation (as of the time the situation unfolded) must again be measured. Furthermore, at least one commentator suggests that the contract, with its promises, benefits and detriments, must border on being inimical to public policy before it can be said to be sufficiently unfair or oppressive. . . . Others suggest that it must be utterly lopsided, that is, there must be no reasonable or subjective parity between the values exchanged.

Yet, regardless of grounds proffered as illustrative of substantive abuse, they must be sufficiently shocking or gross to compel the courts to intercede. Indeed, the same must be said vis-a-vis procedural abuse; the circumstances surrounding the negotiations must be shocking. Anything less would be an invitation to excessive governmental intrusion into our dealings. Our court system cannot act as the mother hen watching over its chicks, standing ready to ameliorate every unpleasant circumstance which might befall them. . . . One's right to negotiate a bargain, to exercise free will, to choose a path, and to even make a bad deal must be admitted and respected. . . . After all, the general responsibility to fend for one's self still lies with one's self. Consequently, only when the negative aspects of the bargaining process and subsequent contract are gross, under the totality of the circumstances, is the court's authority to intercede triggered. . . .

Similarly, it is imperative that the complaining party fall prey to those gross aspects of the deal. That is, the circumstances before him must be such as to compel him to execute the bargain. . . . Again, if the complainant did what he did because of his own motivations, and not those of his opponent, then he must suffer the result of his deal.

Lastly, and to the extent that El Paso argues otherwise, section 2.302 of the Business and Commerce Code does not limit its protections to only those involved in personal, as opposed to commercial, transactions. The doctrine has been invoked with success in the latter setting. Indeed, Campbell Soup Co. v. Wentz, 172 F.2d 80 (3d Cir.1948), a case cited by the legislature in the comments following section 2.302 as indicative of unconscionability, is one such example. There, the court struck down a contract which obligated Wentz, a farmer, to dedicate his entire crop to Campbells even if Campbells did not take or pay for it. ... In citing Wentz, it can be said that the legislature did not intend to ipso facto exclude commercial transactions from the realm of unconscionability. And, we are not in a position to do that which the legislature has not done. ...

Of course, we acknowledge that a claimant's status as a merchant or businessman may be considered in the overall equation. Indeed, the expertise, knowledge, financial strength and such possibly garnered by a businessman may be enough to warrant the conclusion that he or she did not fall prey to supposedly unconscionable activity. ...

B. Application to Case

As previously mentioned, the trial court held unconscionable those portions of the November Termination Letter which effectively waived Minco's claims against El Paso. It did so because of:

> [1] El Paso's admitted policy that it did not voluntarily make take-or-pay payments ... as well as its express and implied representations that it was not obligated to purchase minimum contractual amounts of gas or to pay take-or-pay damages ... and the overall advantage of bargaining power held by El Paso ... [and]

> [2] Minco was required to release all contractual take-or-pay obligations of El Paso in order [to] be able to sell any of its gas ... which El Paso was refusing to purchase....

So too were the provisions of the February Termination Letters which waived liabilities against El Paso avoided. The reasons given, however, differed. Those agreements were set aside because

> [1] [they] represent that it "may be in the best interests of all parties" to sign the agreements and because the stated purpose of the letters [was] the early termination of, in part, the McMordie contracts, and because according to El Paso's own records, the McMordie contracts would terminate at the approximate same time whether Doornbos and Cross–Timbers signed the letters or not [and]

> [2] the effect of such a release of past take-or-pay damages without any corresponding benefit to Plaintiffs ... [was] so one-sided....

We now turn to the question of whether these were sufficient to establish unconscionability.

1. Minco Release

a. Procedural Abuse

We initially note that the court said nothing of Minco's business expertise, financial status, and overall knowledge of the oil and gas trade. Nor did it comment upon the viable alternatives, if any, which were available. To the extent that these factors went unconsidered, it can be said that the court failed to assess the totality of the circumstances as required. And, in not doing that, the court abused its discretion. ... Similarly absent is consideration of whether the indicia cited by the court compelled Minco to do what it did. That too indicates analysis of less than the totality of the circumstances and abused discretion.

Next, the supposed policy referred to by the trial court as illustrative of procedural abuse was used prior to execution of the Amendatory Agreements. Whether it was still in existence three years later when Minco signed the November Termination Letter cannot be garnered from the evidence before us.

Moreover, the record undisputably demonstrates that the subject of terminating the 1979 Agreement was first broached by Minco's president, Gene Hall. He believed it "prudent" to sell his gas and grew frustrated with what he perceived to be El Paso's persistent refusal to live up to its agreement. As he stated at trial:

> You know, I finally reached the point, I believe ... I believe it was in '88 or along there that they [El Paso] hadn't taken gas in some time period. They just hadn't been taking gas.

> And so, at that point I realized that I wasn't going to be able to sell any gas and so, I asked for a release.

The release was needed, Hall testified, to insulate any potential new buyers from suit by El Paso. So, he proposed to El Paso that the relationship between it and Minco come to an end. El Paso responded by drafting the November Termination Letter which included a mutual release of claims. Upon receiving the document, Minco signed it, and within days, the producer had contracted to sell its gas to another company. It may be that El Paso had superior bargaining position due to its size, pocketbook, and ability to prevent sales to third-parties. Yet, we were cited to no evidence, nor did we find any, indicating that Minco objected to the release provision in the November Termination Letter. Nor is there any evidence indicating that it sought to renegotiate that language. Under this state of the record, it can hardly be said that Minco fell prey to El Paso's bargaining power when it did not attempt to test that power or when it simply acquiesced to El Paso's preferences.

Interestingly, the November Letter was not the first contract drafted by El Paso and signed by Minco which contained release provisions. Many such instruments had been executed by the producer since 1985. That the documents also had the effect of releasing or minimizing El Paso's take-or-pay liability was something about which Minco was not "too concerned," despite being "real disappointed" with El Paso. . . .

Additionally, nothing of record indicates that Minco failed to understand the effect of its actions in executing the November Termination Letter. Its president, Hall, was a sophisticated businessman. He had graduated from college, become a certified public accountant, and began acquiring oil and gas interests at least five years before incorporating Minco in the 1960's. Moreover, his venture into the oil patch was sufficiently profitable to induce him, in the 1970's, to leave his accounting practice and pursue the oil trade full-time. And, throughout his career as a professional, he not only drafted various business instruments but knew enough to hire attorneys to draft those which he could not. These circumstances coupled with his admission that he knew what the concept of waiver meant belie any notion that Hall was something less than an astute businessman. It may be, as Minco suggested in its brief, that Hall did not know the extent, if any, of El Paso's potential liability before signing the November Termination Letter. Yet, the undisputed evidence illustrates that not only was Hall disappointed with El Paso's performance but also that he never attempted to investigate the extent of El Paso's potential liability until long after signing the releases.

Furthermore, there existed options to waiving the claims. At the very least, Minco could have tried to end the relationship without releasing El Paso. Or, it could have acted upon its "real disappointment" with El Paso and demanded that El Paso perform. If it did not, then Minco could have also done that which it postponed until the 1990's, that is, sue. After all, when El Paso sent the Termination Letter, Minco stood at the precipice. At that point, Minco could no longer delay the inevitable. It had to decide whether to sign the release or convert its frustration with the company into a law suit. Contrary to Minco's insinuations to the contrary, a lawsuit can be a very viable option when one is finally faced with the choice of either waiving claims or suing upon them.

In sum, we hold that in failing to consider the totality of the circumstances, the trial court abused its discretion in finding that El Paso engaged in gross procedural abuse. So too do we conclude, as a matter of law, that the indicia relied upon by the trial court were alone not enough to illustrate gross procedural abuse. We also find, as a matter of law, that under the totality of the circumstances, Minco did not succumb to any gross procedural abuse in executing the November Termination Letter.

b.   Substantive Abuse

As to the question of substantive abuse, the trial court found same in the fact that Minco had to purportedly release its causes of action before it could sell to other buyers. Though that may be a distasteful option, we hold as a matter of law, that it was not enough to render the release an instance of substantive abuse or an act approaching the violation of public policy. First, there is nothing inimical in releasing claims. Indeed, that is done most every time a legal controversy is settled. Second, in exchange for the release, Minco gained the opportunity to sell its gas to third-parties without hindrance from El Paso. That, in the words of Minco's president, was a "prudent" goal to pursue. Third, Minco undoubtedly considered the claims unimportant at the time since it did not even attempt to investigate their potential existence or extent. Fourth, and as previously discussed, Minco had the option to pursue those claims rather than release them. Given the totality of the circumstances which went unmentioned by the court, we conclude that the latter abused its discretion in finding that Minco was the victim of substantive abuse.

2.   Doornbos/Cross–Timbers Releases—February Termination Letters

a.   Procedural Abuse

As previously mentioned, the trial court found that the February Termination Letters were the result of procedural abuse because 1) El Paso represented in the documents that it " 'may be in the best interests of all parties' to sign the agreement," 2) "the stated purpose of the letters [was] the early termination of, in part, the McMordie contracts," and 3) "according to El Paso's own records, the McMordie contracts would terminate at the approximate same time whether Doornbos and Cross–Timbers signed the letters or not." As can be seen, the trial court did not address the relative bargaining strength of the parties at the time the items were signed or their relative business acumen, knowledge, education, or financial ability. Nor did it discuss the presence or absence of viable business alternatives. To the extent that all these factors were ignored, the court did not permissibly exercise its discretion.

More importantly, it could not be said that the ability of Doornbos or Cross–Timbers to sell gas to others was conditioned upon the execution of either document. Indeed, other findings of the trial court revealed that the producer/buyer relationship once existed between El Paso, and Cross–Timbers ended approximately 14 months before execution of the 1991 releases. So, no approval was needed from El Paso to market their gas elsewhere. Similarly non-existent is evidence indicating that either Doornbos or Cross–Timbers read the releases before signing them, relied upon anything mentioned therein as inducement to sign them, objected to signing the documents, attempted to negotiate the terms of the documents, or felt compelled in any way to sign them for any particular reason. And, though we have no information of record about the financial or educational background of the Cross–Timbers partners or evidence of their relative business acumen, the evidence undisputably characterizes Doornbos as a college educated man of "considerable" wealth, learned in the oil and gas trade, and careful about his business and what he signed. It further depicts him as someone who had sold gas to and dealt with a number of interstate pipelines in his career and knew how and when to obtain legal counsel.

Given the dearth of evidence regarding compulsion by El Paso or reliance upon anything the company said to induce execution of the 1991 releases, as well as the general absence of evidence illustrating lack of viable alternatives, business acumen, financial ability, and knowledge about what was being signed and its effect, the things cited by the trial court as illustrating procedural abuse are inconsequential. So, we hold as a matter of law, that under the totality of the circumstances the court's finding of gross procedural abuse emanated from an exercise of abused discretion.

b.   Substantive Abuse

Next, the court found that the 1991 termination letters were illustrative of substantive abuse since they were "one-sided," that is, they effectively released "past take-or-pay damages without any corresponding benefit to" Doornbos or Cross–Timbers. To the extent that the 1979 Agreement had long since expired and the two producers were free to sell to whomever they chose, it can be said that they got little value in return for releasing El Paso of its potential take-or-pay liability. Yet, as previously mentioned, there is nothing inherently wrong in release agreements. Nor was the incorporation of the waiver terminology such that it could have escaped attention or been misunderstood. And, given the general want of procedural abuse, we hold as a matter of law, that the absence of a quid pro quo was not enough to raise the transaction from the realm of a bad deal into that of unconscionability.

c.   Conclusion

In sum, neither the November nor February Termination Letters, or their release provisions, were unconscionable under the totality of the circumstances. In holding that they were, the trial court abused its discretion. Finally, because each document effectively waived the take-or-pay claims which Minco and Doornbos pursued herein against El Paso, we need not determine whether any other release or modification agreement was unconscionable. So, El Paso's first point of error is sustained.

Point of Error Two—Good Faith

In its second point, El Paso attacks the finding that it acted in bad faith vis-a-vis execution of the amendatory agreements, monthly release letters, and termination letters. The findings were wrong because 1) it allegedly owed no duty of good faith or, in the alternative, 2) they lacked evidentiary support. We overrule the point.

* * *

A.   Duty of Good Faith

El Paso correctly argues that whether one has a duty to act in good faith is a question of law. So too is it correct in saying that no general duty of good faith exists between parties to a contract. ... A statute may impose upon one such an obligation. And, it is the ... situation that concerns us here.

The court's findings of fact and conclusions of law, dated October 23, 1995, allude to the concept of good faith as espoused in sections 1.203 and 2.103(a)(2) of the Texas Business and Commerce Code. ... Additionally, the duties apply not only to the performance of the contract but also to the formation and modification of those agreements. TEX. BUS. & COM. CODE ANN. § 2.209, cmt. 2.

Next, to fall within the ambit of § 2.209 of the Business and Commerce Code, the transaction in question must be one involving goods. ... The buying and selling of oil and gas is such a transaction. ... So, El Paso is wrong when it posits that it had no duty to act in good faith vis-a-vis the modification and performance of the many agreements at bar.

However, breaching the Business and Commerce Code duty of good faith does not provide the injured with an independent cause of action for damages. TEX. BUS. & COM. CODE ANN. § 1.203, cmt. Rather, the complainant may use the wrong to vitiate the agreement tainted by bad faith. For instance, if one used bad faith to secure modification of an agreement, then sections 1.203 or 2.103 could be invoked as a way of avoiding the modification and enforcing the original agreement. Id.

Next, whether the duty has been breached depends upon several factors. For instance, the presence or absence of a legitimate commercial reason for pursuing modification is one indicia, assuming the parties are merchants. See TEX. BUS. & COM. CODE ANN. § 2.209, cmt. 2 (stating that the "extortion of a 'modification' without legitimate commercial reason is ineffective as a violation of the duty of good faith"); ... Another indicia concerns the means by which the modification was obtained. ... That is, one cannot benefit from a change induced by acts tantamount to economic extortion or overreaching. ... 1 J. White & R. Summers, Uniform Commercial Code § 1–6(b), pp. 43–44 (4th ed. 1995). Nor may one enforce a modification when its catalyst was little more than some unfounded dispute manufactured by the party requesting modification. Id. at 44.

Finally, deception can also serve to vitiate the new agreement. Indeed, an aspect of good faith according to the legislature is simple honesty. That is why it initially defined the concept as "honesty in fact in the conduct or transaction concerned." TEX. BUS. & COM. CODE ANN. § 1.201 (19). So, if trick, artifice, or misrepresentation is utilized by a party in obtaining a modification of the contract, for instance, that misconduct can later be the modification's downfall.

B.   Sufficiency of the Evidence

1.   Standard of Review

... [W]ith regard to claims of legal insufficiency, the court examines the record only for evidence supporting the determination. All contradictory evidence is ignored. As to claims of factual insufficiency, we are required to peruse the entire record to see if the supporting evidence is so weak or the contrary evidence so overwhelming as to make the finding clearly wrong and manifestly unjust. Needless to the say, this does not accord us carte blanche authority to do whatever we would care to do. Quite the contrary. The standard is one of deference. We cannot simply substitute our interpretation of the evidence for that of the fact finder. Rather, the latter's factual conclusions must be accepted unless found to be clearly wrong or manifestly unjust, given the entire record.

2.   Application of Standard

In considering the entire record, we find evidence illustrating that the gas market experienced appreciable decline several years after the 1979 Agreements were executed. And, there is no question that the drop in price was caused by factors outside the control of El Paso. Given that, one could say that El Paso had a legitimate commercial reason for endeavoring to ameliorate the situation by modifying its obligations to take-or-pay at the price and quantity set forth in the 1979 Agreements. ...

Yet, the record contains evidence illustrating that El Paso did more than simply approach its producers, inform them of its predicament, and attempt to negotiate a modification. Rather, in 1982, the company unilaterally reduced the amount of gas it took to less than the 80% minimum specified in the 1979 Agreements. Furthermore, it did so without disclosing its intent to Minco. It further decided, unilaterally, to eschew voluntary payment for the gas it did not take. That is, the 1979 Agreements contained a provision specifying the date by which El Paso had to pay for the gas it did not take. However, El Paso simply decided to ignore that provision, again without notifying its producers. Instead, the company opted to remain silent until a producer made inquiry into the situation. And, once that happened, it interposed excuses for its conduct, denied any liability, and forced them into negotiations to resolve the claim.

Furthermore, during the "denial/negotiation" process, the producers like Minco were effectively "boxed in," as another El Paso employee eventually admitted. Again, they had dedicated 100% of their product to El Paso. So, they could not sell it to others without El Paso's consent, and needless to say, El Paso was not consenting to such sales without first being released from potential liability for not performing. This situation was comparable to that in Campbell Soup Co. v. Wentz, 172 F.2d at 83. There, like here, Wentz was bound by an agreement under which his commodity was entirely dedicated to Campbell, and, like here, he too was unable to not sell it to others save with Campbell's approval. After reviewing the circumstances, the appellate court refused to enforce the unfair agreement because it was tantamount to "carrying a good joke too far." Id.

So, having placed Minco in a box which at least one court believed to be unfair, El Paso tendered the Amendatory Agreement to the producer. In the cover letter accompanying the agreement, the buyer represented that it was "firmly committed to solving [the problems facing it] so as to remain capable of marketing your gas." So, El Paso proposed that if Minco would agree to retroactively and prospectively reduce both the price to be paid for gas and quantity to be taken, then the prospects for El Paso taking gas in the future would be enhanced.

As to the change in minimum take-or-pay percentage, El Paso maintained that the agreement was "soft"; that is, the provisions of the original 1979 Agreement could still be invoked to either reduce the percentage or entirely relieve the company of its duty to take-or-pay for a particular period. However, the producer's obligation to dedicate 100% of its gas to El Paso remained. So, in effect, the previously unfair contract was further enhanced in favor of El Paso. For all practical purposes, the latter found a way to escape potential liability for its prior conduct and make it easier for it to avoid, conceivably in toto, its future take-or-pay duties while keeping the producers obligated to dedicate all their gas to it. And, more importantly, all this was done under the pretense of enabling itself to acquire more gas from them.

But, instead of finding that El Paso was buying more, Minco encountered the opposite. Indeed, within a short time, El Paso began to forward to its producers monthly release letters. Though their format varied from time to time, their substance did not. Each informed the producer that El Paso did not intend to or could not buy gas during that month. The reasons given for avoiding its obligations were several. For instance, at times they were told that governmental regulations or the status of the market prevented it from complying. Yet, those two reasons proved less than accurate. For instance, a company representative admitted that no regulation actually prohibited it from taking gas in any particular month. This same representative also conceded that the gas could have actually been taken and paid for.

Another reason why El Paso chose not to perform was its supposed policy barring discrimination among its producers. In other words, since the total amount of gas it was required to take from all its producers exceeded its need, it chose either to forgo taking gas from any or to take a prorated fraction from all. Yet, in applying this policy against discrimination, El Paso again proved to be less than candid. For instance, in none of its monthly release letters did the company disclose to the producers that while it was not taking from them, it was actually buying gas on the spot market (at a reduced price) from its own affiliates. In other words, El Paso was using its anti-discrimination policy in a way to discriminate in favor of it and its own.

And, as to the assurances made in the monthly letters regarding its dedication to helping Minco and the others to "maximize [their] production and revenues," El Paso also omitted to tell them of other adverse affects they would suffer by agreeing to the temporary releases. Admittedly, the producers would gain the option to sell their product on the spot market (at a lesser price most likely). But, they would be extending to El Paso the option to either eliminate its take-or-pay obligation for that month or offset the amount of gas sold against its cumulative take-or-pay obligation. Moreover, El Paso admitted that the option it intended to select would be that most advantageous to it and most disadvantageous to the producer. That suggests a mode of conduct contrary to the supposed desire to maximize the production and revenues of Minco.

Finally tiring of El Paso's ongoing practice, Minco asked to end the contractual relationship. In effect, El Paso was not buying Minco's gas, and Minco could not sell it elsewhere without El Paso's approval.

When viewed as a whole, the record contains sufficient evidence from which it could reasonably be inferred that El Paso acted, with regard to each release and modification secured, like what some call a "dishonest compromiser" or extortionist. 1 J. White, R. Summers Uniform Commercial Code § 1–6(b) (1995). It 1) decided not to voluntarily perform its contractual obligations without informing its producers of same, 2) waited until its conduct was questioned then interjected the unwary producer into the denial/negotiation process, 3) obtained modification of its duties through the use of its power to block sales to others and by dangling hollow promises and representations in front of the producer, and 4) contrived additional reasons to avoid performing its modified duties until the producer eventually capitulated by asking to end the relationship. While this evidence may not illustrate the gross oppression implicit in unconscionability, it is some evidence of El Paso posturing its producers into granting concessions through means which were less than honest in fact. And, we found no evidence of a commercial standard proven at trial which condoned the use of deceit in obtaining modifications and releases like those won here.

Of course, there is evidence indicating that El Paso believed its defenses and posturing were legally justifiable. So too is there evidence indicating that Minco may have benefitted from the modifications and releases; after all it did gain the chance to sell gas on the spot market (at a lesser price) when El Paso could have even denied it that. Yet, this contradictory evidence is not enough to overwhelm the court's finding of bad faith. Consequently, we overrule point two as it relates to Minco.

* * *

NOTES

(1) **Unconscionability.** The trial judge held that the release agreements obtained by El Paso Gas Co. were unconscionable, but the Texas Court of Appeals (an intermediate level appellate court) reversed the trial judge on this point. The appellate court held that the standard of review of the trial court's findings of fact was quite limited. Did the appellate court adhere to that standard in its analysis? What message does this decision give to the advocates, in future disputes, who consider making the contention that a contract or term is unconscionable, or who are defending against such a contention, or to future trial judges who must decide such matters?

(2) **Good Faith.** The appellate court upheld the trial judge's finding that El Paso Gas Co. had not acted in good faith "vis-à-vis the execution of the amendatory agreements, monthly release letters, and termination letters."

The appellate court characterized the issue as a "question of law." Was the court correct in so declaring? Compare the text of UCC 2–302 with the text of UCC 1–203 and 2–103(a)(2). In a jury trial, would the trial judge or the jury, properly instructed, decide whether the obligation of good faith had been met?

The statutory obligation of UCC 1–203 extends only to "performance and enforcement" of sales contracts. There is, by clear implication, no statutory obligation of good faith in negotiation of contracts. Were the release agreements, release letters and termination letters within the scope of UCC 1–203?

(3) **Changed Circumstances.** The obvious basis for the behavior of El Paso Gas Co. was the dramatic fall in the market price for natural gas.

Under what circumstances, if any, would a seller's obligation of good faith in performance or enforcement of a contract lead to the conclusion that the seller should accept a lower price when there has been a sharp break in the market value of goods sold? Under what circumstances, if any, should a sharp break in the market value of goods sold be a legal excuse that allowed a buyer, acting in good faith, to terminate a sales contract without liability?

As a prelude to these questions, you should consider the provision in Article 2 on excuse for impracticability of performance resulting from changed circumstances. UCC 2–615 deals, in text, with possible excuse of sellers from their obligations to buyers. The facts in the problems that follow are drawn from two major cases in which sellers sought relief.

Problem 2.3.1. Aluminum Refining Company agreed to provide Wire Manufacturing Company with its requirements of aluminum over a twenty year period. The agreement established a base price subject to adjustment determined by changes in the Producers' Price Index, which tracks the change in prices of industrial commodities. Five years after the agreement, as a result of oil embargoes and related world developments, the price of energy, including electricity, rose dramatically. The aluminum refining process requires an extraordinary amount of electrical energy. As a result, price adjustments under the contract formula are inadequate to meet the sharply rising costs of Aluminum Refining Company, which faces the prospect of severe loss in performance of the balance of the contract. Wire Manufacturing Company, on the other hand, stands to receive refined aluminum at a cost well below current market prices for that material.

(a) On what legal grounds, if any, may Aluminum Refining Company properly cease performance? Does UCC 2–615 offer relief to seller? See Re Westinghouse Elec. Corp. Uranium Contracts Litigation No. 235 (E.D. Va. Oct. 27, 1978) Do the common-law rules of mistake have any application?

(b) If Aluminum Refining Company seeks a court order to reform the contract, what should be the result? See Aluminum Co. of America v. Essex Group, Inc., 499 F.Supp. 53 (W.D.Pa.1980), vacated, No. 80–1604 (3d Cir. Feb. 5, 1981).

For further reading on these and related matters, see J. Wladis, Impracticality as Risk Allocation: The Effect of Changed Circumstances Upon Contract Obligations for the Sale of Goods, 22 Ga. L. Rev. 503 (1988); R. Scott, Conflict and Cooperation in Long–Term Contracts, 75 Cal. L. Rev. 2005 (1987); S. Halpern, Application of the Doctrine of Commercial Impracticability: Searching for the "Wisdom of Solomon," 135 U. Pa. L. Rev. 1123 (1987); R. Hillman, Court Adjustment of Long–Term Contracts: An Analysis Under Modern Contract Law, 1987 Duke L.J. 1; N. Prance, Commercial Impracticability: A Textual and Economic Analysis, 19 Ind. L. Rev. 457 (1986); C. Gillette, Commercial Rationality and the Duty to Adjust Long–Term Contracts, 69 Minn. L. Rev. 521 (1985); V. Goldberg, Price Adjustments in Long–Term Contracts, 1985 Wis. L. Rev. 527; L. Trakman, Winner Take Some: Loss Sharing and Commercial Impracticability, 69 Minn. L. Rev. 471 (1985); R. Speidel, Court–Imposed Price Adjustments Under Long–Term Supply Contracts, 76 Nw. U. L. Rev. 369 (1981);

Joskow, Commercial Impossibility, the Uranium Market and the Westing-house Uranium Contracts Litigation, 6 J. Legal Studies 119 (1977).

Problem 2.3.2. Producer agreed to sell to Distributor specified quantities of natural gas for fifteen years. The agreement provided that Distributor could take gas as needed and pay the contract price, but if Distributor took less than the minimum annual amount, Distributor would pay the contract price for the difference. In the oil and gas industry, these agreements are commonly referred to as take-or-pay contracts. Two years after the agreement, Distributor's gas sales dropped sharply as a result of a decline in oil prices making oil an attractive alternative to natural gas, successful energy conservation efforts, abnormally warm weather, and economic recession. Distributor was unable to sell the minimum annual quantities of natural gas specified in the agreement with Producer. On what legal grounds, if any, may Distributor be excused from the obligation to pay for that part of the annual minima it had not taken? Does UCC 2–615 have any applicability? See Golsen v. ONG Western, Inc., 756 P.2d 1209 (Okla.1988); Resources Investment Corp. v. Enron Corp., 669 F.Supp. 1038 (D.Colo.1987); Northern Indiana Public Service Co. v. Carbon County Coal Co., 799 F.2d 265 (7th Cir.1986).[4]

Although the text of UCC 2–615 is silent on whether the section allows any relief for buyers, there is basis in the comments for the view that the section can be invoked to protect some buyers. See Comment 9. See also Golsen v. ONG Western, Inc., 756 P.2d 1209 (Okl.1988); Resources Investment Corp. v. Enron Corp., 669 F.Supp. 1038 (D.Colo.1987); Northern Indiana Public Service Co. v. Carbon County Coal Co., 799 F.2d 265 (7th Cir.1986). Could El Paso Gas Co. have obtained relief under UCC 2–615?

(C) INTERNATIONAL SALES LAW

This segment of the Chapter deals primarily with the Convention on Contracts for the International Sale of Goods (CISG). CISG is not, of course, the only body of international sales law, but it has a central role in that sphere. CISG is analogous in many ways to the UCC. Basic legal issues similar to those that we considered under the Code arise under CISG

SECTION 4.   SCOPE OF CISG

Internationality of Transactions. The Convention on Contracts for the International Sale of Goods (CISG) applies only to transactions that have a prescribed international character. Article 1(a) declares that the Convention applies to contracts of sale of goods between parties whose

4. For further reading, see E. Farnsworth, Developments in Contract Law During the 1980's: The Top Ten, 41 Case Western L. Rev. 203, 213–216 (1990); J. Medina, G. McKenzie & B. Daniel, Take or Litigate: Enforcing the Plain Meaning of the Take-or-Pay Clause in Natural Gas Contracts, 40 Ark. L. Rev. 185 (1987); Comment, Take-or-Pay Provisions: Major Problems for the Natural Gas Industry, 18 St. Mary's L.J. 251 (1986).

places of business are in different States ... when the States are Contracting States. CISG 1(a).[1]

A nation[2] becomes a Contracting State by ratification, acceptance, approval or accession, terms that have distinctive meaning in public international law, but the differences are not important for our purposes. The United States became a Contracting State when the Senate gave its advice and consent to the President's signing of the Convention.[3] The Convention went into force on January 1, 1988. The Convention is open for additional nations to join, and the number of nations doing so is growing steadily. As of 1999, the Convention applies to the three nations of North America (the NAFTA nations) and to most of the nations of Western Europe. The United Kingdom, Ireland and Greece are European Union nations that have not ratified CISG. In the Pacific Rim, non-ratifying nations include Japan, South Korea, and Thailand. (Taiwan is not eligible to accede.)

The trigger for application of CISG is international diversity in the places of business of the parties to transactions. It is very important to note that CISG does not refer to the place of incorporation or registration as the determinant of the Convention's scope. Some parties to international sales contracts have only one place of business, but increasingly many enterprises have places of business in more than one nation. One of the most dramatic changes occurring in the global economy is the explosive development of transnational enterprises (TNE), sometimes called multinational enterprises or multinational corporations. The national identity of a large TNE may be hard to find.[4] CISG is not concerned with the national identity of an enterprise, nor with the number of its places of business. When a party to a contract has more than one place of business, CISG refers to the place "which has the closest relationship to the contract and its performance." CISG 10(a).[5]

Goods, Seller and Buyer. CISG applies to "contracts for the sale of goods" (CISG 1), but offers no definition of "goods." (Indeed, the Convention defines none of the terms used in it.) The Convention does not apply to all goods. One important exception is the provision that excludes from coverage sales of goods "bought for personal, family or household use."

1. The Convention may apply to contracts when only one party's place of business is in a Contracting State if the choice of law rules of private international law lead to the application of the law of a Contracting State. CISG 1(b). Under CISG 95, nations are permitted to ratify the Convention without agreeing to be bound by Article 1(b). The United States did so, but most nations did not. See Honnold, International Sales, Appendix B (3d ed. 1999). Germany took a unique position, declaring that its obligation under CISG 1(1)(b) would not apply in circumstances where the other nation had exercised its CISG 95 power. Id.

2. International usage of "state" refers to a nation; another usage is "nation-state."

3. The Convention became part of the law of the United States upon ratification, without need for further implementing legislation by the Congress.

4. The enterprise that resulted from the merger of the Chrysler Corporation and Daimler Benz, although registered under German law, is no longer either an American or a German enterprise.

5. If a party has no place of business, applicability is determined by the party's "habitual residence." CISG 10(b).

CISG 2(a).[6] Although ships, vessels, hovercraft or aircraft are probably "goods," the Convention excludes sales of them from its scope. CISG 2(e). Investment securities, negotiable instruments and money are unlikely to be deemed "goods," but sales of these types of "paper property" are also expressly excluded by CISG 2(d). Contracts for the sale of electricity, whether or not goods, are excluded by CISG 2(f).

The Convention defines neither "seller" nor "buyer," but sales by auction, on execution or otherwise by authority of law are expressly excluded from its scope. CISG 2(b) and (c).

Goods and Services. The Convention expressly recognizes contracts for mixed goods and services and provides for inclusion of some of them. The Convention does not apply if "the preponderant part of the obligations of the party who furnishes the goods consists in the supply of labour and other services." CISG 3(2). By implication, the Convention does apply if supply of materials is the preponderant part of a seller's obligation. Like the UCC, CISG includes within its scope contracts for the supply of goods to be manufactured or produced, with an important proviso that excludes any contract in which the buyer supplies a substantial part of the materials necessary for such manufacture or production. CISG 3(1).

Goods and Information. CISG does not mention transactions in information or intellectual property. It provides no guidance on applicability of the Convention to transactions that are combinations of goods (hardware) and information (software).[7]

Problem 2.4.1. Assume that the contract in *Advent Systems*, between United Kingdom and United States companies, lacked a choice-of-law clause. Assume further (contrary to the facts) that both the United States and the United Kingdom had ratified CISG before the transaction occurred. Would a United States or a United Kingdom court properly conclude that the transaction was governed by CISG?

Goods and Real Property. The Convention is silent on contracts for extraction or severance of property from real estate or for affixing property to real estate. Professor Honnold finds: "Contracts requiring the seller to extract and sever corporeal objects from land and make them available to the buyer seem to be covered by Article 3(1). ... On the other hand, a contract permitting a party to come on land and mine, drill or cut timber does not call for one party to deliver goods to the other; crucial provisions of the Convention on conformity of goods (art. 35), delivery, shipment (Arts. 31–33) and risk of loss (Arts. 66–70) do not address the special circumstances of contracts for mining or other extraction activities."[8]

---

6. Contracts for consumer goods may be governed by the Convention if the seller neither knew nor ought to have known that they were bought for that purpose.

7. A German district court (Landgericht München I) held that a contract for the international sale of a computer program was governed by CISG. CLOUT Case 131 (8 Feb. 1995).

8. Honnold, International Sales § 56 (3d ed.1999). A French Court of Appeal (Grenoble) held that an international contract for the dismantling and delivery of a warehouse building was a transaction within the scope

International Transactions Outside CISG. If an international transaction is a contract for the sale of goods, but is outside CISG because the transaction lacks the requisite internationality of the parties, the governing law would be the domestic law of a nation, chosen by operation of the principles of private international law. Absent a valid choice of law clause in the contract, a court or tribunal might apply the Hague Convention on the Law Applicable to International Sales of Goods, 15 June 1955. Many, but not all European nations have ratified this convention. The United States has not ratified it. If choice of law is not governed by the Hague Convention, courts and tribunals refer to general principles of customary international law. See, e.g., Restatement (Third) of the Foreign Relations Law of the United States (1987). If an international sales transaction is outside the scope of the Convention because the subject of the transaction is not goods, again the governing law will be the domestic law of a nation, not a body of international common law.

Problem 2.4.2. Assume a contract for the sale of goods by a seller, whose place of business is in the United Kingdom and a buyer, whose place of business is in the United States. Recall that the United States but not the United Kingdom has ratified CISG. If the buyer and seller inserted a clause in their agreement that the contract was to be governed by CISG, should a United States court, or a United Kingdom court, or an international arbitrator properly conclude that the clause should be given effect? The Convention does not deal with this question. What body of law is relevant?

Problem 2.4.3. Assume a contract for sale of goods in which both parties are United States companies. If the parties agreed that the contract was to be governed by CISG, should a United States court give effect to that agreement? Would it be significant that the domestic sales contract was a leg in a chain of contracts in which the domestic seller had acquired the goods in an international sales transaction that was governed by CISG?

SECTION 5.   THE RELATIONSHIP OF CISG TO UNDERLYING LAW

CISG, like the UCC, is an incomplete body of law. International commercial law conventions are inevitably bodies of law that presuppose that other law will govern on matters that are not within the ambit of the convention or, if within the ambit of a convention, that are not addressed therein. With international conventions, the inevitable problem of incompleteness is exacerbated by the nature of the other law that will be invoked. The interface between a convention and other law is likely to be a discontinuity involving the international law with a nation's domestic law.

of CISG. CLOUT Case 152 (26 April 1995). The analysis in the abstract does not consider the building as real property; it is focused entirely on the relative importance of the services, dismantling and delivery, and the warehouse. The court concluded, under CISG 3(2) that the supply of services did not constitute the preponderant part of the obligations.

There is no general body in international commercial law that underlies and supplements international agreements.

CISG's treatment of the problem of incompleteness is, first, to invite tribunals to fashion particular solutions from the Convention's general principles. CISG 7(2).

> Questions concerning matters governed by this Convention which are not expressly settled in it are to be settled in conformity with the general principles on which it is based. . . . (CISG 7(2)).

The Convention's approach to gap-filling reflects that established for civil law codes which were designed to displace an entire body of pre-existing law. As the Convention was being drafted, some representatives objected that, since these general principles had not been articulated, reference to them in the Convention injected a high degree of uncertainty as to its meaning. This objection was met with the argument that filling gaps by turning to the domestic law of some nation, the only alternative, was a worse solution that would produce even greater uncertainty and, further, undermine the effort to produce a body of uniform law.

Proponents of a "general principles" statement prevailed in the provision of CISG 7(2) quoted above, but the objectors prevailed in seeking a subordinate reference to some nation's domestic law if a needed general principle cannot be found. Article 7(2) continues:

> . . . or, in the absence of such principles, in conformity with the law applicable by virtue of the rules of private international law.

The "rules of private international law" are the choice-of-law rules which exist apart from the Convention and which designate the domestic law that governs any particular contract dispute.

While only future litigation will reveal authoritatively how the two facets of CISG 7(2) will be applied, the views of respected commentators will be important to that outcome. Professor Honnold outlines an approach to implementation of this provision. He first discusses three problem areas to illustrate how the Convention's "general principles" may be ascertained: reliance on representations of the other party, the duty to communicate information needed by the other party, and the obligation to take steps to avoid unnecessary hardship for the other party. He then propounds a general approach:

> This approach responds to the reference in Article 7(2) to the principles on which the Convention is based by requiring that general principles to deal with new situations be moored to premises that underlie specific provisions of the Convention. Thus, like the inductive approach employed in case law development, the first step is the examination of instances regulated by specific provisions of the Convention. The second step is to choose between these two conclusions: (a) The Convention deliberately rejected the extension of these specific provisions; (b) The lack of a specific provision to govern the case at hand results from a failure to anticipate and resolve the issue. If the latter alternative applies, the third step is to consider whether the

cases governed by the specific provisions of the Convention and the case at hand are so analogous that a lawmaker would not have deliberately chosen discordant results for the group of similar situations. In this event, it seems appropriate to conclude that the general principle embracing these situations is authorized by Article 7(2). In sum, the approach involves the analogical application of specific provisions of the Convention.

See Honnold, International Sales § 102 (3d ed. 1999).

Under the domestic law of the United States, where transactions fall outside the scope of Article 2 of a state's version of the UCC, those transactions are governed by the common law of that state. There is no body of "common law" underlying and surrounding CISG. The UNIDROIT Principles of International Commercial Contracts, promulgated in 1994, are a step in that direction, but that is still a nascent body of law.

Drafters of CISG had no occasion to use legislation to overrule or supersede existing international sales law. The grand purpose of CISG was to displace the wide variety of national laws that might apply to international sales transactions with a single, uniform body of law. It is impossible, in these materials, to canvas the various domestic commercial laws that exist around the world in order to comprehend the extent to which the provisions of CISG depart from some or all variations of domestic law. The treatment of writings, in contract formation and contract interpretation, is a good example of the CISG's approach to underlying domestic laws.

Statute of Frauds. The Convention's primary position on the requirement of a writing as a condition to enforcement of a sales contract was to eschew such a requirement. CISG 11 provides that a contract need not be concluded in or evidenced by a writing. During the preparation of the Convention, representatives of some nations objected to the omission of a requirement of a writing. To meet this objection, CISG 12 was added to permit nations to obviate Article 11 by so declaring at the time of ratification. CISG 96.[1]

Gap Fillers. CISG contains many provisions that supply contract terms if the express agreements of the parties do not deal with those terms. The general obligation of sellers and buyers is found in the requirements of "the contract and this Convention." CISG 30, 53. Many of the "gap fillers" are found in Part III. Thus, CISG 55 deals with the absence of an agreed price term, and CISG 31 and 33 with the absence of terms for place and time of delivery. "Gap fillers" appear throughout the Convention.

Battle of the Forms. The Convention provision on battle of forms is found in the formation articles in Part II. CISG 19 deals with only one factual pattern: a reply to an offer that purports to be an acceptance but contains additional or different terms that do not materially alter the terms of the offer. Immaterial alterations would become terms of the contract,

---

1. For the nations that exercised this power, see Honnold, International Sales, Appendix B (3d ed.1999).

CISG 19(2), but CISG 19(3) defines changes in common contract terms as material alterations.

Written Agreements and Parol Evidence. The Convention approach to the admissibility of evidence of contract terms that add to a written agreement is quite liberal. CISG 11 declares that a contract may be proved by any means, including witnesses. CISG 8 may also be relevant. The following case is instructive.

MCC–Marble Ceramic Center, Inc. v. Ceramica Nuova d'Agostino, S.p.A.

United States Court of Appeals, Eleventh Circuit, 1998.
144 F.3d 1384.

■ Before Edmondson and Birch, Circuit Judges and Fay, Senior Circuit Judge.

■ Birch, Circuit Judge:

This case requires us to determine whether a court must consider parol evidence in a contract dispute governed by the United Nations Convention on Contracts for the International Sale of Goods ("CISG"). The district court granted summary judgment on behalf of the defendant-appellee, relying on certain terms and provisions that appeared on the reverse of a pre-printed form contract for the sale of ceramic tiles. The plaintiff-appellant sought to rely on a number of affidavits that tended to show both that the parties had arrived at an oral contract before memorializing their agreement in writing and that they subjectively intended not to apply the terms on the reverse of the contract to their agreements. The magistrate judge held that the affidavits did not raise an issue of material fact and recommended that the district court grant summary judgment based on the terms of the contract. The district court agreed with the magistrate judge's reasoning and entered summary judgment in the defendant-appellee's favor. We REVERSE.

BACKGROUND

The plaintiff-appellant, MCC–Marble Ceramic, Inc. ("MCC"), is a Florida corporation engaged in the retail sale of tiles, and the defendant-appellee, Ceramica Nuova d'Agostino S.p.A. ("D'Agostino") is an Italian corporation engaged in the manufacture of ceramic tiles. In October 1990, MCC's president, Juan Carlos Mozon, met representatives of D'Agostino at a trade fair in Bologna, Italy and negotiated an agreement to purchase ceramic tiles from D'Agostino based on samples he examined at the trade fair. Monzon, who spoke no Italian, communicated with Gianni Silingardi, then D'Agostino's commercial director, through a translator, Gianfranco Copelli, who was himself an agent of D'Agostino. The parties apparently arrived at an oral agreement on the crucial terms of price, quality, quantity, delivery and payment. The parties then recorded these terms on one of D'Agostino's standard, pre-printed order forms and Monzon signed the contract on MCC's behalf. According to MCC, the parties also entered into a requirements contract in February 1991, subject to which D'Agostino agreed to supply MCC with high grade ceramic tile at specific discounts as long as MCC purchased sufficient quantities of tile. MCC completed a number of additional order forms requesting tile deliveries pursuant to that agreement.

MCC brought suit against D'Agostino claiming a breach of the February 1991 requirements contract when D'Agostino failed to satisfy orders in April, May, and August of 1991. In addition to other defenses, D'Agostino responded that it was under no obligation to fill MCC's orders because MCC had defaulted on payment for previous shipments. In support of its position, D'Agostino relied on the pre-printed terms of the contracts that MCC had executed. The executed forms were printed in Italian and contained terms and conditions on both the front and reverse. According to an English translation of the October 1990 contract, the front of the order form contained the following language directly beneath Monzon's signature:

> The buyer hereby states that he is aware of the sales conditions stated on the reverse and that he expressly approves of them with special reference to those numbered 1–2–3–4–5–6–7–8.

R2–126, Exh. 3 P 5 ("Maselli Aff."). Clause 6(b), printed on the back of the form states:

> Default or delay in payment within the time agreed upon gives D'Agostino the right to . . . suspend or cancel the contract itself and to cancel possible other pending contracts and the buyer does not have the right to indemnification or damages.

Id. P 6.

D'Agostino also brought a number of counterclaims against MCC, seeking damages for MCC's alleged nonpayment for deliveries of tile that D'Agostino had made between February 28, 1991 and July 4, 1991. MCC responded that the tile it had received was of a lower quality than contracted for, and that, pursuant to the CISG, MCC was entitled to reduce payment in proportion to the defects. D'Agostino, however, noted that clause 4 on the reverse of the contract states, in pertinent part:

> Possible complaints for defects of the merchandise must be made in writing by means of a certified letter within and not later than 10 days after receipt of the merchandise. . . .

Maselli Aff. P 6. Although there is evidence to support MCC's claims that it complained about the quality of the deliveries it received, MCC never submitted any written complaints.

MCC did not dispute these underlying facts before the district court, but argued that the parties never intended the terms and conditions printed on the reverse of the order form to apply to their agreements. As evidence for this assertion, MCC submitted Monzon's affidavit, which claims that MCC had no subjective intent to be bound by those terms and that D'Agostino was aware of this intent. MCC also filed affidavits from Silingardi and Copelli, D'Agostino's representatives at the trade fair, which support Monzon's claim that the parties subjectively intended not to be bound by the terms on the reverse of the order form. The magistrate judge held that the affidavits, even if true, did not raise an issue of material fact regarding the interpretation or applicability of the terms of the written contracts and the district court accepted his recommendation to award summary judgment in D'Agostino's favor. MCC then filed this timely appeal.

DISCUSSION

We review a district court's grant of summary judgment de novo and apply the same standards as the district court. . . .

The parties to this case agree that the CISG governs their dispute because the United States, where MCC has its place of business, and Italy, where D'Agostino has its place of business, are both States Party to the Convention. See CISG, art. 1. Article 8 of the CISG governs the interpretation of international contracts for the sale of goods and forms the basis of MCC's appeal from the district court's grant of summary judgment in D'Agostino's favor. MCC argues that the magistrate judge and the district court improperly ignored evidence that MCC submitted regarding the parties' subjective intent when they memorialized the terms of their agreement on D'Agostino's pre-printed form contract, and that the magistrate judge erred by applying the parol evidence rule in derogation of the CISG.

I. Subjective Intent Under the CISG

Contrary to what is familiar practice in United States courts, the CISG appears to permit a substantial inquiry into the parties' subjective intent, even if the parties did not engage in any objectively ascertainable means of registering this intent. Article 8(1) of the CISG instructs courts to interpret the "statements . . . and other conduct of a party . . . according to his intent" as long as the other party "knew or could not have been unaware" of that intent. The plain language of the Convention, therefore, requires an inquiry into a party's subjective intent as long as the other party to the contract was aware of that intent.

In this case, MCC has submitted three affidavits that discuss the purported subjective intent of the parties to the initial agreement concluded between MCC and D'Agostino in October 1990. All three affidavits discuss the preliminary negotiations and report that the parties arrived at an oral agreement for D'Agostino to supply quantities of a specific grade of ceramic tile to MCC at an agreed upon price. The affidavits state that the "oral agreement established the essential terms of quality, quantity, description of goods, delivery, price and payment." . . . The affidavits also note that the parties memorialized the terms of their oral agreement on a standard D'Agostino order form, but all three affiants contend that the parties subjectively intended not to be bound by the terms on the reverse of that form despite a provision directly below the signature line that expressly and specifically incorporated those terms.[9]

The terms on the reverse of the contract give D'Agostino the right to suspend or cancel all contracts in the event of a buyer's non-payment and require a buyer to make a written report of all defects within ten days. As the magistrate judge's report and recommendation makes clear, if these terms applied to the agreements between MCC and D'Agostino, summary judgment would be appropriate because MCC failed to make any written complaints about the quality of tile it received and D'Agostino has established MCC's non-payment of a number of invoices amounting to $108,389.40 and 102,053,846.00 Italian lira.

Article 8(1) of the CISG requires a court to consider this evidence of the parties' subjective intent. Contrary to the magistrate judge's report, which the district court endorsed and adopted, article 8(1) does not focus on interpreting the parties' statements alone. Although we agree with the magistrate judge's conclusion that no "interpretation" of the contract's terms could support MCC's position,[10] article 8(1) also requires a court to consider subjective intent while interpreting the conduct of the parties. The CISG's language, therefore, requires courts to consider evidence of a party's subjective intent when signing a contract if the other party to the contract was aware of that intent at the time. This is precisely the type of evidence that MCC has provided through the Silingardi, Copelli, and Monzon affidavits, which discuss not only Monzon's intent as MCC's representative but also discuss the intent of D'Agostino's representatives and their knowledge that Monzon did not intend to agree to the terms on the reverse of the form contract. This acknowledgment that D'Agostino's representatives were aware of Monzon's subjective intent puts this case squarely within article 8(1) of the CISG, and therefore requires the court to consider MCC's evidence as it interprets the parties' conduct.[11]

9. MCC makes much of the fact that the written order form is entirely in Italian and that Monzon, who signed the contract on MCC's behalf directly below this provision incorporating the terms on the reverse of the form, neither spoke nor read Italian. This fact is of no assistance to MCC's position. We find it nothing short of astounding that an individual, purportedly experienced in commercial matters, would sign a contract in a foreign language and expect not to be bound simply because he could not comprehend its terms. We find nothing in the CISG that might counsel this type of reckless behavior and nothing that signals any retreat from the proposition that parties who sign contracts will be bound by them regardless of whether they have read them or understood them. See e.g., Samson Plastic Conduit and Pipe Corp. v. Battenfeld Extrusionstechnik GMBH, 718 F. Supp. 886, 890 (M.D.Ala.1989) ("A good

and recurring illustration of the problem . . . involves a person who is . . . unfamiliar with the language in which a contract is written and who has signed a document which was not read to him. There is all but unanimous agreement that he is bound. . . .")

10. The magistrate judge's report correctly notes that MCC has not sought an interpretation of those terms, but rather to exclude them altogether.

11. Without this crucial acknowledgment, we would interpret the contract and the parties' actions according to article 8(2), which directs courts to rely on objective evidence of the parties' intent. On the facts of this case it seems readily apparent that MCC's affidavits provide no evidence that Monzon's actions would have made his alleged subjective intent not to be bound by the terms of the contract known to "the under-

II. Parol Evidence and the CISG

Given our determination that the magistrate judge and the district court should have considered MCC's affidavits regarding the parties' subjective intentions, we must address a question of first impression in this circuit: whether the parol evidence rule, which bars evidence of an earlier oral contract that contradicts or varies the terms of a subsequent or contemporaneous written contract, plays any role in cases involving the CISG. We begin by observing that the parol evidence rule, contrary to its title, is a substantive rule of law, not a rule of evidence. ... As such, a federal district court cannot simply apply the parol evidence rule as a procedural matter—as it might if excluding a particular type of evidence under the Federal Rules of Evidence, which apply in federal court regardless of the substantive rule of decision.[13]

The CISG itself contains no express statement on the role of parol evidence. See Honnold, Uniform Law [for International Sales Under the 1980 United Nations Convention] § 110 at 170 [2d ed. 1991] ... It is clear, however, that the drafters of the CISG were comfortable with the concept of permitting parties to rely on oral contracts because they eschewed any statutes of fraud provision and expressly provided for the enforcement of oral contracts. Compare CISG, art. 11 (a contract of sale need not be concluded or evidenced in writing) with U.C.C. § 2–201 (precluding the enforcement of oral contracts for the sale of goods involving more than $500). Moreover, article 8(3) of the CISG expressly directs courts to give "due consideration ... to all relevant circumstances of the case including the negotiations ..." to determine the intent of the parties. Given article 8(1)'s directive to use the intent of the parties to interpret their statements and conduct, article 8(3) is a clear instruction to admit and consider parol evidence regarding the negotiations to the extent they reveal the parties' subjective intent.

Despite the CISG's broad scope, surprisingly few cases have applied the Convention in the United States, see Delchi Carrier SpA v. Rotorex Corp., 71 F.3d 1024, 1027–28 (2d Cir.1995) (observing that "there is virtually no case law under the Convention"), and only two reported decisions touch upon the parol evidence rule, both in dicta. One court has concluded, much as we have above, that the parol evidence rule is not viable in CISG cases in light of article 8 of the Convention. In Filanto, a district court addressed the differences between the UCC and the CISG on the issues of offer and acceptance and the battle of the forms. See 789 F.Supp. at 1238. After engaging in a thorough analysis of how the CISG applied to the dispute before it, the district court tangentially observed that article 8(3) "essentially rejects ... the parol evidence rule." Id. at 1238 n.7. Another court, however, appears to have arrived at a contrary conclusion. In Beijing

standing that a reasonable person ... would have had in the same circumstances." CISG, art. 8(2).

13. An example demonstrates this point. The CISG provides that a contract for the sale of goods need not be in writing and that the parties may prove the contract "by any means, including witnesses." CISG, art. 11. ...

Metals & Minerals Import/Export Corp. v. American Bus. Ctr., Inc., 993 F.2d 1178 (5th Cir.1993), a defendant sought to avoid summary judgment on a contract claim by relying on evidence of contemporaneously negotiated oral terms that the parties had not included in their written agreement. The plaintiff, a Chinese corporation, relied on Texas law in its complaint while the defendant, apparently a Texas corporation, asserted that the CISG governed the dispute. Id. at 1183 n.9. Without resolving the choice of law question, the Fifth Circuit cited Filanto for the proposition that there have been very few reported cases applying the CISG in the United States, and stated that the parol evidence rule would apply regardless of whether Texas law or the CISG governed the dispute. *Beijing Metals*, 993 F.2d at 1183 n.9. The opinion does not acknowledge Filanto's more applicable dictum that the parol evidence rule does not apply to CISG cases nor does it conduct any analysis of the Convention to support its conclusion. In fact, the Fifth Circuit did not undertake to interpret the CISG in a manner that would arrive at a result consistent with the parol evidence rule but instead explained that it would apply the rule as developed at Texas common law. See id. at 1183 n.10. As persuasive authority for this court, the Beijing Metals opinion is not particularly persuasive on this point.

As one scholar has explained:

> The language of Article 8(3) that "due consideration is to be given to all relevant circumstances of the case" seems adequate to override any domestic rule that would bar a tribunal from considering the relevance of other agreements. ... Article 8(3) relieves tribunals from domestic rules that might bar them from "considering" any evidence between the parties that is relevant. This added flexibility for interpretation is consistent with a growing body of opinion that the "parol evidence rule" has been an embarrassment for the administration of modern transactions.

Honnold, Uniform Law § 110 at 170–71. Indeed, only one commentator has made any serious attempt to reconcile the parol evidence rule with the CISG. See David H. Moore, Note, The Parol Evidence Rule and the United Nations Convention on Contracts for the International Sale of Goods: Justifying Beijing Metals & Minerals Import/Export Corp. v. American Business Center, Inc., 1995 BYU L. Rev. 1347. Moore argues that the parol evidence rule often permits the admission of evidence discussed in article 8(3), and that the rule could be an appropriate way to discern what consideration is "due" under article 8(3) to evidence of a parol nature. Id. at 1361–63. He also argues that the parol evidence rule, by limiting the incentive for perjury and pleading prior understandings in bad faith, promotes good faith and uniformity in the interpretation of contracts and therefore is in harmony with the principles of the CISG, as expressed in article 7. Id. at 1366–70. The answer to both these arguments, however, is the same: although jurisdictions in the United States have found the parol evidence rule helpful to promote good faith and uniformity in contract, as well as an appropriate answer to the question of how much consideration to give parol evidence, a wide number of other States Party to the CISG have rejected the rule in their domestic jurisdictions. One of the primary factors motivating the negotiation and adoption of the CISG was to provide parties to international contracts for the sale of goods with some degree of certainty as to the principles of law that would govern potential disputes and remove the previous doubt regarding which party's legal system might otherwise apply. See Letter of Transmittal from Ronald Reagan, President of the United States, to the United States Senate, reprinted at 15 U.S.C. app. 70, 71 (1997). Courts applying the CISG cannot, therefore, upset the parties' reliance on the Convention by substituting familiar principles of domestic law when the Convention requires a different result. We may only achieve the directives of good faith and uniformity in contracts under the CISG by interpreting and applying the plain language of article 8(3) as written and obeying its directive to consider this type of parol evidence.

This is not to say that parties to an international contract for the sale of goods cannot depend on written contracts or that parol evidence regarding subjective contractual intent need always prevent a party relying on a written agreement from securing summary judgment. To the contrary, most cases will not present a situation (as exists in this case) in which both parties to the contract acknowledge a subjective intent not to be bound by the terms of a pre-printed writing. In most cases, therefore, article 8(2) of the CISG will apply, and objective evidence will provide the basis for the court's decision. See Honnold, Uniform Law § 107 at 164–65. Consequently, a party to a contract governed by the CISG will not be able to avoid the terms of a contract and force a jury trial simply by submitting an affidavit which states that he or she did not have the subjective intent to be bound by the contract's terms. ... Moreover, to the extent parties wish to avoid parol evidence problems they can do so by including a merger clause in their agreement that extinguishes any and all prior agreements and understandings not expressed in the writing.

Considering MCC's affidavits in this case, however, we conclude that the magistrate judge and the district court improperly granted summary judgment in favor of D'Agostino. Although the affidavits are, as D'Agostino observes, relatively conclusory and unsupported by facts that would objectively establish MCC's intent not to be bound by the conditions on the reverse of the form, article 8(1) requires a court to consider evidence of a party's subjective intent when the other party was aware of it, and the Silingardi and Copelli affidavits provide that evidence. This is not to say that the affidavits are conclusive proof of what the parties intended. A reasonable finder of fact, for example, could disregard testimony that purportedly sophisticated international merchants signed a contract without intending to be bound as simply too incredible to believe and hold MCC to the conditions printed on the reverse of the contract. Nevertheless, the affidavits raise an issue of material fact regarding the parties' intent to incorporate the provisions on the reverse of the form contract. If the finder of fact determines that the parties did not intend to rely on those provisions, then the more general provisions of the CISG will govern the outcome of the dispute.

MCC's affidavits, however, do not discuss all of the transactions and orders that MCC placed with D'Agostino. Each of the affidavits discusses the parties' subjective intent surrounding the initial order MCC placed with D'Agostino in October 1990. The Copelli affidavit also discusses a February 1991 requirements contract between the parties and reports that the parties subjectively did not intend the terms on the reverse of the D'Agostino order form to apply to that contract either. See Copelli Aff. p. 12. D'Agostino, however, submitted the affidavit of its chairman, Vincenzo Maselli, which describes at least three other orders from MCC on form contracts dated January 15, 1991, April 27, 1991, and May 4, 1991, in addition to the October 1990 contract. See Maselli Aff. P 2, 25. MCC's affidavits do not discuss the subjective intent of the parties to be bound by language in those contracts, and D'Agostino, therefore, argues that we should affirm summary judgment to the extent damages can be traced to those order forms. It is unclear from the record, however, whether all of these contracts contained the terms that appeared in the October 1990 contract. Moreover, because article 8 requires a court to consider any "practices which the parties have established between themselves, usages and any subsequent conduct of the parties" in interpreting contracts, CISG, art. 8(3), whether the parties intended to adhere to the ten day limit for complaints, as stated on the reverse of the initial contract, will have an impact on whether MCC was bound to adhere to the limit on subsequent deliveries. Since material issues of fact remain regarding the interpretation of the remaining contracts between MCC and D'Agostino, we cannot affirm any portion of the district court's summary judgment in D'Agostino's favor.

CONCLUSION

MCC asks us to reverse the district court's grant of summary judgment in favor of D'Agostino. The district court's decision rests on pre-printed contractual terms and conditions incorporated on the reverse of a standard order form that MCC's president signed on the company's behalf. Nevertheless, we conclude that the CISG, which governs international contracts for the sale of goods, precludes summary judgment in this case because MCC has raised an issue of material fact concerning the parties' subjective intent to be bound by the terms on the reverse of the pre-printed contract. The CISG also precludes the application of the parol evidence rule, which would otherwise bar the consideration of evidence concerning a prior or contemporaneously negotiated oral agreement. Accordingly, we REVERSE the district court's grant of summary judgment and REMAND this case for further proceedings consistent with this opinion.

NOTES

(1) **Parol Evidence.** The issue in this case was not typical of parol evidence disputes in which one party offers evidence of terms that were not included in the record or evidence that contradicts a term in the record. Buyer's contention here was that the record contained boilerplate terms, in the seller's form, that the parties agreed were not part of their contract.

The issue, framed this way, is whether the parties had adopted the writing in its entirety. This may explain why the court relied primarily on CISG 8 and referred only incidentally, in a footnote, to CISG 11.

(2) Language of the Agreement. The contract in this case was negotiated face-to-face in Italy by an American buyer, acting through its president who did not speak or understand Italian, and an Italian seller, who may not have understood English. The parties communicated through a translator, an agent of the seller. The parties agreed on the economic terms of their transaction. The agreed terms were then integrated into a document (in Italian?) that contained many printed terms, expressed in Italian. Undoubtedly, these printed terms were seen by the buyer. Without knowing what those terms were, the buyer signed the document.

Should the printed terms be excluded from the contract because the buyer did not speak Italian, and the seller was aware of this impairment? Buyer's counsel "made much" of this argument. How might counsel have distinguished this argument from the argument that the parties intended to exclude the printed terms from the contract? The Court of Appeals found the argument based on the use of Italian "nothing short of astounding." Was the court correct?

SECTION 6. REGULATION OF PRIVATE CONDUCT

The regulatory-like provisions of UCC Article 2 were the provisions that allow courts to strike unconscionable contracts or terms and the parties' general obligation of good faith in their performance or enforcement of sales contracts. CISG contains neither provision. Moreover, CISG declares that parties to contracts that come within the scope of CISG have unfettered power to modify or vary any of the provisions of the Convention. See CISG 6. If there were regulatory provisions in the Convention, authority to derogate from them would not exist.

CISG does not expressly or impliedly address unconscionability as a defense to enforcement of a contract for international sale of goods. No party to an international sales contract could plausibly assert such a defense as a matter of Convention law.

CISG 4(a) does state, however, that the Convention is "not concerned with" the "validity" of the contract or any of its provisions. CISG does not define "validity." In a transaction governed by the CISG, in which the underlying domestic law is United States law, a contention might be made that a contract or term that is unconscionable under UCC 2–302 is not "valid" within the meaning of that term in CISG 4(a). Although "validity" is not defined in CISG, the meaning of that word in the Convention is a matter of Convention law, not domestic law. Scholars of the Convention generally agree that fraud, illegality and incapacity are issues within the term, but do not agree on whether it also encompasses unconscionability.[1]

---

1. Compare Honnold, International Sales § 67 (3d ed. 1999), with C. Gillette & S. Walt, Sales Law: Domestic and International 162–165 (1999).

CISG does not contain a good faith requirement of the kind provided in UCC 1–203 and 2–103(1)(b) or in other bodies of domestic law.[2] Such a provision was included in a draft of the Convention, but that provision was deleted from the final text. Professor Honnold explains: "In 1978, the Commission [UNCITRAL] ... decided that the obligation of 'good faith' should not be imposed loosely and at large, but should be restricted to a principle for interpreting the provisions of the Convention. This compromise was generally accepted and was embodied in the concluding words of Article 7(1)."[3]

2. The German Civil Code (§ 242) states: "The debtor is bound to effect performance according to the requirements of good faith, giving consideration to common usage."

3. Honnold, International Sales § 94 (3d ed. 1999).

CHAPTER 3

TITLE AND QUALITY: SELLERS' RESPONSIBILITY AND BUYERS' RIGHTS

SECTION 1. WARRANTIES OF TITLE

DOMESTIC UNITED STATES LAW

Introduction to Warranties of Title. Buyers of goods ordinarily expect to obtain "good" or "clean" title to the goods they have purchased. Two situations may defeat that expectation: sales of stolen goods and sales of encumbered goods.[1] We explored the case of stolen goods in Problem 1.3.1. In Chapter 3, Section 6(B), we shall consider buyers of goods subject to Article 9 security interests, a type of consensual lien or encumbrance. As we have seen, other encumbrances may arise by action of a third party, usually against the will of the owner. Thus, a judgment creditor may obtain a lien on property of the judgment debtor by the process of attachment or judgment execution. Alternatively, liens may arise by operation of law without a judgment. Examples are the liens that may be obtained by the Internal Revenue Service for unpaid federal taxes ("tax liens") or by repairers of goods for their services ("mechanics' liens").

Having bought and paid for goods, a buyer will be surprised and disappointed to learn that the seller did not own the goods sold or that the goods were encumbered and that the seller did not have authority or power to sell them on behalf of the true owner or free of the encumbrance. As we saw in Chapter 1, Section 3, if there was a thief in the seller's "chain of title," the rightful owner who finds the goods may demand their return from anyone whose claim to them derives from the thief. As we also saw, even a good faith purchaser will not always be protected.

A seller's responsibility to the buyer who is compelled to surrender goods to the rightful owner is stated in UCC 2–312(1)(a). A seller warrants that "the title conveyed shall be good, and its transfer rightful." The warranty against encumbrances is set forth in UCC 2–312(1)(b): "the goods

---

1. For property subject to a patent or trademark or other form of intellectual property, a seller may sell the goods without conveying the right to use them without infringement of the rights of the owner of the intellectual property. Intellectual property law often separates the physical thing from the right to use it. Rights to use are commonly conveyed by license by the patent holder or owner of the intellectual property right. A sellers' warranty with respect to infringement of intellectual property rights is found in UCC 2–312(3). See also UCC 2–607(5)(b).

shall be delivered free from any security interest or other lien or encumbrance of which the buyer at the time of contracting has no knowledge." A seller's warranty can be excluded or modified "by specific language" in the agreement of sale or by certain "circumstances." UCC 2–312(2). We considered ever so briefly the seller's warranty of title in Problem 1.1.3 and Note (5) on the Basic Conveyancing Rules, in Chapter 1, Section 3. This Section considers the seller's warranty of title in more detail.

Colton v. Decker

Supreme Court of South Dakota, 1995.
540 N.W.2d 172.

■ KONENKAMP, JUSTICE.

After his truck was seized by law enforcement officials for having multiple serial numbers the owner sued and recovered damages from the seller. Both parties appeal. We affirm the breach of warranty of title but reverse and remand a portion of the damages award.

FACTS

Lee Decker, an over-the-road trucker, purchased a repossessed 1975 Peterbilt truck, Model 359, from a Minnesota bank in 1984. The truck's history is not completely known, but its rails or frame had apparently been extended from its original length to accommodate a double sleeper and it had also been wrecked at one time. The vehicle identification number (VIN) listed on the Minnesota title was 60596P. Decker transferred the truck's title to South Dakota. Although he claims not to have made any major structural changes, on several occasions Decker has acknowledged he rebuilt the truck "from the frame up."

Over a nine-month period in 1989, John Colton, who worked as a driver for Decker, drove the 1975 Peterbilt nearly 100,000 miles. In late December of that year, he offered to purchase the truck for $22,000. To help obtain financing Decker provided Colton with a list of the truck's features. On the list he wrote, "I spent 3 months rebuilding from the frame up when I first got the truck. 90% of the work was performed by myself." Decker's signature immediately followed. Assured of the truck's good condition, Marquette Bank of Sioux Falls financed Colton's purchase. On March 8, 1990, Decker's South Dakota truck title was transferred to Colton.

On August 22, 1991, Colton was stopped by the Wyoming Highway Patrol near Rock Springs, Wyoming and cited for speeding. After noting discrepancies in his logbook, the trooper inspected the rig and discovered that the VIN stamped on the right frame rail did not match the VIN listed on the registration. Conflicting VINs commonly indicate a stolen vehicle or stolen parts. The truck, but not the loaded trailer, was then impounded. Colton hired another trucker to haul the cargo in his trailer to Salt Lake City and retained a Wyoming attorney, but the attorney could not obtain immediate release of his truck. Colton returned to South Dakota. During the months waiting to recover his vehicle, he found some work driving trucks for other companies.

Meanwhile, Wyoming authorities disassembled Colton's truck in search of other serial numbers. The letter "K" in one conflicting number indicated that a glider kit[2] had been used. A third VIN, stamped with a manufacturer's die, was also discovered. Although more numbers matching the VIN on the title were found at various points on the truck (some hidden beneath paint and body putty), the numbers had not been imprinted by the manufacturer, but had been stamped by hand, apparently with a hardware store die. For example, a VIN matching the title was hand-stamped on a crudely fashioned rectangular piece of tin and affixed to the fire wall just above the clutch pedal.

Upon completing their nine-month investigation, Wyoming authorities determined Colton was indeed the true owner. A Wyoming court ordered a new Wyoming title to be issued clarifying the conflicting serial numbers. The truck would then be released upon payment of a $1,000 storage fee. Colton, who was now behind on loan payments, borrowed the money from Marquette Bank, traveled to Wyoming, and paid it. Unfortunately, the truck was inoperable, because while in Wyoming's possession, it remained dismantled and unsheltered throughout the winter. On April 11, 1992, Colton towed the truck from Wyoming back to Sioux Falls.

Once home, Colton placed the truck in storage until he could raise the money to repair it. Despite the court order, Colton was unable to obtain a new title in Wyoming because Marquette Bank refused to surrender the South Dakota title—its collateral—to Wyoming authorities. The bank also refused to exchange the faulty title for a new South Dakota "rebuilder's" title. Colton filed suit against Decker alleging breaches of warranty of title, warranty of merchantability, and express warranty of description. He also sent Decker a notice of intent to rescind the sale of the truck.

At trial on November 4–5, 1993, Decker disputed that his reconstruction of the truck required a rebuilder's title. ... After noting in its memorandum opinion (incorporated into the findings of fact and conclusions of law) that the man who assisted Decker in rebuilding the truck had noticed differing serial numbers, the trial court wrote:

> [Decker] bought it as a wrecked truck, tore it down and rebuilt it. Even though he did not replace the parts which bore the different VINs, the discrepancies were obvious and discovered at the time he was rebuilding the vehicle.

The court awarded Colton $27,572.71 for breach of warranty of title. His other alleged breaches and offer to rescind were rejected. ...

---

2. Glider kits are parts used to update and replace older equipment on the truck such as frame rails, hood, drive line, and sleeper.

DECISION

I. Warranty of Title

Wyoming authorities challenged the authenticity of Colton's title as the truck had three different VINs engraved at various points. Under these circumstances Colton averred Decker breached the warranty of title under SDCL 57A–2–312:

(1) Subject to subsection (2) there is in a contract for sale a warranty by the seller that

(a) The title conveyed shall be good, and its transfer rightful; and

(b) The goods shall be delivered free from any security interest or other lien or encumbrance of which the buyer at the time of contracting has no knowledge.

(2) A warranty under subsection (1) will be excluded or modified only by specific language or by circumstances which give the buyer reason to know that the person selling does not claim title in himself or that he is purporting to sell only such right or title as he or a third person may have.

Comment 1 to UCC § 2–312 states a buyer is entitled to "receive a good, clear title transferred . . . in a rightful manner so [the buyer] will not be exposed to a lawsuit in order to protect it." A split of authority persists on the scope of § 2–312. Decker relies on those cases which hold that a breach of warranty of title occurs only when an outstanding superior title exists.[3] See, e.g., C.F. Sales, Inc. v. Amfert, Inc., 344 N.W.2d 543 (Iowa 1983); Johnston v. Simpson, 621 P.2d 688 (Utah 1980). Other courts hold that under § 2–312 mere initiation of a colorable challenge, one which is not spurious, regardless of the outcome, is sufficient to violate the warranty of title. Jefferson v. Jones, 286 Md. 544, 408 A.2d 1036, 1042 (Md. 1979) (law enforcement seizure of motorcycle when its VIN did not correspond to VIN in title document was colorable claim thus seller breached title warranty); American Container Corp. v. Hanley Trucking Crop., 111 N.J. Super. 322, 268 A.2d 313 (N.J. 1970) (law enforcement seizure of semi-trailer as stolen sufficient to cast substantial shadow thus violating warranty of good title). "Good title" typically means "the title which the seller gives to the buyer is 'free from reasonable doubt, that is, not only a valid title in fact, but [also] one that can again be sold to a reasonable purchaser . . .' " Jefferson, 408 A.2d at 1040 (quoting Langford v. Berry, 68 Ga. App. 193, 22 S.E.2d 349, 351 (Ga.Ct.App.1942)). We find the latter to be the better rule.

Wyoming Highway Patrol officials questioned Colton's ownership due to contradictory VINs thus casting a colorable challenge to its title. This was sufficient for a breach of title warranty claim. American Container

---

3. Indeed, the UCC drafters flatly stated "The warranty of quiet possession is abolished." Comment 1 UCC § 2–312. Yet the same comment states, "Disturbance of quiet possession, although not mentioned specifically, is one way, among many, in which the breach of the warranty of title may be established."

Corp., 268 A.2d at 318; City Car Sales, Inc. v. McAlpin, 380 So. 2d 865 (Ala.Civ.App.1979); Ricklefs v. Clemens, 216 Kan. 128, 531 P.2d 94 (Kan. 1975). Indeed, the majority view holds that a purchaser can recover for a breach of warranty of title by merely showing the existence of a cloud on the title. Maroone Chevrolet, Inc. v. Nordstrom, 587 So. 2d 514, 518 (Fla.Dist.Ct.App.1991). Once breach of good title is established, good faith is not a defense, nor is a lack of knowledge of the defect. James A. White & Robert S. Summers, UNIFORM COMMERCIAL CODE § 9–12 (3d ed. rev. 1993); Smith v. Taylor, 44 N.C. App. 363, 261 S.E.2d 19 (N.C.Ct.App.1979). Purchasers should not be required to enter into a contest on the validity of ownership over a titled motor vehicle. Frank Arnold Contractors v. Vilsmeier Auction Co., Inc., 806 F.2d 462, 464 (3d Cir.1986); Maroone Chevrolet, 587 So. 2d at 518; American Container, 268 A.2d at 318; Ricklefs, 531 P.2d at 100. As the undisputed facts reveal, Colton was forced into a contest over ownership because of conflicting VINs and an improper title. Thus, we uphold the circuit court's ruling that Decker breached the warranty of title. Maroone Chevrolet, 587 So. 2d at 518.

II.   Damages

Colton was awarded total damages of $27,572.71, consisting of $14,000 for the value of the truck and $13,572.71 for costs incurred retrieving it from Wyoming and storage. Breach of warranty damages are calculated under SDCL 57A–2–714:

> (2) The measure of damages for breach of warranty is the difference at the time and place of acceptance between the value of the goods accepted and the value they would have had if they had been as warranted, unless special circumstances show proximate damages of a different amount.
>
> (3) In a proper case any incidental and consequential damages under § 57A–2–715 may also be recovered.

Truck's Diminution in Value

Ample special circumstances take this case out of the "time of acceptance" provision in SDCL 57A–2–714. Here the measure of damages begins with determining the value of the truck at the time of dispossession. Ricklefs, 531 P.2d at 101; John St. Auto Wrecking v. Motors Insurance, 56 Misc. 2d 232, 288 N.Y.S.2d 281 (1968). Testimony established the truck was worth $22,000 when impounded, meaning it apparently did not depreciate in value during the months between Colton's purchase and the impoundment. Dismantled and unprotected from the Wyoming winter, uncontroverted testimony valued the truck at $8,000 in salvage. The trial court properly considered the "special circumstances" of SDCL 57A–2–714(2) to include the devaluation of the vehicle while in the hands of the Wyoming Highway Patrol and awarded the difference to Colton. Was the truck worth less than $22,000 at the time of impoundment? Could the truck have been worth more than $8,000 at the time it was released? The trial court could not answer those questions, as neither party offered any other estimates.

The $14,000 award on the loss of the truck due to the breach is affirmed. Carlson v. Rysavy, 262 N.W.2d 27 (S.D.1978).

Retrieving the Truck

Of the $13,572.71 awarded for impoundment, retrieval, and storage expenses, Decker does not dispute that $4,810.10 of this amount relates to expenses incurred in connection with the seizure of the truck by Wyoming authorities.[4] Decker argues the remaining expenses cannot be upheld as incidental damages pursuant to SDCL 57A2–715(1):

> Incidental damages resulting from the seller's breach include expenses reasonably incurred in inspection, receipt, transportation and care and custody of goods rightfully rejected, any commercially reasonable charges, expenses or commissions in connection with effecting cover and any other reasonable expense incident to the delay or other breach.

Towing back to Sioux Falls was properly allowed as a reasonably foreseeable expense, not only because the truck was inoperable, but also because driving the still defectively-titled vehicle imposed the risk of another seizure along the route home. White & Summers at § 10–4; Gerwin v. Southeastern Cal. Ass'n of Seventh Day Adventists, 14 Cal. App. 3d 209, 92 Cal. Rptr. 111 (1971). An award based upon a bona fide effort to compensate for consequences of defects that establish a breach of warranty is a remedy the UCC seeks to provide. McGrady v. Chrysler Motors Corp., 46 Ill. App. 3d 136, 360 N.E.2d 818, 4 Ill. Dec. 705 (Ill. App. Ct. 1977). Expenses incurred retrieving the truck from Wyoming were reasonable expenses incident to the breach.

Storing the Truck

Colton spent $2,375 to store the truck near Sioux Falls, a truck worth $8,000 in salvage. Here, the causal link between the breach and the damages became so attenuated the damages were no longer incident to the breach. SDCL 57A–2–715(1); White & Summers at § 10–3. This was unreasonable, unexpected and served only to drive up expenses and devalue the truck. Neither does this expense meet the requirements for consequential damages under SDCL 57A–2–715(2):

> (a) Any loss resulting from general or particular requirements and needs of which the seller at the time of contracting had reason to know and which could not reasonably be prevented by cover or otherwise; and

> (b) Injury to person or property proximately resulting from any breach of warranty.

---

4. This amount is composed of towing fees [in Wyoming], hiring another trucker to haul his load to Salt Lake City, retrieving his trailer from Salt Lake City, retaining a Wyoming attorney to get the truck out of impoundment, postage, a loan from Marquette Bank to pay the storage fee, and the motel and long distance expenses while authorities kept Colton in Wyoming.

The law should not encourage waste. Even though the breach started the chain of events, Colton could not leave the truck in storage for an indefinite time until he had the finances to repair the damage caused in Wyoming. Consequential damages must be reasonably foreseeable by the breaching party at the time of contracting. ... The storage fees fail to qualify as reasonably foreseeable. Once Colton retrieved his truck, his responsibility included mitigating further loss. ... The official comment to UCC § 2–715(2) states recovery is impermissible "unless the buyer could not reasonably have prevented the loss by cover or otherwise."

Attorney Fees

Colton incurred legal fees in South Dakota attempting to clear the title and retrieve the truck from Wyoming. The trial court allowed these fees as damages under SDCL 57A–2–715. As an element of damages, the attorney's fees were reasonable expenses incident to the impoundment for clouded title. ...

In his notice of review Colton argues the trial court erred in not allowing his attorney's fees for prosecuting this suit. Also, Colton contends the trial court should have awarded him the attorney fees his bank incurred. Trying to get the title issue resolved, Marquette Bank paid attorney fees, which it added to Colton's loan balance. Other than referring to the UCC, Colton cites no authority to support these arguments. We conclude the trial court properly declined to award such fees as damages under SDCL 57A–2–715(1) or (2) or as disbursements under SDCL 15–17–38.

* * *

Unawarded Damages

Colton further seeks compensation for repairs to the truck, lost profits, lost investment opportunities, and use of an expert witness. The trial court declined to award these damages or costs. We see no abuse of discretion for omitting these items from incidental and consequential damage consideration. Stormo v. Strong, 469 N.W.2d 816, 820 (S.D.1991).

* * *

Affirmed in part, reversed in part and remanded.

■ AMUNDSON, JUSTICE (concurring in part and dissenting in part).

I disagree with the majority's calculation of damages. The truck was impounded on August 22, 1991, and Colton towed the truck from Wyoming on April 11, 1992, however, the majority glosses over the fact that the Wyoming authorities offered release of the truck in January 1992 if Colton would pay $1,000 storage fee and forfeit the South Dakota title so that a new Wyoming title could be issued. It is undisputed that the value of the truck when impounded was $22,000. Colton could not afford the $1,000 fee so he went to his creditor, Marquette Bank. Marquette Bank refused to extend Colton's credit to pay the $1,000 and also refused to surrender the

South Dakota title. So, from January until April, the dismantled truck endured the Wyoming winter. Decker should not be responsible for the diminution in value of the truck between January and April.

Colton's proper remedy is recovering this loss from Marquette Bank. Forcing Decker to pay for the unreasonable delay caused by Marquette Bank's actions is unjust. Colton had a duty to mitigate his damages, and any damages resulting from his failure to take reasonable steps to mitigate or prevent damages cannot be recovered from Decker. See Wieting v. Ball Air Spray, Inc., 84 S.D. 493, 173 N.W.2d 272 (1969). SDCL 57A–2–715(2) states in part: "(2) Consequential damages resulting from the seller's breach include: (a) Any loss ... which could not reasonably be prevented by cover or otherwise[.]" (Emphasis added.) This loss could have been prevented by Marquette Bank's releasing the title in a timely manner. Surrendering the title in order for a new, clearer and correct title to be issued was the logical step for Marquette Bank to take. Unfortunately, logic does not always play a part in today's world.

The buyer's right to recover for damages is not unlimited. Buyer must take reasonable steps to reduce or minimize his damages. ... However, buyer will be excused from mitigation when his financial condition will not allow him to take mitigating steps. ...

In this case, however, it was not buyer who refused to take mitigating steps, but buyer's creditor, Marquette Bank, who refused to take the necessary steps. The general rule is that a bank is required to maintain a "duty of good faith and fair dealing toward its customers." Garrett v. BankWest, Inc., 459 N.W.2d 833, 846 n. 9 (S.D.1990). Whether or not Marquette Bank acted in good faith is not at issue here, however, Decker should not be punished for the action or inaction of Marquette Bank. Therefore, we should remand in order for the trial court to assess the correct amount of damages.

NOTES

(1) **Stolen Goods; Clouds on Title.** If the truck that Decker sold to Colton had been a stolen vehicle, Decker's breach of the warranty of title would have been clear. See Fischer v. Bright Bay Lincoln Mercury, Inc., 234 A.D.2d 586, 651 N.Y.S.2d 625 (2d Dep't 1996); Curran v. Ciaramelli, 37 UCC Rep. Serv.2d 94 (N.Y.Dist. Ct., Suffolk County 1998). The Wyoming police suspected that Colton was driving a stolen truck, but the suspicion proved to be unfounded. Why did the South Dakota Supreme Court conclude that Decker was in breach of the warranty of title? Is the court's construction of the UCC sound? Is the conclusion supported by the *text* of the section? Is it supported by the Comments? Are the Comments authorized to go beyond the text? Claims that goods have been stolen can range from being clearly plausible to quite fanciful. Where on this spectrum does a sellers' responsibility end?

(2) **Goods Subject to Security Interests; Inventory Finance.** A security interest is an interest in property. A security interest is often

called an encumbrance on the title. If an obligation to pay a loan secured by a security interest is in default, the secured party may repossess the goods, sell them, and apply the proceeds to the debt. Merchants and farmers commonly borrow money to finance their business activities and those who lend money to them often secure their loans by taking security interests in property, including the goods in inventory. Lenders routinely release their encumbrances on merchants' and farmers' inventory at the time of retail sale. They expect that the loans will be repaid from the proceeds of the sales and therefore authorize the merchants or farmers to sell the goods to buyers free of security interests. This commercial practice is reflected in UCC 9–315(a)(1), which provides that a security interest "continues" after a disposition "unless the secured party authorized the disposition free of the security interest."

Problem 3.1.1. Buyer was the winning bidder at an auction sale and agreed to buy 45 head of cattle for $13,000. Unknown to Buyer at the time of the auction sale, there was a valid and perfected security interest in the cattle. Also unknown to Buyer, the secured party had consented to the auction sale of the cattle free and clear of the security interest. Terms of the auction sale required Buyer to pay $1,000 down and the balance within six days. On the day following the auction sale, Buyer was informed by a third party that the cattle were subject to a security interest. Buyer was not informed and did not learn that the secured party had authorized sale of the cattle. Buyer stopped payment on his check for the down payment and refused to take and pay for the cattle. Seller promptly resold the cattle for $3,000 and sued Buyer for $10,000. What should be the result? See Wright v. Vickaryous, 611 P.2d 20 (Alaska 1980). How likely is it that an auction buyer of 45 head of cattle would be so unsophisticated in that marketplace as to be surprised by the information that the secured party authorized the sale? How likely is it that such a buyer would not expect that encumbrances created by the seller would be released?

After buyer refused to accept them, the cattle were resold, in an apparently similar auction, one week after the first auction, but the price obtained in the second auction was sharply lower. Does this suggest that the buyer may have overbid in the first auction and, having realized this, wanted a way to escape the obligation to pay the contract price? If this were buyer's motive, would buyer's action be consistent with the obligation to act in good faith in the performance of the contract?

Problem 3.1.2. The Hammer Auction Company operates a sales barn at which livestock are sold regularly at auction. Hammer sells the livestock on commission for many cattlemen. Bidders are aware that Hammer is not the owner and acts as the agent of some unnamed principal. William Buyer made the high bid on three heifers which had been left with Hammer by Sam Theft. After the purchase, Buyer learned that the heifers were stolen and had to return them to the true owner. Buyer sues Hammer to recover the amount of his bid.

What argument may be made for the defendant, Hammer, based on UCC 2–312(1)? Was Hammer "the seller" of the livestock? See UCC 2–103.

Under common-law agency doctrine, one who contracts as agent for another without disclosing the identity of the principal is not merely an agent, but is deemed a "party to the contract." Restatement (Second) of Agency §§ 321–322. See Jones v. Ballard, 573 So.2d 783 (Miss.1990) (warranty of title); cf. Powers v. Coffeyville Livestock Sales Co., 665 F.2d 311 (10th Cir.1981) (warranty of quality). Does this doctrine from common law apply to transactions under UCC Article 2. Recall UCC 1–103.

What argument may be made for the defendant, Hammer, under UCC 2–312(2)? Does the statute displace the common-law of agency? Is "the seller" in 2–312(1) the same as "the person selling" in 2–312(2)? Should 2–312(2) be read to create an immunity for auctioneers and other agents of partially disclosed or undisclosed principals? See UCC 2–312, Comment 5.

Problem 3.1.3. Charles Creditor held a judgment against Daniel Debtor, and sued out a writ of attachment to levy on Debtor's property. Pursuant to the writ of attachment, Samuel Sheriff seized a tractor in Debtor's possession and sold it at an execution sale; Buyer bought the tractor for $500. Unknown to all parties, the tractor was subject to a security interest held by Leo Lean to secure a $300 debt which Debtor owed Lean. Lean's security interest was not terminated by the sale, and Lean threatens to seize the tractor from Buyer unless Debtor's debt is satisfied. Has Buyer any recourse against Sheriff or Creditor? See UCC 2–312(2); Bogestad v. Anderson, 143 Minn. 336, 173 N.W. 674 (1919). Has Buyer any recourse against Debtor?

(3) Remedy for Breach of the Warranty of Title. The UCC does not provide clearly the measure of damages appropriate when a seller has breached the warranty of title. If a seller had no title to the goods and the rightful owner reclaimed the goods from the buyer, or if the goods were subject to a security interest and the secured party repossessed the goods, the buyer has suffered injury, but the correct measure of damages is disputed.

Buyers who have been deprived of the goods altogether should be allowed to recover the value of the goods of which they have been deprived, but a question that often arises is on what date is value to be measured. A defect in title may be unknown to a buyer for a substantial period of time after goods have been purchased. Between the date of delivery and the date buyer loses possession, the market value of the goods may have changed substantially. The direction of change could be up or down, and the rate of change can be slow or fast. For example, equipment generally depreciates steadily over time, whereas some works of art appreciate, occasionally precipitously, if the reputation of the artist is growing. Other changes in value may be attributable to modifications or improvements made by the buyers.

The UCC contains several remedy provisions that might be invoked to measure buyers' damages when they had to surrender goods to the rightful owners. One possible measure of damages is that provided in UCC 2–714. Subsection (2) deals with "breach of warranty." Under this subsection damages are measured by the value of the goods as warranted "at the time

... of acceptance" unless there are "special circumstances [that] show proximate damages of a different amount." Value-at-the-time-of acceptance is most apt in measurement of damages for breach of a warranty of quality, but the text does not preclude its application to breach of a warranty of title. Neither the text nor the comments expand on the meaning of the "special circumstances" exception. Moreover, Comment 3 declares that subsection (2), while the usual, standard and reasonable method of ascertaining damages, is not an exclusive measure. Subsection (1) deals with "any non-conformity of tender," a phrase that undoubtedly includes tender of goods with a title defect. Subsection (1) defines damages as the loss resulting from seller's breach and allows a tribunal to determine the amount "in any manner which is reasonable." For buyers aggrieved by breach of warranty of title, either subsection (1) or the exception to subsection (2) may be the most appropriate way to measure damages.

A Maryland court faced the problem in a case arising from sale of certain patterns used to produce hardware. The patterns had depreciated in value while in buyer's possession. Buyer contended that UCC 2–714(2) should govern and that the value of the patterns on the date of acceptance should be used to fix the amount of damages. The court wrote:

> Scholars contend that § 2–714(2) does not regulate damages for breach of warranty of title, but that it in fact relates only to breach of warranty of quality.... This is said to be so because § 2–714(2) is based on § 69(6) and (7) of the Uniform Sales Act; those provisions pertained to breaches of warranty of quality, not title....

> It is suggested that because § 2–714(2) does not expressly apply to a breach of warranty of title, a court should look to pre-U.C.C. law in that situation by virtue of the "special circumstances" provision of § 2–714(2) and because the U.C.C. comment to that section indicates it is not intended to provide for the exclusive measure of damages.... Pre–U.C.C. law is not too helpful, however. Under it decisions relating to the measure of damages for breach of warranty of title range from purchase price plus interest to value of the goods at time of dispossession, to value without specifying any time of determination, to value at time of sale (which may or may not be the same as the purchase price).
> . . .

> Other jurisdictions have faced this problem. They have applied § 2–714(2) to breaches of warranty of title.... We shall do likewise. The statute is plain and unambiguous on its face and should be read according to its clear meaning....

> The next question is whether to apply § 2–714(2)'s "difference at the time and place of acceptance between the value of the goods accepted and the value they would have had as warranted" or whether there are "special circumstances [that] show proximate damages of a different amount." We hold that there are special circumstances here.... [Buyer] had use and possession of the patterns for varying periods of time before it had knowledge of any title defects. And the

patterns were unique; they were specially designed to produce castings to particular specifications.

Since we conclude that this case falls within the "special circumstances" clause of § 2–714(2), we must now decide what measure of damages to apply under it. Courts that have considered the question under the U.C.C. have almost uniformly rejected the view that the purchase price of the goods is the proper measure.... The value of the goods at the approximate date of dispossession, or something akin to that, is the measure of damages generally selected.

Metalcraft, Inc. v. Pratt, 65 Md.App. 281, 292–294, 500 A.2d 329, 335–336 (1985).

In *Metalcraft* the value of the goods at the time of dispossession had diminished from their value at the time of sale. Suppose that the goods, prior to discovery of a title defect, had appreciated significantly in value. Should a court interpret UCC 2–714(2) to permit the larger recovery that takes the appreciation into account? See Jeanneret v. Vichey, 693 F.2d 259 (2d Cir.1982); Menzel v. List, 24 N.Y.2d 91, 298 N.Y.S.2d 979, 246 N.E.2d 742 (1969).

In *Colton v. Decker*, buyer was dispossessed of the truck only temporarily. There was no defect in seller's title and the buyer regained possession of the truck. What statutory measure of damages did the South Dakota Supreme Court find to be appropriate? What statutory measure of damages would have been applied by the dissenting justice? Were the actual damages assessed by the majority or avowed by the dissent consistent with the statutory measure?

(4) Warranty of Non–Infringement. Section 2–312(3) provides for a warranty that buyers of goods shall have them free of a "rightful claim" of a third person "by way of infringement or the like." Comment 3 indicates that the purpose of the section is to protect buyers from claims that the goods were made by infringement of a patent or trademark. Many goods today are "smart goods," i.e., they contain semiconductors and computer information that enable the goods to carry out complex functions. Information content, such as computer programs, can be protected by the law of copyright. The Comment is silent on whether sale of goods that, without license from a copyright holder, incorporate copyrighted information would be covered by this subsection.

Unlike the warranty of title, the warranty of non-infringement is made, as a matter of law, only by a seller that is a "merchant regularly dealing in goods of the kind." Merchant is a UCC-defined term.[2]

Section 2–312(3) is rarely litigated. A recent case turned on the allocation of responsibility for infringement when the buyer had supplied a

---

2. UCC 2–104(1). Although "merchant" is statutorily defined, the word is not listed in the Definitional Cross References at the end of the comments to UCC 2–312. The lesson for students is not to rely exclusively on these cross references to signal defined terms.

description of the goods that it wanted the seller to make. Bonneau Co. v. AG Industries, Inc., 116 F.3d 155 (5th Cir.1997).

Problem 3.1.4. Marie Louise Jeanneret, a citizen of Switzerland, is a well-known art dealer in Geneva. Defendants Anna and Luben Vichey, wife and husband, are citizens of the United States. Anna's father, Carlo Frua DeAngeli, had an extensive and internationally recognized private collection of paintings in Milan, Italy. One of these was a painting, Portrait sur Fond Jaune, by the renowned French post-impressionist, Henri Matisse, who was born in 1869 and died in 1954. Title to the Matisse painting ultimately vested in Anna Vichey. In 1970 the Matisse painting was brought to Vichey's apartment in New York City. In January 1973 Mme. Jeanneret began negotiations for the purchase of the painting, and an agreement was reached for its sale for 700,000 Swiss francs, then equivalent to approximately $230,000. Luben Vichey delivered the painting to plaintiff in Geneva in March 1973.

Mme. Jeanneret included the Matisse painting in a large exhibit of 20th century masters at her gallery in Geneva. In November 1974, Mme. Jeanneret encountered Signora Bucarelli, superintendent in charge of the export of paintings from Italy, who declared she had been looking for the Matisse painting because she suspected its illegal exportation from Italy under laws designed to protect that nation's cultural heritage. Subsequently, the Assistant Minister of Culture issued a notification declaring the painting "an important work" of "particular artistic and historical interest" within the meaning of Italian law.

Mme. Jeanneret brought suit against the Vicheys for breach of warranty of title. At trial, John Tancock, a vice-president of Sotheby Parke Bernet auction house and head of its Department of Impressionist and Modern Painting and Sculpture, testified that, but for the question of illegal exportation, he would appraise the painting at $750,000. On the other hand, if the painting lacked "the necessary export documents from any country where it had been located," his opinion was that it would be impossible to sell the painting since "[n]o reputable auction house or dealer would be prepared to handle it." Hence, "on the legitimate market its value is zero."

What should be the result of this action under UCC 2–312? Does Italy's cultural heritage law affect the owners' title to objects possessed in Italy that are restricted as to export? Should the UCC 2–312 provision on infringement be invoked by an export restriction? Were sellers "merchants dealing in goods of the kind"? See UCC 2–104(1). If the trade usage of the reputable art dealers is self-imposed, in that they would incur no liability to the Italian government if they did handle such works, should that affect determination of Mme. Jeanneret's claim under UCC 2–312? See Jeanneret v. Vichey, 693 F.2d 259 (2d Cir.1982).

NOTE

Lease Transactions: Lessor's Warranty. The supplier of goods in a lease transaction does not contract to pass title to the goods. Under the

UCC, " 'lease' means a transfer of the right to possession and use of the goods for a term in return for consideration. . . ." UCC 2A–103(j). The warranty of a lessor analogous to a seller's warranty of title and non-infringement is found in UCC 2A–211:

> (1) There is in a lease contract a warranty that for the lease term no person holds a claim or interest in the goods that arose from an act or omission of the lessor . . . which will interfere with the lessee's enjoyment of its leasehold interest.

> (2) Except in a finance lease there is in a lease contract by a lessor who is a merchant regularly dealing in goods of the kind a warranty that the goods are delivered free of the rightful claim of any person by way of infringement or the like.

What is the purpose of limiting warranty liability under subsection (1) to "an act or omission of the lessor"? There is no such limitation in UCC 2–312(1). What is the purpose of the exception in subsection (2) for a "finance lease"? "Finance lease" is a defined term of considerable importance to the overall pattern of Article 2A. See UCC 2A–103(1)(g). Is it possible that the "act or omission" term in subsection (1) was drafted to apply only to finance leases? See the Comment to this section.

Statute of Limitations for Warranty of Title Claims. The resolution of disputed property rights may give rise to contract claims for breach of warranty of title and the period of limitations applicable to such claims. See Note (4) on the Basic Conveyancing Rules in Chapter 1, Section 3. Under Article 2, an action for breach of any contract of sale must be commenced within four years after the cause of action has accrued, and a breach of warranty occurs when tender of delivery is made regardless of the aggrieved party's lack of knowledge of the breach. UCC 2–725(1) and (2). Are these provisions appropriate to claims for breach of warranty of title? See UCC 2–312, Comment 2: "Whether the breach by the seller is in good faith or bad faith Section 2–725 provides that the cause of action occurs when the breach occurs. Under the provisions of that section the breach of the warranty of good title occurs when tender of delivery is made since the warranty is not one which extends to 'future performance of the goods.' " Could the tolling reference in UCC 2–725(4) be invoked to permit a court to suspend the accrual of a buyer's cause of action to a later date, such as the date of discovery?[3]

INTERNATIONAL SALES LAW

Sellers' Responsibility. The Convention on Contracts for the International Sale of Goods provides that, absent agreement otherwise, a seller must deliver goods that are "free from any right or claim of a third party."[4]

---

3. Proposed Revised Article 2 contains new provisions on the limitations period for breach of warranty of title claims. Under the proposal, the period does not begin to run until a buyer discovers or should have discov-ered the breach. See Proposed Revised § 2–725(c)(4).

4. CISG 41.

The Convention does not use the word "title." Does the Convention's formulation of the sellers' obligation differ from UCC 2–312 in any substantial way?[5]

The parties in *Jeanneret* were from different nations: United States sellers and a Swiss buyer. The buyer was a dealer who purchased the Matisse painting for resale. If this transaction had occurred after the effective date of CISG, would the transaction be within the scope of the Convention?[6] Assuming that the Convention had applied in a case like *Jeanneret*, what would be the outcome?

Good Faith Purchase. Article 4(b) declares that the Convention "is not concerned with the effect which the contract may have on the property in the goods sold." Given CISG 4(b)'s disclaimer of concern with property rights in the goods even between sellers and buyers, not surprisingly the CISG has no provision on the property or ownership rights of third parties. When such issues arise in relation to sales transactions otherwise governed by CISG, what law would apply to resolve conflicting claims to the goods?

Statute of Limitations. CISG has no statute of limitations provisions. The international community has addressed this matter in a separate multilateral Convention on the Limitation Period in the International Sale of Goods, which was adopted several years before CISG. The Limitations Period Convention does not explicitly address the issue of claims for breach of warranty of title. The Convention generally fixes a limitations period of four years (Article 8), and specifies that the period begins to run when a claim accrues (Article 9(1)). Article 10 declares:

1.   A claim arising from a breach of contract shall accrue on the date on which such breach occurs.

2.   A claim arising from a defect or other lack of conformity shall accrue on the date on which the goods are actually handed over to, or their tender is refused by, the buyer.

The United States ratified the Limitations Period Convention effective December 1, 1994.

SECTION 2.   INTRODUCTION TO WARRANTIES OF QUALITY

INTRODUCTORY NOTES

(1) **Historical Background.** The scope of sellers' responsibility for the quality of goods has passed through a remarkable evolution of a curiously cyclical character. In the Middle Ages the authority of the Church and of guilds combined to impose heavy standards of quality upon sellers.[1]

---

5. The Convention's provision on sellers' obligation with respect to intellectual property is found in Article 42.

6. See CISG 2(a)

1. W. Hamilton, The Ancient Maxim Caveat Emptor, 40 Yale L.J. 1133 (1931).

Thereafter, as we shall see, English law came to afford but little protection to buyers: *caveat emptor!* This outlook, in turn, has been reversed in modern law, but some of the quaint language found in current statutes cannot be understood without an appreciation of the history.

The law of sales is here, as at so many points, enmeshed with the larger body of contract law. Students of the history of contracts will recall the reluctance of early common-law courts to enforce simple promises; in a static land economy, legal obligations were not to be assumed lightly. Although the specific undertakings in a document bearing the maker's seal received early legal protection, less formal undertakings had to wait for the ancient action "on the case" to develop beyond its tort ancestry into its contractual descendant, the action of special *assumpsit*.

The reluctance to give legal effect to simple informal statements made by sellers is illustrated by the famous 1625 decision of Chandelor v. Lopus[2] in which a buyer brought an action on the case against a goldsmith for affirming that a stone he sold the buyer was a "bezoar" (or "bezar"), a stone found in the alimentary organs of goats and supposed to have remarkable medicinal qualities. The jury found for the plaintiff. (How the plaintiff proved that this was not a "true" bezoar does not appear.) The Exchequer Chamber set aside the verdict and ruled that the declaration based on this affirmation was insufficient: " ... the bare affirmation that it was a bezar stone, without warranting it to be so is no cause of action."[3] Just how far the seller had to go to "warrant" was not stated; apparently he had to make an explicit statement like "I warrant that ..." or "I agree to be bound that...."

It is striking to find this 17th century decision dominating the New York court's thinking in an 1804 commercial case, Seixas v. Woods.[4] A dealer advertised and sold wood as "brazilletto," a wood valuable for manufacturing a chemical used in making dye; in fact the wood was worthless "peachum." A judgment for the buyer was reversed. Chancellor Kent's concurring opinion stated: "The mentioning the word, as Brazilletto wood, in the bill of parcels, and in the advertisement some days previous to the sale, did not amount to a warranty to the plaintiffs. To make an affirmation at the time of the sale, a warranty, it must appear by evidence to be so *intended*, and not to have been a mere matter of judgment and opinion, and of which the defendant had no particular knowledge. Here it is admitted, the defendant was equally ignorant with the plaintiffs, and could have had no such intention."[5]

---

2. Cro. Jac. 4, 79 Eng. Rep. 3 (1625).

3. In view of the peculiar nature of the commodity, it may be worthwhile to record the further statement of the judges that, " ... every one in selling wares will affirm that his wares are good, or the horse which he sells is sound."

4. 2 Caines 48 (1804).

5. Chief Justice Gibson, of Pennsylvania, used characteristically salty (and extreme) language to similar effect in McFarland v. Newman, 9 Watts 55 (Pa.1839). Gibson also drew a questionable analogy between a sale of goods and the deed for real estate. "A sale is a contract executed, on which, of course, no action can be directly founded." [Why not?] He added that war-

Later in the 19th century, cases like these were overturned. The *Seixas* ("brazilletto") case was rejected in New York in a 1872 case involving a dealer who bought barrels of "blue vitriol" and innocently resold them as such: when the material proved to be "salzburger vitriol" (a less valuable commodity) the dealer was held liable to the purchaser.[6] The opinions in such cases usually did not discuss the reasons of policy that produced the change in approach, but one may surmise that a greater volume and speed of trade called for firmer protection for contractual expectations. The dealer who resold the goods may have been misled by its supplier, but a rule of law that made the dealer liable to its buyer for its representations would normally give the dealer recourse against its supplier.[7]

When Professor Williston came to draft the Uniform Sales Act,[8] one of his principal targets was the emphasis which some cases placed on the seller's "intent"—an offensive manifestation of a "subjective" view of contracts.[9] To obliterate this approach, Section 12 of the Uniform Sales Act provided:

> Any affirmation of fact or any promise by the seller relating to the goods is an express warranty if the *natural tendency* of such affirmation or promise is to induce the buyer to purchase the goods, and if the buyer purchases the goods *relying thereon*.[10]

This language was well chosen to focus attention on the crucial question of reasonable reliance by the buyer on the seller's statements. This formulation also foreclosed difficult (and unprofitable) litigation over whether the seller's statement was a "promise" or an "affirmation of fact."

The UCC in Section 2–313(1)(a) closely follows the above provision of the Uniform Sales Act. However, there is one noteworthy change: There is no reference to reliance by the buyer. Instead, an affirmation or a promise is an express warranty if it "becomes part of the basis of the bargain." The meaning of this novel phrase will be explored later.

(2) Types of Warranties. It is orthodox learning, carried forward from the Uniform Sales Act to the UCC, that warranties of quality come in

---

ranty is "no more a part of the sale than the covenant of warranty in a deed is part of the conveyance." [Is it possible at the same time to convey property and undertake contractual obligations?]

6. Hawkins v. Pemberton, 51 N.Y. 198 (1872).

7. This practical point was emphasized in Jones v. Just, L.R. 3 Q.B. 197 (1868). Defendant sellers argued that they had relied on the selection of the goods by a supplier in Singapore; Mellor, J., replied that defendant sellers "had recourse against [the supplier] for not supplying an article reasonably merchantable."

8. Unlike most of the Uniform Sales Act (USA), Section 12 was not modeled on the British Sale of Goods Act (SGA). Indeed, the USA treatment of warranties of quality departed fundamentally from the provisions on quality in the SGA. See Sales of Goods Act §§ 13 to 15, 62(1).

9. The Commissioners' Note to USA 12 referred to the "intent" concept and stated that " ... the fundamental basis for liability on warranty is the justifiable reliance on the seller's assertions."

10. Emphasis added. USA 12 also included a sentence dealing with statements as to "value" or "opinion." This troublesome provision, and its overgrown offspring in UCC 2–313(2) will be considered later.

various "types." "Express" warranties (UCC 2–313) are to be distinguished from warranties that are "implied." Implied warranties of quality fall in two categories: "merchantable quality" (UCC 2–314), and "fitness for particular purpose" (UCC 2–315).

Consider simple examples of each of the three types of warranties. *Case 1:* B and S, a Ford automobile dealer, sign an agreement of sale for a "new Taurus." After delivery, B discovers that the car had been used as a demonstrator with the odometer disconnected. *Case 2:* A car purchased by B has a defective crankshaft that promptly breaks. *Case 3:* B tells S, a paint dealer, that he wants paint for the outside of his house. S puts on the counter a can of "Lustro" which B buys. This paint is good for interior walls but is washed from exterior walls by the first rain. *Case 1* involves an express warranty (UCC 2–313), *Case 2* the warranty of merchantable quality (UCC 2–314), and *Case 3* the warranty of fitness for particular purpose (UCC 2–315).

In spite of the complexity and diversity of these statutory provisions it may help to consider whether they may be related—and possibly inspired by a common principle. For example, suppose that just before the purchase, the seller had been asked these questions: In *Case 1*, "Has anyone been driving this car before?" In *Case 2*, "Is the crankshaft sound?" In *Case 3*, "Will the paint stand up under a rain?" Would the seller normally have given the undertakings requested by the buyer? If the seller had refused, would the buyer have purchased the goods?

Do buyers normally articulate such questions? If not, why not? Because they are unimportant? Or because the answers "go without saying"?[11] As we watch the results (as contrasted with the language) of the cases it will be useful to analyze the degree of kinship between the terms of the contract (including "express" warranties) and the various "types" of "implied" warranties?[12]

These seemingly simple-minded questions have larger impact than might be evident at first glance, for the answers may be relevant not only in defining the scope of a seller's undertaking but also in determining the effectiveness of contract terms purporting to disclaim and limit implied

---

11. Are there analogous situations, outside the law of sale, where legal effect is given to understandings and expectations that are real, but normally are not fully expressed?

12. Randall v. Newson 2 Q.B. 102 (Court of Appeal, 1877) held a seller liable on the sale of a defective carriage pole. Lord Justice Brett, after referring to various types of warranties that had been mentioned in earlier opinions, stated: "The governing principle . . . is that the thing offered and delivered under a contract of purchase and sale must answer the description of it which is contained in words in the contract, or which would be so contained if the contract were accurately drawn out." This unified approach, however, was not sufficiently dominant in the English cases to be reflected in the drafting of the Sale of Goods Act. As a result, the different "types" of warranties, developed in the typical case-law process of distinguishing unwanted precedents, were cast into statutory form, and were carried into the Uniform Sales Act and on into the Sales article of the UCC. The UCC does provide, however, that "warranties whether express or implied shall be construed as consistent with each other and as cumulative . . . ." UCC 2–317.

"warranties." These questions may even be relevant to the border warfare between the "fields" of sales (contract) and tort.

(3) Breach and Discovery of Breach. Disputes about the quality of goods sometimes arise at the time sellers tender delivery, but warranties of quality are more likely to be invoked in disputes that arise after goods have been received by buyers and after buyers have paid all or part of the price. For purposes of enforcement of quality warranties, the extent to which buyers can refuse to take nonconforming goods and, more basically, can refuse to pay for them is critical. Often, when buyers discover that goods do not conform to sellers' obligations, the goods have been received and the price has been paid. Enforcement of warranties of quality on goods that have been accepted and paid for is the paradigmatic remedial situation to be considered in this Chapter.

(4) Buyers' Remedies for Sellers' Breach of Warranty. The general remedial principle of contract law applies in warranty cases. Aggrieved buyers are entitled to the benefit of their bargains. In simplest terms, this means that buyers' monetary recovery for breach of warranty is measured by the value of goods that would have met sellers' obligation of quality. Since buyers commonly have received goods of *some* value, that value must be taken into account in the formulation of a remedy.

If a buyer keeps the nonconforming goods, the value of those goods should be subtracted from the value of goods as warranted. This formula is set forth in UCC 2–714(2).[13] The market-oriented formula of UCC 2–714(2) is not an exclusive measure of buyers' damages. Buyers may seek recovery measured "in any manner which is reasonable." UCC 2–714(1). If the quality non-conformity is correctable at reasonable expense, a buyer may seek to recover the cost of repairing the defect.[14]

Buyers who accepted goods with non-conformities may not be "made whole" by monetary recovery measured only by the value of goods as warranted or by the cost of repair. The UCC authorizes buyers, "in a proper case," to recover "incidental damages" in UCC 2–715(1), and "consequential damages," in UCC 2–715(2).

A buyer may prefer to return nonconforming goods to the sellers. The law allows some, but not all, aggrieved buyers to force sellers to take back "accepted" goods for quality deficiencies. The UCC term for this is "revoca-

---

13. "Value" in this formulation means "market value" or "market price," the amounts that informed sellers and buyers have set or would have set for goods of the different levels of quality. In active markets for goods of the kind, "market price" is a statistical compilation of many actual contract prices. Where no active market of the precise goods exists, "value" must be determined by extrapolation from other transactions. Sometimes this is done by expert appraisers.

14. See, e.g., Wat Henry Pontiac Co. v. Bradley, 202 Okla. 82, 210 P.2d 348 (1949) (pre-UCC case). The reasonableness limitation no doubt precludes recovery of repair costs that greatly exceed the value added to a non-conforming product. Students may recall studying this as a common-law principle of damages in cases like Peevyhouse v. Garland Coal & Mining Co., 382 P.2d 109 (Okla.1962); Plante v. Jacobs, 10 Wis.2d 567, 103 N.W.2d 296 (1960).

tion of acceptance.'' A buyer is entitled to revoke acceptance only if the nonconformity substantially impairs the value of the goods to the buyer. UCC 2–608(1).[15] A buyer that rightfully revokes acceptance of goods is entitled to monetary damages. UCC 2–711(1). The amount of a buyer's damages can be measured in two ways. The first, analogous to the market-based damages under UCC 2–714(2), allows recovery of the benefit of the bargain, i.e., the value ("market price") of conforming goods less the contract price; buyer is also entitled to get back all or any part of the price paid. The alternative measure of damages is based on buyer's cost of purchasing specific substitute goods ("cover") rather than on the general market price of conforming goods. UCC 2–712.

As we saw with remedies when buyers retain nonconforming goods, buyers who revoke acceptance may recover incidental and consequential damages. UCC 2–712(2); 2–713(1).

(5) Commercial and Consumer Buyers. With few exceptions, judicial decisions involving warranty law emerged historically in transactions between merchant buyers and merchant sellers, such as the "brazilletto" wood case and the "blue vitriol" case.[16] The commercial context of the early cases, in which merchants bought goods for the purpose of resale, explains the use of the rather archaic word, "merchantable," in the basic implied warranty of quality.

Transactions between business sellers and business buyers, usually corporations on both sides of the transactions, continue to be the most frequent source of warranty disputes that have been litigated to the level of appellate courts with reported opinions. In the setting of business-to-business sales, reported cases typically involve sales of equipment rather than of supplies. Ongoing commercial relationships between suppliers and business customers involve repeated sales, a "course of dealing."[17] If a relationship is valuable to both sides, any quality disputes that may arise from time to time will be adjusted amicably, without resort to litigation. The parties to equipment sales tend not to have ongoing relationships. Litigation of disputes that arise in such transactions does not jeopardize a valuable relationship. Moreover, the amount at stake in a dispute over the quality of equipment is often great enough to make it practical for the parties to incur the costs of litigation.

Warranties are commonly made in sales of consumer products by retail dealers to individuals for their personal, family or household use. Reported judicial decisions involving such warranties, however, are rather rare. Part

---

15. The UCC does not attempt to define "substantial impairment," but does indicate that the standard is subjective and turns on a buyer's particular circumstances. See the phrase "to him" in UCC 2–608(1) and Comment 2.

16. The most notable exception was horse trading, perhaps one of the earliest consumer goods transactions. See K. Llewellyn, Across Sales on Horseback, 52 Harv.

L.Rev. 725 (1939); K. Llewellyn, The First Struggle to Unhorse Sales, 52 Harv.L.Rev. 873 (1939).

17. The term is defined in the UCC. See UCC 1–205(1). The UCC looks to the pattern of past dealings for the purpose of interpretation of current expressions and conduct.

of the explanation may be that disputes are resolved within ongoing dealer-consumer relationships, but the amounts at stake in quality disputes regarding consumer products, even a consumer durable product, such as a toaster oven or a washing machine, are generally too small to make litigation practical beyond the level of small-claims courts. A few reported trial and appellate court decisions do arise out of sales of new and used automobiles. When the quality of such goods turns out to be unsatisfactory, the expense of litigation may not be a complete deterrent to a legal action.[18]

Some modern consumer product warranty law has developed by legislation. The statutory platform that existed for warranties of commercial goods was not limited to such goods. The provisions of the Uniform Sales Act and of Article 2 of the UCC apply to all goods, whether bought for commercial purposes or for purposes of personal, family or household use. There are a few special consumer-protection provisions in the UCC's provisions on quality warranties and remedies for breach of these warranties. See UCC 2–318, 2–719(3). Increasingly, warranty legislation has been enacted to protect ordinary consumers outside the UCC. Some of that legislation has become a special part of warranty law, and we will consider some of that law later in Section 5 of this Chapter.

Section 3.   Warranties of Quality: Express and Implied

Domestic United States Law

Royal Business Machines v. Lorraine Corp.

United States Court of Appeals, Seventh Circuit, 1980.
633 F.2d 34.

■ Baker, D.J.

This is an appeal from a judgment of the district court entered after a bench trial awarding ... [Booher] $1,171,216.16 in compensatory and punitive damages against ... [Royal]. The judgment further awarded Booher attorneys' fees of $156,800.00. ... The judgment also granted Royal a set-off of $12,020.00 for an unpaid balance due on computer typewriters.

The case arose from commercial transactions extending over a period of 18 months between Royal and Booher in which Royal sold and Booher purchased 114 RBC I and 14 RBC II plain paper copying machines. [Booher bought the machines for the purpose of leasing them to its customers.] In mid-August 1976, Booher filed suit against Royal in the Indiana courts claiming breach of warranties and fraud. . . .

---

18. One means to increase the amount at stake in litigation over consumer products is to combine many individuals' claims into a single, class action. However, class actions to enforce a quality warranty are relatively rare because quality failures tend to be unique rather than common. An exception would be a condition in manufactured goods that results from the products's design.

The issues in the cases arise under Indiana common law and under the U.C.C. as adopted in Indiana, Ind. Code § 26–1–102 et seq. (1976). ...

EXPRESS WARRANTIES

We first address the question whether substantial evidence on the record supports the district court's findings that Royal made and breached express warranties to Booher. The trial judge found that Royal Business Machines made and breached the following express warranties:

(1) that the RBC Model I and II machines and their component parts were of high quality;

(2) that experience and testing had shown that frequency of repairs was very low on such machines and would remain so;

(3) that replacement parts were readily available;

(4) that the cost of maintenance for each RBC machine and cost of supplies was and would remain low, no more than ½ cent per copy;

(5) that the RBC machines had been extensively tested and were ready to be marketed;

(6) that experience and reasonable projections had shown that the purchase of the RBC machines by Mr. Booher and Lorraine Corporation and the leasing of the same to customers would return substantial profits to Booher and Lorraine;

(7) that the machines were safe and could not cause fires; and

(8) that service calls were and would be required for the RBC Model II machine on the average of every 7,000 to 9,000 copies, including preventive maintenance calls.

Substantial evidence supports the court's findings as to Numbers 5, 7, 8, and the maintenance aspect of Number 4, but, as a matter of law, Numbers 1, 2, 3, 6, and the cost of supplies portion of Number 4 cannot be considered express warranties.

Paraphrasing U.C.C. § 2–313 as adopted in Indiana, an express warranty is made up of the following elements: (a) an affirmation of fact or promise, (b) that relates to the goods, and (c) becomes a part of the basis of the bargain between the parties. When each of these three elements is present, a warranty is created that the goods shall conform to the affirmation of fact or to the promise.

The decisive test for whether a given representation is a warranty or merely an expression of the seller's opinion is whether the seller asserts a fact of which the buyer is ignorant or merely states an opinion or judgment on a matter of which the seller has no special knowledge and on which the buyer may be expected also to have an opinion and to exercise his judgment. ... General statements to the effect that goods are "the best," ..., or are "of good quality," ... or will "last a lifetime" and be "in perfect condition," ... are generally regarded as expressions of the seller's opinion or "the puffing of his wares" and do not create an express warranty.

No express warranty was created by Royal's affirmation that both RBC machine models and their component parts were of high quality. This was a statement of the seller's opinion, the kind of "puffing" to be expected in any sales transaction, rather than a positive averment of fact describing a product's capabilities to which an express warranty could attach. ...

Similarly, the representations by Royal that experience and testing had shown that the frequency of repair was "very low" and would remain so lack the specificity of an affirmation of fact upon which a warranty could be predicated. These representations were statements of the seller's opinion.

The statement that replacement parts were readily available is an assertion of fact, but it is not a fact that relates to the goods sold as required by Ind.Code § 26–1–2–313(1)(a) and is not an express warranty to which the goods were to conform. Neither is the statement about the future costs of supplies being ½ cent per copy an assertion of fact that relates to the goods sold, so the statement cannot constitute the basis of an express warranty.

It was also erroneous to find that an express warranty was created by Royal's assurances to Booher that purchase of the RBC machines would bring him substantial profits. Such a representation does not describe the goods within the meaning of U.C.C. § 2–313(1)(b), nor is the representation an affirmation of fact relating to the goods under U.C.C. § 2–313(1)(a). It is merely sales talk and the expression of the seller's opinion. See Regal Motor Products v. Bender, 102 Ohio App. 447, 139 N.E.2d 463, 465 (1956) (representation that goods were "readily saleable" and that the demand for them would create a market was not a warranty). ...

On the other hand, the assertion that the machines could not cause fires is an assertion of fact relating to the goods, and substantial evidence in the record supports the trial judge's findings that the assertion was made by Royal to Booher. The same may be said for the assertion that the machines were tested and ready to be marketed. ...

As for findings 8 and the maintenance portion of Number 4, Royal's argument that those statements relate to predictions for the future and cannot qualify as warranties is unpersuasive. An expression of future capacity or performance can constitute an express warranty. In Teter v. Shultz, 110 Ind.App. 541, 39 N.E.2d 802, 804 (1942), the Indiana courts held that a seller's statement that dairy cows would give six gallons of milk per day was an affirmation of fact by the seller relating to the goods. It was not a statement of value nor was it merely a statement of the seller's opinion. The Indiana courts have also found that an express warranty was created by a seller's representation that a windmill was capable of furnishing power to grind 20 to 30 bushels of grain per hour in a moderate wind and with a very light wind would pump an abundance of water. Smith v. Borden, 160 Ind. 223, 66 N.E. 681 (1903). Further, in General Supply and Equipment Co. v. Phillips, supra, the Texas courts upheld the following express warranties made by a seller of roof panels: (1) that tests show no deterioration in 5 years of normal use; (2) that the roofing panels won't turn black or discolor ... even after years of exposure; and (3) that the panels will not burn, rot, rust, or mildew. ...

Whether a seller affirmed a fact or made a promise amounting to a warranty is a question of fact reserved for the trier of fact. General Supply and Equip. Co. v. Phillips, supra. Substantial evidence in the record supports the finding that Royal made the assertion to Booher that maintenance cost for the machine would run ½ cent per copy and that this assertion was not an estimate but an assertion of a fact of performance capability.

Finding Number 8, that service calls on the RBC II would be required every 7,000 to 9,000 copies, relates to performance capability and could constitute the basis of an express warranty. There is substantial evidence in the record to support the finding that this assertion was also made.

While substantial evidence supports the trial court's findings as to the making of those four affirmations of fact or promises, the district court failed to make the further finding that they became part of the basis of the bargain. Ind.Code § 26–1–2–313(1) (1976). While Royal may have made such affirmations to Booher, the question of his knowledge or reliance is another matter.[7]

This case is complicated by the fact that it involved a series of sales transactions between the same parties over approximately an 18–month period and concerned two different machines. The situations of the parties, their knowledge and reliance, may be expected to change in light of their experience during that time. An affirmation of fact which the buyer from his experience knows to be untrue cannot form a part of the basis of the bargain. ... Therefore, as to each purchase, Booher's expanding knowledge of the capacities of the copying machines would have to be considered in deciding whether Royal's representations were part of the basis of the bargain. The same representations that could have constituted an express warranty early in the series of transactions might not have qualified as an express warranty in a later transaction if the buyer had acquired independent knowledge as to the fact asserted.

The trial court did not indicate that it considered whether the warranties could exist and apply to each transaction in the series. Such an analysis is crucial to a just determination. Its absence renders the district court's findings insufficient on the issue of the breach of express warranties.

Since a retrial on the questions of the breach of express warranties and the extent of damages is necessary, we offer the following observations. The

---

7. The requirement that a statement be part of the basis of the bargain in order to constitute an express warranty "is essentially a reliance requirement and is inextricably intertwined with the initial determination as to whether given language may constitute an express warranty since affirmations, promises and descriptions tend to become a part of the basis of the bargain. It was the intention of the drafters of the U.C.C. not to require a strong showing of reliance. In fact, they envisioned that all statements of the seller become part of the basis of the bargain unless clear affirmative proof is shown to the contrary. See Official Comments 3 and 8 to U.C.C. § 2–313." Sessa v. Riegle, 427 F.Supp. 760, 766 (E.D.Pa.1977), aff'd without op. 568 F.2d 770 (3d Cir.1978). ...

court must consider whether the machines were defective upon delivery. Breach occurs only if the goods are defective upon delivery and not if the goods later become defective through abuse or neglect. . . .

In considering the promise relating to the cost of maintenance, the district court should determine at what stage Booher's own knowledge and experience prevented him from blindly relying on the representations of Royal. A similar analysis is needed in examining the representation concerning fire hazard in the RBC I machines. The court also should determine when that representation was made. If not made until February 1975, the representation could not have been the basis for sales made prior to that date.

FRAUD AND MISREPRESENTATION

The district court found that beginning in April or May of 1974 and continuing throughout most of 1975, Royal, by and through its agents and employees acting in the course and scope of their employment, persuaded Booher to buy RBC I and RBC II copiers by knowingly making material oral misrepresentations which were relied upon by Booher to his injury.

Under Indiana law, the essential elements of actionable fraud are representations, falsity, scienter, deception, and injury. . . . A fraud action must be predicated upon statements of existing facts, not promises to perform in the future. . . . Nor do expressions of opinion qualify as fraudulent misrepresentations. The district court made no specific findings as to which of the alleged representations it relied upon in finding fraud. If the court held all eight to be fraudulent misrepresentations, the court erred as to Numbers 1, 2, and 6 because, as discussed above, these were merely expressions of the seller's opinion rather than statements of material fact upon which a fraud action could be based. Numbers 3, 4, 5, 7, and 8, on the other hand, readily qualify as material factual representations. . . .

The trial court, however, is silent on the remaining question, that of deception or reasonable reliance by Booher on the representations in the various transactions. . . . This issue is virtually identical to the basis of the bargain question remanded under the express warranty theory.

The district court's finding of fraud, therefore, must be set aside, and the cause remanded for retrial on the questions of the specific misrepresentations relied upon by Booher in each transaction and the reasonableness of that reliance.

With regard to rescission as a remedy for fraud, rescission would be available only for those specific sales to which fraud attached. . . .

IMPLIED WARRANTIES

The district court found that Royal breached the implied warranties of merchantability and of fitness for a particular purpose. We cannot agree that the record supports the court's findings.

A warranty of merchantability is implied by law in any sale where the seller is a merchant of the goods. To be merchantable, goods must, *inter alia*, pass without objection in the trade under the contract description, be of fair average quality, and be fit for the ordinary purposes for which such goods are used. Ind.Code § 26–1–2–314 (1976). They must "conform to ordinary standards, and . . . be of the same average grade, quality and value as similar goods sold under similar circumstances." . . . It was Booher's burden to prove that the copying machines were not merchantable. . . . Booher failed to satisfy his burden of proof as to standards in the trade for either the RBC I or RBC II machine. No evidence supports the trial court's findings of a breach of the implied warranty of merchantability.

An implied warranty of fitness for a particular purpose arises where a seller has reason to know a particular purpose for which the goods are required and the buyer relies on the seller's skill or judgment to select or furnish suitable goods. Ind.Code § 26–1–2–315 (1976). The court found that Royal knew the particular purpose for which all the RBC machines were to be used and, in fact, that Royal had taken affirmative steps to persuade Booher to become its dealer and that occasionally its employees even accompanied Booher on calls to customers. . . .

The district court, however, failed to distinguish between implied warranties on the RBC I and on the RBC II machines. Nor did the court differentiate among the different transactions involving the two machines. On remand the district court should make further findings on Booher's actual reliance on Royal's skill or judgment in each purchase of the RBC I and RBC II machines. We view it as most unlikely that a dealer who now concedes himself to be an expert in the field of plain paper copiers did not at some point, as his experience with the machines increased, rely on his own judgment in making purchases.

* * *

[Judgment reversed. Cause remanded for a new trial.]

NOTES

(1) Express Warranties. The trial court concluded that a set of statements made by a representative of the seller were express warranties. The Court of Appeals reversed as to all. Unpacking and critiquing the analysis of the appellate court is an excellent way to learn some of the subtle intricacies of express warranty law. The court's analysis focused on three separate aspects of the law.

Relate to the Goods. Section 2–313(1)(a) applies only to an affirmation of fact or promise that "relates to the goods."[1] The Court of Appeals reversed the trial court on three statements because they did not relate to the goods: the affirmations that replacement parts were readily available;

---

1. This element is not found in UCC 2–313(1)(b) or (c). Do you understand why it is omitted there? In the taxonomy of warranties in the Uniform Sales Act, these warranties were considered to be "implied." USA §§ 14, 16. The drafters of UCC 2–313 decided to classify these warranties as "expressed." See Comments 1, 5 and 6.

that the cost of supplies was and would remain low, not more than ½ cent per copy; and that the leasing business would return substantial profits. These affirmations do not describe the goods, but do you agree that the affirmations do not "relate to" the goods sold? The Comments are silent on the intended force of "relates to the goods" as a limiting concept.

Assume that the Court of Appeals was correct in holding that the three statements did not relate to the goods. Does it follow that seller is immune for legal liability for made them? The implied premise of the appellate court's holding is that express warranties that do not relate to the goods are not actionable, that the statute precludes the possibility of common-law warranties. Is this premise justified? Recall UCC 1–103. Comment 2, which deals with other aspects of warranty law, recognizes that the UCC is incomplete and leaves matters beyond its scope to the courts.

Part of the Basis of the Bargain. All three subsections of UCC 2–313(1) require that seller's statements or conduct be "part of the basis of the bargain." What does this term mean? Comment 3 declares that the section deals with affirmations of fact by the seller, descriptions of the goods, or exhibitions of samples "exactly as any other part of a negotiation which ends in a contract is dealt with." General contract law doctrine has no analogue for the point that negotiated terms can be treated as not binding if not part of the basis of the bargain. What does the Comment mean? Is the underlying problem different from any general contract inquiry seeking to find the nature of the parties' reasonable expectations?[2]

"Part of the basis of the bargain" had no counterpart in the Uniform Sales Act. USA § 12, which dealt only with affirmations and promises relating to the goods, created warranties only "if the natural tendency of such affirmation or promise is to induce the buyer to purchase the goods, and if the buyer purchases the goods relying thereon." The "natural tendency" and "actual reliance" elements were not used in connection with warranties of description or sample. Drafters of UCC 2–313 did not use "natural tendency" and "actual reliance." In their place, the UCC drafters inserted "part of the basis of the bargain" for all three kinds of express warranties. Comment 3 states: "no particular reliance on [affirmations of fact] need be shown in order to weave them into the fabric of the agreement. Rather, any fact which is to take such affirmations, once made, out of the agreement requires clear affirmative proof." Does the Comment suggest that, while reliance is not a part of a buyer's cause of action for breach of an express warranty, a buyer's non-reliance on a seller's affirmation could be an affirmative defense, if seller can prove that fact?

The Court of Appeals recognized that four affirmations did relate to the goods: that the machines could not cause fires; that the machines were tested and ready to be marketed; that maintenance of the machine would cost ½ cent per copy; and that service calls would be required every 7,000 to

---

2. See J. Murray, Basis of the Bargain,   Rev. 283 (1982). Transcending Classical Concepts, 66 Minn. L.

9,000 copies. The trial court found that the affirmations had been made and the resulting warranties had been breached. The Court of Appeals reversed. It said: "While Royal may have made such affirmations to Booher, the question of his knowledge or reliance is another matter" and concluded: "An affirmation of fact which the buyer from his experience knows to be untrue cannot form part of the basis of the bargain." What experience of buyer was dispositive in the view of the court? How would you evaluate the decision to reverse the trial court on this ground?

Promise or Affirmation of Fact; Affirmation of Value or Seller's Opinion or Commendation. Section 2–313(1) provides that express warranties are created by a promise or an affirmation of fact that relates to the goods and becomes part of the basis of the bargain, but subsection (2) provides that an affirmation "merely of the value of the goods" or a statement "purporting to be merely the seller's opinion or commendation of the goods" does not create a warranty. What is the legislative purpose for the distinction between affirmations of fact and affirmations of value? Does it derive from the concept that matters of opinion cannot be tested for truth or falsity? Comment 8 indicates that the distinction is not based on the extent to which propositions are verifiable, but rather on the psychology of ordinary buyers hearing or reading certain kinds of sellers' statements: "common experience discloses that some statements cannot fairly be viewed as entering into the bargain. Even as to false statements of value, however, the possibility is left open that a remedy may be provided by the law relating to fraud and misrepresentation." Is the Comment referring to the statutory element, "part of the basis of the bargain"? Does your experience correlate with the "common experience" recited in the Comment?[3] Sales pitches of this genre are very common; would sellers continue this practice if it did not influence buyers? Are there reasons of public policy for negating buyers' protection if sellers' affirmations or statements are not true?

Applying the value and opinion provision, the Court of Appeals held that three of seller's affirmations did not create express warranties: that the machines and component parts were of high quality; that frequency of repairs was very low and would remain so; and that the buyers would make substantial profits. The Court of Appeals introduced its analysis with a statement of the "decisive test," which is "whether the seller asserts a fact of which the buyer is ignorant or merely states an opinion or judgment on a

---

3. Professor Page Keeton outlined the wide variations in the impact of statements which might fall under the heading of "opinion." Quoting Learned Hand, Keeton observed that some statements are like the claims of campaign managers before election: "rather designed to allay the suspicion that would attend their absence than to be understood as having any relation to objective truth." P. Keeton, The Rights of Disappointed Purchasers, 32 Tex.L.Rev. 1, 8 (1953). In a slightly different connection, Keeton illus- trated the effect of the nature of the recovery on the framing of the legal rule. A misrepresentation which is innocent ordinarily will not support an action for damages for deceit. But such a misrepresentation may more readily provide a defense to an action to enforce the agreement which it induced and even, in some cases, a basis for rescission of a completed transaction. Id. at 10. Is such shaping of the rule to the remedy feasible under current statutory structures?

matter of which the seller has no special knowledge and on which the buyer may be expected to have an opinion and to exercise judgment." Does the statute provide any basis for any of the elements of this "decisive test"? Why should buyer's ignorance matter? Seller's "special knowledge"?

Could the court's conclusion have been based on other reasoning? Were the affirmations too lacking in specificity to be affirmations of fact and warranties?

(2) Implied Warranty of Merchantability. The trial court found that seller was in breach of the implied warranty of merchantability, under UCC 2–314. The Court of Appeals reversed, holding that the buyer had failed to introduce any evidence to support the trial court's finding. The case was remanded for retrial. Can the appellate court's conclusion be reconciled with its finding (in connection with express warranties) that there was substantial evidence that the copy machines had not been tested and were not ready to be marketed, that the machines were not safe and could cause fires. How could copy machines that are not ready to be marketed "pass without objection in the trade under the contract description"? UCC 2–314(2)(a). How could copy machines that cause fires be "fit for the ordinary purposes for which such goods are used"? UCC 2–314(2)(c). The Court of Appeals said that the buyer failed to satisfy his burden of proof as to "standards in the trade." What kind of trade standards would deem copy machines with such negative qualities to pass without objection and to be fit for ordinary purposes?

(3) Implied Warranty of Fitness for Particular Purpose. The trial court found that seller knew the buyer's "particular purpose" in buying the copy machines and supplied machines that did not satisfy that purpose, thereby being in breach of warranty of fitness for particular purpose under UCC 2–315. The Court of Appeals reversed and remanded for new trial. Among other observations about the claim, the appellate court expressed skepticism that the buyer would be able to prove that he had relied on seller's skill or judgment to select suitable goods.

How does a fitness-for-particular-purpose warranty differ from a fitness-for-ordinary-purpose warranty? The latter, one of the meanings of merchantable quality under UCC 2–314(2), is not constrained by any statutory requirement that the buyer prove reliance on seller's skill and judgment. Is there any reason to believe that the buyer's purpose in buying the copy machines was to use them other than for their ordinary purpose? Should buyer's lawyer have added to the complaint a count under UCC 2–315?

(4) Other "Fields" of Law. As *Royal Business Machines* demonstrates, factual situations giving rise to express warranty claims are likely to give rise as well to claims of fraud or misrepresentation. The latter sound in tort. The Restatement (Second) of Torts (1977) provides:

§ 525.   Liability for Fraudulent Misrepresentation

One who fraudulently makes a misrepresentation of fact, opinion, intention or law for the purpose of inducing another to act or to refrain from action in reliance on it, is subject to liability to the other in deceit for pecuniary loss caused to him by his justifiable reliance upon the misrepresentation.

An illustration to § 525 reveals the close relationship between the tort and the law of express warranty

2. A, in order to induce B to buy a heating device, states that it will give a stated amount of heat while consuming only a stated amount of fuel. B is justified in accepting A's statement as an assurance that the heating device is capable of giving the services that A promises.

The Restatement, § 526, defines "fraudulently" in broad terms. The Restatement adds a provision for "negligent misrepresentation," § 552, and a special provision for "innocent misrepresentation" in certain transactions, including sales or rental of goods:

§ 552C. Misrepresentation in Sale, Rental or Exchange Transaction

(1) One who, in a sale, rental or exchange transaction with another, makes a misrepresentation of a material fact for the purpose of inducing the other to act or to refrain from acting in reliance upon it, is subject to liability to the other for pecuniary loss caused to him by his justifiable reliance upon the misrepresentation, even though it is not made fraudulently or negligently.

"Misrepresentation," as a part of general contract law, permits a party who has been misled by a fraudulent *or* material misrepresentation in the negotiation of a contract to avoid it. Restatement (Second) of Contracts § 164 (1981). See also E. Farnsworth, Contracts §§ 4.10–4.15 (3d ed. 1999).

The trial court in *Royal Business Machines* held that the seller had knowingly made numerous oral misrepresentations which had been relied upon by the buyer. The Court of Appeals set aside the trial court's findings of fact because the judge had treated the statements, made over more than 18 months, in the aggregate and therefore had not made findings of the reasonableness of buyer's reliance as to each representation when it was made. The Court of Appeals noted that the issue, under the common-law of tort, was virtually identical to the basis of the bargain question under the UCC's provision on express warranty.

Should buyer's lawyer have added to the complaint the count alleging the tort of misrepresentation?

(5) Formation of the Contract in *Royal Business Machines.* Underlying the many issues that were litigated in *Royal Business Machines* is the counseling question: how did the parties do such a bad job of contract formation? The facts of the warranty and misrepresentation claims involve oral statements by seller's representatives. Virtually any lawyer, looking back at this dispute, would conclude that it was a serious mistake for the seller, and probably for the buyer, to enter into this contractual relationship without a written agreement that evidenced the bargain. Affirmations of fact that are drafted to be set down in writing are likely to be much less casual than were the oral representations that were found to have been made in this case. Proof of oral representations is made by testimony of witnesses, whose memories of past events and accounts of them may be unreliable. The manifest value of written agreements is so widely recognized that one rarely finds disputes in transactions involving so many goods and so much money without writings. Indeed, as the amount involved in an exchange goes up, lawyer drafted written terms will be found in the agreements. This was undoubtedly true in the case that follows.

McDonnell Douglas Corp. v. Thiokol Corp.

United States Court of Appeals, Ninth Circuit, 1997.
124 F.3d 1173.

■ HUG, CHIEF JUDGE:

Thiokol Corporation contracted to provide Star 48 motors to McDonnell Douglas Corporation for inclusion in McDonnell Douglas' upper-stage Payload Assist Module, which is designed to propel satellites from the Space Shuttle to a geosynchronous orbit 22,000 nautical miles from Earth. In the contract, Thiokol warranted that the motors would be free of defects in material, labor, and manufacture and that the motors would comply with contract drawings and specifications. Following the failure of two satellites to reach their intended orbit, McDonnell Douglas brought this warranty action against Thiokol. The district court entered judgment against McDonnell Douglas after an eleven-day bench trial. We must decide whether Thiokol breached its warranties. We have jurisdiction, 28 U.S.C. § 1291, and we affirm.

Background

In 1976, McDonnell Douglas Corporation ("McDonnell Douglas") entered a contract with the National Aeronautics and Space Administration ("NASA") to develop and market an upper-stage Payload Assist Module ("PAM"). The PAM propels satellites from the Space Shuttle to a geosynchronous orbit some 22,000 nautical miles from Earth. It consists of several components, including: (1) a cradle that links the satellite to the Space Shuttle; (2) a mechanism that deploys the satellite from the Shuttle's cargo bay; (3) an upper-stage motor to move the satellite from the Shuttle's 160 mile parking orbit into a transfer orbit; and (4) a smaller motor to take the satellite from the apogee of the transfer orbit to its intended orbit. In 1976 there were no upper-stage motors in production that suited McDonnell Douglas' needs. To obtain such a motor, McDonnell Douglas completed Specification Control Drawing 1B98497 (the "Specification Control Drawing") on August 18, 1976, which conceptualized a motor that would meet its needs.

In response to the Specification Control Drawing, Thiokol Corporation ("Thiokol") developed a preliminary design for an upper-stage motor. Thiokol's preliminary design incorporated a carbon-carbon exit cone, rather than the more common carbon-phenolic exit cone. The use of the lighter carbon-carbon exit cone was necessary in order to comply with the weight limitations set forth in the Specification Control Drawing. Thiokol sent its preliminary design to McDonnell Douglas for its review. Because of the "young maturity" of carbon-carbon technology, Thiokol also sent a separate preliminary design of the motor's nozzle assembly, which indicated that Thiokol planned to use a carbon-carbon cone.

In 1978, Thiokol and McDonnell Douglas entered a contract for the development and qualification of an upper-stage motor. The motor became known as the Star 48 motor. The development and qualification contract was labeled the 7011 contract. This contract established a rigorous series of development and qualification tests that Thiokol's proposed design had to meet before Thiokol was allowed to begin production.

Before Thiokol could continue with development of the motor under the contract, it had to obtain McDonnell Douglas' approval of the design. The development phase thus called for a preliminary design review in which McDonnell Douglas and Thiokol engineers jointly reviewed the design of the Star 48 motor. McDonnell Douglas gave Thiokol its approval following the preliminary design review. The approval extended to the carbon-carbon exit cone.

After receiving McDonnell Douglas' approval, Thiokol conducted five engine test-firings, all of which were witnessed by McDonnell Douglas engineers. McDonnell Douglas engineers were allowed to inspect the motors following the firings and received reports analyzing the results of the tests.

After a second design review, which focused on whether the motor design complied with the requirements of the Specification Control Drawing, McDonnell Douglas again gave Thiokol its approval. Six more motors were test-fired and a qualification program review was held. The purpose of this review was to obtain McDonnell Douglas' approval of the motor, which was necessary to allow Thiokol to move into the production phase. McDonnell Douglas gave its approval, concluding that the motor met all of the performance and technical requirements of the Specification Control Drawing.

Following qualification of the motor, but before the parties agreed to a production contract, Thiokol test-fired another motor. This test resulted in a motor failure, and an investigation ensued. Although the cause of the failure was not determined with certainty, McDonnell Douglas issued a statement indicating that the most probable cause was a low density/low quality cone. The failure occurred even though the motor met all of the contract's specification and acceptance requirements.

NASA and the United States Air Force conducted and independent investigation of the test failure. Significantly, this investigation concluded, "The state of knowledge about the material properties of carbon/carbon involute exit cones is such that a meaningful margin of safety cannot be established for the Star 48 exit cone." The NASA/Air Force investigation recommended that McDonnell Douglas expand its testing procedures to detect density variations in cones that otherwise met technical and acceptance standards. McDonnell Douglas thus knew that a test firing resulted in a failure, that NASA and the Air Force believed a meaningful margin of safety could not be established, and that its acceptance testing could not detect all density variations. Despite its knowledge, McDonnell Douglas did not adopt the NASA/Air Force recommendations.

McDonnell Douglas and Thiokol entered into a production contract (the "7047 contract") in 1981. The contract required Thiokol to "maintain the system of producing hardware as established under [the 7011 contract]." The contract also incorporated Article 18 of McDonnell Douglas' Terms and Conditions Guide. That article provides:

> Seller warrants the articles delivered hereunder to be free from defects in labor, material and manufacture, and to be in compliance with any drawings or specifications incorporated or referenced herein.... All warranties shall run to [McDonnell Douglas], its successors and assigns, and to its customers and the users of its products.

On February 3, 1984, the Space Shuttle Challenger used the PAM system to deploy WESTAR–VI, a private communications satellite. The WESTAR–VI satellite failed to reach its transfer orbit. An interply density variation, which is an area of reduced density between the layers of carbonized cloth that comprise the carbon-carbon exit cone, caused the Star 48 motor to fail. Three days later, the Challenger deployed the Palapa B–2 satellite, which also failed to reach its transfer orbit because of a motor failure caused by an interply density variation.

On February 7, McDonnell Douglas convened a Failure Investigation Committee to investigate the WESTAR–VI and Palapa B–2 failures (collectively the "failures"). The Committee issued its final report in September 1984, concluding that the most probable cause of the failures were interply density variations, but that the "exact cause of these exit cone failures could not be determined." The Committee further concluded that the "materials, components, and subassemblies of the nozzle assemblies were produced to the established standards and specifications and essentially satisfied all acceptance criteria applicable to the failed motors." Additionally, the Committee found no evidence that the materials, labor, or manufacture of the WESTAR–VI and Palapa B–2 exit cones varied from contract specifications and requirements.

In March, 1985, McDonnell Douglas made a formal written warranty claim against Thiokol. It alleged that Thiokol breached the warranty provisions of the 7047 contract. McDonnell Douglas sought incidental damages of $10,926,000 (costs associated with the failure investigation) and consequential damages of $6,947,000 (the cost of replacing carbon-carbon exit cones with carbon-phenolic cones).

* * *

The district court conducted an eleven-day bench trial. At the conclusion of the trial, the court issued detailed findings of fact and conclusions of law. It entered judgment against McDonnell Douglas. McDonnell Douglas filed a timely notice of appeal.

Standard of Review

We review de novo the district court's application of the principles of contract interpretation to the facts. ... Whether the seller's representations formed part of the basis of the parties' bargain is a question of fact. See Royal Business Machines Inc. v. Lorraine Corp., 633 F.2d 34, 43 (7th Cir.1980) (whether seller affirmed a fact amounting to an express warranty is a question of fact). We review the district court's factual determinations for clear error. ...

Discussion

Under California law, any affirmation of fact or promise relating to the subject matter of a contract for the sale of goods, which is made part of the basis of the parties' bargain, creates an express warranty. Cal. Com. Code § 2313 (a). California courts use a three-step approach to express warranty issues. Keith v. Buchanan, 220 Cal. Rptr. 392, 395, 173 Cal. App. 3d 13 (Ct. App. 1985). First, the court determines whether the seller's statement amounts to "an affirmation of fact or promise" relating to the goods sold. Id. Second, the court determines if the affirmation or promise was "part of the basis of the bargain." Id. Finally, if the seller made a promise relating to the goods and that promise was part of the basis of the bargain, the court must determine if the seller breached the warranty. Id.

Here, McDonnell Douglas argues that Thiokol made two separate promises, both of which constitute express warranties. McDonnell Douglas maintains that Thiokol promised to deliver goods that (1) were "free from defects in labor, material, and manufacture," and (2) complied with "any drawings or specifications incorporated [into] or referenced" by the contract. We analyze each promise separately.

I. Defects in Labor, Material and Manufacture

We turn first to Thiokol's promise to deliver goods free from defects in labor, material, and manufacture. There is no question that this promise relates to the goods and was made a part of the basis of the parties' bargain. It therefore constitutes an express warranty, Cal. Com. Code § 2313, and we move directly to the final step of the analysis. We must determine whether the WESTAR VI and Palapa B–2 satellite motors suffered from defects in labor, material, or manufacture.

The district court concluded that the motor failures were caused by severe and extensive interply density variations. It further concluded such variations did not amount to a breach of Thiokol's warranty because, "where the buyer qualifies and approves product acceptance specifications, a product which satisfies all [such] specifications is not 'defective.'" The district court thus held that the interply density variations could not be considered a defect "because [they] did not [violate] the product acceptance specifications qualified and approved by [McDonnell Douglas]."

A further inquiry is necessary, however, because Thiokol did not limit its warranty to technical compliance with the specifications set forth in the contract. Thiokol made a separate promise—that the goods would be free of defects in labor, material, and manufacture. We must then make the further inquiry of whether, under the terms of the contract, the interply density variations in the motors delivered constitute a defect in labor, material or manufacture.

McDonnell Douglas offers alternative definitions of the term "defect." First, it contends that a defective product is one that "differs from the manufacturer's intended results or from other ostensibly identical units of the same product line." Barker v. Lull Engineering Co., Inc., 20 Cal. 3d 413, 429, 143 Cal. Rptr. 225, 573 P.2d 443 (1978). This argument lacks merit. While this definition of "defect" is firmly rooted in the law of products liability, McDonnell Douglas presented no evidence that the parties intended to incorporate this definition, and all of the social concerns regarding distribution of risk that it connotes, into their contract. In fact, all of the evidence is to the contrary. . . .

McDonnell Douglas advances a second definition of the phrase "defect in labor, material, and manufacture." Relying on S.M. Wilson & Co. v. Smith Int'l, Inc., 587 F.2d 1363, 1372 (9th Cir.1978), McDonnell Douglas maintains that a defect in labor, material, or manufacture is a "defect in quality." McDonnell Douglas argues that Thiokol breached its warranty by delivering motors that contained "severe and extensive interply density variations," which constituted a defect in quality.

McDonnell Douglas' definition of the critical language finds superficial support in our case law. However, a close reading of Lombard Corp. v. Quality Aluminum Products Co., 261 F.2d 336 (6th Cir.1958), the case relied on in S.W. Wilson, demonstrates that a defect in labor, material, or manufacture is a defect or flaw in the quality of the labor, material, or manufacture of the product. See *Lombard*, 261 F.2d at 338 (holding that there was no defect in material where "the steel [used] in the tie rods was of excellent quality"). This definition of defect is compelled by the plain meaning of the terms selected by the parties because it gives meaning to the limiting language "in labor, material, or manufacture." McDonnell Douglas' definition, to the contrary, renders the limiting language superfluous.

We therefore reject McDonnell Douglas' definition of a "defect." We hold that, to prove a breach of Thiokol's warranty against defects in labor, material, or manufacture, McDonnell Douglas had to demonstrate that the WESTAR and Palapa satellite motors suffered from a flaw in the quality of the material used in their construction. See S.W. Wilson, 587 F.2d at 1372. McDonnell Douglas failed to do this.

At trial McDonnell Douglas attempted to prove that the rayon cloth provided by Union Carbide, which was used in the manufacture of Star 48 motors, was "dirty" and of substandard quality. The district court expressly found "no evidence . . . that the cloth supplied by Union Carbide was defective." This conclusion is amply supported by the record and is in accord with the findings of the failure investigation committee. Additionally, there was conflicting evidence regarding the effect of "dirty" cloth. A NASA expert testified that, although NASA pursued the "dirty cloth" theory for a "number of months," it eventually concluded that the condition of the cloth at the beginning of the manufacturing process had no significant effect on the strength of the carbon-carbon exit cone.

The record is otherwise devoid of any evidence that the failures were caused by a defect in labor, material, or manufacture of the carbon-carbon exit cones. There is, rather, substantial evidence to the contrary. The failure investigation committee concluded that "changes and variations in materials or [the manufacturing] process were not a determinative cause of the failures." It also found that "equipment, work procedures, personnel and production and support systems were not proven to be contributory to the failures." Although the committee found that there was a shift in the quality of the exit cones, it concluded that "[a] single cause of density variations has not been isolated."

In light of the foregoing, we conclude that McDonnell Douglas failed to demonstrate that a flaw in labor, material, or manufacture caused the interply density variations which resulted in the failures. Accordingly, the district court properly entered judgment against McDonnell Douglas on this issue.

II.   Failure to Comply with Drawings and Specifications

McDonnell Douglas also contends that Thiokol warranted that all Star 48 motors delivered under the contract would comply "with any drawings or specifications incorporated [into] or referenced" by the 7047 contract. The Specification Control Drawing was attached to the 7047 contract. Section 3.0 of the statement of work, which was attached to the Specification Control Drawing, stated that "all rocket motor components shall be suitable for the purpose for which they are intended." Additionally, section 3.5.4 of the statement of work stated that "the nozzle [which includes the exit cone] shall be capable of withstanding the thermal mechanical loads during motor burn without any detrimental structural failure." McDonnell Douglas argues that these provisions were incorporated into and referenced by the 7047 contract, and that Thiokol breached those provisions.

The essential inquiry is whether these statements in a drawing attached to the contract constitute additional express warranties that were understood and bargained for by the parties. These provisions would constitute performance warranties with serious financial risks involved and it would be very unusual to find the parties intended to tuck them away in drawings attached to the contract. The determinative question is whether the parties intended the warranties to be confined to those expressed in the body of the contract (products free from defects in labor, material, and manufacture) or expanded to performance warranties by drawings attached to the contract.

The district court determined that "it was the true understanding of the parties that a performance warranty ... was not part of the agreement or a basis of [McDonnell Douglas'] bargain." The facts and circumstances surrounding the making of the contract, the testimony of McDonnell Douglas agents, understandings prevalent throughout the aerospace industry, and McDonnell Douglas' own conduct all support the conclusion that McDonnell Douglas did not bargain for a performance warranty. Accordingly, we conclude that the statements in the Specification Control Drawing were not intended to be additional warranties forming a part of the bargain of the parties.

The state-of-the-art of carbon-carbon technology, which is one of the facts and circumstances surrounding the formation of the contract, indicates that a performance warranty was not technically feasible. McDonnell Douglas was aware, at the time it prepared the Specification Control Drawing, of the state-of-the-art of carbon-carbon exit cones. Additionally, McDonnell Douglas knew that the NASA/Air Force investigation of the test failures concluded that a meaningful margin of safety could not be maintained. Finally, McDonnell Douglas knew that the carbon-vapor densification process did not yield uniform density throughout the exit cone. McDonnell Douglas could not have bargained for a performance warranty because it knew that, given the state-of-the-art of carbon-carbon technology, such a promise was impossible to fulfill. See Royal Business Machines, 633 F.2d at 44 ("An affirmation of fact which the buyer from [its] experience knows to be untrue cannot form a part of the basis of the bargain.").

Moreover, juxtaposing the costs of a satellite with the costs of the Star 48 motor, indicates that a performance warranty was economically unfeasible. In an internal memorandum commenting on a NASA inquiry, a McDonnell Douglas employee stated that McDonnell Douglas "decided early on in the PAM program that the financial risks associated with performance warranties were too high considering the price of the satellite compared to the price of the PAM." McDonnell Douglas accordingly wrote its sales contracts "in terms of what the product is, not what it does" because "to prepare a contract in terms of what the hardware does would indeed be a performance warranty." McDonnell Douglas did not include the cost of a performance warranty in the price of its product. Because McDonnell Douglas knew that its profit margin was greater than Thiokol's and it knew what it paid Thiokol for the Star 48 motors, McDonnell Douglas knew that it was not being charged for a performance warranty.

The testimony of John Willacker, the McDonnell Douglas employee who drafted the specification control drawing, also supports the district court's conclusion that the parties did not bargain for a performance warranty. He testified at trial that in 1977 it was McDonnell Douglas' practice to set forth only technical requirements in specification control drawings. Willacker was asked if "it was a standard industry practice that a specification, like a specification control drawing, was not to be used to contain warranty provisions?" Willacker answered, "That's correct." More importantly, Willacker also testified that he intended only to set forth technical requirements in the document. Willacker's testimony further supports the district court's conclusion that the parties did not intend to create a performance warranty by incorporating the "drawings and specifications" of the Specification Control Drawing.

Finally, McDonnell Douglas' post-failure conduct is inconsistent with the understanding of the contract that it now advances. On February 20, 1984, D.H. Hauver, a negotiator/administrator for McDonnell Douglas, wrote to Thiokol, "Should this investigation determine that the PAM–D (STAR 48) rocket motors failed to achieve specified performance levels due to defects in their manufacture, we will expect you to comply with the warranty provisions of our subcontract." (emphasis added). Had McDonnell Douglas understood Thiokol to have provided a performance warranty, it would not have included the limiting language "due to defects in their manufacture" in the letter. This subsequent practical construction of the warranty provisions further supports the district court's conclusion that the affirmations in sections 3.0 and 3.5.4 were [not?] a basis of the parties' bargain.

In sum, McDonnell Douglas did not bargain for a warranty of performance, knew that it was not paying for such a warranty, and acted as if it understood the contract not to include such a warranty. To create a performance warranty under the circumstances of this case, the contract would have to be much more specific. Accordingly, the district court correctly concluded that statements in the Specification Control Drawings were not intended by the parties to be additional performance warranties.

Conclusion

Thiokol did not breach either of its express warranties. The judgment of the district court is

AFFIRMED.

NOTES

(1) Warranty Against Defects in Materials or Workmanship. One of the express warranties in this case was seller's warranty against "defect in labor, material, and manufacture." This warranty is a variant of a common express warranty against defects in materials and workmanship. Such express warranties are found in written agreements, drafted by counsel for sellers, who find this warranty preferable to the implied warranty of merchantability. Note that, in *McDonnell Douglas*, there is no discussion of the merchantability warranty. Undoubtedly, the sales contract contained a disclaimer of that warranty. (We will consider the law of warranty disclaimers in the next Section.) For what reasons would sellers, advised by their lawyers, prefer an express warranty against defects in materials or workmanship to an implied warranty of merchantability? How do the two warranties differ?

The courts in *McDonnell Douglas* held that the warranty against defects in labor, material, and manufacture was not breached. Note the difficulty of the meaning of "defect," a threshold problem for buyer's counsel. Two definitions that were proposed by counsel were rejected by the Court of Appeals. The definition adopted by the Court of Appeals required buyer to identify a specific flaw in the materials used. Evidence that the motor had failed to function properly was not sufficient to prove a breach of warranty. Would the failure of goods to function be sufficient evidence of a breach of a warranty of merchantability?

(2) Warranty of Conformity to Specifications. The goods in *McDonnell Douglas* were goods to be specially manufactured. Article 2 applies to such contracts. UCC 2–105(1). Designs for goods to be specially manufactured may be provided by sellers or buyers. The design of the goods in this case was provided by the seller in engineering drawings and specifications. Accordingly, the contract for production of the Star 48 motor had a term that required the manufacturer-seller to comply with the drawings and specifications. Buyer relied on two provisions that it claimed had been incorporated into the Star 48 motor contract and obligated the manufacturer of the Star 48 motor to underwrite the performance of the motor. The trial court held, and appellate court affirmed, that a performance warranty had not been incorporated by reference. Study carefully the closely-reasoned rationale of the Court of Appeals in arriving at its determination on this critical point.

Sidco Products Marketing, Inc. v. Gulf Oil Corp.

United States Court of Appeals, Fifth Circuit, 1988.
858 F.2d 1095.

■ JONES, CIRCUIT JUDGE:

At issue here is the grant of summary judgment for the defendant [Gulf] concerning claims for breach of express and implied warranties . . . in the sale [by Gulf to Sidco] of a material called "middle layer emulsion" (MLE). Texas law applies in this diversity case. Concluding essentially that Gulf did not misrepresent the nature or qualities of MLE to the ultimate purchaser Sidco, we affirm.

I. BACKGROUND

According to Sidco, this is the story of a pig in a poke. On December 15, 1983, Gulf published a Bid Inquiry in which it invited bids from a selected group of purchasers for a product called "middle layer emulsion." One company on the bid list was Chemwaste, Inc. Several portions of the Bid Inquiry are relevant to our discussion. First, the product was defined as Middle Layer Emulsion [MLE], "a mixture of oil, water and particulate matter." Second, paragraph 10 of the Bid Inquiry afforded any prospective purchaser the opportunity to "inspect the tanks containing MLE and . . . obtain a reasonable sample therefrom for testing." The bid price was to be gauged by the value of recoverable hydrocarbons estimated to be contained in the MLE. Third, a cautionary environmental note appeared as paragraph 14 of the Bid Inquiry:

The solids in the middle layer emulsion are listed by the United States Environmental Protection Agency in 40 CFR Part 261 as a "Hazardous Waste from Specific Sources, Slop Oil emulsion solids from the petroleum refining industry" with an EPA hazardous waste number of K049. If the solids are removed from the middle layer emulsion, then the disposal of these solids are regulated by the Federal Government as well as many state and local governments. It will be the responsibility of the successful bidder to dispose of these solids and any waste water generated in accordance with all applicable Federal, State and local rules and regulations.

Sidco became interested in purchasing MLE for processing and resale of the oil in it when its president, Dirk Stronck, obtained and read a copy of the Bid Inquiry, including paragraph 14. Because Gulf was selling the product only to authorized bidders, Stronck contacted Romero Brothers Oil Exchange, Inc., which acquired from Chemwaste the right to sell MLE. Sidco availed itself of the opportunity to examine MLE chemically and engaged E.W. Saybolt & Company, Inc. for this purpose. Upon receipt of what it believed were satisfactory test results from Saybolt, Sidco signed a contract to purchase the MLE from Romero. The Romero contract was executed for Sidco by Ron Bougere, its then vice-president.

The sale from Gulf to Chemwaste, thence to Romero and Sidco, occurred January 24, 1984. Sidco paid $394,482 for MLE estimated to yield 28,077 barrels of recoverable hydrocarbons. Sidco then entered into a processing agreement with Texas Oil and Chemical Terminal, Inc. [TOCT] for "slop oil" without showing TOCT the Bid Inquiry or advising it that the product was MLE. TOCT's attempts to process MLE encountered serious difficulty—the product first plugged a pump screen and damaged TOCT's heater and later clogged a processing tower.

After further testing, Sidco was led to inquire of the Texas Department of Water Resources whether MLE might be a "hazardous waste" regulated by federal environmental law. The department answered affirmatively. [Sidco] protested this decision, but was ordered to and did remove the MLE from the TOCT refinery, which was not licensed to process hazardous waste, and paid for repairs to TOCT's heater. Nevertheless, hydrocarbon products were eventually extracted and sold by Sidco for gross revenue exceeding $400,000.

Sidco claims to have sustained over $13 million in damages, including $60,000 out-of-pocket costs, over $360,000 in lost revenues, the loss of $5 million in financial backing for proposed slop oil activities, and foregone business opportunities exceeding $8.6 million.

Sidco's lawsuit against Gulf alleged the following causes of action:

    1. Gulf breached an express warranty regarding the nature and quality of MLE, in violation of Tex. Bus. & Com. Code Ann. § 2.313;

    2. Gulf breached the implied warranty of merchantability in that MLE was not fit for the purpose for which slop oil is ordinarily sold, violating Tex. Bus. & Com. Code Ann. § 2.314.

* * *

II. DISCUSSION

The determination most critical to the success of Sidco's position is the nature of the misrepresentations or omissions by Gulf in its Bid Inquiry.

Sidco concedes that the Bid Inquiry constitutes the only relevant communication between Gulf and Sidco's representatives prior to Sidco's purchase of MLE. Sidco charges that Gulf misrepresented three characteristics of the MLE: that it formed an unusually tight emulsion which was not susceptible to ordinary processing methods; that the product was not "ordinary slop oil," and that the product in its totality was a hazardous waste under applicable environmental regulations. Sidco alleges that all of its damages flowed from these misrepresentations. Sidco's breach of warranty claims, and its alleged breach of the DTPA founded on warranty and misrepresentation claims, depend upon the existence of these pleaded and vigorously argued misrepresentations of MLE's qualities.

Try as we may, we are unable to discern in the bare simplicity of Gulf's Bid Inquiry the false representations that Sidco asserts. The pertinent portions of the Bid Inquiry were quoted above. MLE is there described as an emulsion, which the dictionary alerts us is an "intimate mixture" of two incompletely miscible liquids, such as water and oil, or of a semisolid or solid dispersed in a liquid. Webster's Third New Int'l Dictionary. The MLE is defined to contain water, hydrocarbons and particulate matter. Prospective purchasers are offered the opportunity to sample a sufficient quantity of the MLE to determine its qualities. Finally, there is a cautionary note about the hazardous waste nature of solids contained in the MLE. There is, however, no affirmation of fact concerning the susceptibility of MLE to any particular hydrocarbon processing or refining technique. There is no representation that MLE is "ordinary slop oil." The term slop oil appears only once in the Bid Inquiry, as a descriptive term (in paragraph 14) in the title of the EPA regulation governing the nature of the solids. MLE itself is not represented in the Bid Inquiry as either environmentally hazardous or non-hazardous. The Bid Inquiry did, however, put the would-be purchaser on notice that he should sample and test the MLE in order to determine the nature and quantity of its hydrocarbon content and to calculate his bid price. To put the matter briefly, the Bid Inquiry described MLE much as would a want-ad for a "truck," in that it described the product generically and left the rest of the characteristics to be discerned by the purchaser in his test-drive or at his mechanic's shop.

A warranty is a promise or affirmation of fact concerning a product or a description of the product to which the product is represented to conform. Tex. Bus. & Com. Code Ann. §§ 2.313(a)(1) and (2). Gulf's Bid Inquiry made no promise or description of MLE with regard to its processability or its status as either "ordinary slop oil" or an EPA-regulated hazardous waste. Where there is no such representation, promise, or affirmation that becomes part of the basis of the parties' bargain, there is no express warranty to be breached. La Sara Grain Co. v. First National Bank, 673 S.W.2d 558, 565 (Tex.1984).

Sidco responds to this conclusion in two ways, which we believe are but versions of the same argument. Gulf, it says, "by its conduct" as well as by the Bid Inquiry, "acted as if" MLE was ordinary slop oil. Alternatively, the essence of Gulf's duplicitous conduct, Sidco contends, is that Gulf *omitted* to disclose that MLE could not be processed by ordinary refinery means, that it was not ordinary slop oil and that it was, irrespective of the solids it contained, a hazardous waste. Omissions, however, are not affirmative representations of any sort and thus cannot support a warranty claim, because express warranties must be explicit. . . . On the record before us, it appears that Gulf's Bid Inquiry embodied no express warranty concerning the processability of MLE or its status as "ordinary slop oil" or a non-hazardous material.

Sidco also contends that MLE was sold under an implied warranty of merchantability or fitness for the purposes for which "ordinary slop oil" is used. Gulf moved for summary judgment on this issue, asserting that slop oil is bought and sold so that it can be processed to yield valuable petroleum products. Since the MLE did eventually produce $400,000 of such products for Sidco, the implied warranty of merchantability was fulfilled. This argument suffers from the lack of record evidence demonstrating that, if MLE were to be equated to "ordinary slop oil" for implied warranty purposes, the revenue earned for its petroleum contents represented a "quality comparable to that generally acceptable in that line of trade . . ." Official Comment 2 to Tex. Bus. & Com. Code Ann. § 2.314. Alternatively, however, Gulf asserts that there can be no implied warranty of merchantability as requested by Sidco, because Gulf nowhere expressly represented MLE as "ordinary slop-oil." We find this latter rationale convincing and consistent with our previous discussion.

* * *

For these reasons, the summary judgment granted by the district court is AFFIRMED.

NOTES

(1) Merchantable Quality: Fitness for Ordinary Purposes. Goods may be useful for more than one purpose. Flour may be useful for human consumption, but can also be used in the manufacture of ceiling tiles. Cows may be used as dairy animals, for breeding purposes, or for slaughter. What should determine the "ordinary purposes" of goods that have multiple uses? Can the answer be found in the words of the contract of the parties? Are there other sources? Once purposes are identified, how good must goods be to be deemed "fit"? What should determine the minimum standard of "fitness" of goods?

Problem 3.3.1. Buyer purchased a new Mustang automobile from a Ford dealer. After 30 months, during which Buyer had driven the car 75,000 miles, buyer discovered that the taillight assembly gaskets had been installed in a manner that permitted water to enter and cause severe rust damage. Did the dealer breach the warranty of merchantability? On these facts, the Wisconsin Supreme Court held that the rust problem did not render the car unfit for the purpose of driving. "When a car can provide safe, reliable transportation it is generally considered merchantable." Taterka v. Ford Motor Co., 86 Wis.2d 140, 271 N.W.2d 653 (1978). If the car had been a Mercedes, would the same ruling be appropriate?

(2) Merchantable Quality: Pass Without Objection in the Trade. Section 2–314(2)(a) defines merchantability by reference to trade standards. The UCC provides that trade usage (UCC 1–205(2)) becomes, by implication, part of the parties' bargain in fact (UCC 1–201(3)) ("agreement") which results in defining their legal obligations (UCC 1–201(11)) ("contract"). If goods of a certain quality are regularly accepted without objection by buyers in the trade, this provides a contractual standard against which to measure the objection of a particular buyer in the same trade. See Comment 7 to UCC 2–314. Does this suggest that the issue of sellers' responsibility should be decided as a matter of contract interpretation?

(3) Merchantable Quality: Fair Average Quality. UCC 2–314(2)(b) specifies that goods must be such as "in the case of fungible goods, are of fair average quality within the description." Comment 7 implies a limited scope for this provision: " 'Fair average' is a term directly appropriate to *agricultural* bulk products ..." (emphasis added). The statute, of course, extends to non-agricultural fungible goods; "fungible" goods, as defined in UCC 1–201(17), comprise not only various bulk products (like ores) but also most manufactured goods where "any unit is, by nature or usage of trade, the equivalent of any other like unit."

Comment 7 to UCC 2–314 seeks to shed light on the standard by stating that "fair average" means "goods centering around the middle belt of quality, not the least or the worst that can be understood in the particular trade by the designation, but such as can pass 'without objection.' Of course a fair percentage of the least is permissible but the goods are not 'fair average' if they are all of the least or worst quality possible under the description."

Does the text of the statute support the implication that goods fail to be of "merchantable quality" if they are below average quality but are "within the description"? Suppose that buyers had been accepting shipments of sugar which ranged in polarization between 75 and 80, with the various shipments averaging out at 77 ½. Would a shipment in that case which polarized at 75 3/8 fail to meet the statutory standard? If buyers started rejecting shipments below 77 ½, so that the average quality of acceptable sugar rose to 79, would this in turn justify rejection of sugar below a polarization of 79? Can independent meaning be given to paragraph (b)? See 1 N.Y.L.R.C., Study of the UCC 400–01 (1955). Are similar problems latent in paragraph (d)?

Problem 3.3.2. Manufacturer of two-way taxi radios contracted to buy 2500 microprocessors to be used as components in the radios to be delivered in installments. After 1900 had been delivered, buyer notified seller that these items were unsatisfactory. The buyer asserted that it had had 130 (some 8%) of the microprocessors tested by an independent laboratory which reported that 2.6% of those tested had failed to perform. Buyer asserted that its acceptable quality level—the number of devices which can be defective without rendering the entire shipment unacceptable—was 1%. In a suit by buyer for damages for breach of the warranty of merchantability,[4] seller's expert witness testified that a defect rate of less than 5% was sufficient to make the goods conforming. Buyer's technicians testified that, in products containing only five components, a 5% failure rate for each part would result in a probability that one in four of the products had an inadequate component. Did seller breach the warranty of merchantability? See Integrated Circuits Unlimited, Inc. v. E.F. Johnson Co., 691 F.Supp. 630 (E.D.N.Y.1988), aff'd, 875 F.2d 1040 (2d Cir.1989) (held warranty breached).

The court in *Integrated Circuits* also addressed the adequacy of evidence based upon sampling of only 8% of the microprocessors. The court noted that the tests were expensive. While the sample had not been selected randomly, the court found that selection for sampling sufficed because it had been made without bias. The court concluded that the statistical probabilities were high enough and sufficiently reliable to warrant the buyer's action.

(4) Merchantable Quality: Contract Description. In *Sidco*, the advocate for the MLE buyer described the contract as a purchase of "a pig in a poke." Sales in which the parties use no description of the goods are not likely to occur. Normally, the goods would be described verbally.[5] "Any description of the goods which is made part of the basis of the bargain creates an express warranty that the goods shall conform to the description." UCC 2–313(1)(b). What is added to the idea of an *express* warranty by description by the provisions in UCC 2–314(2) that define an *implied* warranty on the basis of the "contract description" (UCC 2–314(2)(a) and (b)) or "the agreement" (UCC 2–314(2)(d) and (c))? Recall the discussion in Section 2 regarding the overlapping relationship of the three warranties of quality.

Section 2–314(2)(c) does not refer on its face to "contract description" or "agreement," but it declares sellers responsible for the ordinary utility of "such goods." To what antecedent could "such" goods refer?[6]

(5) Merchantable Quality of Manufactured Goods: Design Standards. Manufacturers determine their own quality-control standards. Such standards, which may be high or low, are used to decide whether the manufacturer will sell a finished product in the marketplace. (Manufacturers of some goods, e.g., glass crystal or clothing, market some products that

---

4. Buyer contended it had not accepted the goods in question. Much of the legal analysis of the courts addressed the question whether buyer's rejection was rightful. On some microprocessors, the court found for the seller. As to materials rightly rejected, the buyer did not seek damages for seller's breach.

5. In a "present sale" (UCC 2–106(1)) words may be considerably less important

than the parties' focus on the thing itself. So, too, in a sale by sample or model.

6. Proposed Revised Article 2, with a single exception, does recommend any change in UCC 2–314. The exception is to amend UCC 2–314(2)(c) to read "are fit for the ordinary purposes for which goods of that description are used." Proposed Revised 2–314(b)(3).

do not meet the firms' standards as "seconds.") If a manufacturer fails to detect that a product does not conform to its own quality-control standards and, without notice of that fact, sells the product to a buyer, is the product, for that reason, unmerchantable?

Problem 3.3.3. A restaurant patron ordered and was served a platter that includes a portion of fish almondine. While eating, the patron choked on a fishbone, which lodged in his esophagus. The patron was rushed to a hospital where a bone, one centimeter long, was removed. Patron sues Restaurant for breach of the implied warranty of merchantability. (Note that serving food in a restaurant is a sale under UCC 2–314(1).) What result? See Morrison's Cafeteria v. Haddox, 431 So.2d 975 (Ala.1983)(jury verdict for patron reversed; as a matter of law, a one-centimeter bone in a fish fillet does not make the food unmerchantable). Sellers' liability for buyers' personal injuries that result from nonconformity of the goods is considered further in Section 6 infra.

Problem 3.3.4. Seller, a car dealer, showed Buyer a car on display in the showroom. While Buyer was examining the car, Seller described the car as a Model XX–V. Buyer agreed to buy the car and the Seller drew up a written agreement in which the car was described as a Model XX–V. After driving the car for several weeks, Buyer learned that it was a Model XX–J. A Model XX–V has four doors and chrome trim, while a Model XX–J has two doors and no chrome trim. Otherwise the cars are the same. Has Buyer a claim for breach of warranty under UCC 2–313(1)(b)? Under UCC 2–314? See UCC 2–316(3)(b). Cf. Best Buick v. Welcome, 18 UCC Rep. 75 (Mass. Dist.Ct., App.Div.1975) (car erroneously described as "1970" model).

NOTE

Remedies for Breach of Warranty. We turn now to the remedies available to buyers for breach of warranty of quality. The UCC provisions on remedies do not vary with the kind of warranty. The nature of the relief does depend on whether the goods are retained by a buyer or returned to the seller. If the goods are kept by buyers, damages are provided in UCC 2–714. If the goods go back to the seller, by revocation of acceptance, damages are provided in UCC 2–713.

Chatlos Systems v. National Cash Register Corp.

United States Court of Appeals, Third Circuit, 1982.
670 F.2d 1304.

[Chatlos Systems, Inc. (Chatlos) designed and manufactured cable pressurization equipment for the telecommunications industry. In the spring of 1974, Chatlos decided to buy a computer system and contacted several manufacturers, including National Cash Register Corp. (NCR). NCR recommended its 399/656 disc system. NCR's representative said that the equipment would provide Chatlos with six accounting functions: accounts receivable, payroll, order entry, inventory deletion, state income tax, and cash receipts. The representative also told Chatlos that the system would solve inventory problems, result in direct savings of labor costs, and be programmed to be in full operation in six months. On July 24, 1974, Chatlos signed a written agreement in which NCR warranted the equipment "for 12 months after delivery against defects in material, workmanship and operational failure from ordinary use."

[NCR installed the equipment, but never succeeded in making it fully operational. In November 1976, Chatlos instructed NCR to remove the equipment. NCR refused.]

■ PER CURIAM

This appeal from a district court's award of damages for breach of warranty in a diversity case tried under New Jersey law presents two questions: whether the district court's computation of damages under N.J.Stat.Ann. § 12A:2–714(2) was clearly erroneous, and whether the district court abused its discretion in supplementing the damage award with pre-judgment interest. We answer both questions in the negative and, therefore, we will affirm.

Plaintiff-appellee Chatlos Systems, Inc., initiated this action in the Superior Court of New Jersey, alleging, *inter alia,* breach of warranty regarding an NCR 399/656 computer system it had acquired from defendant National Cash Register Corp. The case was removed under 28 U.S.C. § 1441(a) to the United States District Court for the District of New Jersey. Following a nonjury trial, the district court determined that defendant was liable for breach of warranty and awarded $57,152.76 damages for breach of warranty and consequential damages in the amount of $63,558.16. Chatlos Systems, Inc. v. National Cash Register Corp., 479 F.Supp. 738 (D.N.J.1979), aff'd in part, remanded in part, 635 F.2d 1081 (3d Cir.1980). Defendant appealed and this court affirmed the district court's findings of liability, set aside the award of consequential damages, and remanded for a recalculation of damages for breach of warranty. Chatlos Systems, Inc. v. National Cash Register Corp., 635 F.2d 1081 (3d Cir.1980). On remand, applying the "benefit of the bargain" formula of N.J.Stat.Ann. § 12A:2–714(2) (Uniform Commercial Code § 2–714(2)), the district court determined the damages to be $201,826.50, to which it added an award of pre-judgment interest. Defendant now appeals from these damage determinations, contending that the district court erred in failing to recognize the $46,020 contract price of the delivered NCR computer system as the fair market value of the goods as warranted, and that the award of damages is without support in the evidence presented. Appellant also contests the award of pre-judgment interest.

. . . The district court relied . . . on the testimony of plaintiff-appellee's expert, Dick Brandon, who, without estimating the value of an NCR model 399/656, presented his estimate of the value of a computer system that would perform all of the functions that the NCR 399/656 had been warranted to perform. Brandon did not limit his estimate to equipment of any one manufacturer; he testified regarding manufacturers who could have made systems that would perform the functions that appellant had warranted the NCR 399/656 could perform. He acknowledged that the systems about which he testified were not in the same price range as the NCR 399/656. Appellant likens this testimony to substituting a Rolls Royce for a Ford, and concludes that the district court's recomputed damage award was therefore clearly contrary to the evidence of fair market value—which in NCR's view is the contract price itself.

Appellee did not order, nor was it promised, merely a specific NCR computer model, but an NCR computer system with specified capabilities. The correct measure of damages, under N.J.Stat.Ann. § 12A:2–714(2), is the difference between the fair market value of the goods accepted and the value they would have had if they had been as warranted. Award of that sum is not confined to instances where there has been an increase in value between date of ordering and date of delivery. It may also include the benefit of a contract price which, for whatever reason quoted, was particularly favorable for the customer. Evidence of the contract price may be relevant to the issue of fair market value, but it is not controlling. ... Appellant limited its fair market value analysis to the contract price of the computer model it actually delivered.[3] Appellee developed evidence of the worth of a computer with the capabilities promised by NCR, and the trial court properly credited the evidence.[4]

Appellee was aided, moreover, by the testimony of Frank Hicks, NCR's programmer, who said that he told his company's officials that the "current software was not sufficient in order to deliver the program that the customer [Chatlos] required. They would have to be rewritten or a different system would have to be given to the customer." Appendix to Brief for Appellee at 2.68. Hicks recommended that Chatlos be given an NCR 8200 but was told, "that will not be done." Id. at 2.69. Gerald Greenstein, another NCR witness, admitted that the 8200 series was two levels above

---

3. At oral argument, counsel for appellant responded to questions from the bench, as follows:

Judge Rosenn: Your position also is that you agree, number one, that the fair market value is the measure of damages here.

Counsel for Appellant: Yes, sir.

Judge Rosenn: The fair market value you say, in the absence of other evidence to the contrary that is relevant, is the contract price. That is the evidence of fair market value.

Counsel: That's right.

Judge Rosenn: Now seeing that had the expert or had the plaintiff been able to establish testimony that there were other machines on the market that were similar to your machine?

Counsel: Yes.

Judge Rosenn: That the fair market value of those was $50,000, that would have

been relevant evidence but it had to be the same machine—same type machine.

Counsel: Well, I would say that the measure of damages as indicated by the statute requires the same machine—"the goods"—in an operable position.

4. We find the following analogy, rather than the Rolls Royce–Ford analogy submitted by appellant, to be on point:

Judge Weis: If you start thinking about a piece of equipment that is warranted to lift a thousand pounds and it will only lift 500 pounds, then the cost of something that will lift a thousand pounds gives you more of an idea and that may be?

Counsel for Appellee: That may be a better analogy, yes.

Judge Weis: Yes.

the 399 in sophistication and price. Id. at 14.30. This testimony supported Brandon's statement that the price of the hardware needed to perform Chatlos' requirements would be in the $100,000 to $150,000 range.

Essentially, then, the trial judge was confronted with the conflicting value estimates submitted by the parties. Chatlos' expert's estimates were corroborated to some extent by NCR's supporters. NCR, on the other hand, chose to rely on contract price. Credibility determinations had to be made by the district judge. Although we might have come to a different conclusion on the value of the equipment as warranted had we been sitting as trial judges, we are not free to make our own credibility and factual findings. We may reverse the district court only if its factual determinations were clearly erroneous. Krasnov v. Dinan, 465 F.2d 1298 (3d Cir. 1972).[5]

Upon reviewing the evidence of record, therefore, we conclude that the computation of damages for breach of warranty was not clearly erroneous. We hold also that the district court acted within its discretion in awarding pre-judgment interest, Chatlos Systems, Inc. v. National Cash Register Corp., 635 F.2d at 1088.

The judgment of the district court will be affirmed.

■ ROSENN, CIRCUIT JUDGE, dissenting.

The primary question in this appeal involves the application of Article 2 of the Uniform Commercial Code as adopted by New Jersey in N.J.S.A. 12A:2–101 et seq. (1962) to the measure of damages for breach of warranty in the sale of a computer system. I respectfully dissent because I believe there is no probative evidence to support the district court's award of damages for the breach of warranty in a sum amounting to almost five times the purchase price of the goods. The measure of damages also has been misapplied and this could have a significant effect in the marketplace, especially for the unique and burgeoning computer industry.[1]

In July 1974, National Cash Register Corporation (NCR) sold Chatlos Systems, Inc. (Chatlos), a NCR 399/656 disc computer system (NCR 399) for $46,020 (exclusive of 5 percent sales tax of $1,987.50). The price and system included:

The computer (hardware)	$40,165.00
Software (consisting of 6 computer programs)[2]	5,855.00
	$46,020.00

---

5. The dissent essentially is based on disagreement with the estimates provided by Chatlos' expert, Brandon. The record reveals that he was well qualified; the weight to be given his testimony is the responsibility of the factfinder, not an appellate court.

1. Plaintiff's expert, Brandon, testified that generally 40 percent of all computer installations result in failures. He further testified that successful installations of computer systems require not only the computer companies' attention but also the attention of the customers' top management.

2. The six basic computer programs were: (1) accounts receivable, (2) payroll, (3) order entry, (4) inventory deletion, (5) state

NCR delivered the disc computer to Chatlos in December 1974 and in March 1975 the payroll program became operational. By March of the following year, however, NCR was still unsuccessful in installing an operational order entry program and inventory deletion program. Moreover, On August 31, 1976, Chatlos experienced problems with the payroll program. On that same day and the day following NCR installed an operational state income tax program, but on September 1, 1976, Chatlos demanded termination of the lease[3] and removal of the computer.

When this case was previously before us, we upheld the district court's liability decision but remanded for a reassessment of damages, instructing the court that under the purchase contract and the law consequential damages could not be awarded. Consequential damages, therefore, are no longer an issue here.

On remand, the district court, on the basis of the previous record made in the case, fixed the fair market value of the NCR 399 as warranted at the time of its acceptance in August 1975 at $207,826.50. It reached that figure by valuing the hardware at $131,250.00 and the software at $76,575.50, for a total of $207,826.50. The court then determined that the present value of the computer hardware, which Chatlos retained, was $6,000. Putting no value on the accepted payroll program, the court deducted the $6,000 and arrived at an award of $201,826.50 plus pre-judgment interest at the rate of 8 percent per annum from August 1975.

Chatlos contends before this court, as it had before the district court on remand, that under its benefit of the bargain theory the fair market value of the goods as warranted was several times the purchase price of $46,020. . . .

[T]he sole issue before us now is whether the district court erred in fixing the fair market value of the computer system as warranted at the time of the acceptance in August 1975 at $207,826.50.

II.

A.

I believe that the district court committed legal error. . . .

There are a number of major flaws in the plaintiff's attempt to prove damages in excess of the contract price. I commence with an analysis of plaintiff's basic theory. Chatlos presented its case under a theory that

income tax, and (6) cash receipts. The contract price also included installation.

3. Chatlos decided to lease the system rather than purchase it outright. To permit this arrangement, NCR sold the system to Mid Atlantic National Bank in July 1975 for $46,020, which leased the system to Chatlos. Chatlos made monthly payments to Mid Atlantic in amounts which would have totaled $70,162.09 over the period of the lease.

although, as a sophisticated purchaser, it bargained for several months before arriving at a decision on the computer system it required and the price of $46,020, it is entitled, because of the breach of warranty, to damages predicated on a considerably more expensive system. Stated another way, even if it bargained for a cheap system, i.e., one whose low cost reflects its inferior quality, because that system did not perform as bargained for, it is now entitled to damages measured by the value of a system which, although capable of performing the identical functions as the NCR 399, is of far superior quality and accordingly more expensive.

The statutory measure of damages for breach of warranty specifically provides that the measure is the difference at the time and place of acceptance between the value "of the goods accepted" and the "value they would have had if they had been as warranted." The focus of the statute is upon "the goods accepted"—not other hypothetical goods which may perform equivalent functions. "Moreover, the value to be considered is the reasonable market value of the *goods delivered*, not the value of the goods to a particular purchaser or for a particular purpose." KLPR TV, Inc. v. Visual Electronics Corp., 465 F.2d 1382, 1387 (8th Cir.1972) (emphasis added). The court, however, arrived at value on the basis of a hypothetical construction of a system as of December 1978 by the plaintiff's expert, Brandon. The court reached its value by working backward from Brandon's figures, adjusting for inflation.

* * *

Although NCR warranted performance, the failure of its equipment to perform, absent any evidence of the value of any NCR 399 system on which to base fair market value, does not permit a market value based on systems wholly unrelated to the goods sold. Yet, instead of addressing the fair market value of the NCR 399 had it been as warranted, Brandon addressed the fair market value of another system that he concocted by drawing on elements from other major computer systems manufactured by companies such as IBM, Burroughs, and Honeywell, which he considered would perform "functions identical to those contracted for" by Chatlos. He conceded that the systems were "[p]erhaps not within the same range of dollars that the bargain was involved with" and he did not identify specific packages of software. Brandon had no difficulty in arriving at the fair market value of the inoperable NCR equipment but instead of fixing a value on the system had it been operable attempted to fashion a hypothetical system on which he placed a value. The district court, in turn, erroneously adopted that value as the fair market value for an operable NCR 399 system. NCR rightly contends that the "comparable" systems on which Brandon drew were substitute goods of greater technological power and capability and not acceptable in determining damages for breach of warranty under section 2–714. Furthermore, Brandon's hypothetical system did not exist and its valuation was largely speculation.

B.

A review of Brandon's testimony reveals its legal inadequacy for establishing the market value of the system Chatlos purchased from NCR.

Brandon never testified to the fair market value which the NCR 399 system would have had had it met the warranty at the time of acceptance. . . .

Thus, the shortcomings in Brandon's testimony defy common sense and the realities of the marketplace. First, ordinarily, the best evidence of fair market value is what a willing purchaser would pay in cash to a willing seller. . . . In the instant case we have clearly "not . . . an unsophisticated consumer," . . . who for a considerable period of time negotiated and bargained with an experienced designer and vendor of computer systems. The price they agreed upon for an operable system would ordinarily be the best evidence of its value. The testimony does not present us with the situation referred to in our previous decision, where "the value of the goods rises between the time that the contract is executed and the time of acceptance," in which event the buyer is entitled to the benefit of his bargain. . . . On the contrary, Chatlos here relies on an expert who has indulged in the widest kind of speculation. Based on this testimony, Chatlos asserts in effect that a multi-national sophisticated vendor of computer equipment, despite months of negotiation, incredibly agreed to sell an operable computer system for $46,020 when, in fact, it had a fair market value of $207,000. . . .

Fourth, the record contains testimony which appears undisputed that computer equipment falls into one of several tiers, depending upon the degree of sophistication. The more sophisticated equipment has the capability of performing the functions of the least sophisticated equipment, but the less sophisticated equipment cannot perform all of the functions of those in higher levels. The price of the more technologically advanced equipment is obviously greater.

It is undisputed that in September 1976 there were vendors of computer equipment of the same general size as the NCR 399/656 with disc in the price range of $35,000 to $40,000 capable of providing the same programs as those required by Chatlos, including IBM, Phillips, and Burroughs. They were the very companies who competed for the sale of the computer in 1974 in the same price range. On the other hand, Chatlos' requirements could also be satisfied by computers available at "three levels higher in price and sophistication than the 399 disc." Each level higher would mean more sophistication, greater capabilities, and more memory. Greenstein, NCR's expert, testified without contradiction that equipment of Burroughs, IBM, and other vendors in the price range of $100,000 to $150,000, capable of performing Chatlos' requirements, was not comparable to the 399 because it was three levels higher. Such equipment was more comparable to the NCR 8400 series.

* * *

III.

The purpose of the N.J.S.A. 12A:2–714 is to put the buyer in the same position he would have been in if there had been no breach. See Uniform Commercial Code 1–106(1). The remedies for a breach of warranty were intended to compensate the buyer for his loss; they were not intended to give the purchaser a windfall or treasure trove. The buyer may not receive more than it bargained for; it may not obtain the value of a superior computer system which it did not purchase even though such a system can perform all of the functions the inferior system was designed to serve. ...

* * *

VI.

On this record, therefore, the damages to which plaintiff is entitled are $46,020 less $6,000, the fair market value at time of trial of the retained hardware, and less $1,000, the fair market value of the payroll program, or the net sum of $39,020.

Accordingly, I would reverse the judgment of the district court and direct it to enter judgment for the plaintiff in the sum of $39,020 with interest from the date of entry of the initial judgment at the rate allowed by state law.

After the decision by the panel, seller filed a petition for rehearing by the Court of Appeals *en banc*. The court declined to rehear the case. Three judges dissented from that decision. The following opinion expresses the views of the majority and minority in that determination.

SUR PETITION FOR REHEARING

The petition for rehearing filed by appellant in the above entitled case having been submitted to the judges who participated in the decision of this court and to all the other available circuit judges of the circuit in regular active service, and no judge who concurred in the decision having asked for rehearing, and a majority of the circuit judges of the circuit in regular active service not having voted for rehearing by the court in banc, the petition for rehearing is denied. Judges Adams, Hunter and Garth would grant the petition for rehearing.

■ ADAMS, CIRCUIT JUDGE, dissents from the denial of rehearing, and makes the following statement:

Ordinarily, an interpretation of state law by this Court, sitting in diversity, is not of sufficient consequence to warrant reconsideration by the Court sitting in banc. One reason is that if a federal court misconstrues the law of a state, the courts of that state have an opportunity, at some point, to reject the federal court's interpretation. See Chuy v. Philadelphia Eagles Football Club, 595 F.2d 1265, 1286–87 (3d Cir.1979) (in banc) (Aldisert, J., dissenting). In this case, however, the majority's holding, which endorses a measure of damages that is based on what appears to be a new interpretation of New Jersey's commercial law, involves a construction of the Uniform Commercial Code as well. Rectification of any error in our interpretation is, because of the national application of the Uniform Commercial Code, significantly more difficult than it would be if New Jersey law alone were implicated. Moreover, the provision of the Uniform Commercial Code involved here is of unusual importance: the measure of damages approved by this Court may create large monetary risks and obligations in a wide range of commercial transactions, including specifically the present burgeoning computer industry. Because there would appear to be considerable force to the dissenting opinion of Judge Rosenn and because I believe that the principle articulated by the majority should be reviewed by the entire Court before it is finally adopted, I would grant the petition for rehearing in banc.

■ JAMES HUNTER, III and GARTH CIRCUIT JUDGES join in this statement.

NOTES

(1) Benefit of the Bargain: What Was the Bargain? Was it reasonable for Chatlos to expect to receive goods worth five times the contract price? Should the price term be part of the "contract description" of goods sold? Consider Comment 7 to UCC 2–314: "In cases of doubt as to what quality is intended, the price at which a merchant closes a contract is an excellent index of the nature and scope of his obligation under the present section." Would it have been appropriate to probe more deeply into the probable expectations of the parties as to seller's obligation and buyer's remedy in the event that the computer system failed to perform? Should expectations as to (A) performance and (B) redress be considered in relation to each other? Are implied expectations as to redress less permissible that implied expectations as to performance, such as implied warranties of quality? Note that the court, in its earlier decision, gave full effect to the contract provision denying recovery for consequential damages. Does this shed light on the parties' allocation of the risks and benefits of the agreement?

(2) Parol Evidence Rule. In *Chatlos* and in *Royal Business Machines*, sellers were charged with liability for breach of oral statements made by their representatives. When contracts of sale are reduced to writing, frequently sellers include in the document a declaration that the document contains the complete agreement of the parties and that there are no promises or representations not contained therein. These "integration" clauses are meant to invoke the parol evidence rule, which for sales contracts is codified in UCC 2–202. In addition to barring evidence that would *contradict* a writing intended as a final expression of a sales agreement, paragraph (b) bars "consistent additional terms" if the court finds "the writing to have been intended also as a complete and exclusive statement of the terms of an agreement." The parol evidence rule, and its codified sales version, are complex legal issues normally studied in the course on Contracts.

Problem 3.3.5. An agreement was signed for the sale of air conditioning equipment to Buyer. The written contract contained detailed specifications concerning the type of equipment, the horsepower of the motors and the tons of refrigeration to be produced. The machinery met the contract specifications, but it was not sufficiently large or powerful to cool Buyer's building. Seller refused to take back the equipment, and pointed out that Buyer received an efficiently operating unit of precisely the size called for in the contract. Buyer tells his attorney that Seller had recommended the model and size, and had assured Buyer that it would cool Buyer's building. In preparing for trial, Buyer's attorney is concerned that Buyer's testimony with respect to the foregoing statements by Seller would be excluded under the parol evidence rule. The attorney asks you to develop a line of questions that would minimize this danger.

Examine carefully the language of UCC 2–202. Note that "term" is defined (UCC 1–201(42)) as "that portion of an agreement which relates to a particular matter." Compare UCC 1–201(3) ("agreement" is defined as "the bargain of the parties in fact as found in their language or *by implication from other circumstances* ...") with UCC 1–201(11) ("contract" means "the total legal obligation which results from the parties' agreement as affected by this Act and any other applicable rules of law"). Does UCC 2–202 exclude the above evidence if offered to establish an *implied* warranty?

(3) Lease Transactions. The "buyer" in *Chatlos* was actually a lessee. Because Chatlos lacked sufficient credit to purchase the computer system on an installment basis, an intermediary company bought the system from NCR and leased it to Chatlos. The courts treated Chatlos as a buyer for purposes of the litigation. In 1987, Article 2A on Leases was added to the UCC. Under UCC 2A–209(1), a seller's warranties to a lessor extend to the lessee if the lease is a "finance lease" (UCC 2A–103(1)(g)). This provision codifies the result in *Chatlos.*

The buyer of the copying machines in *Royal Business Machines* was an equipment lessor, but the lease was not a finance lease. As to its lessees, such a lessor's warranties of quality are provided in UCC 2A–210,–212, and–213. These sections parallel the warranty provisions in Article 2.

Hemmert Ag. Aviation, Inc. v. Mid–Continent Aircraft Corp.

United States District Court, District of Kansas, 1987.
663 F.Supp. 1546.

■ BROWN, J.

This is a diversity action wherein plaintiff seeks to revoke acceptance and to recover damages arising from its purchase of an agricultural spray plane from the defendant. After hearing the witnesses' testimony and counsels' arguments, examining the evidence and researching the law, the court makes the following findings of fact and conclusions of law as required by Fed.R.Civ.P. 52.

FINDINGS OF FACT

1.   Hemmert Agricultural Aviation, Inc. ("Hemmert Ag"), is a Kansas corporation engaged in the business of agricultural spraying, primarily commercial crop dusting and fertilizer application. Hemmert Ag generally operates within a forty mile radius of Oakley, Kansas, and its typical spray season runs from the first of May until the middle of September each year.

2.   Mark Hemmert (Hemmert) is the President and sole stockholder of Hemmert Ag. He is presently 31 years old. He has fifteen years of general flying experience and approximately ten years of agricultural spraying experience. He personally does most of the flying for Hemmert Ag, but occasionally other pilots and planes are hired on a temporary basis.

3.   Defendant, Mid–Continent Aircraft Corporation (Mid–Continent), is a Missouri corporation in Hayti, Missouri, engaged in the business of commercial crop dusting and aircraft sales. Mid–Continent is an authorized dealer of Ag–Cat spray planes. Ag–Cat spray planes were initially manufactured by Grumman, but the current manufacturer is Schweizer Aircraft Corporation.

4.   Richard Reade is the President and principal stockholder of Mid-Continent.

5.   In 1980, Hemmert purchased a 1977 used "B" model Schweizer Ag–Cat. This plane was the trade-in when the plane in issue was purchased. This 1977 "B" had a 300 gallon hopper and a larger tail and vertical fin than the Model G–164B Ag–Cat 600 Super "B" plane (Super "B"), which is the plane in issue. The Super "B" had a 400 gallon hopper and a raised upper wing. From reading advertisements and talking with Reade, Hemmert believed the raised wing on the Super "B" made it faster and more maneuverable and improved visibility. Terrell Kirk, an engineer and test pilot with Schweizer, testified the raised wing was primarily for visibility purposes.

6.   In 1984, Hemmert called Mid–Continent, as he was interested in trading in his 1977 "B" Ag Cat for a new and bigger plane, Super "B".

7.   In August 1985, Hemmert again contacted Mid–Continent, in particular Richard Reade, about purchasing the Super "B". While satisfied with the performance of his 1977 "B" Ag Cat, he had been having a good year and wanted a plane that was faster to the field, more maneuverable and more productive. Hemmert's trade-in was in good condition other than needing some routine maintenance. Hemmert purchased the Super "B" believing it would make his work easier, safer and more profitable. ...

8.   Hemmert's belief that a Super "B" was more maneuverable than his 1977 Ag–Cat "B" was based in part on an advertisement for the 450 "B" ..., which stated in part: "New raised wing design means more maneuverability; more visibility; more speed." The 450 "B" described in [the advertisement] differs from the Super "B" 600 hp. only in horsepower,

hopper size, and length (4 inches). In fact, ... a Schweizer advertisement brochure stamped with defendant's name and address, explains the Super "B" is powered by either a 450 or 600 horsepower engine. The 450 "B" is identical to the 600 hp. Super "B" in almost all relevant respects, except for engine size and hopper capacity.

9.   Hemmert testified that during the telephone conversation in early August 1985, Richard Reade represented the Super "B" to be faster, more maneuverable, and having better visibility than his 1977 Ag–Cat "B". Reade denied that these representations were made and stated that he only represented the Super "B" as more productive.

10.   The parties struck their bargain over the telephone on August 6, 1985. ... The plane was sold to plaintiff for $128,000.00 total, $75,500.00 in cash plus Hemmert's trade-in. ...

12.   ... Ed Zeeman, a ferry pilot, delivered the Super "B" to Hemmert Ag in Oakley, Kansas, on August 20, 1985. Zeeman arrived in Oakley late in the afternoon, and he was in a hurry to return that afternoon with plaintiff's trade-in.

* * *

16.   Prior to August 6, 1985, Hemmert had not flown the particular Super "B" he purchased nor flown any Super "B". Hemmert made no inquiries to other spray pilots who were using a Super "B". Reade acknowledged that it is not unusual for agricultural spray planes to be sold before the purchaser has actually flown them.

17.   On August 20, 1985, the actual delivery date, Hemmert called Reade saying he was happy but that [certain optional equipment was] not on the aircraft. [Mid–Continent subsequently delivered these items.] Hemmert never had these options installed even though they had arrived and Mid–Continent had agreed to pay the installation cost.

18.   Around August 23, 1985, Hemmert flew the Super "B" with a small load of water in an effort to calibrate the spraying system. Hemmert noticed that the shut-off valve was not developing adequate "suck back" to shut off the flow of water. After his adjustments failed to correct the situation, Hemmert called Reade and told him the valve was defective. Read said a new valve would be sent and it could be installed at Mid–Continent's expense.

19.   At about the same time, Hemmert complained about the performance of the Super "B". Hemmert noted that the plane was unresponsive in pitch, rolled excessively to the right, and lost air speed in turns, giving the pilot the sensation that the aircraft was "falling out from under him." Reade suggested the performance problems could be simply due to a bad engine. Hemmert said he was not satisfied and instructed Reade not to sell his trade-in. Reade represented that the trade-in had been sold. While the sale of the trade-in was not completed until September 6, 1985, at the time of Reade's representation to plaintiff there was an outstanding offer on the plane.

20. When the second spray valve arrived within a couple of days of August 23, 1985, plaintiff and an airport mechanic installed the second valve which also proved to be defective. When Hemmert called Reade about the defective second valve, Reade said additional valves would be sent until an operative one was found.

21. Reade directed Dan Westbrook, a mechanic with Mid–Continent, to drive to Oakley, Kansas, and to replace the engine.... On or about August 26, 1985, Westbrook checked over the plane and replaced the engine. Westbrook then flew the plane empty for 30–40 minutes. Westbrook detected nothing glaringly wrong with the plane's flight characteristics. He believed the plane "flew well" and that it had a "personality of its own."

22. Still dissatisfied with the plane's flight characteristics, Hemmert contacted four other agricultural spray pilots and asked them to fly the Super "B". Each of these four spray pilots were highly experienced, but none had previously flown a Super "B". Each pilot flew the plane before Hemmert related any of his negative feelings regarding the plane. The four spray pilots were Jim Bussen of Sharon Springs, Kansas; Steven Kistler of Colby, Kansas; Kelly Henry of Augusta, Kansas; and Ken Bixeman of Colby, Kansas.

23. Bussen owned a Grumman Ag–Cat with a small fin. He test flew the Super "B" empty and it felt heavy and like it wanted to drop out beneath him. Bussen commented the Super "B" did not turn like his old Ag–Cat. He did not feel safe in the Super "B" and expected it to fly better. The Super "B" was then loaded with 200 gallons of water and Bussen flew it. He said it felt "scary" and that it did not climb like it should have. It took him twice the radius to make the turns and any steep turns caused the feeling of an imminent stall. He said the plaintiff's Super "B" flew "too much differently" to be termed just the personal characteristics of the plane.

24. Kistler flew the Super "B" once for 30–40 minutes with an empty hopper. Kistler's prior experience with Ag–Cats did not include the "big fin" B models. Kistler flew the plane making maneuvers similar to those in spraying a field. He never felt comfortable in the Super "B" as its power drained on right turns. The Super "B" flew seriously different from other Ag–Cats, creating the sensation that it could stall any moment in a turn. He also testified that the Super "B" 's tail configuration resembled that of the "A" models which he had flown.

25. Bixeman and Henry experienced the same sensation of the plane's falling out from underneath them when they flew the Super "B". Henry testified that he had to make wider, easy turns with Super "B" which took extra time. At that point, Henry repeated the appropriate aphorism: "Time is money." Based upon the advertising literature that he had seen, Henry expected the Super "B" to be highly maneuverable.

26. Mark Hemmert also talked with Charles Dykes, an experienced agricultural spray pilot from Coy, Arkansas. He has fourteen Ag–Cat

models including three Super "B" 's. Dykes has never seen nor flown plaintiff's Super "B". When Dykes got his first Super "B" he grew "sick of it", as it did not respond like any other Ag–Cat spray plane that he had owned or flown. At first, Dykes was very unhappy and was scared the first couple of times. After 40–50 hours flying, he started to become accustomed to the Super "B", and after 75 hours flying, he loved his Super "B". Dykes now uses his Super "B" 's to spray fields of much smaller acreages than the fields generally located in Western Kansas. Dykes told Hemmert to "stick with" the Super "B" and he would discover that it was a good plane.

27.   Reade next arranged for Terrill Kirk, chief test pilot for Schweizer Company, to go to Oakley, Kansas, and check out plaintiff's Super "B". Kirk has an engineering degree and has flight tested twelve different models of Ag–Cats. He did all the flight testing necessary for type certification from the Federal Aviation Administration. Kirk has no experience as a commercial agricultural spray pilot. When Kirk arrived in Oakley, he first had Hemmert explain the flying characteristics of the Super "B". Kirk then checked several measurements on the plane. Kirk next flew the plane empty, experiencing nothing unusual and finding it to be a "typical good Ag–Cat." The plane was then loaded with 270–280 gallons of water, and Kirk flew it, noting a tendency for the plane to roll into right hand turns. Kirk testified that this phenomenon could be called a stall, but that it was actually caused by pilot technique in using too much rudder. Kirk considered that technique to be a carryover from flying the big-fin "B" models like plaintiff's trade-in. Kirk thought plaintiff's Super "B" "handled good and flew well." Kirk then observed Hemmert flying the Super "B" and remarked that Hemmert made abrupt maneuvers and advised him to stop "cowboying" the plane and to try smoother turns. Kirk believed pilot technique for flying the Super "B" differs from that used on previous models.

28.   Hemmert is dissatisfied with his Super "B" and has lost his confidence in it. Each pilot that testified at trial acknowledged that a spray pilot's confidence in his aircraft is very important. Because of a spray pilot's maneuvers close to the ground, his confidence is extremely essential.

29.   In the Spring of 1986, Hemmert purchased another Ag–Cat, a 1982 600 horsepower "B" plus. This model did not have a raised wing design as found on the Super "B". Hemmert paid $78,000.00 for this plane and is still using it.

30.   Hemmert was never satisfied with the Super "B". On October 30, 1985, Hemmert's attorney sent a certified letter notifying Mid–Continent of Mr. Hemmert's intent to revoke acceptance of the Super "B" under the Uniform Commercial Code. Reade admitted the plaintiff's complaints in that letter were not new to him.

CONCLUSIONS OF LAW

1.   The Court has jurisdiction over the parties and has subject matter jurisdiction pursuant to 28 U.S.C. Sec. 1332 by reason of diversity of citizenship and the requisite amount in controversy.

2.   The parties have stipulated that the law of Kansas is to be applied. This is a sale of goods governed by the Kansas Uniform Commercial Code, K.S.A. 84–2–102, et seq. . . .

3.   Plaintiff seeks to employ the remedy of revocation of acceptance set forth at K.S.A. 84–2–608: . . . To revoke acceptance is to refuse the delivered goods after they have been accepted and after the time for their rejection has run. . . . While a buyer may nominally reject for any defect, acceptance cannot be revoked absent a substantial nonconformity. The purpose of this remedy is to restore the buyer to the economic status quo which would have been enjoyed if the goods had not been delivered. . . .

4.   Notice. K.S.A. 84–2–608(2) (hereinafter 2–608) requires revocation to occur within a reasonable time after the buyer discovers or should have discovered the grounds for it. What is a reasonable time is obviously a function of circumstances. Typically, the notice of revocation will be given after the general notice of breach required under K.S.A. 84–2–607(3)(a), as the purchaser's wish to revoke is frequently the last resort after the seller's attempts to cure have failed. Because one purpose behind the notice provisions is to allow the seller the chance to cure, the outer limits of the reasonable time period should be flexible to encourage both the buyer and seller to cooperate in an effort to cure. See Murray v. Holiday Rambler, Inc., 83 Wis. 2d 406, 265 N.W.2d 513, 24 U.C.C. Rep. 52, 67–68 (1978); Official Comment 4 to 2–608. Similarly, if the seller continuously assures the buyer that the defects will be remedied, the notice period should be accordingly suspended.

Plaintiff gave notice of revocation within a reasonable time. Plaintiff properly relied on defendant's assurances that any defects would be corrected, and on defendant's subsequent efforts to cure. Hemmert promptly discovered the defects and immediately advised Reade of his complaints.

5.   Elements of Revocation Remedy. . . . As discussed more fully later in this order, the primary issue in this case is whether a substantial impairment exists when the plane's handling characteristics create fear and apprehension in the pilot for the first 50 hours of flying during the execution of maneuvers considered normal for other models of Ag–Cat planes. Substantial impairment is not defined in the Uniform Commercial Code. What constitutes a substantial impairment is considered to be a common sense determination. . . . Kansas courts have followed the interpretation of other courts and have given substantial impairment both a subjective and an objective element. [T]he Kansas Supreme Court adopted the two-step inquiry found in Jorgensen v. Pressnall, 274 Ore. 285, 545 P.2d 1382, 1384–1385 (1976), which is:

> Since ORS 72.6080(1) provides that the buyer may revoke acceptance of goods "whose nonconformity substantially impairs its value to him," the value of conforming goods to the plaintiff must first be determined. This is a subjective question in the sense that it calls for a consideration of the needs and circumstances of the plaintiff who seeks to revoke; not the needs and circumstances of an average buyer. The second inquiry is whether the nonconformity in fact substantially

impairs the value of the goods to the buyer, having in mind his particular needs. This is an objective question in the sense that it calls for evidence of something more than plaintiff's assertion that the nonconformity impaired the value to him; it requires evidence from which it can be inferred that plaintiff's needs were not met because of the nonconformity. In short, the nonconformity must substantially impair the value of the goods to the plaintiff buyer. The existence of substantial impairment depends upon the facts and circumstances in each case. (Emphasis in original.) . . .

Leading commentators have noted:

The only element of objectivity the Jorgensen court required was evidence from which it could be inferred that the buyer's needs were not met because of the nonconformity; that evidence must be something more than the buyer's mere assertion of substantial impairment. The language of cases like Jorgensen, coupled with the subjective phrase "to him" in Section 2–608 and official Comment 2 to that section, gives an aggrieved buyer a strong argument that he has the right to revoke acceptance because of his special sensitivity to the breach of warranty, even though the defects would be considered insubstantial to the average buyer.

Clark and Smith, The Law of Product Warranties, Para. 7.03(3)(a)(1984). While the evidence in this case establishes that not just Hemmert experienced discomfort and fear from the handling characteristics of the Super "B", if Hemmert's sensitivity to the Super "B" had been unique and there had been objective evidence that his needs were not met, revocation would still be consistent with the purpose and interpretation of 2–608. In considering the subjective element, the courts have employed a term, "shaken faith." In determining whether value was substantially impaired, the courts have weighed the cost of repairs, the inconvenience resulting from the nonconformities, and the entire impact the defects had on the buyer's confidence in the goods purchased. Wallach, Buyer's Remedies, 20 Washburn L.J. 20, 34 (1980). Lost confidence has been adopted by a number of courts and labelled as the "shaken faith" doctrine. Where the buyer's confidence in the dependability of the machine is shaken because of the defects and possibly because of seller's ineffective attempts to cure, revocation appears justified. . . .

6.   Nonconformities. A nonconformity includes breaches of warranties (implied and express) as well as any failure of the seller to perform pursuant to his contractual obligation. . . . An express warranty is created by any representation of fact or promise that relates to the goods and becomes a basis of the bargain. K.S.A. 84–2–313. . . . Advertising may form a part of an express warranty. . . . The advertisement for the 450 "B" . . . closely relates to the plane purchased by plaintiff and was relied upon by plaintiff in his decision to purchase the Super "B". Plaintiff reasonably inferred that the advertising representations for the 450 "B" were applicable to the 600 horsepower version that he purchased. The court finds an

express warranty that the Super "B", because of the raised wing design, was more maneuverable and offered better visibility and more speed.

In light of that advertisement and plaintiff's reliance on the same, the court believes that Hemmert did ask Reade if the Super "B" was more maneuverable and faster and that Reade made some representations that assured Hemmert in a reasonable manner that these qualities existed. Defendant expressly warranted that the Super "B" was more maneuverable and faster than former models of Ag–Cat spray planes.

* * *

7. Plaintiff has sustained its burden in establishing nonconformities. The handling characteristics which created fear and apprehension in plaintiff and other experienced spray pilots were directly contrary to express representations of maneuverability and speed. There being no question that Mid–Continent is a merchant as defined at K.S.A. 84–2–104(1), the Super "B" is in breach of the implied warranty of merchantability. Plaintiff has proven that the Super "B" it purchased cannot pass without objection to its handling characteristics in normal turning maneuvers in spraying fields. In a trade as hazardous as crop dusting, a pilot would not reasonably accept without objection a plane that takes some 50 hours of flight time before the pilot's unusual fears and concerns about the particular plane are allayed. This conclusion is particularly appropriate where neither the seller nor manufacturer cautions the purchaser that the particular model handles significantly different from other Ag–Cats.

* * *

9. Substantial Impairment. The relevant law regarding this question has been previously discussed. Plaintiff has proven a substantial impairment. His lost confidence in the Super "B" caused by its handling characteristics, which scare experienced pilots in making normal spraying maneuvers, amounts to a substantial impairment. A spray pilot's activities are considered dangerous in flying at very low altitudes and quickly maneuvering to apply sprays and to avoid obstacles. Undeniably, a spray pilot's confidence in his plane is absolutely crucial. Mr. Dykes' endurance of his "unhappiness" and fear for the first fifty hours of flying the Super "B" does not mean that the same fears and dissatisfaction experienced by Hemmert are not a substantial impairment of value. A pilot's confidence and willingness to undertake dangerous spraying maneuvers in a plane is reasonably destroyed when the pilot consistently experiences the sensation that the plane is about to "fall out from under him" when making normal spraying turns. Similarly, it is unreasonable to expect someone to endure his fears and otherwise operate the plane in his normal spraying business for those fifty hours. A seller's subsequent assurance that the buyer need only modify his flying technique and the sensations will no longer occur is understandably ineffective in rekindling a purchaser's confidence in a plane that he believed would be more maneuverable and faster. These nonconformities substantially impair the value of the Super "B" to plaintiff. The testimony of the four spray pilots and Dykes is evidence other than

plaintiff's assertion which sustains an inference that plaintiff's needs are not met by the Super "B".

* * *

11.   Remedy. When a buyer rightfully revokes his acceptance, he may recover pursuant to K.S.A. 84–2–711 a refund of the purchase price paid and incidental and consequential damages, which may include expenses reasonably incurred in inspection, receipt, transportation and care and custody of goods and any other commercially reasonable charge or expense in effecting cover or caused by delay or other breach. The buyer is also entitled to prejudgment interest from the date that revocation is attempted.
. . .

IT IS THEREFORE ORDERED that judgment is entered in favor of plaintiff and against defendant, and defendant is herein ordered to pay plaintiff the sum of $159,314.14, which are those damages set forth in plaintiff's exhibit 10 modifying the prejudgment interest to commence on September 30, 1985. Upon payment of the entire judgment, plaintiff shall make the Super "B" available upon one week's notice for defendant to pick up the Super "B" at the plaintiff's place of business in Oakley, Kansas.

NOTES

(1) **Substantial Impairment of Value to the Buyer.** Since the right to revoke acceptance under UCC 2–608 is conditioned upon the existence of a non-conformity that substantially impairs the value of the goods to the buyer, there are three steps to the application of this section. Analysis must begin with the criteria of conforming goods. When revocation of acceptance is made on the basis of the quality of the goods, the measure of conformity may be found in express or implied warranties of quality. What warranties of quality did the court find had been breached in *Hemmert Agricultural Aviation*? Was it necessary for the court to cite more than the express warranty?

Analysis must begin with warranties, but UCC 2–608 does not allow a buyer to revoke acceptance for mere breach of warranty. The breach must be of a certain severity, indicated by the substantial impairment term. Did the court in *Hemmert Agricultural Aviation* find, correctly, that the non-conformities in the Super "B" were grave enough to cause substantial impairment of the plane's value? Do the Comments to UCC 2–608 provide any assistance to understanding the meaning of "substantially impairs its value"?

The third element in the analysis is the meaning of the statutory phrase, "to him." The phrase clearly introduces an element of subjectivity to the measurement of the impairment of value. Comment 2 suggests that the legislative intent was to give weight to a buyer's particular circumstances even though the seller did not know of them at the time of the sales contract. Cf. 2–315. How did the court in *Hemmert Agricultural Aviation* deal with the subjective-objective aspect of UCC 2–608 in the context of that case?

(2) Time and Manner of Revocation of Acceptance. Revocation of acceptance occurs when buyers give notice of it to the sellers.[7] UCC 2–608(2). The UCC provides that buyers must give notice "within a reasonable time" after they discover or should have discovered the ground; the time is defined in part by nature of the unsatisfactory quality of the goods. In goods bought for use rather than resale, the unsatisfactory quality may become manifest only after the goods have been used for some time. Was Hemmert Ag's notice timely under this standard?

In many transactions, before buyers elect to revoke acceptance, they complain to the sellers. Sellers, whether or not required by their contracts to try to repair the conditions complained of, often do attempt to satisfy the buyers. Should such events have a bearing on the timeliness of buyers' decision to revoke acceptance? Is there any statutory basis for tolling the running of the "reasonable time" during this period?

The answer may lie, in part, in the two situations in which buyers may revoke acceptance. Sometimes buyers accept goods with full knowledge of their nonconformities because they are assured by the sellers that the nonconformities will be "cured." ("Cure" is a statutory concept, defined in UCC 2–508.) That situation is addressed in UCC 2–608(1)(a). Reasonableness of the time of notice of revocation of acceptance must take into account sellers' unsuccessful efforts to "cure." The second situation deals with nonconformities that manifest themselves after buyers acceptance. "Cure" is not a statutory factor in later-discovered nonconformities, but buyers often allow sellers to try to overcome the nonconformities. Is there any reading of the "reasonable time" requirement in UCC 2–608(2) that would not penalize buyers who allow these efforts to be made?

Buyers are not required to offer to hand back the goods to effect a revocation of acceptance. Buyers who have paid part or all of the price have security interests in the goods that entitle them to keep the goods and, if necessary, to sell them to recover the price paid. UCC 2–711(3), 2–608(3). Note how buyer's security interest was handled by the court's order in *Hemmert Agricultural Aviation.*

(3) Legal Actions Following Revocation of Acceptance. A buyer's decision to revoke its acceptance of goods is entirely within the buyer's control, but to obtain effective relief buyers are often required to follow up notice of revocation of acceptance with legal action against their sellers. Buyers who have paid all or part of the price may seek to recover those sums from the sellers. Even if, as in *Hemmert Agricultural Aviation,* buyer has a security interest in goods held following revocation, buyer may elect not to resell the goods and may choose instead to sue the seller (and others). What might induce buyers to seek recovery through litigation

---

7. This is by inference from the actual language of the UCC, which states that a revocation is "not effective until" a buyer gives notice. UCC 2–608(2).

rather than by self-help relief through foreclosures of their security interests? See UCC 2–711(1).

(4) Buyers' Monetary Remedies After Revocation of Acceptance. UCC 2–608(3) incorporates the "rights" applicable to rejection of goods, which include the right to seek monetary relief. UCC 2–711 allows buyers that justifiably revoke acceptance to recover "so much of the price as has been paid," plus expectation damages under UCC 2–712 or 2–713.[8] These are determined by an actual "cover" transaction or a potential market transaction whereby the buyer obtains or could obtain replacement goods. Both of those provisions allow recovery of incidental and consequential damages under UCC 2–715. Often, it appears, buyers are satisfied to get their money back and be rid of a deal that went bad. Some buyers, however, seek more than recovery of the price. The opinion of the court in *Hemmert Agricultural Aviation* does not recite the elements of buyer's claim for damages, but rather orders that seller pay a substantial sum, in excess of the sales price.

(5) Buyers' Use of the Goods After Revocation of Acceptance. Notice of revocation of acceptance is a declaration that the goods belong to the seller. Often, however, buyers continue to use the goods if the nonconformities are not wholly disabling. UCC 2–608 has no provision that allows buyers to go on using goods after revocation of acceptance. Rather UCC 2–608(3) incorporates the "duties" applicable to rejection of goods, which include the prohibition, in UCC 2–602(2)(a), of "any exercise of ownership" and the duty, under UCC 2–602(2)(b), "to hold" the goods for the seller. Without legislative basis, many courts have found nonetheless that buyers' continued use of goods after revocation of acceptance is not inconsistent with their revocations. See McCullough v. Bill Swad Chrysler–Plymouth, Inc., 5 Ohio St.3d 181, 449 N.E.2d 1289 (1983). The genesis of a rule that allows "reasonable use" is found in the judicial recognition that some buyers, having paid for the goods, have no practical alternative and that their predicaments are not of their making.

At the same time, courts are sometimes unwilling to allow buyers to use goods without charge. In Johnson v. General Motors Corp., 233 Kan. 1044, 668 P.2d 139 (1983), the buyers of a 1979 Chevrolet pick-up truck, after extended and unsuccessful attempts at repair, notified GM that they revoked acceptance and thereafter drove the truck an additional 14,619 miles. The court awarded the buyers a judgment for return of the price less an offset for the value of their use of the truck. In fixing the offset the court relied on a Federal Highway Administration Booklet, "Cost of Owning and Operating Automobiles and Vans 1982." How would the cost of operation compare with rental costs?[9]

---

8. If the buyer "covers," damages are determined by the reasonable price paid. In other cases, damages are measured by the market value of the goods.

9. The proposed revision of Article 2 contains a new subsection on buyers' use of goods after revocation o acceptance. See Proposed Revised 2–508(d). The subsection permits use that is "reasonable under the circumstances" but obligates buyers to pay "the value of the use to the buyer."

(6) Sellers' Right to Cure After Revocation of Acceptance. We noted above that the UCC allows sellers to "cure" nonconformities, UCC 2–508, but the right to cure in that section arises when a buyer rejects goods at the time the seller tenders delivery of them. The UCC has no provision that gives sellers a right to cure after revocation of acceptance. Some courts have held, nonetheless, that there is a post-revocation right to cure, but other courts have disagreed. Compare, e.g., Fitzner Pontiac–Buick–Cadillac, Inc. v. Smith, 523 So.2d 324 (Miss.1988) (recognizing a right to cure) with Gappelberg v. Landrum, 666 S.W.2d 88 (Tex.1984)(no right to cure).

––––––––

Consequential Damages. A problem of large importance in sales transactions is the scope of sellers' liability for buyers' consequential damages. The legal issue is related to general contract law growing out of *Hadley v. Baxendale*.[10] The common-law principle is codified in the UCC at UCC 2–715(2).

Within the context of sales transactions, buyers may suffer many types of consequential damages resulting from non-conformity of goods purchased. However, certain categories of damages tend to arise regularly. Merchants buying inventory may suffer consequential damages in the form of lost revenues. Such a claim was advanced in *Sidco* and may explain the large amount of the compensatory damages awarded by the trial court in *Royal Business Machines*. Persons buying business equipment may incur expenses coping with the fall-out of the equipment's failure. Such a claim was advanced in *Chatlos*. Farmers buying seeds or herbicides may suffer damages in crop failures. We will see such cases later in this Chapter.

A quite different set of consequential losses arises when buyers suffer personal injuries as a result of defects in the goods. This branch of warranty law has become integrally related to the law of strict tort liability and other facets of product liability law. We will consider this issue, along with others, in the later part of this Chapter devoted to special laws of consumer protection.

Carnation Company v. Olivet Egg Ranch

Court of Appeal of California, 1986.First Appellate District, Division Two.
189 Cal.App.3d 809, 229 Cal.Rptr. 261.

■ KLINE, J.

Olivet Egg Ranch [Olivet] ... appeal[s] following jury trial on [its] claims of fraud and breach of various warranties arising out of [its]

––––––––

10. A remarkable study of *Hadley v. Baxendale* discloses that the case, as decided, was not a contract case. See R. Danzig, *Had-* *ley v. Baxendale*: A Study in the Industrialization of the Law, 4 J. Legal Studies 249 (1975).

purchase and use of chicken feed produced by the Albers Milling Division of the Carnation Company [Albers].

* * *

[Olivet] ... controlled and managed an egg producing operation in Northern California.

For approximately five years, Olivet or its predecessors in interest purchased chickenfeed from Albers, which operated a mill in Santa Rosa. After unsuccessfully seeking payment of its bills, Carnation advised appellants they would no longer be allowed to purchase on credit. Appellants executed a note for the $606,382 balance owed to Carnation. When appellants defaulted on the note Carnation commenced this litigation. Appellants cross-complained on various theories, all premised on their assertion that the feed sold them was "misformulated, mis-produced and nutritionally substandard" and, therefore, breached a variety of express and implied warranties made to appellants by Carnation and its employees. Appellants alleged that the feed's nutritional deficiencies had caused a decrease in Olivet's egg production revenues and sought to offset such losses against the amount due Carnation on the note.

After lengthy pretrial discovery, jury trial commenced in October 1979. Because the execution and terms of the note were uncontested, appellants proceeded as if plaintiffs and presented their case first. At the conclusion of Olivet's case Carnation successfully moved for nonsuit as to the loss of goodwill portion of Olivet's damage claim. The court granted a nonsuit on goodwill damages as to the breach of warranty causes of action only on the theory appellants had not met their burden of proving, under California Uniform Commercial Code section 2715, that they had made reasonable efforts to mitigate the damages flowing from the loss of their retail egg marketing accounts.

At the close of evidence Carnation was granted a directed verdict as to a portion of the damages suffered by Olivet's predecessor in interest in 1970.

The jury found that Carnation had breached its warranties and damaged Olivet in the amount of $225,000, but that the claim of fraudulent misrepresentation had not been established.

Separate judgments for both parties were entered and Olivet moved for a new trial on various grounds. ... The court denied the motion for new trial, granted a motion to vacate the two previously entered judgments and ordered nunc pro tunc entry of the net judgment after verdict. This appeal followed.

I.

Burden of Proof Under California Uniform Commercial Code Section 2715, subdivision (2)(a)

The nonsuit as to the $309,000 loss in goodwill appellants claimed due to their inability to service their egg marketing accounts[3] was granted upon the theory that California Uniform Commercial Code section 2715, subdivision (2)(a) places on the aggrieved party the burden of showing it took reasonable steps to mitigate its consequential damages. In granting nonsuit the court necessarily determined that, as a matter of law, Olivet failed to present evidence sufficient to meet its burden. It will be necessary to consider whether Olivet presented evidence sufficient to withstand nonsuit on this issue only if we first determine that the court's imposition of the burden on Olivet was legally correct. Olivet could not be penalized for failing to meet a burden which actually rested with Carnation. Thus, we are squarely faced with a question of first impression in California: which party bears the burden of proving the adequacy or inadequacy of efforts to mitigate consequential damages under California Uniform Commercial Code section 2715, subdivision (2)(a)?

Section 2715, subdivision (2)(a), which was adopted without change from the Uniform Commercial Code (UCC), simply declares that "[c]onsequential damages resulting from the seller's breach include ... [a]ny loss resulting from general or particular requirements and needs of which the seller at the time of contracting had reason to know and which could not reasonably be prevented by cover or otherwise."

The official comment to the parallel provision of the UCC does not shed much light on allocation of the burden of proof. Paragraph 2 of the pertinent UCC comment provides in material part that: "The 'tacit agreement' test for the recovery of consequential damages is rejected. Although the older rule at common law which made the seller liable for all consequential damages of which he had 'reason to know' in advance is followed, the liberality of that rule is modified by refusing to permit recovery unless the buyer could not reasonably have prevented the loss by cover or otherwise. Subparagraph (2) [of the statute] carries forward the provision of the prior uniform statutory provision as to consequential damages resulting from breach of warranty, but modifies the rule by requiring first that the buyer attempt to minimize his damages in good faith, either by cover or otherwise." This comment does not demonstrate, as respondent asserts, that section 2715, subdivision (2)(a) was intended to act as "a restraint on the liberality of the common law."

---

3. Olivet had an arrangement with several large supermarket chains pursuant to which the markets invested in the ranch partnership and purchased all of their requirements directly from the ranch at a retail price. Olivet was thereby provided with an assured outlet for its eggs and was to derive a profit for the processing and marketing, as well as the egg sale. Due to Olivet's shortfall in egg production, it ultimately was unable to keep up with the requirements of its market accounts and Olivet transferred the accounts to Olson Egg Farms. Appellants claimed the loss of the goodwill value of the retail marketing arm of its operation as an additional element of damages.

The nonsuit was granted only as to the loss of goodwill attributable to the claimed breach of warranty. Because the burden of proof on mitigation as to the fraud cause of action is on the party asserting the defense, the court ruled that the issue remained in the case as to that claim.

Paragraph 4 of the UCC comment makes specific reference to the UCC's section on the liberal administration of remedies, indicating that the right to consequential damages should be broadly, not narrowly, construed. Furthermore, while paragraph 4 states that "[t]he burden of proving the extent of loss incurred by way of consequential damage is on the buyer ..." this statement does not determine the allocation of the burden of proof on the mitigation issue. It is entirely possible for the injured party to bear the burden of proving the extent of consequential damages while the breaching party has the duty of proving those items which limit the award of consequential damages.

The UCC's failure to allocate unambiguously the burden of proving mitigation has resulted in conflicting interpretations among those jurisdictions that have considered the question. Unfortunately, these cases are of little value to us since they do not analyze the problem nor explain why the burden should rest with one party or the other. By and large the cases merely state the unembellished conclusion that one or the other party has the burden of proof on this issue.

* * *

While the commentators do not unanimously support allocating the burden to the breaching party, there is substantial support among them for this position. Corbin, for example, declares that "[t]he burden of proving that losses could have been avoided by reasonable effort and expense must always be borne by the party who has broken the contract." (5 Corbin on Contracts (1964) § 1039 ...) White and Summers state that "consequential damages that the *defendant* proves the buyer could have avoided will not be allowed ..." (J. White and R. Summers, Uniform Commercial Code (2d ed. 1980) §§ 6–7, p. 250, italics added.) ...

Placing on the party who breaches the burden of showing that consequential losses could have been avoided is intuitively attractive, since proof that there has been a failure to mitigate adequately will reduce the damages awarded and, therefore, seems more in the nature of a defense than an element of the plaintiff's affirmative case. In this sense, proof of failure to mitigate is analogous to evidence showing comparative negligence in tort law, which must be alleged and proved by the defendant. ... Moreover, it is sensible to require the defendant to prove those items which go to reduce the plaintiff's recovery, as plaintiffs would have little incentive to do so.

Respondent maintains that "[i]t makes more sense to place the burden of proving efforts to mitigate on the party best able to adduce evidence of such efforts." While this argument is on its surface appealing it does not stand up to closer scrutiny. As has been noted "[v]ery often one must plead and prove matters as to which his adversary has superior access to the proof. Nearly all required allegations of the plaintiff in actions for tort or breach of contract relating to the defendant's acts or omissions describe matters peculiarly in the defendant's knowledge. Correspondingly, when the defendant is required to plead contributory negligence, he pleads facts specially known to the plaintiff." (McCormick on Evidence (3d ed. 1984) ch. 36, § 337 at p. 950.)

Moreover, in cases such as this defendants do not genuinely lack the ability to ascertain the pertinent facts. A carefully drafted set of interrogatories could have provided Carnation with all the information it required about Olivet's efforts to mitigate its consequential damages. Since it therefore had access to the relevant evidence we see no reason why this consideration should prevent allocation to Carnation of the burden of showing that appellants failed to adequately mitigate their consequential damages.

For the foregoing reasons, we hold that while the burden of proving the extent of loss incurred by way of consequential damages rests with the injured party, section 2715, subdivision (2)(a) imposes upon the allegedly breaching party the burden of proving the inadequacy of efforts to mitigate consequential damages. Thus, Carnation, not Olivet, properly had the burden of proof on the issue of Olivet's mitigation of the consequential damages arising from Carnation's breach. Olivet therefore had no duty to present evidence of mitigation and the granting of the nonsuit on the basis of Olivet's asserted failure to produce such evidence was error. The nonsuit removed from the jury's consideration a $309,000 damage claim. Since Carnation never presented evidence on this issue there is no way of knowing whether appellants likely would have prevailed if the court had placed the burden of proof on Carnation. Accordingly, the judgment must be reversed.

* * *

■ ROUSE, J., and SMITH, J., concurred.

INTERNATIONAL SALES LAW

Having considered sellers' obligations for the quality of their goods under domestic United States law, we turn to the analogous provisions of the Convention on Contracts for International Sales of Goods (CISG).

(1) Sellers' Obligations. The Convention sets forth sellers' quality obligations in Section II of Chapter II. The primary standards, in Article 35, resemble the warranty provisions of the UCC, but there are substantial differences. The CISG does not use the term "warranty" and does not divide sellers' quality obligations into sub-categories. CISG does not differentiate between express warranties and implied warranties. Compare carefully the provisions in Article 35(2) with their counterparts in the various quality warranties in the UCC. Consider also the UCC provisions for which no explicit counterparts exist in the CISG. What conclusions can be drawn from these comparisons? Are the quality obligations of sellers under CISG greater or less than their obligations under the UCC?

(2) Buyers' Remedies. Buyers' remedies under CISG are stated broadly in Article 45, which cross refers to Articles 46 to 52 and 74 to 77. The latter set of articles deals with monetary damages recoverable for breach. Two of these, CISG 74 and 77 apply to cases in which sellers have breached the CISG 35 obligations of quality but the goods are nonetheless retained by the buyers. CISG allows some aggrieved buyers to require sellers to take back nonconforming goods. The power is termed the power to "avoid" a contract. That power is provided under CISG 49(1)(a), which deals with circumstances in which a seller's breach of contract is "fundamental." "Fundamental breach" is defined in CISG 25. Damages allowed when buyers properly avoid contracts under CISG 49(1)(a) are determined by CISG 75 to 77.

We consider first buyers' remedies when contracts are not avoided. The basic formula for measurement of damages is found in the first sentence of Article 74. Unlike the UCC which deals separately with buyers' damages and sellers' damages, CISG 74 is a general provision that applies to both buyers' and sellers' damages. Therefore, in proceedings involving claims that sellers have breached the quality obligations of CISG 35, buyers' basic damages would be determined by CISG 74. How does this formula compare with UCC 2–714? What is the meaning of "loss ... suffered" by a buyer in the context of a claim for breach of CISG 35? Does this permit a buyer to recover damages determined by the value the goods would have had if they had been conforming, the "benefit of the bargain" principle that undergirds UCC 2–714?

"Loss suffered" is undoubtedly broad enough to include buyers' losses that common law and the UCC characterize as consequential damages. Like the UCC, CISG limits sellers' liability for consequential damages. That limitation is found the second sentence of CISG 74. How does this limitation compare with UCC 2–715(2)? CISG has no express provision for recovery of damages characterized by common law and the UCC as incidental damages, but, again, "loss suffered" is undoubtedly broad enough to include such losses.

Buyers's damages after avoidance of sales contracts are provided by CISG 75–76. These articles deal with the possibility and the reality of buyers' entering into substitute transactions. If a buyer contracts to buy replacement goods, "cover" in the UCC, buyer's basic damages are measured by the difference between the price in the substitute transaction and the contract price, CISG 75. That article adds that buyers are also entitled to any further damages recoverable under CISG 74. If a buyer has not made a purchase under CISG 75, damages are measured by the "current price" for the goods. CISG 76(1).[11] Again buyers may recover further damages under CISG 74.

The UCC lacks a general provision limiting damages for losses that aggrieved parties might have prevented from occurring, the principle of mitigation of damages. The mitigation principle is included in the UCC's criteria for recovery of consequential damages, UCC 2–715(2), the section

---

11. "Current price" is the price prevailing at the place where delivery of the goods should have been made or, absent such price, at another place that is a reasonable substitute. CISG 76(2).

litigated in *Carnation Co. v. Olivet Egg Ranch*. The Convention has a broadly applicable rule that limits all damages that may be sought. CISG 77.

(3) Other "Fields" of Law. The Convention (CISG 4) "governs only" the "obligations of the seller and the buyer arising from [the international sales] contract." Does the CISG displace rules of law that deal with defective goods under rubrics other than "contract"? To what extent is an international sales contract subject to law of fraud, misrepresentation or mistake, like those referred to earlier in United States law? Consider CISG 4(a). What issues are excluded from the CISG as going to the "validity of the contract"? The problems regarding the relationship between the Convention and domestic law are important and difficult. See J. Honnold, Uniform Law for International Sales §§ 64–67, 238–240 (3d ed. 1999).

Delchi Carrier SpA v. Rotorex Corp.

United States Court of Appeals for the Second Circuit, 1995.
71 F.3d 1024.

■ WINTER, CIRCUIT JUDGE:

Rotorex Corporation, a New York corporation, appeals from a judgment of $1,785,772.44 in damages for lost profits and other consequential damages awarded to Delchi Carrier SpA following a bench trial before Judge Munson. The basis for the award was Rotorex's delivery of nonconforming compressors to Delchi, an Italian manufacturer of air conditioners. Delchi cross-appeals from the denial of certain incidental and consequential damages. We affirm the award of damages; we reverse in part on Delchi's cross-appeal and remand for further proceedings.

BACKGROUND

In January 1988, Rotorex agreed to sell 10,800 compressors to Delchi for use in Delchi's "Ariele" line of portable room air conditioners. The air conditioners were scheduled to go on sale in the spring and summer of 1988. Prior to executing the contract, Rotorex sent Delchi a sample compressor and accompanying written performance specifications. The compressors were scheduled to be delivered in three shipments before May 15, 1988.

Rotorex sent the first shipment by sea on March 26. Delchi paid for this shipment, which arrived at its Italian factory on April 20, by letter of credit. Rotorex sent a second shipment of compressors on or about May 9. Delchi also remitted payment for this shipment by letter of credit. While the second shipment was en route, Delchi discovered that the first lot of compressors did not conform to the sample model and accompanying specifications. On May 13, after a Rotorex representative visited the Delchi factory in Italy, Delchi informed Rotorex that 93 percent of the compressors were rejected in quality control checks because they had lower cooling capacity and consumed more power than the sample model and specifications. After several unsuccessful attempts to cure the defects in the compressors, Delchi asked Rotorex to supply new compressors conforming to the original sample and specifications. Rotorex refused, claiming that the performance specifications were "inadvertently communicated" to Delchi.

In a faxed letter dated May 23, 1988, Delchi cancelled the contract. Although it was able to expedite a previously planned order of suitable compressors from Sanyo, another supplier, Delchi was unable to obtain in a timely fashion substitute compressors from other sources and thus suffered a loss in its sales volume of Arieles during the 1988 selling season. Delchi filed the instant action under the United Nations Convention on Contracts for the International Sale of Goods ("CISG" or "the Convention") for breach of contract and failure to deliver conforming goods. On January 10, 1991, Judge Cholakis granted Delchi's motion for partial summary judgment, holding Rotorex liable for breach of contract.

After three years of discovery and a bench trial on the issue of damages, Judge Munson, to whom the case had been transferred, held Rotorex liable to Delchi for $1,248,331.87. This amount included consequential damages for: (i) lost profits resulting from a diminished sales level of Ariele units, (ii) expenses that Delchi incurred in attempting to remedy the nonconformity of the compressors, (iii) the cost of expediting shipment of previously ordered Sanyo compressors after Delchi rejected the Rotorex compressors, and (iv) costs of handling and storing the rejected compressors. The district court also awarded prejudgment interest under CISG art. 78.

The court denied Delchi's claim for damages based on other expenses, including: (i) shipping, customs, and incidentals relating to the two shipments of Rotorex compressors; (ii) the cost of obsolete insulation and tubing that Delchi purchased only for use with Rotorex compressors; (iii) the cost of obsolete tooling purchased only for production of units with Rotorex compressors; and (iv) labor costs for four days when Delchi's production line was idle because it had no compressors to install in the air conditioning units. The court denied an award for these items on the ground that it would lead to a double recovery because "those costs are accounted for in Delchi's recovery on its lost profits claim." It also denied an award for the cost of modification of electrical panels for use with substitute Sanyo compressors on the ground that the cost was not attributable to the breach. Finally, the court denied recovery on Delchi's claim of 4000 additional lost sales in Italy.

On appeal, Rotorex argues that it did not breach the agreement, that Delchi is not entitled to lost profits because it maintained inventory levels in excess of the maximum number of possible lost sales, that the calculation of the number of lost sales was improper, and that the district court improperly excluded fixed costs and depreciation from the manufacturing cost in calculating lost profits. Delchi cross-appeals, claiming that it is entitled to the additional out-of-pocket expenses and the lost profits on additional sales denied by Judge Munson.

DISCUSSION

The district court held, and the parties agree, that the instant matter is governed by the CISG, *reprinted at* 15 U.S.C.A. Appendix (West Supp. 1995), a self-executing agreement between the United States and other signatories, including Italy.[1] Because there is virtually no caselaw under the Convention, we look to its language and to "the general principles" upon which it is based. *See* CISG art. 7(2). The Convention directs that its interpretation be informed by its "international character and . . . the need to promote uniformity in its application and the observance of good faith in international trade." *See* CISG art. 7(1); see generally John Honnold, Uniform Law for International Sales Under the 1980 United Nations Convention 60–62 (2d ed. 1991) (addressing principles for interpretation of CISG). Caselaw interpreting analogous provisions of Article 2 of the Uniform Commercial Code ("UCC"), may also inform a court where the language of the relevant CISG provisions tracks that of the UCC. However, UCC caselaw "is not *per se* applicable." Orbisphere Corp. v. United States, 13 C.I.T. 866, 726 F. Supp. 1344, 1355 (Ct. Int'l Trade 1989).

We first address the liability issue. We review a grant of summary judgment de novo. . . .

Under the CISG, "the seller must deliver goods which are of the quantity, quality and description required by the contract," and "the goods do not conform with the contract unless they . . . possess the qualities of goods which the seller has held out to the buyer as a sample or model." CISG art. 35. The CISG further states that "the seller is liable in accordance with the contract and this Convention for any lack of conformity." CISG art. 36.

Judge Cholakis held that "there is no question that [Rotorex's] compressors did not conform to the terms of the contract between the parties" and noted that "there are ample admissions [by Rotorex] to that effect." We agree. The agreement between Delchi and Rotorex was based upon a sample compressor supplied by Rotorex and upon written specifications regarding cooling capacity and power consumption. After the problems were discovered, Rotorex's engineering representative, Ernest Gamache, admitted in a May 13, 1988 letter that the specification sheet was "in error" and that the compressors would actually generate less cooling power and consume more energy than the specifications indicated. Gamache also testified in a deposition that at least some of the compressors were nonconforming. The president of Rotorex, John McFee, conceded in a May 17, 1988 letter to Delchi that the compressors supplied were less efficient than the sample and did not meet the specifications provided by Rotorex.

---

1. Generally, the CISG governs sales contracts between parties from different signatory countries. However, the Convention makes clear that the parties may by contract choose to be bound by a source of law other than the CISG, such as the UCC. See CISG art. 6 ("The parties may exclude the applica-tion of this Convention or . . . derogate from or vary the effect of any of its provisions.") If, as here, the agreement is silent as to choice of law, the Convention applies if both parties are located in signatory nations. See CISG art. 1.

Finally, in its answer to Delchi's complaint, Rotorex admitted "that some of the compressors ... did not conform to the nominal performance information." There was thus no genuine issue of material fact regarding liability, and summary judgment was proper. ...

Under the CISG, if the breach is "fundamental" the buyer may either require delivery of substitute goods, CISG art. 46, or declare the contract void, CISG art. 49, and seek damages. With regard to what kind of breach is fundamental, Article 25 provides:

> A breach of contract committed by one of the parties is fundamental if it results in such detriment to the other party as substantially to deprive him of what he is entitled to expect under the contract, unless the party in breach did not foresee and a reasonable person of the same kind in the same circumstances would not have foreseen such a result.

CISG art. 25. In granting summary judgment, the district court held that "there appears to be no question that [Delchi] did not substantially receive that which [it] was entitled to expect" and that "any reasonable person could foresee that shipping non-conforming goods to a buyer would result in the buyer not receiving that which he expected and was entitled to receive." Because the cooling power and energy consumption of an air conditioner compressor are important determinants of the product's value, the district court's conclusion that Rotorex was liable for a fundamental breach of contract under the Convention was proper.

We turn now to the district court's award of damages following the bench trial. A reviewing court must defer to the trial judge's findings of fact unless they are clearly erroneous. ... However, we review questions of law, including "the measure of damages upon which the factual computation is based," de novo. ...

The CISG provides:

> Damages for breach of contract by one party consist of a sum equal to the loss, including loss of profit, suffered by the other party as a consequence of the breach. Such damages may not exceed the loss which the party in breach foresaw or ought to have foreseen at the time of the conclusion of the contract, in the light of the facts and matters of which he then knew or ought to have known, as a possible consequence of the breach of contract.

CISG art. 74. This provision is "designed to place the aggrieved party in as good a position as if the other party had properly performed the contract." Honnold, supra, at 503.

Rotorex argues that Delchi is not entitled to lost profits because it was able to maintain inventory levels of Ariele air conditioning units in excess of the maximum number of possible lost sales. In Rotorex's view, therefore, there was no actual shortfall of Ariele units available for sale because of Rotorex's delivery of nonconforming compressors. Rotorex's argument goes as follows. The end of the air conditioner selling season is August 1. If one totals the number of units available to Delchi from March to August 1, the sum is enough to fill all sales. We may assume that the evidence in the record supports the factual premise. Nevertheless, the argument is fallacious. Because of Rotorex's breach, Delchi had to shut down its manufacturing operation for a few days in May, and the date on which particular units were available for sale was substantially delayed. For example, units available in late July could not be used to meet orders in the spring. As a result, Delchi lost sales in the spring and early summer. We therefore conclude that the district court's findings regarding lost sales are not clearly erroneous. A detailed discussion of the precise number of lost sales is unnecessary because the district court's findings were, if anything, conservative.

Rotorex contends, in the alternative, that the district court improperly awarded lost profits for unfilled orders from Delchi affiliates in Europe and from sales agents within Italy. We disagree. The CISG requires that damages be limited by the familiar principle of foreseeability established in *Hadley v. Baxendale*, 156 Eng. Rep. 145 (1854). CISG art. 74. However, it was objectively foreseeable that Delchi would take orders for Ariele sales based on the number of compressors it had ordered and expected to have ready for the season. The district court was entitled to rely upon the documents and testimony regarding these lost sales and was well within its authority in deciding which orders were proven with sufficient certainty.

Rotorex also challenges the district court's exclusion of fixed costs and depreciation from the manufacturing cost used to calculate lost profits. The trial judge calculated lost profits by subtracting the 478,783 lire "manufacturing cost"—the total variable cost—of an Ariele unit from the 654,644 lire average sale price. The CISG does not explicitly state whether only variable expenses, or both fixed and variable expenses, should be subtracted from sales revenue in calculating lost profits. However, courts generally do not include fixed costs in the calculation of lost profits. See Indu Craft, Inc. v. Bank of Baroda, 47 F.3d 490, 495 (2d Cir.1995) (only when the breach ends an ongoing business should fixed costs be subtracted along with variable costs); Adams v. Lindblad Travel, Inc., 730 F.2d 89, 92–93 (2d Cir.1984) (fixed costs should not be included in lost profits equation when the plaintiff is an ongoing business whose fixed costs are not affected by the breach). This is, of course, because the fixed costs would have been encountered whether or not the breach occurred. In the absence of a specific provision in the CISG for calculating lost profits, the district court was correct to use the standard formula employed by most American courts and to deduct only variable costs from sales revenue to arrive at a figure for lost profits.

In its cross-appeal, Delchi challenges the district court's denial of various consequential and incidental damages, including reimbursement for: (i) shipping, customs, and incidentals relating to the first and second shipments—rejected and returned—of Rotorex compressors; (ii) obsolete insulation materials and tubing purchased for use only with Rotorex compressors; (iii) obsolete tooling purchased exclusively for production of units with Rotorex compressors; and (iv) labor costs for the period of May 16–19, 1988, when the Delchi production line was idle due to a lack of compressors to install in Ariele air conditioning units. The district court denied damages for these items on the ground that they "are accounted for in Delchi's recovery on its lost profits claim," and, therefore, an award would constitute a double recovery for Delchi. We disagree.

The Convention provides that a contract plaintiff may collect damages to compensate for the full loss. This includes, but is not limited to, lost profits, subject only to the familiar limitation that the breaching party must have foreseen, or should have foreseen, the loss as a probable consequence. CISG art. 74; see *Hadley v. Baxendale*, supra.

An award for lost profits will not compensate Delchi for the expenses in question. Delchi's lost profits are determined by calculating the hypothetical revenues to be derived from unmade sales less the hypothetical variable costs that would have been, but were not, incurred. This figure, however, does not compensate for costs actually incurred that led to no sales. Thus, to award damages for costs actually incurred in no way creates a double recovery and instead furthers the purpose of giving the injured party damages "equal to the loss." CISG art. 74.

The only remaining inquiries, therefore, are whether the expenses were reasonably foreseeable and legitimate incidental or consequential damages.[2] The expenses incurred by Delchi for shipping, customs, and related matters for the two returned shipments of Rotorex compressors, including storage expenses for the second shipment at Genoa, were clearly foreseeable and recoverable incidental expenses. These are up-front expenses that had to be paid to get the goods to the manufacturing plant for inspection and were thus incurred largely before the nonconformities were detected. To deny reimbursement to Delchi for these incidental damages would effectively cut into the lost profits award. The same is true of unreimbursed tooling expenses and the cost of the useless insulation and tubing materials. These are legitimate consequential damages that in no way duplicate lost profits damages.

The labor expense incurred as a result of the production line shutdown of May 16–19, 1988 is also a reasonably foreseeable result of delivering nonconforming compressors for installation in air conditioners. However, Rotorex argues that the labor costs in question were fixed costs that would have been incurred whether or not there was a breach. The district court labeled the labor costs "fixed costs," but did not explore whether Delchi would have paid these wages regardless of how much it produced. Variable costs are generally those costs that "fluctuate with a firm's output," and typically include labor (but not management) costs. ... Whether Delchi's

---

2. The UCC defines incidental damages resulting from a seller's breach as "expenses reasonably incurred in inspection, receipt, transportation and care and custody of goods rightfully rejected, any commercially reasonable charges, expenses or commissions in connection with effecting cover and any other reasonable expense incident to the delay or other breach." U.C.C. § 2–715(1) (1990). It defines consequential damages resulting from a seller's breach to include "any loss resulting from general or particular requirements and needs of which the seller at the time of contracting had reason to know and which could not reasonably be prevented by cover or otherwise." U.C.C. § 2–715(2)(a).

labor costs during this four-day period are variable or fixed costs is in large measure a fact question that we cannot answer because we lack factual findings by the district court. We therefore remand to the district court on this issue.

The district court also denied an award for the modification of electrical panels for use with substitute Sanyo compressors. It denied damages on the ground that Delchi failed to show that the modifications were not part of the regular cost of production of units with Sanyo compressors and were therefore attributable to Rotorex's breach. This appears to have been a credibility determination that was within the court's authority to make. We therefore affirm on the ground that this finding is not clearly erroneous.

Finally, Delchi cross-appeals from the denial of its claimed 4000 additional lost sales in Italy. The district court held that Delchi did not prove these orders with sufficient certainty. The trial court was in the best position to evaluate the testimony of the Italian sales agents who stated that they would have ordered more Arieles if they had been available. It found the agents' claims to be too speculative, and this conclusion is not clearly erroneous.

CONCLUSION

We affirm the award of damages. We reverse in part the denial of incidental and consequential damages. We remand for further proceedings in accord with this opinion.

NOTES

(1) Consequential Damages. The principal loss suffered was the profit that buyer had expected to make from sales of air conditioners. Seller contested the buyer's right to recover for this loss. The trial court allowed some of buyer's claims. The more difficult issue on appeal was the manner of trial court's calculation of this loss. By excluding fixed costs from the calculation, the courts increased the hypothetical profit. Should fixed costs have been excluded? Is this a question of interpretation of the Convention? Was the Court of Appeals reasoning on this matter a proper method of interpretation of the Convention? The trial court disallowed recovery for expenses that had been incurred by the buyer in unsuccessful efforts to manufacture air conditioners with seller's compressors. The trial court considered these items to be included in the recovery for lost profits. The Court of Appeals disagreed. Was the appellate court correct?

(2) Other Damages. The trial court denied recovery for expenses incurred by the buyer in receiving and then returning the unsatisfactory compressors. The Court of Appeals reversed. Such expenses would be characterized as incidental expenses under the UCC and recoverable under UCC 2–715(1), which the court cited in a footnote. Under what language of CISG 74 are such damages recoverable? The Court of Appeals stressed that these expenses were foreseeable; was that conclusion necessary to buyer's recovery?

(3) Recovery of the Price Paid. The buyer paid the full price for both shipments of compressors. The trial court found that buyer had paid almost $320,000.[12] The compressors were returned to the seller. Was the buyer entitled to refund of the price paid under the CISG? The trial court found that seller's breach was fundamental under CISG 25 and the Court of Appeals affirmed. Was this finding necessary for the courts' determination of the damages under CISG 74? If there had been no finding of fundamental breach, would the measure of damages have changed? Was a finding of fundamental breach necessary for recovery of the price? CISG 81 to 84 provide for the effects of avoidance. Under CISG 81(2), upon avoidance, a party who has performed its obligations under the contract may claim restitution of whatever was paid. Seller must pay interest on the money. CISG 84(1).

(4) Return of the Goods. The buyer sent the nonconforming compressors back to the seller and thereby incurred expenses that were assessed as damages. CISG determines buyers' obligations with respect to the goods after avoidance. Under CISG 81(2), buyers that avoid contracts have the duty to make restitution. They must also account for all benefits derived from the goods. CISG 84(2). Buyers ordinarily lose the right to declare contracts avoided if they cannot make restitution of the goods substantially in the condition in which they were received. CISG 82(1) and (2). Buyers are entitled to retain goods until sellers reimburse them for reasonable expenses, CISG 86(1), a right that the buyer did not insist upon in this case.

Medical Marketing Int'l, Inc. v. Internazionale Medico Scientifica, S.R.L.

United States District Court, Eastern District of Louisiana, 1999.
1999 WL 311945.

■ Duval, Jr., J.

Before the court is an Application for Order Conforming Arbitral Award and Entry of Judgment, filed by plaintiff, Medical Marketing International, Inc. ("MMI"). Having considered the memoranda of plaintiff, and the memorandum in opposition filed by defendant, Internazionale Medico Scientifica, S.r.l. ("IMS"), the court grants the motion.

FACTUAL BACKGROUND

Plaintiff MMI is a Louisiana marketing corporation with its principal place of business in Baton Rouge, Louisiana. Defendant IMS is an Italian corporation that manufactures radiology materials with its principal place of business in Bologna, Italy. On January 25, 1993, MMI and IMS entered into a Business Licensing Agreement in which IMS granted exclusive sales rights for Giotto Mammography H.F. Units to MMI.

---

12.   1994 U.S. Dist. LEXIS 12820.

In 1996, the Food and Drug Administration ("FDA") seized the equipment for non-compliance with administrative procedures, and a dispute arose over who bore the obligation of ensuring that the Giotto equipment complied with the United states Governmental Safety Regulations, specifically the Good Manufacturing Practices (GMP) for Medical Device Regulations. MMI formally demanded mediation on October 28, 1996, pursuant to Article 13 of the agreement. Mediation was unsuccessful, and the parties entered into arbitration, also pursuant to Article 13, whereby each party chose one arbitrator and a third was agreed upon by both.

An arbitration hearing was held on July 13–15, July 28, and November 17, 1998. The hearing was formally closed on November 30, 1998. The arbitrators rendered their decision on December 21, 1998, awarding MMI damages in the amount of $357,009.00 and legal interest on that amount from October 28, 1996. The arbitration apportioned 75% of the $83,640.45 cost of arbitration to MMI, and the other 25% to IMS. IMS moved for reconsideration on December 30, 1998, and this request was denied by the arbitrators on January 7, 1999. Plaintiff now moves for an order from this court confirming the arbitral award and entering judgment in favor of the plaintiff under 9 U.S.C. § 9.

JURISDICTION

The Federal Arbitration Act ("FAA") allows parties to an arbitration suit to apply to the "United States court in and for the district within which such award was made" for enforcement of the award. 9 U.S.C. § 9. As the arbitration in this case was held in New Orleans, Louisiana, this court has jurisdiction over petitioner's Application under 9 U.S.C. § 9. This court also has diversity jurisdiction over the case, as the amount in controversy exceeds $75,000 and the parties are a Louisiana corporation and an Italian corporation.

ANALYSIS

The scope of this court's review of an arbitration award is "among the narrowest known to law." Denver & Rio Grande Western Railroad Co. v. Union Pacific Railroad Co., 119 F.3d 847, 849 (10th Cir.1997). The FAA outlines specific situations in which an arbitration decision may be overruled: (1) if the award was procured by corruption, fraud or undue means; (2) if there is evidence of partiality or corruption among the arbitrators; (3) if the arbitrators were guilty of misconduct which prejudiced the rights of one of the parties; or (4) if the arbitrators exceeded their powers. Instances in which the arbitrators "exceed their powers" may include violations of public policy or awards based on a "manifest disregard of the law." See W.R. Grace & Co. v. Local Union 759, 461 U.S. 757, 766, 103 S. Ct. 2177, 2183, 76 L. Ed. 2d 298 (1983), Wilko v. Swan, 346 U.S. 427, 436–37, 74 S. Ct. 182, 187–88, 98 L. Ed. 168 (1953), overruled on other grounds, 490 U.S. 477, 109 S. Ct. 1917, 104 L. Ed. 2d 526 (1989).

IMS has alleged that the arbitrators' decision violates public policy of the international global market and that the arbitrators exhibited "manifest disregard of international sales law." Specifically, IMS argues that the arbitrators misapplied the United Nations Convention on Contracts for the International Sales of Goods, commonly referred to as CISG, and that they refused to follow a German Supreme Court Case interpreting CISG.

MMI does not dispute that CISG applies to the case at hand. Under CISG, the finder of fact has a duty to regard the "international character" of the convention and to promote uniformity in its application. CISG Article 7. The Convention also provides that in an international contract for goods, goods conform to the contract if they are fit for the purpose for which goods of the same description would ordinarily be used or are fit for any particular purpose expressly or impliedly made known to the seller and relied upon by the buyer. CISG Article 35(2). To avoid a contract based on the non-conformity of goods, the buyer must allege and prove that the seller's breach was "fundamental" in nature. CISG Article 49. A breach is fundamental when it results in such detriment to the party that he or she is substantially deprived of what he or she is entitled to expect under the contract, unless the party in breach did not foresee such a result. CISG Article 25.

At the arbitration, IMS argued that MMI was not entitled to avoid its contract with IMS based on non-conformity under Article 49, because IMS's breach was not "fundamental." IMS argued that CISG did not require that it furnish MMI with equipment that complied with the United States GMP regulations. To support this proposition, IMS cited a German Supreme Court case, which held that under CISG Article 35, a seller is generally not obligated to supply goods that conform to public laws and regulations enforced at the buyer's place of business. Entscheidunger des Bundersgerichtshofs in Zivilsachen (BGHZ) 129, 75 (1995). In that case, the court held that this general rule carriers with it exceptions in three limited circumstances: (1) if the public laws and regulations of the buyer's state are identical to those enforced in the seller's state; (2) if the buyer informed the seller about those regulations; or (3) if due to "special circumstances," such as the existence of a seller's branch office in the buyer's state, the seller knew or should have known about the regulations at issue.

The arbitration panel decided that under the third exception, the general rule did not apply to this case. The arbitrators held that IMS was, or should have been, aware of the GMP regulations prior to entering into the 1993 agreement, and explained their reasoning at length. IMS now argues that the arbitration panel refused to apply CISG and the law as articulated by the German Supreme Court. It is clear from the arbitrators' written findings, however, that they carefully considered that decision and found that this case fit the exception and not the rule as articulated in that decision. The arbitrators' decision was neither contrary to public policy nor in manifest disregard of international sales law. This court therefore finds that the arbitration panel did not "exceed its powers" in violation of the FAA. Accordingly,

IT IS ORDERED that the Application for Order Conforming Arbitral Award is hereby GRANTED.

NOTES

(1) Commercial Arbitration and Judicial Enforcement of Awards. Many parties to international sales contracts elect by a clause in those contracts to have disputes resolved by arbitration. The parties to this transaction included an agreement to arbitrate in their contract. When the dispute arose they went to arbitration as agreed. The arbitrators were a panel of three, one selected by each side and a neutral third panelist. Arbitrators' decisions in favor of claimants are usually called "awards." Awards may be accepted by the losing party without further process, but awards cannot be enforced by the same means available to enforce judgments of courts. Legislation was enacted to give teeth to arbitration awards.[13] The legislation in this case, a federal statute, allows parties that prevail in arbitration to seek the assistance of federal district courts.[14] In that court proceeding, the law allows a few very limited objections to the validity of the arbitrators' decision. This procedure was followed in this case.

(2) CISG and Commercial Arbitration. Contracts governed by the CISG are likely to have arbitration clauses for the resolution of disputes that may arise. While the CISG can be enforced in national and state courts, parties to international sales contracts that choose the neutral substantive law of CISG for their transactions may also choose to refer their disputes to a neutral forum rather than to the domestic court of one of the parties. Commercial arbitration offers advantages other than neutrality, of course, which add to the incentive to include arbitration clauses in sales contracts. A principal disadvantage is that arbitrators are not judges and may not even be lawyers. Persons who seek rigorous enforcement of substantive legal norms may distrust the arbitration process to produce that result.

The seller in this case sought to persuade the district court to refuse to enforce the arbitration award for an error of law allegedly committed by

---

13. International commercial law is considerably developed with regard to enforcement if the initial decision is an arbitration award. The United Nations Convention on the Recognition and Enforcement of Foreign Arbitral Awards, a multilateral treaty of 1958, commonly known as the "New York Convention," commits signatory nations to enforcement of awards. The United States, a party to the New York Convention, fulfilled its obligation by adding chapter 2 to the Federal Arbitration Act, 9 U.S.C. §§ 201–208, in 1970. The New York Convention is reprinted in the notes of United States Code Annotated at § 201.

UNCITRAL has also been active in promoting international arbitration of commercial disputes. In 1976, UNCITRAL issued Arbitration Rules that parties to international contracts can choose to incorporate into their agreements. UNCITRAL promulgated a Model Law on International Commercial Arbitration in 1985. See A. Broches in ICCA, International Handbook on Commercial Arbitration (Arb. Supp. 11, Jan. 1990); H. Holtzmann & J. Neuhaus, Guide to the UNCITRAL Model Law (1989); A. Redfern & M. Hunter, Law and Practice of International Commercial Arbitration 360–404, 416–430 (text of UNCITRAL Rules), 435–449 (text of Model Law)(1986).

14. The courts are authorized by the statute to enter judgments that are based upon arbitration awards. Those judgments can then be executed by public officials to compel payment, if necessary.

the arbitrators. In most legal systems, there is no right to appeal an arbitration award comparable to the right to appeal a trial court's decision. When courts are asked to confirm an arbitration award, losing parties may try to achieve some degree of judicial review of the arbitrators' legal analysis. That of course is what seller tried to do in this case, under the rubric that the arbitrators had acted in "manifest disregard of the law." In the setting of a judicial proceeding to enforce the award, seller's effort failed. It is useful to consider the strength of the seller's legal argument. If the initial decision had been that of a federal district court rather than an arbitration panel, would seller have had valid ground for appeal? The seller's argument appeared to be that a prior decision, by the German Supreme Court, had given CISG 49 a definitive meaning that the United States courts were bound to follow. To what extent should the principle of *stare decisis* apply to judicial construction of CISG articles? Would a different legal principle apply if the original forum is an arbitration panel?

The court does not indicate whether the arbitration in this case was conducted under the auspices of an organization for the facilitation of such dispute resolution. There are several major organizations of this kind.

One is the International Chamber of Commerce, which established, in 1923, what is now called the International Court of Arbitration. Since its founding, the ICC Court has handled more than 6,700 cases. Most of the awards in those cases are unreported. However, since 1974, selected arbitral awards have been published in redacted form. The initial volume looked back over eleven years. Since 1976, the International Council for Commercial Arbitration has been publishing Yearbooks of Commercial Arbitration which contain a selection of arbitral awards and other materials. As time goes by, there will be a growing corpus of ICC arbitration awards involving application of the CISG.

Another arbitration system devoted substantially to arbitration of international commercial disputes is the London Court of International Arbitration (LCIA). The LCIA, which has been in existence for more than a century, is a corporation under the control of its constituent bodies, the Corporation of the City of London, the London Chamber of Commerce, and the Chartered Institute of Arbitrators. Under LCIA rules, arbitral tribunals are required to make their awards in writing; an award must include the reasons on which the award is based unless the parties agree otherwise. The LCIA Rules are annexed to the Report of the ILEX Delegation to International Arbitration Centers: An Update on Commercial Dispute Resolution Developments in London and Paris (ABA Section of International Law and Practice (1995)).

Commercial arbitration is also widely used in the United States and elsewhere for the resolution of commercial disputes not involving international transactions. Domestic commercial arbitration tends to be done with high concern for privacy of the parties and the arbitrators in the United States are generally not expected to write reasoned awards. Although there was a reasoned award in the instant case, it does not appear to have been published. We have no direct way to evaluate the legal analysis of the arbitrators.

NOTE

The following arbitrators' awards, taken from the ICC reports, are indicative of the process in disputes involving the quality of goods delivered. Since these arose before the CISG took effect, they are governed by domestic law. The arbitrators' resolution of the choice of law is also instructive. Would these disputes have been resolved differently if the governing law had been the CISG?

AWARD IN CASE NO. 3779 OF 1981
Collection of ICC Arbitral Awards 1974–85, p. 138

Arbitrator: Prof. Jacques H. Herbots (Belgium)

Parties: Claimant: Swiss seller
                 Respondent: Dutch buyer

Published: Not (yet) published

* * *

[FACTS]

Three contracts were concluded in 1979 between the parties, all three concerning the same type of merchandise [whey powder] of which the quality was described in detail.

The merchandise, coming from a Canadian factory was to be delivered C.I.F. Rotterdam. The contracts were made in French and all contained— except for quantities—the same conditions, including an arbitral clause referring disputes to arbitration under the Arbitration Rules of the ICC. However, only the first two contracts were signed by the parties and executed. The third contract was not signed and before shipment from Canada took place, it was cancelled by the Respondent who complained that the merchandise delivered under the first two contracts was not in accordance with the quality prescribed in the contract.

The Canadian Factory sent one of its technicians, Dr. E., to the Netherlands and samples were taken and examined in an independent laboratory. It appeared that they were in accordance with the contractual requirements when analyzed under the North American method, but not when the European analytic method was used.

Arbitration followed in which the Swiss seller claimed US $55,000 (including *inter alia* $37,500 paid to the Canadian factory) in respect of the cancellation of the third contract. The Dutch buyer introduced a counterclaim of Hfl. 181,645.—covering losses in respect of the first two contracts.

[EXTRACT]

I. Competence of Arbitrator

The clause attributing jurisdiction to the ICC occurs in two preceding and similar contracts that were signed by both parties, as well as in the third contract, that, although it was not signed, was not protested against within a reasonable delay either.

Although the contracts are independent from one another from a juridical point of view, the three contracts form a group from an economic point of view.

If, in principle, silence does not mean acceptance, this meaning is, however, attributed to it in view of the circumstances, in particular, the previous business relations of the parties.

Consequently, within the context of their juridical relation and according to their obligations of good faith, the exception of incompetence does not apply.

II. Law Applicable to the Contract

* * *

In an international sale of goods, when the parties remain silent, the domestic law of the country in which the seller has his place of residence is to be applied (see the Hague Convention on the International Sale of Goods of June 15, 1955); Kahn, J., Rep.Dall., dr. internat., VE Vente commerciale; Lunz, Cours Acad. Dr. Internat. 1965, I, 1; Federal Court of Switzerland, 12th February 1952, R 1953, 390, note Flattet.

The chosen language, the place where the contract was entered into by correspondence together with applying the theory of reception, and the way of payment, all point in the same direction.

Consequently, Swiss law is applicable to the contract in dispute.

* * *

IV. With Respect to the Merits of the Dispute

* * *

3. The misunderstanding

Both parties seem to have acted in good faith.

Actually, the Claimant had immediately declared his willingness to submit samples drawn by both parties to a test by a competent laboratory to be chosen by both parties, and to accept cancellation of the remaining contracts if this analysis proved that the Respondent's allegations had been well-founded.

The Respondent, on his part, also immediately reported the quality problems encountered, asked for an expert and sent samples to the Canadian factory. He agreed to pay for the goods that had already arrived in Rotterdam and he restricted himself to refusing to give any forwarding-instructions or to receive the goods ordered, but not yet loaded on board.

The dispute essentially arises from a misunderstanding.

The following conclusion is essential for understanding the matter: "The main conclusion of Dr. E. during his visit to the Dutch buyer was that the goods sent were not the product the Dutch buyer believed to have bought; the Dutch buyer maintains that, when the Swiss seller initially gave a description of the goods, no mention was made of a method of analysis. The Dutch buyer supposed that, since the description was given by a European firm, the European methods were to be applied ..." (quotation from document 24). To this the Claimant replies: "It goes without saying that the methods to be used should be those of the country of origin or those that are universally accepted, such as the (North American) method" (document 3).

It was only when the quality problems emerged that the Claimant announced the method of analyzing, *inter alia*, the solubility index, viz. the (North American) method that, according to him, is intentionally accepted (document 6 bis).

The Canadian factory was willing to send a technician but made the condition that first agreement should be reached on the method of analysis (document 7).

It is certain that the goods are in accordance with the contractual description, provided that the samples are analyzed according to the (North American) method.

It appears from the proceedings that, although it is not a sale on sample, a sample had been sent to the Respondent prior to the conclusion of the contracts.

The first deliveries were in accordance with this quality, the latter not, although they remained in accordance with the contractual description of the goods, which explains why it was only at a late stage that the misunderstanding came to light.

The misunderstanding is essentially about the solubility degree of the powder delivered.

The method of analysis must be carefully specified in order to be able to determine the solubility degree of the powder.

In Switzerland, methods of analysis are used that are incorporated in the Swiss Manual on Foods, of which Manual the chapter on goods like this particular powder has, unfortunately, not been published yet.

Although the North American method (actually designed for a different type of powder) is better known in the international powder industry involved than a French method, it cannot be considered, however, to be implicitly understood, at least, not on the European market.

The French method differs from the (North American) method with respect to the temperature during the dissolution and the technique of dissolution. The two methods are particularly different with respect to the method of expressing the result in a figure (the solubility index). The Canadian factory took this into account when it was too late, notably, when the Respondent complained about the quality of the goods and the question of analyzing the samples was raised.

4. Shared responsibilities with respect to the origin of the misunderstanding

From a telex from the Canadian factory to the Claimant ... it appears that the factory claims to have been clear as to the description of the goods and the methodology, and that the contractual (possibly insufficient) description of the goods, given by the Claimant to his own clients, does not concern him at all, from which it can be deduced that the factory leaves the total contractual responsibility to the Claimant in the case he had not done likewise with his own principal, that is to say, the Respondent.

The Claimant should have known that there was a possibility of error on the European market with respect to the appreciation of the description of the powder.

One cannot presume that there is agreement on the (North American) method between a Swiss seller and a Dutch buyer.

The Claimant should have mentioned that the contractual description was to be interpreted according to the (North American) method, as the Canadian supplier had done in his contract with the Claimant.

The Claimant should have informed the buyer of the conditions on which he contracted (see T.G.I., Argentan, 15th October 1970, D.S., 1971, p. 718, note of M. Ghestin, quoted by Lucas de Leyssac, *L'obligation de renseignements dans les contrats*, in: *L'information en droit privé*, L.G.D., J., 1978, p. 316).

With respect to the interpretation of the contract, the (also in Swiss law) traditional rule can be applied as well: *"in dubio, contra proferentem."*

As Loysel wrote: "qui vend le pot, dit le mot."

The seller is obliged to state clearly what obligations he is undertaking.

The Respondent, on the other hand, knew very well that the goods were of Canadian origin, because he had had contact with the supplier.

Consequently, the error is equally due to his negligence, for he should have asked about the meaning of the symbols used in the contractual description of the powder, of North American origin.

The dialectics between the right of being informed, and the obligation of informing oneself is thus at the heart of the problem in the present dispute.

The error of the Respondent is due to a negligence shared with the Claimant (in Swiss law one can find the following instances of shared negligence: A and B have concluded a sale, for which the price has been fixed on the basis of a tariff, the rectification of which has been published many times. A and B conclude a contract without informing themselves about the provisions of clearing that are applicable to their deal—see ENGEL, Pierre, *Traité des obligations en droit Suisse*, Neuchatel, 1973, p. 257).

The (North American) method being more frequently used than the other methods, the negligence of the Claimant as to the information seems less than that of the Respondent.

* * *

THEREFORE:

We, Arbitrator, deciding in accordance with the provisions of the ICC Rules of Conciliation and Arbitration, within the limits of our mission, that was extended by decision of the Court of Arbitration;

> observe in the commercial relations of the parties the existence of an arbitration clause to settle the present dispute and consequently declare ourselves competent to decide and award with respect to the claim and the counterclaim;

With respect to the claim

> condemn the Respondent to pay to the Claimant the amount of $27,000 as indemnification for the invalidation (that is to say cancellation) of the third contract.

With respect to the counterclaim

> reject the claim of the Respondent for indemnification because of the non-conformity of the goods delivered under the two preceding contracts.

Order that the costs of the arbitration, including costs and fee of the arbitrator, being $8,300, will be borne by the Claimant for 2/5 and by the Respondent for 3/5.

AWARD MADE IN CASE NO. 2129 IN 1972, Collection of ICC Arbitral Awards 1974–1985, p. 23. A German seller contracted to deliver motor car accessories to a United States buyer. Buyer claimed relief for expenses incurred in altering the goods to make them usable on United States automobiles, which were larger than German automobiles. The arbitrator, applying the Ohio Commercial Code, found for the United States buyer:

> The defendant's equipment had to be fit for the ordinary purposes for which it was to be used. Thus, the equipment manufactured for the German market had to be modified to service the U.S. market. At the time of contracting the defendant knew the purpose for which the equipment was required and the buyer relied upon him to furnish suitable machines. ... This warranty of merchantability and fitness

applies to sales for use as well as to sales for resale and can be invoked by the plaintiff as well as by his customers. The plaintiff is therefore entitled to be reimbursed for the money he spent repairing or altering the defendant's equipment pursuant to an implied warranty of merchantability and fitness.

AWARD OF SEPTEMBER 27, 1983, CASE NO. 3880

(Original in French)

Arbitrators:	Dr. Werner Wenger; Prof. Lucien Simont; Prof. Marcel Storme
Parties:	Claimant: Belgian buyer A Defendant: Belgian seller B
Published in:	110 *Journal du droit international (Clunet)* 1983, p. 897, with note Y. Derains and S. Jarvin, pp. 897–899.

[FACTS]

On January 26, 1979, claimant A and defendant B entered into a contract whereby B undertook to supply A with 150,000 pairs of ladies' boots between April and August 1979. On the same date, B entered into an identical contract (differing only in relation to the price) with a Romanian State trading enterprise C, who was to supply the same quantity of boots to B. When the Romanian enterprise C defaulted, arbitration proceedings were commenced by A who sought damages for late delivery and defective goods. The arbitrators rejected a request by defendant B to join the claim with an arbitration it had commenced separately against its supplier, the Romanian enterprise C, based on that company's default in delivery. Claimant A was successful as to 75% of its claim.

[EXTRACT]

[On *force majeure*:]

... [D]efendant B contends ... that to the extent that the contract obliged it to supply boots made at the factory D in Romania, the source proposed by its supplier, the Romanian enterprise C, the default of the latter constituted an insurmountable obstacle and an extraneous cause relieving it of any liability towards Claimant A.

* * *

It follows that, B's obligations being in the nature of obligations of result, their non-fulfilment places B in default and involves it in liability vis-à-vis A, except for those cases where the latter company cancelled orders without justification....

[On the mitigation of damages:]

B argues, however, that A could have offered its clients in sufficient time merchandise equivalent to the subject-matter of the contract between the parties, in conformity with its obligation to take all appropriate steps to limit its damage and reduce its losses.

The boots which were the subject-matter of the contract have a seasonal character and could not be sold and delivered to A's client except at the beginning of the winter season at the latest. B, on the basis of promises made by its own supplier, had led A to believe, up to August 1979 and, at least for the major part of the order, even up to the first half of September 1979, that it would be in a position to deliver the goods, admittedly late, but before the last moment. Its failure to fulfil these promises only became apparent after it was too late to obtain the merchandise elsewhere. In effect, having regard to the changing fashions to which this type of product is subject, suppliers keep very little in stock. B omits to identify the sources to which A could have turned at the end of September 1979, to obtain merchandise equivalent to that described in the Contract.

In these circumstances it is not appropriate to reduce the compensation for damages suffered by reason of a violation of the creditor to observe its obligation to mitigate its damages.

[On loss of goodwill:]

Having regard to the fact that, out of a total of about 127,000 pairs of boots ordered by A from B, a significant number, 45,509 pairs, or about 35%, were the subject of justifiable complaints about failure to meet delivery dates and defects in quality. This percentage considerably exceeds what would normally be expected to be tolerated. Having regard to the seasonal character of the merchandise, A was only able to satisfy its clients from other sources to a limited extent. One's commercial reputation would seem to be affected when a business finds itself in the position of not being able to fulfil a significant proportion of its orders.

The nature of the effect on its reputation is such as to make it impossible, in the absence of precise criteria, to determine the exact extent of the damage caused by it; that such damage cannot be evaluated. In these circumstances, it appears that for the reasons stated above, and taking all aspects of the case into consideration, particularly the net margin of A and the trading figures with the clients mentioned above from 1980–1982 in comparison with previous years, A's claim can only be deemed to be partly founded, and the sum of Bfrs. 200,000 must be allowed to it as damages for any prejudice to its commercial reputation.

SECTION 4. WARRANTY DISCLAIMERS AND LIMITATION OF DAMAGES CLAUSES

DOMESTIC UNITED STATES LAW

Introduction. Article 2 of the UCC does not require that sellers provide warranties of quality on their goods. This Section considers the means by which sellers can sell goods without warranties of quality. The primary issue that recurs in this Section is the nature and effectiveness of disclaimers of the implied warranty of merchantability.[1] Express warranties arise only if sellers, by their own words or conduct, take affirmative action to create them. Implied warranties of quality arise in a different manner. The warranty of merchantability arises, by implication, in every sales contract in which seller is a merchant that deals in goods of the kind. The merchantability warranty exists unless, by a clause in the sales contract, the merchant-seller has effectively disclaimed it. The UCC allows sellers to disclaim implied warranties of quality if they do so in accordance with prescribed procedures.

The implied warranty provision in UCC 2–314 contains the conditioning language: "unless excluded or modified," which expressly permits the parties to agree that these warranties have been negated. As we will see, the UCC further imposes certain *formal* requirements on sellers who seek to do so. UCC 2–316(2).

Article 2 does not require that the statutory remedies be available for breach of express warranties or breach of implied warranties of quality. The UCC allows the parties to sales contracts to agree to remedies other than the statutory remedies. Contracts may provide remedies in addition to, or in substitution for the statutory remedies. A common contract remedy for breach of warranty is seller's undertaking, for a limited time after delivery, to repair defects in materials or workmanship that are discovered. The primary issue that we will see recurring is the nature and effectiveness of contract clauses obligating sellers to remedy defects and contract clauses excluding sellers' liability for consequential damages that result from breach of warranty.

The UCC's treatment of clauses limiting sellers' liability for damages is found in UCC 2–719. Section 2–719(1)(a) declares that the parties "may provide for remedies in addition to or in substitution for those provided in this Article" and may agree to "limit or alter the measure of damages recoverable under this Article, as by limiting the buyer's remedies to return of the goods and repayment of the price or to repair and replacement of non-conforming goods or parts." Under UCC 2–719(3), consequential damages may be limited or excluded unless the limitation or exclusion is unconscionable.

In modern sales of most durable goods and many non-durable goods, few contracts lack a disclaimer of the implied warranty of merchantability or a damages exclusion clause, or both. In many kinds of transactions, patterns of warranty disclaimers or limitation of damages clauses have become so common that their absence in a given transaction would be remarkable. Counsel to businesses that sell goods typically advise their clients to use warranty disclaimers and damages excluders. This advice is

---

1. Disclaimers of the implied warranty of fitness for particular purpose are not as significant commercially as disclaimers of the implied warranty of merchantability. Note will be taken of disclaimers of fitness-for-purpose warranties as appropriate.

often implemented in lawyer-drafted provisions that are included in the standard contracting forms used by sellers. In the marketplace, would clauses limiting the damages that aggrieved buyers may recover or clauses disclaiming implied warranties be equally significant in the minds of buyers? Do these clauses deal with the same or different economic risks? Which kind of clause is more likely to cause a potential buyer to forego a purchase?

Insurance Co. of North America v. Automatic Sprinkler Corp.

Supreme Court of Ohio, 1981.
67 Ohio St.2d 91, 423 N.E.2d 151.

Appellee, Automatic Sprinkler Corporation of America ("Automatic Sprinkler"), purchased the components of a dry chemical fire protection system from appellant, The Ansul Company ("Ansul"). Both parties understood that Automatic Sprinkler would install this system in a building occupied by Youngstown Steel and Alloy Corporation ("Youngstown Steel").

A representative of Ansul signed a "Proposal," dated February 13, 1970. No one signed the proposal on behalf of Automatic Sprinkler. This document is five pages long. The front of each page includes typewritten or printed information which either describes the goods or states the price. Only the fifth and last page has printing on the back including:

"This sale is subject to the following terms and conditions:

" . . .

"9. The Ansul extinguisher is warranted to the original purchaser for five years from date of delivery against defects in workmanship and material. The Ansul Company will replace or repair any metal parts which in its opinion are defective and have not been tampered with or subjected to misuse, abuse or exposed to highly corrosive conditions. This warranty is *in lieu of* all other warranties express or implied. The Ansul Company assumes no liability for *consequential* or other loss or *damage* whatsoever arising out of injuries to or death of persons and damages to or destruction of property in any manner caused by, incident to, or connected with the use of the equipment, and the Buyer shall *indemnify* and save harmless the Seller from and against all such claims, loss, cost or damage. In addition, unless the Ansul equipment is maintained per Ansul's recommendations, Ansul hereby disclaims all liability whatsoever, including, but not limited to, any liability otherwise attaching under the warranty provisions of this paragraph." (Emphasis added.)

There are 15 paragraphs in all—each without a heading, each without extraordinary capitalization.

Ansul delivered the goods under a "Purchase Order," dated April 14, 1970, "per Ansul Quotation 8674 signed 2–13–70."

A fire occurred on September 9, 1974, at the building occupied by Youngstown Steel. The Ansul fire extinguisher system did not discharge.

None of the aforementioned facts is disputed. Two lawsuits did result, however.

Insurance Company of North America ("INA"), subrogee to the building owner, complained against Automatic Sprinkler and Ansul (case No. 80–619). Automatic Sprinkler ultimately cross-claimed against Ansul. Youngstown Steel and its insurer sued Automatic Sprinkler (case No. 80–620) Automatic Sprinkler then filed a third-party complaint against Ansul. In both cases, the claims alleged breach of warranty and negligence.

Later, the Court of Common Pleas consolidated these cases. The trial judge granted Ansul's motion for summary judgment and dismissed Automatic Sprinkler's claims against Ansul in both cases because (1) Ansul had disclaimed all warranties on sale and limited Automatic Sprinkler's remedies to repair and replacement of defective parts and (2) Automatic Sprinkler agreed to indemnify Ansul and hold it harmless from all claims. The Court of Appeals reversed the trial court, holding that the disclaimer and exclusion of consequential damages fail because they are not conspicuous.

The Court of Appeals also held that "there is no basis for summary judgment in favor of the Ansul Company on the indemnity provision question at this stage of the case," because paragraph 9 is not conspicuous. The court reversed and remanded the cause to the trial court for further proceedings on this issue.

The cause is now before this court pursuant to the allowance of motions to certify the record.

* * *

■ LOCHER, JUSTICE.

This case presents three issues: (1) whether Ansul has effectively disclaimed all implied warranties with Automatic Sprinkler; (2) whether Ansul has effectively excluded all liability for consequential damages; and (3) whether Automatic Sprinkler must indemnify Ansul against all claims arising in this litigation. Resolving each of these issues requires an interpretation of paragraph 9.

We hold that Ansul has neither disclaimed its liability for implied warranties nor excluded its liability for consequential damages.

I.

Ansul attempted to disclaim all liability to Automatic Sprinkler for breach of implied warranties by including the following language in paragraph 9: "This warranty is in lieu of all other warranties express or implied." Automatic Sprinkler argues that this language fails as a disclaimer because it does not mention merchantability and is not conspicuous as required by [UCC 2–316(2)]. Ansul, on the other hand, suggests that the "in lieu of" language is similar to "as is" under [UCC 2–316(3)(a)]. Under

Ansul's view, the disclaimer is effective regardless of whether it is conspicuous or whether it mentions merchantability.

We hold that the "in lieu of" language is not similar to "as is".... The effort to disclaim liability for all implied warranties fails because paragraph 9 is not conspicuous and because the disclaimer does not mention merchantability.

"As is" language describes the *quality of the goods* sold. As an example of "as is" language, [UCC 2–316(3)(a)] expressly includes "with all faults." ... Official Comment 7 ... further explains the intent of the drafters:

> "Paragraph [(a)] deals with general items such as 'as is,' 'as they stand,' 'with all faults,' and the like. Such terms in ordinary commercial usage are understood to mean that the buyer takes the entire risk as to the *quality of the goods* involved. ..." (Emphasis added.)

> . . .

We recognize that the courts have held that "in lieu of" language eliminates implied warranties. ... We reject this conclusion.

Under [2–316(3)(a)] "other language which, in common understanding, calls the buyer's attention to the exclusion of warranties and makes plain that there is no implied warranty" must be language which is consistent with the intention of the drafters and the General Assembly. This language must describe the *quality* of the goods.

Accordingly, the "in lieu of" language in paragraph 9 falls outside [2–316(3)(a)].

This "in lieu of" provision does not qualify, therefore, as a disclaimer of implied warranties under [2–316(2)]. There is no mention of merchantability. In addition, we have held that paragraph 9 is inconspicuous.

[UCC 1–201(10)] defines "conspicuousness" as follows:

> " 'Conspicuous': A term or clause is conspicuous when it is so written that a reasonable person against whom it is to operate ought to have noticed it. A printed heading in capitals (as: NON–NEGOTIABLE BILL OF LADING) is conspicuous. Language in the body of a form is 'conspicuous' if it is in larger or other contrasting type or color. But in a telegram any stated term is 'conspicuous.' Whether a term or clause is 'conspicuous' or not is for decision by the court."

Paragraph 9 appears among 15 other paragraphs on the back of the last page of the Proposal. This is the only page with writing on the back and is unnumbered. None of these paragraphs has a heading, extraordinary capitalization or contrasting type. Furthermore, Ansul alone executed the Proposal which contained paragraph 9 approximately two months before Automatic Sprinkler submitted its purchase order. In light of all these circumstances, therefore, it is clear that paragraph 9 is inconspicuous.

Accordingly, we hold that the "in lieu of" provision in paragraph 9 does not disclaim all implied warranties.

II.

Ansul argues that, even if the purported disclaimer fails, paragraph 9 excludes "liability for consequential or other loss or damage...." We disagree.

[UCC 2–719(3) and 2–316(4)] permit parties to exclude consequential damages without expressly requiring that the exclusion be conspicuous. Nevertheless, courts and commentators have read U.C.C. 2–719[3] and U.C.C. 2–316[4] *in pari materia*. See e.g., Avenell v. Westinghouse Electric Corp. (Cuyahoga Cty., 1974), 41 Ohio App.2d 150, 324 N.E.2d 583; Zicari v. Joseph Harris Co., Inc. (1969), 33 App.Div.2d 17, 304 N.Y.S.2d 918; Nordstrom, Law of Sales, at 276; Special Project—Article Two Warranties in Commercial Transactions, 64 Cornell L.Rev. 30, 224. Nordstrom, supra, explains why these two statutes should be read together, as follows:

> "The requirement that the agreement contain the alteration of basic Code remedies brings into play those ideas discussed in the prior section of this text [dealing with disclaimers of implied warranties]. The limitation [or exclusion of remedies] must be a part of the parties' bargain in fact. If it is contained in a printed clause which was not conspicuous or brought to the buyer's attention, the seller had no reasonable expectation that the buyer understood that his remedies were being restricted to repair and replacement. As such, the clause cannot be said to be a part of the bargain (or agreement) of the parties." (Citation omitted.)

Any other reading of these provisions would permit inconspicuous provisions excluding or limiting damage recovery to circumvent the protection for buyers in [2–316(2)]. ...

Paragraph 9 is inconspicuous in its entirety. The attempt to exclude liability for consequential damages, therefore, is also inconspicuous. Accordingly, Automatic Sprinkler may recover consequential damages from Ansul.

* * *

NOTES

(1) **Bargain in Fact.** Could Automatic Sprinkler Corporation of America contend persuasively that the language in the "Proposal" that disclaimed "all other warranties" was unclear to the buyer as a disclaimer of the warranty of merchantability? Could Automatic Sprinkler contend persuasively that it was reasonably unaware of the clause on Ansul's liability for consequential damages? Do you think it likely or unlikely that corporations like Automatic Sprinkler use such contractual clauses in transactions in which they are sellers?

(2) **Construction of UCC 2–316(2).** Why did the drafters of the UCC include 2–316(2)? What did they intend by the requirement that a seller must "mention merchantability" to disclaim the 2–314 warranty?

The Ohio Supreme Court made no effort to resolve the controversy on the bargain in fact, but rather decided the case on the basis of Ansul's non-compliance with the "mention" clause in UCC 2–316(2) and with the court's implication of a statutory "conspicuousness" requirement in UCC 2–719. What is the public policy rationale of those *formal* requirements? Is it arguable that the legislation was designed to protect consumer buyers and not sophisticated commercial buyers like Automatic Sprinkler? Could a court properly exclude buyers who are large corporations?[2]

Section 2–316(2) treats disclaimers of merchantability and fitness-for-particular purpose rather differently. Disclaimer of merchantability may be oral, but disclaimer of fitness-for-particular-purpose must be in writing. What might explain this difference?

(3) Legislative History. Consider the history of UCC 2–316. In the initial drafts of the UCC, from 1940 to 1952, subsection (2) provided:

> (2) Exclusion or modification of the implied warranty of merchantability or of fitness for a particular purpose must be in specific language and if the inclusion of such language creates an ambiguity in the contract as a whole it shall be resolved against the seller; except that [the three subparagraphs now in (3) followed as exceptions].

Comments to the 1952 draft provided:

> 3.   Disclaimer of the implied warranties of merchantability and of fitness for particular purpose is permitted under subsection (2), but with the safeguard that such disclaimers must be in specific terms and that any ambiguity must be resolved against the seller.
>
> 4.   Implied warranties may not be excluded merely by the use of a clause disclaiming "all warranties express or implied." On the other hand, a clause such as "We assume no responsibility that the goods concerned in this contract are fit for any particular purpose for which they are being bought outside of the general purposes of goods of the description," would normally be sufficient to satisfy the requirement that the disclaimer be in "specific terms."
>
> 5.   The provision of subsection (2) that an ambiguity arising from the co-existence of words of disclaimer and evidence showing the creation of the implied warranties of merchantability or fitness for a particular purpose must be resolved against the seller is intended to pose the true issue in such cases. This section rejects that line of approach which presupposes the original existence of warranty and then attempts to deal with the question of whether it has been disclaimed by language in the agreement. . . .

In 1955, after the UCC had been adopted in Pennsylvania and was under consideration in a number of states, the UCC was revised. The language

---

2. A federal district court, in a recent decision, held that the language denied effect in this case was sufficient to exclude the warranty of merchantability. Lefebvre Inter-graphics, Inc. v. Sanden Machine Ltd., 946 F.Supp. 1358 (N.D.Ill.1996) (sale of a commercial printing press).

above was deleted and the current provision substituted, with the exceptions set off in a new paragraph (3). The Editorial Board, which proposed the revision, gave this brief explanation:

> **Reason.** The purpose of this change is to relieve the seller from the requirement of disclaiming a warranty of fitness in specific language and yet afford the buyer an adequate warning of such disclaimer.

No explanation was given for adding the requirements (i) that a valid disclaimer must "mention merchantability," (ii) that a disclaimer of the warranty of fitness for particular purpose must be in writing and conspicuous, or (iii) that a disclaimer of warranty of merchantability, if in a writing, must be conspicuous. Comments to take account of the 1955 (and 1956) text changes were published in 1957. Comments 3, 4, and 5, in their present form, replaced the earlier comments.

Does this history shed light on the drafters' intention with regard to the necessary form of a disclaimer of the implied warranty of merchantability? What weight should a court place on such history in construing the UCC as adopted by a particular legislature, such as the construction of the Ohio version of the UCC in the *Insurance Company* case?

(4) Conspicuousness of Warranty Disclaimers. UCC 2–316(2) does not require that a disclaimer of the implied warranty of merchantability be in writing, but if a written disclaimer is made the disclaimer must be "conspicuous." Any disclaimer of the warranty of fitness for particular purpose must be in writing and must be "conspicuous." The Definitional Cross References in the Official Comment do not note that this term is defined in Article 1, UCC 1–201(10). The Ohio Supreme Court declared that the paragraph 9 of the Ansul proposal was not "conspicuous," but this followed the primary conclusion that the language of that paragraph was insufficient to operate as a disclaimer. Would otherwise sufficient language be denied legal effect if a court found that the conspicuousness requirement had not been met. Consider the following:

> The owner of a small business agreed to purchase a computer system (hardware and software) to increase bookkeeping efficiency. Buyer signed two separate one-sheet documents, with printing on both sides, prepared by seller. Neither document referred on its face to any warranty of quality. On the document dealing with the hardware, the last line before the place for signatures stated—in all-capital letters—that the buyer had agreed to all terms and conditions, including those on the reverse side. On the face of the software document was a provision that "THE TERMS AND CONDITIONS, INCLUDING THE WARRANTY AND LIMITATION OF LIABILITY, ON THE REVERSE SIDE ARE PART OF THIS AGREEMENT."

On the reverse side of the hardware document, in a separate numbered paragraph (one of 15), appeared the following in bold-face type:

EXCEPT AS SPECIFICALLY PROVIDED HEREIN, THERE ARE NO OTHER WARRANTIES, EXPRESS OR IMPLIED, INCLUDING, BUT

NOT LIMITED TO, ANY IMPLIED WARRANTIES OF MERCHANT-ABILITY OR FITNESS FOR A PARTICULAR PURPOSE.

In the software document, the same language appeared in a separately numbered paragraph (one of 14) under a heading, "WARRANTY," printed in bold face but the paragraph under the heading was not in bold type.

The computer system failed to meet the buyer's needs. Buyer sued seller. The trial court held that warranty exclusion clauses were not sufficiently conspicuous, and the United States Court of Appeals for the Ninth Circuit affirmed. Sierra Diesel Injection Service, Inc. v. Burroughs Corp., 874 F.2d 653 (9th Cir.1989)(2–1). The Court of Appeals said (pp. 658–659):

> Whether a disclaimer is conspicuous is not simply a matter of measuring the type size or looking at the placement of the disclaimer within the contract [document]. A reviewing court must ascertain that a reasonable person in the buyer's position would not have been surprised to find the warranty disclaimer in the contract [document]. ... One factor to consider is the sophistication of the parties. ... Also relevant as to whether a reasonable person would have noticed a warranty disclaimer are the circumstances of the negotiation and signing.
>
> The trial court found that Mr. Cathey was not familiar with computers or with contracts. Mr. Cathey read the front of the [documents], but did not notice the warranty disclaimer clauses on the back. Given Mr. Cathey's lack of sophistication in the field of contracts and the written and oral representations made by Burroughs, it is not surprising that it would require more than a collection of standardized form contracts on various subjects involved in a transaction to notify a reasonable person in Mr. Cathey's position that the [computer] came without any warranty of merchantability.

(5) Construction of UCC 2–719. In what sense is the *Insurance Company* decision a construction of UCC 2–719? Is it conceivable that the drafters of the UCC were unaware of the differences in the formulations of UCC 2–316 and UCC 2–719? Does the court's approach trespass on the legislature's prerogative?

(6) Proposed Revised of Article 2. Revisers of Article 2 have proposed to make substantial changes to UCC 2–316. Most of those changes deal with disclaimers of the implied warranty of merchantability. No revision of UCC 2–719 is proposed.

In many respects, current drafts of Proposed Revised 2–316 would have two sets of rules, one for contracts with ordinary consumer buyers and another for contracts with commercial buyers.

In sales to consumer buyers, an enforceable merchantability disclaimer would have be in a record (writing or electronic record), would have to use statutorily prescribed language, and would have to be conspicuous.[3]

---

3. Proposed Revised 2–316(b). In some respects the draft is unclear.

Universal Drilling Co. v. Camay Drilling Co.

United States Court of Appeals, Tenth Circuit, 1984.
737 F.2d 869.

■ McKay, Circuit Judge.

The parties to this lawsuit are "experienced, sophisticated, intelligent business[men] with vast education and experience in petroleum engineering, ... oil and gas exploration, and ... [the] makeup and operation of oil drilling rigs and equipment." ... In June 1977 they entered into negotiations for the purchase and sale of two drilling rigs referred to by the parties as the Marthens Rig and Rig 10.

The negotiations resulted in a contract dated July 1, 1977, [which contained the following clauses]:

18.01   The assets being purchased and sold hereunder are being sold by [defendant] in an "as-is" condition and without any warranty of operability or fitness.

* * *

26.01   This Agreement and the exhibits hereto and the agreements referred to herein set forth the entire agreement and understanding of the parties in respect of the transactions contemplated hereby and supersede all prior agreements, arrangements and understanding relating to the subject matter hereof. No representation, promise inducement or statement of intention has been made by [defendant] or [plaintiffs] which is not embodied in this Agreement or in the documents referred to herein, and neither [defendant] nor [plaintiffs] shall be bound by or liable for any alleged representation, promise, inducement or statements of intention not so set forth.[*]

... The contract defines the property to be sold as the personal property listed in Exhibits A, B and C to the contract. Rig 10 is defined as

---

With respect to merchant-buyer transactions, proposed subsection (b) gives effect to any language or conduct which in common understanding makes it clear to the buyer that the seller assumes no responsibility for the quality of the goods, but proposed subsection (c) invalidates a disclaimer that does not "mention merchantability." The same lack of clarity is found in current Article 2. Earlier drafts would have removed any mandatory terms for disclaimers of merchantability warranties in business-to-business transactions, but would have given a "safe harbor" to a disclaimer that "mentioned merchantability."

With respect to consumer transactions, proposed subsection (c)declares that a merchant seller's merchantability disclaimer must state: "The seller undertakes no responsibility for the quality of the goods except as otherwise provided in the contract." For disclaimer of fitness-for-particular-purpose warranties in consumer contracts, proposed subsection (c) requires the following: "The seller assumes no responsibility that the goods will be fit for any particular purpose for which you may be buying these goods, except as otherwise provided in the contract." There may be some confusion in the minds of the drafters as to whether the quoted language is the only language that be effective or whether, rather, the quoted language is intended to be a "safe harbor."

* [The court reproduced the contract in a footnote. Eds.]

the property in Exhibit A and the Marthens Rig is defined as the property in Exhibits B and C. [The purchase price was $2,925,000.]

Subsequent to the delivery of the property, plaintiffs complained that the property they received did not conform to the contract alleging that they were to receive two used but nevertheless operable drilling rigs. Defendant, however, relying on the contract, argued that it delivered all of the property listed in the specific exhibits. This diversity lawsuit resulted.

At trial, [t]he trial court ... rejected plaintiffs' theory that there were breaches of express warranties based on the description of the goods contained in the contract. Plaintiffs appeal....

* * *

Breach of Express Warranties by Description

Approaching this issue it must again be remembered that the parties to this suit are experienced in the field of oil and gas exploration and drilling. Furthermore, none of the parties allege that they were in an inferior bargaining position.

Plaintiffs do not dispute the trial court's finding that the contract, specifically paragraph 18.01, effectively disclaimed all implied warranties. Plaintiffs do allege, however, that the description of the assets contained in the contract created an express warranty that the assets would conform to that description. In addition, plaintiffs argue that such an express warranty of description cannot be disclaimed, ... or at least was not effectively disclaimed.

Section 2–316 of the Uniform Commercial Code as adopted in Colorado provides for the modification and exclusion of warranties. Colo. Rev. Stat. § 4–2–315 (1973). In particular it provides that

> [w]ords or conduct relevant to the creation of an express warranty and words or conduct tending to negate or limit warranty shall be construed wherever reasonable as consistent with each other; but subject to the provisions of this article on parol or extrinsic evidence (section 4–2–202), negation or limitation is inoperative to the extent such construction is unreasonable.

Id. § 4–2–316(1). Accordingly, the initial inquiry must be whether express warranties were created under section 4–2–313 and if so how they are affected by section 18.01 of the contract.

Plaintiff argues that this case is controlled by Section 4–2–313(b) which provides that "[a]ny description of the goods which is made part of the basis of the bargain creates an express warranty that the goods shall conform to the description." Colo. Rev. Stat. § 4–2–313(b). The principles underlying section 4–2–313 are set out in comment four to that section:

> 4. In view of the principle that the whole purpose of the law of warranty is to determine what it is that the seller has in essence agreed to sell, the policy is adopted of those cases which refuse except in unusual circumstances to recognize a material deletion of the

seller's obligation. Thus, a contract is normally a contract for a sale of something describable and described. A clause generally disclaiming "all warranties, express or implied" cannot reduce the seller's obligation with respect to such description and therefore cannot be given literal effect under Section 2–316.

This is not intended to mean that the parties, if they consciously desire, cannot make their own bargain as they wish. But in determining what they have agreed upon in good faith is a factor and consideration should be given to the fact that the probability is small that a real price is intended to be exchanged for a pseudo-obligation.

Id. § 4–2–313 comment 4.

Similarly, Professors White and Summers argue that a seller should not be able to disclaim a warranty created by description.

We hope courts will reach similar conclusions and strike down attempted disclaimers in cases in which the seller includes a description of the article which amounts to a warranty and then attempts to disclaim all express warranties. To illustrate further: assume that the sales contract describes machinery to be sold as a "haybaler" and then attempts to disclaim all express warranties. If the machine failed to bale hay and the buyer sued, we would argue that the disclaimer is ineffective. In our judgment, the description of the machine as a "haybaler" is a warranty that the machine will bale hay and, in the words of 2–316, a negation or limitation ought to be "inoperative" since it is inconsistent with the warranty.

J. White & R. Summers, Handbook of the Law Under the Uniform Commercial Code § 12–3 at 433 (2d ed. 1980).

Plaintiff relies principally on two cases that follow this rationale. Century Dodge Inc. v. Mobley, 155 Ga. App. 712, 272 S.E. 2d 502, 504 (1980)(cert. denied); Blankenship v. Northtown Ford, Inc., 95 Ill. App. 3d 303, 420 N.E. 2d 167, 170–71 (1981). In both cases automobile dealers had sold "new" cars which for various reasons did not meet the description of a "new" car. Consequently the courts held that the boilerplate disclaimer provisions of the consumer sales contracts did not relieve the dealers of their responsibility to deliver a "new" car.

We do not question the rationale of the above authorities. Nonetheless, we find them not controlling the instant case. If in this case we were dealing with a consumer transaction, as in the cases just cited, we would be more inclined to follow those authorities. However, as noted in subsequent cases, "the courts are less reluctant to hold educated businessmen to the terms of contracts to which they have entered than consumers dealing with skilled corporate sellers." . . .

Furthermore, both sections 4–2–313 and 4–2–316 express the policy of the statutory scheme to allow parties to make any bargain they wish. Comment four to section 4–2–313 states that if parties consciously desire they can disclaim whatever warranties they wish. Colo. Rev. Stat. § 4–2–313 comment 4 (1973). In addition, comment one to section 4–2–316 explains that its purpose is to "protect a buyer from unexpected and unbargained language of disclaimer." Id. § 4–2–316 comment 1. Consequently, we will not rewrite the contract in this case. The exhibits to the contract which described the goods must be read in conjunction with the contract itself. The contract states that the goods are used and there is no guarantee that they are fit or even *operable*.

If we were to hold the contract in the instant case created undisclaimable express warranties by description, we cannot think of alternative language that would memorialize the intent of the parties—to purchase and sell used "as is" equipment which has value but which may need repairs or additional parts to be fit and operable.

Our holding on this issue does not leave plaintiffs in general without remedy in similar contexts or the plaintiffs in this case with an "empty bargain." If the goods delivered do not meet the description in the contract there is a breach of the contract. In short, if no mast were delivered or if what was delivered was junk metal which in no way resembled a mast, plaintiffs would have a cause of action for breach of the contract.

Finally, plaintiffs did not receive an empty bargain. An appraisal which plaintiffs commissioned valued the goods received at an amount in excess of $3,000,000. . . . The purchase price for the assets was $2,925,000.

The trial court did not err in excluding plaintiffs' evidence regarding breach of warranty.

* * *

AFFIRMED.

NOTES

(1) **"As Is"; "With All Faults."** UCC 2–316(3)(a) declares that "all implied warranties are excluded by expressions like 'as is' [or] 'with all faults.'" Many read this as a declaration that either phrase is effective as a matter of law to disclaim the merchantability warranty. However, this subsection begins with a qualifier: "unless the circumstances indicate otherwise." Would all buyers understand the meaning of the quoted phrases?

Problem 3.4.1. In negotiations that led to the purchase of a mobile home, the seller showed a model mobile home to the buyer. The contract stated in capital letters that the sale was "AS IS." The buyer asserts that the mobile home delivered to him was not like the model. What result? See UCC 2–313(1)(c), 2–316(1); Consolidated Data Terminals v. Applied Digital Data Systems, 708 F.2d 385 (9th Cir.1983).

(2) **Contract Interpretation: UCC 2–316(1).** Buyer's attorney apparently argued, under UCC 2–316(1), that the words of negation of warranty in § 18.01 were "inoperative" in light of the words of description. Could buyer's attorney have made the essential point differently? Suppose counsel had argued that the "operability" language in § 18.01 referred to

future performance of the rigs, but was not intended to declare that the rigs were presently not in operating condition. Would that have been a persuasive argument?

(3) Commercial Sophistication of Buyers. On the surface of the UCC provisions defining sellers' responsibility for quality, the UCC does not differentiate among buyers who are seasoned veterans in buying goods of the kind, buyers who are commercially naive, and buyers in between.[4] Nor does the UCC's provision on exclusion or modification of warranties. What, then, explains the emphasis that the *Universal Drilling* court put on the experience and sophistication of the parties? The buyer relied principally on two decisions involving consumer retail sales of new automobiles. The Tenth Circuit expressed no question about the rationale of those decisions, but found them not controlling. Does the UCC permit such different treatment for consumer retail sales and sales of business equipment?[5]

Western Industries, Inc. v. Newcor Canada Limited

United States Court of Appeals, Seventh Circuit, 1984.
739 F.2d 1198.

■ POSNER, CIRCUIT JUDGE.

Western Industries purchased several custom-built welding machines from Newcor Canada for use in manufacturing microwave oven cavities. The machines did not work right and Western brought this breach of contract action against Newcor, basing federal jurisdiction on diversity of citizenship. Newcor counterclaimed for the unpaid portion of the purchase price of the machines. The jury awarded Western damages of $1.3 million dollars and Newcor about half that (the full unpaid balance of the purchase price of the machines) on its counterclaim. Separate judgments were entered on the two claims and both parties have appealed. The appeals raise a variety of interesting substantive and procedural issues, the former being controlled (the parties agree) by the law of Wisconsin, including the Uniform Commercial Code, which Wisconsin has adopted.

The contract between Western and Newcor grew out of Western's contract with a Japanese manufacturer of microwave ovens, Sharp, to supply Sharp with cavities for microwave ovens. Sharp wanted Western to weld the cavities by a process known as projection welding, because that is how microwave oven cavities are made in Japan; and Western agreed. The projection method is not used in the United States to weld thin metal, such as the cavities of microwave ovens are made of; spot welding is the method used here. So when Western went to Newcor, a leading manufacturer of

---

4. The UCC does differentiate among sellers on the basis of commercial experience in UCC 2–314. Only a seller who is "a merchant with respect to [the] goods" sold makes an implied warranty of merchantability. "Merchant" is defined in UCC 2–104(1).

5. Elsewhere the UCC is sensitive to market levels in sales transactions. The UCC provision on contractual limitation or exclusion of consequential damages sets forth two standards, one for "injury to the person in the case of consumer goods" and another for "loss [that] is commercial." UCC 2–719(3).

specialty welding machines, to explore the possibility of buying machines for use in fulfilling its contract with Sharp, it had to ask Newcor to design and build a type of welding machine that Newcor was unfamiliar with. Newcor agreed to do this, however, and after further discussions Western's director of engineering placed a purchase order by phone for eight machines with Newcor's sales engineer on May 17, 1979. According to the memoranda that both men made of the conversation, no specific terms other than the date of delivery were discussed; price was not discussed, for example. On May 23 Newcor delivered to Western a formal written quotation of terms for the sale. On the back of one page a number of standard contract terms were printed, including one disclaiming all liability for consequential damages. Western did not reply immediately, but in mid July it sent Newcor a formal purchase order, mysteriously pre-dated to May 15, that included on the back a set of printed terms one of which stated that the buyer (Western) was entitled to general as well as special damages in the event of a breach of the seller's warranties. On July 20 Newcor sent Western an acknowledgement form stating, "In conformity with our conditions of sale appearing in [the written quotation . . .] furnished to you by us, this approves and accepts your order." Western did not respond. The parties never discussed any of the printed terms contained in the contract forms that they had exchanged. Three machines were bought later through a similar exchange of forms. The parties treat the sale of all 11 machines as one contract, as shall we.

The machines were built and delivered but turned out to be unusable for making microwave oven cavities. Newcor took the machines back and rebuilt them as spot welding machines, redelivering them to Western a year after the delivery date called for in the contract. As a result of the delay in getting machines that it could use, Western incurred unforeseen expenses in fulfilling its commitment to Sharp; for example, it had to manufacture cavities manually at much higher cost than it would have incurred if it has had proper machines. These expenses are the basis of its damage claim against Newcor.

Newcor's first ground of appeal is that the district judge improperly excluded evidence that the custom of the specialty welding machine trade is not to give a disappointed buyer his consequential damages but just to allow him either to return the machines and get his money back or (for example if the breach consists in delivering them late) keep the machines and get the purchase price reduced to compensate for the costs of delay. . . . Newcor contends that it is not liable for any damages above the purchase price, however those damages are described; and if this is right, then even if Newcor had a contract with Western that it broke it is not liable for any of the damages that Western was awarded.

Although trade custom or usage is a question of fact, see UCC 1–205(2) and Official Comments 4 and 9; . . . the district judge refused to allow Newcor's three principal witnesses on the existence of the alleged trade custom to testify, on the ground that they were incompetent to give such testimony; and having done this the judge later instructed the jury that there was no issue of trade custom in the case. Two of the three witnesses whom Newcor wanted to call were experienced executives of companies that manufacture specialty welding machines (one of them was also the president of those manufacturers' trade association), and between them the two had almost 75 years of experience in selling such machines. The third witness was a former executive of Western and had long experience in buying such machines. These witnesses were prepared to testify that consequential damages were unheard of in their trade. When a machine did not work the manufacturer would spend his own money to fix it or would take it back and refund the purchase price to the buyer, but he would not compensate the buyer for the disruption to the buyer's business caused by the defect.

* * *

Although we are in no position to determine whether the custom alleged by Newcor actually exists, we think it relevant to note that the hypothesis that it exists is certainly not so incredible that testimony on the subject could be excluded by analogy to the principle that excludes testimony in contradiction of the laws of nature. The relevant trade is the manufacture of a particular kind of custom-built machinery. A custom-built machine is quite likely either not to be delivered on time or not to work (not at first, anyway) when it is delivered; anyone who has ever had a house built for him knows the perils of custom design. If a custom-built machine is delivered late, or does not work as the buyer had hoped and expected it would, the buyer's business is quite likely to suffer, and may even be ruined; and as the buyers of these welding machines are substantial manufacturers to whose businesses the machines are essential, the potential costs of defective design or late delivery are astronomical.

. . . [A]ll we need find in order to conclude that Newcor's evidence of trade custom was admissible is that a rational jury could have concluded that, yes, it was the custom for manufacturers of specialty welding machines not to be liable for consequential damages. That contractual liability for such damages (in the absence of special notice) is of relatively recent vintage, that many breaches of contract are (as here) involuntary, that only the sky would be the limit to the amount of consequential damages that manufacturers of machinery indispensable to their customers' businesses might run up, that those manufacturers not only have a better idea of what the potential injury to them might be but also might be able to avert it more easily than their supplier—all these things make it not at all incredible that a custom might have evolved in this industry against a buyer's getting consequential damages in the event of a breach.

If there was such a custom, it would not take the manufacturers of specialty welding machines off the financial hook completely. When they have to take back and resell custom-built machines they face the prospect of a heavy loss. A machine custom-designed to one manufacturer's specifications may not fit any other's. That is no doubt why Newcor spent hundreds of thousands of dollars to rebuild these machines as spot-welding machines that Western could use. That is also why we reject Newcor's argument that Western should be estopped to claim damages because it induced Newcor to rebuild the machines. Newcor rebuilt them in its own interest, to mitigate the loss it would have incurred if it had had to take back the machines and refund the purchase price; if it had taken back the machines it would have had to rebuild them in order to be able to resell them.

But a disclaimer of liability for consequential damages would place some limit on the exposure of the manufacturers of specialty welding machines. It would also give buyers incentives to take their own precautions, which might be efficacious, against the disasters that might befall them if the machines did not work. ... There was much evidence that Western made a serious mistake in agreeing with Sharp (rather casually as it appears) to build microwave oven cavities by projection welding, a process which, it turned out, American safety standards made infeasible. Western would have been less likely to make such mistakes if it had known with certainty that it would not be able to get consequential damages if the machines didn't work.

* * *

Newcor has a second ground of appeal. It wanted to put before the jury not only the theory that trade custom had supplied a silent contractual term excluding liability for consequential damages, but also the theory that the explicit terms of the contract excluded such liability....

* * *

As a practical matter, however, Newcor's alternative theory is not very different from its main theory—that the custom of the trade excluded liability for consequential damages. Given an exchange of inconsistent forms, Newcor would have to present a reason why its form disclaiming liability for consequential damages should be accepted over Western's form asserting such liability; and the reason would have to be the custom of the trade, as that is the only substantial ground that Newcor has for claiming precedence for its disclaimer. ...

* * *

The parties raise some other issues, which we have considered but find to have no merit. The judgment in favor of Western on its claim and the judgment in favor of Newcor on its counterclaim are reversed and the case is remanded for a new trial on both claims, with no costs in this court.

REVERSED AND REMANDED.

NOTES

(1) **Battle of the Forms.** The facts in *Western Industries* illustrate a familiar process in which the representatives of the two contracting firms doing the actual negotiation communicate with each other by inserting the details of the particular deal on their firm's printed standard forms. Who

writes the terms that are printed on such forms? How can the drafters design terms that will fit the unknown particular agreements in which the forms may be used?

The portion of the court's opinion addressed to the battle of the forms has been omitted. Most students study this topic in the course on Contracts. The governing law for domestic United States transactions is the infamous UCC 2–207.

(2) Implied Warranty Disclaimers or Limitation of Damages. The UCC expressly declares that implied warranties can be excluded or modified by course of dealing, course of performance, or usage of trade. UCC 2–316(3)(c). Recall the decision in *Royal Business Machines*, Section 3, supra. No similar provision is found in UCC 2–719. Is the omission significant?

Kunststoffwerk Alfred Huber v. R.J. Dick, Inc.

United States Court of Appeals, Third Circuit, 1980.
621 F.2d 560.

■ WEIS, CIRCUIT JUDGE.

In this diversity case, the district court concluded that under the Uniform Commercial Code the buyer has the burden of establishing that the seller agreed to pay consequential damages when goods proved defective. We hold that to avoid such liability the seller must prove an agreement that limits damages, and, in this instance, the course of dealing between the parties was not adequate to demonstrate such an understanding. Accordingly, we modify a judgment in favor of the plaintiff-seller for goods sold to allow credits for losses on resale incurred by the defendant-buyer.

The plaintiff brought suit in the United States District Court for the Eastern District of Pennsylvania to recover the cost of nylon industrial belting it sold to the defendant. Counterclaims asserted that some of the belting had been defective. After a bench trial, the district court entered judgment for the plaintiff, deducting from the requested damages portions of the amounts sought by two of the defendant's counterclaims.

The defendant, R.J. Dick, Inc., distributes nylon cord belting throughout the United States. Its principal place of business is in Iowa, and it maintains a warehouse in King of Prussia, Pennsylvania. The plaintiff is a sole proprietorship that manufactures nylon cord belting in Offenburg, West Germany under the trade name "Vis."

In September 1967 plaintiff's export manager, Alfred Ziegler, sent a letter to the defendant's president, quoting prices on belting and enclosing terms for delivery and payment. Included in the correspondence was a form entitled "General Terms of Sales II." One paragraph in the form limited the plaintiff's liability for defective merchandise to replacement or price reduction and excluded damages of any kind:

[Reclamations must be made within 10 days after receipt of merchandise and prior to processing or use. Our guaranty is limited to replacement or price reduction and excludes damages of any kind. Also, we do not give a guaranty for specific utilization. Minor deviations do not provide grounds for reclamations.][*]

In the following month, Ziegler and Vis's owner, Alfred Huber, visited King of Prussia and arranged for sale of their product to the Dick Company. At no time were the Vis general terms of sale discussed, and, consequently, Dick did not agree to be bound by the provisions of the form, including the limitation on damages recoverable for defective merchandise.

During the period from 1967 to 1974 there were occasions when the plaintiff's product did not meet the defendant's standards, either on initial inspection or after a period of use by defendant's customers. When the defendant issued a credit to a customer for belting that had manufacturing defects, a claim was made to the plaintiff for replacement or credit. If a difference arose between the parties over whether the defect was attributable to the manufacturer, the claim would be compromised.

In late 1973, Dick's problems with the belting increased, the most frequent being delamination, which made the product unusable. Beginning at that time and continuing through 1974, Ziegler complained about Dick's delay in payments. This suit followed the parties' inability to resolve these difficulties.

At trial, the plaintiff asserted that after making allowances for various credits to which it was agreeable, the defendant owed $30,910.29. Against this figure, however, the defendant asserted four counterclaims.

* * *

The court did allow partial recovery on the third and fourth counterclaims. The defendant contended in the third claim that it was entitled to $7,300.69, the amount it had credited its customers for defective material supplied by the plaintiff in 1974. The Court, however, awarded $3,398.25, a sum representing the price the defendant paid plaintiff. ... The fourth claim was for defective belting that one of Dick's distributors sold to a company called Wesco. Dick issued a credit of $7,092.80 on that transaction, but again the court allowed only the amount the defendant had paid plaintiff for the goods, $3,301.95. ... The defendant appeals.

* * *

The issue underlying the remaining two claims is straightforward: Was the defendant entitled to recover the credits granted customers when the product proved defective? In other words, was the defendant entitled to the profits it would have made on those sales? The parties agree that Pennsylvania law applies, particularly Article 2 of the Uniform Commercial Code.

* * *

* [The court reproduced the contract clause in a footnote.]

There is no dispute that plaintiff was aware of the nature of defendant's business, i.e., that the goods were to be resold. In these circumstances, we conclude that under § 2–715(2)(a) the credits that defendant was obliged to extend to customers are proper consequential damages. ...

The plaintiff does not dispute this proposition but argues that the parties agreed to exclude recovery of such damages under U.C.C. § 2–719(1)(a). That section provides that the agreement between the parties may provide for limiting the measure of damages, as by restricting the buyer's remedy to return of the goods and repayment of the price or to repair and replacement nonconforming goods. Pa. Stat. Ann. tit. 12A, § 2–719(1)(a) (Purdon 1970).

There is insufficient evidence in the record to establish an express agreement to limit damages. The trial judge found that the only communication between the parties bearing on the subject was the form sent by plaintiff to defendant in September 1967. He stated that "Dick never expressly consented to the Huber contract" and therefore could not be held subject to it. Nevertheless, the trial judge reasoned that the form had put the defendant on notice that Huber did not intend to assume liability for consequential damages and that Dick therefore had the burden, which it failed to carry, of informing plaintiff that such damages might be demanded.

* * *

The plaintiff argues ... that there was a "course of performance" under U.C.C. § 2–208(1) which established an agreement to forgo consequential damages. Since there was no single contract between the parties, but rather a series of separate sales, we believe it more accurate to characterize the conduct as a "course of dealing," defined in U.C.C. § 1–205(1). The plaintiff's argument is not weakened by adopting the course of dealing route because the Code specifically permits a course of dealing or a usage of trade, unlike a course of performance, to "give particular meaning to and supplement or qualify terms of an agreement." U.C.C. § 1–205(3), Pa. Stat. Ann. tit. 12A, § 1–205(3) (Purdon 1970) (emphasis added).[6] In Posttape Associates v. Eastman Kodak Co., 537 F.2d 751 (3d Cir.1976), we concluded that a limitation of damages could be imposed by a trade usage; it follows that a course of dealing is a circumstance that may establish this term as part of the bargain of the parties in fact. U.C.C. § 1–201(3), Pa. Stat. Ann. tit. 12A, § 1–201(3) (Purdon 1970).

The inquiry then is whether the record establishes the course of dealing the plaintiff suggests. Initially we observe that the burden is on the

---

6. By its own terms, a course of performance goes no further than being "relevant to determine the meaning of the agreement." U.C.C. § 2–208(1), Pa. Stat. Ann. tit. 12A, § 2–208(1) (Purdon 1970). Nevertheless, courts have generally allowed a course of performance to supplement and qualify the terms of an agreement as well. White & Summers § 3–3 (1972).

plaintiff to prove the limitation agreement, ... especially where it is to be found in a course of dealing.[7]

In its findings the district court did not set out facts that would constitute a course of dealing establishing defendant's agreement to forgo consequential damages. On appeal, the plaintiff does not point to specific parts of the record where such facts may be found, nor has our independent review disclosed such evidence. It is not enough that the defendant accepted replacement or credits for the purchase price in many instances. Obviously, if the defects were detected before resale and supplies of belting were available to fill outstanding orders, the defendant might not have had a claim for lost profits. In other instances it may well be that even after resale, the defendant's customers were content to accept replacement rather than demand a refund. Moreover, the record does show that the parties compromised many of the claims for defects in workmanship.

We find no instances in which the defendant had made a claim for loss of profits on resale transactions other than those underlying the counterclaims. If such claims had been made and then been denied by the plaintiff without protest from the defendant, the argument that a course of dealing established such a limitation might have some force. Cf. U.C.C. § 2–208(1), Pa. Stat. Ann. tit. 12A, § 2–208(1) (Purdon 1970) ("any course of performance accepted or acquiesced in without objection shall be relevant to determine the meaning of the agreement").... Absent such circumstances, however, we cannot say that the plaintiff has met the burden of proving a limitation agreement. Accordingly, the defendant is entitled to recover on the two counterclaims for loss of profits on actual sales.

The total of the two counterclaims is $14,393.49. The parties agree that the increases sought by the defendant and contained in this figure accurately reflect the loss on sales. That total will therefore be deducted from the amount which plaintiff claimed to be due—$30,910.29—thus resulting in an award to the plaintiff of $16,516.80. The case will be remanded to the district court so that it may modify its judgment accordingly.

NOTES

(1) Choice of Forum. The German seller in *Kunststoffwerk* was litigating in a foreign court, the "home" court of the U.S. buyer. What led to this choice of forum? In counselling German or other non-U.S. sellers or buyers dealing with U.S. firms, would you recommend structuring transactions to obtain a more familiar or at least a neutral forum? How could this be done?

---

7. In discussing terms supplied by a course of dealing, a usage of trade, and a course of performance, Professors White and Summers observed:

"Who has the burden of proof? The Code does not say. Yet courts are likely to impose the burden of proof on the party who seeks to benefit from evidence of course of dealing, trade usage, or course of performance."

White & Summers § 3–3, at 88 (1972)(footnote omitted).

(2) Seller's Express Exclusion of Damages. The German seller's standard form would have excluded liability for consequential damages. Why did the court not give effect to this form?

(3) Damages Exclusion by Course of Dealing. Seller's counsel argued that an agreement to exclude liability for consequential damages could be proved by course of performance. The court first corrected counsel's argument, which should have been characterized as based on course of dealing. Should an advocate in the Court of Appeals be expected to know the difference? The appellate court, having recast the argument, rejected it. Was the court's reasoning sound? Was there any conduct inconsistent with the alleged course of dealing? Why is that not sufficient to show agreement?

(4) Oral Express Warranties and Written Negations: Parol Evidence and UCC 2–202. The UCC allows disclaimers only of implied warranties of quality. Purported negation of an express warranty is addressed in UCC 2–316(1). That section directs courts to attempt to give effect to words or conduct that negate express warranties if that construction is consistent, but if consistent construction fails words or conduct that negate or limit the express warranty are inoperative.

The UCC 2–316(1) rule that protects express warranties against negation is expressly subject to the parol evidence rule in UCC 2–202. Transactions frequently occur in which buyers and sellers execute contract documents that contain a clause negating the existence of any express warranties that are not contained in the documents. Buyers often contend later that, before the documents were brought out for signatures, the sellers had made oral affirmations or promises that would constitute express warranties under UCC 2–313. Efforts to introduce that testimony are contested under a claim that the terms in the documents were intended to be complete and exclusive statements of the terms of the agreement and are therefore excluded by UCC 2–202(b). The words of negation in such documents cannot be construed reasonably as consistent with the words allegedly spoken. The UCC 2–316(1) rule would make the words of negation inoperative, but UCC 2–202 reverses that outcome. Terms in a writing that the parties intended as a final expression of their agreement may not be contradicted by evidence of any prior agreement or of a contemporaneous oral agreement.

Absent a clause in a document that negates express warranties that are not incorporated therein, testimonial evidence that seller made oral affirmations and promises could be offered as additional evidence that supplements the document. While UCC 2–202(a) allows other kinds of parol evidence to be admitted to prove consistent additional terms, the section is silent on admission of testimonial evidence of oral express warranties. Should courts admit such evidence?

Sellers' standard documents often have a clause declaring that the writing is a complete and exclusive statement of the terms of the agreement. These clauses are sometimes referred to as "merger clauses," signifying that all the terms that had been negotiated and agreed to have been merged into the terms of the document. Buyers effort to show, by testimony, that sellers made oral warranties of quality might be challenged as inadmissible under UCC 2–202 on two grounds: (1) that the additional evidence contradicts the merger clause and (2) that document on its face declares that it is intended to be a complete and exclusive statement of the terms of the agreement.

For further reading, see E. Farnsworth, Contracts § 7.3 (3d ed. 1999); J. White & R. Summers, §§ 2–9 to 2–12 (5th ed. 2000).

(5) Oral Express Warranties and Merger Clauses; Proposed Revised Article 2. The Study Committee that reviewed Article 2 before the revision process began expressed the following concern about the operation of UCC 2–202 in the context of oral warranties: "To what extent should a 'merger' clause in a standard form contract be permitted to accomplish indirectly what cannot be done directly, e.g., the disclaimer of an express warranty. See § 2–316(1). Other than § 2–302, there is no explicit control over the risk of unfair surprise [in the UCC]. A possible solution is to require that a 'merger' clause in a standard form contract be 'separately signed' by the party against whom the clause operates. See § 2–205." PEB Article 2 Report 60. Would you support the proposed solution? Throughout the revision process, drafting committees have not followed the suggestion of the Study Committee. See Proposed Revised 2–202.

(6) Post–Purchase Disclaimers. In many sales transactions, the parties negotiate and agree to contract by telephone or electronic communications. When the goods are picked up or delivered, sellers attach documents such a delivery receipts to the goods, or sellers send documents such as invoices shortly after delivery. If those documents have clauses that purport to disclaim implied warranties or exclude statutory damages, are those terms enforceable?

Hill v. Gateway 2000, Inc.

United States Court of Appeals, Seventh Circuit, 1997.
105 F.3d 1147.

■ EASTERBROOK, CIRCUIT JUDGE.

A customer picks up the phone, orders a computer, and gives a credit card number. Presently a box arrives, containing the computer and a list of terms, said to govern unless the customer returns the computer within 30 days. Are these terms effective as the parties' contract, or is the contract term-free because the order-taker did not read any terms over the phone and elicit the customer's assent?

One of the terms in the box containing a Gateway 2000 system was an arbitration clause. Rich and Enza Hill, the customers, kept the computer more than 30 days before complaining about its components and performance. They filed suit in federal court.... Gateway asked the district court to enforce the arbitration clause; the judge refused, writing that "the present record is insufficient to support a finding of a valid arbitration agreement between the parties or that the plaintiffs were given adequate notice of the arbitration clause." Gateway took an immediate appeal, as is its right. 9 U.S.C. § 16(a)(1)(A).

The Hills say that the arbitration clause did not stand out: they concede noticing the statement of terms but deny reading it closely enough to discover the agreement to arbitrate, and they ask us to conclude that they therefore may go to court. Yet an agreement to arbitrate must be enforced "save upon such grounds as exist at law or in equity for the revocation of any contract." 9 U.S.C. § 2. . . . A contract need not be read to be effective; people who accept take the risk that the unread terms may in retrospect prove unwelcome. . . . Terms inside Gateway's box stand or fall together. If they constitute the parties' contract because the Hills had an opportunity to return the computer after reading them, then all must be enforced.

ProCD, Inc. v. Zeidenberg, 86 F.3d 1447 (7th Cir.1996), holds that terms inside a box of software bind consumers who use the software after an opportunity to read the terms and to reject them by returning the product. Likewise, Carnival Cruise Lines, Inc. v. Shute, 499 U.S. 585, 113 L. Ed. 2d 622, 111 S. Ct. 1522 (1991), enforces a forum-selection clause that was included among three pages of terms attached to a cruise ship ticket. ProCD and Carnival Cruise Lines exemplify the many commercial transactions in which people pay for products with terms to follow; ProCD discusses others. 86 F.3d at 1451–52. The district court concluded in ProCD that the contract is formed when the consumer pays for the software; as a result, the court held, only terms known to the consumer at that moment are part of the contract, and provisos inside the box do not count. Although this is one way a contract could be formed, it is not the only way: "A vendor, as master of the offer, may invite acceptance by conduct, and may propose limitations on the kind of conduct that constitutes acceptance. A buyer may accept by performing the acts the vendor proposes to treat as acceptance." Id. at 1452. Gateway shipped computers with the same sort of accept-or-return offer ProCD made to users of its software. ProCD relied on the Uniform Commercial Code rather than any peculiarities of Wisconsin law; both Illinois and South Dakota, the two states whose law might govern relations between Gateway and the Hills, have adopted the UCC; neither side has pointed us to any atypical doctrines in those states that might be pertinent; ProCD therefore applies to this dispute.

Plaintiffs ask us to limit ProCD to software, but where's the sense in that? ProCD is about the law of contract, not the law of software. Payment preceding the revelation of full terms is common for air transportation, insurance, and many other endeavors. Practical considerations support allowing vendors to enclose the full legal terms with their products. Cashiers cannot be expected to read legal documents to customers before ringing up sales. If the staff at the other end of the phone for direct-sales operations such as Gateway's had to read the four-page statement of terms before taking the buyer's credit card number, the droning voice would anesthetize rather than enlighten many potential buyers. Others would hang up in a rage over the waste of their time. And oral recitation would not avoid customers' assertions (whether true or feigned) that the clerk did not read term X to them, or that they did not remember or understand it. Writing provides benefits for both sides of commercial transactions. Customers as a group are better off when vendors skip costly and ineffectual steps such as telephonic recitation, and use instead a simple approve-or-return device. Competent adults are bound by such documents, read or unread. For what little it is worth, we add that the box from Gateway was crammed with software. The computer came with an operating system, without which it was useful only as a boat anchor. ... Gateway also included many application programs. So the Hills' effort to limit ProCD to software would not avail them factually, even if it were sound legally—which it is not.

For their second sally, the Hills contend that ProCD should be limited to executory contracts (to licenses in particular), and therefore does not apply because both parties' performance of this contract was complete when the box arrived at their home. This is legally and factually wrong: legally because the question at hand concerns the formation of the contract rather than its performance, and factually because both contracts were incompletely performed. ProCD did not depend on the fact that the seller characterized the transaction as a license rather than as a contract; we treated it as a contract for the sale of goods and reserved the question whether for other purposes a "license" characterization might be preferable. 86 F.3d at 1450. All debates about characterization to one side, the transaction in ProCD was no more executory than the one here: Zeidenberg paid for the software and walked out of the store with a box under his arm, so if arrival of the box with the product ends the time for revelation of contractual terms, then the time ended in ProCD before Zeidenberg opened the box. But of course ProCD had not completed performance with delivery of the box, and neither had Gateway. One element of the transaction was the warranty, which obliges sellers to fix defects in their products. The Hills have invoked Gateway's warranty and are not satisfied with its response, so they are not well positioned to say that Gateway's obligations were fulfilled when the motor carrier unloaded the box. What is more, both ProCD and Gateway promised to help customers to use their products. Long-term service and information obligations are common in the computer business, on both hardware and software sides. Gateway offers "lifetime service" and has a round-the-clock telephone hotline to fulfil this promise. Some vendors spend more money helping customers use their products than on developing and manufacturing them. The document in Gateway's box includes promises of future performance that some consumers value highly; these promises bind Gateway just as the arbitration clause binds the Hills.

Next the Hills insist that ProCD is irrelevant because Zeidenberg was a "merchant" and they are not. Section 2–207(2) of the UCC, the infamous battle-of-the-forms section, states that "additional terms [following acceptance of an offer] are to be construed as proposals for addition to a contract. Between merchants such terms become part of the contract unless...." Plaintiffs tell us that ProCD came out as it did only because Zeidenberg was a "merchant" and the terms inside ProCD's box were not excluded by the "unless" clause. This argument pays scant attention to the opinion in ProCD, which concluded that, when there is only one form, "§ 2–207 is irrelevant." 86 F.3d at 1452. The question in ProCD was not whether terms were added to a contract after its formation, but how and when the contract was formed—in particular, whether a vendor may propose that a contract of sale be formed, not in the store (or over the phone) with the payment of money or a general "send me the product," but after the customer has had a chance to inspect both the item and the terms. ProCD answers "yes," for merchants and consumers alike. Yet again, for what little it is worth we observe that the Hills misunderstand the setting of ProCD. A "merchant" under the UCC "means a person who deals in goods of the kind or otherwise by his occupation holds himself out as having knowledge or skill peculiar to the practices or goods involved in the transaction", § 2–104(1). Zeidenberg bought the product at a retail store, an uncommon place for merchants to acquire inventory. His corporation put ProCD's database on the Internet for anyone to browse, which led to the litigation but did not make Zeidenberg a software merchant.

At oral argument the Hills propounded still another distinction: the box containing ProCD's software displayed a notice that additional terms were within, while the box containing Gateway's computer did not. The difference is functional, not legal. Consumers browsing the aisles of a store can look at the box, and if they are unwilling to deal with the prospect of additional terms can leave the box alone, avoiding the transactions costs of returning the package after reviewing its contents. Gateway's box, by contrast, is just a shipping carton; it is not on display anywhere. Its function is to protect the product during transit, and the information on its sides is for the use of handlers ("Fragile!" "This Side Up!") rather than would-be purchasers.

Perhaps the Hills would have had a better argument if they were first alerted to the bundling of hardware and legal-ware after opening the box and wanted to return the computer in order to avoid disagreeable terms, but were dissuaded by the expense of shipping. What the remedy would be in such a case—could it exceed the shipping charges?—is an interesting question, but one that need not detain us because the Hills knew before they ordered the computer that the carton would include some important terms, and they did not seek to discover these in advance. Gateway's ads state that their products come with limited warranties and lifetime support. How limited was the warranty—30 days, with service contingent on shipping the computer back, or five years, with free onsite service? What sort of support was offered? Shoppers have three principal ways to discover these things. First, they can ask the vendor to send a copy before deciding whether to buy. The Magnuson–Moss Warranty Act requires firms to distribute their warranty terms on request, 15 U.S.C. § 2302(b)(1)(A); the Hills do not contend that Gateway would have refused to enclose the remaining terms too. Concealment would be bad for business, scaring some customers away and leading to excess returns from others. Second, shoppers can consult public sources (computer magazines, the Web sites of vendors) that may contain this information. Third, they may inspect the documents after the product's delivery. Like Zeidenberg, the Hills took the third option. By keeping the computer beyond 30 days, the Hills accepted Gateway's offer, including the arbitration clause.

* * *

. . . The decision of the district court is vacated, and this case is remanded with instructions to compel the Hills to submit their dispute to arbitration.

NOTES

(1) Rolling Contracts. This case is one of the most controversial commercial law decisions of recent years. It has spawned the phrase "rolling contract" to describe a theory of contract formation that makes the point of closure of the bargain later than would otherwise have been found under the formation rules of the UCC. The Court of Appeals does not refer to UCC 2–204 or UCC 2–206. If UCC 2–204 had been applied to the facts set forth in the first paragraph of the opinion, was a contract formed by the end of the telephone call? UCC 2–206(1)(b) provides that an offer to buy goods for prompt shipment shall be construed as inviting acceptance either by a prompt promise to ship or by prompt shipment. If those provisions had been applied, when was buyer's offer accepted?

The Court of Appeals justifies deferral of time of contract formation on two quite different grounds: (1) The court finds that buyers generally are aware (not that the Hills personally were aware) that warranty terms may or will be found in the boxes containing goods purchased, that some consumers highly value the warranties and want to bind the warrantors to those terms. (2) The court finds that, in some negotiation settings, practical considerations preclude sellers from making full disclosures of their contract terms. Are either of these grounds persuasive?

The warranty-in-the-box ground refers to a familiar commercial situation in which buyers contract with retail dealers to buy goods that are delivered with warranties. Often the warranties are not those of the sellers, but are rather manufacturers' warranties. Sometimes, as here, manufacturers sell directly to the end-users. Are warranty obligations that are undertaken after a contract has been formed enforceable or unenforceable under the UCC? Such obligations enlarge the legal rights of buyers, whose tacit assent to that result can be taken for granted and whose subsequent conduct may reflect actual reliance on the warranty terms. Sellers' increased obligations do not require buyers to pay more for the goods, but modification agreements are enforceable without the need for consideration under UCC 2–209(1). Could merchant sellers renege of the warranties and be acting in good faith? Does it follow that buyers' power to enforce post-sale warranties depends on buyers' willingness to be bound by post-sale terms that reduce their contract rights or impair their ability to enforce those rights?

The "practical considerations" rationale for allowing sellers to incorporate contract terms into the boxes is dubious. First, sellers' terms that reduce buyers' contract rights or impair their ability to enforce those rights are not complex. It takes only a moment to say "There is no implied warranty of merchantability. Seller has no liability for incidental or consequential damages. Disputes under this agreement must be submitted to arbitration." There is no practical problem in disclosing, or at least outlining, rights-negating terms at the point of sale in any contracting situation, whether by telephone, email, or in-store. The verbose terms to which the court appears to refer are the (lawyer-drafted?) terms of the sellers' express warranties and related promises, which add to the buyers' contract rights, in ways that the buyers generally expect in transactions of that kind. Second, even if non-disclosure is impractical in an immediate negotiation, is it impractical for sellers to communicate, in full text, all of their required terms before they ship the goods? Before they cash credit card vouchers?

(2) Post–Sale Disclaimers or Damages Excluders. Warranty, disclaimer of implied warranty and damages exclusion were involved only obliquely in *Hill*. The issue before the court was the enforceability of the arbitration clause.[6] The court's decision does not turn on how much buyers may have lost in warranty protection or remedial rights.[7]

In *Hemmert Agricultural Aviation, Inc. v. Mid–Continent Aircraft Corp.*, part of which we considered in Section 3, there was another issue involving seller's disclaimer of the implied warranty of merchantability. Recall that the parties struck their bargain for sale of a crop duster plane over the telephone. A ferry pilot, Zeeman, delivered the plane to Hemmert two weeks later. Zeeman was in a hurry to return that afternoon with buyer's trade-in. Zeeman asked Hemmert to sign a Purchase Order and Delivery Receipt. Hemmert glanced at the documents and then signed them. Immediately above Hemmert's signature the following printed language appears:

> The undersigned PURCHASER agrees that he has read and that he understands the provisions set out on the reverse side and that the same are included in and are a part of this Aircraft Purchase Order all as if fully set forth on the face hereof.

---

6. Gateway's arbitration clause was held to be unconscionable in Brower v. Gateway 2000, Inc., 246 A.D.2d 246, 676 N.Y.S.2d 569 (App.Div. 1st Dept.1998). The New York court followed the Seventh Circuit analysis in *Hill* with respect to contract formation. After striking down the Gateway clause, the appellate court remanded the case to allow the trial court to fashion an arbitration clause that was not unconscionable.

7. The enforceability of a warranty disclaimer packaged with the goods was contested in a case in a trial court in Delaware. The argument of buyers' counsel was based on the requirement, in UCC 2–316(2), that the disclaimer must be conspicuous. The trial court held that the statutory requirement had been met. Rinaldi v. Iomega Corp., Del.Super.Ct., New Castle County, June 4, 1999, 1999 Del.Super.LEXIS 563.

On the backside of the Purchase Order, there was a disclaimer of the implied warranties of merchantability and fitness for particular purpose. The court refused to enforce the disclaimer.[8]

> The parties did not intend the purchase order to be the final expression of their agreement. The plaintiff's order was taken over the telephone, and the parties never signed a negotiated document. This form purchase order is easily susceptible to interpretation as a billing statement rather than a fully integrated contract, the printed language toward the top providing: "The undersigned agrees to complete the contract and accept delivery as stated in the terms, conditions, warranty and limitations of liability printed on the reverse side of this order." This document creates the impression that it serves as acknowledgment of receipt and that the terms of the contract can be found elsewhere. This case is one where unexpected and unbargained for disclaimers appear in a printed form prepared by the seller. . . .

Is *Hemmert* relevant to the decision in *Hill?*

Remedial Promises: Obligation to Repair or Replace. Remedial promises have been part of sales contracts for some time. There is a relationship between sellers' remedial promises and sellers' warranties of quality. A relationship exists, but understanding it requires close legal analysis. Remedial promises are also related to statutory remedies for breach of warranties of quality. The nature of these relationships has been confusing to many lawyers and judges. The core of the analytic difficulties lies in the difference between a contractual obligation, which may or may not be met, and the legal remedy for breach of a contractual obligation. Consider the following contract scenarios:

> *Case 1.* A contract for sale of a printing press is formed without any express warranties of quality and includes effective disclaimers of all implied warranties. The contract has the following clause: "If the printing press is found to be defective in materials or workmanship within one year after it has been delivered to the buyer, seller will, at its option, repair or replace the printing press."

> *Case 2.* A contract for sale of a printing press is formed with effective disclaimer of all implied warranties of quality but including the following express warranty and remedy clauses: "Seller warrants that the printing press is free of defects in materials or workmanship if, and only if, any such defect is brought to seller's attention within one year after delivery. In the event of breach of this warranty, seller's liability shall be limited to the repair or replacement, at seller's option, of the printing press. This is buyer's exclusive remedy. Seller assumes no liability for incidental or consequential damages."

---

8. The court cited Transamerica Oil Corp. v. Lynes, Inc., 723 F.2d at 762–63; Christopher & Son v. Kansas Paint & Color Co., 215 Kan. 185, 523 P.2d 709, modified on other grounds, 215 Kan. 510, 525 P.2d 626 (1974); Van Den Broeke v. Bellanca Aircraft Corp., 576 F.2d 582 (5th Cir.1978).

Functionally, the two contracts are quite similar. Both involve manufactured goods, which have substantial market value and which are expected to have a relatively long useful life. These are the kinds of transactions in which the repair or replace arrangement is likely to be found. Buyers that discover defects in materials or workmanship within the prescribed time have the right to call on the sellers to repair the defects or replace the equipment. From a buyer's perspective, either outcome gives buyer equipment that works as expected, although perhaps not at the date expected, without need to use any legal process. From a seller's perspective, the bargain provides the opportunity to fulfill a contractual obligation by using its own personnel and resources to make post-delivery repair to the original equipment, and, if necessary, to replace the original equipment with another of its products. The cost to seller of repairing or replacing defective goods is likely to be less than the amount of the damages that would be at risk in a legal proceeding for breach of warranty. The contracts have many of the positive aspects of a win-win arrangement.

The win-win outcome does not occur, however, if the seller does not repair defective equipment or replace it with non-defective goods. Seller and buyer now have a legal dispute in which the buyer is the aggrieved party. Neither type of contract has an agreed remedy for this dispute. If the parties do not settle the matter, the dispute will be referred to a court of law. Legally, however, the two cases will be quite dissimilar.

The aggrieved buyer in *Case 1* has a cause of action for seller's breach of a contractual promise,[9] but no claim for breach of warranty. There are no warranties of quality in *Case 1*.[10]

Although the controversy arises out of a sales contract, no provisions in Article 2 are germane.[11] Therefore, under UCC 1–103, the matter would be determined by the underlying principles of law and equity. Under those principles, the aggrieved buyer in *Case 1* is entitled to damages that are measured by the value of the seller's promise to repair or replace, together with incidental and consequential damages for that breach.

There is an express warranty of quality in *Case 2* and that warranty has been breached, but the contract excluded all statutory remedies for that breach of warranty and substituted seller's obligation to repair or replace defective goods. The buyer still has an unsatisfied grievance for breach of the express warranty. Does the buyer have a claim for damages? An answer might be found by interpretation of the sales contract: Did the

---

9. Seller may have contract defenses to a claim of breach. If, for example, buyer refused to allow seller to have access to the goods, seller would not be in breach. Other contract defenses may exist.

10. To underscore this conclusion, assume that the clause in *Case 1* was not in the sales contract, but was rather in a contract with a third party. Such arrangements between buyers and non-sellers, sometimes called something like "extended warranties,"

are often found in the marketplace. The non-sellers have no warranty obligations, but they do have whatever obligations they undertake in their contracts.

11. The proposed revision of Article 2 would adds a set of provisions on remedial promises made by sellers in contracts of sale. See Proposed Revised 2–103(a)(35); 2–313(d); 2–725(b)(3).

buyer and seller intend that, if seller failed to repair or replace defective goods, buyer should be left without any redress? Or did the parties agree, implicitly, that the clause excluding all statutory remedies would become inoperative if seller failed to repair or replace and buyer could seek damages provided by the UCC?

Although the issue might be resolved as a matter of interpretation of the parties' agreement in fact, Article 2 appears to provide an answer as a matter of law. UCC 2–719(1)(a) lists repair or replacement of nonconforming goods as an example of a contract "remedy." UCC 2–719(2) provides: "Where circumstances cause an exclusive or limited remedy to fail of its essential purpose, remedy may be had as provided in this Act."[12] The statutory remedy for breach of warranty is damages, which are ordinarily measured by UCC 2–714. If buyer has the goods repaired by a third party, the cost of repair might be claimed as damages under UCC 2–714(1). Alternatively, the buyer is entitled, under UCC 2–714(2), to damages measured by the difference between the market value of conforming goods and the market value of the delivered goods.

But the buyer may have other legal rights. Consider again the meaning of the sales contract in *Case 2*. Did the buyer and seller intend that seller could repair or replace, if it wished to do so, but could decide to refuse to repair or replace and not thereby incur liability? In simplest terms, did the seller in *Case 2* have a contractual obligation comparable to the seller in *Case 1*? The answer appears to be affirmative. If the sales contract in *Case 2* obligates the seller to repair or replace the goods, that contractual obligation has not been performed.[13] The remedies for breach of that obligation are not the same as the remedies for breach of a warranty of the quality of the goods. The aggrieved buyer in *Case 2*, if enforcing the promise to repair or replace, has the same rights and remedies as the buyer in *Case 1*. An aggrieved buyer in *Case 2* cannot recover damages for breach or warranty and damages for breach of the remedial promise to the extent that the remedies overlap. Courts should and do deny double recovery.

Breach of warranty and breach of remedial promise differ on matters other than remedies. One of these differences involves the statute of limitations. The date on which the period of limitations begins to run for

---

12. The quality of the drafting of this subsection can be criticized on multiple levels. Efforts to interpret the subsection by close attention to its words and syntax are frustratingly difficult. The use of the passive voice is one source of difficulty of obscurity. To what does "circumstances" refer? Does "circumstances" extend to anything other than the seller's action or inaction? A remedy cannot have a "purpose." The persons that place an exclusive remedy clause in a sales contract have purposes, but the purpose of the buyer and the purpose of the seller are probably not the same. Whose purpose is "essential"? Comment 1 states: "... where an apparently fair and reasonable clause because of circumstances fails of its purpose or operates to deprive either party of the substantial value of the bargain, it must give way to the general remedy provisions of this Article." Does the Comment help to give meaning to the text? Does the Comment have substantive provisions that have no textual basis?

13. Failure to repair or replace may not be a breach of contract if the seller has a contract defense.

breach of warranty is different from the date for breach of a remedial promise. Section 2–725(1) has a 4–year limitations period that applies to claims for breach of warranty. Claims for breach of remedial promises may or may not be governed by the statute of limitations in Article 2. These claims may be subject to the general contract limitations period, which is longer than four years in most jurisdictions.

In the cases and materials that follow, buyers are aggrieved by the failure or refusal of sellers to do what they said they would do and are seeking to recover statutory remedies for breach of warranty. The cases are of a kind that resembles *Case 2*. Subsection 2–719(2) is in play. The remedy that the buyers seek, however, is not only damages measured by UCC 2–714. The most contested question is whether buyers can recover consequential damages notwithstanding provisions in the sales contracts that excluded liability for consequential damages.

Milgard Tempering, Inc. v. Selas Corp.

United States Court of Appeals, Ninth Circuit, 1990.
902 F.2d 703.

■ HALL, CIRCUIT JUDGE:

This appeal marks the end of nearly seven years of litigation over a "sure fire" glass tempering furnace purchased over ten years ago. The seller, Selas Corporation of America ("Selas") appeals the judgment of the district court awarding the buyer, Milgard Tempering, Inc. ("Milgard"), damages resulting from its failure to repair serious defects in the furnace. ... We have jurisdiction under 28 U.S.C. § 1291 (1988) and affirm.

I

... On June 11, 1979, [Milgard] entered into a carefully-negotiated contract with appellant/cross-appellee Selas to purchase a horizontal batch tempering furnace. ... Under the contract, Selas agreed to design and manufacture the furnace for $1.45 million. Its design was complex, and in Selas' eyes, experimental. However, Selas marketed it as a working piece of equipment. The contract provided a $50,000 bonus if Selas delivered all the major components before January 31, 1980. It also provided a penalty of $5,000 per week (not to exceed a total of $25,000) for every week of late delivery after March 31, 1980. Selas failed to meet either deadline, having completed delivery of major components in November, 1982.

Selas agreed to assemble the furnace at Milgard's plant and to assist in a "debugging period" that both parties expected would end June or July 1980. The contract also required Selas, in a series of preacceptance tests, to demonstrate that the furnace was capable of achieving designated yield and cycle rates. Section 28.5 of the contract limited Selas' liability for breach of warranty to repair or replacement of the furnace and barred liability for consequential damages. The parties modified the contract and agreed to forego the preacceptance tests and instead place the furnace in commercial production in July, 1980, thus making glass available for the "debugging" process.

By January 1982, Selas continued work on the furnace, but failed to achieve yield and cycle rates that substantially conformed with the contract specifications. Milgard then filed suit against Selas for breach of contract. In March 1982, the parties, without counsel, attempted to enter into a contractual agreement to settle the dispute. Under the proposed agreement, Selas would take over the tempering operation for 60 days to demonstrate the furnace's ability to achieve a 90 yield rate. It would also pay any operating losses Milgard incurred during that period. Then, if Milgard operated the furnace for six months without incident, Selas would "finetune" the furnace to achieve a 95 rate. Selas did the work and paid Milgard's operating losses. Milgard dismissed the suit without prejudice. However, during the six-month period, the furnace failed to perform to the specifications of either the contract or the attempted settlement agreement.

Milgard initiated a second lawsuit on March 4, 1983, alleging breach of contract and breach of warranty. On June 29, 1984, Judge Tanner in the district court granted summary judgment in favor of Selas. ... This court, in Milgard Tempering, Inc. v. Selas Corp. of America, 761 F.2d 553 (9th Cir.1985) [hereinafter Milgard I], reversed and remanded for trial. ...

On remand, after a five-week bench trial, Judge Bryan in the district court found that the furnace had never lived up to the specifications in the contract. He held that the limited repair remedy failed of its essential purpose and that Selas' default was sufficiently severe to expunge the cap on consequential damages. He awarded Milgard $1,076,268 in net damages. . . .

Selas appeals the judgment and denial of its motion for new trial. . . . We affirm.

II

Selas ... argues that the district court erred in ruling that the limited repair remedy failed of its "essential purpose" and that such failure lifted the contractual cap on consequential damages.

A

Section 28.5 of the contract limited Milgard's remedies in the event of breach of warranty to repair or replacement of the defective equipment.

> [In the event of a breach of any warranty, express, implied or statutory, or in the event the equipment is found to be defective in workmanship or material or fails to conform to the specifications thereof, *[Selas']* liability shall be limited to the repair or replacement of such equipment as is found to be defective or non-conforming, provided that written notice of any such defect or non-conformity must be given to Selas within 1 year from the date of acceptance, or 15 months from completion of shipment, whichever first occurs. In the event that acceptance is delayed through the fault of Selas, then the Selas 1 year

warranty shall be applicable and not begin until the date of acceptance. *Selas assumes no liability for no [sic] consequential or incidental damages of any kind (including fire or explosion in the starting, testing, or subsequent operation of the equipment), and the Purchaser assumes all liability for the consequences of its use or misuse by the Purchaser or his employees. In no event will Selas be liable for damages resulting from the non-operation of Purchaser's plant, loss of product, raw materials or production as a result of the use, misuse or inability to use the equipment covered by this proposal* or from injury to any person or property alleged to be caused by or resulting from the use of the product produced with the equipment to be supplied to Purchaser by Selas pursuant to this proposal whether the customer or Purchaser is mediate or immediate. Purchaser hereby releases [Selas] of and from and indemnifies [it] against, all liability not specifically assumed by [it] hereunder. (Emphasis added).][*]

Such limitations on a party's remedies are permitted by Washington's version of the U.C.C., Wash.Rev.Code § 62A.2–719(1)(a) (West Supp. 1989).

An exclusive or limited remedy ... must be viewed against the background of § 62A.2–719(2).... This section requires a court to examine the contract in general and the remedy provision in particular to determine what the remedy's essential purpose is and whether it has failed.

A limited repair remedy serves two main purposes. First, it serves to shield the seller from liability during her attempt to make the goods conform. Second, it ensures that the buyer will receive goods conforming to the contract specifications within a reasonable period of time....

A contractual provision limiting the remedy to repair or replacement of defective parts fails of its essential purpose within the meaning of § 62A.2–719(2) if the breaching manufacturer or seller is unable to make the repairs within a reasonable time period. ... It is not necessary to show negligence or bad faith on the part of the seller, for the detriment to the buyer is the same whether the seller's unsuccessful efforts were diligent, dilatory, or negligent. ...

The district court in this case found that the furnace had never lived up to the specifications of the contract. ... Moreover, the court found that the few successful improvements were not made within a reasonable period of time, taking over two and one-half years. We agree that under these circumstances, the unreasonable delay and ultimate failure in repair made the repair remedy ineffective; thus, the remedy failed of its essential purpose.

Although the contract did not guarantee a specific time for completion of debugging, the court found that the writing was not completely integrated.... Looking at the commercial context, the court found that both parties implicitly agreed that the complete period for start up and "debugging" would take about eight weeks....

---

* [The court reproduced the contract in a footnote.]

B

Washington courts have not addressed the issue of whether failure of a limited repair remedy may serve to invalidate a consequential damages exclusion. Therefore, it is our responsibility to determine how the state's supreme court would resolve it. In undertaking this task, we may draw upon recognized legal sources including statutes, treatises, restatements, and published opinions.... We may also look to "well-reasoned decisions from other jurisdictions." ...

1

We begin our analysis with Fiorito Bros., Inc. v. Fruehauf Corp., 747 F.2d 1309, 1314–15 (9th Cir.1984). In that case, we held that under Washington law, the failure of a repair remedy does not automatically remove a cap on consequential damages. We predicted that Washington courts would take a case-by-case approach and examine the contract provisions to determine whether the exclusive remedy and damage exclusions are either "separable elements of risk allocation" or "inseparable parts of a unitary package of risk-allocation." Id. at 1315 (quoting district court).

If the exclusions are inseparable, we reasoned, a court's analysis should track the Official Washington Comments to § 62A.2–719(2) [hereinafter Washington Comments], which explain that the subsection "relates to contractual arrangements which become oppressive by change of circumstances...." 747 F.2d at 1315. We then affirmed the district court's ruling that the seller's arbitrary and unreasonable refusal to live up to the limited repair clause "rendered the damages limitation clause oppressive and invalid." Id.

Fiorito relied heavily on this circuit's analysis of Cal. Com. Code § 2719(2) (West 1964) in [S.M. Wilson & Co. v. Smith Int'l, Inc.,], 587 F.2d 1363. Wilson involved a contract between commercially sophisticated parties for a tunnel boring machine. The contract contained both a limited repair clause and a cap on consequential damages. After concluding that the repair remedy failed of its essential purpose within § 2719(2), this court held that the bar to consequential damages remained enforceable. We explained:

> Parties of relatively equal bargaining power negotiated an allocation of their risks of loss. Consequential damages were assigned to the buyer, Wilson. The machine was a complex piece of equipment designed for the buyer's purposes. The seller Smith did not ignore his obligation to repair; he simply was unable to perform it. This is not enough to require that the seller absorb losses the buyer plainly agreed to bear. Risk shifting is socially expensive and should not be undertaken in the absence of a good reason. An even better reason is required when to so shift is contrary to a contract freely negotiated. The default of the seller is not so total and fundamental as to require that its consequential damage limitation be expunged from the contract.

Id. at 1375 (emphasis added). However this court in Wilson quickly pointed out that its holding was limited to the facts and was in no way intended to state that consequential damages caps always survive failure of limited repair remedies. Id. at 1375–76.

2

The district court in the instant case found Selas' default "fundamental, but not total." Nonetheless, it found the breach sufficiently fundamental to remove the cap on consequential damages. Selas claims that the court misunderstood the legal standard and that consequential damages may be allowed only when the seller's breach is both total and fundamental.

We agree that the district court's characterization of the case law was flawed. However, the analysis it employed was not. This court has found nothing magical about the phrase "total and fundamental" default in relation to U.C.C. 2–719(2). In Fiorito we eschewed such wooden analysis, leaving "[e]ach case [to] stand on its own facts." Id., 747 F.2d at 1314 (quoting Wilson, 587 F.2d at 1376). We further expressed our distaste for talismanic analysis in Milgard I, finding the "oppressive circumstances" analysis utilized by Fiorito and the Washington Comments and the "total and fundamental" default analysis in Wilson in accord with each other. 761 F.2d at 556.

The task before the district court was to examine the remedy provisions and determine whether Selas' default caused a loss which was not part of the bargained-for allocation of risk.... This was the analysis that the district court actually employed.

We agree with the district court's decision to lift the cap on consequential damages. Milgard did not agree to pay $1.45 million in order to participate in a science experiment. It agreed to purchase what Selas represented as a cutting-edge glass furnace that would accommodate its needs after two months of debugging. Selas' inability to effect repair despite 2.5 years of intense, albeit injudicious,[9] effort caused Milgard losses not part of the bargained-for allocation of risk. Therefore, the cap on consequential damages is unenforceable.

III

Next, Selas challenges the district court's determination of damages. The court had found that for 21 months (April 1, 1980 to December 31, 1982), the furnace was incapable of reaching any of the yield rates outlined in the contract. Thereafter, the furnace could reach a few with some regularity. Accordingly, the district court calculated damages for two time periods. First, it calculated Milgard's lost profits during the 21–month

---

9. Selas exacerbated the repair problem by not providing a qualified process engineer during the initial debugging period and stubbornly refusing to replace the unproven ircon transfer system with more reliable methods that were available. We therefore agree with the district court's conclusion that "Selas did not make a completely open and honest effort to bring the furnace into compliance with the contract requirements." ... However, as noted earlier, the question of Selas' good faith is not dispositive of this appeal.

"damage" period. Second, it calculated losses Milgard did and would incur after December 31, 1982.

* * *

All three tests for loss of profits have been met in this case. First, the district judge made the factual finding that the parties contemplated the possibility of lost profits. Because § 28.5 of the contract refers to such profits, this finding is not clearly erroneous.

Second, the district court found that the failure of the machine to conform to the contract specifications proximately caused Milgard to lose profits. Selas does not challenge this finding and we do not disturb it.

Third, the district court had a sufficient factual basis upon which to make its computation of lost profits. As forecast by Larsen and its progeny, Milgard's sole source of evidence in this area was its expert witness, Dr. Finch. Although the district judge found some of Dr. Finch's figures difficult to swallow, he pointed out that that did not negate them. . . . [T]he court discounted the damage award in accordance with the weight of Finch's testimony. Therefore, we find no error.

* * *

VIII

For these reasons, the judgment of the district court is AFFIRMED.

NOTES

(1) The Case–By–Case Approach. The Ninth Circuit Court of Appeals, in this and the earlier *Fiorito* and *S.M. Wilson* cases, decided to make each case turn on its facts rather than to fashion a general rule by construction of UCC 2–719(2). These were diversity-of-citizenship cases, and the court therefore attributed its decision to the laws of Washington and California, but there were no definitive judgments of the courts of those states. When a seller's repair/replace obligation has not been performed, what kinds of fact issues should determine whether a particular buyer can recover consequential damages for breach of warranty?

In *Milgard*, what facts were determinative? The court declared that buyer "did not agree to pay $1.45 million in order to participate in a science experiment," and that seller had represented the furnace as "a cutting-edge furnace that would accommodate [buyer's] needs after two months of debugging." The court also noted that the degree of certainty of the workability of the design of the furnace in seller's sales talk was not consistent with its private view that the design was experimental. Do such facts have any relevance to the contractual allocation of the risk of consequential damages in the event that the furnace was not as warranted? The court also noted that the seller was unable to effect repair "despite 2.5 years of intense, albeit injudicious effort," which a footnote explained included failure for a time to provide a qualified process engineer and stubborn refusal to replace an unproven system with a more reliable one. The footnote concluded that seller's failure to make "a completely open and honest effort to bring the furnace into compliance" was not "dispositive." Were these facts important, even if not dispositive?

The *Milgard* opinion said nothing about the facts in *Fiorito* and little about the facts that might have been determinative in *S.M. Wilson*. *Fiorito* arose out of a sale of thirteen dump truck bodies to a construction company buyer for use in carrying wet concrete. Before the agreement, seller assured buyer that the bodies were suitable for this purpose. None was able to handle wet concrete. Seller declared that the problems were not covered by its warranty and that they were the result of buyer's misuse. Seller never attempted to repair the truck bodies, much less replace them. The Court of Appeals declared: "It cannot be maintained that it was the parties intention that Defendant be enabled to avoid all consequential liability for breach by first agreeing to an alternative remedy provision designed to avoid consequential harms, and then scuttling that alternative through its recalcitrance in honoring the agreement." Were these facts sufficient to be dispositive? Do you agree with the premise that clauses for repair or replacement are designed to avoid consequential harms?

The *Milgard* court noted a few facts from the *S.M. Wilson* decision, that the product was a tunnel boring machine, and quoted a passage from its opinion in that case: "The seller ... did not ignore his obligation to repair; he simply was unable to perform it." From the full opinion in *S.M. Wilson*, it appears that the seller did repair the tunnel boring machine after failing, for some considerable time, to diagnose the cause of the machine's malfunctioning. The consequential damages sought were losses of revenue incurred during the down time of the machine. Were these facts sufficient to be dispositive?

(2) State Comments to the UCC. The Ninth Circuit in *Milgard* and in *Fiorito* declared that its analysis should track the Official Washington Comments. When the UCC is promulgated by the Uniform State Laws Conference and the American Law Institute for adoption by state legislatures, some states have studies conducted before the legislatures act. Commonly, committees of state bar associations take on this task. In some instances, the studies also produce comments, like the Official Washington Comments. To the extent that the local comments differ from the Official Comments, they compromise the national goal of uniformity. The Official Washington Comment cited by the court "explains" that UCC 2–719 "relates to contractual arrangements which become oppressive by change of circumstances." Does anything in the text UCC 2–719 suggest that it applies to arrangements that "become oppressive"? Should that concept be general approach to the question whether to abrogate clauses that exclude liability for consequential damages in repair/replace contracts? Was it a factor in the Ninth Circuit's decisions?

Smith v. Navistar International Transportation Corp.

United States Court of Appeals, Seventh Circuit, 1992.
957 F.2d 1439.

■ COFFEY, CIRCUIT JUDGE.

Plaintiff-appellant Jeary Smith appeals the district court's grant of partial summary judgment in favor of the defendants after determining that Smith was not entitled to consequential or incidental damages result-ing from a defective truck purchased from the defendants. Smith also appeals the district court's judgment in his favor for the purchase price of the truck. We affirm.

I.

Plaintiff-appellant Jeary Smith brought this action charging the Navis-tar International Transportation Corporation ("Navistar"), Navistar Fi-nancial Corporation ("Navistar Financial") and J. Merle Jones & Sons, Inc. ("Jones"), a truck dealer, located in Ottawa, Illinois, with breach of warranty on the purchase of a truck. In 1984, Smith, an independent owner-operator of long distance trucks, decided to purchase a new truck, and Smith requested a list of sixteen options and/or components on the truck. After discussing the proposed purchase with several dealers, Smith decided to buy the Navistar semi-tractor truck Model 9370 as specified, from Jones (a Navistar authorized dealership), on November 7, 1984. Smith signed a Retail Order at the time of purchase which included the following warranty:

> International Harvester Company's [now Navistar] Promise to You. We promise to you, the first user purchaser, that we will replace or repair any part or parts of your new International motor vehicle which are defective in material or workmanship without charge for either parts or labor during the first year or 12,000 miles of operation, whichever occurs first.
>
> * * *
>
> What You Must Do. We recommend that you bring the vehicle back to the dealership where you purchased it; however, if you are in transit or have moved, take it to the most convenient authorized International Truck Dealer.
>
> * * *
>
> THIS WARRANTY IS IN LIEU OF ALL OTHER WARRANTIES, EXPRESSED OR IMPLIED, INCLUDING WITHOUT LIMITATION, WARRANTIES OF MERCHANTABILITY AND FITNESS FOR PAR-TICULAR PURPOSE, ALL OTHER REPRESENTATIONS TO THE FIRST USER PURCHASER, AND ALL OTHER OBLIGATIONS OR LIABILITIES, INCLUDING LIABILITY FOR INCIDENTAL AND CONSEQUENTIAL DAMAGES ON THE PART OF THE COMPANY OR THE SELLER.

(Capitalization in original).[2] . . .

---

2. Smith later purchased an extended warranty for the Cummins engine in the Navistar truck. Smith's purchase of addition-al warranty protection implies that he had read and understood the terms of the Retail Order warranty.

Upon delivery of the truck Smith received an Owner's Limited Warranty booklet which in pertinent part read:

> International Harvester [now Navistar] will repair or replace any part of this vehicle which proves defective in material and/or workmanship in normal use and service, with new or ReNewed parts, for the first twelve months from new vehicle delivery date or for 50,000 miles (90,000 Km), whichever occurs first, except as specified under "What is Not Covered."

On the second page of the Owner's Limited Warranty booklet are additional warranty disclaimers:

NOTE: DISCLAIMER!

> THERE ARE NO WARRANTIES WHICH EXTEND BEYOND THE DESCRIPTION ON THE FACE HEREOF. THIS WARRANTY IS IN LIEU OF ALL OTHER WARRANTIES, EXPRESSED OR IMPLIED. THE COMPANY SPECIFICALLY DISCLAIMS WARRANTIES OF MERCHANTABILITY AND FITNESS FOR A PARTICULAR PURPOSE, ALL OTHER REPRESENTATIONS TO THE FIRST USER/PURCHASER, AND ALL OTHER OBLIGATIONS OR LIABILITIES. THE COMPANY FURTHER EXCLUDES LIABILITY FOR INCIDENTAL AND CONSEQUENTIAL DAMAGES, ON THE PART OF THE COMPANY OR THE SELLER. No person is authorized to give any other warranties or to assume any liabilities on the Company's behalf unless made or assumed in writing by the seller. (emphasis in original).

These disclaimers are similar to those disclaimers set forth in the Retail Order that Smith signed when executing the bill of sale.

Some nine days after Smith's purchase of the truck, he experienced problems with the truck's braking system. On no fewer than ten separate occasions between November 7, 1984 and April 1985, Smith brought the truck to authorized Navistar dealers for repairs. Thus, the truck was out of service for a period of forty-five days.[3] Smith alleges that throughout the period of repair, the defendants were aware that he had a contract with one firm that he relied upon for his business and that if he was unable to operate his truck he would lose the contract. Notwithstanding Smith's dissatisfaction with the number and frequency of the alleged defects, Smith continued to use the truck during the problem time period and eventually ran up some 48,488 miles on it. On June 6, 1985, Smith sent a letter to the . . . defendants expressing his intention to revoke his contract based upon his dissatisfaction with the final repair effort. . . .

Almost two years later, on May 4, 1987, Smith brought suit against the defendants Navistar and Jones for their alleged breach of express and implied warranties, and breach of contract in the truck purchase. . . . After extensive discovery, the defendants moved for summary judgment, and on

---

3. Neither Navistar nor any of its dealers ever refused to work on Smith's truck, and Smith was never charged for any of the repairs undertaken.

January 27, 1989, the district court denied defendants' motion for summary judgment on the issue of liability, but granted defendants' motion as to damages in an opinion reported at 714 F. Supp. 303 (N.D.Ill.1989). The practical effect of this order was to limit the amount of damages a jury could award to $19,527.70, the amount Smith had paid for the truck prior to the revocation of his acceptance. After repeated attempts by the defendants to pay Smith the full amount of damages Smith was entitled to under the district court ruling, the defendants presented a motion ... offering to have judgment entered against them in the amount of $19,527.70. Over the plaintiff's objection the court granted the defendants' motion for judgment and entered a judgment against the defendants on February 28, 1989. ... Smith appeals.

* * *

III. DISCUSSION

A. Consequential Damages

Illinois law applies in this diversity action, and the transaction is governed under Article 2 of the Uniform Commercial Code. The plaintiff Smith argues that, because this is a diversity action, the district court was required to determine the applicable law of the State of Illinois when determining whether the plaintiff was entitled to consequential damages. The plaintiff contends that because, "the Illinois Supreme Court has not addressed the issue in question, the district court was required to use the predictive approach and in applying this approach, the district court disregarded the sole Illinois appellate decision on point and chose a resolution having no basis in Illinois law."

Our review of the district court's grant of partial summary judgment in favor of the defendants is de novo.... In its denial of partial summary judgment, the district court cited two conflicting cases which dealt with the issue of whether consequential damages could be awarded when a limited warranty failed to provide the protection the buyer expected. The first of these cases was a decision of an intermediate appellate court, Adams v. J.I. Case Co., 125 Ill. App. 2d 388, 261 N.E.2d 1 (4th Dist. 1970). The second was a decision of this court, AES Technology Systems, Inc. v. Coherent Radiation, 583 F.2d 933 (7th Cir.1978). Smith in essence argues that the district court erred in granting partial summary judgment because it chose to follow AES rather than Adams. However, federal courts are not bound by the decision of a lower state court unless the state's highest court in the jurisdiction whose law governs the diversity action has ruled on the matter.
. . .

Smith's signature on the Retail Order would ordinarily constitute an effective waiver of any right to recover incidental and consequential damages arising from the loss of his single employment contract. However, the U.C.C. provides that "where circumstances cause an exclusive or limited remedy to fail of its essential purpose, remedy may be had as provided in this Act." Ill. Rev. Stat. ch. 26, § 2–719(2). In Adams, the Illinois Appellate

Court adopted a categorical approach and held that the seller's breach of a limited warranty to repair or replace defective tractor parts automatically exposes the seller to liability for the buyer's consequential damages despite an otherwise enforceable disclaimer:

> The limitations of remedy and of liability are not separable from the obligations of the warranty. Repudiation of the obligations of the warranty destroyed its benefits. ... It should be obvious that they cannot at once repudiate their obligation under the warranty and assert its provisions beneficial to them.

Adams, 261 N.E.2d at 7–8.

However, in AES, this court rejected the categorical approach enunciated in Adams, and refused to automatically sever a consequential damage disclaimer from a contract merely on the failure of a limited warranty to provide the benefits that the parties bargained for:

> [s]ome courts have awarded consequential damages, when a remedy failed of its essential purpose, in the face of prohibitions in the contract against consequential damages. ... However, we reject the contention that failure of the essential purpose of the limited remedy automatically means that a damage award will include consequential damages. An analysis to determine whether consequential damages are warranted must carefully examine the individual factual situation including the type of goods involved, the parties and the precise nature and purpose of the contract. The purpose of the courts in contractual disputes is not to re-write contracts by ignoring parties' intent; rather, it is *to interpret the existing contract as fairly as possible when all events did not occur as planned.*

AES, 583 F.2d at 941 (footnote omitted) (emphasis added).

Other courts have similarly adopted this case-by-case approach. In Chatlos Systems v. National Cash Register Corp., 635 F.2d 1081 (3d Cir.1980), the court held that the failure of the essential purpose of a limited remedy does not automatically mean that a damage award will include consequential damages:

> New Jersey has not taken a position on this question, so in this diversity case we must predict which view the New Jersey Supreme Court would adopt if the question were presented to it.

> It appears to us that the better reasoned approach is to treat the consequential damage disclaimer as an independent provision, valid unless unconscionable. This poses no logical difficulties. A contract may well contain no limitation on breach of warranty damages but specifically exclude consequential damages. Conversely, it is quite conceivable that some limitation might be placed on a breach of warranty award, but consequential damages would expressly be permitted.

> The limited remedy of repair and a consequential damages exclusion are two discrete ways of attempting to limit recovery for breach of

> warranty. The Code, moreover, tests each by a different standard. The former survives unless it fails of its essential purpose, while the latter is valid unless it is unconscionable. We therefore see no reason to hold, as a general proposition, that the failure of the limited remedy provided in the contract, without more, invalidates a wholly distinct term in the agreement excluding consequential damages. The two are not mutually exclusive.

Id. at 1086 (footnotes and citations omitted).

Similarly, in S.M. Wilson & Co. v. Smith International, Inc., 587 F.2d 1363 (9th Cir.1978) (California law), the court determined that consequential damages were not warranted even though the limited repair warranty failed to achieve its essential purpose:

> The issue remains whether the failure of the limited repair remedy to serve its purpose requires permitting the recovery of consequential damages.... We hold it does not. In reaching this conclusion we are influenced heavily by the characteristics of the contract between [seller] and [buyer] ... .Parties of relatively equal bargaining power negotiated an allocation of their risks of loss. Consequential damages were assigned to the buyer, Wilson. The machine was a complex piece of equipment designed for the buyer's purposes. The seller Smith did not ignore his obligation to repair; he simply was unable to perform it. This is not enough to require that the seller absorb losses the buyer plainly agreed to bear. Risk shifting is socially expensive and should not be undertaken in the absence of a good reason. An even better reason is required when to so shift is contrary to a contract freely negotiated. The default of the seller is not so total and fundamental as to require that its consequential damages limitation be expunged from the contract.

Id. at 1375.

We believe the district court's reliance on AES rather than Adams was correct. The case-by-case approach adopted by AES and the other decisions allows some measure of certainty in that parties of relatively equal bargaining power can allocate all of the risks that may accompany a breach of warranty, and prevents the court from upsetting that allocation upon a breach of contractual duties. Moreover, in those situations where the limited warranty fails to provide the benefits that the buyer expected (i.e., to repair or replace defective parts) and the parties are clearly on unequal terms with respect to relative bargaining power, the case-by-case approach enunciated in AES enables the courts to examine "the intent of the parties, as gleaned from the express provisions of the contract and the factual background" to determine whether consequential damages are warranted, rather than automatically exposing the seller to liability for consequential damages despite an otherwise valid disclaimer. AES, 583 F.2d at 941. Thus, we agree with the district court that the rationale underlying AES and the other decisions adopting the case-by-case approach is more compelling than the categorical approach enunciated in Adams.

Smith also argues that "even if the district court was correct in the approach that it chose, the case-by-case approach, it misapplied that approach." Smith contends that the district court failed to analyze "all of the attendant objective facts and circumstances, including the language of the agreement, the relative bargaining power of the parties and the commercial context of the transaction" in order to determine which party should bear the risk of consequential damages. In our opinion, this argument is without merit as the district court noted that Smith failed to present any evidence in opposition to the damages awarded in the summary judgment motion. Moreover, our review of the record reveals that at the time Smith purchased the truck he was an experienced operator of long-distance trucks and had visited at least six different truck dealers in Indiana and Illinois, and had drawn up a list of sixteen specifications for the truck that he felt met his specific need. Having refused to accept any truck that did not meet his list of sixteen requirements, Smith presented the necessary components and options to defendant Jones, who offered the plaintiff-appellant the Navistar truck that met his specifications. At the time of purchase, Smith signed a Retail Order specifically excluding liability on the part of the seller for incidental and consequential damages:

THIS WARRANTY IS IN LIEU OF ALL OTHER WARRANTIES, EXPRESSED OR IMPLIED, INCLUDING WITHOUT LIMITATION, WARRANTIES OF MERCHANTABILITY AND FITNESS FOR PAR-TICULAR PURPOSE, ALL OTHER REPRESENTATIONS TO THE FIRST USER PURCHASER, AND ALL OTHER OBLIGATIONS OR LIABILITIES, INCLUDING LIABILITY FOR INCIDENTAL AND CONSEQUENTIAL DAMAGES ON THE PART OF THE COMPANY OR THE SELLER.

Moreover, Smith accepted a warranty which also clearly excluded seller liability for incidental and consequential damages in a section set off with the words, "NOTE: DISCLAIMER!." Smith read the terms and conditions of the warranty and failed to ask any questions regarding the terms of the Retail Order or warranty before signing the same. We have failed to discover evidence in the record that the parties intended that the defendants bear the risk of consequential damages or that the parties' relative bargaining power was so unequal that the disclaimer was unconscionable and we refuse to re-write the contract including the Retail Order's clear exclusion of consequential damages.

* * *

IV. CONCLUSION

The decision of the district court is AFFIRMED.

NOTES

(1) Case–By–Case Approach. The Seventh Circuit purports to accept the case-by-case approach to the question of enforcement of clauses excluding liability for consequential damages. Is the approach of the Seventh Circuit (applying Illinois law) the same as that of the Ninth Circuit (applying California and Washington law)? Note that the Seventh Circuit opinion does not cite either *Fiorito* or *Milgard*, but does refer to *S.M. Wilson.*

What facts are apparently dispositive in the Seventh Circuit's case? The opinion has long quotes of the terms of the contract (some more than once). It emphasized that the buyer was "an experienced operator of long-distance trucks," had shopped extensively before agreeing to buy the Navistar truck, and "accepted a warranty which . . . clearly excluded seller liability for incidental and consequential damages. . . . [Buyer] read the terms and conditions of the warranty and failed to ask any questions regarding the Retail Order or warranty before signing the same. We have failed to discover any evidence . . . that the parties' relative bargaining position was so unequal that the disclaimer was unconscionable and we refuse to re-write the contract. . . ." How did this approach compare with that of the Ninth Circuit?

Although not stressed by the Seventh Circuit, its opinion referred to the seller's—and buyer's—conduct when the buyer experienced problems with the truck. The court noted that seller made numerous attempts to repair the truck and never charged buyer for any of the repairs undertaken. Even though buyer said that he was revoking his acceptance, he continued to use the truck and logged over 48,000 miles of travel. After two and a half years, when buyer sued seller, seller tried to give the buyer the entire purchase price, but buyer refused to accept the money. What weight should these facts have in the court's decision?

(2) The Unconscionability Standard. A noted, in the concluding paragraph of the Seventh Circuit opinion, the court found that the clause excluding liability for consequential damages (the court called the clause a "disclaimer") was not unconscionable. Unconscionability appeared in the body of the opinion in the court's reference to the Third Circuit's opinion in the *Chatlos* case.[14] How does the UCC provision on unconscionability become part of the analysis? Does reference to unconscionability indicate the facts that determine whether buyers are entitled to consequential damages when sellers fail to repair or replace defective goods? Recall that unconscionability, under UCC 2–302, is determined entirely by facts that exist at the time of contract formation. Events that occur during performance of contracts are not material. Is UCC 2–302 the appropriate source of the law to be applied in these cases?

Unconscionability has been the ground for striking out clauses excluding consequential damages in a number of cases arising out of sales of equipment and supplies to farmers. See, e.g., Cox v. Lewiston Grain Growers, Inc., 86 Wn.App. 357, 936 P.2d 1191 (1997): A & M Produce Co. v. FMC Corp., 135 Cal.App.3d 473, 186 Cal.Rptr. 114 (1982) (tomato sizing machines); Durham v. Ciba–Geigy Corp., 315 N.W.2d 696 (S.D.1982) (herbicide).

---

14. We studied a later opinion in the *Chatlos* controversy in Section 3.

(3) Remedial Promises: Refund of Price. Many sales contracts are formed with explicit or implicit promises by sellers to take back the goods and refund the price. Most of these involve sales of non-durable goods that have relatively low market value compared with commercial equipment and durable consumer goods. In some instances, price refund is available on request; buyers dissatisfied with the goods for any reason are allowed to have their money back. The commercial explanation for this practice is the good will that sellers generate with repeat customers.

In other sales contracts, price return is an agreed remedy for breach of a warranty of quality. UCC 2–719(1)(a) mentions repayment of the price in its illustrative list of remedies that may be agreed to in place of the UCC's remedies. Price-return agreements are often made without clauses excluding consequential damages for breach of warranty. The nature of goods involved in small-ticket sales does not generally create a risk of significant consequential damages. An important exception is in sales of seeds, fertilizer and herbicide to farmers. Crop losses of considerable magnitude can result from nonconforming seeds, fertilizers and herbicides. We will see that problem in the forthcoming Section on manufacturers' warranties.

INTERNATIONAL SALES LAW

The Convention on Contracts for the International Sale of Goods does not contain regulatory provisions comparable to UCC 2–316 and 2–719. Under CISG 6, the parties may "derogate from or vary the effect of" any of the Convention's provisions. Article 6 therefore permits parties to agree to disclaimers of a quality warranty, that would otherwise arise under CISG 35(2),[15] or to clauses limiting damages otherwise provided by the Convention, particularly by CISG 74. On the surface, therefore, it appears that the regulatory provisions of domestic law, like those of the UCC, would not apply to international sales contracts.

However, the Convention does not purport to exclude application of all domestic laws to international sales contracts. Thus, CISG 4(a) declares that the Convention is not concerned with "the validity of the contract or any of its provisions." Should CISG 4 be construed to permit challenge of warranty disclaimers or clauses limiting damages in international sales contracts as "invalid" under United States or another nation's domestic law?[16]

"The answer should be No. ... It would be awkward to require [an international sales] contract to 'mention merchantability' in order to disclaim an implied obligation under [CISG] 35(2) that ... does not itself refer to 'merchantability.' ...

---

15. CISG 35(2) also contains a provision that the parties may agree otherwise.

16. CISG 7(2) refers to the rules of private international law for choice of law on questions not settled by the Convention. Since questions of "validity" are expressly not governed by the Convention, the law governing such questions would be found by application of the choice of law rules under private international law. In an appropriate case, United States domestic law might be chosen as the governing law.

"The argument [that CISG 4(a) incorporates UCC 2–316(2) and (3)] proves too much for it leads to the conclusion that any domestic rule that denied full literal effect to a contract provision on the ground that it does not accurately represent the parties' understanding would constitute a rule of 'validity.' The reference to domestic rules of 'validity' in Article 4(a) cannot be carried this far without intruding on the Convention's rules for interpreting international sales contracts. More specifically, Article 8 addresses a basic question of interpretation in a manner somewhat similar to the rules of domestic law in UCC 2–316. ... The point is not, of course, that Article 8 of the Convention and UCC 2–316 are identical but rather that both address the same issue. It follows that the reference to 'validity' in Article 4(a) of the Convention may not be read so broadly as to import domestic rules that would supplant articles of the Convention such as Article 8." J. Honnold, Uniform Law for International Sales §§ 233–234 (2d ed. 1991). *Contra*: Note, 53 Fordham L. Rev. 863 (1985).

Whether or not CISG 4(a) incorporates regulatory provisions of the UCC, counsel for sellers engaged in international sales transactions to which United States law may apply would be prudent to advise their clients to contract in accordance with the disclosure requirements of the UCC. However, an international sales contract drafter should not rely on the UCC rules that a disclaimer clause is sufficient if it uses the phrases "as is" or "with all faults." A non-U.S. buyer, relying on CISG 8, could reasonably argue that the full import of these provisions had not been made clear to it.

———

Problem 3.4.2. The parties in *Western Industries* were a United States buyer and a Canadian seller. The transaction occurred before the CISG took effect. If the CISG had applied, would the outcome have changed?

Problem 3.4.3. The parties in *Kunststoffwerk* were a United States buyer and a German seller. The transaction occurred before the CISG took effect. If the CISG had applied, would the outcome have changed?

Section 5.   Manufacturers' Warranties and Remedial Promises to Remote Buyers

Domestic United States Law

This Section addresses warranties and remedial promises of manufacturers that run to remote buyers. Many of the cases in the previous Sections involved warranties and remedial promises that arose in transactions between manufacturers and their immediate buyers. Those warranties and promises were part of contracts of sale. The manufacturers' warranties and remedial promises that we take up in this Section are warranties and promises that are extended by manufacturers to remote buyers, usually persons that buy manufactured goods from retail dealers.

The commercial context for manufacturers warranting their goods to remote buyers and undertaking to remedy defects in those goods has roots in the 19th century, but the practice flowered in the 20th century. Several economic and legal developments contributed to this. One was the capacity of the assembly line to produce large quantities of standardized goods.[1] Another was the development of brand names, which were protected forms of intellectual property and which became powerful tools for marketing of mass-produced goods.[2] Corporations that owned the production facilities and the brand names became large national enterprises, many of which have grown into huge transnational enterprises.

Various distribution systems were set up to move goods from the plant to retail markets across the country: Sometimes goods move to end users through a limited set of dealers "authorized" by the manufacturers to sell to the end users. The automobile industry is a prominent example. Sometimes goods move through independent wholesalers and distributors, unrelated to the manufacturers. Manufacturers of brand named goods spend large sums to advertise their products to potential buyers in order to increase demand in retail markets. (Commercial television, most national magazines and the advertising industry would not exist otherwise.) Brand named goods used for ordinary personal, family and household purposes dominate this field, but many commercial goods are made and distributed in similar manner.

Communication of written warranties and remedial promises from manufacturers to end users takes various routes. Automobile manufacturers with "authorized dealers" require dealers to turn over warranty materials with the vehicles. Typically they also contract with their dealers to perform the manufacturers' remedial promises. Manufacturers of consumer electronic products and appliances and other goods that are delivered in boxes use the technique of packing warranty materials in the boxes. A variant of the card-in-the-box technique is to print a warranty and remedial promise on the box itself, as is done with small goods like photographic film.

Communication of warranties and remedial promises takes place outside of written media as well, including television and radio advertising.

1. References to "manufacturers" in this Section include businesses that assemble components made by others into final products that carry the brand name of the assemblers, such as some makers of desktop computers, as well as businesses that process primary goods into brand named final products, such as oil companies.

2. Some large retail business enterprises, using the marketing power of known brand names, sell goods with brand names owned by the retailers, so-called "store-brands." Store-brand goods are not manufactured by the retailers, but are made for them by manufacturers, usually manufacturers that make and sell similar goods under the manufacturers' own brand names. Sears Roebuck Co. sells many goods of this kind under its brand names, Kenmore and Craftsman. Buyers of store-brand goods are normally unaware of the identity of the manufacturers of the goods. Warranties associated with store-brand goods are warranties of the retailers and not of the manufacturers. These warranties arise within sales contracts and are not warranties to remote buyers.

Traveling representatives of manufacturers of commercial goods seek out prospective buyers of their goods and promote their firm's products.

Where is the legal platform for the creation and enforcement of the warranties or remedial promises that manufacturers have made to remote buyers? All of the warranty provisions of Article 2 of the UCC are addressed to warranties that arise within contracts of sale. Examine carefully the language of UCC 2–313, 2–314, and 2–315. Express warranties exist only if it is part of the basis of the bargain between "the seller" and "the buyer." Comment 1 states that express warranties rest on the "dickered" aspects of individual bargains. The implied warranty of merchantability is implied in "a contract for sale." The implied warranty of fitness for particular purpose cannot arise unless the seller knows the buyer and has reason to know that buyer's purpose, and the buyer knows the seller and is relying on that seller' skill and judgment to furnish suitable goods. The current Article 2 is silent on the enforcement of remedial promises not made within contracts of sale.

Should manufacturers' warranties to remote buyers and remedial promises be governed by common law? The UCC, by its own terms, is incomplete. Many aspects of sales contracts, including remedial promises, are determined by principles of law and equity rather than by Article 2. Warranties and remedial promises that arise outside of sales contracts could be interpreted and enforced under uncodified principles of law and equity.

What is the legal relationship, if any, between manufacturers' warranties to remote buyers and the warranties of the immediate sellers on the same goods? Between remedial promises of manufacturers and remedial promises of retailers on the same goods? Retailers of goods that "come with" manufacturers' warranties and remedial promises sometimes provide, in their sales contracts, that the buyers' sole protection for nonconformities in the goods is in the manufacturers' warranties and remedial promises. As between seller and buyer, goods are sold "as is." In other settings, however, sellers and manufacturers' warranties or remedial promises overlap.

Martin Rispens & Son v. Hall Farms, Inc.

Supreme Court of Indiana, 1993.
621 N.E.2d 1078.

■ KRAHULIK, J.

We grant transfer to address whether defendants, Martin Rispens & Son, and Petoseed Company, Inc. are entitled to summary judgment on certain warranty, negligence and strict liability in tort claims filed by Hall Farms, Inc. Martin Rispens & Son v. Hall Farms, Inc. (1992), Ind. App., 601 N.E.2d 429.

Facts

The facts pertinent to Hall Farms' petition are as set forth in the opinion of the Court of Appeals:

Hall Farms, Inc., farms about 1,400 acres of mostly rented land in Knox County, Indiana. It produces grain, row crops, hay, watermelons, and cantaloupes and raises a few hogs and cows. In 1989, Hall Farms employed between 116 and 170 people; that year's watermelon and cantaloupe crop generated some $440,000 in gross revenues, despite the fruit blotch. Much of Hall Farms' past success in the melon market is attributable to the Prince Charles variety watermelon seed, known for its high yield and resistance to disease. Hall Farms had used the variety since 1982 or 1983.

In August of 1988, Hall Farms ordered 40 pounds of Prince Charles seeds from Rispens at a cost of $85.40 per pound. As requested, Rispens delivered the seeds, packaged in sealed one pound cans, in February 1989. Hall Farms stored the unopened cans until early April, at which time the watermelon seeds were germinated in two greenhouses.

On April 25th Mark Hall noted that about 15 seedlings were spotted with small yellow lesions. Suspecting gummy stem blight, a seed borne disease, Hall contacted a neighbor who, in turn, contacted Dr. Richard Latin, a plant pathologist from Purdue University. After transporting samples to the Purdue laboratory, Dr. Latin concluded the problem was neither gummy stem blight nor any fungus.

The lesions did not affect the plants' growth, however, and no plants died. The asymptomatic seedlings were transplanted to the fields between May 8th and 10th. Mark Hall monitored the plants every three or four days for the next several weeks, as was his custom. Although some looked a little "funny," they were nevertheless "growing like mad.".... On July 5th or 6th, Hall spotted a watermelon blemished by a small purple blotch. By July 15th, the blotch was "spreading like wildfire." ... By harvest time ten days later, a significant portion of the watermelon crop had been ruined.

Hall Farms left most of the blotched Prince Charles watermelons in the fields. They were eventually plowed under in early September in preparation for the planting of oats and then soybeans. Volunteer plants appeared the next summer, but Mark Hall killed them with Blazer, a herbicide, before Dr. Latin could examine them. Hall Farms suffered no watermelon blotch in 1990, even in fields that were infected the year before. During its investigation, Hall Farms learned the Prince Charles variety seeds it planted came from Petoseed's Lot Nos. 1018 and 5024. Lot 1018 was grown in China; lot 5024 was grown in Mexico.

Based on his discussions with Dr. Latin, who was of the opinion the bacteria causing the fruit blotch were introduced into Indiana through the Prince Charles seeds, Hall reasoned the Chinese or Mexican fields must have had the fruit blotch because his plants had it. Petoseed, a part of Hall Farms' argument goes, was therefore culpable to the extent it knew or should have known the fields were infected and yet harvested the seeds of the infected watermelons for resale to businesses like his.

Rispens, 601 N.E.2d at 432–3 (footnote omitted).

Hall Farms sued Rispens (the seed retailer) and Petoseed (the seed grower) seeking a recovery on theories of ... breach of express and implied warranties. After the trial court denied defendants' motions for summary judgment, defendants brought an interlocutory appeal. For Petoseed, the Court of Appeals ordered the trial court to enter summary judgment on the ... breach of warranty claims. ... For Rispens, the Court of Appeals ordered the trial court to enter summary judgment on ... all but one of the warranty counts. Summary judgment was denied with respect to one express warranty claim. Additionally, the Court held that Rispens and Petoseed had effectively limited their liability to the cost of the seed....

Plaintiff Hall Farms seeks reinstatement of the trial court's denial of summary judgment on all issues. ...

I. Warranty Claims

A. Express Warranties

Hall Farms argues that the Court of Appeals erred (1) in deciding the non-existence of certain express warranties as a matter of law, and (2) in holding that certain language on the Petoseed can and the Rispens order form did not create express warranties.

Where an agreement is entirely in writing, the question of whether express warranties were made is one for the court.... Here, all the representations upon which Hall Farms relies were in writing. Therefore, the Court of Appeals correctly determined the existence of express warranties as a matter of law.

Hall Farms' warranty claims arise out of the sale of goods and, thus, those claims are governed by Article 2 of the Uniform Commercial Code ("UCC"), Ind. Code Ann. § 26–1–2–101 through § 26–1–2–725 (West 1980 & Supp. 1992). The UCC provides for the creation of express warranties. Ind. Code § 26–1–2–313.

An express warranty requires some representation, term or statement as to how the product is warranted. Candlelight Homes, Inc. v. Zornes (1981), Ind. App., 414 N.E.2d 980, 983. Stated another way, an express warranty may be created if the seller asserts a fact of which the buyer is ignorant, but not if the seller merely states an opinion on a matter on which the seller has no special knowledge and on which the buyer may be expected also to have an opinion and to exercise his judgment. Royal Business Machines, Inc. v. Lorraine Corp., 633 F.2d 34, 41 (7th Cir.1980). Thus, a seller's factual statement that a machine had a new engine constituted an express warranty. Perfection Cut, Inc. v. Olsen (1984), Ind.

App., 470 N.E.2d 94, 95. Assurances by a seller that carpet would be replaced if any defects surfaced within one year of purchase was sufficient to create an express warranty. Carpetland U.S.A. v. Payne (1989), Ind. App., 536 N.E.2d 306, 308.

By contrast, statements of the seller's opinion, not made as a representation of fact, do not create an express warranty. Thompson Farms, Inc. v. Corno Feed Products (1977), 173 Ind. App. 682, 708, 366 N.E.2d 3, 18; James J. White & Robert S. Summers, 1 Uniform Commercial Code § 9–4, at 445 (3d ed. 1988) (hereafter "White & Summers"). The statement that a product "is the best" is simply puffing which does not create an express warranty. Thompson Farms, 173 Ind. App. at 708, 366 N.E.2d at 18.

Petoseed. The label on the Petoseed cans of Prince Charles watermelon seeds states that they are "top quality seeds with high vitality, vigor and germination." This printed label is the sole basis for Hall Farms' express warranty claims against Petoseed.

Hall Farms equates the phrase "top quality seeds" with the statement that the goods were "in good order, condition and repair," found to be an express warranty in Continental Sand & Gravel, Inc. v. K & K Sand & Gravel, Inc., 755 F.2d 87, 90–91 (7th Cir.1985), and with the statement that a truck was "road ready," held to be an express warranty in Wiseman v. Wolfe's Terre Haute Auto Auction, Inc. (1984), Ind. App., 459 N.E.2d 736, 737. We do not agree. The phrase contains no definitive statement as to how the product is warranted or any assertion of fact concerning the product, but is merely the opinion of Petoseed that the seeds are "top quality." The Court of Appeals correctly concluded that the statement "top quality seeds" is a "classic example of puffery." 601 N.E.2d at 435.

Hall Farms also argues that the Court of Appeals erred in holding that, although the phrase "with high vitality, vigor and germination" constituted an express warranty, Petoseed did not breach this warranty because the growth of the seeds conformed to the affirmation on the label. 601 N.E.2d at 435. This phrase is a promise that the seeds will perform in a certain manner; it is not simply the opinion of the seller. However, we are not able to determine as a matter of law whether this express warranty was breached. On the one hand, Petoseed asserts that the promise made was only that the seeds would germinate and grow, which according to Mark Hall, they did. On the other hand, Hall Farms asserts that the presence of the disease inhibited the vitality and vigor with which the plants grew. We agree with Hall Farms that the issue of whether the seeds which carried the watermelon fruit blotch had the capacity for natural growth and survival is one for the finder of fact. Thus, summary judgment is not appropriate on this express warranty claim.

Rispens. Rispens' purchase order, the sole basis for Hall Farm's express warranty claim against Rispens, stated in pertinent part:

> The seller agrees to deliver such seeds in good merchantable condition as hereinafter defined and of good germination for the crop of the current year. The phrase "in good merchantable condition" is defined

as seeds properly fitted for seeding purposes, by thorough screening, and where necessary by hand picking; approximately free from foreign seeds distinguishable by their appearance.

The parties agree that the language "properly fitted for seeding purposes," created an express warranty, but they assign different meanings to it. Rispens asserts that the warranty is merely that the can contains Prince Charles watermelon seeds and not some other type of seed. Hall Farms asserts that the warranty contains a quality component promising that the seeds would be free of a latent bacteria such as watermelon fruit blight. Although courts decide as a matter of law the existence of express warranties when the representations are in writing, if the writing is ambiguous, then its interpretation is one of fact.... Questions of fact exist as to the meaning of the express warranty and, thus, the Court of Appeals correctly held that Rispens is not entitled to summary judgment on whether this express warranty was breached....

Hall Farms also argues that the phrase, "strictly high grade seeds," which appeared at the top of the purchase order, created an express warranty. The Court of Appeals held that this language may have constituted an express warranty, but Hall Farms failed to meet its burden of proof by presenting evidence about the meaning of this phrase, so Rispens was entitled to summary judgment.... Whether Rispens gave an express warranty which was breached encompasses a question of fact: in the seed industry, does "high grade" connote some promise that the seeds will be free from disease or is it mere puffing. However, it is Rispens' burden, as the movant, to show the absence of material fact. Having failed to do so, Rispens is not entitled to summary judgment on the express warranty claim.

B. Implied Warranties

Hall Farms alleged that both Petoseed and Rispens breached certain implied warranties. The Court of Appeals held that the language on the Petoseed seed can had effectively excluded any implied warranty. ... Hall Farms does not seek transfer [to this court] on that holding.[2]

With respect to Rispens, the Court of Appeals held that, although the language on Rispens' purchase order did not effectively exclude the implied warranty of merchantability, Rispens established such exclusion by usage of trade.... On transfer [to this court], Hall Farms argues that the Court of Appeals erred in deciding usage of trade as a matter of law. We agree.

Unless excluded or modified, a warranty that goods shall be merchantable is implied in a contract for their sale if the seller is a merchant with respect to goods of that kind. Ind. Code § 26–1–2–314; Travel Craft v.

---

2. In addition, we note that the lack of privity between Hall Farms and Petoseed would also defeat any action by Hall Farms against Petoseed for breach of an implied warranty. In Indiana, privity between the seller and the buyer is required to maintain a cause of action on the implied warranties of merchantability, Ind. Code § 26–1–2–315. Prairie Prod., Inc. v. Agchem Div.-Pennwalt Corp. (1987), Ind. App., 514 N.E.2d 1299, 1301; Candlelight Homes, Inc. v. Zornes (1981), Ind. App., 414 N.E.2d 980, 982.

Wilhelm Mende (1990), Ind., 552 N.E.2d 443, 444. Disclaimers of implied warranties are not favored and are strictly construed against the seller for reasons of public policy. Woodruff v. Clark County, 153 Ind. App. at 45, 286 N.E.2d at 196.

Effective disclaimers of implied warranties must be conspicuous; whether a term or clause is conspicuous is a question of law for the court. Jones v. Abriani (1976), 169 Ind. App. 556, 571, 350 N.E.2d 635, 645. Where a purported exclusion of implied warranties was located at the bottom of the reverse page of a contract, which page did not contemplate the signature of the buyer, the court could properly find that the purported disclaimer was not sufficiently conspicuous. Jerry Alderman Ford Sales, Inc. v. Bailey (1973), 154 Ind. App. 632, 645, 294 N.E.2d 617, 619. Usually, to exclude the implied warranty of merchantability, the disclaimer must contain the word "merchantability." Travel Craft, 552 N.E.2d at 444.

Here, the attempted disclaimer (1) did not mention the word merchantability, (2) appeared on the reverse side of the purchase order which did not require a signature, and (3) was not conspicuous. Jerry Alderman, 154 Ind. App. at 645, 294 N.E.2d at 619.

Notwithstanding, Rispens argues that even if the content of the disclaimer did not conform to certain requirements, the warranties were effectively disclaimed by usage of trade. An implied warranty may be excluded or modified by usage of trade. Ind. Code § 26–1–2–316(3)(c). A usage of trade is "any practice or method of dealing having such regularity of observance in a place, vocation or trade as to justify an expectation that it will be observed with respect to the transaction in question." Ind. Code § 26–1–1–205(2). Commercial acceptance of a usage of trade "makes out a prima facie case that the usage is reasonable, and the burden is no longer on the usage to establish itself as being reasonable." Ind. Code § 26–1–1–205, cmt. 6. A buyer need not have actual knowledge of the usage of trade. See Western Industries, Inc. v. Newcor Canada Ltd., 739 F.2d 1198, 1203 (7th Cir. 1984); White & Summers, § 3–3. It is sufficient either that the usage of trade is used in the vocation or trade in which the contracting parties are engaged or that the usage is one of which the parties are or should be aware. Ind. Code § 26–1–1–205(3).

Rispens and Hall Farms are not in the same trade; Rispens is in the business of selling seeds while Hall Farms is in the business of planting seeds and producing crops. Thus, Rispens can effectively negate the implied warranty of merchantability only by establishing that Hall Farms was or should have been aware of the asserted usage of trade. To do so, Rispens submitted affidavits from, among others, the Executive Vice–President of the American Seed Trade Association, which stated that the implied warranty of merchantability is uniformly disclaimed by seed merchants. Hall Farms submitted no evidence suggesting otherwise. To show that Hall Farms should be charged with this knowledge, Rispens submitted purchase orders used by another seed company with whom Hall Farms had dealt in the past which also disclaimed the implied warranty of merchantability. In response, Hall Farms submitted testimony of Mark Hall to the effect that he had never read such disclaimers on the purchase orders. With these conflicting facts, we cannot conclude, as a matter of law, that Hall Farms is charged with the knowledge that seed distributors routinely disclaim implied warranties of merchantability. Therefore, whether the implied warranty of merchantability was disclaimed by usage of trade is a question of fact which must be resolved at trial. Summary judgment on the implied warranty of merchantability is not appropriate for Rispens.

II. Limitation of Liability on Warranty Claims

We next address the validity of the attempts by Petoseed and Rispens to limit the amount recoverable under the warranties that accompanied the sale of the seeds. Petoseed and Rispens assert that they effectively limited Hall Farms' remedy, if any, to the purchase price of the seed. Hall Farms responds that these limitations are unenforceable because they fail in their essential purpose and are unconscionable. We hold that, although such limitations are enforceable generally, there remains a question of fact as to their applicability here.

Buyers and sellers may agree on a limitation of remedy. Ind. Code § 26–1–2–719. A "limitation of remedy" acknowledges the quality commitment of a warranty, but restricts the type or amount of remedy available once a breach has been established. Hahn v. Ford Motor Co. (1982), Ind. App., 434 N.E.2d 943, 952–3. Limitations of remedy are not favored in Indiana and are strictly construed against the seller on the basis of public policy. Id. at 948.

A. Failure of Essential Purpose.

Hall Farms argues that limiting recovery to the cost of the seed fails of its essential purpose because: (l) the presence of the bacteria was a novel circumstance not contemplated by the parties; and (2) Hall Farms bargained for seed which would produce a money crop, it will be deprived of the substantial value of its bargain if the limitation is enforced. We hold that limitation on the measure of damages does not fail of its essential purpose.

Commentators have suggested that § 2–719, as it relates to failure of essential purpose, is not concerned with arrangements which were oppressive at the inception which is a question of unconscionability, but with the application of an agreement to "novel circumstances not contemplated by the parties." White & Summers, § 10–12. In addition, they have suggested that this provision should be triggered when the remedy fails of its essential purpose, not the essential purpose of the UCC, contract law, or of equity. Id. One author suggests that the method used to decide whether a particular limitation fails of its essential purpose is to identify the purpose underlying the provision and determine whether application of the remedy in the particular circumstances will further that purpose. If not, then, and only then, is there a failure of essential purpose. Jonathan A. Eddy, On The "Essential" Purposes of Limited Remedies: The Metaphysics of UCC § 2–719(2), 65 Cal. L. Rev. 28, 36–40 (1978). Thus, for example, where the sale of a car was accompanied by the exclusive remedy of repair and replacement of defective parts but attempted repairs were ineffective in correcting the problems, the purchaser was entitled to recover an amount in excess of the cost of repairs. Riley v. Ford Motor Co., 442 F. 2d 670 (5th Cir.1971). The exclusive remedy of repair and replacement of defective parts failed of its essential purpose because the car could not be repaired so as to operate free of defects as promised in the express warranty. Id.

Petoseed. Here, the label on the Petoseed can stated in pertinent part:

2.   LIMITATION OF LIABILITY: Purchaser's exclusive compensation for loss or damage arising from purchase or use of seed from Petoseed Co., Inc., shall be limited to an amount equal to the purchase price of the seed. There shall not be included any amount for incidental or consequential damages, nor for amounts expended in using or growing such seed, nor for harvesting the produce of such seed. This limitation of liability shall be applicable to any claims presented to Petoseed, regardless of the legal theory forming the basis of such claim, and whether such theory involves negligence, contractual liability, or otherwise.

This provision clearly states that liability is limited to the purchase price of the seed, and does not allow any amount for incidental or consequential damages such as Hall Farms' lost profits. Obviously, the purpose of the limitation was to limit contract liability to the purchase price of the seed. The contract term has not failed of its essential purpose; rather, enforcement of the limitation will serve precisely the purpose intended.

Rispens. Rispens' contract conditions on the reverse side of the invoice provided:

Paragraph 10. . . . In [any] event, however, the seller shall not be liable to the purchaser for any loss or damages in a sum greater than the invoice price of the individual lot of seed which is the cause of the complaint, arbitration or action at law.

Paragraph 11. . . . Our liability, in all instances, is limited to the purchase price of the seed.

The intent of this limitation of liability is also clear. Limiting any warranty recovery to the price of the seed serves the intended purpose of the limitation.

We do not accept Hall Farms' assertion that the presence of the watermelon fruit blotch was a novel circumstance not contemplated by the parties because the fact that the seeds might not conform to the warranties is a possibility that should occur to both buyer and seller.

As to the benefit of the bargain argument, Hall Farms bargained for seed, not, as its argument suggests, for a full-grown crop of watermelons. If Hall Farms deemed recovery of the purchase price inadequate, then it was free to bargain for a more comprehensive remedy. Therefore, the terms limiting Hall Farms' remedy against Petoseed to the purchase price of the seeds have not failed of their essential purpose.

B.   Unconscionability.

Hall Farms also argues that the limitation of liability is substantively unconscionable because farmers will be denied a minimum adequate remedy while giving seed manufacturers and distributors effective immunity from liability in a situation where the defect in the seed was latent. Ind. Code § 26–1–2–719(3) provides that consequential damages may be limited or excluded unless the limitation or exclusion is unconscionable. Unconscionability is a question of law determined on the basis of circumstances existing at the time the contract was made. Ind. Code § 26–1–2–302(1). The party raising the issue bears the burden of proof. Hahn v. Ford Motor, 434 N.E.2d at 950.

"Substantive unconscionability" refers to oppressively one-sided or harsh terms of a contract, and generally involves cases where courts have determined the price to be unduly excessive or where the terms of the contract unduly limit a buyer's remedies. Hahn, 434 N.E.2d at 951. A substantively unconscionable contract is one that no sensible man would make and such as no honest and fair man would accept. Weaver v. American Oil Co. (1972), 257 Ind. 458, 462, 276 N.E.2d 144, 146. Often there are circumstances which show that there was unequal bargaining power at the time the contract was executed which led the party with lesser power to enter it unwillingly or without knowledge of its terms. Dan Purvis Drugs, Inc. v. Aetna Life Ins. (1981), Ind. App., 412 N.E.2d 129, 131; see also Sho–Pro of Indiana, Inc. v. Brown (1992), Ind. App., 585 N.E.2d 1357, 1360.

In keeping with this standard, Indiana courts have rejected claims that contractual limitations of remedy are substantively unconscionable. Carr v. Hoosier Photo Supplies, Inc. (1982), Ind., 441 N.E.2d 450, 454 (film processor's receipt issued to knowledgeable consumer); Hahn, 434 N.E.2d at 952 (automobile warranty issued to consumer); General Bargain Center v. American Alarm Co. (1982), Ind. App., 430 N.E.2d 407, 411 (alarm system contract).

Hall Farms argues that the limitation of remedy was substantively unconscionable because the defect in the seed was latent, not being discoverable until the plants began growing. Once discovered, the growing season was too far along for Hall Farms to replant. Thus, Hall Farms asserts that for the loss occasioned by the infected seeds to fall only upon Hall Farms would be unconscionable. Hall Farms cites Martin v. Joseph Harris Co., Inc., 767 F.2d 296 (6th Cir.1985), and Lutz Farms v. Asgrow Seed Co., 948 F.2d 638, 646 (10th Cir.1991), as examples of latent defects rendering a limitation of remedy unconscionable. There are also cases holding that such limitations are not unconscionable. See, e.g., Estate of Arena v. Abbott & Cobb, Inc. (1990), 158 A.D.2d 926, 551 N.Y.S.2d 715 (remedy limited to the purchase price of seed); and Southland Farms, Inc. v. Ciba–Geigy Corp.

(1990), Ala., 575 So. 2d 1077, 1079–81 (consequential damages limited for agricultural chemical).

We are not persuaded that the limitation is unconscionable simply because the defect is latent. Although a seller may not limit liability for a defect which he knows to be nonconforming to warranties without disclosing that knowledge, the evidence is not conclusive that either Petoseed or Rispens was aware that the seeds carried disease. The possibility that a latent defect may exist is one of the risks present at the time the contract is formed. Had the parties contemplated this possibility, Indiana law would have left them free to allocate that risk as they saw fit. It is not unconscionable for the seed producer and distributor to redistribute such risks.

Left unanswered, however, is whether the parties in fact agreed to redistribute the risk of a latent defect in the seed. The question is whether there was mutual assent to the limitation of liability contained on the Petoseed can and the Rispens purchase order. Contract formation requires mutual assent on all essential contract terms. Carr v. Hoosier Photo, 441 N.E.2d at 455. Without mutual assent, the limitations are ineffective as a matter of law. Hahn, 434 N.E.2d at 948. Assent to a limitation of liability may be assumed where a knowledgeable party enters into the contract, aware of the limitation and its legal effect, without indicating non-acquiescence to those terms.... However, the intention of the parties to include a particular term in a contract is usually a factual question determined from all of the circumstances....

Therefore, we must determine if there is a genuine issue of fact about whether Hall Farms assented to the limitation of liability.

Petoseed. Petoseed's limitation appeared in the printed material on the label affixed to the side of the seed cans. Mark Hall testified that, although he read the printed material on the top of the can which Hall Farms asserts gave an express warranty, he did not read the material on the side of the can relating to the limitation of liability. Thus, whether there was mutual assent to the limitation of liability is a question of fact precluding summary judgment.

Rispens. Rispens' limitation appeared on the reverse side of the purchase order for the seeds. This side of the purchase order did not require Hall's signature and he testified that he did not read it. Therefore, there is a question of fact about whether Hall Farms intended to accept the limitation of liability from Rispens.

* * *

Conclusion

In summary, we grant transfer, vacate the opinion of the Court of Appeals, and remand this case to the trial court with directions to enter summary judgment against Hall Farms on all claims except those of breach of express warranties as to both defendants and breach of the implied warranty of merchantability as to Rispens and to proceed in a manner consistent with this opinion.

NOTES

(1) Multiple Warrantors of the Same Goods. The seed buyer brought this case against two warrantors: the seller from which the buyer purchased the seeds (Martin Rispens & Son) and the upstream manufacturer (processor) which sold the seeds to the immediate seller (Petoseed Co., Inc.). The two defendants are independent businesses. Martin Rispens & Son is an example of the many intermediaries ("middlemen") whose economic *raison d'etre* is to move goods from the makers to the end users. Intermediaries such as Martin Rispens & Son sometimes give express warranties on goods that they sell even though they did not make the goods. Absent effective disclaimers, an intermediary's sales contract has an implied warranty of merchantability. The legal platform for the buyer's warranty claims against Martin Rispens & Son was the subject of Sections 2 and 3. In this Section, we are considering warranty claims by end users, like Hill Farms, Inc., against upstream sellers. For convenience, we refer to those upstream sellers as the manufacturers of the goods.

(2) Manufacturer's Express Warranty; Law Governing. The manufacturer's only express warranties in this case were affirmation printed on the label of the cans containing the seeds in question. Why would manufacturers place such affirmations on containers? At what stage in the retail sales of the goods of this kind would buyers be likely to see the containers? If a buyer saw a container for the first time after the retail sales contract had been formed, should that make the manufacturer's warranty unenforceable?

Alternative theories. The Indiana Supreme Court declared, without any discussion, that the law governing the claim of a manufacturer's express warranty is UCC 2–313. Although the court cites a number of cases in its introduction of the law, it fails to note whether any of those cases involved a manufacturer's warranty to a remote buyer. An alternative characterization of the warranties as matters governed by common law would have been plausible. A well-known 19th century case involved enforcement of a manufacturer's promise to pay money to certain remote buyers, made in newspaper advertisements. A British court construed the advertisement as an offer that was accepted when members of the public bought the advertised product from retailers and used it. Carlill v. Carbolic Smoke Ball Co., [1893] 1 Q.B. 256 (C.A.1892).[3]

---

3. The contract defense raised on behalf of the manufacturer was lack of consideration to support the promise. The British court concluded that it was not necessary for consideration to "move to" the promisor.

In 1932, enforcement of a manufacturer's affirmations of the quality of its goods took on a modern warranty form. The statement in an automobile manufacturer's promotional literature that its windshields were "shatterproof" was held to create an express warranty to a retail buyer. Baxter v. Ford Motor Co., 168 Wash. 456, 12 P.2d 409 (1932). *Baxter* involved personal injury. As will be developed, warranty law, particularly the law of implied warranties, played a significant role in the development of the law regarding manufacturers' liability for the safety of their products.

The principle of *Carbolic Smoke Ball* has been accepted for many years in express warranty cases. The seminal case involved a claim by a garment manufacturer against a chemical company, manufacturer of resins it claimed would make fabrics shrink-proof. The garment manufacturer bought resin-treated fabric from suppliers. The shrink-proof warranty failed. The garment manufacturer was allowed to sue the chemical company, with which it had has no contractual dealings, for breach of warranty.[4]

Implications of the choice of theory. The Indiana Supreme Court held that the manufacturer's affirmation that the seeds were "top quality" was a "classic example of puffery" and therefore not a warranty, but remanded for trial the "high vitality, vigor and germination" affirmation. If the court had concluded that manufacturers' warranties to remote buyers were common-law warranties and not governed by UCC 2–313, should the court have reached a different conclusion on whether the affirmations would be enforced as warranties of the manufacturer?

The choice of characterization of the warranties as statutory or common-law may not have had much significance in the outcome in this case. Would that be true of other aspects of warranty law. Suppose that the manufacturer had raised the defense that its affirmations on the containers were not "part of the basis of the bargain" and were therefore unenforceable.

That defense arose in a case against a cigarette manufacturer which had made affirmations in advertisements published over many years. A smoker contended that the affirmations were express warranties that had been breached. The Court of Appeals for the Third Circuit assumed that the claim was governed by UCC 2–313 and tried to apply the rule that affirmations are not express warranties under that section unless they become part of the basis of the bargain. The court declared:

> The law does not require plaintiff to show that Rose Cipollone specifically relied on Liggett's warranties.
>
> Ordinarily a guarantee or promise in an advertisement or other description of the goods becomes part of the basis of the bargain if it would naturally induce the purchase of the product and no particular reliance by the buyer on such statement needs to be shown. However, if the evidence establishes that the claimed statement cannot fairly be viewed as entering into the bargain, that is, that the statement would not naturally induce the purchase of a product, then no express warranty has been created.
>
> ... We hold that once the buyer has become aware of the affirmation of fact or promise, the statements are presumed to be part of the "basis of the bargain" unless the defendant, by "clear affirmative proof," shows that the buyer knew that the affirmation of fact or promise was untrue. ...

----

4. Randy Knitwear v. American Cyanamid Co., 11 N.Y.2d 5, 181 N.E.2d 399, 226   N.Y.S.2d 363 (1962).

Applying our interpretation of section 2–313 to the case at bar, we conclude that the district court's jury instructions were erroneous for two reasons. First, they did not require the plaintiff to prove that Mrs. Cipollone had read, seen, or heard the advertisements at issue. Second, they did not permit the defendant to prove that although Mrs. Cipollone had read, seen, or heard the advertisements, she did not believe the safety assurances contained therein. We must therefore reverse and remand for a new trial on this issue.

Cipollone v. Liggett Group, Inc., 893 F.2d 541 (3d Cir.1990), reviewed on other grounds, 505 U.S. 504, 112 S.Ct. 2608, 120 L.Ed.2d 407 (1992). How should the question be determined if the advertisements were characterized as creating common-law warranties?

Remedies. The remedies available to remote buyers for manufacturers' breaches of express warranty also depend upon choice of the law governing contracts of this kind.

If the law chosen is UCC Article 2, would buyers' UCC remedies be appropriate? Do the formulae for measuring damages in UCC 2–714, particularly in UCC 2–714(2), fit these circumstances? Do buyers have the choice of "cover" under UCC 2–712? Do buyers have the power to revoke their acceptance of the goods and proceed under UCC 2–608?

If common law applies, buyers' remedies would be fashioned under general contract law. Damages could be measured by the expectation principle that puts the aggrieved party in the position in which it would have been if there had been no breach.

Problem 3.5.1. M, a manufacturer of building materials, markets its products through independent distributors. However, M sends sales engineers to construction companies to explain the uses of M's products and promote their purchase. Following such a visit by one of M's sales engineers, the B construction company buys M's roofing material from distributor, D. B claims that the roofing material does not have the qualities described by M's sales engineer, and sues M for breach of express warranty. What result? See M. Ruud, Manufacturers' Liability for Representations made by their Sales Engineers to Subpurchasers, 8 U.C.L.A. L. Rev. 251 (1961).

(3) Manufacturer's Implied Warranty of Merchantability: Law Governing. The Indiana Supreme Court disposed of the matter of an implied warranty of merchantability by the manufacturer on two grounds: that the warranty had been effectively disclaimed (in text) and that the warranty could not be enforced by a remote buyer which lacked "privity" (in footnote). The court showed no awareness of the peculiarity in the propositions that there was sufficient "privity" for the express warranty to be enforced, and for the disclaimer to be enforced, but not sufficient "privity" for the implied warranty to be enforced.

Privity. One has to look to legal history to appreciate the origin of "privity" as the verbal linchpin for the recognition and enforcement of manufacturers' implied warranties of quality. A doctrine of general contract law allows enforcement of a contract only by the parties to the contract and those in privity with them.[5] "Privity," in that sense, refers not to the lack of a contract, but it came to be the shorthand expression for the enforceability of manufacturers' implied warranties by remote buyers. If breach of warranty was claimed but enforcement was disallowed, the privity requirement was said to be upheld; if breach of warranty was claimed and enforcement was allowed, the privity requirement was said to be abrogated.

Products liability. This issue was central to many early and mid–20th century cases in which consumers sought remedies for deaths and personal injuries caused by unwholesome foods or beverages. In 1960, Professor William Prosser wrote an influential article about the body of cases in which manufacturers' warranties had been recognized and allowed to be enforced by remote buyers. Prosser's literary image was a fall of the citadel of privity that had once shielded manufacturers from consumer warranty actions for personal injuries, but his real purpose was to recharacterize the warranty cases as cases *really* sounding in tort.[6] His article was a great success. Since the 1960s, personal injury litigation in the United States has become largely a question of strict tort liability, currently called products

---

5. "The modern doctrine of privity, . . . a set of rules whereby a contract cannot confer rights or impose liabilities on third parties, was not really known as such until very late in the nineteenth century. . . . There is a sense in which the new doctrine of privity was an important development in the law at a time of increasing complexity in multilateral commercial relationships. The appearance of middlemen in all sorts of commercial situations served to separate the parties at either end of the transaction, and it was generally accepted that no privity existed between them. Economically, this may have served a useful purpose, in that it encouraged the development of a more market-based concept of enterprise liability. But on some occasions the results were not only economically dubious but socially disastrous." P. Atiyah, The Rise and Fall of Freedom of Contract 413–414 (1979).

United States courts never applied the requirement of privity-of-contract with the rigor of British courts. Restatements of contract law in this country did not even use "privity" in their black-letter formulations. See, e.g., Restatement, Contracts (1933); Restatement, Second, Contracts (1981). Rather,United States contract doctrine defines the persons that had the power to enforce contracts which they had no role in forming. Two recognized classes of such persons are assignees and third party beneficiaries.

In U.S. tort law, privity was once a requirement in negligence claims. That requirement was abrogated in a famous opinion of Judge Cardozo, MacPherson v. Buick, 217 N.Y. 382, 111 N.E. 1050 (1916).

6. W. Prosser, The Assault Upon the Citadel (Strict Liability to the Consumer), 69 Yale L.J. 1099 (1960). In the same year, the New Jersey Supreme Court expanded the category of consumer products in which privity would not be required to include automobiles. Henningsen v. Bloomfield Motors, Inc., 32 N.J. 358, 161 A.2d 69 (1960). Two years later, the California Supreme Court announced the strict tort liability. Greenman v. Yuba Power Products, Inc., 59 Cal.2d 57, 27 Cal.Rptr. 697, 377 P.2d 897 (1963). A curious factual coincidence links the New Jersey decision in *Henningsen* and the California decision in *Greenman*. In both cases, the product that caused injury was purchased as a gift and the person injured was the donee.

Fundamental to the new tort was the explicit omission of any requirement that the injured consumer or user have had a contract with the seller or manufacturer. See Restatement (Second) of Torts § 402A(2)(b). The drafters of § 402A issued a caveat on the horizontal privity question whether bystanders or others who were neither users nor consumers should be permitted to recover. See also Restatement of the Law, Torts: Products Liability § 1 (1996).

liability. Warranty theory continues to apply, but plaintiffs generally prefer to base their claims for relief in strict tort. From the birth of strict tort liability, privity was not required.

Fitness for ordinary purpose and "privity." Claims involving only economic loss, particularly claims that goods are not fit for their ordinary purpose, remain matters of warranty law. The warranty claim in *Martin Rispens* was that the watermelon seeds were not fit for the ordinary purpose of seeds of that description.[7] "Privity" continues to be the misleading shorthand expression used by courts for a rule that bars claims by remote buyers against manufacturers for breach of such implied warranties of quality. The real issue is whether a warranty of fitness for ordinary purpose exists and has been breached, not whether a remote buyer is within the circle of those entitled to enforce that warranty. If a warranty of fitness for ordinary purpose did exist and was breached, no one is more appropriate to seek enforcement of that warranty than the end user of the goods.

Silence of Article 2. UCC 2–314 does not recognize a manufacturers' warranty of fitness of goods for their ordinary purposes. That section is explicitly limited to a warranty by "the seller" in a contract of sale. The matter is left therefore to the courts and, in some states, to non-uniform legislation. As indicated in *Martin Rispens*, Indiana courts do not recognize the right of remote buyers to proceed against manufacturers. Without a right to sue, existence of an implied warranty and breach of that warranty are moot questions.[8] As we shall see later in this Section, other states, through statutes or court decisions, have a different position on the requirement of privity. In those states, the issues of the nature and effect of manufacturers' implied warranties arise.

Promise to Refund Price. Paragraph 2 of the label on the container contained an implied promise by the manufacturer to refund an amount equal to the purchase price of the watermelon seeds and a clause excluding liability for consequential or incidental damages. The price-refund sentence does not refer to any theory of legal liability, such as receipt of defective goods. The sentence applies broadly, whenever there is "loss or damage arising from purchase or use of seed." The price-refund sentence can be read, by implication, to obligate the manufacturer to pay the stated amount, but on its face it is only a limitation of "compensation" for loss or damage. The exclusion-of-damages sentence also lacks reference to any

---

7. Of all the branches of the UCC's definition of merchantability in UCC 2–314(2), the one most pertinent to claims by end-use buyers is fitness for ordinary purpose.

8. The *Martin Rispens* manufacturer included a disclaimer of implied warranty of merchantability in the language on the can. The Indiana Court of Appeals held that the disclaimer was valid and the buyer did not press the matter in the Indiana Supreme Court. Would reasonable counsel for a manufacturer that is shielded from remote buyers' suits by the requirement of privity nonetheless advise the manufacturer to include a disclaimer? Is it likely that the manufacturer's products might be sold in more than one state?

theory of legal liability. The openendedness of the possible legal theories to which the paragraph applies is underscored in the last sentence.

The drafter of this paragraph, undoubtedly a lawyer, seemed to be working from this premise: We have not intentionally undertaken any express warranty obligation to end users of our seeds and we don't believe that we have any implied warranty obligation to such end users, but if it turns out that we're wrong about any of that, our liability is limited. If you were counsel to the seed manufacturer, could you do a better job of counseling your client?

Exclusion of Consequential Damages. The Indiana Supreme Court, again without discussion, decided that Article 2 governed the issue of the effectiveness of a clause excluding a manufacturer's liability for consequential damages in a claim by a remote buyer. The court turned to UCC 2–719(2) and framed the issue in terms of failure of purpose of a sales contract remedy. Payment of an amount equal to the purchase price, if that is a "contract" remedy for breach, makes no economic sense as a remedy for a warranty breach that can be discovered only after the seeds have been planted and failed to grow properly. Turning UCC 2–719(2) on its head, the court construed purpose of the price-refund clause to be to protect the manufacturer, not to protect the remote buyer, and held that it served that purpose quite well.

If the court had recognized that Article 2 is silent on all of the issues of the manufacturer's liability, that UCC 2–719 does not apply to these facts, how would a common-law court look at the price-refund and exclusion-of-damages provisions?

Agreement in Fact by the Remote Buyer; Mutual Assent. In the closing paragraphs of the Indiana Supreme Court's opinion, the court held that there was an open question of fact whether there had been "mutual assent to the limitation of liability" in the printed material on the seed containers and remanded the case for trial of this issue. Although phrased as a question of "mutual assent," the question, in the court's view, was only whether the remote buyer had assented to the manufacturer's terms. The court observed that an agent of the buyer testified that, during the retail sale, he had read some of the terms in the label but had not read the entire label.

The Indiana court does not identify any legal rule, statutory or common law, under which the remote buyer's assent or lack of assent to the limitation of liability terms would be a pertinent issue of fact. The court is unaware that no bargaining had occurred between the manufacturer and remote buyer. When the buyer bought the seeds from the retail dealer, the seeds came in cans with the manufacturer's warranty *cum* limitation of liability on the label. There was never an occasion for the buyer to assent to the warranty or to the limitation of liability. What legal effect could lack of assent possibly have in this context?

Unconscionability. The Indiana Supreme Court rejected the remote buyer's argument that the manufacturer's limitation of remedy was substantively unconscionable. The court implied that the ruling would have been otherwise if there had been conclusive evidence that the manufacturer had been aware that the seeds carried disease. Other courts have found manufacturers' limitations of damages clause unconscionable in suits brought by remote buyers. See Durham v. Ciba–Geigy Corp., 315 N.W.2d 696 (S.D.1982). The South Dakota court declared (p. 700):

> [T]he label represents that foxtail will be controlled by the pesticide but the user subsequently discovers that the pesticide is ineffective to control foxtail. To permit the manufacturer of the pesticide to escape all consequential responsibility for the breach of contract by inserting a disclaimer of warranty and limitation of consequential damage clause, such as was used herein, would leave the pesticide user without any substantial recourse for his loss. One-sided agreements whereby one party is left without a remedy for another party's breach are oppressive and should be declared unconscionable. . . .
>
> In this case, loss of the intended crop due to the ineffectiveness of the herbicide is inevitable and potential plaintiffs should not be left without a remedy. Furthermore, the purchasers of pesticides are not in a position to bargain with chemical manufacturers for contract terms more favorable than those listed on the pre-printed label, nor are they in a position to test the effectiveness of the pesticide prior to purchase. . . .
>
> The legislature of this state has spent considerable time and effort in establishing the law of warranty in South Dakota, and the damages that are recoverable for a breach of that warranty. Appellant seeks to restrict and abolish this established law on the label of the product to the point where there is no actionable warranty for the consumer. This is not acceptable.
>
> We agree with the trial court's determination that appellant's disclaimer of warranty and limitation of consequential damages clause is invalid as unconscionable and contrary to the public policy of this state.

Proposed Revised UCC Article 2. The proposed revision of UCC Article 2 contains provisions that deal with manufacturers' warranties that are addressed to remote buyers.[9]

Proposed Revised§ 2–313A deals with manufacturers' affirmations of fact or promises that relate to the goods or manufacturers' descriptions of the goods that are packaged with or accompany the goods to remote buyers. Proposed § 2–313B deals with affirmations, promises or descriptions in advertisements. Under these sections the manufacturers' obligation is determined by the quality of the goods when they left the manufacturers'

---

9. The applicability of the draft provisions is not limited to manufacturers or remote buyers. Although persons in these transactional roles are the parties most likely covered by the draft provisions, the text deals with any upstream seller and with remote purchasers. "Purchaser" is a UCC-defined term that includes but is not limited to a "buyer." See UCC 1–201(32) and (33); UCC 2–103(a).

control. The statutory remedy breach in both instances would be damages measured by the loss resulting in the ordinary course of events determined in any manner that is reasonable, including incidental and consequential damages other than buyers' lost profits.

Both sections have provisions that would allow manufacturers to exclude statutory remedies. Exclusions would be effective, without regard to buyers' assent or lack of assent, if the exclusions are communicated in certain ways. An exclusion is effective if it is contained in the record or advertisement that contains the affirmation, promise or description or if it is furnished to the remote buyer no later than the time of purchase.

(4) Manufacturer's Remedial Promise to Repair or Replace Goods; Law Governing. The only remedial promise in *Martin Rispens* was a promise to refund the price. Performance of that promise was not an issue in the case since the losses at stake were vastly in excess of the price of the seeds. The materials that follow consider manufacturers' promises, made to remote buyers, to repair or replace goods. In transactions of this kind, the value of the goods is the dominant concern, although these transactions may also involve large losses in the form of consequential damages. Consequential damages for personal injuries or death will be considered in Section 6. In this Section the focus remains on buyers' failure to get what they bargained for.

For these cases, the legal platform becomes more complex. A federal statute, the Magnuson–Moss Warranty Act (MMWA), comes into play. Although the MMWA applies only to sales of consumer products, those sales constitute most of the transactions in which manufacturers' repair/replace promises are made to remote buyers. (Manufacturers' repair/replace promises on commercial equipment sold to their immediate buyers were considered in Section 4.)

Magnuson–Moss Warranty Act[10]

Introduction. The Magnuson–Moss Warranty Act (MMWA) applies to any transaction in which a manufacturer undertakes "to refund, repair, replace, or take other remedial action" with respect to a consumer product in the event that the product fails to meet the specifications in the undertaking. Such undertakings, called "written warranties" in the MMWA,[11] are the primary grist for the application of the federal act.[12] The MMWA applies to any "supplier" of a consumer product that provides a

---

10. 15 U.S.C. §§ 2301–2312. The MMWA has been interpreted and supplemented by regulations promulgated by the Federal Trade Commission. 16 CFR Parts 700–703.

11. MMWA 101(6)(B). References to the MMWA in these materials use the section numbers of the Act rather than the section numbers of the U.S. Code. Statutory supple-

ments for law students contain the MMWA with the Act's section.

12. The MMWA has a second definition of a "written warranty." A warranty that a consumer product is defect free or will meet a specified level of performance over a period of time is also a "written warranty." MMWA 101(6)(A). Such written warranties are rare.

"written warranty." "Supplier" refers primarily to manufacturers,[13] but the term would include a retailer if the retailer provided a "written warranty."

A major impetus to this legislation was the view that manufacturers, particularly manufacturers of automobiles, were not making adequate remedial promises and were not living up to the promises that they had made. Through 1960, all United States automobile manufacturers, using virtually identical language, undertook to repair new cars for only 90 days or 4,000 miles of use, whichever came first. In that year, the New Jersey Supreme Court declared that the common remedial promise was inimical to the public good and invalid.[14] Automobile manufacturers began to offer express warranties that differed in terms and duration and that had different remedial promises, but consumer organizations lobbied strongly for stronger legal protection. One result was the 1975 Magnuson–Moss Warranty Act.

The MMWA is a regulatory statute. One of the Act objectives was to induce manufacturers to provide stronger remedial promises. Most of the Act was focused on this primary goal. A second objective was to enhance the ability of aggrieved consumers to enforce remedial promises that were not performed. The Act contains a number of provisions intended to help consumers and their lawyers to obtain judicial relief. The regulatory provisions of the MMWA are built on the underlying state warranty and contract law. The law in this area is thus a complex blend of state and federal law.

Stronger Obligations. The strategy of the MMWA was not to require manufacturers to provide warranties or remedial promises but was, rather, to create market conditions that would induce manufacturers to improve consumer protection. One piece of this strategy was to describe the minimum elements of a satisfactory remedial promise.[15] Any manufacturer that elects to use the congressionally-approved terms was permitted to tout its

---

13. "Supplier" means "any person engaged in the business of making a consumer product directly or indirectly available" to consumers. MMWA 101(4).

14. Henningsen v. Bloomfield Motors, Inc., 32 N.J. 358, 404, 161 A.2d 69, 75–76 (1960):

> The disclaimer of the implied warranty and exclusion of all obligations except those specifically assumed by the express warranty signify a studied effort to frustrate that protection. True, the Sales Act authorizes agreements between buyer and seller qualifying the warranty obligations. But quite obviously the Legislature contemplated lawful stipulations (which are determined by the circumstances of a particular case) arrived at freely by parties of relatively equal bargaining strength. The lawmakers did not

authorize the automobile manufacturer to use its grossly disproportionate bargaining power to relieve itself from liability and to impose on the ordinary buyer, who in effect has no real freedom of choice, the grave danger of injury to himself and others that attends the sale of such a dangerous instrumentality as a defectively made automobile. In the framework of this case, illuminated as it is by the facts and the many decisions noted, we are of the opinion that Chrysler's attempted disclaimer of an implied warranty of merchantability and of the obligations arising therefrom is so inimical to the public good as to compel an adjudication of its invalidity.

15. MMWA 104.

undertaking as a FULL WARRANTY.[16] Other manufacturers were required to give consumers a conspicuous signal that they were offering only a LIMITED WARRANTY.[17] Coupled with the requirement of this highly visible signal, the MMWA required manufacturers to make all of the warranty terms available to prospective buyers, at the point of retail sales, before shoppers committed to become buyers.[18] Congress believed that competition among manufacturers would lead to widespread use of FULL WARRANTIES and that knowledgeable consumers would examine the different terms of manufacturers and buy goods that came with the more attractive remedial promises. The hope that manufacturers of consumer durable goods would offer FULL WARRANTIES has proven to be unfounded.[19]

Stronger Enforcement of Remedial Promises. The MMWA sought, in several ways, to improve enforcement of manufacturers' remedial promises. These provisions have had little practical effect.

The Act created a federal forum for warranty litigation,[20] authorized a special kind of federal class action,[21] and provided that successful claimants could recover attorneys' fees and costs.[22] The Act also provides the consumers may seek relief in state courts.[23] In a state-court action that is "brought" under the federal Act, claimants who prevail are entitled to seek recovery of attorneys' fees and costs.[24] The MMWA also encouraged creation and use of alternative dispute resolution mechanisms for warranty disputes.[25] None of these provisions has been more than marginally successful.

Express Warranties and the MMWA. Although the W in MMWA refers to warranties, the Act has no application to ordinary express warranties of quality. This results from the Act's extremely precise and narrow definition of "written warranty." The word "warranty" is quite misleading. "Written warranty," in practical terms, means a remedial promise. Any manufacturer's ordinary express warranty is outside the scope of the Act.

Shortly after the MMWA was enacted, a class action was brought against General Motors Corp. on behalf of individuals who had purchased new cars advertised by GM as having particular transmissions that would

---

16. MMWA 103(a)(1).

17. MMWA 103(a)(2).

18. MMWA 102. The Act relies extensively on Federal Trade Commission regulations to implement this requirement.

19. A notable exception was American Motors, Co., which offered FULL WARRANTIES on its automobiles in the late 1970s. The manufacturer did not survive.

FULL WARRANTIES are more prevalent in marketing of relatively low-priced consumer products, transactions in which manufacturers are willing to replace the goods or refund the retail price of defective goods.

20. MMWA 110(d)(1)(B) and (d)(3).

21. MMWA 110(d)(3)(C) and (e).

22. MMWA 110(d)(2).

23. MMWA 110(d)(1)(A).

24. State courts have general jurisdiction over such cases without reference to the MMWA. Whether a case is brought under that general jurisdiction or under the MMWA can be difficult to determine. See C. Reitz, Consumer Product Warranties Under Federal and State Laws 134–143 (2d ed. 1987).

25. MMWA 110(a); FTC Reg. 703.

give superior performance. The class action complaint alleged that GM actually used inferior transmissions in cars manufactured between 1976 through 1979. The class action was cognizable only if it was based on the class action provisions of the MMWA. The court dismissed the complaint because the representations of the quality of the transmissions in GM promotional literature did not constitute a "written warranty." Skelton v. General Motors Corp., 660 F.2d 311 (7th Cir.1981). Buyers' rights under GM's express warranty were determined entirely by state law, a matter outside the scope of the MMWA case before the court.

Implied Warranties of Merchantability and the MMWA. The MMWA does not cover manufacturers' express warranties of quality, but does have a few provisions on implied warranties. The Act defines "implied warranty" as an implied warranty arising under state law.[26] None of the "truth in warranting" regulations of the MMWA apply to implied warranties. Indeed, the MMWA is silent on whether a warranty of fitness for ordinary purpose is an implied obligation of manufacturers in transactions that end with retailers' sales of brand name durable consumer products to buyers. However, the MMWA provides that, if a manufacturer markets goods with a "written warranty," the manufacturer is precluded from disclaiming or modifying "any implied warranty." MMWA 108(a) declares in pertinent part:

> No supplier may disclaim or modify any implied warranty to a consumer with respect to [a] consumer product if . . . such supplier makes any written warranty to the consumer with respect to such consumer product.[27]

Section 108(a) does not declare that an implied warranty is created. The Act provides only that, if there is an implied warranty under state law, that warranty cannot be disclaimed by certain manufacturers.

The MMWA provisions on implied warranties were the basis of the court's decision in the following case:

Szajna v. General Motors Corp.

Supreme Court of Illinois, 1986.
115 Ill.2d 294, 104 Ill.Dec. 898, 503 N.E.2d 760.

■ JUSTICE RYAN delivered the opinion of the court:

The plaintiff, John L. Szajna (Szajna), filed a suit in the circuit court of Cook County against the defendant, General Motors Corporation (GM), on his own behalf and on behalf of all others who bought 1976 Pontiac Venturas which were equipped with Chevette transmissions. Count I of his second amended complaint is based on an alleged breach of implied warranty under section 2–314 of the Uniform Commercial Code (UCC) (Ill. Rev. Stat. 1975, ch. 26, par. 2–314) and section 110(d) of title I of the Magnuson–Moss Warranty–Federal Trade Commission Improvement Act (Magnu-

---

26. MMWA 101(7).

27. MMWA 108(a) also applies if a supplier enters into a "service contract," defined in MMWA 101(8).

son–Moss).... Count II is based on an alleged breach of express warranty under section 2–313 of the UCC ... .Count III alleges common law fraud. The trial court granted GM's motion to strike and dismiss the second amended complaint. ... The court did not determine whether the suit could be maintained as a class action. The appellate court affirmed. ... We granted Szajna's petition for leave to appeal....

* * *

The following allegations were common to all three counts of Szajna's second amended complaint. In August 1976, he bought a 1976 Pontiac Ventura from Seltzer Pontiac, Inc. (Seltzer), in Chicago. Seltzer, as agent for GM, gave Szajna a folder which contained two warranties: one entitled a "Limited Warranty On 1976 Pontiac Car" and another entitled "1976 Pontiac Passenger Car Emission Control System." It was alleged that both warranties were made by GM to Szajna. It was also alleged that thousands of the cars sold as 1976 Pontiac Venturas, including Szajna's, were equipped with Chevette transmissions; that the use of Chevette transmissions in Pontiac Venturas necessitates higher amounts of repairs and that they have shorter service lives than do transmissions ordinarily used in Pontiac Venturas because the Chevette transmission was designed for use in a lighter weight car; that use of the Chevette transmission in Pontiac Venturas lessens the value of the cars; and that Szajna paid $375 to have the transmission in his car replaced.

The following allegations were also common to all three counts. GM manufactured, labeled and made available through its Pontiac Division the 1976 Pontiac Ventura. GM designed and engineered a transmission specifically for the 1976 Pontiac Ventura. "Through its brochures, parts catalogues and repair manuals, as well as through the release of automobile news and information from its public relations department," GM "advised the expert observers, testers and reporters of the nature of the '1976 Pontiac Ventura' model as including the transmission designed for that size of car." The public and Szajna, in buying the cars, relied on the experts and on GM for any noteworthy information on GM cars not readily observable. No information was given to the public or the experts that some of the 1976 Pontiac Venturas were equipped with Chevette transmissions.

Count I of Szajna's second amended complaint alleges breach of implied warranty under section 2–314 of the UCC. It alleges that 1976 Pontiac Venturas equipped with Chevette transmissions were not merchantable because they "would not pass without objection in the trade" under the contract description; "were not of fair average quality within the description, did not run within the variations permitted by the agreement of even kind and quality and did not conform to their labels" as Pontiac Venturas. ... (The "description" referred to above was the name 1976 Pontiac Ventura.) Count I also alleges that the failure by GM to deliver 1976 Pontiac Venturas as warranted rendered them nonconforming goods for which Szajna and other purchasers could ... receive damages [under UCC 2–714]. ...

Szajna also alleges in count I breach of implied warranty pursuant to section 110(d) of Magnuson–Moss, which provides that a consumer who is damaged by the failure of a supplier or warrantor to comply with any obligation under an implied warranty may bring suit for damages and other legal and equitable relief in any court of competent jurisdiction in any State. . . .

In dismissing count I of Szajna's second amended complaint, the trial court entered the following conclusions of law. First, privity of contract is a prerequisite in Illinois to a suit for breach of implied warranty alleging economic loss. Second, Magnuson–Moss, in permitting recovery for breach of implied warranty, incorporates State-law privity requirements. (15 U.S.C. sec. 2301(7) (1976).) Third, no privity of contract existed between Szajna and GM. Fourth, the limited written warranty extended by GM, although running to the ultimate purchaser, did not give rise to the implied warranty of merchantability. The appellate court, in essence, adopted the trial court's conclusions of law. It was of the opinion, however, that while Szajna and GM "were in privity for purposes of the provisions in the express limited warranty, they were not in privity for purposes of implied warranties, which were specifically disclaimed by the express warranty." Szajna v. General Motors Corp. (1985), 130 Ill. App. 3d 173, 177.

Szajna urges this court to abolish the privity requirement in suits for breach of an implied warranty when a plaintiff seeks to recover for economic loss. In Suvada v. White Motor Co. (1965), 32 Ill. 2d 612, this court held that lack of privity of contract was no longer a defense in a tort action against the manufacturer in a products liability case. In Suvada this court abandoned the concept of implied warranty in tort and followed the holding of the California court in Greenman v. Yuba Power Products, Inc. (1963), 59 Cal. 2d 57, 377 P.2d 897, 27 Cal. Rptr. 697, and the position taken in Restatement (Second) of Torts section 402A (1965). This court imposed liability on the theory of strict liability in tort. . . .

We need not trace in detail the development of the retreat from the strict privity requirement as it relates to implied warranty and the theories upon which recovery, in the absence of privity, has been allowed. That has been the subject of numerous articles. Its discussion further here would be needless repetition. Dean Prosser appears to have spearheaded the attack on implied-warranty privity in two oft-cited articles. (Prosser, The Assault Upon the Citadel (Strict Liability to the Consumer), 69 Yale L.J. 1099 (1960) (hereafter referred to as Assault); Prosser, The Fall of the Citadel (Strict Liability to the Consumer), 50 Minn. L. Rev. 791 (1966) (hereafter referred to as Fall).) Although Prosser favored abolition of the privity requirement and indeed the concept of implied warranty in a broad area, he nonetheless favored the contractual nature of implied warranty and its privity requirement when recovery for economic loss was sought. (See Fall, 50 Minn. L. Rev. 791, 820–23 (1960).) Much more has been written on the historical development of this subject. . . .

The law, as it applies to recovery for purely economic loss, is far from clear and most certainly is not uniform in all the jurisdictions. . . .

It appears that much of the confusion involving privity as it relates to implied warranty stems from the imprecise use of the term implied warranty. That term, unfortunately and inaccurately, has been used to describe obligations imposed by law as a matter of public policy totally unrelated to any contractual relationship. It has also been used to describe obligations implied because of a privity relationship between contracting parties. We need not develop this distinction further at this time or discuss its many ramifications. We leave that to the legal scholars and commentators. Suffice it to say that in this State we have, for public policy reasons, abolished the requirement of privity in certain noneconomic-loss areas. (See Suvada v. White Motor Co. (1965), 32 Ill. 2d 612; Berry v. G. D. Searle & Co. (1974), 56 Ill. 2d 548.) However, . . ., we held that recovery for economic loss must be had within the framework of contract law. Moorman Manufacturing Co. v. National Tank Co. (1982), 91 Ill. 2d 69, 86.

* * *

[I]n the purchase of a new car the transaction in most instances involves a responsible commercial entity (the dealer) and an individual. The sections of the UCC referred to above create implied warranties running from the dealer to the purchaser. The purchaser of a defective product is not left without a remedy and in most instances is not left without a responsible entity from which the purchaser can recover. It is argued that if a dealer is not financially responsible, the purchaser has no remedy. There is nothing before us that indicates that that is the situation in this case. Also, there is no showing that this condition occurs other than infrequently. . . .

. . . [A] number of States have judicially abolished the privity requirement in economic-loss cases for various reasons. (See Comment, Enforcing the Rights of Remote Sellers Under the UCC: Warranty Disclaimers, The Implied Warranty of Fitness for a Particular Purpose and the Notice Requirement in the Nonprivity Context, 47 U. Pitt. L. Rev. 873, 887–88 (1986) (hereafter referred to as Rights of Remote Sellers).) Some States have legislatively abolished the privity requirement. (See 3 R. Anderson, Uniform Commercial Code sec. 2–314:98 (1985 Supp.).) We need not here consider whether privity or nonprivity jurisdictions are in the majority. Professors White and Summers assert that the majority of courts, absent proof of reliance by the nonprivity buyer upon representations by the remote seller, hold that privity is a requirement in cases seeking recovery for economic loss. (J. White & R. Summers, Uniform Commercial Code sec. 11–5, at 407 (2d ed. 1980).) Szajna, in his brief, argues to the contrary.

* * *

We think it is unnecessary to indulge in the judicial legislation . . . necessary to reconcile nonprivity to the UCC requirements, particularly of notice (section 2–607(3)(a)), requiring buyer to notify seller, and disclaimers and limitations (sections 2–316 and 2–719), both of which are stated in contractual language. Even those who favor the abolition of privity recognize that some judicial adjustments of the UCC must be made to accommodate nonprivity implied warranties. (See Razook, 23 Bus. L.J. 85, 100–05 (notice), 111 (disclaimers and limitations of liability).) We view judicial intervention unnecessary in view of the legislative concern expressed by certain enactments in this field which we will discuss later. We therefore decline to abolish the privity requirement in implied-warranty economic-loss cases.

* * *

Magnuson–Moss, enacted by Congress in 1975, ... does not require that warranty be given, but if there is a *written* warranty, Magnuson–Moss imposes certain requirements as to its contents, disclosures, and the effect of extending a written warranty. ... No supplier may disclaim or modify an implied warranty, except a supplier giving a limited written warranty may limit the duration of an implied warranty to the duration of the written warranty if such limitation is conscionable and is clearly set forth ... In this case we are concerned only with the question of whether, under Magnuson–Moss, Szajna can maintain an action based on an implied warranty against the manufacturer of the automobile. Magnuson–Moss suffers from certain deficiencies insofar as clarity is concerned. (See Skelton v. General Motors Corp. (N.D. 1980), 500 F. Supp. 1181, 1184, rev'd in part on other grounds (7th Cir.1981), 660 F.2d 311.) The provisions of Magnuson–Moss relating to implied warranties are no exception to this observation. Section 2301(7) defines implied warranty as follows:

> The term "implied warranty" means an implied warranty arising under State law (as modified by sections 2308 and 2304(a) of this title) in connection with the sale by a supplier of a consumer product. ...

Focusing on that part of the definition stating the term means "an implied warranty arising under State law," some authors maintain that if the law of the State holds that privity is essential to implied warranty, then an action such as is involved in our case cannot be maintained. (Miller & Kanter, *Litigation Under Magnuson–Moss: New Opportunities in Private Actions*, 13 U.C.C. L.J. 10, 22 (1980).) However, the definition also states that the term means an implied warranty arising under State law "(*as modified by sections 2308 and 2304(a) of this title*)." (Emphasis added.) ... Section 2308 provides:

> "No supplier may disclaim or modify (except as provided in subsection (b) of this section [limiting the duration of an implied warranty to the duration of a 'limited' written warranty]) any implied warranty to a consumer * * * if (1) such supplier makes any written warranty to the consumer * * * or (2) at the time of sale, or within 90 days thereafter, such supplier enters into a service contract with the consumer which applies to such consumer product." ...

This section raises the question as to whether it modifies implied-warranty State-law provisions to the extent that any written warranty given by a manufacturer to a remote purchaser creates an implied warranty by virtue of Magnuson–Moss. At the very least we must acknowledge that the provisions of section 2308 clearly demonstrate the policy of Magnuson–

Moss to sustain the protection afforded to consumers by implied warranties.

The Act broadly defines "consumer" in section 2301(3) as "a buyer (other than for purposes of resale) of any consumer product, any person to whom such product is transferred during the duration of an implied or written warranty * * * and any other person who is entitled by the terms of such warranty * * * or under applicable State law to enforce against the warrantor * * * the obligations of the warranty." ... It has been suggested that this broad definition of "consumer" and the provisions of section 2310(d)(1) ... which section authorizes a "consumer" to maintain a civil action for damages for failure of a "supplier" or "warrantor" to comply with any obligation of a written or implied warranty, effectively abolish vertical privity. (See Comment, *Consumer Product Warranties Under the Magnuson–Moss Warranty Act and the Uniform Commercial Code*, 62 Cornell L. Rev. 738, 755–59 (1977).) We do not think we can focus on any one section of Magnuson–Moss but should read the sections referred to together to accomplish the purpose of Magnuson–Moss of furnishing broad protection to the consumer.

In resolving this murky situation we find helpful, and accept, Professor Schroeder's analysis and suggestion as a reasonable solution. In cases where no Magnuson–Moss written warranty has been given, Magnuson–Moss has no effect upon State-law privity requirements because, by virtue of section 2301(7), which defines implied warranty, implied warranty arises only if it does so under State law. However, if a Magnuson–Moss written warranty (either "full" or "limited") is given by reason of the policy against disclaimers of implied warranty expressed in Magnuson–Moss and the provisions authorizing a consumer to sue a warrantor, the nonprivity "consumer" should be permitted to maintain an action on an implied warranty against the "warrantor." (Schroeder, *Privity Actions Under the Magnuson–Moss Warranty Act*, 66 Calif. L. Rev. 1, 16 (1978).) The rationale of this conclusion, though not specifically articulated by Professor Schroeder in the article, would hold that under Magnuson–Moss a warrantor, by extending a written warranty to the consumer, establishes privity between the warrantor and the consumer which, though limited in nature, is sufficient to support an implied warranty under sections 2–314 and 2–315 of the UCC. The implied warranty thus recognized, by virtue of the definition in section 2301(7) of Magnuson–Moss, must be one arising under the law of this State....

The appellate court in this case held that while the parties were in privity for purposes of the provisions of the express written limited warranty which General Motors had extended, they were not in privity for the purposes of implied warranty. (130 Ill. App. 3d 173, 177.) This holding is in conflict with our holding herein and will therefore be reversed. The appellate court, in the same sentence, stated that implied warranties were "specifically disclaimed by the expressed warranty." (130 Ill. App. 3d 173, 177.) The written warranty in this case limited any implied warranties to the duration of the written warranty. Thus, the part of the warranty referred to by the appellate court as disclaiming implied warranties may properly be referred to as a limitation on the duration of an implied warranty. Such limitation is covered by sections 2304(a)(2) and 2308(b) of Magnuson–Moss. We will not here define how this disclaimer-limitation fits within the contours of section 2–316 of the UCC, which covers "exclusions or modifications of warranties." Szajna here contends that the issue of disclaimer was not raised, briefed or argued by GM in either the circuit or appellate courts and should not have been considered by the appellate court. These issues, it is argued, are affirmative defenses which, because of other provisions of the UCC and Magnuson–Moss, may or may not be applicable to this transaction. GM also has stated that it does not believe the disclaimer-limitation issue can be resolved fully on the basis of the allegations of Szajna's complaint and therefore did not address these questions in its briefs. In light of this, we find that the trial court erred in dismissing count I, and this cause will be remanded to the circuit court of Cook County. So that the trial court will know whether count II and count III remain viable parts of the complaint, we must further consider the propriety of the appellate court's holding that these counts were properly dismissed.

Count II of Szajna's second amended complaint alleges breach of express warranty pursuant to section 2–313 of the UCC. In addition to the allegations mentioned above that were common to all three counts, several others pertained specifically to count II. It was alleged that GM, in labeling and advertising 1976 Pontiac Venturas, made an affirmation of fact and a description of the goods which became part of the basis of the bargain. . . . [UCC 2–313(1)(a), (1)(b).] Also, that in labeling and advertising 1976 Pontiac Venturas, GM warranted that the nature of the material and equipment used was of the kind and quality that could be expected from cars which had the transmissions designed and engineered for use in that car. Finally, it alleged that Szajna and the general public, in purchasing cars, relied on the description of a car by division and model, which meant to them that the component parts of the car were of the kind and quality which GM publicized were part of the car.

The trial court held that, as a matter of law, Szajna had failed to allege the existence of an express warranty by GM that his car would be equipped with a particular transmission. Likewise, the appellate court stated that it did "not believe that defendant's use of a trade name, alone, [could] be extended to encompass a 'description' of the transmission used." 130 Ill. App. 3d 173, 178.

Szajna does not maintain that GM breached the terms of its limited written warranty. Nor does he claim to have seen any express representation by GM pertaining to the transmission used in 1976 Pontiac Venturas or to have relied on any such representation. Rather, count II is based on the contention that the name "1976 Pontiac Ventura" is a description which, under section 2–313 of the UCC, . . . constitutes an express warranty of kind and quality as to the car and its component parts. While Szajna has cited several Illinois cases in support of this contention . . . none of those cases stand for the proposition that a trade name is a description creating an express warranty that the product is of a particular quality or that its component parts are of a particular kind or quality. . . .

The name "1976 Pontiac Ventura" includes characteristics of both a trademark and a trade name. . . . It identifies the manufacturer. It identifies and distinguishes the car (product) from cars produced by other manufacturers. It also serves to identify and distinguish the car from other car models made by GM and from cars of the same model made by GM in other years. However, it does not, alone, describe the transmission used in the car or its quality. In the context of new cars, there is and must be a distinction between a manufacturer's description of its product and a manufacturer's warranty of its product. . . .

Although a trademark or trade name has traditionally been viewed as identifying the origin or source of the goods to which it is affixed, in recent years trademarks and trade names have assumed another function, that of assuring the purchaser of a certain degree of uniformity or quality. (Hanak, The Quality Assurance Function of Trademarks, 43 Fordham L. Rev. 363, 375 (1974).) However, this assurance of uniformity of quality does not preclude all changes in the product. In the article last cited, the author states that purchasers of new automobiles, while unable to discern mechanical changes from prior models, fully expect changes to exist and that variations necessitated by trade discoveries, newer and more economical methods of making the same product, or changed manufacturing conditions are not contrary to the assurance-of-uniformity or quality role of the trademark. (Hanak, The Quality Assurance Function of Trademarks, 43 Fordham L. Rev. 363, 375 (1974); see also Comment, Traffic in Trade—Symbols, 44 Harv. L. Rev. 1210, 1216 (1931).) We hold that the name "1976 Pontiac Ventura," alone does not create an express warranty of the kind or nature of the car's components. . . .

Count III of the second amended complaint is in tort and alleges common law fraud. . . . [T]here are no allegations that GM made the assertion to Szajna or to the public in general that 1976 Pontiac Venturas were all equipped with a transmission that had been specifically designed for that automobile. Szajna alleges that it is "inferred" in the "advertising" that the 1976 Ventura had the transmission designed for it. Thus, Szajna bases his cause of action on an inference of an untrue statement by GM from which inference we are, in turn, asked to infer the necessary fraudulent intent to deceive. We have held above that the use of the trade name "Pontiac Ventura" does not create an express warranty of the quality and nature of the vehicle's components. We likewise now hold that the use of this name as the description of the vehicle does not constitute an untrue statement capable of supplying an inference of intent to deceive. We hold that the allegations of count III do not state a cause of action based on fraud.

* * *

For the foregoing reasons, the judgment of the appellate court, affirming the dismissal of Szajna's second amended complaint is reversed as to count I and the cause is remanded to the circuit court of Cook County. The appellate court's judgment affirming the dismissal of counts II and III of the second amended complaint is affirmed. The judgment of the circuit court with respect to count I is reversed. Its judgment with respect to counts II and III is affirmed.

NOTES

(1) GM's "Written Warranty." Counsel for the buyers made no claim of breach of GM's limited warranty. What is the explanation for omission of that legal claim in the complaint?

(2) GM's Express Warranty. Buyers' counsel framed the complaint for GM's breach of express warranty under UCC 2–313. Counsel argued that the phrase "1976 Pontiac Ventura" was an affirmation of fact (2–313(a)) and a description of the goods (2–313(b)) that became part of the basis of the bargain. Counsel also argued that the words indicated to the general public that the component parts of vehicles with that name were of the kind and quality that GM had advertised. The opinion of the court made no reference to any specific affirmations about the components.

The Illinois Supreme Court held that "1976 Pontiac Ventura" did not describe the transmissions in the cars. Use of Chevette transmissions was not inconsistent with the phrase. Was this decision affected in any way by the legal argument that UCC 2–313 governed? Did the court agree that the UCC applied? Would an argument grounded in common law have been more persuasive?

(3) GM's Implied Warranty. Most of the opinion of the Illinois Supreme Court was devoted to the law underlying the claim of breach of an implied warranty of merchantability, but the opinion contains little of substance on the warranty claim. Counsel for the buyers argued that the governing law was UCC 2–314 and cited three subsections of UCC 2–314(2). Did the Illinois Supreme Court hold that GM had extended such an implied warranty to retail buyers of the Pontiac Venturas? That the implied warranty had been breached? The opinion has no discussion of the UCC 2–314(1) provisions that find the statutory warranty in contracts of sale. On remand of the case to the trial court, could GM raise the defense that UCC 2–314(1), by its terms, does not apply to the circumstances of this case?

How much understanding of the nature and substance of manufacturers' implied warranties of quality can one glean from the (lengthy) opinion in this case? Commentators have noted that the concept of an implied warranty is derivative: the implication must have some source. The court noted that sometimes warranties have been implied from standards of public welfare, as in the implied obligation to sell food and beverages that will not cause personal injury or death. The alternative, in the court's analysis, was a warranty of quality implied from other terms of a contract.

The court fails to assay the nature of a contract that might exist between GM and buyers of Pontiac Venturas.

The court observed that each of the buyers had been party to a sales contract with a retail dealer, deemed to be a responsible commercial entity. The court rejects, as unfounded in the record, that any of the dealers might not be financially responsible. In virtually all contracts for sale of new automobiles, the dealers make no express warranties of quality, provide no "written warranties" of their own, and totally disclaim all implied warranties (carefully mentioning "merchantability").[28] Dealers explain their disclaimers to the buyers with the fact that the buyers are protected by the warranties of the manufacturers (and of some component suppliers). If the court had been aware of the business practice in retail car sales, would its analysis have been changed?

(4) Privity. The dominant issue in the case was the requirement of privity, whether the remote buyers could sue GM for breach of an implied warranty of merchantability under the law of Illinois. Did the court consider this issue as one of common law or statutory interpretation?[29] The Illinois Supreme Court, after much discussion, concluded that Illinois law would continue to prohibit suits by remote buyers. The court then held that the privity barrier had been lowered by the MMWA, reversed the trial court and remanded the case for trial. Is the court's position coherent?

The opinion of the court is quite clear that the implied warranty in this case is a warranty entirely under Illinois state law. The court has said, in effect, that an Illinois buyer can enforce the Illinois warranty if he or she received a "written warranty" from a manufacturer, even though the "written warranty" has not been breached, but absent a "written warranty," an Illinois buyer is barred from relief for breach of the Illinois warranty. If an Illinois warranty exists, why would Illinois courts deny aggrieved Illinois buyers the right to enforce that warranty under the law of Illinois?

The Illinois Supreme Court saw no problem in the idea of remote buyers' enforcement of a GM express warranty. The court found that there was no breach of an express warranty in this case. Suppose, however, that a plausible claim of breach of express warranty had been found. If Illinois buyers, although contractually remote from manufacturers, have the right under Illinois law to enforce an Illinois express warranty, why would those buyers not have the right under Illinois law to enforce an Illinois implied warranty?

---

28. Automobile dealers typically do not make "written warranties" and therefore are not precluded by MMWA 108(a) from disclaiming implied warranties. Sometimes a dealer associates itself too closely with a manufacturer's "written warranty" and becomes a co-warrantor under the MMWA. See Ventura v. Ford Motor Corp., 180 N.J.Super. 45, 433 A.2d 801 (App.Div.1981).

29. In an omitted section of the opinion, the court cited the Illinois version of UCC 2–318 (Alternative A) and declared that the UCC does not directly address vertical privity. The court went on to observe that most of the provisions in UCC Article 2, including the warranty provisions, deal with sellers and buyers directly involved in contracts of sale.

(5) State and MMWA Class Actions. The class action in this case was brought in an Illinois state court under state procedural law. The class action authorized by the MMWA requires that the number of named plaintiffs be at least 100. Efforts by plaintiffs counsel to gather that number of named plaintiffs for a federal MMWA class action have been, in the main, futile.[30] Illinois law did not require 100 named plaintiffs for a class action. However, the trial court had not yet certified a class when the complaint was dismissed.

(6) Buyers' Remedies. In the procedural posture of *Szajna*, none of the courts needed to consider the law governing the remedies if the plaintiffs were to prevail on remand.

Damages. Early in the opinion of the Illinois Supreme Court there is passing reference to UCC 2–714. Assume that the presence of Chevette transmissions in Pontiac Venturas reduced the value of the automobiles, what would be the amount of each owner's damages? Does it matter whether the matter is governed by UCC 2–714 or common law? Is the amount of damages at stake for any one car owner likely to be sufficient to justify the owner seeking judicial relief as a sole plaintiff? The circumstances may demonstrate the practical importance of the class action form of proceeding.

Revocation of Acceptance in Actions Against Manufacturers. Buyers dissatisfied with goods with substantial problems that cannot be repaired may elect to revoke their acceptance of the goods and seek to recover the purchase price. We had a case of that kind in Section 4, *McCullough v. Bill Swad Chrysler–Plymouth, Inc.* The retail dealer was the principal defendant in that case. Buyers sometimes try to revoke acceptance and recover the purchase price from manufacturers, in addition to or instead of suing the immediate sellers. McCullough did so; the trial court dismissed that part of buyer's case and apparently buyer did not appeal. Does UCC 2–608 or the MMWA contemplate or authorize buyers to bring revocation-of-acceptance price-recovery actions against manufacturers? Courts deciding the issue are sharply divided.[31] One set of commentators argues that

30. Abraham v. Volkswagen of America, Inc., 795 F.2d 238 (2d Cir.1986); Alberti v. General Motors Corp., 600 F.Supp. 1026 (D.D.C.1985); Walsh v. Ford Motor Co., 588 F.Supp. 1513 (D.D.C.1984), *vacated and remanded*, 807 F.2d 1000 (D.C.Cir.1986); Lieb v. American Motors Corp., 538 F.Supp. 127 (S.D.N.Y.1982): Watts v. Volkswagen Artiengesellschaft, 488 F.Supp. 1233 (W.D.Ark. 1980).

31. *Compare* Andover Air Ltd. Partnership v. Piper Aircraft Corp., 7 UCC Rep. Serv.2d 1494 (D.Mass.1989); Gasque v. Mooers Motor Car Co., 227 Va. 154, 313 S.E.2d 384 (1984); Seekings v. Jimmy GMC of Tucson, Inc., 130 Ariz. 596, 638 P.2d 210 (1981); Edelstein v. Toyota Motors Distributors, 176 N.J.Super. 57, 422 A.2d 101 (1980); Conte v. Dwan Lincoln–Mercury, Inc., 172 Conn. 112, 374 A.2d 144 (1976); Voytovich v. Bangor Punta Operations, Inc., 494 F.2d 1208 (6th Cir.1974), *with* Fode v. Capital RV Center, Inc., 575 N.W.2d 682 (N.D.1998); Gochey v. Bombardier, Inc., 153 Vt. 607, 572 A.2d 921 (1990); Costa v. Volkswagen of America, 150 Vt. 213, 551 A.2d 1196 (1988); Ford Motor Credit Co. v. Harper, 671 F.2d 1117 (8th Cir.1982); Volkswagen of America v. Novak, 418 So.2d 801 (Miss.1982); Murray v. Holiday Rambler, Inc., 83 Wis.2d 406, 265 N.W.2d 513 (1978); Volvo of America v. Wells, 551 S.W.2d 826 (Ky.App.1977); Durfee v. Rod Baxter Imports, Inc., 262 N.W.2d 349

revocation of acceptance and price recovery from remote sellers should be permitted:

> There is certainly nothing in Article 2 that would be inconsistent with such an approach. Moreover, the concept of "remote revocation" is gaining a foothold elsewhere. In the Magnuson–Moss Federal Warranty Act, a manufacturer who markets consumer products under a "full warranty" heading must permit the consumer/buyer to elect either a refund of the full purchase price or replacement goods if the product contains a "defect" or "malfunction" that cannot be cured after a "reasonable number of attempts" by the manufacturer. Thus, revocation against the remote manufacturer is a remedy under *federal* law in some situations. Similarly, a number of state legislatures are enacting "lemon" statutes that give revocation rights against the manufacturer of a defective motor vehicle without regard to limits in the written warranty accompanying the goods.

B. Clark & C. Smith, The Law of Product Warranties § 7.03(3)(d) (1984). Cf. White & Summers, 330–331 (5th ed. 2000).

"Lemon laws." A large number of states have enacted "lemon laws" that give special protection, including the right to revoke acceptance, when defects in motor vehicles are not corrected within a reasonable time. While non-uniform in their language, these statutes tend to allow consumers to demand that manufacturers either refund the retail purchase price or replace the car. Commonly a buyer's right to relief matures when the "same defect" continues to exist after four unsuccessful attempts to repair it during a statutory time period or the car was out of service for 30 days during the statutory period. See C. Reitz, Consumer Product Warranties Under Federal and State Laws, ch. 14 (2d ed. 1987).

Revocation of Acceptance of Goods Financed. Most consumer buyers of new automobiles do not pay the price in cash. Instead they pay a small part of the price at delivery (including, perhaps, the agreed value of a trade-in) and arrange to pay the balance of the price in installments over a period of four or five years. Commonly, the loans that finance buyers' purchases are made by banks or finance agencies. The buyer in *McCullough* entered into such an arrangement; one of the parties sued was a bank, presumably the bank to which buyer was obligated to make installment payments. What relief would buyers likely seek from lenders? Refund of previous payments? Release from obligation to pay future installments? Damages for breach of warranty? The trial court in *McCullough* dismissed the suit against the bank and apparently buyer did not appeal.

In retail installment-purchase transactions, contracts of sale typically provide for buyers' deferred payments; promptly after the sale, the retailers assign the buyers' debt obligations to a bank or finance company. A Federal Trade Commission rule requires sellers of consumer goods to insert into

(Minn.1977); Asciolla v. Manter Oldsmobile–
Pontiac, Inc., 117 N.H. 85, 370 A.2d 270
(1977).

their contract documents a provision that makes lender-assignees subject to all claims and defenses that buyers could assert against seller-assignors. Preservation of Consumers' Claims and Defenses, 16 C.F.R. § 433. If buyers have claims or defenses against their immediate sellers, lender-assignees would be subject to them as well.[32]

In retail sales of consumer durable goods, retailers commonly advise the buyers that the manufacturers of the goods provide warranties/remedial promises and that this is the buyers' only assurance of the quality of the goods. The retail sales contracts contain no express warranties but do contain disclaimers of implied warranties. The sales contracts are promptly assigned to lenders. Would the FTC rule make lenders subject to buyers' claims or defenses against the manufacturers of the goods? See Smith v. Navistar International Transportation Corp., 714 F.Supp. 303 (N.D.Ill. 1989) (manufacturer, financer, and dealer were part of one corporate family).

Proposed Revised UCC Article 2. The proposed revision of UCC Article 2 would codify the law with respect to manufacturers' remedial promises. Proposed Revised 2–313A and 2–313B, which deal with manufacturers' express warranties, also deal with manufacturers' remedial promises. Under Proposed Revised 2–725(b)(3), a cause of action accrues when a remedial promise is not performed when due.

Morrow v. New Moon Homes

Supreme Court of Alaska, 1976.
548 P.2d 279.

■ RABINOWITZ, CHIEF JUSTICE.

This appeal raises questions concerning personal jurisdiction over, and the liability of, a nonresident manufacturer of a defective mobile home that was purchased in Alaska from a resident seller.

In October of 1969, Joseph R. and Nikki Morrow bought a mobile home from Golden Heart Mobile Homes, a Fairbanks retailer of mobile homes. A plaque on the side of the mobile home disclosed that the home had been manufactured in Oregon by New Moon Homes, Inc. The Morrows made a down payment of $1,800, taking out a loan for the balance of the purchase price from the First National Bank of Fairbanks. The loan amount of $10,546.49, plus interest of 9 percent per year, was to be repaid by the Morrows in 72 monthly installments of $190.13 each.

At the time of the purchase, the Morrows inspected the mobile home and noticed that the carpeting had not been laid and that several windows were broken. Roy Miller, Golden Heart's salesman, assured them that these problems would be corrected and later made good his assurances. Miller also told the Morrows that the mobile home was a "good trailer," " . . . as

---

32. The rule provides that buyer's recovery against a lender "shall not exceed   amounts paid by the debtor hereunder."

warm as ... any other trailer." After the sale, Miller moved the Morrows' mobile home to Lakeview Terrace, set it up on the space the Morrows had rented, and made sure that the utilities were connected. Then the troubles started.

On the first night that the mobile home's furnace was in use, the motor went out and had to be replaced. The electric furnace installed by the manufacturer had been removed by someone who had replaced the original with an oil furnace. The furnace vent did not fit, and consequently the "stove pipe" vibrated when the furnace was running. Subsequent events showed the furnace malfunction was not the primary problem with the mobile home.

About four days after the mobile home had been set up, the Morrows noticed that the doors did not close all the way and that the windows were cracked. The bathtub leaked water into the middle bedroom. In March of 1970 when the snow on the roof began to melt, the roof leaked. Water came in through gaps between the ceiling and the wall panels, as well as along the bottom of the wallboard. A short circuit developed in the electrical system; the lights flickered at various times. When it rained, water came out of the light fixture in the hallway. Other problems with the mobile home included the following: the interior walls did not fit together at the corners; the paneling came off the walls; the windows and doors were out of square; the door frames on the bedroom doors fell off and the closet doors would not slide properly; the curtains had glue on them; and the finish came off the kitchen cabinet doors.

Despite all these problems, the Morrows continued to live in the mobile home and make the loan payments. Golden Heart Mobile Homes was notified many times of the difficulties the Morrows were having with their mobile home. Roy Miller, the Golden Heart salesman with whom the Morrows had dealt, did put some caulking around the bathtub, but otherwise he was of little assistance. Finally, sometime before April 1, 1970, Nikki Morrow informed Miller that if Golden Heart did not fix the mobile home the Morrows wanted to return it. Miller said the Morrows would "[h]ave to take it up with the bank." Subsequently, Golden Heart went out of business.

The First National Bank of Fairbanks was more sensitive to the Morrows' plight. Upon being informed by the Morrows that they intended to make no further payments on the mobile home, bank personnel went out and inspected the home several times. In addition, on May 27, 1970, the bank wrote to New Moon Homes, Inc. in Silverton, Oregon. Its letter informed New Moon of the problems the Morrows were having with their New Moon mobile home and asked whether New Moon expected to send a representative to Fairbanks since Golden Heart, the dealer, was no longer in business. Apparently, New Moon did not respond to the bank's letter.

A short time later the Morrows' counsel wrote a letter to New Moon Homes notifying New Moon that the Morrows intended to hold the company liable for damages for breach of implied warranties. About a month later the Morrows separated, with Nikki Morrow continuing to live in the mobile home. She continued to make payments to First National because she "couldn't afford Alaskan rents." Nikki Morrow eventually moved out of the mobile home but made no effort to sell or rent it because she considered it "not fit to live in." In October of 1971 the Morrows filed this action against both New Moon Homes and Golden Heart Mobile Homes, alleging that defendants had breached implied warranties of merchantability and fitness for particular purpose in manufacturing and selling an improperly constructed mobile home. . . .

The case was tried in July of 1973. No attorney appeared on behalf of Golden Heart Mobile Homes, but the Morrows proceeded to present their evidence against New Moon because they were looking primarily to the manufacturer for recovery. The Morrows offered the testimony of four witnesses which tended to identify the mobile home in question as a New Moon home. Neither side presented any evidence concerning New Moon's business connections with Alaska or the circumstances under which the New Moon mobile home came into Golden Heart's possession. The superior court granted the Morrows a default judgment against Golden Heart, but dismissed their claim against New Moon "for both failure of jurisdiction and failure of privity of contract." The Morrows then appealed from that portion of the superior court's judgment which dismissed their claim against New Moon.

* * *

The principal theory of liability advocated by the Morrows at trial was that New Moon had breached statutory warranties which arose by operation of law with the manufacture and distribution of this mobile home. Specifically, the Morrows rely upon [UCC 2–314] and [UCC 2–315] of the Uniform Commercial Code as enacted in Alaska. The former section provides for an implied warranty of "merchantability" in the sale of goods governed by the Code; the latter establishes an implied warranty that the goods are fit for the particular purpose for which they were purchased. The superior court was of the view that these Code warranties operated only for the benefit of those purchasing directly from a manufacturer or seller. Since the Morrows were not in privity of contract with New Moon, the superior court concluded that a warranty theory based on [UCC 2–314] and [UCC 2–315] could not serve as a basis for liability.

There is little question that the Code applies to the distribution of mobile homes. New Moon qualifies as a "merchant" within the meaning of the relevant section, AS 45.05.042, and mobile homes, being highly movable, are "goods" as defined in AS 45.05.044. . . .

It is equally clear that in this jurisdiction the Morrows, as immediate purchasers, can recover against their seller for breach of the Code's implied warranties. Indeed, this was the theory upon which the default judgment against Golden Heart Mobile Homes was predicated. The critical question in this case is whether the Morrows, as remote purchasers, can invoke the warranties attributable to the manufacturer which arose when New Moon passed title of the mobile home to the next party in the chain of distribution. In other words, do the implied warranties of merchantability and fitness run from a manufacturer only to those with whom the manufacturer is in privity of contract?

Although sometimes criticized, the distinction between horizontal and vertical privity is significant in this case. The issue of horizontal privity raises the question whether persons other than the buyer of defective goods can recover from the buyer's immediate seller on a warranty theory. The question of vertical privity is whether parties in the distributive chain prior to the immediate seller can be held liable to the ultimate purchaser for loss caused by the defective product. The Code addresses the matter of horizontal privity in [UCC 2–318], extending the claim for relief in warranty to any " ... person who is in the family or household of his buyer or who is a guest in his home if it is reasonable to expect that the person may use, consume, or be affected by the goods...." With regard to vertical privity, the Code is totally silent and strictly neutral, as Official Comment 3 to [UCC 2–318] makes eminently clear. The Code leaves to the courts the question of the extent to which vertical privity of contract will or will not be required.

This court has never previously confronted the question whether a requirement of privity of contract will preclude a purchaser from recovering against the original manufacturer on a theory of implied warranties.

. . .

The dispute here is whether the requirement of vertical privity of contract should be abolished in Alaska. This battle has already been waged in many jurisdictions, and the results are well known: the citadel of privity has largely toppled. The course of this modern development is familiar history and we need not recount it at length here. Contrived "exceptions" which paid deference to the hoary doctrine of privity while obviating its unjust results have given way in more recent years to an open frontal assault. The initial attack came in Spence v. Three Rivers Builders & Masonry Supply, Inc., 353 Mich. 120, 90 N.W.2d 873 (1958), but the leading case probably remains Henningsen v. Bloomfield Motors, Inc., 32 N.J. 358, 161 A.2d 69 (1960), in which the New Jersey Supreme Court held liable for personal injuries and property damages both the manufacturer of an automobile and the dealer who sold the vehicle. The rationale for the widespread abolition of the requirement of privity stems from the structure and operation of the free market economy in contemporary society; it was succinctly summed up not long ago by the Supreme Court of Pennsylvania [in Kassab v. Central Soya, 432 Pa. 217, 246 A.2d 848, 853 (1968)]:

> Courts and scholars alike have recognized that the typical consumer does not deal at arms length with the party whose product he buys. Rather, he buys from a retail merchant who is usually little more than an economic conduit. It is not the merchant who has defectively manufactured the product. Nor is it usually the merchant who advertises the product on such a large scale as to attract consumers. We have in our society literally scores of large, financially responsible manufacturers who place their wares in the stream of commerce not

only with the realization, but with the avowed purpose, that these goods will find their way into the hands of the consumer. Only the consumer will use these products; and only the consumer will be injured by them should they prove defective.

The policy considerations which dictate the abolition of privity are largely those which also warranted imposing strict tort liability on the manufacturer: the consumer's inability to protect himself adequately from defectively manufactured goods, the implied assurance of the maker when he puts his goods on the market that they are safe, and the superior risk bearing ability of the manufacturer. In addition, limiting a consumer under the Code to an implied warranty action against his immediate seller in those instances when the product defect is attributable to the manufacturer would effectively promote circularity of litigation and waste of judicial resources. Therefore, we decide that a manufacturer may be held liable for a breach of the implied warranties of [UCC 2–314] and [UCC 2–315] without regard to privity of contract between the manufacturer and the consumer.

The more difficult question before this court is whether we should extend this abolition of privity to embrace not only warranty actions for personal injuries and property damage but also those for economic loss. Contemporary courts have been more reticent to discard the privity requirement and to permit recovery in warranty by a remote consumer for purely economic losses. In considering this issue we note that economic loss may be categorized into direct economic loss and consequential economic loss, a distinction maintained in the Code's structure of damage remedies. One commentator has summarized the distinction:

> Direct economic loss may be said to encompass damage based on insufficient product value; thus, direct economic loss may be "out of pocket"—the difference in value between what is given and received— or "loss of bargain"—the difference between the value of what is received and its value as represented. Direct economic loss also may be measured by costs of replacement and repair. Consequential economic loss includes all indirect loss, such as loss of profits resulting from inability to make use of the defective product.[35]

The claim of the Morrows in this case is one for direct economic loss.

A number of courts recently confronting this issue have declined to overturn the privity requirement in warranty actions for economic loss. One principal factor seems to be that these courts simply do not find the social and economic reasons which justify extending enterprise liability to the victims of personal injury or property damage equally compelling in the case of a disappointed buyer suffering "only" economic loss. There is an apparent fear that economic losses may be of a far greater magnitude in value than personal injuries, and being somehow less foreseeable these

---

35. Note, Economic Loss in Products   917, 918 (1966).
Liability Jurisprudence, 66 Colum.L.Rev.

losses would be less insurable, undermining the risk spreading theory of enterprise liability.

Several of the courts which have recently considered this aspect of the privity issue have found those arguments unpersuasive. We are in agreement and hold that there is no satisfactory justification for a remedial scheme which extends the warranty action to a consumer suffering personal injury or property damage but denies similar relief to the consumer "fortunate" enough to suffer only direct economic loss. . . .

The fear that if the implied warranty action is extended to direct economic loss, manufacturers will be subjected to liability for damages of unknown and unlimited scope would seem unfounded. The manufacturer may possibly delimit the scope of his potential liability by use of a disclaimer in compliance with [UCC 2–316] or by resort to the limitations authorized in [UCC 2–719]. These statutory rights not only preclude extending the theory of strict liability in tort, supra, but also make highly appropriate this extension of the theory of implied warranties. Further, by expanding warranty rights to redress this form of harm, we preserve ". . . the well developed notion that the law of contract should control actions for purely economic losses and that the law of tort should control actions for personal injuries." We therefore hold that a manufacturer can be held liable for direct economic loss attributable to a breach of his implied warranties, without regard to privity of contract between the manufacturer and the ultimate purchaser.[42] It was therefore error for the trial court to dismiss the Morrows' action against New Moon for want of privity.

Our decision today preserves the statutory rights of the manufacturer to define his potential liability to the ultimate consumer, by means of express disclaimers and limitations, while protecting the legitimate expectation of the consumer that goods distributed on a wide scale by the use of conduit retailers are fit for their intended use. The manufacturer's rights are not, of course, unfettered. Disclaimers and limitations must comport with the relevant statutory prerequisites and cannot be so oppressive as to be unconscionable within the meaning of [UCC 2–302]. On the other hand, under the Code the consumer has a number of responsibilities if he is to enjoy the right of action we recognize today, not the least of which is that he must give notice of the breach of warranty to the manufacturer pursuant to [UCC 2–607]. The warranty action brought under the Code must be brought within the statute of limitations period prescribed in [UCC 2–725]. If the action is for breach of the implied warranty of fitness for particular purpose, created by [UCC 2–315], the consumer must establish that the warrantor had reason to know the particular purpose for

---

42. We recognize that the arguments against the abolition of privity are more compelling when the injury alleged is damages of a consequential nature many times the value of the manufacturer's product. See, e.g., Note, Economic Loss in Products Liability Jurisprudence, 66 Colum.L.Rev. 917, 965–66 (1965). We do not speak today to the issue of consequential economic loss, other than to note that [UCC 2–715] governs the recovery of such damages and requires, among other things, that said damages must have been foreseeable by the manufacturer. Adams v. J.I. Case Co., 125 Ill.App.2d 388, 261 N.E.2d 1 (1970).

which the goods were required and that the consumer relied on the seller's skill or judgment to select or furnish suitable goods. In the case of litigation against a remote manufacturer, it would appear that often it will be quite difficult to establish this element of actual or constructive knowledge essential to this particular warranty.

In the case at bar the trial judge failed to enter written findings of fact.... We cannot determine from the record whether the Morrows would have prevailed on a theory of breach of implied warranties had the trial court not erred in raising the barrier of privity.

* * *

... Consequently, we order that this cause be remanded for a new trial in which Morrows will have the opportunity to establish every element of their case....

Reversed and remanded for a new trial in accordance with this opinion.

NOTES

(1) Importance of Manufacturers' Trade Names in Retail Sales. Unlike the transactions in *Martin Rispens* and *Szajna*. the manufacturer in this case made no effort to communicate with the remote buyers. The court does not mention any advertisements of the manufacturer. There was no manufacturer's description of the goods, no express warranty of any kind, no remedial promise, and no MMWA "written warranty." The court noted that a plaque on the side of the mobile home identified it as manufactured by New Moon Homes. If there was a claim that the buyers had seen the plaque before deciding to buy the mobile home, the court did not mention that fact.

If a retail buyer, without knowledge of the identity of the manufacturer, buys a product from a retail dealer and, later, the buyer is dissatisfied with the quality of the product, should the buyer be permitted to recover from the manufacturer on an implied warranty theory?

(2) The Upstream Contract Theory. Counsel for the buyers and the court chose to ground their legal analysis in Article 2 of the UCC and, particularly, on the warranty of merchantability in UCC 2–314(2)(c)(not fit for the ordinary purposes for which such goods are used). The court noted that the manufacturer was a "merchant" and the mobile home was a "good" under Article 2 definitions. The court then stated as the critical question: "whether the Morrows, as remote purchasers, can invoke the warranties attributable to the manufacturer *which arose when New Moon passed title to the next party in the chain of distribution.*"

At this stage, the court's analysis was not based on the retail sales contract. Nor was the analysis based on a contract between the manufacturer and the remote buyers. The contract to which the court referred was a sales contract between the manufacturer and some unknown person, the first contract link in the chain of distribution. That contract was a sales contract, and likely was a sales contract subject to some state's version of the UCC. The privity issue framed by the court was whether the Morrows, though not a party to that upstream sales contract, could be allowed to enforce the terms of that contract.

That novel analytical move is intriguing, but does it support the claim of the Morrows? There are three major problems with the theory: First, the court has no idea of the actual terms of that upstream sales contract. The description of the goods in that contract is unknown. Likely there was an express warranty coupled with a disclaimer of all implied warranties. If the disclaimer of an implied warranty of merchantability was effective against the immediate buyer, a remote buyer—allowed to enforce the contract—has no claim under the warranty of merchantability. Second, the court has no idea whether the quality of the mobile home that was delivered to the first buyer failed to conform to the warranties in the contract. If the first buyer had no valid claim of breach for warranty against the manufacturer/seller, would a remote buyer—privity being waived—have a valid breach of warranty claim under that contract? Third, the losses suffered by the Morrows may not have been caused by breach of the upstream contract. The court noted that the mobile home that was received by the Morrows had been modified by someone, presumably after the first sale by the manufacturer. Did the court consider any of these problems?

(3) Contract Relationship Between the Manufacturer and the Remote Buyers. In a later part of its opinion, the court appears to have strayed from the view that it was merely allowing remote buyers to enforce an upstream contract. The court declared that: "Our decision today preserves the statutory rights of the manufacturer to define his potential liability to the ultimate consumer, by means of express disclaimers and limitations, while protecting the legitimate expectation of the consumer that goods distributed on a wide scale by conduit retailers are fit for their intended use." Is this a reference to warranty disclaimer or clause excluding damages in the upstream contract? The "legitimate expectation of the consumer" must be based on facts reasonably available to consumers. Consumers have no practical way of discovering the terms of remote upstream contracts; nor do retailers unless they were the persons that dealt directly with the manufacturers. Does the court's opinion imply that the disclaimer or damages limitations, to be effective, must be communicated by manufacturers to the ultimate consumers of their products?

(4) Ordinary Damages for Economic Loss. Market value of a product at the retail level is normally considerably higher than the market value as the product first enters the chain of distribution. In a warranty action, a buyer's damages are measured by the value the goods would have had if they had been as warranted. UCC 2–714(2). If a remote manufacturer is held liable to a consumer buyer, which market level establishes the value of the goods as warranted?

Problem 3.5.2. A manufacturer sold brand named goods that were described in the contract of sale as "seconds." Thereafter those goods were sold by a retailer to a consumer buyer. The retail sales contract did not describe the goods as "seconds." Is the manufacturer liable to the consumer buyer for the difference between the retail value of regular merchandise and the retail value of the goods that are "seconds"?

Problem 3.5.3. Manufacturer sold new automobiles to a dealer. Both parties knew that the automobiles were not yet in a satisfactory condition for sale to retail buyers and understand that the dealer will perform certain functions ("dealer-prep" functions) to make the goods ready for delivery to consumers. Is the manufacturer liable for inadequate performance of these tasks by the dealer?

(5) Consequential Economic Losses. In warranty actions by consumers buyers against remote manufacturers, can damages be recovered for buyers' consequential economic losses? The *Morrow* court dealt with this question in an interesting dictum. Was the court's statement an appropriate construction of the UCC? In what circumstances would a manufacturer, at the time of its sale of a product, have reason to know of the general or particular needs of an unknown ultimate consumer?

(6) Components Suppliers. The image of vertical privity has products moving down a chain of distribution from manufacturers to consumers. In many instances, however, the final product contains many components made by others, sold to the manufacturer, and assembled into the final product. Often the components carry brand names that identify the manufacturers of the components. Should consumer buyers be allowed to recover in warranty claims against suppliers of components?

(7) Proposed Revised UCC Article 2. The proposed revision of UCC Article 2 has no text or comment reference to manufacturers' implied warranties of quality and remote buyers. The matter was raised at one meeting of the drafting committee, which determined not to include it in the draft. See C. Reitz, Manufacturers' Warranties of Consumer Goods, 75 Wash.U.L.Q. 357 (1997).

(8) Non–Uniform Departures from the UCC. A number of state legislatures have enacted laws addressed to the problem of privity that has arisen in various situations, including manufacturers' warranties to remote buyers. The legislation is sometimes formulated as a change to some provision in the UCC. Virginia is one of the states to do so. It enacted a non-uniform version of UCC 2–318.

There is no uniform version of UCC 2–318. The "official text" contains three alternatives. All of the alternatives of UCC 2–318 are quite important to claims for injuries to person and wrongful death that result from nonconforming goods. That subject is addressed in the next Section of this Chapter.

The focus of this Section is on manufacturers' obligation to remote buyers for the quality of the goods. The Virginia version of UCC 2–318, which is none of the "official" alternatives, has been cited in claims against manufacturers for failure of the goods to conform to warranties of quality. The Virginia version explicitly refers to actions brought against manufacturers:

Lack of privity between plaintiff and defendant shall be no defense in any action brought against the manufacturer or seller of goods to recover damages for breach of warranty, express or implied, or for negligence, although the plaintiff did not purchase the goods from the defendant, if the plaintiff was a person whom the manufacturer or seller might reasonably have expected to use, consume, or be affected by the goods. . . .

The Virginia statute was construed in the following case, an action by a remote buyer against the manufacturers of plumbing supplies.

Beard Plumbing and Heating, Inc. v. Thompson Plastics, Inc.

United States Court of Appeals for the Fourth Circuit, 1998.
152 F.3d 313.

■ ERVIN, CIRCUIT JUDGE:

In this diversity action, Beard Plumbing and Heating, Inc., (Beard), appeals from a grant of summary judgment to Thompson Plastics, Incorporated (Thompson), and NIBCO, Incorporated (NIBCO) on Beard's claims of negligence and breach of warranty. For the reasons which follow, we affirm the decision of the district court.

* * *

II.

Beard is a Virginia corporation engaged in providing materials and labor related to plumbing and heating. Thompson, an Alabama corporation, and NIBCO, an Indiana corporation, manufacture postchlorinated polyvinyl chloride (CPVC) plumbing components.

In 1992, Beard, engaged as the plumbing subcontractor in a condominium development in Woodbridge, Virginia, installed CPVC plumbing fittings manufactured by Thompson or NIBCO. Beard purchased these fittings from two third-party suppliers, Thomas Somerville Co., which was originally named as a defendant in the case but later non-suited after Thompson and NIBCO were granted summary judgment, and National Plumbing Store, which was never named as a party. There were no contracts between Beard and either manufacturer. When the fittings cracked and subsequently leaked after hot water was used in the system, the general contractor required Beard to replace the fittings and repair the damage sustained by the homes and then dismissed Beard from the job. The general contractor proceeded to sue Beard, which settled for $165,878.93. In addition to that loss, Beard claims it was denied compensation for performing change orders on the site, was denied compensation for the cost of repairs to the damaged buildings, was denied the remainder of its contract price, incurred legal fees, and lost revenue due to damage to its business reputation. . . .

To recover these losses, Beard filed the instant diversity action on June 8, 1995, alleging both breach of warranty and negligence. Beard contends that the CPVC fittings manufactured by Thompson and NIBCO were defective and that certain adapters failed when they attempted to shrink around thermally-expanded metal fittings during cool-down. On November 1, 1995, NIBCO filed for summary judgment, and Thompson followed on November 7, on the ground that Beard could not recover economic losses in these circumstances. The district court ... granted both motions for summary judgment on Beard's contract and tort claims. ... This appeal followed.

III.

Beard seeks to assert three causes of action: a negligence claim sounding in tort, and two warranty claims sounding in contract, one for breach of the warranty of fitness for a particular purpose under Va. Code § 8.2–315 and the other for breach of the implied warranty of merchantability under Va. Code § 8.2–314. The first two claims are barred by Virginia law in these circumstances and will be dealt with first. The final claim of breach of the implied warranty of merchantability is a more difficult question and will be treated last.

* * *

B.

Beard's claim for breach of the warranty of fitness for a particular purpose must also fail. Va. Code § 8.2–315 provides:

> Where the seller at the time of contracting has reason to know any particular purpose for which the goods are required and that the buyer is relying on the seller's skill or judgment to select or furnish suitable goods, there is unless excluded or modified under the next section #AD8E #8.2–316, an implied warranty that the goods shall be fit for such purpose.

The Supreme Court of Virginia has interpreted this section to require the buyer to prove three elements: (1) the seller had reason to know the particular purpose for which the buyer required the goods, (2) the seller had reason to know the buyer was relying on the seller's skill or judgment to furnish appropriate goods, and (3) the buyer in fact relied upon the seller's skill or judgment. Medcom, Inc. v. C. Arthur Weaver Co., 232 Va. 80, 348 S.E.2d 243, 246 (Va. 1986).

Beard has not satisfied the third element, nor can it. Thompson and NIBCO rely principally, but wrongly, on Beard's response to interrogatories that Beard is not aware of any express warranties made by either Thompson or NIBCO to Beard. Section 8.–315, however, provides for an implied warranty; express warranties are treated in § 8.2–313, and Beard's claim is not based on that section. Nevertheless, Beard contends that an implied warranty arises because the "suppliers of the resin used in the manufacture of the CPVC fittings published catalogs which expressly warranted that the female and male adapters were intended for, and could be used in, hot and cold water systems." This statement clearly demonstrates that

Beard did not rely upon Thompson or NIBCO's skill or judgment but rather upon some representation made by a more remote merchant. Whether that representation can pass through Thompson and NIBCO and hold that remote merchant liable on its warranty (whether express or implied) is not at issue here. Because there was never any communication between Beard and Thompson or NIBCO, there can be no genuine dispute that Beard did not, in fact, rely upon Thompson or NIBCO's skill or judgment in furnishing goods suitable for a particular purpose. Beard's reliance on § 8.2–318's abrogation of the privity requirement is misplaced, for that section only provides that lack of privity shall be no defense in certain circumstances. Before even reaching possible defenses, Beard ... must prove as an element of its claim that it in fact relied on Thompson and NIBCO's skill or judgment. Because Beard cannot make a sufficient showing on this essential element, its claim must fail. ... Therefore, summary judgment on this claim was appropriate and the district court's judgment hereon is affirmed.

C.

Beard's final claim of breach of the implied warranty of merchantability is a much more difficult problem. The district court's ruling did not even address this claim. Moreover, the record before this court does not contain the parties' memoranda concerning the summary judgment motion nor other sufficient evidence to fully determine that there is not a genuine dispute as to a material fact. Thus, the grant of summary judgment on this claim can only be upheld if Beard's claim is barred as a matter of law since this court reviews that grant de novo. ...

* * *

Finally, and most problematically, Thompson and NIBCO claim that because Beard suffered only economic losses it cannot recover under Virginia's Commercial Code, in effect, because of lack of privity. In support of this claim, Thompson and NIBCO argue that the Code's damages provisions in §§ 8.2–714 & –715, even read together with § 8.2–318, which apparently abrogates the privity requirement, will not permit economic losses to be recovered for breach of warranty absent privity. However, Thompson and NIBCO cite no case law in support of their argument because there is none.

Beard, on the other hand, claims that § 8.2–318, by its own terms, clearly abolishes the privity requirement.... Indeed, ... it would be odd if economic losses, which result from the frustration of bargained-for expectations, could not be recovered for breach of warranty, notwithstanding the lack of privity, given the especially broad reach of Virginia's § 8.2–318. ...

Having determined that this issue was undecided under Virginia law and having found no case in any jurisdiction jointly construing UCC provisions § 2–318 and § 2–715 with regards to economic loss, we certified the question to the Supreme Court of Virginia on January 17, 1997.

Our question to that court was phrased as follows:

Is privity required to recover economic loss under Va. Code § 8.2–715(2) due to the breach of the implied warranty of merchantability, notwithstanding the language of Va. Code § 8.2–318?

On September 12, 1997, the Virginia Supreme Court answered our question in the affirmative, holding in part:

> To answer this question, we must first determine whether § 8.2–715(2) requires the existence of a contract for the recovery of economic loss damages in breach of warranty cases. . . .

> This section does not address economic loss damages. However, because the Court of Appeals directed its inquiry specifically to this section, we assume that the Court of Appeals concluded that the economic loss damages claimed by Beard were consequential damages rather than direct damages. We also limit our discussion to subparagraph (a), since injury to persons or property is not involved in this case.

> Section 8.2–715(2)(a) is part of the UCC, a comprehensive statutory scheme affecting commercial transactions. Although the UCC is based on a uniform act now adopted by virtually every state, we found no case interpreting the language of § 8.2–715(2)(a) as it relates to the requirement of a contractual relationship between the parties.

> Nevertheless, the language of the section itself contains a presumption that there is a contract between the parties. The phrase "at the time of the contracting" in subparagraph (a) conveys the understanding of a contract between two par ties. To assert, as Beard did at oral argument, that the purpose of the phrase is only to establish the historical moment for judging the seller's foreseeability, does not eliminate the connotation of the existence of a contract inherent in the phrase. Beard's interpretation would require substituting the word "sale" for the word "contracting," and we decline the invitation to rewrite the statute. Therefore, we conclude that § 8.2–715(2)(a) requires a contract between the parties for the recovery of consequential economic loss damages incurred as a result of a breach of warranty by the seller.

> The second part of the certified question asks us to determine whether the provisions of § 8.2–318 supersede the con tract requirement of § 8.2–715(2)(a). Section 8.2–318 provides in pertinent part:

>> Lack of privity between plaintiff and defendant shall be no defense in any action brought against the manufacturer or seller of goods to recover damages for breach of warranty, express or implied, or for negligence, although the plaintiff did not purchase the goods from the defendant, if the plaintiff was a person whom the manufacturer or seller might reasonably have expected to use, consume, or be affected by the goods[.]

> The provisions of this section appear to conflict with § 8.2–715(2)(a) regarding the requirement of a contract for the recovery of consequential damages in a breach of warranty action. Rules of statu-

tory construction, however, resolve the apparent conflict. In construing conflicting statutes, if one section addresses a subject in a general way and the other section speaks to part of the same subject in a more specific manner, the latter prevails. ... Applying this rule, we conclude that, to the extent the two statutes conflict, § 8.2–715(2)(a) prevails.

The general subject of § 8.2–318 is the ability to raise the common law requirement of privity as a defense. We have not previously construed § 8.2–318; however, we have referred to it as modifying the common law privity rule. ...

The contract requirement of § 8.2–715(2)(a), however, is not a privity requirement imposed by the common law. Part 7 of Title 8.2 of the UCC imposes a number of limitations and conditions on the recovery of damages in a breach of warranty claim. See, e.g., §§ 8.2–714 (defining measure of damages),–715(1) (identifying recoverable incidental damages), and–719(b)(3) (ability to exclude consequential dam ages). The contract requirement of § 8.2–715(2)(a) is one of those limitations. Section 8.2–715(2)(a) does not address the general subject of the common law privity requirement's effect on the ability of a litigant to maintain an action for breach of warranty. It is limited to that part of the litigation dealing with the damages which may be recovered and imposes a contract requirement only where recovery of con sequential damages is sought. Applying the rule of statutory construction recited above, the limited contract requirement of § 8.2–715(2)(a) prevails over the general provisions relating to common law privity in § 8.2–318.

Accordingly, because § 8.2–715(2)(a) requires a contract between the parties for recovery of consequential economic loss damages in a claim for breach of the implied warranty of merchantability, we answer the certified question in the affirmative.

Based upon the reasoning of the Virginia Supreme Court, we affirm the grant of summary judgment in favor of Thompson and NIBCO on Beard's claim for breach of implied warranty of merchantability.

IV.

The judgment of the district court is in all respects affirmed.

NOTES

(1) State Law in Federal Courts. This case, like many cases we read previously, was litigated in federal courts. The federal courts have power to hear cases if the citizenship of the parties to the case is diverse, but the law to be applied in diversity cases is state law. In most diversity cases, federal judges seek to find the relevant state law in decisions of state courts, particularly decisions of the highest state court. Federal civil procedure provides an alternative means for ascertaining state law, certified questions. That procedure was invoked by the Court of Appeals in this case. The federal appellate court submitted questions to the Supreme Court of Virginia and relied on that court's replies. Note that the procedure does not transfer the whole case from federal to state court. The inter-court exchange is limited to the specific questions asked and answered.

(2) Virginia's UCC 2–318. What was the effect in this case of Virginia's non-uniform version of UCC 2–318? The Court of Appeals, before framing its question, concluded that the privity requirement had been clearly abolished by the legislation. The manufacturers could not defend on that ground. Of what value was that clear holding to Beard Plumbing & Heating in the case?

Did the trial court or the Court of Appeals find that the plumbing supplies were unmerchantable as sold by the manufacturers? Does the Virginia statute assist counsel for remote buyers in making their case that the goods were unmerchantable? The question certified by the Court of Appeals assumed that there was economic loss due to breach of the implied warranty of merchantability? Should the Court of Appeals have asked whether, in light of the Virginia Code, manufacturers may be obligated to remote buyers for breach of an implied warranty of merchantability?

The question posed by the Court of Appeals asked only about the application of UCC 2–715 in claims by remote buyers against manufacturers. The Virginia legislature did not adopt a non-uniform version of UCC 2–715. The Virginia Supreme Court replied first that the question's phrase "economic loss," often used in tort law analysis, meant "consequential damages," the proper phrase to use in warranty law analysis under UCC 2–715. The Supreme Court then found that UCC 2–715 and UCC 2–318, as enacted in Virginia, were in conflict. The former has an implicit requirement of privity; the latter abrogates the privity requirement generally. Using a principle of statutory interpretation that gives effect to the more specific provision, the Supreme Court stated that a claim for consequential damages resulting from breach of warranty was not permitted in an action by a remote buyer against manufacturers. Was the Virginia Supreme Court's answer a correct interpretation of the Virginia Code?

Was the Virginia Supreme Court's position sound as a matter of economic policy? The court in *Morrow* faced a similar question under Alaska law. Were the analyses similar?

Suppose the only claim in *Beard Plumbing & Heating* had been a claim that the plumbing supplies delivered were not fit for the ordinary purpose for which such goods are used and were therefore worth less than supplies that were merchantable. Under the Virginia UCC, should the buyer be allowed to recover damages for this loss?

———

Remote Buyers' Actions Under Other Law. Remote buyers seeking relief from manufacturers are not limited to claims grounded in the law of warranty. Some buyers may have claims arising under tort law. Some consumer buyers may have claims under non-uniform consumer protection legislation.

Strict Tort Liability. In actions against manufacturers for goods of unsatisfactory quality, counsel for buyers often seek relief on both tort and warranty theories. The principal tort theory on which they rely, once called strict tort liability, has come to be known as product liability.[34] The law of product liability has aspects that are valuable to some buyers: First, the tort has a substantive standard of manufacturers' conduct. The standard is independent of the terms of any contract. The standard is an implementation of a public policy enunciated by courts as a matter of common law. Second, the law of product liability has no privity requirement. Actions against manufacturers can be brought by individuals who suffered certain kinds of injury, whether those individuals were downstream buyers or mere bystanders.

Product liability is not useful to buyers aggrieved by nonconformity of the goods. Product liability is concerned only with harms done by products that injure or kill persons or damage property. This body of tort law is not concerned with goods that are qualitatively disappointing. A fundamental precept of tort law is that tort liability does not extend to "economic losses." The courts in *Szajna* and *Morrow* rejected efforts to ground those buyers' claims in strict tort liability. For a comprehensive history of buyers' efforts to use the theory of product liability to recover damages based upon the expected value of goods purchased, see East River S.S. Corp. v. Transamerica Delaval, Inc., 476 U.S. 858, 106 S.Ct. 2295, 90 L.Ed.2d 865 (1986) (failures of turbines in supertankers not grounds for action under strict tort liability).

Deceptive Acts and Practices Acts. Many states have enacted laws to protect consumers against deceptive acts and practices.[35] As indicated by the title, the statutes deal with wrongdoing in the marketplace. An action under one of these statutes by the buyer of a new BMW automobile became a case of wide national interest because of the size of the initial award of punitive damages.[36]

Dr. Ira Gore purchased a BMW sports sedan for $40,750 from a dealer in Birmingham, Alabama. Shortly after receiving the car, Dr. Gore discovered that the car had been repainted after manufacture. Dr. Gore sued the United States distributor of BMW automobiles for failure to disclose the repainting in violation of Ala. Code § 6–5–102 (1993). The BMW distributor acknowledged it had a policy concerning cars damaged in the course of

---

34. Counsel often add counts in negligence, a claim that can be sustained only if there is evidence of fault on the part of manufacturers.

35. Although these acts are sometimes referred to as "uniform," they are not a product of the National Conference of Commissioners on Uniform State Laws.

36. Section 908(2) of the Restatement, Second, of Torts provides that such damages may be awarded "for conduct that is outrageous, because of the defendant's evil motive or his reckless indifference to the rights of others." In recent years, large punitive damages awards have created concern that there may need to be a limiting principle to define when such awards are excessive.

manufacture or transportation: where cost of repair was less than 3% of the suggested retail price, repairs were made by the distributor without informing retail dealers and such cars were sold as new. The cost of repainting the car later sold to Dr. Gore had been about 1.5% of suggested retail price and the dealer had not been informed. An Alabama jury returned a verdict for compensatory damages of $4,000 and punitive damages of $4,000,000.

The Alabama Supreme Court affirmed the trial court's judgment but reduced the punitive damages to $2,000,000.[37] The Supreme Court of the United States held that the reduced award was still grossly excessive in light of three guideposts on punitive damages: the degree of reprehensibility of the nondisclosure, the disparity between the harm or potential harm suffered by Dr. Gore and the punitive damages award, and the difference between this punitive damages remedy and civil penalties authorized or imposed pursuant to statutes in comparable cases.[38] On remand, the Alabama Supreme Court awarded Dr. Gore punitive damages in the amount of $50,000.[39]

Sharing Responsibility. Criticisms of the courts in the preceding materials should be tempered with some recognition that the analytical fog is not entirely the courts' fault. Undoubtedly, the advocates—on both sides of the case—failed to discern that manufacturers' warranty liability to remote buyers is not governed by the law that is applicable only to sales contracts. The blame cannot be left entirely to courts and lawyers. Commercial law scholars and teachers have also failed, until recently, to provide an adequate base of knowledge to guide the lawyers and judges who are in the trenches of difficult warranty litigation.[40]

International Sales Law

The Convention on International Sales of Goods has no specific provisions regarding privity of contract. With regard to vertical privity, CISG provisions on the responsibilities of sellers and rights of buyers are drafted in terms of "the seller" and "the buyer" and "the contract," language which strongly implies a requirement of contractual privity. Suppose, however, that a manufacturer participates actively in marketing its products by providing dealers with the manufacturer's written "warranty" for delivery to buyers from those dealers. Even if it were held that the "warranty" created a contractual obligation to the ultimate buyers, should the rules of the Convention apply to that contractual relationship?

37. BMW of North America v. Gore, 646 So.2d 619 (Ala.1994).

38. BMW of North America, Inc. v. Gore, 517 U.S. 559, 116 S.Ct. 1589, 134 L.Ed.2d 809 (1996).

39. BMW of North America, Inc. v. Gore, 701 So.2d 507 (Ala.1997).

40. Recent contributions include C. Reitz, Manufacturers' Warranties of Consumer Goods, 75 Wash.U.L.Q. 357 (1997); D.

Clifford, Express Warranty Liability of Remote Sellers: One Purchase, Two Relationships, 75 Wash.U. L.Q. 413 (1997). See also R. Speidel, Warranty Theory, Economic Loss, and the Privity Requirement: Once More Into the Void, 67 Bost.U.L.Rev. 9 (1987); C. Reitz & M. Seabolt, Warranties and Product Liability: Who Can Sue and Where?, 46 Temple L.Q. 527 (1973).

Professor Honnold provided this commentary to CISG:[36]

> In recent decades some legal systems have established contractual rights for buyers against manufacturers for damage or loss caused by defects in goods which the buyer purchased from a retail dealer or other distributor. At the outset this development responded to the plight of consumers who suffer personal injury from dangerous products—an area that lies outside the Convention because of the general exclusion of consumer purchases ... and the further exclusion ... of the liability of "the seller for the death or personal injury caused by the goods to any person:" However, in some legal systems this development has made manufacturers liable, without regard to negligence, for economic loss caused by defective products purchased from a dealer or other distributor.

> The first edition of this work concluded that this development under the Convention was barred by the language of Article 4 that the Convention "governs only the formation of the contract of sale and the obligations of the seller and the buyer arising from such a contract:" See, e.g., B sued manufacturer (M) for defects in a machine B purchased from S. B's suit was dismissed because B had not contracted with M. GER LG Dusseldorf, 31–0–231/94, 23–06–'94. UNILEX D. 1994–16. (For US domestic cases rejecting this approach, see, e.g., Reitz, 75 Wash.U.L.Rev. 357 at 361 (1997).)

> Further reflection calls for reexamination in some commercial settings. For example, some manufacturers (and similar mass distributors such as importers) provide dealers with a written "guarantee" or "warranty" by the manufacturer and instruct dealers to give buyers the manufacturer's "guarantee" in connection with the sale. One purpose is to encourage sales because of the confidence that prospective buyers have in a guarantee to them by a well-known manufacturer. A second, less evident, purpose is to limit their responsibility (*e.g.*) to the replacement of defective parts for a specified limited period and thereby to bar claims for consequential damages caused by defects in the goods.

> The difficult problem is whether the manufacturer is a "seller" within the language of Article 4 in view of the fact that the dealer executed the contract with the buyer, delivered the goods and received the price.

> Some tribunals applying the Convention, like some tribunals applying domestic laws governing the "sale of goods", may be impressed by the fact that the delivery of a "guarantee" through a local dealer was part of a larger setting in which the manufacturer played a dominant role in the sale—by franchise agreements controlling aspects of the dealer's performance and by mass-media advertising addressed to prospective buyers. Indeed, advertising appeals are typically designed to say or imply: "Go to our dealers

---

36. J. Honnold, Uniform Law for International Sales § 63 (3d ed. 1999).

and buy our product. If you do you will get a good product." This in substance is an offer of a unilateral contract: "If you will do X you will get Y."

Of course these facts alone do not make the manufacturer a "seller"—a contract of sale depends on the buyer's completing a transaction with a dealer. But some tribunals may conclude that when such a transaction is completed the manufacturer, although not *"the* seller", has participated with the dealer in a "contract of sale" with the buyer.

The supplier's participation may be more evident—as when a representative of the manufacturer personally contacts the buyer and persuades him to purchase the manufacturer's goods from a local dealer. In many cases participation by the manufacturer is more tenuous, confined to advertising and possibly control of aspects of the dealer's business such as promotion methods, volume, stocking of repair parts, training of mechanics and, in some cases, the price to be charged.

When (as in the usual case) the buyer and dealer are in the same State the Convention would not apply to a claim against the dealer. . . . Similarly, the Convention would not apply to a claim against even a foreign supplier if the supplier's place of business applicable to this transaction . . . is in the same State as the buyer. In any event, when domestic law is favorable and the dealer is financially responsible it usually will be more convenient to confine one's claim to a local action against the dealer. The same may be true even when the claim might jeopardize the dealer's resources since the dealer may be able to bring in the manufacturer to defend the action and to satisfy any judgment. Thus, attempts to extend the Convention to foreign suppliers may be confined to special situations such as financial failure of the local dealer. Even here the rules on jurisdiction, private international law and domestic sales law in the buyer's jurisdiction may meet the buyer's needs.

On the other hand, it seems hasty to conclude that the "buyer-seller" language of Article 4 will be an impassable barrier in cases where the supplier has participated substantially (although not formally) in the sale to the buyer. Domestic experience suggests that legal relations with foreign suppliers may be a field for gradual development.

SECTION 6.   PERSONAL INJURIES AND WARRANTY LAW
DOMESTIC UNITED STATES LAW

Owners of products sometimes suffer traumatic injuries or die when they use or consume the goods they have bought. Until the last turn of a century, redress for such injuries was available only if it could be shown that the suppliers of the goods had failed to exercise due care. Advocates of consumer protection found a legal theory that did not require proof of defendants' fault in the law of warranty. The prototypical injured plaintiff was a buyer who had consumed spoiled or adulterated food.

In cases decided in the late 19th century and early 20th century, courts implied warranties of quality in ordinary retail sales,[1] even in transactional settings where the defendants were sellers of canned or packaged goods that did not know, and had no practical way of finding out the true quality of the goods.[2] Once courts found that a warranty had been breached, they had no difficulty in broadening the injuries compensable as consequential damages from commercial losses, as in *Hadley v. Baxendale*, to personal injuries and property damage. The move toward protection of the health of consumers did not end with establishment of retailers' warranty liability. Injured consumers were allowed to obtain warranty relief directly from remote manufacturers of certain defective consumer goods that caused personal injuries. The list of such goods was confined to food, beverages, and other items of "intimate bodily use." In 1960, in *Henningsen v. Bloomfield Motors*,[3] the New Jersey Supreme Court held that the owner of an automobile, injured when the steering failed, had a warranty claim against the manufacturer.

Shortly after the *Henningsen* decision, courts of many states recognized a new common-law tort, originally known as strict tort liability.[4] The

1.   The British Sale of Goods Act and its United States counterpart, the Uniform Sales Act, posed a problem for buyers: the basic warranty of quality, merchantability, was not "implied" in ordinary retail sales of food or other goods. Caselaw codified by these statutes had found the warranty of merchantability arising in situations where sellers had contracted to supply goods that would fit contract descriptions; Mackensie Chalmers "restated" the cases by limiting merchantability to sales "by description." Protection had to be found under the rubric of fitness for particular purpose.

The change is well illustrated by developments in Massachusetts. Farrell v. Manhattan Market Co., 198 Mass. 271, 84 N.E. 481 (1908) (buyer suffered ptomaine poisoning from a fowl: buyer denied relief); Ward v. Great Atlantic & Pacific Tea Co., 231 Mass. 90, 120 N.E. 225 (1918) (buyer broke a tooth on a stone in a can of baked beans: buyer recovered); Flynn v. Bedell Co., 242 Mass. 450, 136 N.E. 252 (1922) (buyer contracted skin disease from dyed fur collar of coat: verdict for buyer upheld).

Consumers injured by unwholesome food or beverages served by a restaurant or hotel faced an additional legal hazard. At common law, some courts considered such transactions a service ("uttering") rather than a sale and, therefore, not transactions in which a

warranty of quality applied. Compare Friend v. Childs Dining Hall Co., 231 Mass. 65, 120 N.E. 407 (1918), with Nisky v. Childs, 103 N.J.L. 464, 135 A. 805 (1927). The UCC declares that such transactions are sales under Article 2. UCC 2–314(1).

2.   Compare Julian v. Laubenberger, 16 Misc. 646, 38 N.Y.S. 1052 (Sup.Ct.1896) (sale of can of salmon: since both parties knew that seller had not prepared the food, had not inspected it, and was entirely ignorant of the contents of the can, it would be unreasonable to say that the buyer had relied upon the superior knowledge of the seller), with Ward v. Great Atlantic & Pacific Tea Co., 231 Mass. 90, 120 N.E. 225 (1918) (sale of can of baked beans and pork: even though seller is not the manufacturer, seller is in a better position to ascertain the reliability of the manufacturer; the principle of retailers' liability may work apparent hardship in some instances, but that is no reason to change it).

3.   32 N.J. 358, 161 A.2d 69 (1960).

4.   Two years after *Henningsen*, the California Supreme Court recognized a new tort to protect the consumer-owner of a lathe injured when a piece of wood was ejected from the equipment. Greenman v. Yuba Power Products, Inc., 59 Cal.2d 57, 377 P.2d 897 (1963). At this time, the American Law Insti-

new tort became the principal claim advanced by counsel for buyers who had suffered personal injuries that were caused by "defective" products. Warranty claims continued to be made by personal injury lawyers, but these claims were not their preferred cause of action.[5] The law of the tort of strict liability was revised in the 1997 Restatement of the Law of Torts: Products Liability.

Judicial acknowledgment of the new tort did not displace consumers' warranty claims arising out of the same facts. What has emerged, therefore, is that consumer buyers in most states have substantially overlapping theories of possible recovery for personal injuries. Full consideration of the law of products liability is beyond the scope of these materials. However, certain issues that arise in warranty claims for personal injuries should be considered.

One of these is the matter of protection for individuals who did not buy the goods but who suffer injuries attributable to defects in the goods. This issue is commonly described as one of horizontal privity. The claimants are not parties in the chain of distribution of the goods, but are related in some way to the buyers in the last sales of the goods. The other is the preclusive effect of a decision for the defendant in a product liability case on the alternative claim of breach of warranty. The question is whether the two theories are sufficiently different that a decision for a claimant on a

tute was preparing a second edition of the Restatement of Torts. The new tort was inserted into the revision as § 402 A, Special Liability of Seller of Product for Physical Harm to User or Consumer. Reception of § 402A as new common law was rapid and widespread. Only a small number of state supreme courts have rejected strict tort liability. E.g., Cline v. Prowler Industries of Md., Inc., 418 A.2d 968 (Del.1980); Swartz v. General Motors Corp., 375 Mass. 628, 378 N.E.2d 61 (1978); Prentis v. Yale Manufacturing Co., 421 Mich. 670, 365 N.W.2d 176 (1984). In New York, the Court of Appeals initially rejected the new tort. Mendel v. Pittsburgh Plate Glass Co., 25 N.Y.2d 888, 304 N.Y.S.2d 4, 251 N.E.2d 143 (1969). However, the New York court quickly joined the majority of states. Codling v. Paglia, 32 N.Y.2d 330, 345 N.Y.S.2d 461, 298 N.E.2d 622 (1973).

5. A major difference in the two theories lies in the measure of recovery. Plaintiffs proceeding in a tort theory ordinarily are permitted to recover damages for pain and suffering and, in extraordinary cases, may be permitted to recover punitive damages. Proof of a defendant's liability on a strict tort theo-

ry is therefore less difficult than the proof under a warranty theory. The strict tort theory is also more protective of consumers with regard to contractual disclaimers or clauses limiting damages. Comment *m* to § 402A states that the "consumer's" cause of action "is not affected by any disclaimer or other agreement."

Moreover, a consumer who suffers an injury some considerable time after the good was sold may be unable to proceed successfully on a warranty theory while the strict tort theory is still available. The warranty statute of limitations begins to run at the time of delivery of the goods. UCC 2–725(1). If an injury occurs more than four years after delivery, the tort statute may be more favorable to plaintiffs. The tort statute of limitations does not begin to run until the injury.

The warranty statute of limitations may be more favorable to a plaintiff who suffers injury shortly after goods have been delivered but fails to institute legal proceedings within the one-or two-year limitation period generally provided for tort claims. Even though the tort claim is time-barred, the warranty period may not have expired on the date of filing suit.

warranty theory can be sustained if there has been a final decision against the claimant on the products liability theory.

Horizontal Privity

Article 2 of the UCC provides that some non-buyers may recover in breach of warranty actions against sellers of goods. The caption of the section, UCC 2–318, refers to the extended class of potential claimants as third party beneficiaries. General contract law allows contracting parties to agree that the contractual obligations of one contracting party may be enforced by someone other than the other contracting party. A classic example is the contract of life insurance, in which the terms of the policy make the insurer's obligation to pay enforceable by a person designated by the owner of the policy as the beneficiary.

In the UCC now, UCC 2–318 appears with three alternatives. In the 1962 UCC, however, Alternative A was the entire section. Alternatives B and C were put forward by the sponsors of the UCC in 1966.[6] Most states had already adopted the UCC before Alternatives B and C were promulgated and did not revisit the question. According to White and Summers, six states adopted Alternative B and at least eight states have adopted Alternative C or a similar provision.[7] Several states have chosen their own non-uniform variations of UCC 2–318.

Alternative A is the most narrow of the choices. The class of protected beneficiaries extends only to individuals ("natural persons") who are in the family or household of the buyer or are guests in the buyer's home, provided that sellers reasonably expect that these individuals may use, consume or be affected by the goods.[8] Beneficiaries under this provision cannot recover for diminution in the value of the goods or for consequential economic loss. The only harms covered are injury to person or property.[9]

Employees who are injured by equipment that was purchased by their employers are not protected beneficiaries under Alternative A, but would likely be included under Alternative B. That Alternative extends to all natural persons whom sellers may reasonably expect to use, consume, or be

---

6. See Comments 2 and 3.

7. See White & Summers, § 11–3 (5th ed. 2000).

8. An early UCC case involved a young child who was killed when a vaporizer-humidifier malfunctioned. The product had been purchased by the child's aunt, who lived next door. The Pennsylvania Supreme Court held that the child was not in the "family" of the buyer for purposes of UCC 2–318. Miller v. Preitz, 422 Pa. 383, 221 A.2d 320 (1966).

9. In some circumstances, a person other than a buyer of goods may be aggrieved by the loss in value of the goods resulting from breach of a warranty of quality or a remedial promise. Such a case arose in Pennsylvania. The buyer of a new automobile died months after the purchase and his widow inherited it. When the automobile was three years old, it began to exhibit signs of a defective transmission. The widow sued the manufacturer for breach of express and implied warranties of quality. (Apparently the term of the manufacturer's remedial promise had expired. The complaint did not allege breach of such a promise.) The manufacturer argued, under UCC Article 2, that the widow was not the "buyer" of the automobile and, under UCC 2–318, had no standing to sue because her claim was not for injury to the person. The defense was upheld. Johnson v. General Motors Corp., 349 Pa.Super. 147, 502 A.2d 1317 (1986).

affected by the goods. Indeed, the phrase "affected by" may extend protection to individuals, wholly unrelated to buyers, who happened to be in the vicinity of goods that caused their injuries.

Alternative C broadens the protection in two ways. Injury is not limited to personal injury or property damage and protected persons include business entities as well as individuals.

Warranty and Products Liability

Castro v. QVC Network, Inc.

United States Court of Appeals for the Second Circuit, 1998.
139 F.3d 114.

■ CALABRESI, CIRCUIT JUDGE:

In this diversity products liability action, plaintiffs-appellants alleged, in separate causes of action for strict liability and for breach of warranty, that defendants-appellees manufactured and sold a defective roasting pan that injured one of the appellants. The United States District Court for the Eastern District of New York (Leonard D. Wexler, Judge) rejected appellants' request to charge the jury separately on each cause of action and, instead, instructed the jury only on the strict liability charge. The jury found for appellees and the court denied appellants' motion for a new trial. This appeal followed. We hold that, under New York law, the jury should have been instructed separately on each charge, and, accordingly, reverse and remand for a new trial on the breach of warranty claim.

I. BACKGROUND

In early November 1993, appellee QVC Network, Inc. ("QVC"), operator of a cable television home-shopping channel, advertised, as part of a one-day Thanksgiving promotion, the "T–Fal Jumbo Resistal Roaster." The roaster, manufactured by U.S.A. T–Fal Corp. ("T–Fal"), was described as suitable for, among other things, cooking a twenty-five pound turkey. Appellant Loyda Castro bought the roasting pan by mail and used it to prepare a twenty-pound turkey on Thanksgiving Day, 1993.

Mrs. Castro was injured when she attempted to remove the turkey and roasting pan from the oven. Using insulated mittens, she gripped the pan's handles with the first two fingers on each hand (the maximum grip allowed by the small size of the handles) and took the pan out of the oven. As the turkey tipped toward her, she lost control of the pan, spilling the hot drippings and fat that had accumulated in it during the cooking and basting process. As a result, she suffered second and third degree burns to her foot and ankle, which, over time, has led to scarring, intermittent paresthesia, and ankle swelling.

It is uncontested that in their complaint appellants alleged that the pan was defective and that its defects gave rise to separate causes of action for strict liability and for breach of warranty. Moreover, in the pre-charge conference, appellants' counsel repeatedly requested separate jury charges on strict liability and for breach of warranty. The district court, nevertheless, denied the request for a separate charge on breach of warranty. Judge Wexler stated that "you can't collect twice for the same thing," and deemed the warranty charge unnecessary and "duplicative." The court, therefore, only gave the jury the New York pattern strict products liability charge.

The jury returned a verdict for appellees QVC and T–Fal. Judgment was entered on September 14, 1995. Appellants subsequently moved, pursuant to Federal Rule of Civil Procedure 59, that the jury verdict be set aside and a new trial be ordered for various reasons including that the court had failed to charge the jury on appellants' claim for breach of warranty. By order dated July 10, 1996, the district court denied appellants' Rule 59 motion, reasoning that the breach of warranty and strict products liability claims were "virtually the same." This appeal followed.

II. DISCUSSION

We review a district court's denial of a new-trial motion for abuse of discretion. . . .

A. Two Definitions of "Defective" Product Design

Products liability law has long been bedeviled by the search for an appropriate definition of "defective" product design. Over the years, both in the cases and in the literature, two approaches have come to predominate. The first is the risk/utility theory, which focuses on whether the benefits of a product outweigh the dangers of its design. The second is the consumer expectations theory, which focuses on what a buyer/user of a product would properly expect that the product would be suited for.

Not all states accept both of these approaches. Some define design defect only according to the risk/utility approach. . . . Others define design defect solely in terms of the consumer expectations theory.

One of the first states to accept both approaches was California, which in Barker v. Lull Engineering Co., 20 Cal. 3d 413, 573 P.2d 443, 143 Cal. Rptr. 225 (Cal. 1978), held that "a product may be found defective in design, so as to subject a manufacturer to strict liability for resulting injuries, under either of two alternative tests"—consumer expectations and risk/utility. 573 P.2d at 455–56. Several states have followed suit and have adopted both theories. . . .

Prior to the recent case of Denny v. Ford Motor Co., 87 N.Y.2d 248, 662 N.E.2d 730, 639 N.Y.S.2d 250 (1995), it was not clear whether New York recognized both tests. In Denny, the plaintiff was injured when her Ford Bronco II sports utility vehicle rolled over when she slammed on the brakes to avoid hitting a deer in the vehicle's path. See Denny v. Ford Motor Co., 42 F.3d 106, 108 (2d Cir.1994), certifying questions to Denny, 87 N.Y.2d 248, 662 N.E.2d 730, 639 N.Y.S.2d 250. The plaintiff asserted claims for strict products liability and for breach of implied warranty, and the district judge—over the objection of defendant Ford—submitted both causes of action to the jury. The jury ruled in favor of Ford on the strict liability claim, but found for the plaintiff on the implied warranty claim. On appeal, Ford argued that the jury's verdicts on the strict products liability claim and the breach of warranty claim were inconsistent because the causes of action were identical.

This court certified the Denny case to the New York Court of Appeals to answer the following questions: (1) "whether, under New York law, the strict products liability and implied warranty claims are identical"; and (2) "whether, if the claims are different, the strict products liability claim is broader than the implied warranty claim and encompasses the latter."

In response to the certified questions, the Court of Appeals held that in a products liability case a cause of action for strict liability is not identical to a claim for breach of warranty. Moreover, the court held that a strict liability claim is not per se broader than a breach of warranty claim such that the former encompasses the latter. Thus, while claims of strict products liability and breach of warranty are often used interchangeably, under New York law the two causes of action are definitively different. The imposition of strict liability for an alleged design "defect" is determined by a risk-utility standard. . . . The notion of "defect" in a U.C.C.-based breach of warranty claim focuses, instead, on consumer expectations. . . .

B. When Should a Jury be Charged on Both Strict Liability and Warranty Causes of Action?

Since Denny, then, it has been settled that the risk/utility and consumer expectations theories of design defect can, in New York, be the bases of distinct causes of action: one for strict products liability and one for breach of warranty. This fact, however, does not settle the question of when a jury must be charged separately on each cause of action and when, instead, the two causes are, on the facts of the specific case, sufficiently similar to each other so that one charge to the jury is enough.

While eminent jurists have at times been troubled by this issue, the New York Court of Appeals in Denny was quite clear on when the two causes of action might meld and when, instead, they are to be treated as separate. It did this by adding its own twist to the distinction—namely, what can aptly be called the "dual purpose" requirement. Thus in Denny, the Court of Appeals pointed out that the fact that a product's overall benefits might outweigh its overall risks does not preclude the possibility that consumers may have been misled into using the product in a context in which it was dangerously unsafe. And this, the New York court emphasized, could be so even though the benefits in other uses might make the product sufficiently reasonable so that it passed the risk/utility test.

In Denny, the Ford Bronco II was not designed as a conventional passenger automobile. Instead, it was designed as an off-road, dual purpose vehicle. But in its marketing of the Bronco II, Ford stressed its suitability for commuting and for suburban and city driving. Under the circumstances, the Court of Appeals explained that a rational factfinder could conclude that the Bronco's utility as an off-road vehicle outweighed the risk of injury resulting from roll-over accidents (thus passing the risk/utility test), but at the same time find that the vehicle was not safe for the "ordinary purpose" of daily driving for which it was also marketed and sold (thus flunking the consumer expectations test).

That is precisely the situation before us. The jury had before it evidence that the product was designed, marketed, and sold as a multiple-use product. The pan was originally manufactured and sold in France as an all-purpose cooking dish without handles. And at trial, the jury saw a videotape of a QVC representative demonstrating to the television audience that the pan, in addition to serving as a suitable roaster for a twenty-five pound turkey, could also be used to cook casseroles, cutlets, cookies, and other low-volume foods. The court charged the jury that "[a] product is defective if it is not reasonably safe[,] that is, if the product is so likely to be harmful to persons that a reasonable person who had actual knowledge of its potential for producing injury would conclude that it should not have been marketed in that condition." And, so instructed, the jury presumably found that the pan, because it had many advantages in a variety of uses, did not fail the risk/utility test.

But it was also the case that the pan was advertised as suitable for a particular use—cooking a twenty-five pound turkey. Indeed, T–Fal added handles to the pan in order to fill QVC's request for a roasting pan that it could use in its Thanksgiving promotion. The product was, therefore, sold as appropriately used for roasting a twenty-five pound turkey. And it was in that use that allegedly the product failed and injured the appellant.

In such circumstances, New York law is clear that a general charge on strict products liability based on the risk/utility approach does not suffice. The jury could have found that the roasting pan's overall utility for cooking low-volume foods outweighed the risk of injury when cooking heavier foods, but that the product was nonetheless unsafe for the purpose for which it was marketed and sold—roasting a twenty-five pound turkey—and, as such, was defective under the consumer expectations test. That being so, the appellants were entitled to a separate breach of warranty charge.

III.   CONCLUSION

In light of the evidence presented by appellants of the multi-purpose nature of the product at issue, the district court, applying New York law, should have granted appellants' request for a separate jury charge on the breach of warranty claim in addition to the charge on the strict liability claim. Accordingly, we reverse the order of the district court denying the motion for a new trial, and remand the case for a new trial on the breach of warranty claim, consistent with this opinion.

NOTES

(1) Nature of the Warranty Allegedly Breached. The court's references to the warranty do not indicate, for the most part, whether the warranty on which the plaintiff relies is the implied warranty of merchantability or an express warranty. The question certified to the New York Court of Appeals in the *Denny* case referred only to an implied warranty. How would you characterize the warranty in *Denny*? The warranty in this case? Does it matter whether the warranty in issue is an express warranty or an implied warranty?

(2) Goods Not Fit for Ordinary Purposes and Defective Goods. The trial court held that the warranty claim and the products liability claim amounted to the "same thing." If the warranty in question is a warranty that the goods are fit for their ordinary purposes, does it not follow that defective goods which cause personal injuries are not fit for such purposes? The logical force of that proposition is the basis for the conclusion that the two claims are the same thing. But logic does not support the inverse. Goods that are not fit for their ordinary purposes may or may not have a defect sufficient to be actionable under the doctrine of products liability. The reason is that the level of a reasonable buyer's expectation of quality, the warranty obligation, is derivative from the seller's description of the goods. A seller's description can be the basis of a claim under UCC 2–314 or UCC 2–313. The descriptions in *Castro* and *Denny* were of the goods being used in certain particular ways, the kind of descriptions that are appropriately express warranties.

(3) Proposed Revised UCC Article 2. While the drafting committee was at work on the proposed revision of Article 2, the American Law Institute completed work on the Restatement, Third, of Torts: Products Liability. ALI representatives sought to have UCC 2–314 revised to recognize that the elements of the tort were the same as the elements of the warranty of merchantability. The drafting committee proposed no change in the text of UCC 2–314, but accepted a proposed new comment:

> When recovery is sought for injury to person or property, whether goods are merchantable is to be determined by applicable state products liability law. When, however, a claim for injury to person or property is based on an implied warranty of fitness under Section 2–315 or an express warranty under Section 2–313 ..., this Article determines whether an implied warranty of fitness or an express warranty was made and breached, as well as what damages are recoverable under Section 2–715.[10]

Is this comment a sound interpretation of the text of UCC 2–314? Should the comment be approved as part of a revised Article 2?

INTERNATIONAL SALES LAW

The Convention on Contracts for the International Sale of Goods does not apply to goods bought for personal, family or household use, pursuant to CISG 2(a), and does apply to the liability of sellers for death of personal injury caused by the goods to any person, pursuant to CISG 5. Professor Honnold commented:[11]

---

10. Proposed Revised 2–314, Comment 7.

11. J. Honnold, Uniform Law for International Sales §§ 50, 71 (3d ed. 1999).

In UNCITRAL attention was drawn to the development of national legislation and case law designed to protect consumers; it was agreed that the Convention should not supersede these rules. Consideration was given to a provision that the Convention would not override any domestic rule that was "mandatory" or that implemented "public policy" (*ordre public*) but it was found that these concepts carried different meanings in various legal systems; the clearest and safest solution was specifically to exclude consumer purchases from the Convention. . . .

The strong protection that the Convention gives to the international sales contract made it necessary to limit the Convention's scope lest the Convention collide with the special protection that some domestic rules provide for the noncommercial consumer. . . . A similar purpose underlies [CISG 5].

SECTION 7. LEGAL BARS TO ACTIONS FOR BREACH OF WARRANTY

DOMESTIC UNITED STATES LAW

Introduction. A buyer may be barred from litigation of the merits of a warranty claim if the buyer fails to give the seller timely notice of the seller's breach. Even if a buyer's notice is timely, the buyer may be barred from relief if the buyer has not commenced a law suit within the statutory period of limitations. The notice-to-seller requirement is found in UCC 2–607(3)(a). The statute of limitations for transactions in goods is UCC 2–725.

(A) NOTICE OF BREACH

Lawyers representing sellers in warranty litigation are drawn to the "slam dunk" provision that results in buyers' being "barred from any remedy." UCC 2–607(3)(a). A buyer is subject to this catastrophic result if, after acceptance of goods, the buyer fails to notify seller of breach within a reasonable time after the buyer discovered or should have discovered the breach.

M.K. Associates v. Stowell Products, Inc.

United States District Court for the District of Maine, 1988.
697 F.Supp. 20.

■ CARTER, DISTRICT JUDGE.

I. Introduction

M.K. Associates, a seller of wood products, has brought an action to recover the remainder of the purchase price due from a sale of ash dowels to the defendant Stowell Products, Inc. The defendant claims that the plaintiff breached the contract because the dowels were defective. The defendant argues that it is entitled to set off the remaining amount due as damages caused by the defective goods.

The case was tried before the court on September 19, 1988. For the reasons set forth below, the court finds for the plaintiff. The findings of fact and conclusions of law follow.

II.   Findings of Fact

From December, 1986 through February, 1987, Stowell Products, through its purchasing manager, Wayne Curley, made a series of offers for ash dowels from M.K. Associates. The dowels were delivered during the period from December, 1986 to March, 1987. Stowell Products intended to use the dowels to manufacture products to fill a contract with another company, Mirro/Foley Corp., due in late August, 1987. Although Stowell Products made periodic payments to M.K. Associates on these orders up through the fall of 1987, it was substantially in arrears as early as March, 1987. The parties have stipulated that the amount still due for the purchase and delivery of the ash dowels is $10,518.40.

The employee who received the orders from M.K. Associates noticed that some of the dowels were defective because they were "out of round," and he reported this defect to Wayne Curley, the purchasing manager. The factory foreperson, Virginia Johnson, found she was unable to use the dowels because of the defects. From June to September, 1987, Johnson ran the dowels through a "seavey" machine in order to correct the defects. This corrective process enabled Stowell Products to use the dowels for the Mirro/Foley order, although the order was not shipped until September 25, 1987, about a month late.

In the spring of 1987, Wayne Curley, purchasing manager of Stowell Products, and Doug Bucy, general manager, had a series of conversations with M.K. Associates. These conversations discussed the fact that Stowell Products was behind on its payments for the order. Only one conversation, however, made any mention of problems with the dowels. This conversation occurred between Curley and Marshall Kates, owner of M.K. Associates, in March, 1987. At this time, Curley asked Kates if one of the orders could be cancelled because of problems in running the dowels through the production process. Kates answered that he couldn't cancel. They did not discuss the issue further.

Stowell Products made no other attempts to raise the issue of defects in the dowels to M.K. Associates. On September 2, 1987, M.K. Associates filed a complaint in this court for the remainder due from Stowell Products on the dowel order.

III.   Conclusions of Law

The issue in this case is whether Stowell Products is entitled to deduct damages for defects in the dowels purchased from M.K. Associates against the amount owed for the orders. The defendant does not dispute that Stowell Products accepted the dowels from M.K. Associates, and that it did not revoke this acceptance. Instead, the defendant decided to keep the dowels and use them in its business. . . .

Nonetheless, accepting defective goods does not preclude a buyer from pursuing remedies for breach of contract due to defects in goods. 11 M.R.S.A. § 2–607(2). "The buyer on notifying the seller of his intention so to do may deduct all or any part of the damages resulting from any breach of the contract from any part of the price still due under the same contract." 11 M.R.S.A. § 2–717. A buyer claiming a breach of contract after accepting goods must, however, notify the seller of the breach within a reasonable time after discovery of the breach, or the buyer will be barred from any breach of contract remedy. 11 M.R.S.A. § 2–607(3)(a).

The critical question in this case, therefore, is whether the defendant gave timely notice of the breach of contract claim. What constitutes reasonable time depends on the particular circumstances of a case. 11 M.R.S.A. § 1–204. The policies underlying the requirement of timely notice are first, to enable the seller to cure or replace, second, to give the seller an opportunity to prepare for negotiation and litigation, and third, to ensure finality. J. White & R. Summers, Uniform Commercial Code 421–22 (2d ed. 1980). . . . To further these purposes, "reasonable time" for notice is interpreted strictly for commercial buyers. See 11 M.R.S.A. § 2–607, Uniform Commercial Code (U.C.C.) Comment 4.

The defendant argues that notice of the breach was given by Wayne Curley, purchasing manager for Stowell Products, to Marshall Kates, owner of M.K. Associates, in their conversation in March, 1987. In this conversation, Curley told Kates that defects in some dowels were causing production problems, and Kates said he could not cancel the order. The defendant argues that Curley's conversation with Kates was sufficient notice. It is true that "no formality of notice is required." 11 M.R.S.A. § 2–717, U.C.C. Comment 2. "The content of the notification need merely be sufficient to let the seller know that the transaction is still troublesome and must be watched." 11 M.R.S.A. § 2–607, U.C.C. Comment 4. Nevertheless, after Kates responded that he would not be able to cancel the order, Curley let the matter rest and gave Kates no indication that Stowell Products pursued it further. Therefore, the defendant did not give adequate notice that the transaction was still troublesome.

Moreover, the U.C.C. Comments emphasize that notice of a claim of breach is crucial. "The notification which saves the buyer's rights under this Article need only be such as informs the seller that the transaction is claimed to involve a breach, and thus opens the way for normal settlement through negotiation." 11 M.R.S.A. § 2–607, U.C.C. Comment 4. Even if the seller knows of defects in the goods, the buyer must notify the seller of the buyer's claim that the defects constitute a breach. . . . The requirement that a commercial buyer's notice must include an indication that the buyer considers the contract breached is consistent with the policies behind the notice requirement, which include ensuring finality for transactions and allowing the seller to prepare for negotiation and settlement. In the conversation with Kates, however, Curley did not clearly let Kates know that Stowell Products considered the contract breached.

Finally, U.C.C. Comment 2 to 11 M.R.S.A. § 2–717 states that "any language which reasonably indicates the buyer's reason for holding up his payment is sufficient." Despite repeated conversations concerning late payments, no one from Stowell Products suggested to M.K. Associates that payments were being withheld to cover the costs of defects in the dowels.

Therefore, Stowell Products' only notice of the breach was in its answer to the plaintiff's complaint, filed on October 13, 1987, more than five months after the dowels were received and more than three months after the dowels were received and more than three months after the defendant began processing the dowels. The defendant argues that it was reasonable to wait until the Mirro/Foley order was completed in order to determine the total amount of damages.

The U.C.C. does not require, however, that the buyer give notice of the exact amount of damages that will be incurred. . . . At least by June, 1987, the defendant knew of significant costs that would be incurred by correcting the defective dowels. The defendant has given no reason to justify letting several months go by while it used the defective goods for its own business purposes before warning M.K. Associates that it considered the contract breached.

The defendant also claims that the delay was reasonable in light of the purposes of the notice requirement, since ample time for settlement remained after the plaintiff began this litigation. Courts have held, however, that waiting until the seller sues for the purchase price to claim a breach of contract fails to satisfy the requirement of timely notice. . . .

IV.   Conclusion

The defendant accepted and used the dowels from M.K. Associates despite any defects it found. The defendant failed to notify the plaintiff of any claim of a breach of contract until the plaintiff began this litigation. This delay was unreasonable, and therefore the defendant is barred from deducting damages for breach of contract.

Accordingly, the Court hereby ORDERS that judgment in this action be entered for the plaintiff in the amount of Ten Thousand Five Hundred Eighteen Dollars and Forty Cents ($10,518.40), plus interest and costs as provided by law.

NOTES

(1) Understanding the Buyer's Delay. Can you think of a possible explanation for the almost complete failure of the buyer's purchasing manager to mention the problem that the factory was experiencing with the dowels in his series of conversations with the seller's general manager? For his polite inquiry about cancellation rather than complaint about nonconformity? At what point in this transaction does it appear that buyer came to the conclusion that seller was in breach of warranty?[1] Do you think this occurred before seller obtained legal representation?

(2) UCC 2–607(3): Rationale and History. Comment 4 states that "the rule of requiring notification is designed to defeat commercial bad faith. . . ." The court in *M.K. Associates* gives three quite different policies said to underlie the requirement. Does the *text* of 2–607(3)(a) support the positions in the comment or the opinion? What purpose could be important enough to justify totally barring a buyer's claim without regard to the degree of injury, if any, to the interest of the seller? Comment 4 declares that the necessary content of a buyer's notice is minimal: "merely sufficient to let the seller know that the transaction is still troublesome and must be watched . . . , [not] a clear statement of all the objections that will be relied upon by the buyer . . . , and [not] a claim for damages or of any threatened litigation or other resort to a remedy."[2] Can the extreme consequence be reconciled with that minimal information requirement?

As indicated in the comment (Prior Uniform Statutory Provision), 2–607(3) has an antecedent in USA 49, which also barred buyers who failed to give sellers timely notice of breach. But USA 49 had no counterpart in the Sale of Goods Act. Why did the drafters of the United States statute add this element? See S. Williston, The Law Governing Sales of Goods at Common Law and Under the Uniform Sales Act ? 488 (1909). See also John C. Reitz, Against Notice: A Proposal to Restrict the Notice of Claims Rule in UCC § 2–607(a)(3), 73 Cornell L. Rev. 534, 540–541 (1988).

Some civil law jurisdictions impose a requirement of buyers' prompt notice of default. Some nations provide very short periods within which actions must be brought (statutes of limitation or "prescription") or notices given to sellers. G. Treitel, Remedies for Breach of Contract: A Comparative Account 141 (1988). Another technique is used in the German Commercial Code, §§ 377–378. In the case of commercial sales, buyers are required to examine goods promptly after delivery and to give notice of any discernible lack of conformity discovered; if a buyer fails to give such notice, goods are deemed to be in conformity with the contract. Id.

Could UCC 2–607(3)(a), in its present form, be construed to provide relief only if a seller can show that buyer's delay has prejudiced the seller and limiting the bar to recovery to the extent necessary to overcome the prejudice shown? One commentator argues for an affirmative answer:

> Many courts have in effect interpreted the "reasonable time" standard of the rule to reflect a rough balance of the interests of the buyer in obtaining a remedy against the interests [of the seller] served by the notice rule. Because the legislatures have not provided any guidance on the policy goals underlying the notice rule, the courts are free to construe them as broadly or narrowly as they think proper. . . .

1. Recall the effect in the court's reasoning of buyer's continuing to accept further deliveries of copy machines in *Royal Business Machines*, Section 3, supra.

2. Would a notice be sufficient if it stated in entirety: "Your delivery was non-conforming"?

The prejudice least likely to justify barring all of the buyer's claim is loss of opportunity to cure [the nonconformity]. When the seller demonstrates such a loss, the court might use the mitigation principle to justify barring only the costs that the seller could have avoided.

[For the prejudice resulting from seller's loss of the opportunity to gather evidence of the goods conformity, courts should employ an evidentiary presumption in seller's favor.] Traditionally. courts place the burden of production of evidence on the party with the best access to the relevant evidence. Courts should also be free to employ presumptions to prevent the careless or deliberate behavior of one litigant from prejudicing the opposing litigant's defense or prosecution.

J.C. Reitz, supra, 588–589. Do you agree with this analysis?

The PEB Article 2 Study Group stated in its report:

Literal interpretation of the notice requirement should be rejected. Either the text of § 2–607(3)(a) or the comments should be revised to require only that the notice inform the seller that problems have arisen or continue to exist with regard to the accepted goods. Also, the comments should clarify that the buyer has no obligation to notify for breaches of which it has no knowledge.

PEB Article 2 Report 168–169.

Do you agree?

(3) Proposed Revised UCC Article 2. Proposed Revised UCC 2–607(3) would change the consequence of delay in notice of breach. A dilatory buyer would be barred from a remedy "only to the extent that the seller is prejudiced by the failure."[3]

(B) STATUTE OF LIMITATIONS

The UCC generally shortened the period of limitations for warranty actions. The period of limitations for breach of contract is six years in most states. Section 2–725(1) provides a four-year period for breaches of warranties of quality.[4] The period begins to run when a buyer's cause of action accrues, defined for most transactions as the date of tender of delivery.[5] UCC 2–725(2). Buyer's knowledge or lack of knowledge of the breach is not material.

---

3. Proposed Revised UCC 2–607(c)(1).

4. UCC 2–715(1) permits parties to a contract of sale to reduce the limitations period (with a one-year minimum) but not to extend it.

5. Application of UCC 2–715 to sales contracts that obligate sellers not only to deliver goods to buyers, but also to install and test the goods after delivery, has proven to be controversial. See Flagg Energy Devel-opment Corp. v. General Motors Corp., 244 Conn. 126, 709 A.2d 1075 (1998); Washington Freightliner, Inc. v. Shantytown Pier, Inc., 351 Md. 616, 719 A.2d 541 (1998); Baker v. DEC International, 458 Mich. 247, 580 N.W.2d 894 (1998). These cases are discussed in J. Wladis, R. Hakes, M. Kotler, R. Meadows & P. Tauchert, Uniform Commercial Code Survey: Sales, 54 Bus. Law. 1831, 1844–1846 (1999).

This section is addressed to the limitations period on claims of breach of warranties of quality. The statute of limitations on claims of breach of warranty of title were considered in Chapter 1.

Implied Warranties. When does the period of limitations begin to run on seller's breach of implied warranty of merchantability? Of fitness for particular purpose? As might be expected, UCC 2–725(2) provides that a cause of action accrues when "breach occurs," but the section adds that breach of warranty occurs when tender of delivery is made unless there is a warranty that "explicitly extends to future performance of the goods." Explicit extension of warranties can occur only by expression, not by implication. Breach of an implied warranty of quality occurs, therefore, at tender of delivery of the goods.[6]

Could the limitations period expire before a buyer has learned of the breach of an implied warranty? Again UCC 2–725(2) is clear: A cause of action accrues "regardless of the aggrieved party's knowledge of the breach." What is the policy rationale for a rule that will lead, in some cases, to warranty claims being time-barred before buyers are aware that there are any nonconformities in the goods? The Comment to the section provides no explanation. Nor can an answer be found in the Uniform Sales Act, which had no statute of limitations. Prior to adoption of the UCC, the statute of limitations for claims of breach of warranty was the general statute for all contract actions.[7]

Express Warranties. Under UCC 2–725(2), the period of limitations begins to run on seller's breach of an express warranty of quality at the date of tender of delivery of the goods unless the warranty "explicitly

6. In a remote buyer's implied warranty of merchantability claim against a manufacturer, a court may decide that the warranty claim is governed by UCC Article 2 and decide, therefore, that the applicable statute of limitations is UCC 2–725(2). In this situation, a tender of delivery occurred in each link of the distribution chain. Which tender of delivery begins the running of the statute? This problem arose in a New York case in which a remote buyer's claim was based on personal injuries that were allegedly caused by a motorcycle manufactured by the defendant. New York had adopted Alternative B of UCC 2–318. The N.Y. Court of Appeals held that the statute allowed the remote buyer to sue the manufacturer, but that the relevant contract was the manufacturer's sales contract. Tender of delivery under the upstream contract had occurred more than four years before the claim. The Court of Appeals, in a 4–2 decision, held that plaintiff's claim was time-barred. Heller v. U.S. Suzuki Motor

Corp., 64 N.Y.2d 407, 488 N.Y.S.2d 132, 477 N.E.2d 434 (1985).

Would the result change if the court had not decided to apply UCC Article 2 to the dispute?

7. A New York case involved a claim for severe injuries suffered by a child when she ran into a glass door that broke. The injury occurred more than four years after the door had been purchased. Shortly after the accident, the claim made was that the glass door did not conform to the implied warranty of merchantability and that this caused the child's injuries. (New York courts did not recognize the tort of strict liability at the time of this case.) The child's claim was held to be time-barred under UCC 2–725. Mendel v. Pittsburgh Plate Glass Co., 25 N.Y.2d 888, 304 N.Y.S.2d 4, 251 N.E.2d 143 (1969). Within a few years, New York joined the large number of states that allowed tort recovery in cases of this kind. Codling v. Paglia, 32 N.Y.2d 330, 345 N.Y.S.2d 461, 298 N.E.2d 622 (1973).

extends to future performance of the goods and discovery of the breach must await the time of performance." If the exception applies, the four-year period commences "when the breach is or should have been discovered." Interpretation of the quoted language has been a most difficult task for lawyers and judges.

Some contract obligations that extend to future performance of the goods are thought to be clearly covered by the exception UCC 2–725(2). Sales contracts that contain a guarantee that siding will last a "lifetime"[8] or that the roof shingles will serve for 25 years are deemed to extend to future performance. But other contract clauses have also been construed to come within the exception.

———

MOORMAN MANUFACTURING CO. v. NATIONAL TANK CO., 91 Ill.2d 69, 61 Ill.Dec. 746, 435 N.E.2d 443 (1982). In 1966 Moorman purchased a large grain-storage tank from National. The contract of sale contained the following:

> Tank designed to withstand 60 lbs. per bushel grain and 100 m.p.h. winds.

In 1976 a crack developed in the tank; Moorman brought suit against National in 1977. One count of the complaint, based on the quoted language, alleged breach of express warranty. National contended that the claim was barred by the statute of limitations. The trial court, relying on the exception in 2–725(2), held that Moorman's claim was not time-barred. The Illinois Supreme Court reversed.

> The final issue is whether count IV, based upon breach of express warranty, was barred by the statute of limitations. . . .
>
> Several appellate court decisions in this State have held that merely because it is reasonable to expect that a warranty of merchantability extends for the life of a product does not mean that such a warranty "explicitly extends to future performance." . . .
>
> In Binkley Co. v. Teledyne Mid–America Corp. (E.D.Mo.1971), 333 F.Supp. 1183, aff'd (8th Cir.1972), 460 F.2d 276, the seller of a welding machine expressly warranted that a welder would weld at a rate of 1,000 feet per 50–minute hour, which it never did. The court defined "explicit" under 2–725(2) as " '"[n]ot implied merely, or conveyed by implication; distinctly stated; plain in language; clear; not ambiguous; express; unequivocal." ' " Although the warranty expressly stated that the welder would weld at 1,000 feet per hour, the court found that the statute had lapsed because there was no reference to future time in the warranty and, thus, no explicit warranty of future performance. In response to the buyer's argument that he was unable to test the

---

8. Moore v. Puget Sound Plywood, Inc., 214 Neb. 14, 332 N.W.2d 212 (1983) ("According to the parties the description of the goods as 'siding' carried with it the representation that it would last the lifetime of the house.").

product until after delivery the court pointed to the clear language of section 2–725(2) which provides that the breach occurs at the time of delivery "regardless of the aggrieved party's lack of knowledge."

We agree with the decision in that case as well as the appellate decisions in this State adhering to the clear language of the statute.

———

Remedial Promises and Warranties. An especially troublesome question for courts has been the application of UCC 2–715(2) to transactions in which sellers have provided a remedial promise, sometimes along with express or implied warranties of quality and sometimes without any quality warranties. As we learned in Section 4, when remedial promises fail of their essential purpose under UCC 2–719(2), buyers may have remedies provided by the UCC. When does a buyer's cause of action accrue in transactions of this kind? On a claim of breach of warranty? On a claim of breach of the remedial promise? What is the applicable statute of limitations?

Tittle v. Steel City Oldsmobile GMC Truck, Inc.

Supreme Court of Alabama, 1989.
544 So.2d 883.

■ SHORES, JUSTICE.

The plaintiff, Rodney K. Tittle, appeals a summary judgment entered in favor of defendants, Steel City Oldsmobile GMC Truck, Inc. (hereinafter "Steel City"), and General Motors Corporation (hereinafter "General Motors").

Tittle purchased a 1981 Oldsmobile automobile from Steel City on October 9, 1981, and accepted delivery of it the same day. With the purchase of his automobile, General Motors provided Tittle with a document entitled "1981 Oldsmobile New Car Warranty." This writing provided that Steel City, as Tittle's Oldsmobile dealer, would repair and adjust defects in material or workmanship that occurred during the first 12 months or first 12,000 miles in which the car was in use. The document provided, further, that the warranty period would begin on the date the car was first delivered or placed in service. In addition to this warranty, Tittle purchased from General Motors Acceptance Corporation (hereinafter "GMAC"), the company with whom he financed the purchase of the car, a supplemental warranty that extended coverage of the original warranty to 36 months or 36,000 miles.

After Tittle accepted the automobile, he discovered numerous defects in it and repeatedly asked Steel City and GMAC to cure the problems. When Steel City proved unable, after a number of attempts, to repair the vehicle, Tittle met with the zone representative for GMAC, Don Ackerman. Tittle alleges that Mr. Ackerman, as agent for GMAC, offered to extend the existing warranty on the vehicle for an additional 12 months or 12,000 miles if Tittle would allow Steel City another opportunity to repair the defects in the vehicle. Tittle agreed, but following several unsuccessful attempts to repair the vehicle, Tittle returned the car to Steel City.

Tittle sued on January 29, 1986, in Jefferson County Circuit Court, alleging that Steel City, GMAC, and General Motors had breached their respective express warranties as well as implied warranties of merchantability and fitness. Tittle founded his claims upon the federal Consumer Product Warranty Act, known commonly as the Magnuson–Moss Act, 15 U.S.C. § 2301 et seq., and upon Alabama's version of the Uniform Commercial Code (hereinafter "U.C.C."), § 7–1–101 et seq., Ala. Code (1975). In their answers to the plaintiff's complaint, both Steel City and General Motors specifically pleaded the statute of limitations as an affirmative defense.

Steel City and General Motors filed motions for summary judgment based upon the statute of limitations defense. During the hearing on the motions, the trial judge asked the parties to present the court with additional authorities supporting their respective positions. The court requested that the parties submit these authorities on or before April 1, 1988. General Motors responded to the trial court's request by providing it with four cases. Tittle, however, filed both a supplemental brief opposing the defendants' motion for summary judgment and an affidavit containing facts not alleged at the time the court heard the summary judgment motions.

On April 4, 1988, the trial court entered summary judgment in favor of Steel City and General Motors. The court found that Tittle's claims were barred by the statute of limitations at the time his complaint was filed. The trial court specifically noted that the plaintiff's case remained pending as to defendant GMAC, but made its order final with respect to Steel City and General Motors. See, Ala. R. Civ. P. 54(b). It is from this summary judgment that the plaintiff appeals. Apparently anticipating Tittle's argument on appeal, General Motors filed a motion to strike the plaintiff's affidavit from the record, on June 20, 1988.

The issue presented this Court for review is whether the trial court erred in entering summary judgment for these two defendants on the ground that Tittle's claim for breach of an express warranty was barred by the statute of limitations. In arguing this issue, the parties raise five questions this Court must address: first, what statute of limitations applies in cases brought under the Magnuson–Moss Act or the breach of warranty claims brought under Alabama's version of the U.C.C.?; second, does Ala. Code (1975), § 8–2–12, toll the statute of limitations for breach of warranty in consumer cases until the breach is discovered?; third, does the warranty issued by General Motors explicitly extend to the future performance of the vehicle?; fourth, is a repair and replacement warranty breached upon tender of the car or upon refusal or failure to repair an alleged defect?; and fifth, was Mr. Tittle's affidavit properly submitted to the trial court and included in the record on appeal, and, if so, did the affidavit present a genuine issue of material fact precluding the trial court's summary judgment?

I.

The Magnuson–Moss Act authorizes civil actions by consumers in state or federal court when suppliers, warrantors, or service contractors violate its provisions. 15 U.S.C. § 231O(d)(1). The Act, however, does not provide a statute of limitations for claims that arise under this legislation. Where a federal statute grants a cause of action, but does not include a statute of limitations governing the scope of that statute's application, federal common law requires that the court apply the state statute of limitations governing the state action most closely analogous to the federal claim. . . . The state law action most analogous to Tittle's Magnuson–Moss warranty claim is an action for breach of warranty in a contract for sale. Thus, the statute of limitations that appropriately applies to Tittle's state breach of warranty action is the same statute of limitations that appropriately applies to his federal Magnuson–Moss claim. Under Alabama's version of the U.C.C., the statute of limitations that applies to an action for breach of any contract for sale is found in § 7–2–725, Ala. Code (1975).

* * *

III.

Under § 7–2–725(2), a cause of action for breach of warranty accrues when the seller tenders to the buyer the goods made the basis of the warranty. Once the cause of action accrues, the statute provides a four-year limitations period in which the buyer may file suit, subject to two exceptions. First, a cause of action will not accrue, in the case of consumer goods, on a claim for damages for injury to the person until the injury occurs.[*] And, second, where the seller of consumer goods gives the buyer an express warranty that extends to the future performance of the goods, a cause of action will not accrue until the buyer discovers or should have discovered the defect in the goods.

Tittle argues that the trial court erred in entering summary judgment in this case even if the limitations period contained in § 7–2–725 is the one that appropriately applies to his cause of action, because, he says, the warranties given him by Steel City and General Motors explicitly extended to the future performance of his automobile. Consequently, Tittle claims that his cause of action did not accrue until he discovered or should have discovered the breach of the Steel City and General Motors warranties.

While Tittle's argument has been addressed in other jurisdictions, the question of whether a so-called "repair and replacement" warranty extends to the future performance of goods, so as to fall within the limited exception set out in § 7–2–725(2), is a case of first impression for this

---

* [The Alabama version of UCC 2–725 contains a non-uniform amendment that establishes the date of a personal injury as the date on which the period of limitations begins to run with respect to such claims.]

Court. Therefore, a brief analysis of the case law interpreting this section is appropriate. Before we analyze case law, however, it is critical that we consider exactly what the warranties given Tittle purport to guarantee.

Page 2 of Tittle's warranty is entitled, "1981 Oldsmobile New Car Limited Warranty." This document provides that "Oldsmobile Division, General Motors Corporation, warrants each new 1981 car," that "this warranty covers any repairs and needed adjustments to correct defects in material or workmanship," and that "the warranty period begins on the date the car is first delivered or put in use." The warranty further provides, "your Oldsmobile dealer will make the repairs or adjustments, using new or remanufactured parts." The warranty stipulates on page 3 that "it is our intent to repair under the warranty, without charge, anything that goes wrong during the warranty period that is our fault." The warranty then distinguishes the term "defects," which "are covered [under the warranty] because we, the manufacturer, are responsible," from the term "damages," which are not covered by the warranty because the manufacturer has "no control over damage caused by such things as collision, misuse and lack of maintenance which occurs after the car is delivered." . . .

In 1976, in the leading case of Voth v. Chrysler Motor Corp., 218 Kan. 644, 545 P.2d 371 (1976), the Supreme Court of Kansas spoke to Tittle's argument. The warranty in Voth read in pertinent part:

> Chrysler Corporation warrants this vehicle to the first registered owner only against defects in material and workmanship in normal use as follows: (1) the entire vehicle (except tires) for 12 months or 12,000 miles of operation after the vehicle is first placed in service, whichever occurs first, from the date of sale or delivery thereto; and (2) the engine block, head and all internal engine parts, water pump, intake manifold, transmission case and all internal transmission parts, torque converter (if so equipped), drive shaft universal joints, rear axle and differential, and rear wheel bearings for 5 years or 50,000 miles of operation after the vehicle is first placed in service, whichever occurs first, from the date of such sale or delivery. Any part of this vehicle found defective under the conditions of this warranty will be repaired or replaced, at Chrysler's option, without charge at an authorized Imperial, Chrysler, Plymouth, or Dodge dealership.

Voth, 218 Kan. at 647, 545 P.2d at 374–75 (quoting Chrysler's warranty from the record).

This warranty is similar to the warranty issued by General Motors in this case. The Kansas Supreme Court held that the Chrysler warranty did not explicitly extend to the future performance of the vehicle. Moreover, the court found that the warranty did not guarantee performance without malfunction during the term of the warranty, but warranted only that the manufacturer would repair or replace defective parts in the event the car malfunctioned. Voth, 218 Kan. at 648, 545 P.2d at 375. The Kansas court explains its rationale through a quotation from Owens v. Patent Scaffolding Co., 77 Misc.2d 992, 354 N.Y.S.2d 778 (Sup. Ct. 1974), rev'd on other grounds, 50 A.D.2d 866, 376 N.Y.S.2d 948 (1975), in which an argument similar to Tittle's was rejected:

> In this case the warranty does not go to performance of the equipment. To warrant to make needed repairs to leased equipment is not a warranty extending to its future performance. All that the supplier promises is that if the equipment needs repairs he will make them. It does not promise that in the future the goods will not fall into disrepair or malfunction, but only that if it does, the supplier will repair it. [Underlying] the warranty to make needed repairs is the assumption that the goods may fall into disrepair or otherwise malfunction. No warranty that the goods will not, is to be inferred from the warranty to make needed repairs.

Voth, 218 Kan. at 651, 545 P.2d at 378 (quoting Owens, supra, 77 Misc.2d at 999, 354 N.Y.S.2d at 785).

In articulating the distinction between a warranty to repair and a warranty extending to future performance, the court in Owens said:

> A promise to repair is an express warranty that the promise to repair will be honored [citations omitted]. The seller's warranty ... that ... [goods] "will give satisfactory service at all times" is distinguishable from the supplier's warranty to "make modifications, alterations or repairs to the component parts of the equipment" when necessary. [The words in the former warranty] go to the performance of the goods; that it "will give satisfactory service at all times." When the time came that the [goods] did not give satisfactory service, the warranty was breached. [The former warranty] explicitly extended to future performance of the goods, and its breach could only be discovered at the time of such performance.

77 Misc.2d at 998, 354 N.Y.S.2d at 784.

In Ontario Hydro v. Zallea Systems, Inc. 569 F.Supp. 1261 (D.Del. 1983), Chief Judge Latchum expressed the distinction between these two types of warranties in this manner:

> [T]he key distinction between these two kinds of warranties is that a repair or replacement warranty merely provides a *remedy* if the product becomes defective, while a warranty for future performance *guarantees the performance* of the product itself for a stated period of time. In the former case, the buyer is relying upon the warranty merely as a method by which a defective product can be remedied which has no effect upon his ability to discover his breach. In the latter instance, the buyer is relying upon the warranty as a guarantee of future performance and therefore has no opportunity to discover the breach until the future performance has been tested. (Emphasis in original.)

Ontario Hydro, at 1266.

Other courts and authorities support the same conclusion: a promise to repair is not necessarily a promise of future performance. ... See also, W. D. Hawkland, Uniform Commercial Code Service, § 2–725:02 at 480 (the hardship to the buyer that may sometimes be created by the four-year limitations period as measured from tender of delivery is thought to be outweighed by the commercial benefit derived from an established limitations period).

Tittle, in response to the foregoing cases, proffers two cases that he suggests represent substantial authority from other jurisdictions directly contrary to Voth and similar cases. In the first case, Standard Alliance Industries, Inc. v. Black Clawsen Co., 587 F.2d 813 (6th Cir.1978), cert. denied, 441 U.S.923, 99 S.Ct. 2032, 60 L.Ed.2d 396 (1979), the seller of a forging machine, in addition to warranting specific performance levels for the operation of the machine, warranted that "the equipment manufactured by it would be free from defects in workmanship and material" for a period of one year. 587 F.2d at 816–17 (emphasis added). When the manufacturer failed, after numerous attempts, to repair the defective machinery, the buyer brought an action against the seller alleging breach of his express warranty. The Standard Alliance court held that the warranty at issue in the case extended to the future performance of the machine for a period of one year and that the buyer's cause of action accrued when the purchaser discovered or should have discovered that the machine was defective. Id., at 817.

In the second case, R. W. Murray Co. v. Shatterproof Glass Corp., 697 F.2d 818 (8th Cir.1983), the manufacturer's warranty provided:

> Vision and spandrel glass shall be guaranteed by the glass manufacturer for a period of ten (10) years from the date of acceptance of the project to furnish and replace any unit which develops material destruction of vision between the interglass surfaces. This guarantee is for material and labor costs for replacing.

697 F.2d at 821–22 n. 2.

> Shatterproof Glass Corporation warrants its insulating glass units for a period of twenty (20) years from the date of manufacture against defects in material or workmanship that result in moisture accumulation, film formation or dust collection between the interior surfaces, resulting from failure of the hermetic seal. Purchaser's exclusive remedy and Shatterproof's "total" liability under this warranty shall be limited to the replacement of any lite failing to meet the terms of this warranty. Such replacement will be made F.O.B. Detroit to the shipping point nearest the installation.

697 F.2d 822 n. 3. The court construed these warranties as extending to the future performance of the goods for periods of 10 years and 20 years, respectively, and held that the purchaser's cause of action for breach of warranty accrued when the breach was, or should have been, discovered.

Despite the language used in the Shatterproof Glass warranties, guaranteeing for a specified period of time that a product is "free" from defects, as in Standard Alliance, seems to us altogether different from guaranteeing that product "against" defects, as in Voth. In the first instance, the manufacturer guarantees that the product possesses no defect whatsoever, while in the second instance the manufacturer guarantees that where defects emerge, he will remedy them, generally by repairing or replacing the defective part. While Shatterproof Glass used the term "against" in its warranty, we reconcile the holding in that case with Voth and Standard Alliance by noting the explicit nature of the remaining language in the warranty. Had the Shatterproof Glass court held that the warranties fell outside the U.C.C. § 2–725(2) "extends to future performance" exception, then despite the 10–and 20–year periods set out in the warranties, § 2–725(1) would have terminated the plaintiff's right of action four years after tender of the goods. (Section 2–725(1) provides in pertinent part, "By the original agreement the parties may reduce the period of limitation to not less than one year but may not extend it [beyond four years from the date of tender].")

In the present case, the warranty under which Tittle pursued his claim is even more free of ambiguity than that found in Voth and the other cases. The activating language of that warranty provides: "This warranty covers any repairs and needed adjustments to correct defects in material or workmanship." This language clearly does not guarantee that the car will perform free of defects for the term of the agreement. In fact, as the court in Voth recognized, the language of the guarantee anticipates that defects will occur. We, therefore, hold that the warranty provided Tittle upon the purchase of his car did not extend to the car's future performance.

We recognize that, under the analysis adopted by this Court, one might reasonably suggest that the language of the "Emission Components Defect Warranty" places it within our definition of a warranty that extends to future performance, at least within the limited scope of that separate provision. The emissions warranty provides: "Oldsmobile ... warrants ... that the car ... is free from defects in material and workmanship which cause the car to fail to conform with applicable Federal Environmental Protection Agency regulations for a period of use of 50,000 miles or 5 years, whichever comes first." We note, however, that although he enumerates an exhaustive list of defects, Tittle never alleged in his complaint or elsewhere that his vehicle failed to conform to EPA emissions standards. Hence, this provision is not applicable to the case before us.

IV.

Tittle next contends that even if the General Motors and Steel City warranties do not extend to the future performance of the vehicle, the cause of action does not accrue until there is a refusal or failure to repair. This contention, however, directly contradicts the plain meaning of the language in § 7–2–725, which states that a cause of action for breach of any contract for sale accrues when the breach occurs and that the breach occurs upon tender of delivery, regardless of the buyer's knowledge of the breach, unless the warranty explicitly extends to future performance. We have earlier determined that Tittle's warranty does not extend to the future performance of his car. The trial court, therefore, correctly determined that

Tittle's cause of action, by statute and by the express terms of his warranty, accrued at the time Steel City delivered the vehicle to him.

V.

Finally, Tittle argues that even if we affirm the lower court's rulings regarding interpretation of § 7–2–725, the trial court still erred in granting summary judgment because, he says, a material issue of fact exists as to whether the defendants are estopped to assert the statute of limitations based upon their agent's representations.

* * *

... General Motors and Steel City argue that they should not be estopped from raising the statute of limitations defense because, they say, no evidence exists that the misrepresentations made by Mr. Ackerman were intentional or fraudulent, or that Tittle, relying on these representations, was induced not to file a lawsuit. ...

Tittle states in his affidavit that in 1984 a General Motors representative, Mr. Don Ackerman, represented that Steel City would repair the defects in his vehicle; that Mr. Ackerman indicated that if Tittle would allow Steel City another opportunity to repair the car, then Ackerman would extend the warranty 12 months or 12,000 miles; and that based on Mr. Ackerman's representations, he continued to attempt to have the car repaired rather than returning the car to the appellees. We find that a jury might conceivably construe Mr. Ackerman's statements as a promise to make repairs in return for a promise not to sue.

In reviewing a disposition of a motion for summary judgment, we use the same standard as that of the trial court in determining whether the evidence before the court made out a genuine issue of material fact. ... We do not here decide whether these defendants are estopped as a matter of law from asserting the statute of limitations as a defense; rather, we hold that a fact issue exists as to whether Ackerman acted as an agent for General Motors and Steel City and made a statement that Tittle reasonably relied on in delaying the filing of this lawsuit.

We, therefore, reverse the summary judgment in favor of General Motors and Steel City.

REVERSED AND REMANDED

NOTES

(1) The Defendants' Obligations. Counsel for the buyer in *Tittle* elected to join three defendants, the manufacturer of the automobile (General Motors), the retail dealer (Steel City Oldsmobile GMC Truck), and the provider of a "supplemental warranty" (General Motors Acceptance). Only the manufacturer and the retail dealer are parties to the appeal. Although the liability of each of these defendants is separate from the liability of the other two, the court did not distinguish between the cases of the manufacturer and the dealer.

The 1981 Oldsmobile New Car Limited Warranty was provided by the manufacturer. Retail dealers normally deliver such manufacturers' warranties to their customers but do not become co-warrantors under the manufacturers' warranties. In the sales contracts, retail dealers typically make no express warranties of quality and disclaim all implied warranties. Manufacturers commonly use retail dealers to perform the repairs promised by the manufacturers. The Limited Warranty made that arrangement explicit in this case. According to the complaint, the dealer was unable to repair buyer's vehicle. The gravity of the unrepaired problems is not described.

The court's opinion in this case offered no explanation for treating the dealer as if it were a co-warrantor of the New Car Limited Warranty. The defendants were represented by separate counsel before the Alabama Supreme Court, but the opinion did not reflect any difference in the arguments that may have been advanced by each set of attorneys.

(2) Magnuson–Moss Warranty Act. The buyer in *Tittle* based his claim in part on the Magnuson–Moss Warranty Act. Nothing in that Act deals with the statute of limitations. The Alabama court found, properly, that state law provided the limitations period for the federal cause of action. Was UCC 2–725 the proper state law to apply?

(3) Application of UCC 2–725(2). Counsel for buyer argued that the remedial promise in the New Car Limited Warranty brought it within the exception for warranties that extend to future performance. After extensive review of precedents, the court concluded that the language of the Limited Warranty "does not guarantee that the car will perform free of defects for the term of the agreement," and therefore buyer's warranty claims are time-barred under the four-year statute of limitations. Was the court's analysis correct?

In some sales contracts, sellers warrant that the goods are free of defect in materials and workmanship, but that the exclusive remedy for breach of that warranty is a remedial repair promise. The New Car Limited Warranty had only the remedial promise. Is there a substantive difference between the two forms? Should a seller's explicit promise to repair defects, if defects arise within a stated period of time, be construed as implying that the goods would be free of defects for that time? Notice the importance of the legal sophistication of the lawyers who draft warranty documents for their clients.

(4) Warranties of Quality; Remedies. The court noted that the complaint filed by counsel for the buyer had alleged defendants' breach of their respective express warranties as well as breach of implied warranties of merchantability and fitness. The trial court granted summary judgment for the manufacturer and the dealer on the statute of limitations without, apparently, considering the merits of the warranty claims. The case was remanded by the Alabama Supreme Court to consider whether the defendants were estopped from relying on the statute of limitations. Assume that the claim is found not to be time-barred. On the basis of your understanding of transactions of this kind, how would you evaluate the likely success of plaintiff on the various warranty counts? Against the dealer? Against the manufacturer? Against the provider of the "supplemental warranty"? What remedies would be available if the claims are upheld?

(5) Breach of the Remedial Promise. Counsel for the buyer argued that defendants were in breach of the obligations of the remedial repair promise and that this breach occurred when the defendants refused or failed make the repairs. The Alabama Supreme Court dismissed this argument on the ground that it "directly contradicts the plain meaning of the language of [UCC] 2–725." Is there any possible basis for the court's decision?

The "supplemental warranty" obligor was not in the case on appeal, but that "warranty" was described by the Alabama court as a repair promise that became operative after the expiration of the12 months or 12.000 mile period of the promise in the manufacturer's New Car Limited Warranty and extended protection to 36 months or 36.000 miles of usage. When would the statute of limitations begin to run on a claim of breach of the "supplemental warranty"? How could the Alabama Supreme Court distinguish the repair promise in "supplemental warranty" from the repair promise in the New Car Limited Warranty for statute of limitations purposes?

Nationwide Insurance Co. v. General Motors Corp.

Supreme Court of Pennsylvania, 1993.
533 Pa. 423, 625 A.2d 1172.

■ CAPPY, JUSTICE.

This appeal presents the issue of whether an express, 12 month/12,000 mile "New Car Limited Warranty" promising "repairs and needed adjustments" to correct manufacturing defects is a warranty that "explicitly extends to future performance of the goods" for purposes of determining when a cause of action for breach of that warranty accrues under the statute of limitations provision of the Uniform Commercial Code—Sales, 13 Pa.C.S. § 2725. We are also asked to determine whether the implied warranties of merchantability and fitness for a particular purpose so extend. For the following reasons, we hold that the express warranty does explicitly extend to future performance of the goods but that the implied warranties do not. We now reverse in part and affirm in part the decision of the Superior Court.

The essential facts are undisputed. On June 20, 1986, the Appellant, Nationwide Insurance Company, instituted this action against Appellee General Motors Corporation/Chevrolet Motor Division.... According to the Complaint ..., Appellant is the insurance carrier for Michael Joseph Villi, who on January 5, 1982, purchased and accepted delivery of a 1982 Chevrolet Corvette manufactured by Appellee. On November 22, 1982, the car "malfunctioned and/or exhibited a defect, caught fire and was destroyed." Appellant paid Mr. Villi $18,473.00 for damage to the vehicle. The

Complaint alleged that Appellee was liable for this amount because it had breached: (1) a written 12 month/12,000 mile warranty (Count One); (2) an implied warranty of merchantability (Count Two); and (3) an express or implied warranty of fitness for a particular purpose (Count Three).

Appellee filed a motion for summary judgment, which the Court of Common Pleas of Allegheny County initially denied. Upon reargument, however, the court granted the motion on the basis that the action was barred by the four-year statute of limitations at 13 Pa.C.S. § 2725: Although the action had been filed within four years of the date the car allegedly malfunctioned or displayed a defect, it had not been filed within four years of the date of tender of delivery. The trial court deemed the cause of action to have accrued upon tender of delivery because the court specifically found that the express, 12 month/12,000 mile warranty did not "explicitly extend to future performance of the goods" and therefore that the "discovery rule" exception of § 2725 did not apply. The Superior Court affirmed in an unpublished opinion, with Judge Brosky dissenting. 396 Pa.Super. 662, 570 A.2d 1093.[3] This Court granted Appellant's Petition for Allowance of Appeal.

. . . In this case, the question is whether the warranties explicitly extended to future performance of the vehicle so that the cause of action accrued when the breach was discovered (allegedly November 2, 1982),[4] in which case the action was timely filed, or whether the general rule regarding breach of warranty applies and the cause of action accrued upon tender of delivery (January 5, 1982), so that the action was untimely filed.

In the ordinary case, a breach of warranty action accrues on, and suit must be filed within four years of, the date the seller tenders delivery of the goods, even if the breach is not apparent until after delivery has been tendered. Section 2725 sets tender of delivery as the point at which the cause of action accrues because the section "presumes that all warranties, express or implied, relate only to the condition of the goods at the time of sale." Max E. Klinger, The Concept of Warranty Duration: A Tangled Web, 89 Dick.L.Rev. 935, 939 (1985) (hereinafter, "A Tangled Web"). Such warranties are breached, if at all, when the goods are delivered but do not meet that standard. Of course, the deficiency contained in the goods may not be discovered by the buyer within four years of delivery. However,

> [i]n the usual circumstances, . . . defects are apt to surface within that time period, and the few odd situations where this is not the case, resulting in hardship to the buyer, are thought to be outweighed by the commercial benefit derived by allowing the parties to destroy records with reasonable promptness.

---

3. The lower courts did not address Appellee's argument that it was entitled to summary judgment because the express warranty promised only the repair or replacement of defective parts and specifically excluded liability for consequential damages, and that issue is not before us.

4. This point fell within the warranty period because it was less than 12 months from the date the car was "first delivered or put in use" . . ., and the car had been driven less than 12,000 miles.

William D. Hawkland, Uniform Commercial Code Series § 2–725:02, at 480 (1984). See 13 Pa.C.S. § 2725, Uniform Commercial Code Comment (four year period "is most appropriate to modern business practice" because it "is within the normal commercial record keeping period"). Thus, in breach of warranty cases the four-year statute of limitations is essentially a statute of repose.

Section 2725 contains an exception, however, for warranties that "explicitly extend to future performance of the goods" where discovery of the breach must await the time of future performance. Where such a warranty is involved, the cause of action does not accrue until "the breach is or should have been discovered." This exception has caused confusion among courts, lawyers, and commentators for years. See generally, e.g., James J. White & Robert S. Summers, Uniform Commercial Code § 11–9 (3d ed. 1988); Klinger, A Tangled Web, 89 Dick.L.Rev. at 937–950 (discussing conflicting cases). Professors White and Summers have noted that "[a]lthough the time of accrual under [§ 2725] is ordinarily clear—'when tender of delivery is made'—the exception to this general rule poses interpretive difficulties." White & Summers, Uniform Commercial Code § 11–9, at 477. They go on to cite the very type of express warranty at issue here as an agreement that "leaves one in considerable doubt about its true meaning" and that could be interpreted either as a warranty that "explicitly extends to future performance" or as simply an agreement to repair.[5] Id. at 479.

Despite its ambiguity, one thing the plain language of § 2725(b) makes clear is that our analysis of whether the written warranty "explicitly" extends to future performance must focus on the express language of that warranty. It is entitled "1982 Chevrolet New Car Limited Warranty" and provides, in part:

WHAT IS COVERED

CHEVROLET Chevrolet Motor Division, General Motors Corporation, warrants each new 1982 car.

DEFECTS This exclusive warranty covers any repairs and needed adjustments to correct defects in material or workmanship.

REPAIRS Your Chevrolet dealer will make the repairs or adjustments, using new or remanufactured parts.

WHICHEVER COMES FIRST This warranty is for 12 months or 12,000 miles, whichever comes first.

WARRANTY BEGINS The warranty period begins on the date the car is first delivered or put in use.

---

5. The example cited is an agreement in which "the manufacturer promises to repair any defect in a car's drivetrain that occurs within two years or 24,000 miles, whichever occurs first."

NO CHARGE Warranty repairs and adjustments (parts and/or labor) will be made at no charge. A reasonable time must be allowed after taking the car to the dealer.

WARRANTY APPLIES This warranty is for Chevrolets registered and normally operated in the United States or Canada.[6]

Appellant argues that the express warranty explicitly extends to future performance of the goods because the warranty is for a specific duration, "12 months or 12,000 miles, whichever comes first." According to Appellant, such a warranty must contemplate the vehicle's future performance, at least for the stated period following delivery. Appellee, on the other hand, argues that the warranty does not explicitly extend to future performance of the goods because it does not promise that the goods will perform in a particular way in the future.[7]

---

6. The document also states: "ANY IMPLIED WARRANTY OF MERCHANTABILITY OR FITNESS FOR A PARTICULAR PURPOSE APPLICABLE TO THIS CAR IS LIMITED IN DURATION TO THE DURATION OF THIS WRITTEN WARRANTY. CHEVROLET SHALL NOT BE LIABLE FOR CONSEQUENTIAL OR INCIDENTAL DAMAGES RESULTING FROM BREACH OF THIS WRITTEN WARRANTY."

Under "WHAT IS NOT COVERED," the warranty excludes tires; damage due to accidents, misuse, or alterations; damage from the environment; and damage due to lack of maintenance or use of the wrong fuel, oil or lubes. It also states that normal maintenance is the owner's responsibility and that "extra expenses" relating to the loss of use of the car during repairs are not covered.

7. This position has been taken by courts in other states that have considered similar automobile warranties. See, e.g., Tittle v. Steel City Oldsmobile GMC Truck, Inc., 544 So.2d 883 (Ala.1989); Voth v. Chrysler Motor Corp., 218 Kan. 644, 545 P.2d 371 (1976); Stoltzner v. American Motors Jeep Corp., 127 Ill.App.3d 816, 82 Ill.Dec. 909, 469 N.E.2d 443 (1984) (also holding that express disclaimer of implied warranties "for any period beyond the express warranty" did not amount to explicit extension), appeal denied; Poppenheimer v. Bluff City Motor Homes, 658 S.W.2d 106 (Tenn.Ct.App.1983); Muss v. Mercedes–Benz of North America, Inc., 734 S.W.2d 155 (Tex.Ct.App.1987). n construing the same General Motors warranty language that is at issue in this case, the Supreme Court of Alabama stated:

This language clearly does not guarantee that the car will perform free of defects

for the term of the agreement. In fact, as the court in Voth [v. Chrysler Motor Corp., 218 Kan. 644, 545 P.2d 371 (1976)] recognized, the language of the guarantee anticipates that defects will occur. We, therefore, hold that the warranty provided Tittle upon the purchase of his car did not extend to the car's future performance.

Tittle, 544 So.2d at 891.

Decisions of the courts of other states on this issue are influential, given the purposes of the UCC. One of the explicit purposes of the Code in general is "[t]o make uniform the law among the various jurisdictions." 13 Pa.C.S. § 1103(b)(3). Section 2725 is intended specifically to "introduce a uniform statute of limitations for sales contracts." 13 Pa.C.S. § 2725, Uniform Commercial Code Comment. It would, therefore, be both acceptable and tempting simply to follow the lead of other courts. However, we decline to do so because we believe that the other courts' reasoning is flawed and would lead to absurd results if extended to its logical conclusion. For example, carrying through with the analysis described above would lead to a situation where a consumer who purchases a vehicle with a 7 year/70,000 mile warranty would have no cause of action for breach of that warranty if the breach were to occur in the fifth year following the date of delivery. Further, with the exception of the General Motors warranty at issue in Tittle, the warranties involved in the cited cases were worded differently from the warranty in the case sub judice, and some are distinguishable on that basis. The warranties in Stoltzner, Poppenheimer, and Muss, in particular, were

We cannot accept Appellee's position for a number of reasons. First, we do not read the words "explicitly extends to future performance of the vehicle" to require that the warranty make an explicit promise regarding how the goods will perform in the future. We believe that the focus of § 2725 is not on what is promised, but on the duration of the promise—i.e., the period to which the promise extends. Cf. Safeway Stores, Inc. v. Certainteed Corp., 710 S.W.2d 544, 549 (Tex.1986) (Robertson, J., concurring) (pointing out that "explicitly" modifies the words "extends," and not the word "warranty"; therefore, it is the extension that must be explicit). Therefore, we agree with Appellant that the phrase "explicitly extends to future performance" can be interpreted to include a promise that, by its terms, comes into play upon, or is contingent upon, the future performance of the goods. There can be little doubt that an explicit extension has been given where the warranty itself plainly states that it "is for 12 months or 12,000 miles" and that "[t]he warranty periods begins on the date the car is first delivered or put in use." (emphasis added). Logically, a promise to repair or adjust defective parts within the first 12 months or 12,000 miles after delivery cannot be breached until the vehicle requires repair or adjustment, and "discovery of the breach must await the time of [future] performance."

Second, the essence of Appellee's position is that the document here is not a warranty, but a promise to repair or replace defective parts.[9] To be sure, the agreement here is not a model of clear draftsmanship. It could plausibly be interpreted any one of three ways: as creating a warranty that extends for 12 months or 12,000 miles, with a limited remedy of repair or adjustment for breach of the warranty; as creating not a warranty, but a repair agreement that extends 12 months or 12,000 miles; or as creating an "un-extended" warranty with a limited remedy of repair or adjustment if a breach is reported within 12 months or 12,000 miles. However, any difficulty interpreting the agreement must be resolved in favor of the non-drafting party. ... It was the Appellee who drafted the document here, labeled it a "warranty," and included statements such as: "Chevrolet Motor Division, General Motors Corporation, warrants each new 1982 car" and "This warranty is for 12 months or 12,000 miles, whichever comes first." (emphasis added). If the drafter did not intend the document to operate as a warranty—and, more importantly for our purposes, if it did not intend the warranty to "[be] for 12 months or 12,000 miles,"—then it should have stated so more clearly.

more clearly promises to repair or replace defective parts for the stated "warranty" period.

9. Appellee never explicitly argues that the document is not a warranty. Indeed, having drafted the document and labeled it a warranty, Appellee would be hard-pressed to so argue. Instead, Appellee argues, somewhat disingenuously, that this is not a "performance warranty," but a "repair warranty." Section 2725 draws no such distinction. In addition, although Appellee argues that the document makes no promise regarding the condition or performance of the vehicle, its statement that it "warrants each new 1982 car" could be read to provide otherwise.

Moreover, Appellee's attempt to argue, in essence, that this is not really a warranty reveals the internal inconsistency, and hence the weakness, in its position. On the one hand, Appellee's position depends upon calling the document a warranty, because only then can it argue that the cause of action accrued upon tender of delivery. On the other hand, Appellee argues that the "warranty" promises nothing about the condition or performance of the car, but is simply a promise to repair or replace defective parts. If that were the case, then the cause of action would not accrue until the promise to repair were breached.

We recognize that the document does not create a classic warranty that fits neatly within the UCC view of warranties. Although it is a "promise made by the seller to the buyer which relates to the goods," 13 Pa.C.S. § 2313(a)(1), ... it does not "express[ly] warran[t] that the goods shall conform to the ... promise." (emphasis added). However, even if "repair or replace" warranties are viewed as remedies rather than as warranties, they do not fit strictly into the conceptual framework established by the provisions of the UCC, and a conceptually satisfactory resolution cannot be achieved. See generally Klinger, A Tangled Web, 89 Dick.L.Rev. at 943–950 (pointing out difficulty in distinguishing between limited warranty and limited remedy and in applying warranty and remedy provisions of UCC to "repair or replace" warranties). We also note that, although "repair or replace" warranties are not traditional warranties, they do fit within the modern concept of warranty. For example, the federal Magnuson–Moss Warranty Act includes in its definition of "warranty"

> any undertaking in writing in connection with the sale by a supplier of a consumer product to refund, repair, replace, or take other remedial action with respect to such product in the event that such product fails to meet the specifications set forth in the undertaking ...

15 U.S.C. § 2301(6)(B).

Furthermore, we will not permit Appellee and other sellers who draft similar documents to escape the consequences of presenting them to the consumer as "extended warranties." There can be little question that the consumer will consider the length of any warranty offered in determining whether to purchase a particular vehicle: The consumer naturally would believe that the longer the warranty, the greater the protection, and hence, the better the value, he or she is receiving. If Appellee's position were to prevail, the protection afforded the buyer during the latter part of a warranty approaching four years would be largely illusory, as the buyer would have a very short period of time in which to bring a cause of action for breach. Moreover, the longer-term protection afforded by a warranty extending beyond four years would be completely illusory.

Finally, reading the express warranty as one that "explicitly extends to future performance of the goods" will do no violence to the purposes of § 2725. Sellers will still be able to determine the time period for which they should maintain their records, simply by adding the limitation period to the warranty period. In addition, nothing in our analysis would prevent the parties from reducing the period of limitation in accordance with § 2725(a), which provides that "[b]y the original agreement the parties may reduce the period of limitation to not less than one year but may not extend it," provided, of course, that the period is reduced in a way that is not unconscionable.

Because we find that the express warranty "explicitly extends to future performance of the goods" for purposes of applying 13 Pa.C.S. § 2725, we find that the cause of action alleging breach of that warranty was timely filed and reverse the decision of the Superior Court with respect to Count One of the Complaint. We express no opinion, however, as to whether a cause of action has been stated or as to the appropriate remedy for breach of the express warranty.

Although we find the express warranty to explicitly extend to future performance of the goods, we cannot find that the implied warranties of merchantability and fitness for a particular purpose so extend. The warranty contains the following language: "ANY IMPLIED WARRANTY OF MERCHANTABILITY OR FITNESS FOR A PARTICULAR PURPOSE APPLICABLE TO THIS CAR IS LIMITED IN DURATION TO THE DURATION OF THIS WRITTEN WARRANTY." We do not read this language as explicitly extending the terms of any implied warranties, because the document states that any implied warranties are of a duration no longer than that of the express warranty and not that they are of a duration equal to that of the express warranty. The quoted language does not create implied warranties, because such warranties are created not by contract language but by operation of law in certain circumstances. See 13 Pa.C.S. §§ 2314 and 2315. The legal effect of the quoted language is merely to limit the protection that the law might otherwise impose. Therefore, it cannot be read as the type of language that "explicitly extends to future performance" for purposes of § 2725(b). In addition, the great weight of authority takes the position that an implied warranty, by nature, cannot "explicitly" extend to future performance. . . . Anno., What Constitutes Warranty Explicitly Extending to "Future Performance" for Purposes of UCC § 2–725(2), 93 A.L.R.3d 690, § 2 (collecting cases).

Because the implied warranties do not explicitly extend to future performance of the car, we conclude that Counts Two and Three of the complaint, alleging breach of implied warranties, were filed too late.

Accordingly, we reverse the decision of the Superior Court as to Count One and affirm as to Counts Two and Three. The case is remanded to the Court of Common Pleas of Allegheny County for further proceedings consistent with this opinion.

■ LARSEN, JUSTICE, dissenting.

I dissent. I would hold that the implied warranties of merchantability and fitness for a particular purpose also extend to the future performance of the vehicle because these implied warranties are expressly linked temporally to the express warranty by the following language contained in the express warranty at issue: "ANY IMPLIED WARRANTY OF MERCHANTABILITY OR FITNESS FOR A PARTICULAR PURPOSE APPLICABLE

TO THIS CAR IS LIMITED IN DURATION TO THE DURATION OF THIS WRITTEN WARRANTY." Accordingly, I would reverse the decision of the Superior Court as to Counts One, Two and Three, and remand to the Court of Common Pleas.

■ ZAPPALA, JUSTICE, dissenting.

I am compelled to dissent from the opinion of the Court because I believe a number of serious flaws in the reasoning lead the Court to an incorrect result.

First, the majority finds that the warranty in this case, by specifying a 12 month/12,000 mile duration, "explicitly extends to future performance of the goods." I do not follow the logic. Granted, a warranty that explicitly extends to future performance of goods will by definition in most cases specify a certain time period. It does not follow, however, that because a certain time period is specified a warranty necessarily applies to future performance of the goods. The scope of the warranty—what is promised— may be something other than a representation about how the goods will perform and yet still contain a specified time period.

Here, the promise is to repair or adjust defective parts for 12 months or 12,000 miles. This is not the same as a promise that the car and its parts will remain free of defects for 12 months or 12,000 miles. The latter promise "explicitly extends to future performance of the goods;" the former promise does not.

The majority applies a faulty grammatical analysis of the phrase "where a warranty explicitly extends to future performance of the goods" to expand the reach of 13 Pa.C.S. § 2725(b). It is true that the adverb "explicitly" modifies the verb "extends" and not the noun "warranty," and thus it is the extension that must be explicit. In this context, however, the verb "extend" does not merely describe temporal duration, as the majority suggests. Rather, it describes scope or application. The conceptual difficulty with this case is that the Appellant characterized the warranty as a representation "that said vehicle would be free from defects in material and workmanship, for at least 12 months or 12,000 miles," in order to bring this action within the exception of 13 Pa.C.S. § 2725(b), when in fact the warranty was not so worded.

Second, the majority, states that "the essence of Appellee's position is that the document here is not a warranty, but a promise to repair or replace defective parts." In doing so, it sets up a straw man, mis-characterizing the Appellee's position in order to more easily refute it. The essence of the Appellee's argument is not that the document is not a warranty, but that it is not a warranty within the definition of 13 Pa.C.S. § 2313.[1]

---

1. The majority also errs in perceiving an internal inconsistency in the appellee's argument based on its erroneous characterization of the argument. The appellee argues that if the warranty is construed as a promise about the quality or condition of the car, it does not "explicitly extend to future performance," therefore an action under that theory had to be commenced within four years of the date of delivery. If, however, the warranty is construed as a promise to repair, I believe the Appellee would concede that the

In the Uniform Commercial Code, the term "warranty" is given a very specific definition. "Any affirmation of fact or promise made by the seller to the buyer which relates to the goods and becomes a basis of the bargain creates an express warranty that the goods shall conform to the affirmation or promise." 13 Pa.C.S. § 2313(a)(1) (emphasis added). Likewise, "[a]ny description of the goods which is made a part of the bargain creates an express warranty that the goods shall conform to the description," 13 Pa.C.S. § 2313(a)(2), and "[a]ny sample or model which is made part of the basis of the bargain creates an express warranty that the whole of the goods shall conform to the sample or model." 13 Pa.C.S. § 2313(a)(3).

A warranty, in this sense, establishes as a term of the agreement certain qualities of the goods being sold. If the goods actually delivered do not possess such qualities, the buyer has remedies for breach of warranty. It is thus entirely sensible that in setting out when a cause of action accrues, the Code states that "[a] breach of warranty occurs when tender of delivery is made, except that where a warranty explicitly extends to future performance of the goods and discovery of the breach must await the time of such performance the cause of action accrues when the breach is or should have been discovered." 13 Pa.C.S. § 2725(b). Since a warranty as defined by the Code is a promise as to qualities of the goods, if the goods, when tendered, possess the qualities promised, the warranty has been satisfied; if the goods, when tendered, do not possess the promised qualities, the warranty has been breached. In the limited case where the promise is that the goods will have certain qualities, or will perform in a certain way, at a time beyond when the goods are delivered, it cannot be determined at the time of delivery whether the goods possess the promised qualities. Because the promise endures over a period of time, whether a breach has occurred can only be determined when the specified time has passed.

Here, in the document captioned "1982 Chevrolet New Car Limited Warranty", the seller did not promise that the car would perform without defect for twelve months or 12,000 miles; in fact, the "Limited Warranty" contained no specific promise or affirmation of fact relating to the car. The only promise was that any repairs and adjustments to correct defects in materials or workmanship would be made free of charge during the specified period. This promise related to the seller's obligations under the contract, not to the quality of the goods. Although this document is a warranty in the general sense in that it guarantees or promises something, it is not a warranty as to the quality of the car or as to its performance.

Indeed, as the majority notes, "although 'repair and replace' warranties are not traditional warranties, they do fit within the modern concept of warranty," and a document such as the one involved here fits within the definition of "warranty" under the federal Magnuson–Moss Warranty Act, 15 U.S.C. § 2301(6)(b). This, I believe, is the ultimate source of the difficulty in this case. General Motors, selling its product in a national

four year limitation would not have commenced until this promise had been breach-   ed, if the complaint had alleged this as the basis for the action.

market, produces a standard document that includes a promise to repair or adjust defective parts. Under federal law, such a promise is properly captioned a warranty. Unfortunately, it does not "fit[ ] neatly within the UCC view of warranties." When an action is later brought under the UCC, GM suffers the consequence of having the "difficulty interpreting the agreement" be resolved against it, the drafter.

I think it entirely unjust to apply this rule of construction in these circumstances. As noted above, the Appellant mischaracterized the nature of the warranty in order to bring it within the exception to the limitations period under § 2725(b) of the UCC. To my mind, the Appellant is as much responsible for the "difficulty interpreting the agreement" as the Appellee. Had the action been brought under the Magnuson–Moss Warranty Act, 15 U.S.C. § 2310(d)(1)(A), the "difficulty" would not have arisen. The warranty could then have been analyzed as a promise as to the Appellee's conduct and a determination made whether the failure, or practical inability, to repair the vehicle constituted a breach of that promise.

This analysis also avoids the "problem" identified by the majority with respect to warranties of duration longer than four years. Because such warranties set forth promises as to the seller's conduct during a specified period of time, any breach of such promise will occur, and therefore any cause of action for breach of such promise will accrue, only after the lapse of time. Thus, for example, under a seven year/seventy thousand mile "repair and adjust" warranty, if a defect appeared in the fifth year, there would no longer be an action for breach of warranty to claim that the car was not of the quality bargained for, but the seller would still be obligated by the terms of the contract to make the necessary repairs or adjustments. Refusal to do so would be actionable as a breach, the cause of action accruing at the time of the breach and the limitation period extending four years from that point.

In the case presently before the Court, if the defect was such that the car delivered was not in fact possessed of a quality that had been bargained for, a breach of warranty action pursuant to the UCC could have been maintained. Such claim, however, would have to have been brought within four years of the date of delivery. Because this action was not commenced within four years of delivery, the Appellant could no longer make such a claim. Instead, the Appellant attempted to make the seller's promise into something that it plainly is not—a guarantee of the future performance of the car—in order to bring the action within the exception of the statutory limitation period.

Had the Appellant alleged that the seller breached the promise that it had made, the action would have been timely and the grant of summary judgment would have been improper. The Appellant made no such allegation. It was not alleged that the seller refused to make repairs or needed adjustments to correct defects in material or workmanship; nor was it alleged that any such refusal was the cause of the Appellant's damages.

By obligingly adopting the Appellant's transmogrification of this action in order to secure a remedy, the majority has, I fear, thrown the entire law of warranty under the Code in Pennsylvania into confusion.

I dissent and would affirm the grant of summary judgment.

NOTES

(1) Warranty or Remedial Promise. The differences between the analyses in the majority opinion and the dissenting opinion of Justice Zappala are largely differences in characterization of the claim. The majority concluded that the claim was for breach of the manufacturer's express warranty. Justice Zappala decided that the manufacturer's warranty was not a warranty of quality, but was rather a remedial promise that bore the caption of "warranty." What is the consequence, in this case, of the way that this disagreement was resolved?

If the majority had accepted Justice Zappala's view, to what remedy would plaintiff be entitled? Did General Motors breach the remedial promise? Would repair of the burned-out remains have been practical?

What remedy did plaintiff seek in this case? Could that remedy be granted on the basis of the promise to repair? The majority concluded that the plaintiff's express warranty claim was not time-barred. Did the majority conclude that there was an express warranty and that the warranty had been breached?

(2) Rejection of Precedent. A footnote in the majority, after reviewing prior decisions of several courts, including the Alabama Supreme Court's decision in *Tittle*, declared that the court would decline to follow the lead of other courts because "we believe that the other courts' reasoning is flawed and would lead to absurd results of extended to its logical conclusion." Was it necessary for the majority to declare its opposition to decisions like *Tittle*? Could those cases be distinguished from *Nationwide Insurance*?

(3) Duration of Implied Warranties. Justice Larsen's brief dissent, based on the mysterious provision in § 108(b) of the Magnuson–Moss Warranty Act, concluded that a term in the manufacturer's Limited Warranty had the legal effect of postponing, for a year, commencement of the remote buyer's cause of action for breach of implied warranties of quality. The Limited Warranty provided:

> ANY IMPLIED WARRANTY OF MERCHANTABILITY OR FITNESS FOR A PARTICULAR PURPOSE APPLICABLE TO THIS CAR IS LIMITED IN DURATION TO THE DURATION OF THIS WRITTEN WARRANTY.

This sentence, which clearly refers to implied warranties of quality, does not mention the period of limitations. It purports only to limit the "duration" of implied warranties.

The language in the Limited Warranty closely tracks the language in MMWA § 108(b). In most, if not all, limited warranties that have been provided by manufacturers since 1975, the same term has appeared. All of the lawyers who have drafted standard warranty forms for manufacturer clients have decided, it appears, that the term, which is permitted but not required by the MMWA, must have some value to their clients. By now, the term has appeared in untold numbers of limited warranties. What did all those lawyers think that the term means? If they had an inkling that the term might mean that their clients were exposed to more than the four-year limitations period, would they have incorporated the term in the limited warranty forms?[9]

What are the possible meanings of the mysterious concept of duration of an implied warranty? Some years ago, I offered the following analysis:[10]

The notion of limiting duration connotes the shortening of a period of time. Implied warranties of quality do not have any period of existence. An implied warranty is breached or is not breached in the scintilla of time that marks tender of delivery of the goods. A time period begins to run from that moment, the period of the statute of limitations. But plainly an implied warranty is not some kind of continuing promise . . .

At least five possible meanings might be ascribed to terms limiting the duration of implied warranties.

1.   [S]hortening of the statute of limitations period.

2.   [L]engthening the statute of limitations period.

3.   [Defining] the time within which a buyer must give notice of breach or be barred from any remedy under [UCC 2–607(3)].

4.   [Defining] a period of time after which a buyer cannot complain of non-conformities that later come to light even though they could not reasonably have been discovered earlier.

5.   [Defining] a time during which buyer's remedy is to seek seller's repair or other promised post-delivery relief. . . .

None of the suggested meanings . . . is entirely satisfactory as a matter of statutory construction. . . . In my view, the fifth meaning comes closest to the spirit of the . . . Act. It also makes sense in the marketplace.

What are your views?

---

9. Drafters of manufacturers' limited warranties were evidently aware that their clients were not obligated to remote buyers for implied warranties of quality. We considered this issue in Section 5. The drafters of the standard forms tried to avoid language that would clearly acknowledge that implied warranties of quality existed. The duration-limitation term applies to "*any* implied war-

ranty," a verbal formulation that left room for the argument that none existed, but, if any implied warranty were found, it had a limited duration.

10. C. Reitz, Consumer Product Warranties Under Federal and State Laws 82, 86, 95 (2d ed. 1987).

Anderson v. Crestliner, Inc.

Court of Appeals of Minnesota, 1997.
564 N.W.2d 218.

■ KALITOWSKI, JUDGE.

Appellants Barton and Bonnie Anderson challenge the district court's determination that their action against respondent Crestliner, Inc. was barred by the four-year statute of limitations under Minn. Stat. § 336.2–725 (1996).

FACTS

On April 24, 1989, the Andersons purchased a 21–foot Crestliner fiberglass power boat from respondent that came with a 1989 Crestliner warranty that states in relevant part:

Crestliner warrants to the first purchaser at retail that each new boat of Crestliner's manufacture shall be free from any defect in material or workmanship according to the following guidelines.

* * * FIBERGLASS BOATS

The following warranties apply specifically to all fiberglass boats.

1. The warranty period for defects in material or workmanship of the hull and deck structure is 5 years.

EXCLUSIVE REMEDY UNDER CRESTLINER WARRANTY

As the original retail purchaser's sole and exclusive remedy under this warranty, Crestliner, will, at its option, repair or replace without charge any part or parts covered by this warranty and found to Crestliner's satisfaction, to be defective in material or workmanship upon examination at its factory, Little Falls, Minnesota.

Subsequently, appellants began to experience problems with the hull. On October 17, 1991, appellants made a complaint to respondent. In February1992, respondent's employees inspected the boat, but claimed not to have found any hull damage. After the inspection, representatives of respondent met with appellants and agreed to have the hull repaired, which was done in May 1992. On June 7, 1992, appellants complained to respondent regarding the boat, but were told that respondent would not spend any more money on it.

On April 11, 1994, appellants sent a letter to respondent demanding that respondent honor its warranty by repairing the hull. Respondent did not answer appellants' letter. On September 15, 1995, appellants brought a lawsuit against respondent, alleging breach of express warranty, breach of implied warranty, violation of the Magnuson–Moss Warranty Act, and negligence. The negligence claim was later dismissed by the district court. Upon respondent's motion, the district court granted summary judgment on the ground that appellants' action was barred by the four-year statute of limitations under Minn. Stat. § 336.2–725(1).

* * *

I.

... The district court concluded that the Crestliner warranty did not constitute a warranty extending to "future performance of the goods," but was only a repair or replacement commitment within a specified time. As such, the district court held appellants' action for breach of express warranty accrued when the boat was delivered on April 24, 1989, and that appellants' action was barred by the four-year statute of limitations because they did not file the complaint until September 15, 1995.

Appellants argue the district court erred in failing to consider the first paragraph of the warranty together with the warranty language for fiberglass boats. We agree.

The first paragraph of the Crestliner warranty provides that respondent warrants to the first purchaser at retail that each new boat "shall be free from any defect in material or workmanship according to the following guidelines." (Emphasis added.) One of the guidelines for fiberglass boats is that "the warranty period for defects in material or workmanship of the hull and deck structure is 5 years." Reading the warranty as a whole as required by the warranty itself, respondent explicitly warrants to "the first purchaser at retail" that each new fiberglass boat's hull and deck structure shall be free from any defects in material or workmanship for five years.

The warranty in question is similar to the warranty in Church of the Nativity of Our Lord v. WatPro, Inc., 491 N.W.2d 1, 6 (Minn.1992). In that case, the supreme court addressed the question of whether a warranty promising to maintain the roof in a watertight condition for a period of ten years was a warranty that explicitly extended to future performance under Minn. Stat. § 336.2–725. The court held that the guarantees "extended to the future performance of the goods, expressly warranting that the roofs would remain watertight for ten years."

Here, the Crestliner warranty guarantees to the first purchaser at retail that each new fiberglass boat's hull and deck structure shall be free from any defects in material or workmanship for five years. Like the warranty in WatPro, Inc., this warranty explicitly extends to future performance. See ... Docteroff v. Barra Corp. of America, Inc., 282 N.J. Super. 230, 243, 659 A.2d 948, 955 (1995) (holding that a warranty extended to future performance when the supplier guaranteed that it would maintain the roof in a watertight condition for five years).

The following reasoning in Docteroff is instructive in determining whether the warranty here extends to future performance:

There can be little question that the consumer will consider the length of any warranty offered in determining whether to purchase a particular vehicle: The consumer naturally would believe that the longer the warranty, the greater the protection, and hence, the better the value, he or she is receiving. If Appellee's position were to prevail, the protection afforded the buyer during the latter part of a warranty approaching four years would be largely illusory, as the buyer would have a very short period of time in which to bring a cause of action for breach. Moreover, the longer-term protection afforded by a warranty extending beyond four years would be completely illusory.

Docteroff, 282 N.J. Super. at 242, 659 A.2d at 954 (quoting Nationwide Ins. Co. v. General Motors Corp., 533 Pa. 423, 625 A.2d 1172, 1178 (1993)) (emphasis added). Here, the district court's holding that appellants' warranty expired four years after the delivery of the boat is inconsistent with the express language providing for a five-year warranty period.

Further, the district court erred when it construed the warranty as a repair or replacement commitment, rather than a warranty of future performance. A warranty of future performance is different from a repair or replacement warranty. Ontario Hydro v. Zallea Sys., Inc., 569 F. Supp. 1261, 1266 (D.Del.1983).

> A warranty of future performance of a product must expressly provide some form of guarantee that the product will perform in the future as promised. * * *
>
> On the other hand, a repair or replacement warranty does not warrant how the goods will perform in the future. Rather, such a warranty simply provides that if a product fails or becomes defective, the seller will replace or repair within a stated period.
>
> Thus, the key distinction between these two kinds of warranties is that a repair or replacement warranty merely provides a remedy if the product becomes defective, while a warranty for future performance guarantees the performance of the product itself for a stated period of time. In the former case, the buyer is relying upon the warranty merely as a method by which a defective product can be remedied which has no effect upon his ability to discover a breach. In the latter instance, the buyer is relying upon the warranty as a guarantee of future performance and therefore has no opportunity to discover the breach until the future performance has been tested.

Id. "The presence of language limiting the remedy to replacement of defective materials, by itself, is [not] determinative of the exact nature of the warranties in question." Shatterproof Glass Corp., 697 F.2d at 823.

In holding that the Crestliner warranty does not extend to future performance, the district court relied on Zallea Sys., Inc. and Crouch v. General Elec. Co., 699 F. Supp. 585 (S.D.Miss.1988). The court's reliance on these two cases is misplaced. In Zallea Sys., Inc., the warranty provides:

> If at any time up to twelve (12) months after the date of Acceptance of the Equipment by the Engineer, any defect or deficiency should appear due to faulty workmanship, material or design, or if the Equipment or any part thereof fails to meet the requirements of the

Contract, the Company shall restore the Equipment to satisfactory operating condition * * *.

569 F. Supp. at 1264. Nowhere in this warranty does Zallea warrant how the equipment will perform in the future. Rather, the warranty provides a remedy for repair within one year of acceptance if any defects appear as specified in the warranty. This warranty is different from the Crestliner warranty that explicitly promises that the hull and deck structure of each new fiberglass boat shall be free from any defects in material and workmanship for a period of five years.

Similarly, the warranty in Crouch is distinguishable from the Crestliner warranty. In Crouch, the warranty states that the helicopter engines "will, at the time delivery [sic] be free from defects in material and workmanship." Id. at 593 (emphasis added). This "warranty of material and workmanship" does not expressly guarantee the future performance of the helicopter engines; rather, it simply warrants the condition of the goods at the time of delivery. Id. at 594 (emphasis added). In contrast, the Crestliner warranty does not just guarantee the condition of the boat at the time of sale, as argued by respondent. Rather, it promises to the first purchaser at retail that each new boat shall be free from any defect in material or workmanship according to the guidelines set out in the warranty.

II.

Respondent further argues appellants' claims are time-barred even if the Crestliner warranty extends to future performance because appellants commenced this action more than four years after the breach was or should have been discovered. Respondent contends appellants knew or should have known of the breach in 1989, but no later than the summer of 1991. We disagree.

In WatPro, Inc., the supreme court stated that where there is a warranty that explicitly extends to future performance,

> the cause of action accrues and the statute of limitations begins to run "when the plaintiff discovers or should have discovered the defendant's refusal or inability to maintain the goods as warranted in the contract."

WatPro, Inc., 491 N.W.2d at 6. The court in WatPro, Inc. held the breach occurred when the distributor advised the building owner that the manufacturer's agent was unable or unwilling to honor its guaranty. Applying this holding here, the breach of warranty occurred on June 7, 1992, when respondent told appellants it was unwilling to spend more money on the boat. Appellants commenced this action on September 15, 1995, well within the four-year statutory period under Minn. Stat. § 336.2–725.

DECISION

The district court erred in holding that the Crestliner warranty does not explicitly extend to future performance and in dismissing appellants' action as untimely.

Reversed.

INTERNATIONAL SALES LAW

(A) NOTICE OF BREACH

Assume that *M.K. Associates* had been an international sales transaction governed by CISG. Would the result have been the same or different? See CISG 39(1). The answer seems reasonably clear. Like the UCC, CISG imposes a notice requirement with comparable elements of "reasonable time" and buyer's discovery. Instead of "barred from any remedy" CISG uses "loses the right to rely on a lack of conformity." Is there a different meaning?

A perceptive reader of CISG 39(1), familiar with the UCC, would observe that the CISG demands more in the content of a buyer's notice than "of breach." How much factual detail must buyers include to "specify . . . the nature of the lack of conformity"? If multiple non-conformities are discovered, must each be detailed? When a second non-conformity surfaces after a notice has been given, must another notice be sent?

Having worked through the CISG provision and made comparison to the UCC, one might stop the legal analysis. To do so would be to commit a grave error. See CISG 44. What could explain drafting in this style?[11]

The danger continues beyond noticing that CISG 44 modifies CISG 39(1). On the face of CISG 44, a reader might conclude that relief from loss of the right to rely on a lack of conformity is available only if a buyer has not yet paid the full price. "[T]he buyer may reduce the price in accordance with article 50 . . . ." When one turns to CISG 50, however, one learns that a buyer can "reduce" a price "whether or not the price has already been paid." In short, a buyer who is excused under CISG 44 has not only the right to set off damages against the unpaid price, but also has an affirmative right to recover some or all of the price paid.

Fortunately these "traps" are not typical of the drafting of the CISG. However, they should alert those who use the Convention to the need for great care in its application.

The CISG imposes an outside limit on the time for a buyer's notice to the seller specifying the nature of the lack of non-conformity. Buyers must give notice within two years from the date the goods were "actually handed over" to them, whether or not the buyers discovered or ought to have discovered the non-conformities ("in any event"). CISG 39(2). An exception exists if this time limit is "inconsistent with a contractual period of

---

11. In the last days of the diplomatic conference that produced the Convention, there was a major inter-regional disagreement regarding the notice requirement in CISG 39. Proposals by developing countries to relax the requirement had not been adopted. The proponents of modifying CISG 39 were sufficiently dissatisfied that the nec- essary two-thirds vote in favor of the Convention was in jeopardy. A compromise solution was proposed and became CISG 44. It was made a separate article so that the added provision would apply also to the notice requirements of CISG 43(1). J. Honnold, Uniform Law for International Sales § 261 (3d ed. 1999).

guarantee." Note that the CISG 44 excuse provision is not available against the CISG 39(2) time bar.

The UCC has no provision comparable to CISG 39(2).

FINAL AWARD IN CASE NO. 5713 OF 1989

International Chamber of Commerce 15 Y.B. Comm. Arb. 70 (1990)

Facts

In 1979, the parties concluded three contracts for the sale of a product according to certain contract specifications. The buyer paid 90% of the price payable under each of the contracts upon presentation of the shipping documents, as contractually agreed.

The product delivered pursuant to the first and third contracts met the contract specifications. The conformity of the second consignment was disputed prior to its shipment. When the product was again inspected upon arrival, it was found that it did not meet the contract specifications. The product was eventually sold by the buyer to third parties at considerable loss, after having undergone a certain treatment to make it more saleable.

The seller initiated arbitration proceedings to recover the 10% balance remaining due under the contracts. The buyer filed a counterclaim alleging that the seller's claim should be set off against the amounts which the buyer estimates to be payable to the buyer by the seller, i.e., the direct losses, financing costs, lost profits and interest.

Excerpt

I. Applicable Law

The contract contains no provisions regarding the substantive law. Accordingly that law has to be determined by the Arbitrators in accordance with Art. 13(3) of the ICC rules.[12] Under that article, the Arbitrators will "apply the law designated as the proper law by the rule of conflicts which they deem appropriate."

The contract is between a Seller and a Buyer [of different nationalities] for delivery [in a third country]. The sale was f.o.b. so that the transfer of risks to the Buyer took place in [the country of the Seller]. [The country of the Seller] accordingly appears as being the jurisdiction to which the sale is most closely related.

The Hague Convention on the law applicable to international sales of goods dated 15 June 1955 (Art. 3) regarding sales contracts, refers as

---

12. Art. 13 of the ICC Rules of 1975 (Not amended by the 1988 amendments) reads in relevant part:

3. The parties shall be free to determine the law to be applied by the arbitrator to the merits of the dispute. In the absence of any indication by the parties as to the applicable law, the arbitrator

shall apply the law designated as the proper law by the rule of conflict which he deems appropriate.

(. . . .)

5. In all cases the arbitrator shall take account of the provisions of the contract and the relevant trade usages.

governing law to the law of the Seller's current residence....[13] [The country of the Buyer] has adhered to the Hague Convention, not [the country of the Seller]. However, the general trend in conflicts of law is to apply the domestic law of the current residence of the debtor of the essential undertaking arising under the contract. That debtor in a sales contract is the Seller. Based on those combined findings, [the law of the country of the Seller] appears to be the proper law governing the Contract between the Seller and the Buyer.

As regards the applicable rules of [the law of the country of the Seller], the Arbitrators have relied on the Parties' respective statements on the subject and on the information obtained by the Arbitrators from an independent consultant.... The Arbitrators, in accordance with the last paragraph of Art. 13 of the ICC rules, will also take into account the "relevant trade usages."

II.   Admissibility of the Counterclaim

(a) Under [the law of the country of the Seller]

* * *

(b) Under the international trade usages prevailing in the international sale of goods

The Tribunal finds that there is no better source to determine the prevailing trade usages than the terms of the United Nations Convention on the International Sale of Goods of 11 April 1980, usually called "the Vienna Convention." This is so even though neither [the country of the Buyer] nor [the country of the Seller] are parties to that Convention. If they were, the Convention might be applicable to this case as a matter of law and not only as reflecting the trade usage.

The Vienna Convention, which has been given effect to in 17 countries, may be fairly taken to reflect the generally recognized usages regarding the matter of the non-conformity of goods in international sales. Art. 38(1) of the Convention puts the onus on the Buyer to "examine the goods or cause them to be examined promptly." The Buyer should then notify the Seller of the non-conformity of the goods within a reasonable period as of the moment he noticed or should have noticed the defect; otherwise he forfeits his right to raise a claim based on the said non-conformity. Art. 39(1) specifies in this respect that:

> In any event the buyer shall lose the right to rely on a lack of conformity of the goods if he has not given notice thereof to the seller within a period of two years from the date on which the goods were

---

13. Art. 3 of the Hague Convention on the Law Applicable to the International Sales of Goods reads in pertinent part:

In default of a law declared applicable by the parties under the conditions provided in the preceding article, a sale shall be governed by the domestic law of the country in which the vendor has his habitual residence at the time when he received the order....

handed over, unless the lack of conformity constituted a breach of a guarantee covering a longer period.

In the circumstances, the Buyer had the shipment examined within a reasonable time-span since [an expert] was requested to inspect the shipment even before the goods had arrived. The Buyer should also be deemed to have given notice of the defects within a reasonable period, that is eight days after the expert's report had been published.

Tribunal finds that, in the circumstances of the case, the Buyer has complied with the above-mentioned requirements of the Vienna Convention. These requirements are considerably more flexible than those provided under [the law of the country of the Seller]. This law, by imposing extremely short and specific time requirements in respect of the giving of the notices of defects by the Buyer to the Seller appears to be an exception on this point to the generally accepted trade usages.

In any case, the Seller should be regarded as having forfeited its right to invoke any non-compliance with the requirements of Arts. 38 and 39 of the Vienna Convention since Art. 40 states that the Seller cannot rely on Arts. 38 and 39, "if the lack of conformity relates to facts of which he knew, or of which he could not have been unaware, and which he did not disclose." Indeed, this appears to be the case, since it clearly transpires from the file and the evidence that the Seller knew and could not be unaware [of the non-conformity of the consignment to] contract specifications.

* * *

UNCITRAL CLOUT Abstract No. 285

Oberlandesgericht, Koblenz, Germany, 1998.

A Moroccan buyer, plaintiff, purchased raw material for manufacturing plastic PVC tubes (dryblend) from a German seller, defendant. When the buyer discovered that the dryblend was not suitable for use in its manufacturing facilities, the buyer claimed lack of quality and sued for damages.

The court dismissed the claim. It held that the buyer had lost its right to rely on the lack of conformity according to article 39(1) of the CISG. Giving notice to the seller three weeks after delivery was held as being too late. The court said that, if trial processing was necessary to examine the quality of the goods, a period of one week for examination and another week for giving notice would have been reasonable. As to the buyer's argument that it had been unable to examine the goods any earlier because the manufacturing facilities were still under construction, the court held that this did not constitute a reasonable excuse (article 44 CISG). Such an excuse demanded that the buyer acted with reasonable care in providing for prompt examination of the goods, which included the timely supply of machinery necessary for trial processing. The buyer failed to provide particulars that it had acted with such due care. Moreover, disorganisation on the part of the buyer was not an aspect to be considered in determining the period practicable in the circumstances (article 38(1) CISG).

Since the seller was found not to have been aware of the fact that the dryblend was not suitable for producing plastic tubes in the buyer's manufacturing facilities, as the buyer had failed to inform the seller of the kind of equipment in use, the seller did not lose its right to rely on late notification (article 40 CISG). The court said that, although there would be a loss of the right to rely on late notification if the seller had had a duty to warn the buyer or provide additional information about the goods delivered, in this case there had been no such obligation.

NOTES

(1) Frequency of Litigation Involving CISG 39 and 44. Collections of CISG decisions contain a considerable number of cases in which CISG 39 and 44 have been applied. Courts and arbitrators have been rigorous in narrow interpretations of "reasonable time" under CISG 39(1). See the Pace University Law School data base at www.cisg.law.pace.edu.

(2) Waiver by Seller. A court may find that a seller has waived the right to rely on CISG 39. An Austrian buyer sued a German seller for damages caused by surface-protective film that left residues of glue on polished high-grade steel products. After buyer gave seller notice of of the nonconformity of the film, seller and buyer entered into negotiations as to the amount of damages and the manner in which the damages should be paid. Negotiations continued over 15 months but failed to settle the dispute. In the suit, seller contended that buyer had not given timely notice under CISG 39. The court held that seller had waived the defense. UNCITRAL abstract no. 270, Bundesgerichtshof, Germany, 1998.

(B) PERIOD OF LIMITATIONS

CISG contains no period of limitations. That is found in an entirely separate convention, the United Nations Convention on the Limitation Period of the International Sale of Goods. A convention was required to replace the greatly diverse limitation ("prescription") periods and subordinate rules, such as rules on "tolling," among various nations' domestic laws. A sufficient number of nations had ratified this Convention for it to take effect in 1988. The United States is a party to the Convention, which is in force in 23 nations.[14]

Like UCC 2–725, the Convention sets a four-year limitation period.

Article 11 of the Limitation Period Convention contains a provision on extended warranties that differs from the analogous UCC provision:

> If the seller has given an express undertaking relating to the goods which is stated to have effect for a certain period of time, whether expressed in terms of a specific period of time or otherwise, the

---

14. See J. Honnold, Uniform Law for International Sales § 261.1 (3d ed. 1999).

limitation period in respect of any claim arising from the undertaking shall commence on the date on which the buyer notifies the seller of the fact on which the claim is based, but not later than on the date of the expiration of the period of the undertaking.

Is the Convention provision better than that in the UCC?

SECTION 8.   ALTERNATIVE TO WARRANTY LAW AS A MEANS OF ASSURING QUALITY OF GOODS

The law of quality warranties and their enforcement are a kind of *ex post* response to market failures. The question we wish to raise in this Section is whether society would be better served by other mechanisms for assuring the "optimal" quality of goods. Alternatives may include legal mechanisms for quality assurance that are *ex ante*, i.e., that address quality assurance in the production and marketing of goods.

Warranties of quality are enforced after buyers discover that the goods delivered or tendered by sellers are deficient in some respect. Commonly, buyers make this discovery after the goods have been put to use, if the buyer is a consumer or processor, or resold, if the buyer is a dealer in goods of that kind. Certain economic efficiency is attained in that only qualitatively poor goods are subject to warranty enforcement. Buyers have the risk of discovery of any defects in purchased goods and the burden of seeking compensation for their losses. To the extent that aggrieved buyers seek and obtain damages, the costs of marketing suboptimal quality goods is transferred back to sellers; the prospect of this occurring may induce sellers to avoid or minimize these costs by use of better designs or better methods of quality control so that defective goods do not enter the market.

Not all aggrieved buyers will seek and obtain relief for breach of warranties of quality. Various practical reasons for this exist. Moreover, transaction costs of such *ex post* quality assurance, for buyers and sellers, are high. The harm suffered may be so small in relation to transaction costs that the aggrieved party has no incentive to pursue a contractual or legal remedy. The harm suffered may be so great that a seller lacks the financial resources to pay. The question to be considered is whether there are means, better than warranty law, for reaching the desired outcome of optimal quality in good sold. Can the law induce an *ex ante* response by sellers to improve the quality of their goods?

The market already creates powerful *ex ante* economic incentives for sellers to generate higher product quality. To the extent that buyers are informed about aspects of quality and are capable of appreciating their significance, better quality products will command a premium. In theory, sellers will be induced to supply goods of a quality at which the marginal cost for further improvement begins to exceed the marginal benefits to buyers, and the market equilibrium will be efficient.

This economic theory fails if buyers are not adequately informed about aspects of quality or lack ability to appreciate their significance *before purchase*. Economists refer to this as a problem of imperfect information. If buyers cannot cheaply assess the quality of goods for sale, willingness to buy and pay will not adjust to improvements in quality, and the economic incentive to raise quality will be diminished. Because better quality is generally costly to produce, poorer-quality products can outcompete higher-quality products, and the market equilibrium may result in production of suboptimal low-quality products exclusively.

To some extent, markets respond to the problem of imperfect information without the intervention of regulatory law. The development of marketing reputation through word-of-mouth and through investment in brand-name capital is one way that some manufacturers have gained a stake in setting and maintaining quality. Sellers may transmit useful quality related information to potential buyers through advertising, if it is deemed credible. Independent agencies, such as Consumer Reports or Good Housekeeping or Underwriter's Laboratories, may supply useful information as to the quality of goods in the marketplace. For products that are repeatedly purchased, buyers may reward sellers of products perceived—in past use—to be higher in quality. Even sellers' quality warranties may be part of an *ex ante* market response, if prospective buyers perceive the seller's willingness to issue a warranty as a signal of the product's quality.

These market responses, separately or collectively, do not fully solve the problem of imperfect information. One alternative solution would be to create a system for close evaluation o manufacturers' production facilities and processes under standards developed, promulgated, and administered by third-party organizations of unquestioned independence and integrity. Certification of a manufacturer would depend upon finding that its quality-assurance system meets prescribed standards and provides buyers objective evidence on which to base their choice of suppliers. Establishment of such a system probably requires the participation of a government, or set of governments, to assure that it is independent of the manufacturers or sellers and capable of designing and administering quality-assurance standards.

ISO 9000 Standard Series

An example of such an organization is the International Organization for Standardization (ISO), an international body consisting of the representatives of all nations who wish to participate. The impetus for establishment of the ISO in 1947 came from the United Nations. More than 90 countries are represented in ISO. Each nation delegates its own representative to the ISO; the United States is represented by a private entity, the American National Standards Institute, assisted by the American Society for Testing Methods and the American Society for Quality Control. In recent years, after abandoning its earlier practice of requiring unanimity for the creation of standards, the ISO has undertaken a major initiative in quality assurance. The ISO 9000/10011 standard requires the management of a company seeking ISO certification to document formally its policy on quality, to ensure that this policy is understood by all concerned with the company, and to take appropriate steps to see that the policy is fully implemented.

ISO 9000 takes the mystery out of quality. It defines quality chapter by chapter, verse by verse, thereby providing a clearly defined path to set up a world-class quality assurance system that is elemental in its logic and application.

The standards do not apply to products. Instead, they provide assurance—primarily through a system of internal and external audits—that a certified company has a quality system in place that will enable it to meet its published quality standards. . . .

A key characteristic of ISO certification is that it requires third-party registration. The third party in this case is an authorized assessor or registrar who conducts an independent audit of an organization's quality system. . . . If it passes the audit, the system is registered and certified. Regular maintenance audits are conducted to ensure that the system doesn't degrade.

Until recently there were no accredited U.S. registrars, so at Du Pont we've worked with such European firms as the British Standards Institute and Lloyds Register, which are government-accredited in Britain. However, recently an accreditor of U.S. registrars, the Registrar Accreditation Board, was established. It is a subsidiary of the American Society for Quality Control.[1]

A set of ISO standards is being used by the U.S. Department of Defense and by NATO. More importantly, the European Union adopted ISO standards to provide a universal framework for quality assurance within that 15–nation economic area. More than half of European manufacturing companies had received ISO certification by October 1991. "Although U.S. companies were initially slow to react to the ISO 9000/10011 standards, the number of U.S. facilities seeking ISO registration is growing rapidly."[2]

ISO 9000 certification is not a requirement for selling goods in the private sector. Buyers in Europe and elsewhere are free to purchase goods from uncertified sources. However, if several suppliers are trying to land a contract, the one with ISO 9000 certification is likely to have a substantial competitive advantage. The situation is different in sales of goods to governments and public agencies; ISO certification may be mandatory:

Conforming to the standards of ISO 9000/10011 has quickly become a condition of doing business in many parts of the world. For example, firms seeking to sell products to government-controlled indus-

1. Hockman, The Last Barrier to the European Market, Wall Street Journal, Oct. 7, 1991.

2. C. Bell and J. Connaughton, New Global Standards May Guide Industry on Environmental Issues, National Law Journal, Sept. 6, 1993.

tries in Europe typically have to establish quality systems that meet ISO standards.[3]

3. Id. The authors note that the ISO has undertaken a series of global environmental standards.

CHAPTER 4

Execution of Sales Contracts: Manner, Time and Place of Sellers' and Buyers' Performances

Previous Chapters were concerned with the "what" (title and quality) and the "who" (privity) of sales transactions. This Chapter considers "when," "where," and "how" the parties execute the promises made in contracts of sale. Buyers and sellers may fix the terms of time, place and manner of performance by agreement. Terms may be set by express agreement or by implication from trade usage, course of dealing, or course of performance.

It is not uncommon for agreements to confer on one party discretion to determine certain matters regarding particulars of performance, perhaps within stated limits. Thus, an agreement may require seller to ship goods in March, the exact date to be determined by the seller. Under domestic United States law, when an agreement "leaves particulars of performance to be specified by one of the parties, ... specification must be made in good faith and within limits set by commercial reasonableness." UCC 2–311(1).

Buyers and sellers often fail to agree, even by implication, on time, place and manner of each party's performance. Such buyers and sellers look to the law to fill the gaps. One of the functions of modern commercial law is to provide a set of gap-fillers.

Section 1. Local Sales Transactions

Performance of sales contracts is relatively simple when the places of business or the residences of the buyers and sellers are in the same local area. Sellers' obligation is to hand over the goods and buyers' obligation is to pay the purchase price. When the parties are close enough that it is practical for them to meet, their contract obligations can be performed in face-to-face meetings where the goods and the money are exchanged. In the absence of agreement, the law determines where and when those meetings occur and what actions the parties are required to take there. Rules supplied by law are commonly referred to as "default rules."

Contractual terms on when, where and how sales contracts are to be executed are enforceable obligations. A party who fails, without excuse, to meet an obligation when due is in breach of contract, and the aggrieved party will have one or more legal remedies. The terms of parties' agreements or the law's default rules provide the normative standards against which to measure whether sellers' or buyers' acts or omissions were in breach of their obligation to execute sales contracts.

Domestic United States Law

Basic performance obligations and related default rules are stated by the UCC. The UCC provisions are found largely in Parts 3 and 5 of Article 2. You should look at those parts of the UCC to get a general sense of the matters that are covered.

Section 2–301 of the UCC states the general obligation of both parties:

The obligation of the seller is to transfer and deliver and that of the buyer is to accept and pay in accordance with the contract.

"Transfer" refers to title to the goods and "deliver" refers to the goods themselves. On the buyers' side, the general obligation to "pay" is coupled with the obligation to "accept" the goods. This purport of the obligation to "accept" is, on the surface, strange;[1] if sellers are paid, would they care whether buyers "accept" the goods? We will defer further consideration of that matter until the next Chapter.

The parties' 2–301 obligations are elaborated in the operational standards of *tender of delivery* and *tender of payment*. Tender connotes performance by the tendering party that satisfies its obligation and puts the other party in default if it fails to execute its obligation. See UCC 2–507(1) and 2–511(1). The UCC's default rules on time, place and manner of the parties' performance obligations use the concept of tender.

Sellers' Tender of Delivery of Goods. "Tender of delivery requires that the seller put and hold conforming goods at the buyer's disposition and give the buyer any notification reasonably necessary to enable him to take delivery." UCC 2–503(1). The "put and hold" formulation, which by implication excludes "let go," is the essence of the concept of tender of goods. Tender must be at a "reasonable hour" and tendered goods must be kept available for "the period reasonably necessary to enable the buyer to take possession." UCC 2–503(1)(a). "Tender" begins delivery, but effecting completed delivery usually requires a buyer's response.

Place of Sellers' Tender. If the agreement is silent, the default rule establishes the place of delivery at a merchant seller's place of business.

---

1. Students should be cautious to avoid confusing "acceptance of goods" with the concepts of offer and acceptance familiar from general contract law and found in the in UCC 2–206 and 2–207. "Acceptance of an offer" is a way of describing formation of contracts. "Acceptance of goods" is a concept used in connection with buyers' performance of sales contracts. Referring to "acceptance" without indicating whether one is referring to acceptance of an offer or of goods can be confusing, but context usually indicates which type of acceptance is meant. See, e.g., UCC 2–310.

UCC 2–308(a). In this circumstance, a seller tenders by holding the goods at the place of business and notifying buyer that the goods are available.[2] Sellers may agree to take the goods to their buyers; in such transactions, the UCC provides that buyers must furnish facilities reasonably suited to receipt of the goods.[3] UCC 2–503(1)(b).

Time of Sellers' Tender. UCC 2–503(1)(a) provides that sellers' tender must be made at a reasonable hour and for a reasonable duration, but does not have a default rule for the date on which a seller is required to have the goods ready. The UCC's answer is a "reasonable time" standard. UCC 2–309(1). Under this provision, a seller has some leeway before failure to tender delivery becomes a breach of contract. The outside limits of that period of time will be difficult to fix as an exact date.

Time of Payment. Sales contracts are more likely to have express or implied terms regarding buyers' time payment than sellers' tender of delivery. In certain transactions, the contract requires buyers to pay part of the price before seller tenders delivery of the goods. Such payments are often called "down payments." Parties to sales contracts often agree to a payment term that involves sellers' extending credit to the buyers. Sellers willing to extend credit deliver the goods before buyers pay the price. Sometimes the credit period is relatively short, e.g., 10 days after invoice or at the end of the month after delivery. In other transactions, the credit period is quite long. Long-term credit arrangements are often part of secured transactions or other arrangements that reduce the risk of buyers' failure to pay. In contracts that are silent on the time that payment is due, the default rules of the UCC fill that gap and provide further for other incidents of buyers' performance.

Buyers' Tender of Payment. The UCC refers to "tender of payment" in UCC 2–511, but does not define what constitutes such a tender. By analogy to tender of delivery, tender of payment occurs when a buyer "puts and holds" money or other instrument or payment device at the disposition of a seller. If a buyer tenders a personal check,[4] seller may insist on legal tender but must give buyer any additional time needed to procure it. UCC 2–511(2). Many sellers now accept payment in the form of a bank-issued credit card, but no seller is required to take payment in this form. Another form of payment, the debit card, authorizes buyer's bank to make an immediate transfer funds from buyer's bank account to seller's bank

---

2. The UCC has no provision declaring that buyers are contractually obligated to take possession of tendered goods. When sellers put and hold goods at buyers' disposition, in the overwhelming majority of transactions the buyers will dispose of them. They want to have possession of the goods they agreed to buy. That may explain why the UCC is silent on the matter.

3. This provision on buyers' obligation is oddly located in a section defining the manner of sellers' tender of delivery. Comment 4 to 2–503 states that this obligation of the buyer is no part of the seller's tender.

4. Personal checks would likely be considered a means of payment "current in the ordinary course of business." UCC 2–511(2). A buyer's personal check is an order by the buyer to a designated bank to pay money to a designated payee on demand. See UCC 3–104.

account. This mode of payment is quite satisfactory to sellers that have the requisite telecommunication connection.

Place and Time of Buyers' Tender. A buyer's payment is due "at the time and place at which the buyer is to receive the goods...." UCC 2–310(a). If the place of delivery is the merchant seller's place of business, the default rule of UCC 2–308(a), then that is the place of payment as well. If the parties agreed that the goods would be delivered elsewhere, then the place of payment changes accordingly.

When the default rules are applicable, performances by seller and buyer are required to occur simultaneously. UCC 2–511(1) declares that "tender of payment is a condition to the seller's duty to tender and complete any delivery," while UCC 2–507(1) declares that "tender of delivery is a condition to the buyer's ... duty to pay...."

Buyers' Right to Inspect Before Payment. Before paying, a buyer has the right to inspect the goods. UCC 2–513(1) provides that "where goods are tendered or delivered or identified to the contract of sale, the buyer has a right before payment ... to inspect them ... in any reasonable manner." The UCC does not define "inspect." The word could have many different meanings, including simple visual examination, scientific chemical or physical analysis, and trial use. The drafting of UCC 2–513 is a source of further confusion. It ties the right to inspect to three events, stated in the alternative. For present purposes, the difference between "tender" and "delivery" are pertinent.[5] "Tender" means put-and-hold, but not let-go. Tendered goods are still in the seller's control. "Delivery" implies transfer of possession to the buyer. The nature of a possible inspection of goods that are in the buyer's possession is quite different from the nature of an inspection of goods that are in the seller's possession. "The problem with § 2–513(1) is that it does not tell us whether the right to inspect is triggered by the first or the last of the listed events. The use of 'or' suggests that passage of any of them will be sufficient...."[6]

Tender of Delivery in "Lots." Ordinarily, sellers must tender at one time all the goods sold, but the UCC has an exception for partial deliveries.[7]

---

5. Seller's identification of goods to a sales contract is an event that precedes tender. Identification of goods is not an incident of performance. The goods may be identified at the time of contracting if the goods exist then. For "future goods" other than certain agricultural products, identification is done by sellers, unilaterally. See UCC 2–501(1). After goods have been identified to a sales contract, the buyer has an insurable interest in the goods. Id. Identification also gives a pre-paying buyer the right to recover the goods from an insolvent seller. UCC 2–502.

6. C. Gillette & S. Walt, Sales Law: Domestic and International 181 (1999).

7. When a single article has been sold, delivery or tender of that article is the only performance possible. However, sometimes the goods sold are physically divisible into "lots." UCC 2–105(5). Under what circumstances may a seller make a proper delivery or tender of less than all of the goods? The agreement may provide for multiple deliveries. In the absence of express agreement, the circumstances may indicate that this is not only proper but necessary. For example, the buyer of a large quantity of bricks needed to construct a large building may lack space at the site to store all the bricks if delivered at one time; when both seller and buyer are aware of this, multiple deliveries are proper.

If a seller properly delivers goods in installments, in the absence of agreement otherwise, a buyer must pay for each delivery if the contract price can be apportioned; otherwise the buyer can withhold all payment until all the goods have been tendered. UCC 2–307.

Problem 4.1.1. Wire Manufacturer ordered a quantity of certain copper from Copper Trading Co., which agreed to supply it. The sales agreement specified no delivery date. Manufacturer knew that Trading Co. would have to find a source of copper that met Manufacturer's needs, but assumed that no shortage of such copper existed. Trading Co. also assumed that it would have little difficulty locating the needed copper at a favorable price. Trading Co. discovered that the copper market was "tight" and spot prices were high. Trading Co. extended its search for copper to look for a relatively low price in the current market or, if necessary, to wait out what it hopes is a temporary peak in market prices.

(a) Manufacturer, whose inventory of copper is running low, demands that Trading Co. make immediate delivery. Trading Co. responds that it will deliver soon but gives no specific date.

(i) As counsel for Manufacturer, advise it on when Trading Co. was or will be in default.

(ii) As counsel for Trading Co., advise it as to the outside limit of its time for performance without breach.

(b) Manufacturer declares Trading Co. in default and institutes legal action. Which party has the burden of proving that a reasonable time had elapsed before Manufacturer's decision?

Problem 4.1.2. Plastics agreed to manufacture and deliver 40,000 pounds of special high-impact polystyrene pellets at 19 cents a pound for Industries. Industries agreed to accept delivery at the rate of 1000 pounds per day as the pellets were produced. Two weeks after the June 30 agreement, Plastics notified Industries that it was ready to deliver. Industries telephoned to say that labor difficulties and vacation schedules made it impossible to receive any pellets immediately; in that conversation Plastics replied that it would complete production and that it hoped that Industries would start taking delivery soon.

(a) On August 18, Plastics wrote to Industries: "We produced 40,000 pounds of high-impact pellets to your special order. You indicated that you would be using 1,000 lbs. per day. We have warehoused these products for more than forty days. However, we cannot keep these products indefinitely and request that you begin taking delivery. We have done everything that we agreed to do." After another month, Industries has not taken any pellets. Plastics consults you for legal assistance. What advice would you give? Is UCC 2–610 applicable? Compare Multiplastics v. Arch Industries, 166 Conn. 280, 348 A.2d 618 (1974).

The default rule, however, is that all the
goods must be delivered or tendered in a
single lot. UCC 2–307.

(b) Suppose Plastics had consulted you before sending its August 18 letter. Would you have advised changes in the letter? Would you have set a specific date as a deadline for Industries to take delivery? Is UCC 2–311 helpful? Would you advise sending a written demand pursuant to UCC 2–609(1)?

Problem 4.1.3. Consumer and Car Dealer entered into a sales agreement for a new automobile. Three weeks after the agreement, Car Dealer notified Consumer that the specified car had arrived. Consumer went to Car Dealer's place of business, looked at and sat in the car, kicked the tires, lifted the hood and peered at the engine. Consumer asked for the keys in order to "take it for a spin" to see if the car performed satisfactorily. Car Dealer responded that Consumer could have the keys only after he had paid the price. Has Consumer had a reasonable opportunity to inspect? The UCC declares that "tender of payment is a condition of the seller's duty to ... complete any delivery." UCC 2–507(1). Does this support Car Dealer's contention that Consumer's right to inspect includes only what Consumer can learn from examination of the goods while still in the Car Dealer's possession?

Problem 4.1.4. Builder, constructing a new house, ordered appliances from Dealer. The sales contract required Dealer to deliver the appliances to the construction site on February 1. Builder agreed to pay 30 days after delivery. When Dealer's truck arrived, after 5 p.m., Builder's employees had gone home for the night. Dealer's truck driver put the appliances into the garage and locked it. Were Dealer's actions in conformity with the requirements of UCC 2–503? See Ron Mead T.V. & Appliance v. Legendary Homes, 746 P.2d 1163 (Okla.App.1987).

INTERNATIONAL SALES LAW

The Convention on Contracts for International Sale of Goods states the general obligation of buyers and sellers. Article 30 provides:

> The seller must deliver the goods, hand over any documents relating to them and transfer the property in the goods, as required by the contract and this Convention.

Article 53 is the reciprocal provision for buyers:

> The buyer must pay the price for the goods and take delivery of them as required by the contract and this Convention.

The Convention does not use the concept of *tender* for either party's performance.

Because of its scope, CISG is more concerned with sales transactions in which the parties are in different nations and are therefore likely to be at considerable distance from each other. However, the Convention does provide default rules of performance of contracts that do not involve carriage of goods. The default rules apply only to the extent that the agreement of the parties is silent.

Time and Place of Seller's Delivery. Seller's obligation to deliver consists of "placing the goods at the buyer's disposal at the place where the seller had his place of business at the time of the conclusion of the contract," CISG 31(c), unless the parties knew from the circumstances of the contract that the goods would be placed at buyer's disposal at another location. CISG 31(b).

Time and Place of Buyers' Payment. Unless otherwise agreed, "a buyer must pay when the seller places either the goods or documents controlling their disposition at the buyer's disposal in accordance with the contract and this Convention." CISG 58(1). If payment is to be made against the handing over of goods or of documents, a buyer must pay "at the place where the handing over takes place." CISG 57(1)(b). Otherwise, payment must be made "at the seller's place of business." CISG 57(1)(a).

Inspection of Goods Before Payment. Absent agreement to the contrary, buyers are not bound to pay the price until they have had opportunity to examine the goods. CISG 58(3).

SECTION 2.   SHIPMENT CONTRACTS

We turn now to transactions in which sales contracts are performed through an intermediary, a carrier, and the necessary adaptation of agreements and the law governing performance of those contracts. Goods move to their markets on trucks, railroads, airplanes, and ships whose owners are transportation companies that sell a commercial service. Some carriers hold themselves out as available to the public; they are deemed "common carriers" and are regulated by federal and state laws. Others, known as "contract carriers," do not offer their services to the general public.[1]

Sales agreements determine whether sellers are required or authorized to ship the goods to buyers via carriers. The most elementary type of agreement involves simply that, a requirement or authorization to ship. In many circumstances, even though agreements are silent on the matter of shipment, the distance between sellers and buyers makes it evident that the default rules for local transactions are not appropriate and that the shipment of the goods is the implicitly expected method of delivery. Once an agreement authorizes or requires the seller to ship the goods, absent further agreement on the manner and time of shipment, all other elements of performance of the sales contract could be supplied by law. In the jargon of sales law, such contracts are often referred to as "shipment contracts."

DOMESTIC UNITED STATES LAW

When a sales contract is a shipment contract, the default rules for the seller's performance are found in UCC 2–503(2) and UCC 2–504. UCC 2–504(a) and (c) state two basic requirements. A seller must:

---

1. There is a large body of commercial practice and commercial law that deals with contracts for transport of goods. These materials refer to those practices and law only to the extent necessary to understand their effect on sales contracts

(a) put the goods in the possession of the carrier and make a contract for their transportation as may be reasonable having regard to the nature of the goods and other circumstances,[2] and

(c) promptly notify the buyer of the shipment.

In shipment contracts, sellers complete their performance obligations substantially before buyers receive the goods. The simultaneous exchange of performances that occur in local transactions is not feasible. The tender rules, for both sellers and buyers, must accommodate to that fact.

Comment 1 to UCC 2–504 declares that the general principles of the section cover the special cases of "F.O.B. point of shipment contracts." This Comment refers to a trade term that sellers and buyers commonly use in their agreements when they contemplate that the goods will be shipped by railroad.[3] To make commercial sense, an F.O.B. term must refer to a designated place where the goods are to be "free on board." The Comment refers to the place as the "point of shipment," i.e., the place where a seller puts the goods in the possession of a carrier. Often sales contracts that use an F.O.B. point-of-shipment term will identify the point of shipment merely by reference to the city where sellers have their places of business, e.g., "F.O.B. Sellersville." (Parties sometimes use an F.O.B point-of-destination term. The significance of this variant, referred to as "destination contracts," is considered later. For now we will remain focused on shipment contracts.)

Shipment contracts are often performed through use of transportation modes other than rail. Goods may be sent by various ground and air transportation services. The provisions of sales contracts for such means of shipment will vary with the nature of the services used, but are not likely to be expressed in an F.O.B. term.

Manner of Sellers' Tender of Delivery. Designation of the seller's city in the F.O.B. term of a sales contract or use of any other term that authorizes or requires a seller to ship the goods to the buyer has the important legal effect of defining the seller's obligations with respect to tender of the goods.[4] UCC 2–503(2) provides that "tender requires that the seller comply with [UCC 2–504]." The UCC does not elaborate on the criteria for determining the mode of transport or the nature of the "reasonable contract" that a seller must make with a transportation company.[5] The UCC does indicate that the criteria may vary with the

---

2. Specifications and arrangements relating to shipment are at the seller's option unless otherwise agreed. UCC 2–311(2).

3. The meaning of the F.O.B.term, when used in sales contracts, is defined in UCC 2–319(1).

4. This explains why the UCC describes an F.O.B. term as a "delivery term," UCC 2–319(1), and not "merely a price term." Comment 1.

5. The basis of the controversy in *Hadley v. Baxendale* was the decision of transportation company to use water transport rather than rail to carry a piece of broken manufacturing equipment to the place where it could be repaired. Water transport was slower (and perhaps less expensive) than transport by rail. The delay caused the mill to be shut down longer than it would have been. The mill owner sought consequential damages for loss of revenue from the mill during the

nature of the goods. Use of the term F.O.B. place-of-shipment has the added meaning, under UCC 2–319(1)(a) that the seller must "bear the expense and risk of putting the goods into the possession of the carrier."[6]

Time of Sellers' Tender. When sellers are authorized or required to ship goods to buyers via carriers, the matter of time of performance can be broken down into multiple questions: when must seller deliver to carrier, when must seller give notice of shipment to buyer, and when must carrier deliver to buyer? If the sales contract is a "place of shipment" contract, it may provide that seller must ship within a stated time, but in the absence of agreement the reasonable-time standard would apply. UCC 2–309(1). A contract may have a term that requires seller to use the fastest means, such as overnight delivery or air transport, but land and water transportation companies do not generally guarantee dates of arrival. Once a shipment is begun, seller's notification to buyer must be made "promptly." UCC 2–504(c).

Inspection of the Goods. The rule, in UCC 2–513(1), that a buyer has the right to inspect the goods before payment applies to shipment contracts. That subsection declares: "When the seller is required or authorized to send the goods to the buyer, the inspection may be after their arrival." In these elementary shipment contracts, carriers deliver the goods to buyers on arrival. Buyers are thus in possession of the goods to be inspected.

Time, Place and Manner of Buyers' Payment. The UCC contains default rules for the time, place and manner of buyers' payment when goods are delivered by carrier pursuant to an elementary shipment contract. Unless otherwise agreed, payment is due at the time and place at which the buyer is to receive the goods. UCC 2–310(a). This rule applies even though the place of shipment is the place of delivery, e.g., as in F.O.B. point-of-shipment contracts. Buyers ordinarily receive shipped goods at the termination of the carriage. Sellers may designate an agent to receive payment at that time and place, but in the absence of someone authorized to receive payment, buyers must send the money to sellers. This is commonly done by mailing checks but, if the agreements require faster transmittal, by wire transfers of funds.

————

Destination Contracts. When sellers are required or authorized by sales contracts to send goods by carrier, the UCC recognizes two types of

extended down-time. See R. Danzig, *Hadley v. Baxendale*: A Study in the Industrialization of the Law, 4 J. Legal Studies 249 (1975).

6. When, according to the sales contract, the buyer bears the cost of freight, as in an F.O.B. Sellersville contract, the seller may pay the carrier and add the freight charge to the invoice. When, according to the sales contract, the seller bears the cost of freight, as in an F.O.B. Buyersville contract, the price of the goods will be high enough to cover all of the seller's costs, including the costs of freight. Freight costs initially allocated to sellers are likely to be passed through to their buyers.

such contracts. One is the "shipment contract," considered above. A variant is the "destination contract."[7] The default tender rules that apply to destination contracts are different from the default rules that apply to shipment contracts. If a seller is required to deliver the goods *at a particular destination*, the tender rules applicable to local transactions apply, but the locale for performance of both parties is at the place where the carrier holds the goods for delivery to the buyer. UCC 2–503(3). The seller is not likely to be present at that place, but some of its duties could be performed by the transportation company on behalf of the seller.

If the parties use an F.O.B. term and designate "the place of destination," the UCC characterizes this as a contract in which seller is required to deliver *at* a particular destination. A seller must, at its own expense, transport the goods to *"the* place of destination" and *there* tender delivery of the goods to the buyer. UCC 2–319(1)(b). The tender rules are otherwise comparable to rules for sellers' tender in simple, two-party transactions, UCC 2–503(3), except the place of tender is at the destination of the transportation. Seller must tender at that place within the time permitted by the sales contract. In all likelihood, the seller will not be "there" in person to put and hold the goods at buyer's disposition. This is effected by the carrier acting pursuant to seller's instructions.

In destination contracts, absent further agreement, the put-and-hold manner of seller's tender of delivery of the goods would apply if seller has an agent at the place of destination that is able to make tender in that manner. Under the default rules of the UCC, seller would not be obligated to hand over the goods until buyer tendered any payment due and buyer's right to inspect may have to be exercised before the goods are handed over.

Mendelson–Zeller Co. v. Joseph Wedner & Son Co.

U.S. Department of Agriculture, 1970.
29 Agriculture Decisions 476.

■ FLAVIN, JUDICIAL OFFICER.

PRELIMINARY STATEMENT

This is a reparation proceeding under the Perishable Agricultural Commodities Act, 1930, as amended (7 U.S.C. 499a et seq.) A timely complaint was filed in which complainant seeks reparation against respondent in the amount of $2,480.73 in connection with a shipment of cantaloupes and lettuce in interstate commerce.

---

7. On quick and careless reading, the phrase makes little sense. Would not every sales contract that requires a seller to ship via carrier be a destination contract? How can a seller send goods to the buyer via carrier without sending them to a named destination? If a seller is required to send the goods to a buyer at buyer's place of business or residence, would that not be sending them to a particular destination? Such questions misread the key language of the UCC, which speaks of delivery *at*, not delivery *to* a particular designation.

A copy of the formal complaint and of the Department's report of investigation were served upon the respondent, and respondent filed an answer denying liability. The answer included a counterclaim for $2,892.73. Complainant did not file a reply to the counterclaim and therefore it is deemed to be denied pursuant to section 47.9(a) of the rules of practice (7 CFR 47.9(a)).

An oral hearing at the request of respondent was held at Pittsburgh, Pennsylvania, on July 30, 1969. Respondent was represented by counsel at the hearing. One witness appeared for respondent. Complainant filed a brief.

FINDINGS OF FACT

1. Complainant, Mendelson–Zeller Co., Inc., is a corporation whose address is 450 Sansome Street, San Francisco, California. At the time of the transaction involved herein, complainant was licensed under the act.

2. Respondent, Joseph Wedner & Son Co., is a corporation whose address is 2018 Smallman Street, Pittsburgh, Pennsylvania. At the time of the transaction involved herein, respondent was licensed under the act.

3. On or about March 7, 1968, in the course of interstate commerce, complainant contracted orally to sell to respondent, a mixed truckload of produce consisting of 25 cartons of cantaloupes Jumbo size 45 at $17.75 per carton, 85 cartons of cantaloupes Jumbo size 56 at $15.25 per carton, and 574 cartons of lettuce size 24 at $3.45 per carton, delivered Pittsburgh, Pennsylvania. The total delivered price for the truckload, including $15.00 for top ice, was $4,116.55. It was agreed that shipment would begin on March 8. The parties estimated that delivery would be in time for the market of Tuesday morning, March 12, 1968.

4. Complainant shipped the lettuce at 9:40 a.m. March 8, 1968, from El Centro, California, and the cantaloupes were shipped at 10:00 p.m. the same day from Nogales, Arizona, in a truck operated by Arkansas Traffic Service, Inc., of Redfield, Arkansas. At 12:00 a.m. March 12, the truck driver called respondent stating that the truck would arrive about 3:00 or 3:30 p.m. and requesting that respondent's men wait to unload the truck. Respondent checked with its men, who said they would not wait, and then told the truck driver to arrive at 3:00 a.m. the morning of March 13th.

5. The truckload of produce arrived at respondent's place of business at 5:00 a.m., March 13, 1968, approximately 103 hours after leaving Nogales, Arizona.

6. Respondent unloaded and sold the commodities and remitted the net proceeds in the amount of $1,635.82 to complainant.

7. The formal complaint was filed on August 1, 1968, which was within 9 months after accrual of the cause of action.

CONCLUSIONS

Complainant seeks to recover the full delivered price for the truckload of produce sold to respondent and respondent contends that it was justified in remitting only the net proceeds resulting from its resale of the produce. The only material factual dispute relates to whether a delivery time of 3:00 a.m. March 12, 1968, was specified as a condition of the delivered sale contract. Complainant contends that such time was not specified as a contract condition but was merely the estimated time of arrival assuming normal condition, and that a 48 hour leeway is allowable by custom in such cases.

On March 13, 1968, the day the truck actually arrived, respondent's Manager, Norman Wedner, wrote to complainant's Sales Manager, Mr. E. A. Melia, Jr., in part as follows:

> The truck of mixed lettuce and cantaloupes was due for the market of Tuesday morning at 3:00 AM March 12, 1968.

> The truck driver called us at noon Tuesday and said he would be in at 3:00 or 3:30 PM Tuesday afternoon, and asked us to have the men wait to unload him. We held him on the phone and our warehouse men said they could not wait for him. We then told him to be at the warehouse at 3:00 AM Wednesday morning. He said fine, he would be there.

> He didn't arrive until 5:00 AM Wednesday Mar. 13, 1968. The lettuce wasn't available for delivery until 6:30 AM, causing us to miss a large chain store order.

Complainant's Traffic Manager, John Monk testified by deposition and referred to an exhibit which he said was a correct copy of his notes concerning instructions for the shipment of the produce. The exhibit is entitled "Loading and Delivery instructions," and in part gives the following information: "Delivery Date *Tues* Time *3:30 AM.*" Mr. Monk stated that this exhibit reflected the estimated time of arrival and that he "was given no specific instructions as to actual time of delivery other than the delivery was to be planned so that if at all possible it would arrive in Pittsburgh on Tuesday morning." Complainant's Salesman, Irving Raznikov, stated that he was the actual recipient of the telephone order from Mr. Wedner. Although he stated that "Wedner requested a Tuesday a.m. arrival and I indicated to him that under normal circumstances there would be no problem with said delivery schedule," he also stated that he "stressed with Mr. Wedner that we could not and would not guarantee any specific arrival."

Respondent as the party alleging that a specified arrival time was a part of the contract of sale had the burden of proving by a preponderance of the evidence that its allegation was true. In view of the foregoing discussion we conclude that respondent has not met its burden of proof.

Section 2–309(1) of the Uniform Commercial Code provides that the time for delivery in the absence of an agreed time shall be a reasonable time. The load was tendered and accepted at 5:00 a.m. March 13, about 103 hours after the truck left Nogales, Arizona. Under the circumstances, we are unable to say the delivery was not within a reasonable time.

The failure of respondent to pay to complainant the full purchase price of $4,116.55 for the lettuce was in violation of section 2 of the act.

Respondent has already paid net proceeds of $1,635.82 to complainant. Reparation should therefore be awarded to complainant for the balance of the purchase price of $2,480.73, with interest. In the absence of any breach of contract on the part of complainant, respondent's counterclaim should be dismissed.

ORDER

Within 30 days from the date of this order, respondent shall pay to complainant, as reparation, $2,480.73, with interest thereon at the rate of 6 percent per annum from April 1, 1968, until paid.

The counterclaim should be dismissed.

NOTES

(1) **Delay in Buyer's Receipt of the Goods.** This case illustrates how much economic significance can attach to time of performance in certain kinds of sales transactions. Buyer resold lettuce and cantaloupes after 5:00 a.m. for $1,635.82, less than half of the original contract price. Moreover, buyer claimed damages of nearly $2,900.00, presumably profit that buyer allegedly would have made on resale to the large chain store. Assuming that the resale was reasonable[8] and the amount claimed as damages was not exaggerated, goods delivered at 3:00 a.m. were worth $5,000 more than goods delivered at 5:00 a.m.

(2) **Contract Interpretation.** Buyer's counsel apparently contended that the delivery term in the "Loading and Delivery instructions" was binding upon the seller. Was this document part of the contract of sale? On what theory might it reflect on the sales contract?[9]

(3) **Time of Seller's Tender of Delivery.** The judicial officer concluded that the sales contract did not provide the day and hour for buyer's receipt of the goods. The legal issue therefore is whether the seller made timely tender of delivery. Determination of that issue depends upon characterization of the shipping term contract. If the sales contract is a shipment contract, the timeliness of seller's tender of delivery is determined under UCC 2-504(a). The issue turns on the day and hour when the seller put the goods into the carrier's possession in El Centro, California, and Nogales, Arizona. If the sales contract is a destination contract, the timeliness of seller's tender of delivery is determined under UCC 2-503(1). The issue turns on the day and hour that the seller tendered the goods to the buyer at its place of business in Pittsburgh.

8. The opinion does not suggest that the buyer "dumped" the goods at less than their market value at the time of resale.

9. A different legal question is whether the terms of the document were part of the contract of carriage and binding on the carri-

er. Although the buyer was not a named party to the contract of carriage, the buyer might be able to seek a remedy from the carrier for its breach of that contract. Cf. UCC 2-722. In the principal case, of course, the carrier was not a party to the litigation.

Was this sales contract a shipment contract or a destination contract? What was the judicial officer's characterization of the contract? There is no reference in the sales contract to an F.O.B. term or any other trade term in common usage. The opinion noted that the contract price was a "delivered price," i.e., the lump sum included the cost of freight and top ice. Was this relevant? Determinative? Would there have been an issue of the timeliness of seller's tender of delivery if this were a shipment contract?[10]

(4) Construction of UCC 2–309. Accepting for the purpose of further analysis that this sales contract was a destination contract, the seller's performance obligation on time of tender of delivery was found in the default rule of UCC 2–309. Do you agree with the judicial officer's application of that provision to the facts of this case? Note the judicial officer's odd double negative conclusion: "we are unable to say the delivery was not within a reasonable time." Was this equivalent to a conclusion that delivery *was made* within a reasonable time?

The truck driver could have delivered on the afternoon of March 12. Was it not reasonable to require the goods to be delivered at 3:00 a.m. the next morning, in time to make the prime market for that day?

The goods were not delivered on March 12 because the buyer did not have employees who were willing to wait until the truck was expected to arrive, in mid-afternoon. Was the inability of the buyer to take delivery on March 12 pertinent to its claim that the delivery on March 13 was in violation of the seller's obligation? Consider the application of the requirements of UCC 2–503(1)(a) and (b): Tender must be at a reasonable hour and buyer must furnish facilities reasonably suited to the receipt of the goods

---

Distinguishing Between Shipment Contracts and Destination Contracts. If sellers and buyers do not use an F.O.B. term or another trade term that indicates their intent to have a shipment contract or a destination contract, interpretation of the sales contracts on this point can be difficult. A comment to UCC 2–503 offers some guidance to courts. Comment 5 declares that the drafters of the UCC intentionally omitted the rule under prior uniform legislation that a contract term requiring a seller to pay the freight or costs of transportation was equivalent to an agreement

---

10. The law governing the *Mendelson–Zeller* case is the UCC supplemented by a federal statute, the Perishable Agricultural Commodities Act. 7 U.S.C. §§ 499a–499s. The act and regulations issued under it determine the obligations of parties to sales contracts. Many trade terms used in sales agreements for perishable agricultural commodities are specially defined in 7 C.F.R. § 46.43. Nothing in the case turned on provisions of the federal statute.

Under the federal act, when parties use certain trade terms, buyers are precluded from rejecting goods on arrival. Among them are "f.o.b. acceptance final," "rolling acceptance," and "purchase after inspection." See, e.g., L. Gillarde & Co. v. Joseph Martinelli & Co., 169 F.2d 60 (1st Cir.), cert. denied, 335 U.S. 885, 69 S.Ct. 237, 93 L.Ed. 424 (1948).

to deliver to the buyer or at an agreed destination and regard the-place-of-shipment contract as "the normal one." The Comment continues:

> The seller is not obligated to deliver at a named destination ... unless he has specifically agreed so to deliver or the commercial understanding of the terms used by the parties contemplates such delivery.

Does the Comment go beyond the text of the UCC? Does it provide a reasonable interpretation of the text?[11]

Problem 4.2.1. Buyer telephoned Catalogue Seller and ordered a compact disc player. In the conversation, Buyer said: "Please send the CD player by parcel post." Seller accepted the order without more being said about the price or delivery. Is the contract a place-of-shipment or at-a-particular-destination contract? Which party must pay the parcel post charges? See Pestana v. Karinol Corp., 367 So.2d 1096 (Fla.App.1979).

Problem 4.2.2. National Heater Co., located in St. Paul, Minnesota, offered to sell heating units to Corrigan Co. to be used by the buyer in construction of an automobile plant in Fenton, Missouri. National Heater's written proposal of the terms of sale stated the price as $275,640, "F.O.B. St. Paul, Minn. with freight allowed." Corrigan then submitted a purchase order with the following: "Price $275,640—Delivered." National Heater sent an acknowledgment which included: "$275,640 Total Delivered to Rail Siding." Is the contract a place-of-shipment or at-a-particular-destination contract? See National Heater Co. v. Corrigan Co., 482 F.2d 87 (8th Cir.1973).

INTERNATIONAL SALES LAW

As noted in Section 1, the primary duties of sellers and buyers under the Convention on Contracts for International Sale of Goods are stated in CISG 30 and CISG 53. Sellers must deliver the goods and transfer the property as in the goods "as required by the contract and this Convention," and buyers must pay the price and take delivery of the goods "as required by the contract and this Convention."

Manner and Place of Delivery. Sales contracts governed by CISG are between parties from different nations and are, therefore, highly likely to require use of carriers. Absent agreement on the nature of sellers' performance, the Convention provides that sellers' obligation has the following steps: Seller "must make such contracts as are necessary for carriage to the place fixed [by agreement] by means of transportation appropriate in the circumstances and according to the usual terms for such

---

11. The PEB Study Group on UCC Article 2 stated: "Without FOB terms in the agreement, § 2–319(1), it is not clear when a seller who is authorized to ship goods is required to deliver at a particular destination. § 2–503(3). Comment 5 to § 2–503 provides a rule for construction. [We recommend] that this rule of construction be placed in the text of either § 2–319(1) or § 2–503." PEB Article 2 Report 134. See also id. at 115.

The recommendation of the Study Group was not followed. Instead, the drafting committees determined that UCC 2–319, along with the sections on shipment terms that follow 2–319, should be repealed.

transportation." CISG 32(2). Seller must "hand ... the goods over to the first carrier for transmission to the buyer." CISG 31(a). If the goods are not clearly identified to the sales contract, by markings on the goods or by documents or otherwise, when handed over to the carrier, seller must give buyer notice of the consignment, CISG 32(1); the Convention does not require sellers to give notice of shipment in all transactions.[12]

Unlike the UCC the Convention does not distinguish between place-of-shipment and at-a-particular-destination contracts. The latter are not contemplated, no doubt in light of prevailing mercantile practice.

> [E]ven when the seller undertakes to pay freight costs to destination under "C.I.F." and "C. & F." ... quotations, it has long been settled that the seller ... completes his delivery duties ... when the goods are (at the latest) loaded on the carrier.

Honnold, International Sales § 209(1). Moreover, the Convention, unlike the UCC, contains no provisions regarding the meaning of shipment terms.

In their contracts, parties to international sales transactions often refer to a set of trade terms which are known as **Incoterms**. Incoterms are prepared and promulgated by the International Chamber of Commerce (ICC).[13] Incoterms, last revised in 1990, categorize shipping or delivery terms into four principal categories: main carriage paid by seller (e.g., Cost and Freight, CFR, or CIF), main carriage paid by buyer (e.g., FOB, FAS), departure terms (Ex Works), and arrival terms (e.g., Delivered Ex Ship or DES). Incoterms 1990 do not use the FOB term other than at port of shipment. Departure terms do not oblige sellers to contract for carriage. The arrival term, DES, requires a seller to place the goods at the disposal of the buyer on board the vessel at the usual unloading point in the named port of destination.[14]

The ICC noted a growing practice of use of shipment terms in international sales transactions that authorize carriers to deliver the goods to

---

12. As we will see in the next Section, international sales transactions may be documentary transactions in which seller "must ... hand over [to the buyer] any documents relating to [the goods]." CISG 30.

13. The ICC is a non-governmental organization with members from 110 countries. From its wide membership base, the ICC is able to compile information on business practices and to develop expertise in the needs of the marketplace for various shipment terms. Parties to particular contracts can incorporate Incoterms in their agreements as they deem appropriate. The ICC noted that if a buyer and seller specifically refer to one of the Incoterms, "they can be sure of defining their respective responsibilities, simply and safely. In so doing they eliminate any possi-

bility of misunderstanding and subsequent dispute." ICC, Incoterms 1990. Foreword.

14. During the drafting of the Convention, consideration was given to inclusion of a term that would have had the effect of incorporating trade terms in common usage, like *Incoterms*, into all international sales contracts. This proposal was opposed, in part because it would impose trade terms on a party, perhaps one from a developing country, whether or not it knew or ought to have known of them. The Convention's general provision on trade usage would direct tribunals to consider *Incoterms* if both parties knew or ought to have known of them. CISG 9(2). See Honnold, International Sales § 118 and n. 5.

designated consignees, transactions that have been referred to here as elementary shipment transactions.[15]

Time of Delivery. The Convention looks to the parties' contract as the primary source of the time term. CISG 33(a). Often, international sales contracts specify a period of time within which delivery is to occur. The agreement may provide further how an exact date will be set by one or both of the parties. If a period of time is stated without more, CISG 33(b) states a default rule that permits the seller to choose to perform "at any time within that period unless circumstances indicate that the buyer is to choose a date." When the contract is silent on time, CISG 33(c) requires a seller to perform "within a reasonable time after the conclusion of the contract."

Buyers' Payment. The Convention does not have any provisions on the manner of buyers' payment beyond the requirement in CISG 54 that a buyer's obligation includes "taking such steps and complying with such formalities as may be required under the contract or any laws and regulations to enable payment to be made."

Time and Place of Buyers' Payment. Unless otherwise agreed, "a buyer must pay when the seller places either the goods or documents controlling their disposition at the buyer's disposal in accordance with the contract and this Convention." CISG 58(1). If payment is to be made against the handing over of goods or of documents, a buyer must pay "at the place where the handing over takes place." CISG 57(1)(b). Otherwise, payment must be made "at the seller's place of business." CISG 57(1)(a).

Inspection of Goods Before Payment. Absent agreement to the contrary, buyers are not bound to pay the price until they have had opportunity to examine the goods. CISG 58(3). If the contract involves carriage of goods, sellers may dispatch the goods on terms whereby the goods, or documents controlling their disposition, will not be handed over to the buyer except against payment of the price. CISG 58(2). Since examination of goods can occur while goods are in the possession of carriers, before the goods are handed over to buyers, CISG 58(2) does not override CISG 58(3).[16]

Sellers' Duty to Deliver When Buyers' Provide Vessels. In some international transactions that involve transport of large quantities of goods by sea, the parties agree that the buyer will contract to provide a vessel onto which the seller loads the goods at a designated port. Seller cannot deliver until the vessel is in the port, but it is usually important that the goods be available to be loaded as soon as the vessel arrives.

---

15. "In recent years, a considerable simplification of documentary practices has been achieved. Bills of lading are frequently replaced by non-negotiable documents similar to those which are used for other modes of transport than carriage by sea. ... These non-negotiable documents are quite satisfac- tory to use except where the buyer wishes to sell the goods in transit by surrendering a paper document to the new buyer." ICC, Incoterms 1990, Introduction ¶ 19.

16. See Honnold, International Sales § 338.

A transaction of this kind gave rise to a controversy that was litigated in a U.K. court. Seller and Buyer contracted for sale of 12,000 tons of sugar to be delivered at the port of Dunkirk in May or June 1986 on board one or more ships provided by Buyer. The contract required Buyer to give Seller not less than 14 days' notice of the vessels' readiness to load. The contract also incorporated by reference the Rules of the London Refined Sugar Association (LRSA). One LRSA Rule stated: "the seller shall have the sugar ready to be delivered at any time within the contract period." Another LRSA Rule provided: "the buyer, having given reasonable notice, shall be entitled to call for delivery of the sugar between the first and the last working days inclusive of the contract period." A third LRSA Rule stated that the buyer was responsible for costs incurred by the seller if the nominated vessel did not present herself within five days of the date specified in the buyer's notice. On May 15, Buyer gave notice calling on Seller to load the sugar on board the *Naxos*, estimated to arrive in Dunkirk between May 29 and 31. The *Naxos* was at the dock in Dunkirk and ready to load on May 29. Seller informed Buyer that the sugar would be available on June 3.

Applying British domestic sales law, the House of Lords held that seller was bound to have the sugar ready for loading immediately upon the ship's arrival. Seller contended that the contract permitted commencement of loading within a reasonable time after the ship had arrived. The House of Lords construed the notice provision of the agreement and the Rules to require the seller to have the sugar at the dock, ready to be loaded, when the ship arrived. See Compagnie Commerciale Sucres et Denrees v. C. Czarnikow Ltd. (*The Naxos*), [1990] 1 W.L.R. 1337 (H.L.), reversing [1989] 2 Lloyd's Rep. 462 (C.A.).

If the governing law had been the CISG, how should the case have been decided?

SECTION 3.   DOCUMENTARY SALES

Elementary shipment or destination contracts are satisfactory for sales transactions in which sellers are willing to extend short-term credit to buyers. Such contracts are not satisfactory to sellers that are unwilling to allow the buyers to take possession of goods without paying for them. Simultaneous tenders of delivery and of payment eliminate credit risk. In simultaneous exchange transactions, sellers extend no credit to buyers and buyers extend no credit to sellers. Such exchanges are paradigmatic in local sales transactions. They can be replicated, in a more complex legal way, when sellers and buyers are not in the same locales. Documents of title, and the law that undergirds them, are the means to this end.

Elementary shipment or destination contracts are satisfactory for sales transactions in which buyers expect to receive the goods from carriers. In some commercial settings, however, buyers intend to sell the goods while they are en route. Quick resales of goods are a function of intermediaries in the movement of some goods to their ultimate markets. Such volatile markets can be facilitated by the use of documents of title.

Documents of Title. A negotiable document of title is a document that effectively controls the rights to ownership and possession of goods. Documents of title are pieces of paper that, with the proper legal platform, are themselves important items of property. One can "own" a document of title and thereby own the underlying rights in the goods. The person entitled to the rights represented by a document of title is referred to as the "holder" of the document. A holder can transfer a document of title to another holder. Transfer of a document of title, in a certain manner, transfers those key rights to goods.

Order Bills of Lading. A classic example of a document of title is a negotiable or "order" bill of lading. A bill of lading (originally a bill of "loading") is a document that a carrier (e.g., railroad, ship owner, air freight carrier) issues when goods are delivered to it for shipment. Carriers that issue bills of lading may issue either of two kinds of bills of lading, the "order bill of lading" and the "straight bill of lading." Under a "straight" bill, a carrier undertakes to deliver goods at a stated destination to a stated person, e.g., "to Buyer & Co." Under an "order" bill of lading, a carrier agrees to deliver the goods *to the order of* a stated person, e.g., to "the order of Seller & Co." An "order" bill of lading typically provides:

> The surrender of this Original Bill of Lading properly indorsed shall be required before the delivery of the property.

Straight Bills of Lading. A straight bill is a document of title but it does not control the rights to ownership or possession of the goods. Straight bills can be used in elementary shipment or destination contracts of the kind that were considered in Section 2. Order bills are documents of title and have the added dimension that makes a simultaneous exchange feasible even though a seller and a buyer are unable to meet in the same place. The simultaneous exchange involves money and the document.

A bill of lading, in part, embodies the contract between the carrier and the shipper, often termed the *consignor.* A number of terms are printed on the front of printed bills of lading where data describing specific shipments are filled in; the back contains more standard contract terms, often densely packed in small print. The bill of lading identifies the carrier receiving the goods, the shipper or consignor, the goods, the intended destination, the consignee, and possibly other terms.[1]

When parties to sales contracts elect to enter into "documentary transitions," they enlist the aid of banks to accomplish the result. Banks are linked together to provide a communications network that allows funds to be transferred, but the banking system also serves to transport documents of title. Using the mix of transportation services provided by carriers and financial services provided by banks, a seller and a buyer are able to effect simultaneous exchange of a document of title to goods in exchange

---

1. In these materials, we are concerned with only those aspects of carriage contracts that are significant to the performance of sales transactions.

for payment of the price. The payment side of the exchange is facilitated by the use of a common negotiable instrument, a bill of exchange, the negotiable draft.

Drafts. A draft is a negotiable instrument in which one party, the seller (the *drawer*) orders another party, the buyer (the *drawee*) to pay a specified amount of money at a specified time. In a documentary transaction, a draft is drawn *by* a seller *on* a buyer for the amount of money due to the seller under a sales contract.

Sight Drafts. Typically, the seller's draft will order buyer to pay the price when the draft is presented to buyer ("at sight"); drafts payable on demand are called "sight drafts." Sight drafts are used in transactions in which the parties have agreed to the type of simultaneous exchange that occurs in documentary transactions.

Time Drafts. An alternative transaction involves use of a "time draft," which contains an order to the buyer to pay the amount of the draft at the end a specified period of time after the draft has been presented to the buyer. A "time draft" transaction, which extends credit for the specified period, does not accomplish a simultaneous exchange.

For the moment, we will consider a documentary transaction that involves a sight draft and an order bill of lading. The commercial purpose of time drafts in documentary transactions will be considered later.

Carriers' and Banks' Services in a Typical Documentary Transaction. The sequence of steps in performance of a typical documentary transaction utilizes the services of carriers and banks.

A seller first delivers the goods to a carrier and obtains an "order bill of lading" from the carrier. A standard form order bill of lading begins:

> RECEIVED, subject to the classifications and tariffs in effect on the date of issue of this Bill of Lading, the property described below, in apparent good order, except as noted (contents and conditions of contents of packages unknown) marked, consigned and designated as indicated below, which [carrier] agrees to carry to its usual place of delivery at said destination. . . .

The bill of lading has boxes on its face in which the carrier enters the "number of packages", the carrier's "description of the articles, special marks and exceptions," and the weight of the goods.

In a "consigned to" box, after the printed words ORDER OF the carrier enters the name of the consignee provided by the seller. In a documentary sale, a seller typically designates itself as the consignee. In a "destination" box the carrier notes the city to which the goods are to be carried. Below that, in a "notify" box, is the name of the person to be notified by the carrier when goods have arrived. The person listed is the buyer.

Seller then prepares a "sight draft" for the price due under the sales contract. A sight draft looks very much like an ordinary bank check, which is a draft drawn on a bank. A sight draft used in a documentary transaction is drawn on the buyer.

The seller indorses the order bill of lading,[2] attaches the indorsed bill of lading to the sight draft, and delivers both documents to its local bank for transmission to the buyer through normal banking channels. Seller's bank forwards the documents through the network of bank-to-bank relationships that exists for this, and many other purposes.

In due course, the draft and bill of lading arrive at a specified bank in buyer's city, typically the bank with which the buyer has an ongoing banking relationship. It is the function of that bank to effect the exchange of goods for money by turning over the order bill of lading when buyer has paid the amount of the sight draft.

After payment is made, the funds are transferred back to seller's bank and eventually to seller, again through normal banking channels. Once a document of title has been transferred to a buyer, it can surrender the document to the carrier for the goods or it can sell the document of title to a third party.

---

2. Sellers' indorsements are usually "in blank," i.e., the indorsement authorizes any one in possession of the document to negoti- ate it further without indorsement. Blank indorsements facilitate forwarding of the documents through banking channels.

DIAGRAM OF A DOCUMENTARY TRANSACTION

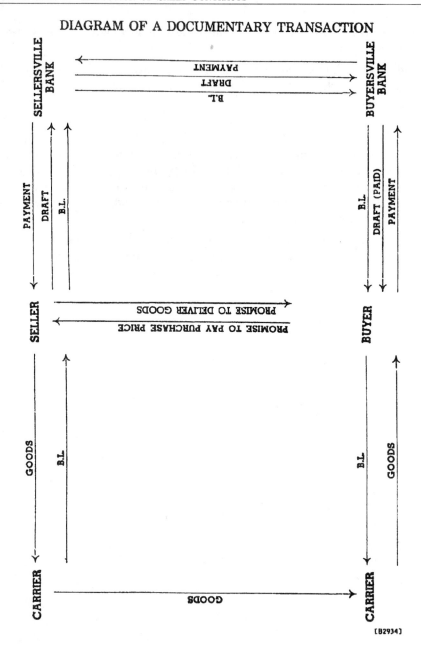

[B2934]

C.O.D. Contracts. A transaction type equivalent in some respects to a documentary transaction is possible if a carrier agrees not only to transport the goods but also to collect payment from the buyer before handing over the goods. Some carriers offer this added service (for an added fee, of course). Transactions of this kind, referred to as collect-on-delivery or C.O.D. transactions, are usually sales in which the price of the goods is relatively small, as in retail sales of consumer goods.

DOMESTIC UNITED STATES LAW

Performance of documentary transactions is quite different from performance of sales contracts that require sellers only to tender delivery of goods and require buyers to tender payment in exchange for tender of delivery of the goods. In documentary transactions, sellers tender delivery of documents of title and buyers are required to make payment in exchange for the documents. The shorthand expression for this exchange is "payment against documents." Goods are not present when a documentary exchange takes place. Indeed the goods are probably still en route to their destination. In these circumstances, buyer's inspection of the goods before making payment is not feasible.

Contracting for Documentary Transactions. Payment against documents is required only if the parties to a sales contract have agreed to this manner of performance. The UCC, together with federal law, assists sellers and buyers to perform their obligations under documentary transactions, but those obligations can arise only if the parties have agreed to this transaction type. It is important to know the nature of the contract terms that have the effect of requiring payment against documents. A common term used for this purpose in sales contracts is: "Sight draft against order bill of lading."

Sales contracts may use certain shipment terms which, by law, have the effect of requiring buyers to pay against documents. The shipment terms that have this effect are terms commonly associated with transport of goods on deep water ships. UCC Article 2 refers to four such terms: C.I.F., C. & F., F.A.S. vessel, and F.O.B. vessel. The term C.I.F. means that the contract price includes, in a single sum, the price of the goods plus cost of insurance and freight to a named destination.[3] C. & F. is similar, but omits insurance.[4] F.A.S. vessel means "free alongside" a ship at a named port.[5] F.O.B. vessel means on board a named vessel.[6] UCC Article 2 declares that, when these terms are used in sales contracts, sellers must obtain negotiable bills of lading.[7] Unless otherwise agreed, the buyers must make payment against tender of the required documents and sellers may not tender nor buyers demand delivery of the goods in substitution for the documents.[8]

---

3. UCC 2–320(1).

4. Id.

5. UCC 2–319(2).

6. UCC 2–319(1)(c).

7. UCC 2–320(2)(a), 2–323(1). The requirement in UCC 2–323(1) is limited to sales contracts that contemplate "overseas ship-ment" of the goods, defined in UCC 2–323(3) to mean any contract that by agreement or trade usage is subject to the commercial, financial or shipping practices of international deep water commerce.

8. UCC 2–319(4); 2–320(4).

Time, Place and Manner of Sellers' Tender of Documents Under UCC Article 2. When a seller, in conformity with a contract of sale, ships goods under an "order" bill of lading, UCC 2–504(b) adds a third requirement to seller's manner of execution of a shipment contract. Seller must tender the bill of lading, properly indorsed so that the buyer is empowered to obtain possession of the goods from the carrier. Tender of any documents needed to obtain possession of goods must be made "promptly" under UCC 2–504(b). UCC 2–503(5)(b) provides that "tender [of such documents] through customary banking channels is sufficient." Through "banking channels" or otherwise, a seller can transmit documents to a buyer. "Properly indorsed" means that the seller must act so that the buyer becomes the holder of the bill of lading, the person entitled to obtain the goods from the carrier.

The default provisions in UCC Article 2 are complemented by other bodies of law: the Federal Bill of Lading Act and Articles 3 and 4 of the UCC.

Federal Bill of Lading Act. The primary law that undergirds negotiable bills of lading and proper indorsement thereof is federal law, the Federal Bill of Lading Act.[9] This Act sets out the criteria for making a bill of lading negotiable and for negotiating such a bill once it has been issued.[10] The provisions most pertinent to the carriers' role in the execution of documentary transactions are the sections on carrier's duty to deliver goods to the holder of a negotiable bill of lading, carrier's liability for delivery of the goods to a person not entitled thereto,[11] and carrier's liability for nonreceipt of the goods described in a bill of lading or misdescription of the goods.[12]

Documentary Drafts Under UCC Articles 3 and 4. The legal platform for the banks' role in execution of documentary transactions is found in Articles 3 and 4 of the UCC. These articles refer to a draft that is accompanied by a bill of lading as a "documentary draft."[13] A bank taking a documentary draft and an order bill of lading from a seller is authorized to present the draft to buyer or to send it via another bank or banks to buyer.[14] Each bank that handles a seller's draft becomes a "collecting bank"[15] with the duties to send forward or to present the draft and accompanying documents.[16] The last bank in the chain of banks is the

---

9. 49 U.S.C. §§ 80101–80116. The federal act applies to bills of lading issued by common carriers for interstate transportation or export of goods. Id. § 80102. The law governing bills of lading for intrastate transportation of goods is found in Article 7 of the UCC.

10. Id. §§ 80103(a), 80104. UCC criteria for making bills of lading negotiable are found in UCC 7–104. Negotiation requirements are set forth in UCC 7–501.

11. Id. §§ 80110, 80113. For carriers' obligation to deliver goods under UCC Article 7, see UCC 7–403, 7–404.

12. Id. § 80113. The comparable provision in the UCC is UCC 7–301.

13. UCC 4–104(6).

14. Banks who handle the paper are agents and subagents of sellers. UCC 4–201.

15. UCC 4–105(d).

16. UCC 4–501.

"presenting bank."[17] Unless otherwise instructed, the bank presenting a "sight draft" is authorized to send buyer a written notice that it holds a draft for payment.[18] A buyer to whom a notice is sent has three banking days from the date the notice was sent to make payment.[19] The bank must deliver the bill of lading accompanying the draft to the buyer "only on payment."[20] Upon receipt of payment, the presenting bank remits the funds to the seller.[21]

Negotiation; Rights of Holders. Both the order bill of lading and the negotiable draft move through these steps by the process of negotiation, not by mere transfer.[22] "Holders" of negotiable documents of title or of negotiable instruments may receive greater legal protection than mere transferees. In Chapter 1, we noted that the concept of good faith purchase has developed in a wider setting than purchase of goods. Commercial law offers very significant legal protection to holders in due course of negotiable instruments,[23], and to holders of negotiable documents of title to whom the documents have been duly negotiated.[24] These protections are often significant to buyers and sellers as well as to the banks whose services they use in carrying out documentary transactions.

Inspection of the Goods and the Documents. Buyers' agreement to documentary sales has severe consequences on their right to inspect the goods before payment. The default rule of UCC 2–513(3)(b) provides that a buyer is not entitled to inspect the goods before payment of the price "when the contract provides for payment against documents of title...."[25]

If the parties to a sales contract agree, an inspection of the goods can be made before or at the time the goods are turned over to the carrier. Buyers are not likely to be at that location, but they may be able to hire independent inspectors to examine the goods. Alternatively, sales contracts can provide that sellers must arrange for inspection of the goods by independent inspectors and that the inspectors' certificates must be tendered along with the bills of lading and drafts.

17. UCC 4–105(6).

18. UCC 4–212(a).

19. UCC 4–212(b). See also UCC 3–502(c).

20. UCC 4–503(1).

21. **Air Freight.** The speed of carriage of goods by air required adaptation of the method of issuing and transmitting bills of lading. Taking a bill of lading at the point of shipment and forwarding it through banking channels to the destination to be exchanged for the price would be too slow. A solution was found by using electronic communications. The UCC permits a carrier, at the request of a consignor, to issue a bill of lading at the point of destination, UCC 7–305(1), and to deliver it to a local bank. Meanwhile, seller (or seller's bank) wires a draft on the buyer to the bank holding the bill. Within hours, the bank notifies buyer who pays the draft and obtains the bill.

22. 49 U.S.C. § 80104, UCC 3–201, 7–501.

23. UCC 3–305.

24. 49 U.S.C. § 80105; UCC 7–502.

25. This is a default rule that is explicitly subject to agreement otherwise. The subsection refers to an exception for transactions in which an agreement provides that payment is due only after the goods are to become available for inspection. See Comment 5.

The inspection provisions of UCC 2–513 are concerned only with inspection of the goods, but, in documentary transactions, buyers will inspect the documents tendered to them when drafts are presented for payment. The right to inspect an instrument upon presentment is stated in UCC 3–501(b)(2).

Time, Place, and Manner of Buyer's Tender of Payment. In documentary transactions, the time, place and manner of buyer's tender of payment are determined by the rules on the proper presentment of sight drafts. Under UCC 2–507(1), "tender of delivery" is a condition of buyer's duty to pay. The section does not specify delivery *of goods* and could be read to mean delivery *of documents*. This alternative reading is explicit in UCC 2–507(2), which refers to payment that is due either on delivery of the goods or documents of title.[26]

Dishonor. If a buyer, presented with a documentary sight draft, fails or refuses to make payment when due, the presenting and collecting banks have further duties. Buyer's failure or refusal is referred to as "dishonor."[27] Upon dishonor, the presenting bank must use diligence and good faith to ascertain the reason for dishonor, must notify its transferor of the dishonor and of the results of its effort to ascertain the reasons therefor, and must request instructions.[28] The bank is under no obligation with respect to the goods represented by the documents of title except to follow reasonable instructions received.[29] Upon learning that the draft has not been paid in due course, each collecting bank must seasonably notify its customer of that fact.[30]

Time, Place, and Manner of Seller's Delivery of the Goods. A sales contract, in the form of a documentary transaction, is not completely executed when a presenting bank, which is seller's agent, delivers a document of title to a buyer and buyer pays the amount of a sight draft. Seller's underlying obligation to tender delivery of the goods is not satisfied by the delivery and acceptance of the document of title. In all likelihood the sales contract is a shipment contract.[31] Seller's obligation in UCC 2–504(b), to tender promptly a document of title is, in addition to the obligations in UCC 2–503(a), to put the goods in the possession of a carrier and contract for their transportation. The time, place, and manner of seller's compliance with the requirements of UCC 2–504(a) and (c) were considered in the previous Section.

---

26. The default provision on seller's duty to tender, UCC 2–511(1), is similarly drafted so that delivery could refer either to goods or documents. See also Comment 1: "in the case of specific transactions such as ... agreements providing for payment against documents, the provisions of this subsection must be considered in conjunction with the special sections of the Article dealing with such terms."

27. UCC 3–502(b)(2), 3–502(c).

28. UCC 4–503(2).

29. UCC 4–503.

30. UCC 4–501.

31. Contracts that require seller to tender goods after they arrive at their destination are not likely to be used in documentary transactions. After a buyer has receive an indorsed negotiable bill of lading, only the buyer can obtain the goods from the carrier.

1. THE SITUATION OF BUYERS

Documentary transactions in the form just described reduce the credit risk for buyer and sellers in many ways, but they leave buyers in a precarious position in a number of respects. The following problems are intended to develop your understanding of the mechanics of documentary transactions and to examine the situation of buyers who are expected to pay the purchase price in exchange for a negotiable bill of lading.

Problem 4.3.1. Seller & Co. of Sellersville, N.Y., agreed to sell a large quantity of paper bags to Buyer & Co., of Buyersville, California, who agreed to pay $10,000.00, F.O.B. Sellersville. The parties agreed to a payment term: "sight draft against order bill of lading." Seller & Co. turned over the goods to Railroad and received a negotiable bill of lading made out to the order of Seller & Co. Seller & Co. prepared a draft for the purchase price, indorsed the bill of lading "in blank,"[32] and forwarded the draft and bill through Sellersville Bank to Buyer & Co.

(a) Before the goods have arrived in Buyersville, Buyersville Bank received the draft and bill of lading. Buyersville Bank promptly notified Buyer & Co. that it had a draft and bill of lading. Buyer & Co. refused to pay the draft on the ground that it had not had an opportunity to inspect the goods. Is Buyer & Co. permitted to refuse to pay pending arrival of the goods and inspection of them? See UCC 2–513(3)(b); see also 2–310(b).

(b) Assume that Buyer & Co. paid when the sight draft was presented and obtained the bill of lading. Subsequently, the railroad car containing the 50 cartons of paper bags arrived in Buyersville and Railroad so notified Buyer & Co.[33] Buyer & Co. surrendered the bill of lading to Railroad and took possession of the goods. Upon opening the boxes, Buyer & Co. discovered that a large percentage of the paper bags had been improperly glued. Is Seller & Co. in breach? What are the remedies of Buyer & Co.? See UCC 2–512(2). To what extent are buyer's rights affected by the fact that it has already paid the price?

(c) Assume that Buyer & Co. paid when the sight draft was presented and obtained the bill of lading. The goods did not arrive within the expected time. When Buyer & Co. asked Railroad for information, Railroad disclosed that the car containing the goods had been attached to the wrong train in St. Louis and had to be rerouted. The goods arrived in California three weeks later than anticipated. Is Seller & Co. in breach? If the sales contract had provided that the goods be shipped F.O.B. Buyersville, would Seller & Co. be in breach?

32. A negotiable document of title running to the order of a named person can be negotiated by indorsement and delivery. An indorsement "in blank" permits further negotiation by delivery alone. 49 U.S.C. § 80104(a); UCC 7–501(1). Negotiation of documents of title within banking channels is facilitated by "in blank" indorsements. This permits a document to move forward without the necessity that each bank sign it and identify the next bank in the chain.

33. Order bills of lading usually indicate the person to be notified upon arrival of the goods at their destination. The "notify" provision does not authorize the carrier to deliver goods to the party listed without surrender of the bill of lading.

(d) On the facts of the previous question, does Buyer & Co. have a cause of action against Railroad for delivering goods that do not conform to the sales contract? If the description of the goods in the bill of lading was "Bags, paper," would that create a basis for carrier liability for the quality of the goods? See 49 U.S.C. § 80113; UCC 7–301(1).

Carriers have some duties regarding the quality and quantity of goods not in packages or sealed containers. Thus a carrier must ascertain the kind and quantity of bulk freight, and may be liable for misdescription or nonreceipt of the goods.[34] To protect themselves against claims that goods were damaged en route, carriers may add notes on bills of lading about the condition of the goods or packages.

2. THE SITUATION OF SELLERS

Sellers who engage in documentary exchange transactions incur certain risks of transaction failure. Vis-à-vis buyers, risk exists that buyers will not make payment against tender of documents. Sellers may want to stop the goods, then en route to buyers' locations, and either get them back or divert them to other destinations. Carriers permit consignors to modify the routing of goods, but sellers lose time and incur expenses in making these changes.

Sellers are dependent upon banks and carriers to carry out their respective services. If they should fail to do so, sellers might be deprived of their goods without having received the promised payments.

Problem 4.3.2. Buyer and Seller agreed on sale of a lathe No. 3X from Seller's current catalogue with payment to be made against documents. The next day, Seller delivered a No. 3X lathe to the railroad, obtained a bill of lading that calls for delivery to "order of Seller," indorsed the bill in blank, and gave it along with a sight draft drawn on Buyer to its local bank for transmittal to Buyer. The documents were forwarded to a bank in Buyer's city, which sent a notice to Buyer that it held these documents for Buyer's payment.

(a) Buyer ignored the notice. What is the nature of the bank's obligation?

(b) Has Buyer dishonored the draft by not responding to the bank's notice? See UCC 3–502(c)?

(c) Is the presenting bank obliged to do more than inform seller of buyer's dishonor? See UCC 4–503(2). What might be the reason for these obligations?

Problem 4.3.3. Assume the facts as above, except that the presenting bank gave Buyer the bill of lading in exchange for the Buyer's uncertified check in the amount of the draft. Before the Buyer's check was paid, Buyer obtained the lathe from the railroad and stopped payment on its check.[35]

(a) What are Seller's rights?

---

34. 49 U.S.C. § 80113; UCC 7–301(2).   **35.** See UCC 4–403(a).

(b) Does Seller have a claim against Railroad? See 49 U.S.C. § 80110; UCC 7–404.

(c) Does Seller have a claim against the presenting bank? See UCC 4–202(1), 4–211(1), 4–103(5). And see Bunge v. First National Bank of Mount Holly Springs, 118 F.2d 427 (3d Cir.1941).

(d) Does Seller have a claim against its local bank for the actions of the presenting bank? See UCC 4–202(3) and Comment 4.

(e) Does Seller have a claim against Buyer? See UCC 2–301, 2–507. Of what practical value to Seller is 2–507(2)?

Problem 4.3.4. Assume the same facts as in preceding problem, except that Buyer, without paying the draft or obtaining the bill of lading, gets possession of the lathe from Railroad.

(a) What are Seller's rights?

(b) Does Seller have a claim against Railroad? See 49 U.S.C. §§ 80110, 80111; UCC 7–403(1). What would be the proper measure of damages? See Alderman Bros. Co. v. New York, etc. R. Co., 102 Conn. 461, 129 A. 47 (1925).

(c) Does Seller have a claim against any bank?

(d) Does Seller have a claim against Buyer?

––––––––

Sellers' Use of Drafts to Obtain Credit. Sellers engaging in documentary transactions sometimes seek to speed up the inflow of cash by getting the amount of the drafts, less a discount, from the banks who take them for collection and presentment. The context of documentary transactions gives banks reasonable assurance that credit extended to sellers will be repaid promptly from proceeds of the drafts. Moreover, the drafts are negotiable instruments on which the sellers are liable as drawers.[36] The banks are holders of indorsed bills of lading and therefore have security for repayment in their control of the goods. Not uncommonly, therefore, banks taking drafts for collection will "discount" them.

Sellers may also "discount" drafts to anticipate payment when underlying documentary transactions require buyers to accept "time drafts" upon presentment rather than make immediate payment. Drafts may be discounted before their presentment. The banks' legal rights in the period before presentment are similar to their rights in discount of sight drafts. The situation changes when buyers "accept" time drafts.[37] Acceptance of a draft establishes a new obligation on a drawee/acceptor.[38] This obligation is independent of the payment obligation in the sales contract and can be

36. UCC 3–414(b).

37. "Acceptance" means the drawee's signed agreement to pay a draft as presented. UCC 3–409(a).

38. UCC 3–413(a).

enforced by subsequent holders of the instrument without regard to the buyer's rights under the sales contract. The drawer is also obligated to pay the amount of the draft to a subsequent holder of the instrument. The drawer's liability is secondary to that of the acceptor.[39] Accepted time drafts arising from documentary transactions are referred to as "trade acceptances." Trade acceptances are very negotiable instruments.

INTERNATIONAL SALES LAW

Documentary transactions of the kind described in this Section are used less in international sales than in domestic United States sales. Part of the explanation, no doubt, is the absence of an international legal platform comparable to the domestic United States laws on negotiable instruments and negotiable documents of title. Given the choice of law rules of private international law, no nation's domestic laws are likely to have sufficient scope of application to provide a legal platform for the execution of documentary transactions in international sales.

Without any legal platform, parties engaged in international trade often understand and accept the reliability of the commitment of ocean carriers, which issue negotiable bills of lading, that goods will be delivered only upon surrender of a properly indorsed bill of lading. International sales contracts that incorporate certain shipping terms are understood to require sellers to obtain and deliver negotiable bills of lading. The ICC noted:[40]

Traditionally, the on board bill of lading has been the only acceptable document to be presented by the seller under [contracts that use the] terms CFR and CIF. The bill of lading fulfills three important functions, namely

— proof of delivery of the goods on board the vessel

— evidence of the contract of carriage

— a means of transferring rights to the goods in transit by the transfer of the paper document to another party.

Transport documents other than the bill of lading would fill the two first-mentioned functions, but would not control the delivery of the goods at destination or enable a buyer to sell the goods in transit by surrendering the paper document to his buyer. Instead, other transport documents would name the party entitled to receive the goods at destination.

In the oil business, crude oil in holds of supertankers steaming across oceans is often bought and sold many times while the ships are en route.

If international sales contracts involve negotiable documents of title, the Convention has a brief provision regarding sellers' duty to deliver the documents. Sellers are bound to hand over documents relating to the goods

---

39. UCC 3–414(b) and (d); but see UCC 3–414(e) (drafts drawn "without recourse").

40. ICC Incoterms 1990, Introduction ¶ 18.

"at the time and place and in the form required by the contract." CISG 34. The Convention has no default rule for when or where this is to occur.

Payment by buyers against documents of title, the essence of domestic documentary transactions is not mentioned by the CISG.[41] In international transactions, payment arrangements typically involve bank letters of credit. Letter of credit transactions are taken up in the next Section.

SECTION 4.   PAYMENT BY LETTER OF CREDIT

Documentary transaction arrangements are useful in producing a kind of simultaneous exchange, but such arrangements do not assure sellers that buyers will make payment against sight drafts or accept time drafts upon presentment. Dishonor is a risk whenever a buyer decides not to fulfill its obligation under the sales contract or the buyer, for some reason, is unable to pay (or accept) the draft. If a buyer dishonors a draft, the seller has not lost ultimate control of the goods, but, when dishonor occurs, the goods are en route to their original destination and must be brought back or diverted. To avoid the risk of dishonor by a buyer on presentment of documents, parties to sales contracts can contract for a payment arrangement whereby a draft and a negotiable document of title, and perhaps other documents, are presented to a bank that is independently obligated to pay (or accept) the draft. Banks commonly undertake such obligations when they issue letters of credit. Bank letters of credit are extraordinarily important payment devices in international sales transactions, but such letters of credit are often used in domestic sales transactions within the United States.

Buyers' obligation to make payment though letters of credit must be bargained for in sales contracts. Use of a letter of credit is not a default obligation. Terms of sales contracts that call for payment by letter of credit provide not only that a letter of credit may be used, but also provide whether the credit is for immediate payment or for acceptance of a time draft and specify in detail the exact documents that will be sufficient to trigger payment by the bank that issued the credit. Banks issue letters of credit of two kinds: revocable or irrevocable. Sellers normally negotiate for buyers to obtain irrevocable letters of credit. Sellers typically require buyers to open letters of credit for an amount in excess of the contract price so that sellers can recover incidental expenses incurred on buyers' behalf. If the date of shipment is uncertain at the time of the sales contract, the parties negotiate for the length of time during which a letter must remain open.

---

41. Common-law courts have long held that an obligation to pay against documents is implicit in certain international sales contracts. The leading case is E. Clemens Horst Co. v. Biddle Bros., [1912] A.C. 18 (H.L.)(sale of hops shipped from San Francisco C.I.F to London, Liverpool, or Hull). This common-law rule was incorporated into the UCC, which provides that contractual use of terms associated with water transport (C.I.F., C. & F., F.A.S., F.O.B. vessel) creates a duty on buyers to pay against documents. UCC 2–319(4), 2–320(4), 2–321(3).

Counsel for buyers should be especially careful in negotiating the letter of credit terms of sales contracts, because they will have almost no control of the banks' conduct when demand for payment is made. Conversely counsel for sellers negotiating these terms should be careful to identify the bank or class of banks that is acceptable as issuer of a letter of credit and specify only documents that the sellers can prepare or obtain.

Once a sales contract calling for payment by letter of credit is concluded, two other independent contracts must be negotiated. First, the buyer must negotiate with a bank for the bank to issue a letter of credit, probably an irrevocable credit, and the terms to be included in the credit. Critical to this negotiation is a method, satisfactory to the bank, for it to be reimbursed. Also to be agreed between the bank and the buyer is the bank's fee for its participation. The second contract, which is not negotiated, is the contract between the bank and the seller that arises when the bank issues its letter of credit to the beneficiary-seller. If a bank issues an irrevocable letter of credit, the bank must pay (or accept) seller's drafts that satisfy the conditions specified in the letter.

Each of the three contracts: the underlying sales contract, the buyer-bank contract, and the bank-beneficiary contract is independent of the others. Obligations to perform the promises in each contract are not conditional on performances or events under the other contracts. Thus, a seller's breach of its obligation under the underlying sales contract or a buyer's breach of its obligation to reimburse the issuing bank is not a defense to the bank's obligation to pay (or accept) under its letter of credit. This is often referred to as the *independence principle* among the congeries of contracts that are involved in letter of credit transactions.

Buyers obligated under sales contracts to *open* letters of credit are likely to want to go to the banks with which they have ongoing banking relationships. Sellers, on the other hand, are likely to want to have letters of credit from banks that are conveniently located for presentment. Letter of credit practice developed two solutions for this situation. In one scenario, sellers are authorized by letters of credit to present their drafts and documents to local banks which forward the paper to the issuing banks. This scenario resembles the arrangement in documentary transactions, but presentment in a letter of credit transaction is to the issuing bank rather than to the buyer.

In an alternative scenario, parties to sales contracts arrange for seller's bank to issue its letter of credit on the strength of a letter of credit issued by buyer's bank. In banking and commercial practice, the bank issuing the second letter is said to *confirm* the first letter of credit. Sellers who want a local bank's commitment must negotiate buyers' obligation to obtain a letter of credit from an issuing bank that will, in turn, secure a confirming bank.[1] If a seller does not negotiate for the commitment of a local bank as a

---

1. In making its commitment to the beneficiary of a confirmed credit, the confirming bank is relying entirely on the credit of the issuing bank. This works better when the banks have a continuing relationship. "It is customary that the issuing bank requests a

confirming bank, enforcement of the issuing bank's obligation may require litigation in a foreign country.[2] The conditions on payment in the two letters of credit are identical. When a confirming bank pays under its letter of credit, it is entitled to reimbursement from the original bank.[3]

DOMESTIC UNITED STATES LAW

UCC Article 2 has one section on the use of letter of credit payments in sales contracts. The section deals in part with interpretation of payment terms in sales contracts and in part with performance of buyers' obligations to furnish letters of credit.

UCC 2–325(3) is pertinent to interpretation of some terms used in sale contract. It provides that contractual reference to "letter of credit" or "banker's credit" obligates a buyer to obtain an irrevocable letter of credit. Moreover, the issuing bank must be a "financing agency of good repute" and, where shipment is to an overseas buyer, the issuing bank must be "of good international repute." A sales contract's reference to a "confirmed credit" means that the credit must carry the direct obligation of a bank that does business in the seller's financial market.

Time, Place and Manner of Buyers' Furnishing Letters of Credit. Sales contracts may provide explicitly the time for buyers to furnish sellers with letters of credit that conform to sales contracts. UCC 2–325(1) implies that a letter of credit must be furnished "seasonally," but does not otherwise elaborate on the time, place or manner of a buyer's performance. Banks that issue letters of credit customarily send them directly to the named beneficiaries as soon as they have accepted buyers' applications.[4]

UCC 2–325(1) declares that failure of the buyer seasonably to furnish an agreed letter of credit is a breach of the sales contract.

Article 5 of the UCC contains domestic United States law on letters of credit. This Article provides a broad legal platform that undergirds letter of credit transactions in sales contracts. Article 5, however, refers to parties only by their roles in a letter of transaction: principally applicant, issuer, confirmer, beneficiary.[5] The independence principle is stated in UCC 5–

---

bank of its choice to advise and, as the case may be, to confirm its credit to the beneficiary." ICC, Case Studies on Documentary Credits, Case 26, p. 39 (J. Dekker 1989).

2. See Pacific Reliant Industries, Inc. v. Amerika Samoa Bank, 901 F.2d 735 (9th Cir.1990)(Oregon seller of building materials to Samoa buyer agreed to letter of credit issued by Samoan bank; seller's suit to enforce the credit in Oregon federal district court dismissed for lack of personal jurisdiction over the bank).

3. For fuller accounts of letter of credit transactions, see J. Dolan, Commercial Law: Essential Terms and Transactions 39–50 (2d

ed. 1997); H. Harfield, Payment Commitments—Banker's Acceptances and Letters of Credit, in Bank Credit 219 (H. Prochnow, ed., 1981).

4. Delivery of a proper letter of credit creates a bank's obligation to honor the credit and suspends buyer's obligation to pay the contract price. UCC 2–325(2). If a letter of credit is dishonored, seller may proceed against the bank or, on seasonable notification, against the buyer. Id.

5. All of these are defined terms under UCC 5–102(a).

103(d). For sales contracts that require payment by letter of credit, Article 5 serves the same purpose as Articles 3 and 4 serve in documentary transactions.[6]

INTERNATIONAL SALES LAW

Although terms requiring letter of credit payment are ubiquitous in international sales transactions, the Convention on Contracts for International Sale of Goods is silent on these terms. CISG 54 provides only that a buyer's obligation "includes taking such steps ... as may be required under the contract...."

Problem 4.4.1. A contract for the sale of 3000 tons of Brazilian groundnuts called for shipment from Brazil to Genoa between February 1 and April 30, at the option of the sellers. The contract further provided: "Payment: By opening of a confirmed, irrevocable, divisible, transmissible and transferable credit opened in favour of the sellers and utilisable by them against delivery of the following documents." The buyer established the letter of credit on April 22. The seller had already resold the goods on the ground that the credit was established too late in the light of the seller's privilege to ship in February or March. Seller sued the buyer for damages. What result under CISG? What evidence of custom and what arguments concerning seller's need for the letter of credit would be relevant?[7]

Problem 4.4.2. If a buyer has the obligation to arrange for shipping and has the privilege of selecting the date for shipment within a designated period, may the buyer delay establishing the letter of credit until the end of the period? What would be the effect of a showing by seller that it was customary in this trade to use the letter of credit in order to raise funds to pay the seller's supplier?[8]

Problem 4.4.3. If a sales contract requires only that buyer furnish a letter of credit, does buyer meet that obligation by obtaining a revocable letter of credit? Domestic United States law, the UCC, declares that buyer must provide an irrevocable letter of credit. UCC 2–325(3). Would the same result follow under CISG?[9]

Uniform Customs and Practices for Documentary Credits. Contracting for payment by letter of credit is greatly aided by the availability of the Uniform Customs and Practices for Documentary Credits (UCP). The UCP are another product of the International Chamber of Commerce

---

6. A leading American treatise is J. Dolan, The Law of Letters of Credit (rev.ed. 1996)

7. See Pavia & Co. v. Thurmann Nielsen, [1952] 1 All E.R. 492 (C.A.).

8. See Ian Stach, Ltd. v. Baker Bosly, Ltd., [1958] 1 All E.R. 542 (interesting and instructive opinion by Diplock, J., on the practical problems presented by using the ultimate buyer's letter of credit to finance "a string of merchants' contracts between the manufacturer or stockist and the ultimate user"); 108 L.J. 388 (1958).

9. A similar, but quite different question arises of interpreting a letter of credit that does not declare whether or not it is revocable.

(ICC). Bankers from throughout the world have established, within the ICC, a Commission on Banking Technique and Practice. The UCP, adhered to by banks in over 145 nations, are practically universal in the scope of their application. The UCP originated in the 1930s and have been revised a number of times. The most recent revision, known as UCP 500, was promulgated in 1993.

The ICC project goes beyond promulgation of the UCP. The Commission on Banking Technique and Practice issues opinions on interpretation of UCP provisions from time to time. The Commission also has a group of experts, the International Centre for Expertise, who respond to queries about the application of the UCP to particular circumstances.[10]

UCP provisions are not law. They constitute an elaborate body of standard contract terms which parties to contracts may elect to incorporate in their agreements. When buyers and sellers specify payment by letter of credit, they commonly add that they intend letters of credit under the UCP. When banks issue or confirm letters of credit, the letters specify that they are subject to the UCP. Contract provisions incorporating the UCP are enforceable to the extent that the domestic laws otherwise governing the transactions give effect to the terms of the contracts.

Although UCP provisions are not law, many of the provisions address matters that are covered by Article 5 of the UCC, which is a statute. The 1960s version of UCC Article clashed with the UCP of that period.[11] The recent revision of Article 5 is very compatible with the UCP. Comment 8 to UCC 5–108 refers to the UCP as a valid source of customs governing letters of credit. "Clearly, the Article 5 drafters intended that their rules parallel the UCP rules."[12]

––––––––

Revocable Letters of Credit. Banking practice developed two types of letters of credit, revocable and irrevocable. Issuing banks and their customers choose whether the customers have power to revoke without the consent of the beneficiaries of the credits. Normally issuing banks are careful to state explicitly whether a letter of credit is revocable or irrevocable. If, however, a bank fails to do so in a credit subject to the UCP, article

10. Opinions of the Banking Commission are published regularly by the ICC. See ICC Publications 371, 399, 434 and 469. For responses to recent queries, see Case Studies on Documentary Credits: Problems, Queries, Answers (C. del Busto, 1995).

11. Four states, including New York, adopted Article 5 with non-uniform amendments providing that the statute would not apply to letters of credit that were issued subject to the UCP. The New York action was particularly significant, since banks in New York City were prominent among United States banks that issued letters of credit. See J. Dolan, Letter of Credit: A Comparison of UCP 500 and the New U.S. Article 5, [1999] J. Bus. L. 521.

12. J. Dolan, Letter of Credit: A Comparison of UCP 500 and the New U.S. Article 5, [1999] J. Bus. L. 521, 523. Professor Dolan concluded, however, that the efforts of the drafters of Article 5 were not entirely successful. He found two areas in which there is some measure of dissonance.

6(c) of UCP 500 provides that the credit is irrevocable.[13] (Note that the UCP provision deals only interpretation of letters of credit and has no application to interpretation of sales contracts when those contracts lack specification as to the revocability or irrevocability of required letters of credit.)

Transferable Letters of Credit; Assignability of Proceeds. Added commercial flexibility may be achieved if the named beneficiary under a letter of credit can transfer or assign its rights to third parties. Article 48(b) of the UCP 500 provides: "A credit can be transferred only if it is expressly designated as 'transferable' by the issuing bank." Article 49 adds that a statement prohibiting transfer does not affect the beneficiary's right to assign any proceeds to which it may be entitled under the credit "in accordance with the provisions of the applicable law." UCC 5–114(a) establishes a rule similar to that in the UCP with respect to "the right *to draw* under a credit." Subsection (b) adds: "A beneficiary may assign its right to a part or all of the proceeds of a letter of credit," but this is immediately qualified by subsection (c): "An issuer ... need not recognize an assignment of proceeds of a letter of credit until it consents to the assignment," and by subsection (d): "... consent may not be unreasonably withheld if the assignee possesses and exhibits the letter of credit and presentation of the letter of credit is a condition to honor." UCC 5–113 adds an exception where transfer occurs by operation of law.

Section 5.   Transactions in Goods not to Be Moved

In some circumstances, owners of goods, having put them into storage, decide to sell the goods to buyers who want to keep the goods where they are. The persons with custody of the goods, often warehouse operators, are characterized legally as bailees. Performance of sellers obligations in sales contracts that concern goods that are not to be moved require, in effect, that the sellers transfer to the buyers the bailees' obligation to surrender the goods.[1]

An example of a market situation in which goods may be sold without intent to move them at the time of sale occurs in sales of propane and natural gas, which are held in huge underground storage facilities. Sellers and buyers perform contracts for sale of the goods by transfer to buyers of commitments to deliver by operators of the storage facilities. See., e.g., Commonwealth Petroleum Co. v. Petrosol International, Inc., 901 F.2d 1314 (6th Cir.1990).

---

13. This provision in UCP 500 is directly opposite to the provision on the same matter in UCP 400.

1. The situation of a sale of goods in possession of bailee is analogous to the situation of a sale of goods in possession of a carrier. The carrier with custody of the goods is not generally characterized as a bailee.

DOMESTIC UNITED STATES LAW

Performance rules for such contracts are provided in UCC 2–503(4) for transactions in which the parties have not specifically described the manner of sellers' performance.

Manner of Sellers' Tender. Some bailees in possession of goods issue negotiable documents of title, similar to negotiable bills of lading issued by carriers, that control the right to obtain possession of the goods.[2] Such documents are called negotiable warehouse receipts. If goods are covered by such a document, a seller performs its obligation under the sales contract by tendering the document in a form that makes the buyer the holder of the document. UCC 2–503(4)(a). Alternatively, a seller performs by procuring the bailee's acknowledgment of the buyer's right to possession of the goods.

UCC 2–503(4) goes on to qualify the tender rules of subsections (a). When goods are stored with a bailee that has not issued a negotiable document of title, tender occurs when a seller tenders a non-negotiable document of title or a written direction to the bailee to deliver the goods to the buyer, unless the buyer objects to tender in this manner. If a buyer does object, seller's tender obligation is met provisionally upon the bailee's receipt of notification of the buyer's rights, but that tender is defeated if the bailee refuses to obey the direction. UCC 2–503(4)(b).

Manner of Buyers' Tender; Inspection. The UCC does not have a default rule for buyers' inspection of the goods or tender of payment of the price in transactions where goods are to be delivered without being moved. Therefore, a buyer has the right to inspect the goods before payment is due under UCC 2–513(1). Seller's tender entitles the seller to payment according to the contract under UCC 2–507(1).

The UCC contains no default rules on the time and place for sellers' tender under UCC 2–503(4) or buyers' tender under UCC 2–507.

INTERNATIONAL SALES LAW

The Convention on Contracts for International Sale of Goods has no provisions on performance of contracts for sales of goods in storage.

---

2. The governing law is Article 7 of the UCC. The prototypical document of title is-sued by a bailee is a warehouse receipt. UCC 1–201(45), 7–202.

CHAPTER 5

Performance Stage Controversies

Introduction. The performance stage of sales contracts is a time in which many diverse controversies can arise. That is not the case in sales contracts where the goods being sold are present and identified at the time the contracts are formed. When performance follows immediately after formation, the likelihood of performance stage controversy is slight.[1] As the period between contract formation and performance grows, the probability of performance-stage controversy increases. A number of reasons exist: A gap between contract formation and performance usually results because the goods contracted for are "future goods."[2] In such transactions, sellers may not be able to make or buy goods that conform completely to contract descriptions. Also, in such transactions, buyers opportunity to see and examine the goods arises when the goods are tendered or delivered. Inspection of the goods may reveal qualities that are not satisfactory to the buyers. Any problems in the manner, time or place of performance become manifest in the performance stage of sales of future goods.

An added factor that causes instability in the performance stage of many sales contracts is reduced commitment to the deal on the part of one of the parties. The values of the exchange anticipated by buyers and sellers at the time of contract formation may not exist at the time of performance. The simplest reason for this is movement in the market value of goods sold for fixed prices. In a market with falling prices for available goods, a buyer may regret its agreement to pay the higher-than-market contract price.[3] Other changes in the situations of buyers, such as their planned use of the goods, may also result in reduced commitment to the contracts. If regrets or changed circumstances lead a buyer to want to escape from its contract obligation without liability for breach, the buyer may become extremely finicky about every aspect of the seller's performance. If the contract conditions on a buyer's duty to pay are not fulfilled, the buyer can walk away without liability. Analogous incentives may exist on the sellers' side

---

1. Nonconformities may exist in present goods, such as breach of a warranty of quality or title, but these nonconformities are likely to be latent and not detected by buyers until performances have been completed. When latent nonconformities are discovered by buyers, their remedies in the post-performance stage were considered in Chapter 3.

2. See UCC 2–105(2).

3. Similarly, in a market of rising prices, a seller may regret its agreement to accept a lower-than-market contract price.

of contracts, but the contract conditions on a seller's duty to deliver goods are different.

Strategic behavior of the kind just discussed in unlikely to occur when the parties have an ongoing and mutually valued commercial relationship.[4] If continuation of a relationship has a sufficient value to both of the parties, neither is likely to raise performance-stage issues in an effort to escape from one unfavorable deal. Indeed, when market breaks occur or circumstances change otherwise, they may have incentives to modify terms of contracts not yet executed to take account of the changes that occurred.

As you consider cases and problems in which performance-stage controversies arise, be aware of the contract relationships between the parties and the extent to which one of the parties may be seeking to escape from a deal that it no longer considers favorable. More personally, consider the role of counsel in advising sellers or buyers in the performance stage of contracts that may be prone to have controversy.

A Preliminary Roadmap of Controversies. Prominent among performance-stage controversies are controversies that arise when sellers' performances do not conform to their contractual obligations or are perceived by buyers not to conform. The first two Sections of this Chapter considers the performance options available to buyers when, in fact, sellers have tendered or delivered nonconforming goods or nonconforming documents or otherwise failed to satisfy their contract obligations, the performance options available to sellers when buyers decide not to accept goods, and the legal remedies that flow from the parties' exercise of their options.

Section 3 examines performance stage controversies that arise in connection with letters of credit.

Another set of controversies stems from some casualty to the goods, e.g., loss or damage, during the performance stage of sales contracts. The loss of value in goods identified to sales contracts is a major risk, which parties may address in their sales contracts. Default rules on "risk-of-loss" are an important part of any body of sales law. These are considered in Section 4.

SECTION 1.   NONCONFORMING PERFORMANCE BY SELLERS: BUYERS' ACCEPTANCE OR REJECTION, AND SELLERS' CURE

DOMESTIC UNITED STATES LAW

(A) ACCEPTANCE

Buyers' Duty to Accept Goods. UCC 2–301 declares that buyers are obligated to "accept" goods delivered by sellers, and UCC 2–507(1) states

---

4. If one of the parties to a long-term contractual relationship determines that the relationship is no longer sufficiently valuable to it, it may seek legal grounds for termi- nation of the long-term contract. See., e.g., Advent Systems, Ltd. v. Unisys Corp., Chapter 2, Section 1(B), supra.

that: "tender entitles the seller to [buyer's] acceptance of the goods...." Although not clearly stated, the UCC's provisions cannot be read reasonably to impose on buyers the obligation to accept nonconforming goods or goods tendered in a manner, time or place that does not conform to sellers' obligation. Implicit in buyers' obligation is the condition that the tender and the tendered goods conform to the contract.

The opposite of acceptance is rejection. Buyers may reject nonconforming goods or documents and may reject goods or documents tendered other than in conformity with the contract. The basic provisions on rejection are found in UCC 2–601 and UCC 2–612(2).

Significance of Acceptance. Acceptance of goods is a significant legal watershed: at that moment the legal positions of a buyer and a seller change substantially. Acceptance precludes rejection. UCC 2–607(2). The buyer must pay at the contract rate for any goods accepted. UCC 2–607(3).

Acceptance of goods does not foreclose buyers from relief if the goods do not conform to the contract. As we learned in Chapter 3, buyers may have claims for breach of warranties of title or quality.[1] In such litigation, the burden is on the buyers to establish any breach with respect to accepted goods. UCC 2–607(4). Unless time-barred under UCC 2–725 or barred for lack of notice under UCC 2–607(3)(a), aggrieved buyers may recover damages under UCC 2–714 and 2–715. As you recall, monetary relief under UCC 2–714 and 2–715 is not the sole remedy for aggrieved buyers. Some are empowered to revoke their acceptances under UCC 2–608 and are entitled to recover the contract price as well as damages.

Manner of Buyers' Acceptance of Goods. The UCC has a three-pronged definition of how buyers' accept goods: (1) overt statements to sellers, (2) estoppel resulting from buyers' handling of the goods, and (3) lapse of time after delivery or tender of delivery. UCC 2–606(1).

In most ordinary commercial and consumer transactions, acceptance is the result of mere lapse of time. Sometimes a buyer may "[signify] to the seller that the goods are conforming or that he will take them or retain them in spite of their non-conformity," UCC 2–606(1)(a), but, more likely, buyers receive goods and simply say nothing to the seller about conformity or nonconformity.[2] Continued silence becomes "failure to make an effective rejection," UCC 2–606(1)(b), because "rejection of goods must be within a reasonable time after their delivery or tender." UCC 2–602(1).[3]

Time of Acceptance: Inspection of Goods Before Acceptance. Acceptance by signification or by lapse of time cannot occur until buyers

---

1. Nearly all the cases and Problems on breach of warranty of quality and breach of warranty of title in Chapter 3 involved buyers who had accepted goods.

2. Businesses courting good will sometimes inquire about customer satisfaction with the goods received. This may produce express responses, but thank-you notes or equivalent are not commonplace occurrences in market transactions.

3. The third prong, "does any act inconsistent with the seller's ownership," UCC 2–606(1)(c), is based on buyers' conduct. Common acts that may fit this prong are buyers' consumption of the goods or transfer of them to a sub-purchaser.

have had "a reasonable opportunity to inspect" the goods. UCC 2–606(1)(a) and (b), 2–513(1). In Chapter 4 we considered buyers' right to inspect before the obligation to pay matured. The same provisions of the UCC condition both the obligation to accept and the obligation to pay with buyers' right to inspect. The UCC declares that buyers may inspect goods "in any reasonable manner," UCC 2–513(1), but offers no criteria for determining what inspection methods are reasonable.

ZABRISKIE CHEVROLET, INC. v. SMITH, 99 N.J.Super. 441, 240 A.2d 195 (1968). Buyer purchased a new car from Dealer. Buyer gave the Dealer his personal check for the price and took possession of the car. After driving 7/10 of a mile from Dealer's showroom, Buyer discovered a non-conformity. Buyer stopped payment on his check. Dealer sued for the purchase price under UCC 2–709(1)(a). Dealer contended that buyer had accepted the car. The court found that Buyer had not accepted. In so deciding, the court concluded that Buyer had not completed his inspection of it when he paid and drove it away: "To the layman, the complicated mechanisms of today's automobiles are a complete mystery. To have the automobile inspected [in the showroom] by someone with sufficient exper-tise to disassemble the vehicle in order to discover latent defects ... is assuredly impossible and highly impractical. ... Consequently, the first few miles of driving become even more significant to the excited new car buyer. This is the buyer's first reasonable opportunity ... to see if it conforms to what it was represented to be.... How long the buyer may drive the new car under the guise of inspection is not an issue in the present case."

(B) REJECTION

Buyers' Right to Reject Goods or Documents. As already noted, the antithesis of acceptance is rejection. The right of buyers to reject goods or documents is set forth in UCC 2–601 for single-delivery sales contracts and in UCC 2–612 for sales contracts in which sellers' performances are divided into installments.

Significance of Rejection. Rejection of goods, if rightful, means that seller has failed to meet its obligation to make due tender of conforming goods. Buyer is released from obligation to pay the contract price, UCC 2–507(1), and, absent cure of the deficiencies in sellers' performance, is entitled to monetary remedies, which are catalogued in UCC 2–711. In addition to recovering any part of the contract price paid, UCC 2–711(1), buyer is entitled to damages measured by the cost of purchasing substitute goods ("cover") from another source, UCC 2–712, or by the differential between market price and contract price, UCC 2–713, together with inci-dental or consequential damages under UCC 2–715. Responsibility for disposition of rejected goods is on seller, although some buyers have the right or duty to act on seller's behalf in disposing of them.

Perfect Tender; Substantial Impairment of Value. The basic standard that differentiates rightful from wrongful rejection is UCC 2–601.[4]

---

4. Buyers are permitted, of course, to accept goods known to be nonconforming. See UCC 2–607(2). There is no concept of wrongful acceptance.

In transactions that involve a single delivery of goods, a buyer is permitted to reject "if the goods or the tender of delivery fail in any respect to conform to the contract." Common legal usage refers to this standard as the "perfect tender rule."[5] Goods or the tender of delivery may fail to conform to the contract in many respects, but four tend to predominate: clouds on title, defects in quality, deficiencies or excesses in quantity, and late deliveries. Section 2–601 is "subject to the provisions of this Article on breach in installment contracts." The perfect-tender rule does not apply to sellers' tenders of goods in installment contracts.

Historians identify a mid–19th century British decision as the origin of the perfect tender rule. Bowes v. Shand, [1876] 1 Q.B.D. 470, [1877] 2 Q.B.D. 112, [1877] 2 App. Cas. 455. Professor Grant Gilmore said that the perfect tender rule in the United States dates from October 26, 1885, when the Supreme Court decided Norrington v. Wright, 115 U.S. 188, 6 S.Ct. 12, 29 L.Ed. 366 (1885), and Filley v. Pope, 115 U.S. 213, 6 S.Ct. 19, 29 L.Ed. 372 (1885). See E. Peters, Commercial Transactions 33 (1971). A high (or low) water mark cited by Professor (later Connecticut Supreme Court Chief Justice) Peters was Frankel v. Foreman & Clark, 33 F.2d 83 (2d Cir.1929) (permitting rejection of a shipment of coats for trivial and inconsequential nonconformities in less than 2% of the coats). Id. at 34. The perfect tender rule was not stated, explicitly in either the Sale of Goods Act or the Uniform Sales Act.[6] For a comprehensive review of court decisions applying the perfect tender rule prior to the UCC, see J. Honnold, Buyer's Right of Rejection, 97 U. Pa. L. Rev. 457 (1949).

The perfect tender rule was codified in early versions of the UCC. After the UCC had been promulgated for adoption by the states, a major study was conducted under the aegis of the Law Revision Commission of the State of New York. That Commission recommended that "the right of rejection as stated in Section 2–601 be limited to material breach." The Editorial Board responsible for revising the UCC following the New York study did not accept this recommendation. That Board relied on two grounds: "first, ... the buyer should not be required to guess at his peril whether a breach is material; second, ... proof of materiality would sometimes require disclosure of the buyer's private affairs such as secret formulas or processes." R. Braucher & E. Sutherland, Commercial Transactions 56 (1964). Other considerations, noted by Professor Honnold in Buyer's Right of Rejection, supra, at 466–72, were : (1) the hazard for buyers of securing redress when full cash payment is demanded on tender of the goods; (2) the difficulty in many cases of measuring, without controversy, the extent of the deficiency in sellers' performance. Are these reasons persuasive?[7] Do the rules of the UCC fit these underlying interests

---

5. Comment 2 to UCC 2–106(2) (definition of "conforming") states: "It is in general intended to continue the policy of exact performance by the seller of his obligations as a condition to his right to require acceptance."

6. See the Prior Uniform Statutory Provision segment of the Comment to UCC 2–601.

7. See W. Lawrence, Appropriate Standards for a Buyer's Refusal to Keep Goods Tendered by a Seller, 35 Wm. & Mary L. Rev. 1635 (1994); J. Sebert, Rejection, Revocation,

as well as is feasible?[8]

The perfect tender rule does not apply to sellers' performances in installment contracts. The substance of the governing provision, UCC 2–612, is closer to the common-law standard for contract performance that entitles those rendering performance to the contract price.[9] However, the text of UCC 2–612 is detailed and complex. We take up its provisions later in this Section.

Manner and Time of Buyers' Rejection of Goods. Rejection of goods must be made before lapse of a reasonable time after tender or delivery, UCC 2–602(1). The only way for a buyer to reject effectively is to notify the seller seasonably. UCC 2–602(1). The UCC does not prescribe the minimum content of an effective rejection notice, but does provide that certain buyers' failure to describe particular defects will preclude them from later relying on unstated defects to justify their rejection or to establish sellers' breach. UCC 2–605.[10]

Cure. Rejection of goods or documents opens another performance option for sellers. UCC 2–508 gives some sellers a second chance to perform.[11]

Responsibility for Rejected Goods. Goods rejected by buyers are not necessarily worthless. Although goods may not conform to the terms of a sales contract, the goods may be useful and marketable under accurate contract descriptions. When a buyer's rejection occurs at or before the seller's tender of delivery, the seller is not likely to complete delivery and the goods remain in the seller's control. The seller can make an alternative disposition of the goods. In sales contracts that involve carriers' transport of the goods, but that require buyers' inspection of the goods before carriers hand them over to the buyers, rejected goods are in the possession of the carriers and can be rerouted or returned on instructions from the sellers.[12]

---

and Cure Under Article 2 of the Uniform Commercial Code: Some Modest Proposals, 84 Nw. U. L. Rev. 375 (1990); W. Lawrence, The Prematurely Reported Demise of the Perfect Tender Rule, 35 Kan. L. Rev. 557 (1987).

8. See E. Peters, Remedies for Breach of Contracts Relating to the Sale of Goods Under the UCC, 73 Yale L.J. 199, 206–27 (1963); G. Priest, Breach and Remedy for the Tender of Nonconforming Goods: An Economic Approach, 91 Harv.L.Rev. 960 (1978); Schmitt & Frisch, 13 Toledo L.Rev. 1375 (1982).

9. See E, Farnsworth, Contracts § 8.16 (3d ed. 1999); Restatement, Second, Contracts §§ 237, 241 (1981).

10. Compare the necessary content of buyers' notices to sellers with regard to non-

conformity of accepted goods. UCC 2–607(3)(a) and Comment 4.

11. There is a common-law doctrine on the right to cure defective performances. The common-law rule was influenced by UCC 2–508. See E. Farnsworth, Contracts § 8.17 (3d ed. 1999)

12. In at-a-particular-destination contracts, when sellers tender goods through carriers *at* the stated place, buyers accept or reject in response to such tenders in the same way as they perform the acceptance obligation in transactions performed without carriers. Within a reasonable time after tender, they must elect to accept or reject the goods. UCC 2–606(1)(b). In the-place-of-shipment contracts, tender may be completed before arrival of the goods, but the time period for a buyer to accept or reject does not begin to

The situation is more complicated, commercially and legally, when rejection decisions are made and communicated after the goods have been received by the buyers. If a non-merchant buyer has taken possession of goods before rejecting them, buyer must hold the goods with reasonable care for a time sufficient to permit seller to remove them, UCC 2–602(2)(b), but has no further obligations with regard to the goods. UCC 2–602(2)(c). A merchant buyer in possession of rejected goods must follow seller's reasonable instructions. UCC 2–603(1). A merchant buyer in possession of perishable goods or goods whose market value may decline speedily, in the absence of seller's instructions, must make reasonable efforts to sell the goods for the seller's account. Id.[13] If sellers give no instructions within a reasonable time after notification of rejection, buyers may store the goods, ship them back to sellers, or sell them for the sellers' accounts. UCC 2–604.

Litigation After Rejection. Buyers must decide to reject goods or documents unilaterally. If in doubt about the rightfulness of their actions, a buyer that is contemplating rejection can seek advice of counsel, but there is no practical way to obtain a judicial ruling that a rejection is legally rightful. Buyers therefore act at some considerable peril that courts will decide later that their actions were wrongful.

Litigation after rejection often takes the form of a price action by sellers. UCC 2–709 allows some sellers to recover the contract price of goods that buyers have wrongfully rejected. Aggrieved sellers have an alternative cause of action for damages. The UCC provisions on sellers' damages for wrongful rejection are found in UCC 2–703, 2–706, and 2–708. The cases in this Section are cases in which sellers sought to recover (or to retain) the price from buyers that based their defenses on the right to reject. In Section 2, we will consider cases involve sellers' claims for damages.

Moulton Cavity & Mold v. Lyn–Flex Industries

Supreme Judicial Court of Maine, 1979.
396 A.2d 1024.

■ DELAHANTY, JUSTICE.

Defendant, Lyn–Flex Industries, Inc., appeals from a judgment entered after a jury trial by the Superior Court, York County, in favor of plaintiff, Moulton Cavity & Mold, Inc. The case concerns itself with an oral contract for the sale of goods which, as both parties agree, is governed by Article 2 of the Uniform Commercial Code, 11 M.R.S.A. §§ 2–101 et seq. For the

---

run until buyer has had an opportunity to inspect the goods. UCC 2–606(1)(b). Unless the agreement designates a different time and place, the inspection opportunity begins when the goods have arrived. UCC 2–513(1). Thus, within a reasonable time after arrival of the goods, buyers must elect to accept or reject the goods. UCC 2–606(1)(b).

13. Resales of goods before rejection would normally constitute acceptances of the goods under the provision that an act inconsistent with sellers' ownership constitutes acceptance. UCC 2–606(1)(c). However, resale of rightfully rejected goods in conformity with the UCC is neither acceptance nor conversion of them. UCC 2–603(3), 2–604.

reasons set forth below, we agree with defendant that the presiding Justice committed reversible error by instructing the jury that the doctrine of substantial performance applied to a contract for the sale of goods. We do not agree, however, that based on the evidence introduced at trial defendant is entitled to judgment in its favor as a matter of law. The appeal is therefore sustained and the case remanded for a new trial.

An examination of the record discloses the following sequence of events: On March 19, 1975, Lynwood Moulton, president of plaintiff, and Ernest Sturman, president of defendant, orally agreed that plaintiff would produce, and defendant purchase, twenty-six innersole molds capable of producing saleable innersoles. The price was fixed at $600.00 per mold. Whether or not a time for delivery had been established was open to question. In his testimony at trial, Mr. Moulton admitted that he was fully aware that defendant was in immediate need of the molds, and he stated that he had estimated that he could provide suitable molds in about five weeks' time. Mr. Sturman testified that "I conveyed the urgency to [Mr. Moulton] and he said 'within three weeks I will begin showing you molds and by the end of five weeks you will have [the entire order].' "

In apparent conformity with standard practice in the industry, plaintiff set about constructing a sample mold and began a lengthy series of tests. These tests consisted of bringing the sample mold to defendant's plant, fitting the mold to one of defendant's plastic-injecting machines, and checking the innersole thus derived from the plaintiff's mold to determine if it met the specifications imposed by defendant. After about thirty such tests over a ten-week period, several problems remained unsolved, the most significant of which was "flashing," that is, a seepage of plastic along the seam where the two halves of the mold meet. Although characterized by plaintiff as a minor defect, Mr. Moulton admitted that a flashing mold could not produce a saleable innersole.

It was plaintiff's contention at trial, supported by credible evidence, that at one point during the testing period officials of defendant signified that in their judgment plaintiff's sample mold was turning out innersoles correctly configured so as to fit the model last supplied by defendant's customer. Allegedly relying on this approval, plaintiff went ahead and constructed the full run of twenty-six molds.

For its part, defendant introduced credible evidence to rebut the assertion that it had approved the fit of the molds. It also noted that Moulton's allegation of approval extended only to the fit of the mold; as Moulton conceded, defendant had never given full approval since it considered the flashing problem, among others, unacceptable.

On May 29, some ten weeks after the date of the oral agreement and five weeks after the estimated completion date, Mr. Sturman met with plaintiff's foreman at the Moulton plant. A dispute exists regarding the substance of the ensuing conversation. Plaintiff introduced evidence tending to show that at that time, Mr. Sturman revoked defendant's prior approval of the fit of the sample mold and demanded that plaintiff redesign the molds to fit the last. Testimony introduced by defendant tended to show that it had never approved the fit of the molds to begin with and that on the date in question, May 29, plaintiff's foreman indicated that plaintiff simply would not invest any more time in conforming the molds to the contract. Mr. Sturman met the next day with Mr. Moulton, and Moulton ratified the position taken by his foreman. Thereupon, Mr. Sturman immediately departed for Italy and arranged to have the molds produced by the Plastak Corporation, an Italian mold-making concern, at a cost of $650.00 per mold. Plaintiff later billed defendant for the contract price of the molds, deducting an allowance for "flashing and shut-off adjustments." Upon defendant's refusal to pay, plaintiff brought this action for the price less adjustments. Defendant counterclaimed for its costs in obtaining conforming goods to the extent that they exceeded the contract price.

At trial, plaintiff's basic theory of recovery was that it had received approval with regard to the fit of the sample mold, that in reliance on that approval it had constructed a full run of twenty-six molds, and that defendant had, in effect, committed an anticipatory breach of contract within the meaning of Section 2–610 by demanding that the fit of the molds be completely redesigned. On its counterclaim, and in response to plaintiff's position, defendant advanced the theory that plaintiff had breached the contract by failing to tender conforming goods within the five-week period mentioned by both parties.

After the presiding Justice had charged the jury, counsel for plaintiff requested at side bar that the jury be instructed on the doctrine of substantial performance. Counsel for defendant entered a timely objection to the proposed charge which objection was overruled. The court then supplemented its charge as follows:

> The only point of clarification that I'll make, ladies and gentlemen, is that I've referred a couple of times to performance of a contract and you, obviously, have to determine no matter which way you view the contract to be, and there might even be a possible third way that I haven't even considered, whether the contract whatever it is has been performed and there is a doctrine that you should be aware of in considering that. That is the doctrine of substantial performance.

> It is not required that performance be in any case one hundred percent complete in order to entitle a party to enforcement of their contractual rights. That is not to say within the confines of this case that the existence of flashing would be excused or not be excused. It is just a recognition on the part of the law when we talk about performance, probably if we took any contract you could always find something of no substance that was not completed one hundred percent. It is for you to determine that whether it has been substantially performed or not and what in fact constitutes substantial performance.

> In your consideration, and as I say in this case, that's not to intimate that something like flashing is to be disregarded or to be considered. It's up to you based upon facts.

The jury returned a verdict in favor of plaintiff in the amount of $14,480.82.

I

In Smith, Fitzmaurice Co. v. Harris, 126 Me. 308, 138 A. 389 (1927), a case decided under the common law, we recognized the then-settled rule that with respect to contracts for the sale of goods the buyer has the right to reject the seller's tender if in any way it fails to conform to the specifications of the contract. We held that "[t]he vendor has the duty to comply with his order in kind, quality and amount." Id. at 312, 138 A. at 391. Thus, in *Smith*, we ruled that a buyer who had contracted to purchase twelve dozen union suits could lawfully refuse a tender of sixteen dozen union suits. Various provisions of the Uniform Sales Act, enacted in Maine in 1923, codified the common-law approach. R.S. (1954) ch. 185, §§ 11, 44. The so-called "perfect tender" rule came under considerable fire around the time the Uniform Commercial Code was drafted. No less an authority than Karl Llewellyn, recognized as the primum mobile of the Code's tender provisions (see, e.g., W. Twining, Karl Llewellyn and the Realist Movement 270–301 (1973); Carroll, Harpooning Whales, of Which Karl N. Llewellyn is the Hero of the Piece; or Searching for More Expansion Joints in Karl's Crumbling Cathedral, 12 B.C.Indus. & Comm.L.Rev. 139, 142 (1970)), attacked the rule principally on the ground that it allowed a dishonest buyer to avoid an unfavorable contract on the basis of an insubstantial defect in the seller's tender. Llewellyn, On Warranty of Quality and Society, 37 Colum.L.Rev. 341, 389 (1937). Although Llewellyn's views are represented in many Code sections governing tender,[6] the basic tender provision, Section 2–601, represents a rejection of Llewellyn's approach and a continuation of the perfect tender policy developed by the common law and carried forward by the draftsmen of the Uniform Sales Act. See Official Comment, § 2–106; Priest, Breach and Remedy for the Tender of Nonconforming Goods Under the Uniform Commercial Code: An Economic Approach, 91 Harv.L.Rev. 960, 971 (1978). Thus, Section 2–601 states that, with certain exceptions not here applicable, the buyer has the right to reject "if the goods or the tender of delivery fail *in any respect* to conform to the contract...." (emphasis supplied). Those few courts that have considered the question agree that the perfect tender rule has survived the enactment of the Code. Ingle v. Marked Tree Equipment Co., 244 Ark. 1166, 428 S.W.2d 286 (1968); Maas v. Scoboda, 188 Neb. 189, 195 N.W.2d 491 (1972); Bowen v. Young, 507 S.W.2d 600 (Tex.Civ.App.1974). We, too, are convinced of the soundness of this position.

In light of the foregoing discussion, it is clear that the presiding Justice's charge was erroneous and, under the circumstances, reversibly so. The jury was informed that "[i]t is not required that performance be in any case one hundred percent complete in order to entitle a party to enforce-

---

6. See, e.g., §§ 2–508 (seller's limited right to cure defects in tender), 2–608 (buyer's limited right to revoke acceptance), and 2–612 (buyer's limited right to reject nonconforming tender under installment contract).

ment of their contractual rights." Under this instruction, the jury was free to find that although plaintiff had not tendered perfectly conforming molds within the agreed period (assuming the jury found that the parties had in fact agreed on a specific time period for completion) it had nevertheless substantially performed the contract within the agreed time frame and was merely making minor adjustments when defendant backed out of the deal. Had the jury been instructed that plaintiff was required to tender perfectly conforming goods—not just substantially conforming goods—within the period allegedly agreed to and had they been instructed that, under Section 2–711, the buyer has the absolute right to cancel the contract if the seller "fails to make delivery," a different verdict might have resulted. Indeed, the supplemental instruction tended to encourage the jury to resolve the question by deciding whether "flashing" was or was not a substantial defect:

> It is not required that performance be in any case one hundred percent complete in order to entitle a party to enforcement of their contractual rights. That is not to say within the confines of this case that the existence of flashing would be excused or not be excused. ... It is for you to determine ... whether [the contract] has been substantially performed or not and what in fact constitutes substantial performance.

We find unpersuasive plaintiff's argument that the presiding Justice's instruction merely informed the jury that if it found that defendant had committed an anticipatory breach of the contract then plaintiff was not thereafter required to complete its performance as a condition precedent to recovery under the contract. Such an instruction might well have been appropriate and would certainly have been supportable under the applicable law. Dehahn v. Innes, Me., 356 A.2d 711, 719 (1976) ("When the other party has already repudiated the agreement, a tender would be a futile act and is not required by law."); §§ 2–610, 2–704. However, an examination of the passage of the charge in question leads us to reject plaintiff's interpretation. Without informing the jury that it must first find that defendant had committed an anticipatory repudiation, the presiding Justice, without qualification, stated that "performance [need not] be ... one hundred percent complete in order to entitle a party to enforcement of their contractual rights." Furthermore, the court drew a distinction between substantial and insubstantial defects, a distinction which, on these facts and under plaintiff's interpretation of the charge, would have been completely irrelevant. Finally, both the presiding Justice and counsel for plaintiff referred to the instruction at side bar as an explanation of the "substantial performance" doctrine. In legal parlance, that doctrine requires a buyer, under certain circumstances, to accept something less than a perfectly conforming tender. See, e.g., Rockland Poultry Co. v. Anderson, 148 Me. 211, 216, 91 A.2d 478, 480 (1952) (construction contract); Jacob & Youngs, Inc. v. Kent, 230 N.Y. 239, 129 N.E. 889 (1921) (Cardozo, J.) (construction contract). As such, it has no application to a contract for the sale of goods, and the jury should not have been permitted to consider it.

II

In his testimony at trial, Mr. Moulton indicated that he was aware that to defendant time was a critical factor. He also stated that he had given defendant an estimated delivery date of five weeks from the date the contract was formed. On appeal, defendant takes the position that the parties agreed on a five-week time period for delivery and that plaintiff's failure to tender conforming goods after ten weeks constitutes a breach as a matter of law and precludes plaintiff from recovering under the contract.

We disagree. While on the one hand Mr. Sturman testified that Mr. Moulton had told him that the goods would be delivered in five weeks, on the other hand Mr. Moulton testified that it was clear that he was merely making an estimate. The testimony thus left the jury at liberty to decide the factual question of whether the five-week time period was an agreed delivery date and thus a term of the contract or merely an estimate. While the interpretation of unambiguous language in a written contract falls within the province of the court, Blue Rock Industries v. Raymond International, Inc., Me., 325 A.2d 66 (1974), questions of fact concerning the terms of an oral agreement are left to the trier of fact, Carter v. Beck, Me., 366 A.2d 520 (1976).

The entry is: Appeal sustained. New trial ordered.

NOTES

(1) **Substantial Performance.** Most students will recall from general contract law that a party is entitled to the full contract price if it has substantially performed its contractual obligations. To the extent that less than exact performance has been rendered, the other party is entitled to recoupment in the amount of any damages. A leading contracts case is Judge Cardozo's opinion in Jacob & Youngs v. Kent, 230 N.Y. 239, 129 N.E. 889 (1921)(the Reading pipe case), cited by the Maine court. See also Restatement (Second) of Contracts §§ 237, 241, which puts the same performance standard in terms of material failure. On request of seller's counsel, the trial court in *Moulton Cavity & Mold* framed the jury charge on the substantial performance standard. What argument could be made in support of the trial court's decision?

(2) **Manner and Time of Buyer's Rejection.** The manner and time of buyer's rejection in *Moulton Cavity & Mold* is unclear. Any legal question of the sufficiency of buyer's actions was masked by the overriding issue of the legal standard for rejection. However, the court's opinion contains a factual account of the behavior of the buyer and the seller as the controversy emerged. Does this account show a clear-cut rejection decision by the buyer and communication of that decision to the seller?

(3) **Seller's Price Action.** The law suit in *Moulton Cavity & Mold* was brought by the seller for the contract price. This is a common litigation position in cases that involve buyers' rejection of goods. Buyers that have paid the purchase price are far less likely to reject goods. Can you articulate

practical reasons for buyers' behavior in this respect? What lessons does this teach in counseling sellers and buyers with respect to terms of sales contracts on the timing of the parties' respective performances?

Problem 5.1.1. Grain Supply and Miller made a contract for the sale to Miller of 1,000 bushels of wheat at $5.00 per bushel. The contract specified that the wheat would be delivered on June 1, and would be of No. 1 milling quality, free of weevil; Miller was to pay the price of $5,000 within 60 days after delivery. On delivery of the wheat, Miller inspected the wheat and found that it was "crawling" with weevils and was totally unfit for milling; he instructed his manager to sell the wheat for chicken feed. The manager suggested that they get in touch with Supply and work out some adjustment. Miller, thoroughly disgusted with Supply's performance, said: "I'm not having anything more to do with that outfit. Just let them try to collect for this rotten stuff." The wheat, sold for chicken feed, brought only $2,000—a fair price under the circumstances. Three months later, Supply called Miller and reminded him that the bill was overdue. Miller said "You should know that I won't pay for such a rotten shipment," and hung up.

Supply brought an action to recover the contract price for the wheat. Miller counterclaimed on grounds of breach of express and implied warranty and demanded damages resulting from the necessity of purchasing the No. 1 wheat elsewhere at $6.00 per bushel.

(a) What result in Supply's action to recover the contract price? UCC 2–709, 2–606.

(b) What result in Miller's counterclaim for damages? UCC 2–607(3)(a).[14]

Problem 5.1.2. Assume that in Problem 5.1.1., when the wheat arrived on June 1, Miller wired Grain Supply, "Wheat defective. Holding you responsible." Supply did not respond. Miller stored the wheat in his warehouse, and two months later (on August 1) Miller wired Supply, "What do you want done with your weevily wheat?" Supply wired back, "You bought the wheat, and I expect you to pay your bill," and brought suit. Miller interposed all available defenses and counterclaims.

By the time of trial, the wheat, which at delivery had been worth $2,000 for chicken feed, had been further damaged by the weevils; and in the meantime the price level for feed grains had dropped so that the shipment was worth only $300.

(a) May Miller defeat the claim for payment of the price on the ground that he has made an effective rejection of the goods? See UCC 2–607(1), 2–606(1)(b), 2–602(1).

(b) Assume that the court finds that Miller's rejection was not effective. What judgment should be entered? Was Miller's brief wire of June 1 adequate to meet the requirements of UCC 2–607(3)(a)? See Comment 4. Who bears the deterioration and price decline that occurred after delivery? See UCC 2–510(1), UCC 2–606(1)(b), UCC 2–714.

---

14. See Economy Forms Corp. v. Kandy, 391 F.Supp. 944 (N.D.Ga.1974).

Plateq Corp. v. Machlett Laboratories

Supreme Court of Connecticut, 1983.
189 Conn. 433, 456 A.2d 786.

■ Ellen Peters, Judge.

In this action by a seller of specially manufactured goods to recover their purchase price from a commercial buyer, the principal issue is whether the buyer accepted the goods before it attempted to cancel the contract of sale. The plaintiff, Plateq Corporation of North Haven, sued the defendant, The Machlett Laboratories, Inc., to recover damages, measured by the contract price and incidental damages, arising out of the defendant's allegedly wrongful cancellation of a written contract for the manufacture and sale of two leadcovered steel tanks and appurtenant stands. The defendant denied liability and counterclaimed for damages. After a full hearing, the trial court found for the plaintiff both on its complaint and on the defendant's counterclaim. The defendant has appealed.

The trial court, in its memorandum of decision, found the following facts. On July 9, 1976, the defendant ordered from the plaintiff two leadcovered steel tanks to be constructed by the plaintiff according to specifications supplied by the defendant. The parties understood that the tanks were designed for the special purpose of testing x-ray tubes and were required to be radiation-proof within certain federal standards. Accordingly, the contract provided that the tanks would be tested for radiation leaks after their installation on the defendant's premises. The plaintiff undertook to correct, at its own cost, any deficiencies that this post-installation test might uncover. The plaintiff had not previously constructed such tanks, nor had the defendant previously designed tanks for this purpose. The contract was amended on August 9, 1976, to add construction of two metal stands to hold the tanks. All the goods were to be delivered to the defendant at the plaintiff's place of business.

Although the plaintiff encountered difficulties both in performing according to the contract specifications and in completing performance within the time required, the defendant did no more than call these deficiencies to the plaintiff's attention during various inspections in September and early October, 1976. By October 11, 1976, performance was belatedly but substantially completed. On that date, Albert Yannello, the defendant's engineer, noted some remaining deficiencies which the plaintiff promised to remedy by the next day, so that the goods would then be ready for delivery. Yannello gave no indication to the plaintiff that this arrangement was in any way unsatisfactory to the defendant. Not only did Yannello communicate general acquiescence in the plaintiff's proposed tender but he specifically led the plaintiff to believe that the defendant's truck would pick up the tanks and the stands within a day or two. Instead of sending its truck, the defendant sent a notice of total cancellation which the plaintiff received on October 14, 1976. That notice failed to particularize the grounds upon which cancellation was based.[3]

---

3. The defendant sent the plaintiff a telegram stating: "This order is hereby ter- minated for your breach, in that you have continuously failed to perform according to

On this factual basis, the trial court, having concluded that the transaction was a contract for the sale of goods falling within the Uniform Commercial Code, General Statutes §§ 42a–2–101 et seq., considered whether the defendant had accepted the goods. The court determined that the defendant had accepted the tanks, primarily by signifying its willingness to take them despite their nonconformities, in accordance with General Statutes § 42a–2–606(1)(a), and secondarily by failing to make an effective rejection, in accordance with General Statutes § 42a–2–606(1)(b). Once the tanks had been accepted, the defendant could rightfully revoke its acceptance under General Statutes § 42a–2–608 only by showing substantial impairment of their value to the defendant. In part because the defendant's conduct had foreclosed any post-installation inspection, the court concluded that such impairment had not been proved. Since the tanks were not readily resalable on the open market, the plaintiff was entitled, upon the defendant's wrongful revocation of acceptance, to recover their contract price, minus salvage value, plus interest. General Statutes §§ 42a–2–703; 42a–2–709(1)(b). Accordingly, the trial court awarded the plaintiff damages in the amount of $14,837.92.

* * *

Upon analysis, all of the defendant's claims of error are variations upon one central theme. The defendant claims that on October 11, when its engineer Yannello conducted the last examination on the plaintiff's premises, the tanks were so incomplete and unsatisfactory that the defendant was rightfully entitled to conclude that the plaintiff would never make a conforming tender. From this scenario, the defendant argues that it was justified in cancelling the contract of sale. It denies that the seller's conduct was sufficient to warrant a finding of tender, or its own conduct sufficient to warrant a finding of acceptance. The difficulty with this argument is that it is inconsistent with the underlying facts found by the trial court. Although the testimony was in dispute, there was evidence of record to support the trial court's findings to the contrary. ... There is simply no fit between the defendant's claims and the trial court's finding that, by October 11, 1976, performance was in substantial compliance with the terms of the contract. The trial court further found that on that day the defendant was notified that the goods would be ready for tender the following day and that the defendant responded to this notification by promising to send its truck to pick up the tanks in accordance with the contract.

On the trial court's finding of facts, it was warranted in concluding, on two independent grounds, that the defendant had accepted the goods it had ordered from the plaintiff. Under the provisions of the Uniform Commercial Code, General Statutes § 42a–2–606(1) "[a]cceptance of goods occurs when the buyer (a) after a reasonable opportunity to inspect the goods

your commitment in spite of additional time given you to cure your delinquency. We will hold you liable for all damages incurred [sic]

by Machlett including excess cost of reprocurement.''

signifies to the seller ... that he will take ... them in spite of their nonconformity; or (b) fails to make an effective rejection."

In concluding that the defendant had "signified" to the plaintiff its willingness to "take" the tanks despite possible remaining minor defects, the trial court necessarily found that the defendant had had a reasonable opportunity to inspect the goods. The defendant does not maintain that its engineer, or the other inspectors on previous visits, had inadequate access to the tanks, or inadequate experience to conduct a reasonable examination. It recognizes that inspection of goods when the buyer undertakes to pick up the goods is ordinarily at the seller's place of tender. See General Statutes §§ 42a–2–503, 42a–2–507, 42a–2–513; see also White & Summers, Uniform Commercial Code § 3–5 (2d Ed.1980). The defendant argues, however, that its contract, in providing for inspection for radiation leaks after installation of the tanks at its premises, necessarily postponed its inspection rights to that time. The trial court considered this argument and rejected it, and so do we. It was reasonable, in the context of this contract for the special manufacture of goods with which neither party had had prior experience, to limit this clause to adjustments to take place after tender and acceptance. After acceptance, a buyer may still, in appropriate cases, revoke its acceptance, General Statutes § 42a–2–608, or recover damages for breach of warranty, General Statutes § 42a–2–714. The trial court reasonably concluded that a post-installation test was intended to safeguard these rights of the defendant as well as to afford the plaintiff a final opportunity to make needed adjustments. The court was therefore justified in concluding that there had been an acceptance within § 42a–2–606(1)(a). A buyer may be found to have accepted goods despite their known nonconformity ... and despite the absence of actual delivery to the buyer. ...

* * *

Once the conclusion is reached that the defendant accepted the tanks, its further rights of cancellation under the contract are limited by the governing provisions of the Uniform Commercial Code. "The buyer's acceptance of goods, despite their alleged nonconformity, is a watershed. After acceptance, the buyer must pay for the goods at the contract rate; General Statutes § 42a–2–607(1); and bears the burden of establishing their nonconformity. General Statutes § 42a–2–607(4)." ... After acceptance, the buyer may only avoid liability for the contract price by invoking the provision which permits revocation of acceptance. That provision, General Statutes § 42a–2–608(1), requires proof that the "nonconformity [of the goods] substantially impairs [their] value to him." ... On this question, ... the trial court again found against the defendant. Since the defendant has provided no basis for any argument that the trial court was clearly erroneous in finding that the defendant had not met its burden of proof to show that the goods were substantially nonconforming, we can find no error in the conclusion that the defendant's cancellation constituted an unauthorized and hence wrongful revocation of acceptance.

Finally, the defendant in its brief, although not in its statement of the issues presented, challenges the trial court's conclusion about the remedial consequences of its earlier determinations. Although the trial court might have found the plaintiff entitled to recover the contract price because of the defendant's acceptance of the goods; General Statutes §§ 42a–2–703(e) and 42a–2–709(1)(a); the court chose instead to rely on General Statutes § 42a–2–709(1)(b), which permits a price action for contract goods that cannot, after reasonable effort, be resold at a reasonable price.[19] Since the contract goods in this case were concededly specially manufactured for the defendant, the defendant cannot and does not contest the trial court's finding that any effort to resell them on the open market would have been unavailing. In the light of this finding, the defendant can only reiterate its argument, which we have already rejected, that the primary default was that of the plaintiff rather than that of the defendant. The trial court's conclusion to the contrary supports both its award to the plaintiff and its denial of the defendant's counterclaim.

There is no error.

NOTES

(1) Seller's Price Action. This is an action by the seller for the contract price of the goods, two steel tanks and appurtenant stands. UCC 2–709 authorizes sellers' recovery of the price in limited circumstances. The trial court held for the seller under UCC 2–709(1)(b), which allows recovery of the price of goods identified to the contract if the seller is unable to resell them at a reasonable price. The steel tanks had been specially manufactured according to buyer's specifications. The trial court found, no doubt, that any reasonable effort by seller to resell these tanks would be unavailing. On appeal, the Supreme Court affirmed, but did so on a totally different legal analysis. Judge Peters found for the seller under the "goods accepted" clause of UCC 2–709(1)(a), which entailed her extensive analysis of the question whether the buyer had accepted the steel tanks. Why did the Supreme Court decline to affirm the trial court on that court's legal theory?

The UCC does not completely integrate its provisions on the performance options of the parties to sales contracts, accept or reject, with its

---

19.   ... It should be noted that § 42a–2–709(1)(b) is not premised on a buyer's acceptance. Instead, it requires a showing that the goods were, before the buyer's cancellation, "identified to the contract." In the circumstances of this case, that precondition was presumably met by their special manufacture and by the defendant's acquiescence in their imminent tender. See White & Summers, Uniform Commercial Code, § 7–5 (2d Ed.1980). The defendant has not, on this appeal, argued the absence of identification.

It should further be noted that § 42a–2–709(1)(b), because it is not premised on acceptance, would have afforded the seller the right to recover the contract price even if the trial court had found the conduct of the buyer to be a wrongful rejection (because of the failure to give the seller an opportunity to cure) rather than a wrongful revocation of acceptance.

remedial provisions. The provisions on rejection are keyed to sellers' conforming or not conforming to their contract obligations. UCC 2–601 allows a buyer to reject for nonconformity in any respect. The price remedy provision is silent on the issue of conformity of sellers' performance. Does UCC 2–709(1)(b) allow a seller to recover the price of unsaleable goods if the goods did not conform to the contract? Does the "goods accepted" provision of UCC 2–709(1)(a) allow a seller to recover the price of goods that did not conform to the contract? You should now understand why Judge Peters did not affirm on the trial court's legal analysis.

(2) Buyer's Acceptance. UCC 2–606(1) gives three different scenarios that constitute a buyers's acceptance of goods. Which of the three was the basis of the decision of the Connecticut Supreme Court?

The trial court found ("secondarily" according to Judge Peters) that buyer had failed to make an effective rejection under UCC 2–602(1). Failure to make an effective rejection occurs under UCC 2–602(1) when a buyer fails to act within a reasonable time after delivery or tender of delivery of the goods. A buyer is not obligated to choose between acceptance and rejection before the seller has at least tendered delivery. Did the seller tender delivery of the steel tanks?

Can a buyer accept nonconforming goods under UCC 2–606(1)(a)? Can a buyer accept nonconforming goods before seller tenders delivery under UCC 2–606(1)(a)? Judge Peters' analysis is built on the premise that the answer to these questions is "yes" and that the buyer in this case not only could accept nonconforming goods before tender but that it did so. The trial court also found such an acceptance. Was this decision sound as a matter of statutory construction? Did the court reach the right result in this case?

T.W. Oil, Inc. v. Consolidated Edison Co.

Court of Appeals of New York, 1982.
57 N.Y.2d 574, 457 N.Y.S.2d 458, 443 N.E.2d 932.

■ Fuchsberg, Judge.

In the first case to wend its way through our appellate courts on this question, we are asked, in the main, to decide whether a seller who, acting in good faith and without knowledge of any defect, tenders nonconforming goods to a buyer who properly rejects them, may avail itself of the cure provision of subdivision (2) of section 2–508 of the Uniform Commercial Code. We hold that, if seasonable notice be given, such a seller may offer to cure the defect within a reasonable period beyond the time when the contract was to be performed so long as it has acted in good faith and with a reasonable expectation that the original goods would be acceptable to the buyer.

The factual background against which we decide this appeal is based on either undisputed proof or express findings at Trial Term. In January, 1974, midst the fuel shortage produced by the oil embargo, the plaintiff (then known as Joc Oil USA, Inc.) purchased a cargo of fuel oil whose sulfur content was represented to it as no greater than 1%. While the oil was still at sea en route to the United States in the tanker *M T Khamsin*, plaintiff received a certificate from the foreign refinery at which it had been processed informing it that the sulfur content in fact was .52%. Thereafter, on January 24, the plaintiff entered into a written contract with the defendant (Con Ed) for the sale of this oil. The agreement was for delivery to take place between January 24 and January 30, payment being subject to a named independent testing agency's confirmation of quality and quantity. The contract, following a trade custom to round off specifications of sulfur content at, for instance, 1%, .5% or .3%, described that of the *Khamsin* oil as .5%. In the course of the negotiations, the plaintiff learned that Con Ed was then authorized to buy and burn oil with a sulfur content of up to 1% and would even mix oils containing more and less to maintain that figure.

When the vessel arrived, on January 25, its cargo was discharged into Con Ed storage tanks in Bayonne, New Jersey. In due course, the independent testing people reported a sulfur content of .92%. On this basis, acting within a time frame whose reasonableness is not in question, on February 14 Con Ed rejected the shipment. Prompt negotiations to adjust the price failed; by February 20, plaintiff had offered a price reduction roughly responsive to the difference in sulfur reading, but Con Ed, though it could use the oil, rejected this proposition out of hand. It was insistent on paying no more than the latest prevailing price, which, in the volatile market that then existed, was some 25% below the level which prevailed when it agreed to buy the oil.

The very next day, February 21, plaintiff offered to cure the defect with a substitute shipment of conforming oil scheduled to arrive on the *S.S. Appollonian Victory* on February 28. Nevertheless, on February 22, the very day after the cure was proffered, Con Ed, adamant in its intention to avail itself of the intervening drop in prices, summarily rejected this proposal too. The two cargos were subsequently sold to third parties at the best price obtainable, first that of the *Appollonian* and, sometime later, after extraction from the tanks had been accomplished, that of the *Khamsin*.

There ensued this action for breach of contract, which, after a somewhat unconventional trial course, resulted in a nonjury decision for the plaintiff in the sum of $1,385,512.83.... To arrive at this result, the Trial Judge, while ruling against other liability theories advanced by the plaintiff, which, in particular, included one charging the defendant with having failed to act in good faith in the negotiations for a price adjustment on the *Khamsin* oil (Uniform Commercial Code, § 1–203), decided as a matter of law that subdivision (2) of section 2–508 of the Uniform Commercial Code was available to the plaintiff even if it had no prior knowledge of the nonconformity. Finding that in fact plaintiff had no such belief at the time of the delivery, that what turned out to be a .92% sulfur content was "within the range of contemplation of reasonable acceptability" to Con Ed, and that seasonable notice of an intention to cure was given, the court went on to hold that plaintiff's "reasonable and timely offer to cure" was improperly rejected (sub nom. Joc Oil USA v. Consolidated Edison Co. of N.Y., 107 Misc.2d 376, 390, 434 N.Y.S.2d 623 [Shanley N. Egeth, J.]). The Appellate Division, 84 A.D.2d 970, 447 N.Y.S.2d 572, having unanimously affirmed the judgment entered on this decision, the case is now here by our leave. . . .

In support of its quest for reversal, the defendant now asserts that the trial court erred (a) in ruling that the verdict on a special question submitted for determination by a jury was irrelevant to the decision of this case, (b) in failing to interpret subdivision (2) of section 2–508 of the Uniform Commercial Code to limit the availability of the right to cure after date of performance to cases in which the seller knowingly made a nonconforming tender and (c) in calculating damages on the basis of the resale of the nonconforming cargo rather than of the substitute offered to replace it. For the reasons which follow, we find all three unacceptable.

I

[The court rejected objection (a).]

II

We turn then to the central issue on this appeal: Fairly interpreted, did subdivision (2) of section 2–508 of the Uniform Commercial Code require Con Ed to accept the substitute shipment plaintiff tendered? In approaching this question, we, of course, must remember that a seller's right to cure a defective tender, as allowed by both subdivisions of section 2–508, was intended to act as a meaningful limitation on the absolutism of the old perfect tender rule, under which, no leeway being allowed for any imperfections, there was, as one court put it, just "no room . . . for the doctrine of substantial performance" of commercial obligations (Mitsubishi Goshi Kaisha v. Aron & Co., 16 F.2d 185, 186 [Learned Hand, J.]; see Note, Uniform Commercial Code, § 2–508; Seller's Right to Cure Non–Conforming Goods, 6 Rutgers–Camden L.J. 387–388).

In contrast, to meet the realities of the more impersonal business world of our day, the code, to avoid sharp dealing, expressly provides for the liberal construction of its remedial provisions (§ 1–102) so that "good faith" and the "observance of reasonable commercial standards of fair dealing" be the rule rather than the exception in trade (see § 2–103, subd. [1], par. [b]), "good faith" being defined as "honesty in fact in the conduct or transaction concerned" (Uniform Commercial Code, § 1–201, subd. [19]). As to section 2–508 in particular, the code's Official Comment advises that its mission is to safeguard the seller "against surprise as a result of sudden technicality on the buyer's part" (Uniform Commercial Code, § 2–106, Comment 2; see, also, Peters, Remedies for Breach of Contracts Relating to the Sale of Goods under the Uniform Commercial Code: A Roadmap for Article Two, 73 Yale L.J. 199, 210; 51 N.Y.Jur., Sales, § 101, p. 41).

Section 2–508 may be conveniently divided between provisions for cure offered when "the time for performance has not yet expired" (subd. [1]), a precode concept in this State (Lowinson v. Newman, 201 App.Div. 266, 194 N.Y.S. 253), and ones which, by newly introducing the possibility of a seller obtaining "a further reasonable time to substitute a conforming tender" (subd. [2]), also permit cure beyond the date set for performance. . . .

Since we here confront circumstances in which the conforming tender came after the time of performance, we focus on subdivision (2). On its face, taking its conditions in the order in which they appear, for the statute to apply (1) a buyer must have rejected a nonconforming tender, (2) the seller must have had reasonable grounds to believe this tender would be acceptable (with or without money allowance), and (3) the seller must have "seasonably" notified the buyer of the intention to substitute a conforming tender within a reasonable time.

In the present case, none of these presented a problem. The first one was easily met for it is unquestioned that, at .92%, the sulfur content of the *Khamsin* oil did not conform to the .5% specified in the contract and that it was rejected by Con Ed. The second, the reasonableness of the seller's belief that the original tender would be acceptable, was supported not only by unimpeached proof that the contract's .5% and the refinery certificate's .52% were trade equivalents, but by testimony that, by the time the contract was made, the plaintiff knew Con Ed burned fuel with a content of up to 1%, so that, with appropriate price adjustment, the *Khamsin* oil would have suited its needs even if, at delivery, it was, to the plaintiff's surprise, to test out at .92%. Further, the matter seems to have been put beyond dispute by the defendant's readiness to take the oil at the reduced market price on February 20. Surely, on such a record, the trial court cannot be faulted for having found as a fact that the second condition too had been established.

As to the third, the conforming state of the Appollonian oil is undisputed, the offer to tender it took place on February 21, only a day after Con Ed finally had rejected the *Khamsin* delivery and the *Appollonian* substitute then already was en route to the United States, where it was expected in a week and did arrive on March 4, only four days later than expected. Especially since Con Ed pleaded no prejudice (unless the drop in prices could be so regarded), it is almost impossible, given the flexibility of the Uniform Commercial Code definitions of "seasonable" and "reasonable" . . ., to quarrel with the finding that the remaining requirements of the statute also had been met.

Thus lacking the support of the statute's literal language, the defendant nonetheless would have us limit its application to cases in which a seller *knowingly* makes a nonconforming tender which it has reason to believe the buyer will accept. For this proposition, it relies almost entirely on a critique in Nordstrom, Law of Sales (§ 105), which rationalizes that, since a seller who believes its tender is conforming would have no reason to think in terms of a reduction in the price of the goods, to allow such a seller to cure after the time for performance had passed would make the statutory reference to a money allowance redundant.[8] Nordstrom, interestingly enough, finds it useful to buttress this position by the somewhat dire prediction, though backed by no empirical or other confirmation, that, unless the right to cure is confined to those whose nonconforming tenders are knowing ones, the incentive of sellers to timely deliver will be undermined. To this it also adds the somewhat moralistic note that a seller who is mistaken as to the quality of its goods does not merit additional time (Nordstrom, *loc. cit.*). Curiously, recognizing that the few decisions extant on this subject have adopted a position opposed to the one for which it contends, Con Ed seeks to treat these as exceptions rather than exemplars of the rule (e.g., Wilson v. Scampoli, 228 A.2d 848 (D.C.App.) [goods obtained by seller from their manufacturer in original carton resold unopened to purchaser; seller held within statute though it had no reason to believe the goods defective]; Appleton State Bank v. Lee, 33 Wis.2d 690, 148 N.W.2d 1 [seller mistakenly delivered sewing machine of wrong brand but otherwise identical to one sold; held that seller, though it did not know of its mistake, had a right to cure by substitution]).

That the principle for which these cases stand goes far beyond their particular facts cannot be gainsaid. These holdings demonstrate that, in dealing with the application of subdivision (2) of section 2–508, courts have been concerned with the reasonableness of the seller's belief that the goods would be acceptable rather than with the seller's pretended knowledge or lack of knowledge of the defect (Wilson v. Scampoli, supra; compare Zabriskie Chevrolet v. Smith, 99 N.J.Super. 441, 240 A.2d 195).

It also is no surprise then that the aforementioned decisional history is a reflection of the mainstream of scholarly commentary on the subject (e.g., 1955 Report of N.Y.Law Rev.Comm., p. 484; White & Summers, Uniform Commercial Code [2d ed.], § 8–4, p. 322; 2 Anderson, Uniform Commercial Code [2d ed.], § 2–508:7; Hogan, The Highways and Some of the Byways in the Sales and Bulk Sales Articles of the Uniform Commercial Code, 48 Cornell L.Q. 1, 12–13; Note, Uniform Commercial Code, § 2–508: Seller's Right to Cure Non–Conforming Goods, 6 Rutgers–Camden L.J. 387, 399; Note, Commercial Law—The Effect of the Seller's Right to Cure on the Buyer's Remedy of Rescission, 28 Ark.L.Rev. 297, 302–303).

White and Summers, for instance, put it well, and bluntly. Stressing that the code intended cure to be "a remedy which should be carefully cultivated and developed by the courts" because it "offers the possibility of conforming the law to reasonable expectations and of thwarting the chisel-

---

8. The premise for such an argument, which ignores the policy of the code to prevent buyers from using insubstantial remedial or price adjustable defects to free themselves from unprofitable bargains (Hawkland, Sales and Bulk Sales Under the Uniform Commercial Code, pp. 120–122), is that the words "with or without money allowance" apply only to sellers who believe their goods will be acceptable with such an allowance and not to sellers who believe their goods will be acceptable without such an allowance. But, since the words are part of a phrase which speaks of an otherwise unqualified belief that the goods will be acceptable, unless one strains for an opposite interpretation, we find insufficient reason to doubt that it intends to include both those who find a need to offer an allowance and those who do not.

er who seeks to escape from a bad bargain" (op. cit., at pp. 322–324), the authors conclude, as do we, that a seller should have recourse to the relief afforded by subdivision (2) of section 2–508 of the Uniform Commercial Code as long as it can establish that it had reasonable grounds, tested objectively, for its belief that the goods would be accepted (ibid., at p. 321). It goes without saying that the test of reasonableness, in this context, must encompass the concepts of "good faith" and "commercial standards of fair dealing" which permeate the code (Uniform Commercial Code, § 1–201, subd. [19]; §§ 1–203, 2–103, subd. [1], par. [b]).[10]

* * *

Judgment affirmed.

NOTES

(1) Sellers' Power to Cure After Rejections of Goods. In a substantial departure from prior law, the UCC authorizes sellers to make a second tender or delivery of goods if the first is rightfully rejected. UCC 2–508(1). Complementing UCC 2–508 is the estoppel provision in UCC 2–605(1), which has the effect of requiring rejecting buyers to inform sellers of nonconformities that were reasonably ascertainable by inspection and that could have been cured. To what extent do these provisions overcome the vices perceived by critics of the perfect tender rule?

(2) Substitute Goods as Cure. When a seller exercises the right to cure by making a tender of substitute goods, the buyer has a second opportunity to accept or reject these goods. With respect to the quality of the goods, what standard applies to buyer's option? May a buyer reject the new goods if they do not conform to the contract *in every respect*? With respect to the time of seller's second tender, UCC 2–508(1) differs from UCC 2–508(2). A second tender of goods under subsection (1) conforms to the time term of the contract. A second tender under subsection (2) does not. What is the policy justification for requiring some buyers to accept later deliveries? Comment 2 refers to avoidance of injustice to the seller by reason of a "surprise rejection" by the buyer. What is a "surprise rejection"?

In *T.W. Oil*, buyer was found to have rejected the *Khamsin* oil rightfully, but its subsequent rejection of the *Appollonian* oil was wrongful. The opinion stated that "the conforming state of the *Appollonian* oil is

---

10. Except indirectly, on this appeal we do not deal with the equally important protections the code affords buyers. It is as to buyers as well as sellers that the code, to the extent that it displaces traditional principles of law and equity (§ 1–103), seeks to discourage unfair or hypertechnical business conduct bespeaking a dog-eat-dog rather than a live-and-let-live approach to the marketplace (e.g., §§ 2–314, 2–315, 2–513, 2–601, 2–608). Over- all, the aim is to encourage parties to amicably resolve their own problems (Ramirez v. Autosport, 88 N.J. 277, 285, 440 A.2d 1345; compare Restatement, Contracts 2d, Introductory Note to Chapter 10, p. 194 ["the wisest course is ordinarily for the parties to attempt to resolve their differences by negotiations, including clarification of expectations [and] cure of past defaults"]).

undisputed.'' Did this statement mean more than that the oil conformed to the sulfur-content term of the sales contract? The opinion did not indicate the nature of the time term of the contract. Delivery of the *Khamsin* oil, which was made on January 25, was not challenged as untimely. Tender of the *Appollonian* oil, which was made on February 21, was rejected, presumably because it believed that the time for performance had expired. The court implicitly agreed (perhaps on concession of seller's counsel) that the February 21 tender was nonconforming with respect to the time term and proceeded to the question whether seller was allowed added time under UCC 2–508(2).

The principal issue decided by the court involved interpretation of the statutory predicate for allowing sellers more time to perform than would have been permitted under their contracts. The predicate in UCC 2–508(2) is that the seller, when making the original nonconforming tender, ''had reasonable grounds to believe [that the nonconforming tender] would be acceptable with or without monetary allowance.'' Was the court's construction of this language sound? The court did not agree with the view, attributed to Professor Nordstrom, that its decision would undermine the incentive of sellers to perform within the time limits set by contracts. Was the court correct on this point? The court did not consider the consequences its decision would have on the legislative intent manifest in the structure of UCC 2–508(1) and (2). In light of *T.W. Oil* what is the effect of lapse of the time to cure under UCC 2–508(1)? Under what circumstances would any seller be barred from claiming the right to added time under UCC 2–508(2)? Does the predicate in UCC 2–508(2) have any meaning?

The consequence of the court's decision in *T.W. Oil* was the determination that the buyer's rejection of the *Appollonian* oil was wrongful and the buyer was therefore in breach. The portion of the opinion dealing with seller's remedy was omitted here. We will consider sellers' remedies for wrongful rejection later in this Chapter.

(3) Repair of Goods or Replacement of Components as Cure. In a sale of a manufactured product that is rejected for nonconformity with respect to quality, would seller's repair of the goods or replacement of a defective component a cure under UCC 2–508? In circumstances where nonconforming goods are repaired or have new components installed, do buyers have a second opportunity to accept or reject the goods? With respect to the quality of the goods, what standard applies to buyer's option? May a buyer reject the new goods if they do not conform to the contract *in every respect*? What is the time allowed for repair or component replacement? Should the statute be construed to permit cure by repair or replacement of components more liberally in sales of business equipment than in sales of ordinary consumer goods?

Should it matter whether the person that does the repair or installs the replacement component is the manufacturer or the retailer? Suppose that a new automobile was rejected by an ordinary consumer because of transmission problems and the car dealer replaced the transmission in its own service department. Must buyer accept the car on second tender? See Zabriskie Chevrolet, Inc. v. Smith, 99 N.J.Super. 441, 240 A.2d 195 (1968) (dealer's replacement did not effect cure).

(4) Cure and Warranty Service. How does sellers' repair or replacement of rightfully rejected goods under UCC 2–508 relate to sales contracts under which sellers undertake to repair or replace goods during a specified warranty period?

(5) Price Adjustment as Cure. In some trade settings, particularly sales of fungible goods, sellers offer to take a lower price when goods may be rightfully rejected and buyers agree. Could a practice of this kind be the basis for concluding that trade usage permits sellers to cure defective tenders by price adjustment? Counsel for seller in *T.W. Oil* argued, in the trial court, that buyer should be held liable for breach of a duty to bargain in good faith for a price adjustment on the *Khamsin* oil. This argument was rejected by the trial court and is mentioned only in passing by the court of appeals. Does this argument have force under the present UCC? Should the UCC be amended to provide generally that sellers may cure by price adjustment?

(6) Sellers' Power to Cure After Rejections of Tenders of Documents. UCC 2–508 is not limited to rejections of goods. Subsection (1) applies also to rejections of documents tendered in documentary transactions. Buyers' obligation to disclose ascertainable nonconformities, under UCC 2–605, is not limited to rejections of goods. Recall also the discussion of the responsibilities of presenting banks under UCC 4–503 to use diligence to ascertain the reasons for dishonor of documentary drafts. What would constitute cure of nonconformities in documents? Should the added time provisions of UCC 2–508(2) be applied after rejection of documents?

———

Proposed Revised UCC Article 2. Drafters of the proposed amendments to UCC Article 2 would retain the substance of the first subsection of UCC 2–508, but change the predicate in the second subsection to allow additional time to any seller "that has performed in good faith." The amendments would also modify the period of additional time for cure to action that is "appropriate and timely under the circumstances." Finally, the amendments would add a requirement, in both subsections, that sellers must compensate buyers for all expenses caused by sellers' breach and subsequent cure.[15]

Midwest Mobile Diagnostic Imaging v. Dynamics Corp. of America

United States District Court, Western District of Michigan, 1997.
965 F.Supp. 1003.

■ ENSLEN, CHIEF JUDGE.

I. INTRODUCTION

Plaintiff Midwest Mobile Diagnostic Imagining, L.L.C. [hereinafter "MMDI"] brings this diversity action against defendant Ellis & Watts,

---

15. Proposed Revised 2–508. The proposed amendments would extend the power to cure, beyond rejections, to revocations of acceptance.

d/b/a Dynamics Corporation of America [hereinafter "E & W"], seeking damages for ... breach of a sales contract for the purchase of four mobile MRI units[1].... Defendant, the seller, counterclaims for damages, alleging that the buyer is in breach. Having considered the evidence submitted and the legal arguments of the parties made during a three-day bench trial, and having reviewed the exhibits submitted, the Court enters the following Findings of Fact and Conclusions of Law pursuant to Federal Rule of Civil Procedure 52(a). ...

* * *

III. CONTENTIONS OF THE PARTIES

MMDI contends that, after its rightful rejection of a nonconforming trailer tendered by E & W on December 13, 1995, E & W repudiated the contract in its entirety. E & W's repudiation whether anticipatory or not, destroyed whatever right to cure E & W may have had and gave MMDI the right to cancel the contract, which it then did. Having rightfully canceled the contract, MMDI argues it is entitled to damages.

E & W counters that its tender on December 13, 1995 was both timely and in conformity with contract specifications. Consequently, MMDI's rejection was wrongful. E & W continues that, even if the trailer were not conforming, E & W had a right to cure pursuant to Uniform Commercial Code [hereinafter "UCC"] § 2–508, and MMDI could not cancel the contract without first requesting adequate assurances from E & W in writing pursuant to UCC § 2–609. Since plaintiff did not satisfy § 2–609 and a reasonable time for performance had not expired, MMDI's cancellation of the contract on December 18, 1995 constituted anticipatory repudiation.

IV. FACTS

Plaintiff Midwest Mobile Diagnostic Imaging, L.L.C. ("MMDI") is a Delaware limited liability company, with offices in Kalamazoo, Michigan, engaged in the business of furnishing equipment and personnel for magnetic resonance imaging (MRI) scans to hospitals in southwestern Michigan. In 1995, MMDI had three mobile MRI units servicing area facilities.

Defendant Ellis & Watts ("E & W") is a New York corporation whose principal place of business is in Cincinnati, Ohio, which engineers, designs, and manufactures trailers for mobile medical uses, including mobile MRI systems. ...

In April 1995, plaintiff commenced negotiations with defendant to purchase four mobile MRI trailers, each designed to house a state-of-the-

---

1. A mobile MRI unit is, in effect, a mobile MRI clinic. It is a semi tractor trailer which contains an MRI scanner and the computer equipment necessary to operate such a machine. It is designed to function as a temporary extension of the hospital which it is serving, with an interior which generally matches the hospital environment.

art, ACS NT 1.5T MR scanner system, which plaintiff would purchase separately from Philips. During these initial negotiations, E & W became aware that MMDI had an immediate need for the first trailer because of the growing demand for its services. As a consequence, the parties agreed that delivery of the first trailer would occur in September 1995 with the rest to follow in monthly installments. However, during final negotiations in Kalamazoo on August 10, 1995, the parties agreed to delete a clause in the written contract requiring that all four trailers be delivered in 1995. While no specific delivery dates were ultimately included in the written contract, E & W understood that early delivery of the first trailer was of great importance to MMDI. At the time of signing, the parties expected delivery of the trailers to occur in October, November, December, 1995 and January, 1996. The delivery dates were, however, contingent upon coordination with Philips and agreement of the parties.

In addition to the timing of the project, during negotiations the parties also made representations concerning the design of the trailer. On April 17, 1995, Robert Freudenberger of E & W, faxed a signed purchase agreement to Jerry Turowski of MMDI. Attached to the form contract were two drawings. One of the drawings depicted a three-dimensional illustration of the interior of a mobile MRI system trailer upon which was written: "Spacious, efficient layout with clean, aesthetically pleasing interior." In addition, these drawings, and all others reviewed by MMDI both before and after contract signing, did not depict a bracing structure surrounding the scanner magnet.

On August 10, 1995, Mr. Turowski and Mr. Freudenberger executed a purchase agreement for four E & W trailers. With the signing of the contract, MMDI paid E & W a deposit in the amount of $63,000. On August 11, 1995, Mr. Andrew Pike, President of E & W, countersigned the purchase agreement in Cincinnati, Ohio. Under the parties' agreement, E & W was to construct the four trailers in accordance with Philips' specifications. Once certified by Philips, the trailers could be delivered.

On September 7, 1995, plaintiff and defendant met in Kalamazoo to discuss the delivery schedule. On September 21, 1995, MMDI sent a letter indicating that, as a result of that meeting, MMDI expected delivery of the first trailer on November 6, 1995. The letter also noted the parties' understanding that the trailer would be "show" ready for MMDI's open house in Kalamazoo, Michigan, on November 3, 1995. E & W did not respond to this letter. During the course of construction, the parties discussed several alterations to the trailer and consequently, again renegotiated the delivery date for the first trailer. Ultimately, the parties agreed upon a December 1, 1995 delivery date. Under the expectation that the trailer would be delivered on that date, MMDI scheduled patients assuming the trailer would be ready for use beginning December 4, 1995.

On November 3, 1995, indicating that the trailer was cosmetically complete, E & W presented the trailer to MMDI to show at its open house in Kalamazoo, during which representatives of MMDI and many of its customers, inspected the trailer. At that time, the scanner magnet was free from any metal, bracing structures. The trailer was then returned to E & W for final adjustments and testing.

As of mid-November 1995, the first E & W trailer was fully fabricated and substantially all equipment was installed and ready for testing by Philips. In anticipation of the December 1 delivery date, E & W invoiced MMDI on November 10, 1995 for the full purchase price of the first trailer. On November 16, 1995, E & W sent a follow-up letter requesting payment prior to shipment of the trailer on November 30 in accordance with the purchase agreement. MMDI paid $321,500 to E & W on November 17, 1995.

On November 28, 1995, the first trailer failed to meet contract specifications in a test conducted by Philips. The test indicated that the trailer did not comply with Philips' specifications for magnetic shielding in the sidewalls of the trailer. This failure occurred despite the fact that, throughout the construction of the trailer, Philips had repeatedly noted the importance of the proper fabrication of this feature in its correspondence with E & W.

When the parties discovered that the trailer had failed the test, they met to discuss potential solutions to the situation. At that time, E & W stated unequivocally that: 1) the trailer was defective; 2) the defect was entirely its fault and responsibility; and 3) it would cure the problem. E & W also indicated a willingness to reimburse MMDI for at least part of the expenses it might incur in renting another trailer to substitute for the one that E & W had not completed. As a result of the need for a cure, E & W failed to tender a conforming trailer on the December 1 delivery date and MMDI was forced to cancel appointments which had been scheduled with patients for December 4, 1995.

During the following two weeks, E & W designed a reinforcement structure to contend with the wall-flexing problem. The solution consisted of multiple, large, steel beams placed around the scanner magnet in a cage-like structure which prevented removal of the magnet's outer covers and dramatically changed its appearance. Such a bracing structure had never been used with a mobile MRI scanner by any manufacturer. During this period, E & W exchanged multiple letters and sketches with Philips in which Philips' representatives indicated several concerns with the bracing structure. E & W made adjustments to address some of these concerns. Ultimately, Philips approved the design as a temporary solution to the wall-flexing problem.

On December 7, 1995, E & W sent MMDI a schedule indicating that the decision whether to proceed with this design would be made on December 12, 1995. The letter indicated: "if no go at this point, alternate plans established." Although MMDI had reviewed drawings of the interior during the course of construction, E & W did not include a sketch of the reinforcement design in this correspondence.

On December 12, 1995, Philips' representatives retested the trailer with the bracing structure in place and found that the flexing problem had been remedied. Thus, the trailer was approved for use on a temporary basis. However, because the structure impaired service of the scanner magnet, Philips would not certify the trailer for permanent use with the structure in place.

On December 13, 1995, Mr. Turowski of MMDI arrived at E & W to inspect the new design for the first time. After viewing the trailer and speaking with Philips' representatives, Mr. Turowski concluded that the bracing structure was unacceptable for several reasons. Mr. Turowski and Mr. Andrew Pike of E & W then placed a telephone conference call to Dr. Azzam Kanaan and Dr. Ilydio Polachini at MMDI. At that time, Mr. Turowski indicated that, with the bracing structure, the trailer did not conform to the contract obligations because: 1) service of the scanner magnet would be impeded and, in cases, would be more dangerous; 2) its appearance was objectionable; and 3) the resale value of the trailer would be diminished.

Mr. Pike countered that the structure in place conformed to the parties' agreement, that this was the design that met the Philips' specification, that it had been approved by Philips, and told MMDI to accept it the way it was. Further, Mr. Pike stated that the materials had already been purchased to install this design in the second trailer, that this was the best design that one could come up with, and that he did not know if it could be done it any differently. Finally, Mr. Pike refused to pay rent for a replacement unit or to refund MMDI's previous payment.

The following day, December 14, 1995, Mr. Pike sent a letter to Dr. Kanaan at MMDI, indicating that E & W was working with "this design" to see if it could be made more aesthetically pleasing. The letter made no reference to the servicing problems, safety concerns, or concerns about a potential diminution in resale value resulting from the use of the bracing structure. Mr. Pike again asserted the validity of the contract, and refused to refund MMDI's payment for the trailer.

On December 18, 1995, acting in good faith, MMDI advised E & W in writing that the Purchase Agreement was canceled. On December 19, 1995, MMDI rented a mobile MRI unit to replace the one it had expected to receive from E & W. On December 21, 1995, MMDI executed a contract with a third party for the manufacture and construction of two trailers to house two of the Philips 1.5T MR scanner systems.

On December 22, 1995, Mr. Freudenberger sent a letter to Mr. Turowski, reiterating that the first trailer was ready for shipment and requesting instructions on how to ship it. In addition, the letter indicated that E & W was finalizing the design for an alternative bracing structure which would neither impede the servicing of the magnet components nor negatively impact the aesthetics of the trailer interior. Mr. Freudenberger also suggested that, after final testing and seeking MMDI's input regarding the aesthetics of the design, the design "would be considered the permanent solution" for the trailer. The design would then be incorporated into the second trailer at which time the first trailer would be returned to E & W and retrofitted with the new design at no cost to MMDI. E & W, however, maintained that the purchase agreement was still effective and continued to refuse to refund MMDI's payment. Soon after this correspondence, the parties ceased communication. Ultimately, E & W did remove the offending reinforcement structure and replaced it with an alternative design which was approved for permanent use by Philips. In the time since this replacement solution was fabricated and installed, E & W has sold two of the trailers to a third party.

On January 9, 1996, MMDI filed the instant suit for damages resulting from breach of contract and misrepresentation. E & W retained payments made by MMDI in the amount of $384,500. Further, MMDI incurred expenses in the amount of $185,250 for the lease of a mobile MRI scanner and trailer between December 19, 1995 and April 20, 1996.

V. ANALYSIS

A. Breach of contract

The primary issue for resolution by the Court is whether MMDI rightfully rejected E & W's tender of the first trailer and then subsequently canceled the contract, or if its actions in mid-December constituted anticipatory repudiation of the contract. Having previously determined that Michigan law controls in the instant case, the Court simply notes that the Michigan version of the Uniform Commercial Code [hereinafter the "UCC"] applies to this sales contract. MCLA §§ 440.1101 et seq.

1. Installment Contract

Before turning to the specific questions of rejection and cancellation, the Court must first resolve a threshold issue. Under the UCC, the parties' rights to reject, cure, and cancel under an installment contract differ substantially from those defined under a single delivery contract. Consequently, resolution of whether the contract is an installment contract is of primary concern. Section 2–612(1) defines an "installment contract" as "one which requires or authorizes the delivery of goods in separate lots to be separately accepted...." The commentary following this section emphasizes that the "definition of an installment contract is phrased more broadly in this Article [than in its previous incarnation as the Uniform Sales Act] so as to cover installment deliveries tacitly authorized by the circumstances or by the option of either party." § 2–612, cmt. 1.

Plaintiff argues that the contract between itself and E & W does not constitute an installment contract because it authorizes delivery in commercial units, and not lots, as required by subsection (1). However, upon review of the Code section defining those terms, it becomes clear that those terms are not mutually exclusive. Section 2–105 defines a "lot" as a "parcel or single article which is the subject matter of a separate sale or delivery, whether or not it is sufficient to perform the contract." The same section defines a commercial unit as "such a unit of goods as by commercial usage is a single whole for purposes of sale and division of which materially impairs its character or value on the market or in use. A commercial unit may be a single article (as a machine) or a set of articles (as a suite of furniture or an assortment of sizes) or a quantity (as a bale, gross, or carload) or any other unit treated in use or in the relevant market as a single whole." Thus, a lot, which is the measure of goods that the contract states will be delivered together in one installment, can be a single commercial unit. Consequently, § 2–612 applies wherever a contract for multiple items authorizes the delivery of the items in separate groups at different times, whether or not the installment constitutes a commercial unit.

The contract between MMDI and E & W for the sale of four trailers authorizes the delivery of each trailer separately. While the written contract does not explicitly state this delivery schedule, it does authorize separate delivery. Paragraph 2 of the contract assumes separate delivery dates by setting out a payment schedule wherein the balance for each unit is due at the time of shipment. Furthermore, based on the parties testimony it is clear that both parties understood the trailers would be delivered in separate installments. Indeed, neither party disputes that they agreed to have the trailers delivered at four separate times. Therefore, the Court finds that the contract in dispute is an installment contract.

2. Right of Rejection

Section 2–612, therefore, is the starting point for the Court's analysis of MMDI's actions on December 13, 1995. ... Under § 2–612, the buyer's right to reject is far more limited than the corresponding right to reject under a single delivery contract defined under § 2–601. Under § 2–601, a buyer has the right to reject, "if the goods or tender of delivery fail in any respect to conform to the contract...." Known as the "perfect tender" rule, this standard requires a very high level of conformity. Under this rule, the buyer may reject a seller's tender for any trivial defect, whether it be in the quality of the goods, the timing of performance, or the manner of delivery. To avoid injustice, the Code limits the buyer's correlative right to cancel the contract upon such rejection by providing a right to cure under § 2–508. § 2–508, cmt. 2. Under § 2–508, the seller has a right to cure if s/he seasonably notifies the buyer of the intent to do so, and either 1) the time for performance has not yet passed, or 2) the seller had reason to believe that the goods were in conformity with the contract. Thus, § 2–508's right to cure serves to temper the buyer's expansive right to reject under a single delivery contract. ...

Section 2–612 creates an exception to the perfect tender rule. ... Under subsection (2), a buyer may not reject nonconforming tender unless the defect substantially impairs the value of the installment. In addition, "if the nonconformity is curable and the seller gives adequate assurances of cure," the buyer must accept the installment. § 2–612, cmt. 5. But even if rejection is proper under subsection 2, cancellation of the contract is not appropriate unless the defect substantially impairs the value of the whole contract. § 2–612(3), cmt. 6. Because this section significantly restricts the buyer's right to cancel under an installment contract, there is no corresponding necessity for reference to § 2–508; the seller's right to cure is implicitly defined by § 2–612.[6]

a.   Delivery Date

Before proceeding with the analysis of MMDI's December 13 rejection, the Court initially notes that E & W's tender on December 13 constituted a cure attempt for the wall-flexing defect which delayed the delivery of the first trailer beyond the agreed upon delivery date. Although under § 2–612 the delivery date does not cut off the seller's right to cure, it does have an effect on the rights of the parties. . . .

In the instant case, the original, written contract included no definite delivery date. Instead, the contract left the delivery term to be agreed upon at a later date. At the time of execution, the parties both expected delivery of the first trailer to take place in October. During the months after the execution of the contract, however, the parties modified the deadline for the first installment of the contract on several occasions. As noted above, upon review of the testimony and documentary evidence, the Court finds that, whatever delivery date the parties had agreed upon prior to November 1995, by early November they had renegotiated their agreement to establish a December 1, 1995 delivery date. See § 2–209 (sales contract may be modified by oral or written agreement without consideration, so long as agreement does not state otherwise).

Defendant argues, however, that, even if the parties had at one point agreed upon a December 1, 1995 deadline, when the first trailer failed the Philips road test on November 28, 1995, the parties renegotiated the delivery term to allow E & W a reasonable time to cure the defect. While E & W is correct that, as of December 1, it had a reasonable time in which to cure the wall-flexing problem, the Court disagrees that MMDI's willingness to wait for a cure constitutes an agreement to extend the delivery deadline. Because the parties believed that the defect was curable and E & W, without solicitation, unequivocally promised to cure it, under § 2–612, MMDI had no choice but to accept an offer of cure. To reject the installment on November 28 would have constituted a violation of § 2–612. The Court, therefore, finds that any negotiations the parties engaged in regarding delivery after discovery of the wall-flexing problem, did not constitute a modification of the delivery date for the first installment, but rather involved negotiation regarding cure. Since no specific date for delivery of a

---

6. Courts of other jurisdictions have reached differing conclusions with regard to the interaction between §§ 2–612 and 2–508. See, e.g., Arkla Energy Resources v. Roye Realty & Dev., Inc., 9 F.3d 855 (10th Cir. 1993); Bodine, 493 N.E.2d at 713; Bevel–Fold, Inc. v. Bose Corp., 9 Mass. App. Ct. 576, 402 N.E.2d 1104, 1108 (Mass.App.Ct.1980); Continental Forest Prods., Inc. v. White Lumber Sales, Inc., 256 Ore. 466, 474 P.2d 1, 4 (Or.1970). This Court does not find the arguments of these other courts persuasive, however, and notes that their decisions are not binding on this Court. Nevertheless, the Court also notes that, since the time for delivery of the first installment had already passed on December 1, 1995 (see infra § 2(a)) and defendant could not have reasonably believed and, in fact, did not believe that the trailer was in conformity with the contract on that date, defendant had no right to cure under § 2–508.

cure was agreed upon during those negotiations, under section 2–309(1), E & W had a reasonable time to effectuate a cure. Although there is some question as to whether further delay would have been reasonable, the Court finds that, as of December 13, 1995, a reasonable time had not yet passed. Therefore, defendant's tender of a cure was timely.

b. Substantial Impairment of the Installment

The Court's conclusion that E & W's December 13 tender was an attempt to cure the November 28 breach raises another question: which standard of conformity applies to cure under an installment contract, perfect tender or substantial impairment? Looking to the rationale behind § 2–612, the Court notes that the very purpose of allowing the seller time to cure under this section is to permit it additional time to meet the obligations of the contract. The assumption is that, because the parties have an ongoing relationship, the seller should be given an opportunity to make up the deficiency. This section was not designed to allow the seller to have a never-ending series of chances to bring the item into conformity with the contract. Nor was it enacted to force the buyer to accept a nonconforming product as satisfaction of the contract. Consequently, it is logical that a tender of cure should be required to meet the higher "perfect tender" standard. On its face, however, § 2–612, which generally defines a buyer's right to reject goods under an installment contract, requires only substantial impairment in this context as well. Thus, there is some question as to which is the appropriate standard. The answer is not crucial, however, since the trailer in this case fails under both standards. Because a decision on this point will not effect the ultimate outcome in this case, the Court declines to address the issue. Instead, the Court proceeds with the substantial impairment analysis provided by § 2–612.

To establish substantial impairment of the value of an installment, the buyer " 'must present objective evidence that with respect to its own needs, the value of the goods was substantially impaired.' " Arkla Energy Resources v. Roye Realty & Dev., Inc., 9 F.3d 855, 862 (10th Cir.1993) (quoting Bodine Sewer, Inc. v. Eastern Illinois Precast, Inc., 143 Ill. App. 3d 920, 493 N.E.2d 705, 713, 97 Ill. Dec. 898 (Ill. App. Ct. 1986)). See also § 2–612, cmt 4. The existence of such nonconformity depends on the facts and circumstances of each case, and "can turn not only on the quality of the goods but also on such factors as time . . . , and the like." § 2–612, cmt. 4. . . . Finally, whether nonconformity rises to the level of substantial impairment may be judged by reference to the concept of material breach under traditional contract law. . . .

In the instant case, plaintiff alleges several aspects in which defendant's December 13 tender failed to conform to contract obligations. Plaintiff contends that the trailer tendered on December 13 with the bracing structure did not conform to the parties' agreement because: 1) it was not and could not be certified by Philips without conditions for use with the 1.5T scanner and 2) its interior design did not conform with the parties' agreements. Because of these defects, MMDI argues that the value of trailer was reduced substantially. Defendant, on the other hand, contends that the contract required only that the trailer meet the technical specifications provided by Philips, and that, therefore, the December 13 trailer was in complete compliance with its terms.

The written contract signed by the parties in this case is relatively skeletal and thus, requires interpretation. The Court's fundamental purpose in interpreting the terms of the contract is to give effect to the intent of the parties as it existed at the time the agreement was made. ... " 'The meaning of the agreement of the parties is to be determined by the language used by them and by their action, read, and interpreted in the light of commercial practices and other surrounding circumstances.' " 1 WILLISTON ON SALES § 10–2, 431 (quoting 1 CORBIN ON CONTRACTS § 2.9 (rev. Ed.)). See also § 1–203 (setting out the requirement of good faith and requiring the Court to interpret "contracts within the commercial context in which they are created, performed, and enforced[]"). Furthermore, the Code explicitly authorizes courts to look to the parties' course of dealings and performance and to the usage of terms in trade in interpreting the terms of the contract. §§ 1–205, 2–202, and 2–208.

As instructed by the commentary to § 2–612, the Court begins the substantial impairment analysis by looking to the "normal and specifically known purposes of the contract." § 2–612, cmt. 4. Reviewing the evidence presented, the Court finds that the primary purpose of the contract was to provide the plaintiff with four trailers for use with the Philips 1.5T scanner. With that in mind, the parties agreed that the trailers would be constructed in accordance with the specifications provided by Philips and that the trailer would be not be ready for delivery until Philips certification had been received. Philips did not, however, ever certify the trailer for unconditional use with the bracing structure. Because the bracing structure prevented normal service of the scanner magnet, it was only approved as a temporary fix.

The general rule in cases where third party approval is required as a condition of performance is one of strict compliance. See generally J. Calamari and J. Perillo, THE LAW OF CONTRACTS 399, § 11–17 (2d ed. 1977). Such conditions will only be excused where the third party acts in bad faith or dishonestly. Id. In the instant case, there was no credible evidence presented that Philips acted in bad faith by withholding approval. On the contrary, there was extensive evidence presented detailing the inherent problems with the long-term use of such a bracing solution, which demonstrated the reasonableness of Philips' refusal to certify the trailer. The bracing structure's shape and orientation prevented removal of the outer panels from the scanner magnet and made some repairs to the magnet more difficult and more dangerous. Furthermore, in order to perform certain repairs, the steel brace would have to be unbolted and removed. Once removed, the scanner magnet would have to be recalibrated and retested. Consequently, Philips' decision to refuse certification was entirely justified. Having found no evidence of bad faith or dishonesty on the part of Philips, the Court finds that defendant's failure to meet this condition constituted a breach of the parties' agreement. . . . Given that the central purpose of the trailer was to house a Philips 1.5T scanner, the failure to meet the standard for Philips' certification substantially impaired the value of the trailer. The Court, therefore, finds that this failure to conform to the parties' agreement, in and of itself, constituted a material breach.

In addition to violating the requirement that the trailer receive certification from Philips, plaintiff correctly asserts that defendant breached yet another term of the contract. The Court notes that the bracing structure also violated the parties' implied agreement regarding the design of the interior of the trailer. During the course of the parties' dealings both before and after the contract signing, MMDI reviewed numerous representations of the trailer's interior layout and design. Many of these drawings showed the location of the scanner and detailed the location of every structure in the trailer. None of them, however, depicted a cage-like brace made up of multiple, large, steel beams surrounding the scanner magnet. These drawings, when coupled with E & W's own statement that the trailer was cosmetically complete without the brace when it was presented at the open house, convince the Court that there was an implied agreement that the trailer would not have such a structure.

Furthermore, it is clear that, when the contract was executed, the parties both understood that the trailer's interior was meant to be aesthetically pleasing. It is the very nature of a mobile MRI trailer to function as an extension of the hospital it services. Since E & W was in the business of constructing trailers for mobile medical uses, it no doubt understood that the appearance of the trailer's interior could impact the comfort of MMDI's patients. Indeed, it is apparent that E & W realized such aesthetics were important to the value of the trailer, since, in its initial negotiations with MMDI, E & W included a cut-away drawing of the interior of a mobile unit which read: "Spacious, efficient layout with clean, aesthetically pleasing interior." The Court, therefore, finds that the agreement between the parties required that the interior of the trailer be aesthetically pleasing.

Such a condition of satisfaction by one of the parties to the contract will only be excused if approval is withheld unreasonably. . . . In the instant case, upon review of photographs of the bracing structure and testimony of those experienced in this industry, and in light of the fact that the interior of the trailer should match that of a hospital and not a construction site, the Court finds that plaintiff's refusal to approve the aesthetics of the design was commercially reasonable. Given that an integral aspect of the trailer's function is to serve as a clinic for patients undergoing medical procedures, and given MMDI's clients' expectations after having viewed the trailer at the open house, such a defect in the trailer's interior also reduced the value of the trailer substantially.

Upon review of the evidence, the Court finds that the bracing structure substantially impaired the value of the first trailer. Although the trailer met the express technical Philips' specifications for wall-flexing, it was never certified by the manufacturer. The failure of this condition does not relieve defendant of liability because it was defendant's failure to properly construct the trailer that prevented certification. In light of the specific facts and circumstances of this case, the Court finds that this deficiency substantially impaired the value of the installment. When coupled with the trailer's failure to conform with the aesthetic requirements of the contract and the delay caused by the cure attempt, the Court holds that the cure attempt clearly constitutes a substantial breach within the meaning of § 2–612(2).

Substantial impairment, however, does not in itself justify rejection of the installment. As noted above, the buyer must still accept tender if the defect can be cured and the seller gives adequate assurances. Under § 2–612, as opposed to § 2–609, it is incumbent upon the seller to assure the buyer that cure would be forthcoming. ... Defendant has failed in this regard. The Court notes that neither E & W's statements during the December 13 conference call nor the letter sent the following day constituted adequate assurances. On the contrary, during the December 13 conference call, Andrew Pike, the President of E & W denied the existence of a defect, disclaimed any continuing obligation to cure under the contract, and stated that he did not believe a better design could be made which would remedy the wall-flexing problem. Furthermore, on December 14, Mr. Pike again ignored the servicing problems that the bracing structure had caused, ignored the fact that the bracing structure had not been approved for permanent use by Philips, and reiterated his doubt that the design could be constructed in a more aesthetically pleasing manner. Under these circumstances, the Court finds that MMDI's rejection of E & W's cure on December 13 constituted a rightful rejection under § 2–612(2).[10]

3. Cancellation

a. Substantial Impairment of Contract as a Whole

The fact that rejection of one installment is proper does not necessarily justify cancellation of the entire contract. Under § 2–612(3) the right to cancel does not arise unless the nonconforming goods substantially impair the value of the entire contract. Indeed, as noted above, the very purpose of the substantial impairment requirement of § 2–612(3) is to preclude parties from canceling an installment contract for trivial defects. Emanuel Law

---

10. Defendant argues that, as of December 13, it still had a right to cure under § 2–508 and that it was not required to give assurances unless plaintiff requested them in writing under § 2–609. The Court reiterates that, under § 2–508, defendant's right to cure was cut off on December 1. Furthermore, § 2–612, unlike § 2–609, does not require the aggrieved party to request assurances. In an installment contract, where the seller's right to cure is more expansive it stands to reason that the burden would fall on the seller to show that it had the present ability and the intent to cure any remaining defect. ... In the instant case, defendant gave no indication that it either had the capability to satisfy the contract or the will to do so. On the contrary, E & W's President, gave MMDI the impression that cure was not possible and indicated clearly that he was not required to do anything more under the contract. Under such circumstances, MMDI's rejection was rightful.

Outlines v. Multi–State Legal Studies, 899 F. Supp. 1081, 1088 (S.D.N.Y. 1995).

Whether a breach constitutes "substantial impairment" of the entire contract is a question of fact. ... Ultimately, "whether the non-conformity in any given installment justifies cancellation as to the future depends, not on whether such non-conformity indicates an intent or likelihood that future deliveries will also be defective, but whether the non-conformity substantially impairs the value of the whole contract." § 2–612, cmt. 6. Thus, the question is one of present breach which focuses on the importance of the nonconforming installment relative to the contract as a whole. If the nonconformity only impairs the aggrieved party's security with regard to future installments, s/he "has the right to demand adequate assurances but [] not an immediate right to cancel the entire contract." § 2–612, cmt. 6. The right to cancel will be triggered only if "material inconvenience or injustice will result if the aggrieved party is forced to wait and receive an ultimate tender minus the part or aspect repudiated." § 2–610, cmt.3 (noting the test for anticipatory repudiation under § 2–610 is the same as the test for cancellation under § 2–612(3)).

In the instant case, there is substantial evidence that one of the primary purposes of this contract was to provide MMDI with a fourth mobile MRI trailer so that it could meet the growing demand for its services. Thus, impairment of one of the four installments would have a substantial negative impact on MMDI. Moreover, an early delivery time was of primary importance to MMDI, as E & W was well aware. By failing to cure the November 28 breach on the first installment, E & W substantially delayed completion of the remainder of the contract which delayed MMDI's ability to begin use of the 1.5T MRI trailer it had promised to its customers at the open house on November 3. Having found that substantial injustice would be done to plaintiff if it were required to accept the remaining three trailers after substantial delay as satisfaction of the contract, the Court finds that plaintiff rightfully canceled the contract on December 18, 1995.

4.   Damages

Having found that plaintiff rightfully rejected defendant's tender of cure on December 13, 1995, and subsequently properly canceled the contract, the Court finds that plaintiff is entitled to damages. Plaintiff has requested reimbursement of the amount it already paid for the nonconforming installment in the amount of $384,500 as well as damages in the amount of $185,250 incurred for the lease of a rental mobile MRI trailer between December 19, 1995 and April 20, 1996, to replace the trailer E & W failed to produce. Under § 2–711, a buyer who has rightfully canceled a contract may recover, among other things: 1) the amount that has already been paid, 2) damages for "cover" as defined in § 2–712, and 3) any damages of nondelivery, including consequential and incidental damages, as defined by § 2–715. Under § 2–715, incidental damages include "any [] reasonable expense incident to the delay or other breach." Thus, plaintiff is clearly entitled to return of the amount already paid for the item it never received. Plaintiff is also entitled to recover the amount paid for a replacement rental unit. Though this amount does not constitute cover it is allowable as incidental to the delay produced by E & W's breach. Had E & W made conforming tender on December 13, 1995, plaintiff would not have been forced to contract with another company for the trailers and to wait until spring for the first one. The Court, therefore, finds plaintiff is entitled to both expectation and consequential damages under the Code and awards plaintiff a sum total of $569,250 for the breach of contract claim.

* * *

VI. CONCLUSION

For the foregoing reasons, plaintiff is awarded expectation and incidental damages in the amount of $569,250. . . .

NOTES

(1) Installment Sales: A Different Set of Standards. The standards governing buyers' power to reject tendered goods change dramatically if the sales contract "requires or authorizes the delivery of goods in separate lots to be separately accepted," UCC 2–612(1), language which the drafters of the UCC intended to have considerable breadth.[16] Such sales, termed "installment contracts," are not governed by the perfect tender rule in UCC 2–601. As each lot is tendered in a simple, two-party sale, a buyer may reject that lot only if "the non-conformity substantially impairs the value of that installment and cannot be cured." UCC 2–612(2).[17] Section 2–612(3) deals with a different matter, cancellation of the "whole contract." Although the meaning of "whole contract" is somewhat uncertain, the most obvious meaning is the current installment and prospective installments that have not yet been tendered.

(2) History of the Installment Sales Rules. The Uniform Sales Act had a provision analogous to UCC 2–612(3), but had no antecedent to UCC 2–612(2). USA § 45(2) allowed installment contract buyers, when sellers have made one or more defective deliveries, to refuse to proceed further and sue for damages for breach of the entire contract if the breach was

---

16. Section 2–307 permits delivery in several lots "where the circumstances give either party the right to make or demand delivery in lots." The issue in 2–307, whether a seller may demand payment for partial deliveries, is not the same as the issue in 2–612(1), whether a seller may demand acceptance of partial deliveries. Comment 1 to 2–612 states that drafters of the UCC intended to define installment contracts more broadly than did pre-UCC law, and Comment 2 adds that provision for separate payment for each lot is not essential to an installment contract.

17. In an unusual "belt and suspenders" style of drafting, 2–612(2) continues to define circumstances in which a buyer "must accept an installment." Conceptually under the UCC, buyers must accept goods that they may not reject. Therefore, the criteria for "may reject" should be the same as the criteria for "must accept." However, as stated the drafters failed to make the two clauses complementary. Consider a tender of nonconforming goods by a seller who has the ability to cure the nonconformity but who fails to give adequate assurance of doing so.

sufficiently material. Buyer's power to reject a single installment, like buyer's power to reject goods in a single-delivery contract, was not codified. Karl Llewellyn, principal drafter of UCC Article 2, believed that some buyers should have limited power to reject single installments.[18]

(3) Rejection or Acceptance of an Installment: Cure. UCC 2–612(2) is a single sentence with two independent clauses that pose interpretation difficulties. The operative language in the clause that precedes the semicolon is that a seller "may reject" an installment under certain circumstances. The operative language in the clause that follows the semicolon is that a seller "must accept" an installment under certain circumstances. The circumstances in the two clauses are not the same. This leads to a series of analytic problems in *Midwest Mobile Diagnostic Imaging*.

With respect to the tender on November 28, the court applied the first clause and concluded that the buyer could not reject the goods. The court did not discuss the second clause. Did the "must accept" clause apply to the events on November 28? If the buyer had accepted the goods on November 28, may the buyer reject those goods on December 13? What is the application to accepted installments of the provision on revocation of acceptance in UCC 2–608?

The court seemed to treat the issue of cure, in this installment sale, as if the issue was one of cure following rejection of a single delivery under UCC 2–601. The court found that the seller's offer of cure had been volunteered, rather than induced by buyer's rejection, and was binding on the buyer without determining whether the nonconformity was of a nature that it could not be cured under the first clause or whether the offer of cure was an "adequate assurance" under the second clause. The court also found that the expiration of the time term of the contract did not foreclose seller's later cure without determining whether the conditions of UCC 2–508(2) had been met. If the court had focused on these issues under UCC 2–612(2) and UCC 2–508(2), how would the analysis have changed?

The court held that buyer had the option, under the first clause of UCC 2–612(2), to reject seller's second tender of the goods on December 13. Did the facts show an effective rejection of the goods tendered on December 13? Does UCC 2–612(2) provide any support for the court's determination that buyers have the option to reject goods after sellers' attempt to cure?

---

18. Llewellyn wrote: "Except for open term contracts, market risks are invariably placed upon the buyer. The installment contract runs over a longer period than does the single delivery agreement. The longer the parties are bound, the greater the possibility of market variation during the contract term. A problem presents itself. If B attempts rejection of a shipment admittedly, but not grossly, defective, which (as evidenced by his conduct in prior installments) he would have accepted had the market behaved as he expected, it there not good reason for the court to limit him to damages? . . . The other policy aspects of the question are fairly clear: is S to lose his whole contract, without chance to repair damage, because of one or two minor technical defaults, which the course of business justifies him in assuming that B would treat as negligible. or at least, as only founding a claim for adjustment?" K. Llewellyn, Cases and Materials on the Law of Sales 543 (1930).

The court's reasoning led to the question of the standard to be applied in rejection after seller's attempt to cure. Without reference to UCC 2–612, the court suggested that the perfect tender rule might apply, but declined to decide that question because the goods tendered on December 13 could be rejected under the substantial-impairment-of-value standard of the first clause of UCC 2–612. How persuasive were the court's findings on the level of impairment of the first installment? If the nonconformities in the goods tendered on December 13 had not been grave enough to impair the value substantially, should the buyer have been permitted to reject the goods?

Seller's counsel argued that seller had a further right to cure after buyer's putative rejection of the goods tendered on December 13. In footnote 10 of the opinion, the court gave several reasons for its rejection of that argument. The court declared that the time for cure had lapsed on December 1. Was that correct? The court declared that seller had the burden of showing present ability and intent to cure any remaining defect. Was that correct?

(4) Cancellation of the Whole Contract. UCC 2–612(3) deals with the power of installment buyers to cancel contracts. The power to reject an installment and the power to cancel the whole are different powers. One manifestation of the difference would be transactions in which repeated tenders of nonconforming installments, no one of which was or could have been rejected, might in the aggregate be sufficient to justify cancellation of further deliveries.

In *Midwest Mobile Diagnostic Imaging*, buyer advised seller in writing on December 18 that the purchase agreement was canceled. The court declared that the standard for cancellation of future installments was not the same as the standard for rejection of an installment that had been tendered. How persuasive were the court's findings on the grounds for cancellation of the whole contract?

(5) Damages. *Midwest Mobile Diagnostic Imaging* is the first case in this Section to consider buyer's recovery of damages after rightful rejection of goods. In prior cases, the primary claim litigated was an action by a seller for the unpaid price of the goods. Although references were made to counterclaims by some of those buyers, the substance of the counterclaims was not determined. Where market prices have fallen, buyers that succeed in rightful rejection of goods do not have a claim for expectation damages resulting from sellers' breach; released from their contract obligations, the buyers can obtain substitute goods at prevailing market prices that are lower than the contract prices.

The rejection of the first installment in *Midwest Mobile Diagnostic Imaging* occurred after the price had been paid and did not occur in a falling market. The procedural posture was therefore quite different. Buyer sought to recover the price paid and, in addition, damages based on a temporary replacement of the goods. The UCC provisions mentioned by the court were UCC 2–711, UCC 2–712, and UCC 2–715. The court found that the rental cost of the replacement unit was not recoverable under UCC 2–

712. Was the court correct? Are rental costs for temporary replacements properly recoverable under UCC 2–715?

Problem 5.1.3. Sellers that sell goods in quantities that could be delivered at once can escape from the rigors of the perfect tender rule by eliciting from buyers express or tacit consent to divide full performance into more than one "lot." In making such arrangements, buyers may or may not be aware that they are surrendering a significant amount of leverage over the sellers when the time comes for performance. If you were counsel to a firm regularly engaged in selling or buying goods in quantities that could be divided, what advice would you give on standard contracting terms?

Problem 5.1.4. Seller and Buyer have a long-term trading pattern whereby Buyer submits orders frequently for goods to be delivered some time later. Within the delivery time necessary for an order, Buyer usually makes one or more additional orders. Each purchase order results in a single delivery by Seller. Is Buyer's right to reject tendered goods governed by UCC 2–601 or 2–612(2)?

INTERNATIONAL SALES LAW

The Convention on International Sale of Goods does not use the concept of buyers' rejection or acceptance of goods found in the UCC or for sellers' cure of rejected goods. The Convention has no provision for revocation of acceptance or for installment sales. The CISG provision most comparable to the UCC provisions for rejection or revocation of acceptance is the provision in CISG 49 that permits aggrieved buyers to *avoid* contracts.[19]

Fundamental Breach. CISG 49(1)(a) permits buyers to avoid contracts on the ground that the goods delivered are nonconforming only if the nonconformities are sufficiently grave as to constitute *fundamental breach*. A breach is "fundamental" if the detriment in performance substantially deprives the aggrieved party of what it was entitled to expect under the contract. CISG 25. Professor Honnold noted that, in developing the Convention, there was no significant support for allowing buyers to avoid contracts for insubstantial deviations from contracts:[20]

> Stricter avoidance (or "rejection") rules in some domestic laws failed to take account of the special circumstances of international trade, such as the fact that claims that the goods are defective often are made only after expensive transport to the buyer's place of business when avoidance for immaterial defects might needlessly lead to wasteful reshipment or redisposition of the goods in a foreign country. Moreover, the power to avoid the contract for immaterial defects in performance may

---

19. The word "reject" is used in CISG 86(1) and 86(2), but probably refers to buyer's refusal to keep goods after avoidance of contracts. See Honnold, International Sales § 455.

20. Honnold, International Sales § 181.2.

tempt the ... buyer (after a price decline) to avoid the contract and thus reverse the allocation of the effect of price changes which the contract contemplated.

Of course, these factors will not always be present and in many cases only avoidance will adequately protect the aggrieved party. In transactions where a party is concerned that Article 25 is too lax or too strict or that a tribunal might improperly apply the law, the contract can provide for stricter (or looser) grounds for avoidance (Article 6).

Decision of the Bundesgerichtshof, Germany

CLOUT Abstract No. 171, UNILEX D. 1996–4.

The Dutch plaintiff was the assignee of a Dutch company, which had sold four different quantities of cobalt sulphate to the [buyer], a German company. It was agreed that the goods should be of British origin and that the plaintiff should supply certificates of origin and of quality. After the receipt of the documents, the [buyer] declared the contracts to be avoided since the cobalt sulphate was made in South Africa and the certificate of origin was wrong. The [buyer] also claimed that the quality of the goods was inferior to what was agreed upon. The plaintiff demanded payment. The German Supreme Court held that there were no grounds for avoidance of the contract and thus found for the plaintiff.

According to the Court, the declaration of avoidance could not be based on article 49(1)(b) CISG since the plaintiff had effected delivery. The delivery of goods which do not conform with the contract either because they are of lesser quality or of different origin does not constitute non-delivery.

The Court also found that there was no fundamental breach of contract since the [buyer] failed to show that the sale of the South African cobalt sulphate in Germany or abroad was not possible (article 49(1)(a) CISG). Thus, the [buyer] failed to show that it was substantially deprived of what it was entitled to expect under the contract (article 25 CISG).

Lastly, the Court held that the delivery of wrong certificates of origin and of quality did not amount to a fundamental breach of contract since the [buyer] could obtain correct documents from other sources. Accordingly, the [buyer] could not refuse payment under article 58.

———

Manner of Avoiding. If goods received are so nonconforming that sellers' performance amounts to fundamental breach, buyers may declare contracts avoided. CISG 49(1). For a declaration of avoidance to be effective, it must be made by notice to the seller. CISG 26.[21]

21. Notices under the Convention are effective, whether or not received, if dis-   patched "by means appropriate in the circumstances." CISG 27.

Time of Avoidance. A buyer's time to decide whether to declare a contracted avoided for fundamental breach is determined by the time needed to discover the deficiency. Power to avoid for quality or quantity defects expires a reasonable time after buyer knew or ought to have known of the breach. CISG 49(2)(b)(i). Power to avoid for late delivery that constitutes fundamental breach expires a reasonable time after buyer has become aware that delivery has been made. CISG 49(2)(a).

Effect of Avoidance. Avoidance of a contract generally releases both parties from their obligations under it. CISG 81(1). The aggrieved buyer is entitled to damages that have accrued prior to avoidance, but must account to the seller for benefits derived from the goods. CISG 84. A party who has performed the contract in whole or in part may claim restitution. CISG 81(2). A buyer that elects to avoid must be able generally to return the goods delivered substantially in the condition in which it received them. CISG 82(1). Exceptions exist (1) if buyer is unable to return the goods and the impossibility is not due to its act or omission, or (2) if the goods were sold in the normal course of business or consumed or transformed by the buyer before it discovered or ought to have discovered the lack of conformity, or (3) if the goods deteriorated or perished as a result of buyer's examination of them. CISG 46(2). A buyer must act, on behalf of the seller, to preserve goods in the buyer's possession or placed at its disposal at their shipping destination. CISG 86. The buyer may warehouse the goods. CISG 87. A buyer need not return goods if seller fails to repay the price or the cost of preservation of the goods. CISG 88(1). If seller delays unreasonably in taking the goods back, buyer may sell them by any appropriate means, CISG 88(1), and must do so if the goods are subject to rapid deterioration or their preservation would involve unreasonable expense. CISG 88(2).

Cure of Nonconforming Deliveries. In contracts governed by the CISG, buyers are without power to reject goods and have only limited power to avoid contracts. Buyers are, therefore, not in a strong position to use self-help to compel sellers to cure nonconforming deliveries. However, the Convention permits buyers to seek court orders compelling sellers to perform. CISG 46(1). Article 46 differentiates between court orders to compel delivery of substitute goods and court orders to repair. Substitute goods may be ordered only if the deficiency in the original delivery was a fundamental breach. CISG 46(2). An order to repair is permitted unless repair is unreasonable in the circumstances. CISG 46(3).

The Convention's authorization of court-ordered relief may be of little value to buyers in the United States or other common-law nations where equitable relief, by injunction or specific performance, is denied if the aggrieved party has an adequate remedy at law, i.e. monetary damages. See, e.g., UCC 2–716. The Convention accepts that some nations' laws limit parties' access to specific relief. CISG 28.

Even if not faced with buyers' avoidance or not ordered to cure nonconforming deliveries, sellers may elect to try to remedy failures in their performances. Buyers must permit sellers to do so if the sellers act without unreasonable delay and without causing buyers unreasonable inconvenience. CISG 48(1). What might motivate sellers to act in this way? Professor Honnold explained:[22]

> It would be easy to over-estimate the importance of the Convention's rules on "requiring" performance. Buyers seldom need to coerce sellers to replace or repair defective goods.... Replacement and repair are opportunities sought by sellers—to preserve good will, reduce damage liability and avoid the drastic remedy of avoidance of the contract.

Problem 5.1.5. Telecommunications Company (TCo) in an African country contracted to buy a high power microwave amplifier (HPA) from a United States supplier (SCo). The agreement contained extensive technical specifications for the HPA. The agreement provided, further, that SCo would install and test the HPA at the site in Africa within 15 months. When the HPA had been manufactured, TCo inspected it at the factory and found that it met the contract specifications. SCo installed the HPA in Africa. Before the HPA was operational, TCo again inspected the equipment and indicated that it was satisfactory. After six months of SCo's effort to get the HPA into service, SCo realized that it would not work because it had been designed for a grounded neutral power supply system, whereas the power supply at the site was an isolated neutral power system. The contract specifications were silent on the nature of the power supply. Rebuilding the HBA to operate with the available power supply would delay installation for more than a year. Assuming that the contract is governed by the CISG, may TCo avoid the contract?[23]

Problem 5.1.6. Buyer and seller contracted for sale of a computer. Seller shipped the computer to buyer. On arrival, buyer discovered that three major components of the equipment were defective. Buyer immediately informed seller of the defects and of its election to avoid the contract. Seller wired back: "All defects can be promptly and completely corrected. Will send top-level team next week." Assume that the deficiencies in the computer, as delivered, would constitute fundamental breach. If the seller has the ability to correct the problems without unreasonable delay and without causing buyer unreasonable convenience, may it do so despite buyer's declaration of avoidance? What is the meaning of "subject to article 49" in CISG 48(1)? According to Professor Honnold:[24]

> [T]he seller's right to cure should also be protected if, ... where cure is feasible, the buyer hastily declares the contract avoided before the seller has an opportunity to cure the defect. ... [W]here cure is feasible and where an offer of cure can be expected, one cannot conclude that the breach is 'fundamental' until one knows the answer to this question: Will the seller cure?

---

22. Honnold, International Sales § 286.

23. See Awards of June 1984 and May 1985 in Case No. 4567, 11 Yearbook Commercial Arbitration 143 (1986). This ICC arbitration case, on the facts set forth in the Problem, was decided under United States law. The arbitration panel, one member dissenting, found that the buyer was entitled to revoke its acceptance of the HPA and to recover damages.

24. Honnold, International Sales § 296.

Several reported cases from France, Germany and Swiss courts, as well as opinions of other commentators, support Professor Honnold's view.[25]

Problem 5.1.7. In performance of a contract for the sale of sugar with an average polarization of 78, seller shipped sugar which buyer tested and determined to average 73. Buyer immediately wired seller a notice that the sugar received did not conform to contract specifications on polarization. What purpose would this notice serve? Recall CISG 39(1). Would this notice constitute an effective declaration of avoidance under CISG 26? May sellers combine, in one communication, notice of a lack of conformity and declaration of avoidance? What content would such a communication have? Must a buyer use the word "avoid"? Professor Honnold offered this analysis:[26]

> A notice specifying a "lack of conformity" in accordance with Article 39 would not, without more, constitute a "declaration of avoidance" under Article 26. A buyer who specifies nonconformity ... may, and often does, choose to retain the goods and claim a reduction in the price or other damages to compensate for the deficiency. Avoidance of the contract is a different and much more drastic remedy. In the setting of tender of delivery of defective goods "avoidance of the contract" by the buyer means that the buyer will not accept or keep the goods, and that the seller has the responsibility to take over their disposition A buyer's declaration of *avoidance*, to be effective under Article 26, must inform the seller that the buyer will not accept or keep the goods.

Problem 5.1.8. Buyer received goods that are sufficiently deficient in quality that seller has committed a fundamental breach. Buyer sent notice to the seller specifying the lack of conformity (CISG 39) and declaring the contract avoided (CISG 26). One week later, buyer sought a court order directing the seller to deliver substitute goods on the ground that seller had delivered goods whose lack of conformity constitutes a fundamental breach and that buyer was entitled to "require" seller to deliver substitute goods under CISG 46(2). Seller counters that its obligations under the contract were released when buyer declared the contract avoided. Is seller correct? See Honnold, International Sales § 440.2.

Litigation After Avoidance. Price actions are likely to be less frequent in international sales transactions than in domestic United States transactions. International sales transactions are commonly structured by the parties so that the price is paid by banks that issued letters of credit payable on submission of documents. In such transactions, buyers exercise the right to avoid in the circumstance that sellers have the money. After avoidance, buyers would have to sue the sellers for restitution of the price.[27]

---

25. Id.

26. Honnold, International Sales § 187.2.

27. As already noted, a buyer that rightfully avoids a contract is entitled to res-

titution of the price paid under CISG 81(2), but is obligated to return the goods to the seller. CISG 82 declares that a buyer loses the right to declare a contract avoided if it is impossible to make restitution of the goods

The Convention does contain a provision that authorizes price recovery by sellers. CISG 62 declares that a seller may require a buyer to "pay the price, take delivery or perform his other obligations" unless the seller has resorted to a remedy that is inconsistent with this requirement. See Honnold, International Sales § 345.

SECTION 2.   BUYERS' WRONGFUL REJECTION: SELLERS' DAMAGES

DOMESTIC UNITED STATES LAW

If buyers reject wrongfully and have not paid the full contract price, sellers are entitled to various remedies, catalogued in UCC 2–703.

Price Actions. One of the remedies that is sometimes available is the UCC 2–709 price remedy, which we considered in Section 1. Sellers that elect to pursue the price remedy are committed, at least initially, to deliver or redeliver the goods to the buyers. If buyers are compelled to pay the price, they are entitled to receive the goods. UCC 2–709(2). The UCC does not require a seller to hold on to to goods pending the ultimate judgment in a price action. A sellers is permitted to sell the goods "if resale becomes possible." Proceeds of the resale are credited against the judgment for the price.

Actions for Damages. Sellers have another set of remedies that are premised on the outcome that the rejected goods, even though wrongfully rejected, will remain under the sellers' control. In these circumstances, aggrieved sellers make alternative disposition of the goods and seek monetary damages from the buyers.

The UCC provides for two remedies based upon sellers' actual or possible substitute transactions. A seller may resell the goods and recover monetary damages measured by the differential between the contract price and the net proceeds of the resale, UCC 2–706, or measured by the difference between the contract price and the market price of the goods, UCC 2–708(1).

The "wild card" remedy available to aggrieved sellers under the UCC is recovery of damages measured by the "profit" the seller would have made if buyer had not rejected. UCC 2–708(2). "Profit" under this section is akin to the accounting formula of contract price less variable costs-of-goods-sold; "overhead" or so-called fixed costs are not included in calculating "profit."

substantially in the condition in which they were received as a result of an act or omission of the buyer. Restitution is also excused, under CISG 82(c), if the buyer either resold the goods in the normal course of business, or consumed or transformed the goods in the course of normal use, before discovery of the lack of conformity.

Apex Oil Co. v. Belcher Co. of New York, Inc.

United States Court of Appeals, Second Circuit, 1988.
855 F.2d 997.

■ WINTER, CIRCUIT JUDGE:

This diversity case, arising out of an acrimonious commercial dispute, presents the question whether a sale of goods six weeks after a breach of contract may properly be used to calculate resale damages under Section 2–706 of the Uniform Commercial Code, where goods originally identified to the broken contract were sold on the day following the breach. Defendants The Belcher Company of New York, Inc. and Belcher New Jersey, Inc. (together "Belcher") appeal from a judgment, entered after a jury trial before Judge McLaughlin, awarding plaintiff Apex Oil Company ("Apex") $432,365.04 in damages for breach of contract and fraud in connection with an uncompleted transaction for heating oil. Belcher claims that the district court improperly allowed Apex to recover resale damages and that Apex failed to prove its fraud claim by clear and convincing evidence. We agree and reverse.

BACKGROUND

Apex buys, sells, refines and transports petroleum products of various sorts, including No. 2 heating oil, commonly known as home heating oil. Belcher also buys and sells petroleum products, including No. 2 heating oil. In February 1982, both firms were trading futures contracts for No. 2 heating oil on the New York Mercantile Exchange ("Merc"). In particular, both were trading Merc contracts for February 1982 No. 2 heating oil—i.e., contracts for the delivery of that commodity in New York Harbor during that delivery month in accordance with the Merc's rules. As a result of that trading, Apex was short 315 contracts, and Belcher was long by the same amount. Being "short" one contract for oil means that the trader has contracted to deliver one thousand barrels at some point in the future, and being "long" means just the opposite—that the trader has contracted to purchase that amount of oil. If a contract is not liquidated before the close of trading, the short trader must deliver the oil to a long trader (the exchange matches shorts with longs) in strict compliance with Merc rules or suffer stiff penalties, including disciplinary proceedings and fines. A short trader may, however, meet its obligations by entering into an "exchange for physicals" ("EFP") transaction with a long trader. An EFP allows a short trader to substitute for the delivery of oil under the terms of a futures contract the delivery of oil at a different place and time.

Apex was matched with Belcher by the Merc, and thus became bound to produce 315,000 barrels of No. 2 heating oil meeting Merc specifications in New York Harbor. Those specifications required that oil delivered in New York Harbor have a sulfur content no higher than 0.20%. Apex asked Belcher whether Belcher would take delivery of 190,000 barrels of oil in Boston Harbor in satisfaction of 190 contracts, and Belcher agreed. At trial, the parties did not dispute that, under this EFP, Apex promised it would deliver the No. 2 heating oil for the same price as that in the original contract—89.70 cents per gallon—and that the oil would be lifted from the vessel Bordeaux. The parties did dispute, and vigorously so, the requisite maximum sulfur content. At trial, Belcher sought to prove that the oil had to meet the New York standard of 0.20%, while Apex asserted that the oil had to meet only the specifications for Boston Harbor of not more than 0.30% sulfur.

The Bordeaux arrived in Boston Harbor on February 9, 1982, and on the next day began discharging its cargo of No. 2 heating oil at Belcher New England, Inc.'s terminal in Revere, Massachusetts. Later in the evening of February 10, after fifty or sixty thousand barrels had been offloaded, an independent petroleum inspector told Belcher that tests showed the oil on board the Bordeaux contained 0.28% sulfur, in excess of the New York Harbor specification. Belcher, nevertheless continued to lift oil from the ship until eleven o'clock the next morning, February 11, when 141,535 barrels had been pumped into Belcher's terminal. After pumping had stopped, a second test indicated that the oil contained 0.22% sulfur—a figure within the accepted range of tolerance for oil containing 0.20% sulfur. (Apex did not learn of the second test until shortly before trial.) Nevertheless, Belcher refused to resume pumping, claiming that the oil did not conform to specifications.

After Belcher ordered the Bordeaux to leave its terminal, Apex immediately contacted Cities Service. Apex was scheduled to deliver heating oil to Cities Service later in the month and accordingly asked if it could satisfy that obligation by immediately delivering the oil on the Bordeaux. Cities Service agreed, and that oil was delivered to Cities Service in Boston Harbor on February 12, one day after the oil had been rejected by Belcher. Apex did not give notice to Belcher that the oil had been delivered to Cities Service.

Meanwhile, Belcher and Apex continued to quarrel over the portion of the oil delivered by the Bordeaux. Belcher repeatedly informed Apex, orally and by telex, that the oil was unsuitable and would have to be sold at a loss because of its high sulfur content. Belcher also claimed, falsely, that it was incurring various expenses because the oil was unusable. In fact, however, Belcher had already sold the oil in the ordinary course of business. Belcher nevertheless refused to pay Apex the contract price of $5,322,200.27 for the oil it had accepted, and it demanded that Apex produce the remaining 48,000 barrels of oil owing under the contract. On February 17, Apex agreed to tender the 48,000 barrels if Belcher would both make partial payment for the oil actually accepted and agree to negotiate as to the price ultimately to be paid for that oil. Belcher agreed and sent Apex a check for $5,034,997.12, a sum reflecting a discount of five cents per gallon from the contract price. However, the check contained an endorsement stating that "[t]he acceptance and negotiation of this check constitutes full payment and final settlement of all claims" against Belcher. Apex refused the check, and the parties returned to square one. Apex demanded full payment; Belcher demanded that Apex either negotiate the check or remove the discharged oil (which had actually been sold) and replace it with 190,000 barrels of conforming product. Apex chose to take the oil and replace it, and on February 23 told Belcher that the 142,000 barrels of discharged oil would be removed on board the Mersault on February 25.

By then, however, Belcher had sold the 142,000 barrels and did not have an equivalent amount of No. 2 oil in its entire Boston terminal. Instead of admitting that it did not have the oil, Belcher told Apex that a dock for the Mersault was unavailable. Belcher also demanded that Apex either remove the oil *and* pay terminalling and storage fees, or accept payment for the oil at a discount of five cents per gallon. Apex refused to do either. On the next day, Belcher and Apex finally reached a settlement under which Belcher agreed to pay for the oil discharged from the Bordeaux at a discount of 2.5 cents per gallon. The settlement agreement also resolved an unrelated dispute between an Apex subsidiary and a subsidiary of Belcher's parent firm, The Coastal Corporation. It is this agreement that Apex now claims was procured by fraud.

After the settlement, Apex repeatedly contacted Belcher to ascertain when, where and how Belcher would accept delivery of the remaining 48,000 barrels. On March 5, Belcher informed Apex that it considered its obligations under the original contract to have been extinguished, and that it did not "desire to purchase such a volume [the 48,000 barrels] at the offered price." Apex responded by claiming that the settlement did not extinguish Belcher's obligation to accept the 48,000 barrels. In addition, Apex stated that unless Belcher accepted the oil by March 20, Apex would identify 48,000 barrels of No. 2 oil to the breached contract and sell the oil to a third party. When Belcher again refused to take the oil, Apex sold 48,000 barrels to Gill & Duffus Company. This oil was sold for delivery in April at a price of 76.25 cents per gallon, 13.45 cents per gallon below the Belcher contract price.

On October 7, 1982, Apex brought this suit in the Eastern District, asserting breach of contract and fraud. The breach-of-contract claim in Apex's amended complaint contended that Belcher had breached the EFP, not in February, but in March, when Belcher had refused to take delivery of the 48,000 barrels still owing under the contract. The amended complaint further alleged that "[a]t the time of the breach of the Contract by Belcher the market price of the product was $.7625 per gallon," the price brought by the resale to Gill & Duffus on March 23. ... In turn, the fraud claim asserted that Belcher had made various misrepresentations—that the Bordeaux oil was unfit, and unusable by Belcher; and that consequently Belcher was suffering extensive damages and wanted the oil removed— upon which Apex had relied when it had agreed to settle as to the 142,000 barrels lifted from the Bordeaux. Apex asserted that as a result of the alleged fraud it had suffered damages of 2.5 cents per gallon, the discount agreed upon in the settlement.

The case went to trial before Judge McLaughlin and a jury between February 3 and February 13, 1986. As it had alleged in its pleadings, Apex asserted that its breach-of-contract claim was based on an alleged breach occurring *after* February 11, 1982, the day Belcher rejected the oil on board the Bordeaux. Judge McLaughlin, however, rejected this theory as a matter of law. His view of the case was that Belcher's rejection of the Bordeaux oil occurred under one of two circumstances: (i) either the oil conformed to the proper sulfur specification, in which case Belcher breached; or (ii) the oil did not conform, in which case Apex breached. Judge McLaughlin reasoned that, if Belcher breached on February 11, then it could not have breached thereafter. If on the other hand Apex breached, then, Judge McLaughlin reasoned, only under the doctrine of cure, see N.Y.U.C.C. § 2–508 (McKinney 1964), could Belcher be deemed to have breached. Apex, however, waived the cure theory by expressly disavowing it (perhaps because it presumes a breach by Apex). Instead, Apex argued that, regardless of whether the Bordeaux oil had conformed, Belcher's refusal throughout February and March 1982 to accept delivery of 48,000 barrels of conforming oil, which Belcher was then still demanding, had constituted a breach of contract. Judge McLaughlin rejected this argument, which he viewed as simply "an attempt to reintroduce the cure doctrine."

In a general verdict, the jury awarded Apex $283,752.94 on the breach-of-contract claim, and $148,612.10 on the fraud claim, for a total of $432,365.04. With the addition of prejudgment interest, the judgment came to $588,566.29.

Belcher appeals from this verdict. Apex has not taken a cross-appeal from Judge McLaughlin's dismissal of its post-February 11 breach theories, however. The parties agree, therefore, that as the case comes to us, the verdict concerning the breach can be upheld only on the theory that, if Belcher breached the contract, it did so only on February 11, 1982, and that the oil sold to Gill & Duffus on March 23 was identified to the broken contract.

DISCUSSION

* * *

Belcher's principal argument on appeal is that the district court erred as a matter of law in allowing Apex to recover resale damages under Section 2–706. Specifically, Belcher contends that the heating oil Apex sold to Gill & Duffus in late March of 1982 was not identified to the broken contract. According to Belcher, the oil identified to the contract was the oil aboard the Bordeaux—oil which Apex had sold to Cities Service on the day after the breach. In response, Apex argues that, because heating oil is a fungible commodity, the oil sold to Gill & Duffus was "reasonably identified" to the contract even though it was not the same oil that had been on board the Bordeaux. We agree with Apex that, at least with respect to fungible goods, identification for the purposes of a resale transaction does not necessarily require that the resold goods be the exact goods that were rejected or repudiated. Nonetheless, we conclude that as a matter of law the oil sold to Gill & Duffus in March was not reasonably identified to the contract breached on February 11, and that the resale was not commercially reasonable.

Resolving the instant dispute requires us to survey various provisions of the Uniform Commercial Code. ... The Bordeaux oil was unquestionably identified to the contract under Section 2–501(b), and Apex does not assert otherwise. Nevertheless, Apex argues that Section 2–501 "has no application in the context of the Section 2–706 resale remedy," because Section 2–501 defines identification only for the purpose of establishing the point at which a buyer "obtains a special property and an insurable interest in goods." N.Y.U.C.C. § 2–501. This argument has a facial plausibility but ignores Section 2–103, which contains various definitions, and an index of other definitions, of terms used throughout Article 2 of the Code. With regard to "[i]dentification," Section 2–103(2) provides that the "definition[] applying to *this Article*" is set forth in Section 2–501. Id. § 2–103 (emphasis added).

Section 2–501 thus informs us that the Bordeaux oil was identified to the contract. It does not end our inquiry, however, because it does not exclude as a matter of law the possibility that a seller may identify goods to a contract, but then substitute, for the identified goods, *identical* goods that are then identified to the contract. ... Belcher relies upon Section 2–706's statement that "the seller may resell the *goods concerned*," N.Y.U.C.C. § 2–706(1) (emphasis added), and upon Section 2–704, which states that "[a]n aggrieved seller ... may ... identify to the contract conforming goods *not already identified* if at the time he learned of the breach they are in his possession or control." Id. § 2–704(1) (emphasis added). According to Belcher, these statements absolutely foreclose the possibility of reidentification for the purpose of a resale. Apex, on the other hand, points to Section 2–706's statement that "it is not necessary that the goods be in existence or that any or all of them have been identified to the contract before the breach." Id. § 2–706(2). According to Apex, this language shows that "[t]he relevant inquiry to be made under Section 2–706 is whether the resale transaction is reasonably identified to the breached contract and not whether the goods resold were originally identified to that contract." Apex Br. at 25.

None of the cited provisions are dispositive. First, Section 2–706(1)'s reference to reselling "the goods concerned" is unhelpful because those goods are the goods identified to the contract, but which goods are so identified is the question to be answered in the instant case. Second, as to Section 2–704, the fact that an aggrieved seller may identify goods "not already identified" does not mean that the seller may not identify goods as substitutes for previously identified goods. Rather, Section 2–704 appears to deal simply with the situation described in Section 2–706(2) above, where the goods are not yet in existence or have not yet been identified to the contract. Belcher thus can draw no comfort from either Section 2–704 or Section 2–706(1). Third, at the same time, however, Section 2706(2)'s reference to nonexistent and nonidentified goods does not mean, as Apex suggests, that the original (prebreach) identification of goods is wholly irrelevant. Rather, the provision regarding nonexistent and nonidentified goods deals with the special circumstances involving anticipatory repudiation by the buyer. See N.Y.U.C.C § 2–706 comment 7. Under such circumstances, there can of course be no resale remedy unless the seller is allowed to identify goods to the contract after the breach. That is obviously not the case here.

* * *

[F]ungible goods resold pursuant to § 2–706 must be goods identified to the contract, but need not always be those *originally* identified to the contract. In other words, at least where fungible goods are concerned, identification is not always an irrevocable act and does not foreclose the possibility of substitution. ... Nevertheless, as [§ 2–706] expressly states, "[t]he resale must be *reasonably* identified as referring to the broken contract," and "every aspect of the sale including the method, manner, time, place and terms must be commercially reasonable." Moreover, because the purpose of remedies under the Code is to put "the aggrieved party ... in as good a position as if the other party had performed," id. § 1–106(1), the reasonableness of the identification and of the resale must be determined by examining whether the market value of, and the price received for, the resold goods "accurately reflects the market value of the goods which are the subject of the contract." Servbest [Foods, Inc. v. Emssee Industries, Inc., 82 Ill. App. 3d 662,] 671, [403 N.E.2d 1], 8.

* * *

Apex's delay of nearly six weeks between the breach on February 11, 1982 and the purported resale on March 23 was clearly unreasonable, even if the transfer to Cities Service had not occurred. Steven Wirkus, of Apex, testified on cross-examination that the market price for No. 2 heating oil on February 12, when the Bordeaux oil was delivered to Cities Service, was "[p]robably somewhere around 88 cents a gallon or 87." (The EFP contract price, of course, was 89.70 cents per gallon.) Wirkus also testified on redirect examination that the market price fluctuated throughout the next several weeks:

Q. Sir, while you couldn't remember with particularity what the price of oil was on a given day four years ago, is it fair to say that prices went up and down?

A. Definitely that's fair to say.

Q. From day-to-day?

A. Yes.

Q. Towards the end of February prices went down?

A. That's correct.

Q. Then in early March it went back up?

A. In early March, yes.

Q. Then they went back down again towards the middle of March; isn't that correct?

MR. GILBERT: I object to the form of this, your Honor, on redirect.

THE COURT: Yes.

Q. Did they go back down in mid March, Mr. Wirkus?

A. My recollection, yes.

Q. In late March what happened to the price?

A. Market went back up.

Moreover, Wirkus testified that, on March 23, in a transaction unrelated to the resale, Apex purchased 25,000 barrels of No. 2 oil for March delivery at 80.50 cents per gallon, and sold an equivalent amount for April delivery at 77.25 cents per gallon. Other sales on March 22 and 23 for April delivery brought similar prices: 100,000 barrels were sold at 76.85 cents, and 25,000 barrels at 76.35 cents. The Gill & Duffus resale, which was also for April delivery, fetched a price of 76.25 cents per gallon—some eleven or twelve cents below the market price on the day of the breach.

In view of the long delay and the apparent volatility of the market for No. 2 oil, the purported resale failed to meet the requirements of Section 2–706 as a matter of law. . . .

. . . Apex's only asserted justification, which the district court accepted in denying Belcher's motion for judgment notwithstanding the verdict, was that the delay was caused by continuing negotiations with Belcher. We find that ruling to be inconsistent with the district court's view that Belcher's breach, if any, occurred on February 11. The function of a resale was to put Apex in the position it would have been on that date by determining the value of the oil Belcher refused. The value of the oil at a later date is irrelevant because Apex was in no way obligated by the contract or by the Uniform Commercial Code to reserve 48,000 gallons for Belcher after the February 11 breach. Indeed, that is why Apex's original theory, rejected by the district court and not before us on this appeal, was that the breach occurred in March.

The rule that a "resale should be made as soon as practicable after . . . breach," . . . should be stringently applied where, as here, the resold goods are not those originally identified to the contract. In such circumstances, of course, there is a significant risk that the seller, who may perhaps have already disposed of the original goods without suffering any loss, has identified new goods for resale in order to minimize the resale price and thus to maximize damages. That was not the case in Servbest, for example, where the resale consisted of the first sales made after the breach. See 82 Ill. App. 2d at 675, 403 N.E.2d at 11. Here, by contrast, the oil originally identified to the contract was sold the day after the February 11, 1982 breach, and no doubt Apex sold ample amounts thereafter in the six weeks before the purported resale. . . . Because the sale of the oil identified to the contract to Cities Service on the next day fixed the value of the goods refused as a matter of law, the judgment on the breach-of-contract claim must be reversed.

We turn finally to Apex's fraud claim. . . . Belcher claims that the evidence was insufficient to support the jury's finding that Apex, in agreeing to the settlement with Belcher, had relied upon Belcher's misrepresentations in ignorance of their falsity and had suffered injury accordingly.

In support of the finding of reliance, Apex relies primarily, if not exclusively, upon the testimony of its president, Anthony Novelly. Novelly testified that he had delegated the task of negotiation to in-house counsel, Harold Lessner. Lessner nevertheless kept Novelly abreast of Belcher's various demands and representations because it was Novelly, as president, "who had to approve the settlement ultimately." To this effect, Novelly testified as follows:

Q. During your discussion with Mr. Lesner [sic], did he say anything to you concerning whether Belcher had used the oil?

A. No, he said the oil was off spec and not useable.

Q. He said that is what Belcher had told him?

A. Correct.

Q. During your conversation with Mr. Lesner [sic], did he tell you anything about whether Belcher was claiming damages, as a result of the delivery?

A. Yes, they were.

Q. And did you rely on all the matters that were conveyed to you in approving the settlement?

A. Yes, I did.

According to Apex, this testimony regarding its alleged reliance is "unrebutted." That may be true so far as other witnesses are concerned, but Novelly candidly modified his testimony on cross-examination as follows:

Q. At the time you approved the settlement, one of the terms was that Belcher was going to get a discount off the agreed price for the BORDEAUX oil of two and a half cents per gallon, is that correct?

A. Yes.

Q. Did you believe they were intitled [sic] to a two and a half cent per gallon discount based on the facts you know?

MR. WEINER: Objection.

THE COURT: Overruled.

A. Not really.

Q. You did not believe that?

A. No.

Q. Did you believe they were intitled [sic] to any discount?

A. I wouldn't have thought so.

Q. You agreed to the settlement for other reasons, did you not?

A. I agreed to the settlement to get the thing settled.

Q. You wanted to get it behind you, is that correct?

A. Yes.

Q. You had a number of items?

A. Whole bunch of them.

Q. You didn't like to leave all these open items?

A. I didn't want a mess hanging around.

Q. You wanted to get everything cleaned up?

A. That's correct.

Q. You had another idea—withdrawn. You had another motivation, didn't you sir?

A. Coastal [Belcher's parent] was a big company, I don't like to have problems with big companies. I try to settle things and avoid litigation.

Q. You want to get all the open items closed, for you to do business with Coastal and its subsidiaries, is that correct?

A. That is a good statement, yes.

* * *

Q. At the time you were discussing the settlement with Mr. Lesner [sic] or anybody else you talked about it with, did you have the belief that the oil delivered to Belcher aboard the BORDEAUX was in fact not useable by Belcher?

A. I never had that belief, no.

However much this display of refreshing candor ought to be rewarded, we must conclude that, in light of the concessions that Novelly was seeking a compromise of all outstanding disputes and did not believe Belcher's misrepresentations as to the oil delivered on February 11, a reasonable jury could not find by clear and convincing evidence that Apex believed and relied upon Belcher's misrepresentations.

Reversed.

NOTES

(1) Commodities Futures. This case illustrates how products may be traded through "exchanges" that permit buyers and sellers to anticipate future deliveries of certain standardized products. Many participants in these futures markets have no expectation of either delivering or receiving goods under their contracts; before the closing date, these traders take offsetting buy-sell positions so that no performance occurs. These participants may be investors seeking profits from changes in market prices of the commodities or merchants "hedging" planned transactions against shifts in market prices. The buyer and seller in *Apex Oil* did not close out their positions and were "matched" by the N.Y. Mercantile Exchange as seller and buyer. Once "matched" the parties became obligated as if they had chosen to contract with each other. Thereafter, they negotiated a modification of the place of performance for part of the oil.

(2) Construction of UCC 2–706 and 2–708. Seller's counsel sought unsuccessfully to fix damages under UCC 2–706 by the March 23 sale to Gill & Duffus. Why was that claim denied? When a seller claims but fails to qualify for relief under 2–706, may recovery be had under UCC 2–708(1)? Under 2–708(2)? See Comment 2 to UCC 2–706.

Should counsel for a seller-plaintiff draft the initial pleading as a claim for damages under all possible statutory provisions in the alternative? Should counsel introduce evidence on each of the alternative claims?

The segment of the opinion dealing with damages was omitted in *T.W. Oil*, which we read in the previous Section. In that case, the buyer rightfully rejected the initial delivery of oil from the *Khamsin* but wrongfully rejected the substitute delivery of the *Appollonian* oil. The trial judge measured seller's damages as the difference between the contract price and the proceeds of resale of the *Khamsin* oil more than two months after wrongful rejection of the *Appollonian* oil.[1] Was this an appropriate application of UCC 2–706? The Court of Appeals declined to entertain appeal on the issue of damages because the issue had not be properly presented to the appellate court.[2]

Problem 5.2.1. Suppose seller in *Apex* had sought damages measured by UCC 2–708(1). Buyer countered that seller's damages should be measured, under UCC 2–706, by the price of the resale to Cities Service. Is there any statutory basis for an argument that seller may not recover a larger amount under 2–708(1) than it would be entitled to receive if damages were measured by 2–706? See J. Sebert, Remedies Under Article Two of the Uniform Commercial Code: An Agenda for Review, 130 U. Pa. L. Rev. 360, 380–383 (1981).

R.E. Davis Chemical Corp. v. Diasonics, Inc.

United States Court of Appeals, Seventh Circuit, 1987.
826 F.2d 678.

■ CUDAHY, CIRCUIT JUDGE.

Diasonics, Inc. appeals from the orders of the district court denying its motion for summary judgment and granting R.E. Davis Chemical Corp.'s

---

1. Joc Oil USA, Inc. v. Consolidated Edison Co., 107 Misc.2d 376, 434 N.Y.S.2d 623 (N.Y. 1980).

2. "As to the damages issue raised by the defendant, we affirm without reaching the merits. At no stage of the proceedings before the trial court did the defendant object to the plaintiff's proposed method for their calculation, and this though the plaintiff gave ample notice of that proposal by means of a preliminary statement and pretrial memorandum filed with the court. So complete was defendant's acquiescence in the theory thus advanced that the plaintiff was permitted to introduce its proof of the *Khamsin* resale alone, and without opposition. Furthermore, in consensually submitting the four jointly framed advisory questions that went to the jury, the language of one of them, which was damages-related, indicates that both parties were acting on the assumption that the *Khamsin* oil was the one with which the court was to be concerned. And, even after the decision at nisi prius revealed that the Judge had acted on such an assumption, so far as the record shows, no motion was ever made to correct it." 57 N.Y.2d 587.

summary judgment motion. ... We ... reverse the grant of summary judgment in favor of Davis and remand for further proceedings.

I.

Diasonics is a California corporation engaged in the business of manufacturing and selling medical diagnostic equipment. Davis is an Illinois corporation that contracted to purchase a piece of medical diagnostic equipment from Diasonics. On or about February 23, 1984, Davis and Diasonics entered into a written contract under which Davis agreed to purchase to equipment. Pursuant to this agreement, Davis paid Diasonics a $300,000 deposit on February 29, 1984. ... Davis ... [subsequently] refused to take delivery of the equipment or to pay the balance due under the agreement. Diasonics later resold the equipment to a third party for the same price at which it was to be sold to Davis.

Davis sued Diasonics, asking for restitution of its $300,000 down payment under section 2–718(2) of the Uniform Commercial Code (the "UCC" or the "Code"). Ill. Rev. Stat. ch. 26, para. 2–718(2) (1985). Diasonics counterclaimed. Diasonics did not deny that Davis was entitled to recover its $300,000 deposit less $500 as provided in section 2–718(2)(b). However, Diasonics claimed that it was entitled to an offset under section 2–718(3). Diasonics alleged that it was a "lost volume seller," and, as such, it lost the profit from one sale when Davis breached its contract. Diasonics' position was that, in order to be put in as good a position as it would have been in had Davis performed, it was entitled to recover its lost profit on its contract with Davis under section 2–708(2) of the UCC. Ill. Rev. Stat. ch. 26, para. 2–708(2) (1985). ...

The district court ... entered summary judgment for Davis. The court held that lost volume sellers were not entitled to recover damages under 2–708(2) but rather were limited to recovering the difference between the resale price and the contract price along with incidental damages under section 2–706(1). Ill. Rev. Stat. ch. 26, para. 2–706(1) (1985). ... Davis was awarded $322,656, which represented Davis' down payment plus prejudgment interest less Diasonics' incidental damages. Diasonics appeals the district court's decision respecting its measure of damages as well as the dismissal of its third-party complaint.

II.

We consider first Diasonics' claim that the district court erred in holding that Diasonics was limited to the measure of damages provided in 2–706 and could not recover lost profits as a lost volume seller under 2–708(2). Surprisingly, given its importance, this issue has never been addressed by an Illinois court, nor, apparently, by any other court construing Illinois Supreme Court would resolve this issue if it were presented to it. Courts applying the laws of other states have unanimously adopted the position that a lost volume seller can recover its lost profits under 2–708(2). Contrary to the result reached by the district court, we conclude that the

Illinois Supreme Court would follow these other cases and would allow a lost volume seller to recover its lost profit under 2–708(2).

We begin our analysis with 2–718(2) and (3). Under 2–718(2)(b), Davis is entitled to the return of its down payment less $500. Davis' right to restitution, however, is qualified under 2–718(3)(a) to the extent that Diasonics can establish a right to recover damages under any other provision of Article 2 of the UCC. Article 2 contains four provisions that concern the recovery of a seller's general damages (as opposed to its incidental or consequential damages); 2–706 (contract price less resale price); 2–708(1) (contract price less market price); 2–708(2) (profit); and 2–709 (price). The problem we face here is determining whether Diasonics' damages should be measured under 2–706 or 2–708(2). To answer this question, we need to engage in a detailed look at the language and structure of these various damage provisions.

The Code does not provide a great deal of guidance as to when a particular damage remedy is appropriate. The damage remedies provided under the Code are catalogued in section 2–703, but this section does not indicate that there is any hierarchy among the remedies. One method of approaching the damage sections is to conclude that 2–708 is relegated to a role inferior to that of 2–706 and 2–709 and that one can turn to 2–708 only after one has concluded that neither 2–706 nor 2–709 is applicable.[6] Under this interpretation of the relationship between 2–706 and 2–708, if the goods have been resold, the seller can sue to recover damages measured by the difference between the contract price and the resale price under 2–706. The seller can turn to 2–708 only if it resells in a commercially unreasonable manner or if it cannot resell but an action for the price is inappropriate under 2–709. The district court adopted this reading of the Code's damage remedies and, accordingly, limited Diasonics to the measure of damages provided in 2–706 because it resold the equipment in a commercially reasonable manner.

---

6. Evidence to support this approach can be found in the language of the various damage sections and of the official comments to the UCC. See § 2–709(3) ("a seller who is held not entitled to the price under this Section shall nevertheless be awarded damages for non-acceptance under the preceding section [§ 2–708]"); UCC comment 7 to § 2–709 ("if the action for the price fails, the seller may nonetheless have proved a case entitling him to damages for non-acceptance [under § 2–708]"); UCC comment 2 to § 2–706 ("failure to act properly under this section deprives the seller of the measure of damages here provided and relegates him to that provided in Section 2–708"); UCC comment 1 to § 2–704 (describes § 2–706 as the "primary remedy" available to a seller upon breach by the buyer); see also Commonwealth Edison Co. v. Decker Coal Co., 653 F. Supp. 841, 844 (N.D.Ill.1987) (statutory language and case law suggest that "§ 2–708 remedies are available only to a seller who is not entitled to the contract price" under § 2–709); Childres & Burgess, Seller's Remedies: The Primacy of UCC 2–708(2), 48 N.Y.U. L. Rev. 833, 863–64 (1973). As one commentator has noted, 2–706 "is the Code section drafted specifically to define the damage rights of aggrieved reselling sellers, and there is no suggestion within it that the profit formula of section 2–708(2) is in any way intended to qualify or be superior to it." Shanker, The Case for a Literal Reading of UCC Section 2–708(2) (One Profit for the Reseller), 24 Case W. Res. 697, 699 (1973).

The district court's interpretation of 2–706 and 2–708, however, creates its own problems of statutory construction. There is some suggestion in the Code that the "fact that plaintiff resold the goods [in a commercially reasonable manner] does *not* compel him to use the resale remedy of § 2–706 rather than the damage remedy of § 2–708." Harris, A Radical Restatement of the Law of Seller's Damages: Sales Act and Commercial Code Results Compared, 18 Stan. L. Rev. 66, 101 n.174 (1965) (emphasis in original). Official comment 1 to 2–703, which catalogues the remedies available to a seller, states that these "remedies are essentially cumulative in nature" and that "whether the pursuit of one remedy bars another depends entirely on the facts of the individual case." See also State of New York Report of the Law Revision Comm'n for 1956, 396–97 (1956).[7]

Those courts that found that a lost volume seller can recover its lost profits under 2–708(2) implicitly rejected the position adopted by the district court; those courts started with the assumption that 2–708 applied to a lost volume seller without considering whether the seller was limited to the remedy provided under 2–706. None of those courts even suggested that a seller who resold goods in a commercially reasonable manner was limited to the damage formula provided under 2–706. We conclude that the Illinois Supreme Court, if presented with this question, would adopt the position of these other jurisdictions and would conclude that a reselling seller, such as Diasonics, is free to reject the damage formula prescribed in 2–706 and choose to proceed under 2–708.

Concluding that Diasonics is entitled to seek damages under 2–708, however, does not automatically result in Diasonics being awarded its lost profit. Two different measures of damages are provided in 2–708. Subsection 2–708(1) provides for a measure of damages calculated by subtracting the market price at the time and place for tender from the contract price.[8]

---

7. UCC comment 2 to 2–708(2) also suggests that 2–708 has broader applicability than suggested by the district court. UCC comment 2 provides: "This section permits the recovery of lost profits in all appropriate cases, which would include all standard priced goods. The normal measure there would be list price less cost to the dealer or list price less manufacturing cost to the manufacturer."

The district court's restrictive interpretation of 2–708(2) was based in part on UCC comment 1 to 2–704 which describes 2–706 as the aggrieved seller's primary remedy. The district court concluded that, if a lost volume seller could recover its lost profit under 2–708(2), every seller would attempt to recover damages under 2–708(2) and 2–706 would become the aggrieved seller's residuary remedy. This argument ignores the fact that to recover under 2–708(2), a seller must first

establish its status as a lost volume seller. . . .

The district court also concluded that a lost volume seller cannot recover its lost profit under 2–708(2) because such a result would negate a seller's duty to mitigate damages. This position fails to recognize the fact that, by definition, a lost volume seller cannot mitigate damages through resale. Resale does not reduce a lost volume seller's damages because the breach has still resulted in its losing one sale and a corresponding profit. . . .

8. There is some debate in the commentaries about whether a seller who has resold the goods may ignore the measure of damages provided in 2–706 and elect to proceed under 2–708(1). Under some circumstances the contract-market price differential will result in overcompensating such a seller. See J. White & R. Summers, Handbook of the Law under the Uniform Commercial Code

The profit measure of damages, for which Diasonics is asking, is contained in 2–708(2). However, one applies 2–708(2) only if "the measure of damages provided in subsection (1) is inadequate to put the seller in as good a position as performance would have done...." Ill. Rev. Stat. ch. 26, para. 2–708(2) (1985). Diasonics claims that 2–708(1) does not provide an adequate measure of damages when the seller is a lost volume seller. To understand Diasonics' argument, we need to define the concept of the lost volume seller. Those cases that have addressed this issue have defined a lost volume seller as one that has a predictable and finite number of customers and that has the capacity either to sell to all new buyers or to make the one additional sale represented by the resale after the breach. According to a number of courts and commentators, if the seller would have made the sale represented by the resale whether or not the breach occurred, damages measured by the difference between the contract price and market price cannot put the lost volume seller in as good a position as it would have been in had the buyer performed. The breach effectively cost the seller a "profit," and the seller can only be made whole by awarding it damages in the amount of its "lost profit" under 2–708(2).

We agree with Diasonics' position that, under some circumstances, the measure of damages provided under 2–708(1) will not put a reselling seller in as good a position as it would have been in had the buyer performed because the breach resulted in the seller losing sales volume. However, we disagree with the definition of "lost volume seller" adopted by other courts. Courts awarding lost profits to a lost volume seller have focused on whether the seller had the capacity to supply the breached units in addition to what it actually sold. In reality, however, the relevant questions include, not only whether the seller could have produced the breached units in addition to its actual volume, but also whether it would have been profitable for the seller to produce both units. Goetz & Scott, Measuring Sellers' Damages: The Lost—Profits Puzzle, 31 Stan. L. Rev. 323, 332–33, 346–47 (1979). As one commentator has noted, under the economic law of diminishing returns or increasing marginal costs[,] ... as a seller's volume increases, then a point will inevitably be reached where the cost of selling each additional item diminishes the incremental return to the seller and eventually makes it entirely unprofitable to conclude the next sale. Shanker, supra, at 705. Thus, under some conditions, awarding a lost volume seller its presumed lost profit will result in overcompensating the seller, and 2–708(2) would not take effect because the damage formula provided in 2–708(1) does place the seller in as good a position as if the buyer had performed. Therefore, on remand, Diasonics must establish, not only that it had the capacity to produce the breached unit in addition to the unit resold, but also that it would have been profitable for it to have produced and sold both. ...

§ 7–7, at 271–73 (2d ed. 1980); Sebert, Remedies under Article Two of the Uniform Commercial Code: An Agenda for Review, 130 U. Pa. L. Rev. 360, 380–83 (1981). We need not struggle with this question here because Diasonics has not sought to recover damages under 2–708(1).

One final problem with awarding a lost volume seller its lost profits was raised by the district court. This problem stems from the formulation of the measure of damages provided under 2–708(2) which is "the profit (including reasonable overhead) which the seller would have made from full performance by the buyer, together with any incidental damages provided in this Article (Section 2–710), due allowance for costs reasonably incurred and due credit for payments or *proceeds of resale*." Ill. Rev. Stat. ch. 26, para. 2–708(2) (1985) (emphasis added). The literal language of 2–708(2) requires that the proceeds from resale be credited against the amount of damages awarded which, in most cases, would result in the seller recovering nominal damages. In those cases in which the lost volume seller was awarded its lost profit as damages, the courts have circumvented this problem by concluding that this language only applies to proceeds realized from the resale of uncompleted goods for scrap. See, e.g., Neri, 30 N.Y.2d at 399 & n.2, 285 N.E.2d at 314 & n.2; see also J. White & R. Summers, Handbook of the Law under the Uniform Commercial Code § 7–13, at 285 ("courts should simply ignore the 'due credit' language in lost volume cases") (footnote omitted). Although neither the text of 2–708(2) nor the official comments limit its application to resale of goods for scrap, there is evidence that the drafters of 2–708 seemed to have had this more limited application in mind when they proposed amending 2–708 to include the phrase "due credit for payments or proceeds of resale." We conclude that the Illinois Supreme Court would adopt this more restrictive interpretation of this phrase rendering it inapplicable to this case.

We therefore reverse the grant of summary judgment in favor of Davis and remand with instructions that the district court calculate Diasonics' damages under 2–708(2) if Diasonics can establish, not only that it had the capacity to make the sale to Davis as well as the sale to the resale buyer, but also that it would have been profitable for it to make both sales. Of course, Diasonics, in addition, must show that it probably would have made the second sale absent the breach.

* * *

NOTES

(1) Subsequent Decision. On remand, Diasonics proved its average costs of manufacturing through expert testimony by accountants. It introduced evidence that the contract price was $1,500,000 but offered no specific evidence of the cost of manufacturing the equipment intended for Davis and resold to the third party. Using average cost data, the district court found that Diasonics profit would have been $453,000. The court of appeals affirmed. 924 F.2d 709 (7th Cir.1991).[3]

---

3. The court of appeals remanded for further consideration of a contract term that buyer contended would have lowered the pur- chase price by a post-payment rebate of $255,000.

(2) Construction of 2–708(2). As indicated in the court's opinion, the academic debate about the proper reading of UCC 2–708(2) has been and continues to be vigorous. Some explanation must be found for the enormous difference in the amount of damages recoverable in a case like *Davis*, under 2–708(2) ($453,000), under 2–706 ($–0–), under 2–708(1) (probably $–0–). The remarkably laconic Comment to 2–708(2) gives no indication of appreciating the sheer force of this section. Much of the academic debate is in the mode of law-and-economics analysis, based upon models of "lost volume" sellers. Others argue that the basic remedial principle requires putting an aggrieved seller into as good a position as buyer's performance would have done, UCC 1–106, and that market-based damages under 2–706 and 2–708(1) fail to mirror full performance. In addition to the materials referred to by the court, see J. Sebert, Remedies Under Article Two of the Uniform Commercial Code: An Agenda for Review, 130 U. Pa. L. Rev. 360 (1981); V. Goldberg, An Economic Analysis of the Lost–Volume Retail Seller, 57 S. Cal. L. Rev. 283 (1984); R. Cooter and M. Eisenberg, Damages for Breach of Contract, 73 Cal. L. Rev. 1434 (1985); White & Summers §§ 7–8 to 7–14 (3d ed. 1988); R. Scott, The Case for Market Damages: Revisiting the Lost Profits Puzzle, 4 U. Chi. L. Rev. 1155 (1990).

Although the 2–708 Comment states that the section is a rewriting of a provision in the Uniform Sales Act, that act had no provision comparable to UCC 2–708(2). The cited section, USA 64, provided generally for recovery of loss resulting in the ordinary course of events from buyer's breach (64(2)) and stated the specific formula of market-based damages in 64(3); it added in 64(4):

> (4) If, while labor or expense of material amount are necessary on the part of the seller to enable him to fulfill his obligations under the contract to sell or the sale, the buyer repudiates the contract or the sale, or notifies the seller to proceed no further therewith, the buyer shall be liable to the seller for no greater damages than the seller would have suffered if he did nothing towards carrying out the contract or the sale after receiving notice of the buyer's repudiation or countermand. The profit the seller would have made if the contract or the sale had been fully performed shall be considered in estimating such damages.

The UCC revised the USA 64(4) allocation of risk if a manufacturing seller elects, upon repudiation, to complete the process. UCC 2–704(2). The manufacturer who exercises reasonable commercial judgment for the purposes of avoiding loss and "effective realization" is protected even if the value added thereby is less than the costs incurred.

Was it accurate to describe UCC 2–708 as a rewriting of USA 64?

(3) Proposed Revised UCC Article 2. The PEB Study Group on UCC Article 2 recommended revision of UCC 2–708(2) to state, explicitly, that a seller may invoke the profit-measure of damages (1) when seller can show "lost volume," i.e., that but for the breach seller would probably have made two sales, or (2) or when a "middleman" seller reasonably stopped performance before the goods were obtained or a manufacturing seller stopped performance before the goods were completed. PEB Article 2 Report 214–216. The Study Group recommended, further, that different measures by used for these two categories: The "due allowance ... due credit ..." clause should apply only to "stopped performance" cases and not to "lost volume" cases, but consideration should be given to economic analyses of declining margins of profit in multiple transactions. Id. 217–218. Do you agree?

The 2001 draft of proposed amendments to Article 2 would make several changes in UCC 2–708(2). The drafters propose deletion of the phrase "due allowance for costs reasonably incurred and due credit for payments or proceeds of resale."[4]

Colonel's Inc. v. Cincinnati Milacron Marketing Co.

United States Court of Appeals, Sixth Circuit, 1998.
149 F.3d 1182.[5]

■ NORRIS, CIRCUIT JUDGE.

This dispute arises out of a transaction involving the sale of equipment between plaintiff The Colonel's Inc., a Michigan corporation, and defendant Cincinnati Milacron Marketing Company, an Ohio corporation. Plaintiff appeals the district court's grant of summary judgment to defendant on both plaintiff's breach of contract claim and defendant's counterclaim. Defendant cross-appeals the district court's damages calculation and its denial of attorney fees, costs, and interest. We affirm.

I.

Plaintiff and defendant entered into a written contract under which plaintiff agreed to purchase two plastic injection molding machines to assist in the production of automobile replacement parts (hereinafter "Machine 1" and "Machine 2"). Machine 1 was a typical plastic injection molding machine, but Machine 2 was uniquely configured. To be usable where it would be placed in plaintiff's plant, the operator's controls were located opposite and ten feet higher than where defendant usually placed them. Machine 2 was the only machine defendant ever manufactured with this configuration. Both machines were designed to have 140.2 inches of "daylight," the opening necessary to allow molds to be inserted and finished parts removed. Plaintiff contracted to purchase each machine for $1,290,871. Delivery of Machine 1 was scheduled for December 1993, and Machine 2 was to be delivered the following February. Plaintiff made an advance payment on each machine.

---

4. Proposed Revised 2–708(b).

5. This opinion was not recommended for full-text publication. Sixth Circuit Rule 24 limits citation to specific situations. See Rule 24 before citing in a proceeding in a court in the Sixth Circuit. If cited, a copy must be served on other parties and the court. This notice is to be prominently displayed if this decision is reproduced.

After receiving shipment of Machine 1, plaintiff discovered that because 140.2 inches of daylight was not available when the machine's ejector box was in place, the machine would not open far enough to accommodate fabrication of the company's largest automobile parts. Accordingly, it rejected Machine 1 and refused to accept Machine 2, claiming that the machines did not conform to the specifications outlined in the sales agreement, and refused to pay the balance due for the two machines. Plaintiff then sued defendant in Michigan state court, seeking two machines that conformed with their specifications. Defendant removed the case to federal court based upon diversity of citizenship.

Defendant notified its sales personnel that it had a configured injection molding machine and to offer Machine 2 to their customers. Because the machine was uniquely designed for plaintiff, it was difficult to market. After efforts to resell Machine 2 failed, defendant filed a counterclaim for the contract price. The parties settled their dispute over Machine 1. Defendant ultimately rebuilt Machine 2 for an existing customer, selling it for more than plaintiff's contract price.

Defendant moved for summary judgment on plaintiff's complaint for specific performance, arguing that the parol evidence rule barred any extrinsic evidence that the two machines did not conform to the parties' agreement. The district court agreed and dismissed plaintiff's claims. Defendant then sought summary judgment on its counterclaim, arguing that the earlier summary judgment removed any defense plaintiff could raise regarding its right to reject the machines. The district court once again granted summary judgment in favor of defendant. The district court then concluded that because defendant had resold Machine 2 for more than it had bargained for with plaintiff, even after allowing for the additional costs of reconfiguration, it was owed no damages. The court later awarded defendant pre-judgment interest and denied attorney fees.

Leaving no stone unturned, the parties appeal each adverse ruling by the district court.

II.

The first two issues on appeal concern the summary judgments dismissing plaintiff's breach of contract claim and finding plaintiff liable on defendant's counterclaim for breach of contract. We review the district court's grant of summary judgment de novo. . . . We will affirm the district court if the evidence, viewed in the light most favorable to the non-moving party, shows that no dispute of material fact exists and that the moving party is entitled to judgment as a matter of law. . . . We review the district court's interpretation of Ohio law de novo. . . .

Plaintiff's breach of contract claim rests upon its contention that the agreement entered into by the parties includes ambiguous language. Plaintiff asserts that it relied upon one of defendant's publications which, in mentioning maximum daylight of 140.2 inches, is unclear as to whether that clearance exists only when the ejector box is not used. In view of that ambiguity, plaintiff argues, the court should have looked to parol evidence, including statements allegedly made by defendant's sales representative, to determine the specifications called for by the parties' agreement. Plaintiff then argues that a reasonable person could conclude that, in light of comments made by defendant's sales representative, the machines were to have 140.2 inches of daylight when the ejector box was in place.

Under Ohio law, when a court determines whether a contract is ambiguous, it is to consider the whole instrument and give the words in the contract their natural and ordinary meaning. ... A contract is ambiguous only if its terms are susceptible to more than one meaning so that reasonable persons may fairly and honestly differ in their construction of the terms. ... A contract is not ambiguous merely because the parties disagree over its meaning. ... While parol evidence may be used to clarify an ambiguous contract, a party cannot use parol evidence to create an ambiguity or to show that an obligation is other than that expressed in the written instrument. ...

The sales agreement provided that defendant would provide two injection molding machines as described in the customer order and the proposal to purchase the machines. The proposal included specifications that point out that the maximum daylight available with an ejector box installed would be 111.6 inches, 140.2 inches with the ejector box left out. Plaintiff's controller, who signed the sales contract, acknowledged that he read all of the pertinent documents and that they were in accordance with what plaintiff intended to order. Because the agreement is clear on its face, parol evidence cannot be used to read into the contract something which it does not say.

Further, parol evidence cannot be used to modify or contradict the unambiguous terms of a written contract purporting to incorporate the whole agreement between the parties. ... The contract between plaintiff and defendant contained an integration clause, which is a strong indication that the parties intended for the agreement to be complete and final. ... Under these circumstances, we conclude that the contract was complete and unambiguous and that, under the terms of the contract, the machines were delivered in an acceptable configuration.

Because plaintiff's only evidence in opposition to defendant's counterclaim consists of the parol evidence underlying its breach of contract claim, we also affirm the district court's summary judgment on the counterclaim.

* * *

IV.

We next consider defendant's claim that the district court erred in refusing to award damages pursuant to U.C.C. § 2–708(2), the lost volume seller provision. Defendant claims on appeal that § 2–709, the provision the district court relied upon in calculating damages, does not provide an adequate measure of damages when the seller is a lost volume seller, and that, thus, the district court erred.

Article 2 contains four provisions that concern the recovery of a seller's general damages (as opposed to its incidental or consequential damages): § 2–706 (contract price less resale price); § 2–708(1) (contract price less market price); § 2–708(2) (profit); and § 2–709 (price). Section 2–709 allows the seller to recover the price of the goods if the goods have been identified to the contract and after reasonable efforts fail to result in a sale of the goods at a reasonable price. Further, § 2–709(3) provides that the seller can pursue a remedy under § 2–708 only if he is not entitled to bring an action for the price under § 2–709.

In its counterclaim, defendant sought the full price of Machine 2. Several weeks later, after settling several other claims with plaintiff, defendant still maintained that it was suing for payment in full and that its counterclaim was an "action for the price." Subsequently, defendant identified Machine 2 to the Davidson Textron contract, and partially disassembled and reconfigured the machine. Nevertheless, defendant did not attempt to amend or supplement its pleadings. It was not until almost a year later, when filing its proposed joint pretrial order, that defendant announced its intention to seek damages pursuant to § 2–708.

Defendant originally sought the full price of Machine 2 pursuant to § 2–709, and never attempted to introduce its "lost volume seller" theory until over a year after discovery had begun. Under these circumstances, we are unable to say that the district court erred in concluding that defendant was bound by its election to pursue remedies under § 2–709.

* * *

VI.

For the reasons outlined above, the orders of the district court are affirmed.

INTERNATIONAL SALES LAW

Sellers' remedies under CISG when buyers' wrongfully declare contracts avoided or, without making a declaration, refuse to accept and pay for the goods, are similar to sellers' remedies under the UCC. For convenience, we will use the term, wrongful avoidance, to refer to situations in which buyers declared contracts avoided without justification as well as situations in which buyer received goods but refused to accept and pay for them. The structure of the remedies provisions of the Convention is quite different from the structure of the remedies provisions in the UCC. Two fundamental differences should be noted. First, the CISG combines buyers' and sellers' damages remedies in the same articles. Second, many of CISG's remedies articles apply only to contracts that have been avoided.

CISG 61(1) summarizes the remedies of a seller if the buyer "fails to perform any of his obligations under the contract or this Convention." As already discussed in Section 1, one of the remedies, in CISG 62, allows an aggrieved seller to recover the contract price. This CISG remedy is not conditioned in the way that the UCC limits price actions under domestic

United States law. In circumstances of wrongful avoidance by buyers that have not paid the price, it is reasonable to expect that counsel for sellers will seek a remedy under CISG 62. This is particularly likely if the goods have been shipped to the buyer and are in the buyer's possession or control at the time of the purported avoidance.

If sellers have possession or control of the goods and elect not to seek the price, their basic damages remedies, listed in CISG 61(1)(b), are provided in CISG 74 to 77. These formulae in these four articles apply to buyers' and sellers' damages, but our concern here is for the application of these articles to sellers' claims. The most basic provisions are CISG 74 and CISG 77. Both apply to all situations of breach. The former states a general formula for measurement of damages; the latter states the principle of mitigation of damages. Under CISG 74, an aggrieved seller is entitled to "a sum equal to the loss, including loss of profit, suffered . . . as a consequence of the breach." Professor Honnold referred to this standard as "brief but powerful."[5] Under CISG 77, an aggrieved seller "must take such measures as are reasonable in the circumstances to mitigate the loss, including loss of profit, resulting from the breach."

The basic damages provision of CISG 74 is complemented by two other damages provisions, CISG 75 and CISG 76, that apply only if an aggrieved seller has avoided the contract.[6] CISG 75 allows an aggrieved seller that has resold the goods to recover "the difference between the contract price and the price in the substitute transaction." CISG 76(1), which applies if a seller has not made a resale under CISG 75, allows an aggrieved seller to recover "the difference between the price fixed by the contract and the current price at the time of avoidance." "Current price" is defined in CISG 76(2) to mean, primarily, the prevailing price at the place where delivery of the goods should have been made. Both CISG 75 and CISG 76 allow sellers to recover further damages under CISG 74. These CISG remedies resemble the resale remedy under UCC 2–706 and the market-damages remedy under UCC 2–708(1), but careful reading of the CISG and UCC provisions reveals important differences. UCC 2–706 has significant conditions on a seller's right to fix damages by resale that are not contained in CISG 75. UCC 2–708(1) measures market damages at the time and place of tender, while CISG 76 uses the time of avoidance and the place of delivery. UCC 2–708(1).

The mitigation principle in CISG 77 applies to sellers claims of damages under CISG 74, CISG 75, and CISG 76. Application of the mitigation

---

5. Honnold, International Sales § 403.

6. An aggrieved seller is not allowed to claim damages under CISG 75 or CISG 76 unless the seller has declared the contract avoided. A seller has he right to avoid a contract, under CISG 64(1)(a), if the buyer's failure to perform its obligations amounts to a fundamental breach of the contract. A buyers' wrongful avoidance is likely to be suffi-

ciently serious as to constitute a fundamental breach. But avoidance is not automatic. Under CISG 26, avoidance does not occur unless the aggrieved party declares the contract avoided and gives a required notice. Sellers aggrieved by buyers' wrongful avoidance are likely to meet the procedural requirements of CISG 26 only in conjunction with arbitration or litigation proceedings.

requirement to aggrieved sellers in possession or control of goods means that sellers must make reasonable efforts to redispose of the goods and credit the net proceeds to reduce the loss. That result is explicit in the damages measure of CISG 75 and implicit in the credit for current price in CISG 76(1). Mitigation by resale can be applied without difficulty to the general "loss suffered" standard of CISG 74.

What, then, is the CISG remedy for a lost-volume seller of the kind that is allowed to recover under UCC 2–708(2)? CISG 74 refers to loss of profit, but that phrase, drafted to cover sellers' and buyers' damages, has its most obvious application to buyers' consequential damages. Moreover, CISG 77 requires mitigation of any loss, including loss of profit. There is no general mitigation requirement in the UCC. UCC 2–708(2) damages are not consistent with a strong general mitigation principle. However, Professor Honnold has taken the view that lost-volume sellers may have a remedy under the CISG that is comparable to the profit recovery allowed by UCC 2–708(2).[7]

SECTION 3.   PERFORMANCE UNDER LETTERS OF CREDIT

Performance issues in letter of credit transactions arise on each of the three independent contracts that form the triad of all payment letter of credit transactions: the bank-beneficiary contract embodied in the letter of credit, the customer-bank contract that causes a bank to agree to issue a letter of credit, and the sales contract in which the buyer agrees to make payment by letter of credit. If more than one bank is involved in performance of a letter of credit transaction, issues arise in the relationship between the issuing bank and a confirming bank, or between the issuing bank and an advising bank.

DOMESTIC UNITED STATES LAW

Hanil Bank v. Pt. Bank Negara Indonesia (Persero)

United States District Court, Southern District of New York, 2000.
2000 WL 254007.

■ JOHN F. KEENAN, UNITED STATES DISTRICT JUDGE:

Before the Court are cross-motions for summary judgment, pursuant to Fed. R. Civ. P. 56. For the reasons discussed below, the Court grants Defendant's motion for summary judgment and denies Plaintiff's motion for summary judgment.

The Parties

Plaintiff Hanil Bank ("Hanil") was, at all times relevant to this action, a banking corporation organized under the laws of the Republic of Korea, with an agency in New York, New York.

---

7. See Honnold, International Sales § 415.

Defendant PT. Bank Negara Indonesia (Pesero) ("BNI") is a banking corporation organized under the laws of Indonesia, with an agency located in New York, New York.

Background

On July 27, 1995, PT. Kodeco Electronics Indonesia ("Kodeco") applied to BNI to issue a letter of credit (the "L/C") for the benefit of "Sung Jun Electronics Co., Ltd." ("Sung Jun"). On July 28, 1995, BNI issued the L/C ... in the amount of $170,955.00 but misspelled the name of the beneficiary as "Sung Jin Electronics Co. Ltd." The beneficiary did not request amendment of the L/C to change the name of the beneficiary. On August 2, 1995 Sung Jun negotiated the L/C to Hanil. Hanil purchased the L/C and the documents submitted by Sung Jun thereunder from Sung Jun for $157,493.00, the face amount of the draft, less Hanil's commission. On August 2, 1995, Hanil submitted the documents, a draft, a commercial invoice, bill of lading, insurance policy, a packing list, and a fax advice, to BNI for payment. On August 16, 1995, BNI rejected the documents tendered by Hanil and refused to pay under the L/C. BNI alleges that it compared the documents with the L/C and identified four discrepancies, and based upon those discrepancies, refused the documents and demand for payment. The alleged discrepancies are as follows:

1.   The Name of the Beneficiary: The L/C identifies the beneficiary as Sung Jin Electronics Co. Ltd. instead of Sung Jun Electronics Co. Ltd.

2.   The Packing List: BNI claims that the packing list did not show the contents of each carton as required by the L/C.

3.   "Export Quality": BNI claims that the packing list also fails to specify that the goods were of "export quality."

4.   The Bill of Lading: BNI claims that Hanil supplied a "Freight Bill of Lading" instead of the required "Ocean Bill of Lading."

BNI alleges that before it issued its notice of refusal on August 16, 1995, it contacted Kodeco to ask whether it would accept the discrepancies and approve the requested payment, but Kodeco declined to do so. BNI further alleges that it continued to ask Kodeco to waive the discrepancies after August 16, but that Kodeco continued to refuse to waive the discrepancies. BNI then returned the entire original package of documents back to Hanil on September 4, 1995.

Hanil contends that BNI decided to reject the documents presented by Hanil after consulting with, and on the instructions of, Kodeco. In support of this contention, Hanil points to a letter from BNI to Hanil, dated October 4, 1995, which stated that "we are acting at the request and on the instruction of the applicant, i.e., PT. Kodeco Electronics Indonesia. We will, anyhow make a final attempt to have the applicant reconsider their determination and to accept the discrepancies and give as the approval [sic] for payment of the documents." BNI denies the contention that it acted on the instructions of Kodeco when BNI refused to pay because of the alleged discrepancies.

Plaintiff brought suit in New York State court on April 19, 1996, asserting claims for breach of contract, breach of the Uniform Customs and Practice for Documentary Credits (1993 Revision) International Chamber of Commerce Publication No. 500 (the "UCP"), unjust enrichment, and breach of an implied covenant of good faith and fair dealing, and seeking $157,493 in damages, plus interest. Defendant then removed the case to this Court. Both parties now move for summary judgment.

Discussion

* * *

Letters of Credit and the UCP

The principles of letter of credit law are embodied in the Uniform Customs and Practice for Documentary Credits (1993 Revision) International Chamber of Commerce Publication No. 500 (the "UCP"). The UCP is a compilation of internationally accepted commercial practices. ... Although it is not law, the UCP commonly governs letters of credit by virtue of its incorporation into most letters of credit. See id. In this case, the L/C provides that it is governed by the UCP and both parties agree that the provisions of the UCP govern the L/C in this case. The New York Uniform Commercial Code (the "U.C.C.") provides that if a letter of credit is subject in whole or part to the UCP, as in this case, the U.C.C. does not apply. See N.Y. U.C.C. § 5–102(4).

Typically, in a letter-of-credit transaction, the letter of credit substitutes the credit of the opening bank for that of the account party. International letters of credit permit quick and easy financing of international transactions by reducing the risks of non-payment. ...

A fundamental tenet of letter of credit law is that the obligation of the issuing bank to honor a draft on a credit is independent of the performance of the underlying contract. ... See Marino Indus. v. Chase Manhattan Bank, N.A., 686 F.2d 112, 115 (2d Cir.1982); E & H Partners, 39 F. Supp. 2d at 280. "The duty of the issuing bank to pay upon the submission of documents which appear on their face to conform to the terms and conditions of the letter of credit is absolute, absent proof of intentional fraud...." E & H Partners, 39 F. Supp. 2d [275,] at 280 [S.D.N.Y 1998], (citing Beyene v. Irving Trust Co., 762 F.2d 4, 6 (2d Cir.1985)). Because the credit engagement is concerned only with documents, "the essential requirements of a letter of credit must be strictly complied with by the party entitled to draw against the letter of credit, which means that the papers, documents and shipping description must be as stated in the letter." Marino Indus., 686 F.2d at 114 ... Even under the strict compliance rule, however, "some variations ... might be so insignificant as not to relieve the issuing or confirming bank of its obligation to pay," for example, if there were a case where "the name intended is unmistakably clear despite what is obviously a typographical error, as might be the case if, for example, 'Smith' were misspelled 'Smithh.'" Beyene, 762 F.2d at 6. The Court will now consider the alleged discrepancies in this case.

The Name of the Beneficiary

As set out above, the name of the beneficiary in this case was Sung Jun. Kodeco's application to BNI for the issuance of the L/C requested that the L/C be issued to Sung Jun. BNI, however, issued the L/C identifying the beneficiary as Sung Jin. BNI argues that under Beyene v. Irving Trust Co., 762 F.2d 4 (2d Cir.1985) and Mutual Export Corp. v. Westpac Banking Corp., 983 F.2d 420 (2d Cir.1993) this discrepancy was a proper basis to reject the letter of credit presentation. Hanil argues, however, that the strict compliance rule does not permit an issuing bank to dishonor a letter of credit based on a discrepancy such as the misspelling in this case which could not have misled or prejudiced the issuing bank. For the reasons discussed below, the Court agrees with BNI.

In *Beyene*, Plaintiffs brought suit seeking damages for the alleged wrongful refusal of the defendant trust company, Irving Trust Co. ("Irving"), to honor a letter of credit. The district court granted Irving's motion for summary judgment because the bill of lading presented to Irving misspelled the name of the person to whom notice was to be given of the arrival of the goods, listing the name of the party as Mohammed Soran instead of Mohammed Sofan. As a result, the district court found that the bill of lading failed to comply with the terms of the letter of credit and that Irving was under no obligation to honor the letter of credit. The Second Circuit agreed, finding that "the misspelling in the bill of lading of Sofan's name as 'Soran' was a material discrepancy that entitled Irving to refuse to honor the letter of credit" and stating that "this is not a case where the name intended is unmistakably clear despite what is obviously a typographical error, as might be the case if, for example, 'Smith' were misspelled 'Smithh.'" 762 F.2d at 6. The Second Circuit also noted that it was not claimed that in the Middle East, where the letter of credit was issued, that "Soran" would be obviously recognized as a misspelling of the surname "Sofan." The Court finds the misspelling in the present case to be similar to the misspelling in *Beyene* and notes that Hanil likewise does not claim that Sung "Jin" would be obviously recognized as a misspelling of Sun "Jun."

Plaintiff argues that *Beyene* is distinguishable from the present case because in *Beyene* the beneficiary made the error, while in the present case, the issuing bank made the error. However, the Second Circuit has made it clear that under letter of credit law, "the beneficiary must inspect the letter of credit and is responsible for any negligent failure to discover that the credit does not achieve the desired commercial ends." Mutual Export, 983 F.2d at 423. Thus, in *Mutual Export*, even though the issuing bank had issued a letter of credit with an incorrect termination date, the Second Circuit reversed the district court's finding that the letter of credit should be reformed to reflect the appropriate date, and held that the beneficiary was responsible for failure to discover the error. The *Mutual Export* court explained that this rule is important because

the beneficiary is in the best position to determine whether a letter of credit meets the needs of the underlying commercial transaction and to request any necessary changes. . . . "it more efficient to require the beneficiary to conduct that review of the credit before the fact of performance than after it, and the beneficiary that performs without seeing or examining the credit should bear the costs."

See id. (citation omitted).

Pursuant to *Beyene* and *Mutual Export*, this Court concludes that BNI properly rejected payment on the ground that the documents improperly identified the beneficiary of the letter of credit. Although Hanil contends that BNI should have known that the intended beneficiary was Sung Jun, not Sung Jin, based on the application letter in BNI's own file, the Second Circuit has stated that in considering whether to pay, "the bank looks solely at the letter and the documentation the beneficiary presents to determine whether the documentation meets the requirements in the letter." See Marino Indus., 686 F.2d at 115; see also UCP 500 Art. 13(a) (stating that compliance is to be determined from the face of the documents stipulated in the letter of credit).

Although Plaintiff argues that Bank of Montreal v. Federal Nat'l Bank & Trust Co., 622 F. Supp. 6 (W.D.Okla.1984), allowed recovery when the error was greater than the misspelling of a single letter, in *Bank of Montreal*, the letter of credit contained two, internally inconsistent, statements of the name of one of the entities whose indebtedness was secured. The letter of credit referred to "Blow Out Products, Ltd." in its first paragraph and to "Blow Out Prevention, Ltd." in its second paragraph. Based on this inconsistency on the face of the letter of credit itself, the court found that the letter of credit was ambiguous and resolved the ambiguity against the issuer. There is no internal inconsistency or ambiguity in the L/C at issue in the present case, however.

Having found that BNI properly refused payment based on the improper identification of the beneficiary of the L/C, the Court need not address the three remaining alleged discrepancies.

Finally, as to Hanil's argument that BNI dishonored the L/C at the instruction of Kodeco and thereby violated its duty of good faith and fair dealing, the Court again disagrees. As noted above, the issuing bank's obligation under the letter of credit is independent of the underlying commercial transaction. Thus, BNI had an obligation to independently review Hanil's submissions to determine if there were any discrepancies. However, under the UCP, BNI is permitted to approach the payor of the letter of credit, in this case Kodeco, for a waiver of any discrepancies with or without the beneficiary's approval. See UCP, Art. 14(c); E & H Partners, 39 F. Supp. 2d at 284; see also Alaska Textile [Co., Inc. v. Chase Manhattan Bank, N.A., 982 F.2d 813,] at 824 (2d Cir.1992) (noting that allowing the issuer to seek waiver from the payor is efficient because the account party typically waives the discrepancies and authorizes payment). In this case there is no evidence that BNI communicated with Kodeco other than to ask whether Kodeco would accept the discrepancies and approve the requested payment. As a result, the Court finds that Hanil has not set forth facts showing there is a genuine issue as to whether BNI breached its duty of good faith and fair dealing by dishonoring the L/C. Summary judgment for BNI is therefore appropriate.

Conclusion

For the reasons discussed above, the Court grants BNI's motion for summary judgment and denies Hanil's motion for summary judgment. . . .

NOTES

(1) Choice of Forum; Choice of Law. The bank that issued the letter of credit was an Indonesian bank, acting on the application of an Indonesian company, which had bought goods from the beneficiary. The beneficiary was apparently a Korean firm, which had sold goods to the Indonesian buyer. What might explain the plaintiff's choice to sue in a federal district court in the United States? The federal district court proceeded on the premise that the law governing this letter of credit was New York law. What might explain the court's assumption that New York law governed?[1]

(2) The New York Version of UCC Article 5. New York adopted the former UCC Article 5 with a non-uniform exception providing that Article 5, in its entirety, did not apply to letters of credit that incorporated the ICC Uniform Customs and Practices for Documentary Credits (UCP). The letter of credit in this case incorporated the UCP and, therefore, the court held that the case was not within the New York version of Article 5. The governing law was therefore the common law of New York.

(3) UCP 500. The court noted that the letter of credit was subject to UCP 500, but did not quote or cite any UCP provision in its analysis of the sufficiency of the documents submitted to the issuing bank. UCP 13(a) provides:

> Banks must examine all documents stipulated in the Credit with reasonable care, to ascertain whether or not they appear, on their face, to be in compliance with the terms and conditions of the Credit. Compliance of the stipulated documents on their face with the terms and conditions of the Credit, shall be determined by international standard banking practice as reflected in these Articles.

The issuing bank communicated with the applicant before refusing to honor the draft presented to it. UCP 14(c), cited by the court, allows issuing banks to do this. It provides:

---

1. Former UCC Article 5 did not contain a provision on choice of law. UCC 1–105(1), the Code's general choice of law provision, allowed parties to a Code transaction to choose the law of a state, such as New York, if the transaction bears a reasonable relation to that state. Current Article 5 has a quite different choice of law provision, UCC 5–116. Parties to a letter of credit transaction are permitted to choose the law of any jurisdiction, whether or not that jurisdiction has any relation to the transaction. Absent agreement, however, UCC 5–116(b) provides that the liability of an issuing bank is governed by the law of the jurisdiction in which the bank is located. The subsection adds that a bank is located at the address indicated in the letter of credit.

If the Issuing Bank determines that the documents appear on their face not to be in compliance with the terms and conditions of the Credit, it may in its sole judgment approach the Applicant for a waiver of the discrepancy(ies). This does not, however, extend the period mentioned in sub-Article 13(b).

Sub–Article 13(b) provides:

The Issuing Bank ... shall ... have a reasonable time, not to exceed seven banking days following the date of receipt of the documents, to examine the documents and determine whether to take up or refuse the documents and to inform the party from which it received the documents accordingly.

Why was UCP 14(c) drafted to allow issuing banks to decide whether to approach applicants when with respect to non-conforming documents? Do banks have an interest in the performance or failure of the transactions underlying letters of credit? Would applicants prefer that issuing banks approach them in these circumstances?

In *Hanil Bank* the issuer approached the applicant, Kodecko, and Kodecko refused to waive the nonconformities. What might explain Kodecko's decision? Is it likely that the Kodecko would have acted on the basis of the misspelled name alone? From Kodecko's perspective, how serious were the various nonconformities?

(4) Transfer of the Letter of Credit. The plaintiff in *Hanil Bank* was not the beneficiary of the letter of credit. The opinion noted that the letter of credit, together with the supporting documents, was sold to Hanil Bank, which paid the face amount of the draft less the bank's commission. Beneficiaries of letters of credit commonly use intermediary banks to present requests for payment to issuing banks. In this case, the beneficiary not only used an intermediary bank, but the bank also discounted the draft and made payment to the beneficiary before presentment to the issuing bank. Hanil Bank's right to payment of the letter of credit by the issuing bank was no stronger than the beneficiary's right to payment.

(5) Aftermath of Dishonor. Upon dishonor by BNI, Hanil Bank elected to sue BNI on the ground that BNI's dishonor was wrongful and the court ultimately held for BNI. What alternatives actions were available to Hanil Bank? What might have led Hanil Bank to sue BNI rather than proceed against Sung Jun?

After an issuing bank rightfully dishonors a draft drawn on a letter of credit, what happens to the bill of lading and the other documents presented to the issuer? The payment term of the underlying sales contract has not been performed. What are the respective rights and obligations of the seller and buyer under that contract?

Upon an issuing bank's dishonor of a draft, what is the effect on the applicant's duty to reimburse the issuing bank?

Petra Int'l Banking Corp. v. First Amer. Bank of Va.

United States District Court, Eastern District of Virginia. 1991.
758 F.Supp. 1120.

■ ELLIS, DISTRICT JUDGE.

This dispute grows out of the use of two documentary letters of credit to finance the purchase of T-shirts by a Virginia corporation from the manufacturer in Amman, Jordan. In essence, following the delivery of poor quality T-shirts, the purchaser refused to pay the issuing bank and the issuing bank then refused to pay the confirming bank, which had honored drafts drawn under the letters of credit. The purchaser and the issuing bank rely on their receipt of technically nonconforming documents under the letters as grounds for nonpayment. The purchaser and the manufacturer settled their dispute over the poor quality T-shirts, but the remaining parties were not able to resolve their differences. Thus, here the confirming bank seeks recovery against the issuing bank and the purchaser for payments it made under the letters of credit, and the issuing bank seeks recovery against the purchaser for any sums it must pay to the confirming bank.

Before the Court are cross-motions for summary judgment. The motions raise, inter alia, the seldom litigated issue of what remedy an account customer has when an issuing bank inadvertently accepts nonconforming documents under a letter of credit. All material facts are undisputed. These facts, the terms of the letters of credit, other relevant contractual agreements, and existing law require that defendant First American Bank, the issuer of the letters, reimburse the confirming bank for payments made under the letters, and that First American Bank's account customer, the purchaser of the T-shirts, reimburse First American. Both First American and the purchaser, by failing to object to documentary inconsistencies in timely fashion, have waived their right to do so. All other issues raised in this case with the exception of costs and attorney's fees are also disposed of on summary judgment.

Facts

In 1987 Dameron International, Inc., a Virginia corporation ("Dameron"), purchased T-shirts from National Marketing–Export Co. ("National Marketing") of Amman, Jordan. To facilitate the transaction, Dameron sought issuance of two letters of credit by First American Bank of Virginia ("First American"). To this end, Dameron executed two documents, each entitled Application and Agreement for International Commercial Letter of Credit ("the Agreements"), and signed two commercial notes, each in the amount of $135,000.00, to secure the letters of credit. Richard Pitts, the president of Dameron, and his wife, son, and daughter-in-law, executed continuing guaranties to further secure any debts of Dameron owed to First American. First American issued its Irrevocable Letters of Credit Nos. 1–629 and 1–630 ("the Letters"), each for $135,000, on December 17, 1987. The Letters stated that they were issued "in favor of National Marketing–Export Co.," of Amman, Jordan and "for the account of Dameron Intl.,

Inc." of McLean, Virginia. The Letters authorized drafts to be drawn on First American within thirty days of submission to First American of specific, listed documents. At the request of National Marketing and National's bank in Jordan, Petra Bank, the Letters were amended on December 22, 1987, to provide that drafts under the Letters could be drawn directly on Petra International Banking Corporation of Washington, D.C. ("PIBC"), Petra's American affiliate. In the vernacular of letters of credit transactions, PIBC became a "confirming bank," First American an "issuing bank," Dameron the "account customer," and National Marketing the "beneficiary" of the Letters.

When initially issued, the Letters required that an "inspection certificate from [an] independent inspector certifying number and quality of pieces per sample" of the T-shirts be among the documents presented for payment. This provision subsequently was amended to require both a certificate from a specific independent inspection company and a "statement by the beneficiary," National Marketing, attesting to the quality of the T-shirts.

Dameron received several T-shirt shipments from National Marketing in 1988. Several corresponding payments were made under the Letters by PIBC to National Marketing. In late September 1988, another shipment was begun and National Marketing made a demand for payment under the Letters. This demand was relayed from Petra Bank in Amman to PIBC as two documentary time drafts drawn against the Letters in the aggregate amount of $95,904. PIBC sent a telex to First American on October 7, 1988, noting certain discrepancies between the documents submitted and those required by the Letters, including the fact that the certificate from the independent inspection company was missing. First American forwarded PIBC's telex to Dameron, which waived the discrepancies listed by PIBC on condition that the drafts were drawn 150 days from the date of the bill of lading, i.e., from the date of shipment. First American sent a telex message to PIBC on October 19, 1988, stating "ACCOUNT PARTY HAS WAIVED ALL DISCREPANCIES PROVIDED DRAFTS ARE DRAWN AT 150 DAYS BILL OF LADING." First American sent a second telex message on October 24, 1988, stating in relevant part: "DISCREPANCIES HAVE BEEN WAIVED BY A/P [i.e., Dameron]. PLEASE ACCEPT DRAFT AND FORWARD DOCS TO US." Between receipt of the first and second telexes, on October 21, 1988, PIBC discounted and accepted the documentary time drafts. On October 25, 1988, PIBC sent a telex to First American that confirmed receipt of First American's telex of October 24th, informed First American that the drafts had been accepted with the proviso that they be drawn 150 days from the date of the bill of lading, i.e., on February 21, 1989, and transmitted the documents to First American. First American forwarded the documents to Dameron shortly after receiving them. Dameron kept the documents and took possession of the T-shirts. On November 16, 1988, First American sent an acknowledgment letter to PIBC stating that the documentary drafts for $95,904 were "accepted and, at maturity, we will remit proceeds according to your cover letter."

Dameron was dissatisfied with the quality of the T-shirts received from National Marketing. It undertook negotiations with National concerning the $95,904 payment. As the February 21, 1989 deadline for drawing on the time drafts approached, Dameron requested that First American obtain an extension of payment. First American then sent a telex to PIBC requesting an extension to May 21, 1989. The telex stated that National Marketing had agreed to this delay in receiving payment. PIBC informed First American that it would delay and refinance the payment provided that First American pay interest during the delay at the prime rate plus two percent. Dameron and First American agreed. As the new May 21, 1989 deadline drew near, Dameron requested that First American seek an additional extension of thirty days. First American requested the extension, explaining that "SPECIAL ARRANGEMENTS REGARDING THESE PAYMENTS WERE MADE BY BUYERS AND SELLERS ALLOWING THE 30 DAY EXTENSION." PIBC agreed to this second extension on the condition that it continue to receive interest at prime plus two percent, and First American and Dameron accepted this requirement.

In June or July, 1989, Richard Pitts informed First American that Dameron did not want to pay National Marketing because of the poor quality of the T-shirts. William von Berg of First American informed Pitts that First American would be obligated to pay under the Letters unless the bank were sued by Dameron and enjoined from doing so. While the parties are uncertain as to when this conversation occurred, it is clear that in late June, when Dameron requested a third extension, Dameron and National Marketing continued to be hopeful that they would settle their differences concerning the $95,904. Dameron planned to obtain additional T-shirts of suitable quality from National at a reduced price, and it so informed First American. On June 20, 1989, Richard Pitts requested that First American seek a third extension. On the same day, Bassem Farouki, the principal of National Marketing, informed PIBC that Dameron would be requesting an additional thirty-day extension. Although PIBC initially took the position that First American should finance Dameron, it eventually agreed to an extension to July 21, 1989, under the same interest payment conditions as were attached to the previous two extensions.

Dameron's negotiations with National Marketing did not bear fruit. On July 20, 1989, Dameron obtained an Order of Attachment from the Fairfax County Circuit Court, directing First American not to pay PIBC under the Letters. First American claims that it did not immediately learn of the existence of the writ. Nevertheless, First American did not pay PIBC on July 21, 1989. Rather, on that day, at Dameron's request, First American requested an extension of payment to the following week. PIBC responded by demanding payment. Payment was not made. Instead, on July 28th, First American informed PIBC that it had been enjoined by the Fairfax County Circuit Court from making payments under the Letters until further notice.

From July 20, 1989 until April 13, 1990, Dameron pursued a law suit against National Marketing in the Fairfax County Circuit Court. In the course of this litigation, and more than one year after its receipt of the documents, Dameron noticed and then informed First American that the "Statement of the Beneficiary" was not among the documents that First American forwarded pertaining to the $95,904 shipment. First American informed Dameron that it had forwarded all documents it had received. The absence of the Statement of the Beneficiary from the documents was not noted as a discrepancy by PIBC or First American when each had examined the documents. Both Dameron and First American agree that the Statement of the Beneficiary was never among the documents presented by National Marketing to PIBC, and that PIBC, First American, and Dameron each inadvertently failed to notice the missing Statement of the Beneficiary when each received the documents.

Dameron and National Marketing eventually settled their suit. Dameron kept the T-shirts, but received an undisclosed amount of cash from National Marketing related, it appears, to the shipment here at issue and to other shipments and disputes between the parties. The precise terms of the settlement remain confidential and have not been disclosed to the Court. On April 13, 1990, the Fairfax County Circuit Court vacated the Order of Attachment. On the same day, PIBC requested payment from First American of $95,904 of principal and $14,079.24 of interest. First American has refused to make the payment, relying primarily on PIBC's alleged failure to note the missing Statement of the Beneficiary. Dameron, in turn, has refused to reimburse First American if payment is made under the Letters, despite having signed the Agreements and commercial notes, kept the documents accompanying the relevant drafts, taken possession of the T-shirts, and recovered settlement compensation from National Marketing. The Pitts, in turn, have refused First American's demands for reimbursement under the Continuing Guarantees.

* * *

I. First American's Obligation to Pay PIBC

PIBC requests summary judgment on Count I of its Complaint, which alleges that First American wrongfully refused to honor the Letters and pay the $95,904 plus interest to PIBC. First American contends that PIBC's failure to note the missing Statement of the Beneficiary relieves it of any obligation to honor the drafts drawn under the Letters. The threshold issue is the choice of governing law. The Letters state on their face that they are to be governed by the Uniform Customs and Practices for Documentary Credits (1983 Revision), International Chamber of Commerce Publication No. 400 ("the UCP"). Given this, the Court finds that the UCP should be applied in this case. Neither PIBC nor First American objects to application of the UCP, though they differ in interpreting its provisions.

The pertinent UCP provision is Article 16, which states that if an issuing bank desires to "refuse documents," it must do so "without delay" by stating the discrepancies it has found and "holding the documents at the disposal of, or ... returning them to, the presentor (remitting bank or the beneficiary, as the case may be)." If the issuing bank fails to perform these requirements, it "shall be precluded from claiming that the documents are not in accordance with the terms and conditions of the credit."[26] Numerous courts have held that Article 16 and its predecessor, Article 8 of the 1974 UCP, preclude an issuing bank from asserting the noncompliance of documents presented by a beneficiary where the bank delays in raising this claim. Bank of Cochin v. Manufacturers Hanover Trust Co., 808 F.2d 209 (2d Cir.1986), a case precisely on point, presents a striking example of this principle in operation between an issuing and a confirming bank. There, the issuing bank, on the very day of its receipt of a documentary draft from the confirming bank, telexed its intention to dishonor the draft. But the issuing bank did not supply the confirming bank with a reason for the dishonor until twelve-to-thirteen-days later. This delay, the Court found, violated Article 8(d)'s command that an issuing bank intending to dishonor a documentary draft "notify [the confirming bank] 'expeditiously' and 'without delay' of specific defects and of the disposition of the documents, and ... precluded [the issuing bank] from asserting noncompliance...." Id. at 213. The same result should obtain here because the issuing bank's notice was delayed even longer than in Bank of Cochin. In the instant case, First American received the documents on or about October 25, 1988. Not only did it fail to note any discrepancies or to hold the documents at PIBC's disposal, it transferred the documents to its account customer and formally notified PIBC on November 16, 1988 that "the transaction was accepted

---

26. The full text of Article 16 of the UCP is as follows:

(a) If a bank so authorized effects payment, or *incurs a deferred payment undertaking*, or accepts or negotiates *against documents which appear on their face to be in accordance with the terms and conditions of a credit*, the party giving such authority *shall be bound* to reimburse the bank which has effected payment, or incurred a deferred payment undertaking, or has accepted or negotiated, and *to take up the documents*.

(b) If, upon receipt of the documents, the issuing bank considers that they appear on their face not to be in accordance with the terms and conditions of the credit, *it must determine, on the basis of the documents alone, whether to take up such documents, or to refuse them* and claim that they appear on their face not to be in accordance with the terms and conditions of the credit.

(c) The issuing bank shall have *a reasonable time* in which to examine the documents and to determine as above whether to take up the documents or to refuse the documents.

(d) *If the issuing bank decides to refuse the documents. it must give notice*

to that effect *without delay* by telecommunication or, if that is not possible, by other expeditious means, to the bank from which it received the documents (the remitting bank), or to the beneficiary, if it received the documents directly from him. *Such notice must state the discrepancies* in respect of which the issuing bank refuses the documents *and must also state whether it is holding the documents at the disposal of, or is returning them to, the presentor* (remitting bank or the beneficiary, as the case may be). The issuing bank shall then be entitled to claim from the remitting bank any refund of any reimbursement which may have been made to that bank.

(e) *If the issuing bank fails* to act in accordance with the provisions of paragraphs (c) and (d) of this article and/or fails *to hold the documents at the disposal of*, or to return them to, *the presentor, the issuing bank shall be precluded from claiming that the documents are not in accordance with the terms and conditions of the credit.*

(Emphasis added.)

and, at maturity, we will remit proceeds...." First American did not mention any discrepancies to PIBC until more than one year after receipt of the documents. In the interim, it made several promises to pay in exchange for extensions of time. First American is therefore precluded by Article 16 from asserting noncompliance.

First American seeks to avoid application of Article 16 by arguing that Article 16 applies to drafts passing from beneficiaries or advising banks to issuing banks, but not to drafts passing from confirming banks to issuing banks. In support, First American points to Virginia Code § 8.5–107(2), which states that a confirming bank "becomes directly obligated on the credit to the extent of its confirmation, *as though it were its issuer* and acquires the rights of an issuer." (Emphasis added.) From this, First American argues that it should be viewed as PIBC's account customer in the transaction at issue, while PIBC should be deemed to be the issuing bank subject to Article 16. It is true that PIBC, upon becoming a confirming bank, has the rights and duties of an issuing bank and is therefore subject to Article 16. It is also true that First American may be viewed as PIBC's customer. Even so, neither of these points changes First American's status as an issuing bank nor relieves it from its Article 16 duties. In short, as one or more confirming banks are inserted in the chain between the original issuing bank and the beneficiary, each bank, including the original issuer, is an issuing bank subject to Article 16. This conclusion finds support in the language of Article 16 and makes good commercial sense. On its face, Article 16 uses broad language, the plain meaning of which covers documentary draft transfers between confirming and issuing banks. Sensible policy considerations support this construction. To hold otherwise and accept First American's reading of Article 16 would render the UCP devoid of standards governing transactions between confirming and issuing banks. This would make no business sense. For similar reasons, the Court rejects First American's odd claim that PIBC's acceptance of the documentary drafts before First American had received and reviewed the documents should absolve First American of its obligation to honor the draft.[32] Finally, even if the Court were to find that First American should be treated as a "customer" of PIBC, First American would still be liable for the reasons given below in Part III for holding Dameron liable to reimburse First American.

* * *

32. Under the scheme of Article 16, it appears that a confirming bank becomes obligated to pay a documentary credit when it transfers documents on to the issuing bank. The confirming bank may, if it finds discrepancies, dishonor a documentary draft and return the documents to the beneficiary or to a prior confirming or advising bank in the chain of transfer. The confirming bank, like the issuing bank, appears to be required to accept or reject the documents "on the basis of the documents alone." Article 16(b). It is not permitted to pass them on perfunctorily to the issuing bank to obtain that bank's opinion on the documents' compliance with the letter of credit. If it could so operate, it would be no more than an advising bank. Furthermore, First American can claim no harm from PIBC's acceptance of the draft before First American received the documents. Under Article 16, First American was still entitled to review the documents upon receipt and to reject and return them as nonconforming to PIBC. . . .

III.   Dameron's Obligation to Reimburse First American

Having found that PIBC has a legal right to payment from First American, ... the Court turns next to First American's claim that Dameron must reimburse it for any amount it must pay PIBC under the Letters. First American relies on the Agreements executed by Dameron to obtain the Letters. In the Agreements, Dameron pledged to indemnify First American for the latter's acts with respect to the Letters as long as such acts were taken in good faith. And, First American correctly notes that Dameron has not shown any bad faith on the part of First American with respect to accepting the documents. Dameron argues, however, that the good faith standard in the Agreements violates Virginia law and hence is void. Therefore, Dameron continues, First American's failure to note the missing Statement of the Beneficiary, though not a breach of good faith, nevertheless relieves Dameron of any obligation to reimburse First American.

It is not necessary to reach the unsettled, thorny question whether the Agreements, which appear to be standard form contracts employed by First American, violate Virginia law. Even assuming first that the Agreements run afoul of Virginia law, next that First American is obligated, as Dameron contends, by Virginia Code § 8.5–109(2) to "examine documents with care so as to ascertain that on their face they appear to comply with the terms" of the Letters, and finally that First American breached this duty by failing to note the absence of the Statement of the Beneficiary, the Virginia UCC and the common law of letters of credit still bar Dameron's claim because Dameron accepted the documents and used them to gain control of the T-shirts. Under these circumstances, Dameron cannot rely on documentary discrepancies to avoid honoring its Agreements with First American.

The Agreements between First American and Dameron state that they shall be governed by Virginia law. Title 8.5 of Virginia's UCC, which pertains to Letters of Credit, contains no provision governing an account customer's remedies for wrongful honor by an issuing bank. Section 8.5–102(3), however, frankly admits that Title 8.5 "deals with some but not all of the rules and concepts of letters of credit...." The section invites the application of "rules or concepts ... developed prior to this act or ... hereafter" to "a situation not provided for ... by this title." Id. ... Thus, in ascertaining Dameron's remedies as an account customer for First American's wrongful honor, this Court is directed by Virginia law to apply the "fundamental theory" of letters of credit and the "canon of liberal interpretation" in Virginia Code § 8.1–102. ...

A review of the few existing, apposite cases indicates that under the common law of letters of credit an account customer, by accepting documents from the issuing bank and subsequently "surrendering the documents [to shippers or customs officials] and accepting a substantial portion of the goods ... waives its right to seek strict enforcement of the letter of credit." Dorf Overseas Inc. v. Chemical Bank, 91 A.D.2d 895, 457 N.Y.S.2d 513, 514 (N.Y.App.Div.1983). This result "is the only one consistent with principle and common sense." H. Harfield, Bank Credits and Acceptances 107 (5th ed. 1974). Fundamental to letter of credit transactions is the principle that both the letter of credit and also the separate agreement between account customer and issuing bank are transactions in documents entirely independent from the underlying sale of goods. . . . An account customer, if it desires to claim discrepancies, has a duty to return documents to the issuing bank rather than use them to obtain control over the goods. The documents provide some compensation to a bank which has inadvertently honored nonconforming documents. "The bank's loss will be the amount of the payment which it has made under the credit less any amount which it may realize from disposition of the documents which it has purchased." Id. at 105. The result is equitable. The beneficiary/seller is paid by the bank for the goods; the bank owns the documents and title to the goods; and the account customer has avoided paying for goods that, because of discrepancies in the documents, it feared accepting. This rule also avoids the inequitable result of a windfall for the account customer in the form of obtaining goods never paid for. While some commentators have favored less stringent rules with respect to an account customer's acceptance of documents,[42] the rule just stated has gained the widest acceptance

---

42. Harfield, quoted in the text, presents the most in-depth analysis found of an account customer's remedies for an issuing bank's inadvertent acceptance of nonconforming documents. Harfield's conclusion, discussed supra, is that an account party must reject and return nonconforming documents within a reasonable period or be deemed to have waived its right to object to documentary inconsistencies. . . . Some commentators have favored other rules.

In an early treatise, Finkelstein contended that an account customer should be able to accept nonconforming documents, reimburse the issuing bank, but deduct any direct or consequential damages flowing from the bank's acceptance of nonconforming documents. Finkelstein likened this to a buyer's ability to keep nonconforming goods, retain its right of action against the seller for breach of contract, and recover consequential damages. Finkelstein, Legal Aspects of Commercial Letters of Credit 195–97 (1930). . . .

More recently, Kozolchyk took a middle ground between Finkelstein and Harfield. Kozolchyk, Commercial Letters of Credit in the Americas 322–26 (1966). Kozolchyk . . . believed . . . that an account customer might be permitted to receive "direct and foreseeable" damages, and urged American courts to adopt the practice found in some other countries of permitting an account customer to accept documents while expressly reserving a

right of action against the bank for document inconsistencies. Id. at 316, 324. See also J. White and R. Summers, Handbook of the Law Under the Uniform Commercial Code § 19–8 at 864–65 (3d ed. 1988) (suggesting that an account customer might recover damages pertaining to defective goods from an issuing bank that wrongfully honors a draft, but providing no case law or reasons for this conclusion and observing that "because customers are so infrequently successful in suing issuing banks for wrongful honor, the law here is quite undeveloped"); Dolan, The Law of Letters of Credit para. 9.03 at 9–35, 9–36 (1984) (observing merely that disputes between issuing banks and account parties should be governed by "contract remedy rules" unless such rules are inadequate). . . .

[E]ven if the Court were to accept the notion that an account customer should be able to accept documents and goods and then sue for direct damages resulting from a bank's acceptance of nonconforming documents, it would not permit Dameron to reduce the payment owed to First American by any damages stemming from National Marketing's delivery of faulty goods. Such damages stem from the seller's breach, not First American's. Moreover, even if the court were to hold that an account customer could receive damages from the issuing bank stemming from the receipt of faulty goods, Dameron has already been compensated for such

in American case law and best reflects the fundamental theory underlying letters of credit.

The undisputed facts of this case are that shortly after October 25, 1988, First American transferred the documents at issue to Dameron. Dameron did not note any discrepancies; rather, it used the documents to take possession of the T-shirts. Until July 1989, when it brought suit against National Marketing, Dameron attempted to sell the T-shirts, apparently with disappointing results, and to work out a deal with National to compensate Dameron for the nonconforming goods. On three occasions during this period, Dameron pledged to reimburse First American for honoring the drafts related to the T-shirts in exchange for extensions of time for payment. Furthermore, Dameron obtained a court order attaching payment of the drafts, which order was not lifted until Dameron had settled its law suit with National Marketing. The terms of this settlement have been kept confidential by Dameron, although it stated that it received some monetary compensation under the settlement. It is reasonable to assume that a portion of the settlement was intended to compensate Dameron for the substandard quality of the T-shirts. Not until approximately a year or more after receipt of the documents and goods, did Dameron raise the issue of the missing Statement of the Beneficiary. The undisputed facts therefore show that Dameron delayed informing First American of any discrepancies for more than a reasonable period of time. It failed to return the documents to First American and instead took control of the goods. By these acts, Dameron waived its right to reject nonconforming documents and bound itself to reimburse First American for the amount of the drafts. ... First American's cross-claim against Dameron should be granted, and Dameron will be ordered to reimburse First American for the amount of the drafts plus interest.

* * *

NOTES

(1) UCP 400 and 500. UCP 500, the current version, was promulgated in 1993. The UCP in effect at the time of the transaction in *Petra* was the earlier version, UCP 400. We will refer to both versions of the UCP in these Notes.

(2) Issuing and Confirming Banks. This case illustrates the role of confirming banks in letter of credit transactions. As originally structured, letters of credit were issued by First American Bank of Virginia (First American) in favor of National Marketing Export Co. of Amman, Jordan. The seller's bank in Jordan, Petra Bank, was not a party to the letter of credit, but seller probably anticipated that Petra Bank would transmit documents, through banking channels, to First American. The letter of

receipt through its settlement with National Marketing. There is no reason in this case for Dameron not to reimburse First American for the full amount First American paid for the goods.

credit arrangement was altered to add a confirming bank, Petra International Banking Corp. (PIBC), an American affiliate of Petra Bank. With the addition of a confirming bank, that bank became the entity to which seller would submit the documents required under the letter of credit. Undoubtedly, Petra Bank in Jordan determined that it would be more efficient to have the seller's documents submitted to its American affiliate. The typical reason for introducing a confirming bank into a transaction is to facilitate the beneficiary's access to the banks.

Article 9 of UCP 500 addresses the liability of issuing and confirming banks. Article 9(b) provides:

> A confirmation of an irrevocable Credit by another bank (the "Confirming Bank") upon the authorization and request of the Issuing Bank, constitutes a definite undertaking of the Confirming Bank, in addition to that of the Issuing Bank, provided that the stipulated documents are presented to the Confirming Bank ... and that the terms and conditions of the Credit are complied with.

A similar provision appeared in Article 10(b) of UCP 400. The UCP provisions are mirrored by provisions in UCC Article 5. Former UCC 5–107(2) declared: "A confirming bank by confirming a credit becomes directly obligated on the credit to the extent of its confirmation as though it were its issuer and acquires the rights of an issuer." Current UCC 5–107(a) is similar.

Both the issuing bank and the confirming bank were involved in handling the presentment of seller's drafts and supporting documents in *Petra*. The confirming bank, PIBC, noted discrepancies in the documents and telexed the issuing bank, First American, which in turn telexed the applicant, Dameron. Dameron's waiver, conditioned on change in the time of payment, was communicated to First American, which informed PIBC. Based on this message, PIBC accepted seller's drafts. PIBC then forwarded the supporting documents to First American, which turned them over to Dameron. Among the documents was the bill of lading that Dameron surrendered to the carrier in exchange for the goods.

Neither the UCP nor the UCC deals with the right or the duty of confirming banks to seek guidance from issuing banks when non-conforming documents are presented to the confirming banks. UCP 500 14(c), which we considered in *Hanil Bank*, refers only to issuing banks approaching applicants. What might explain PIBC's decision to telex First American to seek guidance on whether to accept the non-conforming documents?

(3) Time and Sight Drafts; Accepted Drafts. The letters of credit first issued in this case did not call for immediate payment by the issuing bank, but rather for payment within 30 days of submission of specified documents. Subsequently, at the request of the applicant, the letters of credit were modified to require payment 150 days after the date of the bill of lading. As provided in the letters of credit, the beneficiary presented time drafts, negotiable instruments that called for the bank's future payment. On presentment of the time drafts, after the exchange of telex messages, the confirming bank "accepted" them. Acceptances of time drafts, defined in UCC 3–409, creates an obligation to pay the amount of the drafts under UCC 3–413(a). The liability of a bank that has accepted a time draft is independent of the bank's obligation under a letter of credit. If the letter of credit requires a bank to accept a time draft, the bank's obligation under the letter of credit is discharged by rightful acceptance of a draft. UCC 3–310(c).

Letter of credit transactions that permit the use of time drafts delay payment for the periods of time stated in the drafts. Why would sellers, having contracted for buyers' payment by letter of credit, be willing to allow use of time drafts rather than sight drafts? Without any transfer of funds, buyers obtain the documents of title that give them control or possession of the goods. As this case indicates, time drafts can be dishonored when presented for payment. What explains sellers' willingness to hand over goods to buyers while this risk exists? Note that the obligation to pay an accepted time draft is the unconditional obligation of the bank, not of the buyer, and the bank's obligation is not contingent on buyer's willingness or ability to reimburse the bank. Banks are not prone to dishonor their legal obligations.

PIBC did not dishonor the accepted time drafts in *Petra* when the drafts were presented for payment. The court stated, somewhat inaccurately, that PIBC made payments under its letter of credit. The payments were made pursuant to the independent obligation of the accepted time drafts.

(4) Bank-to-Bank Relationships. The principal claim in the case is by PIBC against First American. The precise nature of the claim is somewhat unclear.

The *Petra* court relied on Article 16 of UCP 400, which it set forth in full in a footnote with much emphasis of certain words and phrases. Article 16 dealt generally with the obligation of issuing banks when presented with documents by remitting banks or by beneficiaries directly, particularly the obligations to give notice of discrepancies without delay and the consequence of failure to act. Nothing in that Article refers explicitly to the relationship between a confirming bank and an issuing bank. Counsel for First American argued, therefore, that Article 16 did not authorize a claim by a confirming bank. The court rejected the argument: "To ... accept First American's reading of Article 16 would render the UCP devoid of standards governing transactions between confirming banks and issuing banks. This would make no business sense." Was the court's analysis sound? Was it First America's reading of Article 16 or the language of the Article itself that rendered UCP 400 devoid of standards governing transactions between confirming banks and issuing banks?

The void in UCP 400 has not been filled in UCP 500. Article 14 of UCP 500, the analog of Article 16 of UCP 400, does not refer to claims by confirming banks against issuing banks.

If the UCP is silent on the rights of issuing and confirming banks *inter sese*, the issue becomes one for the law underlying the transaction. If domestic United States law applies, the legal rule may be found in UCC Article 5. The *Petra* court referred to Former UCC 5–107(2), but that section provides only for the duties of confirming banks. It is as silent as the UCP on the rights of confirming banks.

Current Article 5 adds a new provision, in UCC 5–107(a):

> The confirmer also has rights against and obligations to the issuer as if the issuer were the applicant and the confirmer had issued the letter of credit at the request and for the account of the issuer.

If this provision had been in effect in *Petra*, would it have been a basis for PIBC's claim against First American? First American's letters of credit called for presentment of time drafts. Did PIBC present time drafts to First American? As noted, PIBC ultimately paid against its accepted time drafts. Those payments were not documentary conditions in First American's letter of credit.

(5) Nature of Terms Conditioning Banks' Obligations. In theory, the parties to letter of credit transactions could make any fact or event the condition that unlocks a bank's duty to pay or accept a demand for payment. Banking practice, however, has strongly favored limiting the fact or event to the presentation of described documents. Article 4 of UCP 500, identical to UCP 400, declares: "In credit operations all parties deal in documents, and not in goods, services and/or other performances to which the documents may relate."

The parties in *Petra* established a documentary requirement that seller provide a statement from a specified independent inspection company certifying the number and quality of the goods per sample and the seller's own statement that the goods shipped were of the quality of the samples on which buyer had relied.

The statement of the independent inspection company was a document of potentially great importance to the buyer, since the letters of credit would be honored before the buyer had any opportunity to inspect the goods shipped. The statement was not presented. When informed of this by the issuing bank, the buyer waived the discrepancy. What might explain the buyer's decision to waive this requirement?

The second statement, which the court refers to as the Statement of the Beneficiary, was also not presented to PIBC. This, too, was waived by the buyer. Of what value to buyer would such a documented statement be?

(6) Bills of Lading: "Clean" and "Foul." Bills of lading are obviously important to buyers concerned that payments may be made for goods not shipped. Letters of credit usually call for "clean" bills of lading; in any event, such a requirement may be implied. British Imex Industries Limited v. Midland Bank Limited, [1958] 1 Q.B. 542. If a carrier receives a shipment in torn or leaky cartons, it will note that fact on the bill of lading to protect itself from the claim that it damaged the goods. A bill of lading with such a notation is not "clean," and a bank need not pay under a letter of credit when such bills of lading are tendered.

Article 32 of UCP 500 deals with this question as follows:

a. A clean transport document is one which bears no clause or notation which expressly declares a defective condition of the goods and/or the packaging.

b. Banks will refuse transport documents bearing such clauses or notations unless the credit expressly states the clauses or notations which may be accepted.

Suppose that a bill of lading covering a shipment of oil well casing and tubing is tendered under a letter of credit. In the bill of lading the phrase "in apparent good order and condition" has been deleted and the following inserted: "Ship not responsible for kind and condition of merchandise." The bill also bears the stamped notation, "Ship not responsible for rust." If UCP 500 is applicable, may the bank decline to pay under the letter of credit?[2]

Problem 5.3.1. Seller, in London, agreed to sell "Coromandel groundnuts" to a Danish buyer. Pursuant to the contract Bank opened a letter of credit in Seller's favor. Seller tendered documents to Bank which included a commercial invoice that described the goods as "Coromandel groundnuts" in the manner called for in the letter of credit. The bill of lading tendered to Bank described the goods as "machine shelled groundnut kernels." Bank refused to honor Seller's draft because of the discrepancy between the bill of lading and the letter of credit. In action by Seller against the Bank, Seller proved that, in the London produce market, the two terms referred interchangeably to the same commodity.[3]

What result under the UCP? UCP 500 Article 37(c) provides:

The description of the goods in the commercial invoice must correspond with the description in the Credit. In all other documents the goods may be described in general terms not inconsistent with the description of the goods in the Credit.

Were the goods described in "general terms" in the bill of lading?

Will the distinction drawn by UCP 37(c) be recognized under the UCC? See Former UCC 5–109; current UCC 5–108(a).

(7) Bills in a Set. A practice of carriers' issuing bills of lading in a set of parts grew up in overseas transportation in an era when the transmission of any document across the ocean was more hazardous than it is today.[4] To cope with the risk of non-arrival of the documents, each part of the set could be sent separately. If only one part arrived, the carrier would

---

2. See Liberty National Bank & Trust Co. v. Bank of America National Trust & Savings Ass'n, 218 F.2d 831 (10th Cir.1955), affirming 116 F.Supp. 233 (W.D.Okl.1953).

3. See Rayner & Co. v. Hambros Bank, [1942] 2 All E.R. 694 (C.A.).

4. Bills of lading, if governed by UCC 7–304, may be issued in sets only for overseas transportation.

honor it. Once bills of lading are issued in more than one copy, the separate parts can be negotiated to different persons.[5] When sellers and buyers have agreed to payment by letter of credit, the question arises of the banks' treatment of bills in a set when only one part of the set is presented for payment. Commercial banking practice developed whereby issuing or confirming banks would pay against presentation of part of the set, even though the letter of credit presentation of the "full set," provided the presenting bank agreed to indemnify the paying banks against loss.[6]

Article 23(a)(iv) of UCP500 provides that banks will accept a transport document which "consists of a sole original bill of lading or, if issued in more than one original, the full set as so issued." The ICC group of experts, responding to an inquiry about how to determine the number of parts to a set, replied that the number of originals must be ascertainable from each copy of the bill of lading itself. ICC Case Studies on Documentary Credits 82 (J. Dekker 1989).

The UCC took account of bills in a set only in Article 2. Tender rules, as between seller and buyer, are set forth in UCC 2–323(2). The UCC takes no position as to whether banks are subject to a similar rule under letters of credit.

(8) Bank–Customer Relationships. The second part of *Petra* was the claim of the issuing bank against the applicant. The court noted that this was primarily a matter of the agreement between the bank and the applicant when the latter sought to obtain the letters of credit. The UCP is silent on bank-customer relationships. So, too, was former UCC Article 5. The court was persuaded to follow the general principles of interpretation in UCC 1–102.

Current UCC 5–108(i) adds a subsection on the rights of issuers that have rightfully honored a presentation. Such an issuer "(1) is entitled to be reimbursed by the applicant in immediately available funds not later than the date of its payment of funds." If this provision had been in effect in *Petra*, would it have been a basis for First American's claim against Dameron?

---

5. Some of the problems associated with this possibility are addressed in UCC 7–304(3) and (5).

6. In a World War II era case, an issuing bank in New York refused to pay against part of the set. The Court of Appeals held that the bank's refusal was wrongful:

It is absolutely essential to the expeditious doing of business in overseas transactions in these days when one part of the bill of lading goes by air and another by water. Unless an indemnity can be substituted for the delayed part, not only does quick clearance of such transactions become impossible but also the universal practice of issuing bills of lading in sets loses much of its purpose.

Dixon, Irmaos & Cia v. Chase Nat. Bank, 144 F.2d 759, 762, cert. denied, 324 U.S. 850, 65 S.Ct. 687, 89 L.Ed. 1410 (1945). The *Dixon* case was sharply criticized and defended. Backus & Harfield, Custom and Letters of Credit: The Dixon, Irmaos Case, 52 Colum. L. Rev. 589 (1952); J. Honnold, Letters of Credit, Custom, Missing Documents and the Dixon Case: A Reply to Backus and Harfield, 53 Colum. L. Rev. 504 (1953).

Andina Coffee, Inc. v. National Westminster Bank, USA

Supreme Court of New York, Appellate Division, First Department, 1990.
160 A.D.2d 104, 560 N.Y.S.2d 1.

■ Milonas, J.

Plaintiff Andina Coffee, Inc., a New York corporation, was engaged in the importation of coffee from defendant Gonchecol, Ltda., at one time a major Columbian exporter of coffee. To pay for its purchases, Andina delivered to Gonchecol letters of credit which it obtained from a number of commercial banks in New York, including defendants National Westminster Bank USA (NatWest) and Cooperatieve Centrale Raiffeisenboerenleenbank B.A. (Rabobank). As the beneficiary of the letters of credit, Gonchecol apparently used all or some of the funds to borrow money from defendant Banco Credito y Commercio de Columbia (BCCC) and other Colombian banks in order to finance its business operations. In June 1986, BCCC advanced $2,100,000 to Gonchecol in exchange for which it was to be reimbursed through a $2,100,000 check drawn on a Panamanian bank. However, Gonchecol's check bounced, and BCCC was left with an unpaid $2,100,000 loan. According to NatWest and Rabobank, this event could only have served to confirm what BCCC had already learned from its own sources; that is, that Gonchecol had already lost millions of dollars and was experiencing severe financial difficulties. As was the situation with most of the moneys made available by BCCC to Gonchecol, the source of repayment would have to be proceeds from the letters of credit provided to Gonchecol from the issuing banks.

Beginning in May of 1986, coffee financed under the various letters of credit, which were to be paid on the presentation of interior truck bills of lading, failed to materialize. Consequently, representatives of the New York banks were dispatched to Colombia in August of 1986 when it was discovered that Gonchecol had caused fraudulent truck bills of lading to be furnished for large quantities of coffee which were, in fact, never shipped, thereby resulting in substantial financial losses to New York banks. The four letters of credit involved here are the last outstanding instruments which were not drawn against prior to the disclosure of the exporter's dishonest practices. In that regard, NatWest and Rabobank had each supplied two of the letters of credit, one for $2,104,000 and the other three in the amount of $1,000,000, pursuant to which they agreed to make payment upon the presentation within a specified period of time of drafts and certain documents, among which were to be the "original railroad and/or truck bill of lading." The bill of lading was supposed to show that the coffee was actually in existence, that it had left the control of the growers and that it was in the hands of the shipper and en route from the interior of Colombia to a seaport.

On July 9, 1986, 15 days after BCCC had already advanced $2,100,000 to Gonchecol against the latter's bad check, it received from NatWest a letter of credit in the amount of $2,104,000. The following day, almost six weeks before the earliest possible date for presentment under that instrument, BCCC accepted from Gonchecol its draft and accompanying documents. These documents included truck bills of lading which were dated August 22, 1986, almost six weeks after the date submitted to BCCC, and purported to show that 8,000 bags of coffee had been delivered to a trucking company for transport to a Colombian port. BCCC sent the draft and documents to NatWest with a cover letter dated July 15, 1986. By telex dated July 22, 1986, NatWest advised BCCC that it would not pay under the letter of credit because of four enumerated discrepancies in the documents, including the fact that the draft and documents were presented prior to the earliest date mentioned in the letter of credit and that the truck bills of lading were postdated.

BCCC thereupon requested that the bills of lading and other documents be returned to it by mail. It then reviewed the documents received under the other three letters of credit and perceived that the bills of lading in those instances were similarly postdated. Consequently, it sent all of the bills of lading back to Gonchecol so that the exporter could revise the dates to comply with the letters of credit. Indeed, some of the changes were made twice in an attempt to bring the documents into conformity with both the form and date mandates of the letters of credit. Thus, it appears that the documents were designed more to effect payment under the letters of credit than to reflect accurately the business transactions that they were intended to evince. In any event, by the time that the documents had been altered and realtered, the full extent of Gonchecol's fraud had been detected, and payment was rejected by NatWest and Rabobank on the ground that, in part, the bills of lading were postdated and fraudulent.

The instant appeal concerns respective motions and cross motions for summary judgment with respect to the letters of credit. The Supreme Court, in granting BCCC's cross motion for summary judgment and denying the motions of NatWest and Rabobank for the same relief, was persuaded that BCCC took the drafts for value, in good faith and without any knowledge of any fraud defenses and was, therefore, a holder in due course entitled to payment under the letters of credit. In the view of the court, there is no evidence to support the assertions by NatWest and Rabobank that BCCC possessed actual knowledge of Gonchecol's fraud and that it did not accept the drafts in good faith. Finally, the court concluded that the "transactions involved in this case must be considered against a background of haphazard permissive and careless negotiations and payment of prior letters of credit by the issuing banks over a year and a half period. First of all, it is not denied that the same discrepancies alleged in the documents submitted by BCCC were the same one [sic] which the banks had accepted for the aforementioned period.... Secondly, it cannot be denied that the letters of credit involved are not based upon underlying arms-length transactions." The court proceeded to criticize the issuing banks for assuming a high risk by merely demanding trucking bills of lading rather than on-board bills of lading, since it "appears that the port forwarder and the trucking company were all part of Gonchecol's enterprises and that the importer, Andina Coffee, Inc., although a separate corporate entity, belonged to the same overall organization as the exporter."

Yet, notwithstanding the questionable nature of the financing arrangement undertaken by NatWest and Rabobank, and, certainly, the record is replete with indications of dubious business judgment by the various issuing banks, the soundness of the lenders' financial practices is not at issue here. What is crucial is whether BCCC accepted drafts drawn upon letters of credit "under circumstances which would make it a holder in due course" (Uniform Commercial Code 5–114[2][a]). . . .

The mere fact that the documents presented in connection with the letters of credit may have been complete forgeries and that no coffee was delivered to the trucker for export is insufficient to avoid payment under the letter of credit. . . . What is critical is whether the bills of lading complied with the requirements of the letters of credit or whether BCCC possessed actual knowledge of the fraud . . . or otherwise acted in bad faith. . . . But when a required document does not conform to the necessary warranties or is forged or fraudulent or there is fraud in the transaction, an issuer acting in good faith may, but is not required to, refuse to honor a draft under a letter of credit when the documents presented appear on their face to comply with the terms of the letter of credit. Further than that, a customer may also enjoin an issuer from honoring such a draft if the issuer fails to do so on its own. . . . Notwithstanding this exception, if the person presenting a draft drawn on a letter of credit is a holder in due course . . . the issuer must pay the draft, whether it has notice of forgery or fraud or not.

It is settled that New York law mandates strict compliance with the terms of a letter of credit. . . . The postdating of bills of lading is not only a departure from the requirements of the letters of credit but also constitutes a form of fraudulent practice. Contrary to the Supreme Court's characterization that the objections to the accompanying documents raised by NatWest and Rabobank were frivolous and highly technical, the discrepancies were, in reality, material. At the very least, they would have had the effect of concealing the actual shipment dates (even assuming that they had represented genuine, and not fictitious, transactions) and, in fact, did not, as required by the letters of credit, "evidence shipment" of the coffee. Further, while there is authority that by its previous acceptance of nonconforming documents, as admittedly occurred herein, the issuing bank does not waive the right to reject future defects . . . and the preclusion rule contained in the UCP (Uniform Customs and Practice for Documentary Credits) is by no means absolute, at most the failure to assert an objection on a previous occasion presents a question of fact as to whether there was a waiver. . . .

Unless the postdating was expressly allowed under the letters of credit, and there is no indication that this is the situation, or the parties' prior course of conduct conclusively demonstrates otherwise, the documents provided under the letters of credit did not comply with the terms thereof, and BCCC may not compel payment. Equally significant is the BCCC's apparently active role in obtaining the revisions of the documents, particularly after it was confirmed with definite proof of Gonchecol's financial instability in the form of a bad check, raises questions of fact as to whether it was acting in good faith and without actual knowledge of the exporter's fraud. The record of the present matter clearly presents sufficient unresolved matters precluding summary judgment as to whether BCCC participated in a scheme whereby the bills of lading were altered simply to render them in conformity with the letters of credit. Once it has been "shown that a defense exists a person claiming the rights of a holder in due course has the burden of establishing that he or some person under whom he claims is in all respects a holder in due course" (Uniform Commercial Code 3–307 [3]). Since NatWest and Rabobank have demonstrated a viable defense with respect to the letters of credit, BCCC must now prove that it is a holder in due course, and, consequently, summary judgment in its favor is not warranted.

NOTES

(1) Injunction Against Payment Under a Letter of Credit. The UCC allows some buyers a small chance to stop payment by an issuing bank. The opportunity is predicated on a showing by buyers that they are the potential victims of fraudulent activities by the sellers. Prospective breach of the underlying sales contracts is not sufficient. The harm must be the result of serious fault.

The *Andina Coffee* case was decided under the former UCC Article 5. UCC 5–114(2)(b) refers to circumstances of "fraud, forgery or other defect not apparent on the face of the documents." The subsection provides that an issuing bank, acting in good faith, may honor a draft or demand for payment despite receipt of notification of these circumstances. The key word here is "may." The implication is that an issuing bank may dishonor, but nothing in the section obligates a bank to do so. If a bank does dishonor a draft or demand for payment, the presenter may sue and compel the bank to defend its action. If a bank informs its customer that it intends to honor the draft or demand, the customer's recourse is to seek a court order enjoining the bank from honoring its obligation. UCC 5–114(2)(b) declared, laconically, that "a court of appropriate jurisdiction may enjoin such honor." The statute did not provide substantive or procedural standards for such suits. The court in *Andina Coffee* accepted plaintiff's argument that the circumstances were sufficient for injunctive relief. The controverted issue was whether the relief was available against the defendant bank, BCCC, which had discounted seller's drafts before presentment to the issuing bank.

UCC 5–114(2)(a) provided that an issuing bank must honor a draft or demand for payment by a person that took the draft or demand under circumstances which would make it a holder in due course under UCC 3–302 and, by implication, a court may not enjoin a bank from its obligation. The crux of the case in *Andina Coffee* is whether BCCC qualified as such a protected person. The trial court found that BCCC was protected but the appellate court reversed. What facts or circumstances were critical to the appellate court's decision?

(2) Current UCC Article 5. The problem presented in *Andina Coffee* is addressed in current UCC 5–109(b). If current Article 5 were the governing law, would the result in the case have been the same?

(3) Other Injunctive Remedies; Attachment of Proceeds of Letters of Credit. Some aggrieved buyers proceed on multiple remedial paths: injunction against the bank to stop payment, injunction against the beneficiary from drawing against a letter of credit, and seizure of the seller's bank accounts, including proceeds of an issuing bank's payment of a letter of credit before transmission of the funds to the seller. See Daye Nonferrouse Metals Co. v. Trafigura Beheer B.V., 1997 WL 375680 (S.D.N.Y.1997), vacated in part, 152 F.3d 917 (2d Cir.1998).

INTERNATIONAL SALES LAW

The ICC Uniform Customs and Practices for Documentary Credits (UCP) are a compilation of international banking practices for letter of credit transactions, but the UCP provisions are not positive law. They apply to letter of credit transactions by agreement of the parties to letters of credit. The Convention on Contracts for International Sale of Goods has no provisions on performance of letter of credit transactions. There is no body of international commercial law comparable to Article 5 of the UCC.

SECTION 4. CASUALTY TO GOODS; RISK OF LOSS

Introduction. Casualty to goods—as by fire, theft, or flood—may occur at any one of several stages in the performance of the sales contract. Goods may be lost or stolen. The casualty or loss may occur while the goods are on the seller's premises, either after the making of a contract for the sale of specific (identified) goods or after the seller has identified goods as those intended for performance of the contract. More frequently, the loss occurs while the goods are in transit or after their arrival but before the buyer takes possession. Problems can arise even after the buyer receives the goods if casualty occurs during a period of testing or inspection, or following the buyer's rejection (or revocation of acceptance) of the goods on the ground that they were not in conformity with the contract.

Dispute between the seller and buyer is often avoided by the availability of insurance coverage, and sometimes by the legal responsibility of the carrier for damage occurring during transit. Even in these situations, problems may arise as to whether the seller or the buyer has the responsibility to take over and salvage damaged goods, press a claim against the insurer or carrier, and bear any loss from inadequacy in insurance coverage or from limitations on the liability of the carrier. The point at which the risk of loss passes is thus of greater practical significance than would be indicated by the volume of litigation.

In addition, rules on risk of loss may determine whether the seller has performed its warranty and other contractual obligations. Suppose, for instance, that a contract calls for No. 1 wheat and that water damage during the rail shipment makes the wheat grade only No. 4; in such a case the rules on risk of loss in transit will determine whether the buyer has a claim against the seller for breach of contract. Anglo–American statutory formulations do not bother to express this obvious relationship between rules on risk and warranty; the Convention on International Sale of Goods is more articulate: "The seller is liable . . . for any lack of conformity which exists at the time when the risk passes to the buyer, even though the lack of conformity becomes apparent only after that time."[1]

Historical Background. English law, at an early stage, seemed to conclude that risk of loss did not pass to a buyer until the goods were delivered. Such was the view expressed in the thirteenth century by Bracton in De Legibus, " . . . because in truth, he who has not delivered a thing to the purchaser, is still himself the lord of it;" Bracton illustrated the point with the death of an ox and the burning of a house prior to delivery to the buyer.[2]

Long before the first codification of English sales law, a different approach had developed. This change probably was not designed to accelerate the transfer to buyers of risk of loss, but rather to strengthen buyers' remedies against sellers and against third persons who may attempt to take the goods. The difficulty stemmed from the fact that buyers had no common law remedy to take the goods from recalcitrant sellers, or from third persons (such as a seller's creditors), unless buyers could be said to have "property" or "title." A claim for damages against a seller who is plagued by creditors is, of course, of little value; what is needed is a remedy to seize the goods, or a legal claim (e.g., for conversion) against a third person that is not judgment-proof. There is evidence that, to mitigate this deficiency in the common law remedial system, courts at an early date developed the view that when a contract is made for the sale of specific (identified) goods, the buyer thereupon has the "property."[3]

Once it was concluded that a buyer had "property" in the goods, it seemed to follow that it bore the risk if "its" goods were destroyed. A famous 1827 King's Bench decision in Tarling v. Baxter involved the sale of a stack of hay which burned prior to the time for delivery and payment.[4]

---

1. CISG 36(1); see also CISG 36(2), 66.

2. Bracton, De Legibus, Twiss Ed.1878, Ch. XXVII, p. 493. Compare Glanville, Laws and Customs (cir. 1187–89) Book X, Ch. XIV, 216 (Beames ed. 1900). The joint treatment of goods and realty did not survive later developments in the common law, but to some extent has persisted in civil law formulations.

3. Holdsworth, History of English Law 355–56 (3d ed. 1923). Holdsworth suggests that such remedies led to "the doctrine that a contract of sale of specific goods passes the property in the goods." See also: Blackburn, The Contract of Sale 188–189 (1845); 2 Pollock & Maitland, History of English Law 210 (2d ed. 1898); P. Atiyah, The Rise and Fall of Freedom of Contract 103, 106 (1979) (present ownership, with possession postponed, used as tool for effective future planning).

4. 6 B & C 360, 108 Eng.Rep. 484 (K.B. 1827).

The opinion by Bayley, J., opened with the basic premise: "It is quite clear that the loss must fall upon him in whom the property was vested at the time when it was destroyed by fire." All that remained was to find where "the property" was located. The answer was that "the property" vested in the buyer when the contract was made, even though the buyer did not have possession and would not have even the right to possession until he paid (or tendered) the price. The opinion recognized that more was at stake than risk of loss: "*All* the consequences resulting from the vesting, of the property follow, *one* of which is, that if it be destroyed, the loss falls upon the vendee." (Emphasis added.)

"Property" and Risk of Loss in the Sale of Goods Act and the Uniform Sales Act. The use of the "property" concept was brought to the New World as part of the common-law heritage, and dominated the handling of sales problems in both England and the United States long before the onset of codification. Mackensie Chalmers conscientiously transcribed the case-law rules in preparing the (British) Sale of Goods Act (1893). Under Section 20, unless the parties have agreed otherwise, when "the property" in goods "is transferred to the buyer, the goods are at the buyer's risk whether delivery has been made or not." Under Section 17, where there is a contract for the sale of "specific or ascertained" goods, the property is transferred when the parties so intend. Section 18 laid down five rules (when no different intention appears) "for ascertaining the intention of the parties as to the time at which the property in the goods is to pass to the buyer." Rule 1 codified the approach of *Tarling v. Baxter*:

> Where there is an unconditional contract for the sale of specific goods, in a deliverable state, the property in the goods passes to the buyer when the contract is made, and it is immaterial whether the time of payment or the time of delivery, or both, be postponed.

In preparing the Uniform Sales Act, the reporter, Professor Samuel Williston, closely followed the British model. The general rule that risk of loss passes when "the property" is transferred was placed in Section 22; the rules for ascertaining the parties' intent appear in Article 19—with the rule of *Tarling* reproduced as Rule 1.[5] The Uniform Sales Act retained the crucial role of "property" in other settings. For example, under Section 66, where the property has passed, the buyer may "maintain any action allowed by law to the owner of goods of similar kind when wrongfully converted or withheld;" under Section 63(1) the seller may bring an action to recover the price (as contrasted with damages for breach of contract) where "the property has passed to the buyer." Thus, the solution of a variety of sales problems under the Uniform Sales Act was entangled with the question whether "the property" in the goods remained with the seller or whether "it" had passed to the buyer.

---

5. The Uniform Sales Act made a significant (and unfortunate) deviation from the British Act by adding as Rule 5 a provision holding risk in transit on the seller where the contract "requires the seller to deliver the goods to the buyer ... or to pay the freight or cost of transportation to the buyer. ..."

Difficulty with the "Property" Concept. "Property" in goods is, of course, a legal conclusion and can serve as a tool for decision only when it is implemented by rules referring to events, such as the making of a contract, completion of an agreed performance, delivery to a carrier, or receipt by a buyer. The "property" concept was highly malleable, and probably would have served as well as any other label for the development of rules addressed to a single problem such as risk of loss. Difficulty, however, developed because one concept was employed to solve different problems which sometimes called for different solutions. For instance, there was reason to speed the passage of "property" to buyers to provide them with effective remedies against recalcitrant sellers. Very different practical considerations bear on the question as to who should bear casualty loss while the goods are still held by sellers. The use of "property" in sales law thus suffered from a difficulty that has arisen in various parts of the legal structure when a single concept is pressed into service to solve disparate problems.

DOMESTIC UNITED STATES LAW

The most radical departure of the Sales Article of the UCC from the approach of the Uniform Sales Act was the UCC's virtual abandonment of "property" (or "title") as a vehicle for deciding sales controversies. Instead, the UCC provided separate rules to govern risk, replevin rights, recovery of the full price, and other problems which the Uniform Sales Act referred to the "property" concept. The UCC's provisions on risk of loss are found in UCC 2–509 and UCC 2–510.[6]

(A) LOCAL TRANSACTIONS

We begin with losses that occur in the performance stage of local transactions, that is, transactions in which the goods are to be delivered by a seller to a buyer directly without the use of an independent carrier.

Problem 5.4.1. John Smith, a dairy farmer, usually grows a small amount of alfalfa hay to feed to his dairy cows. This summer his alfalfa field did unusually well and he found he had a stack of hay he did not need. On June 1, a neighbor, Brown, came and looked at the stack of hay in Smith's field, and a contract was made for the sale of the stack to Brown for $400; Brown was to pay for the hay and remove it during the first week in July. On June 15, the stack burned.

(a) Smith sues Brown to recover the agreed price of $400. What result? See UCC 2–509; 2–104(1) and the *Martin* case, infra.

---

6. Professor Williston characterized this step as "the most objectionable and irreparable feature" of the Sales Article; even apart from other objections, this was sufficient reason for rejecting Article 2. S. Williston, The Law of Sales in the Proposed Uni- form Commercial Code, 63 Harv.L.Rev. 561, 569–71 (1950). Most commentators came to a different conclusion. E.g., A. Corbin, The Uniform Commercial Code—Sales; Should it be Enacted? 59 Yale L.J. 821, 824–27 (1950).

(b) At the trial, Smith's lawyer calls Smith to the stand and asks questions that would elicit testimony that Brown specifically requested and received assurances that Smith "would hold the hay in the pasture for Brown and would not sell it to anyone else." Brown's lawyer objects to the evidence as irrelevant. Smith's lawyer answered that the evidence was relevant to show that Brown had received the goods under UCC 2–509(3). What ruling? See UCC 2–103(1)(c).

(c) Suppose the fire had occurred on July 10? See UCC 2–503, 2–510.

(d) Assume that the fire (as in (c), above) occurred on July 10, but that the seller is the Smith Alfalfa Company. What result?

Martin v. Melland's Inc.

Supreme Court of North Dakota, 1979.
283 N.W.2d 76.

■ ERICKSTAD, CHIEF JUSTICE.

The narrow issue on this appeal is who should bear the loss of a truck and an attached haystack mover that was destroyed by fire while in the possession of the plaintiff, Israel Martin (Martin), but after certificate of title had been delivered to the defendant, Melland's Inc. (Melland's). The destroyed haymoving unit was to be used as a trade-in for a new haymoving unit that Martin ultimately purchased from Melland's. Martin appeals from a district court judgment dated September 28, 1978, that dismissed his action on the merits after it found that at the time of its destruction Martin was the owner of the unit pursuant to Section 41–02–46(2), N.D.C.C. (Section 2–401 U.C.C.). We hold that Section 41–02–46(2), N.D.C.C., is inapplicable to this case, but we affirm the district court judgment on the grounds that risk of loss had not passed to Melland's pursuant to Section 41–02–57, N.D.C.C. (Section 2–509 U.C.C.).

On June 11, 1974, Martin entered into a written agreement with Melland's, a farm implement dealer, to purchase a truck and attached haystack mover for the total purchase price of $35,389. Martin was given a trade-in allowance of $17,389 on his old unit, leaving a balance owing of $18,000 plus sales tax of $720 or a total balance of $18,720. The agreement provided that Martin "mail or bring title" to the old unit to Melland's "this week." Martin mailed the certificate of title to Melland's pursuant to the agreement, but he was allowed to retain the use and possession of the old unit "until they had the new one ready." The new unit was not expected to be ready for two to three months because it required certain modifications. During this interim period, Melland's performed minor repairs to the trade-in unit on two occasions without charging Martin for the repairs.

Fire destroyed the truck and the haymoving unit in early August, 1974, while Martin was moving hay. The parties did not have any agreement regarding insurance or risk of loss on the unit and Martin's insurance on the trade-in unit had lapsed. Melland's refused Martin's demand for his new unit and Martin brought this suit. The parties subsequently entered into an agreement by which Martin purchased the new unit, but they reserved their rights in any lawsuit arising out of the prior incident.

The district court found "that although the Plaintiff [Martin] executed the title to the . . . [haymoving unit], he did not relinquish possession of the same and therefore the Plaintiff was the owner of said truck at the time the fire occurred pursuant to [UCC 2–401]."

Martin argues that the district court erroneously applied . . . [§ 2–401 U.C.C.], regarding passage of title, to this case and that . . . [§ 2–509 U.C.C.], which deals with risk of loss in the absence of breach, should have been applied instead. Martin argues further that title (apparently pursuant to [UCC 2–401(1)]) and risk of loss passed to Melland's and the property was then merely bailed back to Martin who held it as a bailee. Martin submits that this is supported by the fact that Melland's performed minor repairs on the old unit following the passage of title without charging Martin for the repairs. Melland's responds that [UCC 2–401(2)], governs this case and that the district court's determination of the issue should be affirmed.

One of the hallmarks of the pre-Code law of sales was its emphasis on the concept of title. The location of title was used to determine, among other things, risk of loss, insurable interest, place and time for measuring damages, and the applicable law in an interstate transaction. This single title or "lump" title concept proved unsatisfactory because of the different policy considerations involved in each of the situations that title was made to govern. Furthermore, the concept of single title did not reflect modern commercial practices, i.e. although the single title concept worked well for "cash-on-the-barrelhead sales," the introduction of deferred payments, security agreements, financing from third parties, or delivery by carrier required a fluid concept of title with bits and pieces held by all parties to the transaction.

Thus the concept of title under the U.C.C. is of decreased importance. The official comment to Section 2–101 U.C.C. [§ 41–02–01, N.D.C.C.] provides in part:

> The arrangement of the present Article is in terms of contract for sale and the various steps of its performance. The legal consequences are stated as following directly from the contract and action taken under it without resorting to the idea of when property or title passed or was to pass as being the determining factor. The purpose is to avoid making practical issues between practical men turn upon the location of an intangible something, the passing of which no man can prove by evidence and to substitute for such abstractions proof of words and actions of a tangible character. Uniform Commercial Code (U.L.A.) § 2–101.

Section 41–02–46, N.D.C.C. (§ 2–401 U.C.C.), which the district court applied in this case, provides in relevant part:

> Each provision of this chapter with regard to the rights, obligations and remedies of the seller, the buyer, purchasers or other third

parties applies irrespective of title to the goods except where the provision refers to such title. Insofar as situations are not covered by the other provisions of this chapter and matters concerning title become material the following rules apply . . .

[UCC 2–509] is an "other provision of this chapter" and is applicable to this case without regard to the location of title. Comment one to Section 2–509 U.C.C. provides that "the underlying theory of these sections on risk of loss is the adoption of the contractual approach rather than an arbitrary shifting of the risk with the 'property' in the goods."

* * *

Before addressing the risk of loss question in conjunction with [UCC 2–509], it is necessary to determine the posture of the parties with regard to the trade-in unit, i.e. who is the buyer and the seller and how are the responsibilities allocated. It is clear that a barter or trade-in is considered a sale and is therefore subject to the Uniform Commercial Code. . . . It is also clear that the party who owns the trade-in is considered the seller. [UCC 2–304] provides that the "price can be made payable in money or otherwise. If it is payable in whole or in part in goods each party is a seller of the goods which he is to transfer." . . .

Martin argues that he had already sold the trade-in unit to Melland's and, although he retained possession, he did so in the capacity of a bailee (apparently pursuant to [UCC 2–509(2)]). White and Summers in their hornbook on the Uniform Commercial Code argue that the seller who retains possession should not be considered bailee within Section 2–509:

> The most common circumstance under which subsection (2) will be applied is that in which the goods are in the hands of a professional bailee (for instance, a warehouseman) and the seller passes a negotiable or a non-negotiable document of title covering the goods to the buyer. That case is simple enough. One question remains, however. Can the seller ever be a "bailee" as the word is used in subsection (2)? The facts in a pre-Code case . . . well illustrate the problem. There seller had reached an agreement with buyer for the sale of a colt. The parties had agreed that the seller would hold the colt for the buyer and, depending upon the terms of the payment of the price, would or would not charge him a fee for stabling the colt. The colt was killed without any fault on the part of the seller, and the seller sued the buyer for the purchase price. In such a case the seller could certainly argue that he was a bailee and that risk had passed since he had acknowledged the buyer's "right" to possession of goods under (2)(b). The case would be a particularly appealing one for that argument if the seller were receiving payment from the buyer for the boarding of the horse.

> We believe that such an interpretation of the word bailee should be rejected by the courts, and except in circumstances which we cannot now conceive, a seller should not ever be regarded as a bailee. To allow sellers in possession of goods already sold to argue that they are bailees

and that the risk of loss in such cases is governed by subsection (2) would undermine one of the basic policies of the Code's risk of loss scheme. As we have pointed out, the draftsmen intended to leave the risk on the seller in many circumstances in which the risk would have jumped to the buyer under prior law. The theory was that a seller with possession should have the burden of taking care of the goods and is more likely to insure them against loss.

If we accept such sellers' arguments, that is, that they are bailees under subsection (2) because of their possession of the goods sold or because of a clause in the sale's agreement, we will be back where we started from, for in bailee cases the risk jumps under (2)(b) on his "acknowledgment" of the buyer's right to possession. By hypothesis our seller has acknowledged the buyer's right and is simply holding the goods at buyer's disposal. Thus, to accomplish the draftsmen's purpose and leave risk on the seller in possession, we believe that one should find only non-sellers to be "bailees" as that term is used in 2–509(2). Notwithstanding the fact that a seller retains possession of goods already sold and that he has a term in his sale's contract which characterizes him as a "bailee" we would argue that he is not a bailee for the purposes of subsection (2) of 2–509 and would analyze his situation under subsection (1) or subsection (3) of 2–509.

J. White & R. Summers, Handbook of the Law Under the Uniform Commercial Code, 144–45 (1972) . . .

It is undisputed that the contract did not require or authorize shipment by carrier pursuant to [UCC 2–509(1)]; therefore, the residue section, subsection 3, is applicable:

> In any case not within subsection 1 or 2, the risk of loss passes to the buyer on his receipt of the goods if the seller is a merchant; otherwise the risk passes to the buyer on tender of delivery.

Martin admits that he is not a merchant; therefore, it is necessary to determine if Martin tendered delivery of the trade-in unit to Melland's. Tender is defined in [UCC 2–503(1)]. . . .

It is clear that the trade-in unit was not tendered to Melland's in this case. The parties agreed that Martin would keep the old unit "until they had the new one ready." . . .

We hold that Martin did not tender delivery of the trade-in truck and haystack mover to Melland's pursuant to (§ 2–509 U.C.C.); consequently, Martin must bear the loss.

We affirm the district court judgment.

NOTES

(1) Relevance of Insurance Coverage. Comment 3 to UCC 2–509 declares that the underlying theory of subsection (3) is based on expectations as to casualty insurance coverage on the goods. Merchants, it is said, can be expected to have effective coverage on merchandise in their possession, while buyers cannot be expected to have insurance on property purchased but not yet delivered. This follows from standard fire and casualty insurance policies, sold to business concerns, that provide broad coverage for specified buildings that includes, generally, all contents of those buildings. Policies typically include expressly "property sold but not removed."[7]

Casualty insurance policies rarely cover the full market value of the property insured. One reason is the concern, commonly referred to as moral hazard, that insureds who do not bear some of the risk of loss may not take sufficient care to protect the property and, in extreme circumstances, may cause casualties to occur. Does the text of UCC 2–509(3) or the Comment's theoretical explanation state or imply that merchant-sellers that have insurance should obtain relief for losses from their insurance carriers primarily? Exclusively?

The "seller" of the trade-in haystack mover in *Martin* was not a merchant-seller of the kind envisioned in Comment 3. He was a farmer who, at the time of the contract of sale, had insurance coverage on that equipment. He allowed the insurance to lapse while he continued to use it. Therefore, when the fire occurred, the seller had no insurance. It is reasonable to infer that the dealer also lacked insurance that covered the equipment in the farmer's possession. The dealer's insurance on buildings and contents would not apply to property located elsewhere. The property in this situation was therefore totally uninsured. Should UCC 2–509(3) be adapted to take into account the total lack of insurance and the reasons therefor? The opinion notes that the sales contract lacked any terms on insurance or risk of loss. What commercially reasonable terms might have been added to the contract? Should either the dealer or the farmer be responsible for the omission of such terms?

The property in *Martin* was covered by a "certificate of title." Pursuant to the sales contract, the farmer had delivered the certificate to the dealer before the fire. This fact was mentioned by the court but was not significant to the court's analysis. Why did the contract require surrender of the certificate of title? Should this fact have played a part in allocation of the risk of loss?

The message of *Martin* for lawyers who counsel clients on transactional matters is quite clear. In many circumstances, insurance and risk of loss clauses must be considered as essential terms of sales contracts.

(2) Insurable Interest in the Goods. Counselors should also be aware that persons in the position of the dealer in *Martin* can obtain insurance on goods that they have bought but have not yet received. UCC 2–501(1) declares that a buyer obtains an "insurable interest" in goods when the goods are "identified" to the contract and continues with rules on when identification occurs. For reasons related to concerns of moral haz-

---

7. In recent years, business concerns have had access to even broader insurance coverage through "multiple line" or "package" policies.

ard, only persons with something at stake, i.e., an insurable interest, may obtain casualty insurance on goods. During the performance stage of sales contracts, both sellers and buyers may have an insurable interest in the goods. UCC 2–501(1) specifies when a buyer's insurable interest arises, often a date well before the delivery date under the contract.

(3) Litigation Posture; Price Actions. Risk of loss cases commonly arise when buyers refuse to pay the price of goods destroyed in the performance stage of sales contracts. UCC 2–709(1)(a) provides that a seller has an action for the price of conforming goods lost or damaged after risk of their loss has passed to the buyer.

The litigation posture in *Martin* is complicated by the offsetting contracts for sale of the new equipment and trade-in of the old equipment. The farmer-seller of the old equipment demanded that the dealer-buyer credit the agreed price of the trade-in against the higher price of the new equipment. In trade-in transactions, however, each party is both a seller and buyer of the separate goods involved. See UCC 2–304(1). When the dealer refused to pay for the trade-in, the parties entered into a new contract which allowed the farmer to obtain the new equipment without giving up the right to sue for the price of the trade-in.

(4) Insurance Carrier Subrogation. A seller who suffers loss or casualty to goods on which it has effective insurance coverage is likely to submit a claim under the insurance policy even if the risk of loss has passed to the buyer. If an insurance company pays a claim, may it seek to be subrogated to seller's claim for the price under UCC 2–709(1)? Would seller be entitled to the proceeds of the policy from the insurance company and recovery of the price from the buyer? Should it matter whether the buyer caused the loss or casualty? These interrelated questions have been answered most clearly in the context of real property transactions. In an executory contract, if only the vendor has effective insurance on property that suffers loss or casualty after risk of loss has passed to the vendee, the vendor's insurance should ultimately benefit the vendee. See R. Keeton & A. Widiss, Insurance Law 324 (1988).[8]

(5) Construction of UCC 2–509(3). The *Martin* court held that the governing law was UCC 2–509(3), accepted the contention of the farmer that he was not a merchant, and therefore concluded that risk of loss passed upon tender of delivery of the trade-in equipment. Without analysis, the court declared that it was "clear" that the trade-in unit had not been tendered. Do you agree that this proposition was "clear"? Tender of delivery, under UCC 2–503(1), occurs when a seller puts and holds goods at the buyer's disposition. Did the farmer put and hold the trade-in equipment at the dealer's disposition? What delayed the "let go" of those goods? If a non-merchant seller tenders conforming goods and the buyer does not

---

8. We have seen examples of subrogation of casualty insurance companies to rights under sales contracts in circumstances where insurers have paid buyers for goods and then sought to recover from the sellers on the basis of the buyers' warranty rights. Insurance Co. of North America v. Automatic Sprinkler Corp., Chapter 3, Section 4; Nationwide Insurance Co. v. General Motors Corp., Chapter 3, Section 7.

tender the price, does risk of loss pass to the buyer? Was the dealer's failure to tender the new equipment tantamount to failure to tender the price?

The *Martin* court characterized the farmer's assertion that he was not a merchant as an "admission." Would the farmer's case under UCC 2–509(3) have been stronger or weaker if he were deemed to be a merchant?[9]

(6) Seller in Possession of Goods Sold as Bailee; UCC 2–509(2). The litigation strategy of counsel for the farmer was to escape from UCC 2–509(3) rather than rely on that section. Counsel argued that the case was governed by UCC 2–509(2). The court, after quoting extensively from a treatise, rejected that argument. Should this argument have prevailed?

(7) Effect of Casualty on Sellers' Contract Obligations: UCC 2–613. The UCC does not declare, in UCC 2–509, that sellers are discharged of obligation to deliver because certain goods have been lost or damaged while the risk of loss was on sellers. Under contracts of sale, there are a number of possibilities that bear on the question of discharge. (a) The goods lost or damaged were the only goods that the seller might have tendered properly under the contract. (b) The goods lost or damaged were part of a supply of substitutable goods, any of which the seller might have tendered properly under the contract, but the seller had identified the specific goods lost or damaged as those it planned to deliver. (c) The goods lost or damaged were among a supply of substitutable goods, but the seller had not yet identified any specific goods lost or damaged as those it planned to deliver. Should seller be discharged from its contractual obligation in any or all of these circumstances?

The UCC provides a partial answer in UCC 2–613, which provides that contracts may be totally or partially "avoided" depending upon the degree of the physical loss. When contracts are avoided, according to Comment 1, the parties are relieved from obligation. Section 2–613 fits, to large extent, the first of the three circumstances we hypothesized. Would UCC 2–613 apply on the facts of *Martin*?[10] If so, did the dealer have a claim against the farmer for breach of his promise to deliver the used haystack mover?

What line of reasoning leads to the conclusion that the dealer should be excused from performing its promise to deliver the new haystack mover? If the farmer had not allowed the insurance coverage to lapse and had tendered the insurance proceeds plus $18,720 (the agreed cash balance owed) to the dealer, could the dealer have refused to deliver the new haystack mover without being in breach of contract?

9. The PEB Article 2 Study Group recommended that the UCC be revised to eliminate the distinction between merchant and non-merchant sellers. "We assume that the non-merchant seller in possession will be in a much better position than the buyer to obtain insurance." PEB Article 2 Report 148. That change has been included in drafts of the proposed amendments. Proposed Revised 2–509(c).

10. Query: Could Melland's Inc. argue persuasively that Martin's allowing the insurance coverage to lapse was a "fault" that should deprive him of the protection of 2–613?

What happens to the contract obligations of sellers who bear the risk of loss of goods but whose contracts are not avoided under 2–613? See UCC 2–615.

Problem 5.4.2. S Company made a contract for the sale to B of a specified machine tool which S had been using in its manufacturing operations; prior to this transaction S had never sold a machine tool. The contract permitted B to remove the tool within a month. One week after the contract was made, the tool was destroyed by a fire in S's plant. Both S and B are insured under the standard fire policy. How should the interests of the parties be adjusted?

United Air Lines v. Conductron Corp.

Appellate Court of Illinois, First District, 1979.
69 Ill.App.3d 847, 26 Ill.Dec. 344, 387 N.E.2d 1272.

■ GOLDBERG, PRESIDING JUSTICE:

United Air Lines, Inc. (plaintiff), brought an action for breach of contract against Conductron Corporation, McDonnell Douglas Electronics Company, a subsidiary of McDonnell Douglas Corporation, and McDonnell Douglas Corporation (defendants). . . . The case involves sale by defendants to plaintiff of an aircraft flight simulator. This machine was destroyed by fire while on plaintiff's property. [At the time of the fire, plaintiff had paid $1,043,434.33 as partial payment of the purchase price. Plaintiff sought recovery of its payments, liquidated damages for defendants' breach of contract, and interest.] The trial court entered summary judgment in favor of plaintiff for $1,326,573.20. Defendants appeal.

Defendants contend that the trial court erred in entering summary judgment for plaintiff because the risk of loss of the simulator was upon plaintiff at the time of its destruction. . . .

Plaintiff contends that at the time the simulator was destroyed the risk of loss was upon defendants. In this regard, plaintiff urges that defendants defaulted under the terms of the contract by failing to deliver a conforming aircraft flight simulator; this default was never cured; the simulator was never accepted by plaintiff because of its deficiencies and plaintiff at all times retained the right of rejection. . . .

Many of the facts which appear from the pleadings, interrogatories, depositions, and affidavits are undisputed. The purchase agreement between plaintiff and defendants, some 65 pages in length, was executed on December 30, 1966. The agreement contains 19 articles and was supplemented by a number of change orders. It required defendants to deliver a Boeing 727 digital flight simulator to plaintiff on January 13, 1968. A flight simulator is a highly sophisticated electro-mechanical device operated by computers. It is designed to simulate the experiences of a pilot in the cockpit of a jet airplane during flight. As flight simulators are used for training pilots, they must meet the requirements necessary for approval by the Federal Aviation Administration (FAA). The contract so provided. In addition the contract provided that the simulator would conform to plaintiff's specifications.

The original contract provided for inspection and testing of the simulator by plaintiff at defendants' plant prior to its shipment to plaintiff's Flight Training Center in Denver, Colorado. The defendants agreed to correct any deficiency or discrepancy appearing from such inspection. The agreement further provided that when delivery of the simulator was made title would pass to plaintiff but that such delivery would not constitute acceptance of the simulator by plaintiff. Final acceptance by plaintiff was subject to satisfactory completion and also to certification by the FAA.

Defendants failed to complete fabrication of the simulator by the agreed upon date. This resulted in a request by plaintiff that the simulator be delivered to the plaintiff's training center in Colorado for the testing process which, under the original agreement, could have been completed at defendants' plant. On February 20, 1969, the parties entered into a modification of the contract referred to as Change Order Number 3. This order provided for disassembly of the machine, its delivery to plaintiff by common carrier not later than February 28, 1969, and reassembly by defendants on plaintiff's premises not later than March 15, 1969. From July 1, 1969 to August 1, 1969, the simulator was to be available to plaintiff for demonstration purposes and for correction by defendants of deviations noted by plaintiff in the above mentioned testing. The documents stated that in the event the defendants were unable satisfactorily to correct all deviations prior to November 1, 1969, the plaintiff would have the right to cancel the agreement and receive a refund of all payments made to the defendants as buyer plus liquidated damages. The Change Order also gave plaintiff the right to use the simulator for personnel training purposes.

While the simulator was still in possession of defendants upon their facilities, plaintiff's personnel noted some 647 deficiencies in its operation. These difficulties were recorded and reported to defendants by means of written reports referred to as "squak sheets." The simulator was delivered to plaintiff's facility and was reassembled by defendants on March 14, 1969, in accordance with Change Order Number 3. Since the machine had not received FAA approval, it could not be used as an aircraft flight simulator. It was used for training purposes to acquaint and familiarize pilots with instrument location in the cabin of a Boeing 727 aircraft.

On April 18, 1969, the simulator was tested for 10 hours by two of plaintiff's test pilots. About 10 p.m. a fire was discovered in the machine. The simulator was substantially damaged. The origin of the fire is unknown. After the fire, plaintiff requested that defendants dismantle and ship the simulator back to their plant for repairs at plaintiff's expense. On May 16, 1969, plaintiff notified defendants that they considered there was a breach by defendants of the warranties contained in the purchase agreement. On June 4, 1969, the parties amended the agreement by Change

Order Number 4. This document provided that the plaintiff would receive $60,000 as liquidated damages for the late delivery of the simulator to be deducted from the remaining payments due defendants. Plaintiff commenced this action on May 11, 1973, seeking rescission of the contract and damages. On January 28, 1977, plaintiff filed Count VII as an amendment to the complaint. This amendment alleged that the risk of loss of the simulator was upon defendants at the time it was destroyed.

... Summary judgment in favor of plaintiff was entered by the trial court based on the theory that the simulator had never been accepted by plaintiff and, therefore, the risk of loss remained upon defendants. The order allowed plaintiff $1,043,434.33 as a refund of partial payments made, $60,000 as liquidated damages for delay and prejudgment interest of $223,138.78; a total of $1,326,573.20. No issue is raised on computation of these damages.

* * *

III.

We turn next to the merits of summary judgment in favor of plaintiff based on the theory that defendants should bear the risk of loss for the destruction of the simulator. ...

To evaluate the risk of loss issue, attention must be given to the impact of both the Uniform Commercial Code and the contract terms. Section 2–510 of the Code (Ill.Rev.Stat.1977, ch. 26, par. 2–510(1)), provides:

> (1) Where a tender or delivery of goods so fails to conform to the contract as to give a right of rejection the risk of their loss remains on the seller until cure or acceptance.

Few cases involve this section of the Code and those that do merely cite the Code with little explanation. ... The official Uniform Commercial Code Comment provides some guidance by stating that the purpose of this section is to make clear that "the seller by his individual action cannot shift the risk of loss to the buyer unless his action conforms with all the conditions resting on him under the contract." (S.H.A. ch. 26, par. 2–510(1) at page 398.) Of primary importance, then, is the determination of whether or not the simulator so failed to conform to the contract provisions as to vest the right of rejection in plaintiff and whether or not there was acceptance of the simulator by plaintiff.

The purchase agreement provided in part that the simulator would "accurately and faithfully simulate the configuration and performance of ..." a certain specified Boeing aircraft and that final acceptance of the simulator would be "subject to satisfactory completion of the reliability demonstration requirements ..." and to Federal Aviation Administration certification. The affidavit of John Darley, an employee of plaintiff who tests and evaluates flight simulators to determine whether they meet plaintiff's and the FAA specifications, states that the simulator at no time met those requirements and that plaintiff was never able to begin acceptance testing. His affidavit states clearly that the machine was destroyed by fire "before that time when United [plaintiff] was to begin acceptance testing …" The affidavit of Phil C. Christy, employed by plaintiff as a technical assistant regarding simulators, reaffirms that as late as February 1969 there were "numerous discrepancies" in the operation of the simulator. These affidavits stand uncontradicted by counteraffidavit. Therefore they "are admitted and must be taken as true." … On February 23, 1977, J.M. Gardner, Director of Contracts & Pricing for defendant McDonnell Douglas Electronics Company wrote a letter to plaintiff's attorney in which he stated that the simulator was "destroyed prior to final acceptance."

Defendants contend that Change Order Number 3, which provided for delivery of the simulator at plaintiff's training center in Denver, resulted in waiver of plaintiff's right to object to predelivery nonconformities. We reject this contention. The Change Order simply provides that the testing and inspection, which under the original agreement would have occurred at defendants' plant, would take place in Denver. Sections of the original agreement which provide that delivery does not constitute acceptance remain unchanged by this Change Order Number 3. Also, the language of the Change Order that testing and inspection would be completed in Denver and that the seller would have access to the simulator to demonstrate compliance are inconsistent with the idea that plaintiff had waived the right to object to nonconformity of the simulator.

Defendants do not contest the fact that there were technical difficulties with the simulator, as evidenced by the hundreds of discrepancy reports, actually 645, prepared by plaintiff's employees during the testing period. Instead, defendants stress the complex nature of the device and urge that plaintiff accepted the simulator despite its manifest deficiencies. In support of this contention defendants look to the six week period of inspection of the simulator in Denver and cite Uniform Commercial Code section 2–606 (Ill.Rev.Stat.1977, ch. 26, par. 2–606), which provides:

Acceptance of goods occurs when the buyer

(a) after a reasonable opportunity to inspect the goods signifies to the seller that the goods are conforming or that he will take or retain them in spite of their non-conformity; or

(b) fails to make an effective rejection (subsection (1) of Section 2–602), but such acceptance does not occur until the buyer has had a reasonable opportunity to inspect them; or

(c) does any act inconsistent with the seller's ownership; but if such act is wrongful as against the seller it is an acceptance only if ratified by him.

Defendants thus wish this court to hold that plaintiff had a reasonable opportunity to inspect the simulator and to reject it prior to its destruction. This approach completely ignores the terms of the contract. The purpose of the Uniform Commercial Code is set forth in section 1–102 (Ill.Rev.Stat. 1977, ch. 26, par. 1–102), which states that the provisions of the act may be varied by agreement. This court expressed the same principle in First Bank

& Trust Co., Palatine v. Post (1973), 10 Ill.App.3d 127, 131, 293 N.E.2d 907, 910, where we stated:

> [t]he Uniform Commercial Code was enacted to provide a general uniformity in commercial transactions conducted in this state and was never intended to be used by courts to create a result that is contrary to the clearly understood intentions of the original parties.

The clear intent of the parties before this court, as stated in the purchase agreement, was that physical delivery of the simulator and payments received by the defendants were not to constitute acceptance of the simulator. Acceptance was to be predicated on successful completion of acceptance testing and also upon receipt of FAA certification. The contract terms definitely anticipated and sanctioned use of the simulator by plaintiff to enable it to determine whether this complex and expensive device met the contract specifications. If use of goods is necessary to allow proper evaluation of them, such use does not constitute acceptance. . . .

This record shows that the simulator at no time conformed to the specifications agreed to in the purchase agreement and it remained nonconforming until its destruction. Although plaintiff had use and possession of the simulator for six weeks that arrangement was expressly sanctioned by the contract to allow testing. Retention of the simulator for testing purposes did not constitute acceptance so as to shift the risk of loss to the plaintiff. The simulator was destroyed before completion of acceptance testing and before receipt of FAA certification. Both were conditions precedent to acceptance of the simulator. In this situation the risk of loss remained on the defendants as seller. On the issue of risk of loss, there is no genuine issue regarding any material fact. On the contrary, in our opinion, plaintiff's right to summary judgment in this regard is clear beyond question. We conclude that the plaintiff is entitled to summary judgment as a matter of law.

* * *

Judgment affirmed.

NOTES

(1) Risk of Loss After Buyers Have Received Goods. Assuming that UCC 2–509(3) governs passage of the risk of loss on the facts of *United Air Lines*, the merchant-seller provision provides that risk passes to the buyer on "receipt of the goods." "Receipt" means "taking physical possession" of goods. UCC 2–103. Without referring to 2–509, the court analyzed the case not in terms of buyer's receipt of the simulator, but in terms of buyer's acceptance of it. On what basis could the court determine that risk of loss remained upon sellers until buyer accepted the simulator? Should UCC 2–509(3) be read to mean that risk of loss passes to a buyer only upon receipt of *conforming* goods? See the caption to UCC 2–509 and UCC 1–109.

The court in *United Air Lines* based its opinion on UCC 2–510(1). Does this section apply to the facts of that case? When Conductron delivered the simulator to United Air Lines pursuant to Change Order Number 3, did the parties expect that it would conform to the contract requirements? Was Conductron then in breach? Was Conductron in breach when the fire occurred on April 18? If Conductron was not in breach, is UCC 2–510 pertinent? (We will consider UCC 2–510 further after the following case.)

If neither 2–509(3) nor 2–510(1) is applicable, what risk of loss rule does apply?

(2) Alternative Analysis Under UCC 2–711(1). Why should risk-of-loss analysis be used at all in a case like *United Air Lines*? Buyer seeks to recover so much of the price as has been paid plus damages, remedies available under UCC 2–711(1) "where the seller fails to make delivery ... or the buyer rightfully rejects [the goods]." United Air Lines would not accept the fire-damaged simulator; if Conductron tendered the simulator in that condition, United Air Lines would certainly reject it. If Conductron fails to tender a conforming simulator within the time permitted under the contract, it will have failed to make delivery. Is application of UCC 2–711(1) affected by risk-of-loss rules?

Problem 5.4.3. B agreed to buy a mobile home of S. In accordance with the agreement, S put the mobile home in place on B's lot and made the sewer and gas connections. B moved into the home. S had not yet made the furnace and electrical hook-ups when a gas explosion and an ensuing fire destroyed the mobile home. Who bears the loss?[11]

Problem 5.4.4. The S Chevrolet Company delivered a car to B under a conditional sales contract. B paid S $1700 in cash and in the contract agreed to pay the balance of $15,000 in 36 monthly installments. The contract provided that S held a security interest in the car which S could exercise to enforce its right to receive payment. In addition, the contract provided:

> It is expressly understood and agreed that the title to the above-described automobile shall remain in the seller until the aforesaid sums of money shall be paid as herein provided, and that the seller may at any time, either personally or by agent, using so much force as is necessary, enter in or upon the premises where said automobile may be, with or without the issuance of any writ of replevin, and take possession of said automobile on default in any of the payments herein provided or on failure to comply with one or all of the conditions of this contract.

A month after delivery, the car is wrecked beyond repair without any fault by B. Must he continue to make the payments to S? Does the language of the conditional sales contract evidence an intent by the parties to exercise their power, under UCC 1–102(3), to vary by agreement the UCC's rules on risk of loss? Can the policy of the UCC be drawn, by analogy, from UCC 2–505; UCC 2–509(1)(a); UCC 1–201(37) (second sen-

---

11. See Southland Mobile Home Corp. v. Chyrchel, 255 Ark. 366, 500 S.W.2d 778 (1973); Wilke v. Cummins Diesel Engines, 252 Md. 611, 250 A.2d 886 (1969).

tence)? What, apart from constructional aids in the statute, is the most sensible reading of this language?

In normal commercial practice, unless there has been some mishap in the drafting, printing or assembling of the forms typically used in installment sales contracts, the documents will provide expressly that the buyers bears all casualty risks and agree to maintain fire and casualty insurance.

Ron Mead T.V. & Appliance v. Legendary Homes, Inc.

Oklahoma Court of Appeals, Division Three, 1987.
746 P.2d 1163.

■ HANSEN, PRESIDING JUDGE.

Plaintiff, Ron Mead, is a retail merchant selling household appliances. Defendant, Legendary Homes, is a home builder. Defendant purchased appliances from Plaintiff for installation in one of its homes. The appliances were to be delivered on February 1, 1984. At five o'clock on that day the appliances had not been delivered. Defendant closed the home and left. Sometime between five and six-thirty Plaintiff delivered the appliances. No one was at the home so the deliveryman put the appliances in the garage. During the night someone stole the appliances.

Defendant denied it was responsible for the loss and refused to pay Plaintiff for the appliances. This suit resulted.

After a non-jury trial the court issued a "Memorandum Opinion" finding § 2–509 of the Uniform Commercial Code, 12A O.S. 1981 controlled. This section provides: "The risk of loss passes to the Buyer on his receipt of the goods." The trial court found Defendant had not received the goods, thus the risk of loss remained with Plaintiff. Plaintiff appeals the judgment rendered in favor of Defendant.

* * *

Plaintiff ... submits the trial court erred in concluding Plaintiff did not establish usage of trade in leaving appliances unattended at a building site. The trial court found the record was void of any evidence which would show the method of delivery used by Plaintiff was pursuant to a "course of dealing" between the parties which would waive or excuse the requirements of 12A O.S. 1981 § 2–503.

Section 1–205(2) defines "usage of trade" as any "practice or method of dealing having such regularity of observance in a place, vocation or trade as to justify an expectation that it will be observed with respect to the transaction in question." Although there was testimony some builders allow deliveries to be made to unattended job sites, nothing indicated such practice was uniformly observed after working hours unless specifically agreed to by the parties.

Although there was conflicting testimony between witnesses whether Defendant advised Plaintiff to deliver the appliances before noon, nothing appears in the record to indicate there was any agreement the appliances would be accepted after hours.

Section 2–103 defines "receipt" of goods as taking physical possession of them. We agree with the trial court "(t)he act by the deliveryman of placing the goods in an unlocked garage, in a house under construction, and then locking the door did not give the Buyer the opportunity to take physical possession (of them)."

Credibility of witnesses and weight and value to be given to their testimony is for the trial court on waiver of a jury, and conclusions there reached will not be disturbed on appeal, unless appearing clearly to be based upon caprice or to be without any reasonable foundation. Accordingly, the trial court is affirmed.

* * *

■ HUNTER, J. and BAILEY, J. concur.

NOTES

(1) Basis of the Decision: Analytical Confusion. The problem presented in this case can be analyzed in three ways: under the UCC's rules for tender of delivery or under the UCC's two rules allocating risk of loss. The Oklahoma courts, and presumably the lawyers arguing the case, did not resolve which of these standards they were applying.

If seller had not made a tender of delivery, buyer had no duty to pay the price. UCC 2–507(1). Seller tried and failed to establish a course of dealing or trade usage that permitted tender of delivery by the method it employed. Thus, buyer's duty to pay the price never matured.

Alternatively, the case can be analyzed under the risk of loss rules in UCC 2–509(3). Since seller unquestionably was a merchant, risk of loss would pass only on receipt of the goods. The appellate court, citing UCC 2–103, concluded that "receipt" had not occurred. Seller's action for the price depended on risk of loss passing. UCC 2–709(1)(a). Absent receipt, risk of loss did not pass, and the price action must fail.

A third line of analysis has been offered:

> Although the court manages to properly conclude that the risk of loss had not passed to the buyer, it does so despite misapplication of the Code's risk of loss provisions. Both the trial court and the court of appeals incorrectly cited section 2–509 as the controlling section. Because of the improper tender by the seller, the risk of loss issue in this case should have been resolved by application of section 2–510(1). Regardless of whether the goods have been received, under section 2–510(1) the buyer does not bear risk of loss where the tender is no nonconforming as to give a right of rejection. ... One must wonder how this case would have ended if, all other things being the same, the court had decided that the buyer had received the goods. In view of the court's apparent ignorance of both section 2–510 and the immateriality

of the possession issue, it would seem that, notwithstanding the defective tender, the seller would have wrongfully prevailed.

D. Frisch and J. Wladis, Uniform Commercial Code Annual Survey: General Provisions, Sales, Bulk Transfers, and Documents of Title, 44 Bus. Law. 1445, 1467 (1989).

Which of these lines of analysis is more sound?[12]

See also Howard, Allocation of Risk of Loss Under the UCC: A Transactional Evaluation of §§ 2–509 and 2–510, 15 U.C.C.L.J. 334 (1983).

(2) Sellers' Price Action. The remedy sought in *Ron Mead* was the contract price for the appliances. On what basis could seller seek to recover the price of the stolen appliances? See UCC 2–709(1)(a). Could seller argue successfully that it was entitled to the price on the ground that the appliances were "conforming goods" even though the manner of their tender did not conform to the contract?

Multiplastics v. Arch Industries

Supreme Court of Connecticut, 1974.
166 Conn. 280, 348 A.2d 618.

■ BOGDANSKI, J.

The plaintiff, Multiplastics, Inc., brought this action to recover damages from the defendant, Arch Industries, Inc., for the breach of a contract to purchase 40,000 pounds of plastic pellets. From a judgment rendered for the plaintiff, the defendant has appealed to this court.

The facts may be summarized as follows: The plaintiff, a manufacturer of plastic resin pellets, agreed with the defendant on June 30, 1971, to manufacture and deliver 40,000 pounds of brown polystyrene plastic pellets for nineteen cents a pound. The pellets were specially made for the defendant, who agreed to accept delivery at the rate of 1000 pounds per day after completion of production. The defendant's confirming order contained the notation "make and hold for release. Confirmation." The plaintiff produced the order of pellets within two weeks and requested release orders from the defendant. The defendant refused to issue the release orders, citing labor difficulties and its vacation schedule. On August 18, 1971, the plaintiff sent the defendant the following letter: "Against P.O. 0946, we produced 40,000 lbs. of brown high impact styrene, and you have issued no releases. You indicated to us that you would be using 1,000 lbs. of each per day. We have warehoused these products for more than forty days, as we agreed to do. However, we cannot warehouse these products indefi-

---

12. The PEB Study Group on UCC Article 2 found numerous flaws in 2–510 and recommended that it be repealed. PEB Article 2 Report 149. The Study Group noted that the section requires no showing of any causal connection between the breach and the loss and may allocate risk from the party in the best position to insure the goods to the party who is not. Moreover, the Study Group declared, the section is "complex, incomplete and difficult to apply." Id. This recommendation has not been followed in recent drafts, which retain UCC 2–510. See Proposed Revised 2–510.

nitely, and request that you send us shipping instructions. We have done everything we agreed to do." After August 18, 1971, the plaintiff made numerous telephone calls to the defendant to seek payment and delivery instructions. In response, beginning August 20, 1971, the defendant agreed to issue release orders but in fact never did.

On September 22, 1971, the plaintiff's plant, containing the pellets manufactured for the defendant, was destroyed by fire. The plaintiff's fire insurance did not cover the loss of the pellets. The plaintiff brought this action against the defendant to recover the contract price.

The trial court concluded that the plaintiff made a valid tender of delivery by its letter of August 18, 1971, and by its subsequent requests for delivery instructions; that the defendant repudiated and breached the contract by refusing to accept delivery on August 20, 1971; that the period from August 20, 1971, to September 22, 1971, was not a commercially unreasonable time for the plaintiff to treat the risk of loss as resting on the defendant under General Statutes § 42a–2–510(3), and that the plaintiff was entitled to recover the contract price plus interest.

General Statutes § 42a–2–510, entitled "Effect of breach on risk of loss," reads, in pertinent part, as follows: "(3) Where the buyer as to conforming goods already identified to the contract for sale repudiates or is otherwise in breach before risk of their loss has passed to him, the seller may to the extent of any deficiency in his effective insurance coverage treat the risk of loss as resting on the buyer for a commercially reasonable time." The defendant contends that § 42a–2–510 is not applicable because its failure to issue delivery instructions did not constitute either a repudiation or a breach of the agreement. The defendant also argues that even if § 42a–2–510 were applicable, the period from August 20, 1971, to September 22, 1971, was not a commercially reasonable period of time within which to treat the risk of loss as resting on the buyer. The defendant does not claim that the destroyed pellets were not "conforming goods already identified to the contract for sale," as required by General Statutes § 42a–2–510(3), nor does it protest the computation of damages. With regard to recovery of the price of goods and incidental damages, see General Statutes § 42a–2–709(1)(a).

The trial court's conclusion that the defendant was in breach is supported by its finding that the defendant agreed to accept delivery of the pellets at the rate of 1000 pounds per day after completion of production. The defendant argues that since the confirming order instructed the defendant to "make and hold for release," the contract did not specify an exact delivery date. This argument fails, however, because nothing in the finding suggests that the notation in the confirming order was part of the agreement between the parties. Since, as the trial court found, the plaintiff made a proper tender of delivery, beginning with its letter of August 18, 1971, the plaintiff was entitled to acceptance of the goods and to payment according to the contract. General Statutes §§ 42a–2–507(1), 42a–2–307.

The defendant argues that its failure to issue delivery instructions did not suffice to repudiate the contract because repudiation of an executory promise requires, first, an absolute and unequivocal renunciation by the promisor, and, second, an unambiguous acceptance of the repudiation by the promisee. ... Anticipatory repudiation is now governed by General Statutes §§ 42a–2–609 to 42a–2–611, which in some respects alter the prior law on the subject. The present case does not involve repudiation of an executory promise, however, since the defendant breached the contract by failing to accept the goods when acceptance became due.

The defendant next claims that the plaintiff acquiesced in the defendant's refusal to accept delivery by continuing to urge compliance with the contract and by failing to pursue any of the remedies provided aggrieved sellers by General Statutes § 42a–2–703. In essence, the defendant's argument rests on the doctrines of waiver and estoppel, which are available defenses under the Uniform Commercial Code. General Statutes §§ 42a–1–103, 42a–1–107, 42a–2–209; Mercanti v. Persson, 160 Conn. 468, 477–79, 280 A.2d 137.... The defendant has not, however, shown those defenses to apply. Waiver is the intentional relinquishment of a known right. ... Its existence is a question of fact for the trier. ... The trial court did not find that the plaintiff intentionally acquiesced in the defendant's breach of their agreement, thereby waiving its right to take advantage of that breach. Indeed, the plaintiff's repeated attempts to secure compliance seem inconsistent with the possibility of waiver. ...

Nor has the defendant made out a case of estoppel. "The two essential elements of estoppel are that 'one party must do or say something which is intended or calculated to induce another to believe in the existence of certain facts and to act on that belief; and the other party, influenced thereby, must change his position or do some act to his injury which he otherwise would not have done.' Dickau v. Glastonbury, 156 Conn. 437, 441, 242 A.2d 777; Pet Car Products, Inc. v. Barnett, 150 Conn. 42, 53, 184 A.2d 797." Mercanti v. Persson, supra, 477. Neither element of estoppel is present in the record of this case. The plaintiff's requests for delivery instructions cannot be said to have misled the defendant into thinking that the plaintiff did not consider their contract breached. In fact, General Statutes § 42a–2–610, entitled "Anticipatory repudiation," specifically provides that the aggrieved seller may "resort to any remedy for breach as provided by section 42a–2–703 ..., even though he has notified the repudiating party that he would await the latter's performance and has urged retraction." Although the present case is not governed by General Statutes § 42a–2–610, that section does demonstrate that the plaintiff's conduct after the defendant refused to accept delivery was not inconsistent with his claim that the contract was breached.

The remaining question is whether, under General Statutes § 42a–2–510(3), the period of time from August 20, 1971, the date of the breach, to September 22, 1971, the date of the fire, was a "commercially reasonable" period within which to treat the risk of loss as resting on the buyer. The trial court concluded that it was "not, on the facts in this case, a commercially unreasonable time," which we take to mean that it was a commercially reasonable period. The time limitation in § 42a–2–510(3) is designed to enable the seller to obtain the additional requisite insurance coverage. ... The trial court's conclusion is tested by the finding. ... Although the finding is not detailed, it supports the conclusion that August 20 to September 22 was a commercially reasonable period within which to place the risk of loss on the defendant. As already stated, the trial court found that the defendant repeatedly agreed to transmit delivery instructions and that the pellets were specially made to fill the defendant's order. Under those circumstances, it was reasonable for the plaintiff to believe that the goods would soon be taken off its hands and so to forego procuring the needed insurance.

We consider it advisable to discuss one additional matter. The trial court concluded that "title" passed to the defendant, and the defendant attacks the conclusion on this appeal. The issue is immaterial to this case. General Statutes § 42a–2–401 states: "Each provision of this article with regard to the rights, obligations and remedies of the seller, the buyer, purchasers or other third parties applies irrespective of title to the goods except where the provision refers to such title." As one student of the Uniform Commercial Code has written: "The single most important innovation of Article 2 [of the Uniform Commercial Code] is its restatement of ... [the parties'] responsibilities in terms of operative facts rather than legal conclusions; where pre-Code law looked to 'title' for the definition of rights and remedies, the Code looks to demonstrable realities such as custody, control and professional expertise." This shift in approach is central to the whole philosophy of Article 2. It means that disputes, as they arise, can focus, as does all of the modern law of contracts, upon actual provable circumstances, rather than upon a metaphysical concept of elastic and endlessly fluid dimensions." Peters, "Remedies for Breach of Contracts Relating to the Sale of Goods Under the Uniform Commercial Code: A Roadmap for Article Two," 73 Yale L.J. 199, 201.

There is no error.

In this opinion the other judges concurred.

(B) SHIPMENT CONTRACTS

In many sales transactions, sellers are authorized or required to ship goods to buyers via carriers. While en route, goods may suffer loss or damage. The principal subject in this subsection is the allocation of risk of such losses between sellers and buyers. A subordinate question is the extent of the carriers' liability for goods that suffer casualty while in their possession.

Shipment and Destination Contracts. In Chapter 4, we learned that sales contracts that contemplate delivery of goods by carrier are generally characterized as place-of-shipment or at-a-particular-destination contracts. In the former, the cost of transportation is borne by the buyer; in the latter, freight charges are paid by the seller. Risk of loss is allocated in the same characterization. UCC 2–509(1).

Under UCC 2–319, sales contracts that use the F.O.B. term are shipment contracts if the term is F.O.B. the place of shipment; seller bears the risk of putting the goods into the carrier's possession. UCC 2–319(1)(a). Risk passes when the goods are duly delivered to the carrier. UCC 2–509(1)(a). Conversely, if the contract term is F.O.B. the place of destination, seller must at its own risk transport the goods to that place. UCC 2–319(1)(b). Risk passes when the goods are there duly tendered. UCC 2–509(1)(b).

Shipping terms commonly associated with deep water transport pose difficult problems for risk of loss. Even though the price includes the cost of transportation, sellers expressly bear the risk of putting the goods into the carriers' possession, loading the goods on board, or delivering them alongside a vessel, as the terms require. UCC 2–319(1)(b) and (2), 2–320(2) and (3). Contracts that use the terms F.O.B. vessel or F.A.S. can be recognized as shipment contracts; thus the risk passing provision of UCC 2–509(1)(a) applies. However contracts that use the terms C.I.F. and C. & F. cannot easily be characterized as shipment contracts. Nor is it plausible to construe them as destination contracts with risk passing at the place of destination.[13] A different result follows if the term used is "delivery ex-ship." UCC 2–322.

Risk of loss and contract performance problems tend to arise when sales contracts are ambiguous as to whether they are shipment or destination contracts.

Problem 5.4.5. Seller Manufacturing Company, in Sellersville, Pennsylvania, has distributed a catalogue giving descriptions and prices for a line of garden tractors which Seller makes and sells. Buyer Garden Supply Company, in Birmingham, Alabama, an enterprise with stores in various cities in Alabama, wired Seller, "Please ship to us in Birmingham, 10 Garden Tractors, Catalogue No. 103X, priced at $1,430 each." Seller replied: "Order accepted. Tractors being shipped this week." Neither the catalogue nor the correspondence dealt with methods or costs of delivery.

Seller promptly hauled the 10 garden tractors in his truck to the freight station of the CSX Railroad in Sellersville and delivered them to the freight agent in the freight yards. Seller received a "straight" (non-negotiable) bill of lading providing that the goods were "Consigned to Buyer Garden Supply Co., Birmingham, Ala." Freight costs of $310 were noted on the bill of lading as "C.O.D." (Collect on Delivery).

One of the tractors was stolen from the CSX freight yard in Sellersville. Another was damaged in a freight car en route to Birmingham.

(a) Buyer paid for eight tractors, but refused to pay for the tractor that was stolen or for the damaged tractor. Seller sues for the price of the two tractors. Buyer interposes all available defenses to the price action and, in addition, counterclaims for the freight costs of $610 which he had to pay the railroad in order to receive delivery of the tractors. What result? See

---

13. The UCC provision on the C.I.F. term imposes a duty on sellers to contract for casualty insurance for the benefit of the buyers. UCC 2–320(2)(c).

UCC 2–509, UCC 2–504, UCC 2–709(1)(a); Pestana v. Karinol Corporation, infra.

(b) Suppose Seller's truck had overturned and burned while the tractors were being taken from Seller's factory to the freight yards. May Seller recover the price for the tractors destroyed by fire?

Pestana v. Karinol Corp.

District Court of Appeal of Florida, Third District, 1979.
367 So.2d 1096.

■ HUNNART, JUDGE.

This is an action for damages based on a contract for the sale of goods. The defendant seller and others prevailed in this action after a non-jury trial in the Circuit Court for the Eleventh Judicial Circuit of Florida. The plaintiff buyer appeals.

The central issue presented for review is whether a contract for the sale of goods, which stipulates the place where the goods sold are to be sent by carrier but contains (a) no explicit provisions allocating the risk of loss while the goods are in the possession of the carrier and (b) no delivery terms such as F.O.B. place of destination, is a shipment contract or a destination contract under the Uniform Commercial Code. We hold that such a contract, without more, constitutes a shipment contract wherein the risk of loss passes to the buyer when the seller duly delivers the goods to the carrier under a reasonable contract of carriage for shipment to the buyer. Accordingly, we affirm.

A

The critical facts of this case are substantially undisputed. On March 4, 1975, Nahim Amar B. [the plaintiff Pedro P. Pestana's decedent herein] who was a resident of Mexico entered into a contract through his authorized representative with the Karinol Corporation [the defendant herein] which is an exporting company licensed to do business in Florida and operating out of Miami. The terms of this contract were embodied in a one page invoice written in Spanish and prepared by the defendant Karinol. By the terms of this contract, the plaintiff's Amar agreed to purchase 64 electronic watches from the defendant Karinol for $6,006. A notation was printed at the bottom of the contract which, translated into English, reads as follows: "Please send the merchandise in cardboard boxes duly strapped with metal bands via air parcel post to Chetumal. Documents to Banco de Commercio De Quintano Roo S.A." There were no provisions in the contract which specifically allocated the risk of loss on the goods sold while in the possession of the carrier; there were also no F.O.B., F.A.S., C.I.F. or C & F terms contained in the contract. See §§ 672.319, 672.320, Fla.Stat. (1977). A 25% downpayment on the purchase price of the goods sold was made prior to shipment.

On April 11, 1975, there is sufficient evidence, although disputed, that the defendant Karinol delivered the watches in two cartons to its agent American International Freight Forwarders, Inc. [the second defendant herein] for forwarding to the plaintiff's decedent Amar. The defendant American insured the two cartons with Fidelity & Casualty Company of New York [the third defendant herein] naming the defendant Karinol as the insured. The defendant American as freight forwarder strapped the cartons in question with metal bands and delivered them to TACA International Airlines consigned to one Bernard Smith, a representative of the plaintiff's decedent, in Belize City, Belize, Central America. The shipment was arranged by Karinol in this manner in accord with a prior understanding between the parties as there were no direct flights from Miami, Florida to Chetumal, Mexico. Mr. Smith was to take custody of the goods on behalf of the plaintiff's decedent in Belize and arrange for their transport by truck to the plaintiff's decedent Amar in Chetumal, Mexico.

On April 15, 1975, the cartons arrived by air in Belize City and were stored by the airline in the customs and air freight cargo room. Mr. Smith was duly notified and thereupon the plaintiff's decedent made payment on the balance due under the contract to the defendant Karinol. On May 2, 1975, Mr. Smith took custody of the cartons after a certain delay was experienced in transferring the cartons to a customs warehouse. Either on that day or shortly thereafter, the cartons were opened by Mr. Smith and customs officials as was required for clearance prior to the truck shipment to Chetumal, Mexico. There were no watches contained in the cartons. The defendant Karinol and its insurance carrier the defendant Fidelity were duly notified, but both eventually refused to make good on the loss.

The plaintiff Pedro P. Pestana, as representative of the Estate of Nahim Amar B., deceased, filed suit against the defendant Karinol as the seller, the defendant American as Karinol's agent freight forwarder, and the defendant Fidelity as the defendant Karinol's insurer. The complaint alleged that the defendant Karinol entered into a contract to ship merchandise from Miami, Florida to Chetumal, Mexico with the plaintiff's decedent, that the defendant American as freight forwarder and agent of the defendant Karinol accepted shipment of such merchandise, that the merchandise was lost, stolen or misplaced while in the care and custody of the defendant Karinol and the defendant American, that the defendants Karinol and American failed to make delivery to the plaintiff's decedent at Chetumal, Mexico, and that there existed a liability policy with the defendant Fidelity for the benefit of the plaintiff's decedent. The complaint sought damages together with court costs and reasonable attorneys fees. All the defendants duly filed answers to the complaint wherein liability was denied. The defendant Karinol filed a cross-complaint against the defendant American. The trial court after a non-jury trial found for all of the defendants in this cause. This appeal follows.

B

There are two types of sales contracts under Florida's Uniform Commercial Code wherein a carrier is used to transport the goods sold: a shipment contract and a destination contract. A shipment contract is considered the normal contract in which the seller is required to send the subject goods by carrier to the buyer but is not required to guarantee delivery thereof at a particular destination. Under a shipment contract, the seller, unless otherwise agreed, must: (1) put the goods sold in the possession of a carrier and make a contract for their transportation as may be reasonable having regard for the nature of the goods and other attendant circumstances, (2) obtain and promptly deliver or tender in due form any document necessary to enable the buyer to obtain possession of the goods or otherwise required by the agreement or by usage of the trade, and (3) promptly notify the buyer of the shipment. On a shipment contract, the risk of loss passes to the buyer when the goods sold are duly delivered to the carrier for shipment to the buyer. §§ 672.503 (Official U.C.C. comment 5), 672.504, 672.509(1), Fla.Stat. (1977). . . .

A destination contract, on the other hand, is considered the variant contract in which the seller specifically agrees to deliver the goods sold to the buyer at a particular destination and to bear the risk of loss of the goods until tender of delivery. This can be accomplished by express provision in the sales contract to that effect or by the use of delivery terms such as F.O.B. (place of destination). Under a destination contract, the seller is required to tender delivery of the goods sold to the buyer at the place of destination. The risk of loss under such a contract passes to the buyer when the goods sold are duly tendered to the buyer at the place of destination while in the possession of the carrier so as to enable the buyer to take delivery. The parties must explicitly agree to a destination contract; otherwise the contract will be considered a shipment contract. §§ 672.319(1)(b), 672.503 (Official U.C.C. comment 5), 672.509(1), Fla.Stat. (1977). . . .

Where the risk of loss falls on the seller at the time the goods sold are lost or destroyed, the seller is liable in damages to the buyer for non-delivery unless the seller tenders a performance in replacement for the lost or destroyed goods. On the other hand, where the risk of loss falls on the buyer at the time the goods sold are lost or destroyed, the buyer is liable to the seller for the purchase price of the goods sold. White and Summers, Uniform Commercial Code 134 (1972).

C

In the instant case, we deal with the normal shipment contract involving the sale of goods. The defendant Karinol pursuant to this contract agreed to send the goods sold, a shipment of watches, to the plaintiff's decedent in Chetumal, Mexico. There was no specific provision in the contract between the parties which allocated the risk of loss on the goods sold while in transit. In addition, there were no delivery terms such as F.O.B. Chetumal contained in the contract.

All agree that there is sufficient evidence that the defendant Karinol performed its obligations as a seller under the Uniform Commercial Code if this contract is considered a shipment contract. Karinol put the goods sold in the possession of a carrier and made a contract for the goods safe transportation to the plaintiff's decedent; Karinol also promptly notified the plaintiff's decedent of the shipment and tendered to said party the necessary documents to obtain possession of the goods sold.

The plaintiff Pestana contends, however, that the contract herein is a destination contract in which the risk of loss on the goods sold did not pass until delivery on such goods had been tendered to him at Chetumal, Mexico—an event which never occurred. He relies for this position on the notation at the bottom of the contract between the parties which provides that the goods were to be sent to Chetumal, Mexico. We cannot agree. A "send to" or "ship to" term is a part of every contract involving the sale of goods where carriage is contemplated and has no significance in determining whether the contract is a shipment or destination contract for risk of loss purposes. ... As such, the "send to" term contained in this contract cannot, without more, convert this into a destination contract.

It therefore follows that the risk of loss in this case shifted to the plaintiff's decedent as buyer when the defendant Karinol as seller duly delivered the goods to the defendant freight forwarder American under a reasonable contract of carriage for shipment to the plaintiff's decedent in Chetumal, Mexico. The defendant Karinol, its agent the defendant American, and its insurer the defendant Fidelity could not be held liable to the plaintiff in this action. The trial court properly entered judgment in favor of all the defendants herein.

Affirmed.

NOTES

(1) Allocation of Freight Costs as Allocation of Risk of Loss. If freight from Sellersville to Buyersville is $12 per ton, quotations of "$100 F.O.B. Sellersville," "$112 F.O.B. Buyersville," and "$112 F.O.B. Sellersville, freight allowed" all have the same effect with respect to the buyer's costs. However, the first and third allocate transit risk to the buyer, while the second allocates transit risk to the seller. It seems likely that the parties, in negotiating the contract, are more likely to concentrate on immediate cost and return factors rather than on the relatively unusual feature of risk of loss. Hence, there is ground for skepticism that choice among the above forms of quotation reflects an express agreement as to risk.

Price quotations that include freight may, on occasion, be employed to meet competition from a seller that is close to the buyer. If a seller wishes to be in a position to quote prices that include freight, but with transit risk allocated to the buyer, how could the order forms be structured? Would it be adequate to include a form clause dealing with risk of loss? Since negotiating agents cannot be expected to remember technical instructions, should the form include a special notation at the point where the price is to be inserted? What would you recommend?

(2) Policy Considerations Relevant to Risk Allocation Rules.
Comment 5 to UCC 2–503 regards the "shipment" contract as normal and
the "destination" contract as a variant. Under UCC 2–509(1) the "normal"
shipment contract places transit risks on the buyer. Are there considerations of policy that bear on this result?

In considering risk allocation while sellers remain in possession, we
considered whether sellers or buyers have the better opportunity to guard
against casualty and to insure against loss. Are these considerations significant in transportation cases? It has been suggested that sellers should bear
transit loss since they are in a better position to select and bargain with
carriers. In evaluating this argument would it be relevant to inquire into
the amenability of railways, truckers and ocean carriers to negotiate
concerning the terms and conditions for transport?

Would it be relevant to consider which party can more readily cope
with the consequences of transit damage? At which point in the transaction
will transit damage be discovered? Are sellers or buyers in a better position
to salvage the goods, assess the damage, and press a claim against the
carriers or insurers? Would the answer be the same for (a) raw materials,
such as cotton shipped to a textile manufacturer and (b) a complex machine
manufactured by a seller?

Note that considerations of policy as to who can most efficiently handle
transit losses is relevant not only in the construction of ambiguous contracts but also in the process of negotiating and drafting contract provisions.

Problem 5.4.6. Seller agreed to sell Buyer an accumulation of brass
scrap, with terms "f.o.b. Seller's city, payable by sight draft on arrival."
Seller shipped and took a bill of lading running to "Seller or order." The
brass was stolen during transit. Must Buyer pay the price? Does the fact
that the bill of lading is a "document of *title*" and ran in Seller's name
affect the risk of loss? See UCC 2–509(1)(a) ("even though the shipment is
under reservation").

What considerations of policy underlie this result?

Problem 5.4.7. Seller in Seattle, Washington, and Buyer in Boise,
Idaho, made a contract calling for Seller to ship Buyer one hundred bags of
"No. 1 Cane Sugar," F.O.B. Seattle. When the shipment was unloaded at
Buyer's place of business Buyer inspected the sugar and immediately wired
Seller "Sugar grades No. 2, will hold you responsible for reduced value of
shipment." The next day the sugar was destroyed by a fire in the buyer's
warehouse.

(a) On the above facts, who has risk of loss? See UCC 2–510(1), UCC
2–606(1)(a).

(b) Suppose the buyer had wired: "Sugar grades No. 2. Will reject
sugar unless you allow price reduction of 50 cents per hundredweight." If
the casualty occurred before Seller replied, who would bear the risk?

Problem 5.4.8. Seller is a sugar refiner located in San Francisco, California; Buyer is a Boston, Massachusetts, candy manufacturer. Seller and Buyer made a contract for the sale to Buyer of 1000 tons of No. 1 beet sugar at $160 per ton. The contract terms were "C.I.F. Boston, ocean carriage via the Panama Canal. Shipment during June; payment 60 days after arrival of ship in Boston."

During the ocean voyage, water leaked into the hold and seriously damaged half of the sugar. On arrival Buyer noticed not only the water damage, but also concluded that the sugar had been poorly refined and that it contained excessive impurities, so that the sugar graded No. 2 and was unsuitable for use in making candy. The sugar undamaged by water would bring $110 per ton; the water-soaked sugar was worthless. Buyer rejected the entire shipment and refused to pay the price.

(a) Seller sues for the price, and claims that the sugar conformed to the contract when it was loaded on board in San Francisco. Seller also contends that, in any event, the loss from the water damage fell on the Buyer, and that the Buyer may not reject since he cannot return the goods to the Seller in the same condition as when risk of loss passed to the Buyer. What result? See UCC 2–320, UCC 2–509, UCC 2–510, UCC 2–601, UCC 2–709(1)(a).

(b) Assume that Seller delivered No. 1 sugar to the ocean carrier, but had completed delivery to the ship on July 3. As in the above problem, the sugar is seriously damaged in transit by ocean water. Seller sues Buyer for the price. What result?

Problem 5.4.9. Rheinberg, a German wine exporter, and Vineyard, a North Carolina wine distributor, made a contract for Rheinberg to sell 620 cases of wine to Vineyard. The contract called for Rheinberg to ship the wine to Vineyard, but Vineyard was to pay the freight. The sales contract also provided: "Insurance to be covered by purchaser." On 29 November, Rheinberg delivered a container containing the wine to an ocean carrier for shipment to Wilmington, Delaware, freight payable by Vineyard at destination. Early in December the shipment left Germany via the M.S. Munchen, which in mid-December was lost in the North Atlantic with all hands and cargo. Vineyard received no notice of the shipment until after the ship and cargo had been lost.

Vineyard refused to pay for the wine, and Rheinberg sued for the price in a North Carolina court. Assume that domestic United States law applies. What should be the outcome? See UCC 2–504(c); Rheinberg–Kellerei GMBH v. Vineyard Wine Co., 53 N.C.App. 560, 281 S.E.2d 425 (1981). In *Rheinberg-Kellerei,* judgment for the buyer was affirmed by the Court of Appeals. The transfer of risk of loss to buyer was negated by UCC 2–504(c) since the seller did not "promptly notify the buyer of the shipment." It would not be practical "to attempt to engraft into [2–504] a rigid definition of prompt notice ... which must be determined on a case-by-case basis, under all the circumstances." However, in this case Vineyard was not notified "within the time in which its interest could have been protected by insurance or otherwise"; the notice had not been "prompt."

The opinion in *Rheinberg-Kellerei* did not discuss the ambiguities latent in the last phrase of UCC 2–504(c): "if material loss or delay *ensues*." On these facts, would loss have ensued from the failure to notify if the buyer had been covered by insurance under a blanket policy? Or did loss ensue from the loss at sea of the ship and cargo? Who should have the burden to show that loss had ensued?

(3) Liability of Domestic United States Carriers; UCC 2–722. When goods suffer casualty or loss when in the custody of carriers, the carrier may be liable for some or all of the loss. The legal obligations of carriers vary with the kinds of carriers involved. Many of the laws on duties of carriers are complex and cannot be considered in any depth in these materials.

When a carrier is liable for injury to goods that are the subject of a sales contract, the carrier's liability can be enforced by the seller or the buyer. The party that bears the risk of loss under the contract of sale is more likely to be the claimant against the carrier. The UCC provides, in UCC 2–722(a), that a right of action is in either party to the sales contract that has title or a special property or an insurable interest in the goods. The section adds that, if the goods have been destroyed or converted, a right of action is in the party that either bore the risk of loss under the contract for sale or that has assumed that risk as against the other party to the contract. UCC 2–722(c) provides that either seller or buyer may, with the consent of the other, sue a carrier for the benefit of "whom it may concern."

(4) Insurers v. Carriers. The seller or the buyer may have insurance that covers damage to the goods that occurs during transit. In cases where rules of law provide that the carrier is also responsible for the damage, interesting jockeying for position has occurred to determine whether the loss should fall ultimately on the insurer or on the carrier. The situation has been summarized by Professors Robert E. Keeton and Alan I. Widiss as follows:

> For many years insurers and common carriers (such as truckers and railroads) engaged in an extended struggle with regard to the insurers' assertion of claims against carriers for damage to goods covered by insurance obtained by shippers. The following description of some main events in this struggle indicates the nature of the controversy and its relation to subrogation.
>
> One of the early events in the conflict was the adoption by carriers of a bill-of-lading clause giving a carrier the benefit of insurance effected by a shipper. Insurers responded to this clause in the bill-of-lading with a policy clause providing for nonliability of an insurer upon shipment under a bill of lading that gave a carrier the benefit of a shipper's insurance. Since carriers then had nothing to gain and shippers had much to lose by retention of the clause previously used in bills of lading, the carriers modified the bill-of-lading clause to give a carrier the benefit of any insurance effected on the goods so far as this did not defeat the insurer's liability. This strategic retreat by the

carriers still left the insurers with a problem. If an insurer paid a shipper, would it be a "volunteer" and therefore not entitled to subrogation to the shipper's claim against the carrier? If it did not pay the shipper, how could it maintain good business relations with an insured who wanted prompt payment from somebody and did not like waiting for the carrier and insurer to resolve a dispute as to ultimate responsibility for the loss? To avoid this problem, insurers resorted to loan receipts: an insurer paid a shipper an amount equal to the promised insurance benefits, but the transaction was cast as a loan repayable out of the prospective recovery from the carrier. The effectiveness of a loan receipt in preserving rights against a common carrier has been recognized in a number of judicial decisions. Thus, at least as reflected in such precedents, the insurers prevailed in the struggle with carriers over form provisions concerning responsibility for losses of insured property during shipment. And this result is also fortified by decisions that a "benefit of insurance" clause in a bill of lading is invalid under statutory prohibitions against rate discrimination, since a carrier would be receiving greater compensation from a shipper who had insurance than from one who did not.

R. Keeton & A. Widiss, Insurance Law 250–251 (1988).[14]

INTERNATIONAL SALES LAW

Convention on Contracts for International Sale of Goods. The CISG provisions on risk of loss are found in Chapter IV of the Convention. The most important articles are CISG 67 and CISG 69. Article 67 applies when the sales contract involves carriage of goods; the special situation of goods sold while in transit is covered in CISG 68. Article 69 applies when the sales contract requires the buyer to come to the seller for the goods.[15]

(A) LOCAL TRANSACTIONS

Sales transactions that do not involve shipment of goods by carriers, while not typical of international sales, may nonetheless occur in some circumstances. The Convention on Contracts for International Sale of Goods establishes risk of loss rules for this type transaction in Article 69. The general principle is that risk passes when a buyer "takes over the goods." CISG 69(1). This phrase is more clear in its connotation of positive buyer action than is the UCC's "receipt." Recall, for example, the conceptual difficulty posed in applying UCC 2–509(3) in the *United Air Lines* case. Moreover the Convention standard applies to all sellers. The Convention does not contemplate non-merchant sellers.

---

14. Copied with permission of the authors and of the West Publishing Company.

15. For a useful account of the Convention's rules, see P. Roth, The Passing of Risk, 27 Am. J. Comp. L. 291 (1979). See also

Berman & Ladd, Risk of Loss or Damage in Documentary Transactions Under the Convention on the International Sale of Goods, 21 Cornell Int'l L.J. 423 (1988).

The Convention also addresses the possibility that buyers, having opportunity to do so, will fail to "take over" goods. Although the Convention does not generally use the concepts of tender of delivery, it incorporates a similar idea here only for the purpose of allocating risk of loss to such buyers. Risk of loss thus remains on sellers until buyers' failure to take over goods placed at their disposal is breach of contract.

The Convention explicitly relates buyers' duty to pay to the risk of loss rules. Buyers' duty to pay is not discharged if casualty or loss occurs after risk of loss has passed. CISG 66. An inference can be drawn that payment obligations are discharged if risk of loss had not passed.[16] The Convention has no counterpart provision that relates sellers' duty to deliver to the rules of risk of loss. However, the Convention provides broadly that sellers (and buyers) may not be liable for failures to perform if the failures were due to impediments beyond their control. CISG 79.[17]

Problem 5.4.10. On June 1, Seller handed over goods to Buyer. Buyer's inspection on June 2 disclosed that the goods were not in conformity with the contract. On June 3 a fire in Buyer's warehouse injured the goods.

(a) Buyer claims damages from Seller for the nonconformity of the goods and for the injury to the goods. What result under CISG? See CISG 36(1), 69(1), 74.

(b) Buyer contends that the nonconformity was so substantial as to constitute a fundamental breach and, on June 4, declares the contract avoided. Assuming that Buyer is correct in characterizing the nonconformity as a fundamental breach, to what remedies is Buyer entitled under CISG? See CISG 70, CISG 81, and CISG 84. See also Honnold, International Sales § 383.

(B) SHIPMENT CONTRACTS

Problem 5.4.11. Seller in San Francisco, California, made a contract with Buyer in Bombay, India, for the sale of a machine to Buyer. The contract included the provision: "Price $10,000. CIF Bombay." The machine was damaged during the ocean voyage. If CISG applies, which party to the sales contract bears the risk of loss?

For purposes of applying CISG 67(1), is Seller "bound to hand [the goods] over at a particular place," i.e., Bombay? Compare CISG 31.

The matter is dealt with more clearly if the parties have incorporated the ICC Incoterms into their sales contracts. Incoterms (1990) specify when risk of loss passes in three categories of common shipping terms, which the ICC categorizes as "F" terms, "C" terms, and "D" terms. The "F" category are the terms in which the contract price does not include cost of

---

16. Under CISG 66, a buyer is discharged from the obligation to pay the price if the loss or damage is due to an act or omission of the seller.

17. CISG 79 adds other conditions that sellers must meet to be protected from liability.

carriage (e.g., FOB or FAS). In the "C" category are terms under which sellers must paid the costs of carriage (e.g., CFR and CIF). Under any of the "F" or the "C" terms of CFR and CIF, risk of loss passes at the time of shipment. A different result follows if the parties use other "C" terms, such as CPT (carriage paid to place of destination) or CIP (carriage and insurance paid to place of destination) or "D" terms, such as DES (delivered ex ship), DEQ (delivered ex quay), and DDP (delivered duty paid). Sellers bear risk of loss until the goods are delivered at the specified place.

Does CISG allocate the responsibility to purchase casualty insurance on goods in transit? If the sales contract incorporates ICC Incoterms (1990), use of the term, CFR,[18] (cost and freight to a named port of destination), means (p. 44):

> The seller must . . . contract on usual terms at his own expense for the carriage of the goods to the named port of destination by the usual route in a seagoing vessel (or inland waterway vessel as appropriate) of the type normally used in the transport of goods of the contract description, [but seller has] no obligation [as to purchase of insurance]

If the parties use the term, CIF, Incoterms 1990 has a different set of sellers' obligations (pp. 50, 52):

> The seller must . . . obtain at his own expense cargo insurance as agreed in the contract, that the buyer, or any other person having an insurable interest in the goods, shall be entitled to claim directly from the insurer and provide the buyer with the insurance policy or other evidence of insurance cover.

> The insurance shall be contracted with underwriters or an insurance company of good repute and, failing agreement to the contrary, be in accordance with the minimum cover of the Institute Cargo Clauses (Institute of London Underwriters) or any similar set of clauses. . . . When required by the buyer, the seller shall provide at buyer's expense war, strikes, riots and civil commotion risk insurances if procurable. The minimum insurance shall cover the price provided in the contract plus ten per cent (i.e. 110%) and shall be provided in the currency of the contract.

Precision in Defining the Moment of Risk Passing. Loading and offloading goods pose special risks of damage to the goods in that process. Allocation of this risk of loss between buyer and seller requires precision in knowing exactly when risk passes.

In an FOB vessel contract, for example, risk passes when the goods pass the ship's rail. This traditional usage is retained in ICC Incoterms (1990) at 38. The same point is designated in CFR and CIF contracts. Id. at

---

18. Incoterms (1990) does not use the term, C. & F., found in UCC 2–320, 2–321. The ampersand, which could be replaced by an "A", would be confusing in international usage. In French, the English "insurance" translates to "assurance." Without knowing which language is implied, use of CAF creates unnecessary ambiguity. Thus the ICC uses CFR in lieu of C. & F.

46, 52. In an FAS contract, risk passes when the goods have been placed alongside the vessel on the quay or in lighters. Id. at 32.

Use of other terms puts the moment of risk passing when goods are delivered into the possession of carriers, including delivery to a terminal facility, e.g., FCA (free carrier). Id. at 26–28. In the "D" terms, sellers bear the risks of offloading under the term, DEQ (delivered ex quay), but not under DES (delivered ex ship). Id. at 74, 82.

Liability of Carriers in International Transport Under International Law. A substantial body of international law deals with the liability of carriers. Attempts to establish the liability of ocean carriers culminated, at the Fifth International Conference on Maritime Law held in Brussels in 1924, in an international convention usually called the "Hague Rules." The United States Government and many other countries signed this Convention. However, ratification by the United States Senate was delayed until 1936, and was then given in connection with the enactment by Congress of the Carriage of Goods by Sea Act, 1936, 46 U.S.C. 1300–15. This Act followed the language of the 1924 Brussels Convention, with a few minor modifications. The Brussels Convention has now been ratified by most of the important commercial countries.[19] Problems resulting from the restricted responsibility of the ocean carrier may be solved but are not necessarily simplified by purchase of a marine insurance policy. Rules for liability for international air shipments were prescribed by the Warsaw Convention of 1929. The Convention has now been accepted by the United States and over 90 other countries.

19. One accustomed to the heavy responsibility of domestic rail carriers will be surprised at the rules which govern ocean carriers. For example, Article 4 the Brussels Convention (as embodied in Section 4(2) of the Carriage of Goods by Sea Act) sets forth a "catalogue" of seventeen grounds for exempting the carrier from liability.

The special exemptions for the carrier in The Hague Rules of 1924 were virtually eliminated from the United Nations Convention on the Carriage of Goods by Sea, finalized in 1978 at Hamburg ("The Hamburg Rules") The United States was one of the twenty-seven States that signed the Convention, but ratification by the United States and several other signatories has been delayed by opposition from ocean carriers. The twentieth ratification needed to bring the Hamburg Convention into force occurred on October 7, 1991; the Convention entered into force for these twenty States on 1 November 1992. With few exceptions, the initial parties to the Convention are small, developing countries.

CHAPTER 6

INTRODUCTION TO SECURED FINANCING

The remainder of this book deals primarily with consumers and businesses that need credit and the lenders and credit sellers who extend credit to them. In particular, the focus is on transactions in which creditors obtain consensual liens—"security interests"—on personal property (both goods and intangibles). Chapter 1's treatment of basic precepts of personal property law—security of property and good faith purchase, in particular—considers the rights of secured creditors as purchasers of personal property. This Chapter takes a broader and more systematic view of secured credit. Section 1 describes the contexts in which extensions of credit take place and the patterns and participants involved. Section 2 provides an overview of the principal statute that regulates security interests, Article 9 of the Uniform Commercial Code. Finally, Section 3 considers the variety of roles lawyers play in secured transactions.

SECTION 1. SECURED FINANCING IN CONTEXT

(A) UNSECURED AND SECURED CREDIT

Although the following materials focus primarily on the legal regulation of secured credit, the legal regime can be understood only by approaching secured credit as a subset of credit extensions generally. Why is credit sought and given? The likely intuitive answer of most North American consumers would be essentially correct: Both consumers and businesses need funds, goods, or services *now*, not later, and often they choose to enjoy the fruits of credit while paying over time. Creditors extend credit not only to increase profit directly, by earning interest, but also indirectly, by increasing the sale of their goods and services.

Many of the problems in this part of the book focus on the Prototype transaction described in Chapter 7, Section 1, infra. As you will see, the Prototype includes detailed examples of both consumer and business credit transactions. In the Prototype, Lee Abel purchased a new car from Main Motors under an **installment purchase** arrangement. After making a down payment (consisting of a trade-in), Abel signed an agreement containing a promise to pay the balance of the purchase price, plus **carrying charges** (comparable to interest charges on a loan) and certain other charges. Main Motors, on the other hand, itself required financing in order to buy the car that it sold to Abel as well as the other cars in its inventory. On average, Main Motors maintains an inventory of cars that cost (wholesale) about $3,500,000; it does not have capital sufficient to enable it to invest that much money for extended periods. Consequently, Main buys automobiles with funds that it borrows from Firstbank.

In the Prototype, Lee Abel granted a security interest in the new car to Main Motors in order to secure the obligations under the installment purchase contract. Similarly, Main Motors granted a security interest in its automobile inventory to Firstbank in order to secure its obligation to repay the loan. Although it is clear enough why Abel and Main Motors needed credit, why was the credit given to Abel and Main *secured*, as opposed to *unsecured*, credit? Before venturing an answer to that question, one must consider three aspects of secured and unsecured credit: (i) enforcement against the borrower or buyer (the "debtor"), (ii) priorities among creditors and buyers competing to satisfy their claims from the same property of the debtor, and (iii) enforcement of the security interest in a bankruptcy proceeding of the debtor.

We saw in Chapter 1 that a secured creditor with an Article 9 security interest has the right to satisfy its claim against the debtor from the collateral (the property subject to the security interest). The Article 9 secured party's rights include the right to take possession of the collateral upon the debtor's default in payment or performance of the obligation secured. See R9–609. We also considered the more limited rights of unsecured creditors; unsecured creditors have *no* property rights in the debtor's property. Their remedies generally depend on first obtaining a judgment against the debtor and subsequently obtaining a lien through the judicial process. Only at that time would a formerly unsecured creditor become secured by the **judicial lien**. See Chapter 1, Section 1, supra.[1]

In general, an Article 9 secured party can acquire rights in the debtor's personal property that are senior to later-in-time secured creditors (including judicial lien creditors) and buyers. (Note, however, that much of Article 9—and consequently much of these materials—is concerned with conditions, qualifications, and exceptions to this generalization.) An unsecured creditor, on the other hand, is subject to the "race of diligence"—it generally is junior to earlier-in-time secured creditors and must obtain a judicial lien in order to take priority over later-in-time secured creditors. See Chapter 1, Section 1, supra.

How does a debtor's bankruptcy affect security interests and other liens? Bankruptcy law is complex and interesting enough to be the subject of a separate course. Although the following brief overview of bankruptcy is greatly simplified, it will suffice for our immediate purposes. Chapter 10 details many of the ways in which a debtor's bankruptcy affects Article 9 secured parties.

---

1. The rights of other kinds of secured creditors, such as holders of **statutory liens** and mortgagees of real property (land and buildings), vary enormously according to the law of each state. Those creditors may enforce some of their rights against the debtor's property only through judicial proceedings.

The substantive law of bankruptcy is contained in the federal Bankruptcy Code (title 11, U.S. Code). Enacted in 1978, the Bankruptcy Code superseded the Bankruptcy Act of 1898, which had been amended many times and substantially overhauled in 1938. The filing of a petition by or against a debtor commences a bankruptcy case (see BC 301; BC 302(a); BC 303(b)), and creates an "estate" comprised of all the legal and equitable interests of the debtor in property as of the commencement of the case. BC 541(a). When the petition is filed under Chapter 7 of the Bankruptcy Code, which contemplates liquidating the debtor's nonexempt assets and distributing the proceeds to creditors, the United States trustee[2] appoints an interim trustee, who will continue to serve as *the* trustee in bankruptcy unless the creditors elect another person to the position. See BC 701; BC 702.

The bankruptcy trustee is a representative of creditors, primarily unsecured creditors. The trustee is charged with the duty, inter alia, of collecting and reducing to money the property of the estate and distributing the money to creditors. See BC 704. The Bankruptcy Code affords to the trustee the power to avoid (i.e., undo) certain valid prebankruptcy transactions, including those that have the effect of improperly preferring one creditor to another and those that are fraudulent. See generally BC 544–548; Chapter 10, infra.

Chapter 11 cases contemplate that the debtor's enterprise will be reorganized; that is, the enterprise will continue and the claims against the debtor will be scaled down or extended or both. In Chapter 11, the debtor's management ordinarily remains in control of the enterprise as the "debtor in possession." A trustee normally is appointed only when management has been guilty of fraud, dishonesty, incompetence, or gross mismanagement. See BC 1104(a). The debtor in possession enjoys the avoiding powers of a trustee. See BC 1107(a).

One important, and immediate, effect of a bankruptcy filing is the automatic stay of virtually all activities of creditors directed toward collection of their debts. See BC 362(a). This means that the state law "race of diligence" for unsecured creditors ends when the debtor enters bankruptcy.

Except for some special priority rules for certain types of claims, unsecured creditors share pro rata in their common debtor's bankruptcy. In contrast, federal bankruptcy law generally respects a secured creditor's claim to the value of its collateral. The following example may assist in comparing the treatment of secured and unsecured claims in bankruptcy:[3]

A debtor in a bankruptcy case has three creditors, each owed $100, for a total of $300 of debt. One creditor is secured by $100 of assets (i.e., fully secured), and the other two creditors are unsecured. The debtor's

---

2. The Attorney General appoints one United States trustee and one or more assistant United States trustees for each of 21 regions. See 28 U.S.C. §§ 581; 582. The United States trustee serves for a term of five years and, like the assistants, is subject to removal by the Attorney General. Id.

3. The treatment of secured claims in bankruptcy is dealt with in detail in Chapter 10, infra.

trustee in bankruptcy sells all the assets for cash and, after payment of all fees and expenses, $150 in cash (of which $100 is attributable to the property that was subject to the security interest) remains. What result? The fully secured creditor would have its claim satisfied in full, leaving $50 to be distributed between the two remaining creditors, each of which claims $100. Each unsecured creditor, then, would receive a distribution of $25 or "25 cents on the dollar," i.e., $50 (assets) â $200 (claims).

Given these obvious advantages of secured credit for creditors, it is easy to see why in the Prototype Main Motors and Firstbank preferred to have a security interest in collateral. Because Abel's purchase of a new automobile and Main Motors' automobile inventory purchases represent very large dollar amounts when compared with their respective net worths and incomes, they had little choice but to agree to give collateral as a condition to obtaining the credit. Virtually all consumer automobile install-ment financing and automobile dealer inventory financing is done on a secured basis. Even if unsecured credit had been available, the absence of collateral could have resulted in a much higher interest rate to compensate the financers for the additional risk.

These observations lead to yet other questions: Why do some creditors extend unsecured credit? By conferring senior status (in and out of bank-ruptcy) on Firstbank, would Main Motors' unsecured creditors charge higher interest rates that would offset any reductions in interest rates paid by Main Motors to Firstbank as a result of providing collateral? Suffice it to observe, for now, that factors such as disparities in bargaining power and information, profit margins of sellers of goods and providers of services on unsecured credit, the relative size and duration of credit extensions, the costs of creating secured financings, disparities among creditors in their ability to monitor the debtor's financial activities and use of collateral, and market competition all serve to explain current financing patterns, to be addressed shortly, which involve a mix of secured and unsecured credit.

A related question should be raised here, although its answer must be deferred. A positive explanation of why debtors sometimes give and credi-tors sometimes take secured credit under current law does not provide a normative justification for the advantages the current legal regime affords to secured claims. Secured credit imposes costs, particularly on the hapless unsecured creditors of a financially distressed debtor. As we shall see, whether and how the social benefits conferred by secured credit can justify those costs has inspired a lively scholarly debate. See Chapter 11, Section 6, infra.

Although collateral provides important advantages for a creditor, its significance in the extension of credit should not be overemphasized. For example, a lawyer who thinks that the security interest is the most important part of a credit transaction will be corrected quickly by a banker or merchant. From the point of view of a lender or seller, the most important safeguard for the credit is the likelihood that the debtor will pay voluntarily. Evaluation of this likelihood requires mature judgment of the debtor's character, ability, and financial status, and sometimes of the business outlook generally. Recourse to the most ironclad security interest is sure to be costly. Executives and lawyers must spend valuable time to enforce the security interest (perhaps fighting off claims of other creditors in the process) and dispose of such diverse collateral as steel, oil, cattle, and blouses—unwieldy merchandise for a banker, whose stock in trade is money. Indeed, enforcement of a security interest in collateral represents a serious breakdown of the financing operation, whose profit depends on a rapid and routine flow of money. Creditors regard the opportunity to enforce a security interest with something of the zest with which a merchant regards the opportunity to file a claim under an insurance policy.

This does not suggest that security arrangements are without value or that bankers and merchants so regard them. The most canny banker or credit manager makes errors in judgment; business conditions shift. While recourse to security ranks far below voluntary payment, it stands well above loss of the entire claim or receipt of a small dividend at the conclusion of extended bankruptcy proceedings. In addition, in consumer transactions the security device often is used as leverage against the debtor. The threat of depriving the debtor of goods that he or she needs or prizes (such as a refrigerator or an automobile) often encourages "voluntary" payment, even though the used goods would realize little for the creditor upon sale. In 1985 the Federal Trade Commission sought to limit the "hostage value" of certain consumer collateral by prohibiting as an unfair trade practice the taking of security interests in household goods unless the secured party maintains possession of the collateral or has extended the credit that enabled the debtor to acquire it. See FTC Rule on Credit Practices, 16 C.F.R. § 444.2(a)(4).

(B) PATTERNS OF FINANCING

Recent decades witnessed profound changes in the patterns of consumer and business financing and in the financial services industry generally. Nonetheless, some useful generalizations about financing patterns remain possible.

Unsecured Consumer Credit. "Consumer credit" generally refers to credit extended to natural persons for personal, family, or household purposes. Much consumer credit is unsecured. Examples are credit extended pursuant to bank and other **lender credit card** arrangements,[4] credit extended by department stores and gasoline companies under **seller credit cards** or charge accounts,[5] and personal or **signature loans** extended by

---

4. Charges made pursuant to lender credit cards constitute loans by the card issuer to the cardholder. The loans are advanced when the card issuer pays, or becomes obligated to pay, the merchant who accepts the credit card in connection with the sale of goods or services.

5. Some "private label" credit cards nominally issued by sellers of goods actually are issued by third-party lenders who may or may not be affiliated with the seller. Also, some credit cards and charge account arrangements provide that the seller receives a

finance companies, banks, thrift institutions, and credit unions. Consumer credit usually is extended with the expectation that it will be repaid from the consumer's future earnings, an expectation often based on satisfactory credit reports obtained from private credit reporting services.

Unsecured Business Credit; Trade Credit. Many business borrowers also obtain unsecured credit. The most creditworthy corporations issue short-term (i.e., 30–to 90–day) debt instruments known as **commercial paper**. Holders of these instruments who wish to dispose of them before they become due can trade (sell) them in a secondary market. As long as the issuer's credit remains satisfactory (according to **rating agencies** such as Moody's and Standard & Poor's), the debt typically is repaid by issuing and selling new commercial paper as the old paper matures. Corporations also issue longer-term debt securities (**bonds** or **debentures**), many of which are publicly traded.

Creditworthy business borrowers obtain both medium-and long-term financing from commercial banks, as well. Bank credit is extended in a variety of forms. Arrangements known as **revolving credits** ("revolvers") allow a borrower to borrow, repay, and reborrow amounts as needed during an agreed time period, provided that the aggregate unpaid amount of loans does not at any time exceed the agreed cap. Some revolvers obligate the bank to extend loans (a **committed credit facility**), subject to certain conditions precedent (such as the absence of any default by the borrower). Others create a **line of credit**, pursuant to which the lending bank is not obligated to lend. The line of credit agreement ("line letter") governs the terms and conditions of the loans that the borrower requests and the lender, in its discretion, elects to make from time to time. Loans outstanding under lines of credit often are to be repaid on the lender's demand or within a relatively short time following demand. Under other credit arrangements, known as **term loans**, the loan advances are to be paid back in installments over a period of time.[6] Some revolvers automatically convert into term loans after a specified period of time, such as two or three years.

Bank credit agreements typically contain provisions dealing with (i) the amount of credit, interest rate, commitment fee, repayment terms, and the like; (ii) conditions precedent (in committed facilities); (iii) affirmative covenants (e.g., the borrower will comply with the law, pay all taxes, give financial statements to the lender periodically); (iv) negative covenants (e.g., the borrower will not incur debt or create security interests except within agreed limits, will not merge with another entity, will not sell substantially all of its assets); (v) events of default (e.g., bankruptcy, nonpayment of the loan when due, default on debt owed to another lender); and (vi) remedies (e.g., acceleration of entire amount of loan).

security interest in goods sold to secure the price.

6. Many term loans also are made by insurance companies, although the transac-

tions usually are structured as a purchase of a note by the insurance company—a "private placement."

For most businesses, the banks, finance companies, and other professional lenders are not the most significant source of short-term credit. Instead, the most important providers of short-term credit are other businesses that typically give extended terms (usually 30 to 90 days) for payment for goods and services—**trade credit**.[7] Most businesses not only receive trade credit in their purchases of goods and services but also grant trade credit in connection with sales of their own goods and services. Principal advantages of trade credit are its general availability and the absence of costly negotiations or formalities associated with longer-term arrangements such as bank credits. From the standpoint of the trade creditor, the credit extensions facilitate the sales of goods and services to those who are not in a position to pay cash or who otherwise would patronize a competitor.

Secured Financing of Sales of Goods. As we have seen, unsecured credit is common and important in both the consumer and the business environments. We shall see, next, that the same can be said of secured credit. We turn first to secured financing in its most familiar (at least to consumers) and historically significant role—secured credit extended to buyers of goods (including consumer goods, equipment used in business, and inventory held for sale or lease).

Consumer Goods. Lee Abel was not unique in entering into a secured installment purchase of a car; most automobiles are sold on a secured, installment basis. Consider the volume of consumer credit extended in the United States. By year-end 1999, outstanding consumer credit obligations stood at over $1,460 billion, with more than one-half of that amount being automobile and other installment credit.[8] This staggering figure is even more startling when compared with $4.5 billion in 1939, $15 billion in 1951, and $750 billion in 1990.[9] Increases in these figures reflect both inflation and the expansion of the economy.[10] For example, annual disposable income rose from $226.1 billion in 1951 to $6.775 trillion in 1999, an increase of more than 2,900%.[11] But in 1951 installment credit was equal to approximately 6.6% of disposable income; and in 1999 the percentage was 21%.[12] United States consumers obviously have been increasingly willing to encumber their future earnings.

---

7. Of course, many consumers also receive short-term, unsecured credit from businesses such as the electric company, lawn care service, plumber, cable TV company, and newspaper delivery service.

8. Fed. Res. Stat. Rel. G19 (August 7, 2000). The figure includes both secured and unsecured credit; however, consumer automobile financing typically involves secured credit. Also, the figure includes installment credit extended in connection with services; it is not limited to goods-related credit.

9. 77 Fed. Res. Bull., May, 1991, at A38, A53; 42 Fed. Res. Bull., Dec., 1956, at 1352, 1370.

10. The dollar amounts mentioned in this paragraph have not been adjusted to take account of inflation, but nonetheless suffice to illustrate substantial increases and expansion.

11. Bur. of Econ. Anal., Surv. of Curr. Bus. 46 (August 2000); 42 Fed. Res. Bull., Dec., 1956, at 1352, 1370.

12. 86 Fed. Res. Bull. 624, Sept., 2000, at 624; 42 Fed. Res. Bull., Dec., 1956, at 1352, 1370.

In the case of consumer goods, secured credit commonly is extended by the seller (dealer), who retains a security interest in the goods to secure payment of the purchase price (or the balance of the price remaining after a down payment). Because dealers usually prefer to obtain the sale price immediately after the sale, rather than in installments over time, dealers commonly enter into an arrangement with a secured financer, such as a bank or finance company, whereby the dealer assigns to the financer the buyer's payment obligation and the security interest and the financer pays the dealer the unpaid portion of the purchase price for the goods. To facilitate this arrangement, which is similar to the automobile chattel paper financing discussed in Chapter 7, Section 1, infra, the financer usually supplies the dealer with the form of credit application and retail install-ment sale-security agreement and often approves the consumer's credit before the dealer makes the sale. The Prototype transaction presents the entire operation (secured sale by the dealer and assignment to the financer) in greater detail in the concrete setting of automobile financing. When expensive consumer goods, such as motor vehicles and boats, are involved, it is not unusual for a third-party lender to make a secured loan directly to the buyer to cover a substantial portion of the purchase price. For example, instead of obtaining credit from Main Motors, Abel might have obtained a secured purchase-money loan from Abel's regular bank: the bank would have provided funds for the specific purpose of enabling Abel to pay for the new car, and Abel would have secured the repayment obligation by giving the bank a security interest in the new car.

An increasingly varied group of creditors holds consumer installment credit obligations. Probably the most significant trend during the last several decades has been the growing dominance of commercial banks in the installment credit market. More recently, deregulation has permitted savings institutions to enter the consumer installment credit market. Perhaps the most striking aspect of Table 1 is the amount of the install-ment credit obligations held in "pools of securitized assets."[13] By 1990 almost 10% of the obligations were held in these "pools," although this category of holdings was not even listed in the 1982 figures. And by the end of 1999 that share had grown to more than 35%. The following table reflects the shifting market shares in the consumer installment credit market.[14]

Table 1

Type of Institution	Credits Outstanding (In Millions)						
	1940	**1950**	**1960**	**1970**	**1982**	**1990**	**1999**
Commercial Banks	1,452	5,798	16,672	45,398	152,069	351,695	499,800
Finance Companies	2,278	5,315	15,435	27,678	94,322	136,154	181,600
Credit Unions	171	590	3,923	12,986	47,253	91,203	167,900
Retail Outlets	1,596	2,898	6,295	13,900	51,154	46,858	80,300
Savings Institutions						49,594	61,500
Pools of Securitized Assets						75,437	435,100

13. Securitization is discussed below in this Section.

14. Fed. Res. Stat. Rel. G19 (August 7, 2000); 77 Fed. Res. Bull., May, 1991, at A38; 69 Fed. Res. Bull., Nov., 1983, at A40; 60 Fed. Res. Bull., May, 1974, at A50.

The legal regulation of consumer credit is extensive and complex enough to warrant a separate course at many law schools. Special consumer protection rules are discussed in several Chapters of this book.

Business Equipment. When consumer goods are bought on credit the financing necessarily anticipates that the debtor will earn income from other sources, usually wages or salary. Business equipment (taxicabs, trucks, computers, commercial refrigerators), however, is intended to assist in generating income that will help repay the credit and even leave a profit for the user. The installment financing of sales of business equipment does not match the mammoth scope of consumer financing, but it has played an important role in aiding productive activity—particularly by small businesses.[15] The financing patterns for buyers of business equipment are similar in many respects to those for consumer buyers. Both dealer-arranged financing, in which the dealer takes the security interest and assigns it to a secured financer, and third-party direct secured lending to buyers are common.

Inventory. Sellers of goods extend secured credit routinely to wholesalers and dealers who hold the goods for sale as their inventory; however, seller-financed sales of inventory are much less common than seller-financed sales of consumer goods and business equipment. Sellers of expensive items that will become the buyer's inventory (e.g., the manufacturers of construction equipment and automobiles) normally insist on cash payment of the purchase price upon delivery. Other sellers, as we have seen, typically extend unsecured, short-term trade credit to buyers of inventory. Dealers and wholesalers who need longer-term inventory financing typically look to third-party secured financers, much as Main Motors looked to Firstbank for inventory financing in the Prototype.

Other Secured Financing. Much secured credit is extended for purposes other than to finance buyers' purchases of consumer goods, business equipment, and inventory. Many business, large and small, must supplement their capital by borrowing, in order to obtain adequate funds to remain in operation. Funds borrowed under **working capital** or **operating capital** lending arrangements may be used for payment of salaries, rent, utilities, and other expenses of operation as well as for the purchase of equipment, supplies, and inventory. Many of these financings are secured, especially in cases of small-to medium-sized borrowers. These loans frequently are structured as uncommitted lines of credit or as revolving credit arrangements that, at some point, convert into term loans, not unlike the unsecured credit arrangements discussed above. Other secured financings

---

15. Secured financing has been significant in aiding smaller business enterprises to buy a wide range of equipment, such as printing presses, laundry equipment, mining and oil field equipment, drink dispensing and bar equipment, commercial refrigerators, machine tools, power shovels, cranes, road- building equipment of all types, agricultural equipment, bottling machines, electronic data processing equipment, dental and medical equipment, hairstyling equipment, trucks, diesel engines, and generators. This list can only suggest the wide variety of equipment involved.

are highly specialized and bear little resemblance to traditional unsecured lending arrangements.

Following are descriptions of some typical financing patterns that, although common, are particularly complex. They are included here with a view toward giving you a "taste" for the diverse contexts in which secured financing plays a central role and introducing you to some transactions about which you may have heard or read and in which you someday may play a role. We do not expect you to memorize these materials, or even to understand them fully at first reading. As will become apparent, the descriptions present only the basics; important details and qualifications have been omitted in the interest of brevity and comprehensibility. Please remember that while the essential elements of many transactions conform to these descriptions, the variations in terms, structure, collateral, and purposes of these secured financings are infinite.

Inventory and Receivables Financings. Consumer goods and business equipment, both of which are purchased for use, must be contrasted with goods held for sale. Goods held for sale include not only inventory, such as cars, trucks, and refrigerators in a dealer's showroom or warehouse, but also raw materials and components awaiting or in the course of manufacture: nuts and bolts to be used for assembly and bales of cotton held by a spinner or going through the spindles. The distinctive fact about inventory, and one that creates complex and fascinating legal problems, is that all parties hope for rapid turnover and liquidation of the goods into cash. The goods often will be (re)sold on credit, thereby creating an account receivable to which the secured creditor's security interest may be transferred.

In many cases creditors who make loans secured by inventory and receivables rely heavily on the collateral as their "way out"—their source of repayment. The current jargon used to refer to transactions in which the lender relies heavily on the value of its collateral is **asset-based financing**. In a typical arrangement a borrower would be required to maintain at all times a **borrowing base** value of inventory and qualifying (not in default) receivables that is at least equal to the outstanding loan balance. Normally the borrowing base would be a percentage (say, 60%) of the book value of inventory plus a percentage (say, 75%) of the face amount of receivables. The excess of collateral value over the outstanding loan balance provides the lender with a "cushion" that offers protection if the borrower defaults. Reporting requirements and, in some cases, inspections of inventory put the lender in a position to monitor the collateral and act to protect its interests if the borrower experiences a financial downslide. In many instances a borrower's receivables, which usually represent its most liquid assets (other than cash), are the principal collateral on which secured lenders rely.[16] The receivables financing Prototype in Chapter 9, Section 1(B), provides a detailed illustration of a "borrowing base" financing secured by accounts and inventory.

---

16. The general setting for receivables financing is developed in detail in Chapter 9,   Section 1, infra.

"All Assets" Secured Financing. A pattern has emerged in certain credit markets whereby lenders routinely take a security interest in all of a borrowers assets.[17] A typical example is a commercial bank loan to a small business. The individual controlling shareholders of a closely-held corporate borrower generally are required to give a guaranty of payment as additional security. Compared to asset-based lenders, these "all assets" lenders may place relatively slight reliance on the collateral's value and the individuals' guaranties as a source of repayment. Instead, they tend to rely heavily on the borrower's predicted cash flow and overall ability to pay. Like those financers who take consumer goods collateral for its hostage value instead of its market value, the "all asset" lenders probably look to the collateral and guaranties primarily as a tool for obtaining power over the borrower so as to inhibit business decisions and investments that could undermine their position.[18]

Acquisition Financing: Leveraged Buyouts. Another financing pattern involves obtaining a security interest in virtually all of a debtor's assets, but that is its only similarity to the "all assets" financings just mentioned. The "takeover" phenomenon of the 1980's fueled demand for secured credit to finance acquisitions of controlling interests in publicly held corporations. Although the transaction structures were and remain quite varied, these **leveraged buyouts** ("LBO's") exhibit certain common patterns. Usually a substantial percentage of the purchase price of the corporate stock of the entity to be acquired (the "target") is borrowed (hence, the **leverage**); those borrowings typically are secured by substantially all of the assets of the *target*, once it is acquired.[19] Many of these secured loans, usually made by **syndicates** of commercial banks, have involved hundreds of millions of dollars and, in some cases, billions. The LBO secured lenders typically rely heavily on collateral value. In many cases unsecured debt also is incurred in order to fund a portion of the purchase price. Because of the high leverage and the dominant position of the secured lender, this unsecured debt became known as **junk bonds** (or, even more bluntly, "junk").[20]

"Special Purpose Vehicle" Financing: Leveraged Leasing. Some very innovative forms of receivables financings involve the use of a type of borrower called a **special purpose vehicle** ("SPV"). In these financings the SPV, which may be a corporation, partnership, or trust, is organized for

17. The borrower's real property may or may not be taken as collateral, depending on its value and the attendant costs.

18. Professor Robert Scott has dubbed these lenders "relational" creditors because the value of the collateral seems to be primarily in its impact on the relationship between the borrower and the lender. See Scott, A Relational Theory of Secured Financing, 86 Colum.L.Rev. 901 (1986).

19. Because the assets of the target are used as collateral, these transactions have long been known as "bootstrap" transactions, reflecting the notion that the target seems to be "buying itself." The vanities of the 1980's investment bankers being what they were, the "bootstrap" label was replaced by the "LBO" nomenclature.

20. The investment bankers, of course, prefer another term: "high-yield securities."

the specific purpose of participating in the financing.[21] **Leveraged leasing** is one such form of financing.

A business entity may choose to lease equipment instead of buying it for a variety of reasons (often including its inability to use the tax benefits of ownership, such as accelerated depreciation, because it lacks sufficient taxable income). For example, long-term leasing is a typical means by which airlines obtain the use of commercial aircraft. The lessor often will be an SPV (typically a trust) formed by "equity" investors who (through the SPV) invest in the equipment and lease it to the lessee. These investors often wish to obtain, through the SPV, the tax benefits of ownership that the lessee cannot use. The investors capitalize the SPV with only a portion (say, 20%) of the funds necessary to purchase the equipment. The SPV then borrows the additional necessary funds, pays for the equipment, and enters into a lease with the lessee. By causing the SPV to borrow a substantial portion of the purchase price (i.e., "leveraging" the invest- ment), the investors achieve 100% of the tax benefits of ownership by putting up only a fraction of the cash necessary to buy the equipment. As collateral for its borrowing, the SPV grants to the lender a security interest in the equipment (subject to the lessee's rights under the lease, of course) and in the lease itself (including the rental stream, payable over time by the lessee).

Because the equipment and the lease are the SPV's only assets, the lender must be satisfied with the value of the equipment and the creditwor- thiness of the lessee.[22] The lessee is instructed to make the lease payments directly to the lender, as assignee of the lease, and those payments are applied by the lender against the SPV's secured debt. If for any reason (such as the lessee's default combined with unanticipated obsolescence of the equipment) the equipment and the lease are not adequate to satisfy the SPV's debt, then the lender will suffer a loss. It will have no recourse against any of the investors. If the lessee does not default and the secured debt is satisfied, then the SPV (and, indirectly, the investors) will be entitled to the **residual value** of the equipment at the end of the lease. The investors expect that value (combined with any tax savings arising out of the SPV's ownership of the equipment, which are passed on to the investors) to be sufficient for them to recover their investments and enjoy a return thereon. Depending on the value of the equipment at the end of the lease term, however, that expectation may or may not be realized. Because the lender's repayment turns on its ability to collect the rental stream from the lessee and on the value of the equipment, the lender must be assured

---

21. Hence the "vehicle" denomination, reflecting the SPV's role as an tool or imple- ment necessary for the financing structure.

22. In some transactions the lessor is not an SPV but is an operating company that has other assets and other liabilities. In those transactions the debt of the lessor to the lender normally is **limited recourse** debt. That is, the lending agreement provides that the lender is entitled to look only to the collateral—the equipment and the lease—for satisfaction of the debt. The lender is not entitled to satisfy the debt out of other assets of the lessor.

that its security interest will withstand attack by any creditor of, or trustee in bankruptcy for, the SPV, any investor, or the lessee.

"Special Purpose Vehicle" Financing: Securitization. **Securitization** transactions (sometimes called "structured finance") are similar in some respects to leveraged leasing transactions, but there are some important distinctions. First, securitization involves the creation of debt securities that are backed by "pools" of receivables (rights to payment); traditional leveraged leasing transactions involve one or more equipment leases to the same lessee. Almost any kind of receivable can support securitization financings; the types seem to increase daily. For example, the future royalties of David Bowie and other recording artists have been securitized, and leveraged leases themselves have been pooled for this purpose. Second, whereas professional lenders (usually banks and finance companies) typically engage in leveraged leasing transactions, securitization involves the issuance of debt securities that can be sold to other kinds of investors. Third, the receivables involved in a securitization transaction initially are owned by a non-SPV operating company, whereas in a leveraged lease the SPV-lessor normally is the original lessor.

A typical securitization transaction begins with a business entity that originates receivables. For example, the originator could be a bank that holds consumer installment sale contracts (as Firstbank holds Lee Abel's contract in the Prototype) or it could be a financial institution that generates credit card receivables (rights to payment from holders of credit cards issued by the institution). The first receivables used in securitization transactions were home mortgage loans secured by residential real estate. These transactions probably remain the most commercially significant securitizations as measured by dollar volume.

> The first structured financing came in 1970 when the newly created Government National Mortgage Association began publicly trading "pass-through" securities. In a mortgage pass-through security, the investor purchases a fractional undivided interest in a pool of mortgage loans, and is entitled to share in the interest income and principal payments generated by the underlying mortgages. Mortgage lenders originate pools of mortgages with similar characteristics as to quality, term, and interest rate. The pool is placed in a trust. Then, through either a government agency, a private conduit, or direct placement, certificates of ownership are sold to investors. Income from the mortgage pool passes through to the investors.[23]

A similar pattern is followed in most other securitizations: The originator transfers a large number of receivables (usually referred to as a "pool") to an SPV, and the SPV issues debt securities. As in the leveraged leasing transaction, because the SPV's only assets are the receivables, collections of the receivables are the only source of payment of interest on, and repayment of principal of, the securities. The funds generated by the sale of the securities are used to pay the originator for the receivables it sells to the

---

23. S. Schwarcz, Structured Finance 4 (2d ed. 1993).

SPV. (The financial intermediaries that arrange the transaction take their shares of the funds as well.) Although the investors are not necessarily knowledgeable enough to evaluate, on their own, the quality of the receivables, disclosure documents provide information concerning the quality of the receivables (e.g., past history of collections of similar receivables, nature and quality of the collateral (if any) securing the assigned receivables) and the risks that the investors are undertaking. Investors in publicly traded securities also may be guided by a rating agency's ratings of the securities.

Before making their investment, the investors must be assured that neither the SPV's nor the originator's insolvency will interfere with the collection of the receivables and the application of those collections to payments to the investors. But, the fact that the receivables originally were owned by the originator, an operating company with liabilities, creates a problem that the lender in a typical leveraged lease transaction does not encounter: making sure that the SPV and the operating company are not linked and that the transfer of the receivables to the SPV will be effective against creditors of the operating company (i.e., making sure that the SPV is **bankruptcy remote** from the originator). Indeed, in securitization transactions it is not unusual for the SPV's obligations to the investors, on the securities, to be *un*secured. It is the transfer of the receivables from the originator to the SPV that is of particular concern.[24]

Securitization can provide an originator with a lower cost of funds than a conventional loan secured by the receivables. Even the fully secured, conventional secured lender faces a variety of risks in the event of a borrower's bankruptcy or other financial distress. By removing the receivables entirely from the asset base of the originator, however, securitization of the receivables may produce less risk and, consequently, lower financing costs for the originator.

Agricultural Financing. The agricultural industry, including the proverbial "family farmers," the large, corporate "agri-business" concerns, and the myriad other businesses in the chain of production, processing, and distribution, depends heavily on secured credit. Farms, like many other businesses, need expensive equipment; what has been observed above about financing sales of business equipment applies as well to farm equipment. Agricultural financing also presents some unique characteristics:

Like Caesar's Gaul, agricultural lending is divided into three parts: (1) long-term credit to finance the purchase or improvement of real estate by a farmer or rancher; (2) intermediate production credit to finance the purchase of equipment and livestock; and (3) short-term loans to cover current operating expenses, including annual crop production. . . .

The variety of collateral put up by farmers and ranchers as security for loans is very broad; it includes the farmland itself, fixtures, growing and future crops (including those pledged to landowner-lessors), products of crops (such as harvested grain), livestock, equipment, and a wide assort-

---

24. As we shall see in Chapter 9, Section 1(D), infra, applicable law may characterize the transfer as a sale or transfer for security.

ment of intangibles, including accounts receivable and U.S. Department of Agriculture "entitlements."[25]

Article 9 and a wide variety of other statutes, both state and federal, contain rules specifically addressing some perceived special problems of agricultural financing.

Secured Financing in the Securities Markets. Secured financing plays an indispensable role in modern securities markets. The transactional patterns vary widely, and most cannot be explained and understood in the absence of a broad and deep treatment of the operations of securities markets. However, some very general examples follow:

> (i) An individual investor who has physical possession of a stock certificate registered in the investor's own name with the issuing corporation wishes to borrow from a local bank and **pledge** (i.e., grant a security interest in) the stock certificate to the bank.
>
> (ii) An individual investor who has a securities account with a stockbroker wishes to borrow from a local bank and pledge to the bank stocks and bonds "in" the investor's account.
>
> (iii) In order to buy securities on **margin**, an individual investor who has a securities account with a stockbroker wishes to obtain credit from the stockbroker and pledge to the stockbroker the securities to be purchased.
>
> (iv) A stockbroker wishes to obtain an "overnight" secured loan from a bank in order to obtain funds needed to settle (pay) its end-of-day payment obligations to other professional securities industry participants.

In the securities markets, secured financing, including **repo** financing,[26] involves truly staggering amounts each day, especially in the United States government securities markets. In late 1999 primary dealers reported approximately $1.2 trillion in repos on their balance sheets.[27] The legal

---

25. B. Clark, The Law of Secured Transactions Under the Uniform Commercial Code ¶ 8.01, at 8–1 to 8–2.

26. "Repurchase agreements," or "repos," are an important means of financing, especially for government securities dealers.

In a repo, a seller of a security (a funds borrower) transfers the security to a buyer (a funds lender) under an arrangement whereby the securities seller agrees to repurchase the security on a specified date (often the next day) at a specified price, and the securities buyer agrees to resell the security back to the seller. From the perspective of the buyer, the transaction is a reverse repurchase agreement (reverse repo). Repos serve the function of secured borrowings and loans, although they are denominated as sales and resales. The economics of the transaction are such that when the seller (funds borrower) pays the repurchase price (i.e. repays the loan), the buyer (funds lender) receives a profit (a return on the money loaned). The legal characterization of repos . . . is not clear.

Mooney, Beyond Negotiability: A New Model for Transfer and Pledge of Interests in Securities Controlled by Intermediaries, 12 Cardozo L. Rev. 305, 324 n. 51 (1990).

27. 85 Fed Res. Bull, Dec., 1999, at 797. This figure double-counts the transactions by adding both sides of each trade. Nevertheless, because it includes figures only for primary dealers, it probably approximates the aggregate volume. See M. Stigum, The Repo and Reverse Markets 7–8 (1989).

and operational aspects of taking collateral in the third and fourth examples mentioned above are likely to be encountered only by securities market professionals and their specialized counsel; however, lenders and their lawyers confront the first two examples with great frequency. We shall consider them in Chapter 9, Section 3, infra.

(C) Real Property Collateral, Guaranties of Payment, and Other Credit Enhancements

Although the focus here is on personal property collateral, one must keep in mind that both consumers and businesses also obtain credit on the strength of real property collateral, e.g., through home mortgage loans, second mortgage "home equity" loans, construction loans, long-term "permanent" mortgage loans, etc. Moreover, there are other means of supporting an extension of credit, such as a third-party's guaranty of payment or a bank's letter of credit. In many cases personal property collateral is taken in a transaction that also involves real property collateral, guaranties of payment, or other credit enhancements. The interplay between the law governing security interests in personal property (Article 9) and that governing the other aspects of the transaction can give rise to some interesting problems. See Chapter 11, Section 4, infra; Chapter 12, Section 3(A), infra.

Section 2.   A Roadmap to Secured Transactions Under Uniform Commercial Code Article 9

(A) Background

Article 9 of the Uniform Commercial Code substantially rewrote the law of secured transactions; it was the most revolutionary of the Articles of the UCC. By virtually abandoning the concept of "title," UCC Article 2 required a drastic change in the focus of legal thinking about sales. But Article 9 even more sharply changed the focus of legal thought about secured transactions.

Prior to the UCC, a creditor seeking security had to choose among a bewildering variety of legal "devices"—pledge, chattel mortgage, conditional sale, trust receipt, assignment of accounts receivable, factor's lien. Each "device" operated within complex (and often unclear) rules governing its scope and the procedures for its validation and enforcement; the choice of the wrong "device" was subject to perils reminiscent of common-law pleading.

The UCC swept away the separate security "devices." The old names (pledge, conditional sale) may still be used, but the label does not control the result. Instead, Article 9 prescribes general rules for all secured transactions, with some variations depending on the type of transaction.

The decision to establish a unitary approach to secured transactions was one of the UCC's most important contributions to the legal system. The important questions that remain relate, for the most part, to whether the maximum possible benefit has been gained from what most agree was a brilliant idea.

Article 9 was the first part of the UCC to undergo significant revision by the UCC's sponsors. Although for a time the UCC's sponsors held the line against most proposed improvements in the UCC, by 1966 the pressure to modify Article 9 became irresistible. The work of the Article 9 Review Committee began in 1967; its efforts culminated in the 1972 Official Text. Without affecting the basic structure of Article 9, the 1972 revisions effected numerous changes (some of them very important) to the Article. The 1978 Official Text made additional material changes to Article 9 as it dealt with securities and other investment property. Article 9's treatment of investment property was overhauled in conjunction with the revision of Article 8 in 1994; its treatment of letters of credit was adjusted in conjunction with the revision of Article 5 in 1995.

In 1999 the UCC's sponsors approved Revised Article 9. Revised Article 9 is the product of nearly a decade of work—first by a Permanent Editorial Board study committee, which in December, 1992, issued a report recommending revision, and then by a drafting committee that met fifteen times from 1993 to 1998. Even after Revised Article 9 was officially promulgated, the work continued: As interested persons stumbled across stylistic and other minor errors and occasionally spotted an error that was more substantive, the sponsors responded by correcting the Official Text and Comments. Following an intensive and unprecedented effort, Revised Article 9 has been enacted in all 50 states and the District of Columbia. It became effective in all but four of the enacting jurisdictions on July 1, 2001. By January 1, 2002 it will be effective in each enacting jurisdiction.

Like the early drafting efforts and the 1972 revision, Revised Article 9 is informed by commercial practice. The conflicting interests affected by Article 9 have had able and alert representatives who invested time and energy to participate in the drafting and otherwise work toward improving the legal regulation of those interests. (Comparatively speaking, very few worry about sales law under Article 2; at least between commercial parties, the problems usually can be solved by contract.)

We turn now to an overview of the substance of Revised Article 9. You should read through this overview several times, to glean a general understanding of the principal terms and concepts. As the course progresses and the details mount up, reference to the overview may restore a needed perspective.

(B) SCOPE OF ARTICLE 9; SECURITY INTERESTS IN COLLATERAL

Article 9 "applies to ... a transaction, regardless of its form, that creates a security interest in personal property or fixtures by contract."

R9–109(a)(1). This provision makes sense only if we consult R1–201(37), which defines the term "security interest," in pertinent part, as "an interest in personal property or fixtures which secures payment or performance of an obligation."[1] The broad reach of Article 9 is limited by various exclusions set forth in R9–109(c) and (d). The scope of Article 9 is discussed in Chapter 8, infra.

Article 9 tells us nothing about the obligation that is secured, leaving that to other law. Although we usually think of the obligation as being a contractual promise to repay a loan or to pay the price of goods bought, in theory a security interest could secure virtually any obligation—liquidated or unliquidated, contingent or noncontingent.

"[T]he property subject to a security interest" is the "collateral." R9–102(a)(12). Property can be "carved up" in many ways. Two or more persons might own property "in common," as owners of undivided fractional interests. Or, property can be divided temporally, as in a lease, where the lessee owns the right to use and possession during the lease term and the lessor owns the residual interest that remains at the end or the term. See UCC 2A–103(1)(m), (1)(q) (defining "leasehold interest" and "lessor's residual interest"). A security interest that secures an obligation, however, can be measured in two dimensions at any given point in time: the *value of the collateral* and the *amount of the obligation secured*. The following figure illustrates these two dimensions:

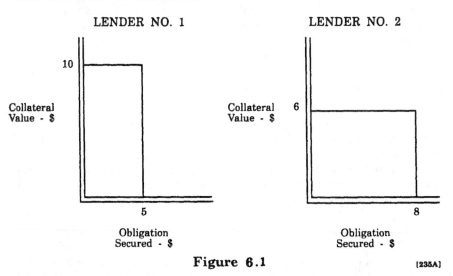

Figure 6.1

[235A]

As you can see, Lender #1 has a security interest in collateral valued at $10 and is owed $5; at this point in time Lender #1 is **oversecured**. Lender #2, on the other hand, is owed $8 but its security interest extends only to

---

1. Certain other transactions—consignments and sales of accounts, chattel paper, payment intangibles, and promissory notes—also are embraced by the definition of "security interest" and by Article 9's basic scope provision, R9–109(a). We shall defer consideration of those transactions for now and focus on interests that secure obligations.

collateral with a value of $6; Lender #2 is **undersecured**. Keep in mind that the value of collateral securing an obligation can change (e.g., by appreciation, depreciation, or the acquisition of additional collateral), as can the amount of the obligation secured (e.g., by additional borrowings, the accrual of interest, and repayments).

(C) THE CAST OF CHARACTERS

The chief protagonists in a secured transaction are the "debtor" and the "secured party." The secured party is "a person in whose favor a security interest has been created." R9–102(a)(72). The debtor is the "person having an interest, other than a security interest or other lien, in the collateral." R9–102(a)(28). Usually, the debtor is the sole owner of the collateral as well as the only person who owes the obligation that the collateral secures. However, there are many possible variations from this straightforward scenario. For example, a corporation might grant a security interest in collateral it owns to secure the indebtedness of its subsidiary. In this situation, the corporation is the debtor; the subsidiary, which owes the secured debt, is a non-debtor "obligor." See R9–102(a)(59) (defining "obligor"). Or, parents might cosign a promissory note with their child, thereby becoming obligated for the same debt as the child, while the child gives a security interest in collateral that he or she owns. Here, the child, who owns the collateral, is the debtor; each parent is an obligor, as is the child. See R9–102, Comment 2.a.

The UCC also deals with the rights of some, but not all, third parties who may claim an interest in collateral covered by a security interest. We already have considered priority contests between a secured party, as a good faith purchaser, and a seller seeking to reclaim goods from a debtor-buyer who has voidable title. See Chapter 1, Section 3, supra. We also have taken note of the trustee in bankruptcy—often a significant player in secured credit when the debtor becomes financially distressed. Other third parties whose rights Article 9 addresses will be mentioned shortly in the discussion of priorities.

(D) CREATION OF A SECURITY INTEREST: ATTACHMENT

The creation of a security interest under Article 9 is embodied in the concept of "attachment." "A security interest attaches to collateral when it becomes enforceable against the debtor with respect to the collateral." R9–203(a). R9–203(b) sets forth three conditions to enforceability, and thus to attachment. These conditions may be met in any order. First, "value" (UCC 1–201(44)) must have been given. Second, the debtor must have "rights in the collateral." Third, the debtor must agree that a security interest will attach *and* either the collateral must be in the secured party's possession or control or the debtor must have signed a security agreement (R9–102(a)(73)) containing a description of the collateral (R9–108). Until all these elements have been satisfied, a security interest does not attach and is not enforceable against the debtor or third parties with respect to the collateral. See R9–203(a), (b). See generally Chapter 7, Section 2, infra.

Although not mentioned as a condition to attachment, the debtor's agreement must address the obligation that is secured by collateral— otherwise one of the two dimensions that mark the borders of a security interest would be missing. Article 9 affords the parties considerable freedom to determine which obligations are secured: "A security agreement may provide that collateral secures . . . future advances or other value." R9–204(c). In addition, "a security agreement may create or provide for a security interest in after-acquired collateral." R9–204(a).[2] But recall that no security interest can attach to the collateral under R9–203(b) until the debtor has "rights" in it.

(E) TYPES OF COLLATERAL

Although Article 9's "unitary" approach to security interests generally treats all security interests the same, different types of collateral receive different treatment in several respects. Before mentioning some of those differences, which derive primarily from differences in the nature of the collateral and in the related financing patterns, it will be useful to identify the various "types" of Article 9 collateral. "Goods" are subdivided into "consumer goods," "equipment," "farm products," and "inventory." Intangible collateral includes "accounts," "deposit accounts," and "general intangibles." Types of paper representing or embodying intangible rights include "chattel paper," "documents," and "instruments," although "chattel paper" may be electronic rather than paper-based. Likewise, "investment property" such as stocks and bonds may be evidenced by paper or may be intangible. Goods affixed to real estate can become "fixtures," although Article 9 leaves to real estate law the determination of what constitutes fixtures. See generally Chapter 11, Section 4, infra. Property acquired by a debtor upon the exchange or disposition of collateral, such as the account (right to payment) that arises when inventory is sold on unsecured credit, constitutes "proceeds." See generally Chapter 7, Section 5, infra.

Although we shall revisit the various types of collateral later in these materials (most of them on several occasions), it would be useful for you to review the statutory definitions in R9–102(a) at this point in your reading. The Comments to R9–102, particularly Comments 4, 5, and 6, contain additional explanations of the terms.

(F) PERFECTION AND PRIORITY

A secured party who wishes to rely on the benefits of a security interest in collateral will be concerned about whether conflicting claims to the collateral could come ahead of its security interest. A baseline rule of

---

2. R9–204(b) limits security interests in after-acquired consumer goods and commercial tort claims.

Article 9 can be found in R9–201: "Except as otherwise provided in [the Uniform Commercial Code], a security agreement is effective according to its terms between the parties, against purchasers of the collateral, and against creditors." That (somewhat awkward) statement generally is understood to mean that an attached security interest in collateral will be senior to conflicting claims unless a provision in the UCC provides otherwise. Much of the remainder of this book is devoted to an examination of the substantial number of provisions otherwise.

In many cases a security interest's priority over other conflicting claims to collateral will depend on whether the security interest is "perfected." Perfection occurs when a security interest has attached and when the applicable steps specified in Article 9, Part 3 (specifically, R9–310 through R9–316) have been taken. R9–308(a). If those steps are taken before attachment, perfection occurs upon attachment. Id. Although there are some specialized means of perfection, the two principal means are (i) the filing of a "financing statement" and (ii) the secured party's taking possession of the collateral. A security interest in some types of collateral can be perfected by either filing or possession (e.g., goods); other types can be perfected only by filing (e.g., accounts) or only by the possession (e.g., money). See generally Chapter 7, Section 3, infra.

Part 5 of Article 9 deals with filing. Of particular importance are R9–502 (dealing with what to file—the contents of a financing statement) and R9–501 (dealing with where to file). See also R9–301 through R9–307 (dealing with what state's law governs perfection and the effect of perfection or non-perfection). See generally Chapter 7, Section 4, infra.

Article 9 includes several important priority rules. For example, under R9–317 certain non-ordinary course, good-faith buyers of collateral take free of an attached but unperfected security interest. Perhaps more important, the same section provides that an attached but unperfected security interest is subordinate to the rights of a "lien creditor." (A "lien creditor" is a creditor with a judicial lien. See R9–102(a)(52). We shall see in Chapter 10 that a debtor's trustee in bankruptcy can assume the seniority of a judicial lien creditor and set aside security interests that are unperfected when the debtor enters bankruptcy.) Under Article 9's priority rules, even perfected security interests are not perfect. For example, they usually are subordinate to competing Article 9 security interests under the first-in-time rule of R9–322(a)(1), which, however, is subject to long list of exceptions. See generally Chapter 7, Section 6(A), infra. Also, perfected security interests in goods can be cut off by a "buyer in ordinary course of business." R1–201(9); R9–320(a). See generally Chapter 7, Section 6(B), infra.

Notwithstanding the apparent breadth of the baseline priority rule in R9–201 and the large number of priority rules found elsewhere in the Article, many priority contests between Article 9 security interests and competing claimants to collateral are not addressed in Article 9 (or elsewhere in the UCC). Examples are priority contests with federal tax liens and a growing variety of other statutory liens. See generally Chapter 11, Section 5, infra.

(G) ENFORCEMENT

The right and ability of a secured party to satisfy its claim out of the collateral already has been mentioned in general terms. Part 6 of Article 9 regulates in detail a secured party's enforcement rights. See generally Chapter 12, infra. These rights arise upon a debtor's "default." Just as Article 9 is silent concerning the nature and scope of the obligation secured by a security interest, so Article 9 does not define what constitutes a default in that obligation. Defining default is left primarily to the agreement of the debtor and secured party. In addition to failure to make a payment when due, sometimes with a grace period, typical defaults include the debtor's insolvency, bankruptcy, and breach of a loan covenant, and the existence of a conflicting lien on the collateral.

A menu of the rights and remedies of secured parties and debtors after default appears in R9–601. Notwithstanding the UCC's general deference to freedom of contract, see UCC 1–102, Article 9 prohibits debtors from waiving certain of their rights before default. R9–602. As an empirical matter, the secured party's most important enforcement tools are its rights (i) to collect on intangible collateral, such as accounts, from the obligors (called "account debtors"), (ii) to take possession of collateral on default, and (iii) to dispose of collateral (typically, by sale or lease). R9–102(a)(3) (defining "account debtor"); R9–607 (secured party's collection rights); R9–609 (secured party's right to take possession); R9–610 (disposition of collateral). In the case of collections and dispositions, the secured party is entitled to apply funds received to the obligation secured, leaving an obligation for a "deficiency" should the funds be insufficient. R9–608(a)(4); R9–615(d). The debtor is entitled to any "surplus" that remains after satisfaction of the secured obligation and certain junior security interests. Id. In addition, a secured party may propose to accept collateral in full or (except in consumer transactions) partial satisfaction of the secured debt, but the debtor and certain junior secured parties are entitled to object to that proposal, thereby forcing the secured creditor to turn to another remedy, such as disposition. R9–620.

To increase the likelihood that a fair price will be obtained upon the disposition of collateral, the secured party must give advance notice of the disposition to the debtor and certain junior secured parties, see R9–611(b), and every aspect of the disposition must be "commercially reasonable." R9–610(b). Similarly, collections on intangible collateral must be undertaken in a commercially reasonable manner. R9–607(c).

A debtor is entitled to "redeem" collateral at any time before the secured party disposes (or contracts to dispose) of the collateral, collects upon the collateral, or accepts the collateral in satisfaction of the secured obligation. R9–623. This redemption right derives from the "equity of redemption" developed by the English courts of equity with respect to real estate. It recognizes that at some point the debtor's equitable right must be "foreclosed." Even today, people commonly use the term "debtor's equity" to refer to the positive remainder obtained when the amount of the secured obligation is subtracted from the value of the collateral and usually speak of "foreclosure" as the means of enforcing a lien. These terms can be traced historically to the foreclosure of a debtor's equity of redemption.

Depending on the circumstances, a secured party who fails to comply with Article 9 can be held liable to a debtor in damages, deprived of some or all of its claim for a deficiency, or subjected to judicial restraint. R9–625; R9–626. In consumer and consumer-goods transactions, noncomplying secured parties may be subjected to losses that bear no relationship to the amount of actual harm or damage (if any) caused by the noncompliance. See R9–625(c)(2); R9–626(b).

SECTION 3.   THE ROLES OF LAWYERS IN SECURED TRANSACTIONS

We have met tax lawyers, litigators, securities lawyers, and patent lawyers, but we have never met a self-styled "secured transactions" lawyer. To be sure, we have met many who held themselves out as experts on secured transactions (and most of them really were). But the law governing secured transactions never represents more than one slice of any pie, significant and complex as that slice may be.

Consider, for example, a large, syndicated bank financing, in which several banks in a "syndicate" are extending credit to a corporation under the same credit agreement. The lawyers who represent each of the parties in such a large, sophisticated transaction well might refer to themselves as "financing lawyers" or "commercial lawyers," but would be just as likely, perhaps, to observe that they are "corporate lawyers" who "do deals." As counsel for the lenders and the borrower, they would be expected to prepare and negotiate the wording of the documentation and render formal, written legal opinions on the enforceability of the documentation and on various other aspects of the transaction. Counsel would consult frequently with their clients and advise them concerning legal risks. Counsel almost certainly would need not only a sound understanding of business matters, such as how the banks obtain funds to make their loans and the accounting principles featured in various covenants, but also expertise in diverse areas of the law: regulations affecting the bank lenders, restrictions on interest rates that can be charged, rights of setoff against bank accounts, liens arising out of the Employee Retirement Income Security Act ("ERISA"), federal and state tax liens and a variety of other federal and state lien statutes, securities regulation laws affecting the borrower, conflict of laws, equitable principles that limit the enforceability of agreements, tort law relating to the behavior of lenders, the effects of the borrower's or lender's insolvency, etc. (the list could go on and on). The collateral may be an indispensable part of the transaction and may occupy much of the time of the lawyers involved, but it is only one part of the deal.

Assume now that the borrower in our syndicated bank financing becomes financially distressed; it is in default under that financing, as well as under various other financings, and is behind in paying its trade debt. If the borrower is not in bankruptcy, counsel for many of the creditors and counsel for the debtor might undertake negotiations (usually called a **workout**) leading to a restructuring of credit extensions. Much of the same expertise and many of the same lawyering skills brought to bear in the original financings will be called upon in the workout context. If the borrower becomes a debtor under the Bankruptcy Code, the nature of the work of many of the lawyers will be essentially the same as in the out-of-court workout. However, some disputes or claims may require litigation, in which case lawyers skilled in trial practice will be utilized.

Now consider an individual consumer's purchase of an automobile financed by a commercial bank. The bank will present several "forms" to the individual borrower for signature (e.g., credit application, promissory note, security agreement). It would be quite rare for the bank's loan officer or the borrower to retain and consult counsel to assist in this financing. Indeed, it is unlikely that the bank would agree to one-time changes to its forms under any circumstances. Although the parties need not worry about securities laws that apply to the borrower or about complicated financial covenants, it would be a serious mistake to think that lawyers had not played an essential role in this consumer transaction. Federal and state regulation of consumer credit (including disclosure requirements and mandatory and prohibited practices and terms) is so complex and pervasive that only highly specialized and knowledgeable counsel are equipped to prepare and approve consumer credit forms.[1]

If the consumer buyer defaults in the monthly payments or files for bankruptcy, the bank may retain a "collection" lawyer who specializes in collections of consumer debts. The lawyer might resort to legal proceedings or, if the debtor is in bankruptcy, might assist the bank in obtaining possession of the collateral or in working out a mutually acceptable resolution between the borrower and the bank. At that stage, the borrower also might have retained a lawyer (if the borrower could afford the cost); the borrower's lawyer would be sure to examine closely the transaction with the bank to uncover potential attacks on the validity of the bank's claim and security interest and any possible counterclaim against the bank arising out of regulatory noncompliance or otherwise.

In sum, the roles of legal counsel in financings, including secured financings, involve much more than the ex post analysis of facts for the purpose of predicting (or advocating) an appropriate judicial resolution (i.e., *A* sues *B*; who wins?). As you work your way through the following materials, from time to time you will be asked to identify problems and propose ex ante solutions. You will also have an opportunity to consider how you might counsel your client in a variety of circumstances.

---

1. We have seen the FTC's anti-holder in due course rule in Chapter 1, Section 4, supra, and its rule prohibiting nonpossessory, non-purchase-money security interests in household goods in Section 1 of this Chapter.

CHAPTER 7

ESTABLISHMENT AND PERFECTION OF SECURITY INTERESTS

SECTION 1. FINANCING AUTOMOBILES: A PROTOTYPE

The preceding Chapter briefly mentioned some aspects of the automobile financing transactions illustrated in this Section. The following Prototype portrays in more detail the legal and related business practices employed in financing the marketing of automobiles.[1] This picture may suggest ways to avoid legal pitfalls through proper handling of business transactions generally; it also provides a good setting for dealing with the legal problems that arise in this and other important types of financing. You should read this Section quickly at this point to get an overview of the basic transactions. We shall return to this Prototype at various points later in these materials when dealing with specific problems.

The following pages present a typical example of automobile financing at two levels: (i) while the dealer holds the automobiles (in this case, cars and light trucks) as inventory (financing the acquisition of a dealer's inventory of durable goods sometimes is called **floorplanning**) and (ii) upon the sale of one of the automobiles to an individual consumer who buys the automobile "on time." The dealer is Main Motors, Inc., a Chevrolet dealer; credit for the dealer's inventory financing is supplied by a lending institution named Firstbank. The consumer buyer is Lee Abel; secured credit for Abel's purchase also is provided by Firstbank, but in a transaction that is separate and distinct from the inventory financing for Main Motors.

The Prototype assumes that Revised Article 9 has become effective in Pennsylvania (and in any other relevant jurisdiction).

(A) FINANCING THE DEALER'S INVENTORY: THE SETTING

Main Motors sells about 700 new Chevrolets each year at a retail value of close to $14,750,000; Main's sales of used automobiles (most taken by Main as "trade-ins" on new automobiles) come to about one-third of this amount. To meet varied tastes for model, color, and combinations of accessories, and to facilitate sales to eager buyers, Main carries an invento-

---

1. This Prototype was prepared with the generous assistance of William B. Solomon, Jr., and Thomas J. Buiteweg of General Motors Acceptance Corporation. It does not necessarily describe the practices of any particular bank, automobile dealer, or automobile manufacturer.

ry averaging 175 new automobiles, with a wholesale cost to Main of about $3,500,000. Main has a physical plant (land and buildings, including showroom, service facility, and parking lots; tools and other equipment; etc.) valued at $2,800,000, and carries about $400,000 worth of parts and accessories required for its service department. More than one-half of Main's sales of new automobiles are installment credit sales; for used automobiles the proportion is greater. Most of the installment contracts for new automobiles run 48 months, and for used automobiles 30 months. Consequently, without financing assistance, Main's investment in new automobiles would be tied up for extended periods even after their sale. Like most automobile dealers, Main lacks capital to meet all of these needs and relies heavily on financing.

Firstbank has field representatives who solicit dealers to establish financing arrangements. One of them contacts Main Motors and proposes terms on which the bank will (i) finance (floorplan) Main's inventory of new automobiles, thereby enabling Main to acquire automobiles on credit, and (ii) purchase the consumer installment contracts generated by Main's installment sales, thereby eliminating Main's burden of waiting for payment until each installment comes due.

Finding the terms of Firstbank's proposal more attractive than Main's existing financing arrangements with another lender, Main's management indicates its willingness to accept Firstbank's terms.

(B) CREATING AND PERFECTING FIRSTBANK'S SECURITY INTEREST

At this point, Main signs several documents, including a *financing statement* and a *security agreement*.

The Financing Statement. Firstbank will file a financing statement (Form 7.1) in the appropriate filing office;[2] the completed form is designed to meet the requirements of R9–502.

The Security Agreement. You will recall that perfection of a security interest requires, in addition to filing a financing statement, that the security interest attach. R9–308(a). Recall as well that one element of attachment is that the debtor sign (or otherwise authenticate) a security agreement describing the collateral. R9–203(b)(3)(A). The security agreement signed by Main Motors is a detailed, **blanket lien** (i.e., very broad coverage) agreement, the "Dealer Inventory Security Agreement" (Form 7.2). This comprehensive contract between the parties includes language not only evidencing the bank's continuing security interest in Main's inventory and related collateral (see ¶ 5), but also authorizing the bank to endorse notes and sign financing statements on behalf of Main (see ¶ 6). It also contains provisions relating to the terms of the lending arrangements (see ¶¶ 1, 2, and 8), defining the "Events of Default" (see ¶ 12), and setting forth Firstbank's remedies (see ¶ 13).

---

2. For the place of filing within a state, see R9–501(a); as to the applicability, here, of Pennsylvania law, see R9–301(1) and Section 4, infra. Firstbank will file with the Secretary of State of the Commonwealth of Pennsylvania, in Harrisburg.

FORM 7.1
FINANCING STATEMENT

UCC FINANCING STATEMENT
FOLLOW INSTRUCTIONS (front and back) CAREFULLY

A. NAME & PHONE OF CONTACT AT FILER [optional]

P. A. SYSTEM, ESQ. - 800-111-2222

B. SEND ACKNOWLEDGMENT TO: (Name and Address)

SYSTEM LAW OFFICES
125 SPRAWL OFFICE PARK
MALVERN, PA 19355

THE ABOVE SPACE IS FOR FILING OFFICE USE ONLY

1. DEBTOR'S EXACT FULL LEGAL NAME - insert only one debtor name (1a or 1b) - do not abbreviate or combine names

1a. ORGANIZATION'S NAME			
MAIN MOTORS, INC.			

1b. INDIVIDUAL'S LAST NAME	FIRST NAME	MIDDLE NAME	SUFFIX

1c. MAILING ADDRESS	CITY	STATE	POSTAL CODE	COUNTRY
237 NORTH SEVENTH STREET	PHILADELPHIA	PA	19116	USA

1d. TAX ID #: SSN OR EIN	ADD'L INFO RE ORGANIZATION DEBTOR	1e. TYPE OF ORGANIZATION	1f. JURISDICTION OF ORGANIZATION	1g. ORGANIZATIONAL ID #, if any	
1234567		CORP	PENNSYLVANIA	PA12345	☐ NONE

2. ADDITIONAL DEBTOR'S EXACT FULL LEGAL NAME - insert only one debtor name (2a or 2b) - do not abbreviate or combine names

2a. ORGANIZATION'S NAME			

2b. INDIVIDUAL'S LAST NAME	FIRST NAME	MIDDLE NAME	SUFFIX

2c. MAILING ADDRESS	CITY	STATE	POSTAL CODE	COUNTRY

2d. TAX ID #: SSN OR EIN	ADD'L INFO RE ORGANIZATION DEBTOR	2e. TYPE OF ORGANIZATION	2f. JURISDICTION OF ORGANIZATION	2g. ORGANIZATIONAL ID #, if any	
					☐ NONE

3. SECURED PARTY'S NAME (or NAME of TOTAL ASSIGNEE of ASSIGNOR S/P) - insert only one secured party name (3a or 3b)

3a. ORGANIZATION'S NAME			
FIRSTBANK, N.A.			

3b. INDIVIDUAL'S LAST NAME	FIRST NAME	MIDDLE NAME	SUFFIX

3c. MAILING ADDRESS	CITY	STATE	POSTAL CODE	COUNTRY
BROAD & SPRUCE STREETS	PHILADELPHIA	PA	19116	USA

4. This FINANCING STATEMENT covers the following collateral:

ALL OF THE FOLLOWING, WHETHER NOW OWNED OR HEREAFTER ACQUIRED:
ACCOUNTS; CHATTEL PAPER; GENERAL INTANGIBLES; INSTRUMENTS (INCLUDING
PROMISSORY NOTES); INVENTORY; LETTER-OF-CREDIT-RIGHTS; PAYMENT
INTANGIBLES; SUPPORTING OBLIGATIONS; CONTRACTS OF LEASE, SALE, RENTAL
OR OTHER DISPOSITIONS OF INVENTORY; BOOKS AND RECORDS; RIGHTS IN
CONNECTION WITH THE RESIDUAL VALUE OF INVENTORY LEASED, RENTED, SOLD,
OR OTHERWISE DISPOSED OF, INCLUDING PROCEEDS OF ANY THIRD PARTY'S
EXERCISE OF AN OPTION TO PURCHASE; REPLACEMENTS OR SUBSTITUTIONS OF
ANY OF THE FOREGOING, CASH PROCEEDS AND NONCASH PROCEEDS THEREOF,
AND PROCEEDS OF PROCEEDS.

5. ALTERNATIVE DESIGNATION (if applicable):	☐ LESSEE/LESSOR	☐ CONSIGNEE/CONSIGNOR	☐ BAILEE/BAILOR	☐ SELLER/BUYER	☐ AG. LIEN	☐ NON-UCC FILING

6. ☐ This FINANCING STATEMENT is to be filed [for record] (or recorded) in the REAL ESTATE RECORDS. Attach Addendum [if applicable]	7. Check to REQUEST SEARCH REPORT(S) on Debtor(s) [ADDITIONAL FEE] [optional]	☐ All Debtors	☐ Debtor 1	☐ Debtor 2

8. OPTIONAL FILER REFERENCE DATA

FILING OFFICE COPY — NATIONAL UCC FINANCING STATEMENT (FORM UCC1) (REV. 07/20/08)

FORM 7.2
DEALER INVENTORY SECURITY AGREEMENT

FIRSTBANK, N.A., a national banking association with a place of business located at Broad & Spruce Streets, Philadelphia, Pennsylvania

("Bank"), and   Main Motors, Inc.   a   Pennsylvania corporation   whose principal place of business is

  237 North Seventh Street, Philadelphia, PA 19116   ("Dealer"), intending to be legally bound, hereby agree as follows:

1. BACKGROUND.

Dealer hereby requests Bank from time to time to make loans and advances to Dealer ("Loan(s)") acceptable to Bank to finance the purchase of Inventory, as that term is defined herein, from suppliers thereof ("Suppliers") for sale or lease in the ordinary course of Dealer's business. Subject to the terms and conditions of this agreement ("Agreement"), Bank expects to finance Dealer's purchase of Inventory, but reserves in its sole discretion, the right to decline to make any Loan(s) requested by Dealer for any reason. Loan(s) may be disbursed either directly to Dealer, to Dealer's demand deposit account at Bank, or by Bank's paying, at Dealer's request and for Dealer's account, drafts of, or other demands for payment by, a Supplier properly presented to Bank when accompanied by the manufacturer's invoice or bill of sale and adequate documentation of proper ownership.

2. LOAN(S) AND NOTE.

Subject to the terms and conditions hereof, and Bank's continuing satisfaction with the financial and other conditions of Dealer, Bank will from time to time during the continuance of the Agreement make Loan(s) to Dealer, as Dealer may from time to time request, on not less than five (5) days prior notice, by submitting to Bank a properly completed Loan Request Form in the form attached hereto ("Loan Request Form") (or by complying with any other means of requesting Loans as may be agreed upon by Bank and Dealer in writing), to finance Dealer's purchase of Inventory, provided, however, the aggregate principal amount outstanding of such Loan(s) shall not, at any one time, exceed the sum of $3,500,000.   ("Loan Limit"). Bank may, from time to time, raise or lower the Loan Limit upon five (5) days' written notice to Dealer. Bank expressly reserves, in its sole discretion, the right to decline to make any Loan(s) requested by Dealer for any reason. Dealer agrees to execute and deliver to Bank a demand note in an amount equal to the Loan Limit, in the form attached hereto ("Note(s)") and, at Bank's request, to execute from time to time such additional or substituted Note(s) as are necessary to evidence any change in the Loan Limit. The actual amount due under the Note(s) shall be that amount as shown on the Bank's books and records. Bank will from time to time render to Dealer statements of all amounts due Bank under the Note(s) which statements shall be deemed conclusive and irrefutable evidence of the actual amounts due Bank, unless Dealer notifies Bank in writing to the contrary within fifteen (15) days of Bank's sending such statements to Dealer.

3. INVENTORY.

For purposes of this Agreement, "Inventory" means any new or used inventory (as that term is defined in the Pennsylvania Uniform Commercial Code (the "UCC"), Article 9) that is owned or possessed by Dealer and shall include all tangible personal property held by Dealer for sale or lease or to be furnished under contracts of service, tangible personal property that the Dealer has so leased or furnished, tangible personal property held by others for sale on consignment for the Dealer, tangible personal property sold by the Dealer on a sale or return or consignment basis, tangible personal property returned to the Dealer or repossessed by the Dealer following a sale thereof by Dealer, and tangible personal property represented by a document of title, including, but not limited to, automobiles, parts and accessories, together with all materials, additions, equipment, accessions, accessories and parts installed in, related, attached or added thereto or used in connection therewith and all substitutions and exchanges for and replacements thereof whether installed prior to receipt or after receipt by Dealer. An item of Inventory financed hereunder is an "Item".

4. FINANCING TERMS.

The percentage of the purchase price of any Item that Bank, in its discretion, elects to lend to Dealer to finance the purchase thereof pursuant to this Agreement will be established by Bank from time to time by prior written notice to Dealer ("Financing Terms").

5. GRANT OF SECURITY INTEREST.

As security for the prompt and punctual payment and performance of all liabilities and obligations of Dealer to Bank, including, but not limited to, the Note(s), and the performance by Dealer of all of Dealer's obligations as set forth herein and/or in any and all documents and instruments executed or delivered in conjunction herewith, and the complete satisfaction of all existing and future liabilities and obligations of Dealer to Bank or of Dealer and others to Bank of any nature whatsoever, whether matured or unmatured, absolute or contingent, direct or indirect, sole, joint or several, and any extensions, modifications or renewals thereof, including, but not limited to, all of Bank's expenses incurred in connection with the collection and performance of Dealer's liabilities and obligations hereunder, Bank's reasonable attorney's fees and the costs of curing any Event of Default (as specified below in paragraph 12) that Bank elects to cure, all of which Dealer hereby agrees to pay (collectively, "Dealer's Liabilities to Bank"), Dealer hereby grants and conveys to Bank a continuing lien upon and security interest in all of Dealer's property described below now owned or hereafter acquired:

(a) Inventory;

(b) Accounts, chattel paper, general intangibles, and instruments (each as defined in the Pennsylvania UCC, Article 9) and all obligations of sureties and guarantors for the payment and satisfaction thereof;

(c) Contracts of lease, sale, rental or other disposition of Inventory in which Dealer has an interest;

(d) Books and Records (herein defined to mean all books and records of original or final entry, including, without limitation: invoices; receipts; instruments; documents; account ledgers and journals (both due and payable); minutes; resolutions; correspondence with regard to the Collateral; tax returns; bank checks; receipts and financing statements; contracts; agreements; and any other books and records maintained by Dealer in the normal course of Dealer's business, including all such books and records as have been photocopied, reduced to film images or otherwise, or encoded into electronic or mechanical impulses in or upon computer tapes, programs, software, and data banks associated therewith, or accounting or recording machines or the like, and without regard to whether such books and records are maintained at Dealer's place of business or elsewhere);

(e) Rights in connection with the residual value of any of Dealer's Inventory leased, rented, sold or otherwise disposed of, including but not limited to the proceeds of any third party's option to purchase any portion of Dealer's Inventory;

(f) Balances on deposit with or held in any capacity by Bank at any time and any other property of any nature of Dealer that Bank may at any time have in its possession wherever located, now or hereafter acquired; and

(g) All replacements and substitutions of all or any of the foregoing, all cash and non-cash proceeds thereof, proceeds of proceeds thereof, all insurance thereon, and all proceeds of such insurance, including, but not limited to trade-ins, returned, and/or repossessed goods.

Bank's rights in all of the above property (collectively, "Collateral") shall be independent of any right of set-off or appropriation that Bank may have or acquire under paragraph 13 hereof or otherwise.

6. POWER OF ATTORNEY.

Dealer hereby appoints any employee, officer or agent of Bank as Dealer's true and lawful attorney-in-fact, with power:

(a)   To endorse the name of Dealer upon:

    (i)   Any Note(s), security agreement, UCC financing statement and continuations thereof, certificates of origin and certificates of title to any motor vehicle or other property evidenced by such a certificate and any other instrument or document required by Bank to perfect or continue perfection of the liens and security interests granted to Bank hereunder or otherwise in connection with Loan(s);

    (ii)   Any and all other notes, checks, drafts, money orders or other instruments of payment;

    (iii)   Instruments received by Dealer in connection with the sale or other disposition of any Collateral;

    (iv)   Any check that may be payable to Dealer on account of returned or unearned premiums or the proceeds of insurance (and any amount so collected may be applied by Bank toward satisfaction of any of Dealer's Liabilities to Bank).

(b)   To sign and endorse the name of Dealer upon any: drafts against all persons obligated to pay, directly or indirectly any account, chattel paper, general intangible, or instrument ("Account Debtors"); assignments, verifications and notices in connection with any Collateral; and invoices, freight or express bills, bills of lading, and storage or warehouse receipts relating to any Collateral;

(c)   To give written notices in connection with accounts, chattel paper, general intangibles, or instruments;

(d)   To give written notices to officers and officials of the United States Postal Service to effect a change or changes of address so that all mail addressed to Dealer may be delivered directly to Bank (Bank will return all mail not related to the Dealer's Liabilities to Bank or the Collateral to Bank); and

(e)   To open all such mail.

Dealer hereby grants unto said attorney full power to do any and all things necessary to be done with respect to the above as fully and effectively as Dealer might or could do with full power of substitution and hereby ratifies and confirms all its said attorney or its substitute shall lawfully do or cause to be done by virtue hereof. This power of attorney shall be deemed to be coupled with an interest and irrevocable until all of Dealer's Liabilities to Bank are paid or performed in full, and shall survive any dissolution, termination or liquidation of Dealer.

7. DOWN PAYMENT; ASSIGNMENT OF TITLE.

Dealer agrees that on or before accepting delivery of any Item it will pay Supplier, in cash and not by credit whether extended by Supplier or any other person, the amount(s) required pursuant to the Financing Terms. Dealer hereby requests and authorizes Bank to pay the proceeds of the Loan(s) to Supplier. Dealer acknowledges that it acquires each Item subject to Bank's lien and security interest therein and Dealer hereby irrevocably authorizes Supplier to deliver to Bank, upon Bank's written request, a certificate of origin, certificate of title or other evidence of ownership evidencing a first perfected security interest in favor of Bank in or unencumbered title to each Item and all other documents and certificates necessary to evidence the same.

8. DEALER'S PAYMENTS TO BANK.

Without Bank's prior written consent, Dealer will not sell any Item for a price less than the then outstanding principal balance of the Loan(s) plus accrued and unpaid interest thereon made to enable Dealer to acquire that Item ("Release Price"). When Dealer sells an Item it will promptly pay to Bank the Release Price of such Item.

Dealer agrees to make such payments to Bank from time to time to reduce the principal balance of any Loan(s) made hereunder to enable Dealer to purchase an Item that Dealer has not sold as Bank and Dealer shall agree to, in writing, from time to time.

Provided, however, that nothing herein shall be construed to amend in any way the terms of the Note(s) which is, and is intended to remain, payable ON DEMAND, it being understood that Bank may demand payment at any time of the Note(s). Without first paying Bank in full the Release Price, Dealer will not return for credit, exchange or consign any Item.

9. INVENTORY RISKS.

Bank assumes no responsibility for the existence, character, quality, quantity, condition, value and/or delivery of any Item. Dealer shall not be relieved of any of Dealer's Liabilities to Bank because any Item fails to conform to the manufacturer's, Supplier's, or Dealer's warranties, or because any Item may be lost, stolen destroyed or damaged. Dealer will promptly notify Bank of the loss, theft or destruction of or damage to any Item and will forthwith pay to Bank the Release Price of such Item.

10. INDEMNIFICATION.

Dealer agrees to comply with all requirements of the federal Truth in Lending Act and the federal Equal Credit Opportunity Act, and Regulations Z and B of the Board of Governors of the Federal Reserve System, Trade Regulation Rules of the Federal Trade Commission, the federal Fair Debt Collection Practices Act and Fair Credit Reporting Act, the Pennsylvania Model Act for the Regulation of Credit Life Insurance and Credit Accident and Health Insurance, the Pennsylvania Unfair Trade Practices and Consumer Protection Law, the Motor Vehicle Sales Finance Act, the Goods and Services Installment Sales Act, and all regulations promulgated by all governmental units and agencies thereunder, and all other applicable state, federal and local laws, regulations and ordinances regulating the credit sale of goods and/or services by Dealer and at all times to carry on its business in a lawful manner. Dealer hereby agrees to indemnify, defend and hold Bank harmless from and against all liability and claims asserted against Bank by any person in connection with:

(a)   any sale, lease, enforcement or other disposition of any Collateral;

(b)   any alleged violation of any law, regulation or ordinance by Dealer or Bank in connection with this Agreement or any other contract between Dealer and Bank;

(c)   any personal injury alleged to have been suffered by any person in connection with any sale, lease, enforcement or other disposition of any Collateral;

(d)   any claim by any person arising out of Dealer's breach of warranty or failure to perform any of Dealer's obligations under any contract regarding the sale, lease, enforcement or disposition of any Collateral; or

(e)   any claim by any person arising from a claim made by a consumer under the Federal Trade Commission's Trade Regulation Rule to Preserve Consumer Defenses on any loan made by Bank to said consumer, whether referred to Bank by Dealer or not.

Dealer further agrees to reimburse Bank for all interest, counsel fees and costs expended by Bank in connection with the foregoing, including, but not limited to, those incurred in any bankruptcy or insolvency proceedings, and any subsequent proceedings or appeals from any order or judgment entered therein. This indemnification shall survive termination of this Agreement.

11. WARRANTIES, REPRESENTATIONS AND COVENANTS.

To induce Bank to enter into this Agreement and to extend credit, Dealer warrants, represents and covenants (which warranties, representations and covenants shall survive termination of this Agreement) that:

(a)   Dealer will keep complete and accurate Books and Records and make all necessary entries thereon to reflect all transactions respecting the Collateral. Dealer will keep Bank informed as to the location of all Books and Records and will permit Bank, its officers, employees and agents, to have access to all Books and Records and any other records pertaining to Dealer's business and financial condition that Bank may request and, if deemed necessary by Bank, permit Bank, its officers, employees and agents, to remove them from Dealer's places of business or any other places where the same may be found for the purposes of examining, auditing and copying same. Any Books and Records so removed by Bank will be returned to Dealer by Bank as soon as Bank shall have completed its inspection, audit or copying thereof.

(b)   Dealer's jurisdiction of organization (if any), the location of Dealer's chief executive office, all of Dealer's offices where it keeps its Books and Records concerning the Collateral, all locations at which it keeps its Inventory, and all locations at which it maintains a place of business are listed in Schedule A attached hereto. Dealer will not change its jurisdiction of organization (if any) unless it gives Bank at least 30 days' prior written notice. Dealer will promptly notify Bank in writing of any change in the locations of its chief executive office, Books and Records, of the Collateral, of any place of business or of the closing or establishment of any new place of business. If any of the Collateral or any Books and Records are at any time to be located on premises leased by Dealer or on premises owned by Dealer subject to a mortgage or other lien, Dealer will obtain and deliver or cause to be delivered to Bank, prior to delivery of any Collateral or Books and Records to such premises, an agreement, in form and substance satisfactory to Bank, waiving the landlord's, mortgagee's or lienholder's rights to enforce any claim against Dealer for monies due under the landlord's lien, mortgagee's mortgage, or other lien by levy or distraint, or other similar proceedings against the Collateral or Books and Records and assuring Bank's ability to have access to the Collateral and Books and Records in order to exercise Bank's rights to take possession thereof and to remove them from such premises.

(c)   Dealer has, and at all times will have, good, marketable and indefeasible title to the Collateral, free and clear of all liens or encumbrances (except for taxes not in default or contested in good faith, for which adequate reserves have been set aside, and Bank's liens and security interests). All accounts, chattel paper, general intangibles, and instruments included in the Collateral arose in the ordinary course of Dealer's business and are not subject to any defense, set-off, or counterclaim.

(d)   Dealer will, at its sole cost and expense, preserve the Collateral and Dealer's rights against Account Debtors free and clear of all liens and encumbrances, except those created pursuant hereto, and take such further actions as may be necessary to maintain the perfection and first priority of Bank's security interest in the Collateral. Dealer will not grant to anyone other than Bank any lien upon or security interest in the Collateral nor allow any person other than Bank to obtain a lien upon the Collateral. At Dealer's sole expense, Dealer will keep the Collateral in good condition and repair at all times.

(e)   Dealer will at all times keep itself and the Collateral insured against all hazards in such amounts and by such insurers as are satisfactory to Bank together with full casualty and extended coverage in amount not less than one hundred ten percent (110%) of the Loan Limit. Dealer will cause Bank's security interests in the Collateral to be endorsed on all policies of insurance thereon in such manner that all payments for losses will be paid to Bank as loss payee and Dealer will furnish Bank with evidence of such insurance and endorsements. Such policies shall be payable to Dealer and Bank as their respective interests appear and shall contain a provision whereby they cannot be cancelled except after ten (10) days' written notice to the Bank. In the event that Dealer fails to pay any such insurance premiums when due, Bank may, but is not required to, pay such premiums and add the costs thereof to the amounts due Bank by Dealer under the Note(s), which costs Dealer hereby agrees to pay to Bank with interest at the rate specified in the Note(s). Dealer hereby assigns to Bank any returned or unearned premiums that may be due Dealer upon cancellation of any such policies for any reason whatsoever and directs the insurers to pay Bank any amounts so due.

(f)   Dealer will promptly notify Bank if there is any change in the status or physical condition of any Collateral or the ability of any Account Debtor to pay or preserve the Collateral, or of any defense, set-off, or counterclaim asserted by any person. If any Collateral is sold, leased, rented, released for demonstration, transferred or otherwise moved from the place where such Collateral is normally kept by Dealer, Dealer will notify Bank forthwith.

(g)   Dealer will permit Bank to inspect and audit the Collateral at all reasonable times. In the event that Bank and Dealer cannot agree within seventy-two (72) hours as to what shall be a reasonable time to inspect and audit Collateral, Bank's decision shall be controlling, and upon oral notice, Dealer will permit such inspection and audit.

(h)   Dealer hereby irrevocably assigns to Bank all of its rights of stoppage in transit with respect to any Item sold on credit to any Account Debtor, which rights shall be paramount to Dealer's.

(i)   Dealer will, at such intervals as Bank may require, submit to Bank:
   (i)   a schedule reflecting, in form and detail satisfactory to Bank, the names and addresses of all Account Debtors together with the amounts due for all of Dealer's outstanding accounts; and
   (ii)   copies of all invoices evidencing the sale or lease of any Item or Items to Account Debtors pertaining to any or all of its accounts, with evidence of shipment of the Item or Items, the sale or the leasing of which have given rise to such accounts.

(j)   Dealer will file all tax returns that Dealer is required to file and pay when due all taxes and license and other fees with respect to the Collateral and Dealer's business, except taxes contested in good faith and for which adequate reserves have been established by Dealer.

(k)   If a certificate of title is required to be issued for any Item, Dealer will file all documents necessary to obtain such a certificate from the appropriate governmental authority within three (3) days after the date of the Loan made to enable the Dealer to purchase that item. Dealer will cause a notation of the Bank's lien and security interest to be made and noted on such certificate at Dealer's sole expense. If Dealer fails or refuses to so file such document or note Bank's liens and security interests thereon, Bank may, at Dealer's expense, file such documents as Bank, in its sole discretion, deems appropriate to perfect its lien and security interest.

(l)   The proceeds of each Loan will be used solely to finance the purchase price of Inventory in accordance with the Financing Terms.

(m)   Dealer, if a corporation, is duly organized, validly existing and in good standing under the laws of the state of its incorporation, has the power and authority to make and perform this Agreement, and is duly qualified in all jurisdictions in which it conducts its business or where such qualification is required. The execution, delivery and performance of this Agreement, and the execution and delivery of the Note(s) and all other documents required hereunder have been duly authorized and will not violate any provision of law or regulation or of the articles of incorporation, by-laws or partnership agreement of Dealer or of any agreement, indenture or instrument to which Dealer is a party, or result in the creation or imposition of any security interest, lien or encumbrance in any of the Collateral. This Agreement, the Note(s) and all other documents related hereto, when executed and delivered by Dealer, will be valid and binding obligations of Dealer, enforceable against Dealer in accordance with their terms.

(n)   Within ninety (90) days after the end of each fiscal year of Dealer, Dealer will furnish Bank with annual financial reports relating to the financial condition of Dealer and its affiliates (including but not limited to consolidated and consolidating balance sheets, earnings or profit or loss statements and surplus statements), each in reasonable detail and prepared by an independent certified public accountant ("CPA") in accordance with generally accepted accounting principles consistently applied. In addition, Dealer will obtain from such independent CPA and deliver to Bank, within ninety (90) days after the close of each fiscal year, such CPA's written statement that in making the examination necessary to the certification, the CPA has obtained no knowledge of the occurrence or imminent occurrence of any Event of Default (as specified in paragraph 12 below) by Dealer hereunder, or disclosing all Events of Default of which such CPA has obtained knowledge; provided, however, that in making the examination such CPA shall not be required to go beyond the bounds of generally accepted auditing procedures for the purposes of certifying financial statements. Bank shall have the right, from time to time, to discuss Dealer's affairs directly with Dealer's independent CPA after notice to Dealer and opportunity for Dealer to be present at any such discussions. Dealer agrees that the CPA selected by Dealer shall be acceptable to Bank, it being agreed that Bank will not unreasonably withhold its consent of the accountants selected by Dealer.

(o)   On or before the fifteenth (15th) day of each month Dealer will furnish to Bank (in form satisfactory to Bank) unaudited statements of the financial condition and operations of Dealer and its affiliates for the preceding calendar month.

(p)   Dealer will furnish Bank promptly with such information in addition to that specified in subparagraphs (n) and (o) above respecting the financial condition and affairs of Dealer and its affiliates as Bank may, from time to time, reasonably require.

(q)   No Event of Default, as specified in paragraph 12 below, has occurred or is about to occur and no event has occurred or is about to occur that, with the passage of time or giving of notice or both, could be an Event of Default.

(r)   There are no suits in law or equity or proceedings before any tribunal or governmental instrumentality now pending or, to the knowledge of Dealer, threatened against Dealer or any guarantor or surety for Dealer's Liabilities to Bank, the adverse result of which would in any material respect affect the property, finances or operations of Dealer or of any surety or guarantor for Dealer, or their ability to satisfy Dealer's Liabilities to Bank.

(s)   No statement, warranty, representation, covenant, information, document or financial statement made, presented or asserted by Dealer to Bank in connection with this Agreement or as an inducement to Bank to make Loan(s) hereunder was or is incorrect, incomplete, false or misleading in any material respect nor has Dealer failed to advise Bank of any information affecting materially Dealer's business, operations or financial condition.

(t)   In the event that Bank, for any reason, determines that the value of the Collateral is insufficient to secure adequately the actual amount due Bank under the Note(s), Dealer will, upon ten (10) days' written notice:
   (i)   deliver or cause to be delivered to Bank additional Collateral in an amount sufficient, in Bank's sole discretion, to secure adequately such amounts due Bank; or
   (ii)   reduce the outstanding aggregate balance of Loan(s) by an amount satisfactory to Bank.

(u)   Dealer will not permit:
   (i)   any of the Collateral to be levied or distrained upon under any legal process;
   (ii)   any of the Collateral to become a fixture unless that fact has been disclosed to Bank in advance in writing; or

(iii)   any Item to be subject to any lease or rental agreement if the Account Debtor's obligations thereon have not been assigned to Bank pursuant to the provisions hereof, unless Dealer has paid Bank in full the Loan made to enable Dealer to purchase that Item.

12. EVENTS OF DEFAULT.

Dealer shall be in default hereunder upon the occurrence of any one or more of the following ("Events of Default"):

(a)   The failure of Dealer at any time to observe or perform any of its agreements, warranties, representations, covenants or obligations contained in this Agreement, the Note(s) or any other document related hereto, or if any statement, warranty, representation, covenant, signature or information made herein or contained in any application, exhibit, schedule, statement, certificate, financial statement or other document executed or delivered pursuant to or in connection with this Agreement or the Note(s), was or is incorrect, incomplete, false or misleading;

(b)   The failure of Dealer to furnish promptly to Bank such financial or other information as Bank may reasonably request;

(c)   The failure to pay the outstanding balance of Loan(s) and all accrued interest thereon to Bank UPON DEMAND by Bank or the nonpayment when due of any amount payable on any of Dealer's Liabilities to Bank of whatsoever nature;

(d)   The failure of Dealer to observe or perform any agreement of any nature whatsoever with Bank or any other party; or the occurrence of any event of default, or any event that, with the passage of time or giving of notice or both, would be an event of default by Dealer under any other agreement;

(e)   Dealer, or any surety or guarantor for Dealer's Liabilities to Bank, becomes insolvent, or makes any assignment for the benefit of creditors, or any petition is filed by or against Dealer, or any surety or guarantor for Dealer's Liabilities to Bank, under the federal Bankruptcy Code or under any provision of any other law or statute alleging that Dealer, or any surety or guarantor for Dealer's Liabilities to Bank, is insolvent or unable to pay debts as they mature;

(f)   The entry of any judicial or tax lien against Dealer, or any surety or guarantor for Dealer's Liabilities to Bank, or against any of their respective properties, whether such lien is junior or senior to Bank's security interest, or the appointment of any receiver, trustee, conservator or other court officer over the Dealer, or any surety or guarantor for Dealer's Liabilities to Bank, or against any of their respective properties, for any purpose, or the occurrence of any change in the financial condition of Dealer or any surety or guarantor for Dealer's Liabilities to Bank, which, in the sole judgment of Bank, is materially adverse;

(g)   The Collateral or any rights therein shall be subject to or threatened with any judicial process, condemnation or forfeiture proceedings;

(h)   The dissolution, merger, consolidation or reorganization of Dealer;

(i)   A substantial change, as determined by Bank in its sole judgment, in the identity, ownership, control or management of Dealer;

(j)   The cancellation, termination or other loss of any franchise held by Dealer, or any restriction on such franchise that affects adversely, as determined by Bank in its sole judgment, Dealer's continued existence, operations or financial condition;

(k)   The borrowing of any money by Dealer from any source other than Bank, whether or not subordinate to this Agreement or the Note(s) executed in conjunction herewith, without Bank's prior written consent;

(l)   Bank believes, in good faith, subject only to its own business judgment, that the prospect of any payment or performance of any obligation hereunder is or may become impaired.

13. BANK'S RIGHTS UPON DEFAULT.

Upon the occurrence of any Event of Default, Bank may, without notice and at its option, do any or all of the following:

(a)   Exercise from time to time any and all rights and remedies available to Bank under the UCC or otherwise available to Bank, including the right to collect, settle, compromise, adjust, sue for, foreclose or otherwise realize upon any of the Collateral and to dispose of any of the Collateral at public or private sale(s) or other proceedings, and Dealer agrees that Bank or its nominee may become the purchaser at any such public sale(s) and that ten (10) days' prior notice of any such disposition constitutes reasonable notification. The proceeds of any Collateral shall be applied to the payment of Dealer's Liabilities to Bank, in such order as Bank may, in its sole discretion, elect. Dealer waives and releases any right to require Bank to collect any of Dealer's Liabilities to Bank from any other Collateral under any theory of marshaling of assets or otherwise, and specifically authorizes Bank to apply any Collateral in which Dealer has any right, title or interest against any of Dealer's Liabilities to Bank in any manner that Bank may determine.

(b)   Declare all of Dealer's Liabilities to Bank to be immediately due and payable.

(c)   Reduce Dealer's Liabilities to Bank to judgment.

(d)   Appropriate, set-off, and apply, on account of any of Dealer's Liabilities to Bank, all balances of Dealer on deposit with, or held in any capacity by Bank at any time, and any other property of any nature of Dealer that Bank may at any time have in its possession, including but not limited to, certificates of deposit and savings, demand and other deposit accounts, securities and personal property.

(e)   Take possession of all or any Collateral with or without legal process, for the purpose of which Bank through its representatives may enter any premises wherein the Collateral may be found and Dealer, on Bank's request, will assemble the Collateral and make it available to Bank at a place designated by Bank that is reasonably convenient to both Dealer and Bank.

(f)   Bank may send notices in Dealer's name or instruct Dealer to send notices and Dealer agrees to send such, advising any and all Account Debtors that the accounts have been assigned to Bank and that all payments thereon are to be made directly to Bank.

14. MISCELLANEOUS.

(a)   This Agreement shall inure to the benefit of and is and shall continue to be binding upon the parties, their successors, representatives, receivers, trustees, heirs and assigns, but nothing contained herein shall be construed to permit Dealer to assign this Agreement or any of Dealer's rights or obligations hereunder without first obtaining Bank's express written approval.

(b)   Until all of Dealer's Liabilities to Bank are paid in full and all of Dealer's obligations hereunder are satisfactorily performed in full, all obligations, representations, warranties, covenants, undertakings and agreements of Dealer hereunder and under the Note(s) and all other documents executed in connection herewith or related hereto shall remain in full force and effect.

(c)   This Agreement and the Note(s) have been executed pursuant to, delivered in and shall be governed by and construed under the laws of the Commonwealth of Pennsylvania. The parties acknowledge the jurisdiction of the state, federal and local courts located within the Commonwealth of Pennsylvania over controversies arising from or relating to this Agreement.

(d)   If any provision of this Agreement shall for any reason be held to be invalid or unenforceable, such invalidity or unenforceability shall not affect any other provision hereof.

(e)   All rights, powers and remedies of Bank hereunder or under any other obligation are cumulative and not alternative and shall not be exhausted by any single assertion thereof. The failure of Bank to exercise any such right, power or remedy will not be deemed a waiver thereof nor preclude any further or additional exercise of such right, power or remedy, now or in the future, upon any obligation of Dealer. The waiver of any default hereunder shall not be a waiver of any subsequent default. This paragraph shall be applicable to Dealer and any person liable with respect to any of Dealer's obligations.

(f)   All notices provided for herein shall be deemed to have been given:

(i)   if by Bank to Dealer, when deposited in the mail or delivered to a reputable courier addressed to:

```
MAIN MOTORS, INC.
237 NORTH SEVENTH STREET
PHILADELPHIA,   PA   19116
```

; and

(ii)   if by Dealer to Bank upon receipt by Bank at:

```
FIRSTBANK, N.A.
DEALER FINANCE DEPARTMENT
BROAD AND SPRUCE STREETS
PHILADELPHIA, PA 19116
```

(g)   This Agreement:

(i)   is the complete written Agreement of the parties hereto, supersedes any prior understandings or written agreement; and

(ii)   cannot be varied, changed or otherwise modified except by written permission of Bank; and no oral promises, conditions or representations made by either party shall vary the terms and conditions herein.

(h)   This Agreement:

(i)   may be executed in any number of counterparts and all of such counterparts taken together shall be deemed to constitute one and the same document; and

(ii)   shall become effective when each of the parties hereto shall have signed a copy hereof (whether the same or different copies) and shall have delivered the same to Bank or shall have sent to Bank a facsimile or electronic message stating that the same has been signed and mailed to it. Complete sets of counterparts shall be lodged with Dealer and with Bank.

IN WITNESS WHEREOF, the parties have hereunto caused this Agreement to be executed and sealed by their proper and duly authorized representatives as of this ____19th____ day of _____March_____ 20 _02_ .

FIRSTBANK, N.A.   NAME OF DEALER____MAIN MOTORS, INC.____

By: _____   By: _____
        Vice President   G. S. Gessel, President

                                                      (Name and Title)

                                      Attest: _____
                                              Stacey Scribe, Secretary

                                                      (Name and Title)

(If a corporation, Dealer's corporate seal must be affixed and its Secretary, Assistant Secretary, Treasurer or Assistant Treasurer must sign on the line marked "Attest".)

The Dealer's Line of Credit; The Demand Note. A "Demand Note" (Form 7.3) is issued in conjunction with the Dealer Inventory Security Agreement (see ¶ 2). This note evidences the obligation of Main Motors to repay loans made to it under the **line of credit** arrangement (Firstbank makes each advance in its discretion, not pursuant to a commitment). The maximum amount of the line of credit set by the bank and reflected in the Dealer Inventory Security Agreement and the Demand Note is $3,500,000.

Main executes only one note throughout the course of this business relationship with Firstbank. However, should the principal amount of Firstbank's loans to Main Motors rise above the stipulated principal amount, the Demand Note (second paragraph) and the Dealer Inventory Security Agreement (¶ 2) protect Firstbank by virtue of Main's promise therein to repay the actual amount of the loans "as shown on the bank's books and records."[3]

"Picking Up" a Floor Plan. Main Motors decided to change its financing relationship from its current lender (Old Bank) to Firstbank. When this happens, Firstbank is said to "pick up a floor plan."

Before picking up the floor plan Firstbank performs a physical inspection of Main Motors' premises. The bank's representative checks all units in stock by listing the vehicle identification number of each unit and examining all invoices held by the dealer. These invoices reflect the wholesale price that has been paid for each unit. Old Bank will send Firstbank a list of all units upon which Main has an outstanding indebtedness, and Firstbank will compare this list with the list compiled by its own representative. When the two lists match dollar for dollar and cent for cent, Main completes a "Loan Request Form" (Form 7.4). Firstbank requires this document only when it refinances an outstanding indebtedness of a dealer; the form functions as a record of those units in which Firstbank initially takes a security interest.

---

3. Firstbank and other lenders require borrowers to execute and deliver promissory notes largely by custom. For most purposes Firstbank's position would be identical if it were to rely only on a borrower's agreement to repay contained in a Dealer Inventory Security Agreement.

FORM 7.3
DEMAND NOTE

<u> March 19, 2002 </u>
Philadelphia, Pennsylvania

$<u> * * * 3,500,000.00 * * * </u>

FOR VALUE RECEIVED AND INTENDING TO BE LEGALLY BOUND HEREBY, the undersigned (each jointly and severally if more than one and jointly and severally referred to as "Dealer") promises to pay to the order of FIRSTBANK, N.A., Philadelphia, Pennsylvania ("Bank") in lawful money of the United States of America, at any of its banking offices, the principal sum of

THREE MILLION FIVE HUNDRED THOUSAND AND NO/100

Dollars ("Loan Limit") to be repaid ON DEMAND, but until such time as demand is made by Bank, to be repaid in accordance with the terms and conditions of a certain Dealer Inventory Security Agreement between Dealer and Bank dated   March 19, 2002   ("Agreement") together with interest on the outstanding principal balance hereof payable monthly, as billed, at a fluctuating rate per annum equal at all times to   one percent (1)   % per annum over the rate of interest announced by the Bank publicly, from time to time, in Philadelphia, Pennsylvania, as the Bank's base rate, but in no event in excess of the maximum rate permitted by applicable law. Each change in the fluctuating rate shall take effect simultaneously with such change in the Bank's base rate. Interest shall be calculated hereunder for the actual number of days that the principal balance is outstanding, based on a year of three hundred sixty (360) days, unless otherwise specified in writing.

The principal balance due hereunder plus all accrued interest due thereon at any time and from time to time shall be that amount as shown on the Bank's books and records and the statements submitted to Dealer by Bank in accordance with paragraph 2 of the Agreement, which shall, if no timely objection is made, be conclusive and irrefutable evidence of the amount of principal and interest due Bank.

THE AGREEMENT. This Note is the Note(s) referred to in and is issued in conjunction with and under and subject to, the terms and conditions of the Agreement, and is secured by, among other things, the Collateral, as that term is defined in the Agreement and a mortgage on all the real property of   N/A   . Upon the happening of an Event of Default, as specified in the Agreement, Bank will be entitled to all of Bank's Rights Upon Default as specified in the Agreement.

PREPAYMENT. The principal sum due under this Note may be repaid by Dealer in whole or in part without penalty at any time.

MISCELLANEOUS. Dealer hereby waives protest, notice of protest, presentment, dishonor and notice of dishonor. In addition to all other amounts due hereunder, Dealer agrees to pay to Bank all costs (including reasonable attorney's fees) incurred by Bank in connection with the enforcement hereof. The rights and privileges of Bank under this note shall inure to the benefit of Bank's successors and assigns forever. All obligations shall bind Dealer's heirs, successors and assigns forever. If any provision of this Note shall be held to be invalid or unenforceable, such invalidity or unenforceability shall not affect any other provision hereof, but this Note shall be construed as if such invalid or unenforceable provision had never been contained herein. This Note has been delivered in, shall be construed in accordance with, and shall be governed by the laws of the Commonwealth of Pennsylvania. The waiver of any default hereunder shall not be a waiver of any other or subsequent default.

Dealer has duly executed this Note the day and year first above written and has hereunto set hand and seal.

IF INDIVIDUAL(S), SIGN BELOW

_____

_____

_____

IF GENERAL OR LIMITED PARTNERSHIP,
SIGN BELOW

_____(SEAL)

_____(SEAL)

_____(SEAL)

IF A CORPORATION, SIGN BELOW

NAME OF CORPORATION: MAIN MOTORS, INC.

BY: *G. S. Gessell*_____(SEAL)   (AFFIX CORPORATE SEAL HERE)
    G. S. Gessel, President

(NAME AND TITLE)

ATTESTED: *Stacey Scribe*_____
    Stacey Scribe, Secretary

(SIGNATURE AND TITLE)

Upon completion of the Loan Request Form, Firstbank will pay Old Bank (by check or electronic funds transfer) for the total debt on all listed units. In return, Old Bank will sign a release, by which it releases all interest in the units listed, and will provide for filing a *termination statement* (see R9–513) to the effect that it no longer claims a security interest in connection with its financing statement.

FORM 7.4
LOAN REQUEST FORM

<u>March 19</u>, 20<u>02</u>
(Date)

<u>MAIN MOTORS, INC.</u>
(Dealer Name)

<u>237 North Seventh Street</u>
(Street Address)

<u>Philadelphia</u>   <u>PA 19116</u>
(City or Town)   (State)

Dealer hereby requests FIRSTBANK, N.A., Philadelphia, Pennsylvania ("Bank") to make the following Loan(s), as the term Loan(s) is defined in a certain Dealer Inventory Security Agreement and Power of Attorney between Dealer and Bank dated   March 19, 2002 ("Agreement"), in accordance with and under and subject to the terms and conditions of the Agreement. Pursuant to the Agreement, Dealer confirms that it has granted to Bank and hereby affirms and grants to Bank a lien and security interest in the Items of Inventory described below together with all materials, additions, equipment, accessions, accessories and parts installed in, related, attached or added thereto or used in connection therewith and all substitutions and exchanges for and replacements thereof as security for all of "Dealer's Liabilities to Bank".

Loan No.	Description of Item	VIN.	New or Used	Dealer Cost	Less Down Payment	Loan Amount
871	Chevrolet	903399	New	16,123.22	None	16,123.22
871	Chevrolet	803821	New	15,839.44	None	15,839.44
871	Chevrolet	921874	New	25,256.12	None	25,256.12
871	Chevrolet	804745	New	18,740.20	None	18,740.20
871	Chevrolet	800215	New	23,839.44	None	23,839.44
871	Chevrolet	907704	New	21,252.50	None	21,252.50

TOTAL   121,049.92

This Loan Request Form is the Loan Request Form referred to in Paragraph 2 of the Agreement and is issued in conjunction with and under and subject to the terms and conditions of the Agreement. All terms used herein shall be defined as such terms are defined in the Agreement. The Loan(s) requested hereunder are the Loan(s) referred to in Paragraph 2 of the Agreement and the Items of Inventory described herein are the Items of Inventory referred to in the Agreement, which is part of the Collateral as that term is defined in the Agreement.

As an inducement to Bank to make the Loan(s) requested hereby, Dealer hereby reaffirms and restates all of Dealer's agreements, liabilities, representations, warranties, covenants and obligations under the Agreement and further covenants that if the Loan(s) requested hereunder are made by Bank they are and will be received by Dealer under and subject to all the terms and conditions of the Agreement.

IF INDIVIDUAL(S), SIGN BELOW

_____

_____

_____

IF GENERAL OR LIMITED PARTNERSHIP,
SIGN BELOW

_____(SEAL)

_____(SEAL)

_____(SEAL)

IF A CORPORATION, SIGN BELOW

NAME OF CORPORATION: __MAIN MOTORS, INC.__

BY:___*G.S. Gessel*_____(SEAL)   (AFFIX CORPORATE SEAL HERE)
      G. S. Gessel, President

(NAME AND TITLE)

ATTESTED:___*Stacey Scribe*_____
      Stacey Scribe, Secretary

(SIGNATURE AND TITLE)

Figure 7.1 diagrams the documentation and payment involved when Firstbank picks up Main Motors' floor plan from Old Bank.

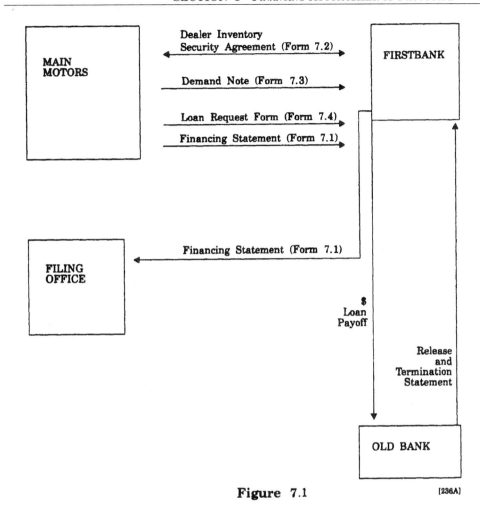

Figure 7.1   [236A]

Financing of New Deliveries. Firstbank will make loans to finance new deliveries of automobiles from the Chevrolet Motor Division of General Motors Corporation by advancing the wholesale price of each automobile directly to General Motors. The details of that procedure are addressed below.

(C) DELIVERY OF AUTOMOBILES: ASSURING THE MANUFACTURER OF PAYMENT

General Motors, like all other automobile manufacturers, does not extend credit to automobile dealers in connection with the purchase of automobiles. Consequently, General Motors must either be paid or be assured of payment before delivery.

At one time it was customary to ship new automobiles by rail, and to send a **sight draft** (instruction to pay upon presentment), accompanied by a negotiable bill of lading, to a local bank that would release the bill of lading to the dealer upon the dealer's payment of the draft. Today, new automobiles usually are delivered by highway trailer. These vehicle haul-away carriers, unlike the railroads, typically do not have facilities to store automobiles during periods of delay that may occur when negotiable bills of lading, with sight drafts attached, pass through banking channels into the hands of the dealer. This relatively cumbersome method of controlling delivery until payment is unnecessary because of the assurance of payment that Firstbank's letter of credit (described next) affords General Motors.

Bank Letter of Credit; Dealer Inventory Security Agreement. In order to provide assurance of payment, Firstbank issues a **letter of credit** in favor of General Motors. The letter of credit provides that from time to time, subject to a stated limitation on amount per week, upon receipt of General Motors' (paper or electronic) draft drawn on Firstbank accompanied by an automobile invoice for the automobiles being shipped, Firstbank will pay to General Motors the amount of the invoice. Of course, under the Dealer Inventory Security Agreement, Main Motors agrees to reimburse Firstbank for all amounts advanced to General Motors under the letter of credit and further agrees that all such amounts constitute loans made under the line of credit established under the Dealer Inventory Security Agreement (Form 7.2) and the Demand Note (Form 7.3).

On receipt of an order for new automobiles from Main Motors, General Motors sends the automobiles and the related manufacturer's certificates of origin[4] directly to Main Motors and, through the bank collection system, sends to Firstbank information describing the shipment (giving models, vehicle identification numbers, and prices of automobiles) and its draft calling on Firstbank to pay under the letter of credit. Upon receipt of these documents, Firstbank pays General Motors by sending funds to General Motors' bank, for credit to General Motors' account. Under an alternative arrangement, General Motors would maintain a bank account with First-bank and, upon receipt of the documents, Firstbank would credit that account.

Figure 7.2 diagrams the documentation and payment involved each time Firstbank makes an advance for a new delivery of automobiles by General Motors to Main Motors.

---

4. The function of the manufacturer's certificates of origin is explained below in connection with financing sales to consumers.

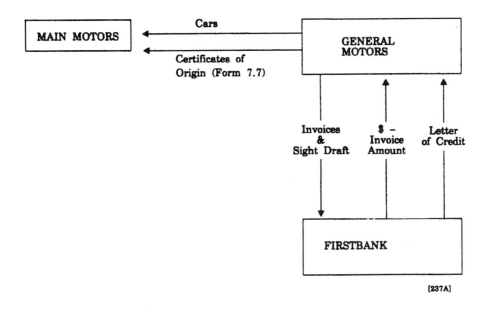

Figure 7.2

Option to Repurchase. Although the letter of credit arrangement just described provides General Motors with assurance of payment, General Motors also has an interest in protecting its reputation and its products in the marketplace. Specifically, General Motors wishes to ensure that new General Motors automobiles are sold only by authorized dealers who maintain certain standards. Consequently, General Motors requires its dealers to obtain secured financing from lenders who enter into an agreement affording General Motors a repurchase option. Under that agreement (which is not to be confused with securities "repos," discussed in Chapter 6 Section 1(B), supra), if Main Motors defaults and Firstbank takes possession of its inventory of automobiles, then General Motors will have an option to repurchase the automobiles for the original wholesale price. Firstbank is not averse to that arrangement; General Motors' exercise of its option to repurchase would provide a convenient means for Firstbank to recover the principal amount of its outstanding loans on new automobiles. General Motors is unique in this respect; automobile inventory financers such as Firstbank typically insist on and receive a repurchase *obligation* from other automobile manufacturers.

(D) DIAGRAM OF AUTOMOBILE DEALER INVENTORY FINANCING

Figure 7.3 diagrams all of the transactions and documentation involved in the Prototype automobile dealer inventory financing.

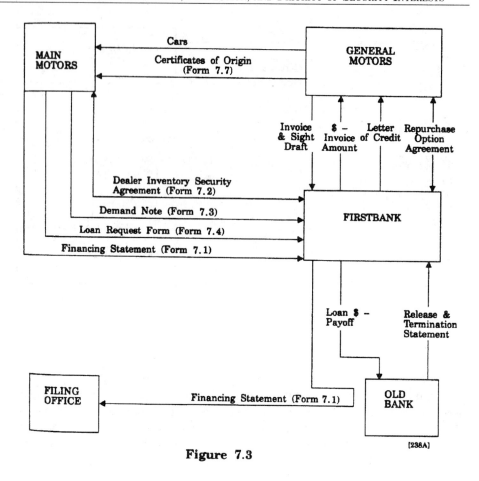

Figure 7.3

(E) SALES TO CONSUMERS

Lee Abel drives a 1995 Mazda Miata to Main's showroom and, after negotiating a $10,556 trade-in allowance for the used car, reaches an agreement with one of Main's salespersons for the purchase of a 2001 Chevrolet Blazer for a cash price of $27,056. (Actually, the negotiations focused on the amount by which the cash price would exceed the trade-in allowance for the Miata; Abel was satisfied with the difference of $16,500, making the trade-in allowance and cash price generally irrelevant to Abel.) Like most automobile buyers, Abel will buy on credit.

The Credit Decision. The relationship between Firstbank and Main Motors concerning consumer installment sales agreements is developed in detail below. For the moment, recall that Main Motors is not in a position to wait for Abel to pay for the new automobile over 48 months. It follows that Main's decision to sell to Abel on credit depends on whether a third-party financer (here, Firstbank) is willing to purchase Abel's installment obligation from Main, thereby putting Main in funds at the inception of the transaction.

Main Motors asks Abel to fill out an "Instalment Credit Application" supplied by Firstbank. That form calls for information concerning Abel's place and length of employment, salary, number of dependents, banking relationships, and other credit outstanding, as well as other information relevant to Firstbank's credit decision. Main Motors then faxes the application to Firstbank's consumer credit department. Firstbank's staff reviews the application, obtains information about Abel's credit history and credit-worthiness from a centralized **credit reporting agency**, and (within a matter of hours) reaches a decision about whether to extend credit to Abel.

Typically Firstbank's credit investigation shows that the prospective buyer is a satisfactory risk for the amount of credit requested. If so, Firstbank agrees to purchase the installment contract, provided that the amount of the down payment and other terms meet its standard requirements. One typical requirement is that the down payment reduce the amount owing for the automobile to not more than the dealer's cost. In this case, the trade-in allowance of $10,556 for Abel's used car reduces the unpaid balance to $16,500—comfortably less than the $25,256 wholesale cost of the new Chevrolet. Nevertheless, the present case does deviate from the customary pattern in that the credit investigation shows that Abel, although honest and reliable, occasionally has been slow in meeting installment obligations.

Alternative Assignment Plans. The method for dealing with this problem depends in part upon the underlying arrangement between a dealer and a purchaser of installment paper for the allocation of the risk of default by buyers. There are five common forms of agreements between a dealer and an assignee of installment credit contracts: (1) without recourse, (2) repurchase, (3) partial guaranty, (4) limited repurchase, and (5) full guaranty. The details of each of these alternatives are found in an "Assignment and Repurchase Agreement" (Form 7.5).

Note that Form 7.5 refers to an arrangement called the "Firstbank Retail Plan." That arrangement consists of a set of standard provisions that Firstbank and Main Motors (and Firstbank's other dealer customers) have agreed will apply to all purchases of consumer installment contracts. It contemplates that in the normal case Firstbank would purchase contracts of buyers on a **non-recourse** basis (i.e., Firstbank will not look to the dealer-assignor in the event of a buyer's nonpayment), thereby relieving Main Motors of liability or risk by reason of a buyer's failure to pay. In this case, however, because of the "slow pay" reports on Abel, Firstbank and Main Motors agree to allocate the risk of default differently. Firstbank requests Main to execute the "repurchase" portion of the Assignment and Repurchase Agreement.

FORM 7.5
ASSIGNMENT AND REPURCHASE AGREEMENT

A. For value received, the undersigned does hereby sell, assign and transfer to Firstbank, N.A. his, its or their entire right, title and interest in and to the attached contract, herewith submitted to Firstbank, N.A. for acceptance, and the property covered thereby, described as follows:

DESCRIPTION OF CONTRACT

Type of Contract	Date of Contract	Customer's Name
Motor Vehicle Installment Sales Contract	7/09/02	Lee Abel

Covering the following property

Year	Make	New or Used	Model	Vehicle Identification No.
2001	Chevrolet	New	Blazer	1FMES24VS2921874

and authorizes Firstbank, N.A. to do every act and thing necessary to collect and discharge obligations arising out of or incident to said contract and assignment. In order to induce Firstbank, N.A. to accept assignment of the contract, the undersigned warrants that: the contract arose from the sale of the within described property; the contract was complete in all respects and the undersigned made all disclosures required by law, including all disclosures required by Title 1 of the Consumer Credit Protection Act of 1968, as amended, and by local law; prior to execution thereof by the Customer, the Customer is not a minor and has capacity to contract; the contract and personal guaranty by third party, if any, are genuine, legally valid and enforceable and comply with all applicable requirements of state and federal law; title to the contract is vested in the undersigned free of all liens and encumbrances and the undersigned has the right to assign the contract; the property is as represented to the Customer by the undersigned, statements made by the Customer in the contract are true to the best of the undersigned's knowledge and belief, and the undersigned has no knowledge of any fact that would impair the validity or value of the contract; the down payment paid by the Customer and received by the undersigned was as stated in the contract; a certificate of title to the property showing the lien or encumbrance for the benefit of Firstbank, N.A. or the undersigned has been or will be applied for forthwith, if permitted by law. If there is a breach of any such warranty, without regard to the undersigned's knowledge or lack of knowledge with respect thereto or Firstbank, N.A.'s reliance thereon, the undersigned hereby agrees unconditionally, notwithstanding the numbered paragraph below executed by the undersigned, to purchase said contract from Firstbank, N.A. upon demand, for the full amount then unpaid whether said contract shall then be, or not be, in default. The undersigned further agrees that in the event the Customer or any other person or governmental agency makes a claim against Firstbank, N.A. alleging facts which, if true, would constitute a breach of any of the foregoing warranties or representations, the undersigned shall assume the defense of such claim and shall indemnify and save Firstbank, N.A. harmless from all loss, cost and expenses arising therefrom, and, at Firstbank, N.A.'s option, the undersigned will repurchase the contract for the full amount then unpaid. Liability of the undersigned arising out of or incident to this assignment shall not be affected by any indulgence, compromise, settlement, extensions, or variations of terms of said contract effected with, or by, the discharge or release of the obligation of the Customer or any other person interested, by operation of law or otherwise. The undersigned waives notice of acceptance of this assignment and notices of non-payment and non-performance of the contract. The acceptance or approval of the contract by Firstbank, N.A. shall not constitute an agreement, representation or warranty by Firstbank, N.A. as to the legal sufficiency thereof or of the disclosures therein contained or a waiver of Firstbank, N.A.'s right to rely on the foregoing warranties or representations with respect thereto

B. As part of the foregoing assignment, the undersigned's obligations are further defined in the particular numbered paragraph below executed by the undersigned, and signature of any such numbered paragraph shall constitute signature of the entire assignment.

---

1. "Without Recourse" (See paragraphs A and B above)
The assignment of said contract is and shall be without recourse against the undersigned, except as otherwise provided above and by the terms of the Firstbank, N.A. Retail Plan in effect at the time this assignment is accepted.

Seller Signs_____By_____
(If corporation or partnership) (Title)

---

2. "Repurchase" (See paragraphs A and B above)
The undersigned guaranties payment of the full amount remaining unpaid under said contract, and covenants if default be made in payment of any instalment thereunder to pay the full amount then unpaid to Firstbank, N.A., upon demand, except as otherwise provided by the terms of the Firstbank, N.A. Retail Plan in effect at the time this assignment is accepted.

Main Motors, Inc.

Seller Signs *G.S. Gessell*   By G. S. Gessell, President
(If corporation or partnership) (Title)

---

3. "Partial Guaranty" (See paragraphs A and B above)
Notwithstanding the terms of the Firstbank, N.A. Retail Plan, the undersigned unconditionally guaranties payment of the full amount remaining unpaid under said contract, and agrees to purchase said contract from Firstbank, N.A. upon demand for the full amount then unpaid whether said contract shall then be, or not be, in default, provided, however, at the time of any such demand by Firstbank, N.A. the undersigned may, at his election, pay to Firstbank, N.A. the sum of $_____ in consideration of being released from such guaranty obligation, and in such event, the assignment of said contract is without recourse against the undersigned, except as otherwise provided above and by the terms of the Firstbank, N.A. Retail Plan in effect at the time this assignment is accepted.

Seller Signs_____By_____
(If corporation or partnership) (Title)

---

4. "Limited Repurchases" (See paragraphs A and B above)
The undersigned guaranties payment of the full amount remaining unpaid under said contract, and covenants if default be made in payment of any instalment thereunder to pay the full amount then unpaid to Firstbank, N.A. upon demand, except as otherwise provided by the terms of the Firstbank, N.A. Retail Plan in effect at the time this assignment is accepted provided, that if the Customer satisfactorily pays each of the first _____ instalments coming due under the within contract, this assignment shall thereafter be without recourse against the undersigned, except as otherwise provided above and by the terms of the Firstbank, N.A. Retail Plan in effect at the time this assignment is accepted.

Seller Signs_____By_____
(If corporation or partnership) (Title)

---

5. "Full Guaranty" (See paragraphs A and B above)
Notwithstanding the terms of the Firstbank, N.A. Retail Plan, the undersigned unconditionally guaranties payment of the full amount remaining unpaid under said contract, and agrees to purchase said contract from Firstbank, N.A., upon demand, for the full amount then unpaid, whether said contract shall then be, or not be, in default.

Seller Signs_____By_____
(If corporation or partnership) (Title)

NOTE: If a corporation, assignment must be executed in the name of the corporation by an officer having proper authority from the Board of Directors. If a partnership, assignment must be executed by a partner.

Under the "repurchase" terms, if a default occurs under Abel's contract, Main Motors agrees to repurchase the contract from Firstbank by paying the entire unpaid amount thereunder. Although not reflected in the Assignment and Repurchase Agreement, the terms of the Firstbank Retail Plan provide that Main would not be required to repurchase the contract until after Firstbank takes possession of the car from Abel. Thus this arrangement divides the burdens and risks of default between Firstbank and Main Motors: Firstbank assumes the burden of repossession and also the risk of loss in the event the automobile cannot be located for repossession; Main Motors assumes the burdens and losses involved in any foreclosure proceedings and in collecting any deficiency from Abel.

The Dealer's Contract With the Consumer. With financing arrangements completed, Main Motors is in a position to make delivery to Abel. As we have seen, Main Motors and Abel have agreed on a cash price of $27,056 for the Chevrolet. Main has agreed to take Abel's 1995 Miata for a trade-in credit of $10,556, leaving a balance of $16,500. In addition, Abel must pay state sales taxes ($1,036.50) and fees ($29.00) and a documentation fee to Main Motors ($40.00). Abel also has elected to purchase an extended warranty contract ($775.00). These costs bring Abel's unpaid obligation for the car to $18,380.50.

Abel also must pay a finance charge. In this instance, Abel agrees to pay an Annual Percentage Rate of 9.5% on the amount financed, which amounts to $3,784.74 for the four years the contract is to run. This finance charge brings the total of payments to $22,165.24, payable in 48 installments of $461.79. Main Motors and Abel sign an "Instalment Sale Contract" (Form 7.6) that evidences this obligation. Certain provisions of Form 7.6, such as disclosure of the Total Sale Price and the Annual Percentage Rate, are included in order to comply with the Truth In Lending Act, 15 U.S.C. §§ 1601–1667f. (Form 7.6 would not be used in an actual transaction in Pennsylvania because it does not contain certain disclosures required under Pennsylvania law. We have assumed away these provisions of Pennsylvania law in order to simplify the Prototype).

In addition to providing for Abel's payment obligations, the Instalment Sale Contract also contains a security agreement in which Abel grants a security interest in the new car to Main Motors to secure those payment obligations. When the assignment by Main to Firstbank is effected, Firstbank becomes Abel's creditor and is the new secured party in the transaction.[5] (Accordingly, as discussed below, Firstbank will promptly send Abel a notification of the assignment and instruct Abel to make all payments under the Instalment Sale Contract directly to Firstbank.)

---

5. You may note that at the bottom of the face of the Instalment Sale Contract there is a brief assignment form that refers to the Firstbank Retail Plan agreement, as does the Assignment and Repurchase Agreement (Form 7.5). Because the parties elected the "repurchase" option in Form 7.5, Main Motors has signed the "without recourse or with limited recourse" form of assignment on the Instalment Sale Contract.

FORM 7.6
FORM OF INSTALMENT SALE CONTRACT

RETAIL INSTALMENT SALE CONTRACT

Dealer Number	Contract Number

Buyer (and Co-Buyer) – Name and address (include county and zip code)	Creditor (Seller name and address)
LEE ABEL 123 EAST 10TH STREET PHILADELPHIA, PA 19116	MAIN MOTORS, INC 237 NORTH 7TH STREET PHILADELPHIA, PA 19116

You, the Buyer (and Co-Buyer, if any), may buy the vehicle described below for cash or on credit. The cash price is shown below as "cash price." The credit price is shown below as "Total Sale Price." By signing this contract, you choose to buy the vehicle on credit under the agreements on the front and back of this contract. You agree to pay us, the Creditor, the Amount Financed and Finance Charge according to the payment schedule shown below.

New or Used	Year	Make and Model	Vehicle Identification No.	Primary Use for Which Purchased
NEW	2001	CHEVROLET BLAZER	1FMES23VS292187	☒ personal, family, or household ☐ agricultural ☐ business ☐

Your trade-in is a: Year _____   Make _____   Model _____

FEDERAL TRUTH-IN-LENDING DISCLOSURES

ANNUAL PERCENTAGE RATE The cost of your credit as a yearly rate.	FINANCE CHARGE The dollar amount the credit will cost you.	Amount Financed The amount of credit provided to you or on your behalf.	Total of Payments The amount you will have paid after you have made all payments as scheduled.	Total Sale Price The total cost of your purchase on credit, including your downpayment of $10556
9.50 %	$ 3784.74	$ 18380.50	$ 20277.60	$ 30833.60

Insurance. You may buy the physical damage insurance this contract requires (see back) from anyone you choose who is acceptable to us. You are not required to buy any other insurance to obtain credit.

If any insurance is checked below, policies or certificates from the named insurance companies will describe the terms and conditions.

Your Payment Schedule Will Be:

Number of Payments	Amount of Payments	When Payments Are Due	Or as Follows
48	$ 461.79	Monthly beginning 8/24/01	N/A

Late Charge. If a payment is not received in full within 10 days after it is due, you will pay a late charge of 5% of the part of the payment that is late, with a minimum charge of $1.
Prepayment. If you pay off all your debt early, you may be entitled to a refund of part of the finance charge.
Security Interest. You are giving a security interest in the vehicle being purchased.
Additional Information: See this contract for more information including information about nonpayment, default, any required repayment in full before the scheduled date, prepayment refunds and security interest.

Check the insurance you want and sign below:

Optional Credit Insurance.

☐ Credit Life: ☐ Buyer   ☐ Co-Buyer   ☐ Both
☐ Credit Disability (Buyer Only)

Premium:
   Credit Life $ _____
   Credit Disability $ _____

_____
(Insurance Company)

_____
(Home Office Address)

ITEMIZATION OF AMOUNT FINANCED

1 Cash price (including any accessories, services, and taxes)	$ 27056.00	(1)
2 Total downpayment = (If negative enter "0" and see line 4H below)		
Gross trade-in $ 10556 –payoff by seller $ 0		
= net trade-in $ 10556 – cash $ 0		
+ other (describe) $	$ 10556.00	(2)
3 Unpaid balance of cash price (1 minus 2)	$ 16500.00	(3)
4 Other charges including amounts paid to others on your behalf (Seller may keep part of these amounts.):		
A Cost of optional credit insurance paid to the insurance company or companies.		
Life $		
Disability $	$ N/A	
B Other insurance paid to the insurance company	$ N/A	
C Official fees paid to government agencies	$ 5.00	
D Taxes not included in cash price	$ 1036.50	
E Government license and/or registration fees (identify)	$ 4.00	
F Government certificate of title fees	$ 20.00	
G Other charges (Seller must identify who is paid and describe purpose)		
to GMPP for 60 mos/60,000 mi $ 775.00		
to Main Motors for Doc Fee $ 40.00		
to _____ for _____ $		
H Net trade-in payoff to $		
Total other charges and amounts paid to others on your behalf	$ 1880.50	(4)
5 Amount financed (3 + 4)	$ 18380.50	(5)

Credit life insurance and credit disability insurance are not required to obtain credit. They will not be provided unless you sign and agree to pay the extra cost. Credit life insurance and credit disability insurance are for the term of this contract unless a different term for the insurance is shown below.

Other Insurance.

☐ _____
  Type of Insurance   Term

Premium $ _____

_____
(Insurance Company)

_____
(Home Office Address)

I want the insurance checked above.

_____
Buyer Signature   Date

_____
Co-Buyer Signature   Date

ANY INSURANCE REFERRED TO IN THIS CONTRACT DOES NOT INCLUDE COVERAGE FOR PERSONAL LIABILITY AND PROPERTY DAMAGE CAUSED TO OTHERS.

HOW THIS CONTRACT CAN BE CHANGED. This contract contains the entire agreement between you and us relating to this contract. Any change to the contract must be in writing and we must sign it. No oral changes are binding. Buyer (and any Co-Buyer) initials _____

If any part of this contract is not valid, all other parts stay valid. We may delay or refrain from enforcing any of our rights under this contract without losing them. For example, we may extend the time for making some payments without extending the time for making others.

See back for other important agreements.

You agree to the terms of this contract and confirm that you received a completely filled-in copy when you signed it.

Buyer Signs _Lee Abel_   Date _7/9/02_   Co-Buyer Signs _____   Date _____

Co-Buyers and Other Owners – A co-buyer is a person who is responsible for paying the entire debt. An other owner is a person whose name is on the title to the vehicle but does not have to pay the debt. The co-buyer or other owner knows that we have a security interest in the vehicle and consents to the security interest.

Other owner signs here _____   Address _____

Creditor Signs   MAIN MOTORS, INC   Date 7/9/2002   By _B. Fald_   Title Sales Manager

Seller assigns its interest in this contract to Firstbank, N.A. under the terms of the Firstbank, N.A. Retail Plan agreement.

Assigned with recourse			Assigned without recourse or with limited recourse		
			MAIN MOTORS, INC _B. Falc._		Sales Manager
Seller	By	Title	Seller	By	Title

Notice: See Other Side

(FACE)

OTHER IMPORTANT AGREEMENTS

1. YOUR OTHER PROMISES TO US

a. **If the vehicle is damaged, destroyed, or missing.** You agree to pay us all you owe under this contract even if the vehicle is damaged, destroyed, or missing.

b. **Using the vehicle.** You agree not to remove the vehicle from the U.S. or Canada, or to sell, rent, lease, or transfer any interest in the vehicle or this contract without our written permission. You agree not to expose the vehicle to misuse, seizure, confiscation, or involuntary transfer. If we pay any repair bills, storage bills, taxes, fines, or charges on the vehicle, you agree to repay the amount when we ask for it.

c. **Security interest.** You give us a security interest in:
   1. The vehicle and all parts or goods installed in it;
   2. All money or goods received (proceeds) for the vehicle;
   3. All insurance or service contracts we finance for you; and
   4. All proceeds from insurance or service contracts we finance for you. This includes any refunds of premiums.

   This secures payment of all you owe on this contract. It also secures your other agreements in this contract. You will make sure the title shows our security interest (lien) in the vehicle.

d. **Insurance you must have on the vehicle.** You agree to have physical damage insurance covering loss or damage to the vehicle for the term of this contract. The insurance must cover our interest in the vehicle. If you do not have this insurance, we may, if we decide, buy physical damage insurance. If we decide to buy physical damage insurance, we may either buy insurance that covers your interest and our interest in the vehicle, or buy insurance that covers only our interest. If we buy either type of insurance, we will tell you which type and the charge you must pay. The charge will be the premium for the insurance and a finance charge at the highest rate the law permits.

   If the vehicle is lost or damaged, you agree that we may use any insurance settlement to reduce what you owe or repair the vehicle.

e. **What happens to returned insurance or service contract charges.** If we obtain a refund of insurance or service contract charges, we will apply the refund and the unearned finance charges on the refund to as many of your payments as they will cover beginning with the final payment. We will tell you what we do.

2. YOU MAY PREPAY IN FULL

You may prepay all of your debt and get a refund of part of the Finance Charge.

How we will calculate your Finance Charge refund. We will figure the refund by the Rule of 78's if the term of this contract is 61 months or less. If the term of this contract is more than 61 months, we will figure the refund by the Actuarial Method using the payment dates in this contract. We will not pay you a refund if it is less than $1.

3. IF YOU PAY LATE OR BREAK YOUR OTHER PROMISES

a. **You may owe late charges.** You will pay a late charge on each payment we receive more than ten days late. The charge is on the front. Acceptance of a late payment or late charge does not excuse your late payment or mean that you may keep making late payments. If you pay late, we may also take the steps described below.

b. **You may have to pay all you owe at once.** If you break your promises (default), we may demand that you pay all you owe on this contract at once. Default means:
   1. You do not pay any payment on time;
   2. You start a proceeding in bankruptcy or one is started against you or your property; or
   3. You break any agreements in this contract.

   In figuring what you owe, we will give you a refund of part of the Finance Charge as if you had prepaid in full.

c. **You may have to pay collection costs.** If we hire an attorney to collect what you owe, you will pay the attorney's fee and court costs, as the law allows.

d. **We may take the vehicle from you.** If you default, we may take (repossess) the vehicle from you if we do so peacefully and the law allows it. If your vehicle has an electronic tracking device, you agree that we may use the device to find the vehicle. If we take the vehicle, any accessories, equipment, and replacement parts will stay with the vehicle. If any personal items are in the vehicle, we may store them for you at your expense. If you do not ask for these items back, we may dispose of them as the law allows.

e. **How you can get the vehicle back if we take it.** If we repossess the vehicle, you may pay to get it back (redeem). We will tell you how much to pay to redeem. Your right to redeem ends when we sell the vehicle.

f. **We will sell the vehicle** if you do not get it back. If you do not redeem, we will sell the vehicle. We will send you a written notice of sale before selling the vehicle.

   We will apply the money from the sale, less allowed expenses, to the amount you owe. Allowed expenses are expenses we pay as a direct result of taking the vehicle, holding it, preparing it for sale, and selling it. Attorney fees and court costs the law permits are also allowed expenses. If any money is left (surplus), we will pay it to you. If money from the sale is not enough to pay the amount you owe, you must pay the rest to us. If you do not pay this amount when we ask, we may charge you interest at the highest lawful rate until you pay.

g. **What we may do about optional insurance or service contracts.** This contract may contain charges for optional insurance or service contracts. If we repossess the vehicle, you agree that we may claim benefits under these contracts and cancel them to obtain refunds of unearned charges to reduce what you owe or repair the vehicle.

4. WARRANTIES SELLER DISCLAIMS

Unless the Seller makes a written warranty, or enters into a service contract within 90 days from the date of this contract, the Seller makes no warranties, express or implied, on the vehicle, and there will be no implied warranties of merchantability or of fitness for a particular purpose.

This provision does not affect any warranties covering the vehicle that the vehicle manufacturer may provide.

5. Used Car Buyers Guide. The information you see on the window form for this vehicle is part of this contract. Information on the window form overrides any contrary provisions in the contract of sale.

Spanish Translation:
Guía para compradores de vehículos usados. La información que ve en el formulario de la ventanilla para este vehículo forma parte del presente contrato. La información del formulario de la ventanilla deja sin efecto toda disposición en contrario contenida en el contrato de venta.

6. APPLICABLE LAW

Federal and Pennsylvania law apply to this contract.

NOTICE: ANY HOLDER OF THIS CONSUMER CREDIT CONTRACT IS SUBJECT TO ALL CLAIMS AND DEFENSES WHICH THE DEBTOR COULD ASSERT AGAINST THE SELLER OF GOODS OR SERVICES OBTAINED PURSUANT HERETO OR WITH THE PROCEEDS HEREOF. RECOVERY HEREUNDER BY THE DEBTOR SHALL NOT EXCEED AMOUNTS PAID BY THE DEBTOR HEREUNDER.

The preceding NOTICE applies only to goods or services obtained primarily for personal, family, or household use. In all other cases, Buyer will not assert against any subsequent holder or assignee of this contract any claims or defenses the Buyer (debtor) may have against the Seller, or against the manufacturer of the vehic' .r equipment obtained under this contract.

(REVERSE)

Figure 7.4 diagrams the documentation and deliveries involved when Main Motors sells the new car to Lee Abel and assigns Abel's Instalment Sale Contract to Firstbank.

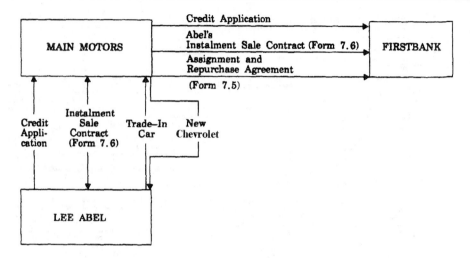

Figure 7.4

[239A]

(F) PERFECTING THE SECURITY INTEREST IN THE NEW CAR; THE CERTIFICATE OF TITLE

One of the terms of Firstbank's purchase of Abel's Instalment Sale Contract is that the security interest in Abel's Chevrolet is to be perfected. (This is a warranty that Main Motors makes under the Firstbank Retail Plan agreement.) All states now have "certificate of title" laws; although these laws vary materially, in general they provide that the normal method of perfecting a security interest in an automobile (or other vehicle required to be titled) is by causing the security interest to be reflected on the certificate of title issued by a central state office (e.g., in Pennsylvania, the Bureau of Motor Vehicles). An exception is made for vehicles in a dealer's inventory, as to which the usual financing statement filing rules apply. See R9–311(d).

Certificates of Origin and Control Over Dealer Operations. For each new vehicle, the manufacturer issues a manufacturer's certificate of origin (Form 7.7) (sometimes referred to as an "MCO").

In most states, because a certificate of title for a new vehicle cannot be issued without presenting a certificate of origin, the latter document is a useful device to ensure that a dealer is operating in conformity with its financing agreement. For this reason, some lenders hold certificates of origin in their own files until they receive word from a dealer that a particular automobile has been sold. Firstbank, like many other lenders, has decided that holding each certificate of origin for each automobile would be too cumbersome; Firstbank also is satisfied with the integrity of Main Motors' operation. Consequently, Firstbank has notified General Motors that these documents are to be delivered directly to Main Motors.

At least once a month Firstbank does a floorplan check at each dealership it finances. During the check the bank's representative looks at every new automobile listed on the invoices it has received from the manufacturer (i.e., all of the automobiles it has financed). After checking the collateral, the representative matches the serial numbers of the units with the serial numbers printed on the certificates of origin kept in the dealer's files. This is done to make sure that each automobile on the floorplan financing remains untitled. If either a certificate of origin or a automobile is missing, Firstbank probably should have been paid by the dealer.[6]

---

6. Under the terms of the Dealer Inventory Security Agreement (Form 7.2, ¶ 8), a dealer is required to repay immediately the amount loaned to finance an automobile (here, the wholesale price) when an automobile is sold. The absence of an automobile or a certificate of origin would be an indication that a sale may have occurred.

FORM 7.7
MANUFACTURER'S CERTIFICATE OF ORIGIN

(FACE)

Each undersigned seller certifies to the best of his knowledge, information and belief under penalty of the law that the vehicle is new and has not been registered in this or any state at the time of delivery and the vehicle is not subject to any security interests other than those disclosed herein and warrant title to the vehicle.

FOR VALUE RECEIVED I TRANSFER THE VEHICLE DESCRIBED ON THE FACE OF THIS CERTIFICATE TO:

DISTRIBUTOR-DEALER ASSIGNMENT NUMBER 1

NAME OF PURCHASER(S)_____

ADDRESS_____

I certify to the best of my knowledge that the odometer reading is _____ No Tenths

DEALER _____ BY_____
NAME OF DEALERSHIP   DEALER'S LICENSE NUMBER

Being duly sworn upon oath says that the statements set forth are true and correct. Subscribed and sworn to me

State of_____ before this _____ day of_____ 19____

County of_____ Notary Public

USE NOTARIZATION ONLY IF REQUIRED IN TITLING JURISDICTION

DISTRIBUTOR-DEALER ASSIGNMENT NUMBER 2

NAME OF PURCHASER(S)_____

ADDRESS_____

I certify to the best of my knowledge that the odometer reading is _____ No Tenths

DEALER _____ BY_____
NAME OF DEALERSHIP   DEALER'S LICENSE NUMBER

Being duly sworn upon oath says that the statements set forth are true and correct. Subscribed and sworn to me

State of_____ before this _____ day of_____ 19____

County of_____ Notary Public

USE NOTARIZATION ONLY IF REQUIRED IN TITLING JURISDICTION

DISTRIBUTOR-DEALER ASSIGNMENT NUMBER 3

NAME OF PURCHASER(S)_____

ADDRESS_____

I certify to the best of my knowledge that the odometer reading is _____ No Tenths

DEALER _____ BY_____
NAME OF DEALERSHIP   DEALER'S LICENSE NUMBER

Being duly sworn upon oath says that the statements set forth are true and correct. Subscribed and sworn to me

State of_____ before this _____ day of_____ 19____

County of_____ Notary Public

USE NOTARIZATION ONLY IF REQUIRED IN TITLING JURISDICTION

DISTRIBUTOR-DEALER ASSIGNMENT NUMBER 4

NAME OF PURCHASER(S)_____

ADDRESS_____

I certify to the best of my knowledge that the odometer reading is _____ No Tenths

DEALER _____ BY_____
NAME OF DEALERSHIP   DEALER'S LICENSE NUMBER

Being duly sworn upon oath says that the statements set forth are true and correct. Subscribed and sworn to me

State of_____ before this _____ day of_____ 19____

County of_____ Notary Public

USE NOTARIZATION ONLY IF REQUIRED IN TITLING JURISDICTION

ODOMETER DISCLOSURE FOR RETAIL SALE

Federal law requires you to state the odometer mileage in connection with the transfer of ownership. Failure to complete or provide a false statement may result in fines and / or imprisonment.

I certify to the best of my knowledge that the odometer reading is the actual mileage of the vehicle unless one of the following statements is checked. Odometer Reading _36_ No Tenths. ☐ The mileage stated is in excess of its mechanical limits ☐ The odometer reading is not the actual mileage.

WARNING ODOMETER DISCREPANCY

Signature(s) of Seller(s) _____ , Sales Mgr

Printed Name(s) of Seller(s) **Main Motors, Inc.** Dealer's No. **6075**

Date of Statement _7/9/02_ Date of Sale _7/9/02_

Being duly sworn upon oath says that the statements set forth are true and correct. Subscribed and sworn to me

Signature of Purchaser(s) _Lee Abel_

before this _____ day of _____ 19____

Printed Name of Purchaser(s) _Lee Abel_

Notary Public

Company Name (if Applicable) _____

State of_____

Address of Purchaser(s) _123 E. 10th, Phila., PA 19116_

County of_____

USE NOTARIZATION ONLY IF REQUIRED IN TITLING JURISDICTION

LIENHOLDER

1st lien in favor of_____ **Firstbank, NA**

whose address is **Broad & Spruce Streets, Philadelphia, PA 19116**

2nd lien in favor of_____

whose address is _____

GM521 REV. 3-91

(REVERSE)

In the event that Firstbank finances a dealer with serious financial problems, Firstbank will be particularly careful to see that it gets paid for each automobile sold. Firstbank's physical inventory checks will be more frequent—perhaps even daily. In protecting its interests, one of the first things that Firstbank will do is take possession of all certificates of origin. Because a dealer cannot title automobiles it sells without such certificates, Firstbank thereby achieves some comfort that it will be paid upon a dealer's sale of each vehicle.

Issuance of the Certificate of Title. Main Motors, as seller, executes an assignment of the Certificate of Origin to Abel, indicating that Firstbank is to have a lien (security interest) in the new car (see the reverse side of Form 7.7). (If Main were going to retain the contract it would list itself as lienholder.) Main Motors then sends the Certificate of Origin to the Bureau of Motor Vehicles, which, in turn, issues a Certificate of Title (Form 7.8). Here, the Certificate of Title is issued in the name of Lee Abel, and it states that the vehicle is subject to an encumbrance in favor of Firstbank. The Certificate of Title is then forwarded to Firstbank.[7]

7. In some states the certificate of title is forwarded to the owner, not the lienholder, and in others a duplicate is forwarded to the owner.

FORM 7.8
CERTIFICATE OF TITLE

COMMONWEALTH OF PENNSYLVANIA

DEPARTMENT OF TRANSPORTATION
CERTIFICATE OF TITLE FOR A VEHICLE

10,098

9620400018002692-001

| 1FMES24VS2921874 | 01 | CHEVROLET | 49895484201 MO |
| VEHICLE IDENTIFICATION NUMBER | YEAR | MAKE OF VEHICLE | TITLE NUMBER |

| SW | D | | 07/27/02 | 000036 | D |
| BODY TYPE | DUP | SEAT CAP | PRIOR TITLE STATE | ODOM PROCD DATE | ODOM MILES | ODOM STATUS |

| 07/27/02 | 07/27/02 | | | | |
| DATE PA TITLED | DATE OF ISSUE | UNLADEN WEIGHT | GVWR | GCWR | TITLE BRANDS |

ODOMETER STATUS
0 = ACTUAL MILEAGE
1 = MILEAGE EXCEEDS THE MECHANICAL LIMITS
2 = NOT THE ACTUAL MILEAGE
3 = NOT THE ACTUAL MILEAGE-ODOMETER TAMPERING VERIFIED
4 = EXEMPT FROM ODOMETER DISCLOSURE

TITLE BRANDS
A = ANTIQUE VEHICLE
C = CLASSIC VEHICLE
F = OUT OF COUNTRY
G = ORIGINALLY MFGD FOR NON-U.S. DISTRIBUTION
H = AGRICULTURAL VEHICLE
L = LOGGING VEHICLE
P = FORMERLY A POLICE VEHICLE
R = RECONSTRUCTED
S = STREET ROD
T = RECOVERED THEFT VEHICLE
V = VEHICLE CONTAINS REISSUED VIN
W = FLOOD VEHICLE
X = FORMERLY A TAXI

REGISTERED OWNER(S)
LEE ABEL
123 EAST 10TH STREET
PHILADELPHIA, PA 19116

FIRST LIEN FAVOR OF
FIRSTBANK, N.A.

SECOND LIEN FAVOR OF

FIRST LIEN RELEASED _____ DATE

BY_____
AUTHORIZED REPRESENTATIVE

If a second lienholder is listed upon satisfaction of the first lien, the first lienholder must forward this Title to the Bureau of Motor Vehicles with the appropriate form and fee

SECOND LIEN RELEASED _____ DATE

BY_____
AUTHORIZED REPRESENTATIVE

MAILING ADDRESS
FIRSTBANK, N.A.
BROAD & SPRUCE STREETS
PHILADELPHIA, PA 19116

I certify as of the date of issue the official records of the Pennsylvania Department of Transportation reflect that the person(s) or company named herein is the lawful owner of the said vehicle.

BRADLEY L MALLORY
Secretary of Transportation

D. APPLICATION FOR TITLE AND LIEN INFORMATION –

TO BE COMPLETED BY PURCHASER WHEN VEHICLE IS SOLD AND THE APPROPRIATE SECTIONS ON THE REVERSE SIDE OF THIS DOCUMENT ARE COMPLETED

SUBSCRIBED AND SWORN
TO BEFORE ME
MO DAY YEAR

When applying for title with a co-owner other than your spouse, check one of these blocks if no block is checked, title will be issued as "Tenants in Common"
A ☐ Joint Tenants with Right of Survivorship (on death of one owner, title goes to the surviving owner)
B ☐ Tenants in Common (on death of one owner, interest of deceased owner goes to his or her heirs or estate)

SIGNATURE OF PERSON ADMINISTERING OATH

LIEN DATE		IF NO LIEN CHECK BOX ☐
FIRST LIENHOLDER		
NAME		
STREET		
CITY		
STATE		ZIP

SEAL

The undersigned hereby makes application for Certificate of Title to the vehicle described above subject to the encumbrances and other legal claims set forth here

SIGNATURE OF APPLICANT OR AUTHORIZED SIGNER

LIEN DATE		IF NO LIEN CHECK BOX ☐
SECOND LIENHOLDER		
NAME		
STREET		
CITY		
STATE		ZIP

SIGNATURE OF CO-APPLICANT/TITLE OF AUTHORIZED SIGNER

STORE IN A SAFE PLACE – IF LOST APPLY FOR A DUPLICATE – ANY ALTERATION OR ERASURE VOIDS THIS TITLE

THE FACE OF THIS DOCUMENT HAS A COLORED BACKGROUND ON WHITE PAPER

09444053

(FACE)

PE OR PRINT) Certificate of Title must be submitted within 20 days, unless the purchaser is a registered dealer holding the vehicle for resale.

WARNING — FEDERAL AND STATE LAWS REQUIRE THAT YOU STATE THE MILEAGE IN CONNECTION WITH THE TRANSFER OF OWNERSHIP. FAILURE TO COMPLETE OR PROVIDING A FALSE STATEMENT MAY RESULT IN FINES AND/OR IMPRISONMENT.

ASSIGNMENT OF TITLE— Registered dealer's must complete forms MV27A or MV27B as required by law. If purchaser is NOT a registered dealer, Section D on the front of this form must be completed.

I/We certify, to the best of my/our knowledge that the odometer reading is _____ TENTHS _____ miles and reflects the actual mileage of the vehicle unless one of the following boxes is checked.

☐ Reflects the amount of mileage in excess of its mechanical limits   ☐ Is NOT the actual mileage WARNING: Odometer discrepancy

I/We further certify that the vehicle is free of any encumbrance and that ownership is hereby transferred to the person(s) or the dealer listed.

SUBSCRIBED AND SWORN TO BEFORE ME _____ MO _____ DAY _____ YEAR

SIGNATURE OF PERSON ADMINISTERING OATH

SEAL — DO NOT NOTARIZE UNLESS SIGNED IN PRESENCE OF A NOTARY AND PURCHASER'S NAME IS LISTED

PURCHASER OR FULL BUSINESS NAME — LAST / FIRST / M.I.
CO-PURCHASER
STREET ADDRESS
CITY
STATE / ZIP / PURCHASE PRICE OR DIN
PURCHASER SIGNATURE
CO-PURCHASER SIGNATURE
PURCHASER AND/OR CO-PURCHASER MUST HANDPRINT NAME HERE
SIGNATURE OF SELLER
SIGNATURE OF CO-SELLER
SELLER AND/OR CO-SELLER MUST HANDPRINT NAME HERE

RE-ASSIGNMENT OF TITLE BY REGISTERED DEALER— If purchaser listed in Block A is NOT a registered dealer Section D on the front of this form must be completed.

I/We certify, to the best of my/our knowledge that the odometer reading is _____ TENTHS _____ miles and reflects the actual mileage of the vehicle, unless one of the following boxes is checked.

☐ Reflects the amount of mileage in excess of its mechanical limits   ☐ Is NOT the actual mileage WARNING: Odometer discrepancy

I/We further certify that the vehicle is free of any encumbrance and that ownership is hereby transferred to the person(s) or the dealer listed.

SUBSCRIBED AND SWORN TO BEFORE ME _____ MO _____ DAY _____ YEAR

SIGNATURE OF PERSON ADMINISTERING OATH

SEAL — DO NOT NOTARIZE UNLESS SIGNED IN PRESENCE OF A NOTARY AND PURCHASER'S NAME IS LISTED AND SELLER IS A DEALER

PURCHASER OR FULL BUSINESS NAME — LAST / FIRST / M.I.
CO-PURCHASER
STREET ADDRESS
CITY
STATE / ZIP / PURCHASE PRICE OR DIN
PURCHASER SIGNATURE
CO-PURCHASER SIGNATURE
PURCHASER AND/OR CO-PURCHASER MUST HANDPRINT NAME HERE
SIGNATURE OF SELLER
SELLER MUST HANDPRINT NAME HERE

RE-ASSIGNMENT OF TITLE BY REGISTERED DEALER— If purchaser is NOT a registered dealer Section D on the front of this form must be completed.

I/We certify, to the best of my/our knowledge that the odometer reading is _____ TENTHS _____ miles and reflects the actual mileage of the vehicle, unless one of the following boxes is checked.

☐ Reflects the amount of mileage in excess of its mechanical limits   ☐ Is NOT the actual mileage WARNING: Odometer discrepancy

I/We further certify that the vehicle is free of any encumbrance and that ownership is hereby transferred to the person(s) or the dealer listed.

SUBSCRIBED AND SWORN TO BEFORE ME _____ MO _____ DAY _____ YEAR

SIGNATURE OF PERSON ADMINISTERING OATH

SEAL — DO NOT NOTARIZE UNLESS SIGNED IN PRESENCE OF A NOTARY AND PURCHASER'S NAME IS LISTED AND SELLER IS A DEALER

PURCHASER OR FULL BUSINESS NAME — LAST / FIRST / M.I.
CO-PURCHASER
STREET ADDRESS
CITY
STATE / ZIP / PURCHASE PRICE OR DIN
PURCHASER SIGNATURE
CO-PURCHASER SIGNATURE
PURCHASER AND/OR CO-PURCHASER MUST HANDPRINT NAME HERE
SIGNATURE OF SELLER
SELLER MUST HANDPRINT NAME HERE

RE-ASSIGNMENT OF TITLE BY REGISTERED DEALER— If purchaser is NOT a registered dealer Section D on the front of this form must be completed.

I/We certify, to the best of my/our knowledge that the odometer reading is _____ TENTHS _____ miles and reflects the actual mileage of the vehicle unless one of the following boxes is checked.

☐ Reflects the amount of mileage in excess of its mechanical limits   ☐ Is NOT the actual mileage WARNING: Odometer discrepancy

I/We further certify that the vehicle is free of any encumbrance and that ownership is hereby transferred to the person(s) or the dealer listed.

SUBSCRIBED AND SWORN TO BEFORE ME _____ MO _____ DAY _____ YEAR

SIGNATURE OF PERSON ADMINISTERING OATH

SEAL — DO NOT NOTARIZE UNLESS SIGNED IN PRESENCE OF A NOTARY AND PURCHASER'S NAME IS LISTED AND SELLER IS A DEALER

PURCHASER OR FULL BUSINESS NAME — LAST / FIRST / M.I.
CO-PURCHASER
STREET ADDRESS
CITY
STATE / ZIP / PURCHASE PRICE OR DIN
PURCHASER SIGNATURE
CO-PURCHASER SIGNATURE
PURCHASER AND/OR CO-PURCHASER MUST HANDPRINT NAME HERE
SIGNATURE OF SELLER
SELLER MUST HANDPRINT NAME HERE

☐ CHECK HERE IF APPLICATION FOR DEALER TITLE AND COMPLETE SECTION D. TITLING FEES $ _____

ALL SELLERS SIGNATURES ON THIS SIDE MUST BE NOTARIZED. SIGN ONLY IN THE PRESENCE OF AN OFFICER EMPOWERED TO ADMINISTER OATHS.

(REVERSE)

Figure 7.5 diagrams the assignment of the certificate of origin and the issuance of the certificate of title.

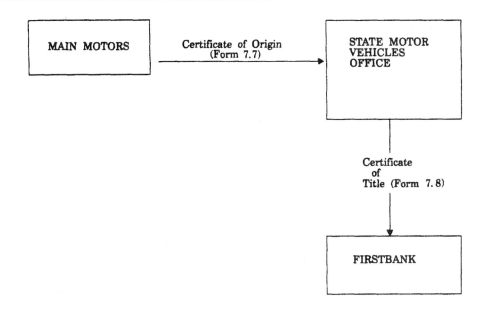

Figure 7.5

[240A]

(G) REPAYMENT OF INVENTORY LOAN AND ASSIGNMENT OF CONSUMER PAPER; NOTIFICATION OF ASSIGNMENT AND PAYMENT INSTRUCTIONS

In the Dealer Inventory Security Agreement (Form 7.2, ¶ 8) Main Motors agreed that when it sells one of the automobiles in which Firstbank holds a security interest, it will pay the amount advanced by Firstbank for that automobile. Main's cost for Abel's Chevrolet, advanced by Firstbank, was $25,256. Had Abel paid cash for the car, Main Motors would send its check for $25,256 to Firstbank. In the more typical situation, as in this sale to Abel, Main Motors has sold the automobile under an Instalment Sale Contract.

In order to obtain funds to pay Firstbank, Main has assigned the contract to a purchaser. Main well might have obtained funds by assigning Abel's contract to a purchaser *other* than Firstbank (e.g., a finance company or another bank). However, Main "just happens" to have assigned the contract to Firstbank, and Firstbank "just happens" to be the inventory financer that is owed payment upon the sale of the car. For this reason, Firstbank can make entries in Main's bank account with Firstbank to effectuate both *Firstbank's payment of the purchase price of Abel's contract* and *Main's repayment to Firstbank of the inventory loan.* Main sends Abel's contract to Firstbank, and Firstbank credits Main's account with the price it is to pay for the contract. The $10,556 allowance given for Abel's trade-in reduced the Unpaid Balance of Cash Price for the car to $16,500. That amount, plus the amount of the state taxes and fees, documentation fee, and extended warranty contract (a total of $18,380.50) approximates the amount that Firstbank will pay to Main as the purchase price for Abel's contract, inasmuch as Firstbank expects to earn the finance charges that Abel is to pay. After crediting Main's account in that amount, the Bank then debits the account for the amount due on the inventory loan. Note that the amount of the debit ($25,256), (which Firstbank advanced to Main against the car) substantially exceeds the amount Firstbank pays for an assignment of the contract. Under these circumstances Main will be expected to enclose its check, or authorize Firstbank to debit its account, for the difference.

Main has not yet received as much cash for the Chevrolet sold to Abel as it has paid for that car. It is evident that Main's profit on this transaction will depend in part on the price it gets from the sale of Abel's 1995 Miata, which Main took in trade. Not so obvious is the opportunity for further profit that Main Motors enjoys. Competition among banks and finance companies to purchase installment sale contracts leads to arrangements with a dealer that enhance the dealer's return. The reasons for this competition become evident when one considers the relatively high finance charges that can be charged on consumer automobile installment paper (9.5% on Abel's contract).

Firstbank may make an informal arrangement for sharing this return with Main Motors. The portion of the finance charges returned to Main (**dealer participation**) will depend on factors such as the level of interest rates generally, the level of the dealer's residual liability, the volume of business provided by the dealer, the bank's cost of funds, and the degree of competition to obtain financing arrangements with Main. Now we can see that it was not a pure coincidence that Firstbank purchased Abel's contract and also provided Main Motors with inventory financing. Many banks and finance companies provide inventory financing, sometimes even as a "loss leader," in order to get the first opportunity to acquire the lucrative retail installment contract financing.

On receipt of Abel's contract, Firstbank writes to Abel and directs that payments are to be made to Firstbank; along with the letter is a coupon book containing coupons to be enclosed with each of the 48 installment payments. When (and if) Abel completes the payments, Firstbank will return the Certificate of Title, marked "encumbrance satisfied."

Figure 7.6 diagrams (i) Firstbank's payment to Main Motors for Abel's Instalment Sale Contract; (ii) Main's payment to Firstbank of the amount of the inventory loan made against the Chevrolet;[8] (iii) Firstbank's communication to Abel, notifying Abel that the contract has been assigned to Firstbank, instructing Abel to make all payments to Firstbank, and enclosing payment coupons; and (iv) Abel's monthly payments.

---

8. As the text observes, Firstbank and Main Motors effect payments to one another by debits and credits to the bank account Main Motors maintains with Firstbank.

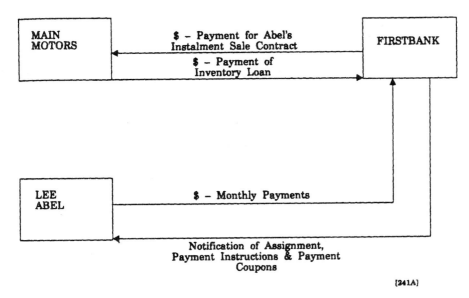

[241A]

Figure 7.6

(H) DIAGRAM OF AUTOMOBILE INSTALMENT SALE CONTRACT FINANCING

Figure 7.7 diagrams all of the transactions and documentation featured in the Prototype installment sale contract financing.

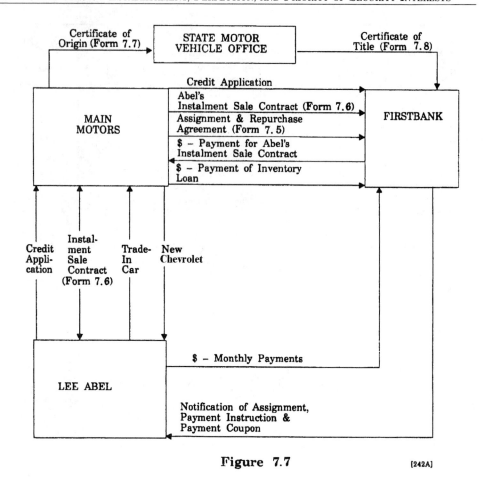

Figure 7.7

[242A]

(I) THE CONSUMER FAILS TO PAY

At this point the transaction with Lee Abel departs from the typical pattern, in which the buyer makes the payments when due. We now shall assume that after 12 months Abel is unable to keep up the monthly payments.

Collection Efforts. If Abel does not respond to one or two dunning letters from Firstbank, a collector calls Abel on the telephone to encourage prompt payment; if letters and telephone calls fail, the collector may demonstrate Firstbank's seriousness of purpose by making a house call. (In special circumstances, the creditor and debtor may execute a new contract (a **refinancing agreement**) that reduces the amount of each monthly payment by extending the payments over a longer period.)

Repossession. In this case we shall assume that there is no hope for prompt improvement in Abel's financial position; Firstbank takes steps to repossess the Chevrolet. Three methods are available: (i) voluntary surrender by the debtor, (ii) self help, and (iii) judicial proceedings such as a replevin action. In most cases creditors employ self help as the less expensive method. Often debtors voluntarily surrender collateral upon the secured creditor's request. Otherwise, an employee of the secured creditor or of a third-party collection service normally will be able to locate the automobile and take it away.

After Abel's car is repossessed, Firstbank sends Abel a notification to the effect that Firstbank has taken the car. The notification also informs Abel of the right to redeem the car upon payment of the balance due (including any late fees, costs of repossession, and expenses of making the car ready for disposition) and of a proposed disposition of the car if that amount is not forthcoming. This letter follows as Form 7.9. (As in the case of the Instalment Sale Contract (Form 7.6), for simplicity Form 7.9 omits several items required under Pennsylvania law.)

FORM 7.9
NOTIFICATION OF REPOSSESSION AND DISPOSITION

FIRSTBANK, NA.
Broad & Spruce Streets
Philadelphia, PA 19116

September 10, 2003

NOTICE OF OUR PLAN TO SELL PROPERTY

Lee Abel
123 East 10th Street
Philadelphia, PA 19116

Subject: Contract Number 81347

We have your vehicle (a 2001 Chevrolet Blazer with VIN 1FMES24VS292187), because you broke promises in our agreement.

We will sell your vehicle at private sale sometime after September 25, 2003. A sale could include a lease or license.

The money that we get from the sale (after paying our costs) will reduce the amount you owe. If we get less money than you owe, you will still owe us the difference. If we get more money than you owe, you will get the extra money, unless we must pay it to someone else.

You can get the property back at any time before we sell it by paying us the full amount you owe (not just the past due payments), including our expenses. To learn the exact amount you must pay, call us at 215-800-0000.

If you want us to explain to you in writing how we have figured the amount that you owe us, you may call us at 215-800-0000 or write us at Broad & Spruce Streets, Philadelphia, PA 19116 and request a written explanation. [We will charge you $10.00 for the explanation if we sent you another written explanation of the amount you owe us within the last six months.]

If you need more information about the sale call us at 215-800-0000 or write us at Broad & Spruce Streets, Philadelphia, PA 19116.

We are sending this notice to the following other people who have an interest in your vehicle or who owe money under your agreement:

None.

FIRSTBANK, N.A.

L. Null

L. Null
Consumer Lending Department

At this point Firstbank calls upon Main Motors to repurchase the contract as Main agreed to do under the terms of the assignment. Main then assumes the rights and duties of a secured party. After the specified notice period expires, Main will sell the automobile. The rights of parties in these situations are developed more fully in Chapter 12 infra.

SECTION 2.   ATTACHMENT OF SECURITY INTERESTS

Problem 7.2.1. The transaction followed precisely the steps described in the Prototype. Main Motors defaults on its obligations under the Demand Note (Form 7.3, supra). What are Firstbank's remedies? See R9–203(b); R9–601(a); Chapter 1, Section 1, supra; R9–609(a), (b); R9–610(a), (b); R9–607(a); Dealer Inventory Security Agreement (Form 7.2, supra) ¶ ¶ 12(a), 17.

Problem 7.2.2. Assume that the only document signed by Main Motors was a simple promissory note. Firstbank paid General Motors for a trailerload of new cars delivered to Main. Main's president, G.S. Gessel, orally agreed that Firstbank had a security interest in the cars.

(a) If Main defaults on its obligations under the note, may Firstbank enforce its security interest by seizing the cars and selling them? See R9–203(b); R9–102(a)(73); UCC 1–201(3); R1–201(37) (1st sentence); R9–102(a)(7); UCC 1–201(39); R9–102(a)(69); Notes (1) and (2) on Attachment, infra.

(b) Would Firstbank have an enforceable security interest if the promissory note signed by Main contained the notation: "Collateral: Motor Vehicles"? See In re Bollinger Corp., infra.

(c) Would Firstbank have an enforceable security interest if Main's oral agreement that Firstbank had a security interest the cars was recorded on Firstbank's voice messaging system ("voice mail")? If so, would you advise Firstbank to extend credit to Main in reliance on this agreement?

(d) Would Firstbank have an enforceable security interest if Gessel sent Firstbank an e-mail message stating, "This confirms that you have a security interest in our existing and future inventory"? Below the message, Gessel's e-mail program automatically inserted the following:

G.S. Gessel, President

Main Motors, Inc.

gsgessel@mainmotorsinc.com

Would you advise Firstbank to extend credit to Main in reliance on this message? Would your answer change if the e-mail program inserted, instead, the following?

G.S. Gessel

Problem 7.2.3. Assume that, in the course of negotiating the financing arrangements, Firstbank sent Main Motors a letter, to which the Financing Statement (Form 7.1, supra) was attached. The letter stated, "In connection with our inventory financing of Main Motors, it will be necessary for us to file the attached financing statement. Kindly sign the enclosed copy of this letter and return it to us at your earliest convenience." Main signed a copy of the letter and returned it, with the Financing Statement attached, to Firstbank. Firstbank promptly filed the Financing Statement in the proper filing office.

Thereafter, Main signed a simple promissory note, and Firstbank paid General Motors for a trailerload of new cars delivered to Main. Does Firstbank have an enforceable security interest in the cars? See R9–203(b)(3)(A); R1–201(3), R9–102(a)(73), R9–102(a)(7); Note (2) on Attachment, infra. Why would anyone authorize the filing of a financing statement without intending to create a security interest? See R9–502(d); R9–322(a)(1).

Problem 7.2.4. Assume that by error a new Chevrolet Cavalier was omitted from the Loan Request Form (Form 7.4, supra), and that this form and a simple promissory note were the only documents executed by Main.

(a) Does Firstbank have an enforceable security interest in the omitted Cavalier, for which it has paid Old Bank? See R9–108; R9–203(b)(3); Note (3) on Attachment, infra.

(b) Would the Dealer Inventory Security Agreement cover the slip-up? See Dealer Inventory Security Agreement (Form 7.2, supra) ¶ 5.

(c) Would your answer to part (b) be the same if the Dealer Inventory Security Agreement covered only "motor vehicle inventory located at Dealer's address set forth above" and, in fact, the omitted Cavalier was stored at another location? Should the reference to location be construed as a limitation on the collateral covered or merely a reference to the location where the parties expected the collateral to be kept? Compare In re Little Puffer Billy, Inc., 16 B.R. 174 (Bkrtcy.D.Or.1981) (collateral described as "[a]ll inventory of [debtor], Valley River Center, Eugene, Oregon" included inventory at other locations; location intended merely as place of inquiry) with In re California Pump & Manufacturing Co., 588 F.2d 717 (9th Cir.1978) (collateral described as "[a]ll furniture . . . located at" a specified address did not include collateral never located at that address).

(d) Would your answer to part (b) be the same if paragraph 5 of the Dealer Inventory Security Agreement contained no subparagraphs and covered only "all Dealer's personal property, of every kind and nature whatsoever"? See R9–203(b)(3); R9–108.

(e) Would your answer to part (b) be the same if paragraph 5 of the Dealer Inventory Security Agreement contained no subparagraphs and covered only "certain motor vehicles"? Note that Revised Article 9 classifies goods into four types: consumer goods, equipment, farm products, and inventory. See R9–102, Comment 4.a. See generally Note (3) on Attachment, infra.

Problem 7.2.5. Assume that Firstbank "picked up" the floorplan financing for Main Motors as described in the Prototype. Subsequently, Firstbank paid General Motors for a new shipment of cars to Main Motors.

Does Firstbank have an enforceable security interest in the newly arrived cars? See R9–203(a), (b); R9–204(a); Dealer Inventory Security Agreement ¶ 5. Would it make any difference if the only references to collateral in the Dealer Inventory Security Agreement and the Financing Statement were to "all inventory"? See R9–108 & Comment 3; Note (3) on Attachment, infra.

Problem 7.2.6. The facts are as in the Prototype, except that paragraph 5 of the Dealer Inventory Security Agreement (Form 7.2, supra) covered only "Inventory."

(a) Does Firstbank's security interest in the cars in Main's inventory extend to the vast array of software used to keep major systems (e.g., exhaust, brakes) in the cars operating properly? Or does Firstbank's security interest attach only to the frames, engines, and other tangible aspects of the cars? See R9–102(a)(48), (a)(44), (a)(75); Dealer Inventory Security Agreement ¶ 3.

(b) Does Firstbank's security interest in Main's inventory extend to electronic repair manuals, car-racing computer games, and other computer software that Main sells as a sideline? If not, how should the security agreement describe this kind of property? See R9–108; R9–102(a)(42), (a)(44), (a)(48), (a)(75).

(c) Does Firstbank hold a security interest in Main's "loaners" (cars that Main Motors allows its customers to use while their cars are being serviced)? See R9–102(a)(33), (a)(23), (a)(34), (a)(48); Dealer Inventory Security Agreement ¶ 3.

(d) Does Firstbank hold a security interest in the Chevrolet Monte Carlo that Main owns but allows Main's president, G.S. Gessel, to use as part of his compensation?

Problem 7.2.7. Main Motors leases from Office!Office! a variety of sophisticated office equipment on a three-year lease. Main may terminate the lease without penalty, for any reason, upon giving 30 days' advance notice to Office!Office!.

(a) Can Main create an enforceable security interest in the equipment? See R9–203(b); Note (1) on Attachment, infra. If so, would you advise a lender to extend credit to Main in reliance on a security interest in the equipment?

(b) The lease contains the following provision: "Lessee [Main] agrees not to assign this lease or its rights hereunder. Any purported assignment shall be void and shall constitute a default resulting in the immediate termination of this lease." Does this provision affect your answers to part (a)? See R9–401(a); R9–407; Note (1) on Attachment, infra. (Note: We shall return to the question of the alienability of a debtor's interest in collateral and the relationship, in this context, between Article 9 and non-Article 9 law in Chapter 9, Sections 1(F) and 6.)

In re Bollinger Corp.[*]

United States Court of Appeals, Third Circuit, 1980.
614 F.2d 924.

■ ROSENN, CIRCUIT JUDGE. This appeal from a district court review of an order in bankruptcy presents a question that has troubled courts since the enactment of Article Nine of the Uniform Commercial Code (UCC) governing secured transactions. Can a creditor assert a secured claim against the debtor when no formal security agreement was ever signed, but where various documents executed in connection with a loan evince an intent to create a security interest? The district court answered this question in the affirmative and permitted the creditor, Zimmerman & Jansen, to assert a secured claim against the debtor, bankrupt Bollinger Corporation, in the amount of $150,000. We affirm.

I

The facts of this case are not in dispute. Industrial Credit Corporation (ICC) made a loan to Bollinger Corporation (Bollinger) on January 13, 1972, in the amount of $150,000. As evidence of the loan, Bollinger executed a promissory note in the sum of $150,000 and signed a security agreement with ICC giving it a security interest in certain machinery and equipment. ICC in due course perfected its security interest in the collateral by filing a financing statement in accordance with Pennsylvania's enactment of Article Nine of the UCC.

Bollinger faithfully met its obligations under the note and by December 4, 1974, had repaid $85,000 of the loan, leaving $65,000 in unpaid principal. Bollinger, however, required additional capital and on December 5, 1974, entered into a loan agreement with Zimmerman & Jansen, Inc. (Z & J), by which Z & J agreed to lend Bollinger $150,000. Z & J undertook as part of this transaction to pay off the $65,000 still owed to ICC in return for an assignment by ICC to Z & J of the original note and security agreement between Bollinger and ICC. Bollinger executed a promissory note to Z & J, evidencing the agreement containing the following provision:

"Security. This promissory note is secured by security interests in a certain security agreement between Bollinger and Industrial Credit Company ... and in a financing statement filed by [ICC] ..., and is further secured by security interests in certain security agreement to be delivered by Bollinger to Z and J with this promissory note covering the identical machinery and equipment as identified in the ICC security agreement and with identical schedule attached in the principal amount of Eighty–Five Thousand Dollars ($85,000)."

No formal security agreement was ever executed between Bollinger and Z & J. Z & J did, however, in connection with the promissory note, record a new financing statement signed by Bollinger containing a detailed list of the machinery and equipment originally taken as collateral by ICC for its loan to Bollinger.

* [The court's citations are to the applicable pre–1972 version of the UCC.]

Bollinger filed a petition for an arrangement under Chapter XI of the Bankruptcy Act in March, 1975 and was adjudicated bankrupt one year later. In administrating the bankrupt's estate, the receiver sold some of Bollinger's equipment but agreed that Z & J would receive a $10,000 credit on its secured claim.

Z & J asserted a secured claim against the bankrupt in the amount of $150,000, arguing that although it never signed a security agreement with Bollinger, the parties had intended that a security interest in the sum of $150,000 be created to protect the loan. The trustee in bankruptcy conceded that the assignment to Z & J of ICC's original security agreement with Bollinger gave Z & J a secured claim in the amount of $65,000, the balance owed by Bollinger to ICC at the time of the assignment. The trustee, however, refused to recognize Z & J's asserted claim of an additional secured claim of $85,000 because of the absence of a security agreement between Bollinger and Z & J. The bankruptcy court agreed and entered judgment for Z & J in the amount of $55,000, representing a secured claim in the amount of $65,000 less $10,000 credit received by Z & J.

Z & J appealed to the United States District Court for the Western District of Pennsylvania, which reversed the bankruptcy court and entered judgment for Z & J in the full amount of the asserted $150,000 secured claim. The trustee in bankruptcy appeals.

II

Under Article Nine of the UCC, two documents are generally required to create a perfected security interest in a debtor's collateral. First, there must be a "security agreement" giving the creditor an interest in the collateral. Section 9–203(1)(b) contains minimal requirements for the creation of a security agreement. In order to create a security agreement, there must be: (1) a writing (2) signed by the debtor (3) containing a description of the collateral or the types of collateral. Section 9–203, Comment 1. The requirements of § 9–203(1)(b) further two basic policies. First, an evidentiary function is served by requiring a signed security agreement and second, a written agreement also obviates any Statute of Frauds problems with the debtor-creditor relationship. Id. Comments 3, 5. The second document generally required is a "financing statement," which is a document signed by both parties and filed for public record. The financing statement serves the purpose of giving public notice to other creditors that a security interest is claimed in the debtor's collateral.

Despite the minimal formal requirements set forth in § 9–203 for the creation of a security agreement, the commercial world has frequently neglected to comply with this simple Code provision. Soon after Article Nine's enactment, creditors who had failed to obtain formal security agreements, but who nevertheless had obtained and filed financing statements, sought to enforce secured claims. Under § 9–402, a security agreement may serve as a financing statement if it is signed by both parties. The question arises whether the converse is true: Can a signed financing statement operate as a security agreement? The earliest case to consider this question was American Card Company v. H.M.H. Co., 196 A.2d 150, 152 (R.I.1963) which held that a financing statement could *not* operate as a security agreement because there was no language *granting* a security interest to a creditor. Although § 9–203(1)(b) makes no mention of such a grant language requirement, the court in American Card thought that implicit in the definition of "security agreement" under § 9–105(1)(h) was such a requirement; some grant language was necessary to "create or provide security." This view also was adopted by the Tenth Circuit in Shelton v. Erwin [In re Shelton; Gassaway v. Erwin], 472 F.2d 1118, 1120 (8th Cir.1973). Thus, under the holdings of these cases, the creditor's assertion of a secured claim must fall in the absence of language connoting a grant of a security interest.

The Ninth Circuit in In Re Amex–Protein Development Corporation, 504 F2d 1056 (9th Cir.1974), echoed criticism by commentators of the American Card rule. The court wrote: "There is no support in legislative history or grammatical logic for the substitution of the word grant for the phrase creates or provides for." Id. at 1059. It concluded that as long as the financing statement contains a description of the collateral signed by the debtor, the financing statement may serve as the security agreement and the formal requirements of § 9–203(1)(b) are met. The tack pursued by the Ninth Circuit is supported by legal commentary on the issue. See G. Gilmore, Security Interests in Personal Property, § 11.4 at 347–48 (1965).

Some courts have declined to follow the Ninth Circuit's liberal rule allowing the financing statement alone to stand as the security agreement, but have permitted the financing statement, when read in conjunction with other documents executed by the parties, to satisfy the requirements of § 9–203(1)(b). The court in In re Numeric Corp., 485 F2d 1328 (1st Cir.1973) held that a financing statement coupled with a board of directors' resolution revealing an intent to create a security interest were sufficient to act as a security agreement. The court concluded from its reading of the Code that there appears no need to insist upon a separate document entitled "security agreement" as a prerequisite for an otherwise valid security interest.

> "A writing or writings, regardless of label, which adequately describes the collateral, carries the signature of the debtor, and establishes that in fact a security interest was agreed upon, would satisfy both the formal requirements of the statute and the policies behind it."

Id. at 1331. The court went on to hold that "although a standard form financing statement by itself cannot be considered a security agreement, an adequate agreement can be found when a financing statement is considered together with other documents." Id. at 1332. See In re Penn Housing Corp., 367 F Supp 661 (W.D.Pa.1973); but see Union National Bank of Pittsburgh v. Providence Washington Insurance Co., (WD Pa 1977).

More recently, the Supreme Court of Maine in Casco Bank & Trust Co. v. Cloutier, 398 A2d 1224, 1231–32 (Me.1979) considered the question of whether composite documents were sufficient to create a security interest within the terms of the Code. Writing for the court, Justice Wernick allowed a financing statement to be joined with a promissory note for purposes of determining whether the note contained an adequate description of the collateral to create a security agreement. The court indicated that the evidentiary and Statute of Frauds policies behind § 9–203(1)(b) were satisfied by reading the note and financing statement together as the security agreement.

In the case before us, the district court went a step further and held that the promissory note executed by Bollinger in favor of Z & J, standing alone, was sufficient to act as the security agreement between the parties. In so doing, the court implicitly rejected the American Card rule requiring grant language before a security agreement arises under § 9–203(1)(b). The parties have not referred to any Pennsylvania state cases on the question and our independent research has failed to uncover any. But although we agree that no formal grant of a security interest need exist before a security agreement arises, we do not think that the promissory note standing alone would be sufficient under Pennsylvania law to act as the security agreement. We believe, however, that the promissory note, read in conjunction with the financing statement duly filed and supported, as it is here, by correspondence during the course of the transaction between the parties, would be sufficient under Pennsylvania law to establish a valid security agreement.

III

We think Pennsylvania courts would accept the logic behind the First and Ninth Circuit rule and reject the American Card rule imposing the requirement of a formal grant of a security interest before a security agreement may exist. When the parties have neglected to sign a separate security agreement, it would appear that the better and more practical view is to look at the transaction as a whole in order to determine if there is a writing, or writings, signed by the debtor describing the collateral which demonstrates an intent to create a security interest in the collateral. In connection with Z & J's loan of $150,000 to Bollinger, the relevant writings to be considered are: (1) the promissory note; (2) the financing statement; (3) a group of letters constituting the course of dealing between the parties. The district court focused solely on the promissory note finding it sufficient to constitute the security agreement. Reference, however, to the language in the note reveals that the note standing alone cannot serve as the security agreement. The note recites that along with the assigned 1972 security agreement between Bollinger and ICC, the Z & J loan is "further secured by security interests in a certain Security Agreement *to be delivered* by Bollinger to Z & J with this Promissory Note, . . ." (Emphasis added.) The bankruptcy judge correctly reasoned that "[t]he intention to create a separate security agreement negates any inference that the debtor intended that the promissory note constitute the security agreement." At best, the note is some evidence that a security agreement was contemplated by the parties, but by its own terms, plainly indicates that it is not the security agreement.

Looking beyond the promissory note, Z & J did file a financing statement signed by Bollinger containing a detailed list of all the collateral intended to secure the $150,000 loan to Bollinger. The financing statement alone meets the basic § 9–203(1)(b) requirements of a writing, signed by the debtor, describing the collateral. However, the financing statement provides only an inferential basis for concluding that the parties intended a security agreement. There would be little reason to file such a detailed financing statement unless the parties intended to create a security interest. The intention of the parties to create a security interest may be gleaned from the expression of future intent to create one in the promissory note and the intention of the parties as expressed in letters constituting their course of dealing.

The promissory note was executed by Bollinger in favor of Z & J in December 1974. Prior to the consummation of the loan, Z & J sent a letter to Bollinger on May 30, 1974, indicating that the loan would be made "provided" Bollinger secured the loan by a mortgage on its machinery and equipment. Bollinger sent a letter to Z & J on September 19, 1974, indicating:

> "With your [Z & J's] stated desire to obtain security for material and funds advanced, it would appear that the use of the note would answer both our problems. Since the draft forwarded to you offers full collateralization for the funds to be advanced under it and bears normal interest during its term, it should offer you maximum security."

Subsequent to the execution of the promissory note, Bollinger sent to Z & J a list of the equipment and machinery intended as collateral under the security agreement which was to be, but never was, delivered to Z & J. In November 1975, the parties exchanged letters clarifying whether Bollinger could substitute or replace equipment in the ordinary course of business without Z & J's consent. Such a clarification would not have been necessary had a security interest not been intended by the parties. Finally, a letter of November 18, 1975, from Bollinger to Z & J indicated that "any attempted impairment of the collateral would constitute an event of default."

From the course of dealing between Z & J and Bollinger, we conclude there is sufficient evidence that the parties intended a security agreement to be created separate from the assigned ICC agreement with Bollinger. All the evidence points towards the intended creation of such an agreement and since the financing statement contains a detailed list of the collateral, signed by Bollinger, we hold that a valid Article Nine security agreement existed under Pennsylvania law between the parties which secured Z & J in the full amount of the loan to Bollinger.

IV

The minimal formal requirements of § 9–203(1)(b) were met by the financing statement and the promissory note, and the course of dealing between the parties indicated the intent to create a security interest. The judgment of the district court recognizing Z & J's secured claim in the amount of $150,000 will be affirmed.

Each side to bear their own costs.

NOTES ON ATTACHMENT

(1) The Conditions for Attachment. "Attachment" is one of the fundamental concepts in Article 9. When the conditions giving rise to an enforceable security interest are satisfied, then a security interest attaches. See R9–203(a), (b). A security interest is an interest in property. See R1–201(37). Unless and until a security interest attaches to particular property, the secured party has no enforceable security interest—and thus no enforceable property right—in the collateral. That is, until the security interest attaches, the secured party is, as a practical matter, unsecured.

R9–203(b) provides that "a security interest is enforceable against the debtor or third parties with respect to the collateral only if" the three conditions specified in therein occur. They may occur in any order, but until all occur, a security interest is not enforceable.

Value. One condition for attachment is that "value has been given." R9–203(b)(1). By definition, a security interest "secures payment or performance of an obligation." R1–201(37). Before a security interest can attach, there must be an obligation (usually a money debt) to secure. The "value" condition normally is satisfied easily; that the secured party extended credit usually is clear. See UCC 1–201(44) (defining "value" to include not only present consideration but also antecedent debt). Any issue that arises with respect to the "value" condition is likely to concern *which* debt is secured rather than whether *any* debt is outstanding. See Problem 7.2.8, infra.

Rights in Collateral. A second condition for attachment is that "the debtor has rights in the collateral or the power to transfer rights in the collateral to a secured party." R9–203(b)(2). The first aspect of this condition ("rights in the collateral") is best conceptualized and understood as a specialized aspect of the familiar principle of *nemo dat quod non habet* (one cannot give what one does not have): A debtor can give a security interest in collateral only if it has rights in that collateral. See Chapter 1, Section 3(A), supra. Straightforward as this may seem, more than a few courts and commentators have confounded the application of the "rights in the collateral" condition in the context of Former Article 9's basic conveyancing principles.

One source of the confusion has been the first sentence of F9–201: "Except as otherwise provided by this Act a security agreement is effective according to its terms between the parties, against purchasers of the collateral and against creditors." (This sentence appears almost verbatim as R9–201(a).) This principle often has been paraphrased to the effect that a security interest in collateral is "good as against the world" except as the UCC provides otherwise. Broad as this statement may be, it is important to mind its limitations. We discuss below, particularly in Section 6, many of the specific instances where the UCC expressly limits the operation of R9–201. For present purposes you should realize that *R9–201 generally operates only with respect to the debtor's rights in collateral—however limited or expansive they might be.* For example, assume that Debtor is the owner of a 25% undivided interest in an item of equipment. Having "rights in the collateral," Debtor can cause a security interest to attach to that item of equipment. Assume further that Debtor signs a security agreement purporting to grant a security interest in the equipment to Bank to secure a loan. Does R9–201 afford Bank a security interest "good against the world" in the 75% interest that Debtor does not own as well as the 25% interest owned by Debtor? Of course not. The "collateral" addressed by R9–201 consists only of the debtor's rights in the equipment. Again, the *nemo dat* principle applies; Debtor cannot give more than it has.

We have seen that sometimes the law affords a person the power to transfer greater rights than the person has. See Chapter 1, supra. If the transferee of these rights can be a secured party, then one condition for attachment and enforceability of a security interest would be satisfied. We shall see examples of how this rule works in Chapter 8, Section 1(B) (consignments) and Chapter 9, Section 1(D) (sales of receivables).

Applicable law sometimes restricts a person from transferring its interest in property or makes an attempted transfer ineffective. Revised Article 9 generally does not override non-Article 9 law to the effect that property is inalienable; a security interest cannot be created in otherwise inalienable property merely because security interests in that type of property are within the scope of the Article. See R9–401(a). This result was implicit under Former Article 9. Id., Comment 4. R9–401(a) specifies exceptions, however. One exception is found in subsection (b). For an example and discussion of the operation of subsection (b) in a typical setting, see R9–401, Comment 5. Other specified exceptions are R9–406 through R–9–409. See Chapter 9, Sections 1(F) and 6.

Debtor's Agreement. A third condition to attachment is the debtor's agreement that a security interest be created. See R9–203(b)(3). The following Note examines this condition.

(2) Article 9's "Statute of Frauds." A security interest cannot attach in the absence of the debtor's security agreement. See R9–203(b)(3); R9–102(a)(73) (defining "security agreement" as "an agreement that creates or provides for a security interest"). Because the attachment of a security interest is a transfer—a conveyance—of a property interest from the debtor to the secured party, the necessity for the debtor's agreement is apparent (at least in a system that respects private property). However, not every agreement that provides for a security interest satisfies the requirements of R9–203(b)(3). That section requires that the requisite agreement be manifested in one of four specified ways. The Comments refer to these as "evidentiary requirement[s] in the nature of a Statute of Frauds"—i.e., formal requisites that both enhance the veracity of claims to secured party status and serve to caution a debtor. R9–203, Comment 3; see E.A. Farnsworth, Contracts § 6.1, at 366 (3d ed. 1999) (discussing functions of Statute of Frauds).

In the vast proportion of secured transactions, the requirements of R9–203(b)(3) are satisfied when the debtor signs a written security agreement describing the collateral. It is not difficult to satisfy this requirement in the usual case; nonetheless, slip-ups do occur. The courts generally have applied the (relatively forgiving and broad) definition of "signed" in UCC 1–201(39) in cases where the debtor's signature on a security agreement has been called into question. As to how an inanimate business entity may sign a security agreement, one must resort to non-UCC law of partnerships, corporations, or agency. See UCC 1–103. Normally, such an organization signs through a individual, e.g., an officer of a corporate debtor or the general partner of a partnership debtor. Good lawyers avoid litigation over the sufficiency of the debtor's signature in these circumstances by making sure that the security agreement identifies the organization as the debtor and the individual as its agent. See, e.g., Main Motors' signature on Forms 7.2, 7.3, and 7.4, supra. They also make sure that the individual purporting to sign on behalf of the debtor is in fact authorized by the debtor to do so.

Revised Article 9 does not require that a security agreement be in writing. R9–203(b)(3)(A) is satisfied when "the debtor has *authenticated* a security agreement." The definition of "authenticate" in R9–102(a)(7) means not only to "sign" (which requires a writing, see UCC 1–201(39) (defining "signed")) but also "to execute or otherwise adopt a symbol . . . with the present intent of the authenticating person to identify the person and adopt or accept a *record*." Thus, a security agreement may be in any authenticated "record," i.e., it may be "inscribed on a tangible medium or . . . stored in an electronic or other medium," provided that the information is "retrievable in perceivable form." See R9–102(a)(69). This definition is very broad, but it excludes information in unrecorded oral communications. Can you think of another type of information that is not a "record"? We can anticipate that the case law will develop the outer reaches of the concepts of "record" and "authentication" as they apply to security agreements that are not in writing.[1]

Under R9–203(b)(3)(B), (b)(3)(C), and (b)(4)(D), even an oral security agreement is sufficient if the secured party is in possession or control of the collateral pursuant to that agreement. A secured creditor who fails to obtain an authenticated security agreement, but is in possession or control of the collateral, nonetheless must provide evidence that its possession or control is "pursuant to the debtor's security agreement." As used in the UCC, "control" has a technical meaning. See R9–104 (deposit accounts); R9–105 (electronic chattel paper); R9–106 (investment property), discussed below in Chapter 9, Sections 4, 2, and 3, respectively.

Printed forms of security agreements are readily available; when properly completed and signed they easily satisfy the minimal requirements

---

1. Some of the case law may arise under UETA or the E–SIGN (discussed in the General Introduction, (E)(2), supra), each of which contains a definition of "record" that is virtually identical to the definition in Article 9. See UETA 2(13); E–SIGN § 106. However, UETA does not apply to a transaction to the extent it is governed by Article 9, and the provisions of E–SIGN validating electronic signatures and electronic contracts do not apply to a contract or other record to the extent it is governed by Article 9. UETA 3(b)(2); E–SIGN § 103.

of R9–203(b)(3)(A). Moreover, a security agreement need not contain any "magic words" to create a security interest. The courts generally have been generous to secured parties who have used inartful language. Nevertheless, the debtor's failure to sign or otherwise authenticate an "agreement that creates or provides for a security interest" normally will be fatal to the assertion of an attached (enforceable) security interest. For example, many cases decided under Former Article 9 have held that a debtor's signature on a financing statement alone does not satisfy F9–203(1)(a) when the financing statement meets only the minimum requirements for a financing statement (see F9–402) and does not contain additional language constituting an appropriate "agreement." See UCC 1–201(3) (defining "agreement" as "the bargain of the parties in fact as found in their language or by implication from other circumstances").

Does a debtor's written authorization of the filing of a financing statement create an "implication" that the debtor has agreed to create a security interest? A "technical" answer is found in R9–502(d): "A financing statement may be filed before a security agreement is made or a security interest otherwise attaches." Why else would a debtor authorize the filing a financing statement if not to create a security interest? As a practical matter, prospective secured parties frequently file before a secured loan or sale is consummated (i.e., they "pre-file") so that a filing office search report reflecting the filed financing statement can be obtained before value is given. That a financing statement is filed does not necessarily mean that any security interest has been or will be created. See R9–502, Comment 2.

Why do putative secured parties sometimes fail to take the relatively simple step of requiring a debtor to sign a security agreement? The reported decisions, at least, indicate that inadvertence and clerical or administrative errors are most often to blame (although examples of mistakes by truly "amateur" creditors also can be found). In the slightly altered words of a famous bumper sticker: "It happens."

Compliance with the requirement that a debtor sign or otherwise authenticate a security agreement is easy enough when a modest amount of care is taken or properly-completed, well-drafted forms are employed. When mistakes are made, however, the results can be disastrous for a putative secured party, even when the debtor's subjective intention to grant a security interest is apparent. The failure of secured creditors to use standard-form security agreements has engendered scores of reported decisions under Former Article 9. In many of these cases the creditors have argued successfully that a group of writings, taken together, are sufficient to comprise a security agreement. In re Bollinger, supra, is typical of these cases. See also In re Numeric Corp., 485 F.2d 1328 (1st Cir.1973) (board of directors' resolution recognizing that agreement existed and financing statement itemizing collateral satisfied Statute of Frauds and identification of collateral functions and, together, comprised adequate security agreement); Komas v. Future Systems, Inc., 71 Cal.App.3d 809, 139 Cal.Rptr. 669 (1977) (adequate security agreement consisted of signed financing statement, loan application, and promissory note). Those arguments sometimes have failed, however. See In re Harmon, 6 U.C.C. Rep. Serv. 1280 (Bkrtcy.D.Conn.1969) (application for automobile certificate of title that named putative secured party as lienholder was analogized to financing statement and, when considered with other insufficient documents (including promissory note), did not constitute a security agreement); In re Taylor Mobile Homes, Inc., 17 U.C.C. Rep. Serv. 565 (Bkrtcy.E.D.Mich.1975) (debtor's execution of note and financing statement held not sufficient to constitute a security agreement; secured party had prepared a security agreement, and the note made reference to a security agreement, but the debtor did not sign it). These cases are important not only for their specific outcomes, but as a reminder of how easy it would have been for the secured parties involved to have avoided the problems.

Finally, consider the situation where *A* grants a security interest in *A*'s property to secure the indebtedness of *B*. (This transaction often is referred to as a **hypothecation**.) Who is the "debtor" whose security agreement is required? R9–102(a)(28) provides that the "debtor" is "a person having an interest, other than a security interest or other lien, in the collateral," regardless of whether the person owes the obligation that the collateral secures. There is little doubt that the debtor is *A*—the owner of the collateral. If collateral is jointly owned, each co-owner would be a debtor with respect to that owner's interest in the collateral.

(3) Description of the Collateral; After–Acquired Property. A security agreement authenticated by the debtor must "provide[ ] a description of the collateral" to satisfy R9–203(b)(3)(A). R9–108(a) contains the general rule: "[A] description of personal or real property is sufficient, whether or not it is specific, if it reasonably identifies what is described." Comment 2 to R9–108 indicates that a description in a security agreement must "do the job assigned to it: *make possible* the identification of the collateral described," while rejecting the notion that a description must be "exact and detailed (the so-called 'serial number' test)" as applied in pre-UCC chattel mortgage cases. R9–108, Comment 2 (emphasis added). As the Comment explains, a security agreement provides evidence that a security interest *in fact* has been created in certain collateral. (The identification function also is served by the alternative of possession or control by the secured party; these alternatives serve as evidentiary proxies for a security agreement that describes the collateral.)

Is it necessary for a description to identify the collateral itself? Or, is a description sufficient if it provides enough information so that someone, by *additional* investigation or with *additional* information, *could* identify it? Whether a security interest in fact has been created may become relevant in the event that the debtor disputes the secured party's claim of a security interest in particular property. The description requirement helps minimize the likelihood of such a dispute. The debtor and secured party may not be the only interested persons; the creation of a security interest may be relevant also to a third party (e.g., a buyer, competing secured party, or judicial lien creditor) who claims an interest in the property. Under these circumstances, the debtor and secured party may have an incentive to extend the coverage of the security agreement beyond their original agreement. The description requirement helps protect the third party from such after-the-fact collusion.

One should place the risk of a collusive "reinterpretation" of a security agreement in proper perspective. As a general matter, third parties are ill-advised to rely on information contained in a security agreement. Any comfort drawn from that information could be illusory, and any protection might be fleeting. Other security agreements covering additional collateral or securing other indebtedness might then exist or thereafter be entered into, and it is the date of *filing a financing statement*—not the date of a security agreement—that generally determines priorities. See Section 6, infra.

R9–108(b) indicates a variety of ways in which a description might "reasonably identif[y]" collateral. Subsection (b)(3) follows the prevailing interpretation under Former Article 9 and expressly validates descriptions by Article 9 "type," such as "equipment" or "inventory." The case law under Former Article 9 was divided over the question whether "super-generic" collateral descriptions, such as "all personal property" and "all assets," are sufficient for purposes of a security agreement. Although generally such "super-generic" descriptions have been held to be sufficient (see White & Summers § 22–3, at 760), R9–108(c) follows those cases that held them to be insufficient. When it is determined that the bargain-in-fact of the parties is that the security agreement covers all personal property of the debtor, why should it be necessary to resort to more detail? In nearly *every* case where attachment is in dispute it will be necessary to determine that a debtor has "rights in the collateral." R9–203(b)(2). If all personal property is to be covered, then, the distinguishing factor between collateral and non-collateral is the existence of those rights.

Why do you suppose the drafters opted for invalidating "super-generic" descriptions? Perhaps the drafters subscribed to the view that, absent overreaching or the debtor's failure to appreciate the full implications of an agreement to encumber everything the debtor has, no one would enter into such an agreement. If so, do you agree with that view? Another possible explanation is that R9–108(c) is designed to increase the likelihood that a debtor actually appreciates that the security agreement creates a security interest in all the debtor's personal property. Which do you think is more likely to drive this point home—an agreement that provides for a security interest in "all debtor's personal property," or an agreement that provides for a security interest in "all Collateral," defined as "accounts, chattel paper, general intangibles, documents, inventory, equipment, deposit accounts, letter-of-credit rights, instruments, and investment property"? Might the drafters have intended to induce secured parties to consider carefully the collateral they take, rather than relying on boilerplate "all assets" collateral descriptions? A more cynical possibility is that some supporters of R9–108(c) simply hoped that secured parties might omit a category or two from the collateral descriptions, thereby making it more likely that property would remain unencumbered.

R9–108 does not resolve one important issue that arose often under Former Article 9: does a description such as "all of debtor's equipment" cover not only equipment of the debtor at the time the security agreement is entered into but also equipment subsequently acquired by the debtor? The question is not whether Article 9 gives effect to a security agreement that encumbers after-acquired property; clearly, it does: "a security agreement may create or provide for a security interest in after-acquired collateral." R9–204(a). Rather the question is whether a particular security agreement that does not expressly refer to after-acquired property nevertheless creates a security interest in that property. Whether conceptualizing the issue as one concerning the adequacy of the collateral description or as one concerning whether the parties agreed to cover after-acquired collateral, some courts have refused to uphold claims to after-acquired property in the absence of an explicit reference in the security agreement. Others have been more generous, especially when the collateral concerned has been accounts or inventory, which turn over continually and for which it would make little commercial sense for the parties to limit the collateral to that on hand at the inception of the transaction. Comment 3 to R9–108 explains: "This question is one of contract interpretation and is not susceptible to a statutory rule (other than a rule to the effect that it is a question of contract interpretation). Accordingly, this section contains no reference to descriptions of after-acquired collateral."

More generally, should courts apply ordinary principles of contract interpretation to discern the meaning of a description in a security agreement? Is there anything special about a security agreement that would justify special treatment? See UCC 1–103 (unless displaced, principles of law supplement the UCC); UCC 1–201(3) (defining "agreement"); UCC 1–205 (roles of course of dealing, usage of trade, and express terms in construing an agreement); In re Wolsky, 68 B.R. 526 (Bkrtcy.D.N.D.1986) (terms of security agreement "strictly construed against the drafter consistent with fundamental rules of contract construction").

Problem 7.2.8. Several months after Firstbank and Main Motors established the inventory financing arrangements as described in the Prototype, Main fell behind in payments to its unsecured trade creditors. Main requested a short-term (60–day) loan from Firstbank in the amount of $100,000. Firstbank agreed and advanced that sum to Main. The only documentation was a promissory note signed by Main. The note contained no reference to any of the inventory financing documentation. Main failed to pay the note when due and also defaulted under the inventory financing arrangement. Subsequently, Lean, a judgment creditor of Main, caused the sheriff to levy on Main's automobile inventory.

As counsel for Lean, you conclude that Lean's execution lien is junior to Firstbank's security interest. However, you learn that the value of the automobile inventory probably is sufficient to satisfy all amounts outstanding on Main's inventory loans from Firstbank, with surplus value available for Lean. On the other hand, if the automobile inventory secures not only the inventory loans but also the $100,000 term loan, there would be little, if anything, left for Lean.

(a) What are the best arguments that the automobile inventory does not secure the $100,000 loan? See R9–204(c) & Comment 5; Dealer Inventory Security Agreement (Form 7.2, supra) ¶ 5; Note on Obligations (Including Future Advances) Covered by Security Agreements, infra.

(b) Assuming that the $100,000 loan would be secured, what result if Main's $100,000 obligation to Firstbank arose not out of a loan but out of an accident in which one of Main's tow-trucks ran through Firstbank's plate glass window, into its lobby, and over its president?

(c) As Firstbank's counsel, how could you draft the Dealer Inventory Security Agreement so as to ensure that the collateral would secure Main's obligations to Firstbank in both of these circumstances?

NOTE ON OBLIGATIONS (INCLUDING FUTURE ADVANCES) COVERED BY SECURITY AGREEMENTS

The term "security interest" is defined in R1–201(37) to include "an interest in personal property or fixtures which secures payment or performance of an obligation." The UCC leaves it to the parties to agree as to what obligations are secured by a security interest. Although the UCC does not define or regulate generally the obligations that are secured, R9–204(c) does address one aspect of the obligations that may be secured by a security interest: "A security agreement may provide that collateral secures ... future advances or other value, whether or not the advances or value are given pursuant to commitment." This provision might seem superfluous, were it not for the pre-UCC treatment of future advance provisions in the courts. Comment 5 to F9–204 noted that "[a]t common law and under chattel mortgage statutes there seems to have been a vaguely articulated prejudice against future advance agreements comparable to the prejudice against after-acquired property interests." The following passage reveals the source and flavor of at least some of that prejudice:

> **Validity of future advance arrangements under pre-Code law: The "dragnet" cases.** A convenient starting point will be the type of situation which regularly calls down the thunderings of judicial wrath: the lender's claim that obligations of the mortgagor [debtor] which are in no sense related to the financing transaction which the mortgage [security interest] was given to secure are, nevertheless, covered by the mortgage. Cases of this type, which often are indistinguishable from cases of outright fraud, keep coming along in numbers just sufficient to keep fresh in the judicial mind the ease with which the future advance device can be exploited by the overreaching mortgagee [secured party] to crush the impoverished but no doubt honest debtor.
>
> A standard boiler-plate clause provides in substance: the mortgaged property [collateral] shall stand as security for any indebtedness

of any sort which may now or hereafter be owing by mortgagor to mortgagee. In polite society this is sometimes referred to as a "cross-security" clause; it can serve many useful and legitimate purposes. A court which proposes to invalidate a claim asserted under such a clause will refer to it less politely as a "dragnet" clause, with the remark that such clauses "are not highly regarded in equity. They should be 'carefully scrutinized and strictly construed.'" Or as the Arkansas court [Berger v. Fuller, 180 Ark. 372, 21 S.W.2d 419, 421 (1929)] put it in a colorful passage:

> Mortgages of this character have been denominated "Anaconda mortgages" and are well named thus, as by their broad and general terms they enwrap the unsuspecting debtor in the folds of indebtedness embraced and secured in the mortgage which he did not contemplate ...

> What often happens in dragnet cases is that a mortgagee who holds a mortgage given to secure a small claim on an otherwise impoverished debtor's one valuable piece of property—which may be his homestead—buys up, no doubt at a large discount, other claims against the mortgagor and adds these to the mortgage debt. A variant is that the mortgagee, after his debt has been largely paid, will assign the mortgage to another creditor, who asserts that his previously unsecured claim is now, by virtue of the dragnet clause, the debt secured.

2 Gilmore, Security § 35.2, at 917–18.

It is clear enough that the UCC itself legitimizes future advance provisions and puts no restrictions on what obligations can be secured. Yet Professor Gilmore argued that the pre-UCC law survived the enactment of Former Article 9, at least to the extent that only future advances that are similar and related to an initial, principal obligation should be given the benefit of broad future advance and "all obligations" provisions. Id. § 35.5, at 932. Numerous cases have taken the approach urged by Professor Gilmore. See, e.g., Community Bank v. Jones, 278 Or. 647, 566 P.2d 470 (1977) (citing, inter alia, Gilmore, Security; applying "general test" of whether indebtedness was of same class as primary obligation); In re Fassinger, 246 B.R. 513 (Bkrtcy.W.D.Pa.2000). In *Fassinger* the bankruptcy court refused to enforce "dragnet clauses" contained in separate security agreements, because the agreements failed the "Four–Part Test" applicable to determine whether they violated the "relatedness" doctrine. The court quoted earlier case law for the "Four–Part Test":

> "(1) Whether the other indebtednesses allegedly covered by the ... [security agreement containing said dragnet clause] are [specifically expressed] therein ...; (2) Whether the other indebtednesses allegedly covered are 'of the same class' as the debt referenced in the ... [security agreement] ...; (3) Whether the other indebtednesses were intended to be separately secured ...; and (4) Whether the ... [secured party] relied on the clause in making further loans...."

Id. at 269 (bracketed language in original).

If the bargain-in-fact of the parties is that a security agreement is to secure all of a debtor's obligations, should that bargain be disregarded merely because a putative secured obligation is somehow dissimilar or unrelated to earlier obligations? (See part (2) of the "Four–Part test," just quoted.) If so, the result would offend the freedom-of-contract principle that the UCC appears to respect in the context of what obligations are to be secured. Cf. UCC 1–102(2)(b) (providing that an underlying purpose and policy of the UCC is to permit the continued expansion of commercial practices through agreement of the parties); UCC 1–102(3) (affording parties substantial freedom to vary UCC provisions and to agree on standards of performance).

As may be the case when determining what collateral is covered by a security agreement, a better approach might be to apply conventional rules of contract interpretation to the task at hand. See, e.g., In re Public Leasing Corp., 488 F.2d 1369 (10th Cir.1973) (parol evidence should not have been admitted to construe a "cross-collateralization clause" that was "clear and unambiguous"). Comment 5 to R9–204 adopts this approach:

> Determining the obligations secured by collateral is solely a matter of construing the parties' agreement under applicable law. This Article rejects the holdings of cases decided under former Article 9 that applied other tests, such as whether a future advance or other subsequently incurred obligation was of the same or a similar type or class as earlier advances and obligations secured by the collateral.

Experience shows that the courts' distrust of broad cross-collateralization agreements may die slowly, notwithstanding this clear instruction in Comment 5. Nevertheless, it seems likely that in many cases the same results would obtain regardless of the approach taken.

SECTION 3. PERFECTION OF SECURITY INTERESTS

(A) PERFECTION BY FILING

We saw in Section 2 that a security interest is not enforceable against the debtor or third parties, and does not attach, until the three conditions in R9–203(b) are satisfied. In this Section we shall see that even if a security interest is enforceable, the secured party does not necessarily prevail over holders of competing claims to the collateral.

Problem 7.3.1. The transaction followed precisely the steps described in the Prototype in Section 1, supra. Lean, the holder of a judgment against Main Motors, subsequently caused the sheriff to levy on the cars in Main's inventory. Is Lean's execution lien senior or junior to Firstbank's security interest in the cars? See R9–201; R9–203(a), (b); R9–317(a)(2); R9–308(a); R9–102(a)(52); R9–310; R9–502(a); R9–102(a)(48); R9–501(a); R9–311(d); Notes (1) and (2) on Perfection by Filing, infra.

Problem 7.3.2. The transaction followed precisely the steps described in the Prototype, except that one of Firstbank's clerks neglected to file the Financing Statement (Form 7.1, supra). On May 1, 2002, Lean, the judgment creditor, caused the sheriff to levy on Main's inventory of cars. Is Lean's execution lien senior or junior to Firstbank's security interest? See R9–317(a)(2); R9–310.

Problem 7.3.3. The transaction followed precisely the steps described in the Prototype, except that, instead of filing the Financing Statement with the Pennsylvania filing office as required by R9–301(1) and R9–501(a)(2), one of Firstbank's clerks mistakenly filed the Financing Statement in the New Jersey filing office. Lean, the judgment creditor, caused the sheriff to levy on Main's inventory of cars. Is Lean's execution lien senior or junior to Firstbank's security interest? See R9–317(a)(2); R9–310. (The proper place of filing is considered in more detail in Section 4, infra.)

Problem 7.3.4. Firstbank obtained the documentation and followed the procedures in the Prototype. However, after Firstbank delivered the Financing Statement to the proper filing office, an error in the process of inputing data into a computer resulted in the Financing Statement's being erroneously indexed so as to reflect Firstbank as *debtor* and Main Motors as *secured party*. This error was reflected in a receipt mailed to Firstbank by the filing office, but none of Firstbank's staff noticed the error.

(a) Secondbank becomes interested in providing floorplan financing to Main Motors and wishes to learn whether Main's inventory may be subject to a security interest. Would Secondbank be able to discover the Financing Statement? See R9–519(c); R9–523(c).

(b) Was the filing effective to perfect Firstbank's security interest? See R9–516(a); R9–517; In re Flagstaff Foodservice Corp., 16 B.R. 132 (Bkrtcy. S.D.N.Y.1981) (filing officer's complete failure to index financing statement did not impair effectiveness of filing, notwithstanding that three years after the filing the secured party had not yet received a copy of the filed financing statement and its check for the filing fee had not cleared). What result better promotes the purposes of the filing system?

(c) Do other creditors or lienholders who may be damaged by the erroneous indexing have any recourse other than to attack the effectiveness of the security interest? See R9–519(c); R9–523(c); Mobile Enterprises, Inc. v. Conrad, 177 Ind.App. 475, 380 N.E.2d 100 (1978) (complaint against Indiana's Secretary of State and Director of the UCC Division for negligent failure to disclose to plaintiff the existence of a filed financing statement was sufficient to withstand a motion to dismiss).

Problem 7.3.5. Firstbank established the financing arrangement with Main Motors as described in the Prototype. Subsequently, Secondbank became interested in providing floorplan financing to Main Motors. Secondbank asks you, its counsel, to check the public record to discover whether, and to what extent, Main's assets may be subject to security interests.

(a) What does the public record reveal? Does it show whether any motor vehicles in fact are subject to Old Bank's or Firstbank's security interest and, if so, which ones? Does it show whether Main is obligated to Old Bank or Firstbank and, if so, the amount of the obligation? See Financing Statement (Form 7.1, supra); R9–522(a); R9–515(a), (c).

(b) If the only reference to collateral were "inventory," would the Financing Statement be adequate to perfect a security interest in the automobiles in Main's inventory as of the time the Financing Statement was filed? Would it be adequate to perfect a security interest in inventory that Main acquired after the Financing Statement was filed? See R9–502(a)(3); R9–504; R9–108. If so, how can an interested party such as Secondbank discover the relevant facts? See R9–210. (Do not overlook the obvious while pondering this question!)

(c) Would the Financing Statement be adequate to perfect a security interest in Main's inventory of automobiles if the only reference were to "certain motor vehicles"? Is "certain motor vehicles" a "description" of the collateral? See Problem 7.2.4(e), supra. If not, would "certain motor vehicles" nevertheless satisfy the requirements of R9–502(a)(3)? See R9–504, Comment 2; Note (4) on Perfection by Filing, infra. If "certain motor vehicles" is not a sufficient "description" for a security agreement but is a sufficient "indication" for a financing statement, what policy explains the difference in result?

(d) The Financing Statement filed by Firstbank appears on the "uniform form" set forth in R9–521. Would the Financing Statement be legally sufficient if it lacked the information requested in boxes 1.c. through 1.g. and 3.c.? If so, would you advise Firstbank to adopt a cost-saving policy of leaving those boxes blank? See R9–502(a); R9–520(a); R9–516(b)(4), (b)(5); 9–520(c); Note (4) on Perfection by Filing, infra.

(e) Should the UCC require more complete information to appear in the public record? Should the answer turn on the purpose(s) of Article 9 filing? See Note (3) on Perfection by Filing, infra. Should the answer turn on the type of collateral involved? Would it be feasible to require more detailed filing in the setting of inventory financing like that involved in the Prototype? See R9–502, Comment 2.

On the other hand, insofar as filing is intended to alert interested parties to the possibility that the secured party may claim a security interest, how could anyone be misled by a filing covering "all debtor's personal property, of every kind and nature"? Would such an indication of collateral be sufficient? See R9–504. Would it suffice as a description of collateral for a security agreement? See Problem 7.2.4(d), supra. What policy explains the difference?

Problem 7.3.6. On March 19 Main executed and delivered the documents described in the Prototype and Firstbank advanced funds to General Motors for a trailer-load of new cars. The new cars were delivered to Main on March 23; that same day Lean levied on the newly-delivered cars. On March 26 Firstbank filed the Financing Statement in the proper office. Is Lean's execution lien senior or junior to Firstbank's security interest? See

R9–317(a)(2); R9–317(e); R9–103(b), (a); Notes (1) and (2) on Perfection by Filing, infra.

Problem 7.3.7. Firstbank established the financing arrangement with Main Motors as described in the Prototype. Subsequently, Secondbank became interested in providing floorplan financing to Main Motors.

(a) If Secondbank were to extend financing to Main Motors secured by Main's existing inventory, and if Secondbank failed to "pick up" Firstbank's floor plan by satisfying Main's indebtedness to Firstbank, would Secondbank's security interest in the cars be senior or junior to Firstbank's security interest? See R9–322(a)(1);[1] Note (2) on Perfection by Filing, infra.

(b) Now assume that Secondbank refuses to advance funds to Main Motors in the face of the financing statement filed in favor of Firstbank, notwithstanding both Main's and Firstbank's assurances that Firstbank has been paid in full and has made no commitment whatsoever to extend more credit to Main. (We shall see below in Section 6 that Secondbank is not acting unreasonably.) What would you advise Main to do? See R9–513(c) and (d).

Problem 7.3.8. The documentation and procedures in the Prototype were followed, except that the Financing Statement filed by Firstbank set forth the name of the debtor as "Main Motors"; Main's exact corporate name is "Main Motors, Inc." Lean, Main's judgment creditor, caused the sheriff to levy on all the cars. Is Lean's execution lien senior or junior to Firstbank's security interest? See R9–317(a)(2); R9–502; R9–503(a)(1); R9–102(a)(70); R9–102(a)(50); R9–506(a)–(c); Note (4) on Perfection by Filing, infra.

Problem 7.3.9. In the context of the Prototype, assume that Main's business is operated (i.e., signs, letterhead, business forms, telephone listing, advertising) under the **trade name** "Center City Chevrolet Sales and Service." Would the filing against "Main Motors, Inc." be sufficient to perfect Firstbank's security interest? Would a filing against "Center City Chevrolet Sales and Service" be sufficient? See R9–502(a); R9–503(a)–(c); Note (4) on Perfection by Filing, infra.

Problem 7.3.10. In the context of the Prototype, assume that Firstbank's operations are carried out under the trade name "Phirst of Philly" and that the Financing Statement set out that trade name in the box for the secured party's name. Is the Financing Statement sufficient? See R9–102(a)(72); R9–502(a); R9–506(a) & Comment 2; Note (4) on Perfection by Filing, infra.

Problem 7.3.11. In the context of the Prototype, assume that Firstbank assigned its security interest and the obligations of Main Motors that it secures to Secondbank, but nothing indicating the assignment is filed

---

1. Section 6, infra, focuses in detail on priorities among conflicting Article 9 security interests, including the baseline, first-to-file-or-perfect rule of R9–322(a)(1). In that connection, we shall see that a secured party who acquires a purchase-money security interest (as defined in R9–103) may qualify for priority over earlier-filed secured parties. See R9–324; Section 6(B)(II), infra.

with the filing office (i.e., the financing statement naming Firstbank as secured party remains unchanged).

(a) Does the Financing Statement remain sufficient to perfect the security interest (now) held by Secondbank? See R9–310(c).

(b) Assume further that one of Firstbank's clerks, having become aware that Firstbank no longer has any outstanding loans to Main on its books, sends a termination statement to the filing office. What is the effect, if any, on Secondbank's security interest? See R9–513(d); R9–514(b); R9–511; R9–509(d).

Problem 7.3.12. Assume that the line of credit in the Prototype was extended to Main Motors not by Firstbank alone but by a group (**syndicate**) of banks, including Firstbank, and that the Dealer Inventory Security Agreement (Form 7.2, supra) named all of these banks as secured parties. As part of an **intercreditor agreement**, the banks agreed among themselves that the Financing Statement would show only Firstbank as secured party and that Firstbank would act as agent for the banks in its capacity as the secured party of record. Is the Financing Statement sufficient? See R9–503(d) and Comment 3; Note (4) on Perfection by Filing, infra.

Problem 7.3.13. Most other documents placed in the public record, including financing statements filed under Former Article 9 (see F9–402(1)) and mortgages, are ineffective unless they are signed. However, a financing statement is sufficient under Revised Article 9 even if it is not signed. See R9–502(a).

(a) Why does Revised Article 9 eliminate the signature requirement? See R9–502 & Comment 3; R9–510(a); R9–509(a); Note (4) on Perfection by Filing, infra.

(b) What course of action would you recommend to a client against whom a financing statement had been filed (purportedly by a secured party named "Donald Duck") for the purpose of impairing the client's ability to obtain secured credit? See R9–510(a); R9–509(a); R9–625(e)(3); R9–509(d); R9–102(a)(72), (a)(79); R9–513(c), (d); R9–518; R9–625(e)(4), R9–511.

(c) Do you expect that the elimination of the signature requirement will increase the likelihood that malefactors will use the filing system to impair the ability of others to get secured credit? See R9–625(b), (e)(3).

Problem 7.3.14. Firstbank obtained the documentation and followed the procedures in the Prototype, except that the Dealer Inventory Security Agreement (Form 7.2, supra) did not include paragraph (5)(b).

(a) Lean, the holder of a judgment against Main Motors, subsequently caused the sheriff to levy on the cars in Main's inventory. Is Lean's lien junior to Firstbank's security interest in the cars? Or, does the fact that Main did not authorize the filing of a financing statement covering accounts, chattel paper, or general intangibles render the filed financing statement ineffective? See R9–317(a)(2); R9–510(a) & Comment 2; R9–509(a), (b).

(b) Lean, the holder of a judgment against Main Motors, caused the sheriff to serve a garnishment summons on several persons who owed debts to Main and thereby obtained a judicial lien on certain of Main's accounts. Is Lean's lien senior or junior to Firstbank's security interest in the accounts? See R9–317(a)(2); R9–203(b).

NOTES ON PERFECTION BY FILING

(1) The Concept of Perfection. We have seen in our discussion of attachment that, as a general matter, "a security agreement is effective according to its terms between the parties, against purchasers of the collateral, and against creditors." R9–201(a). We also have seen that even if a security interest has been created, it is enforceable against the debtor and third parties only if the three conditions for attachment—value, rights in the collateral, and the debtor's security agreement—have been satisfied. R9–203(b). But even an enforceable (attached) security interest is unlikely to be effective against third parties claiming an interest in the collateral unless it is "perfected."

A security interest is "perfected" when the security interest has attached *and* "all of the applicable requirements for perfection in Sections 9–310 through 9–316 have been satisfied." R9–308(a). For the most part, these "applicable requirements" consist of methods by which a secured party gives public notice of its security interest. The filing of a financing statement is the most common method—so common, in fact, that R9–310(a) provides that "[a] financing statement must be filed to perfect all security interests," with certain specified exceptions. Section 3(B) of this Chapter deals with many important exceptions, including perfection by possession under R9–313. Chapter 9 deals with perfection by control under R9–314.

The various elements of perfection and attachment can occur in any order. For example, a secured party first might comply with R9–310 by filing a financing statement. (Firstbank did so in the Prototype.) Next, the debtor might sign a security agreement describing collateral (say, inventory) in which the debtor already has rights. Finally, the secured party might give value (e.g., by making a loan) to the debtor. In this example, upon the occurrence of the last step, the giving of value, the security interest simultaneously would attach and become perfected. Now assume that, subsequent to the initial attachment and perfection as to the debtor's existing inventory, the debtor acquires a new item of inventory. If the security agreement covers "after-acquired" as well as existing collateral, e.g., "all inventory now owned or hereafter acquired," then immediately upon the debtor's acquisition of rights in the new inventory, the security interest would attach and become perfected in the new inventory. As to the after-acquired inventory, the last step giving rise to a perfected security interest would be the debtor's acquisition of "rights in the collateral."

(2) Priority Rules and Conveyancing Principles. For practical purposes, a secured party who fails to take the "applicable steps" for perfection is likely to be no better off than one whose security interest did not attach. Although an attached but unperfected security interest is enforceable against the debtor, such a security interest may be defeated by the claims of several different types of claimants. In particular, an unperfected security interest is vulnerable to the rights of a "lien creditor," such as a creditor who obtains an execution or other judicial lien. See R9–317(a)(2) (unperfected security interest is subordinate to lien creditor); R9–102(a)(52) (defining "lien creditor"). Even worse, from the secured party's perspective, is that an unperfected security interest will not be effective when it is needed most—in the debtor's bankruptcy. See BC 544(a)(1); R9–317(a)(2); R9–102(a)(52); Chapter 10, Section 2(A), infra.[2]

The priority rule of R9–317(a)(2) constitutes an important exception to the general rule of R9–201. It also represents an exception to the *nemo dat* principle. Although the debtor already has conveyed an enforceable (attached) security interest to an unperfected secured party, the lien creditor can achieve rights that are senior to those of the secured party, thereby receiving greater rights than those of the debtor!

R9–317(e) creates an exception to R9–317(a)(2). It creates a grace period for purchase-money security interests, whereby a security interest perfected by filing "before or within 20 days after the debtor receives delivery of the collateral" is senior to the interest of a person who becomes a lien creditor (or buyer or lessee) "between the time the security interest attaches and the time of filing." R9–317(e). R9–103 defines "purchase-money security interest" to include a security interest retained by a seller to secure the price of collateral sold, such as Main's security interest (which subsequently was assigned to Firstbank) in the car sold to Lee Abel in the Prototype. That term also embraces a security interest taken by a third-party lender who advances funds to enable a debtor to acquire the collateral, such as Firstbank's advances to General Motors for cars bought by Main in the Prototype. The priority rule in R9–317(e) balances the interests of purchase-money financers, who may find it inconvenient or impossible to file before the debtor receives possession of collateral, against those of (presumably) nonreliance lien creditors. Is the balance struck an appropriate one? (The rights of a purchase-money secured party when the debtor's bankruptcy intervenes before the secured party has filed a financing statement are considered in Chapter 10, Section 2, infra.)

Consideration of another priority rule rounds out this overview of Article 9's basic conveyancing principles. Assume that *SP*–1 extends credit to Debtor and receives a security interest in Debtor's equipment pursuant to a written security agreement, and further assume that *SP*–1 fails to perfect its security interest by filing or otherwise. Next, assume that, for whatever reason, Debtor grants an enforceable security interest in its equipment to another secured party (*SP*–2); *SP*–2 perfects its security interest by a proper filing. Under the "first-to-file-or-perfect" rule that generally applies among conflicting Article 9 security interests, *SP*–2's

---

2. An unperfected security interest also is subordinate to the rights of certain good-faith buyers and other transferees. R9–317(1)(b)–(d); see Section 6(B), infra.

security interest is senior to that of *SP*–1, even though *SP*–1's security interest was created and attached first and even if *SP*–1 eventually files a financing statement. See R9–322(a). Once again, the subordination of *SP*–1's security interest reflects an exception to the general rule of R9–201 as well as to the *nemo dat* principle. Although Debtor's rights in its equipment were subject to *SP*–1's (unperfected) security interest, Debtor conveyed greater rights to *SP*–2.

(3) Fraud, Ostensible Ownership, and Filing. Why does the filing of a proper (R9–502(a)) financing statement play such an important role in the Article 9 priority scheme? What purpose or purposes motivated the UCC drafters to impose a filing system? Do the actual benefits of that system outweigh the costs? The answers to these and related questions are complex and uncertain, as the following brief exploration of the historical background of the filing system suggests.

Retention of Possession and the "Fraud in Law" Doctrine. Consider the following facts:

> *P* was indebted both to *C* and *T*. *C* brought an action on the debt against *P*. In the meantime, *P* transferred all of *P*'s personal property to *T* in full satisfaction of *P*'s debt to *T*. However, *P* retained possession of the personal property and continued to use it and treat it as *P*'s own, with *T*'s acquiescence. Subsequently, *C* obtained a judgment against *P* and the sheriff attempted to levy on *P*'s property. *P*'s friends resisted the levy, claiming that the property had been transferred to *T* for good consideration.

These are the facts of Twyne's Case, 76 Eng. Rep. 809 (Star Ch. 1601), in which *T* (Twyne) was held convicted of a violation of the Statute of 13 Elizabeth, ch. 5. That statute provided that transfers made with the "intent[] to delay, hinder or defraud creditors and others" were void, provided for the recovery from the transferee of the "whole value of . . . goods and chattels" transferred, and provided criminal sanctions against the parties to the transfer. *Twyne's Case* is best known for setting forth what have become known as "badges of fraud"—in particular, a seller's retention of possession of personal property after its sale. The court in *Twyne's Case* simply could not believe that *P* (Pierce) and Twyne really contemplated the general transfer of all of Pierce's personal property ("without exception of his apparel"—underwear, toothbrush, and all) to Twyne; in short, the transaction was a sham.

The Statute of 13 Elizabeth was either received into the common law or expressly adopted by statute in most jurisdictions in the United States. See, e.g., Sturtevant v. Ballard, 9 Johns. 337 (N.Y.Sup.Ct.1812) ("[A] voluntary sale of chattels, with an agreement . . . that the vendor may keep possession, is, except in special cases, and for special reasons, to be shown to and approved of by the court, fraudulent and void, as against creditors."). Subsequent to the *Sturtevant* case, New York law (after various vicissitudes) became more favorable to buyers who could establish their good faith. See 2 Williston, Sales § 385 (rev. ed. 1948). Several other states, however, continued to articulate the view that a seller's retention of tangible personal property constituted "fraud *per se*." Other jurisdictions rejected this "fraud in law" approach in favor of a more lenient, "fraud in fact" version of the vendor-in-possession doctrine. Modern "fraudulent conveyance" or "fraudulent transfer" law, epitomized by the Uniform Fraudulent Transfer Act (UFTA), adopts the "fraud in fact" approach. Under this approach, the seventeenth-century "badges of fraud" retain their vitality. UFTA 4(b)(2) provides that, in determining whether a transfer is made "with actual intent to hinder, delay, or defraud any creditor of the debtor" and, thus, whether an aggrieved creditor may be able to set the transfer aside, the court may consider various factors, including "whether ... the debtor retained possession or control of the property transferred after the transfer."

Common-law courts typically viewed a transfer for security purposes, such as a mortgage, as a species of sale, which was to be scrutinized for fraud and possibly avoided (set aside) based upon the debtor-transferor's continued possession. Clow v. Woods, 5 Serg. & Rawle 275 (Pa.1819), is an early example. Relying on the rule of the Statute of 13 Elizabeth, the court held a mortgage of all of a tanner's equipment and inventory to be "fraudulent and void" where the debtor was to remain in possession, in the absence of default, under the terms of the mortgage. The court was concerned primarily with the potential for such a transaction to be used for dishonest purposes: "I do not suppose the parties had in fact a fraudulent view, but as such a transaction might be turned to a dishonest use, it was their duty, as far as in their power, to secure the public against it."

Cases like *Clow* proved to be most inconvenient for debtors and secured parties. To be absolutely sure that a creditor could not obtain a judicial lien senior to its interest in the collateral, the creditor could have taken the collateral into its possession; however, for many kinds of collateral (e.g., the bark, tools, skins, and unfinished leather in *Clow*) a possessory security interest (**pledge**) would have been most impractical. Do you see why?

The Problem of "Ostensible Ownership." The potential for a sham transaction—perhaps a conveyance by the debtor that the transferee (a friendly relative or creditor) would assert only if creditors attempted to levy on the debtor's assets—is but one aspect of the fraud that concerned judges from *Twyne's Case* through the early twentieth century. During the same period, reported decisions and commentary dealing with a seller's or debtor's retention of possession typically intermixed expressions of concern about bogus transactions with apprehension about another perceived problem—"ostensible ownership." The ostensible ownership problem involves the risk that a debtor's retention of possession will deceive its creditors into believing that the debtor owns the property free of conflicting claims.

A sham transaction presents a problem distinct from that engendered by ostensible ownership. In the former, the debtor "really" owns the goods free and clear but attempts to deceive creditors into believing that the goods have been conveyed to a third party; in the latter, a third party really has an interest in the goods, but the debtor's continued possession deceives creditors into believing that the debtor owns the goods free and clear.[3] Notwithstanding this distinction, the courts and commentators frequently failed to draw a clear line between the two aspects of fraud, often referring to them interchangeably when determining that a secured transaction constituted a fraudulent conveyance.

Consider, on the one hand, the points made by two judges in *Clow v. Woods*: "In every case where possession is not given, the parties must leave *nothing* unperformed, within the compass of their power, to secure third persons from the consequences of the apparent ownership of the vendor." (Gibson, J.) "There is no way of coming at the knowledge of who is the owner of goods, but by seeing in whose possession they are." (Duncan, J.). On the other hand, the court indicated that it would have approved an arrangement whereby the mortgagee would have bought the goods and leased them to the mortgagor:

> The object of the parties might have been attained without any (at least with less) risk to the public, by the landlord [mortgagee] himself becoming the purchaser in the first instance, and permitting the tenant [mortgagor] to have the use of the property: in which case, the transaction would have been a safe and fair one; and that course should have been pursued.

5 Serg. & Rawle at 280 (Gibson, J.). Thus, Justice Gibson would have been content with the **sale-leaseback** arrangement, even though it would have created the same problem of ostensible ownership as the "secret" mortgage created.[4] Perhaps leases and other bailments, which already had become

---

3. The distinction can be seen particularly clearly when intangibles, rather than chattels, are the subject of the challenged transfer. For example, in Benedict v. Ratner, 268 U.S. 353, 45 S.Ct. 566, 69 L.Ed. 991 (1925), the Court struck down as fraudulent a financing arrangement involving the assignment of accounts receivable, pursuant to which the debtor-assignor was permitted to collect the receivables and use the proceeds in the usual course of its business without accounting to the lender-assignee. The Court held that the fraud consisted of "the reservation [by the debtor] of dominion inconsistent with the effective disposition of title and the creation of a lien." In other words, as in *Twyne's Case*, the perceived inconsistency between what the debtor *did* and what the debtor *said* it was doing, led the Court to conclude that the purported financing arrangement was a sham. Much to the chagrin of the District Court (L. Hand, J.), whose decision was reversed, the Court specifically denied that the fraud rested "upon seeming ownership because of possession retained." Indeed, any fraud concerning assignments of intangibles, which by their nature cannot be possessed or observed, could not derive from misleading appearances. An analogous genre of deception could result, however, when a debtor's books are not marked to reflect an earlier assignment.

4. Commentary likewise failed to come to grips fully with the sham-ostensible ownership dichotomy. For example, Garrard Glenn argued that the relationship between the English reputed ownership doctrine—never widely adopted by statute in the United States—and the avoidance of fraudulent conveyances based on the vendor-in-possession doctrine, was grounded in estoppel. See 1 G. Glenn, Fraudulent Conveyances and Preferences §§ 346–48, at 606–07 (rev. ed. 1940). But Glenn was forced to concede that the courts, in their application of the vendor-in-possession doctrine, were less than faithful to the ostensible ownership rationale. For a brief account of the development of filing statutes and their relationship to fraud and ostensible ownership concerns, see Mooney, The Mystery and Myth of "Ostensible Ownership" and Article 9 Filing: A Critique of Proposals to Extend Filing Requirements to Leases, 39 Ala. L. Rev. 683, 725–38 (1988).

established commercial devices, seemed a less hospitable environment for sham transactions.

The judiciary's concern for unsecured creditors and hostility toward nonpossessory security devices (i.e., devices in which the debtor remains in possession of the collateral) extended beyond ostensible ownership and fraud (more generally). At least some courts feared that, rather than facilitate commerce, the widespread use of these devices would wreak economic havoc, depriving debtors of their ability to pay unsecured claims and, perhaps, of their ability to obtain credit in the first instance.[5]

We will never know the extent to which nonpossessory security devices actually posed serious risks to creditors. We do know that, more than a century and a half ago, one court expressed skepticism about the empirical basis for the doctrine of ostensible ownership and concern over the impediments to commerce that the doctrine itself might impose:

> The truth is, there is something rather loose and indefinite in the idea of a delusive credit gained by the possession of personal property. Such inconvenience may spring from this source, to be guarded against by prudent enquiries on the part of those concerned, and to some extent by legislative enactments, tending to a degree of notoriety in regard to the title. More than this seems to me a remedy worse than the disease; and it is obvious that to prohibit altogether the separation of the title from the possession of personal property, would be incompatible with an advanced state of society and commerce, and productive of much inconvenience and injustice in the pursuits and business of life.

Davis v. Turner, 45 Va. (4 Gratt.) 422, 441 (1848).

Dispelling Fraud Through "Public Notice." Although the judiciary's approach to nonpossessory security interests was somewhat muddled, the legislative responses have been abundantly clear. Beginning with the chattel mortgage statutes in the early nineteenth century and culminating with UCC Article 9, state legislatures enacted statutes that legitimized a wide variety of personal property security devices, including chattel mortgages, conditional sales, accounts receivable financings, and trust receipt financings. These statutes generally imposed (under penalty of avoidance or subordination) an obligation of what came to be known as "public notice," requiring the secured creditor to make a filing or recording in a public office as a substitute, or proxy, for taking possession of the collateral. Article 9's provision for perfection by filing (R9–310(a)) is a direct descendant of these earlier statutes.

---

5. See, e.g., Zartman v. First Nat'l Bank of Waterloo, 189 N.Y. 267, 82 N.E. 127 (1907) (refusing to give effect to chattel mortgage on after-acquired inventory "if the result would deprive the general creditors ... of their only chance to collect debts"; observing that "[i]f it is understood that a corporate mortgage given by a manufacturing corporation may take everything except accounts and debts, such corporations, with a mortgage outstanding, will have to do business on a cash basis or cease to do business altogether.").

The Role of Public Notice in the New Millennium. Perhaps it is of no great moment (but surely it is of historical interest) whether the judicial hostility toward nonpossessory security interests and the demonstrated legislative bias toward "public notice" were motivated primarily by general fraud concerns or by more narrowly focused concerns about ostensible ownership (even if such motivations actually could be identified). However, for those who would evaluate the Article 9 scheme and for those who must interpret and live with that scheme, it is important to obtain the broadest possible understanding of what Article 9's "public notice" requirements actually achieve and fail to achieve. Professors Baird and Jackson see the Article 9 filing system as little more than a solution to the problem of "ostensible ownership." Their somewhat narrow view leads them to argue for an expanded reach of the Article 9 filing regime:

> [O]nce one realizes that these [ostensible ownership] problems have a common source, simple solutions to them become apparent. In proposing these simple solutions to problems that have consumed hundreds of pages of law review commentary, we are not advocating a radical departure from established wisdom. Rather, we are urging only that rulemakers apply more generally the principle that has shaped the law of security interests in personal property for four hundred years: A party who wishes to acquire or retain a nonpossessory interest in property that is effective against others must, as a general matter, make it possible for others to discover that interest.
>
> ... An ostensible ownership problem ... exists whenever there is a separation of ownership and possession. Article 9's treatment of the ostensible ownership problem created by secured credit naturally leads one to ask whether the ostensible ownership problem created by leases or other bailments is different. We believe the answer is simple: The two ostensible ownership problems are not different in any relevant respect. They impose the same costs on third parties, and if a filing system is an appropriate response to the first problem, it is an equally appropriate response to the second.

Baird & Jackson, Possession and Ownership: An Examination of the Scope of Article 9, 35 Stan.L.Rev. 175, 178, 186 (1983). As you ponder the attributes of the Article 9 filing system, addressed next, consider whether this "simple" analysis is a useful, or sufficient, normative baseline. Does it expose all of the costs and benefits? On what empirical assumptions does it depend?

The Attributes of Article 9 Filing. A brief consideration of the operation of the Article 9 filing regime may provide useful insight into the "theory" and "purpose" of that system. Benefits that tend to justify or explain the filing system derive from the following attributes:

> (i) The system *provides useful information to prospective purchasers* of personal property—both buyers and secured parties. For example, a prospective non-ordinary course buyer of an item of equipment[6]

---

6. See R9–315(a)(1) (security interest normally continues notwithstanding sale); R9–317(b)(2) (buyer not in ordinary course of business sometimes takes free of unperfected

or a prospective secured lender can, by searching the proper files, determine whether a security interest in the equipment may have been perfected by filing. The absence of a filing thereby allows the prospective transferor to offer some evidence tending to establish a negative—that no (perfected) security interest has been given to another party. Even if no filing is found, however, the prospective purchaser of tangible personal property also must ascertain that the property is not in the possession of a secured party. See R9–313. Moreover, even a "clean" search does not provide comfort that the prospective transferor owns the equipment or that it acquired its title free of claims that would be senior to those of the prospective purchaser. Finally, the UCC filing records generally cover only security interests; they do not reveal many other claims to the property, including tax and most other statutory liens that may be senior to the rights of the prospective purchaser.

(ii) The filing system also *provides information to existing and prospective creditors generally.* This attribute is related to the preceding one; the filing system reduces the costs of obtaining information. (And, if one believes that prospective creditors and purchasers are misled by a debtor's possession of personal property, the information provided by filing can be viewed as reducing the "problem of ostensible ownership.") That unsecured creditors somehow are "entitled" to accessible information concerning claims of secured creditors may explain, in part, the priority rule that subordinates unperfected security interests to judicial liens. See R9–317(a)(2). Yet no one really knows the extent to which unsecured creditors use or rely upon the filing system. The position of unsecured creditors is unlike that of purchasers, who normally take steps to ensure their seniority to later-arising claims to the purchased property. Ascertaining that there is no filing against a debtor would not provide an existing or prospective unsecured creditor with any protection against the debtor subsequently encumbering some or all of its assets.[7] Unsecured creditors sometimes may be interested in whether there are filings against a debtor for other reasons, however. For debtors in some lines of business a filing against receivables or inventory may be seen by trade creditors as a signal of financial distress, whereas a filing against equipment would be viewed differently. On the other hand, debtors in other lines of business may be expected to give a security interest in "all assets" as a routine matter. The market for secured loans is somewhat stratified, with some secured lenders catering to less creditworthy borrowers. The unexpected filing of a financing statement that names such a secured party may prompt trade creditors to reconsider their credit policy with

---

security interest); R1–201(9) (defining "buyer in ordinary course of business").

7. An unsecured creditor might bargain for the debtor's agreement not to create security interests in its property; however, any security interest created in violation of this agreement ordinarily will be valid. Cf. R9–401(b).

respect to the debtor. Interestingly, reports issued by business credit reporting agencies such as Dun & Bradstreet frequently include information concerning Article 9 filings.

(iii) Article 9's priority rules based on the time of filing also *reduce evidentiary costs and disputes in connection with determination of security interest priorities*. The public office filing system memorializes the time of filing and constitutes a visible and (generally) reliable "scoreboard."

(iv) Article 9's filing rules *create a hurdle that a secured party must clear in order to justify its entitlement to collateral at the expense of a debtor's unsecured creditors*. It is arguable that, as a normative matter, the benefits of security should not be easily obtained. However, this "hurdle" argument is a poor justification for a filing requirement; most would support the provisions of Revised Article 9 that make compliance with filing requirements less difficult and costly.

(v) No matter how simple Article 9's requirements may have become, secured parties from time to time will fail to comply with the filing rules—either by failing to file in the proper location or by filing a defective financing statement. In many cases this noncompliance results in the subordination of security interests to lien creditors or, more often, to trustees in bankruptcy. Consequently, the Article 9 filing rules *enable unsecured creditors to capture assets that otherwise would be allocated to secured parties*. This distributional attribute of the filing regime is related to the "hurdle" rationale just mentioned; seniority to unsecured creditors requires that a secured party "play the game according to the rules." Although those who benefit from the inevitable instances of noncompliance undoubtedly would oppose the abolition of filing requirements, it seems wrong to characterize the inevitability of noncompliance and resulting subordination as a "benefit" of filing. Similar results could be obtained more directly, e.g., by requiring that each debtor maintain a pool of unencumbered assets.[8]

Please continue to ponder the rationale and effects of the Article 9 filing rules as you consider, next, issues concerning the adequacy of financing statements and other issues of compliance and noncompliance with those rules.[9]

(4) What to File: The Adequacy of Financing Statements. The three formal requisites for a financing statement are found in R9–502(a). Except with respect to filings covering collateral related to specific real property, "a financing statement is sufficient only if it (1) provides the name of the debtor; (2) provides the name of the secured party or a representative of the secured party; and (3) indicates the collateral covered

---

8. Exemption laws are intended to preserve a pool of assets for individual (i.e., human) debtors; however, otherwise exempt property ordinarily may be encumbered by a purchase-money security interest.

9. The characteristics of filing rules also are considered in the context of what transactions are and ought to be subjected to those rules. See Chapter 8, Section 1, infra.

by the financing statement." This seemingly straightforward system of "notice filing" derives from the notice filing system of Former Article 9, which was borrowed in large part from the Uniform Trust Receipts Act, promulgated in 1933. It is surprising, perhaps, that determining the adequacy of financing statements under Former Article 9 proved perplexing to courts, commentators, and practitioners alike. In an effort to reduce the uncertainty that developed under the case law and commentary construing F9–402(1), R9–503 expounds upon the first two requirements, and R9–504 expounds upon the third. R9–506 provides additional guidance with respect to errors.

The preceding Note summarizes several plausible positive explanations for what the filing system actually does and does not do. The courts, however, generally have measured the adequacy of financing statements under Former Article 9 against a narrow paradigm consisting of an interested person who wishes to discover whether there are filings against a debtor and, if there are filings, the collateral that they cover. Can an interested person find the financing statement in question? Is the information contained in the financing statement sufficiently complete and meaningful? Revised Article 9 likewise adopts this general approach.

Debtor's Name. Filing officers index financing statements "according to the name of the debtor." R9–519(c)(1). Consequently, whether an interested person can find a financing statement is a function of (i) the debtor's name as it appears on the financing statement, (ii) the name against which the interested person requests a search of the filing office's records, and (iii) the financing statements disclosed by the filing office as a result of that search request.

R9–503(a) explains how to satisfy the requirement that a financing statement provide "the name of the debtor." R9–502(a)(1). If the debtor is a corporation or other "registered organization" (as defined in R9–102(a)(70)), a financing statement sufficiently provides the name of the debtor "only if the financing statement provides the name of the debtor indicated on the public record of the debtor's jurisdiction of organization which shows the debtor to have been organized." R9–503(a)(1). These public records are readily available; some states afford electronic access to them.

If past practice is any indication, secured parties will make errors even in corporate names. Minor errors ordinarily do not render a financing statement ineffective, unless the error makes the financing statement seriously misleading. See R9–506(a). However, when it comes to errors in debtors' names, Revised Article 9 generally is unforgiving: Any name that does not comply with the requirements of R9–503(a) ordinarily is seriously misleading as a matter of law, see R9–506(b), unless "a search of the records of the filing office under the debtor's correct name, using the filing office's standard search logic, if any, would disclose a financing statement." R9–506(c). Cases decided under Former Article 9 reveal many errors in the debtor's name that seem trivial and harmless. See, e.g., In re Tyler, 23 B.R. 806 (Bkrtcy.S.D.Fla.1982) (filing against "Tri–State Moulded Plastics, Inc."

(emphasis added); correct corporate name was "Tri–State Molded Plastics, Inc."); In re Raymond F. Sargent, Inc., 8 U.C.C. Rep. Serv. 583 (Bkrtcy. D.Me.1970) (filing against "Raymond F. Sargent *Co.*, Inc." (emphasis added); correct corporate name was "Raymond F. Sargent, Inc."). Would the financing statements in these cases be effective under Revised Article 9? Do you need more information to answer this question?

Assuming the names implicated in the question just posed do not comply with the requirements of R9–503(a) (i.e., are inaccurate), R9–506(b) requires one bit of necessary additional information—whether a search under the correct name would have uncovered the financing statements "using the filing office's standard search logic, if any." In some filing offices, search requests are processed by individuals who search the files for filings against the name(s) submitted by a party requesting a search. In such a system, whether a search request for filings against "A.B.C. Corp." (the "real" name) would result in identification of filings against other variations (e.g., "ABC Corp.," "A. B. C. Corp.," "ABC," "A.B.C. Systems") will depend on the formal or informal procedures adopted by that office and, perhaps, the judgment of the particular employee conducting the search. Because all filing systems now are "computerized" to some extent, one cannot determine whether a financing statement benefits from R9–506(b) without taking into account the filing office's search logic. Although the search logic *per se* is not a matter of public record in most states, one can determine whether the search logic will uncover a given financing statement by searching under the debtor's correct name and seeing the results of the search.

Apart from inaccuracies in the debtor's name, there is the problem of "trade names," under which individuals, partnerships, and corporations may choose to conduct business. (For example, the Chicago National League Ball Club, Inc., has adopted the trade name "Chicago Cubs.") Although Former Article 9 does not provide for this result explicitly, a majority of the reported cases indicate that use of a trade name instead of a "real" name is insufficient. See, e.g., Greg Restaurant Equipment & Supplies, Inc. v. Valway, 144 Vt. 59, 472 A.2d 1241 (1984) (filing against trade name ("Ricardo's") that differed materially from debtor's actual name ("Richard M. Valway") was ineffective); In re Covey, 66 B.R. 459 (Bkrtcy.D.N.H.1986) (filing against debtor's trade name ("RBF Industries") instead of actual name ("George R. Covey") was ineffective because a third party searching the files against the actual name would not discover the trade name filing). Other courts have reached a different conclusion. See, e.g., In re Glasco, Inc., 642 F.2d 793 (5th Cir.1981) (applying Florida law) (filing against "Elite Boats, Division of Glasco, Inc." was effective to perfect security interest notwithstanding that debtor's correct corporate name was "Glasco, Inc.," because a "reasonably prudent creditor" would have searched against "Elite Boats," the debtor's trade name).

R9–503(c) addresses the issue explicitly: a financing statement that provides only the debtor's trade name does not sufficiently provide the name of the debtor. Nevertheless, under some circumstances a financing statement may be sufficient even if it provides only a trade name for the debtor; however, the sufficiency of a trade name is determined by the same rules for determining the sufficiency of any other incorrect name. See R9–506(b), (c). How would the cases in the preceding paragraph be decided under Revised Article 9?

Names of individual (human) debtors are particularly problematic: Consider an individual whose birth certificate refers to Kelly Livingston Jones, who normally goes by "K. Livingston Jones" for personal affairs and "K. L. Jones" for professional and business purposes, and who is called "Kelly Jones" by friends. What is the "individual . . . name" of this person, as the phrase is used in R9–503(a)(4)(A)? Can a single debtor have more than one name for purposes of R9–502(a)(1) and R9–503(a)(4)(A)? Is a filing that names "Kelly Jones" sufficient?

Professor Julianna Zekan proposed that Article 9 require filings against the "legal name" of a debtor, which she would define as "the official name (appellation) of an individual . . . as stated on an official document such as the birth certificate, passport, registration . . . as modified, supplemented or amended of record with the appropriate judicial or other governmental authorities." Zekan, The Name Game—Playing to Win Under § 9–402 of the Uniform Commercial Code, 19 Hofstra L. Rev. 365, 440–41 (1990). Revised Article 9 does not adopt this proposal. Should it have done so? Are there situations in which an individual debtor could have more than one "legal" name? Although R9–503 substantially clarifies the analysis for names of registered organizations and certain other entities, it preserves the perplexing issues surrounding individual names that existed under Former Article 9.

Under these circumstances, what should a court do? If a financing statement fails to provide "the individual . . . name of the debtor" as required by R9–503(a)(4), then the standard search logic of the filing office is relevant to whether the financing statement is sufficient. See R9–506(b). If, for example, the debtor's name is K. L. Jones, then the search logic will determine whether a search under that name will disclose a filing against K L Jones; KL Jones, Kelly L. Jones, or Kelly Jones; any financing statement that the search discloses satisfies the debtor's-name requirement. But one cannot apply R9–506(b) without first knowing "the individual . . . name of the debtor" under R9–503(a)(4), and R9–503(a)(4) gives no guidance in determining which name (or names) is "the individual . . . name of the debtor." R9–503(a)(4). Should courts, following an approach some courts took under Former Article 9, treat as "the individual . . . name of the debtor" *every* name under which a *reasonable searcher* would search? Is this approach circular: Can one know the names under which a reasonable searcher would search without first knowing which names are sufficient under R9–503? Revised Article 9 rejects the "reasonable-searcher" approach with respect to the name of registered organizations. Does this mean that imposing such a burden on searchers with respect to individual debtors conflicts with the policy of R9–503 and R9–506?

To what extent should Article 9 place the risks and burdens of investigating and listing the exact name of a debtor on the secured party who files? To what extent should the risks of investigating and searching against trade names and names similar to a debtor's "real" name lie with those who search? Is it possible to generalize about which class of parties—secured parties who file or searchers—can protect themselves better against these risks and burdens? For which class of parties is such protection less costly? In answering the foregoing questions, is the frequency with which filings and searches occur relevant?

Finally, in considering the adequacy of a debtor's name on a financing statement, it is worth remembering the need to ascertain the identity of the debtor. R9–102(a)(28) defines "debtor" to include "a person having a [non-security interest or non-lien] interest in the collateral, whether or not the person is an obligor." This, of course, makes perfect sense in the present context. The filing system is designed to provide publicity about possible claims against a debtor's property.

Secured Party's Name; Secured Party of Record. The second formal requirement for a sufficient financing statement is that it must "provide[] the name of the secured party or a representative of the secured party." R9–502(a)(2). The person whose name is provided is the "secured party of record." R9–511(a). The secured party of record has the power to authorize certain amendments to a filed financing statement, including the power to terminate the financing statement's effectiveness. See R9–509(d)(1).

When there is one secured party, the financing statement usually provides the secured party's name. That is, the "secured party" and the "secured party of record" are the same person. An error in this name will not render the financing statement ineffective. See 9–506, Comment 2. In large loans, it is not uncommon for several financial institutions to provide funds that are secured by a security interest. Sometimes each lender is a "secured party," i.e, "a person in whose favor a security interest is created or provided for under a security agreement." R9–102(a)(72). Sometimes a security interest is created in favor of one of the lenders, who serves as the **collateral agent** and holds the security interest for the benefit of itself and the other lenders, usually for a fee. This lender is the "secured party." Sometimes the secured party is a non-lender third party who serves as collateral agent for a fee. Where many lenders are involved, Revised Article 9 affords considerable flexibility in satisfying R9–502(a)(2). Providing the name of all the secured parties is sufficient and will create multiple secured parties of record, each of which has the power to affect its own rights. In the alternative, a financing statement may provide the name of a "representative" (as defined in UCC 1–201(35)) of the secured parties. A financing statement that provides the name of the collateral agent or other representative satisfies R9–502(a)(2), even if it fails to indicate that the name provided is that of a representative and not that of the secured party itself. R9–503(d). A secured party should choose its representative carefully. As the secured party of record, the representative has the power to impair the secured party's rights, e.g., by terminating the effectiveness of the financing statement and thereby rendering the security interest unperfected. See R9–509(d)(1).

The flexibility and margin for error that Article 9 affords with respect to names of secured parties provides a dramatic contrast with the considerable precision that Article 9 requires with respect to debtors' names. Article 9's treatment of post-filing changes makes this contrast even starker. Post-filing changes in the secured party's name do not affect perfection, whereas in certain circumstances a financing statement becomes ineffective to perfect a security interest unless it is amended to reflect a change in the debtor's name. See R9–507(b), (c); Problems 7.3.15 and 7.3.16; Note on Post–Filing Changes, infra.

Why is Article 9 so much more exacting with respect to debtors' names? The principal explanation is that Article 9 filing systems normally provide no system for searching against a *secured party's* name. See R9–519(c); R9–523(c). Rather, the secured party's name must be provided so that notices can be sent to the secured party. See, e.g., R9–324(b). In addition, the secured party's name provides a potential source of information concerning the transaction.

References to Collateral. A secured party must do more than ensure that a financing statement correctly states the debtor's name and provides its own name or the name of its representative. A financing statement also must "indicate the collateral covered by the financing statement." R9–502(a)(3). As Comment 2 explains,

> This section adopts the system of "notice filing." What is required to be filed is not, as under pre-UCC chattel mortgage and conditional sales acts, the security agreement itself, but only a simple record providing a limited amount of information (financing statement). . . .
>
> The notice itself indicates merely that a person may have a security interest in the collateral indicated. Further inquiry from the parties concerned will be necessary to disclose the complete state of affairs.

R9–502, Comment 2.

As a general matter, "[a]n indication is sufficient if it satisfies the purpose of conditioning perfection on the filing of a financing statement, i.e., if it provides notice that a person may have a security interest in the collateral indicated." R9–504, Comment 2. R9–504 provides two safe harbors. First, a "description" of collateral under R9–108–i.e., an indication that "reasonably identifies" the collateral—is a sufficient "indication" of collateral for purposes of R9–502(a)(3). See R9–504(1). In particular, a financing statement that lists the items of collateral (e.g., "two Techno A–32 power lathes, serial numbers 54–0958–98 and 54–0921–98"), identifies the collateral by category (e.g., "motor vehicles"), or refers to collateral by a defined UCC type (e.g., "all equipment") provides a sufficient indication. See R9–108(b). Second, an indication that a financing statement covers all assets or all personal property is a sufficient indication of collateral for a financing statement. See R9–504(2). In this respect, R9–504 rejects the overwhelming majority of cases decided under Former Article 9 which refused to uphold financing statements containing only "super-generic" indications. Is anyone likely to be misled by the use of a "super-generic" indication? Given how little information is conveyed by a financing statement and the permissible use of generic terms, is the informational value of filing reduced by the use of "super-generic" indications that clearly include *all* types of personal property?[10]

Although they suffice as an indication of collateral for purposes of a financing statement, "all debtor's assets" and words of similar import are insufficient as a "description" in a security agreement. See R9–108(c). In this respect, R9–108 rejects the view of those cases decided under Former Article 9 which held that such an indication could "reasonably identify" the collateral. Is there an inherent conflict between the rules in R9–504(a)(2) and R9–108(c)? Even if not, is there a need for two different standards for referring to collateral? If different standards are appropriate, who chose the right standards—the drafters of Revised Article 9 or the judges whose opinions the drafters rejected?

Authorization. A debtor has a strong interest in the content of the public records that disclose possible claims against the debtor's property. To protect this interest, F9–402(1) required that a financing statement be "signed by the debtor." In considering ways in which to facilitate electronic filing of financing statements, the drafters of Revised Article 9 realized that the debtor's interest could be protected by requiring that the debtor authorize the filing of a financing statement, even if the authorization itself (the debtor's signature) does not appear in the public record. Thus a financing statement need not be signed to be sufficient. See R9–502(a). However, a financing statement is not effective unless the filing is authorized by the debtor in an authenticated record. See R9–509(a).

A debtor's authorization of a filing is easy enough to understand in the case of a debtor who is a natural person. When another entity (e.g., a corporation or partnership) is involved, agency law and the law regulating acts taken by the particular entity (e.g., corporate law or partnership law) determine whether the entity authorized a filing. See UCC 1–103; R9–502, Comment 3; R9–509, Comment 3.

A person who creates a security interest ordinarily does not object to the filing of a financing statement covering the collateral. (Indeed, the person may even covenant to take whatever steps may be necessary to perfect and maintain the perfected status of the security interest.) R9–509(b) reflects this phenomenon by providing that the debtor's authentica-

---

10.   In the words of Judge William Hillman:

>   One of the basic words in English is "all." It is actually easier to understand "all" than a compilation of all of the U.C.C. generics. Why must a security document state 1 + 1 + 1 when 3 is easily understood?

In re Legal Data Systems, Inc., 135 B.R. 199, 201 (Bkrtcy.D.Mass.1991). In a footnote, Judge Hillman observed: "There is a T-shirt available in resort areas with the legend: 'What part of NO don't you understand?'." Judge Hillman served on the Drafting Committee to Revise Article 9.

tion of a security agreement *ipso facto* constitutes the debtor's authorization of the filing of a financing statement covering the collateral described in the security agreement. See R9–509(b)(1).

Additional Information. Former Article 9 required that a financing statement give the addresses of the debtor and secured party in addition to their names. The courts generally have imposed a less exacting standard for addresses than they have with respect to debtors' names and identifications of collateral. Indeed, although contrary authority exists, there is support for upholding the sufficiency of financing statements even when addresses are missing entirely. Revised Article 9 adopts this approach and provides that a financing statement may be sufficient even if it does not provide addresses. See R9–502(a).

Although they did not think that providing addresses in a financing statement should be a condition of perfection, the drafters of Revised Article 9 recognized that the addresses serve a useful function. The debtor's address helps a searcher eliminate from consideration financing statements filed against debtors (in particular, individual debtors) whose names are the same as the person against whom the search was conducted. The actual usefulness of an address in eliminating "false positives" depends on the circumstances. For example, an address may be of great assistance to one who is searching against the name "John Smith," and considerably less so to one searching against, say, Phineas T. Bluster or Microsoft Corporation. As for the address of the secured party, Article 9 contemplates circumstances in which one secured party will send notification to the holder of a conflicting security interest. See, e.g., R9–324(b); R9–610(b), (c). A financing statement that provides the secured party's address substantially increases the likelihood that the notification will reach the right person. Sometimes interested third parties seek information, or seek confirmation of information provided by the debtor, from secured parties who have filed. The secured party's address helps direct the seeker to the appropriate person. (Of course, a secured party who receives a request for information from a third party should resolve any confidentiality concerns before responding. See R9–210, Comment 3.)

Revised Article 9 reflects the drafters' appreciation of the utility that addresses may provide. It supplies a strong incentive for a filer to provide the relevant addresses: The filing office is required to reject a financing statement that does not provide an address for each of the parties. See R9–520(a); R9–516(b)(4), (b)(5)(A). Other information that might help distinguish the debtor from another person having the same or a similar name is treated the same way. Thus, R9–520(a) and R9–516(b) require the filing office to reject a financing statement that does not indicate whether the debtor is an individual or an organization. If the financing statement indicates that the debtor is an organization, the filing office must reject the filing unless it provides for the debtor a type of organization (e.g., corporation or partnership), a jurisdiction of organization, and an organizational identification number (or indicates that the debtor has none). See R9–520(a); R9–516(b)(5)(B), (b)(5)(C).

What is the legal effect, if any, of a financing statement that the filing office is obligated to reject but nevertheless files? If the financing statement satisfies the formal requirements of R9–502(a) and the filing is authorized under R9–509(a), then the filed financing statement is effective. See R9–520(c).

(5) Filing Systems. Personal property filing systems based upon an index of debtor names have been utilized at least since the time of the chattel mortgage laws of the nineteenth century. The "modern" system of "notice filing" embraced by Article 9 dates back to the promulgation of the Uniform Trust Receipts Act in 1933—nearly seventy years ago. Although "computerized" systems became common under Former Article 9, there developed a consensus that the filing systems generally did not work well and failed to take full advantage of the benefits of existing technology. See Report of the Uniform Commercial Code Article 9 Filing System Task Force to the Permanent Editorial Board's Article 9 Study Committee 6–10 (1991) (reporting results of an empirical study of the Article 9 filing system and finding many filing offices to be unacceptably slow and inaccurate and to impose unnecessary costs on users.)

One of the principal goals of Revised Article 9 was to improve the operations of the filing offices. To this end, the revision makes clear that, should it choose to do so, a filing office may accept filings only in electronic form. In addition, as we explain elsewhere,

> Revised Article 9 contains several provisions that promote efficiency and uniformity in the operations of filing offices. For example, Revised sections 9–516 and 9–520 underscore that filing offices serve a ministerial, rather than regulatory, function. Taken together, they contain an exclusive list of grounds for rejecting a financing statement or other record that is communicated to a filing office and require a filing office that rejects a record to promptly inform the filer of the fact of and reason for the rejection. To further insure that filers of written financing statements are not burdened by idiosyncratic requirements imposed by individual filing offices, Revised section 9–521 contains forms for initial financing statements and amendments which each filing office must accept (assuming it accepts written records). Revised section 9–519(f) facilitates searches of the public records by requiring a filing office to be capable of retrieving an initial financing statement and all amendments and other filed records relating to it either by the debtor's name or by the file number assigned to the initial financing statement. Revised section 9–523 increases the utility of responses to search requests by requiring a filing office to respond to requests promptly and with current and complete information.

> The Drafting Committee realized that dictating the minimum services a filing office must provide and setting the minimum performance standards for providing those services are appropriate subjects for legislation, but specifying the details of day-to-day filing-office operations is not. Detailed procedures specified in statutes cannot be changed easily enough to enable filing offices to adjust to changes in filing load, personnel, and technology. Particularly given the substan-

tial differences among Article 9 filing offices (in their current operations, in the quantity of filings processed, and in the number of employees who do the processing), imposing absolute uniformity of practices and procedures would be both unnecessary and unwise. Yet, because filers and searchers often deal with many filing offices, great value would come from having filing-office practices and procedures be harmonious with one another. Revised section 9–526 is a useful step toward realizing that value. This section requires the adoption and publication of filing-office rules after consultation with other filing offices and after consideration of the rules and practices of, and technology used by, other Article 9 filing offices. Revised section 9–526 requires the rule-adopting official or agency also to consult the Model Rules promulgated by the International Association of Corporate Administrators ("IACA"), an organization of administrators responsible for statewide corporate and UCC filings.

Harris & Mooney, How Successful Was the Revision of UCC Article 9?: Reflections of the Reporters, 74 Chi.–Kent L. Rev. 1357, 1382–84 (1999).

Whether Revised Article 9 will result in a filing system that is fast, accurate, and inexpensive remains to be seen. The early signs are mixed. Although several filing offices modernized and improved their operations in anticipation of Revised Article 9's effective date, others reached that date in a state of unpreparedness.

Problem 7.3.15. Assume that Firstbank "picked up" the floorplan financing for Main Motors, on September 3, 2001, as described in the Prototype, and that, effective October 1, 2001, Main changed its corporate name from "Main Motors, Inc." to "Center City Chevrolet Sales and Service, Inc." Main received new shipments of cars on November 15 and December 20, 2001, and on February 14, 2002. Firstbank took no action to perfect its security interest subsequent to filing the original Financing Statement (Form 7.1, supra). Lean, Main's judgment creditor, caused the sheriff to levy on all the remaining cars in Main's inventory on February 20, 2002. Is Lean's execution lien senior or junior to Firstbank's security interest? See R9–507(b), (c); Note on Post–Filing Changes, infra. Does the answer depend on whether Firstbank knew that Main had changed its name? Should it?

Problem 7.3.16. You are an attorney in Firstbank's office of legal counsel. Two years after the transactions described in the Prototype, the general counsel informs you that Firstbank plans to change its name to Phirst of Philly, N.A., and asks whether the bank risks becoming unperfected on all its secured loans if it fails to amend each of the several thousand filed financing statements that show the bank's name as Firstbank, N.A. What advice do you give? See R9–507(b); Note on Post–Filing Changes, infra.

NOTE ON POST–FILING CHANGES

The world is always changing. As Problems 7.3.15 and 7.3.16, supra, suggest, information in a financing statement that is correct when the financing statement is filed may become incorrect thereafter. How do post-filing changes affect the legal sufficiency of the financing statement?

Consider the case of a debtor whose name changes after a financing statement is filed. One can imagine a legal regime in which the financing statement becomes ineffective, and the security interest unperfected, immediately upon the name change. Such a rule would impose upon the secured party the burden of discovering the change and amending the financing statement to reflect the debtor's new name. The opposite rule—a financing statement containing correct information remains effective notwithstanding that the information becomes incorrect—is equally imaginable. This rule would impose a risk upon a searcher who fails to ascertain not only the debtor's current name but also its past names.

The debtor's name is not the only information whose change might be relevant to the continued utility of a filed financing statement. For example, the collateral might be put to a different use. A computer dealer might take a computer from inventory and use it in the business. Should a financing statement covering "inventory" remain effective to perfect a security interest in collateral that has become "equipment"?

Revised Article 9 generally imposes no burden to correct information in a filed financing statement. See R9–507(b). However, a secured party who fails to amend a financing statement to reflect a change in the debtor's name risks being unperfected with respect to some collateral. See R9–507(c). What accounts for imposing a greater burden with respect to the debtor's name than with respect to the secured party's name or indication of collateral?

Observe that the rule in R9–507(c) takes an intermediate position between the two extreme positions described above. As to certain collateral, the "old name" financing statement remains effective, whereas it is ineffective as to other collateral. Professor Jay Westbrook thought the predecessor of this rule (to the extent a secured party is absolved indefinitely from providing the debtor's new name in the public record) and of the rule that appears in R9–507(a) created a "loophole" that is "inconsistent with the entire statutory scheme." See Westbrook, Glitch: Section 9–402(7) and the U.C.C. Revision Process, 52 Geo. Wash. L. Rev. 408, 411, 416–17 (1984). R9–507(a) is considered in Section 6(B), infra. Professor Stephen Knippenberg, on the other hand, has argued that the provision may be grounded on the assumption that there are very few second-in-time searchers who would be misled by "old name" financing statements and many first-in-time secured parties whose perfection would be jeopardized by a system that requires them to monitor name changes. See Knippenberg, Debtor Name Changes and Collateral Transfers Under 9–402(7): Drafting From the Outside–In, 52 Mo.L.Rev. 57, 113–115 (1987).

Does R9–507(c) strike an appropriate balance between the burden imposed on the filer and the burden imposed on the searcher? What reasons can you think of for imposing more diligence on a secured party at the time a filing is made (i.e., get the debtor's name *right*) than is imposed on a secured party subsequently?

We shall have occasion to consider the way in which Article 9 deals with other changes that affect the utility of a financing statement. See, e.g., Problems 7.4.3 and 7.4.4, infra (concerning a debtor who relocates and thereby changes the jurisdiction in which a financing statement should be filed); Note (2) on Authorized and Unauthorized Dispositions, Section 6(B), infra (discussing situations in which collateral is sold to a new owner).

(B) PERFECTION BY MEANS OTHER THAN FILING

Problem 7.3.17. Lee Abel purchased a Chevrolet from Main Motors and executed a motor vehicle Instalment Sale Contract (Form 7.6, supra). Main assigned to Firstbank its rights under this contract, and the parties followed the other procedures described in the Prototype. Note that no financing statement naming Abel as debtor was filed with respect to Abel's new Chevrolet.

(a) Friendly Finance, a judgment creditor of Abel's, caused the sheriff to levy on the car. Is Friendly's execution lien senior or junior to First-bank's security interest? See R9–317(a)(2); R9–310(a), (b)(2); R9–309(1); R9–103(b)(1), (a); R9–102(a)(23); R9–311(a), (b); Uniform Motor Vehicle Certificate of Title and Anti–Theft Act §§ 20, 3. Is the result consistent with the policy of requiring public notice as a condition to prevailing over judicial liens and the claims of many other third parties?

(b) The facts are the same, except that Abel purchased a tractor for use on a farm that Abel operates. Under the applicable Motor Vehicle Code, the tractor is not a motor vehicle that must be licensed, registered, or covered by a certificate of title. Again, no financing statement was filed, and Friendly caused the sheriff to levy on the tractor. Is Friendly's execution lien senior or junior to Firstbank's security interest in the tractor? See R9–317(a)(2); R9–310(a), (b)(2); R9–309(1); R9–103(b)(1), (a); R9–102(a)(23), (a)(33); R9–311(a).

(c) The facts are the same as in part (b), except that Abel, who lives in a house surrounded by several acres of rolling lawn, bought the tractor to pull a lawn mower. Is Friendly's execution lien senior or junior to First-bank's security interest? See R9–317(a)(2); R9–310(a), (b)(2); R9–309(1); R9–103(b)(1), (a); R9–102(a)(23); R9–311(a). Can you reconcile the result with the result in part (b)? With Article 9's policy in favor of public notice? Are Abel's other creditors likely to assess the tractor differently under the facts of part (c) than under the facts of part (b)? Federal law views nonpossessory, non-purchase-money security interests in consumer goods with disfavor. See FTC Rule on Credit Practices, 16 C.F.R. 444.2(a)(4) (taking a nonpossessory, non-purchase-money security interest in house-hold goods constitutes an "unfair act or practice" under Federal Trade Commission Act § 5); BC 522(f) (nonpossessory, non-purchase-money secu-rity interests in certain consumer goods can be avoided in bankruptcy).

(d) The facts are the same as in part (c), except that after having used the tractor around the house for a few months, Abel decided that it could be put to better use at the farm. Thereafter, Abel used the tractor exclusively for farming operations. As in part (b), the sheriff levied on the tractor at the farm. Is Friendly's execution lien senior or junior to Firstbank's security interest? See R9–317(a)(2); R9–310(a), (b)(2); R9–309(1); R9–103(b)(1), (a); R9–102(a)(23); R9–311(a). When is the use of collateral determined for purposes of classifying collateral? See R9–102(a)(23) ("used or bought for use"). What is the effect of a change in use? Cf. R9–507(b). See also R9–628(c) (nonliability of secured party that reasonably relies on debtor's or obligor's representation concerning use of collateral or purpose for which obligation incurred).

Problem 7.3.18. Dooley, an amateur numismatist, applied to Castle Finance Company for a loan. In response to Castle's request for security, Dooley delivered to Castle a valuable coin collection and received a loan for $25,000.

(a) Lean, a judgment creditor of Dooley, levies on the coin collection held by Castle. Who has priority? Does Castle even have an interest in the coins? See R9–201; R9–317(a)(2); R9–308(a); R9–203(a), (b); R9–310(a), (b)(6); R9–313(a); UCC 1–201(24); R9–102(a)(44).

(b) What result if Castle filed a financing statement conforming to R9–502(a) but did not take delivery of the coins? See R9–312(b); UCC 1–201(24); R9–102(a)(44); R9–203(b).

(c) What result if Castle itself did not take delivery of the coin collection but instead appointed Dooley its agent for the purpose of holding the coins on its behalf? Dooley's lawyer? See R9–313(a) & Comment 3; In re Copeland & Notes following, infra; Note (2) on Perfection by Possession, infra.

Problem 7.3.19. Assume that Dooley's coin collection in the preceding Problem consisted of coins issued by the 18th century Republic of Vermont and was on display at the Money Museum. Advise Castle on the steps it should take to protect its security interest in the coins, given the size of the transaction (a $25,000 loan). Assume alternatively that the museum is cooperative and that the museum is uncooperative. In particular, consider:

(i) How should Castle perfect its security interest while the coins are on display and thereafter? See R9–312(b); R9–313(a), (c), (d), (f).

(ii) How will Castle be able to enforce its security interest if Dooley defaults on its obligation? See R9–609; R9–610; R9–313(g).

Problem 7.3.20. Recall that in the Prototype, Firstbank filed a financing statement (Form 7.1, supra) to perfect its security interest in Main's inventory of automobiles. Given that Firstbank took possession of the manufacturer's certificates of origin (Form 7.7, supra), was the filing unnecessary? See In re Haugabook Auto Co., 9 U.C.C. Rep. Serv. 954 (Bkrtcy.M.D.Ga.1971) (possession of certificates of origin held not to constitute possession of motor vehicles); cf. Lee v. Cox, 18 U.C.C. Rep. Serv. 807 (M.D.Tenn.1976) (possession of registration papers for Arabian horses held not to constitute possession of horses). If the filing perfects Firstbank's security interest, then what purpose, if any, is served by Firstbank's taking possession of the certificates of origin? See Section 1(F), supra; Note (3) on Perfection by Possession, infra.

Problem 7.3.21. Diggins Construction Company entered into a contract to build a small office building for Realty for a total price of $10,000,000. The contract called for step-by-step progress payments to Diggins as the building reached specified stages of completion. Firstbank is willing to lend Diggins $8,000,000, to be secured by a security interest in the contract with Realty and the payments due and to become due under the contract.

Diggins prefers not to reveal this transaction to the public, and so it suggests to Firstbank that no financing statement be filed. It proposes instead that (i) the security agreement be entitled "Pledge of Contract," (ii) the original signed contract with Realty be delivered to Firstbank by way of pledge, and (iii) upon Diggins's default, Firstbank would have the right to notify Realty to make payments directly to Firstbank.

As counsel to Firstbank, how would you respond to this suggestion? See R9–102(a)(2), (a)(47), (a)(11), (a)(61), (a)(3), (a)(42) & Comment 5.a.–d.; R9–310(a), (b)(6); R9–313(a); R9–607.

Problem 7.3.22. Equipco is in the business of selling construction equipment. It sells to its very best customers on unsecured credit: the customer pays 20 percent down and gives a negotiable promissory note for the balance. To secure a line of credit, Firstbank took a security interest in "all Equipco's existing and after-acquired rights to payment in every form whatsoever, whether or not represented by a writing, and including, without limitation, accounts receivable, general intangibles, chattel paper, and instruments." The security agreement obligates Equipco to deliver to Firstbank all writings evidencing rights to payment within seven days after Equipco receives them. Firstbank filed a financing statement containing the same description of the collateral. On July 1, Equipco files a bankruptcy petition.

(a) On June 15 Equipco sold and delivered a backhoe to Butcher, a customer. Though inadvertence, the only document Butcher signed was a purchase order. Is Firstbank's security interest in Equipco's right to payment perfected as of the commencement of the bankruptcy case? See R9–310(a). (Do not assume that, if the security interest is perfected, it necessarily will be valid in bankruptcy. The ability of the trustee in bankruptcy to avoid security interests, both perfected and unperfected, is discussed in Chapter 10, Sections 2 and 3, infra.)

(b) Also on June 15 Equipco received a promissory note from Baker, another customer, but neglected to turn over the note to Firstbank. Is Firstbank's security interest perfected as of the commencement of the bankruptcy case? See R9–310(a); R9–312(a); R9–102(a)(47).

(c) On June 19 Equipco sold some equipment to Chandler on secured credit: Chandler paid 10 percent down, signed a promissory note for the balance, and signed a security agreement covering the equipment. Again, Equipco failed to deliver the note and security agreement to Firstbank. Is

Firstbank's security interest perfected as of the commencement of the bankruptcy case? See R9–310(a); R9–312(a); R9–102(a)(11).

(d) What answer in the preceding parts if the financing statement had not been filed? See R9–310(a), (b)(5); R9–312(e); R9–102(a)(57). Would it make any difference if the transaction documents entered into between the buyers and Equipco had been delivered to Firstbank? See R9–310(a), (b)(6); R9–313(a).

Problem 7.3.23. Delgado imports whiskey in large quantities, which Delgado stores in storage tanks at a warehouse bonded by the U.S. Customs Service. (Under applicable law, the whiskey may remain in a bonded warehouse for up to five years before Delgado is obligated to pay the import duty. See 19 U.S.C. § 1557(a).) Each time Delgado stores a quantity of whiskey, Delgado receives a warehouse receipt running "to the order of Delgado."

(a) Firstbank is willing to take the whiskey as collateral for a loan and asks you for advice on how to perfect its security interest. Among the possibilities are (i) filing a financing statement; (ii) taking delivery of the warehouse receipts; and (iii) notifying the warehouse of Firstbank's security interest. What do you recommend? See R9–102(a)(30); UCC 1–201(15); R9–312(c), (a); R9–313(a), (c); UCC 7–502(1); R9–331; R9–312(e), (f).

One way to approach this question is to begin by determining which, if any, of the possibilities would satisfy the requirements of R9–310. Next, consider the potential advantages and disadvantages of each course of action. For example, does one approach afford Firstbank the most protection against claims of third parties? Does one approach enhance Delgado's ability to obtain needed access to the whiskey, e.g., when Delgado wishes to bottle some of it?

(b) Assume that Firstbank decides to perfect its security interest by filing a financing statement. How should Firstbank indicate the collateral?

(c) Assume that Firstbank decides to perfect its security interest by taking delivery of the warehouse receipt. Should Firstbank require Delgado to indorse the warehouse receipt before delivery? See UCC 7–502; UCC 7–501; UCC 7–504. If Delgado delivers the warehouse receipt to Firstbank but neglects to indorse it, is Firstbank perfected? See R9–312(c); R9–313(a). If Firstbank wishes to take possession of the whiskey upon Delgado's default, see R9–609, will the warehouse permit Firstbank to remove the whiskey without Delgado's indorsement? See UCC 7–403. If Firstbank makes the loan and later wishes to obtain Delgado's indorsement, what can Firstbank do? See UCC 7–506.

In re Copeland[*]

United States Court of Appeals, Third Circuit, 1976.
531 F.2d 1195.

■ Seitz, Chief Judge.

This is a consolidated appeal from two separate orders of the district court in a Chapter XI bankruptcy proceeding instituted by Lammot du-

_____

* [The court's citations are to the applicable pre–1972 version of the UCC.]

Pont Copeland, Jr. (hereinafter "Copeland" or "debtor"). The appeals are united by a common factual basis. In July of 1967, Copeland personally guaranteed payment on a $2,700,000 loan by Pension Benefit Fund, Inc. ("Pension Benefit") to two corporations and entered into an agreement which required him to pledge as collateral security 18,187 shares of Christiana Securities Co. stock. An "escrow agreement" was simultaneously executed between Copeland, Pension Benefit and Wilmington Trust Company ("Wilmington Trust") which designated Wilmington Trust as escrow holder of the pledged stock. [The stock was thereupon delivered to Wilmington Trust.]

Nearly three years later, in April, 1970, there was a default on the loan. Following written demand upon the principal corporations for payment, Pension Benefit notified Copeland and Wilmington Trust by letter of September 11, 1970 of the uncured default and of its intention to demand the surrender of the escrowed stock in accordance with the pledge agreement. Copeland did not respond to this letter, but on October 20, 1970, filed a petition for an arrangement under Chapter XI of the Bankruptcy Act, 11 U.S.C. §§ 701 et seq., and an application to stay enforcement of Pension Benefit's lien on the Christiana stock. Thereafter, Copeland withdrew his objection to the delivery of the stock to Pension Benefit, and the stock was turned over by Wilmington Trust on December 1, 1970. ...

[D]ebtor filed an independent application for an order requiring Pension Benefit to surrender the stock itself and dividends received with respect thereto. Debtor's application was denied by the district court, sitting as a bankruptcy court, by order dated February 3, 1975. Debtor and the Statutory Creditors' Committee appealed.

I.   DEBTOR'S APPEAL

We shall consider first the issues raised in debtor's appeal since, if he is successful in recovering the stock, Pension Benefit's appeal will be rendered moot.

Copeland asserts a superior right to possession of the stock by virtue of his status as debtor-in-possession which enables him to exercise all the powers of a trustee in bankruptcy, Bankruptcy Act § 342 [the predecessor to Bankruptcy Code § 1107], and specifically, to avail himself of all rights and remedies of any creditor—real or hypothetical—who had or could have obtained a lien on the debtor's property on the date of bankruptcy. Bankruptcy Act § 70c [the predecessor to Bankruptcy Code § 544(a)]. The rights of a lien creditor must be determined by reference to state law. Pertinent here is § 9–301(1)(b) of the Uniform Commercial Code as enacted in Delaware, 6 Del. C. § 9–301(1)(b), which provides:

> "(1) Except as otherwise provided in subsection (2), an unperfected security interest is subordinate to the rights of

"(b) a person who becomes a lien creditor without knowledge of the security interest and before it is perfected."

Since under § 70c of the Bankruptcy Act the trustee has all rights of an ideal lien creditor under § 9–301(1)(b) of the Code, his rights in the stock are superior to Article 9 claimants whose interests were unperfected as of the date of bankruptcy.

Copeland contends that Pension Benefit's security interest in the Christiana stock was unperfected on the date of bankruptcy. He asserts that the district court therefore erred in denying his application for an order requiring Pension Benefit to surrender the stock and dividends received with respect thereto.

A. Attachment

Copeland first argues that Pension Benefit's security interest was unperfected because it had not attached as of October 20, 1970, the date on which debtor filed his Chapter XI petition. The district court determined to the contrary.

Section 9–303 provides that a "security interest is perfected when it has attached and when all of the applicable steps required for perfection have been taken." Attachment occurs under § 9–204 [UCC 9–203(1)] when there is an agreement that the security interest attach, value is given, and the debtor has rights in the collateral. A security interest attaches immediately upon the happening of these events "unless explicit agreement postpones the time of attaching." § 9–204(1) [UCC 9–203(2)]. Although the aforementioned prerequisites to attachment had been fulfilled on the date the pledge agreement was executed in 1967,[3] Copeland contends that the parties explicitly agreed to postpone the time of attachment. In support of this contention, he relies upon paragraph 8 of the pledge agreement which states:

> "8. In the event there is a default by the Pledgor in the performance of any of the terms of this Agreement, or if there is a default in the payment of the loan as provided in the note and if such default continues for a period of fifteen (15) days, the Pledgee shall have the right, upon fifteen (15) days notice, sent by registered mail to the Pledgor, to call upon The Wilmington Trust Company to forthwith deliver all of the stock and stock powers which it is holding as security hereunder to Pledgee, or such other party as Pledgee may designate, and thereupon, without any liability for any diminution in price which may have occurred, and without further consent by the Pledgor, the said Pledgee may sell all or part of the said stock in such manner and for such price or prices as the said Pledgee may be able to obtain. At any bonafide public sale, the Pledgee shall be free to purchase all or

---

3. The pledge and escrow agreements together constituted the requisite agreement. Value was given by Pension Benefit's binding commitment to extend credit. § 1–201(44). The debtor had rights in the collateral in that he remained owner of record and was empowered to vote the shares and receive the dividend income even after the stock was transferred to Wilmington Trust.

any part of the pledged stock. Out of the proceeds of any sale, the Pledgee shall retain an amount equal to the entire unpaid principal and interest then due on the loan plus the amount of the actual expenses of the sale and shall pay the balance to the Pledgor. In the event that the proceeds of any sale are insufficient to cover the entire unpaid principal and interest of the loan plus the expenses of the sale, the Pledgor shall be liable for any deficiency.''

Copeland argues that by the terms of this paragraph, Pension Benefit's security interest did not attach until each of the following events had occurred: (1) the debtor had defaulted; (2) default had continued for fifteen days; (3) fifteen days written notice by registered mail had been sent to the debtor by Pension Benefit; (4) proper demand had been made upon Wilmington Trust to deliver the stock and stock powers; and (5) the stock and stock powers had been delivered to Pension Benefit. Since the stock was not turned over to Pension Benefit until December 1, 1970, he maintains that the security interest had not attached, and consequently was not perfected, on the pivotal date of bankruptcy, October 20, 1970.

We believe that the relevant language of paragraph 8 which debtor urges postpones the date of attachment merely establishes an orderly procedure for enforcement of the security interest upon default. It is understandable that debtor would seek to protect his stock to the fullest extent possible from hasty and premature foreclosure attempts by Pension Benefit. Indeed, § 9–501 of the Code, with exceptions not here relevant, specifically recognizes the right of parties to a security agreement to agree among themselves as to the duties and responsibilities of a secured party when default occurs. To read paragraph 8 as anything other than an attempt to safeguard debtor's interest in the valuable pledged stock against unwarranted claims of default and improper attempts to enforce the security interest would distort the nature of the transaction envisioned by the parties and would render Pension Benefit's security for repayment of the loan largely meaningless. We say this because Pension Benefit's interest in the stock would be subordinate to any intervening creditors who had obtained and perfected a security interest in the stock after Pension Benefit but before bankruptcy, a result clearly not intended by either party. We therefore conclude that the pledge agreement was not intended to delay the date of attachment of Pension Benefit's security interest, but rather was designed to protect debtor's interest in the stock from improper attempts by Pension Benefit to obtain its possession in the event there was a claim of default.

B. Perfection

Relying on § 9–304(1) and § 9–305, Copeland next argues that even assuming the security interest had attached, it was not properly perfected on the date of bankruptcy. Section 9–304 provides that a security interest in instruments, defined in § 9–105(g) and § 8–102 to include corporate securities such as the Christiana stock, can only be perfected by the secured party's taking possession. Section 9–305 modifies this rule by permitting a secured party to perfect his security interest through the possession of his bailee. Section 9–305 states in pertinent part:

"A security interest in letters of credit and advices of credit (subsection (2)(a) of Section 5–116), goods, instruments, negotiable documents or chattel paper may be perfected by the secured party's taking possession of the collateral. If such collateral other than goods covered by a negotiable document is held by a bailee, the secured party is deemed to have possession from the time the bailee receives notification of the secured party's interest...."

Debtor maintains that Pension Benefit's security interest was not perfected by Wilmington Trust's possession of the stock because Wilmington Trust was the agent of both parties. He asserts that this position is inconsistent with the degree of possession needed to perfect under the "bailee with notice" provision of § 9–305. To satisfy the requirement of this section, he urges, possession must be maintained by an agent under the sole control of the secured party.

In support of this contention, debtor places considerable emphasis upon what would have been the nature of the relationship between the parties at common law. Since the stock was held by Wilmington Trust as agent for both parties, he argues that the arrangement must be characterized as an escrow, rather than a perfected pledge which requires possession by the pledgee or an agent under his absolute dominion and control. Citing In re Dolly Madison Industries, Inc., [351 F.Supp. 1038 (E.D.Pa.1972) aff'd mem., 480 F.2d 917 (3d Cir.1973),] he further stresses that the simultaneous existence of an escrow and a pledge is a legal impossibility. Since the transaction fails as a common law pledge for lack of possession by the pledgee or his agent, and since the Code, he asserts, has incorporated the requirement of the common law pledge that the pledgee or an agent under his absolute control maintain possession of the collateral, Pension Benefit's security interest was unperfected under § 9–304 and § 9–305 on the date of bankruptcy.

Although concluding that Wilmington Trust was an escrow agent at common law and hence incapable of becoming Pension Benefit's agent for the purpose of perfecting the pledge, the district court held that the provision of § 9–305 permitting perfection by a "bailee with notice" had been satisfied, and that the security interest was consequently perfected under the Code. The court rejected debtor's argument that § 9–305 had incorporated the restrictive possession requirement of the common law pledge, finding that an acceptance of this proposition would frustrate the parties' intent to collateralize the loan as against third party creditors, would be in disregard of the policy considerations underlying both the law of pledge and the Code, and would unduly restrict the use of the escrow device.

We find it unnecessary to consider the parties' rights at common law because we believe that the language and policy underlying § 9–305 support the district court's conclusion that Pension Benefit's security interest was perfected upon delivery of the stock to Wilmington Trust in July, 1967.

While it is true that the Code does not wholly displace the common law, § 1–103, nor abolish existing security devices, Official Comment 2, § 9–102,[4] Article 9 simplifies pre-Code secured financing by providing for the unitary treatment of all security arrangements. It eliminates many of the antiquated distinctions between various security devices in favor of a single "security interest", §§ 9–102, 1–201(37), and a single set of rules regarding creation and perfection, designed to govern "any transaction (regardless of its form) which is intended to create a security interest in personal property or fixtures including goods, Documents, Instruments...." § 9–102. Since neither party denies that the pledge and escrow agreements were intended to create a security interest in the stock within the meaning of the Uniform Commercial Code, we attach no particular significance to the common law distinctions between the pledge and the escrow which debtor stresses, except insofar as they bear on the question of whether Pension Benefit's security interest was properly perfected under § 9–305 of the Code through Wilmington Trust's possession of the stock.

It is to that question which we now turn. Historically and prior to the Code, possession of collateral by a creditor or third party has served to impart notice to prospective creditors of the possessor's possible interest therein. The Code carries forward the notice function which the creditor's possession formerly provided. Notice to future lenders is furnished under the Code by a filed financing statement, § 9–302, or by the possession of the property subject to the security interest by a secured party or his agent, §§ 9–304, 9–305, depending upon the nature of the collateral.

Where the Code requires perfection by possession of the secured party or his bailee, it is clear that possession by the debtor or an individual closely associated with the debtor is not sufficient to alert prospective creditors of the possibility that the debtor's property is encumbered. See, In re Black Watch Farms, Inc., 9 UCC Rep.Serv. 151 (Ref. Dec. S.D.N.Y.1974). Thus, Official Comment 2 to § 9–305 states:

> "Possession may be by the secured party himself or by an agent on his behalf: it is of course clear, however, that the debtor or a person controlled by him cannot qualify as such an agent for the secured party. ..."

It does not follow from this statement or from the policy underlying § 9–305, however, that possession of the collateral must be by an individual under the sole dominion and control of the secured party, as debtor urges us to hold. Rather, we believe that possession by a third party bailee, who is not controlled by the debtor, which adequately informs potential lenders of the possible existence of a perfected security interest satisfies the notice function underlying the "bailee with notice" provision of § 9–305.

---

4. While Delaware has not adopted the Official Comments prepared by the drafters of the Uniform Commercial Code, these comments are nevertheless useful in interpreting the Code, as it is to be applied in Delaware, in view of the Code's expressed purpose of making uniform the law among the various jurisdictions. § 1–102(2)(c)....

In the case presently before us, the collateral was held by Wilmington Trust pursuant to the terms of both the pledge and escrow agreements. Regardless of whether Wilmington Trust retained the stock as an escrow agent or as a pledge holder, its possession and the debtor's lack of possession clearly signaled future creditors that debtor's ownership of and interest in the stock were not unrestricted. As an independent, institutional entity, Wilmington Trust could not be regarded automatically as an instrumentality or agent of the debtor alone. There was consequently no danger that creditors would be misled by its possession.

The fact that debtor remained owner of record and was empowered to vote the shares and receive current income does not compel a different finding. The location of title to collateral is immaterial with respect to the rights and obligations of the parties to a security transaction. § 9–202; Barney v. Rigby Loan & Investment Co., 344 F.Supp. 694 (D.Idaho 1972).

Nor do we believe our summary affirmance of the district court's decision in *In re Dolly Madison Industries, Inc.*, supra, dictates a contrary conclusion. In reversing a decision by the referee denying the trustee's application for a turnover order, the district court in *Dolly Madison* rested its decision on a finding that the security agreement ... postponed the attachment of the security interest asserted by a creditor of the bankrupt until after bankruptcy. In support of this decision, the court noted that the parties had evidenced their intent to delay attachment by placing the collateral in the neutral custody of an escrow agent pending payment or default. Statements by the court indicating that the simultaneous existence of an escrow and a pledge is a legal impossibility were merely intended to underscore the parties' deliberate choice of the escrow device rather than a pledge in order to assure that attachment would be postponed. Since the district court found that attachment had been delayed by specific agreement of the parties, it was not called upon to determine whether an attached security interest had been perfected. Hence, any statements suggesting that the placement of collateral in escrow precludes a creditor from perfecting his security interest for lack of sufficient possession under § 9–305 are mere uncontrolling dicta.

Having found that Wilmington Trust's possession of the stock afforded the requisite notice to prospective creditors, we conclude that it was a "bailee with notice" within the meaning of § 9–305 and that its possession therefore perfected Pension Benefit's security interest. Hence, perfection occurred in July, 1967, more than three years in advance of bankruptcy, on the date the stock was delivered to Wilmington Trust with notification of Pension Benefit's interest therein. For this reason, the district court correctly concluded that debtor's interest in the stock as debtor-in-possession was subordinate to that of Pension Benefit and properly denied debtor's application for a turnover order.

NOTES ON *IN RE COPELAND*

(1) The Role of Pre–UCC Law. Counsel for Copeland "placed considerable emphasis on what would have been the nature of the relationship between the parties at common law." They argued that the escrow would have failed as a common-law pledge "for lack of possession by the pledgee or his agent." Does the court disagree with this assessment? Assuming that counsel's assertions about the common-law rules were correct, what justifies the court's departure from the common law? See UCC 1–102; UCC 1–103; R9–205(b) (substantially similar to F9–205).

(2) The Effect of Post–*Copeland* Amendments to the UCC. The rules governing security interests in investment property (e.g., stocks and bonds) have changed several times since *Copeland* was decided. The Note on Perfection of Security Interests in Investment Securities, Chapter 9, Section 3, infra, discusses these rules in some detail. For present purposes, please observe that, under Revised Article 9, possession of a security certificate by or on behalf of the secured party remains an effective method by which to perfect a security interest in securities represented by a certificate. See R9–313(a); R8–301(a). Thus, *Copeland*'s discussion of perfection by possession remains "good law." See R9–313(a), Comment 6 ("The second sentence of subsection (a) reflects the traditional rule for perfection of a security interest in certificated securities.").

Revised Article 9 carries forward the rule, first introduced to the UCC in 1994, that perfection of a security interest in certificated securities may be achieved by filing a financing statement. See R9–310(a). As we shall see, filing and taking possession each has its advantages, as does perfecting by having control. See Chapter 9, Sections 3 and 4.

NOTES ON PERFECTION BY POSSESSION

(1) The Pledge. Under R9–313(a), a security interest in most tangible collateral, including goods, may be perfected by the secured party's taking possession of the collateral. The possessory security interest, or **pledge**, was the prototypical common-law security device. In contrast to nonpossessory arrangements, where the debtor remained in possession of the collateral, the pledge was thought not to give rise to significant ostensible ownership or other fraud problems. Possession by the secured party put to rest any notion that the debtor owned the property free and clear; it also was consistent with the secured party's assertion that it was relying on the collateral for repayment of its claim against the debtor. See generally Note (3) on Perfection by Filing, supra.

(2) Possession by Agents and Bailees. It is not much of a stretch to conclude that if possession by the secured party is sufficient for an effective pledge, then possession by its agent would suffice as well. Article 9 apparently adopts this common-law view. See R9–313, Comment 3 ("In determining whether a particular person has possession, the principles of agency apply."). See also UCC 1–103 (unless displaced by particular provisions of the UCC, principles of principal and agent apply). Of course, possession by certain agents—most notably, the debtor itself—would not alleviate one's concerns that the purported secured transaction is a sham or that other creditors might mistakenly rely on the debtor's possession as an indication that the debtor's ownership rights were unencumbered. See R9–313, Comment 3; Restatement of Security § 11 & Comment *b* (1941).

R9–313, Comment 3, indicates that,

> under appropriate circumstances, a court may determine that a person in possession is so closely connected to or controlled by the debtor that the debtor has retained effective possession, even though the person may have agreed to take possession on behalf of the secured party. If so, the person's taking possession would not constitute the secured party's taking possession and would not be sufficient for perfection. See also Section 9–205(b). In a typical escrow arrangement, where the escrowee has possession of collateral as agent for both the secured party and the debtor, the debtor's relationship to the escrowee is not such as to constitute retention of possession by the debtor.

Consider what happens when the collateral consists of property that a third party (Bailee) holds for the debtor. The secured party may wish to perfect a security interest by taking possession of the collateral but without dispossessing Bailee. One way to accomplish this result is for Bailee to become the secured party's agent. Another is for Bailee to authenticate a record acknowledging that it holds possession of the collateral for the secured party's benefit.[11] As R9–313, Comment 4, suggests,

> [i]n some cases, it may be uncertain whether a person who has possession of collateral is an agent of the secured party or a non-agent bailee. Under those circumstances, prudence might suggest that the secured party obtain the person's acknowledgment to avoid litigation and ensure perfection by possession regardless of how the relationship between the secured party and the person is characterized.

In what way is Bailee's acknowledgment akin to possession by the secured party? Does the acknowledgment adequately allay concerns that the purported security interest is merely a sham? The fact that a (presumably disinterested) third party has been informed of a secured transaction would seem to lend credence to the secured party's assertion that the parties actually contemplated one. The acknowledgment makes it less likely that the parties are engaging in after-the-fact fabrication.

Does Bailee's acknowledgment address the ostensible ownership problem? Does it make the debtor less of an ostensible owner than does the original bailment? Suppose Lender wishes to extend credit to the debtor and seeks to determine whether the debtor owns the bailed goods free and clear. Lender could ask the debtor, but the perfection rules of Article 9 are designed to afford creditors a means to obtain information without having to rely solely on the debtor's honesty. (In fact, the drafters of Former Article 9 rejected an early proposal to scrap public files and introduce appropriate safeguards to protect people misled by false or incomplete financial statements. See 1 Gilmore, Security § 15.1, at 464–65.) Lender

---

11. R9–313(c) does not apply to certificated securities or goods covered by a document of title. Instead, R8–301 applies to the former, and R9–312(c) and (d) apply to the latter.

could ask Bailee. Does Bailee's acknowledgment that it holds possession for the benefit of the secured party impose upon Bailee a legal duty to confirm the acknowledgment to third parties with whom it has not contracted? Not unless Bailee agrees or law other than Article 9 provides. See R9–313(g). If Bailee has no legal duty to confirm the acknowledgment, does it have a duty to refrain from affirmatively misleading third parties, e.g., by denying the fact that it has acknowledged? If not, would it be a sufficient solution to the ostensible ownership problem that most bailees tell the truth most of the time, even if they are not legally bound to do so?

A secured party is concerned not only about achieving perfection but also about maintaining the perfected status of its security interest. If Bailee delivers the collateral to the debtor, then the security interest will become unperfected unless it was perfected also by a method other than possession. R9–313(g)(2) makes clear that Bailee's acknowledgment imposes upon Bailee no duty to the secured party, unless Bailee agrees otherwise or law other than Article 9 imposes a duty. Thus, there may be major practical differences between actual possession by the secured party (or its agent) and "deemed" possession by Bailee: Unless the secured party voluntarily relinquishes the collateral in its actual possession, the debtor cannot retake it without engaging in theft; however, Bailee's acknowledgment does not ipso facto deprive the debtor of its right to take possession of, and dispose of, the bailed property. Rather, the debtor may maintain control over the goods notwithstanding Bailee's acknowledgment. Conversely, if the debtor defaults and the secured party demands that Bailee relinquish the collateral, Bailee may be under no duty to obey the secured party's demand.

Does the foregoing lead inexorably to the conclusion that only a foolish secured party would rely upon perfection through a bailee under R9–313(c)? Or, do you see a way in which the secured party could reduce substantially the risk that the bailee will deliver the goods to the debtor or ignore the secured party's instructions?

(3) Other Benefits of Taking Possession of Collateral; Field Warehouses. A secured party can perfect a security interest in all types of tangible collateral, except "money" (as defined in UCC 1–201(24)), by a method other than taking possession. Even when a security interest is perfected by another method, e.g., by filing a financing statement, a secured party may insist upon taking possession of collateral. One reason for doing so is to facilitate enforcement in the event of the debtor's default. Although a secured party has a right to take possession of collateral after default, the secured party may not breach the peace in doing so. See R9–609(a). If the debtor remains in possession and refuses to turn over the collateral to the secured party after default, the secured party must resort to the judicial process to recover any value from the collateral. Taking possession before default reduces this risk.

A more important reason for the secured party's taking possession of collateral is that taking possession (or, more accurately, depriving the debtor of possession) prevents the debtor from disposing of the collateral, either outright or to the holder of a senior security interest. On the other hand, the collateral may have much greater value being used by the debtor than sitting in storage with the secured party. For example, a secured party will not take possession of machinery used in the debtor's manufacturing operations. Not only is the risk of the debtor's wrongfully disposing of the collateral normally very small, but also the benefit to the debtor of retaining possession is quite high. (Without the equipment, how would the debtor earn funds with which to satisfy the secured obligation?) A secured party is much more likely to take possession of a negotiable instrument. Because negotiable instruments are so liquid, the risk of the debtor's wrongful disposition may be substantial, and the benefit to the debtor of retaining the collateral often is negligible.

What can a secured party do if it is concerned that the debtor will wrongfully dispose of collateral, but taking possession of the collateral would impair the debtor's ability to pay the secured obligation? For example, although filing can perfect a security interest in inventory, it does not prevent the debtor from selling the inventory and absconding with or dissipating the proceeds. The lender may not have the skills and resources needed to keep a close watch on the assets of a borrower of questionable financial standing or integrity. Under such circumstances, the secured party may contract with a specialist in watching over the ebb and flow of inventory. Historically, these specialists established a complex and colorful "pledge" arrangement known as a "field warehouse."

Field warehouses developed under the common law, in response to the law's requirement that a secured party take possession of collateral in order to enjoy a property right that was valid against other creditors. The notion of a field warehouse derives from the creative application of the principle that a secured party may take possession of collateral through its agent, which might be a warehouse. Rather than suffer the adverse consequences of moving the debtor's inventory to a warehouse, inventory lenders moved the warehouse to the inventory. Typically, the debtor's inventory was placed in a fenced area (the "warehouse") within its premises. The "warehouse" usually was the debtor's stockroom, but might be a tank of oil or whiskey with a padlock on the outlet vale or a fenced-in pile of coal; there have been an astonishing variety of settings. More recent uses have included "field warehouse feedlots," in which cattle are held, and leased rooms for warehousing a variety of "instruments," as to which possession was the exclusive means of perfection under Former Article 9.

Under the traditional arrangement, a specialized field warehouse company leased the premises from the debtor for a nominal amount, posted signs indicating that the goods in the fenced area were in the custody of the warehouse, and administered the flow of goods in and out of warehouse. Typically, the company issued non-negotiable warehouse receipts naming the secured party as the person entitled to delivery. As such, the secured party could cause the warehouse to release inventory by issuing written delivery orders (or a single, standing delivery order). See UCC 7–403.

Neither Former nor Revised Article 9 relaxes the common-law rules on the degree and extent of possession that are necessary to constitute a valid field warehouse. See R9–205(b). Nevertheless, the UCC has had an indirect, but basic, impact on field warehousing. By providing for the perfection of security interests in fluctuating assets by the filing of a simple financing statement, Former Article 9 undercut the principal reason for the establishment of the field warehouse. Thus, in 1963, Lawrence Systems, then the leading operator of field warehouses, in a dramatic reversal of policy, began to encourage lenders holding its receipts to file under Article 9. The basic reason was the danger that the holder of a competing security interest who filed would have a prior claim to new assets. See F9–312(5)(a); R9–322(a)(1). (The rules governing priority of competing security interests will be examined more fully in Section 6(A), infra.)

Widespread adoption of Former Article 9 deprived the field warehouse of a significant "perfection" function; however, there was still a need for "certified (or 'verified') inventory control." "Certified inventory control" eliminates the bailment trappings, such as the fence and signs. It replaces the warehouse receipt with a certificate or statement to the lender that certifies to the value of the inventory on the borrower's premises; the certifier by contract engages to comply with the lender's delivery instructions and also accepts liability for any loss that may result from reliance on the certificates or from failure to observe the lender's delivery instructions. Day-to-day administration of the program is conducted by a "custodian" on the borrower's premises—usually a former employee of the debtor who was placed on the payroll of the field warehouse (subject, of course, to reimbursement by the debtor).

(4) Rights and Duties of Secured Party in Possession of Collateral. R9–207 affords certain rights to, and imposes certain duties upon, a secured party who perfects a security interest by possession. The most significant of these duties is a requirement to "use reasonable care in the custody and preservation of collateral in the secured party's possession." R9–207(a). As with all obligations of care in the UCC, that duty "may not be disclaimed by agreement." UCC 1–102(3).

SECTION 4.   MULTIPLE-STATE TRANSACTIONS: LAW GOVERNING PERFECTION AND PRIORITY

One generally acknowledged purpose of the Article 9 filing system is to provide information to third parties. See Note (3) on Perfection by Filing, Section 3(A), supra. A well-fashioned system affords prospective purchasers of the collateral (including prospective secured parties) the opportunity to discover, with relative ease, whether the debtor may have encumbered particular property with a security interest. But a prospective purchaser or other searcher will be unable to commence a search of the public records to determine whether a financing statement has been filed against a debtor without first knowing which records to search.

The UCC is state law; each state maintains its own filing offices. Thus, before starting to search, a searcher must determine not only the state in which a financing statement would have been filed but also the particular office within that state in which a financing statement would have been filed. And because a financing statement that is filed in the wrong place is insufficient to perfect a security interest, a secured party who attempts to perfect by filing likewise must make the same determinations. The following materials address Revised Article 9's answers to the problems of where to file and search.

(A) WHERE TO FILE A FINANCING STATEMENT

NOTES ON CHOICE OF LAW

(1) The Need for Choice-of-Law Rules. Owner sells or mortgages Blackacre to Purchaser. Owner lives in State X; Blackacre is in State Y; Purchaser lives in State Z. Where should the transaction be placed on the public record? What law governs perfection of Purchaser's interest against third persons? The answer is clear: the law of the place where Blackacre is (*lex rei sitae*). See Restatement (Second) of Conflict of Laws § 223 (1969). This rule is so firmly established that it may seem to be "in the nature of things," but its strength lies in its practicality. Even if Owner and Purchaser move, Blackacre stays. The rules and the records at the place where Blackacre is located provide a reliable point of reference.

For personal property the answer is not so easy or intuitive. Debtor sells goods on credit to Buyer; to secure a loan, Debtor assigns the account (right to payment) to Secured Party. Debtor is in State X, Buyer is in State Y, and Secured Party is in State Z. Where should notice of the transaction be filed? Which law applies? Those used to thinking about transactions in land may say, "wherever the *res* is." But where is the debt that Buyer owes Debtor? In State X with Debtor, the obligee? In State Y with Buyer, the obligor? Or in State Z with Secured Party, the assignee? The questions multiply when each of the three parties is a corporation with offices in several states.

Even tangible goods—cotton, furniture, railroad cars—present vexing problems. The goods may be moving from state to state at the time of the transaction, or they may be moved after the transaction. They may be resold to a buyer in another, possibly distant, state. And goods usually leave no trail, in the public records or elsewhere, that will disclose where they have been or what has happened.

These problems carry us into a large field (known as conflict of laws, choice of law, and private international law) where, for the most part, solutions must be sought in an amorphous and evolving body of case law. However, statutes on substantive rules sometimes deal with "conflicts" problems by specifying when the statute's rules are applicable to transactions that have contacts with other states. Even after general adoption of "uniform" laws, these conflicts rules are useful because of the proclivity of both legislatures and courts to develop local variations in the "uniform" law.

UCC 1–105(1) contains two general choice-of-law rules: the parties enjoy the right to agree that the law of any state bearing a "reasonable relation" to the transaction shall govern their rights and duties; absent such agreement, the UCC as enacted by the state in which the litigation is brought "applies to transactions bearing an appropriate relation to [such] state." These general rules may be suitable for controversies between the debtor and creditor, e.g., to determine which state's version of Article 9 applies to the exercise of the secured party's rights on default. They are wholly unsuitable for controversies concerning the effectiveness of a security interest against third parties, i.e., controversies whose outcome depends on whether a security interest is perfected. For the Article 9 filing system to work effectively, searchers must be able to determine where to search. Enabling the parties to the transaction to agree between themselves as to the applicable law would be foolhardy. How could a searcher discover whether any such agreement had been made? And even if a searcher could assure itself of the absence of such an agreement, how could the searcher predict which state's law a court would apply in the event of litigation?

Recognizing that the debtor and secured party should not be able to choose the applicable law so as to affect the rights of third parties, the UCC's drafters created a special set of rules that determine the law applicable to perfection and the effect of perfection or non-perfection of security interests. These rules are in R9–301 through R9–307, whose provisions govern notwithstanding an agreement of the parties to the contrary. See R1–105(2).

(2) An Approach to Solving Choice–of–Law Problems. Thinking about choice-of-law problems under the UCC is subject to a subtle trap. In the classroom we have in our hands only one statute book—the "uniform" UCC. We can easily forget that the conflicts rules we see in our version of R9–301 may invoke "perfection" rules that are quite different from those we see in our version of R9–301 and R9–501. State legislatures routinely have made the UCC nonuniform. For example, several states have gagged at the rule of F9–302(1)(d) that perfects purchase-money security interests in consumer goods without filing. The process of enacting Revised Article 9 likewise has seen numerous examples of nonuniform provisions. Some of these provisions are intended to square Revised Article 9 with other, non-UCC state laws. California, for example, added a nonuniform subsection (f) to R9–108, which deals with descriptions of collateral: "A description of investment property collateral also shall meet the applicable requirements of Section 1799.103 of the Civil Code. A description of consumer goods also shall meet the applicable requirements of Section 1799.100 of the Civil Code." Other nonuniform provisions seek to implement a particular policy of the enacting state. As enacted in Texas, R9–109(d)(11) excludes from the scope of Revised Article 9 not only leases of real property and rents relating to real property but also "the interest of a vendor or vendee in a contract for deed to purchase an interest in real property [and] the interest of an optionor or optionee in an option to purchase an interest in real property." Moreover, we may not safely forget that all the world does not have Article 9: Goods may move into the UCC domain from foreign countries that have a wide variety of rules governing what we (but not they) call the "perfection" of "security interests"; debtors may be owed money by persons located in foreign jurisdictions whose law invalidates the assignment of the right to payment.

In short, having only one "uniform" code in our hands can seduce us into forgetting what we are doing in this area—working with *two* legal systems. In law practice we would not fall into this trap, for we would work with at least two different statute books on our desks: (1) one with the conflicts rules of R9–301 through R9–307 and (2) a second with the "perfection" rules (e.g., R9–310, R9–501) of the jurisdiction whose law is made applicable by the conflicts rules of the first book. In the classroom it may help those of us who are visually-minded to imagine that (as in practice) we are working with these two statute books.

Applying Article 9's conflicts rules is not easy, even when one has recourse to two statute books. Thinking about the relationship between two legal systems requires some intellectual strain, as we shall see again in Chapter 10 and Chapter 11, Section 5(D), when we try to mesh state property law with the federal bankruptcy law and the federal tax lien law, respectively.

The wide range of assets—tangible and intangible—embraced by Article 9 and the extent to which financing transactions straddle many states generate problems of amazing subtlety and complexity. Many of the problems cannot be tackled here. The most that is feasible is to lay a foundation for thinking about multiple-state problems, to see the UCC's approach to them in a few common situations, and to appreciate the crucial importance of the UCC's choice-of-law rules both to planning a secured transaction and to litigating over perfection and priority.

Problem 7.4.1. Binary Bits, Inc. (BB), borrowed $50,000,000 from EZ Credit Co. BB is a conglomerate that is incorporated in Indiana, has plants and offices in 21 states, and has its headquarters in Cleveland, Ohio. EZ is incorporated in Delaware but has its headquarters in New Jersey and has representatives in all 50 states. The security agreement, which is governed by the law of California, covers and adequately describes all BB's existing and after-acquired personal property.

(a) In which office(s) should EZ file a financing statement to perfect its security interest? See R9–301; R9–307; R9–102(a)(70); UCC 1–201(28); R1–105(2); R9–501(a). (Recall that, for certain kinds of collateral, the filing of a financing statement does not perfect a security interest. See R9–311(a); R9–312(b)(1); Problem 7.3.18, supra. See also R9–109.).

(b) Assume that BB is a general partnership. In which office(s) should EZ file a financing statement to perfect its security interest? See R9–301; R9–307; R9–102(a)(70); UCC 1–201(28); R9–501(a).

(c) Assume that BB is a German corporation. Does U.S. law apply to this transaction? See UCC 1–105. If so, in which office(s) should EZ file a financing statement to perfect its security interest? See R9–301; R9–307;

R9–102(a)(70); R9–501(a). What result if BB's headquarters are in Hamburg, Germany, and not Cleveland, Ohio?

(d) Assume that BB is incorporated under both the law of Delaware and the law of Germany. In which office(s) should EZ file a financing statement to perfect its security interest? See R9–301(1); R9–307; R9–102(a)(70); R9–501(a).

(e) Assume that BB is Bobby Baker, who owns (as a sole proprietor) Mustard's Last Stand. BB lives in Hammond, Indiana, and the hot dog stand is in South Chicago, Illinois. In which office(s) should EZ file a financing statement to perfect its security interest? (The collateral includes both business assets and property held for personal use.) See R9–301; R9–307; R9–501(a).

Problem 7.4.2. The facts are as in the preceding Problem (i.e., BB is an Indiana corporation). EZ "prefiled" a proper financing statement in the Ohio filing office on July 15, 2001. BB authenticated the security agreement and funds were advanced on July 24. Thereafter, on July 28, Lean, a judgment creditor of BB's, acquired an execution lien on the manufacturing equipment in BB's plant in Taylor, Michigan.

(a) Which state's law governs priority between Lean's lien and EZ's security interest? See R9–301. This question may become important if different versions of Article 9 are in force in different states or if different states have different priority rules for nonconsensual liens. See R9–301, Comment 7.

(b) Is EZ's security interest senior or junior to Lean's lien? Assume the state whose law governs priority has enacted R9–317(a)(2), so that the answer turns on whether EZ filed in the proper filing office. Did EZ file in the proper filing office? Which state's law dictates the filing office in which to file? See R9–301; R9–307.

––––––––

The preceding Problems required you to apply the choice-of-law rules in a static situation. In the two Problems that follow, the facts that determine the applicable law change as time passes: Upon the debtor's relocation, a financing statement that was filed in the "right" jurisdiction becomes a financing statement filed in the "wrong" jurisdiction.

We have seen analogous situations in which the utility of a properly filed financing statement is compromised because of post-filing changes. See, e.g., Problem 7.3.15, supra. As the Note on Post–Filing Changes, Section 3(A), supra, explains, to the extent that Article 9 removes from the filer the burden to update the public record immediately, Article 9 imposes a corresponding burden on potential searchers to discover the facts not only as they are but also as they were, and to search accordingly. After working the following Problems, consider this question: When the debtor relocates, does Article 9 appropriately allocate risk between the secured party who filed in the old location and a subsequent searcher?

Problem 7.4.3. The facts are as in Problem 7.4.1, except that BB is a general partnership. EZ filed a proper financing statement in the Ohio filing office on July 15, 2001. In June, 2002, without EZ's knowledge or consent, BB moved its headquarters from Cleveland to Los Angeles. On November 19, 2002, Buyer bought and took delivery of certain used manufacturing equipment from BB in Taylor, Michigan.

(a) Which state's law governs perfection of EZ's security interest? See R9–301.

(b) Which state's law governs priority between Buyer and EZ's security interest? See R9–301; R9–307.

(c) It is now December 1, 2002, and EZ has yet to discover the removal of BB's headquarters or the sale of the equipment. Does Buyer take free of or subject to EZ's security interest? See R9–316(a), (b). (The rights of buyers are discussed in Section 6(B), infra. For purposes of this Problem, you may assume that a buyer takes free of unperfected security interests but subject to perfected security interests.) What could the losing party have done to protect itself?

(d) What result in part (c) if Buyer bought and took delivery of the equipment on July 20, 2002? What could the losing party have done to protect itself?

(e) What result in part (c) if Buyer bought and took delivery of the equipment on May 15, 2002? What could the losing party have done to protect itself?

(f) Does the result in any of the preceding parts change if BB is a Delaware corporation and EZ filed in the Delaware filing office? If so, how? Will the passage of time affect the rights of EZ and Buyer? See R9–316(a)(3).

Problem 7.4.4. The facts are as in Problem 7.4.1, except that BB is a general partnership. EZ filed a proper financing statement in the Ohio filing office on July 15, 2001. In June, 2002, without EZ's knowledge or consent, BB moved its headquarters from Cleveland to Los Angeles. On July 20, 2002, Elsie, who held a judgment against BB, acquired an execution lien on certain manufacturing equipment at BB's plant in Taylor, Michigan.

(a) It is now August 1, 2002, and EZ has yet to discover the removal of BB's headquarters. Is EZ's security interest senior or junior to Elsie's lien? See R9–317(a)(2); R9–316(a).

(b) It is now December 1, 2002, and EZ has yet to discover the removal of BB's headquarters. Is EZ's security interest senior or junior to Elsie's lien? See R9–317(a)(2); R9–316(a), (b); R1–201(33), (32). What could the losing party have done to protect itself?

(c) Can you reconcile R9–316's treatment of Elsie with the treatment it affords to Buyer in the preceding Problem?

(d) Does the result in part (a) or (b) change if BB is a Delaware corporation and EZ filed in the Delaware filing office? If so, how?

(e) Does the result in part (a) change if BB acquired the manufacturing equipment in early July, after the relocation of its headquarters? When was the security interest in the equipment "perfected"? See R9–316(a) & Comment 2; R9–308(a); R9–203(b)(2).

NOTE ON THE PROSPECTS FOR A NATIONWIDE FILING SYSTEM

Many of the problems associated with determining where to file and whether and when to refile could be solved by scrapping state filing systems and adopting a single, nationwide system. One way to establish a nationwide system would be through preemptive federal legislation. A less intrusive (and probably more feasible) route would be through developments in the private sector: one or more corporations might provide search and filing systems and services to states pursuant to contract. Even if several such nongovernmental systems were to be developed, a de facto nationwide system might emerge if the systems were to share their information. R9–523(f), which requires states to offer to sell or license to the public on a nonexclusive basis, in bulk, copies of all Article 9 filings, may be the first step in that direction.

Why do you suppose the UCC's sponsors did not propose a national filing system?

NOTE ON PART 7 TRANSITION RULES AND CONTINUING RELEVANCE OF CHOICE-OF-LAW RULES UNDER FORMER ARTICLE 9

Part 7 of Revised Article 9 contains a set of detailed rules that govern the transition from pre-revision law to full application of the revised Article. R9–701 provides that the effective date of Revised Article 9 will be July 1, 2001. The effective date represents a substantial delay, inasmuch as more than half the states already had enacted Revised Article 9 by August, 2000. This delay afforded interested persons time to become fully familiar with the revised Article. In addition, it allowed Revised Article 9 to become effective simultaneously in all but four jurisdictions. A detailed coverage of the transition rules is beyond the scope of a basic course in Secured Transactions. However, the Official Comments to the sections of Part 7 and their extensive use of examples provide a good overview.

Anyone who wishes to deal competently with Article 9 during the transition period *must* understand the choice-of-law rules for perfection and priority under Former Article 9. These rules, found in F9–103, differ in many important respects from those of Revised Article 9. Under Part 7 of the revised Article, the "old" choice-of-law rules will continue to be relevant until at least June 30, 2006. The length of the transition period is explained by the drafters' desire to minimize the burden on secured parties whose financing statements are filed before July 1, 2001. These financing statements generally remain effective until they lapse, five years after they are filed.

Briefly summarized, the choice-of-law rules in F9–103 provided that, for tangible collateral, including documents, instruments, and most goods, the law governing perfection and the effect of perfection or nonperfection was that of the jurisdiction in which the collateral was located. However, if the parties understood at the time a purchase-money security interest attached to goods located in one jurisdiction that the goods would be moved to another jurisdiction, the law of the other (destination) jurisdiction would govern those issues. Perfection and the effect of perfection of security interests in intangible collateral was governed by the law of the jurisdiction in which the debtor was located. The same rule (debtor's location determines the law governing perfection and the effect of perfection) applied to security interests in "mobile goods," i.e., mobile equipment and mobile inventory leased or held for lease by the debtor to others, if the equipment or inventory was of a type normally used in more than one jurisdiction. Note, however, that the location of a debtor under Former Article 9 was not necessarily the same as the debtor's location under Revised Article 9. Under F9–103(3), a debtor's location normally was its place of business. If the debtor had more than one place of business, the debtor was located at its chief executive office. For individuals with no place of business, the debtor's residence was the debtor's location for choice-of-law purposes.

F9–401(1) provided that financing statements governing certain types of collateral were to be filed with the Secretary of State or other central filing office, whereas financing statements governing other types of collateral (collateral related to real property and, in many states, consumer goods and collateral relating to agriculture) were to be filed with a county or other local filing office. In some states, F9–401(1) provided that, under certain circumstances, a financing statement was ineffective unless it was filed in both the central and a local filing office.

To take account of the fact that financing statements filed pursuant to Former Article 9 will remain effective even after Revised Article 9 takes effect, a secured party contemplating a loan secured by equipment, for example, might search the records and file its financing statement in each jurisdiction in which equipment is located, in case the situs rule of F9–103(1) is applied. In addition, the secured party might search and file in the debtor's location in case R9–301 is applied. Fortunately, the widespread and prompt enactment of Revised Article 9 has dramatically reduced the burdens attendant to transition.

(B) Motor Vehicles and Certificates of Title

INTRODUCTORY NOTE

We have seen that a security interest in automobiles and other goods covered by a certificate of title normally may not be perfected by filing a financing statement; rather, it may be perfected only by compliance with a certificate-of-title statute. See R9–311(a), (b); Problem 7.3.17, supra. But which jurisdiction's certificate-of-title statute must be complied with? R9–

303(c) answers this question. The answer should not surprise you: the law of the jurisdiction under whose certificate of title the goods are covered. For example, in the Prototype, Lee Abel's Chevrolet was covered by a Pennsylvania certificate of title. For this reason, Firstbank perfected its security interest in Lee Abel's Chevrolet by compliance with the Pennsylvania certificate-of-title statute. See Form 7.8, supra.

Just as the basic choice-of-law rules become more complicated when the debtor changes its location, so the choice-of-law rules applicable to goods covered by a certificate of title become more complicated when the goods are re-titled in another jurisdiction. Further complications may arise when the debtor engages in fraud. As Comment 6 to R9–303 notes:

> Ideally, at any given time, only one certificate of title is outstanding with respect to particular goods. In fact, however, sometimes more than one jurisdiction issues more than one certificate of title with respect to the same goods. This situation results from defects in certificate-of-title laws and the interstate coordination of those laws, not from deficiencies in [Revised Article 9]. As long as the possibility of multiple certificates of title remains, the potential for innocent parties to suffer losses will continue. At best, [Revised Article 9] can identify clearly which innocent parties will bear the losses in familiar fact patterns.

R9–303, Comment 6.

The following Problems present some "familiar fact patterns" that feature duplicitous debtors. To what extent does Revised Article 9 "identify clearly which innocent parties will bear the losses"? Are losses imposed on the "right" innocent parties?

Please assume that, unless otherwise specified, each jurisdiction in the following Problems has enacted the Uniform Motor Vehicle Certificate of Title and Anti–Theft Act ("UMVCTATA").

Problem 7.4.5. On March 1, Bilk, a resident of New Mexico, purchased a car in Arizona with money loaned by Firstbank. The following week, the State of Arizona issued a certificate of title noting Firstbank's security interest and sent the certificate to Firstbank. On March 15 Bilk, by means of a fraudulent affidavit, obtained a clean Arizona certificate. On June 16 Bilk moved to California, driving the car, which still had Arizona license plates.

(a) On August 1, Lean, the holder of a judgment against Bilk, acquires an execution lien on the car.

(i) Which state's law governs priority between Lean's lien and Firstbank's security interest? See R9–303; R9–102(a)(10).

(ii) Is Firstbank's security interest senior or junior to Lean's lien? See R9–317(a)(2); R9–311. See UMVCTATA § 20.

(iii) What could the losing party have done to protect itself?

(b) What result in part (a) if Lean acquires the execution lien on November 15?

(c) Using the clean Arizona certificate, on July 15, Bilk sold the car to Bushing, a used car dealer. Does Bushing take free of or subject to Firstbank's security interest? (The rights of buyers are discussed in Section 6(B), infra. For purposes of this Problem, you may assume that a buyer takes free of unperfected security interests but subject to perfected security interests.) What could the losing party have done to protect itself?

(d) What result in part (c) if Bilk moved to California on June 15 but did not sell the car to Bushing until November? What could the losing party have done to protect itself?

(e) Would it make any difference in part (c) if Bilk sold the car to Broom, a laborer, who bought the car for personal use in November? What could the losing party have done to protect itself?

Problem 7.4.6. On June 1, Bilk purchased a car in Arizona with money loaned by Firstbank. The following week, the State of Arizona issued a certificate of title noting Firstbank's security interest and sent the certificate to Firstbank. On July 1, Bilk registered the car in Pennsylvania, obtained Pennsylvania license plates for the car, and, using a false affidavit, applied for a clean Pennsylvania certificate of title. Under Pennsylvania law, a security interest in a motor vehicle is perfected when the Commonwealth issues a certificate of title showing the security interest. On July 15, the clean Pennsylvania certificate of title was issued.

Luciano, the holder of a judgment against Bilk, acquires an execution lien on the car on July 5.

(a) Which state's law governs priority between Luciano's lien and Firstbank's security interest? See R9–303.

(b) Is Firstbank's security interest senior or junior to Luciano's lien? See R9–317(a)(2); R9–316(d), (e); R1–201(33), (32).

(c) What could the losing party have done to protect itself?

(d) Would the result in part (b) change if Luciano acquires the execution lien on December 5? If so, how?

Problem 7.4.7. The facts are as in the preceding Problem, except that Luciano did not acquire a lien. On July 5, Bilk sold the car to Broucher, a used car dealer.

(a) Does Broucher take free of or subject to Firstbank's security interest? You may assume that the general rule is that a buyer takes free of unperfected security interests but subject to perfected security interests. See R9–311; R9–316(d), (e); R1–201(33), (32); R9–337.

(b) What could the losing party have done to protect itself?

(c) What result if the sale to Broucher occurred on November 1? What could the losing party have done to protect itself? In this setting, is Broucher more or less deserving of protection than was Bushing in Problem 7.4.5? Is Firstbank more or less deserving?

(d) Would it make any difference in part (a) or (c) if the Pennsylvania certificate of title stated that the car may be subject to other liens not noted on the certificate?

(e) Would it make any difference in part (a) or (c) if Bilk had sold the car to Brice, a laborer, who bought the car for personal use? Assume that Brice and Firstbank litigate their rights in Pennsylvania. Would the same result obtain if litigation proceeds in Arizona?

Problem 7.4.8. The facts are as in Problem 7.4.6, except that Luciano did not acquire a lien. On July 5, Bilk created a security interest in the car in favor of Secondbank, which perfected its security interest shortly thereafter by notation on a replacement Pennsylvania certificate of title.

(a) Which security interest, Firstbank's or Secondbank's, has priority in the car? See R9–322(a); R9–311; R9–316(d), (e); R1–201(33), (32); R9–337. What could the losing party have done to avoid the loss?

(b) Would the result in part (a) change if Bilk created the security interest in favor of Secondbank on May 1, but Secondbank did not perfect its security interest until July?

SECTION 5.   PROCEEDS OF COLLATERAL

Introduction. Creditors who have ongoing relationships with business debtors often secure their loans with interests in the debtor's inventory. The Prototype automobile financing transaction that opened this Chapter is an example. When, as both parties hope and expect, the inventory is sold, the creditor's security interest rarely can be asserted against the buyer. See R9–320(a); Section 6(B), infra. Instead, the secured party must enforce its security interest against the "proceeds" of its collateral—whatever is received upon the sale. See R9–102(a)(64); R9–315(a)(2).

Financers of inventory and accounts expect that their collateral will be sold or collected. For them, the creation of proceeds is a normal—indeed, desirable—aspect of the financing; proceeds are the means by which the debtor will be able to repay the loan. In contrast, for those who finance the acquisition of equipment, the creation of proceeds may signal a breakdown in the financing relationship; it may mean that the debtor has disposed of the collateral in violation of the security agreement. Even though the security interest in the equipment may survive the sale, see R9–315(a)(1) (discussed in Section 6(B), infra), the secured party may be unable to locate the collateral to enforce its security interest. Under those circumstances, the secured party's only remaining hope for protection may lie in the proceeds.

The problem of wrongful dispositions is not confined to security interests. In a wide variety of settings in which *B* wrongfully disposes of *A*'s property, basic remedial principles have accorded *A* a property interest in traceable proceeds—not only proceeds held by *B* but also those held by third persons who do not have a strong claim for protection, e.g., persons who lack the reliance interest of a good faith purchaser. For a discussion of the legal tools used to protect *A*'s interest, including the doctrines of "constructive trust" and "equitable lien," see Restatement of Restitution § 202 (1937); D. Dobbs, Remedies §§ 4.3, 5.18 (1993).

As you work through the following materials, it will be useful to consider the extent to which the detailed "proceeds" rules of Article 9 (R9–315) constitute particularized responses to a basic and pervasive remedial problem and the extent to which the rules serve to fill gaps in the articulated bargain between the debtor and the secured party.[1]

Problem 7.5.1. In the setting of the Prototype transaction, a new Chevrolet financed by Firstbank was traded by Main Motors for a Lincoln. Subsequently, Main traded the Lincoln for a Cadillac.

(a) Does the Dealer Inventory Security Agreement (Form 7.2, supra) create a security interest in the Cadillac in favor of Firstbank? If so, is the security interest perfected? See R9–204(a); Financing Statement (Form 7.1, supra); R9–310(a); R9–311(d).

(b) Suppose that both the Security Agreement and the Financing Statement covered only the motor vehicles financed by Firstbank (here, the Chevrolet). Does Firstbank have a security interest in the Cadillac? If so, is it perfected? See R9–203(f); R9–102(a)(64); R9–315(a), (c).

Problem 7.5.2. Firstbank financed the purchase of new cars by Main Motors in the manner described in the Prototype transaction, except that the financing statement referred to the collateral as "Motor Vehicles." On June 1 Main sold to Computer Storehouse, Inc. (CSI), a computer dealer, a new Chevrolet that had been financed by Firstbank. CSI paid for the Chevrolet, in part, by delivering to Main certain computer equipment; CSI installed the equipment in Main's office.

(a) On June 25 one of Main's trade creditors, LC Co., had the sheriff levy on all of Main's office equipment, including the computer equipment. Does Firstbank's security interest extend to the computer equipment? If so, is Firstbank's security interest senior to LC's execution lien? See R9–315(a), (c); R9–102(a)(64); R9–317(a)(2); Notes on Security Interests in Proceeds, infra.

(b) Now assume that instead of swapping the computer equipment for a portion of the price of the Chevrolet, CSI paid cash for the Chevrolet. The next day, June 2, Main Motors used a portion of the cash to purchase the computer equipment. Firstbank took no further action to perfect a security interest in the computer equipment. LC then had the sheriff levy on June 25. Do the results in part (a) change? See R9–315(d).

(c) The facts are as in part (b), except that LC levied ten days earlier, on June 15. Is Firstbank's security interest senior to LC's execution lien?

---

1. Bankruptcy and other insolvency proceedings pose special risks and afford special protection for claims to proceeds. Those matters are addressed in Chapter 10, Section 3(B), infra. This section focuses on the treatment of proceeds claims outside of insolvency proceedings.

Are the relative rights of LC and Firstbank fixed as of the date of levy, or can they change as time passes? Cf. R9–515(c) (security interest that becomes unperfected upon lapse is deemed never to have been perfected as against a purchaser for value); R9–316(b) (security interest that becomes unperfected after debtor changes location is deemed never to have been perfected as against a purchaser for value).

Howarth v. Universal C.I.T. Credit Corp.[*]

United States District Court, Western District of Pennsylvania, 1962.
203 F.Supp. 279.

■ Marsh, District Judge. The plaintiff, trustee in bankruptcy of Spohn Motor Company, Inc. (Spohn), brought this action, pursuant to § 60 of the Bankruptcy Act, as amended March 18, 1950, 11 U.S.C.A. § 96 (1961 Supp.), to recover from the defendant, Universal C.I.T. Credit Corporation (UCIT) the value of property transferred to UCIT from Spohn within four months of filing the petition in bankruptcy.

The underlying facts stipulated by the parties are adopted by the court. From these facts it appears that an involuntary petition in bankruptcy was filed against Spohn on January 6, 1958, and it was adjudicated a bankrupt on February 13, 1958.

On February 5, 1957, pursuant to a Loan Agreement (Ex. H), UCIT advanced to Spohn the sum of $75,000. On the same day, Spohn executed a Chattel Mortgage (Ex. I) covering certain chattels. Shortly thereafter UCIT perfected a security interest therein by properly filing a Financing Statement (Ex. J) under the provisions of the Uniform Commercial Code—Secured Transactions, Act of April 6, 1953, P.L. 3, § 9–101 et seq. . . . (hereinafter referred to as U.C.C.).

Prior to September 28, 1957, Spohn also executed in favor of UCIT used car Trust Receipts (Ex. D) and assigned to UCIT certain Bailment Leases (Ex. E).

During August of 1957, and for some months prior thereto, UCIT had advanced to Spohn, or to Ford Motor Company for the benefit of Spohn pursuant to an Agreement for Wholesale Financing (Ex. A), dated December 13, 1954, the principal sum of $437,972.84 for 201 new motor vehicles, each secured under the terms of new car Trust Receipts (Ex. G). On March 3, 1955, UCIT perfected a security interest in, inter alia, new and used motor vehicles, equipment, accessories or replacement parts, and proceeds by properly filing a Financing Statement (Ex. B).

Prior to September 28, 1957, 110 of the new motor vehicles had been sold out of trust by Spohn, leaving 91 new vehicles which UCIT repossessed and sold for $188,268.32, leaving a remainder of $249,704.52 due by Spohn to UCIT for new vehicles sold out of trust.

---

* [The court's citations are to the applicable pre–1972 version of the UCC.]

Between September 28, 1957 and October 31, 1957, Spohn being thus indebted to UCIT, transferred to it the following items, to which the plaintiff-trustee concedes he has no claim: the proceeds of the sale of 15 vehicles subject to bailment leases; office furniture, fixtures and equipment; shop equipment; accounts receivable from UCIT; accounts receivable from Ford Motor Company for wholesale incentive; warranty and policy claims receivable from Ford Motor Company; and other receivables from Ford Motor Company. The facts show conclusively that UCIT had a perfected security interest in each of these items.

In addition to these items, during the same period, Spohn transferred to UCIT, either voluntarily or involuntarily the following: bank cash, shares of stock, customers receivables, 70 used vehicles, and motor parts and accessories. These transfers were made by Spohn for its antecedent debts, at a time when Spohn was insolvent and UCIT had reason to so believe. The plaintiff-trustee contends that these transfers constituted preferences within the meaning of § 60 of the Bankruptcy Act, since their effect was to enable UCIT to obtain a greater percentage of its debt that Spohn's unsecured creditors, except as to those items in which UCIT held a perfected security interest.

We take up the disputed items seriatim.

BANK CASH

Spohn's bank account in the Peoples First National Bank & Trust Company in the sum of $6,734.21 was garnisheed and transferred to UCIT pursuant to a writ of attachment execution issued on a judgment in favor of UCIT in the sum of $75,000. The lien against the bank cash obtained by the attachment within four months of bankruptcy and while Spohn was insolvent is null and void. Section 67 of the Bankruptcy Act, 11 U.S.C.A. § 107.

Spohn's bank account was not under the control of UCIT, and the source of this money has not been identified. Apparently UCIT has not been able to trace any of the money in the bank to proceeds from the sales of collateral on which it held a security interest. The defendant argues that the money must have come from the sale of property in which it had a security interest. This is an unwarranted assumption for all of it could have come from services rendered, sale of Spohn's common stock, or loans to Spohn.

The court may not assume the source of the money in the bank. The burden is upon UCIT to trace cash proceeds received by Spohn from the disposition of secured collateral into the bank deposits. This it has not done. This cash was received by Spohn, the debtor, and deposited more than 10 days prior to the bankruptcy proceeding (cf. U.C.C. § 9–306(2) [R9–315(a)]); it is not identifiable cash proceeds received from the sale or disposition of any collateral. Thus it is free from any security interest of UCIT and is subject to the claims of general creditors represented by the plaintiff-trustee.

We hold the bank cash garnisheed by UCIT is a voidable preference and the plaintiff-trustee is entitled to recover $6,734.21.

ACCOUNTS RECEIVABLE

Spohn collected customers receivables by cash and checks in the sum of $10,847.75 and transferred this amount to UCIT within four months of bankruptcy. Of this sum $1,100.00 was identified as cash proceeds from the sale of two new vehicles on which UCIT held a perfected security interest, leaving in dispute the sum of $9,747.75. This remainder comprises commingled cash proceeds arising from the sale of motor vehicles, parts and services.

From the Stipulated Facts and Exhibit L, it cannot be ascertained whether any of the articles sold were covered by a perfected security interest in favor of UCIT. Exhibit L gives only the name of the person owing the account, the amount paid, and the date the money was transferred to UCIT. Moreover, even if it were to be assumed that some of the accounts arose from the sale of parts and vehicles, it still could not be ascertained whether or not any portion of any account arose from services performed by Spohn. As UCIT did not hold a security interest in proceeds received from the sale of services, it is not entitled to retain proceeds which may have come from this source.

Furthermore, as we understand the Uniform Commercial Code, in insolvency proceedings the secured creditor is only entitled to commingled cash when it is received as proceeds of collateral within ten days of the filing of the petition.

For these reasons, we hold that the plaintiff-trustee is entitled to $9,747.75.

17 USED VEHICLES

These 17 used vehicles were taken in trade by Spohn toward the purchase price of 17 new vehicles. On each of the new vehicles sold, UCIT held a perfected security interest by virtue of the Agreement for Wholesale Financing (Ex. A), new car Trust Receipts (Ex. G), and Financing Statement (Ex. B). The 17 new vehicles were sold out of trust by Spohn.[**] . . .

The plaintiff-trustee contends that according to the Motor Vehicle Code no lien can be obtained on a "trade-in" unless the lien is noted on the title certificate. It is the opinion of the court that a finance company such as UCIT engaging in wholesale financing of new and used vehicles held for resale by a dealer, and having obtained a security interest in new vehicles

---

** [Selling inventory "out of trust" is an expression frequently used in financing circles, perhaps because of appealing connotations that the sale was a breach of "trust" that should invoke the powerful remedies available against defalcating trustees. (The debtor actually was denominated a "trustee" under the Uniform Trust Receipts Act, which governed much pre-UCC inventory financing. See generally 1 Gilmore, Security ch. 4.) However, as you probably surmised, there was nothing wrong with the *sale* of the cars; the only thing that went wrong was that the *dealer failed promptly to pay* the debt to UCIT attributable to the vehicles that it sold.]

and the proceeds thereof, may perfect its security interest in the proceeds by filing in compliance with § 9–302(1) of the U.C.C. [R9–310(a)], and, in view of § 207(c) of the Motor Vehicle Code, need not require the dealer to procure title certificates for each "trade-in" on which to show its lien. . . .

The security interest of UCIT in these proceeds was created at the times the Agreement and the Trust Receipts were executed and perfected by the filing of the Financing Statement in March, 1955. Pursuant to § 9–306(1) of the U.C.C. [R9–315], this security interest continued up to the time UCIT took possession, within four months of bankruptcy, of the 17 "trade-ins", i.e., identifiable proceeds. In our opinion § 9–306(1) is not in conflict with § 60 of the Bankruptcy Act, and the perfected security interest of UCIT in these proceeds is enforceable.

We hold that UCIT is entitled to retain the money received from the sale of the 17 used vehicles.

42 USED VEHICLES

These 42 used vehicles were taken in trade for new vehicles, which had been financed by UCIT, under the terms of the Agreement for Wholesale Financing (Ex. A) and the Trust Receipts (Ex. G). These vehicles must also be regarded as identifiable proceeds in which, as previously shown, UCIT had perfected a security interest by filing the Financing Statement (Ex. B).

It was not stipulated that the new vehicles were sold out of trust by Spohn. However, as we interpret the pertinent security agreements, UCIT created a security interest in *all proceeds*, which would include these 42 "trade-ins", until *all the indebtedness* due by Spohn to UCIT was paid. As heretofore quoted, the Agreement for Wholesale Financing (Ex. A) provided that until payment in full, Spohn would hold all proceeds separately and in trust for UCIT. Likewise, the Trust Receipts (Ex. G), after providing that UCIT could accelerate all indebtedness then owing to it by Spohn in the event of insolvency, further provided that UCIT "may require the respective amount on any chattel to be paid to it in cash. Until such payment we [Spohn] will hold *all proceeds* of sale separately and in trust for * * * Universal C.I.T." (Emphasis supplied.) Since Spohn owed UCIT upwards of $400,000 on all the chattels which it had financed at the time of the transfers, we think these 42 used cars were proceeds to which UCIT is entitled.

The other arguments advanced by the plaintiff-trustee to recover the value of these used vehicles have been disposed of in the preceding section of this opinion.

We hold that UCIT is entitled to retain the money received from the sale of the 42 used vehicles. . . .

NOTES ON SECURITY INTERESTS IN PROCEEDS

(1) "Automatic," Perfected Security Interests. Revised Article 9 follows the 1972 amendments to Former Article 9 and affords the secured party an automatic right to proceeds. See R9–203(f). A claim to proceeds of the collateral is considered so basic that (like implied warranties) this understanding "goes without saying." See F9–306, Reasons for 1972 Change, Uniform Commercial Code, 1999 Official Text with Comments, App. II, at 1032 ("automatic right to proceeds" based on the "theory that this is the intent of the parties, unless otherwise agreed"). Moreover, like the 1972 amendments to Former Article 9, Revised Article 9 treats a filing against the original collateral as a filing against the proceeds. See R9–315(c). The drafters apparently thought the absence of a claim to proceeds in a financing statement would not mislead third persons; however, they recognized some limits to this principle, as the following Note explains.

(2) Security Interests in Proceeds and in After–Acquired Property: A Comparison. In many cases a perfected security interest in proceeds could be achieved simply by covering after-acquired property of the appropriate type in the security agreement and financing statement. For example, the security agreement of an inventory financer might (and often does) cover after-acquired accounts. However, the "automatic right to proceeds" affords additional benefits to a secured party if after-acquired property qualifies as "proceeds." As explained in the preceding Note, a secured party has an automatic security interest in proceeds even if (through oversight or otherwise) the security agreement does not cover the proceeds as original collateral. Does this benefit represent more than statutory generosity? In addition to rescuing some secured parties from careless omissions, might the "automatic" approach save the costs of extended negotiations? Might it also inhibit abuse and overreaching by some secured parties who, if it were necessary to protect one's claim to proceeds in the security agreement, might use unnecessarily broad language?

As to perfection, R9–315(c) provides that "[a] security interest in proceeds is a perfected security interest if the security interest in the original collateral was perfected." But the security interest in proceeds becomes unperfected "on the 21st day after the security interest attaches to the proceeds," subject to three exceptions.

The first exception, R9–315(d)(1), generally makes it unnecessary for a financing statement to cover the type or items of collateral that proceeds represent (except when proceeds are acquired with cash proceeds). For example, a filing covering inventory is sufficient to ensure continued perfection in proceeds consisting of accounts, as long as financing statements covering inventory and accounts are to be filed in the same office, which they are. See R9–301; R9–501(a); Section 4, supra. Of course, when proceeds are of a type in which a security interest can be perfected by filing, a secured party could achieve the same result as that provided by R9–315(c) and (d)—continued long-term perfection—merely by filing a financing statement covering that type of collateral. If authorized by the debtor, such a filing may be made in advance. Even if not authorized, it ordinarily may be made after the security interest attaches to the proceeds. See R9–509(b)(2).

Another exception to the 20–day limitation is made for "identifiable cash proceeds." R9–315(d)(2). A security interest in "cash proceeds" (R9–102(a)(9)) consisting of an instrument (for example, a checks) may be perfected by filing; however, a filing does not perfect a security interest in other types of cash proceeds as original collateral. Specifically, a security interest in a non-consumer deposit account (as original collateral) may be perfected only by control, and consumer deposit accounts are excluded from Article 9 (as original collateral) altogether. See R9–312(b)(1); R9–109(d)(13). A security interest in money may be perfected only by taking possession. See R9–312(b)(3). It follows that the continued perfection conferred by R9–315(d)(2) provides greater protection for cash proceeds, as such, than would be available under the after-acquired property approach.

The third exception, R9–315(d)(3), permits continued perfection beyond the 20–day period if the security interest in proceeds is perfected (other than automatically under R9–315(c)) before the period expires. A security interest in after-acquired property other than proceeds also can be perfected following the debtor's acquisition of the property; but the temporary perfection provided by R9–315(d)(3) can be important for purposes of priority. See, e.g., R9–317(b), R9–322(b)(1). If a secured party acts within the 20–day period, there will be no "gap" during which the security interest is unperfected. Again, to the extent proceeds consist of property not excluded from the scope of Article 9, and in which a security interest can be perfected by filing, the same advantage could be had by an initial filing covering the after-acquired property. Moreover, unless the debtor cooperates or the secured party monitors the debtor's activities closely, the secured party is not likely to discover the need to perfect in proceeds prior to the expiration of the 20–day period.

The distinction between proceeds and after-acquired, non-proceeds collateral can be particularly important if the debtor enters bankruptcy. Generally speaking, a security interest in property acquired during a bankruptcy case is not subject to a security interest created by a pre-bankruptcy security agreement; however, property that constitutes proceeds (or the like) of pre-bankruptcy collateral is subject to the security interest. See BC 552; Chapter 10, Section 3(B), infra.

Problem 7.5.3. Continental Construction Co. bought a new backhoe; Palmetto Bank loaned Continental the purchase price, and perfected a security interest in the backhoe by filing.

(a) An employee of Iceberg Masonry, Inc., negligently dropped a load of bricks on the backhoe at a job site; the damaged backhoe was beyond repair. Continental's insurer, Everystate Insurance Co., sent its check covering the value of the backhoe ($100,000) to Continental. Does Palmetto's security interest extend to the check? See R9–315(a); R9–102(a)(64). If so, is it perfected? See R9–315(c), (d).

(b) Would the result in part (a) be the same if the $100,000 check had been sent by *Iceberg's* liability insurance carrier? What result if the check had been sent by Iceberg itself?

(c) Suppose instead that the backhoe malfunctioned and that Continental pressed a claim against Manufacturer for damages resulting from negligent design and breach of implied warranty; the claim included evidence of damage resulting from the malfunctions and loss of profits resulting from loss of use of the backhoe. Manufacturer settled for $50,000 and sent a check to Continental for that sum. Palmetto Bank claims the check as proceeds of its collateral. What result? See Note on What Constitutes Proceeds, infra.

(d) Now suppose that the backhoe was not damaged. Instead, a sluggish economy reduced Continental's business and its equipment needs. Continental leased the backhoe to Deep Dig Corp. for a one-year term pursuant to a written lease. Does Palmetto's security interest extend to the lease? To checks sent to Continental by Deep Dig as lease payments? Would the answers be different if the lease had been an oral one, not reduced to writing? Would it matter if the lease were for a day or a month instead of a year?

Problem 7.5.4. United Entertainment Group, Inc. (UEG), operates coin-operated music and entertainment machine "routes." UEG supplies coin-operated jukeboxes, video games, pool tables, and the like to establishments (called "joints," in the trade) such as restaurants, taverns, and clubs. The operators of the joints receive no interest in the machines (other than the right to possession) and pay nothing for the machines. However, once or twice each week, an employee of UEG stops by each joint. The joint manager and the UEG employee "rob" the machine and, together, count the money. The joint keeps one half of the money and UEG takes the other half. Either party can terminate the arrangement for any reason upon five-days' notice.

Firstbank has a security interest in UEG's existing and after-acquired equipment, inventory, and accounts, perfected by filing. Does Firstbank acquire a security interest in the funds obtained from the machines? If so, is the security interest perfected?

Problem 7.5.5. Busy Bee Co. operates an interstate bus company. Firstbank has a security interest in Busy's existing and after-acquired equipment, inventory and accounts, perfected by filing. Every day, thousands of riders pay Busy and independent travel agents for tickets. Does Firstbank acquire a security interest in these payments? If so, is the security interest perfected? What could Firstbank have done to improve its position? See R9–312(a); R9–102(a)(49).

Problem 7.5.6. On June 1, Dale Bookbinder obtained a short-term (six-month) loan from Firstbank in the amount of $25,000. Bookbinder delivered to Firstbank, as collateral, a certificate for 2,000 shares of General Motors Corporation (GMC) common stock.

(a) On June 3 GMC declared (i.e., undertook to pay) a stock dividend: each stockholder became entitled to receive one additional share of stock for each four shares owned. Because Bookbinder remained the registered owner of the shares, GMC mailed a new certificate for 500 shares directly to Bookbinder, who received it on July 15. Does Firstbank acquire a security interest in the new certificate? If so, is the security interest perfected? See R9–315(a); R9–102(a)(64) & Comment 13.a.; Note on What Constitutes Proceeds, infra; R9–315(c), (d). What could Firstbank have done to improve its position?

(b) Would your answers to part (a) change if GMC had declared a cash dividend instead of a stock dividend? Assume that it is now August 15 and the dividend check is sitting in Bookbinder's desk drawer. Next assume that it is now July 4 and that GMC has declared the dividend but has not yet issued the check.

NOTE ON WHAT CONSTITUTES PROCEEDS: EXCHANGE AND REPLACEMENT; PROPERTY CLOSELY ASSOCIATED WITH ORIGINAL COLLATERAL

The definition of proceeds is transactional. Each of the triggering events specified in R9–102(a)(64) contemplates that proceeds are to some extent acquired in place of and in substitution for the original collateral, which has been disposed of or reduced in value (such as by collections). This "replacement" standard is most clear in the case of dispositions, such as sales, leases, licenses, and exchanges under subsection (a)(64)(A).[2] But it also is apparent with respect to the other triggering events as well.

Another plausible way to conceptualize what are or should be proceeds of collateral does not depend on the exchange concept. Instead, one can view proceeds as property that is so necessarily and obviously associated with an interest in the original collateral that a security agreement and financing statement ought not to be required to mention them explicitly. After all, "automatic" attachment and perfection are the principal effects that flow from classifying property as proceeds. If the debtor, by virtue of its interest in the original collateral, is necessarily entitled to additional property, then a secured party likewise would be entitled to the additional property as proceeds. Claims for damage or loss of collateral seem to fit this characterization. The same could be said for all forms of distributions on account of securities, partnership interests, and other intangibles (which may or may not be covered "collections" proceeds), certain government subsidies, and other rights that do not, technically, involve an "exchange" or disposition.

F9–306(1) defined proceeds to include "whatever is received upon the sale, exchange, collection or other disposition of collateral or proceeds." It also included "insurance payable by reason of loss or damage to collateral." Arguably, the former definition could have been construed to include all proceeds covered by the new definition, R9–102(a)(64), but in some cases the "exchange" and "collection" formulations probably were too narrow to support that construction. Even when the formulations were ample, courts

---

2. Although the proceeds may replace the original collateral, in many cases the security interest continues to exist in the original collateral as well. See R9–315(a)(1).

occasionally were reluctant to construe them as broadly as they might have. The revised definition more easily accommodates and more clearly mandates a broad view of proceeds.

Of course, even the more explicit and broader revised definition of proceeds has limits. Can you imagine the acquisition of assets by a debtor, due in part to a disposition or diminution in value of collateral, to be too attenuated to be considered proceeds of that collateral? For example, would anyone think that accounts generated by a construction contractor would (or should) be considered proceeds of the contractor's construction equipment, even though the equipment depreciates as a result of its use in earning the accounts? Similarly, would (or should) inventory fabricated by a debtor's factory equipment be considered proceeds of that equipment? What about cash earned from music or video machines? Has the equipment merely provided a service, or is the better analogy that of a short-term rental? Should the result turn on whether the equipment user has acquired a *property* interest in the machine under non-UCC law?

Problem 7.5.7. Firstbank has a security interest, perfected by filing, in all of the restaurant equipment of The Bus Corp., the operator of a small restaurant. The Bus wrongfully sold a used oven to the operator of another restaurant, The Light Dog Co. (Because the sale by The Bus was not authorized, Firstbank's security interest in the oven continued and The Light Dog's interest remains subject to that security interest. See R9–315(a)(1); Section 6(B), infra.) Light Dog then resold the oven to another restaurant operator, The New Neck, Inc. In payment, New Neck gave Light Dog its check for $1,500.

(a) Does Firstbank have a security interest in the $1,500 check? See R9–315(a); R9–102(a)(64); R9–102(a)(12). R9–102(a)(64)(A) is one of the few places in which Revised Article 9 uses the passive voice ("whatever is acquired"). Why didn't the drafters use the active voice to identify the acquirer? See R9–102, Comment 13.d.; F9–306(2).

(b) Assuming an affirmative answer in part (a), is Firstbank's security interest perfected? See R9–315(c), (d).

(c) Now assume that the collateral involved was not an oven but was a delivery van, in which Firstbank perfected its security interest by complying with the relevant motor vehicle certificate of title law. Does Firstbank have a perfected security interest in the $1,500 that New Neck paid for the van? See R9–315(d); R9–311(b).

Problem 7.5.8. Finco extended a line of credit to Lappin Leather Ltd. Lappin secured its obligations to Finco with all its existing and future accounts. Finco perfected its security interest by filing. Under the transaction documents, Lappin is obligated to deposit all checks received in payment of accounts into a special "proceeds" account maintained with Local Bank.

(a) Does Finco have a perfected security interest in the bank account, which contains nothing but proceeds of Lappin's accounts? See R9–102(a)(64); R9–315(a), (c), (d), (e).

(b) Lappin draws a $2500 check to Supplier, and Local properly pays the check from the bank account. May Finco recover the payment or hold Supplier liable for money had and received? See R9–332.

(c) Lappin draws a $500 check as a charitable contribution to the local United Way. Local properly pays the check from the bank account. May Finco recover the payment or hold the United Way liable for money had and received? Is the United Way deserving of protection even if it did not give value or otherwise act in reliance on receipt of the funds? See R9–332 & Comment 3.

––––––

The *Howarth* case, supra, illustrates the consequence of a secured party's inability to demonstrate that the collateral it claims constitutes "identifiable proceeds": loss of a security interest. The problem of security interests in proceeds of collateral takes new twists when the proceeds are cash, or its equivalent, deposited in the debtor's bank accounts and commingled with other funds. The remaining portion of this Section explores these twists

Problem 7.5.9. In the setting of the automobile financing Prototype, assume that Firstbank's security interest in Main's inventory was perfected by a filed financing statement that referred to the collateral only as "Motor Vehicles" (as in Problem 7.5.2, supra). Moreover, the security agreement covered only new motor vehicles financed by Firstbank, not used vehicles.

Main deposited cash received from the sale of new and used cars and from its repair department into a checking account maintained with Firstbank. As in the Prototype, when financed cars were sold, Main promptly sent Firstbank a check covering the amount Firstbank had advanced to the manufacturer for those cars. However, in June, when Main owed $1,500,000 to Firstbank, Main became short of cash and used proceeds from the sale of financed cars to meet payroll, rent, utilities, and other pressing obligations. On June 1 Main had a balance of $1000 in its checking account. The following table shows the deposits (+) and withdrawals (-) for the first few days of June; "PC" indicates proceeds of collateral subject to Firstbank's security interest.

June		Debit or Withdrawal		Balance E.O.D.
1				$ 1,000.
2	+	$15,000.	Sale of one new Chevrolet (PC)	16,000.
3	+	9,000.	Sale of one new Chevrolet (PC)	25,000.
4	–	4,000.	Rent on off-site storage lot	21,000.
5	–	12,000.	Payroll	9,000.
6	–	2,000.	Fuel oil	7,000.
7	–	1,000.	Telephone; electricity	6,000.
8	+	2,000.	Collections for body repairs	8,000.
9	+	6,000.	Sale of used cars (Not PC)	14,000.
10	+	12,000.	Loan from relative	26,000.

During this period Main made no payments to Firstbank.

On June 12 Caesar, a creditor of Main with a judgment for $50,000, garnished the checking account by serving a garnishment summons on Firstbank. Is Caesar's garnishment lien senior to Firstbank's security interest in Main's checking account? If so, to what extent? See R9–315(b) & Comment 3; Universal C.I.T. Credit Corp. v. Farmers Bank of Portageville, infra; Note on Tracing and Commingled Cash Proceeds, infra. (Ignore, for now, any right of setoff that Firstbank may enjoy. Setoffs are considered in Chapter 11, Section 5(C), infra.)

Universal C.I.T. Credit Corp. v. Farmers Bank of Portageville[*]

United States District Court, Eastern District of Missouri, 1973.
358 F.Supp. 317.

■ WEBSTER, DISTRICT JUDGE. Plaintiff, a Delaware corporation, brings this action against defendant Farmers Bank of Portageville, a Missouri banking corporation. Jurisdiction is founded upon diversity of citizenship under 28 U.S.C. § 1332. The amount in controversy exceeds $10,000.

Plaintiff's amended complaint is in three counts. In the first count, plaintiff seeks to recover $22,390.19 as the unpaid balance on checks drawn to plaintiff as payee and thereafter endorsed and presented to defendant, which refused payment. In count II plaintiff contends that it had a perfected security interest in the proceeds of sales of certain automobiles, which proceeds were deposited in the debtor's account in defendant bank and which plaintiff contends were thereafter permitted by defendant to be withdrawn with knowledge of plaintiff's claim. The third count, denominated "alternative for improper failure and refusal to honor drafts" was abandoned at the trial.

Facts

Gerald W. Ryan, doing business as Ryan–Chevrolet and Olds Co., a proprietorship, operated an automobile dealership in Portageville, Missouri. On or about June 18, 1968, Ryan entered into an agreement with plaintiff for wholesale financing, commonly known as floor plan financing. Under the terms of this agreement, plaintiff from time to time advanced funds to pay the manufacturer's invoice on new automobiles, acquiring a security in such automobiles. As each automobile was sold by Ryan, he was required to remit plaintiff's advance. These remittances were in the form of checks drawn on Ryan's checking account at defendant's bank. The financing statements filed in New Madrid County reflect the security interest in the proceeds of the sale of the automobiles. Proper filing is not disputed.

---

* [The court's citations are to the applicable pre–1972 version of the UCC.]

Toward the end of 1969, plaintiff decided for reasons of policy, but primarily because it had not been supplied with current financial statements, to terminate the floor plan arrangement. Ryan was notified that the floor plan would be terminated December 31, 1969.

Sometime after 3:00 p.m. on January 15, 1970, Ryan had a conversation with Richard L. Saalwaechter, President of defendant bank. Ryan told Saalwaechter that he was being put out of business by plaintiff since plaintiff had revoked the floor plan, and that he wanted to be sure that the bank got paid, He said "let C.I.T. be last—they put me out of business." Ryan discussed his debt to the bank on a demand promissory note. He told Saalwaechter that he wanted the bank to be safe on its loan. Ryan asked Saalwaechter to debit his account and credit the bank with $12,000 from his checking account. Saalwaechter then verified Ryan's checking account and determined that there was a balance of $16,340.00. When Saalwaechter suggested that Ryan write a check to the bank, Ryan told him that he preferred that the bank run a debit against the account because C.I.T. was after him and he didn't know what they could do to him. Ryan further told Saalwaechter that C.I.T. had checks out, and that he wanted to make a cash withdrawal to keep C.I.T. from getting its checks. Thereupon, although the bank's business day had closed at 3:00 p.m., Saalwaechter debited Ryan's account in the amount of $12,000.00. The next morning, January 16th, Ryan came to the bank and made a cash withdrawal of $3,100.00. Saalwaechter testified that he had no knowledge that any of Ryan's checks to C.I.T. were in the bank until after the debit and the withdrawal.

The funds in dispute derive from the sale by Ryan of six motor vehicles. In some cases, a trade-in was involved with which we are not concerned. In each case, Ryan received a check from the purchaser in payment of the cash portion of the deal. Each check was deposited in Ryan's account with defendant bank and he received full credit therefor. Each automobile sold and the proceeds thereof were subject to plaintiff's security interest. The checks representing the proceeds of the six automobiles sold by Ryan were all deposited on or prior to January 15, 1970 and aggregate $18,112.44. . . .

Liability Under Count I

Plaintiff contends that defendant bank failed to give timely notice of dishonor or make timely settlement and is therefore liable for the full amount of the checks under the applicable provisions of the Uniform Commercial Code in force in Missouri.

[The court rejected the plaintiff's contentions based on Count I.]

Liability Under Count II

It is not disputed that plaintiff had a continuously perfected security interest in six automobiles and their proceeds. See § 400.9–306(3) V.A.M.S. [R9–315(c), (d)]. Ryan sold separately each of these automobiles and deposited the amount received on each sale in his checking account at the defendant bank. Funds from other sources were deposited in the checking account prior to and contemporaneously with such deposits. Numerous checks were issued on the account between the time of the first and last sale. Plaintiff contends that the defendant bank was not entitled to debit Ryan's checking account in the amount of $12,000 on January 15, 1970, relying upon Section 400.9–306(2), which provides:

> "Except where this article otherwise provides, a security interest continues in collateral notwithstanding sale, exchange or other disposition thereof by the debtor unless his action was authorized by the secured party in the security agreement or otherwise, and also continues in any *identifiable* proceeds including collections received by the debtor." (Emphasis supplied.)

Defendant contends that the proceeds from the sales of the six automobiles were not "identifiable" within the meaning of § 400.9–306(2). Defendant argues that when the proceeds were deposited and thereby commingled with other funds in Ryan's account and thereafter substantial withdrawals were made exceeding the amount of the deposited proceeds, the proceeds completely lost their identity. No Missouri case defines the term "identifiable" as used in this section. It is provided in § 400.1–103 that all supplemental bodies of law continue to apply to commercial contracts except insofar as displaced by the particular provisions of the Uniform Commercial Code. Applying § 400.1–103, this court concludes that proceeds are "identifiable" if they can be traced in accordance with the state law governing the transaction. Missouri has recognized in an analogous situation—suits to impose a constructive trust—that special funds may be traced into commingled funds. Perry v. Perry, 484 S.W.2d 257 (Mo.1972). The mere fact that the proceeds from the sales of the six automobiles were commingled with other funds and subsequent withdrawals were made from the commingled account does not render the proceeds unidentifiable under Missouri law. As the court said in Perry v. Perry, supra at 259:

> "... where a defaulting trustee has first commingled the trust funds with his own and then paid them out in satisfaction of his own debts, it will be presumed that the payment was made from his own contribution to the commingled fund, 'and not out of the trust money,' so that whatever is left is the money for which he is accountable in his fiduciary capacity. Lolordo v. Lacy, 337 Mo.1097, 88 S.W.2d 353, 358; Cross v. Cross, 362 Mo.1098, 246 S.W.2d 801, 803." Perry v. Perry, 484 S.W.2d 257, 259 (Mo.1972).

Before tracing the proceeds, it is necessary to decide whether under the circumstances in this case the defendant bank was entitled to debit Ryan's checking account if the account contained proceeds from the sales of the six automobiles. Comment 2(c) to § 400.9–306 provides:

> "Where cash proceeds are covered into the debtor's checking account and paid out in the operation of the debtor's business, recipients of the funds of course take free of any claim which the secured party may have in them as proceeds. What has been said relates to payments and transfers in ordinary course. *The law of fraudulent conveyances would*

no doubt in appropriate cases support recovery of proceeds by a secured party from a transferee out of ordinary course or otherwise in collusion with the debtor to defraud the secured party." (Emphasis supplied)

There are no Missouri cases on point. However, Missouri has long recognized that one indicia of a fraudulent conveyance is a transaction outside the usual course of doing business. Bank of New Cambria v. Briggs, 236 S.W.2d 289, 291 (Mo.1951). In Missouri, "fraud, like any other fact, may be established by circumstantial evidence [and][t]here are circumstances which have come to be recognized as indicia or badges of fraud, one of which circumstances alone may not prove fraud, but may warrant an inference of fraud, especially where there is a concurrence of several indicia of fraud." Id. Ryan told Saalwaechter that plaintiff had revoked the floor plan and that he wanted the bank to be safe on its loan. Ryan asked Saalwaechter to debit his account. When Saalwaechter suggested that Ryan write a check to the bank, Ryan indicated that he preferred the bank run a debit against the account and further informed Saalwaechter that he had issued checks to plaintiff and wished to keep plaintiff from collecting on the checks. All of these events, including the debit to Ryan's account, transpired after the close of business on January 15, 1970. These facts clearly show that the debit of Ryan's account was not in the ordinary course of business. Although, as indicated above, there are no Missouri cases directly on point, this court concludes that the Missouri courts would not, under these circumstances, permit the defendant bank to retain the amount debited outside the usual course of business and thereby defeat the security interest of plaintiff in the identifiable proceeds of the sale of the six automobiles.

Support for this conclusion is also found in the law governing a bank's right of set-off. As a general rule an account constituting a general deposit is subject to the bank's right of set-off. First National Bank of Clinton v. Julian, 383 F.2d 329, 338 (8th Cir.1967), applying Missouri law and following Adelstein v. Jefferson Bank & Trust Company, 377 S.W.2d 247, 251 (Mo.1964). An exception to that general rule is that a bank is not entitled to a set-off where it has "sufficient knowledge of facts relating to the interests of others in the account as to put the bank on inquiry to ascertain the trust character of the account." Northern Ins. Co. v. Traders Gate City National Bank, 239 Mo.App. 132, 186 S.W.2d 491, 497 (1945) following Brown v. Maguire's Real Estate Agency, 343 Mo. 336, 121 S.W.2d 754 (1938). The *Northern Insurance Company* case indicates that the bank's knowledge of the "trust character" of a deposit can be shown by indirect evidence or by showing that the bank would have sufficient information to put it on inquiry as to the trust character of the deposit. 186 S.W.2d at 498. The bank's knowledge that Ryan had floor plan financing with plaintiff, that Ryan had issued checks to plaintiff which Ryan did not want collected by plaintiff, and Ryan's insistence that the bank run a debit against his account, coupled with the communication of such facts after banking hours, were sufficient to put the bank on inquiry as to the possible trust character of all or part of the funds deposited in Ryan's account....

This court's final task is to trace the proceeds of the sales of the six automobiles to determine if they were taken by the bank when it debited Ryan's account after the close of business on January 15, 1970. As indicated above, Perry v. Perry, supra, 484 S.W.2d at 259, stated the general rule that in tracing commingled funds it is presumed that any payments made were from other than the funds in which another had a legally recognized interest. This is commonly referred to as the "lowest intermediate balance" rule. Restatement of Trusts, Second, § 202, Comment *j* provides in pertinent part:

> "*j. Effect of withdrawals and subsequent additions.* Where the trustee deposits in a single account in a bank trust funds and his individual funds, and makes withdrawals from the deposit and dissipates the money so withdrawn, and subsequently makes additional deposits of his individual funds in the account, the beneficiary cannot ordinarily enforce an equitable lien upon the deposit for a sum greater than the lowest intermediate balance of the deposit. . . ."

Illustration 20 to Comment *j* is as follows:

> "*A* is trustee for *B* of $1,000. He deposits this money together with $1000 of his own in a bank. He draws out $1500 and dissipates it. He later deposits $1000 of his own in the account. He is entitled to a lien on the account for $500, the lowest intermediate balance." Comment *j*, Illustration 20, Restatement of Trusts § 202 at 544 and Restatement of Trusts, Second, § 202 at 451.

The situation in the instant case differs from Comment *j* and the Illustration in one respect. We have not one, but six, separate deposits of funds of a "trust character" spanning a period of nearly a month, during which time a substantial number of withdrawals and deposits of other funds were made in the account. Comment *m* to the Restatement of Trusts, Second, § 202 at 453 provides:

> "*m. Subsequent additions by way of restitution.* Where the trustee deposits trust funds in his individual account in a bank, and makes withdrawals from the deposit and dissipates the money so withdrawn, and subsequently makes additional deposits of his individual funds in the account, *manifesting an intention to make restitution* of the trust funds withdrawn, the beneficiary's lien upon the deposit is not limited to the lowest intermediate balance.

> "Where the deposit of trust funds and of his individual funds was *in an account in the name of the trustee as such, and not in his individual account,* and he withdraws more than the amount of his individual funds, and subsequently deposits his individual funds in the account, the beneficiary's lien upon the deposit is not limited to the lowest intermediate balance since the new deposit will be treated as *made by way of restitution of the trust funds previously withdrawn.*" (Emphasis supplied.)

Thus, individual funds subsequently deposited to a trust account by the trustee are presumed to be by way of restitution. Perry v. Perry, supra at

259. Subsequent deposits by the trustee to his own account, on the other hand, are not so treated unless the trustee "manifests an intention to make restitution." No such manifestation of intent was shown in this case. Therefore, subsequent deposits of funds not relating to the proceeds from the sales of the six automobiles in Ryan's individual d/b/a account will not be treated as made by way of restitution of trust funds previously withdrawn.

However, each deposit of the proceeds of the sales of the six automobiles will be treated as additions to the trust fund, and the lowest intermediate balance theory will be followed.

It was stipulated at trial that the following deposits were received by Ryan from the sale of the six automobiles and their proceeds in which plaintiff held a continuously perfected security interest:

	Vehicle	Serial No.	Purchaser	Date of Deposit	Amount
1.	1969 Chev.	866578	Campbell	12–19–69	$5,700.00
2.	1970 Olds.	217371	Faulkner	12–20–69	4,125.00
3.	1969 Chev.	890453	Hunter	1–09–70	1,599.94
4.	1970 Chev.	138013	Carlisle	1–12–70	2,237.50
5.	1970 Olds.	160314	Rone	1–15–70	2,700.00
6.	1970 Chev.	141638	Hendricks	1–15–70	1,750.00

The court has examined the banking records of the Ryan account and finds that the identifiable proceeds in which plaintiff held a continuously perfected security interest on January 15, 1970 prior to the bank's $12,000 debit entry was $11,429.11. This amount may be traced according to the following summarization:

Date		"Proceeds" Deposited	End Balance	"Proceeds" Remaining in Account
12–18–69			$ 710.74	
12–19–69	(1)	$5,700.00	9,100.58	$ 5,700.00
12–20–69	(2)	4,125.00	9,709.90	*9,709.90
12–24–69			6,201.41	*6,201.41
1–02–70			4,715.30	*4,715.30
1–09–70	(3)	1,599.94	11,987.65	6,315.24
1–12–70	(4)	2,237.50	15,426.72	8,552.74
1–14–70			6,979.11	*6,979.11
1–15–70	(5)	2,700.00		
	(6)	1,750.00	16,340.00	11,429.11

* Lowest Intermediate Balance

On January 15, 1970, the bank debited against the Ryan account checks aggregating $516.65 and in addition made the $12,000.00 debit entry in its favor. The $12,000.00 debit entry was made at 3:00 p.m. after the close of business. It may, therefore, be inferred that the checks aggregating $516.65 were received prior thereto in the ordinary course on January 15, 1970 during banking hours. The pro forma balance prior to the $12,000.00 debit entry was, therefore, $15,823.35. Subtracting from this amount the "proceeds" remaining in the account ($11,429.11), the amount which the bank was entitled to debit was $4,394.24. Accordingly, plaintiff is entitled to recover from the bank the excess amount debited, or $7,605.76.

That amount is identified as proceeds in which plaintiff had a perfected security interest, and plaintiff is entitled to recover this amount, together with interest at 6% from October 26, 1970, the filing date of the complaint. The Clerk will enter judgment in favor of plaintiff on Count II in accordance with this Memorandum.

This Memorandum constitutes the court's Findings of Fact and Conclusions of Law.

So ordered.

NOTE ON TRACING AND COMMINGLED CASH PROCEEDS

We have seen that a security interest attaches to "any *identifiable* proceeds" of collateral and remains perfected in "*identifiable* cash proceeds" beyond the 20–day period. R9–315(a)(2) & (d)(2). Problems 7.5.1 through 7.5.8 involved proceeds (or putative proceeds)—goods, intangibles, and cash proceeds such as money or checks—that clearly were "identifiable." Problem 7.5.9 and the *Farmers Bank* case, however, considered deposit accounts in which proceeds and non-proceeds had been commingled. As you know, a depositor has no property interest in specific coins or currency deposited in a bank or other depositary institution. Clearly, then, once cash proceeds are deposited in a deposit account containing non-proceeds, the cash proceeds are not "identifiable" in the same sense as the proceeds considered earlier in this section. They become even less "identifiable" as the debtor makes withdrawals from, and deposits into, the deposit account.

Former Article 9, under which *Farmers Bank* was decided, did not explain exactly what it meant for proceeds to be "identifiable." The *Farmers Bank* court reached for a legal fiction—the "lowest intermediate balance rule" ("LIBR")—in order to identify what otherwise would not have been identifiable. Courts have developed tracing rules, including LIBR, in an effort to afford an equitable, restitutionary remedy to victims of wrongdoing. Is the case for tracing as strong in the context of proceeds of a secured creditor's collateral as it is when, for example, a trustee has misappropriated trust funds? Might the courts easily have concluded that cash proceeds lose their identity upon commingling? In his treatise on Former Article 9, Professor Gilmore took the position that proceeds cease to be identifiable upon deposit in a commingled bank account, and there is some early authority supporting that result. 2 Gilmore, Security § 27.4, at 735–36; Morrison Steel Co. v. Gurtman, 113 N.J.Super. 474, 274 A.2d 306 (App.Div.1971) ("Generally, as is true here, proceeds will have been rendered unidentifiable by having been commingled with other funds in a single bank account.") (dictum). But since 1973 the reported cases uniformly have allowed a secured party to employ tracing principles in order to claim a continuing perfected security interest in a commingled deposit account. But cf. In re Littleton, 106 B.R. 632 (Bkrtcy.9th Cir.1989) (secured party who allowed debtor to commingle proceeds in a general account rather than segregate them in separate account as required by security agreement held to have waived security interest in proceeds and made identifiability impossible), affirmed on other grounds (per curiam) 942 F.2d 551 (9th Cir.1991). The case law all seems to be directly or indirectly traceable to the *Farmers Bank* case, and the cases generally invoke LIBR as the tracing principle.

Application of LIBR in the commingled deposit account context has provoked considerable scholarly debate. In general, the commentary gives the approach mixed reviews. Notwithstanding their abundance, the scholarly critiques seem to have had little, if any, influence on the judiciary; nor have there been other indications of dissatisfaction with the current state of the law. Unlike Former Article 9, Revised Article 9 specifically addresses the question of commingled funds. See R9–315(b)(2) & Comment 3. What, exactly, does it mean? When *may* a court use LIBR? When *must* it do so?

Commingled cash proceeds in deposit accounts is not the only example of commingling that can affect Article 9 security interests. The identity of goods can be lost through manufacturing or production (e.g., flour that has become part of baked goods) as well as by commingling with other goods from which they cannot be distinguished (e.g., ball bearings). R9–336 explains the extent to which a security interest attaches to the product or mass into which "commingled goods"—whether original collateral or proceeds—have been commingled.

––––––

Problem 7.5.10. In the setting of the Prototype, assume that Lee Abel had just turned 18 and had never applied for credit before. As a condition of extending purchase-money credit, Main and Firstbank required that a person with a good credit history undertake the obligation to repay the debt secured by the Chevrolet. Lee Abel's aunt, Bea, signed a guaranty, in which she agreed to perform Lee's obligations under the Instalment Sale Contract (Form 7.6, supra).

(a) Why did Main and Firstbank require a guaranty? Wouldn't the security interest in the Chevrolet insure the full repayment of Abel's debt? See Note on Supporting Obligations, infra.

(b) Why do you suppose Bea Abel agreed to sign the guaranty?

(c) Does Firstbank have a security interest in Main's rights under the guaranty? If so, is the security interest perfected? See R9–102(a)(77), (a)(71); R9–203(f); R9–308(d).

NOTE ON SUPPORTING OBLIGATIONS

As in Problem 7.5.10, extenders of credit not infrequently require, as a condition of extending credit, that a financially responsible third party guaranty payment of the debt. Apparently Abel's credit rating and income were not adequate to justify the extension of $18,380.50 credit, even though the credit was secured by a Chevrolet having a retail price of $27,056. Do you see why? In business settings, the shareholders and officers of a closely-held corporation typically are required to guaranty loans made to the corporation. In many cases this is not so much to have a "deep pocket" to which the lender may turn if the debtor becomes insolvent; the fortunes of the shareholders and officers are likely to rise and fall with that of the corporation. Instead, it is an effective and persuasive mechanism to keep the individuals on the job and interested in the success of the venture.

In Revised Article 9 terminology, a third-party guarantor is a "secondary obligor."[3] A secondary obligor's secondary obligation is a "supporting obligation" if it supports one of the types of collateral specified in the definition of the term. R9–102(a)(77).[4] For example, in the setting of the Prototype and Problem 7.5.10, the secondary obligation of Lea Abel's Aunt Bea is a supporting obligation because it supports Lee Abel's payment and performance obligations under the Instalment Sale Contract, which is chattel paper. Recall that in the Prototype Firstbank advanced funds against the chattel paper, the collateral. Naturally, Firstbank expects that its perfected security interest in the chattel paper will extend to collections—proceeds of the chattel paper. But what are Firstbank's rights with respect to collections from Aunt Bea? Former Article 9 did not specifically address supporting obligations for collateral. However, most would agree that collections from Aunt Bea under her guaranty of Abel's obligations under the chattel paper would have been proceeds of the chattel paper itself under Former Article 9. See R9–203, Comment 8 ("[A] security interest in a "supporting obligation" . . . automatically follows from a security interest in the underlying, supported collateral. This result was implicit under former Article 9."). Revised Article 9 makes this result explicit for supporting obligations. R9–203(f). Moreover, if the security interest in the underlying collateral is perfected, then the security interest in the supporting obligation is perfected as well. R9–308(d).

SECTION 6.   CONFLICTING CLAIMS TO COLLATERAL: ARTICLE 9'S BASIC PRIORITY RULES

The preceding Sections of this Chapter dealt primarily with whether a security interest is enforceable against the debtor and would withstand attack from judicial lien creditors. This Section deals with other claims to the collateral: claims by holders of conflicting security interests and by buyers and lessees of the collateral from the debtor. The last subsection provides another look at the relative rights of a secured party and the holder of a judicial lien.

---

3. Secondary obligors and the law of suretyship, which governs secondary obligations, are addressed in more detail in Chapter 12, Section 3(A), infra.

4. A letter-of-credit right (defined in R9–102(a)(51)) also may be a supporting obligation.

(A) COMPETING SECURITY INTERESTS

Introductory Note. Prior to enactment of the UCC, conflicts between security interests had to be resolved under circumstances that approached anarchy. Only some of the security "devices" (chattel mortgage, conditional sale, trust receipt, assignment of accounts, factor's lien) had the benefit of statutory priority rules; even these rules almost invariably were rudimentary and were confined to conflicts between security interests created by the same "device." When separate security worlds would collide (e.g., conditional sale vs. trust receipt; assignment of accounts vs. factor's lien), the outcome was wildly unpredictable. The total effect was bearable only for one who had a taste for case-law improvisation or for chaos.

In bringing all personal property security under one roof, the UCC exposed the wide variety of priority problems that had been lurking in the crannies among the various types of chattel security; the drafters met a scene that makes one think of Noah when he came to the room in the Ark reserved for snakes.

Even in the initial version of Article 9, by a happy marriage of theory and practical experience, the drafters developed a priority system that created a kind of order. Experience and further thought during the UCC's first two decades produced significant refinements that were reflected in the 1972 revision of the great priority schema, F9–312.

Most of the significant priority problems that experience and lively imaginations have exposed seem susceptible of solution under the 1972 version of Article 9. However, the study of that Article identified several examples of priority contests that warranted additional refinements. Many of these refinements are reflected in the priority rules of Revised Article 9. Revised Article 9 also carries forward, with minor changes, the special priority rules governing security interests in investment property which accompanied the 1994 revision of UCC Article 8. These rules were adapted to govern the priority of security interests in deposit accounts. See Chapter 9, Sections 3 and 4, infra (discussing priority of security interests in investment property and deposit accounts).

Interestingly, Article 9 does not define or explain (at least not directly) the concept of "priority." What does it mean to say that one claim has "priority" over another or that one claim is "senior" or "junior" to another? One answer is that the claimant with priority, the senior claimant, is entitled to have its claim satisfied first from the value of the collateral involved. The junior claimant, then, could look to the remaining value, if any. However, as we shall consider in Chapter 12, Section 3(B), even in the absence of any action or participation by a senior claimant, a junior claimant sometimes can enforce its security interest by collecting or disposing of collateral after the debtor's default.

(I) THE FIRST–TO–FILE–OR–PERFECT RULE

Problem 7.6.1. On June 1 *D*, a dealer in mink pelts, obtained a $50,000 loan from *SP*–1 and as security delivered to *SP*–1 pelts of equivalent value. *SP–1* did not file a financing statement.

On July 1 D obtained a $50,000 loan from SP–2 and executed a security agreement granting to SP–2 a security interest in all mink pelts owned by D. SP–2 immediately filed a financing statement covering "mink pelts."

(a) D defaults on the debts to SP–1 and SP–2. D's principal assets are the pelts delivered to SP–1. Do both SP–1 and SP–2 have a security interest in the pelts? Is each security interest perfected? Whose security interest is senior? See R9–322(a)(1) & Comment 4; R9–310(a), (b)(6); Notes (1) and (2) on the First-to-File-or-Perfect Rule, infra. What could the losing party have done to avoid the loss?

(b) Reverse the order of the transactions in part (a): The transaction with SP–2 (including filing) occurred on June 1, and the transaction with SP–1 occurred on July 1. In this setting whose security interest is senior? What could the losing party have done to avoid the loss?

(c) Now assume that SP–2 filed the financing statement on June 1 but did not make the loan or obtain a security agreement at that time. On July 1 the transaction with SP–1 occurred (including the loan and delivery of the pelts). On August 1 SP–2 made the loan to D and D signed the security agreement. Whose security interest is senior? What could the losing party have done to avoid the loss? See R9–513(c), (d); R9–339.

Problem 7.6.2. On June 1 D, a dealer in soybeans, borrowed $200,000 from SP–1. D granted to SP–1 a security interest in all soybeans that D then owned or might thereafter acquire, to secure the $200,000 loan and any other indebtedness of D to SP–1 that might arise in the future. SP–1 filed a financing statement covering "soybeans, now owned or hereafter acquired." On June 1 D owned and held in its granaries approximately 50,000 bushels of soybeans with a market price of $5.00 per bushel (i.e., with an aggregate value of $250,000). During the summer and fall D made many purchases and sales of soybeans, but the amount held in the granaries remained in the vicinity of 50,000 bushels; also, the price remained in the neighborhood of $5.00 per bushel.

By September 1 D's payments to SP–1 had reduced the debt from $200,000 to $25,000. On that date D applied to SP–2 for a loan and showed SP–2 cancelled checks showing payments to SP–1 and current statements from SP–1 to D that accurately reported the current balance of $25,000 owing to SP–1. SP–2 thereupon loaned D $150,000, took a written security agreement covering D's soybeans, and filed a financing statement.

On September 15 SP–1 made a further loan to D of $175,000; SP–1's financing statement of June 1 remained on file throughout.

(a) On October 1 D defaulted on the loans to both SP–1 and SP–2. Who has the senior security interest in the 50,000 bushels of soybeans in D's granaries? See R9–204(c); R9–322(a)(1); R9–323(a) & Comment 3; Note (3) on the First-to-File-or-Perfect Rule, infra. What should the losing party have done to protect itself? See R9–339; R9–513(c), (d); R9–514(b); R9–511(b).

(b) Would the result in part (a) change if, on September 1, *SP*–2 gave written notice of its transaction to *SP*–1? See R9–322(a)(1); R9–323(a).

(c) Would the result in part (a) change if, on September 1, when *SP*–2 made the loan of $150,000 to *D*, *D*'s debt to *SP*–1 had been reduced to zero? (As above, the financing statement remained on file, and on September 15 *SP*–1 made a further loan of $175,000.) See R9–322(a)(1); R9–323(a).

(d) Would the result in part (a) change if *SP*–1's security agreement secured payment of "all amounts due and to become due under D's promissory note in the amount of $200,000 of even date herewith" and *SP*–1's September 15 loan was evidenced by a new promissory note in the amount of $175,000? If so, what should the losing party have done to protect itself?

(e) In preparing to apply for a loan from *SP*–2, *D* presented to *SP*–1 on September 1 a signed "request regarding a statement of account" under R9–210. The request indicated what *D* believed to be the aggregate amount of unpaid obligations secured by collateral on September 1 of $25,000 and reasonably identified the transaction. *D* requested that *SP*–1 approve or correct the statement and return it to *D*. *SP*–1 wrote "approved" on the statement, signed it, and returned it to *D*. *D* showed this statement to *SP*–2 in applying for the $150,000 loan that *SP*–2 thereupon extended to *D*. On September 15 *SP*–1 extended to *D* a further loan of $175,000, as described above. On *D*'s default on October 1, who has the senior security interest in *D*'s 50,000 bushels of soybeans? What should the losing party have done to protect itself?

NOTES ON THE FIRST–TO–FILE–OR–PERFECT RULE

(1) Article 9's Basic Rule on Priority Among Competing Security Interests: A Complex Excursus to Explain a Basic Rule. R9–322(a)(1) gives legal priority to a security interest that is prior in time with respect to either "filing or perfection." It may seem odd, at first glance, that legal priority is given to the interest that is first in time with respect to *either* filing *or* perfection. Wouldn't the party who *files* first also be first as to *perfection* of a security interest? If so, why not omit the reference to perfection? To state the basic rule solely in terms of who files first would not be adequate, since in some situations security interests can be perfected without filing. See Section 3, supra.

A more complex question is this: Why doesn't Article 9 simply say that legal priority is given to the security interest that is *perfected* first? Why is there also a reference to filing? For most ordinary security transactions, the simpler first-to-perfect rule would be adequate. But in many common commercial transactions, particularly those in which the collateral includes after-acquired property (see, e.g., Problem 7.6.2, supra), filing may precede "perfection."

This distinction between filing and perfection results from the interplay of R9–308 and R9–203. R9–308(a) provides that a security interest is not "perfected" unless it has "attached." R9–203(b) lays down a series of requirements for enforceability and thus for "attachment": (a) authentication of a security agreement (or the secured party's possession or control of the collateral pursuant to a security agreement); (b) the giving of value by the secured party; and (c) the debtor's having rights in the collateral. Consider the following example: Bank files a financing statement on June 1 and makes a secured loan (i.e., gives "value" and takes an authenticated security agreement) to Debtor on July 1. R9–203(b) tells us that the security interest did not "attach" until July. And we have just learned from R9–308(a) that a security interest must "attach" before it is "perfected." Thus, "perfection" did not occur until July 1, although filing took place a month earlier.

Why does Article 9 go to such lengths to provide that "perfection" of a security interest, in some circumstances, will not occur at filing? Was all this designed to lead to the result that a security interest that is filed before any other security interest will be subordinate to a security interest that is filed later but is the first to reach "perfection"? Quite the contrary. Let us return to the basic priority rule in R9–322(a)(1): "Conflicting perfected security interests ... rank according to priority in time of filing *or* perfection." Suppose that *A* files on June 1, that *B* files and makes a secured loan on June 15, and that *A* makes a secured loan on July 1. Under the basic rule of R9–322(a)(1), the prevailing security interest is the one that is first *either* to file *or* to perfect. *A* filed before *B* either filed *or* perfected. Consequently, *A*'s security interest prevails over *B*'s. See R9–322, Comment 4, Example 1.

The drafters thought these intricacies necessary to address the setting of continuing financing arrangements where credits and collateral ebb and flow—the "floating lien." (The financing of Main Motors' inventory in the Prototype is an example of the "floating lien." This type of financing is discussed in detail in Chapter 10, Section 3(A), infra.) Moreover, in many ordinary financings the creditor extends "value" at a time when the other elements of "attachment" (R9–203) and "perfection" (R9–308) have been satisfied. When filing and perfection occur together, there is no occasion to distinguish between the separate elements in the basic rule of R9–322(a)(1): filing *or* perfection. Perhaps it would have been better to state Article 9's basic rule on priority in a way so that it could be applied to simple financing transactions without worrying about the significance of language that was designed for more complex (albeit not uncommon) situations. Be that as it may, the current rule affords secured parties the opportunity to fix their place in line by filing a financing statement even before the details of a secured loan have been finalized.

(2) Guarding Against Prior Security Interests: The Two–Step Ideal. Assume that Bank is considering making a loan to Debtor, and that the loan will be extended only if secured by certain assets of Debtor. How can Bank be sure that there is no outstanding security interest that will take priority? As we have seen from Section 3(B), supra, and from R9–310(b), checking the public records will not, alone, give Bank the assurance it desires. But let us suppose that the cautious Bank takes two steps: (1) It ascertains that Debtor is in possession of the collateral; and (2) it checks the public records and finds that no other creditor has filed a financing statement.[1] Under these circumstances is Bank safe from outstanding security interests? The answer is: Yes—in most situations, but not in all. For instance, a creditor who wants to be sure there is no outstanding security interest that will receive priority also will need to consider whether the collateral, or the situation, is of a type that might fall within one of the other exceptions from the filing requirement that are listed in R9–310(b). Happily, most of these exceptions are limited either as to type of collateral or as to the period of temporary perfection.

(3) Future Advances. As we have seen, collateral may secure future as well as past or present advances if the parties so agree. See R9–204(c); Section 2, supra. A strict application of the first-to-file-or-perfect rule of R9–322(a)(1) would seem to leave no room for determining priority of security interests based on the time that value is given, except when a financing statement was not filed and the advance is the giving of value as the last step for attachment and perfection. (Of course, if a first-filed secured party *never* gives value, it will not be entitled to any of the benefits of a security interest.)

As a general matter, then, all advances securing a security interest enjoy the same priority under R9–322(a)(1). However, R9–323(a) sets forth the only circumstances under which the priority of an advance does not date from the time of filing or perfection:

> when the security interest is perfected only automatically under Section 9–309 or temporarily under Section 9–312(e), (f), or (g), and the advance is not made pursuant to a commitment entered into while the security interest was perfected by another method. Thus, an advance has priority from the date it is made only in the rare case in which it is made without commitment and while the security interest is perfected only temporarily under Section 9–312.

R9–323, Comment 3.[2]

As we have seen, some courts evidenced a hostility to future advance clauses by construing them narrowly. See Note on Obligations (Including

---

1. Checking the public record may prove to be easier said than done. We have seen several Article 9 provisions under which financing statements remain effective even though the facts governing the location of the filing and the content of the statement have changed. See, e.g., R9–316(a) (financing statement remains effective after debtor changes its location) (discussed in Section 4, supra); R9–315(d) (financing statement covering one type of collateral may be effective to perfect a security interest in another type of collateral constituting proceeds) (discussed

in Section 5, supra); R9–507(c) (financing statement remains effective as to certain collateral even after debtor's name changes) (discussed in Section 3(A), supra, and Chapter 11, Section 1, infra).

2. As we shall see, the timing of advances can be relevant to sorting out priorities between secured parties and certain buyers (see R9–323(d), considered in Section 6(B), infra), lien creditors (see R9–323(b), considered in Section 6(C), infra), and the United States (see Chapter 11, Section 5(D), infra).

Future Advances) Covered by Security Agreements, Section 2, supra. This hostility also was evidenced in decisions denying priority to future advances, even if made by the first–filed secured party. Consider an example:

> On March 1, 2002, D entered into a security agreement granting to SP–1 a security interest in an item of equipment to secure a new $100,000 loan. SP–1 perfected by filing on March 2 a financing statement covering "all equipment now owned or hereafter acquired." By December 1, 2002, D paid the loan in full. There was no commitment by SP–1 to give further value, and the entire transaction between SP–1 and D came to an end. On February 3, 2003, D obtained a $500,000 loan from SP–2 and entered into a security agreement granting to SP–2 a security interest in all of D's equipment. SP–2 perfected by filing a financing statement on the same day. On January 15, 2006, D obtained another $100,000 loan from SP–1 and entered into a new security agreement granting to SP–1 a security interest in all of D's equipment.

Whose security interest has priority? Both R9–322(a) and its predecessor, F9–312(5), could not be more clear on this point. By virtue of having the first-filed financing statement, filed back in 2002, SP–1 holds the senior security interest. That the parties' intention and motivation for the filing arose in connection with a long-since completed transaction under a security agreement that did not secure future advances has no impact on application of the first-to-file-or-perfect rule. Nonetheless, some early cases refused to give SP–1 its due priority. In one notorious opinion, the court expressed concern that affording priority to SP–1 "places a lender in an unusually strong position, vis-a-vis, the debtor and any subsequent lenders. In fact, it gives the lender a throttle hold on the debtor." Coin–O–Matic Service Co. v. Rhode Island Hospital Trust Co., 3 U.C.C. Rep. Serv. 1112, 1116 (R.I.Super.Ct.1966). Was that a legitimate concern? Most later cases were to the contrary. What went wrong for SP–2 was not the harshness of the first-to-file-or-perfect rule. It was, instead, either SP–2's careless failure to search the filing office or its foolishness in proceeding in the face of SP–1's filing. Observe that had SP–2 insisted that SP–1's filing be terminated, SP–1 would have been obliged to terminate the financing statement had D made an authenticated demand on SP–1 to do so. See R9–513(c).

Problem 7.6.3. SP–1 perfected a security interest in certain collateral by filing a financing statement in May, 2002. It is now July, 2007.

(a) In April, 2007, the debtor created a security interest in the same collateral in favor of SP–2, who immediately perfected the security interest by filing. SP–2 had actual knowledge of SP–1's security interest. Which security interest is senior? See R9–515(a), (c) & Comment 3. What, if anything, could the holder of the junior security interest have done to prevent the loss? See R9–515(c), (d); R9–102(a)(27); R9–521(b).

(b) Should one inclined toward the "good faith" principle, discussed in the *Shallcross* and *Lowry* cases, infra, apply that principle to preserve SP–

1's priority over *SP*–2 notwithstanding R9–515(c) or its predecessor, F9–403(2)? Cf. Frank v. James Talcott, Inc., 692 F.2d 734 (11th Cir.1982) (under 1962 UCC 9–403, lapse of first-filed financing statement rendered secured party unperfected and subordinate to second-to-file secured party; the latter's knowledge of the earlier-in-time security interest was not relevant). Has *SP*–2 acted dishonestly, violated reasonable commercial standards of fair dealing, or otherwise misbehaved in any way that would warrant continued subordination of *SP*–2's security interest notwithstanding the lapse of *SP*–1's financing statement? See UCC 1–203; R9–102(a)(43).

(c) The facts are as in part (a). In March, 2007, Elsie acquired an execution lien on the collateral. How should the three competing claims be ranked? See R9–317(a)(2); R9–515(c) & Comment 3; R1–201(32); Note (4) on the Role of Knowledge in Priority Contests, infra.

Problem 7.6.4. John Brown owns, as a sole proprietor, a shoe store. Brown created a security interest in the store's inventory in favor of Lender, who filed a financing statement covering "inventory." Due to a clerical error by one of Lender's paralegals, the financing statement indicated that Brown's mailing address was "2425 Chicago Ave., Springfield IL." The correct address was "2425 Springfield Ave., Chicago, IL." Sometime thereafter, Brown approached Finco for inventory financing. Before closing the loan, Finco sought and received from the filing office information concerning all financing statements naming "Brown, John" as debtor. See R9–523(c). The filing office provided information concerning dozens of such financing statements, including the one filed by Lender. After reviewing the information provided by the filing office, Finco proceeded to close the inventory loan.

(a) Is Lender's security interest perfected? See R9–502(a).

(b) Which security interest has priority? See R9–338.

(c) Would the results in parts (a) and (b) change if Lender's financing statement had failed to provide any mailing address for the debtor? See R9–520(c), (a); R9–516(b)(5)(A); R9–502(a).

(d) Would the results in parts (a) and (b) change if Finco had requested information concerning financing statements naming "Brown, John" of 2425 Springfield Ave., Chicago, IL, as debtor? See R9–338; R9–523(c).

————

The following two cases test whether a secured party's knowledge or conduct may deprive the secured party of the benefits of the first-to-file-or-perfect rule under F9–312(5). Although the cases were decided under Former Article 9, the discussions remain relevant to the first-to-file-or-perfect rule of R9–322(a)(1).

Shallcross v. Community State Bank & Trust Co.[*]

Superior Court of New Jersey, Law Division, 1981.
180 N.J.Super. 273, 434 A.2d 671.

■ LONG, J. S. C.

This case involves a novel issue arising out of a priority dispute between two secured creditors. The facts are as follows:

Plaintiff is Lawrence Shallcross, the president of Shallcross and Pace Sheet Metal Works. In February 1977 Shallcross had a discussion with Raymond Dunphey, president of R. Dunphey Sheet Metal Works, Inc., concerning a Wysong shear owned by Shallcross and an RAS shear owned by Dunphey. According to Shallcross, Dunphey wanted to purchase plaintiff's shear but could not then afford it. It was agreed that Shallcross would deliver the Wysong shear to Dunphey, and if Dunphey paid the purchase price of $13,500 within six months, Shallcross would transfer title to him. It was also agreed that if Dunphey sold its RAS shear within the six-month period, Shallcross was to be paid at that time. Dunphey took possession of the Wysong shear on or about February 25, 1977 and the terms of the above oral agreement were set forth in a letter dated March 4, 1977.

In January 1978 Dunphey sold its RAS shear and Shallcross sought payment for the Wysong shear. In June, 1978, Shallcross and Dunphey renegotiated the price of the Wysong shear downward to $11,250 when Dunphey indicated that only $10,000 had been received for its RAS shear. Dunphey agreed to make monthly payments of $356.95. On June 29, 1978 a bill of sale, promissory note, financing statement and security agreement were signed by plaintiff and Dunphey, and on July 12, 1978 the financing statement was filed. Dunphey made three of the monthly payments and then defaulted.

In the interim, defendant Community State Bank and Trust Company (hereinafter, the bank) entered into a loan transaction and security agreement with Dunphey on June 19, 1978. The Wysong shear was listed as one of the items of collateral for the loan, and the security agreement contained an after-acquired property clause. Pursuant to this agreement the bank loaned Dunphey $50,000 on the date of the agreement and an additional $40,000 on December 15, 1978, in accordance with the provision for future advances. This security agreement was filed on June 23, 1978. Dunphey defaulted in the payment of the loan and the shear was sold by the bank to offset the debt under the terms of this security agreement. When Shallcross attempted to satisfy Dunphey's obligation to him by obtaining possession of the shear, he found that the collateral was no longer available. Shallcross has sued the bank for wrongful conversion of the shear. The bank now moves for summary judgment, claiming that there are no genuine issues of fact and that it clearly had priority in the collateral under the provisions of Article 9 of the Uniform Commercial Code, N.J.S.A. 12A:9–101 et seq.

---

* [The court's citations are to the applicable pre–1972 version of the UCC.]

Article 9 lays out the framework upon which competing security interests can be evaluated and priorities established. In this regard, N.J.S.A. 12A:9–312(5) provides in relevant part that

> In all cases not governed by other rules stated in this section (including cases of purchase money security interests which do not qualify for the special priorities set forth in subsections (3) and (4) of this section), priority between conflicting security interests in the same collateral shall be determined as follows: (a) in the order of filing if both are perfected by filing, regardless of which security interest attaches first under 12A:9–204(1) and whether it attaches before or after filing.…

Here, it is undisputed that the bank filed first in time and therefore perfected its security interest prior to Shallcross. Shallcross maintains that this provision does not establish the relative positions of the parties, for several reasons which will be discussed serially.

Shallcross must … proceed under the general priority rules of N.J.S.A. 12A:9–312(5). As has previously been noted, that statute clearly provides that the priority is to be determined by the order of filing when both security interests are perfected by filing. In order to avoid the effect of the statute, Shallcross has suggested that the bank's knowledge of his prior interest in the collateral prevents the bank from obtaining a priority. Factually, Shallcross asserts that the bank knew of his interest in the shear before it loaned Dunphey the money and accordingly took the shear as collateral subject to his interest. In support of this position, Shallcross claims that he was present in Dunphey's shop when a representative of the bank came to inspect the shop and equipment, and that he personally heard Dunphey inform the representative that he still owed Shallcross money on the shear.

Although no New Jersey court has yet to pass on this issue, a review of the statute, decisions from other jurisdictions and the Official Code Comments adopted by the New Jersey Study Commission leads to the conclusion that knowledge of a prior interest does not affect the priority provisions of the act.

First, it should be noted that there is no suggestion in the language of N.J.S.A. 12A:9–312(5) that knowledge or notice of a prior interest is a bar to the invocation of the priorities established therein. The absence of a notice provision in this section of the act is particularly significant since the drafters of the act saw fit to specifically include knowledge or notice provisions in other sections of it. One such example is N.J.S.A. 12A:9–301(1)(b), dealing with the priority between an unperfected security interest and a lien creditor.

> Except as otherwise provided in subsection (2), an unperfected security interest is subordinate to the rights of … (b) a person who becomes a lien creditor without knowledge of the security interest and before it is perfected.

[The 1972 amendments to Former Article 9 eliminated the knowledge test from F9–301(1)(b).]

Obviously, the drafters contemplated that, in certain cases, knowledge of another interest would bar the subsequent interest from obtaining priority. Had they intended that this be an element of N.J.S.A. 12A:9–312(5), they would have specifically provided so. Even in N.J.S.A. 12:9–312(3), which governs a purchase money security interest in inventory collateral, there is a notice provision. There is, however, no such provision in clause (5). Hence, it seemed clear that the failure to set forth a "knowledge" or "notice" provision in 9–312(5) was intentional and that such a provision is not to be implied. This conclusion is consistent with the weight of decisional authority. First Nat'l Bank and Trust Co. v. Atlas Credit Corp., 417 F.2d 1081 (10 Cir.1969); In re Smith, 326 F.Supp. 1311 (D.Minn.1971); National Bank of Sarasota v. Dugger, 335 So.2d 859 (Fla. App.1976); Madison Nat'l Bank v. Newrath, 261 Md. 321, 275 A.2d 495 (Ct.App.1971); Bloom v. Hilty, 427 Pa. 463, 234 A.2d 860 (Sup.Ct.1967); Noble Co. v. Mack Financial Corp., 107 R.I. 12, 264 A.2d 325 (Sup.Ct.1970).

The leading out-of-state case on the subject is *In re Smith*, supra, where the court discussed these issues at length. There, Smith purchased an automobile, and a conditional sales contract was executed by the dealer and subsequently assigned to the First National Bank of Minneapolis. No financing statement was filed. A few months later Community Credit Co. lent Smith money and Smith executed a chattel mortgage on the automobile and a financing statement was filed. Community Credit Corp. had actual knowledge of the unperfected security interest held by First National in the automobile. Id. at 1312. The court concluded that prior knowledge was irrelevant for several reasons equally applicable here. First, the court discussed the integrity of the filing system, a point raised by Professor Gilmore in his treatise, Security Interests in Personal Property, § 34.2 (1965). The court commented:

> It is desirable that perfection of interests take place promptly. It is appropriate then to provide that a secured party who fails to file runs the risk of subordination to a later but more diligent party. In this regard it should be pointed out that filing is of particular importance with respect to notice to other parties. It is agreed that where the later party has actual notice there is no need to rely upon a filing to notify him of a prior interest. The problem, however, cannot be analyzed in this narrow context. Some parties may rely on the record in extending credit and obtaining a security agreement in collateral. Although they will prevail over the unperfected prior interest in time if a dispute arises, it is entirely possible that they wanted to avoid the dispute altogether. In other words, they may not have relied in ultimately prevailing in the event of a dispute but they may have relied on the complete absence of a prior interest perfected or otherwise out of which a dispute could arise. The only way this kind of record expectation can be protected is by prompt perfection of all security interests. [326 F.Supp. at 1313–1314].

In conjunction with this, the *Smith* court also recognized the evidentiary problems created by a knowledge requirement, which is subjective and is much more difficult to establish than an objective criterion such as the date of filing. Id. at 1314. Finally, the court in *Smith* analyzed the Official Comments accompanying the Code and determined that they supported the view that knowledge is not an element for consideration in this connection.

The official comments to § 9–312 contain several examples which illustrate the resolution of priority disputes under clause (5). These examples, adopted by the New Jersey Study Commission in its comment to the section, comport with the conclusion in *Smith*. Example 2 is perhaps closest in point.

> A & B [make] non-purchase money advances against the same collateral. The collateral is in the debtor's possession and neither interest is perfected when the second advance is made. Whichever secured party first perfects his interest (by taking possession of the collateral or by filing) takes priority and *it makes no difference whether he knows of the other interests at the time he perfects his own.* [Emphasis supplied]

The language of this example is clear—it makes no difference whether the secured party knows of the other's interest at the time he perfects his own. The point of the example and the statutory scheme itself is to encourage the prompt perfection of security interests as an unequivocal method of establishing priorities with certainty and without opening the flood gates of litigation, no more or no less.

Nothing in this interpretation can be considered to controvert the good faith requirement of N.J.S.A. 12A:1–203. For this record is devoid of any evidence to show a leading on, bad faith or inequitable conduct on the part of the bank which would justify what in essence is estoppel against the assertion of a priority. This is not to say that the priorities established under N.J.S.A. 12A:9–312(5) would never be affected by a showing of bad faith. That is simply not the question presented here.

For the foregoing reasons the motion for summary judgment is hereby granted.

General Insurance Co. v. Lowry[*]

United States District Court, Southern District of Ohio, 1976. 412 F.Supp. 12.
Affirmed 570 F.2d 120 (6th Cir.1978).

■ CARL B. RUBIN, DISTRICT JUDGE.

This is an action to compel specific performance of an agreement. It was heard on June 20, 1975, for purposes of a preliminary injunction and on the merits on February 2, 1976. In accordance with Rule 65(a)(2), evidence presented at the hearing for preliminary injunction was deemed to be evidence on the merits as well and has been considered by the Court in reaching its determination. Pursuant to Rule 52 of the Federal Rules of Civil Procedure the Court does submit herewith its findings of fact and conclusions of law.

* [The court's citations are to the applicable pre–1972 version of the UCC.]

I
FINDINGS OF FACT

1.   Prior to January 14, 1972, plaintiff General Insurance Company of America issued surety bonds on which George A. Hyland, Edward F. Lowry and C. M. Dingledine were indemnitors. Pursuant to obligations credited by such bonds the plaintiff paid out various sums of money for which it sought indemnity from the named indemnitors.

2.   On January 14, 1972, a cognovit note in the sum of $564,566.79 was executed by the three named indemnitors. Twelve items of collateral security were given to secure such promissory note. For purposes of this litigation, only one such is of any significance. Item III in the list of collateral securities is stated to be "shares of common stock owned by Edward F. Lowry in Pico, Inc., an Ohio corporation." On the same date the above indemnitors executed a Memorandum Agreement (Plaintiff's Exhibit 1) which contained the following language:

> Hyland, Lowry and Dingledine each agree that he will do no act which will reduce or impair the security listed and that each will cooperate in the preparation and execution of the instruments necessary to perfect the security.

3.   Subsequently on October 12, 1972, and on July 3, 1973, other notes were executed by the indemnitors and in each instance Item III of the collateral security was a pledge of shares of common stock owned by Edward F. Lowry in Pico, Inc. (Plaintiff's Exhibits 2 and 3). At no time were the shares of stock ever delivered to the plaintiff and no further written agreement regarding such shares was ever executed by the defendant.

4.   Throughout these proceedings defendant was represented by attorney Jacob Myers, both as an individual practitioner and as President and sole shareholder in Kusworm & Myers Company, LPA. Mr. Myers attended the meeting of January 14, 1972, examined the documents signed by his client and actively represented defendant Lowry throughout the time involved in this litigation. Subsequent meetings of the parties were held in July, 1972, September, 1972, and May, 1973. Mr. Myers attended the meetings of September 27, 1972, and May 8, 1973, but did not attend the meeting in July of 1972. Other than a letter in January of 1972 from counsel for plaintiff to Mr. Myers requesting delivery of the shares of stock, no other written demand for such shares was ever made by plaintiff's counsel.

5.   On January 8, 1974, Edward Lowry executed a promissory note to Kusworm & Myers Company, LPA, in the sum of $12,555.65 (Joint Exhibit I). To secure such note defendant Lowry likewise signed an agreement pledging 19 shares of stock in Pico Development Company, Inc. to Kusworm & Myers Company, LPA, (Joint Exhibit IV) and endorsed at the appropriate place Certificate No. 4 of Pico Development Company (Joint Exhibit II). The stock was subsequently transferred on the books of such company to the name of Kusworm & Myers Company, LPA, and Jacob

Myers individually had knowledge of the agreements that had been signed, the reference to the stock in Pico Development Company and the fact that such shares had not been transmitted to plaintiff. The note signed by Edward Lowry to Kusworm & Myers Company, LPA, was given for valuable consideration, to-wit: attorney fees rendered and to be rendered by both Kusworm & Myers Company, LPA, and Jacob Myers.

6. Pursuant to preliminary injunction issued by this Court on June 26, 1975, physical possession of 19 shares of Pico Development Company still remain with Jacob A. Myers, conditioned upon an injunction against sale, assignment, transfer, hypothecation or other disposition without prior approval of this Court.

OPINION

Were it not for the unusual circumstances surrounding this case, its resolution would be a simple matter. The Memorandum of Agreement and the list of collateral which it incorporates by reference from the note fulfill the requirements of a binding security agreement.... General Insurance Company gave value for this security interest. Lowry had rights in the stock and accordingly the security interest did attach under [F9–204]. But since this was a security interest in an instrument as defined in [F9–105], and General Insurance never took possession of the Pico stock, the security interest was never perfected under [F9–304].

By taking possession of Lowry's stock pursuant to its 1974 pledge agreement, Kusworm & Myers, LPA, did perfect their security interest. Under [F9–312] defendants' rights in the stock prevail over the plaintiff's unperfected security interest, even though they had knowledge of the plaintiff's interest. In re Smith, 326 F.Supp. 1311 (D.Minn.1971).

If the integrity of the concept of "good faith" is to be maintained, we do not believe that such a result can be tolerated. Defendant Myers is not merely a disinterested creditor who attempted to protect his commercial interests. He is the [defendant's] attorney and he and his client as witness and obligor respectively signed the memorandum of agreement. Under the circumstances herein, when the parties signed that agreement and executed the note, the plaintiff obtained an equitable lien against the 19 shares of Pico stock superior in priority to the later perfected security interest held by Kusworm & Myers, LPA.

Although courts should hesitate to invoke equity powers to disturb the operation of a statute, nothing in the Uniform Commercial Code precludes the imposition of an equitable lien in narrowly-circumscribed situations. Aetna Casualty & Surety Co. v. Brunken & Son, Inc., 357 F.Supp. 290 (D.S.D.1973); Warren Tool Company v. Stephenson, 11 Mich.App. 274, 161 N.W.2d 133 (1968); see [UCC 1–103].

All of the prerequisites to the establishment of an equitable lien by plaintiff are present here: all of the parties intended that the Pico stock then in Lowry's possession be given to the plaintiff as security for the debt; an instrument was signed by the parties memorializing this intent; and the present holder of the stock, Mr. Myers, had knowledge of the agreement. The defendants may not use their own dereliction in failing to turn over the stock to the plaintiffs as a defense of their actions.

Faced with facts similar to the instant case, the Supreme Court of Ohio imposed an equitable lien on stock which a defendant failed to deliver according to its agreement with the plaintiff stating that:

> *What good conscience requires, equity should require*, and while we are able to find no adjudicated case upon parallel facts, we are persuaded from the nature of the transaction, the relations and rights of the parties, good conscience and sound morals among men in every-day business, that Klaustermeyer should have his lien for his loan. (emphasis added)

Klaustermeyer v. Cleveland Trust Company, 89 Ohio St. 142, 105 N.E. 278 (1913).

The Court finds this reasoning sound and adopts it *in toto*.

CONCLUSIONS OF LAW

A.   This Court has jurisdiction in accordance with 28 U.S.C. § 1332.

B.   Where defendant Edward F. Lowry as first party for consideration agrees to secure a bond issued by plaintiff General Insurance Company of America as second party with collateral security and agrees further not to impair such security, he creates an equitable lien on such collateral in favor of such second party.

C.   The Uniform Commercial Code does not preclude the imposition of an equitable lien under appropriate circumstances.

D.   Defendants Jacob A. Myers and Kusworm & Myers, LPA, as third party with full knowledge of the agreements referred to in Conclusion of Law B and occupying an attorney-client relationship to first party may not under the circumstances of this case obtain by pledge under the U.C.C. a security interest superior to the equitable lien of second party General Insurance Company of America.

E.   The prayer of the amended complaint should be and is hereby GRANTED. Defendant Edward F. Lowry is hereby ordered to pledge the shares of Pico, Inc., referred to herein to Plaintiff. Defendant Jacob A. Myers and Kusworm & Myers, LPA, are hereby directed to endorse, transfer and deliver to plaintiff the shares of Pico, Inc.

Costs to be assessed against defendants.

Let Judgment Issue in Accordance With the Foregoing.

[The opinion of the United States Court of Appeals, affirming the District Court, included the following]:

■ PHILLIPS, CHIEF JUDGE.

The issue in this diversity suit is whether the priority provision of the Ohio Uniform Commercial Code, Ohio Rev.Code Ann. § 1309.31 [F9–312], precludes the imposition of an equitable lien under the unusual facts of the present case. In comprehensive findings of fact and conclusions of law, District Judge Carl B. Rubin allowed an equitable lien under the "narrowly-circumscribed" situation here presented. General Insurance Company of America v. Lowry, 412 F.Supp. 12 (S.D.Ohio 1976). Reference is made to the reported decision of the district court for a detailed recitation of pertinent facts.

In diversity cases, federal courts must apply the law of the State as pronounced by its highest court. See Erie R. R. v. Tompkins, 304 U.S. 64, 58 S.Ct. 817, 82 L.Ed. 1188 (1938). We conclude that because of the peculiar circumstances involved in this case, the Supreme Court of Ohio would uphold the imposition of an equitable lien notwithstanding the priority provisions of [F9–312]. We reach this conclusion based upon two considerations.

First, § 1301.09 (UCC 1–203) provides: "Every contract or duty within [Chapter 1309] of the Revised Code, imposes an obligation of good faith in its performance of enforcement." Section 1301.01(S) defines good faith as "honesty in fact in the conduct or transaction concerned." See In re Samuels & Co., 526 F.2d 1238, 1243–44 (5th Cir.1976) (en banc), cert. denied, Stowers v. Mahon, 429 U.S. 834, 97 S.Ct. 98, 50 L.Ed.2d 99 (1976). In Thompson v. United States, 408 F.2d 1075, 1084 (8th Cir.1969), the Eighth Circuit held that the good faith provision of the UCC "permits the consideration of the lack of good faith . . . to alter priorities which otherwise would be determined under Article 9."

The district court emphasized that this case involves the attorney for one of the parties, not a disinterested creditor attempting to protect his commercial interests. We agree with the district court that the record discloses facts which do not meet the good faith standards of the Uniform Commercial Code.

Second, an equitable lien was created by appellants in favor of appellee. In 1913, the Supreme Court of Ohio dealt with facts strikingly similar to the present suit. In Klaustermeyer v. The Cleveland Trust Co., 89 Ohio St. 142, 105 N.E. 278 (1913), each member of the Board of Directors of Euclid Avenue Trust Company loaned $5,000 to the company when the trust company began having financial difficulties. Stock owned by the company was to be delivered to the directors as security for each member of the Board of Directors of Euclid Avenue Trust for the benefit of creditors to the Cleveland Trust Company before the stock was delivered to Klaustermeyer, one of the board members. The Supreme Court of Ohio held that Klaustermeyer had an "equitable lien on the securities in the possession of the Euclid Avenue Trust Company, which were assigned and transferred to The Cleveland Trust Company. . . ." 89 Ohio St. at 144, 105 N.E. at 279. In holding that the trust company had a duty to deliver the securities to Klaustermeyer, the court said:

> In modern times the doctrine of equitable liens has been liberally extended for the purpose of facilitating mercantile transactions, and in order that the intention of the parties to create specific charges may be

justly and effectually carried out. Bispham's Principles of Equity (8 ed.), Section 351.

What good conscience requires, equity should require, and while we are able to find no adjudicated case upon parallel facts, we are persuaded from the nature of the transaction, the relations and the rights of the parties, good conscience and sound morals among men in everyday business, that Klaustermeyer should have his lien for his loan. 89 Ohio St. at 153, 105 N.E. at 282.

We disagree with appellants' argument that the enactment of the Uniform Commercial Code overruled *Klaustermeyer* and eliminated equitable liens in all situations. Section 1301.03 (UCC 1–103) states in pertinent part: "Unless displaced by the particular provisions of [Chapter 1309] of the Revised Code, the principles of law *and equity* ... shall supplement its provisions." (emphasis added).

Discussing the doctrine of equitable liens and citing *Klaustermeyer*, the Ohio Court of Appeals held in Syring v. Sartorious, 28 Ohio App.2d 308, 309–10, 277 N.E.2d 457, 458 (1971):

The doctrine may be stated in its most general form that every express executory agreement in writing whereby a contracting party sufficiently indicates an intention to make some particular property, real *or personal*, or fund, therein described or identified, *a security for a debt* or other obligation, or whereby the party promises to convey, assign, or transfer the property as security, creates an equitable lien upon the property so indicated, which is enforceable against the property in the hands not only of the original contractor, but of his purchasers or encumbrancers with notice. Under like circumstances, a merely verbal agreement may create a similar lien upon personal property. The doctrine itself is clearly an application of the maxim "equity regards as done that which ought to be done." Cf. Klaustermeyer v. Cleveland Trust Co., 89 Ohio St. 142, 105 N.E. 278. (emphasis added).

This court has recognized the continuing validity of *Klaustermeyer*. See In re Easy Living, Inc., 407 F.2d 142, 145 (6th Cir.1969). See also In re Troy, 490 F.2d 1061, 1065 (6th Cir.1974).

Construing Texas law, the Fifth Circuit implicitly found that the existence of an equitable lien does not conflict with Article Nine of the UCC. See Citizens Co–Op Gin v. United States, 427 F.2d 692, 695–96 (5th Cir.1970). Other Circuits construing various state laws have recognized the doctrine of equitable liens. See Casper v. Neubert, 489 F.2d 543, 547 (10th Cir.1973); Arkwright Mutual Insurance Co. v. Bargain City, U.S.A., Inc., 373 F.2d 701 (3d Cir.1967); Cherno v. Dutch American Mercantile Corp., 353 F.2d 147, 151–53 (2d Cir.1965). But cf. Shelton v. Erwin, 472 F.2d 1118 (8th Cir.1973).

We, therefore, are convinced that the Ohio Supreme Court, if it were deciding this case, would follow its earlier opinion in *Klaustermeyer* holding that General Insurance Company is entitled to an equitable lien on the Pico stock in possession of appellant Myers.

Affirmed.

NOTES ON THE ROLE OF KNOWLEDGE IN PRIORITY CONTESTS

(1) The "Pure Race" Priority Rule of R9–322(a)(1). In holding that knowledge of an earlier, unperfected security interest is irrelevant to a priority contest governed by the first-to-file-or-perfect rule of F9–312(5)(a), the *Shallcross* case is in accord with the majority of reported decisions that have considered the issue. The commentary also generally supports that reading of the statute. Like the first-to-file-or-perfect rule of F9–312(5)(a), the first-to-file-or-perfection rule of R9–322(a)(1) is silent concerning the effect, if any, of knowledge; however, the Examples in Comment 4 to R9–322 suggest that knowledge is irrelevant to a priority contest governed by R9–322(a). A recording system (such as R9–322(a)(1)) that awards priority to the first party to file irrespective of that party's knowledge of an unfiled, earlier-in-time interest is called a "pure race" system. The priority rule of R9–317(a)(2), which affords priority to a person who becomes a lien creditor before a competing security interest is perfected and before a financing statement is filed, whether or not the lien creditor knows of the security interest, is another "pure race" rule.

(2) "Notice" and "Race–Notice" Priority Systems. Some of Article 9's priority rules are not "pure race" rules, but are more accurately described as "notice," or perhaps "race-notice," rules. In a "notice" system, a subsequent purchaser who takes with notice of an earlier-in-time claim is subordinated to that claim even if the earlier-in-time claimant has failed to give any public notice, such as by filing. As we have seen, R9–337(1) affords priority to certain buyers of goods covered by a certificate of title only if they act "without knowledge of the security interest." See Section 4(B), supra. In a similar vein, R9–317(b), (c), and (d) give certain non-secured party transferees priority over an unperfected security interest only if the transferees do not have "knowledge of the security interest" at the specified relevant time. See Section 6(B)(II), infra.

In a "race-notice" system, a subsequent claimant becomes senior to an earlier, unperfected security interest only if the subsequent party takes its interest without notice (or knowledge) of the earlier interest and *also* is the first to perfect its interest. Revised Article 9 has eliminated the "race-notice" rule contained in Former Article 9; however, if one conceptualizes the "delivery" requirement in R9–317(b) and (c) as a form of compliance with a "public notice" requirement, then those provisions arguably fall within the "race-notice" category.

(3) Non–temporal Priority Systems. As we shall see, a number of the priority rules in Revised Article 9 are non-temporal, i.e., they afford priority without regard to when a security interest was perfected. Most of these rules relate to specialized collateral, such as deposit accounts and investment property, and are discussed in Chapter 9, infra. Non-temporal priority of security interests in goods is discussed in Section 6(A)(II), infra.

(4) Circular Priority. Peculiar priority problems may arise when more than two creditors claim an interest in particular collateral. Assume, for example, that under the applicable priority rules, *C*–1 takes priority over *C*–2 and *C*–2 takes priority over *C*–3. One might be tempted to jump to the conclusion that *C*–1 takes priority over *C*–3. One ought not yield to this temptation. The transitive law of mathematics (i.e., if $A > B$ and $B > C$, then $A > C$) does not necessarily apply to priority rules. It is possible that *C*–1 prevails over *C*–2, *C*–2 prevails over *C*–3, and *C*–3 prevails over *C*–1! This unhappy state of affairs is called a "circular priority."

Circular priorities can arise under Revised Article 9. Consider, for example, the facts of Problem 7.6.3(c), supra. *SP*–2's security interest is senior to *SP*–1's because the effectiveness of *SP*–1's financing statement lapsed. See R9–515(c). *SP*–1's security interest was perfected before Elsie became a lien creditor, and so is senior to Elsie's execution lien. R9–317(a)(2). (R9–515(c) is of no assistance to Elsie, who is not a "purchaser." See R1–201(32); Chapter 1, Section 3(B), supra.) However, Elsie's lien is senior to *SP*–2's security interest under R9–317(a)(2). *SP*–2 beats *SP*–1, *SP*–1 beats Elsie, and Elsie beats *SP*–2 (who beats *SP*–1, who beats Elsie, who beats *SP*–2 . . .).

"Race-notice" and "notice" systems are particularly likely to generate circular priorities because they can enable a later claimant to take priority over some, but not all, earlier claims. R9–338 presents a similar possibility. Suppose, for example, that in the setting of Problem 7.6.4, supra, Bank took and perfected a security interest after Lender filed but before Finco. If Bank did not reasonably rely on the incorrect information in Lender's financing statement, then Lender would be senior to Bank under the first-to-file-or-perfect rule. See R9–322(a)(1). Likewise, Bank would be senior to Finco. See id. However, Finco would be senior to Lender if Finco reasonably relied on the incorrect mailing address in Lender's financing statement. See R9–338. Lender beats Bank, Bank beats Finco, and Finco beats Lender.

Although Article 9 creates circular priority puzzles, it provides no solution for them. In the absence of a controlling statutory rule, how should a court determine the priority? Possibilities might include allocating the value of the collateral pro rata and subordinating the party (or parties) that the court deems least deserving (because of carelessness or some other reason that the court finds compelling).

(5) Certainty, Good Faith, and Extra–UCC Principles. A few commentators have called for tempering the "pure race" rule of F9–312(5)(a) with some sort of knowledge qualification. See Felsenfeld, Knowledge as a Factor in Determining Priorities Under the Uniform Commercial Code, 42 N.Y.U.L.Rev. 246 (1967); Nickles, Rethinking Some U.C.C. Article 9 Problems, 34 Ark. L. Rev. 1, 72–103 (1980). Professors Baird and Jackson, on the other hand, have defended the "pure race" rule. Baird &

Jackson, Information, Uncertainty, and the Transfer of Property, 13 J. Legal Stud. 299 (1984).

Baird and Jackson argue that judicial inquiries into the question of knowledge would be costly and would cause delay. Among the costs of "notice" systems are the costs of determining whether and when a person acquired knowledge of a competing claim and the uncertainty costs arising from the possibility that a court would make an erroneous determination. Baird and Jackson also argue that knowledge of an earlier-in-time interest is not equivalent to bad faith. In their view, parties should not be penalized for obtaining knowledge; acquiring knowledge should be encouraged. They point out that "notice" systems do not provide any incentive for a knowledgeable second-in-time party to cause the public records to be corrected so as to reflect the earlier, unfiled security interest.

By way of contrast, Professor Carlson's study offers the harshest critique of the "pure race" rule. Carlson, Rationality, Accident, and Priority Under Article 9 of the Uniform Commercial Code, 71 Minn.L.Rev. 207 (1986). To Carlson, a knowledgeable second-in-time party who achieves seniority under F9–312(5)(a)'s first-to-file-or-perfect rule is much like a thief. Carlson explains that cost-benefit analyses such as those of Baird and Jackson fail to consider all of the pertinent costs, including the costs to the parties who are subordinated and the social costs of a rule that is inconsistent with well-accepted morality. Moreover, his analysis of the drafting history suggests that the drafters of F9–312(5) may not have intended to create a strict "pure race" rule!

Interestingly, Carlson stops short of proposing a modification of what generally has been construed to be a "pure race" statutory scheme. Instead, he seems satisfied that courts can import, through UCC 1–103, extra-UCC doctrine that is sufficient to deprive the truly bad-faith actors of the fruits of their wrongful actions. The *Lowry* case is an example.

One hopes that the case-by-case application of extra-UCC doctrines to a "pure race" reading of F9–312(5) and R9–322(a)(1) will result in a just, workable, and sufficiently predictable system of priorities. To a considerable extent, the success of the system depends on the ability of judges to override the first-to-file-or-perfect rule judiciously, i.e., only in appropriate cases and only with appropriate techniques. In the *Lowry* case, the court resorted to the doctrine of "equitable lien" to justify subordinating the perfected security interest of Kusworm & Myers's. That doctrine carries with it a considerable amount of baggage, including a set of priority rules that may have been appropriate for the case at bar but inappropriate in another Article 9 case. (See the excerpt from Syring v. Sartorious quoted in the opinion of the Sixth Circuit.) Rather than giving the unperfected secured party an additional property right (an "equitable lien") that took priority over Kusworm & Myers's perfected security interest, could the court have reached the same result by applying the good faith requirement of UCC 1–203 to subordinate Kusworm & Myers's perfected security interest? Would that approach have created fewer potential problems?

As Baird and Jackson point out, acting with knowledge that an earlier-in-time interest exists is not *necessarily* equivalent to bad faith. Indeed, what Carlson condemns is acting with the knowledge that achieving seniority over that interest is *wrongful* as to the earlier-in-time claimant. The knowledgeable second-in-time secured party may be exposed to liability for tortious interference with the contractual relations between the earlier-in-time secured party and the common debtor. See First Wyoming Bank v. Mudge, 748 P.2d 713 (Wyo.1988) (imposing liability for tortious interference on bank that took security interest with knowledge that transaction caused debtor to violate a covenant in agreement between debtor and another creditor). Well-drafted credit agreements typically contain provisions requiring debtors to maintain the perfection and priority of security interests and prohibiting debtors from giving senior interests (and often *any* competing interests) to other parties. For an example, see ¶ 11(d), Form 7.2, supra. In most cases, then, one might argue that knowledge of the earlier, unperfected interest is essentially equivalent to knowledge that subordination of the earlier party's interest is wrongful. Does this argument give knowledge too great a role to play in rearranging the "pure race" priorities of R9–322(a)(1)?

We will return to these issues again when we consider the special priority rules applicable to chattel paper and instruments. See Chapter 9, Section 2, infra. These rules regulate priority in part on the basis of whether a purchaser acts "without knowledge that the purchase violates the rights of the secured party." See R9–330(b), (d).

(II) PURCHASE–MONEY SECURITY INTERESTS

Problem 7.6.5. On June 1 *D*, a construction company, obtained a $100,000 loan from *SP*–1, and executed in favor of *SP*–1 a security agreement covering "all construction equipment now owned or hereafter acquired" by *D*. *D* owned construction equipment such as bulldozers, cranes and trucks. *SP*–1 immediately filed a financing statement covering "construction equipment."

(a) On July 1 *D* bought a new Cletrac bulldozer from the manufacturer, *M*, and paid *M* the price of $100,000. On July 2 *D* obtained a $90,000 loan from *SP*–2, and executed to *SP*–2 a security agreement covering the new bulldozer. *SP*–2 promptly filed a financing statement covering the Cletrac bulldozer (bulldozers are not subject to the relevant certificate-of-title act). *D* defaulted on the loans to *SP*–1 and *SP*–2. Who has priority as to the new bulldozer? See R9–322(a)(1); R9–324(a); R9–103(a), (b).

(b) Suppose that *D* on July 1 had told *SP*–2 of the need for a loan to buy the new bulldozer from *M*. *SP*–2 then made a loan to *D* in the form of a $90,000 check payable jointly to *D* and *M*; *D* then endorsed the check to *M* and paid *M* the remaining $10,000 of the price. On July 2 *M* delivered the bulldozer to *D*. *SP*–2 filed on July 8. Who has priority as to the new bulldozer? See R9–324(a); R9–103(a), (b). What, if anything, could the losing party have done to avoid the result?

(c) What policy considerations underlie the legal rules that decide parts (a) and (b)? See R9–324, Comment 4; Note (2) on Purchase–money Priority and the Definition of "Purchase–money Security Interest," infra.

(d) Would the results in parts (a) and (b) change if the security agreement in favor of *SP*–1 contained the following provision?

> Debtor shall not create or suffer to exist any security interest (including any purchase-money security interest) in any collateral that is, at any time, covered by this agreement, and any such prohibited security interest that Debtor may attempt to create shall be null and void.

See R9–401.

Problem 7.6.6. The facts are as in part (b) of the preceding Problem. In August, SP–2 made an additional $25,000 loan to D. The loan agreement, signed by D, provided that the new loan was secured by the Cletrac bulldozer. Is SP–1's security interest in the bulldozer senior to SP–2's? If so, to what extent? See R9–103(b), (f); Note (4) on Purchase–money Priority and the Definition of "Purchase–money Security Interest," infra.

Problem 7.6.7. The facts are as in Problem 7.6.5(b). By August, *D* was having difficulty making the monthly payments on the loan from *SP*–2. *SP*–2 agreed to extend a new loan to *D* to be secured by the Cletrac bulldozer. The new loan was in the amount of $70,000, which was sufficient to pay off the remaining balance of the original $90,000 loan and give *D* an additional $10,000. By the end of November, *D* had reduced the loan balance to $65,000. Is *SP*–1's security interest in the new bulldozer senior to *SP*–2's? If so, to what extent? See R9–103(b), (f), (e); Note (4) on Purchase–money Priority and the Definition of "Purchase–money Security Interest," infra.

Problem 7.6.8. The facts are as in Problem 7.6.5(b). By August, *D* was having difficulty making the monthly payments on the loan from *SP*–2. *SP*–3 agreed to extend a new loan in the amount of $70,000 to *D*, to be secured by the Cletrac bulldozer. The loan was for the purpose of paying off the balance of the original $90,000 loan from *SP*–2 and affording *D* some additional working capital. After using the loan proceeds to pay off the loan from *SP*–2, $10,000 remained for *D*'s use. By the end of November, *D* had reduced the loan balance to $65,000.

(a) Is *SP*–3's security interest in the new bulldozer senior to *SP*–1's? If so, to what extent?

(b) Would the result in part (a) differ if *SP*–2 had assigned to *SP*–3 *SP*–2's loan balance and security interest?

(c) Would the result in part (a) differ if *SP*–3 had paid $60,000 of the loan proceeds directly to *SP*–2?

(d) Would the result in part (a) differ if *SP*–3 had made a working capital loan to *D* and *D* used the loan proceeds to pay off the loan from *SP*–2?

Problem 7.6.9. *D*, a wholesaler, sells textiles to retail stores from substantial stocks of textiles maintained in *D*'s warehouse.

On June 1 D obtained a $100,000 loan from SP–1 and executed a security agreement granting a security interest to SP–1 in all the textiles that D then owned or might thereafter acquire. SP–1 immediately filed a financing statement covering "textiles."

Late in June D needed to purchase $20,000 worth of additional textiles from the manufacturer, M. M would not sell to D on credit. D lacked the necessary cash and SP–1 refused to enlarge the existing $100,000 loan.

Because of these difficulties, on July 1 D applied to SP–2 for a loan to pay M for the textiles. SP–2 agreed and made out a check for $20,000 payable jointly to D and M; D endorsed the check to M. On July 2 SP–2 filed a financing statement. On July 5 M delivered the textiles to D, who placed them in the warehouse.

Shortly after the $20,000 shipment of textiles arrived, D defaulted on the loans to SP–1 and SP–2. Whose security interest is senior as to this shipment of textiles? See R9–322(a)(1); R9–324(b), (c); R9–103(a), (b). What, if anything, could the losing party have done to improve its position?

Problem 7.6.10. D is a wholesale distributor of toys. On June 1 D obtained a $100,000 loan from SP–1 and signed a security agreement covering "all inventory now owned or hereafter acquired." On June 2 SP–1 properly filed a financing statement.

On July 1 D signed a security agreement in favor of SP–2, a toy marble manufacturer, covering "all marbles that SP–2 sells to Customer from time to time" and securing "the purchase price of marbles sold from time to time by SP–2 to Customer." That same day SP–2 properly filed a financing statement and sent a notice to SP–1 in compliance with the requirements of R9–324(b).

On July 15, at D's request, SP–2 shipped 100,000 marbles to D in 1,000 bags containing 100 marbles each, and sent D an invoice for $1,000 (a unit price of 1 cent per marble). On July 30 SP–2 filled another order from D by shipping another 100,000 marbles, packaged in 100 boxes of 1,000 marbles each. SP–2 then sent to D an invoice for another $1,000.

After making three payments in the aggregate amount of $700, D failed to make further payments to SP–2. It is now September 1 and D is in possession of 350 bags of marbles from the first order and 25 boxes of marbles from the second order—the other marbles having been sold.

Is SP–2's perfected security interest in the marbles senior to the security interest of SP–1? If so, to what extent? Do you need additional facts to determine the priority issue? See R9–103(b) & Comment 4; R9–324(b), (c); Southtrust Bank of Alabama, National Association v. Borg–Warner Acceptance Corp., infra; Note (4) on Purchase–money Priority and the Definition of "Purchase–money Security Interest," infra.

Problem 7.6.11. You represent Bigstore Co., which owns and operates a national chain of appliance stores. Bigstore frequently sells appliances to its customers (mainly for personal and household use) on the basis of installment sale agreements that grant a security interest to Bigstore to secure the price. (For an example of such an agreement in another setting, see the Instalment Sale Contract, Form 7.6, supra.) Bigstore never files financing statements against its customers. Often a single customer will enter into multiple installment sale agreements at different times in connection with different sales transactions. The manager of Bigstore's credit department consults you about a proposed modification of its standard form of installment sale agreement. The manager would like the agreement to provide that the collateral it covers will secure all indebtedness of the customer to Bigstore, including any debt owed in connection with the customer's *other* installment sales agreements. The manager believes that the modified version will be especially useful for Bigstore in connection with customers who fall behind on their payments and request an extension or "refinancing" of their obligations under multiple agreements.

Bigstore's general counsel has heard that Revised Article 9 is much more friendly to purchase-money financings than was Former Article 9. In particular, the general counsel has asked you for advice about (i) the agreements and procedures necessary to implement the proposed modification and (ii) the procedures for consolidating multiple agreements of a customer into a single refinancing arrangement. What advice do you give the general counsel? See R9–103(a), (b), (e)–(h) & Comments 7 & 8; Notes (4) and (6) on Purchase–money Priority and the Definition of "Purchase–money Security Interest," infra.

The following case discusses the concept of purchase-money security interest in a commercial setting. How would it be decided under R9–103?

Southtrust Bank v. Borg–Warner Acceptance Corp.[*]

United States Court of Appeals, Eleventh Circuit, 1985.
760 F.2d 1240.

■ TUTTLE, SENIOR CIRCUIT JUDGE:

Borg–Warner Acceptance Corporation ("BWAC") appeals from a decision of the district court denying its motion for summary judgment and granting summary judgment to Southtrust Bank ("the Bank") in a diversity suit. The Bank filed a declaratory judgment action to ascertain which of the parties has priority in the inventory of four debtors, Molay Brothers Supply Company, Inc., Gulf City Distributors, Inc., Standard Wholesale Supply Company and Crest Refrigeration, Inc. These debtors, which are no longer in existence, defaulted on obligations they owed to one or the other party.

* [The court's citations are to the pre–1972 version of Alabama's UCC and to the 1972 version of Georgia's UCC.]

Both the Bank and BWAC have perfected security interests in the inventory of the debtors. In each case, the Bank filed its financing statement first. BWAC contends that as a purchase money lender it falls within the purchase money security interest exception to the first to file rule and therefore is entitled to possession of the inventory.[2] The Uniform Commercial Code (UCC) as adopted in both Alabama and Georgia, provides in pertinent part:

A security interest is a "purchase money security interest" to the extent that it is:

(a) Taken or retained by the seller of the collateral to secure all or part of its price; or

(b) Taken by a person who by making advances or incurring an obligation gives value to enable the debtor to acquire rights in or the use of collateral if such value is in fact so used.

Ala.Code § 7–9–107 (1975); O.C.G.A. § 11–9–107 (1981).

BWAC engages in purchase money financing. Here, BWAC purchased invoices from vendors who supplied inventory items to the debtors in question. The security agreements between BWAC and each of the debtors contained the following provision:

In order to secure repayment to Secured Party of all such extensions of credit made by Secured Party in accordance with this Agreement, and to secure payment of all other debts or liabilities and performance of all obligations of Debtor to Secured Party, whether now existing or hereafter arising, Debtor agrees that Secured Party shall have and hereby grants to Secured Party a security interest in all Inventory of Debtor, whether now owned or hereafter acquired, and all Proceeds and products thereof.

The term "Inventory" was defined as "all inventory, of whatever kind or nature, wherever located, now owned or hereafter acquired ... when such inventory has been financed by Borg–Warner Acceptance Corporation."

BWAC and the debtors employed a scheduled liquidation arrangement to reduce the debt owed BWAC. Under this arrangement a debtor was permitted to pay a percentage of the invoice each month, without regard to whether the item was actually sold. If an unpaid item was sold, then the remaining inventory served as collateral to secure the unpaid balance.

The key issue for decision by this Court is whether inclusion of an after-acquired property clause and a future advances clause in BWAC's security agreements converted its purchase money security interest (PMSI) into an ordinary security interest.

The district court held that inclusion of after-acquired property and future advances clauses ("the clauses") in the security agreement convert-

---

2. A purchase money security interest in inventory has priority over a conflicting security interest in the same inventory. Ala. Code § 7–9–312(3) (1975); O.C.G.A. § 11–9–312(3) (1981).

ed BWAC's PMSI into an ordinary security interest. The court relied on In re Manuel, 507 F.2d 990 (5th Cir.1975) (holding, in a consumer bankruptcy context, that PMSI must be limited to the item purchased at time of the agreement and cannot exceed the price of that item); In re Norrell, 426 F.Supp. 435 (M.D.Ga.1977) (same); and In re Simpson, 4 U.C.C.Rep.Serv. 243 (W.D.Mich.1966) (inclusion of future advances clause in security agreement for farm equipment destroys PMSI).

BWAC argues that the cases relied on by the court are distinguishable. First, BWAC notes that almost all the cases following the "transformation" rule (i.e., inclusion of the clauses transforms a PMSI into an ordinary security interest) are consumer bankruptcy cases. It argues that the rationale of those cases, which is to protect the consumer, does not apply in commercial cases such as the case at bar. See In re Mid–Atlantic Flange, 26 U.C.C.Rep.Serv. 203, 208 (E.D.Pa.1979). BWAC argues that the policy considerations in a commercial setting, promoting commercial certainty and encouraging credit extension, do not support the application of the transformation rule. According to BWAC, applying the transformation rule to inventory financiers would require them to police inventory constantly and to see that inventory corresponds on an item-by-item basis with debt.

The Bank argues that the transformation rule is not a product of special bankruptcy considerations, and that if the drafters had intended to limit the rule to consumer transactions, they would have said so, as they did in other sections of the Code. The Bank contends that a holding that inclusion of the clauses destroys a PMSI would not have a serious negative effect on inventory financiers. It points out that such financiers could retain priority by obtaining a subordination agreement from the first-to-file creditor.

We see no reason to limit the holding of In re Manuel to consumer bankruptcy cases. In that case, the Fifth Circuit stated:

> A plain reading of the statutory requirements would indicate that they require the purchase money security interest to be in the item purchased, and that, as the judges below noted, the purchase money security interest cannot exceed the price of what is purchased in the transaction wherein the security interest is created....

Id. at 993. Nothing in the language of U.C.C. § 9–312(3) or § 9–107 distinguishes between consumer and commercial transactions or between bankruptcy and nonbankruptcy contexts. We see no policy reasons for creating a distinction where the drafters have not done so.

Second, BWAC contends that the cases supporting the transformation rule involve situations in which the clauses were actually exercised, e.g., Manuel (agreement covered preexisting debt); Simpson (future advances actually made). BWAC argues that mere inclusion of the clauses does not void a PMSI. In re Griffin, 9 B.R. 880 (Bankr.N.D.Ga.1981) (when creditor is seller, mere existence of unexercised future advances clause does not destroy PMSI); Mid Atlantic Flange (same). We need not reach the issue of whether mere inclusion of unexercised future advances and after-acquired property clauses voids a PMSI because we find that BWAC exercised the clauses here. After entering the security agreements with the debtors, BWAC regularly purchased inventory for the debtors and now claims that the debtors' BWAC-financed inventory secures these purchases. This is an exercise of the future advances clause. Similarly, BWAC claims as collateral not only the inventory purchased at the time the security agreements were entered, but all BWAC-financed inventory. This is an exercise of the after-acquired property clause. We hold, therefore, that BWAC's exercise of the future advances and after-acquired property clauses in its security agreements with the debtors destroyed its PMSI.

We note, as did the district court, that BWAC retains a security interest in the goods. It merely loses its priority status as a purchase money secured lender. The concept of the floating lien under the U.C.C. remains intact. We hold, merely, that such a floating lien is inconsistent with a PMSI. A PMSI requires a one-to-one relationship between the debt and the collateral.

BWAC's final argument is that the court should adopt a "to the extent" rule, based on the literal language of UCC, § 9–107:

> A security interest is a "purchase money security interest" *to the extent* that it is ... (b) Taken by a person who by making advances or incurring an obligation gives value to enable the debtor to acquire rights in or the use of collateral if such value is in fact so used. (emphasis added.)

Some courts have held that the clauses, even if exercised, do not invalidate a PMSI if there is some method for determining the extent of the PMSI. For example, in re Staley, 426 F.Supp. 437 (M.D.Ga.1977), the court held that the PMSI was valid because the security agreement specified that payments be allocated first to items bought first. Thus, it was easy for the court to ascertain which items had been fully paid for and hence no longer served as collateral. Here, however, nothing in the contract or in state law allocates payments to particular items of inventory. BWAC, in fact, claims all BWAC-financed inventory as its collateral without regard to payments made by the debtors. We agree with the court in In re Coomer, 8 B.R. 351, 355 (Bankr.E.D.Tenn.1980), that

> Without some guidelines, legislative or contractual, the court should not be required to distill from a mass of transactions the extent to which a security interest is purchase money.

Unless a lender contractually provides some method for determining the extent to which each item of collateral secures its purchase money, it effectively gives up its purchase money status.

Because we hold that BWAC's exercise of the after-acquired property and future advances clauses in its security agreements voided its PMSI, we need not reach the other issues raised by the Bank. We also do not reach the issue raised by BWAC concerning the district court's reference to proceeds from sales of the inventory being held "in trust." Whether the proceeds are held "in trust" is relevant only to the issue of damages. The district court entered final judgment only on the claim for declaratory relief and referred the damage claim to a magistrate. Because no final judgment has been entered as to damages, that issue is not properly before this Court.

AFFIRMED.

NOTES ON PURCHASE–MONEY PRIORITY AND THE DEFINITION OF "PURCHASE–MONEY SECURITY INTEREST"

(1) Contexts in Which the Distinction Between "Purchase-money Security Interests" and Non–purchase–money Security Interests Is Relevant. Whether a security interest meets the definition of "purchase–money security interest" ("PMSI") in R9–103 is important in several contexts. We saw above in Section 3(A), that a PMSI perfected by filing "before or within 20 days after the debtor receives delivery of the collateral" receives priority over the interests of lien creditors which arise "between the time the security interest attaches and the time of filing." UCC 9–317(e). Observe also that R9–317(e) also subordinates to a PMSI the interests of buyers and lessees whose interests arise during the "gap" between attachment and filing. We also saw that PMSI's in most consumer goods are "automatically" perfected without filing or possession by the secured party. See R9–309(1) (discussed in Section 3(B), supra).

This Section of the materials addresses the priority of PMSI's as against competing security interests. In particular, it looks at priority rules that provide exceptions to the first-to-file-or-perfect rule of R9–322(a)(1), thereby allowing qualifying PMSI's to achieve seniority over security interests perfected by earlier-in-time filings. See Note (2), infra. In Chapter 11, Section 4, infra, we shall see that Article 9 affords a similar "super-priority" to PMSI's in fixtures. See R9–334(d).

(2) Purchase–Money Priority Under R9–324. A set of PMSI priority rules in R9–324 overrides the otherwise-applicable first-to-file-or-perfect rule of R9–322(a)(1). To qualify for these special rules, a PMSI must meet the definition in R9–103, which is discussed more fully in the following Notes. In addition, PMSI priority is conditioned on the satisfaction of certain procedural requirements, discussed below in this Note. When these requirements are not met, R9–322(a) governs the priority of a PMSI.

Eligible Collateral. A PMSI can arise in only two types of collateral, goods and software. See R9–103(b), (c). However, in many cases a "second-in-time" secured party can achieve priority in "paper collateral" (such as documents, instruments, and chattel paper) and other intangible collateral (such as investment property and deposit accounts) under other special priority rules. See, e.g., R9–312(c)(2); R9–327; R9–328; R9–330; R9–331. See generally Chapter 1, Sections 4 and 5, supra; Chapter 9, Sections 2, 3 and 4, infra.

Timing of Perfection. Each of the PMSI priority rules establishes a temporal standard for perfection. For goods other than inventory and livestock, the security interest must be "perfected when the debtor receives possession of the collateral or within 20 days thereafter." R9–324(a). The standard for inventory collateral is less flexible. An inventory PMSI must be "perfected when the debtor receives possession of the inventory"; there is no 20–day period of grace. R9–324(b)(1). The same requirement applies to livestock. See R9–324(d)(2).

Notification to Competing Secured Parties. For inventory collateral, R9–324(b) provides a detailed scheme that requires a PMSI financer to give a written notification to certain competing secured parties (see R9–324(c)).[3] The notification must be received by those parties before (but not more than five years before) the debtor receives possession of the inventory (see paragraph (b)(3)). Finally, the notification must state that the PMSI financer has or may obtain a PMSI in specified items or types of inventory (see paragraph (b)(4)). You should study these notification requirements with care.

Comment 4 to R9–324 explains the rationale for the notification requirement of subsections (b) and (c) as follows:

The arrangement between an inventory secured party and its debtor typically requires the secured party to make periodic advances against incoming inventory or periodic releases of old inventory as new inventory is received. A fraudulent debtor may apply to the secured party for advances even though it has already given a purchase-money security interest in the inventory to another secured party. For this reason, subsections (b)(2) through (4) and (c) impose a second condition for the purchase-money security interest's achieving priority: the purchase-money secured party must give notification to the holder of a conflicting security interest who filed against the same item or type of inventory before the purchase-money secured party filed or its security interest became perfected temporarily under Section 9–312(e) or (f). The notification requirement protects the non-purchase-money inventory secured party in such a situation: if the inventory secured party has received notification, it presumably will not make an advance; if it has not received notification (or if the other security interest does not qualify as purchase-money), any advance the inventory secured party may make ordinarily will have priority under Section 9–322. Inasmuch as an arrangement for periodic advances against incoming goods is unusual outside the inventory field, subsection (a) does not contain a notification requirement.

Do you find this explanation of the notification requirement persuasive? Should that requirement be extended to other collateral, such as equipment? See Baird & Jackson, Possession and Ownership: An Examination of the Scope of Article 9, 35 Stan.L.Rev. 175, at 194–96 (1983), where the authors argue that a notification requirement should be added to F9–312(4) for non-inventory PMSI's. Apparently they believe that the reliance

---

3. The rules applicable to PMSI's in livestock are similar to those applicable to PMSI's in inventory. See R9–324(d), (e).

of secured creditors on after-acquired equipment warrants a notification requirement. Although they base their argument on ostensible ownership grounds, they fail to address the empirical question of whether secured creditors typically are aware of debtors' possession of after-acquired equipment. For a different view of reliance on after-acquired equipment, see Harris, A Reply to Theodore Eisenberg's *Bankruptcy in Law Perspective*, 30 UCLA L. Rev. 327, at 338 n.66 (1982) (defending the application of the two-point test in BC 547(c)(5) only to accounts and inventory):

> [T]hose who take equipment as collateral typically expect the original collateral to remain in the debtor's possession so that he can use it to generate income that will enable him to repay the loan. Although they may easily take a security interest in after-acquired equipment, ordinarily these lenders do not expect to rely upon it and would be protected without it.

Why Purchase–Money Priority? The most commonly advanced justification for PMSI priority is that it provides a means for a debtor to obtain additional secured financing when the first-to-file secured party is unwilling to provide it. In this sense, PMSI priority ameliorates the "situational monopoly" of a first-to-file secured creditor who has the benefit of an after-acquired property clause. See Jackson & Kronman, Secured Financing and Priorities Among Creditors, 88 Yale L.J. 1143, at 1167 (1979) ("Although the after-acquired property clause saves costs, it also creates what economists call a 'situational monopoly,' in that a creditor with a security interest in after-acquired property enjoys a special competitive advantage over other lenders in all his subsequent dealings with the debtor.").

It is understandable that a debtor might prefer the flexibility that purchase-money financing affords. What price does the first-to-file secured party (and, indirectly, the debtor) pay for this flexibility? Do the PMSI priority rules place a substantial risk on the first-to-file secured creditor? If so, does the first-to-file secured creditor react to the risk by charging higher rates (in effect, discounting the value of collateral) to offset the risks? In fact, several safeguards are available to first-to-file lenders who might otherwise perceive that the PMSI priority rules present material risks to their positions. For example, we already have seen that inventory lenders are entitled to notification from later PMSI financers. That notification puts the inventory lender in a position to protect itself by not relying on the PMSI-financed collateral. Also, first-to-file financers can bargain for covenants and events of default that restrict or prohibit the debtor from obtaining PMSI financing. Although these contractual obligations and remedies do not entirely eliminate the risk (see R9–401(b)), they are considered important nonetheless in the credit markets.

There is a more fundamental reason why PMSI priority does not seriously impair the position of first-to-file secured creditors. The PMSI financer contributes new value that *in fact is used by the debtor to acquire a new asset*. The debtor's balance sheet reflects both a new debt and a new asset. Neither the first-to-file secured creditor's existing collateral nor its overall position are affected. (This rationale also assumes that non-notified, first-to-file secured creditors do not rely materially to their detriment on after-acquired, non-inventory collateral.) This explanation highlights the importance of the tracing requirement in R9–103(b)'s definition of PMSI, discussed below in Note (3). Consider the effect of a rule to the contrary, under which a debtor could borrow funds, fail to acquire a new asset, and confer on the lender a super-priority in a first-to-file secured creditor's existing collateral: it would undercut the core basis of secured credit. Would the result of that sort of "last-in-time" priority rule be that no one would go the trouble of obtaining collateral? Would all credit be unsecured credit? An affirmative answer to each of these questions is developed in Jackson & Kronman, Secured Financing and Priorities Among Creditors, 88 Yale L.J. 1143, at 1162–64 (1979).

(3) Definition of "Purchase–money Security Interest"; The Tracing Requirement. R9–103(b)(1) contains the basic definition of a PMSI in goods: "A security interest in goods is a purchase-money security interest . . . to the extent that the goods are purchase-money collateral with respect to that security interest." Working through the definitions of "purchase-money collateral" and "purchase-money obligation," one finds that R9–103(b)(1) provides for two types of PMSI's in goods: those held by a seller to secure "an obligation . . . incurred as all or part of the price of the collateral," and those taken by a lender to secure "an obligation . . . incurred . . . for value given to enable the debtor to acquire rights in or the use of the collateral if the value is in fact so used." R9–103(a)(2).

For a security interest taken by a lender to qualify as a PMSI, the value (i.e., the loan—or **enabling loan** as it often is called) (i) must be given for the purpose of enabling the debtor to acquire the collateral and (ii) must actually be used for that purpose. It follows from the second component of this rule that, to achieve PMSI status, a secured lender must trace the loaned funds and establish that they actually were used to pay the purchase price for the collateral. The secured lender typically accomplishes this by advancing the loaned funds directly to the seller of the collateral or by issuing a check payable jointly to the seller and the buyer-debtor. Does the rationale of the purchase–money priority rules, considered above in Note (2), explain this strict tracing requirement? Normally there is no tracing problem when a PMSI is created in favor of a seller.

Does PMSI status require a close temporal connection between the incurrence of purchase-money obligation and the attachment and perfection of the security interest? Suppose, for example, that a seller sells goods on unsecured credit (an **open account**) or a lender makes an unsecured enabling loan. Sometime (months, or even years) later, the buyer gives the seller (or the enabling lender) a security interest in the goods to secure the balance of the purchase price (or unpaid balance of the loan). Is the security interest a PMSI? Comment 3 to R9–103 indicates that it is not: "a security interest does not qualify as a purchase-money security interest if a debtor acquires property on unsecured credit and subsequently creates the security interest to secure the purchase price." Is the Comment consistent with the text of R9–103? Even if the security interest is a PMSI, in many cases the delay would disqualify the security interest from enjoying pur-chase–money *priority* under R9–324. See Note (2) supra; Note on Debtor's Receipt of Possession of Collateral, infra.

(4) The "Transformation" and "Dual Status" Rules. R9–103(b)(1) provides that a security interest in goods is a PMSI "to the extent" that the goods are purchase-money collateral, i.e., to the extent that the secure a purchase-money obligation incurred with respect to those goods. The implication of the quoted phrase is that a security interest in the PMSI-financed collateral is *not* a PMSI "to the extent" that it also secures debt other than the price or an enabling loan. Likewise, that language suggests that a security interest in collateral other than the PMSI-financed collateral is not a PMSI even though it secures a purchase-money obligation with respect to other collateral.

The words "to the extent" in R9–103(b) derive from the definition of "purchase money security interest" in F9–107. Several cases construing F9–107 have supported the retention of PMSI status for a security interest in PMSI-financed collateral when that collateral also secures obligations other than the purchase-money obligation. Those cases recognize security interests having a "dual status": they are part PMSI (i.e., to the extent that they secure the price or an enabling loan) and part non-PMSI (i.e., to the extent that they secure other indebtedness). However, there is a substantial body of Former Article 9 case law holding that what otherwise would be a PMSI is "transformed" into a non-PMSI whenever the PMSI-financed collateral secures any obligations other than the price or an enabling loan or whenever other collateral, in addition to the PMSI-financed collateral, secures the purchase-money obligation.

A number of cases construing F9–107 also have applied this "transfor-mation" rule to deny PMSI status when the purchase-money obligation (the price or an enabling loan) has been **refinanced** (i.e., extended or combined with other indebtedness), even when the secured party could identify a portion of the collateral as PMSI-financed collateral and a portion of the secured indebtedness as the price or as an enabling loan for that collateral. In re Matthews, 724 F.2d 798 (9th Cir.1984), is typical of those cases. In *Matthews*, the debtors owed $3,902.64 to Transamerica. The debt was secured by a PMSI in a piano and a stereo. The parties agreed to refinance the loan: the term was extended and the monthly payment was reduced in amount. Transamerica's books showed a new secured loan to the debtors in the amount of $4,245.01, of which $3,902.64 was applied to pay off the old delinquent loan. The court observed that the debtors did not use the proceeds of the new loan to acquire rights in or the use of the piano or stereo; they already owned them. "The new security interest in the piano and stereo taken by Transamerica at the time of the refinancing was therefore not a 'purchase money security interest' as [Former Article 9] has defined it."

Which approach—transformation or dual-status—is more consistent with the policies that underlie Article 9? Consider two important principles of the Article 9 scheme that seem to be well-accepted. First, parties are given great flexibility to agree as to what collateral (any combination of now-owned and after-acquired property) will secure what obligations (any combination of now-existing or later-arising debt). See R9–204. But see R9–204(b)(1) (limiting the effect of an after-acquired property clause with respect to consumer goods). Second, PMSI's are given favored treatment. See, e.g., R9–317(e); R9–309(1); R9–324. Should parties to a secured transaction be forced to sacrifice flexibility for PMSI treatment or PMSI treatment for flexibility? Should consensual refinancing and restructuring of debt, including secured debt, be discouraged by the threat of losing PMSI status? See In re Billings, 838 F.2d 405 (10th Cir.1988) (transformation rule discourages creditors holding PMSI's from helping their debtors work out of financial problems without the need to enter bankruptcy or surrender collateral).

For non-consumer-goods transactions, R9–103(f) straightforwardly rejects the "transformation" rule. In those transactions, a PMSI does not lose its status as such, even if the purchase-money collateral also secures an obligation that is not a purchase-money obligation, collateral that is not purchase-money collateral also secures the purchase-money obligation, or the purchase-money obligation has been renewed, refinanced, consolidated, or restructured. R9–103(f). Most cases that have confronted the issue under Former Article 9, including *Matthews*, supra, have concerned consumer goods. Revised Article 9's treatment of PMSI's in consumer-goods transactions is discussed in Note (6), infra.

The "dual status" rule, which R9–103(f) adopts, can prove troublesome to apply. For example, suppose Bank holds a PMSI in an item of equipment to secure an enabling loan of $50,000 and all present and future obligations of Debtor to Bank. When the loan is reduced to $35,000, Bank extends an additional $10,000 to Debtor. To what extent is the security interest a PMSI? The answer is easy to intuit: to the extent of $35,000. Gleaning the answer from the statute is a bit more difficult. The security interest is a PMSI only to the extent the equipment is purchase-money collateral. R9–103(b)(1). The equipment is purchase-money collateral if it secures a purchase-money obligation with respect to the equipment. See R9–103(a)(1). Of the obligations secured by the equipment, only $35,000 is a purchase-money obligation. See R9–103(a)(2). To the extent that the equipment secures the $10,000 non-purchase-money obligation, the security interest is not a PMSI.

Now suppose that Debtor pays Bank $5,000, leaving a balance of $40,000 secured by the equipment. To what extent is the security interest a PMSI? The answer depends on the amount of the purchase-money obligation, which in turn depends on how much, if any, of the $5,000 payment was applied towards satisfaction of the $35,000 purchase-money obligation and how much, if any, was applied towards satisfaction of the $10,000 non-purchase-money obligation. Cases decided under Former Article 9 generally required the secured party to prove that amount. In non-consumer-goods transactions, R9–103(g) adopts this approach. (Consumer-goods transactions are discussed in Note (6), infra.) To assist the secured party in meeting this burden, R9–103(e) permits the parties in non-consumer-goods cases to agree to an allocation formula and provides rules of allocation applicable in the absence of an agreement.

(5) "Cross–Collateralization" and Purchase–money Financing of Inventory. Problem 7.6.10, supra, presents a common fact pattern: Debtor creates a security interest in all its inventory, existing and after-acquired, in favor of a lender (*SP*–1). Thereafter, *SP*–2 periodically sells inventory to Debtor on secured credit (or, *SP*–2 might be another lender, who makes a series of secured loans that enable Debtor to acquire inventory). Debtor and *SP*–2 also enter into a **cross-collateral** agreement; that is, they agree that each item of inventory secures not only its own price but also the aggregate unpaid price of all other inventory financed by *SP*–2.

As we have seen, the fact that an item of inventory secures not only its own price but also other obligations does not destroy the purchase–money status of a security interest. See R9–103(f). However, under R9–103(b)(1), *SP*–2 has a PMSI in each item of inventory only to the extent that the item secures a purchase-money obligation incurred with respect to that item of collateral. This rule may present serious practical problems for *SP*–2. Suppose that some of the *SP*–2–financed inventory has been sold and some of the debt to *SP*–2 has been paid. To establish its PMSI under R9–103(b)(1), and thus its priority under R9–324(b), *SP*–2 would have to allocate each payment towards a particular purchase-money obligation incurred with respect to particular collateral. When inventory is financed in bulk, as when *D* acquired 1,000 bags of marbles in Problem 7.6.10, must *SP*–2 work this calculation shipment by shipment? Bag by bag? Marble by marble? And, when *SP*–2 has financed multiple shipments of fungible inventory, how is *SP*–2 to determine which inventory has been sold and which remains?

When *SP*–2 has sold all the marbles to Debtor on a purchase-money basis, should the extent of its priority depend on which inventory has been sold and how payments have been allocated? When confronted with this problem under Former Article 9, a number of institutional lenders agreed that the answer should be "no." They entered into an **intercreditor agreement** affording priority to each purchase-money financer in the inventory that it had financed. Revised Article 9 adopts this approach. R9–103(b)(2) provides that, if inventory subject to a PMSI secures not only its own price (or enabling loan) but also the price of (or enabling loan with respect to) other purchase-money inventory, then the security interest in the inventory is a PMSI not only to the extent the inventory secures its own price but also the price of the other inventory. In other words, by cross-collateralizing PMSI's in inventory, the parties create a PMSI in each item of inventory that secures the aggregate of the purchase-money obligations. See R9–324, Comment 4.

In the commercial setting, the purchase–money secured party's concerns relate primarily to priority under R9–324. In the consumer setting, a series of transactions between the debtor and a purchase-money financer may implicate perfection under R9–309(1) and also raise the consumer-protection issues discussed in the following Note.

(6) The "Dual Status" Rule, "Cross–Collateral" Agreements, and Payment Allocation Formulas in Consumer Transactions. As Note (4) above indicates, R9–103(f) rejects the "transformation" rule for non-consumer-goods transactions. Most of the cases that raised the issue under Former Article 9 have concerned consumer goods. They have arisen largely under BC 522(f), which permits the avoidance (nullification) in bankruptcy of certain non-purchase-money security interests in, inter alia, certain consumer goods,[4] or under BC 544(a), which permits the avoidance in bankruptcy of unperfected security interests.[5] Despite the salience of the issue, Revised Article 9 is aggressively agnostic concerning the "dual status" rule in consumer-goods transactions. See R9–103(h) & Comment 8. Absent subsection (h), would there be any statutory basis for the application of one rule or the other? See R9–103(b)(1), (b)(2) ("to the extent"). Does subsection (h) create a statutory basis for the "transformation" rule where none would exist otherwise? Do you think a court confronted with the issue will rely on cases decided under F9–107, or will it consider the issue anew? Do you think the revision of Article 9 will affect the outcome in cases construing BC 522(f)? Should it? See R9–103, Comment 8.

The Federal Trade Commission's Rule on Credit Practices makes it an unfair practice for lenders or retail installment sellers to receive nonpossessory, non-PMSI's in household goods. See 16 C.F.R. 444.2(a)(4). This Rule, like that of BC 522(f), recognizes that used home furnishings and other used consumer goods bring relatively little at liquidation sales when compared with their use value to the installment buyer. Both the Rule and BC 522(f) reduce the "hostage value" aspect of collateral consisting of consumer goods. As the FTC explained it, the Rule seems to reject the "transformation" rule, at least with respect to refinancing and consolidations:

> When a purchase money loan is refinanced or consolidated, we intend that, for purposes of this rule, the security collateralizing the prior loan can continue to secure the new loan, even if the new loan is for a larger amount or is in other respects a non-purchase money loan.

49 Fed. Reg. 7740, 7767 (March 1, 1984). To what extent, if any, is the FTC's construction of the concept of a PMSI relevant to the construction of the Bankruptcy Code or the UCC?

Assuming that the "dual status" rule applies in consumer-goods transactions, on what basis are payments allocated? As we saw above in Note

---

4. BC 522(f)(1)(B) permits debtors to avoid "nonpossessory, nonpurchase-money security interest[s]" in certain types of exempt property. The significance of this avoidance power is limited by the FTC's Rule on Credit Practices, which restricts the taking of certain nonpossessory, non-PMSI's. See 16 C.F.R. § 444.2(a)(4) (making it an unfair practice for lenders or retail installment sellers to obtain from consumers nonpossessory security interests, other than PMSI's, in household goods).

5. Recall that a security interest in consumer goods is automatically perfected upon attachment. See R9–309(1); F9–302(1)(d). Automatic perfection is lost, and the security interest can be avoided, if a PMSI is transformed into a non-PMSI and no perfection step (e.g., filing) is taken. BC 544(a) is discussed in Chapter 10, Section 2(A), infra.

(4), R9–103(e) contains rules concerning the allocation of payments between PMSI's and non-PMSI's in non-consumer-goods transactions. Yet, as with the "dual status" rule itself, Revised Article 9 is agnostic on the issue of application of payments. See R9–103(h).

In leaving the court free to fashion the applicable legal rule, R9–103(h) permits the court to "apply established approaches." Cases decided under Former Article 9 approved different methods for determining the extent of purchase-money obligations. For a case upholding the parties' agreement on a formula for allocating payments, see In re Breakiron, 32 B.R. 400 (Bkrtcy.W.D.Pa.1983). In some jurisdictions there is a statutory method of allocation. See, e.g., Pristas v. Landaus of Plymouth, Inc., 742 F.2d 797 (3d Cir.1984) (applying formula provided by Pennsylvania's Goods and Services Installment Sales Act to a dual-status security interest). In the absence of explicit agreement or statutory guidance, some courts have devised a method of allocation. See, e.g., In re Conn, 16 B.R. 454 (Bkrtcy.W.D.Ky. 1982) (allocation based on first-in, first-out method). Which approach should a court apply? Uniform Consumer Credit Code (U3C) 3.303, which has not been widely enacted, deals with this problem by providing that payments shall be "applied first to the payment of the debts arising from the sales first made." Is this a reasonable and appropriate regulation of the parties' freedom to contract?

The FTC Rule would appear to have the effect of prohibiting **cross-collateral** provisions—agreements whereby each item of collateral secures not only its own price (and, absent application of the transformation rule, would be subject to a PMSI to that extent) but also the price of other items of collateral sold by the financer (to that extent, a non-PMSI). The explanation of the Rule, quoted above, seems to point in the opposite direction. Moreover, the FTC has taken the position that, for purposes of the FTC Rule, state law should govern the determination of the extent of the purchase-money security interest. If under applicable state law an interest is in part a purchase-money security interest at the time a contract is signed, the FTC has stated that the contract does not violate the Rule, even if the purchase-money portion of the security interest is exhausted before the end of the contract.

Secured parties may be able to preserve much of the leverage that comes from the threat of repossessing many of the debtor's most valued consumer goods without violating the FTC regulations, if each item secures only its own price but the system of allocating installment payments among a series of purchases means that the debt for none of the goods is paid until all debts are paid. For example, a consumer buyer and a secured seller (or secured enabling lender) could agree that each payment made by the buyer would be allocated proportionately among the outstanding balances for all items purchased. In this way, any default in payment would constitute a default under each transaction, and the secured creditor would be entitled to take possession of all of the items of collateral.

This type of arrangement with a consumer debtor was attacked as "unconscionable" in the famous case of Williams v. Walker–Thomas Furniture Co., 350 F.2d 445 (D.C.Cir.1965) (remanded to trial court for factual determinations on issue of unconscionability). The court in In re Breakiron, supra, held that this kind of allocation agreement did not transform PMSI's into non-PMSI's, for purposes of BC 522(f), because each item secured only its own price. The court was influenced by a Pennsylvania statute that contains a similar allocation formula. See 69 Pa. Cons. Stat. Ann. § 1802.

Why do you suppose R9–103(h) leaves to courts the decision whether to apply the allocation rules in subsection (f), or other rules, or no rules at all (e.g., to hold that cross-collateralization results in the loss of PMSI status, thereby obviating any need to allocate payments between PMSI's and non-PMSI's)? Does the continued absence of a clear statutory rule help or hurt consumers?

(7) Purchase–money Security Interests in Software. F9–107 was ambiguous concerning the type of collateral eligible to be the subject of a PMSI, although F9–312's receipt-of-possession requirement appeared to exclude from eligibility purely intangible collateral. R9–103 makes it clear that a PMSI may be created only in goods and, in limited circumstances, software. To be eligible to be the subject of a PMSI, software must be associated with goods in the manner specified in R9–103(c): the debtor must acquire an interest in the software in an integrated transaction in which the debtor acquires an interest in the goods, and the debtor must acquire an interest in the software for the principal purpose of using the software in the goods. This rule permits a person who finances a debtor's acquisition of the goods and related software to take a PMSI in both. (Take care not to confound this approach with the concept of a computer program "embedded" in goods; such an "embedded" program actually is a part of the goods under R9–102(a)(44). See Problem 7.2.6, supra.) The priority of a PMSI in software is the same as that of the goods in which the software was acquired for use. See R9–324(f).

Problem 7.6.12. Dragon purchased a combine (harvesting machine) from Retailer, a dealer in farm implements. Dragon gave Retailer a check for half the purchase price and agreed to pay the balance over time. Dragon secured its obligation to Retailer with a security interest in the combine. Unbeknownst to Retailer, the check was drawn on an account containing only the proceeds of a loan from Bank. Bank advanced the loan for the purpose of enabling Dragon to buy the combine, which secured the loan. Bank perfected its security interest by filing three days after Dragon took delivery of the combine. Retailer perfected its security interest by filing ten days thereafter (i.e., 13 days after delivery). Which security interest has priority? See R9–324(a), (g) & Comment 13; Note on Competing Purchase-money Security Interests in the Same Collateral, infra. What could the losing party have done to avoid the result?

NOTE ON COMPETING PURCHASE–MONEY SECURITY INTERESTS IN THE SAME COLLATERAL

Problem 7.6.12, supra, presents a scenario in which a debtor acquires goods subject to two PMSI's. What is the relative priority of two PMSI's in the same collateral, each of which qualifies for priority under R9–324(a)? Whereas Former Article 9 provided no clear answer, Revised Article 9 affords priority to the seller of the goods. See R9–324(g).

Is there any reason to favor one secured party over the other? One might argue that the two PMSI's should enjoy equal priority, inasmuch as each secured party has some reason to believe that it enjoys first priority. Moreover, as a practical matter, in many cases it is likely that a PMSI financer will be unable to discover the filing (or, in the case of consumer goods, the automatically perfected security interest) of its competitor before it takes and perfects its own security interest. On the other hand, there may be good reasons to prevent a "tie" and award priority to one secured party or the other. In particular, a rule of equal priority could create unnecessary complications when one secured party tries to enforce its security interest.[6] Assuming that security interests of equal rank are undesirable, is the rule favoring sellers, R9–324(g), preferable to the first-to-file-or-perfect rule of R9–322(a)(1)? Consider, in this regard, that in the case of PMSI's in consumer goods, attachment, and consequently perfection, of a seller's security interest and a lender's security interest may occur simultaneously upon the debtor's acquisition of rights in the collateral. See R9–203(b)(2); R9–309(1). Consider also that the first-to-file-or-perfect rule governs the priority of conflicting PMSI's where neither is held by a seller. See R9–324(g).

Problem 7.6.13. Lee is in the data processing business. *SP*–1 has a perfected security interest in "all equipment now owned or hereafter acquired" by Lee. On June 1, 2002, Lee and Lor entered into a "true lease" of a computer for a three-year term. The lease agreement provides that Lee, as lessee, has an option to purchase the computer at the end of the lease term for its "fair market value." In accordance with the lease, on May 1, 2005, Lee notified Lor of Lee's intention to exercise that option. Thereafter Lee and Lor reached agreement that the fair market value of the computer—and therefore the sale price—is $1,000.

Lee requests financing from your client, *SP*–2, for Lee's purchase of the leased computer. Your search of the records uncovers *SP*–1's financing statement covering "all equipment." Lee is reluctant to ask *SP*–1 to subordinate its security interest to that of *SP*–2 because Lee does not want to pay the fees that *SP*–1's lawyers will charge for drawing up the subordination agreement. However, Lee has assured your client that Lee's agreement with *SP*–1 permits Lee to give PMSI's in equipment to other financers.

How can you assure *SP*–2 that it will achieve purchase–money priority? See R9–102(a)(28), (a)(12); R9–103(a), (b); R9–324(a) & Comment 3; Note on Debtor's Receipt of Possession of Collateral, infra.

---

6. See Chapter 12, Section 3(B), infra, which considers the duties that secured parties who enforce their security interests owe to other secured parties.

NOTE ON DEBTOR'S RECEIPT OF POSSESSION OF COLLATERAL

We have seen that a PMSI does not qualify for purchase–money priority under R9–324(b) unless it is perfected "when the debtor receives possession of the inventory." Likewise, purchase–money priority in collateral other than inventory and livestock under R9–324(a) depends on perfection of the PMSI "when the debtor receives possession of the collateral or within 20 days thereafter." The UCC does not define "possession" for these purposes, nor does the text of Revised Article 9 explain what it means for the debtor to "receive[ ] possession of the collateral." Cf. R9–313 (explaining when secured party takes possession of collateral).

Delivery of various components of a product to a buyer, over a period of time, is one circumstance in which the determination of the beginning of the 20–day period can be perplexing. This is especially so when the seller is required to assemble and test the goods before the buyer becomes obligated to accept them. Courts have reached differing results in these situations under F9–312(4), which provided for a 10–day period. Compare In re Ultra Precision Industries, Inc., 503 F.2d 414 (9th Cir.1974) (10–day period did not begin to run until testing of machines was completed and financing arrangements were made, because those events were conditions precedent to buyer's obligation to buy) with In re Vermont Knitting Co., 98 B.R. 184 (Bkrtcy.D.Vt.1989) (10–day period began when machines were delivered to buyer and was not delayed until after machines had been set up by seller's technician) and In re Michaels, 156 B.R. 584 (Bkrtcy.E.D.Wis.1993) (applicable 20–day period began when equipment came under the recipient's "physical control"). Comment 3 to R9–324 attempts to give guidance under this circumstance. Is Comment 3 persuasive? Is it an appropriate use of the Comments?

The courts also have struggled with the scenario presented by Problem 7.6.13, supra, in which a prospective debtor in a PMSI transaction is *already* in possession of collateral in a capacity other than that of buyer-owner. Comment 3 to R9–324 addresses this issue, as well. Relying on the reference in R9–324(a) to the debtor's receiving "possession of the *collateral,*" Comment 3 indicates that "the 20–day period in subsection (a) does not commence until a the goods become 'collateral' (defined in Section 9–102), i.e., until they are subject to a security interest." The result urged by Comment 3—that the 20–day period starts to run only once the debtor has created a security interest—is consistent with cases decided under Former Article 9; however, the Former Article 9 cases were decided based on whether the person in possession was a "debtor" as defined in F9–105(1)(d). See, e.g., Color Leasing 3 v. FDIC, 975 F.Supp. 177 (D.R.I.1997). Does delaying the commencement of the 20–day period undercut the policy of favoring public notice and the policy against "secret" liens? Or, is this approach better characterized as being consistent with current law that does *not* require public notice in the case of leases and various other bailments? We shall see in Chapter 8, Section 1, infra, that there is disagreement over whether some of those transactions should be subjected to Article 9's filing regime. But, inasmuch as filing is not required, isn't it appropriate to delay commencement of the 20–day period until the relationship of the parties falls within the scope of Article 9?

Does the statutory argument presented in Comment 3 prove too much? Consider the following case: A seller sells equipment to a buyer on unsecured credit, or an enabling lender extends unsecured credit that enables the buyer to acquire equipment. Subsequently—say, one year later—a security agreement is signed covering the equipment and, within 20 days thereafter, a financing statement is filed. Does the secured party enjoy purchase–money priority status under R9–324(a)? If the 20–day period does not start running until the debtor receives possession of the "collateral," and the equipment is not "collateral" as defined in R9–102(a)(12) until the security agreement is authenticated, then arguably the secured party enjoys priority under R9–324(a).

Is this result consistent with the underlying purposes and policies of purchase-money priority? If not, can one fairly read Revised Article 9 to yield a different result? The special priority in R9–324 applies only to PMSI's. One never reaches the priority issue if the security interest in question is not a PMSI. As mentioned in Note (3) on Purchase–money Priority and the Definition of "Purchase–Money Security Interest," Comment 3 to R9–103 states definitively that the security interest would not be a PMSI in the case under discussion; however, the cases decided under Former Article 9 go both ways. Compare In re Cerasoli, 27 B.R. 51 (Bkrtcy.M.D.Pa.1983) (security interest taken to secure enabling loan several months after enabling loan was made, held a PMSI) with In re Brooks, 29 U.C.C. Rep. Serv. 660 (Bkrtcy.D.Me.1980) (security interest taken several months after the making of enabling loans, held not a PMSI). Although there are few cases, the result in *Brooks* appears to reflect the prevailing view.

(III) PROCEEDS

Problem 7.6.14. The facts are as in Problem 7.6.5(b), supra: *SP*–1 holds a security interest in present and future construction equipment; *SP*–1 filed on June 1. *SP*–2 holds a security interest in the new Cletrac bulldozer purchased in July with the loan from *SP*–2. *SP*–2 filed on July 8.

Late in July *D* found that, to meet the special requirements of a new construction job, *D* needed a bulldozer with a power attachment that the Cletrac bulldozer lacked. On August 1, without consulting *SP*–1 or *SP*–2, *D* traded the Cletrac bulldozer for a used Caterpillar bulldozer that met *D*'s needs.

Shortly thereafter *D* ran out of cash and defaulted on the debts to *SP*–1 and *SP*–2. Who has priority as to the Caterpillar bulldozer? See R9–322(a), (b); R9–315(a); R9–102(a)(64); R9–324(a).

Problem 7.6.15. *D* is a wholesaler of textiles whose business is like that described in Problem 7.6.9, supra. *D* makes many sales on credit to retail stores. The retail stores, in a period of recession, began to take more and more time to pay, with the result that *D* ran short of operating funds.

On June 1, when accounts receivable due *D* from retail stores amounted to $60,000, *D* applied to *SP*–1 for a loan. *SP*–1 extended *D* a loan of $50,000, and *D* executed a security agreement covering "all present and future accounts." *SP*–1 promptly filed a financing statement covering "accounts receivable currently existing or arising hereafter."

On July 1, finding itself in need of additional funds, *D* applied to *SP*–2 for a loan. *D* offered its inventory as collateral. *SP*–2 searched the files and found only *SP*–1's financing statement covering accounts, not inventory. *SP*–2 made a loan of $20,000 to *D*, and *D* executed a security agreement covering "all inventory now owned or hereafter acquired." *SP*–2 promptly filed a financing statement covering "inventory."

In September *D* defaulted on the loans to *SP*–1 and *SP*–2. At that time there were on hand (i) inventory valued at $5,000; (ii) accounts (that arose out of the sale of inventory) valued at $25,000; and (iii) a bank account containing $5,000 that came from the collection of accounts.

(a) Who has the senior security interest in each of these three groups of property? See R9–322(a), (b); Note on Conflicting Security Interests of Accounts Financers and Inventory Financers, *infra*.

(b) Now assume that *SP*–2 was the first to file a financing statement. What result?

NOTE ON CONFLICTING SECURITY INTERESTS OF ACCOUNTS FINANCERS AND INVENTORY FINANCERS

Before concluding that the answers to Problem 7.6.15 are the result of accident or whimsy, read the following excerpts from a 1973 panel discussion by some of the drafters of the 1972 revisions to UCC 9–312.[7]

PROFESSOR KRIPKE: ... A prospective debtor goes to the bank and asks, "Will you lend me $1,000,000 on my accounts receivable?" The bank asks its counsel to check the filings against the debtor. He finds no filings of any kind against this debtor, and the bank is prepared as a matter of credit to make the loan, but it says to its counsel, "Are you sure that we'll have a first security interest on these accounts?" and counsel says, "Yes, of course, there's nothing on file against this debtor. You will therefore be first." Then the counsel says, "On second thought I don't know, because even though you now file first on accounts, I don't know what the answer will be if someone else later files on inventory and claims the accounts as proceeds." That problem exists today under the Code and we think we have a very serious problem if counsel can't give that opinion. ... From my point of view, next to the fixture problem which was causing a great deal of public difficulty, the solution to this problem before it got into the cases was the principal reason for undertaking this amendment pro-

---

7. A Second Look at the Amendments   1001–03 (1974).
to Article 9 of the UCC, 29 Bus. Law. 973,

cess. It was not a purely theoretical question. Sitting in New York as I do where a number of the commercial lenders are situated, every time they get a difficulty under the Code they call me up and bawl me out for it. This was one of the particular problems that they constantly came back to—this whole group of problems as to the relationship between inventory financing and accounts receivable financing.

The first step to solve it was to do something about the two different rules for priority problems which are contained in the existing [1962] Code in Section 9–312(5). One of those rules is the first to file rule and the other is the first to perfect rule. One can never see ahead to the answers to priority problems unless he can visualize what the rules of the game are going to be. Here are two different rules of the game and you don't know which game you're going to play. ...

We collapsed the effect of filing and the effect of perfection, and the basic principle is that the priority ranks from the time at which either of these events occurs.... Applying this to the simple fact situation that I have suggested, if the accounts receivable secured party lends on accounts and files before anything else happens, he will win even though someone else enters the chain of production earlier and files on inventory and its proceeds. Similarly, if someone files on inventory and has through it a claim to proceeds, he will have the first right to accounts even though someone else later comes along and claims accounts. In that latter case the inventory financer has it because he gets there first by perfecting a claim to inventory through possession or through filing. We rejected the notion that I think caused this difficulty and which is implied in certain writings under the Code that the person who handles inventory has a prior claim simply because inventory precedes accounts in the cycle of a business. We thought that if we recognized such a principle we could never give an accounts financer any certainty as to his position. It was important to give him certainty so we make the inventory right depend on his first filing or perfection and not on the fact that inventory comes ahead of accounts in the cycle of a business.

... It's more important to have a clear rule that everyone can accommodate to than it is to have a vague rule that no one is sure of even though you might argue that some different rule is theoretically correct.

MR. COOGAN: I would stress again that this is a purely empirical answer. I think everybody said that if one could practically protect the financer who furnishes new inventory, without cutting the heart out of accounts financing, we would have been willing to do it, but the difficulty is that if you protected the inventory financer you make the accounts financing so problematical that you cut off the most likely source of cash that is going to be used to pay the inventory financer.

MR. HAYDOCK: It does seem unfair to some people where an inventory financer comes in later with a purchase money security interest to have him defeated, when we have adopted a different rule with respect to other types of collateral.

SOMEONE IN AUDIENCE: In the case of an inventory financer would you ever go into inventory financing if you had checked the records and knew that there was an accounts receivable financing statement on file?

MR. HAYDOCK: No.

PROFESSOR KRIPKE: I think there are people who do that.

AUDIENCE: Is it normal business procedure? Would you ever advise your client to do inventory financing without getting a waiver on it? When they do it they take a credit risk.

PROFESSOR KRIPKE: They take a credit risk. That raises a point that I think is worth mentioning and which was the subject of a quite vehement attack on our drafting on the floor of the American Law Institute. A gentleman from Massachusetts said in substance: "When we agreed to the Code, we understood that there could be purchase money priorities as to inventory, and I took it for granted that the priority would flow through to the receivables. My orientation is in favor of unsecured trade creditors, but it was on this assumption that I was willing to go along with the Code. Now you say that the inventory security interest does not carry through to receivables." His ultimate point was just like yours: "What good is the inventory financing if it doesn't carry through to the receivables." Now Bob Braucher and I answered him on the floor of the Institute, and I think the answer is still applicable and is sound. The answer is: "If you were right that your inventory financing carried through to the receivable, there wouldn't be any receivables financing and you wouldn't get paid until the receivable was paid. You'd have to extend your credit a great deal longer. By permitting receivables financing to occur, you're going to get paid when the sale occurs. You'll get paid a lot earlier, you're a trade creditor, you're not in the financing business, you need your own working capital, and you want to limit the duration of your own extensions of credit." Now, if the inventory parties are seriously concerned about the problem, they can, of course, insist on some kind of an arrangement with the receivables party that he pay them, or they'll refuse to do the inventory financing. I recall another meeting at which this question was thrashed out. Persons presently actively engaged in financing said that a number of Japanese trading companies are doing substantial amounts of inventory financing in the United States on the goods which they ship over here, knowing that others will be picking up the receivables financing and being content to lose their security interest when the goods are sold.

MR. HAYDOCK: I see that our time is up. Thank you very much.

———

Problem 7.6.16. *D* is a wholesaler of textiles whose business is like that described in Problems 7.6.9 and 7.6.15.

As in Problem 7.6.15, on June 1, when accounts receivable due *D* from retail stores amounted to $60,000, *D* applied to *SP*–1 for a loan. *SP*–1 extended *D* a loan of $50,000, and *D* executed to *SP*–1 a security agreement covering "all present and future accounts, and all inventory now owned or hereafter acquired." *SP*–1 promptly filed a financing statement covering "accounts receivable currently existing or arising hereafter, and all inventory now owned or hereafter acquired."

On July 1 *D* wanted to purchase $20,000 worth of additional stocks of textiles from manufacturer *M*. In response to *D*'s request *SP*–2 made a $20,000 loan to *D* by a check payable jointly to *D* and *M*; *D* indorsed the check to *M*. *D* executed a security agreement covering the new shipment. *SP*–2 immediately filed a financing statement covering "textiles, now owned or hereafter acquired." In addition, *SP*–2 immediately gave *SP*–1 written notice of the transaction. Shortly thereafter *M* delivered the textiles to *D*.

In September *D* defaulted on the loans to *SP*–1 and *SP*–2. In the meantime, textiles purchased from *M* under the July transaction had been sold to retail stores, generating (i) unpaid accounts of $15,000; (ii) a separate deposit collateral account containing $5,000, which came from payments by retail stores of such accounts; and (iii) a check for $4,000 received as an advance payment for an order of textiles that were subsequently shipped to the buyer.

(a) Who has priority with respect to (i) the unpaid accounts of $15,000; (ii) the $5,000 in the deposit account; (iii) the $4,000 check? See R9–322(a), (b); R9–324(a)–(c); R9–102(a)(9). What explains the result?

The proper resolution of the foregoing priority disputes was hotly contested under the 1962 version of Article 9. Although the drafters of the 1972 version (reflected in Former Article 9) addressed the problems, they communicated their solutions in a somewhat subtle fashion. Revised Article 9 takes a similar approach. It may help to take the following steps: (a) Is the purchase-money priority under R9–324(a) applicable to this case? (b) Does the purchase-money priority for inventory under R9–324(b) carry through to proceeds in the form of accounts? (Note: "identifiable *cash* proceeds.") (c) As to the identifiable cash received from the payments of accounts, note the language of R9–324(b): "cash proceeds . . . received *on or before* the delivery of the inventory to a buyer." (d) Is any of the "special" rules in R9–322(c)–(f) applicable to these proceeds? If not, what result follows from the general rules of R9–322(a) and (b)?

(b) Would the priorities be resolved differently if *SP*–1 had taken and perfected a security interest only in inventory and not in accounts?

(B) Buyers of Goods

Introduction. We have seen that R9–201(a) provides secured lenders with powerful words of comfort: "Except as otherwise provided in [the

Uniform Commercial Code], a security agreement is effective ... against *purchasers* of the collateral, and against creditors." Of course, Article 9 does "otherwise provide[ ]" if the security interest is not perfected; certain buyers of goods (and instruments, documents, tangible chattel paper, and security certificates) can prevail under R9–317(b). See Section 6(B)(II), infra. But when the security interest *is* perfected (usually by filing), then R9–201, especially when read in conjunction with R9–315(a)(1), stands as a serious threat to buyers. In many circumstances a buyer who fails to check the public records will have only itself to blame if its ownership interest is encumbered by a security interest.

(I) PERFECTED SECURITY INTERESTS AND BUYERS OF GOODS

This part deals with priority contests between buyers of goods and secured parties with *perfected* security interests.

Problem 7.6.17. Gadget Construction Co. is in the road construction business. Gadget has a line of credit with Wowsers State Bank ("Bank"), secured by all of Gadget's construction equipment. Bank's security interest is perfected by filing. The security agreement signed by Gadget strictly prohibits Gadget from selling, leasing, or otherwise disposing of any of the collateral without first obtaining Bank's written permission.

Gadget's business was slow during the winter months. On February 1 Gadget sold two of its front-end loaders to Penny, Inc., another construction company. Penny did not check the UCC records and had no knowledge of Bank's security interest or Gadget's agreement not to dispose of the equipment. Gadget used the cash received from Penny to pay various unsecured creditors.

Gadget is in default, and Bank has made demand on Penny to deliver the two loaders to Bank.

(a) Is Bank's security interest senior to Penny's interest in the loaders? See R9–315(a)(1).

(b) Assume that Bank's security interest continued in the loaders following the sale to Penny (i.e., that Penny bought the loaders *subject to* Bank's security interest).

(i) Does Bank's security interest continue to be perfected as against creditors of Penny? Is Bank under a duty to file a new financing statement against Penny? Should it be? If Bank is under no duty to refile, how can Penny's creditors discover that Penny owns the loaders subject to Bank's "secret" security interest? See R9–507(a) & Comment 3; PEB Commentary No. 3; Note (2) on Authorized and Unauthorized Dispositions, infra.

(ii) If Bank's security interest continues to be perfected, for how long does the perfected status last? See R9–316(a). What additional information do you need to answer the preceding question?

(c) What result in part (a) if the security agreement permits Gadget to sell collateral free of the security interest "on the condition that, immediately following any such sale, Gadget remits the net proceeds of the sale to

Bank." See R9–315(a)(1) & Comment 2; National Livestock Credit Corp. v. Schultz, infra; Notes on Authorized and Unauthorized Dispositions, infra. Would your answer be different if Penny had *known* about the foregoing "condition"?

(d) What result in part (a) if the security agreement permits Gadget to sell collateral on the condition that Bank's security interest will continue in the collateral (i.e., sales are to be *subject to*, instead of *free of*, the security interest)? See R9–315(a)(1) & Comment 2; PEB Commentary No. 3.

(e) What result in part (a) if, during the last two years, Gadget has sold unneeded equipment on several occasions, and Bank, which was aware of those dispositions, raised no objection with Gadget? What difference, if any, would it make if Penny had been a party to several of these sales? See UCC 1–103; UCC 1–205; Note (3) on Authorized and Unauthorized Dispositions, infra.

Problem 7.6.18. The facts are as in the preceding Problem. Assume that Bank's security interest continued in the loaders following the sale to Penny and that, on February 1 (the date of Penny's purchase), $25,000 was outstanding on the line of credit. Unaware of the sale, Bank extended an additional $5,000 on the line of credit on March 1 and an additional $10,000 on April 1.

(a) Can Bank enforce its security interest in the loaders to recover the entire $40,000? See R9–322(a); R9–323(d), (e). (The equitable doctrine of "marshaling," discussed in Chapter 12, Section 3(B), infra, may affect the result.)

(b) What result in part (a) if Bank had learned of the sale to Penny on February 15?

This Problem concerns the priority of "future advances." Problem 7.6.2, supra, raises a similar priority dispute; however, the competing claimant in that Problem is not a buyer, but another secured party. Compare your answers to this Problem with your answer to Problem 7.6.2. Can you explain any differences in result? (The 45–day periods in R9–323(b), (d), and (f) derive from the Federal Tax Lien Act. See Chapter 11, Section 5(D), infra.)

National Livestock Credit Corp. v. Schultz[*]

Court of Appeals of Oklahoma, 1982.
653 P.2d 1243.

■ BRIGHTMIRE, JUDGE.

The major question raised by this appeal is whether the terms of a cattle security agreement regarding sale of the cattle, designed for perfected lender's protection, were waived by the creditor's long-term course of conduct inconsistent with the protective provisions. A secondary issue is whether a secured party is estopped to deny authorization of the sale in a

---

* [The court's citations are to the applicable pre–1972 version of the UCC.]

suit for conversion against the buyer based upon a detrimental reliance theory. The trial court resolved both issues against the loan company. We affirm.

I

The facts are not disputed. G.W. "Bill" Schultz and his son were the general and limited partners of Schultz Cattle Co., that ran and grazed cattle until 1973 when it began a so-called "fat cattle" operation.[1] Beginning in April 1964, Schultz Cattle Co. financed its operation with funds from loans obtained through National Livestock Credit Corporation. The financial arrangement was such that in April 1964 a note was executed in excess of $400,000 payable to National in one year. In each of the succeeding years a new note was executed representing the carry over indebtedness of the cattle company from the preceding year's operations. The last such note, and the one that forms the basis of the present suit, was executed on July 27, 1973, in the principal sum of $586,639.02, payable on July 1, 1974. G.W. Schultz signed the note as co-maker with Schultz Cattle Co. and both executed a security agreement to National giving it a security interest in the herd, including after-acquired cattle and proceeds. Also executed was a loan agreement that, among other things, allowed Schultz to draw whatever money he needed over the course of the year to operate his business. Through this type of arrangement there would be no need for Schultz to retain any portion of the proceeds received from sales of cattle to meet business expenses.

> The security agreement also provided: "The Debtor will care for and maintain the crops and property herein described in a good and husbandlike manner and will not further encumber, conceal, remove or otherwise dispose of the same without the written consent of the Secured Party; however, permission is granted for the Debtor to sell the property described herein for the fair market value thereof, providing that payment for the same is made jointly to the Debtor and to the Secured Party...."

The loan agreement contained no conditional consent provision, but did say that "Borrower agrees to remit all funds from sale of secured property directly to National" to apply toward the indebtedness.

Between 1973 and 1974, Schultz sold portions of the collateral cattle to various packers without the prior written consent or knowledge of National. In every instance, the check was made payable to Schultz Cattle Co. only. Schultz, in turn, either mailed the check to National or deposited the packer's check into the Cattle Co.'s account and then issued a new check to National to pay off the note indebtedness. National concedes that it never rebuked Schultz for ignoring the terms of the security agreement relating to sales of secured cattle. As a matter of fact, it admits this procedure was

---

1. That is, cattle were raised and fed at a feedlot and sold for slaughter at a higher rate of return.

customarily followed by all its loan account clients and by the industry as a whole.

In 1974 and 1975, Schultz, along with the entire cattle industry, began experiencing severe financial problems. By a letter dated April 19, 1974, National's then manager, Harley Custer, informed Schultz that several loans would have to be "shaken down fairly well," including the Schultz Cattle Co. loan and that this loan would be discussed at the next board meeting. On June 20, 1974, Custer again wrote Schultz saying there would be no renewal of the loan, due July 1, 1974, because National's bank would approve no more loans and National could not carry the loan unless it were discounted. Custer told Schultz that the loan could be extended an additional 60 to 90 days if Schultz could reduce the loan amount by $200,000. National, however, agreed to a plan by Schultz to liquidate the herd as "fat cattle" over a period of several months instead of immediately selling the cattle as feeders—the expectation was that this plan would increase the value of the herd by $100,000.

It was anticipated, said Custer, that under this program cattle would be sold out of the feedlot to a packer buyer beginning in September 1974 and that National was leaving it solely up to Schultz to decide to whom he would sell the cattle. And, according to Custer, the procedure for handling the proceeds of the sales was to be the same as it had been in the past, i.e., packer would send check to Schultz Cattle Co. in its or Schultz' name and then the cattle company would forward the check to National.

Schultz could not sell the cattle during the fall of 1974 and this spawned weekly calls from Custer to Schultz expressing the lender's concern that no sales had been made. "We had fulfilled our part of the plan in advancing this money [additional money for feed, and extending the note's due date]," he once said, "and we did want him to get to selling these cattle...."

Eventually, some sales were made to a small processing plant owned by Schultz (Schultz Farms), and the proceeds of these sales were remitted to National in the usual manner. On January 5, 1975, Wilson and Company bought 34 steers and 42 heifers from Schultz on a grade and yield basis[2] for a total fair market value of $29,089. Wilson acquired 42 more heifers on January 6 for which it paid a grade and yield price of $14,609. On January 8, Schultz sold 140 heifers to Iowa Beef Processors (IBP) for $50,330.24 and on January 19 sold another 148 head to IBP for $51,121.73. With the exception of the last draft paid by IBP,[3] all of the checks were made payable to Schultz Cattle Co. or Schultz Industries, as directed by Schultz. The proceeds, however, were not transmitted to National, but rather to some of Schultz' feed suppliers.

2. The sales price for cattle bought on a grade and yield basis as opposed to live weight basis is not determined until after the cattle are slaughtered.

3. At this point in time, National had learned of the sales and Schultz' failure to pay it the proceeds. National instructed IBP to make the last check jointly payable to Schultz Cattle Co. and National, and IBP complied.

Upon learning of the sales and Schultz' application of the proceeds to grain bills, National liquidated the remaining herd and otherwise attempted to salvage what it could to reduce the loan balance. National also made demand of Wilson and IBP for payment, which demand, of course, was refused. Schultz, in the meantime, had filed bankruptcy. On March 3, 1976, National filed this action against Wilson and IBP claiming the unauthorized sales to them were in derogation of its security interest and filed financing statements and constituted conversion.

Defendants in their answer admitted the respective purchases of cattle and that they rejected National's demand for the purchase price, but denied they had converted the cattle. IBP also raised the affirmative defenses of waiver and estoppel. Wilson alleged, among other things, "that a pattern and practice of dealing was developed over many years whereby [National] allowed ... Schultz ... to keep possession of all [secured] cattle," sell them without National's knowledge or consent and remit the proceeds of the sale to National; therefore, National waived the consent terms in the security agreement, relinquished its security interest in the cattle and is estopped to assert any claim against Wilson. Both defendant buyers specifically asked for reasonable attorney's fees.

Cross-motions for summary judgment were filed by plaintiff and defendants. By letter order dated July 10, 1980, the trial court granted summary judgment in favor of the defendants after finding that National waived the sale restriction terms of the security agreement through a "course of performance" that allowed Schultz to remit only the proceeds of such sales to National. "Thus," the court said, "National authorized Schultz to sell the cattle to IBP and Wilson without restriction and they took title free and clear of National's security interest." Moreover, the court concluded, National was estopped to demand literal compliance with the payment provisions of its security agreement on a detrimental reliance theory on the authority of Poteau State Bank v. Denwalt, Okl., 597 P.2d 756 (1979). Finally, the trial judge denied the defendants' prayer for attorney's fees upon the theory that 12 O.S.1979 Supp. § 940(A) does not apply to conversion of property causes of action.

National timely filed its petition in error challenging the judgment. ...

II

The arguments raised by National in its voluminous brief boil down to this: only the provisions of general Article One of the Uniform Commercial Code and of secured transactions Article Nine govern security agreements, and therefore, the trial court erred in finding that the course of performance and waiver provisions of Article Two can be invoked to undermine express terms of a security agreement. It further argues there were no transactions between National and defendant packing companies that could act to estop National from asserting its security interest in the cattle.

Since we affirm the trial court's order as to the waiver issue, it becomes unnecessary to address the detrimental reliance theory.

National concedes, as it must, that the uniform code expressly provides that its provisions shall be supplemented by principles of law and equity unless these principles have been displaced by particular provisions of the act. 12A O.S.1981 § 1–103. The code, too, explicitly provides that it is to be liberally construed and applied to promote its underlying purposes and policies, one of which is "to permit the continued expansion of commercial practices through custom, usage and *agreement of the parties.*" 12A O.S. 1981 § 1–102(1) & (2)(b) (emphasis added).

The principal code provision having application to the present appeal is 12A O.S.1981 § 9–306, which provides in part:

"(2) Except where this Article otherwise provides, a security interest continues in collateral, notwithstanding sale, exchange or other disposition thereof, *unless the disposition was authorized by the secured party in the security agreement or otherwise,* and also continues in any identifiable proceeds including collections received by the debtor." (emphasis added)

Clearly, the statute continues the secured party's security interest both in the collateral in the hands of a buyer as well as the proceeds received by the borrower from the unauthorized sale of the collateral. The security interest can be lost, however, and is lost if the sale is authorized by the secured party in the "security agreement or otherwise."

The trial court found the undisputed facts to be that National's prior conduct and its actions in regard to the sales at issue here constituted a waiver of its contractual rights. While National does not deny the facts are undisputed, it does disagree with the court's conclusion on the ground that the doctrine of waiver cannot be applied to a U.C.C. security agreement. More specifically National contends that the court impermissibly applied an Article Two concept to an Article Nine transaction, and in advancing this thesis it assumes that the only statutory basis for the decision is 12A O.S.1981 § 2–208.[5]

We think National misapprehends the basis of the trial court's decision and the effect the separate articles of the uniform code have on one another as well as the effect supplemental principles of law and equity have on commercial transactions. Another provision in Article One, which is applicable to all sections of the code, amply supports the trial court's legal conclusions.

---

5. This section, entitled "Course of Performance or Practical Construction," provides:

"(1) Where the contract for sale involves repeated occasions for performance by either party with knowledge of the nature of the performance and opportunity for objection to it by the other, any course of performance accepted or acquiesced in without objection shall be relevant to determine the meaning of the agreement.

. . .

"(3) Subject to the provisions of the next section [2–209] on modification and waiver, *such course of performance shall be relevant to show a waiver* or modification *of any term inconsistent with such course of performance.*" (emphasis added)

As at least one court has quite correctly pointed out, the definitions in Article One (12A O.S.1981 § 1–201) are automatically made a part of each article in the code and thus a "security agreement" must first be an "agreement" as defined in § 1–201. And, since an agreement is defined by the code as "the bargain of the parties in fact as found in their language or by implication from other circumstances including ... course of performance as provided in this Act (Section ... 2–208)," this has to include security agreements. Therefore, a certain course of performance can result in the waiver of an express term in a security agreement.

There is yet another U.C.C. basis for the invocation of the waiver theory. Section 9–306(2) contemplates extinguishment of a security interest if disposition of collateral is authorized by a secured party "in the security agreement *or otherwise*." The italicized language cannot be considered as mere surplusage and, in fact, the connective "or" gives it at least as much substantive value as the express terms of a security agreement. National's course of conduct certainly has to be considered as an "otherwise" authorization of the sale that resulted in defendant purchasers taking the cattle free from National's security interest.

Finally, apart from the interconnections among the various articles and sections of the code, the previously mentioned §§ 1–103 and 1–102—which allow for supplementation of the code with principles of law and equity in determining rights of the parties—require the court to look not only at the words used by the parties but to analyze their conduct as well in determining what agreement they actually made and what the equities should be. Certainly the facts of this case lend themselves to the application of one time honored maxim of equity: "Where one of two innocent persons must suffer by the act of a third, he who has enabled such third person to occasion the loss must suffer." Pettis v. Johnston, 78 Okl. 277, 190 P. 681 (1920).

Assuming National is an innocent party, it made no effort to alter the customary financial practices of prosperous times after the cattle business turned sour. This "business as usual" attitude made it possible for Schultz to misapply the funds in question and, therefore, from an equitable standpoint National should bear the loss.

[Judgment affirmed.]

NOTES ON AUTHORIZED AND UNAUTHORIZED DISPOSITIONS

(1) "Authorized" Dispositions. R9–315(a)(1) provides that "a security interest ... continues in collateral notwithstanding sale, lease, license, exchange, or other disposition thereof unless the secured party authorized the disposition free of the security interest." Thus a disposition of the collateral causes a security interest to terminate if the secured party has authorized the disposition *free and clear* of the security interest, but the security interest survives a disposition of the collateral if the secured party has authorized the disposition *subject to* the security interest. Is this a sensible rule? Is it reasonable to require a transferee to investigate the details of any authorization given by its transferor's secured party? (Keep in mind that the transferee normally will be able to identify the secured party by searching the appropriate public records.)

(2) Consequences of an Unauthorized Disposition: Remedies Against Collateral and Proceeds; Continued Perfection. A secured party whose security interest survives an unauthorized disposition is entitled to exercise its rights against the collateral, such as the right to take possession from the debtor, the purchaser, or any other junior party following the debtor's default. See R9–609; see generally Chapter 12, infra. (Note that in the typical case the unauthorized disposition itself would constitute a default.) This is, of course, the clear implication of the continuation of the security interest. R9–315(a)(2) also makes it clear that the secured party is entitled not only to the continued security interest in the original collateral *but also* to the identifiable proceeds of that collateral. Does this give the secured party a "windfall"? A "double recovery"? Keep in mind that the secured party will be entitled to only one satisfaction of the secured debt.

A secured party's continuing security interest following an unauthorized disposition also will be effective against the purchaser's creditors and transferees. Under R9–507(a) a financing statement continues to be effective following a disposition of collateral "even if the secured party knows of or consents to the disposition." R9–507(a). (Of course, if a secured party "consents" to a disposition *free of* the security interest, the security interest will not continue and the effectiveness of the financing statement will not matter. See Note (1), supra.) It follows that when a security interest is perfected by filing and continues following a disposition, the security interest may remain perfected until and unless the financing statement lapses. The secured party is not obliged to file a new financing statement, even though no one searching against the buyer's name would discover the filing against the original debtor. Earlier in these materials we noted Professor Westbrook's criticism of this rule and the operation of the second sentence of F9–402(7) (insofar as a secured party need not refile against a new name following a debtor's name change.) See Westbrook, Glitch: Section 9–402(7) and the U.C.C. Revision Process, 52 Geo. Wash. L. Rev. 408 (1984); Section 3(A), supra. See also Chapter 11, Section 1, infra (considering some troublesome priority contests arising from the operation of R9–507(a)).

Article 9's choice-of-law rules may temper the effects of R9–507(a) to some extent. As we saw in Section 4, supra, when collateral is sold or otherwise transferred to a person who becomes an Article 9 debtor, how long the security interest retains its perfected status depends on where the buyer or other transferee is located (within the meaning of R9–307). If the buyer is located in the jurisdiction in which the financing statement has been filed, then the security interest remains perfected until lapse. But if the buyer is located in another jurisdiction, the security interest becomes unperfected one year after the transfer, unless the security interest is perfected under the law of the transferee's jurisdiction before the year expires. R9–316(a), (b). When a security interest becomes unperfected under these circumstances, not only third parties are affected; the buyer, too, may benefit. If within the year the secured party fails to file (or otherwise perfect) in the jurisdiction where the buyer is located, the security interest is "deemed never to have been perfected as against a purchaser of the collateral for value." R9–316(b). Thus, a buyer who bought subject to a security interest that was perfected normally will take free of the security interest, which becomes unperfected. See R9–316(b); R9–317(b); Problems 7.4.3 & 7.4.4, supra; Section 6(B)(II), infra.

(3) Waiver, Estoppel, Course of Performance, and Course of Dealing. R9–315(a)(1) does not prescribe the manner by which a secured party must authorize the disposition of collateral free of its security interest. The statutory silence on this point invites a buyer of goods covered by a perfected security interest to assert that the disposition was "authorized" by the secured party. Even in the absence of R9–315(a)(1), a buyer could attempt to prove that the secured party had waived or subordinated its security interest. Cf. R9–339. In many situations, however, the buyer will be unable to marshal evidence sufficient to establish, through UCC 1–103, a common-law waiver. See, e.g., Weidman v. Babcock, 241 Va. 40, 400 S.E.2d 164 (1991) (" 'Waiver is the voluntary, intentional abandonment of a known legal right, advantage, or privilege.' Essential elements of the doctrine are both knowledge of the facts basic to the exercise of the right and the intent to relinquish that right. A waiver of legal rights will be implied only upon clear and unmistakable proof of the intention to waive such rights; the essence of waiver is voluntary choice."). In a proper case a secured party also might be estopped from asserting that its security interest continues in collateral following a disposition. But, as with waiver, buyers often cannot prove the reasonable reliance on the secured party's actions or omissions that is necessary to establish an estoppel. "A well-established principle of estoppel doctrine provides that in order for silence and inaction to estop a person from pressing some right or claim, there must have been a timely opportunity for the person to speak or act and, in addition, an obligation to do so." Hillman, McDonnell & Nickles, Common Law ¶ 22.04[2][d], at 24–54 to 24–55 (citing 3 J. Pomeroy, Equity Jurisprudence § 808a (S. Symons 5th ed. 1941)).

Because buyers usually lack the clear evidence necessary to establish a true waiver or an estoppel, they often argue that an authorization should be inferred from a secured party's conduct. (Keep in mind that a buyer asserting that a disposition was authorized typically will not have known, at the time of sale, about the facts relevant to the issue of authorization; rather, the buyer will be making the assertion "after the fact.") Indeed, an alternative holding in the *Schultz* case, supra, is that the secured party's conduct—repeatedly failing to insist on the debtor's compliance with a requirement that checks for livestock sold be made jointly payable to the debtor and the secured party—constituted an authorization under F9–306(2) (R9–315(a)(1)). The *Schultz* court also pointed to the secured party's conduct as evidence of a "course of performance" sufficient to constitute a waiver of the offended provisions of the security agreement, citing UCC 2–

208. The cases that have inferred authorizations from the secured party's conduct reflect the following common-sense approach: "A secured party deserves no protection from the terms of a security agreement that he himself ignores." Hillman, McDonnell & Nickles, Common Law ¶ 22.02[1][b][iv], at 22–27.

A "course of dealing" may provide another rationale for finding an authorization. See UCC 1–205(1) ("A course of dealing is a sequence of previous conduct between the parties to a particular transaction which is fairly to be regarded as establishing a common basis of understanding for interpreting their expressions and other conduct."). But when a course of dealing and the "express terms of an agreement" cannot reasonably be construed "as consistent with each other," the express terms control. UCC 1–205(4). Consequently, some courts have declined to allow a course of dealing to overcome an inconsistent provision of a security agreement, especially if the security agreement provides that a consent to a disposition must be in writing.

What seems to be missing in the UCC, the case law, and the commentary is a principled approach to putative authorizations. Should a court stretch to find an authorization, thereby diluting the value of a security interest, or should it practice a contrary bias? It is important to note, here, that the case law construing F9–306(2) may be contaminated by the over-representation of cases in which the buyer was a *buyer in ordinary course of business* ("BIOCOB") of *farm products*. See F1–201(9) (definition of "buyer in ordinary course"); F9–109(3) (definition of "farm products"). Buyers of inventory in ordinary course of business take free of security interests granted by their sellers. See F9–307(1); R9–320(a) (considered in more detail in Problem 7.6.19 and the Note on the "Buyer's Seller" Rule and the Interplay Between UCC 2–403(1) and R9–320(a), infra). However, buyers of farm products—even if in the ordinary course—are exempted from the cleansing benefits of F9–307(1) and R9–320(a). See Note (5), infra. To the extent that reported cases involve sales of farm products in the ordinary course of business (excluded from the benefits of F9–307(1)), they may not provide useful precedents for non-ordinary course dispositions of other types of collateral.[8]

(4) Conditional Authorization of Sales. Recall that the security agreement in the *Schultz* case gave the debtor permission "to sell [collateral] ... for the fair market value thereof, providing that payment for the same is made jointly to the Debtor and to the Secured Party." Implicit in the court's opinion is the belief that when a debtor fails to comply with the condition, a buyer acquires the goods subject to the security interest. Otherwise, the court's reliance on the secured party's conduct as authorizing the sale would not have been necessary.

---

8. Most buyers of inventory from merchants need not rely on R9–320(a) alone: Inventory financers often expressly authorize the debtor's ordinary-course sales of inventory free of the security interest. Agricultural lenders, however, normally insist on restricting the debtor's authority to sell farm products collateral.

The effectiveness (as against the debtor's transferee) of these "conditional authorizations" also was upheld in Southwest Washington Production Credit Association v. Seattle–First National Bank, 92 Wn.2d 30, 593 P.2d 167 (1979) (sale was not authorized because debtor failed to comply with condition of authorization requiring debtor to pay over proceeds of disposition to secured party). Consider the following critique of the result and reasoning of that case:

The reasoning of the court in *Southwest* is problematic, however. First, the only unauthorized aspect of the debtor's disposition in such a case is the failure to remit the sale proceeds. The sale itself is authorized. Moreover, even if such a disposition is properly deemed unauthorized, the reasoning in *Southwest* runs counter to well-established principles of agency law that should apply directly to cases such as *Southwest*. The secured party's consent never is required for a debtor to sell his own rights in collateral. The true significance, therefore, of authorizing a debtor to dispose of collateral is to empower him to sell the secured party's own interest in the property. The debtor in effect becomes the secured party's agent for this purpose. When an agent acts for his principal, the rights acquired by one who deals with the agent are unaffected by the agent's failure to follow secret instructions of his principal even though the principal is disclosed. Further, the law is clear that when an agent is authorized to deal with chattels, the "interests of the principal are affected by an unauthorized transaction of the same kind as that authorized."[132] Professor Seavey wrote that for this reason, if an agent's authority to sell is conditioned on the agent holding the proceeds for his principal, "the rights of a transferee can not, of course, be taken away by his [the agent's] failure to perform the condition subsequent."[133]

The court's reasoning in the *Southwest* case also ignores the predicament of the debtor's transferee. As observed by the court in *First National Bank v. Iowa Beef Processors*,[134] when a secured party consents to a sale of collateral in the debtor's own name provided the debtor remits the proceeds to the secured party,

such a condition makes the buyer an insurer of acts beyond its control. The . . . [secured party] has made performance of the debtor's duty to remit proceeds . . . a condition of releasing from liability a third party acting in good faith. [The buyer from the debtor] could not ascertain in advance whether this condition would be met . . . ; nor did [this buyer] . . . have any control over the performance of the condition, as long as it paid . . . [the debtor].[135]

---

132. [Restatement (Second) Agency] §§ 175(2) (disclosed principal), 201(2) (undisclosed principal) [1958].

133. W. Seavey, Handbook of the Law of Agency § 66 at 115 (1964).

134. 626 F.2d 764 (10th Cir.1980).

135. Id. at 769.

These considerations led to the conclusion in *Iowa Beef* that "even though the secured party conditions consent on receipt of the proceeds, failure of this condition will not prevent that consent from cutting off the security interest under [Former] Section 9–306(2)."[136]

Hillman, McDonnell & Nickles, Common Law ¶ 22.02[2], at 22–28 to 22–29. A majority of the cases, like *Iowa Beef*, do not give effect to similar conditions placed on authorizations to dispose of collateral; they treat dispositions as being authorized even when the conditions are not satisfied.

The facts surrounding the "conditional authorization" may be determinative. Consider, for example, Baker Production Credit Association v. Long Creek Meat Co., 266 Or. 643, 513 P.2d 1129 (1973), which involved more than $88,000 of proceeds of the sale by a debtor, Cattle Feeders, of livestock from a large herd in which Baker PCA held a security interest. The court stated, "[t]he evidence is clear and undisputed that Baker PCA was aware that Cattle Feeders was selling cattle to Meat Company and had no objection to those sales"; however, the PCA's consent was "on condition that payment was received when the cattle left the feed lot for delivery to Meat Company." Both Meat Company and its financer, Bank, knew about the arrangement between Cattle Feeders and Baker PCA; specifically, both knew that the PCA's consent to disposition of the cattle was conditional.

Bank refused to honor drafts that Meat Company drew on Bank to pay Cattle Feeders for the cattle; instead, Bank applied the proceeds in the account to overdue debt that Meat Company owed to Bank. The court concluded (i) that the sale of the cattle by Cattle Feeders was not authorized because the condition for authorizing the sale was broken by nonpayment and (ii) that Bank was liable to Baker PCA for conversion of the funds.

In the above-quoted passage, Professors Hillman, McDonnell, and Nickles express concern about "the agent's [i.e., the debtor's] failure to follow secret instructions of his principal." Nevertheless, they would reach a different result where the debtor's transferee *knows* of the conditional authorization and, consequently, is in a position to ensure compliance (such as by remitting proceeds directly to the secured party). For this reason, they approve of the result in the *Baker PCA* case. Hillman, McDonnell & Nickles, Common Law ¶ 22.02[2], at 22–30 n. 141.

Comment 2 to R9–315 indicates that Revised Article 9 does not "address the frequently litigated situation in which the effectiveness of the secured party's consent to a disposition is conditioned upon the secured party's receipt of the proceeds. In that situation, subsection (a) leaves the determination of authorization to the courts, as under Former Article 9." Does R9–315(a)(1) admit of a construction that would render a conditional authorization effective to cut off a security interest when the transferee does not know of the condition but ineffective when the transferee knows of the condition? Would it be reasonable to insist instead that prospective transferees identify secured creditors (by searching the financing statement

136. Id.

records) and confirm the existence or nonexistence of (and any conditions on) the secured party's authorization of dispositions? (Again, the "ordinary course" nature of sales of farm products may engender additional sympathy for the plight of the farm products transferee.)

(5) Farmers and Farm Products: Amendments to F9–307(1); The Food Security Act; R9–320(a). We mentioned above that farm products were excluded from the general rule of F9–307(1) that protected buyers in ordinary course of business. Responding to a large volume of litigation and widespread dissatisfaction with the farm products exception in F9–307(1), several states repealed (or limited) the farm products exception. Mr. Clark's withering barrage of questions, quoted below, offers some insight into the nature and extent of the criticisms of the farm products exception.

> The farm products rule was something of an anomaly. Marketing agents, auctioneers, and packers argued with force that Article 9 gives unusual protection to agricultural financers at the expense of buyers in the ordinary course of business. If buyers of automobile inventory take free of a security interest, why should not the same rule apply to ordinary course buyers of cattle and crops? Is this not a case where the urban-oriented drafters of Article 9 mistakenly viewed farmers and ranchers as other than sophisticated borrowers? Does the farm products exception not encourage lack of diligence on the part of lenders in policing their loans, because they can always collect from the auctioneer or packer if their debtor defaults and fails to turn over proceeds from the sale of farm products collateral? Is it fair that an innocent auctioneer, selling as a mere agent for the debtor, should be liable in conversion under the farm products exception? Does local filing of financing statements covering farm products not aggravate the problem, because secret liens can come into play so easily? Is it right for the courts to allow agricultural financers to ignore so often the "prior written consent" boilerplate in their security agreements? Instead of enforcing these restrictions, is it not the custom to trust the debtor to sell the cattle or crops, collect the proceeds, and remit them to the secured party? Should the buyers in ordinary course assume the risk of the debtor's default, or is this a risk that agricultural lenders are in a better position to assume and distribute by adjusting the cost of credit? Is not the lender adequately protected in that its security interest carries over into proceeds? Has the farm products exception not led some courts to invoke too stingily the common-law concepts of implied consent, waiver, and estoppel? Should the purchaser have to show an express consent in order to carry the day? Why should the law protect a secured party who knows that the debtor is selling cattle or crops without prior written consent, but who does not object to the practice?

Clark, Secured Transactions ¶ 8.08[4][a], at 8–99 to 8–100.

In 1985 Congress intervened. Section 1324 of the Food Security Act of 1985, Pub. L. No. 99–198, § 1324, 99 Stat. 1535 (1985) (codified at 7 U.S.C. § 1631) preempts the farm products exception of F9–307(1) and R9–320(a).

Under the federal statute, ordinary course buyers take free of security interests in farm products—subject to two significant exceptions. (The Act also protects commission merchants and selling agents.)

The first exception applies when (i) a buyer has received a notification that contains certain details (specified in the statute) concerning a security interest, including "any payment obligations imposed on the buyer by the secured party as conditions for waiver or release of the security interest" and (ii) "the buyer has failed to perform the payment obligations." 7 U.S.C. § 1631(e)(1)(A)(v), (e)(1)(B). For example, if a buyer has received a conforming notification stating that a security interest will be released upon a buyer's delivery to the debtor of a check that is jointly payable to the debtor and the secured party, and the buyer fails to comply with that "payment obligation," then the buyer will take its interest subject to the security interest. To take advantage of this exception, agricultural lenders typically require their debtors to provide a list of prospective buyers and send a notification to each of those prospective buyers.

The second exception applies to certain buyers who buy "a farm product produced in a State that has established a central filing system." 7 U.S.C. § 1631(e)(2). (Nineteen states have established such a system.) The statute specifies the attributes of a qualifying "central filing system." 7 U.S.C. § 1631(c)(2). In general, a "central filing system" involves two lists. One list relates to "effective financing statements" that are filed by secured parties and that contain certain information (specified in the statute) concerning security interests in farm products. (Inasmuch as the "central filing system" is wholly separate from the regular UCC filing system, filing an "effective financing statement" has nothing to do with "perfection" of a security interest.) The other list contains information concerning prospective buyers of farm products who have registered by filing a form in the system. To qualify, the system must require a state's Secretary of State to match up, on a regular basis, buyers whose forms have named particular debtors and the effective financing statements filed against those debtors, and to send to the registered buyers information concerning the relevant effective financing statements. Id. Under the operative priority rule, the buyer will take subject to a security interest if (i) the buyer has failed to register in the system and the secured party has filed an "effective financing statement," or (ii) the buyer has received a notice from the Secretary of State concerning that security interest and the buyer has not complied with the requirements for a waiver or release of the security interest. 7 U.S.C. § 1631(e)(2), (e)(3).

Why does the priority rule for buyers of farm products collateral warrant such a complicated (some might say, convoluted), federally imposed system? Why, as Mr. Clark's questions suggest, cannot agricultural financers live with the same rules applicable to inventory financing generally? One answer is suggested by the inherent characteristics of agricultural production and marketing. Unlike inventory generally, many farm products are marketed only a few times each year—e.g., at harvest-time or after cattle are fattened. Moreover, sales frequently may involve a large proportion (sometimes all) of the farm products owned by a debtor at the time. These factors indicate that the prospects for a secured lender to be left "high and dry" are materially greater in the case of agricultural financing. (UCC Article 6, which regulates "bulk sales" of a large proportion of a merchant's inventory, reflects similar concerns; however, Article 6 is primarily for the benefit of unsecured creditors. See generally Notes on Bulk Sales, infra.)

In the face of nonuniform state approaches to the problem, it is understandable that buyers of farm products would seek a federal solution. A well-drafted statute easily could deal with the principles embraced by the Food Security Act. However, as written, the statute is fraught with problems. It contains internal inconsistencies and appears to have been drafted without the benefit of an understanding of past and present systems of public notice and secured financing. It fails to acknowledge or deal with many matters that are adequately dealt with by the UCC. For example, it largely ignores the issues and problems raised by multi-state transactions. It also makes possible circular priorities that otherwise would not appear. Consequently, it is not surprising that its detractors hold it up as a prime example of the dangers of creeping federal encroachment on commercial law. For another example, see 7 U.S.C. § 196, which deals with reclamation rights of sellers of livestock.

R9–320(a) protects buyers in ordinary course of business in much the same fashion as did F9–307(1). Yet despite the fact that several states repealed or limited the farm products exception to F9–307(1), and despite the enactment of the Food Security Act, R9–320(a) carries forward the farm products exception. That R9–320(a) retains the approach to farm products taken by F9–307(1) does not necessarily reflect widespread satisfaction. Instead, it probably indicates the absence of a strong consensus for change and the realization that achieving uniformity among the states on this issue is unlikely in any event.

Problem 7.6.19. The Diapason Music Company is a retail store that sells electric organs, grand pianos, and other expensive musical instruments. Diapason's inventory has been purchased with the aid of loans from Castle Finance Company. Diapason has executed in Castle's favor a security agreement covering its inventory, both existing and after-acquired. Castle filed a financing statement that described the collateral as "organs, pianos and other musical instruments."

(a) Diapason, without consulting Castle, sold and delivered an organ to Customer, a consumer, for $4,000 cash, and used the money to pay rent, utilities, and other pressing bills. Promptly upon learning the facts, Castle brings a replevin action for the organ against Customer. What result? See R9–315(a)(1); R9–320(a); R1–201(9). (If you are not sure whether subsection (a) or subsection (b) of R9–320 applies to this Problem, see R9–320, Comment 5.) What considerations underlie the UCC's rule on this point? Whose expectations does the rule reflect?

(b) Suppose that the security agreement in part (a) included the following covenant: "Diapason agrees that, under no circumstances, will it complete a sale of any of its inventory without Castle's prior approval. In the event of such approval, Diapason will immediately turn over to Castle any cash, chattel paper or other proceeds resulting from such sale." Suppose also that the financing statement added the sentence, "Sale of collateral not authorized without Castle's prior approval." Would the result change? See R9–320(a); R9–401(b). Does the UCC's rule make sense?

(c) Would the result in part (a) change if Diapason delivered the organ to Customer under a month-to-month lease? See R9–321(c); UCC 2A–103(1)(o).

(d) Clef, a similar music store in the same city, needed a particular model of organ in order to make prompt delivery to a customer. Diapason had such an organ in stock. In accordance with past arrangements between the two firms, Diapason sold the organ to Clef for $3,000 cash, which was slightly more than wholesale cost. Clef knew that Diapason had inventory financing with Castle. As in part (a), Diapason dissipated the cash received for the organ. Castle brings a replevin action against Clef. What result? See R9–315(a)(1); R9–320(a); R1–201(9). What difference, if any, would it make if the past arrangements between Clef and Diapason were highly unusual among music stores?

(e) Diapason owed $4,000 to Creditor, who was pressing for payment. Diapason delivered one of the organs in the store to Creditor in satisfaction of the debt. Castle brings a replevin action against Creditor. What result? What could the losing party have done to protect itself?

(f) Assume that, in part (e), Creditor also was in the business of selling organs. Before Castle learned that Creditor was in possession of the organ, Creditor sold and delivered the organ to Bass, who had no idea how Creditor acquired the organ. Castle brings a replevin action against Bass. What result? What could the losing party have done to protect itself?

(g) What result in part (f) if, several weeks before Creditor sold the organ to Bass, Castle had learned that Creditor was in possession of the organ but had raised no objection with Diapason or Creditor? See R9–320(a) ("A buyer in ordinary course of business . . . takes free of a security interest *created by the buyer's seller*") & Comment 3, Example 2; UCC 2–403(2), (3); UCC 2–402(3); Note on the "Buyer's Seller" Rule and the Interplay Between UCC 2–403(1) and R9–320(a), infra.

NOTE ON THE "BUYER'S SELLER" RULE AND THE INTERPLAY BETWEEN UCC 2–403(1) AND R9–320(a)

R9–320(a) contains a curious limitation: a buyer in ordinary course of business takes free only of security interests that are "created by the buyer's seller." This means that an inventory financer takes the risk that *its own debtor* will cut off the security interest by selling to a buyer in ordinary course of business, but does not risk losing its security interest if the collateral is sold by some other merchant. For example, assume that *A*, a merchant dealer in goods of that kind, sells inventory to *B*, another merchant, and that *B* is *not* a buyer in ordinary course of business (say, because the sale was in "bulk" and not in "ordinary course"). *B* then sells to *C*, who *is* a BIOCOB. *C* would cut off *SP–B*, *B*'s inventory financer, but not *SP–A*, *A*'s inventory financer.

R9–320(a) seems to be an analogue to UCC 2–403(2) in that an inventory financer typically can be said to have "entrusted" the collateral to the merchant-dealer. But what result obtains if *C*, in the example, could show that *SP–A* entrusted the goods to *B* ? See UCC 2–403(3) (" 'Entrusting includes ... any acquiescence in retention of possession[.]' "). As the most straightforward example, imagine that a secured party takes possession of inventory after the debtor's default (R9–609) and then delivers an item of the inventory to another merchant dealer for repairs. The non-debtor merchant dealer then sells to a BIOCOB. If the sale would cut off the rights of an *owner*-entruster—and it would under UCC 2–403(2)—why should the secured party's rights remain intact?

Under Former Article 9, some courts have permitted a BIOCOB to cut off a security interest under UCC 2–403(2) when the "his seller" requirement of F9–307(1) was not satisfied, so long as it could be shown the secured party itself was an entruster to the selling merchant. Other courts have insisted on strict observance of the "his seller" limitation in UCC 9–307(1). There was some support for the latter view in the statute and the Comments (even if not in logic or policy).

Revised Article 9 leaves no doubt as to the appropriate resolution: R9–315(a) makes clear that UCC 2–403(2) is an exception to the general rule that a security interest survives disposition of the collateral. Under the facts in the example above, *C* would take free of the security interest, even though *SP–A* did not authorize the disposition to *C* free of the security interest. See R9–315, Comment 2; R9–320, Comment 3, Example 2.

Problem 7.6.20. Manufacturer delivered mobile homes to Dealer on credit and, by filing, perfected a security interest in that inventory. Buyer agreed in writing to purchase one of the mobile homes, for Buyer's personal use as a residence, and Buyer made a substantial down payment to Dealer. Before Buyer took possession, Dealer defaulted on its debt to Manufacturer and Manufacturer repossessed the mobile homes held by Dealer, including the trailer that Buyer had agreed to purchase.

(a) Does R9–320(a) protect Buyer? See R1–201(9); R2–502; R9–320(e); Notes on Buyers Who Do Not Take Possession, infra. Can Buyer prevail despite R9–320(e) and Comment 8? (Hint: Did Buyer become a BIOCOB *before* Manufacturer took possession?)

(b) Is there a basis other than Manufacturer's security interest for Manufacturer to attack Buyer's interest? See UCC 2–402(2); Uniform Fraudulent Transfer Act §§ 4(a)(1), 4(b)(2), 7, 8(a); Note (6) on Buyers Who Do Not Take Possession infra.

(c) Suppose that Buyer made a substantial down payment to Dealer for a mobile home to be ordered from Manufacturer. The mobile home was delivered to Dealer but was seized by Manufacturer before Buyer took possession. Should this modification of the facts change the result?

(d) Would the result in part (a) or (c) change if the mobile home had been "specially" constructed to Buyer's specifications, such that if Buyer were to order a similar, specially constructed mobile home from another dealer, delivery to Buyer would be delayed at least six months? See R1–201(9); R2–716. Assuming that Buyer's right to take delivery (as against Dealer) is contingent on Buyer's payment of the remaining balance of the purchase price, could Buyer become a BIOCOB before making the payment?

(e) Would the result in part (a) or (c) change if Buyer had agreed to buy the mobile home for use as a business office? See R1–201(9); R2–502; R2–716.

NOTES ON BUYERS WHO DO NOT TAKE POSSESSION

(1) In General. In Chapter 1, Section 3(A), we considered whether taking possession was necessary for protection, under UCC 2–403(1), as a good faith purchaser for value from a seller with voidable title. In that setting, the interest at risk was the general (or "beneficial") ownership interest of a person who enjoyed a right to reclaim goods that the person had sold to the seller. Our current concern is with a putative BIOCOB under R9–320(a) as against a secured party with a security interest in the goods. In particular, we consider the role of possession in determining when a buyer achieves the status of "buyer in ordinary course of business" under R1–201(9). As we saw in Chapter 1, the significance of taking possession has been the subject of doubt and contention.

(2) "Temporal Definition" of "Buyer in Ordinary Course of Business." The stage of a sale transaction at which a buyer becomes eligible to be a BIOCOB was a primary issue raised in both the commentary and the cases interpreting F9–307(1) and F1–201(9). Some have suggested that one cannot be a BIOCOB under Former Article 9 until there has been a sale, i.e., until title has passed. See UCC 2–106 ("A 'sale' consists in the passing of title from the seller to the buyer for a price (Section 2–401)."). Others have suggested that BIOCOB status may arise as soon as the buyer acquires an interest in the goods—i.e., once the goods are identified to the contract and the buyer acquires a "special property" in them. See UCC 2–501; UCC 2–401; UCC 2–103(1)(a) (" 'Buyer' means a person who buys *or contracts to buy* goods."). Some have argued that one cannot be a BIOCOB under Former Article 9 until delivery of the goods. See F1–201(9) (" 'Buying' . . . includes receiving goods . . . under a pre-existing contract for sale. . . .").

Revised Article 9 goes a long way towards resolving this issue: "Only a buyer that takes possession of the goods or has a right to recover the goods from the seller under Article 2 may be a buyer in ordinary course of business." R1–201(9). This approach rejects all the approaches described in the preceding paragraph and instead adopts the resolution proposed by

Professor Frisch in the following passage (references to UCC 2–502 and UCC 2–716 do not reflect the amendments accompanying Revised Article 9):

V.   A Suggested Temporal Definition

This Article has looked at the several contemporary views of when buyer status attaches and has found that each lacks a persuasive justification for its adoption. But the separate criticisms heaped upon each fail to suggest a convincing alternative. It is only when the deficiency common to all accepted definitions is realized that the necessary materials for constructing a theoretically sound temporal definition become apparent.

Kwikset Division of Emhart Industries v. Mohawk Industrial Design Enterprises (In re Pennsylvania Conveyor Co.)[243] may clarify the problem. Kwikset had contracted to purchase a customized press from Mohawk Industrial Design Enterprises, for a price of $69,375.25. When the press was substantially completed and after Kwikset had paid $54,377.25 toward the purchase price, the press was repossessed by Mohawk's secured creditor, PennBank. Kwikset brought suit seeking possession of the press upon payment of the remainder of the purchase price. PennBank argued that Kwikset had no right of possession because the stringent prerequisites of section 2–502 had not been satisfied.

The bankruptcy court found for Kwikset. In so doing, it drew a sharp distinction between rights under section 2–502 and rights under section 9–307(1) [R9–320(a)]. Acknowledging Kwikset's inability to recover from its seller under section 2–502, the court concluded that if Kwikset were to pay the balance of the purchase price it would qualify for buyer in ordinary course protection under section 9–307(1).

The *Kwikset* approach illustrates how courts and commentators have consistently failed to perceive the anomaly that one can be a buyer in ordinary course absent the availability of a possessory remedy against the immediate seller. Had Mohawk remained in possession of the press, Kwikset, because it failed to meet the requirements of section 2–502, would have been relegated to that hapless class of unsecured creditors for whom full recovery is seldom a reality. Instead, because of the fortuitous circumstance of PennBank's repossession, Kwikset was assured the benefit of its original bargain.

Another version of the same objection to the separability of a possessory remedy from the rights of a buyer in ordinary course views the situation from the secured party's perspective. Before the repossession, PennBank, not Kwikset, had a property interest in the press. And PennBank, not Kwikset, had the legal right of possession. But all this changed once the right of possession was exercised. When PennBank exercised its exclusive right to repossess the printing press, the exclu-

---

243. 31 Bankr. 680 (Bankr.W.D.Pa. 1982).

sivity of that right was destroyed. In other words, once a secured party with the sole and exclusive right of possession repossesses the collateral, its right to retain possession is lost. This is not only bad policy, but also logically inconsistent and linguistically incoherent.

A second argument in favor of defining buyer status in terms of buyer remedies is that such a definition, more than any other, comports with the scope and purpose of the good faith purchase doctrine embodied in the Code. Because the doctrine seeks to facilitate market trading by reducing title uncertainty, its application is premised on the implicit assumption that a point in the sales transaction has been reached at which the buyer has a title expectation needing protection. In assessing where that point lies, it is helpful to think of a sale as the movement of a variety of property sticks from seller to buyer. Absent a stick in the buyer's bundle that give the right to take possession of the goods, the state of the seller's title is immaterial. If the seller breaches, the buyer's expectations are satisfied by an award of monetary damages. If there is no breach, more sticks will come and the cleansing of the seller's title can wait. The buyer's title concerns crystallize, however, once the buyer obtains the legally cognizable right to compel the seller's performance. It is with this stick in hand that the buyer's legitimate claim to good faith purchase treatment materializes.

To see why this is so, one need only understand the Code's approach to buyer's remedies. A central assumption of Article 2 is the homogeneity of goods. If the seller does not deliver the goods, the buyer will, most often, be able to obtain similar goods elsewhere. As a result, the buyer's expectation interest is fully vindicated by a damages award based on an imagined or actual substitute purchase. There are, however, situations, sufficiently out of the ordinary, in which protection of the buyer's expectation demands that the remedy be the right to obtain possession of the goods from the seller. Thus, the buyer has the limited right to recover the goods in certain insolvency situations under section 2–502, the right to specific performance under section 2–716(1), and the right to replevin under section 2–716(3).

Observe the similarity of purpose between the good faith purchase doctrine and the Code's possessory remedies. The essence of both is the perceived utility of protecting the buyer's expectation interest. As a matter of logical consistency, it is impossible to square this common goal with a decision to withhold buyer in ordinary course status until some time after the buyer becomes legally entitled to the goods. Odd indeed would be a legal regime that bestows a possessory right to protect the expectation interest but, at the same time, leaves that right unprotected because of the inapplicability of a doctrine specifically designed to protect that very same interest. Conversely, if one is unwilling to say that the buyer, not the seller, has the superior right of possession, what justification is there for terminating, in favor of that same buyer, third party claims to the goods? It is this constant interplay between remedies and expectations that calls for a definition of buyer status based on remedies. Only when the buyer's expectation interest requires, for its satisfaction, an award of a possessory remedy, should buyer status be recognized.

Frisch, Buyer Status under the U.C.C.: A Suggested Temporal Definition, 72 Iowa L. Rev. 531, 568–572 (1987).

To understand more fully the thinking behind R1–201(9), consider the implications of permitting a putative buyer (*B*) of goods to become a buyer in ordinary course of business from Seller (*S*) *before* it obtains possessory rights against *S*. That normally would produce the anomalous result that *B* could cut off the rights of *S*'s secured party (*SP*) under R9–320(a) even though *B* has no right to possession of the goods as against *S*! As discussed more fully in Note (3), infra, Article 2 would provide pre-delivery possessory rights to *B* only under the limited circumstances set forth in R2–502 and R2–716. Even *S*'s *unsecured* creditors can obtain rights in the goods (e.g., by execution lien) that are senior to those of *B* until such time as *B* obtains possessory rights against *S*. See UCC 2–402(1). *SP*, on the other hand, does have a right to possession as against *S* (albeit a right that normally is contingent on *S*'s default). See R9–609.

Consider also the implications of permitting a buyer to become a BIOCOB and take free of a security interest when the seller (Article 9 debtor) remains in possession of the goods. Can one reconcile such a result with one of Article 9's principal themes: that a secured party ordinarily must give public notice of its interest in order to prevail over competing claimants to the collateral? Should the UCC have been revised to provide that a buyer becomes a BIOCOB only if it either removes the goods from the seller-debtor's possession or notifies the secured party of its purchase? The answer would seem to turn, at least in part, on whether inventory financers actually rely on the debtor's possession of particular items of inventory.

(3) Buyer's Right to Recover Goods from Seller. The temporal aspect to the definition of BIOCOB in R1–201(9) compels one to focus on the circumstances under which a disappointed buyer has an *in rem* rather than an *in personam* remedy against a defaulting seller. R2–716(1) affords a right to specific performance of the sale contract "where the goods are unique or in other proper circumstances." UCC 2–716(3) affords a right to replevin of goods identified to the contract in two limited circumstances: the buyer is unable to effect cover for the goods (or the circumstances reasonably indicate that such effort will be unavailing) or the goods have been shipped under reservation and satisfaction of the security interest in them has been made or tendered.

What are the rights of a buyer who actually has paid for the goods? The secured party has a claim to the payment as proceeds of its collateral. Moreover, if the sale is in the seller' (debtor's) ordinary course of business, the secured party fully expects that the goods will be replaced by the proceeds. As between the prepaying buyer and the seller's secured party, shouldn't the buyer be entitled to the goods? The answer may surprise you: Until the recent revision of Article 9, the fact that a buyer prepaid for goods would appear to have been legally relevant to the buyer's right to recover the goods in only a narrow band of cases. F2–502 afforded a reclamation right "if the seller becomes insolvent within ten days after receipt of the first installment on their price," and then only if the buyer made and kept good a tender of any unpaid portion of the price. If the seller became insolvent before, or more than ten days after, receipt of the first installment, then this reclamation right was unavailable. In practice, however, prepaying buyers may have fared much better. Following is Professor Frisch's analysis:

Consider *Proyectos Electronicos, S.A. v. Alper.*[266] Proyectos had ordered certain electronics equipment from Ram Manufacturing. The full purchase price was paid and the equipment was segregated from the rest of Ram's inventory. Unfortunately for Proyectos, Ram's bankruptcy occurred before the equipment was shipped. Recognizing Proyectos' right to recover the goods from the trustee in bankruptcy, the district court specifically considered the cumulative effect of prepayment and insolvency:

In this case Proyectos has already paid the debtor the full price for the goods. To require Proyectos to cover would require it to pay for identical goods a second time and then stand in line with other unsecured creditors of the debtor, now bankrupt, with the illusory hope that it would get reimbursed for the difference between the cost of cover and the original contract price, plus the money already paid to debtor. Such a result would not be in keeping with the purpose of the Commercial Code to make a non-breaching party whole.

If it were possible to characterize the opinion in *Proyectos* as typical, the inquiry would be at an end and one would be a bit wiser for having made the effort. One would know that a buyer can establish a right to possession, at least against an insolvent seller, by showing a substantial prepayment. The buyer in ordinary course cases could then be viewed as a reaffirmation and extension of this principle, despite the dissimilarity of rhetoric, to similar situations distinguishable only as to the identity of the party contesting the buyer.

Although this logic deduces a pervasive judicial bias in favor of the prepaying buyer, the deduction is premised on the typicality of *Proyectos*. Yet, the majority of courts continue to couch their opinions on possessory remedies in the traditional orthodoxy of uniqueness or peculiarity. The fact remains, however, that prepayment and insolvency are recurrent factual themes in most cases in which the buyer is, for some other stated reason, awarded possession; and prepayment and insolvency are absent in most cases in which possession is withheld. Because this alignment of result is not inevitable, the proposition that the buyer in ordinary course and the right to possession cases are readily explicable as a consequence of a preexistent bias is only

---

266. 37 Bankr. 931 (E.D.Pa.1983).

tentatively offered. Yet, until courts articulate the relevancy, if not the determinacy, of prepayment and insolvency, intuition suggests that these facts have a part to play in determining buyer status, and that the best guess is that they play the leading role.

Frisch, Buyer Status under the U.C.C.: A Suggested Temporal Definition, 72 Iowa L. Rev. 531, 573–74 (1987).

The conflict between the paltry rights that the UCC affords to a prepaying buyer on one hand and what Professor Frisch describes as "a pervasive judicial bias in favor of the prepaying buyer" on the other may soon be resolved. In conjunction with the revision of Article 9, R2–502 was revised to afford considerably greater protection to prepaying buyers of consumer goods: a buyer of consumer goods who has paid a part or all of the price of goods identified to the contract has a right to recover the goods from a seller who repudiates or fails to deliver, if the buyer makes and keeps good a tender of any unpaid portion of the price. R2–502(1)(b). If Article 2 is revised, it is likely to treat non-consumer buyers in a similar way.

(4) The _Tanbro_ Debate. One of the most controversial cases concerning the right of a BIOCOB to take free of a security interest under F9–307(1) is Tanbro Fabrics Corp. v. Deering Milliken, Inc., 39 N.Y.2d 632, 385 N.Y.S.2d 260, 350 N.E.2d 590 (1976). The case concerned unfinished textile fabrics ("greige goods") manufactured by Deering Milliken. Deering sold these goods and others to Mill Fabrics on a "bill and hold" basis; i.e., the goods would be paid for but remain in Deering's warehouse to be delivered as Mill Fabrics instructed. Mill Fabrics agreed that the goods, even if paid for, would secure the obligations of Mill Fabrics to Deering. Mill Fabrics resold the goods to Tanbro, also on a bill and hold basis. Deering refused to deliver the goods to Tanbro on Tanbro's instruction because, although these goods had been paid for, there was an open account balance due Deering from Mill Fabrics, which had become insolvent. Tanbro brought an action in conversion against Deering.

The New York Court of Appeals affirmed the judgment for Tanbro (the court's citations are to the applicable pre–1972 version of the UCC):

> .... Mill Fabrics' sale to Tanbro was in the ordinary course of business, even though its predominant business purpose was, like Tanbro's, the converting of greige goods into finished fabrics. All the Uniform Commercial Code requires is that the sale be in ordinary course associated with the seller's business [F9–307(1)]. The record established that converters buy greige goods in propitious markets and often in excess of their requirements as they eventuate. On the occasion of excess purchases, converters at times enter the market to sell the excess through brokers to other converters, and converters buy such goods if the price is satisfactory or the particular goods are not available from manufacturers. Both conditions obtained here.
>
> Tanbro and Mill Fabrics were customers of Deering for many years. Goods would be purchased in scale on a "bill and hold" basis,

that is, the goods would be paid for and delivered as the buyers instructed. When the goods were needed, they were delivered directly where they were to be converted, at the buyers' plants or the plants of others if that would be appropriate. Pending instructions, the sold and paid for goods were stored in the warehouses of the manufacturer, both because the buyers lacked warehousing space and retransportation of the goods to be processed would be minimized.

. . .

A former Mill Fabrics' employee testified that there were times when Mill Fabrics, like all converters, found itself with excess goods. When it was to their business advantage, they sold the excess fabrics to other converters. Although these sales were relatively infrequent they were nevertheless part of and in the ordinary course of Mill Fabrics' business, even if only incidental to the predominant business purpose. Examples of a nonqualifying sale might be a bulk sale, a sale in distress at an obvious loss price, a sale in liquidation, a sale of a commodity never dealt with before by the seller and wholly unlike its usual inventory, or the like. . . .

The combination of stored, paid for goods, on a hold basis, and the retention of a security interest by Deering makes commercial sense. Mill Fabrics' capacity to discharge its obligation to Deering was in part made possible because it sold off or converted the goods held at the Deering warehouse. Mill Fabrics, as an honest customer, was supposed to remit the proceeds from resale or conversion to Deering and thus reduce, and eventually discharge its responsibility to Deering. Thus, so long as it was customary for Mill Fabrics, and in the trade for converters, to sell off excess goods, the sale was in the ordinary course of business. Moreover, on an alternative analysis, such a sale by Mill Fabrics was therefore impliedly authorized under the code if its indebtedness to Deering was to be liquidated (see Official Comment to [F]9–307, par. 2; Draper v. Minneapolis–Moline, 100 Ill.App.2d 324, 329, 241 N.E.2d 342).

All [F9–307(1)] requires is that the sale be of the variety reasonably to be expected in the regular course of an on-going business. . . . This was such a case.

Tanbro Fabrics Corp. v. Deering Milliken, Inc., 39 N.Y.2d 632, 634–37, 385 N.Y.S.2d 260, 350 N.E.2d 590, 591–93 (1976).

The *Tanbro* case became a *cause celebre* that generated dispute among specialists in secured financing. Professor Kripke thought that the case was wrongly decided and that the buyer should bear the risk that inventory is encumbered with a possessory security interest:

It is irrelevant to argue that it is not commercially feasible for the law to require buyers to inspect the goods and ascertain that the seller has them, and that therefore the secured party as the person best able to bear the risk should bear it. Of course, I do not contend that every buyer should inspect the goods. Trust in fair dealing and honesty is the foundation of all forms of business, but when there is a mistaken reliance on the seller to have unseen goods, it is obvious that there is not always a likely victim to bail out the buyer who thinks that he is in ordinary course of business. As we have seen, the buyer who thinks that he is in ordinary course is out of luck if the seller never had the goods or if he has sold them or if a secured party has repossessed them and thus taken title in himself or another. Why should a secured party who has done everything that he could, namely, taken them into his possession and eliminated any apparent ownership by the merchant, be the one victim required to bail out the improvident or unlucky buyer?

When a secured party has taken possession in himself, he has done everything he could to preclude the existence of a buyer in ordinary course. In my opinion, the Code should not make it impossible to have a loan on goods which are not in fact available for exhibition, sale and delivery by the merchant, without running the risk of losing the security through sales to purported buyers in ordinary course, just because the goods are classified as inventory. The fact that the goods are not in the buyer's possession, but are held by the secured party under an adverse claim of right, makes them very different from ordinary inventory.

Kripke, Should Section 9–307(1) of The Uniform Commercial Code Apply Against a Secured Party in Possession?, 33 Bus.Law. 153, 159 (1977). Both the *Tanbro* opinion and Professor Kripke's article provoked others to address the issue at some length.

Revised Article 9 resolves the debate by rejecting *Tanbro*. R9–320(e) provides expressly that the "BIOCOB-takes-free" rule of R9–320(a) "do[es] not affect a security interest in goods in the possession of the secured party under Section 9–313."[9]

(5) Buyer's Nonpayment. Assume that *B*, in a *cash sale* transaction, has a right to specific performance under UCC 2–716(1). Notwithstanding *B*'s right to specific performance, does *B* actually have a possessory right against *S* before *B* pays the price? See UCC 2–511(2); UCC 2–511(1). If not, and if *B*'s interest is (consequently) subordinate to *S*'s inventory financer, *SP*, what remedy does *B* have against *S*? See UCC 2–711; UCC 2–713.

(6) Fraudulent Transfer Implications of Seller's Retention of Possession; UCC 2–402(2). Recall the discussion of *Twyne's Case* and the "Fraud in Law" doctrine in Note (3) on Perfection by Filing (Section 3, supra). We noted there that modern fraudulent transfer law adopts the "fraud in fact" approach, whereby a seller's retention of possession of goods is merely a factor to be considered in determining whether the seller has made the transfer "with actual intent to hinder, delay, or defraud any

---

9. The revised definition of "buyer in ordinary course of business," under which only a buyer who takes possession of the goods or has a right to recover the goods from the seller under Article 2 may be a BIOCOB, drastically limits the significance of the *Tanbro* debate. See R1–201(9). However, it does not resolve the debate entirely. For example, *B* might have a pre-delivery possessory right in goods by way of an entitlement to specific performance under UCC 2–716(1) even though *SP* is in possession of the goods.

creditor." Uniform Fraudulent Transfer Act §§ 4(a)(1), 4(b)(2). The UCC generally leaves the matter of fraudulent transfers to non-UCC law. However, UCC 2–402(2) does provide a safe harbor for "retention of possession in good faith and current course of trade by a merchant-seller for a commercially reasonable time after a sale or identification." Detailed treatment of fraudulent transfers is beyond the scope of these materials.

NOTES ON BULK SALES

(1) Regulation of Bulk Sales. According to the definition of "buyer in ordinary course of business," "[a] person that acquires goods in a transfer in bulk ... is not a buyer in ordinary course of business." R1–201(9). Pre–1988 Article 6 governed certain transfers in bulk. That Article defined "bulk transfer" as "any transfer in bulk and not in the ordinary course of the transferor's business of a major part of the materials, supplies, merchandise or other inventory ... of an enterprise subject to this Article." UCC 6–102(2) (pre–1988). "The enterprises subject to this Article are all those whose principal business is the sale of merchandise from stock, including those who manufacture what they sell." UCC 6–102(3) (pre–1988).

In 1988, the sponsors of the UCC recommended that Article 6 be repealed and not replaced. The following excerpt from the Prefatory Note to the Repealer of Article 6 explains the history of bulk sales legislation and the reasons for eliminating Article 6 from the UCC:

> **Background.** Bulk sale legislation originally was enacted in response to a fraud perceived to be common around the turn of the century: a merchant would acquire his stock in trade on credit, then sell his entire inventory ("in bulk") and abscond with the proceeds, leaving creditors unpaid. The creditors had a right to sue the merchant on the unpaid debts, but that right often was of little practical value. Even if the merchant-debtor was found, in personam jurisdiction over him might not have been readily available. Those creditors who succeeded in obtaining a judgment often were unable to satisfy it because the defrauding seller had spent or hidden the sale proceeds. Nor did the creditors ordinarily have recourse to the merchandise sold. The transfer of the inventory to an innocent buyer effectively immunized the goods from the reach of the seller's creditors. The creditors of a bulk seller thus might be left without a means to satisfy their claims.

> To a limited extent, the law of fraudulent conveyances ameliorated the creditors' plight. When the buyer in bulk was in league with the seller or paid less than full value for the inventory, fraudulent conveyance law enabled the defrauded creditors to avoid the sale and apply the transferred inventory toward the satisfaction of their claims against the seller. But fraudulent conveyance law provided no remedy against persons who bought in good faith, without reason to know of the seller's intention to pocket the proceeds and disappear, and for

adequate value. In those cases, the only remedy for the seller's creditors was to attempt to recover from the absconding seller.

State legislatures responded to this perceived "bulk sale risk" with a variety of legislative enactments. Common to these statutes was the imposition of a duty on the buyer in bulk to notify the seller's creditors of the impending sale. The buyer's failure to comply with these and any other statutory duties generally afforded the seller's creditors a remedy analogous to the remedy for fraudulent conveyances: the creditors acquired the right to set aside the sale and reach the transferred inventory in the hands of the buyer.

Like its predecessors, [pre–1988] Article 6 ... is remarkable in that it obligates buyers in bulk to incur costs to protect the interests of the seller's creditors, with whom they usually have no relationship. Even more striking is that Article 6 affords creditors a remedy against a good faith purchaser for full value without notice of any wrongdoing on the part of the seller. The Article thereby impedes normal business transactions, many of which can be expected to benefit the seller's creditors. For this reason, Article 6 has been subjected to serious criticism.

In the legal context in which [pre–1988] Article 6 ... and its nonuniform predecessors were enacted, the benefits to creditors appeared to justify the costs of interfering with good faith transactions. Today, however, creditors are better able than ever to make informed decisions about whether to extend credit.... A search of the public real estate and personal property records will disclose most encumbrances on a debtor's property with little inconvenience.

In addition, changes in the law now afford creditors greater opportunities to collect their debts.... Moreover, creditors of a merchant no longer face the choice of extending unsecured credit or no credit at all. Retaining an interest in inventory to secure its price has become relatively simple and inexpensive under Article 9.

Finally, there is no evidence that, in today's economy, fraudulent bulk sales are frequent enough, or engender credit losses significant enough, to require regulation of all bulk sales, including the vast majority that are conducted in good faith. ...

Recommendation. The National Conference of Commissioners on Uniform State Laws and the American Law Institute believe that changes in the business and legal contexts in which sales are conducted have made regulation of bulk sales unnecessary. The Conference and the Institute therefore withdraw their support for Article 6 of the Uniform Commercial Code and encourage those states that have enacted the Article to repeal it.

The Conference and the Institute recognize that bulk sales may present a particular problem in some states and that some legislatures may wish to continue to regulate bulk sales. They believe that [pre–1988] Article 6 has become inadequate for that purpose. For those states that are disinclined to repeal Article 6, they have promulgated a revised version of Article 6. The revised Article is designed to afford better protection to creditors while minimizing the impediments to good-faith transactions.

As of this writing, 42 states are without a bulk sales law; four states and the District of Colombia have adopted revised Article 6; the remainder have retained the pre–1988 Article or a variant thereof.

(2) Does a Buyer's Compliance With Article 6 Affect Its Rights?
Bulk sales legislation was enacted primarily for the benefit of *unsecured* creditors of the seller. But for this legislation, these unsecured creditors would have no right to satisfy their claims against the seller from the property of the buyer (i.e., from the inventory sold in bulk). See generally Chapter 1, Section 3, supra (discussing the *nemo dat* principle).

In contrast, the seller's secured party (inventory financer) would seem to have little need for the protection Article 6 affords. Inasmuch as a "person that acquires goods in a transfer in bulk" is not a "buyer in ordinary course," R1–201(9), a person who buys the seller's inventory at a bulk sale would not take free of perfected security interests in the inventory. See R9–315(a)(1); R9–320(a). Nevertheless, one court suggested repeatedly, albeit in dictum, that compliance with the notice and other requirements of pre–1988 Article 6 would enable a non-ordinary course buyer to take free of perfected security interests. In re McBee, 714 F.2d 1316 (5th Cir.1983). For strong criticism of this, and other, aspects of the case, see Harris, The Interaction of Articles 6 and 9 of the Uniform Commercial Code: A Study in Conveyancing, Priorities, and Code Interpretation, 39 Vand.L.Rev. 179 (1986). For a somewhat less disapproving view of *McBee*, see Carlson, Bulk Sales Under Article 9: Some Easy Cases Made Difficult, 41 Ala. L. Rev. 729, 736–48 (1990).

Problem 7.6.21. Lender obtained a perfected security interest in all existing and after-acquired inventory of Poss.

(a) Poss is now in the process of assembling components into a finished widget that Nonposs has agreed to buy. Nonposs has made advance payments to Poss under the written sale contract. Is Lender's security interest in the components senior to the interest claimed by Nonposs? Can a judgment creditor of Poss acquire an execution lien on the components? If so, is the lien senior to the interest claimed by Nonposs in the goods? What, if anything, could Nonposs have done to ensure its seniority? See generally Notes on Buyers Who Do Not Take Possession, supra.

(b) Would the results in part (a) change if Nonposs had loaned funds to Poss, the seller, in order to enable Poss to acquire the components and complete the manufacture of the widget? See Note on the "Financing Buyer," infra.

(c) Instead of agreeing to buy a widget from Poss, Nonposs agrees to buy, directly from third-party suppliers, all of the raw materials and components necessary to build a widget. Under the terms of the purchase orders, Nonposs will advance funds directly to the suppliers of the materials and components, although the goods are to be delivered directly to Poss's factory. Poss and Nonposs enter into a "service agreement" under which Poss is to manufacture the widget using the supplies "bought and paid for" by Nonposs. Is there an economic difference between this arrangement and Nonposs's prepayment under a contract of sale and the use of those funds by Poss to buy the components? Would each transaction appear in the same fashion on Poss's balance sheet? Should the result here differ from the results in (a) and (b) above? See Notes on Bailments for Processing, Chapter 8, Section 1(C), supra.

NOTE ON THE "FINANCING BUYER"

We have seen that a prepaying buyer is in a precarious position until it takes delivery or obtains pre-delivery possessory rights against a seller. See Notes on Buyers Who Do Not Take Possession, supra; UCC 2–402(1), (2); R2–502; R2–716.

There are many reasons why one who contracts to buy goods might be called upon to pay before delivery. The seller may require a down payment (or even prepayment of the price in full) to offset the risk that the seller will acquire or manufacture the goods only to discover that the buyer cannot or will not pay. But what of the situation where the buyer prepays to "finance" the seller's costs of manufacturing the goods to be sold to the buyer? (Among these costs might be the costs of labor, materials, rent, and utilities.) The buyer could achieve priority over subsequent lien creditors by taking and perfecting a security interest in the seller's relevant materials and in the work in process as manufacturing proceeds. The security interest could be made to secure all of the seller's obligations under the sales contract. But, assuming that there is an earlier-filed financing statement made by the seller's inventory financer (as often is the case), the buyer is left with two choices. One choice is to seek to obtain a subordination agreement from the seller's inventory financer. See R9–339. The other alternative is to ensure that the security interest is a purchase-money security interest ("PMSI") and that all of the steps necessary for PMSI priority under R9–324(b) are taken.

In many transactions the time and expense of obtaining a subordination agreement may make that alternative infeasible. Obtaining a PMSI also may be impractical; in addition, the PMSI may not provide the buyer with the protection it desires. For example, to comply with the strict tracing requirement of R9–103(a)(2), the buyer would be required to advance funds directly to the seller's suppliers. Even then, PMSI status would be available only to the extent of the cost of the raw components, and buyer's damages for the seller's non-delivery could exceed that amount. See generally Section 6(A)(II), supra. Problems also could arise from the commingling of PMSI-financed goods with other supplies and materials of the seller-debtor. See R9–336.

Professors Jackson and Kronman recognized that the purchase-money financer and the financing buyer perform a similar economic function and that Article 9 affords scant protection to the latter. The following excerpt reflects their proposed solution:

The financing buyer may be elevated to parity with the purchase money lender in two ways. The first would simply be to abolish the strict tracing requirement of § 9–107(1)(b) [R9–103(a)(2)] by deleting the words "if such value is in fact so used." Although the elimination of the § 9–107(b) tracing requirement may be desirable, it is also certain to be controversial.

A more conservative solution would be to add a new subsection (c) to § 9–107 . . . , which would read as follows:

A security interest is a "purchase money security interest" to the extent that it is . . .

(c) taken by a buyer who makes advances to a seller to enable the seller to manufacture, assemble or process goods for the buyer during the period of one year following the advance, and the collateral securing the advance consists of (i) materials acquired after the advance has been made which are necessary for the manufacture, assembly or processing of the contract goods, and (ii) goods manufactured, assembled, or processed after the advance has been made which could be used to satisfy the contract (whether or not in a deliverable state).[147]

No further change in the Code would be necessary; the new subsection would give the financing buyer a purchase money security interest in the goods he had contracted for, thereby making him eligible for the special priority of § 9–312(3) [R9–324(b)]. In this way, the financing buyer would be endowed with the rights and charged with the duties, of a purchase money lender.

Although the latter approach lacks simplicity and elegance, it achieves the same result, so far as the financing buyer is concerned, as the abolition of the strict tracing requirement. Whichever approach is preferred, the time has come to improve the status of the financing buyer. Indeed, as we have suggested, the elevation of the financing

---

147. The proposed section limits the priority to materials received or manufacturing steps taken after the advance of the money. This is to ensure that the financing buyer is, indeed, a "financing," and not merely a prepaying, buyer. The ordinary prepaying buyer does nothing to allow the manufacturer to move forward in the completion of the contract, and should not receive a special priority in the completed goods.

The relevant test should be, not the strict tracing requirement itself, but rather a test that looks to see if the financing money has actually been used in a manner that arguably enabled the debtor to progress towards completion of its contract with the financing buyer. This test is, itself, a kind of "tracing" requirement. It looks to any manufacturing steps taken after the receipt of the money from the financing buyer that further the production of goods that are for, or arguably could be for, the financing buyer. The existence of such a continuing manufacturing process signals that the money has been used in an "enabling" sense for that contract. The equities that attach to the purchase money lender, as a consequence, also attach here.

buyer is dictated by the Code's own policy of giving new money priority protection over old. By promoting the financing buyer to parity with the purchase money lender, the Code can cure a longstanding anomaly in commercial law and effectuate the fair and uniform application of one of its own underlying policies.

Jackson & Kronman, A Plea for the Financing Buyer, 85 Yale L.J. 1, 36–37 (1975).

Professors Jackson and Kronman apparently have recanted as to the plausibility of eliminating generally the tracing requirement for PMSI's. See Jackson & Kronman, Secured Financing and Priorities Among Creditors, 88 Yale L.J. 1143, 1176 (1979) (arguing that eliminating the tracing requirement would result in a "last-in-time" priority rule leading to all credit being unsecured credit); Note (3) on Purchase-money Priority and the Definition of "Purchase-money Security Interest," Section 6(A)(II), supra.

Does their proposed UCC 9–107(c) have merit? Although it solves some of the commingling and tracing problems, it elevates the "new money" above the interest of first-to-file secured party as to *all* of the qualifying goods. Those goods might be of a value considerably in excess of the amount of the financing buyer's advances, thereby giving the financing buyer a greater "equity cushion" than the normal PMSI financer. Would this "last-in-time" priority rule have deleterious effects on the utility of secured credit similar to (even if not so significant as) those that the authors later argued would follow from generally eliminating the tracing requirements for PMSI's? Would the proposed solution exacerbate the problem of commingling in cases of multiple financing buyers who claim the same collateral? Is the plight of the financing buyer limited to so few transactions that the alternative of obtaining subordination agreements is more cost-effective than creating additional complexity in the statute?

(II) UNPERFECTED SECURITY INTERESTS AND BUYERS OF GOODS

Problem 7.6.22. On June 1 *SP* loaned $50,000 to *D*. On the same day, to secure the loan, *D* granted a security interest to *SP* by signing a security agreement covering "all equipment now owned or hereafter acquired." *SP* inadvertently failed to file a financing statement.

On July 1 *D* sold an item of equipment (a used backhoe) to *B–1*, a competitor, for $5,000 cash. That same day *B–1* came to *D*'s place of business and picked up the backhoe and took it away. *B–1* knew nothing of *SP*'s security interest.

(a) On July 15 *SP* discovered the error and demanded that *B–1* deliver the backhoe to *SP*. Advise *B–1*. See R9–317(b); R9–310(a), (b).

(b) On July 15 *SP* discovered the error and filed the financing statement in the proper office. On August 1, *B–1* sold the backhoe to *B–2*. Whose rights are senior, *SP*'s or *B–2*'s? See UCC 2–403(1).

(c) Now assume that *SP* did not file a financing statement. However, *SP* found out about the sale to *B*–1 as well as the imminent sale to *B*–2. On August 1, while *B*–2 was at *B*–1's place of business preparing to load the backhoe on *B*–2's truck, *SP* showed up and said to *B*–2, "Don't go through with that sale. I want the backhoe; I have a security interest in it!" *B*–2 ignored the demand and took the backhoe away. Whose rights are senior, *SP*'s or *B*–2's?

Problem 7.6.23. On June 1 *SP*, with *D*'s authorization, filed a financing statement covering "equipment." The following day *D* sold an item of equipment (a used backhoe) to *B*, a competitor, for cash. That same day *B* came to *D*'s place of business, picked up the backhoe, and took it away. *B* did not conduct a UCC filing search. On June 15 *SP* loaned $50,000 to *D*. On the same day, to secure the loan, *D* granted a security interest to *SP* by signing a security agreement covering "all equipment now owned or hereafter acquired."

(a) On July 15 *SP* discovered the sale to *B* and demanded that *B* deliver the backhoe to *SP*. Advise *B*. See R9–317(b); R9–308(a).

(b) Would your advice to *B* change if *D* had signed the security agreement on June 1?

(c) Under the facts of part (b), would your advice to *B* change if on June 1 *SP* also had made the $50,000 loan to *D* and then made another $50,000 loan on June 15? See R9–323(d), (e). Do you need additional facts to answer this question?

Problem 7.6.24. Your client, *B*, is interested in buying, for cash, a large quantity of used construction equipment from *S*, a contractor that is going out of business. What precautions would you take to ensure that your client gets good title to the equipment free of all Article 9 security interests? How would you structure the closing of the transaction (i.e., payment and delivery of the equipment)? See R9–317(b), (e).

NOTES ON UNPERFECTED SECURITY INTERESTS AND BUYERS OF COLLATERAL

(1) The "Delivery" Requirement. R9–317(b) conditions a buyer's taking free of an unperfected security interest on both the giving of value and the receipt of delivery of the property "without knowledge of the security interest ... and before it is perfected." How can a buyer ensure its seniority? Consider the prospective buyer who searches, turns up no filed financing statements against the seller (or its predecessors in interest), and then pays the seller. What result if the buyer learns of the unperfected security interest, or if the secured party files, during the gap (which might be very short) between payment and delivery? What result if the security interest is a purchase-money security interest and the financing statement is filed shortly after the buyer pays for the goods and takes delivery?

(2) Buyers of Certain Intangible Collateral. R9–317(d) applies to licensees of general intangibles and buyers of certain types of intangible collateral. For the most part, the subsection parallels R9–317(b). Observe, however, that subsection (d) contains no "delivery" requirement. Unlike the collateral covered by subsection (b), the types of collateral covered by subsection (d) (i.e., accounts, electronic chattel paper, general intangibles, and investment property other than a certificated security) cannot be delivered or possessed.

(C) LIEN CREDITORS

In Section 3, supra, we saw a few fact patterns in which a security interest came in conflict with a judicial lien. This Section considers a few other fact patterns.

Problem 7.6.25. In the setting of the Prototype (Section 1, supra), Lean, the holder of a judgment against Main, caused the sheriff to levy on Main's inventory of cars. Lean obtained the writ of execution and the sheriff levied after the parties had executed the Dealer Inventory Security Agreement (Form 7.2) and the Financing Statement (Form 7.1) had been filed. After the levy, Firstbank "picked up" the floorplan financing by advancing funds to Old Bank pursuant to Loan Request Form (Form 7.4), as described in the Prototype.

(a) Who has a better claim to the cars, Lean or Firstbank? See R9–317(a)(2); R9–203(a), (b); R9–308(a); UCC 1–201(44); Dealer Inventory Security Agreement ¶ 5. What could the losing party have done to avoid the loss?

(b) Would the answer to part (a) change if the deal "cratered" because of the levy (i.e., if Firstbank never provided financing to Main)?

(c) What result in part (a) if the parties executed the Dealer Inventory Security Agreement after Lean obtained the writ? What could the losing party have done to avoid the loss?

Problem 7.6.26. On March 19 Main Motors executed and delivered to Firstbank the Dealer Inventory Security Agreement and Demand Note (Forms 7.2 and 7.3) described in the Prototype (Section 1, supra). Immediately thereafter, pursuant to paragraph 2 of the Dealer Inventory Security Agreement, Main gave to Firstbank a Loan Request Form, requesting that Firstbank advance funds to General Motors for a trailerload of new cars. Should Firstbank make the loan as requested, even though the Financing Statement has not been filed? See R9–317(a)(2); R9–317(e); R9–103(b), (a).

Problem 7.6.27. Using the proceeds of a loan from Credit Union, on March 1 Dombrowski, a resident of Delaware, purchased and took delivery of a car. The loan was secured by a security interest in the car. Dombrowski's application for a Pennsylvania certificate of title arrived at the Pennsylvania department of motor vehicles on March 3. The application indicated Credit Union's security interest. On March 22, the certificate of title, which indicated Credit Union's security interest, was mailed to Credit Union. Assume that under both Delaware and Pennsylvania law, a security interest in a motor vehicle is perfected when the state issues a certificate of title showing the security interest. In the meanwhile, on March 15, Eck, a judgment creditor of Dombrowski's, acquired an execution lien on the car.

(a) Which state's law governs priority between Eck's lien and Credit Union's security interest? See R9–301; R9–303.

(b) Is Credit Union's security interest senior or junior to Eck's lien? See R9–311(b); R9–317(e) & Comment 8.

Problem 7.6.28. To secure a line of credit, Party Press, a printer, created a security interest in all its inventory and equipment, existing and after-acquired, in favor of Carton Credit Co. Carton perfected the security interest by filing. On February 1 Elsie, who held a judgment against Party, caused the sheriff to levy on two of Party's presses. At the time of the levy, $250,000 was outstanding on the line of credit. Unaware of the levy, Carton extended an additional $50,000 on the line of credit on March 1 and an additional $100,000 on April 1.

(a) Who has the senior claim to the presses, Carton or Elsie? See R9–317(a)(2); R9–323(a), (b).

(b) What result in part (a) if Carton had learned of the levy on February 15?

This Problem concerns the priority of "future advances." Problems 7.6.2 and 7.6.18, supra, raise similar priority disputes in which the competing claimant is a competing secured party and a buyer, respectively. Compare your answers to this Problem with your answers to the others. Can you explain any differences in result? (Hint: See R9–323, Comment 4.)

CHAPTER 8

THE SCOPE OF ARTICLE 9

The discussion in Chapter 7 of the law governing attachment, perfection, and priorities was premised upon the assumption that Article 9 applies to the transactions. Article 9 does not, however, apply to *all* secured transactions. And some of its provisions apply to transactions that do not create security interests. This Chapter examines more closely the scope of Article 9.

Substance, rather than form, controls whether a transaction is within the scope of Article 9. Article 9 applies "to a transaction, *regardless of its form*, that creates a security interest in personal property or fixtures by contract." R9–109(a)(1). What exactly is the substance of a "security interest"? When does a transaction that the parties consider not to be for security nevertheless create a security interest?

To understand which transactions give rise to a "security interest," one must consult the definition of the term in R1–201(37). The length of the definition (it runs nearly two pages) suggests the difficulty of defining the term. The first sentence explains that a security interest is "an interest in personal property ... which secures payment or performance of an obligation." As Professor Gilmore pointed out, "[t]his, like most definitions of basic terms, is essentially a declaration of faith." 1 Gilmore, Security § 11.1, at 334.

Declarations of faith, however, are not meaningless. Section 1 of this Chapter focuses on interests in goods; it explores how courts have attempted to discern the line between security interests, as to which Article 9 applies, and other, similar property interests that are not security interests and as to which Article 9 generally is inapplicable. It not only attempts to refine the definition of "security interest" but also examines the legal treatment of nonpossessory interests in goods that are not "security interests." Section 2 addresses briefly transactions in rights to payment (receivables): accounts, chattel paper, payment intangibles, and promissory notes. (A fuller discussion of rights to payment appears in Chapter 9, Section 1, infra.) As we shall see in each of the first two Sections, the definition of "security interest" and the scope of Article 9 extend beyond interests that secure an obligation; that is, certain interests in goods and receivables are "security interests" governed by Article 9 even though they do not "secure[ ] payment or performance of an obligation." See R1–201(37) (2d sentence); R9–109(a)(3); R9–109(a)(4).

Whereas the scope of Article 9 generally is limited to interests created by contract, Article 9 nevertheless applies to statutorily-created "agricultural liens." See R9–109(a)(2); R9–102(a)(5). Section 3 introduces you to these liens, which are discussed more fully in Chapter 11, Section 5(B), infra. Finally, Section 4 looks at transactions that Article 9 excludes from its scope, even though they do create security interests.

Section 1.   Bailments

INTRODUCTORY NOTE

Much of Article 9 addresses problems that may arise when one person claims an interest in goods in the possession of another. Secured transactions are not the only occasion for nonpossessory interests in goods. These interests arise in a wide variety of settings. Individuals often leave goods with third parties: watches are repaired; clothing is cleaned; tools are loaned to neighbors; film is developed. Commercial transactions, too, often give rise to nonpossessory interests: grain is stored and milled; cattle are fattened in feed lots and sold; metals are refined; construction equipment is leased.

Many of these interests may pose problems similar to those posed by nonpossessory security interests: they may be sham transactions; they may create "ostensible ownership" problems. See generally Chapter 7, Section 3(A), supra. The priority rules contained in Part 3 of Article 9 provide the Article's "solution" to the problems of nonpossessory security interests. As you know, security interests as to which no public notice has been given generally are unperfected, see R9–308(a), and unperfected security interests generally are subordinate to the rights of third parties who claim an interest in the collateral. See, e.g., R9–317(a)(2), (b); R9–322(a)(2). See also Chapter 7, Section 6, supra. To what extent does the UCC impose this solution on transactions that create nonpossessory interests in goods but that are not for security? To what extent should it do so? These are two of the questions that are the focus of this Section.

The law applicable to most nonpossessory interests in goods contains no public notice requirement akin to the Article 9 perfection rules. Rather, third parties take subject to a nonpossessory interest even if the holder of that interest does not publicize it. But see, e.g., UCC 2–403(2) (buyer in ordinary course takes rights of entruster of goods) (discussed in Chapter 7, Section 3(C), supra). Debtors and secured parties desirous of avoiding the application of Article 9's filing and priority rules may be tempted to document a secured transaction in another way (say, as a lease). Similarly, a secured party who has failed to perfect a security interest may argue in retrospect that the transaction does not create a security interest and so the failure to perfect (e.g., file) was irrelevant.

The law distinguishes between security interests and most other nonpossessory interests in goods not only with respect to perfection and priority rules but also with regard to the enforcement rights of the person not in possession. Article 9 affords debtors certain rights and imposes upon secured parties certain duties that cannot be waived. See R9–602; Chapter 12, infra. The law applicable to other, similar transactions may afford no such protection to the person in possession of the goods. This disparity, too, may prompt secured parties to assert that their interests are not security interests.

The scope provisions of Article 9 preclude debtors and secured parties from overriding the substantive provisions of the Article (whether relating to the secured party's remedies or the relative rights of competing claimants to the collateral) by characterizing what is in essence a security interest as something else. To determine whether to reject the parties' characterization of a particular transaction, however, one must have an idea of what a security interest is.

Many of the transactions that create nonpossessory interests in goods are bailments. A commonly used definition of "bailment" is that of Justice Story: "a delivery of a thing in trust for some special object or purpose, and upon a contract express or implied, to conform to the object of the trust." J. Story, Commentaries on the Law of Bailments § 2 (6th ed. 1856). Professor Williston defined bailment even more broadly as "the rightful possession of goods by one who is not the owner." 4 Williston & Thompson, Law of Contracts § 1032 (rev. ed. 1936). This Section examines several common types of bailments with a view toward determining (i) whether the transaction creates a "security interest" and (ii) if not, what law regulates the nonpossessory interest.

(A) LEASES

INTRODUCTORY NOTES

(1) The Role of Personal Property Leasing. A firm that wishes to acquire equipment may be reluctant (or unable) to pay with cash on hand. One option is to acquire the equipment on secured credit. Even a firm with strong credit may prefer, however, to acquire the use of the equipment by entering into a lease. The following are among the reasons that prompt firms to lease goods: the lessor may be able to purchase equipment in large quantity at advantageous rates and may have efficient outlets for disposing of used equipment; the lessor (Xerox and IBM are examples) may have special skill in servicing technical equipment; a leasing arrangement may give the lessee a higher tax deduction than the rate of depreciation on equipment that it purchases; the lessee may have promised other creditors (e.g., in a credit agreement or bond indenture) that it would not grant security interests in its property. In some situations leasing has tax advantages for the lessor, who is able to pass a portion of the tax savings along to the lessee. For example, a lessor who has substantial income from other sources may wish to take advantage of tax deductions for accelerated depreciation.

These various factors have produced in recent decades a tremendous growth in equipment leasing. For example, during the 1990's business investment in leased equipment in the United States nearly doubled—from 388 billion dollars in 1990 to an estimated 738 billion dollars in 1999. The annual volume of equipment leases in the United States rose during that period from 124 billion dollars in 1990 to an estimated 226 billion dollars in 1999. Of the new equipment currently accepted for delivery in the United States, nearly one-third is leased. Leasing also plays an important role in the acquisition of consumer goods. These transactions range from week-to-week "rent to own" leases of television sets to long-term leases of expensive automobiles.

(2) The Legal Consequences of Distinguishing Leases From Secured Transactions. One might argue that the lessor's interest under a lease "secures payment or performance of an obligation" and is therefore always a "security interest" within the meaning of R1–201(37): If the lessee fails to comply with its obligations under the lease, e.g., fails to pay rent, then the lessor may retake the goods. Despite this potentially broad reading of "security interest," the second, third, and fourth paragraphs of the definition in R1–201(37), which are devoted to distinguishing between leases and security interests, make clear that not every lease creates a security interest.

How does one determine whether Article 9 applies to a particular transaction that has been documented as a lease? Before answering this important question, it is useful to have in mind some of the consequences of the distinction between putative leases that are within the scope of Article 9, and other ("true") leases.

A lease for security is nothing other than an Article 9 secured transaction dressed up in lease terminology. The "lessee," who is obligated to make periodic payments, is an Article 9 "debtor." The "lessor," who is entitled to payment and who enjoys the right to recover the leased goods upon the "lessee's" default, is an Article 9 secured party. The attachment, perfection, priority, and remedial rules of Article 9 apply to the transaction, just as if the parties had used the secured transaction form and terminology.

In contrast, a "true lease" is not an Article 9 transaction. Article 2A governs the rights of the lessor and lessee in a true lease transaction. To some extent, Article 2A also governs the rights of third parties.

The need to distinguish between a lease for security and a true lease arises in a variety of contexts. Of primary importance is that the "lessor's" interest in goods under a lease for security is an Article 9 security interest. To protect its interest against the claims of third parties, the "lessor" must file a financing statement; otherwise, the "lessor's" security interest will be unperfected and the competing claimant probably will take priority over the "lessor." See R9–317(a)(2), (b); R9–322(a)(1). (Perfecting by taking possession of the goods is an alternative to filing, but it is of virtually no practical use in a transaction, like a lease for security, which is characterized by the debtor ("lessee") using the goods.) In contrast, absent a statute to the contrary, filing is irrelevant as to true leases.

If the "lessee" under a lease for security enters bankruptcy, the "lessor's" failure to file a financing statement will result in the avoidance (nullification) of the "lessor's" interest by the bankruptcy trustee. See BC 544(a)(1) (discussed in Chapter 10, Section 2(A), infra). The failure of a lessor under a true lease to file a financing statement will not affect the lessor's rights in bankruptcy.

Another consequence of the application of Article 9 to leases for security is that the "lessor" under such a lease must comply with Part 6 of Article 9 upon the "lessee's" default. (Part 6 is discussed in Chapter 12, infra.) In contrast, the rights and obligations of a lessor under a true lease upon the lessee's default are described in UCC 2A–523 to 2A–532. In those very few jurisdictions where Article 2A has not yet been enacted, the rights and obligations of a lessor under a true lease are uncertain; in particular, case law is confused and conflicting in its resolution of such basic issues as whether the lessor who repossesses upon the lessee's default must dispose of the goods and the measure of the lessor's damages.

R1–201(37), which defines "security interest," affords some guidance on the question whether a particular lease is a security interest subject to Article 9 or is a lease (i.e., a "true lease") subject to Article 2A. Coincident with the promulgation of Article 2A in 1987, the definition was amended to clarify the distinction between secured transactions and leases. (The definition was amended again, in conjunction with the revision of Article 9. The most recent amendment can be found in Appendix I to Revised Article 9. It does not affect the lease/security interest distinction.)

The following Problems address the lease/security interest distinction.

Problem 8.1.1. Smith and Jones entered into a written agreement concerning a machine having a useful life of ten years. No financing statement was filed with respect to the machine. Six months after Jones took possession, Lean, one of Jones's creditors, acquired an execution lien on the machine. Under which of the following scenarios, if any, is Lean's lien senior to Smith's interest? In any case where Lean's lien is senior, what, if anything, could Smith have done to avoid the loss?

(a) Smith agreed to sell the machine to Jones for $120,000, payable $10,000 monthly. Smith retained title until Jones made all 12 payments. See R1–201(37) (5th sentence); R9–109(a)(1); R9–317(a)(2); R9–310(a); UCC 2A–307(1).

(b) Smith agreed to lease the machine to Jones for one year at $10,000 per month. The lease gives Jones the option to buy the machine at the end of the year for $10.

(c) Smith agreed to lease the machine to Jones for one year at $1,200 per month. The lease gives Jones the option to buy the machine at the end of the year for $110,000.

(d) Smith agreed to lease the machine to Jones for ten years at $1,200 per month. At the end of the lease term, Jones must return the goods to Smith.

(e) Smith agreed to lease the machine to Jones for one year at $10,000 per month, with an option to renew the lease at $1 per month for each of the following nine years. At the end of the lease term, Jones must return the goods to Smith.

(f) Smith agreed to lease the machine to Jones for ten years at $10,000 per month for the first year and $1 per month thereafter. At the end of the lease term, Jones must return the goods to Smith.

Problem. 8.1.2. Grace agreed to lease a bread wrapping machine to Royer's Bakery for one year at $10,000 per month. Royer's has the option to purchase the machine at the end of the lease term for $1. Royer's also has the right to terminate the lease at any time without penalty, provided it gives thirty days' advance notice to Grace. No financing statement was filed with respect to the machine.

(a) At the end of the first month of the lease, Lean acquired an execution lien on Royer's interest in the machine. Is the execution lien senior or junior to Grace's interest?

(b) Assume that the transaction creates a security interest in favor of Grace and that Royer's defaults after making only one monthly payment. If the property is sold pursuant to R9–610 for $110,000, how are the proceeds of the sale to be allocated? (Under R9–615(d)(1), the debtor is entitled to any surplus after satisfaction of the secured obligation and any related costs of sale. What is the size of the secured obligation?)

(c) Would your answer to part (a) change if Lean acquired the lien during the eleventh month?

(d) If you believe that Grace's interest is junior in part (a) or part (c), what could Grace have done to avoid the loss?

Problem. 8.1.3. Manufacturer agreed to lease a $6 million aircraft to Airline for three years at $2.3 million a year. Airline has the option to purchase the aircraft at the end of the lease term for $500,000.

(a) Is Manufacturer an Article 9 secured party?

(b) Assume that the transaction creates a security interest in favor of Manufacturer and that Airline defaults after making the payment for year two.

(i) If the property is sold pursuant to R9–610 for $4 million, how are the proceeds of the sale to be allocated? (Under R9–615(d)(1), the debtor is entitled to any surplus after satisfaction of the secured obligation and any related costs of sale. What is the size of the secured obligation?)

(ii) If the property is sold pursuant to R9–610 for $2.2 million, what is the size of Manufacturer's deficiency claim; i.e., how much more, if anything, does Airline owe Manufacturer? See R9–615(d)(2) (obligor is liable for any deficiency).

Problem. 8.1.4. Developer was constructing a new office building. A local ordinance required Developer to install sprinklers throughout the building. Developer agreed to lease a sprinkler system from Wetco for three years at $1,000 per month. No financing statement was filed with respect to the sprinkler system. Developer has the option to purchase the system at the end of the lease term for $10,000. If Developer does not exercise the purchase option, then it must return the system to Wetco. To remove the system from the building, Developer would incur costs (including the costs of repairing the damage to the building caused by the removal) totaling approximately $50,000.

Lean acquires an execution lien on Developer's interest in the sprinkler system.

(a) Is the execution lien senior or junior to Wetco's interest?

(b) If you believe that Lean's lien is senior in part (a), what, if anything, could Wetco have done to avoid the loss?

In re Marhoefer Packing Co.[*]

United States Court of Appeals, Seventh Circuit, 1982.
674 F.2d 1139.

■ PELL, CIRCUIT JUDGE. This appeal involves a dispute between the trustee of the bankrupt Marhoefer Packing Company, Inc., ("Marhoefer") and Robert Reiser & Company, Inc., ("Reiser") over certain equipment held by Marhoefer at the time of bankruptcy. The issue presented is whether the written agreement between Marhoefer and Reiser covering the equipment is a true lease under which Reiser is entitled to reclaim its property from the bankrupt estate, or whether it is actually a lease intended as security in which case Reiser's failure to file a financing statement to perfect its interest renders it subordinate to the trustee.

I

In December of 1976, Marhoefer Packing Co., Inc., of Muncie, Indiana, entered into negotiations with Reiser, a Massachusetts based corporation engaged in the business of selling and leasing food processing equipment, for the acquisition of one or possibly two Vemag Model 3007–1 Continuous Sausage Stuffers. Reiser informed Marhoefer that the units could be acquired by outright purchase, conditional sale contract or lease. Marhoefer ultimately acquired two sausage stuffers from Reiser. It purchased one under a conditional sale contract. Pursuant to the contract, Reiser retained a security interest in the machine, which it subsequently perfected by filing a financing statement with the Indiana Secretary of State. Title to that stuffer is not here in dispute. The other stuffer was delivered to Marhoefer under a written "Lease Agreement."

The Lease Agreement provided for monthly payments of $665.00 over a term of 48 months. The last nine months payments, totaling $5,985.00,

---

* [The court's citations are to the applicable pre–1972 version of the UCC. The pre–1987 version of UCC 1–201(37) was substantially similar to the pre 1972 version and is found in the appendix to most compilations of commercial statutes.]

were payable upon execution of the lease. If at the end of the lease term the machine was to be returned, it was to be shipped prepaid to Boston or similar destination "in the same condition as when received, reasonable wear and tear resulting from proper use alone excepted, and fully crated." The remaining terms and conditions of the agreement were as follows:

1. Any State or local taxes and/or excises are for the account of the Buyer.

2. The equipment shall at all times be located at

   Marhoefer Packing Co., Inc.
   1500 North Elm & 13th Street
   Muncie, Indiana

   and shall not be removed from said location without the written consent of Robert Reiser & Co. The equipment can only be used in conjunction with the manufacture of meat or similar products unless written consent is given by Robert Reiser & Co.

3. The equipment will carry a ninety-day guarantee for workmanship and materials and shall be maintained and operated safely and carefully in conformity with the instructions issued by our operators and the maintenance manual. Service and repairs of the equipment after the ninety-day period will be subject to a reasonable and fair charge.

4. If, after due warning, our maintenance instructions should be violated repeatedly, Robert Reiser & Co. will have the right to cancel the lease contract on seven days notice and remove the said equipment. In that case, lease fees would be refunded pro rata.

5. It is mutually agreed that in case of lessee, Marhoefer Packing Co., Inc., violating any of the above conditions, or shall default in the payment of any lease charge hereunder, or shall become bankrupt, make or execute any assignment or become party to any instrument or proceedings for the benefit of its creditors, Robert Reiser & Co. shall have the right at any time without trespass, to enter upon the premises and remove the aforesaid equipment, and if removed, lessee agrees to pay Robert Reiser & Co. the total lease fees, including all installments due or to become due for the full unexpired term of this lease agreement and including the cost for removal of the equipment and counsel fees incurred in collecting sums due hereunder.

6. It is agreed that the equipment shall remain personal property of Robert Reiser & Co. and retain its character as such no matter in what manner affixed or attached to the premises.

In a letter accompanying the lease, Reiser added two option provisions to the agreement. The first provided that at the end of the four-year term, Marhoefer could purchase the stuffer for $9,968.00. In the alternative, it could elect to renew the lease for an additional four years at an annual rate of $2,990.00, payable in advance. At the conclusion of the second four-year term, Marhoefer would be allowed to purchase the stuffer for one dollar.

Marhoefer never exercised either option. Approximately one year after the Vemag stuffer was delivered to its plant, it ceased all payments under the lease and shortly thereafter filed a voluntary petition in bankruptcy. On July 12, 1978, the trustee of the bankrupt corporation applied to the bankruptcy court for leave to sell the stuffer free and clear of all liens on the ground that the "Lease Agreement" was in fact a lease intended as security within the meaning of the Uniform Commercial Code ("Code") and that Reiser's failure to perfect its interest as required by Article 9 of the Code rendered it subordinate to that of the trustee. Reiser responded with an answer and counterclaim in which it alleged that the agreement was in fact a true lease, Marhoefer was in default under the lease, and its equipment should therefore be returned.

Following a trial on this issue, the bankruptcy court concluded that the agreement between Marhoefer and Reiser was in fact a true lease and ordered the trustee to return the Vemag stuffer to Reiser. The trustee appealed to the district court, which reversed on the ground that the bankruptcy court had erred as a matter of law in finding the agreement to be a true lease. We now reverse the judgment of the district court.

II

The dispute in this case centers on section 1–201(37) of the Uniform Commercial Code, I.C. 26–1–1–201.[1] In applying this section, the bankruptcy court concluded that "the presence of the option to renew the lease for an additional four years and to acquire the Vemag Stuffer at the conclusion of the second four-year term by the payment of One Dollar ($1.00) did not, in and of itself, make the lease one intended for security."

The district court disagreed. It held that the presence of an option to purchase the stuffer for one dollar gave rise to a conclusive presumption under clause (b) of section 1–201(37) that the lease was intended as security. Although it acknowledged that the option to purchase the stuffer for only one dollar would not have come into play unless Marhoefer chose to renew the lease for an additional four-year term, the district court concluded that this fact did not require a different result. "It would be anomalous," said the court, "to rule that the lease was a genuine lease for

---

1. Section 1–201(37) of the Uniform Commercial Code states:

"Security interest" means an interest in personal property or fixtures which secures payment or performance of an obligation. . . . Unless a lease or consignment is intended as security, reservation of title thereunder is not a 'security interest' but a consignment is in any event subject to the provisions on consignment sales. Whether a lease is intended as security is to be determined by the facts of each case; however, (a) the inclusion of an option, to purchase does not of itself make the lease one intended for security, and (b) an agreement that upon compliance with the terms of the lease the lessee shall become or has the option to become the owner of the property for no additional consideration or for a nominal consideration does make the lease one intended for security.

four years after its creation but was one intended for security eight years after its creation."

Reiser, relying on Peter F. Coogan's detailed analysis of section 1–201(37), Coogan, Hogan & Vagts, Secured Transactions Under the Uniform Commercial Code, ch. 4A, (1981) (hereinafter "Secured Transactions Under U.C.C."), argues that the district court erred in construing clause (b) of that section as creating a conclusive presumption that a lease is intended as security where the lease contains an option for the lessee to become the owner of the leased property for no additional consideration or for only nominal consideration. It contends that by interpreting clause (b) in this way, the district court totally ignored the first part of that sentence which states that "[w]hether a lease is intended as security is to be determined by the facts of each case." Reiser claims that because the totality of facts surrounding the transaction indicate that the lease was not intended as security, notwithstanding the presence of the option to purchase the stuffer for one dollar, the district court erred in reversing the bankruptcy court's determination.

We agree that the district court erred in concluding that because the Lease Agreement contained an option for Marhoefer to purchase the Vemag stuffer at the end of a second four-year term, it was conclusively presumed to be a lease intended as security. However, in our view, the district court's error lies not in its reading of clause (b) of section 1–201(37) as giving rise to such a presumption,[2] but rather in its conclusion that clause (b) applies under the facts of this case.

The primary issue to be decided in determining whether a lease is "intended as security" is whether it is in effect a conditional sale in which the "lessor" retains an interest in the "leased" goods as security for the purchase price. 1C Secured Transactions Under U.C.C. § 29A.05[1][C], p. 2939. By defining the term "security interest" to include a lease intended as security, the drafters of the Code intended such disguised security interests to be governed by the same rules that apply to other security interests. See U.C.C., Art. 9. In this respect, section 1–201(37) represents the drafter's refusal to recognize form over substance.

Clearly, where a lease is structured so that the lessee is contractually bound to pay rent over a set period of time at the conclusion of which he automatically or for only nominal consideration becomes the owner of the

---

2. This reading of section 1–201(37) is not without support in the reported cases. In Peco v. Hartbauer Tool & Die Co., 262 Or. 573, 500 P.2d 708 (1972), for example, the court noted that

> [a]t first glance the provisions of . . . section [1–201(37)] may be somewhat confusing, probably because they are stated in the inverse order of importance. However, upon a careful reading of the entire section it is clear that the first question to be answered is that

posed by clause (b)—whether the lessee may obtain the property for no additional consideration or for a nominal consideration. If so, the lease is intended for security. If not, it is then necessary to determine "by the facts of each case" whether . . . the fact that the lease contains an option to purchase "does not (of itself) make the lease one intended for security." Id. at 575, 500 P.2d at 709–10, quoting Ore.Rev.Stat. § 71–2010(37) (1969).

leased goods, the transaction is in substance a conditional sale and should be treated as such. It is to this type of lease that clause (b) properly applies. Here, however, Marhoefer was under no contractual obligation to pay rent until such time as the option to purchase the Vemag stuffer for one dollar was to arise. In fact, in order to acquire that option. Marhoefer would have had to exercise its earlier option to renew the lease for a second four-year term and pay Reiser an additional $11,960 in "rent." In effect, Marhoefer was given a right to terminate the agreement after the first four years and cease making payments without that option ever becoming operative.

Despite this fact, the district court concluded as a matter of law that the lease was intended as security. It held that, under clause (b) of section 1–201(37), a lease containing an option for the lessee to purchase the leased goods for nominal consideration is conclusively presumed to be one intended as security. This presumption applies, the court concluded, regardless of any other options the lease may contain.

We think the district court's reading of clause (b) is in error. In our view, the conclusive presumption provided under clause (b) applies only where the option to purchase for nominal consideration necessarily arises upon compliance with the lease. *See* 1C Secured Transactions Under U.C.C. § 29.05[2][b] pp. 2947–49. It does not apply where the lessee has the right to terminate the lease before that option arises with no further obligation to continue paying rent. But see In re Vaillancourt, supra, 7 U.C.C. Rep. 748; In re Royer's Bakery, Inc., 1 U.C.C. Rep. 342 (Bankr.E.D.Pa.1963). For where the lessee has the right to terminate the transaction, it is not a conditional sale.

Moreover, to hold that a lease containing such an option is intended as security, even though the lessee has no contractual obligation to pay the full amount contemplated by the agreement, would lead to clearly erroneous results under other provisions of the Code. Under section 9–506 of the Code, for example, a debtor in default on his obligation to a secured party has a right to redeem the collateral by tendering full payment of that obligation. The same right is also enjoyed by a lessee under a lease intended as security. A lessee who defaults on a lease intended as security is entitled to purchase the leased goods by paying the full amount of his obligation under the lease. But if the lessee has the right to terminate the lease at any time during the lease term, his obligation under the lease may be only a small part of the total purchase price of the goods leased. To afford the lessee a right of redemption under such circumstances would clearly be wrong. There is no evidence that the drafters of the Code intended such a result.

We therefore hold that while section 1–201(37)(b) does provide a conclusive test of when a lease is intended as security, that test does not apply in every case in which the disputed lease contains an option to purchase for nominal or no consideration. An option of this type makes a lease on intended as security only when it necessarily arises upon compliance with the terms of the lease.

Applying section 1–201(37), so construed, to the facts of this case, it is clear that the district court erred in concluding that the possibility of Marhoefer's purchasing the stuffer for one dollar at the conclusion of a second four-year term was determinative. Because Marhoefer could have fully complied with the lease without that option ever arising, the district court was mistaken in thinking that the existence of that option alone made the lease a conditional sale. Certainly, if Marhoefer had elected to renew the lease for another term, in which case the nominal purchase option would necessarily have arisen, then the clause (b) test would apply.[6] But that is not the case we are faced with here. Marhoefer was not required to make any payments beyond the first four years. The fact that, at the conclusion of that term, it could have elected to renew the lease and obtain an option to purchase the stuffer for one dollar at the end of the second term does not transform the original transaction into a conditional sale.

This fact does not end our inquiry under clause (b), however, for the trustee also argues that, even if the district court erred in considering the one dollar purchase option as determinative, the lease should nevertheless be considered a conditional sale because the initial option price of $9,968 is also nominal when all of the operative facts are properly considered. We agree that if the clause (b) test is to apply at all in this case, this is the option that must be considered. For this is the option that was to arise automatically upon Marhoefer's compliance with the lease. We do not agree, however, that under the circumstances presented here the $9,968 option price can properly be considered nominal.

It is true that an option price may be more than a few dollars and still be considered nominal within the meaning of section 1–201(37). Because clause (b) speaks of nominal "consideration" and not a nominal "sum" or "amount," it has been held to apply not only where the option price is very small in absolute terms, but also where the price is insubstantial in relation to the fair market value of the leased goods at the time the option arises.[7]

Here, however, the evidence revealed that the initial option price of $9,968 was not nominal even under this standard. George Vetie, Reiser's treasurer and the person chiefly responsible for the terms of the lease, testified at trial that the purchase price for the Vemag stuffer at the time the parties entered into the transaction was $33,225. He testified that the initial option price of $9,968 was arrived at by taking thirty percent of the purchase price, which was what he felt a four-year-old Vemag stuffer would be worth based on Reiser's past experience.

---

6. Reiser concedes that had Marhoefer elected to renew the lease after the first term, the transaction would have been transformed into a sale.

7. The trustee argues that the determination of whether the option price is nominal is to be made by comparing it to the fair market value of the equipment at the time the parties enter into the lease, instead of the date the option arises. Although some courts have applied such a test, In re Wheatland Electric Products Co., 237 F.Supp. 820 (W.D.Pa.1964); In re Oak Mfg., Inc., 6 U.C.C. Rep. 1273 (Bankr.S.D.N.Y.1969), the better approach is to compare the option price with the fair market value of the goods at the time the option was to be exercised. In re Universal Medical Services, Inc., 8 U.C.C. Rep. 614 (Bankr.E.D.Pa.1970). See 1C Secured Transactions Under U.C.C. § 29A.05[2][b].

The trustee, relying on the testimony of its expert appraiser, argues that in fact the stuffer would have been worth between eighteen and twenty thousand dollars at the end of the first four-year term. Because the initial option price is substantially less than this amount, he claims that it is nominal within the meaning of clause (b) and the lease is therefore one intended as security.

Even assuming this appraisal to be accurate, an issue on which the bankruptcy court made no finding, we would not find the initial option price of $9,968 so small by comparison that the clause (b) presumption would apply. While it is difficult to state any bright line percentage test for determining when an option price could properly be considered nominal as compared to the fair market value of the leased goods, an option price of almost ten thousand dollars, which amounts to fifty percent of the fair market value, is not nominal by any standard.

Furthermore, in determining whether an option price is nominal, the proper figure to compare it with is not the actual fair market value of the leased goods at the time the option arises, but their fair market value at that time as anticipated by the parties when the lease is signed. 1C Secured Transactions Under U.C.C. § 29A.05[2][b], p. 2953. Here, for example, Vetie testified that his estimate of the fair market value of a four-year-old Vemag stuffer was based on records from a period of time in which the economy was relatively stable. Since that time, a high rate of inflation has caused the machines to lose their value more slowly. As a result, the actual fair market value of a machine may turn out to be significantly more than the parties anticipated it would be several years earlier. When this occurs, the lessee's option to purchase the leased goods may be much more favorable than either party intended, but it does not change the true character of the transaction.

We conclude, therefore, that neither option to purchase contained in the lease between Marhoefer and Reiser gives rise to a conclusive presumption under section 1–201(37)(b) that the lease is one intended as security. This being so, we now turn to the other facts surrounding the transaction.

III

Although section 1–201(37) states that "[w]hether a lease is intended as security is to be determined by the facts of each case," it is completely silent as to what facts, other than the option to purchase, are to be considered in making that determination. Facts that the courts have found relevant include the total amount of rent the lessee is required to pay under the lease, Chandler Leasing Corp. v. Samoset Associates, supra, 24 U.C.C. Rep. at 516; whether the lessee acquires any equity in the leased property, Matter of Tillery, 571 F.2d 1361, 1365 (5th Cir.1978); the useful life of the leased goods, In re Lakeshore Transit–Kenosha, Inc., 7 U.C.C. Rep. 607 (Bankr.E.D.Wis.1969); the nature of the lessor's business, In re Industro Transistor Corp., 14 U.C.C. Rep. 522, 523 (Bankr.E.D.N.Y.1973); and the payment of taxes, insurance and other charges normally imposed on ownership, Rainier National Bank v. Inland Machinery Co., 29 Wash.

App. 725, 631 P.2d 389 (1981). *See generally* 1C Secured Transactions Under U.C.C. § 29A.05[2][e]; and Annot., 76 ALR 3d 11 (1977). Consideration of the facts of this case in light of these factors leads us to conclude that the lease in question was not intended as security.

First, Marhoefer was under no obligation to pay the full purchase price for the stuffer. Over the first four-year term, its payments under the lease were to have amounted to $31,920. Although this amount may not be substantially less than the original purchase price of $33,225 in absolute terms, it becomes so when one factors in the interest rate over four years that would have been charged had Marhoefer elected to purchase the machine under a conditional sale contract.[8] The fact that the total amount of rent Marhoefer was to pay under the lease was substantially less than that amount shows that a sale was not intended. 1 Secured Transactions Under U.C.C. § 4A.01.

It is also significant that the useful life of the Vemag stuffer exceeded the term of the lease. An essential characteristic of a true lease is that there be something of value to return to the lessor after the term. 1C Secured Transactions Under U.C.C. § 29A.05[2][c], p. 2959. Where the term of the lease is substantially equal to the life of the leased property such that there will be nothing of value to return at the end of the lease, the transaction is in essence a sale. In re Lakeshore Transit–Kenosha, Inc., supra. Here, the evidence revealed that the useful life of a Vemag stuffer was eight to ten years.

Finally, the bankruptcy court specifically found that "there was no express or implied provision in the lease agreement dated February 28, 1977, which gave Marhoefer any equity interest in the leased Vemag stuffer." This fact clearly reveals the agreement between Marhoefer and Reiser to be a true lease. See Hawkland, The Impact of the Uniform Commercial Code on Equipment Leasing, 1972 Ill. L. Forum 446, 453 ("The difference between a true lease and a security transaction lies in whether the lessee acquires an equity of ownership through his rent payments."). Had Marhoefer remained solvent and elected not to exercise its option to renew its lease with Reiser, it would have received nothing for its previous lease payments. And in order to exercise that option, Marhoefer would have had to pay what Reiser anticipated would then be the machine's fair market value. An option of this kind is not the mark of a lease intended as security. See In re Alpha Creamery Company, 4 U.C.C. Rep. 794, 798 (Bankr.W.D.Mich.1967).

Although Marhoefer was required to pay state and local taxes and the cost of repairs, this fact does not require a contrary result. Costs such as taxes, insurance and repairs are necessarily borne by one party or the

8. The bankruptcy court found that Reiser was originally willing to sell Marhoefer the stuffer under a conditional sale contract the terms of which would have been $7,225 down and monthly installments of $1,224 over a twenty-four month period. The total payments under such an agreement would have amounted to $36,601, substantially more than the amount Marhoefer was required to pay over four years under the lease.

other. They reflect less the true character of the transaction than the strength of the parties' respective bargaining positions. See also Rainier National Bank, supra, 631 P.2d at 395 ("The lessor is either going to include those costs within the rental charge or agree to a lower rent if the lessee takes responsibility for them.").

IV

We conclude from the foregoing that the district court erred in its application of section 1–201(37) of the Uniform Commercial Code to the facts of this case. Neither the option to purchase the Vemag stuffer for one dollar at the conclusion of a second four-year term, nor the initial option to purchase it for $9,968 after the first four years, gives rise to a conclusive presumption under clause (b) of section 1–201(37) that the lease is intended as security. From all of the facts surrounding the transaction, we conclude that the agreement between Marhoefer and Reiser is a true lease. The judgment of the district court is therefore reversed.

NOTES ON DISTINGUISHING LEASES FROM SECURED TRANSACTIONS[1]

(1) The "Factors" Approach. Few commercial law issues have spawned as much litigation and provided as much uncertainty as the determination whether a purported lease of goods creates a security interest or a true lease. The pre–1987 version of UCC 1–201(37) stated that "[w]hether a lease is intended as security is to be determined by the facts of each case...." Although the courts usually took cognizance of the facts of the cases before them, they often exhibited great difficulty in determining which facts are relevant and which are not.

The scores of reported cases on the subject identify no fewer than two dozen factors that courts have used in drawing the lease/security interest distinction. Most of these factors are consistent with both a lease and a secured transaction. These factors include the lessor's disclaimer of warranties; the lessor's right to repossess the goods on the lessee's default; the lessee's obligation to repair, maintain, and insure the goods; the lessor's lack of storage facilities; the lessee's selection of specific goods for acquisition by the lessor; and the manner in which the parties treated the transaction for tax or accounting purposes. Unfortunately, few courts have shown the courage to dispense with what seems to have become an obligatory recitation of a list of factors. Even in the course of expressing regret over other courts having relied on factors that are "basically irrelevant" and that "merely add to confusion" in analyzing transactions, one court felt compelled to reproduce a "laundry list" of factors, "in recognition that they have been mentioned by some courts." In re Loop Hospital Partnership, 35 B.R. 929 (Bkrtcy.N.D.Ill.1983).

1. These Notes are drawn substantially from Harris, The Interface Between Articles 2A and 9 Under the Official Text and the California Amendments, 22 UCC L.J. 99, 104–110 (1989).

As revised in 1987, UCC 1–201(37) does not draw a precise line between true leases and security interests. Instead, it continues to state that whether a transaction creates a lease or security interest is determined by the facts of each case. Nevertheless, the 1987 amendments go a long way toward clarifying the distinction between the two transactions. One of their major contributions is to state unequivocally that some of the factors upon which courts have relied in holding that a transaction creates a security interest *do not, of themselves, create a security interest*. These factors, which appear in R1–201(37) (second a)–(e), are:

• the discounted present value of the rental stream equals or exceeds the fair market value of the goods at the time the lease is entered into (often known as a "full-payout" lease);

• provisions whereby the lessee assumes risk of loss of the goods, or agrees to pay taxes, insurance, filing, recording, or registration fees, or service or maintenance costs with respect to the goods (these provisions are commonly found in "net" leases);

• an option for the lessee to renew the lease, including an option for a fixed rent that equals or exceeds the reasonably predictable fair market rent at the time the option is to be performed; and

• an option for the lessee to become the owner of the goods, including an option for a fixed price that equals or exceeds the reasonably predictable fair market value of the goods at the time the option is to be performed.

(2) The Irrelevance of the Parties' Subjective Intent. A second major contribution of the 1987 amendments to UCC 1–201(37) is the substitution of the term "security interest" for the phrase "intended as security." That phrase prompted some courts to distinguish between leases and security interests by reference to the subjective intentions of the parties rather than by analysis of the economics of the transaction. For example, in Carlson v. Tandy Computer Leasing, 803 F.2d 391 (8th Cir.1986) (construing Missouri law), the court relied in part on the "intent of the parties, as expressed in the written document, to create nothing more than a lessor-lessee relationship." The court noted that the document "consistently uses 'lease language' " and "states in clearest terms that the agreement is only a lease." Id. Because the characterization of the transaction may affect the rights of third parties, reliance upon the subjective intentions of the parties to the lease transaction is inappropriate. Rather, as *Marhoefer* recognizes, the economic substance of the transaction should determine its characterization. (In *Carlson*, the "lessee" was obligated to pay an amount substantially in excess of the purchase price and had the right to use the property for its entire economic life. As the following Notes suggest, these facts are indicative of a secured transaction.)

(3) The Importance of the Lessee's Contractual Obligation. In explaining the difference between a lease and a security interest, the 1987 amendments to UCC 1–201(37) focus on economic realities. They set forth four specific cases in which a transaction creates a security interest. Each case is characterized by two elements, the first of which is the existence of a debt owed by the "lessee" to the "lessor." Without a debt to secure, there can be no security interest. The statute states this point as follows: "the consideration the lessee is to pay the lessor . . . is an obligation for the term of the lease not subject to termination by the lessee." Although the Uniform Conditional Sales Act contained a similar requirement, pre–1987 UCC 1–201(37) contained none. The better cases, including *Marhoefer*, have recognized that an obligation of this kind is a necessary but not sufficient condition to the existence of a secured transaction; however, some courts have failed to grasp this important principle. See, e.g., In re J.A. Thompson & Son, Inc., 665 F.2d 941 (9th Cir.1982) (holding that a nominal purchase option establishes conclusively that a transaction is a secured transaction, even if the "lessee" unilaterally may terminate its obligation to pay the "lessor").

(4) The Importance of a Meaningful Residual Interest for the Lessor. In addition to an unconditional obligation to pay, each secured transaction described in the 1987 amendments to UCC 1–201(37) includes a second element—the absence of a meaningful residual interest for the lessor. In a true lease, the lessor is the owner of the goods. The lessee acquires the right to use the goods for a limited period of time. When the lease term ends, the lessor expects the property to be returned so that the lessor can use it, relet it, or otherwise dispose of it. The lessor's interest in the goods after expiration, cancellation, or termination of the lease is called the "lessor's residual interest." See UCC 2A–103(1)(q). In contrast, if the lease affords the lessee the right to use the goods for their entire economic life, then the lessee (and not the lessor) is in effect the owner of the goods. The goods have been sold to the lessee, and the lessor does not expect to recover them unless the lessee fails to pay for them. In other words, the lessor has only a security interest.

Determining whether the lessor retains a meaningful residual interest in the goods can be difficult. R1–201(37) (first a)-(d) sets forth four specific cases in which the lessor lacks a meaningful residual interest and that, therefore, create security interests if the lessee has a noncancellable obligation to pay. These cases are:

• the original term of the lease equals or exceeds the remaining economic life of the goods;

• the lessee is bound to renew the lease for the remaining economic life of the goods or is bound to become the owner of the goods;

• the lessee has an option to renew the lease for the remaining economic life of the goods for no additional consideration or nominal additional consideration upon compliance with the lease agreement; and

• the lessee has an option to become the owner of the goods for no additional consideration or nominal additional consideration upon compliance with the lease agreement.

In the first two cases the lessee acquires the right to use the goods until the goods have no further economic life. At the end of the lease term or renewal term, the goods will have no value to the lessor, who therefore is a secured party.

The third and fourth cases address an issue with which the courts have grappled, with varying degrees of success, under pre–1987 UCC 1–201(37): the effect of renewal and purchase options. The fourth case follows pre–1987 UCC 1–201(37), and the third case is a variation on the same theme. But rather than refer to an option to become the owner, the third case refers to its equivalent—an option to renew the lease for the remaining economic life of the goods.

Although not specifically mentioned in R1–201(37), the remedies that a "lease" affords to the "lessor" upon the "lessee's" default may deprive the "lessor" of its residual and thus be indicative of a secured transaction. Consider a lease that requires the lessor to sell the property upon the lessee's default and to apply the proceeds of sale to the lessee's obligation under the lease. The proceeds of the sale represent the value of the use of the goods for their entire useful life. The useful life consists of two portions—the portion covered by the lease term, for which the lessee bargained, and the portion commencing with the expiration of the lease, which the lessor retains as the lessor's residual interest. A lessor who credits to the lessee the entire amount of the proceeds received upon a sale following the lessee's default has, in effect, allocated none of the value of the property to its residual interest. This suggests that the lessor never enjoyed a residual interest (businesses rarely give away property for other than eleemosynary purposes), which, in turn, suggests that the transaction was not really a lease to begin with. Cf. In re Tulsa Port Warehouse Co., 690 F.2d 809 (10th Cir.1982) (lease held to be security interest where termination and default provisions provided for (i) sale of automobile by lessor, (ii) application of proceeds of sale to "agreed depreciated value," and (iii) lessee's liability for any deficiency and entitlement to any surplus).

(5) The Meaning of "Nominal Consideration." Although pre–1987 UCC 1–201(37) spoke of "nominal consideration," it failed to define the term. When confronted with option prices that are not nominal in absolute terms, courts adopted a variety of tests, some of which overlap. The 1987 amendments to UCC 1–201(37) follow the better-reasoned case law. R1–201(37)(x) provides that "[a]dditional consideration is nominal if it is less than the lessee's reasonably predictable cost of performing under the lease agreement if the option is not exercised." "Reasonably predictable" costs "are to be determined with reference to the facts and circumstances at the time the transaction is entered into." R1–201(37)(y). In other words, if it would appear to the parties at the outset of the lease that it would cost the lessee less to exercise the option than not to exercise it, one reasonably can assume that the lessee will exercise the option and become the owner of the goods, leaving no meaningful residual for the lessor.

R1–201(37)(x) also gives two examples of when additional consideration is not nominal:

- when the consideration for an option to renew is stated to be the fair market rent for the use of the goods for the term of the renewal, determined at the time the option is to be performed; and

- when the consideration for an option to become the owner of the goods is stated to be the fair market value of the goods determined at the time the option is to be performed.

A lessee faced with either of these "fair-market" options cannot necessarily be expected to exercise them and deprive the lessor of a residual interest. For a well-reasoned case analyzing an option to purchase at fair market value, see In re Celeryvale Transport, Inc., 44 B.R. 1007 (Bkrtcy. E.D.Tenn.1984), affirmed per curiam 822 F.2d 16 (6th Cir.1987).

Detailed as it is, the revised definition does not consider all possible variations and combinations of factors. See R1–201, Comment 37 (penultimate paragraph). Consider, for example, a "lease" containing a renewal option at a nominal renewal rate *coupled* with a nominal purchase option at the end of the renewal term. That structure highlights the weak link in the otherwise sound reasoning of *Marhoefer*. See Reisman & Mooney, Drafting, Negotiating, and Construing the Equipment Lease, in B. Fritch, A. Reisman, & I. Shrank, Equipment Leasing–Leveraged Leasing 36 n. 108 (1988) ("The [*Marhoefer*] court did not explore whether the renewal option rentals were 'nominal.' Nominal renewal rentals would indicate an economic compulsion on the lessee to renew the lease and thereby become entitled to the one dollar purchase option.").

(6) Dealing With Uncertainty. Although the 1987 amendments to UCC 1–201(37) have reduced the confusion and uncertainty that prevailed in the cases construing its predecessor, some uncertainty has remained. This uncertainty derives not only from unavoidable infelicities of drafting but also from the decision of the drafters not to draw a precise line between security interests and leases or to create safe harbors for transactions that meet certain requirements. One can anticipate that close cases will continue to arise in which, for example, reasonable people might differ over whether the lessee enjoys an option to become the owner of the goods for "nominal consideration." The extensive case law construing the pre–1987 version is likely to provide another source of uncertainty, as is the fact that many of the reported opinions emanate from bankruptcy courts, where the economics of litigating sometimes results in issues not being briefed as fully as they otherwise might be.

A cautious lessor may wish to plan in advance for the possibility that a court will recharacterize what the lessor believes to be a "lease" as a secured transaction. The lessor's principal concern in this regard is that, if its interest in the goods is held to be a security interest, then its failure to file a financing statement would render the security interest unperfected. The lessor might be reluctant to file a financing statement using the terms "debtor" and "secured party"; a court might consider the use of those terms as evidence that the transaction creates a security interest. R9–505 suggests the solution: File a precautionary financing statement using the terms "lessee" and "lessor" instead of "debtor" and "secured party." The fact of filing "is not of itself a factor in determining whether the collateral secures an obligation." However, "[i]f it is determined for another reason that the collateral secures an obligation, a security interest held by the ... lessor ... which attaches to the collateral is perfected by the filing...." R9–505(b). Box 5 on the uniform financing statement form accommodates this practice. See R9–521(a).

NOTE ON LEASES AND "OSTENSIBLE OWNERSHIP"

One way to eliminate much of the litigation over the lease/security interest distinction would have been to create a set of rules under which third parties take free of a lessor's interest as to which there had been no public notice (e.g., by filing a financing statement). Indeed, the imposition of a filing requirement for leases has been urged by prominent members of the current generation of Article 9 scholars as well as by some of those who were present at the creation of Article 9. These commentators generally have argued that a lessor's nonpossessory interest in leased goods gives rise to the same problems of "ostensible ownership" as does a nonpossessory security interest. From the perspective of third parties, goods held subject to lease appear identical to goods held subject to a security interest. Creditors of the lessee, like creditors of an Article 9 debtor, may be misled into thinking that the person in possession of the goods owns them free and clear. Why, then, should the rights of third parties differ, depending on whether the holder of the nonpossessory interest enjoys a meaningful residual interest and the unconditional right to receive payment for the goods?

The Article 2A drafting committee was not moved by this strong support for the imposition of a filing requirement for leases. Rather, Article 2A generally reflects the longstanding common-law rule that creditors of, and other transferees from, the lessee take subject to the lessor's interest in the goods, regardless of whether the lessor's interest has been publicized. See, e.g., UCC 2A–307(1) (creditors); UCC 2A–305 (buyers and sublessees).

Can one develop a principled justification of the drafting committee's decision? Is it simply a response to pressures brought by the leasing industry, or perhaps the reflection of unthinking conservatism? Consider the premise of those who would extend the filing system to leases: Do leases and secured transactions present equivalent problems of ostensible ownership? Were the Article 9 filing system to be abolished, would it be as difficult to determine whether a person in possession of goods in fact is the owner as it would be to determine whether the person owns them free of a security interest? The absence of an outcry from creditor groups suggests that the secret interests held by lessors of personal property have not resulted in losses to third parties claiming through lessees.

Imposing a filing requirement is easier than articulating the consequences that flow from a failure to file. For example, would the non-filing lessor lose its residual interest, which it may never have agreed to convey and which may be of substantial value relative to the lessee's rights under the lease? To the extent that the consequences of failing to file with respect to a true lease would differ from that those with respect to a security interest, parties will retain the incentive to litigate over the characterization of the transaction, and a major incentive for imposing a filing requirement would be lost.

(B) CONSIGNMENTS

Introductory Note. The preceding part of this Chapter explored leases—bailments in which the bailee was to *use* the goods. As we saw, these bailments bear a resemblance (sometimes a very close resemblance) to purchase-money security interests in *equipment*. This part of the Chapter addresses consignments—bailments in which the bailee is to *sell* the goods. These bailments resemble purchase-money security interests in *inventory*. As you work through the following materials, you will see that the UCC's treatment of consignments differs considerably from its treatment of leases. Should the drafters have afforded the same treatment to both consignments and leases? If so, what should that treatment have been?

Problem 8.1.5. The Corona Company has just developed what it believes to be its crowning achievement: Cal–Trak, a portable instrument that can measure and record calories as they are expended. Corona wishes to market this product to joggers and others concerned with fitness. It entered into the following agreement with Spartners: Corona will deliver a specified quantity of Cal–Traks to Spartners "on consignment." Title will remain in Corona. Spartners will use best efforts to sell the Cal–Traks to retail stores. Spartners has no obligation to pay for the Cal–Traks until they are sold, at which time Spartners will remit the sale price, less its commission. Spartners may return unsold Cal–Traks at any time without penalty and must return them upon Corona's demand.

Two months later, one of Spartners' judgment creditors caused the sheriff to levy upon all its inventory, including 10,000 Cal–Traks. Corona seeks to recover the Cal–Traks from the sheriff, arguing that they are not property of the judgment debtor's (i.e., of Spartners').

(a) What result? See R1–201(37) (2d & 5th sentences); R9–109(a)(1), (4); R9–102(a)(20), (21), (72), (19), (28); R9–319; R9–317(a)(2); In re Zwagerman, infra; Notes on Consignments, infra.

(b) What could the loser have done to avoid the loss? See R9–310(a); R9–505.

(c) Suppose that, prior to taking delivery of the Cal–Traks, Spartners had granted a security interest in all its inventory, existing and after-acquired, to Bank. Would Bank's security interest attach to the Cal–Traks (which, recall, are still owned by Corona)? See R9–319; R9–203(b). (Do not assume that, if Bank's security interest attaches then Bank necessarily defeats Corona. See Note (1) on Attachment, Chapter 7, Section 2, supra (discussing "rights in the collateral"). As to the relative priority of Corona's ownership interest and Bank's security interest, see R9–103(d); R9–324(a); Note (4) on Consignments, infra.)

(d) Would the result in part (a) change if Spartners were required to obtain Corona's approval of the terms of each sale?

(e) Would the result in part (a) change if Spartners were free to determine the price at which the Cal–Traks were sold?

Problem 8.1.6. Corona (of Problem. 8.1.5) entered into the following agreement with Wholesaler: Wholesaler will take delivery of 10,000 Cal–Traks "on consignment" and will use best efforts to sell the Cal–Traks to retail stores. Wholesaler will pay the wholesale price 30 days after delivery; however, after three months Wholesaler may return to Corona any goods that Wholesaler is unable to sell. Wholesaler will receive a refund for these returned goods.

Two months later, one of Wholesaler's judgment creditors caused the sheriff to levy upon all its inventory, including 8,000 unsold Cal–Traks. Corona seeks to recover the Cal–Traks from the sheriff, arguing that they are not property of the judgment debtor, Wholesaler.

(a) What result? See R2–326(1), (2).

(b) What could the loser have done to avoid the loss? Does Corona retain a "security interest" in the Cal–Traks that it sold to Wholesaler? Does it retain another type of interest in the goods? See R1–201(37) (5th sentence); Note (5) on Consignments, infra.

Problem 8.1.7. Corona entered into the following agreement with Distributor: Distributor will take delivery of 10,000 Cal–Traks "on consignment" and will use best efforts to sell the Cal–Traks to retail stores. Distributor will pay the wholesale price 30 days after delivery; if Distributor fails to pay, Corona may demand return of all unsold Cal–Traks.

Two months later, one of Distributor's judgment creditors caused the sheriff to levy upon all its inventory, including 8,000 unsold Cal–Traks. Corona seeks to recover the Cal–Traks from the sheriff, arguing that they are not property of the judgment debtor, Distributor.

(a) What result? See Note (2) on Consignments, infra.

(b) What could the loser have done to avoid the loss?

Problem 8.1.8. Crispin is a stereophile who acquires new speakers every six months or so. Crispin leaves the old speakers with Dealer, who agrees to try to sell them on commission. Acting pursuant to an execution writ issued at the request of one of Dealer's judgment creditors, the sheriff levies on the speakers. Is the levy effective against Crispin? If so, then the sheriff's sale would cut off Crispin's ownership interest.

In Chapter 1, Section 3(C), supra, we saw that Factor's Acts and UCC 2–403(2) empower Dealer to make even an unauthorized sale of the speakers free of Crispin's ownership interest. Is Crispin a consignor? See R9–102(a)(21). Is Crispin's ownership interest also subject to the claims of

Dealer's creditors? See R9–109(a)(4); R9–102(a)(20); Note (4) on Consignments, infra.

———

As the Notes on Consignments, infra, explain in some detail, Revised Article 9 applies to certain transactions in which goods are delivered to a merchant "for the purpose of sale," even if the goods do not secure a debt or other obligation. R9–102(a)(20) (defining "consignment"). The quoted phrase derives from F2–326(3), which likewise described a set of transactions (referred to as "consignments") in which goods are delivered to a person "for sale." The *Zwagerman* case, which follows, reveals how courts have attempted to distinguish transactions in which goods have been delivered "for sale" from those in which they have been delivered other than "for sale." Under F9–326, the owner's interest in goods delivered to a person "for sale" was vulnerable to claims of the person's creditors unless the owner takes a specified step (which might be the filing of a financing statement) to publicize its ownership interest.

In re Zwagerman

United States Bankruptcy Court, W.D. Michigan, 1990.
115 B.R. 540, affirmed 125 B.R. 486 (W.D.Mich.1991).

OPINION

■ DAVID E. NIMS, JR., BANKRUPTCY JUDGE.

This case comes before the court on the complaint filed by James D. Robbins, the Trustee in this estate, for a determination as to the respective interests in proceeds from the sale of cattle present on the farm of Gordon and Joan Zwagerman, doing business as Zwagerman Farms, the Debtors herein, at the time of the filing of the petition. . . .

FACTS

Gordon and Joan Zwagerman filed their Chapter 7 bankruptcy petition on December 30, 1985. Other than at a 341 Meeting held on February 5, 1986, the Debtors have refused to testify, claiming their privilege against self-incrimination. David Bradley claims that all proceeds belong to him because he owned the cattle on the Debtors' farm. Comerica Bank–Detroit, the Bank herein, argues that based on their properly perfected security interest in the cattle, they are entitled to the proceeds.

Since approximately 1969, the Debtors operated a farm at which they fattened hogs and cattle and then sold them for slaughter. Originally, the Debtors fattened livestock which they personally owned. At some point in the early 1980's the Debtors apparently had a cash flow problem and started to bring some cattle into their feedlots[1] in which they did not have

---

1. A "feed lot" is an area where the operator keeps his cattle while fattening them. A "custom feed lot" physically appears the same, but the operator does not own the cattle.

an ownership interest. Those cattle were furnished by David Bradley, a man the Debtor met while buying cattle out of the South. Bradley agreed to deliver cattle to the Zwagerman farm in order for the cattle to be fattened. The first delivery to the Debtors was on or about November 27, 1981. Both the number of head per shipment and the number of shipments per month were sporadic. Each shipment was accompanied by a contract, generally including the following pertinent provisions:

1. That Red River will deliver a specified number of cattle on a specified date, with the expense of hauling to be paid by Red River.

2. Zwagerman agrees to feed such cattle and to be paid fifty-five (55) cents per pound for the poundage the cattle gain after being delivered.

3. Any loss of cattle by death shall be borne by Zwagerman.

4. Zwagerman agrees to feed the cattle until the weights reach approximately one thousand one hundred (1,100) pounds and when sold, the proceeds will be delivered to Red River. Red River will send to Zwagerman its check for the number of pounds gained by the cattle from time of delivery to Zwagerman to time of sale.

5. The parties agree that should any dispute arise in this agreement that the forum for settling such dispute will be Sumner County, Tennessee.

. . .

Bradley never visited the farm, but called the Debtor two to six times a week to discuss the best time to sell based on the market and cattle conditions. Although no amount of time was set for the fattening of the cattle, Bradley estimated that it took 90–140 days. The purchasers made checks out to the Debtor who then deposited the check into one of his personal checking accounts. Pursuant to the contract, the Debtor was supposed to send a check to Bradley for the full amount of the sale. Once Bradley received a check for the sale of cattle, he would send a weight gain check in return to the Debtor. . . .

In the spring of 1983, the Debtor contacted Phillip Roberts, an agricultural loan officer at Comerica Bank, to pursue the refinancing of his debt to P.C.A. and F.M.B. The cattle on the farm were to be part of the security for the Comerica loan, just as they were for the existing P.C.A. loan. In deciding to recommend to the loan committee that a revolving credit loan for $1,300,000.00 and a term loan for $200,000.00 be given to the Debtor, Roberts testified that he took many things into consideration. He went out to the farm and saw cattle which the Debtor referred to as "my cattle." Parties mentioned on the various documents were contacted for verification, including Michigan Livestock Exchange which informed the Bank that Zwagerman bought cattle through them. Lien searches were done at the

Register of Deeds. Various financial records, including bank statements and tax returns, were reviewed. A balance sheet paralleling statements dated 12/31/82 and 3/31/83, accompanied by an earnings work sheet, was submitted by the Debtor. Production of the Bills of Sale for the cattle was not required since Comerica was refinancing a debt owed to P.C.A.

The balance sheet bearing dates of 12/31/82 and 3/31/83 indicated in the assets section an increase of 715 cattle in three months and a decrease in liabilities. Roberts commented that it is typical for banks to have problems interpreting the figures submitted by farmers, particularly those who do a large amount of buying and selling, as farmers are usually poor bookkeepers. Therefore, it was left up to an analyst to reconcile the figures. The accompanying earnings work sheet showed "custom cattle" as an entry separate from "cattle" in the amount of $208,232.00 for the period ending 3/31/83. Roberts admitted that in 1983 he knew the term "custom cattle" meant that the farmer didn't own the cattle, but rather would be compensated for feed and care of the cattle pursuant to an agreement with the owner. Furthermore, he stated that he would have red flagged any documents with such an entry to require more information regarding ownership. The only explanation Roberts proffered to the Court was that when the loan application was being reviewed in 1983, no one from the Bank, including himself, caught the entry.

On November 10, 1983, a note and security agreement were signed. The security agreement purportedly gave the Bank a security interest in the livestock. The following paragraph was also contained within that document,

> 2.4 At the time any Collateral becomes subject to a security interest in favor of Bank, Debtor shall be deemed to have warranted that (i) Debtor is the lawful owner of such Collateral and has the right and authority to subject the same to a security interest in Bank ...

A financing statement was filed by the Bank on November 17, 1983.

. . .

On December 3, 1985, Bradley received a call from Gordon Zwagerman who disclosed that many Bradley cattle had been sold without accounting for them to Bradley. ... The 90–140 day turnaround period had become a 13–14 month turnaround period. No cattle were shipped and no checks were sent or received by Bradley after that December 3, 1985, telephone call. A few days later, the Zwagermans' attorney told Bradley that approximately 458 cattle were on the farm. In contrast, Bradley's records showed that 3,141 cattle should have been on the farm.

On December 11, 1985, Comerica was contacted by the Zwagermans' attorney who relayed that the Zwagermans had encountered financial difficulties due to losses in the commodity futures market, the number of cattle presently on the farm was much lower than the Bank records reflected, and a David Bradley owned at least some of the cattle. Two days later the Bank "took possession" of the cattle, but actually left them on the farm and paid Gordon Zwagerman $500.00 a week to take care of them.

. . .

DISCUSSION

Bradley contends that because he retained ownership in the cattle and the relationship between himself and the Debtor was only a bailment, the proceeds are held for his benefit by constructive trust. Comerica claims that the Bradley/Debtor relationship was not a bailment, but rather a consignment subject to [UCC 2–326], and therefore their properly perfected security interest gives them an interest in the proceeds which has priority over Bradley. The Trustee argues that the nature of Bradley's interest is either a consignment subject to [UCC 2–326] or a security interest, and not a bailment. Thus, the Trustee asserts that Comerica has a superior interest in the proceeds, or in the alternative, based on his status as hypothetical lien creditor under 11 U.S.C. § 544,[*] the proceeds are property of the estate; and all the payments the Debtors made to Bradley for cattle sales within ninety days of the bankruptcy are preferences.

Although Count I of the Complaint suggested that the contract between Zwagerman and Bradley created a security interest under Article 9 of the U.C.C., I assume that such a claim has been abandoned since there were no arguments at trial advancing that position. In addition, the evidence does not indicate that there was any intent between the contracting parties that Bradley would retain a security interest in the cattle.

Bailment

. . .

A bailment is nothing more than a delivery of goods for some purpose, upon a contract, express or implied, to be redelivered to the bailor upon fulfillment of the purpose or to be dealt with according to the bailor's direction. Similarly, an agency is a relationship arising from a contract, express or implied, by which one of the parties confides to the other the transaction or management of some business or other activity in his name, or on his behalf, and whereby the other party assumes so to act and to render an account thereof. Thus in both situations, the title to the property remains in the bailor or principal, and the bailee or the agent holds the property under the bailment or agency for the owners' benefit. Consequently, it became well settled under the Bankruptcy Act that absent state statutory enactment to the contrary, if property was in a debtor's hands as bailee or agent, the trustee held it as such, and the bailor or principal could recover the property or its proceeds.

4 Collier on Bankruptcy § 541.08[2] (15th ed. 1990). Bradley has suggested in his briefs that Zwagerman was an agister and the contract was an agistment. The term agistment is an ancient one derived from the old

* [BC 544 is discussed in Chapter 10, Section 2(A), infra.]

Germanic word *giest* meaning guest. The Random House Dictionary of the English Language (1973) indicates agistment as being an obsolete word meaning the act of feeding or pasturing for a fee. Black's Law Dictionary 61 (5th ed. 1979) defines agistment as:

> Agistment. A contract whereby a person, called an agister, has control of animals and retains possession of land. The taking in and feeding or pasturing of horses, cattle, or similar animals for a reward and is a species of bailment.

Delivery of animals pursuant to a contract of agistment has been held to be a bailment of the animals.

> "Bailment," in its ordinary legal signification, imports the delivery of personal property by one person to another in trust for a specific purpose, with a contract, express or implied, that the trust shall be faithfully executed and the property returned or duly accounted for when the special purpose is accomplished.

The contracts and the practice of the parties seem to clearly indicate their intent. Bradley had cattle to be fed. Zwagerman had good feed. Not only was Michigan grass superior to Tennessee grass but also Zwagerman had access to good silage and even discarded cookies. Bradley delivered the cattle to Zwagerman who fed them until they reached a certain weight. Then, by mutual agreement they were sold at an agreed price. Zwagerman, as a bailee or agister, never had title to the cattle.

Effect of U.C.C. § 2–326

The Bank and Trustee claim that because of Bradley's failure to give notice under Uniform Commercial Code (U.C.C.) § 2–326, his interest is subordinate to theirs. The written contracts seem to imply that Tennessee law will apply. However, both Tennessee and Michigan have adopted the U.C.C. and I find no material differences between Tenn. Code Ann. § 47–2–326 (1989) and Mich. Comp. Laws § 440.2326 (1989) . . . .

· · ·

Section 2–326(1) is limited to transactions where delivered goods may be returned by the buyer even though they conform to the contract. There was never any intent that Zwagerman could return the cattle to Bradley. Costs, together with the shrinkage loss, would have made a return economically unfeasible.

In this case, delivery was never made to a buyer. U.C.C. § 2–103(1)(a) provides: "(1) In this article unless the context otherwise requires (a) 'Buyer' means a person who buys or contracts to buy goods." The U.C.C. does not seem to define "buy." Black's Law Dictionary 181 (5th ed. 1979) defines "buy" as "to acquire the ownership of property by giving an accepted price or consideration therefor; or by agreeing to do so; to acquire by the payment of a price or value; to purchase."

There was no agreement between Bradley and Zwagerman that Zwagerman would acquire ownership in the cattle. No price was agreed upon. Sale was not to take place until sometime in the future at which time

Zwagerman would sell as agent for Bradley, at a price agreeable to Bradley, and the entire proceeds of the sale would be sent to Bradley less a shrinkage fee.

Section 2–326(1)(b) would restrict the operation of § 2–326 "Sale or return" transactions to those instances where the goods were delivered "primarily" for resale. The word "primarily" is not defined in the U.C.C. XII The Oxford English Dictionary 472 (2d ed. 1989) defines "primarily" as "[w]ith reference to other temporal order: In the first place, first of all, preeminently, chiefly, principally; essentially."

In this case I find that delivery was not primarily for resale. The cattle were shipped for feeding and fattening. If it were primarily for resale, it would have been much more reasonable to sell them in Tennessee and avoid the expense of transporting, shrinkage, and other loss unless an unusual market condition existed in the Southwestern Michigan area; and there were no proofs to that effect.

Thus, for all the reasons stated, the court finds that this case does not involve a "sale or return" under § 2–326(1).

This brings us to [former] § 2–326(3). Undisputedly, the exclusions found in subsections 2–326(3)(a), (b), and (c) do not affect this case. No applicable sign law exists, the Debtors were not known by their creditors to be engaged in selling the goods of others, and Bradley stipulated that he did not file a financing statement. Therefore, a determination must be made as to whether or not the facts of this case fall within the parameters of U.C.C. § 2–326(3).

The court finds that the goods were not delivered to Zwagerman "for sale." It is not clear whether "for sale" refers to the sale to the buyer or resale by the buyer to third parties. But, delivery was not "for sale" in either event. As stated above, the delivery was for the care, feeding, and fattening the cattle. It would have been far more economical for Bradley to sell or to have someone in Tennessee sell the cattle and save shipping and shrinkage costs.

. . .

I do not find a definition of consignment in the code. A "consignment contract" is defined in Black's Law Dictionary 278 (5th ed. 1979) as "[c]onsignment of goods to another (consignee) for sale under agreement that consignee will pay consignor for any sold goods and will return any unsold goods." A consignment contract, as defined above, is common. This type of consignment has not given courts a lot of trouble, and is the subject of many of the cases cited to by the Trustee and the Bank. I have read and agree with the conclusion of those cases.

BFC Chemicals, Inc., v. Smith–Douglas, Inc., 46 Bankr. 1009 (E.D.N.C. 1985) is slightly different from the cases noted above. A certain chemical was placed by BFC, the creditor, in a large storage tank from which the debtor withdrew its needs from time to time to formulate agricultural chemicals for resale to its customers. The debtor then paid BFC for chemical taken. The debtor filed under Chapter 11. BFC filed what was treated by the bankruptcy judge as a motion for relief from stay [in order to recover the chemicals]. This was denied. The district judge held that N.C.G.S. § 25-2-326 was applicable because the goods were delivered "for sale" and the matter was remanded for reconsideration and a determination whether BFC complied with N.C.G.S. 25-2-326(3)(a). While this is somewhat different than the above cited consignment cases, I believe I would be inclined to agree with the district judge.

In Simmons First National Bank v. Wells, 279 Ark. 204, 650 S.W.2d 236 (1983), the bank had a perfected security interest in inventory and after acquired property of Western Rice Mills. Western defaulted on its loan and a receiver was appointed. Wells intervened. Until about four months prior to the receivership, Wells sold his rice to Western which milled and resold it. But, because of Western's financial inability to buy the rice outright, Wells had orally agreed that Western would mill for a certain price, market at an agreed price, and turn over the proceeds less Western's charge for milling. The trial court held for Wells. The state supreme court held that here was a clear consignment but remanded to determine whether Wells was protected by the state statute pertaining to grain warehousemen. This case differs from our case in that Western marketed the rice at an agreed minimum price. It could be said that in the Wells case delivery was primarily for resale.

O'Brien v. Chandler, 765 P.2d 1165 (N.M.1988) involved an oral agreement between McCoy, a cattle dealer, and Chandler, a cattle broker, whereby McCoy agreed to ship cattle to a feedlot for delivery to Chandler. Delivery was made and McCoy furnished invoices to Chandler which set out the sales price. Without knowledge to McCoy, Chandler obtained a loan from a bank and pledged the cattle as security. This security interest was perfected. The bank claimed that it had no knowledge of any interest of McCoy. McCoy sued to recover the cattle. The trial court held that the bank had a perfected security interest superior to any rights of McCoy. The New Mexico Supreme Court affirmed, holding that the contract was a sale. This case differs from ours in two important facts. First, a price was set, and secondly, invoices were furnished. If the bank had requested proof of ownership, Chandler had the proof in the invoices. In our case, if any creditor had requested proof of ownership, all Zwagerman could have furnished would have been contracts that indicated that he had no interest in the cattle.

. . .

In Eastman Kodak Co. v. Harrison (In re Sitkin Smelting & Refining, Inc., 639 F.2d 1213 (5th Cir.1981), reh'g en banc denied, 645 F.2d 72 (1981)), Sitkin entered into an agreement with Eastman by which it would process film waste and purchase the silver content recovered. Sitkin filed under Chapter XI. Eastman filed an adversary proceeding against the trustee in bankruptcy and C.I.T. Corp., a secured creditor. The bankruptcy referee held that possession should be entrusted to the [sic] C.I.T. The court of appeals reversed, concluding that the agreement between Kodak and Sitkin provided for a bailment of the unprocessed waste, and therefore, Kodak was entitled to reclaim possession. The court stated:

> The transaction between Kodak and Sitkin is not a sale or return within the meaning of section 2–326, since the goods were not delivered for resale with an option to return. C.I.T., then, fails to overcome the presumption against the application of section 2–326.

Id. at 1218. I would agree with the result reached in Sitkin but not on the basis for the decision. Even if this was a "sale or return," the print waste was not "delivered primarily for resale."

In Union State Bank of Hazen v. Cook (In re Cook), 63 Bankr. 789 (Bankr.D.N.D.1986), parents, a son and his wife, and a partnership of which the father and son were partners filed petitions under Chapter 11. These debtors operated a family farm on which they raised Angus cattle and maintained a custom feed lot. Another son, Tom, did not stay on the farm but cattle he had raised as part of a 4–H project were left on the farm. He spent about one week each year on the farm. The court found that the business relationship between Tom and the debtors was quite loose. Tom's cattle were not separated from the debtors' cattle. The debtors were allowed to cull and market Tom's cattle, and even retain some of the proceeds of his cattle, but he never gave them authority to mortgage his cattle. The plaintiff bank was granted a security interest by the debtors in all livestock owned by them, including the increase thereof. The bank was not aware of Tom's interest until the bankruptcy was filed. Partnership schedules indicated 36 head were held for Tom, valued at approximately $22,000.00. While there were other issues before the court in determining ownership, the court noted that the cattle were all branded with the partnership brand. Although North Dakota has a branding statute, a brand is only prima facie evidence of ownership. N.D. Cent. Code § 36–09–19 (1980). The testimony of Tom and his brother was found to be convincing and supported by the fact that some of the cattle were registered by the American Angus Association in Tom's name. The court held that the parties' intent was crucial, and the intent was that Tom retain ownership. The burden was on the bank to demonstrate that the debtors possessed sufficient rights in Tom's cattle for the security interest to attach. The debtors' authority to sell Tom's cattle did not give them the authority to encumber the cattle.

In *Cook*, as in our case, the bank was casual about its loan. Although the bank representative made inspections of the operation, he never counted the cattle. The bank's officer admitted that other cattle besides debtors' could have been on the ranch and that he relied only on the financial statements submitted. The court held that Tom's cattle were not subject to the bank's lien.

In First National Bank of Blooming Prairie v. Olsen, 403 N.W.2d 661 (Minn.Ct.App.1987), Olsen owned and operated a feedlot for which the bank provided financing. The bank had a perfected security interest in Olsen's farm property including livestock. There were approximately 2,500 cattle on the farm, all of which were owned by third-party investors. The owner-investors did not perfect under § 2–326. The bank filed a replevin action and the trial court held that § 2–326 did not apply because the cattle were not delivered for sale. The court of appeals held that the § 2–326 did apply, relying on the official comment that "Subsection (3) resolves all reasonable doubts as to the nature of the transaction in favor of the general creditors of the buyer." However, the court found for the investors because the bank had actual knowledge that Olsen custom-fed a substantial number of cattle.

. . .

In Walter E. Heller & Co. S.E. v. Riviana Foods, Inc., 648 F.2d 1059 (5th Cir.1981) Riviana entered into a warehouse agreement with Amos Brokerage Company to store and eventually deliver the goods to Riviana's customers. Amos was not permitted to sell these goods but did maintain a place where it sold like goods under another name. Heller and Amos entered into an inventory security agreement and accounts financing security agreement. Subsequently, Amos filed bankruptcy. The court held that the goods were not delivered "for sale" as required by U.C.C. § 2–326 for a "sale and return." It drew a comparison to Allgeier v. Campisi, 117 Ga.App. 105, 159 S.E.2d 458 (1968), where the plaintiff entrusted her car to a dealer who was authorized to receive offers but lacked authority to sell without the approval of the plaintiff. The defendant, a security interest holder in the plaintiff dealer's inventory, sought possession of the car. The court held for the plaintiff since the car was not delivered "for sale" under U.C.C. § 2–326.

As can be noted from the cases mentioned above, there has been little uniformity in the court decisions on § 2–326. There is much to be said for extension of the section to situations that were not anticipated or intended by the drafters of the law. If I could interpret the law as I think it should be written, I would probably hold that 2–326 should be applied to every situation where there may be secret interests in property which would be harmful to those dealing with the person having possession. One of the purposes of Article 9 was to eliminate the secret lien, and an aim of 2–326 was to protect third parties in consignment cases. However, cattle cases are not as serious as some of the situations faced by courts in the cases above. Any prudent, prospective lender or purchaser is well aware that cattle may be custom fed or cows may be leased. More disturbing are the inventory cases in which it is not common practice to deliver goods while retaining title.

I am well aware of the provision in § 1–102 of the U.C.C. which provides that, "This Act shall be liberally construed and applied to promote its underlying purposes and policies." Nevertheless, radical changes in the unambiguous provisions of the law should not be made by judicial interpretation. The result would be to uproot the drafters' intent to promote uniformity and certainty. It is much better that such changes be brought about by legislation after much discussion both inside and outside the legislative bodies concerned. It was no accident that the Michigan U.C.C. Act of 1962, 1962 Mich. Pub. Acts 174, did not become effective until over a year later on January 1, 1964. Those of us who were around at that time can recall the many seminars which were held for lawyers, accountants, financial institutions, trade associations, and many others to prepare the commercial world for this new law. Because the U.C.C. was so superior to what it replaced it was not surprising that some lawyers and jurist expected a miraculously all-encompassing statute. However, the U.C.C. has been amended many times and I am sure it will be amended many more times in the future.

R. Anderson, Anderson on the Uniform Commercial Code § 1–102:20–21 (1981) states:

> When a section of the code is clear and unambiguous there is "no occasion" to engage in statutory construction.
>
> Contrary to the rule of liberal construction stated in the preceding sections, there is some authority that the Code is to be strictly construed where in derogation of the common law, and a statute should be construed in harmony with the common law unless there is a clear legislative intent to abrogate the common law. In many states there are special statutory construction acts that expressly repudiate this principle of statutory construction, so that it is extremely doubtful whether strict construction should be made solely because of conflict with the common law.
>
> A better reason for strict construction is that if the court does not adhere to the letter of the Code, the objective of certainty will be defeated. Thus where the Code is unambiguous, it should be applied according to its letter, as to do otherwise would merely produce confusion in the business world.
>
> When the provisions of the Code are unambiguous they are to be followed by the courts....
>
> A court should adhere strictly to the provisions of the Code in order to achieve stability, consistency, and predictability. And an "overly" liberal interpretation of the Code should be avoided as creating uncertainty among businessmen and their legal advisors who believe themselves to be entering into transactions on the basis that the Code means what it says.
>
> Loose construction of the Code cannot be justified on the basis of the direction to construe the Code liberally as a mandate for liberal construction is not a "license to legislate."

Later Anderson continues:

> The certainty of commercial practices and relations is essential to furthering trade. Consequently as a variant of the objective of furthering trade, a court should so interpret the Code as to further certainty in commercial dealings.

The dangers of expanding the boundaries of § 2–326 cannot be better illustrated than the case before us. Bradley, at the time of trial, was an 80 year old man who had been in the cattle business his entire life except for a

few years in service during World War II. He had also served as a vice
president of a local bank. While he was aware of the practice of custom
feeding of cattle, he never actually engaged in it before his arrangement
with the Debtors. He then did what any prudent businessman should do—
he visited his lawyer who "was good," according to Bradley, because he
subsequently became a judge. His lawyer set up a group of forms to be used
and instructed Bradley as to the procedure to be followed, but he never
instructed Bradley to perfect his transaction by filing with a register of
deeds. Bradley had never heard of requiring the filing of a financing
statement as to these transactions. Testimony during the trial indicated
that there was little custom feeding going on in Michigan at the time
Zwagerman and Bradley entered into their joint undertaking. In the fall of
1986, Michigan Livestock, a large cattle dealer, commenced delivering their
cattle for feeding in an operation similar to that of Bradley and Zwagerman. It is possible they may have heard of Bradley's operation and
problems by this time. Before that, most of the custom lots were carried out
by the big lots out West. Michigan Livestock filed a sort of financing
statement; the form used did not comply with the U.C.C. but did give
notice. However, testimony indicated that most persons delivering cattle for
custom feeding did not file financing statements.

Twenty states have branding laws and dispose of title matters as to
cattle through these laws. Neither Michigan or Tennessee have adopted
such a statute.

From the clear terms of § 2–326, related sections of the U.C.C., the
general commercial practice, and the fact that a number of states have felt
that control in this area should be by a separate branding statute outside of
the U.C.C., I find that the transaction with which we are concerned is not a
"sale or return" under the meaning of § 2–326 and that the title to the
cattle delivered to the Zwagermans by Bradley remained in Bradley.

[In the remainder of the opinion, the court determined which cattle
were Bradley's and whether certain pre-bankruptcy payments from Zwagerman to Bradley were recoverable as preferences under BC 547. Preferences are discussed in Chapter 10, Section 2(B), infra.

The District Court affirmed on both the consignment issue and the
preference issue. Its conclusion as to the former was as follows: "While the
question is a close one, the factual finding that the delivery was not 'for
sale' is not clearly erroneous and will not be upset on appeal."]

NOTES ON CONSIGNMENTS

(1) **Consignments Under Pre–UCC Law.** The delivery of goods on
"consignment" has an ancient and honorable history. The consignee (sometimes called a "factor") was a selling agent who did not undertake
entrepreneurial risks. To the extent the consigned goods were sold, the
consignee received a commission or a margin above a stated price; unsold
goods could be returned to the owner.

The agreement between consignor and consignee clearly provided that the consignor remained the owner of the goods; when the consignee, as selling agent, effected a sale to a buyer, title passed from the consignor to the buyer. Under this arrangement, creditors of the *consignor* could, of course, levy on the goods while they were held by the consignee. By the same token, most courts held that creditors of the *consignee* had no right to levy on the consignor's goods. Possession often did not imply ownership. On the other hand, courts usually would rebel when the agreement made the "consignee" an entrepreneur rather than a selling agent, as when the agreement required the consignee to pay for the goods even though the consignee was unable to sell them. See 1 Gilmore, Security § 3.5.

The law of a few states reflected a wider concern for creditors of the consignee by enacting the "Trader's Acts." These Acts typically dealt with the situation where a person transacted business "as a trader" in its own name and without disclosing the name of its principal or partner by a conspicuous sign at the place of business. In these circumstances, all the property used in the business was made liable for the debts of the "trader." The model for such legislation was a Virginia statute first enacted in 1839; this Virginia statute was repealed in 1973.

(2) Consignments Under the UCC: "True" Consignments versus Consignments for Security. Does Article 9 govern an orthodox ("true") consignment, where the consignee has no obligation to pay for the goods? It is difficult to conclude that the consignor's ownership of the goods is an "interest in personal property ... which secures payment or performance of an obligation." R1–201(37). The duty of a bailee to return bailed goods is not the kind of obligation that supports a security interest. If it were, then *all* bailments would create security interests; we know this is not the case.

The drafters of the UCC recognized, however, that *some* "consignments" might secure payment or performance of an obligation, i.e., that the parties to inventory financing might describe the transaction in their documents as a "consignment." You have seen that the common law provided an incentive to do so: By retaining title, a consignor immunized the goods from the reach of the consignee's creditors.[2] The UCC follows pre-UCC law in treating as secured transactions those "consignments" that are for security. R9–109(a)(1). For example, a "consignment" that requires the "agent-consignee" to pay for goods that the consignee is unable to sell is likely to be characterized as securing an obligation. If so, then the transaction creates an Article 9 security interest and is subject to Article 9 in its entirety; the rules concerning attachment, perfection, priority, and remedies all apply. See, e.g., In re Oriental Rug Warehouse Club, Inc., 205

---

2. In addition, because the consignor remained the owner of the consigned goods, the consignor was free to set the resale price charged to the ultimate consumer. However, a consignor who sets the resale price should be aware that if a court later determines that there was not a genuine consignment relationship between the consignor and consignee, the consignor could be liable for violating antitrust laws against price fixing. Simpson v. Union Oil Co., 377 U.S. 13, 84 S.Ct. 1051, 12 L.Ed.2d 98 (1964).

B.R. 407 (Bkrtcy.D.Minn.1997). In that case, a rug manufacturer put rugs in retailer's possession under a "consignment agreement." The court held that the manufacturer actually retained only a security interest because (i) the retailer was entitled to set its own prices, (ii) the manufacturer billed the retailer upon shipment of the rugs, not on the sale of the rugs by the retailer, (iii) the retailer commingled both the rugs and the proceeds of sale with its own property, and (iv) the retailer was entitled to obtain a profit on its sales instead of a commission.

(3) "True" Consignments before the 1999 Revision of Article 9. For true consignments, the drafters of the UCC rejected the common-law rule, which provides that creditors of the consignee cannot reach the consignor's (owner's) interest in the consigned goods. They concluded instead that, even in true consignments, creditors of a consignee deserve protection from a consignor's undisclosed interest in goods. This protection now appears in Revised Article 9; before the 1999 revision of Article 9, protection was found in Article 2.

F2–326(3) specified circumstances where consigned goods were "deemed to be on sale or return," i.e., where the creditors of the consignee (who held only the limited interest of a bailee) could reach the consignor's ownership interest. That section afforded the three methods by which a cautious consignor could shield the goods from the reach of the consignee's creditors. One was a litigator's nightmare: The consignor must "establish [cf. UCC 1–201(8) (definition of 'burden of establishing')] that [the consignee] is *generally* known by his creditors to be *substantially* engaged in selling the goods of others." F2–326(3)(b). Would you have advised a client to rely on this subsection?

A second method by which a consignor may protect its ownership interest against creditors of the consignee under Former Article 9 was to comply with "an applicable law providing for a consignor's interest or the like to be evidenced by a sign." F2–326(3)(a). Resort to this method was likely to be futile: There is authority to the effect that the phrase "applicable law" refers only to a statute and not to a common-law rule, see, e.g., Vonins, Inc. v. Raff, 101 N.J.Super. 172, 243 A.2d 836 (App.Div.1968), and "there are few states if any that have enacted a sign law that would protect a consignor." Clark, Secured Transactions ¶ 1.06[1], at 1–70.

The only realistic alternative for a consignor under Former Article 2 was to "compl[y] with the filing provisions of the Article on Secured Transactions (Article 9)." F2–326(3)(c). Former Article 9 permitted a consignor to file a financing statement showing itself as "consignor" and the party in possession as "consignee" without prejudicing the determination whether the transaction was a consignment or a security interest. See F9–408. For purposes of priority, Former Article 9 treated a perfected consignment (i.e., one where the consignor had filed a financing statement) much like a purchase-money security interest. See F9–114.

(4) "True" Consignments under Revised Article 9. The drafters of Revised Article 9 found favor with most of the results of the pre–1999 approach to consignments; however, they took exception to the drafting approach. Revised Article 9 replaces the consignment provisions of F2–326 with Article 9 provisions intended to have much the same effect.

Scope of Revised Article 9; "Consignment." We have seen that Revised Article 9 applies to a consignment for security, which is a garden-variety security interest. See Note (2), supra. Revised Article 9 also applies to a "consignment." R9–109(a)(4). This term, which is defined in R9–102(a)(20) and discussed below, includes many, but not all, "true" consignments and excludes purported consignments where the goods secure an obligation. See R9–102(a)(20)(D). The term "security interest" now includes the ownership interest of a consignor in a transaction that is subject to Article 9. R1–201(37) (2d sentence). Thus the term "security interest" encompasses a true consignment, where the consignor is a bailor whose ownership interest does not secure payment or performance of an obligation, as well as a purported consignment that secures an obligation.

In the case of a (true) consignment under Revised Article 9, the consignor is a "secured party," and the consignee is a "debtor." See R9–102(a)(72)(C), (a)(28)(C). A consignment is not enforceable against the consignee unless the requirements for attachment in R9–203(b) are satisfied, and the consignor must give public notice to insulate its ownership interest from claims of the consignee's creditors. The primary purpose of subjecting true consignments to Revised Article 9 is to regulate the relative rights of a consignor and creditors of the consignee. Because consigned goods do not secure an obligation owed by the consignee to the consignor, it would make no sense to apply Article 9's remedial scheme to a consignee's breach of a consignment agreement. Accordingly, law other than Article 9 governs a consignor's remedies against the consignee. See R9–601(g); Note (4) on Distinguishing Leases From Secured Transactions, Section 1(A), supra.

The (true) consignments to which Revised Article 9 applies are to some extent the same as those described in F2–326(3): transactions in which a person delivers goods to a merchant for the purpose of sale, and the merchant deals in goods of that kind under a name other than the name of the person making delivery. See R9–102(a)(20) (defining "consignment"). As the *Zwagerman* case, supra, indicates, courts construing F2–326(3) have had difficulty determining whether a particular transaction meets this description: Were the goods delivered "for the purpose of sale"? Does the person in possession (the putative consignee) deal in goods of that kind "under a name other than the name of the person making delivery"?

What purpose do these phrases serve? Comment 2 to F2–326(3) suggested that public notice is required for transactions where creditors of the consignee may reasonably be deemed to have been misled by the secret reservation of title in the consignor. Did the *Zwagerman* court, which professed to be sympathetic to "ostensible ownership" concerns, construe these requirements too narrowly?

The Article 2 Study Group recommended that the phrase "delivered to a person for sale" in F2–326(3) "should be expanded to include all deliveries of goods pursuant to which the parties expect the consignee ultimately to sell to others, even though further processing or prior consent to sale is required." PEB Article 2 Report 122. Does R9–102(a)(20) (delivered "for *the purpose of* sale") accomplish this result? Would the italicized words have changed the result in *Zwagerman*? Comment 14 to R9–109 appears to capture the Article 2 Study Group's recommendation. Is the Comment consistent with the statutory text? Would it have changed the result in *Zwagerman*?

As mentioned above in Note (3), F2–326(3) protected a consignor from claims of creditors of a consignee who is generally known by its creditors to be substantially engaged in selling the goods of others. Although this rule may present problems of interpretation and proof, Revised Article 9 retains it. See R9–102(a)(20)(A)(iii). In addition, Revised Article 9 is inapplicable (and the common-law rule favoring the consignor applies) to goods delivered to auctioneers and goods having a value of less than $1,000. See R9–109(a)(20)(A), (a)(20)(B). What justifies these exclusions?

The definition of "consignment," and thus the scope of Revised Article 9, also excludes true consignments of consumer goods. Although F2–326, literally applied, subjected consumer consignors, like Crispin in Problem. 8.1.8, supra, to the risk that their goods would be used to satisfy debts owed by their consignees, Professor John Dolan has observed that the cases generally protect the consumer consignor. See Dolan, The UCC Consignment Rule Needs an Exception for Consumers, 44 Ohio St. L.J. 21 (1983). Professor Dolan approves of the results of those cases but not their reasoning, which does not depend on the fact that the consignor was a consumer. He argues that contemporary credit practices no longer justify rules based on ostensible ownership concerns. Whatever validity remains in requiring consignors to file financing statements derives from antifraud concerns not present when consumers are the consignors: There is little risk that a consumer is cloaking what is essentially inventory financing in the guise of a consignment. Are you persuaded by Professor Dolan's argument? Even if not, can you justify Revised Article 9's exclusion of consumer-goods consignments?

Conflicting Claims to Consigned Goods. Like pre–1999 Article 2, Revised Article 9 contains a rule that violates the *nemo dat* principle and enables creditors of the consignee (who has a bailee's limited interest in the goods) to reach the consignor's (ownership) interest in the goods: "while the goods are in the possession of the consignee, the consignee is deemed to have rights and title to the goods identical to those the consignor had or had power to transfer." R9–319(a). Thus, if the consignor's security interest is unperfected, creditors of the consignee may acquire a senior judicial lien on the consigned goods. See R9–317(a)(2). Similarly, the consignee may create an enforceable security interest not only in its own (bailee's) interest but also in the consignor's (ownership) interest. See R9–203(b)(2) (debtor has power to transfer a security interest in the collateral to a third party).

A consignor may perfect its security interest by filing. Like a lessor (see Note (6) on Distinguishing Leases from Secured Transactions, Section (1)(A), supra), a consignor may file a financing statement showing itself as "consignor" and the party in possession as "consignee" without prejudicing the determination whether the transaction is actually a consignment. See R9–505. If the consignor's security interest is perfected and has priority over a conflicting claim to the goods, then law other than Article 9 determines the rights and title of the consignee. R9–319(b). For example, at common law a true consignee was merely a bailee-agent of goods owned by the consignor-principal. See R. Brown, The Law of Personal Property at 247–48 (Raushenbush ed., 3d ed. 1976).

In determining whether a consignor's security interest has priority over a conflicting claim to the goods, do not ignore the teaching of R9–103(d): a consignor's security interest in consigned goods is a purchase-money security interest in inventory. In some settings, purchase-money status may be advantageous. See R9–317(e) (PMSI takes priority over the rights of a lien creditor that arise between the time the security interest attaches and the time of filing, if filing occurs before or within 20 days after the debtor receives delivery of the collateral); Chapter 7, Sections 3(A) and 6(C), supra. On the other hand, to enjoy priority over the holder of a "floating lien" on the consignee's inventory, the consignor must comply with the notification requirement of R9–324(b). See Note (2) on Purchase–Money Priority and the Definition of "Purchase–Money Security Interest," Chapter 7, Section 6(A)(II), supra.

Most people would agree that, in their pre–1999 incarnation, "[t]he Uniform Commercial Code's provisions regarding consignments are not models of draftsmanship." In re State Street Auto Sales, Inc., 81 B.R. 215 (Bkrtcy.D.Mass.1988). Are the consignment provisions of Revised Article 9 an improvement?

(5) "Sale or Return" Transactions. What is the effect of filing a financing statement against a buyer in a transaction that is a "sale or return," i.e., a transaction where goods are delivered to a buyer primarily for resale, which goods the buyer may return even though they conform to the contract? See UCC 2–326(1). Unlike a true consignment, where the person in possession of the goods is a bailee, a "sale or return" is a sale to a buyer. Is a "sale or return" simply an unsecured sale that provides an alternative method (i.e., return of the goods) by which the buyer can discharge its obligation for the price? If so, then the filing of a financing statement would be irrelevant. On the other hand, does the buyer's privilege of returning unsold goods for credit against its obligation for the purchase price create an interest in the goods in favor of the seller? If so, what is the nature of that interest? Can it be anything more than a security interest, given UCC 2–401(1) (second sentence) and R1–201(37) (fifth sentence)?

(C) BAILMENTS FOR PROCESSING

The UCC directly addresses two prototypical types of bailments: leases and consignments. But many transactions in which one person is in possession of goods "owned" by another do not fit within these prototypes. Among these are arrangements whereby the person in possession is to return the goods (or something extracted from them) to the owner—or deliver them to a third party—only after the goods are repaired, processed, refined, fabricated, or similarly dealt with. Regardless of the form these arrangements take (and they may take an infinite variety of forms), if the "owner's" interest in the goods "secures payment or performance of an obligation" (R1–201(37)), then the "owner" holds a security interest subject to Article 9. See R9–109(a)(1). As observed above, if the *only* performance that the goods secure is the obligation to return them to the owner, then the transaction would not be a security interest; otherwise, all bailments would be Article 9 transactions.

As the following materials suggest, drawing the lines among secured transactions, consignments, and other bailments is quite difficult.

Problem 8.1.9. Grower delivers rice to Miller. Miller agrees to pay for the rice in three installments. Concerned about Miller's ability to make the payments, Grower retains title to the rice.

(a) Is this transaction a security interest or a bailment?

(b) The sheriff levies on the rice pursuant to an execution writ procured by Elsie, a judgment creditor of Miller's. Whose rights are senior, Grower's or Elsie's? Recall that a judicial lien creditor ordinarily acquires no better rights to the goods than its debtor enjoyed, see Chapter 1, Section 3(B), supra; however, under R9–317(a)(2) an unperfected security interest often will be subordinate to the rights of a person who becomes a lien creditor.

Problem 8.1.10. Grower delivers rice to Miller. Miller agrees to mill it for a fee and return it to Grower.

(a) Is this transaction a security interest or a bailment?

(b) While Miller is in possession of the rice, the sheriff levies on it pursuant to an execution writ procured by Elsie, a judgment creditor of Miller's. Whose rights are senior, Grower's or Elsie's?

(c) Assume that Lender holds a security interest in all Miller's existing and after-acquired inventory and equipment. Will the security interest attach to the rice? See R9–203(b); Note (1) on Attachment, Chapter 7, Section 2, supra. If so, will Lender be able to cut off Grower's interest in the rice? See UCC 2–403(1) (1st sentence); Note on Bailments for Processing, infra.

Problem 8.1.11. Grower delivers rice to Miller. Miller agrees to mill it for a fee and deliver it at Grower's direction to Grower's customers. The customers are to pay Miller, who will deduct the milling fee and remit the balance to Grower.

(a) Is this transaction a security interest or a bailment? If it is a bailment, is it a consignment subject to Article 9?

(b) While Miller is in possession of the rice, the sheriff levies on it pursuant to an execution writ procured by Elsie, a judgment creditor of Miller's. Whose rights are senior, Grower's or Elsie's?

Problem 8.1.12. What results in Problem. 8.1.11 if Miller delivers the rice to its own customers, rather than Grower's? See Simmons First National Bank v. Wells, 279 Ark. 204, 650 S.W.2d 236 (1983) (holding arrangement whereby miller was obligated to sell at an agreed minimum price to be subject to F2–326(3); this case was described, and distinguished, in *Zwagerman*, supra).

NOTE ON BAILMENTS FOR PROCESSING

Article 9 applies to secured transactions; it does not apply to bailments (other than certain consignments).[3] Two important consequences follow from this observation. First, if the person in possession of goods claimed by another is a bailee, then the bailor's ownership interest in the goods generally is enforceable against third parties even in absence of public notice. See UCC 2–403(1) (1st sentence) (*nemo dat* principle). But see UCC 2–403(2) (entrustment rule). See also Chapter 1, Section 3, supra (discussing these rules).[4] If, however, the person in possession is an Article 9 debtor, then the secured party must file a financing statement to protect its security interest against most third parties. See, e.g., R9–317(a)(2), (b) (lien creditors, certain buyers); R9–322(a)(2) (perfected secured parties).[5] Second, a bailor's remedies against the bailee and the bailed goods are determined by common law and scattered statutes, whereas Article 9 governs a secured party's remedies against the debtor and the collateral.

As we have seen, the UCC expounds at length about the distinction between leases ("bailments for hire" at common law) and security interests, see UCC 1–201(37) (last three paragraphs), and it singles out certain types of consignments (bailments for sale) for special treatment. See R9–109(a)(4); R9–102(a)(20). The UCC does not, however, give any other guidance for distinguishing between bailments and security interests. Some cases are easy to characterize: No one would seriously contend that a security interest is created when, for example, Lee Abel brings the Chevrolet to Jiffy Lube for an oil change or Benny Stulwicz brings Arnie Becker's suits to the cleaners. But as one moves away from the "pure" bailment, characterizing the transactions becomes more difficult and the results become harder to predict.

---

3. The possessory security interest (**pledge**), whereby a debtor's property is delivered to a secured party to secure an obligation, is a bailment that is subject to Article 9; however, the pledge differs from the bailments under consideration in this Chapter. Unlike a pledge, if any of the "bailments" discussed here creates a security interest, the person in possession of the goods would be the debtor, not the secured party.

4. In some cases, the common law of accession and confusion may operate to sub-

ordinate the rights of the bailor to claims of creditors of, and purchasers from, the bailee. See R. Brown, The Law of Personal Property ch. VI (Raushenbush ed., 3d ed. 1976).

5. Of course, if a putative bailment is a secured transaction, the secured party will have no enforceable security interest unless the requirements for attachment are met. See R9–203(a), (b) (discussed in Chapter 7, Section 2, supra).

As with the lease/security interest distinction, courts have looked to a variety of factors when distinguishing between a bailment for processing and a secured transaction. Two of these factors seem particularly irrelevant. First, some courts appear to have been influenced by the perception that creditors of the bailee (including Article 9 secured parties) may rely to their detriment on the bailee's possession of bailed goods. Although one might argue, as some commentators have, that public notice of bailments *should* be required as a prerequisite for protection against creditors and purchasers, the law simply is not to that effect: Bailors generally are not required to cure any "ostensible ownership" problems by filing or otherwise. It follows that the "ostensible ownership" of the goods provides no illumination whatsoever concerning the lease/security interest distinction.

Second, courts may become concerned with the subjective intentions, or purposes, of the parties. The learning in the context of leases is relevant here: Because the characterization of the transaction affects not only the rights of the parties but also the rights of third parties, subjective intentions should be irrelevant. See Note (2) on Distinguishing Leases from Secured Transactions, Section 1(A), supra. Nevertheless, some reported decisions attempt to divine the "intention," "motivation," or "purpose" of the parties.

Rohweder v. Aberdeen Production Credit Association, 765 F.2d 109 (8th Cir.1985), is a fine example of this phenomenon. The facts of *Rohweder* were described in the *Zwagerman* opinion, supra, as follows:

> ... Rohweder turned over certain cows to Bellman with an option to purchase for an agreed price. Bellman bred the cows with his bulls, calved them out, pastured, and cared for all of the cows and calves. Bellman was to receive 40% of calf crop and Rohweder was to retain the rest. The Rohweder cattle were pastured with Bellman's. Bellman branded some of the cows with his brand and ear tagged the calves. Rohweder instructed Bellman to sell off some of the older and poorer cows. Some sale barns paid Bellman, who then paid Rohweder, and others paid Rohweder directly. Bellman had given PCA a security interest in all of his cattle and after acquired cattle. Bellman then filed under Chapter 11. PCA seized all of the cattle, resulting in Rohweder suing PCA for conversion. The district court ruled that Bellman had sufficient rights for attachment of a security interest and granted a directed verdict at the close of plaintiff's proofs.

115 B.R. at 552.

In dismissing the judgment and remanding the proceedings for trial by jury, the Eighth Circuit concluded that Rohweder was entitled to the cattle only if he was a bailor, not if he was a secured party.

> The crucial question in this regard is the parties' intent. If Rohweder intended to make a conditional sale when he delivered the cows to Bellman, he retained only a security interest and Bellman had sufficient rights for PCA's security interest to attach. On the other hand, if the parties intended to create a bailment, with Rohweder retaining

complete ownership of the cows and relinquishing only possession, Bellman would not have sufficient rights for attachment of PCA's lien and, in the absence of an estoppel, Rohweder should prevail. While the factors of control over the cattle, including the right of sale, and the option to purchase do not necessarily constitute "rights in collateral," they are relevant evidence for the jury in determining the parties' intent to transfer an ownership interest to Bellman.

765 F.2d at 113.[6]

What can a putative bailor do to protect itself against the risk that a court will determine its interest in the goods to be a security interest? The easiest step is to file a financing statement; in the event the arrangement is held to be a secured transaction, the security interest will be perfected. (Under some loan agreements, the filing of a financing statement against the debtor is a default; if the bailee is a debtor under such an agreement, a bailor who files a financing statement without the bailee's authorization would face liability to the bailee.) Will the fact that a financing statement has been filed affect the court's characterization of the transaction? To reduce this risk, a bailor might file a financing statement referring to itself as "bailor" and to the person in possession as "bailee." See R9–505.

A filed financing statement will protect the "bailor's" interest against lien creditors of the "bailee" and, as we shall see in Chapter 10, Section 2(A), against the "strong arm" of the "bailee's" bankruptcy trustee. But, as Chapter 7, Section 6(A), supra, makes clear, perfection of a security interest does not guarantee priority over conflicting security interests. The bailment-security interest issue often is litigated between a putative bailor and the "bailee's" inventory financer. In that setting, if the arrangement is characterized as a secured transaction rather than a bailment, the "bailor's" security interest may be subordinate to that of the inventory financer. See R9–324(b) (discussed in Chapter 7, Section 6(A)(II), supra).

SECTION 2.   SALES OF RIGHTS TO PAYMENT

As we have seen, questions as to the applicability of Article 9 to transactions in goods are dominated by the concept of "security interest." This unitary approach is expressed in the basic rule of R9–109(a)(1): Article

---

6. The *Rohweder* court's concern with the subjective intentions of the parties is not its only error. The court mistakenly assumed that PCA's security interest cannot attach to bailed goods because bailees do not have "rights in the collateral" within the meaning of F9–203(1). Unfortunately, the court is not unique in this regard. See, e.g., In re Sitkin Smelting & Refining, Inc., 639 F.2d 1213 (5th Cir.1981); In re Zwagerman, 125 B.R. 486 (W.D.Mich.1991) (quoting *Rohweder*). Of course bailees have rights in bailed goods! At a minimum they have the right to possession as against the entire world, other than the owner.

Note that to challenge the court's assumption is not necessarily to disagree with its conclusion. Even if Bellman had rights in the cattle, PCA ordinarily would acquire no greater rights than Bellman had. See UCC 2–403(1) (1st sentence). Thus the court was correct that resolution of the conflicting claims turned on whether Rohweder was a bailor or an Article 9 secured party.

9 applies "to a transaction, regardless of its form, that creates a *security interest*." We also have seen that the term "*security* interest" can be misleading. It encompasses not only an interest that "*secures* payment or performance of an obligation" but also "any interest of a consignor . . . in a transaction that is subject to Article 9." R1–201(37). See R9–109(a)(4); Section 1(B), supra.

Article 9 also applies to certain transactions in rights to payment that do not secure payment or performance of an obligation. Specifically, "[t]he term ['security interest'] also includes any interest of . . . a buyer of accounts, chattel paper, a payment intangible, or a promissory note in a transaction that is subject to Article 9." Article 9 applies to most sales of these rights to payment. See R9–109(a)(3) (Article 9 applies to "a sale of accounts, chattel paper, payment intangibles, or promissory notes"). But see R9–109(d)(4) though (7) (excluding certain sales of rights to payment from Article 9).

The implications of Article 9's including sales of rights to payment are discussed more fully in Chapter 9, Section 1(D), infra.

SECTION 3. AGRICULTURAL LIENS AND UCC LIENS

Article 9 is designed primarily for consensual transactions: transactions that create a security interest by contract, including consignments and sales of receivables. See R9–109(a)(1), (a)(3), (a)(4). However, Article 9 also applies to liens arising under other articles of the UCC. See R9–109(a)(5), (a)(6). The application of Article 9 to security interests arising under Article 4 (in favor of a bank that takes an item for collection) and Article 5 (in favor of an issuer of, or nominated person with respect to, a letter of credit) is limited by UCC 4–210 and R5–118, respectively. The application of Article 9 to security interests arising under Article 2 (in favor of a seller or buyer of goods) or 2A (in favor of a lessee of goods) is limited by R9–110.

Notwithstanding its general inapplicability to statutory liens, Revised Article 9 (unlike Former Article 9) also governs the perfection, priority, and enforcement of a large variety of statutorily-created "agricultural liens" on farm products. See R9–109(a)(2); R9–102(a)(5) (defining "agricultural lien"). Non–Article 9 law governs the creation of agricultural liens, and the circumstances giving rise to the liens vary widely from state to state. We discuss agricultural liens in Chapter 11, Section 5(B), infra.

SECTION 4. EXCLUSIONS FROM ARTICLE 9 OR ITS FILING PROVISIONS

We have seen that Article 9 applies not only to interests that "secure[ ] payment or performance of an obligation," R1–201(37), but also to many sales of accounts, chattel paper, payment intangibles, and promissory notes and to agricultural liens. See R9–109(a)(2), (3); Sections 2and 3, supra. And, as we saw in Section 1(B), supra, Article 9's attachment, perfection, and priority provisions apply to true consignments.

This Section discusses two other aspects of the scope of Article 9: transactions that create security interests, but as to which Article 9 nevertheless is inapplicable in whole or in part; and transactions that create security interests covered by Article 9, but as to which public notice is given by filing or recording in a non-Article 9 system.

R9–109 excludes certain types of transactions from Article 9. Many of the exclusions follow directly from the basic scope provision, R9–109(a)(1). For example, Article 9 applies to "a transaction . . . that creates a security interest in personal property or fixtures." R9–109(d)(11) reflects the converse: Article 9 generally "does not apply to . . . the creation or transfer of an interest in or lien on real property" other than fixtures. Security interests in real property (i.e., mortgages and trust deeds) are governed by real property law. We shall consider fixtures and the applicability of Article 9 to other real property-related collateral in Chapter 11, Section 4, infra.

In a similar fashion, R9–109(a)(1) provides that Article 9 applies to security interests created "by contract,"[1] and R9–109(d) specifically excludes from the applicability of Article 9 two types of nonconsensual liens: landlord's liens, see R9–109(d)(1), and liens given by statute or other rule of law for services or materials (other than agricultural liens). See R9–109(d)(2). The creation, priority, and enforcement of most nonconsensual, nonagricultural liens is governed by the statutory and common law of each jurisdiction. However, Article 9 contains a provision governing priority contests between an Article 9 security interest and a nonagricultural lien for services or materials. This provision, R9–333, is discussed in Chapter 11, Section 5(B), infra. When R9–333 does not apply, non-UCC law governs priorities; that law often is not well developed.

Another exclusion that one might think to be self-evident is that of R9–109(c)(1): Article 9—state law—does not apply "to the extent that a statute, regulation, or treaty of the United States preempts this article." The phrase "to the extent that" is a signal that the provision creates delicate problems of meshing state and federal law. The federal statutes that touch on security interests—e.g., those governing copyrights, patents, ships, and aircraft—do not contain a complete set of rules governing creation, perfection, priority, and enforcement. (For a recent list of such statutes, see White & Summers § 21–10.) The courts must determine the extent to which any particular federal statute touching upon a secured transaction governs the specific issue in question. Suppose the statute, as often is the case, is not explicit. Courts choosing to apply Former Article 9 typically have justified their decision on one of two grounds: They have concluded that Congress did not (or constitutionally could not) preempt the

---

1. Recall that Article 9 also applies to statutory "agricultural liens" on farm products and to security interests arising under Articles 2, 2A, 4, and 5. See R9–109(a)(2), (a)(5), (a)(6); R9–102(a)(5); Section 3, supra.

field, so that state law governs. See, e.g., Johnston v. Simpson, 621 P.2d 688 (Utah 1980) (Federal Aviation Act has preempted field of recordation of conveyances of aircraft but not validity of conveyances or determination of title or ownership). Or they have concluded that Congress did intend to preempt the field but did not enact a rule governing the issue before them, in which case they have created a federal rule modeled after Article 9. See, e.g., Interpool Ltd. v. Char Yigh Marine (Panama) S.A., 890 F.2d 1453 (9th Cir.1989), modified and rehearing denied 918 F.2d 1476 (1990) (UCC is taken as indicative of federal law of admiralty). However, at least one case holds that, under F9–104(a), Article 9 ceded the field to the United States. See In re Peregrine Entertainment, Ltd., 116 B.R. 194 (C.D.Cal.1990) (F9–104 provides for "voluntary step back" of Article 9 to the extent federal law governs the rights of the parties). The reference to preemption in R9–109(c)(1) is intended to reject this view and make clear that Revised Article 9 "steps back" *only to the extent required by the Constitution.*

A more detailed discussion of R–109(c)(1) would require greater familiarity with particular federal statutes. Two points nevertheless are worthy of note. First, the integration of Former Article 9 with federal statutes often has been confused and unpredictable. For example, the cases hold that a security interest in patents and trademarks may be perfected without recording in the Patent and Trademark Office. See, e.g., City Bank & Trust Co. v. Otto Fabric, Inc., 83 B.R. 780 (D.Kan.1988) (patents); In re Roman Cleanser Co., 43 B.R. 940 (Bkrtcy.E.D.Mich.1984), affirmed 802 F.2d 207 (6th Cir.1986) (trademarks). But a secured party seeking to perfect a security interest in registered copyrights must record in the Copyright Office. See In re Peregrine Entertainment, Ltd., 116 B.R. 194 (C.D.Cal.1990); In re World Auxiliary Power Co., 244 B.R. 149 (Bkrtcy. N.D.Cal.1999) (limiting *Peregrine* to registered copyrights; holding that an unregistered copyright can be perfected under Article 9).

Second, many of the federal statutory recording schemes are not designed to accommodate contemporary financing. For example, the records of the Copyright Office are arranged by copyrighted work. A financer who wishes to perfect a security interest in, say, the film library of a motion picture studio, must make a separate filing against each title in the Copyright Office. In contrast, a single financing statement filed in the appropriate Article 9 filing office would suffice to perfect a security interest in unregistered copyrights, which are not subject to the federal statute. Efforts at making federal intellectual-property law more conducive to contemporary patterns of commercial finance began in the mid–1980's. The American Bar Association Joint Task Force on Security Interests in Intellectual Property, comprised of lawyers from the Sections of Business Law and Intellectual Property Law (formerly the Section of Patent, Trademark and Copyright Law), has been preparing drafts of acts that would govern security interests in all federally regulated intellectual property, including copyrights, patents, and trademarks. More recently, the Commercial Finance Association, an international trade association for financial institutions engaged in commercial secured lending and factoring, has been supporting the enactment of the Security Interests in Copyrights Financing

Protection Act. As the name implies, this a more modest reform effort than that of the ABA Task Force.

Related, but not identical, to the exclusion from the *applicability* of Article 9 in R9–109(c) and (d) is the exclusion from the Article 9 *filing system* in R9–311(a)(1). The filing of a financing statement under Article 9 is unnecessary and ineffective to perfect a security interest in property subject to "a statute, regulation, or treaty of the United States whose requirements for a security interest's obtaining priority over the rights of a lien creditor with respect to the property preempt Section 9–310(a)." Rather, perfection under Article 9 is to be accomplished by compliance with the requirements of the federal statute, regulation, or treaty. R9–311(b). Which federal requirements must be complied with? The "requirements . . . for obtaining priority over the rights of a lien creditor." Id. Even if federal law governs perfection, Article 9 would continue to apply to questions other than perfection (unless, of course, R9–109 excludes the transaction to a greater extent).

R9–109 excludes certain transactions the drafters thought were governed adequately by other law. (Others, who must find, and make decisions based on, this other law, sometimes disagree.) Subsections (c)(2) and (3) exclude security interests *granted* by a government or governmental subdivision or agency, but only to the extent that another statute expressly governs the creation, perfection, priority, or enforcement of the security interest.[2] Subsection (d) excludes security interests in wages, salary, or other compensation; they "present important social issues that other law addresses." R9–109(d)(3), Comment 4. (Since 1984, most wage assignments have been prohibited by the Federal Trade Commission. See FTC Rule on Credit Practices, 16 C.F.R. § 442.2(3).)

Comment 7 to F9–104 observed that "[r]ights under life insurance and other policies . . . are often put up as collateral." Nevertheless, security interests in this type of property were excluded from Former Article 9, except insofar as the property constituted proceeds of other collateral. See F9–104(g); Chapter 7, Section 5, supra (discussing proceeds). With one exception, discussed below, the exclusion continues in Revised Article 9. See R9–109(d)(8). As a consequence, a lender who takes a consensual lien on the debtor's rights under an insurance policy must consult non-UCC law to

---

2. Federal law governs the rights of the United States as *creditor*, including as secured party. In United States v. Kimbell Foods, Inc., 440 U.S. 715, 99 S.Ct. 1448, 59 L.Ed.2d 711 (1979), the Supreme Court adopted Former Article 9, as enacted by the appropriate state, as the federal law applicable to security interests held by the Small Business Administration and the Farmers Home Administration. The opinion left room for the adoption, in appropriate cases, of a federal rule of law that is not borrowed from Article 9, e.g., when the federal program in question by its nature must be uniform in character throughout the nation or when application of state law would frustrate specific objectives of the federal program in question. Some courts have taken advantage of this leeway, most notably in cases involving the Department of Defense. See, e.g., In re American Pouch Foods, Inc., 769 F.2d 1190 (7th Cir.1985), cert. denied 475 U.S. 1082, 106 S.Ct. 1459, 89 L.Ed.2d 716 (1986) (refusing to apply F9–301(1)(b) [R9–317(a)(2)] to the government's interest, which would have been an unperfected security interest under state law).

determine whether its lien has attached and is protected against the competing claims of third parties. Non–UCC law also regulates the enforcement of these liens. The law applicable to these transactions may be difficult to find; it is likely to be incomplete.

Can one justify the exclusion of security interests in insurance policies from Article 9, especially given the UCC's goals of simplifying, clarifying, and modernizing the law governing commercial transactions, and of making uniform the law among the various jurisdictions? See UCC 1–102(2)(a), (c). Comment 7 to F9–104 explained that "[s]uch transactions are often quite special, do not fit easily under a general commercial statute and are adequately covered by existing law." Do you find that explanation persuasive? Is a more cogent, albeit equally unsatisfying, explanation, that the drafters bowed to pressure from the insurance industry to exclude these transactions? See 1 Gilmore, Security § 10.7, at 315 (the exclusion of insurance policies "was politically inspired"). Professor Gilmore recalled that the attitude of counsel for the insurance companies "was not that any provision of the Article was incorrect, harmful, or disadvantageous to their clients, but was rather that they were disinclined to flee to evils that they knew not of." Id.

Insurers that make payments under their policies understandably do not want to face liability for paying the wrong party; in particular, they do not want to be caught in the cross-fire between their customers and their customers' secured parties. In what ways, if any, do the concerns of insurers differ from those of other persons who owe a debt to an Article 9 debtor? Would it be possible to incorporate insurance policies into Article 9 in a manner that facilitates their use as collateral but still affords appropriate protection for the insurers?

The Article 9 Drafting Committee was inclined answer the question just posed in the affirmative. As the following excerpt explains, the Drafting Committee ultimately decided not to proceed along these lines:

> [Former] Article 9 excluded transfers of "an interest in or claim in or under any policy of insurance," except as proceeds of other collateral. Consistent with the [Article 9 Study Committee] Report's recommendation, early drafts of Revised Article 9 narrowed the exclusion substantially. Certain sectors of the insurance industry, most notably the life insurance industry, objected to the potential inclusion of insurance as original collateral. [As Reporters, we] met with representatives of the life insurance industry to discuss their concerns, nearly all of which related to the insurer's status as an obligor. In essence, the insurers wanted to be able to determine with certainty whom to pay to discharge their obligations under their policies, and they wanted to continue making that determination in accordance with existing procedures.

The Article 9 Drafting Committee was inclined answer the question just posed in the affirmative. As the following excerpt explains, the Drafting Committee ultimately decided not to proceed along these lines:

[Former] Article 9 excluded transfers of "an interest in or claim in or under any policy of insurance," except as proceeds of other collateral. Consistent with the [Article 9 Study Committee] Report's recommendation, early drafts of Revised Article 9 narrowed the exclusion substantially. Certain sectors of the insurance industry, most notably the life insurance industry, objected to the potential inclusion of insurance as original collateral. [As Reporters, we] met with representatives of the life insurance industry to discuss their concerns, nearly all of which related to the insurer's status as an obligor. In essence, the insurers wanted to be able to determine with certainty whom to pay to discharge their obligations under their policies, and they wanted to continue making that determination in accordance with existing procedures. The Drafting Committee agreed with us that some of these concerns were unwarranted (*e.g.*, the concern that an insurer would need to consult the UCC filings before deciding whom to pay) and that others (*e.g.*, the concern that the insurer would be obligated to pay the secured party upon receipt of a notification of assignment) could be addressed with special rules that would not require insurers to change their way of doing business. At is meeting in June, 1996, the Drafting Committee voted 5–3 in favor of including insurance within the scope of Revised Article 9.

Immediately following the vote, we asked for guidance on the substance of some of the special rules that might be needed. These preliminary discussions highlighted the complexity that might be necessary to bring insurance-related collateral into Revised Article 9 without upsetting current practices and prompted the Drafting Committee to reconsider its decision. On reconsideration, apparently motivated by the substantial thought required to address this complex subject properly and the limited time in which to do so, the Drafting Committee voted 9–0 in opposition to including insurance policies within the scope of Revised Article 9. We were asked, however, to consider any special scope or other provisions that might be necessary to facilitate the financing of what Revised Article 9 now calls "health-care-insurance receivables," *i.e.*, rights to payment for health-care goods or services which arise under an insurance policy.

Harris & Mooney, How Successful was the Revision of UCC Article 9?: Reflections of the Reporters, 74 Chi.-Kent L. Rev. 1357, 1374–75 (1999).

As the excerpt intimates, Revised Article 9 has narrowed the insurance exclusion somewhat, by bringing within Article 9's scope any assignment of "health-care-insurance receivables" by or to a health-care provider. See R9–109(d)(8); R9–102(a)(46) (defining "health-care-insurance receivable"). Thus, Revised Article 9 applies to assignments of health insurance policy benefits by a patient to a doctor, hospital, or other health-care provider; however, these assignments are automatically perfected. See R9–309(5). Revised Article 9 applies as well as to assignments of these receivables from the health-care provider to its lender. From the perspective of the health-care provider, these receivables are the equivalent of traditional accounts—

rights to payment for goods sold or services rendered. For this reason, Revised Article 9 classifies "health-care-insurance receivables" as "accounts." See R9–102(a)(2). But see R9–408 (special rules governing assignments of otherwise non-assignable health-care-insurance receivables).

Insurers are not the only institutions that often owe debts to a large number of claimants; a bank may owe a debt to tens of thousands of depositors. Former Article 9 did not apply to security interests in deposit accounts. The Comments explained this exclusion on the same ground offered for the exclusion of insurance policies. See F9–104, Comment 7. As we shall see in Chapter 9, Section 4, the drafters expanded the scope of Revised Article 9 to encompass deposit accounts as original collateral in transactions other than consumer transactions. See R9–109(d)(13). This change has been controversial; some believe that the expansion of Article 9's scope is ill-advised, whereas others contend that it did not go far enough (i.e., that Article 9 should govern security interests in all deposit accounts, even those in consumer transactions).

F9–104, Comment 8, explained that Former Article 9 did not apply to security interests in certain "types of claims which do not customarily serve as commercial collateral: judgments under paragraph (h), set-offs under paragraph (i) and tort claims under paragraph (k)." R9–109(d)(9) retains the exclusion of judgments (other than judgments taken on a right to payment that itself was collateral under Article 9). R9–109(d)(12) narrows somewhat the broad exclusion of transfers of tort claims under F9–104(k). Revised Article 9 applies to assignments of "commercial tort claims" as well as to security interests in tort claims that constitute proceeds of other collateral (e.g., a right to payment for negligent destruction of the debtor's inventory). As defined in R9–102(a)(13), "commercial tort claim" includes all tort claims held by a corporation, partnership, or other organization, and those tort claims of individuals that arise in the course of the individual's business or profession (except claims for damages arising out of personal injury or death).

Professor Gilmore, the principal drafter of Former Article 9, had the following observations about the exclusion for **setoffs**:[3]

> This exclusion is an apt example of the absurdities which result when draftsmen attempt to appease critics by putting into a statute something that is not in any sense wicked but is hopelessly irrelevant. Of course a right of set-off is not a security interest and has never been confused with one: the statute might as appropriately exclude fan dancing. A bank's right of set-off against a depositor's account is often loosely referred to as a "banker's lien," but the "lien" usage has never led anyone to think that the bank held a security interest in the bank account. Banking groups were, however, concerned lest someone, someday, might think that a bank's right of set-off, because it was called a

---

3. The ability of an assignee of a right to payment to take free of the obligor's right to set off is discussed in Note (2) on Defenses to Payment Obligations, Chapter 1, Section 4, supra.

> lien, was a security interest. Hence the exclusion, which does no harm
> except to the dignity and self-respect of the draftsmen.

1 Gilmore, Security § 10.7, at 315–16. Professor Gilmore may not have
recognized all the costs of excluding "any right of set-off" from Former
Article 9. As we shall see in Chapter 11, Section 5(C), infra, the meaning of
the exclusion has been litigated with some frequency; the outcomes have
not been altogether consistent. R9–109(d)(10) retains and clarifies the
exclusion.

The foregoing exclusions relate to the scope provision in R9–109(a)(1):
transactions that create a security interest by contract. Two limitations of
the other scope provisions are worthy of mention. First, the definition of
"consignment" excludes from Article 9 certain "true" consignments, such
as consignments of consumer goods. See R9–102(a)(20); Section 1(B), supra.
Second, although Article 9 applies to most sales of receivables, R9–
109(d)(4)–(7) excludes from Article 9 "certain sales . . . of receivables that,
by their nature, do not concern commercial financing transactions." R9–
109, Comment 12. See generally Chapter 9, Section 1(D) (discussing sales of
receivables).

CHAPTER 9

SECURITY INTERESTS IN RIGHTS TO PAYMENT, INVESTMENT PROPERTY, AND OTHER INTANGIBLES

This Chapter is concerned with security interests in intangible property, including rights to payment of various kinds (referred to colloquially as "receivables"), investment property (such as stocks and bonds), and deposit accounts (such as checking and savings accounts). Although the extension of credit secured by goods goes back to ancient times, the use of intangible property as collateral is largely a product of the twentieth century. Over the past fifty years, the relative importance of intangible property as a source of wealth has grown substantially. This dramatic change is reflected in Revised Article 9; the revised Article contains many new provisions applicable only to one or more types of intangible collateral.

The financing of intangible property raises many of the same considerations as the financing of goods, and many of the same legal rules apply. The financer must insure that its security interest is enforceable, i.e., that the conditions for attachment in R9–203 have been met. See Chapter 7, Section 2, supra. To prevail over subsequent judicial lien creditors and secured parties, the security interest must be perfected, often by filing a financing statement. See R9–317(a)(2); R9–322(a)(1); R9–310(a); Chapter 7, Section 3, supra. We have seen that Article 9 contains special rules governing security interests in goods. See, e.g., R9–324; (governing PMSI's). That Article 9 likewise contains special rules governing security interests in various forms of intangible property should come as no surprise. One also would expect that the Article would contain provisions that reflect the vast array of types of intangible property. While a franchisee's rights under a franchise agreement, a stockholder's rights against the corporation, and a merchant's right to payment for goods sold share certain attributes, they are in many ways dissimilar; Article 9 reflects some of these dissimilarities. Even rights to payment come in a variety of forms. Rights secured by personal property (as evidenced by the Instalment Sale Contract, Form 3.6), rights secured by real property (as evidenced by a mortgage), bank accounts, negotiable and nonnegotiable promissory notes, and rights to insurance proceeds are just a few examples.

SECTION 1.   FINANCING RECEIVABLES

(A)   BACKGROUND

The following bird's-eye-view of accounts receivable financing was written, on the basis of first-hand practical experience, shortly after the completion of the UCC. As you might imagine, some details have become dated and some new practices have developed during the nearly 50 years since the following was written; however, the terminology retains its vitality, and the discussion of the mechanics of receivables financing, including the allocation of risks between the assignor and assignee, retains its utility as an introduction to the field.

Kupfer, Accounts Receivable Financing: A Legal and Practical Look–See

Prac. Law., Nov. 1956, at 50, 50–65.

Less than half a century ago, a mere moment of transit in our Anglo–Saxon legal and economic history, accounts receivable financing was virtually unknown. It now approximates an annual volume of ten billion dollars. The office of this paper will be to dissect the economic structure of the mechanism and to analyze the details of the legal blueprints that make it tick. . . .

Purposes of Accounts Receivable Financing. A borrower normally will first seek unsecured credit to the extent to which he can obtain it. But the overwhelming majority of our industrial and commercial units constitute "small business," and require accommodation for which unsecured credit is not readily available. They may require liquid funds for more working capital; or for expansion purposes; or to take discounts on merchandise purchased. For these needs, they will usually resort to their most liquid asset other than cash—their accounts receivable.

Generally speaking, because of its inherently self-liquidating and revolving nature, accounts receivable financing is not an apt permanent source of capital, although it is frequently so employed on a temporary basis. . . .

The greater part of accounts receivable financing covers sales of manufacturers and merchants, and, historically, it was confined, in its early development, to that area. In recent years, however, its operation has been expanded into much wider, and at times greener, fields. Illustrations are the financing of deferred-payment sales and the leasing plans of commercial and industrial equipment; the financing, for department stores, of retail budget-instalment and charge accounts; the rediscounting of the paper of small-loan companies and the smaller consumer-finance companies; and even the financing of mergers and acquisitions of businesses. Its operation in the purely service field is by no means unknown, although the author has yet to hear of lawyers' accounts receivable being accepted as collateral! It could, however, happen, and probably will before we know it.

The Different Types of Accounts Receivable Financing:

The Parties. To every accounts receivable operation there are necessarily three parties: (1) the lender upon, or purchaser of, the accounts; (2) the borrower upon, or seller of, them; and (3) the debtor upon the accounts assigned. For semantic uniformity and brevity, these three parties will be respectively called the *"assignee,"* the *"assignor,"* and the *"account-debtor,"* unless the context otherwise indicates. (Occasionally, the words *"lender"* or *"secured creditor"* will connote the assignee, and the word *"borrower,"* the assignor. Only exceptionally—and then obviously—will there be any departure from the use of *"account-debtor."*)

The Two Basic Forms. There are two essential requirements to the payment of any account receivable. First, the assignor must comply with the terms of his agreement with, or the order of, the account-debtor, and secondly, the latter must be financially able and willing to pay. The first requirement is called the "merchandise risk," and the second, the "credit risk." And out of this dichotomy arise the two basic forms of accounts receivable financing. These are respectively known as *"recourse"* and *"non-recourse"* financing, and the terminology in itself differentiates them.

In *both,* the assignor necessarily retains the *merchandise* risk, because the fabrication of the goods or the rendition of the service in accordance with his commitment to the account-debtor at all times rests solely within his control.

In *recourse* financing, the *assignor* also retains the *credit* risk; he guarantees to the assignee that the account will be paid at its maturity. Therefore, both in economics and in law, the financing transaction, however the contract may be set up, constitutes a loan upon the security of the assigned accounts.

In the *non-recourse* operation, the *assignee* assumes the *credit* risk, and, in legal consequence, the operation constitutes a purchase. (Non-recourse financing is sometimes called *"factoring."* Historically, factoring was first associated solely with inventory financing. When accounts receivable financing—usually on a non-recourse basis—developed as an adjunct to inventory financing, the term was originally applied to the combined operation. Latterly, it is occasionally used to cover both recourse and non-recourse accounts receivable financing, with or without a precedent inventory loan. Therefore, except to the highly initiated and in the context of a specific operation, the use of the term is only apt to confuse, and will be eschewed in this paper.)

The distinction between recourse and non-recourse financing is of great importance in the application of interest and usury laws.

Combining With Inventory Financing. Inventory financing can be combined with either the non-recourse or recourse financing of accounts; traditionally, it was more intimately associated with the former, although it may, but need not, be employed in connection with either type, as the economic "lead line" which ultimately becomes solely the accounts receivable operation. When inventory financing is absent, the operation is called "pure" accounts receivable financing, and this is the more usual form that it takes. . . .

Function of Banks. The function of banks in accounts receivable financing is also a matter of considerable interest. In the first place they constitute the wholesalers of credit to the account receivable companies. Secondly, a number of them are engaged directly in the accounts receivable field. The competition is not at all unwelcome to finance companies, although, from the standpoint of the banks, it presents both advantages and disadvantages which are beyond the ambit of this paper. And finally, the banks frequently participate with finance companies in specific operations because it minimizes the risk and puts at their disposal the specialized know-how of accounts receivable companies, thus reducing the overall cost of the lending operation. . . .

Implementation of the Operation:

The Underlying Contract and the Assignments. Every accounts receivable operation starts with the execution of an underlying contract between the assignor and the assignee. It spells out in detail the rights of the parties, and its contents have become more or less standard.

When the accounts to be assigned have been created by the assignor, they are listed on assignment forms or "schedules." Since the assigned accounts constitute the very lifeblood of the assignee's security, all the material documents pertaining to the assigned accounts must accompany the assignment schedule and be contemporaneously delivered to the assignee at the time when it makes its advance to the assignor upon them. These documents vary with the nature of the assigned accounts but must always include copies of the relevant invoices; the original bills of lading or express receipts evidencing the delivery of the merchandise or (where applicable) proof of the rendition of the service; and all other papers necessary to effect collection of the assigned accounts. It is vital that the assignee satisfy himself as to the authenticity and legal competence of these documents.

The assignment-schedules as a rule must cover specific accounts; in most jurisdictions [prior to the UCC], blanket assignments [were] of little, if any, legal value. See, illustratively, State Factors Corp. v. Sales Factors Corp., 257 App.Div. 101, 12 N.Y.S.2d 12 (1st Dep't 1939). However, under the so-called "floating lien" provisions of the Uniform Commercial Code ([Former] §§ 9–108 and 9–204 [R9–204]) . . . general, or blanket, assignments are permitted and recognized. . . .

Indirect and Direct Collections. There are two methods—indirect or direct, so-called, for the actual collection of the assigned accounts.

In the indirect collection program, the account-debtors are not notified of the assignments, and remittances are made to the assignor, who is obligated promptly to endorse and transmit them in specie to the assignee—customarily on the day of their receipt. If it has not already become apparent, we shall, a little later, appreciate the economic and legal necessity [prior to the UCC] for the imposition of this requirement.

In the direct collection program, the account-debtors are forthwith notified of the assignments, and are instructed to make their remittances directly to the assignee.

Indirect collection is much more frequently found in recourse financing, and direct collection in non-recourse financing, but the association is by no means inevitable. Indeed, one of the larger and most respected financing agencies has recently instituted a non-notification, non-recourse program, for assignors whose operations and standing make it adaptable to their business.

In all accounts receivable programs, the assignee, at periodic intervals (usually monthly) makes an audit of the assignor's books and operations, through one of the members of its own staff. In addition, when the collection program is indirect, the assignee causes periodic spot verification to be made of the existence of the assigned accounts and the amounts due upon them. This is accomplished by direct correspondence between an auditing concern and a random selection of the account-debtors.

Causes of Loss. Experience has demonstrated that the incidence of loss in an accounts receivable operation is minimal, almost to the vanishing point, if: the adaptability of the assignor's business to accounts receivable financing has been soundly analyzed and conceived; the credit standing of the account-debtors has been sensibly evaluated at the time when the assignments are tendered for advances upon them; and the operation is properly conducted within the framework above outlined. Of course, losses do take place, but, when they do, they are attributable, largely, if not solely, to what, in air-travel, would be called "pilot failure" in one of three aspects:

(1) Over-concentration. The first such cause, over-concentration, is purely economic and is by no means indigenous to the accounts receivable field. It is basic (a) that the assignee should diversify, as among the types and selection of assignors whose business he finances, and (b) that the accounts receivable of any one assignor should be diversified as much as the nature of its business permits. If the author were charged with operational responsibility (which none of his clients has ever "threatened" to entrust to him), he would view, with a highly piscatorial eye, financing a borrower who had only three large customers, however, financially "good" these customers might be. All of this is purely an economic matter, but a very important one.

(2) Fictitious Accounts. The second cause of loss—the assignment of fictitious accounts—brings us into the legal area. Obviously, if an assignor ships goods on consignment or, worse yet, purports to assign "accounts" against "account-debtors" to whom no merchandise has been shipped at all, the assignee has no security for his advances. Neither the nature of the operation nor the rates charged for it permit the assumption of any such

hazard, and it is this signpost which points the path to the importance of checking the shipping and other documents adverted to above. . . .

One final feature of this whole matter is so obvious as merely to require mention. If the account-debtor, without notice of either of the duplicate assignments, pays the assignor or either of the assignees, he is fully protected and naturally need not pay any of them, all over again.

(3) Conversions. The last cause of loss is the conversion by the assignor of the proceeds of assigned accounts. It can occur only when the collection method is indirect. . . .

Although there is no substitute for watchfulness, relatively simple techniques exist to guard against and obviate the hazard of over-concentration, fictitious accounts and duplicate assignments, and conversions. Assuming the original soundness of the assignor's business operation, no financing assignee who makes a reasonable realistic check of the account-debtor's credit is apt to sustain any serious loss if he will just watch these three matters.

(B) FINANCING RECEIVABLES: A PROTOTYPE

You have seen many examples of how Article 9 reflects prevailing patterns of financing. One of the basic patterns is receivables financing. The following Prototype portrays in some detail the legal and related business practices employed in the financing of receivables arising from both the retail sale of inventory and the provision of services.[1] In reviewing the Prototype, consider the ways in which the practices and documentation differ from those in the Prototype on financing automobiles in Chapter 7, Section 1, supra. To what extent do these differences appear to stem from differences in the nature of the collateral? To what extent from differences in the applicable law? To what extent from custom in the industry?

Carguys, Inc., is a Delaware corporation that is a nationwide retail and wholesale seller of automobile parts. Carguys sells auto parts from stores in all 50 states; it also operates full-service automobile repair facilities at each of its store locations.

Most of Carguys' customers are consumers. However, many commercial customers also patronize Carguys. Some utilize Carguys' repair and maintenance services; they include taxi and limousine operators, car and truck rental companies, delivery services, and corporate employers that provide automobiles to their employees. Other commercial customers, who operate their own repair and maintenance operations, buy auto parts from Carguys. These customers also buy and lease sophisticated automobile diagnostic equipment from Carguys.

Carguys' consumer customers pay for goods and services at the time they are received. They use cash, checks, and credit cards. Unlike its

---

1. This Prototype was prepared with the generous assistance of Edwin E. Smith of Bingham Dana LLP. It does not necessarily describe the practices of any particular finance company or seller of auto parts.

arrangements with consumer customers, Carguys extends credit to its commercial customers. It provides repair and maintenance services and sells parts and equipment on **open account**—i.e., on unsecured credit. Carguys sends bills (**invoices**) to its commercial customers monthly for services and parts purchased during the preceding month. The credit terms require the customers to pay the outstanding charges within 30 days after the date of the invoice.

Not unlike Main Motors in the Prototype on financing automobiles, Chapter 7, Section 1, supra, Carguys requires financing. It lacks the capital necessary to extend credit to its commercial customers while also meeting its operating expenses and other current obligations, including its obligations to suppliers, employees, and landlords.

Revolving Credit Agreement; Revolving Credit Note. Effective July 2, 2001, Carguys established a new credit relationship with Eastinghome Credit Corporation. The essential aspects of the relationship are embodied in a Revolving Credit Agreement (Form 9.1), which is reproduced below (with some provisions omitted and summarized).

FORM 9.1
REVOLVING CREDIT AGREEMENT

REVOLVING CREDIT AGREEMENT

This **REVOLVING CREDIT AGREEMENT** (this "Agreement") is made as of July 1, 2001, by and between CARGUYS, INC. (the "Borrower"), a Delaware corporation having its principal place of business at 1313 West Rosannadanna Boulevard, Los Angeles, California, and EASTINGHOME CREDIT CORPORATION (the "Lender"), a New York corporation having its office at 94 Wintershire Drive, Territown, New York.

1. DEFINITIONS:

Certain capitalized terms are defined below:

Accounts: All rights of the Borrower to any payment of money for goods sold, leased or otherwise marketed in the ordinary course of business or for services rendered in the ordinary course of business, whether evidenced by or under or in respect of a contract or instrument, and all proceeds thereof.

Agreement: This Agreement as amended and in effect from time to time.

Base Accounts: Those Accounts (net of any finance charges, late charges, credits, commissions, contras or other offsets or counterclaims) (i) that the Borrower reasonably determines to be collectible, (ii) the account debtors in respect of which purchased the goods or services from Borrower at arms' length, are deemed creditworthy by the Lender, are solvent, and are not affiliated with the Borrower, (iii) that are not outstanding for more than sixty (60) days past the earlier to occur of (A) the date of invoice and (B) the date of shipment (as to goods) or of provision (as to services), (iv) in which the Lender has a valid and perfected first-priority security interest, and over which there is no other lien, (v) that are in payment of fully performed and undisputed obligations, and (vi) that are payable in U.S. currency from an office within the United States.

Base Inventory: Inventory (i) that is owned, possessed and held for sale or lease by the Borrower within the United States but not yet shipped, (ii) that is not held on land leased by, or in a warehouse of a warehouseman other than, the Borrower, absent delivery to the Lender of a waiver of the lien of the lessor or warehouseman in form an substance satisfactory to the Lender, (iii) as to which a valid and perfected first-priority security interest in favor of the Lender has been created and on which there is no other lien, and (iv) that the Lender deems neither obsolete nor unmarketable.

Base Rate: The annual rate of interest announced from time to time by Firstbank, N.A., at its office as the that bank's "base rate."

Borrower: See preamble.

Borrowing Base: An amount equal to the sum of 75% of the Base Accounts and 60% of the Base Inventory.

-2-

Borrowing Base Report: A report, in form and with supporting details satisfactory to the Lender, setting forth the Borrower's computation of the Borrowing Base.

Business Day: Any day on which banks in New York, New York, are open for business generally.

Collateral: All of the property, rights and assets of the Borrower that are or are intended to be subject to the security interest created by the Security Documents.

Commitment: The obligation of the Lender to make Loans to the Borrower up to an aggregate outstanding principal amount not to exceed Twenty-Five Million Dollars ($25,000,000), as such amount may be reduced from time to time or terminated under this Agreement.

Default: An event or act which with the giving of notice and/or the lapse of time, would become an Event of Default.

Drawdown Date: In respect of any Loan, the date on which such Loan is made to the Borrower.

Event of Default: Any of the events listed in §7 hereof.

Indebtedness: In respect of any entity, all obligations, contingent and otherwise, that in accordance with generally accepted accounting principles should be classified as liabilities, including without limitation (i) all debt obligations, (ii) all liabilities secured by liens, (iii) all guarantees, and (iv) all liabilities in respect of bankers' acceptances or letters of credit.

Inventory: All goods now owned or hereafter acquired by the Borrower which are held for sale or lease.

Lender: See preamble.

Loan: Any loan made or to be made to the Borrower pursuant to §2 hereof.

Loan Documents: This Agreement, the Note, and the Security Documents, in each case as from time to time amended or supplemented.

Loan Request: See §2.1.

Margin: Two percent (2%) per annum.

-3-

Materially Adverse Effect: Any materially adverse effect on the financial condition or business operations of the Borrower or material impairment of the ability of the Borrower to perform its obligations under this Agreement or under any of the other Loan Documents.

Maturity Date: July 1, 2004, or such earlier date on which all Loans may become due and payable pursuant to the terms hereof.

Note: See §2.1.

Obligations: All indebtedness, obligations and liabilities of the Borrower to the Lender, existing on the date of this Agreement or arising thereafter, direct or indirect, joint or several, absolute or contingent, matured or unmatured, liquidated or unliquidated, secured or unsecured, arising by contract, operation of law or otherwise, arising or incurred under this Agreement or any other Loan Document or in respect of any of the Loans or the Note or other instruments at any time evidencing any thereof.

Security Documents: The Security Agreement dated as of the date hereof between the Lender and the Borrower, pursuant to which the Borrower grants to the Lender a security interest in the Borrower's existing and after-acquired personal property and fixture assets, the Perfection Certificate dated as of the date hereof and executed and delivered by the Borrower, all financing statements authorized by the Borrower under the Security Agreement, and any other documents delivered by Borrower in connection with the Security Agreement.

2. **REVOLVING CREDIT FACILITY.**

2. 1. **Commitment to Lend.**

(a)   Upon the terms and subject to the conditions of this Agreement, the Lender agrees to lend to the Borrower such sums that the Borrower may request, from the date hereof until but not including the Maturity Date, provided that the sum of the outstanding principal amount of all Loans (after giving effect to all amounts requested) shall not exceed the lesser of (i) the Commitment and (ii) the Borrowing Base. Loans shall be in the minimum aggregate amount of Two Hundred Fifty Thousand Dollars ($250,000) or an integral multiple thereof.

(b)   The Borrower shall notify the Lender in writing or telephonically not later than 12:00 noon New York time on the day of the Drawdown Date (which must be a Business Day) of the Loan being requested and of the principal amount of the Loan (a "Loan Request"). Subject to the foregoing, so long as the Commitment is then in effect and the applicable conditions set forth in §5 hereof have been met, the Lender shall advance the amount requested to the Borrower's Lender account no.

-4-

081347-012060 at Firstbank, New York, New York, in immediately available funds not later than the close of business on the Drawdown Date.

(c)   The obligation of the Borrower to repay to the Lender the principal of the Loans and interest accrued thereon shall be evidenced by a promissory note (the "Note") in the maximum aggregate principal amount of Twenty-Five Million Dollars ($25,000,000) executed and delivered by the Borrower and payable to the order of the Lender, in form and substance satisfactory to the Lender.

2. 2. Interest. So long as no Event of Default is continuing, the Borrower shall pay interest on the Loans at a rate per annum which is equal to the sum of (i) the Base Rate, and (ii) the Margin, such interest to be payable in arrears on the first day of each calendar month for the immediately preceding calendar month, commencing with the first such day following the date hereof. While an Event of Default is continuing, amounts payable under any of the Loan Documents shall bear interest (compounded monthly and payable on demand in respect of overdue amounts) at a rate per annum which is equal to the sum of (i) the Base Rate, and (ii) three percent (3%) above the Margin until such amount is paid in full or (as the case may be) the Event of Default has been cured or waived in writing by the Lender (after as well as before judgment).

2.3. Repayments and Prepayments. The Borrower agrees to pay the Lender on the Maturity Date the entire unpaid principal of and interest on all Loans. The Borrower may elect to prepay the outstanding principal of all or any part of any Loan, without premium or penalty, in a minimum amount of Two Hundred Fifty Thousand Dollars ($250,000) or an integral multiple thereof, upon written notice to the Lender given by 10:00 a.m. New York time on the date of the prepayment, of the amount to be prepaid. The Borrower shall be entitled to reborrow before the Maturity Date such amounts, upon the terms and subject to the conditions of this Agreement. Each repayment or prepayment of principal of any Loan shall be accompanied by payment of the unpaid interest accrued to date on the principal being repaid or prepaid. If at any time the outstanding principal amount of the Loans shall exceed the lesser of (i) the Commitment and (ii) the Borrowing Base, the Borrower shall immediately pay the amount of the excess to the Lender for application to the Loans. The Borrower may elect to reduce or terminate the Commitment by a minimum principal amount of Two Hundred Fifty Thousand Dollars ($250,000) or an integral multiple thereof, upon written notice to the Lender given by 10:00 a.m. New York time at least two (2) Business Days prior to the date of such reduction or termination. The Borrower shall not be entitled to reinstate the Commitment following the reduction or termination.

-5-

3. FEES AND PAYMENTS.

Contemporaneously with execution and delivery of this Agreement, the Borrower shall pay to the Lender a closing fee in the amount of Twenty-Five Thousand Dollars ($25,000). The Borrower shall pay to the Lender, on the first day of each calendar quarter hereafter, and upon the Maturity Date or the date upon which the Commitment is no longer in effect, a commitment fee calculated at a rate per annum which is equal to one and one-half percent (1-1/2%) of the average daily difference by which the Commitment amount exceeds the aggregate of the outstanding Loans during the preceding calendar quarter or portion thereof. All payments to be made by the Borrower under this Agreement or under any of the other Loan Documents shall be made in U.S. dollars in immediately available funds at the Lender's office at 94 Wintershire Drive, Territown, New York, without set-off or counterclaim and without any withholding or deduction whatsoever. If any payment under this Agreement is required to be made on a day which is not a Business Day, it shall be paid on the immediately succeeding Business Day, with interest and any applicable fees adjusted accordingly. All computations of interest or of the commitment fee payable under this Agreement shall be made by the Lender on the basis of actual days elapsed and on a 360-day year.

4. REPRESENTATIONS AND WARRANTIES.

The Borrower represents and warrants to the Lender on the date hereof, on the date of any Loan Request, and on each Drawdown Date that:

[This section of the Agreement sets forth various facts as to which the Borrower makes representations and warranties. The "reps and warranties" relate to matters such as the Borrower's due organization and good standing, its power and authority to enter into the Loan Documents, the validity and enforceability of the Loan Documents, various aspects of the Borrower's business, the Borrower's financial condition and the absence of a Materially Adverse Effect, legal proceedings affecting the Borrower, the Borrower's compliance with various agreements, corporate restrictions, and laws, and the perfection and priority of the Lender's security interest.]

5. CONDITIONS PRECEDENT.

In addition to the Borrower's foregoing representations and warranties and the delivery of the Loan Documents and such other documents and the taking of such actions as the Lender may require at or prior to the time of executing this Agreement, the obligation of the Lender to make any Loan to the Borrower under this Agreement is subject to the satisfaction of the following further conditions precedent:

-6-

(a)   each of the representations and warranties of the Borrower to the Lender herein, in any of the other Loan Documents or any documents, certificate or other paper or notice in connection herewith shall be true and correct in all material respects as of the time made or deemed to have been made;

(b)   no Default or Event of Default shall be continuing;

(c)   all proceedings in connection with the transactions contemplated hereby shall be in form and substance satisfactory to the Lender, and the Lender shall have received all information and documents as it may have reasonably requested; and

(d)   no change shall have occurred in any law or regulation or in the interpretation thereof that in the reasonable opinion of the Lender would make it unlawful for the Lender to make such Loan.

6. COVENANTS.

6. 1. Affirmative Covenants. The Borrower agrees that until the termination of the Commitment and the payment and satisfaction in full of all the Obligations, the Borrower will comply with its obligations as set forth throughout this Agreement and to:

[This section of the Agreement sets forth various affirmative covenants, including the Borrower's obligation to provide the Lender with audited financial statements and other reports, to keep accurate books and records, to maintain its existence and lines of business, to comply with the law, to use the proceeds of the Loans for specified purposes, and to insure the Collateral and keep it free of competing liens.]

6. 2. Negative Covenants. The Borrower agrees that until the termination of the Commitment and the payment and satisfaction in full of all the Obligations, the Borrower will not:

[This section of the Agreement sets forth various negative covenants, including restrictions on the Borrower's incurrence of Indebtedness, creation of liens, investments, distributions of capital (e.g., dividends), and combinations (e.g., mergers) with other entities.]

6. 3. Financial Covenants. The Borrower agrees that until the termination of the Commitment and the payment and satisfaction in full of all the Obligations, the Borrower will not:

-7-

[This section of the Agreement sets forth various covenants relating to the financial condition of the Borrower. They include a restriction on capital expenditures and an obligation to maintain specified minimum or maximum levels of certain indicators of financial health, e.g., the ratio of total liabilities to tangible net worth, the amount of tangible net worth, the ratio of current assets to current liabilities, and the ratio of operating cash flow to total debt service. Credit agreements normally contain detailed definitions of the financial terms used in financial covenants. However, these definitions have been omitted here.]

7. **EVENTS OF DEFAULT; ACCELERATION.**

If any of the following events ("Events of Default") shall occur:

(a)   the Borrower shall fail to pay when due and payable any principal of the Loans when the same becomes due;

(b)   the Borrower shall fail to pay interest on the Loans or any other sum due under any of the Loan Documents within two (2) Business Days after the date on which the same shall have first become due and payable;

(c)   the Borrower shall fail to perform any term, covenant or agreement contained in [here the Agreement lists certain important covenants contained in Section 6, such as those relating to reporting requirements, use of Loan proceeds, and the negative and financial covenants];

(d)   the Borrower shall fail to perform any other term, covenant or agreement contained in the Loan Documents within fifteen (15) days after the Lender has given written notice of such failure to the Borrower;

(e)   any representation or warranty of the Borrower in the Loan Documents or in any certificate or notice given in connection therewith shall have been false or misleading in any material respect at the time made or deemed to have been made;

(f)   the Borrower shall be in default (after any applicable period of grace or cure period) under any agreement or agreements evidencing Indebtedness owing to the Lender or any affiliates of the Lender or any other Indebtedness in excess of Twenty-Five Thousand Dollars ($25,000) in aggregate principal amount, or shall fail to pay such Indebtedness when due, or within any applicable period of grace;

(g)   any of the Loan Documents shall cease to be in full force and effect,

-8-

(h) the Borrower (i) shall make an assignment for the benefit of creditors, (ii) shall be adjudicated a bankrupt or insolvent, (iii) shall seek the appointment of, or be the subject of an order appointing, a trustee, liquidator or receiver as to all or part of its assets; (iv) shall commence, approve or consent to, any case or proceeding under any bankruptcy, reorganization or similar law and, in the case of an involuntary case or proceeding, such case or proceeding is not dismissed within forty-five (45) days following the commencement thereof, or (v) shall be the subject of an order for relief in an involuntary case under federal bankruptcy law;

(i) the Borrower shall be unable to pay or generally shall cease to pay its debts as they mature;

(j) there shall remain undischarged for more than thirty (30) days any final judgment or execution action against the Borrower that, together with other outstanding claims and execution actions against the Borrower exceeds Twenty-Five Thousand Dollars ($25,000) in the aggregate;

THEN, or at any time thereafter:

(1) In the case of any Event of Default under clause (h) or (i), the Commitment shall automatically terminate, and the entire unpaid principal amount of the Loans, all interest accrued and unpaid thereon, and all other amounts payable under this Agreement and under the other Loan Documents shall automatically become forthwith due and payable, without presentment, demand, protest or notice of any kind, all of which are hereby expressly waived by the Borrower; and

(2) In the case of any Event of Default other than under clause (h) or (i), the Lender may, by written notice to the Borrower, terminate the Commitment and/or declare the unpaid principal amount of the Loans, all interest accrued and unpaid thereon, and all other amounts payable under this Agreement and under the other Loan Documents to be forthwith due and payable, without presentment, demand, protest or further notice of any kind, all of which are hereby expressly waived by the Borrower.

No remedy herein conferred upon the Lender is intended to be exclusive of any other remedy and each and every remedy shall be cumulative and in addition to every other remedy under this Agreement, now or hereafter existing under the other Loan Documents, at law or in equity, or otherwise.

-9-

8. <u>SETOFF</u>.

Regardless of the adequacy of any collateral for the Obligations, any sums credited by or due from the Lender to the Borrower may be applied to or set off against any principal, interest and any other amounts due from the Borrower to the Lender at any time without notice to the Borrower, or compliance with any other procedure imposed by statute or otherwise, all of which are hereby expressly waived by the Borrower.

9. <u>MISCELLANEOUS</u>.

The Borrower agrees to indemnify and hold harmless the Lender and its officers, employees, affiliates, agents, and controlling persons from and against all claims, damages, liabilities and losses of every kind arising out of the Loan Documents, including without limitation, against those in respect of the application of environmental laws to the Borrower absent the gross negligence or willful misconduct of the Lender. The Borrower shall pay to the Lender promptly on demand all costs and expenses (including any taxes and reasonable legal and other professional fees and fees of its commercial finance examiner) incurred by the Lender in connection with the preparation, negotiation, execution, amendment, administration, or enforcement of any of the Loan Documents. Any communication to be made under this Agreement shall (i) be made in writing, but unless otherwise stated, may be made by telex, facsimile transmission or letter, and (ii) be made or delivered to the address of the party receiving notice which is identified with its signature below (unless such party has by five (5) days written notice specified another address), and shall be deemed made or delivered, when dispatched, left at that address, or five (5) days after being mailed, postage prepaid, to such address. This Agreement shall be binding upon and inure to the benefit of each party hereto and its successors and assigns, but the Borrower may not assign its rights or obligations under this Agreement. This Agreement may not be amended or waived except by a written instrument signed by the Borrower and the Lender, and any such amendment or waiver shall be effective only for the specific purpose given. No failure or delay by the Lender to exercise any right under this Agreement or any other Loan Document shall operate as a waiver thereof, nor shall any single or partial exercise of any right, power or privilege preclude any other right, power or privilege. The provisions of this Agreement are severable and if any one provision hereof shall be held invalid or unenforceable in whole or in part in any jurisdiction, such invalidity or unenforceability shall affect only such provision in such jurisdiction. This Agreement expresses the entire understanding of the parties with respect to the transactions contemplated hereby. This Agreement and any amendment hereto may be executed in several counterparts, each of which shall be an original, and all of which shall constitute one agreement. In proving this Agreement, it shall not be necessary to produce more than one such counterpart executed by the party to be charged. **THIS AGREEMENT AND THE OTHER LOAN DOCUMENTS ARE CONTRACTS UNDER THE LAWS OF THE STATE OF NEW YORK AND SHALL BE CONSTRUED IN**

-10-

ACCORDANCE THEREWITH AND GOVERNED THEREBY. THE BORROWER AGREES THAT ANY SUIT FOR THE ENFORCEMENT OF ANY OF THE LOAN DOCUMENTS MAY BE BROUGHT IN THE COURTS OF THE STATE OF NEW YORK OR ANY FEDERAL COURT SITTING THEREIN. The Borrower, as an inducement to the Lender to enter into this Agreement, hereby waives its right to a jury trial with respect to any action arising in connection with any Loan Document.

IN WITNESS WHEREOF, the undersigned have duly executed this Revolving Credit Agreement as a sealed instrument as of the date first above written.

CARGUYS, INC., a Delaware corporation
1313 West Rosannadanna Boulevard
Los Angeles, California 90210
Attention: Angie Boombox, President
Tel: 999-674-1022
Fax: 999-674-1023

By: *Angie Boombox*
      Name: Angie Boombox
      Title: President

EASTINGHOME CREDIT
CORPORATION, a New York corporation
94 Wintershire Drive
Territown, New York 10156
Attention: Tabb Collar, III, President
Tel: 666-785-2133
Fax: 666-785-2134

By: *Tabb Collar, III*
      Name: Tabb Collar, III
      Title: Vice-President

As you can see, the Revolving Credit Agreement creates a **committed credit facility** in favor of Carguys—i.e., Eastinghome has made a binding agreement to lend an amount up to its "Commitment" (see the definition in § 1 of the Agreement and the commitment to lend in § 2.1) of $25,000,000. (This arrangement is to be contrasted with the discretionary **line of credit** that Firstbank provided to Main Motors in the automobile financing Prototype in Chapter 7.) However, under § 2.1, Eastinghome's commitment is further limited to the *lesser* of the Commitment and the "Borrowing Base," which is the sum of 75% of the "Base Accounts" and 60% of the "Base Inventory" (see § 1 for the definitions of these terms and "Accounts" and "Inventory"). Under this structure, Eastinghome is not required to lend more than its Commitment and, depending on the value of the Base Accounts and Base Inventory, may be obligated to lend only a smaller amount. In any event, Eastinghome is assured that it will have a **collateral value cushion** over and above the amount of its Loans of 25% in the case of Base Accounts and 40% in the case of Base Inventory. The Agreement also contains another set of important lender protections. Eastinghome is obliged to make a Loan only if the Conditions Precedent (pronounced preh-SEE-dent, and not to be confused with a PREH-seh-dent) specified in § 5 are satisfied.

This arrangement is called a **revolving credit facility** or **revolver** because Carguys is entitled to borrow, repay, and reborrow throughout the term of the facility, so long as the aggregate outstanding loan balance does not exceed the lesser of the Commitment or the Borrowing Base at any time (see § 2.3). However, on the Maturity Date, July 1, 2004 (three years after the Agreement became effective), Carguys is obliged to repay the Loans in full. In reality, however, Eastinghome is likely to renew the arrangement for an additional term if Carguys remains a viable and creditworthy enterprise and continues to need financing. In the alternative, Carguys might arrange for a new facility with a new lender that would **take out** Eastinghome (not unlike the situation in the automobile financing Prototype in Chapter 7, in which Firstbank "picked up the floor plan" from Main Motors' earlier lender, Old Bank).

The Note (see § 2.1(c) of the Agreement) evidences the outstanding Loans under the Revolving Credit Agreement. A "grid" or table attached to the Note is designed to reflect the various advances and repayments of Loans. In the Note, Carguys authorizes Eastinghome to make the relevant notations on the grid, which Carguys agrees will be *prima facie* evidence of the various Loans and repayments. With respect to each Loan and repayment, Eastinghome will enter on the grid the date and amount, the resulting outstanding principal balance, and the name of the person making the notation. In actuality, of course, the grid is redundant; Eastinghome will have computerized business records of all transactions with respect to the Loans. Nevertheless, as a general matter a note is customary but not necessary.

In addition to interest charges on outstanding Loans (see § 2.2 of the Agreement), Carguys has agreed to pay certain fees to Eastinghome. The fees consist of a one-time "closing fee" of $25,000 and a "commitment fee" of one and one-half percent (1–1/2%) per annum on the unused portion of Eastinghome's Commitment (see § 3). The commitment fee reflects the principle that Eastinghome should be compensated for its ongoing obligation to extend credit.

The Revolving Credit Agreement also specifies "Events of Default" in § 7(a)–(j). Upon the occurrence of certain Events of Default Eastinghome's obligation to extend credit will be terminated and the Loans and all other amounts owed by Carguys automatically become due and payable (i.e., these amounts will be automatically **accelerated**). See § 7(1). Other Events of Default provide Eastinghome with the option to terminate its obligations and to accelerate the payment obligations of Carguys. See § 7(2). Finally, in § 4 Carguys makes various representations and warranties of fact and law, and in § 6 it makes certain covenants (promises).

Security Agreement; Perfection Certificate. The Security Documents, including a Security Agreement, are among the Loan Documents to be delivered by Carguys as a condition precedent to the making of Loans. See §§ 1 and 5 of the Revolving Credit Agreement. Pertinent portions of the Security Agreement are set forth below:

FORM 9.2
SECURITY AGREEMENT

SECURITY AGREEMENT

This **SECURITY AGREEMENT** (this "Agreement") is made as of July 1, 2001, by and between CARGUYS, INC. (the "Company"), a Delaware corporation having its principal place of business at 1313 West Rosannadanna Boulevard, Los Angeles, California, and EASTINGHOME CREDIT CORPORATION (the "Lender"), a New York corporation having its office at 94 Wintershire Drive, Territown, New York.

WHEREAS, the Company has entered into a Revolving Credit Agreement dated as of July 1, 2001 (as amended and in effect from time to time, the "Credit Agreement"), with the Lender, pursuant to which the Lender, subject to the terms and conditions contained therein, is to make loans to the Company; and

WHEREAS, it is a condition precedent to the Lender's making any loans to the Company under the Credit Agreement that the Company execute and deliver to the Lender a security agreement in substantially the form hereof; and

WHEREAS, the Company wishes to grant a security interest in favor of the Lender as herein provided;

NOW, THEREFORE, in consideration of the promises contained herein and for other good and valuable consideration, the receipt and sufficiency of which are hereby acknowledged, the parties hereto agree as follows:

1. Definitions. All capitalized terms used herein without definitions shall have the respective meanings provided in the Credit Agreement. The term "State", as used herein, means the State of New York. All terms defined in the Uniform Commercial Code of the State and used herein shall have the same definitions herein as specified therein; provided, however, that the term "instrument" shall be such term as defined in Article 9 of the Uniform Commercial Code of the State rather than Article 3. The term "Obligations", as used herein, means all of the indebtedness, obligations and liabilities of the Company to the Lender, individually or collectively, whether direct or indirect, joint or several, absolute or contingent, due or to become due, now existing or hereafter arising under or in respect of the Credit Agreement, this Agreement, any promissory notes or other instruments or agreements executed and delivered pursuant thereto or in connection therewith or this Agreement, or any other Loan Documents.

2. Grant of Security Interest. The Company hereby grants to the Lender, to secure the payment and performance in full of all of the Obligations, a security interest in and so pledges and assigns to the Lender the following properties, assets and rights of the Company, wherever located, whether now owned or hereafter acquired or arising, and all proceeds and products thereof (all of the same being hereinafter called the "Collateral"): all personal and fixture property of every kind and nature including without limitation all goods (including inventory, equipment and any accessions thereto), instruments (including promissory notes), documents, accounts (including health-care-insurance receivables), chattel paper (whether tangible or electronic), deposit accounts, letter-of-credit rights (whether or not the letter of credit is evidenced by a writing), commercial tort claims, securities and all other investment property, supporting obligations, any other contract rights or rights to the payment of money, insurance claims and proceeds, tort claims, and all general intangibles including, without limitation, all payment intangibles, patents, patent applications, trademarks, trademark applications, trade names, copyrights, copyright applications, software, engineering drawings, service marks, customer lists, goodwill, and all licenses, permits, agreements of any kind or nature pursuant to which the Company possesses, uses or has authority to possess or use property (whether tangible or intangible) of others or others possess, use or have authority to possess or use property (whether tangible or intangible) of the Company, and all recorded data of any kind or nature, regardless of the medium of recording including, without limitation, all software, writings, plans, specifications and schematics.

3. Authorization to File Financing Statements. The Company hereby irrevocably authorizes the Lender at any time and from time to time to file in any Uniform Commercial Code jurisdiction any initial financing statements and amendments thereto that (a) indicate the Collateral (i) as all assets of the Company or words of similar effect, regardless of whether any particular asset comprised in the Collateral falls within the scope of Article 9 of the Uniform Commercial Code of the State or such jurisdiction, or (ii) as being of an equal or lesser scope or with greater detail, and (b) contain any other information required by part 5 of Article 9 of the Uniform Commercial Code of the State for the sufficiency or filing office acceptance of any financing statement or amendment, including (i) whether the Company is an organization, the type of organization and any organization identification number issued to the Company and, (ii) in the case of a financing statement filed as a fixture filing or indicating Collateral as as-extracted collateral or timber to be cut, a sufficient description of real property to which the Collateral relates. The Company agrees to furnish any such information to the Lender promptly upon request.

4. Other Actions. Further to insure the attachment, perfection and first priority of, and the ability of the Lender to enforce, the Lender's security interest in the Collateral, the Company agrees, in each case at the Company's own expense, to take the following actions with respect to the following Collateral:

4.1. Promissory Notes and Tangible Chattel Paper. If the Company shall at any time hold or acquire any promissory notes or tangible chattel paper, the Company shall forthwith endorse, assign and deliver the same to the Lender, accompanied by such instruments of transfer or assignment duly executed in blank as the Lender may from time to time specify.

4.2. Deposit Accounts. For each deposit account that the Company at any time opens or maintains, the Company shall, at the Lender's request and option, pursuant to an agreement in form and substance satisfactory to the Lender, either (a) cause the depositary bank to agree to comply at any time with instructions from the Lender to such depositary bank directing the disposition of funds from time to time credited to such deposit account, without further consent of the Company, or (b) arrange for the Lender to become the customer of the depositary bank with respect to the deposit account, with the Company being permitted, only with the consent of the Lender, to exercise rights to withdraw funds from such deposit account. The Lender agrees with the Company that the Lender shall not give any such instructions or withhold any withdrawal rights from the Company, unless an Event of Default has occurred and is continuing, or, after giving effect to any withdrawal not otherwise permitted by the Loan Documents, would occur. The provisions of this paragraph shall not apply to (i) any deposit account for which the Company, the depositary bank and the Lender have entered into a cash collateral agreement specially negotiated among the Company, the depositary bank and the Lender for the specific purpose set forth therein and (ii) deposit accounts specially and exclusively used for payroll, payroll taxes and other employee wage and benefit payments to or for the benefit of the Company's salaried employees

4.3. **Investment Property**. If the Company shall at any time hold or acquire any certificated securities, the Company shall forthwith endorse, assign and deliver the same to the Lender, accompanied by such instruments of transfer or assignment duly executed in blank as the Lender may from time to time specify. If any securities now or hereafter acquired by the Company are uncertificated and are issued to the Company or its nominee directly by the issuer thereof, the Company shall immediately notify the Lender thereof and, at the Lender's request and option, pursuant to an agreement in form and substance satisfactory to the Lender, either (a) cause the issuer to agree to comply with instructions from the Lender as to such securities, without further consent of the Company or such nominee, or (b) arrange for the Lender to become the registered owner of the securities. If any securities, whether certificated or uncertificated, or other investment property now or hereafter acquired by the Company is held by the Company or its nominee through a securities intermediary or commodity intermediary, the Company shall immediately notify the Lender thereof and, at the Lender's request and option, pursuant to an agreement in form and substance satisfactory to the Lender, either (i) cause such securities intermediary or (as the case may be) commodity intermediary to agree to comply with entitlement orders or other instructions from the Lender to such securities intermediary as to such securities or other investment property, or (as the case may be) to apply any value distributed on account of any commodity contract as directed by the Lender to such commodity intermediary, in each case without further consent of the Company or such nominee, or (ii) in the case of financial assets or other investment property held through a securities intermediary, arrange for the Lender to become the entitlement holder with respect to such investment property, with the Company being permitted, only with the consent of the Lender, to exercise rights to withdraw or otherwise deal with such investment property. The Lender agrees with the Company that the Lender shall not give any such entitlement orders or instructions or directions to any such issuer, securities intermediary or commodity intermediary, and shall not withhold its consent to the exercise of any withdrawal or dealing rights by the Company, unless an Event of Default has occurred and is continuing, or, after giving effect to any such investment and withdrawal rights not otherwise permitted by the Loan Documents, would occur.

4.4. **Collateral in the Possession of a Bailee**. If any goods are at any time in the possession of a bailee, the Company shall promptly notify the Lender thereof and, if requested by the Lender, shall promptly obtain an acknowledgement from the bailee, in form and substance satisfactory to the Lender, that the bailee holds such Collateral for the benefit of the Lender and shall act upon the instructions of the Lender, without the further consent of the Company. The Lender agrees with the Company that the Lender shall not give any such instructions unless an Event of Default has occurred and is continuing or would occur after taking into account any action by the Company with respect to the bailee.

    4.5.   **Electronic Chattel Paper and Transferable Records**. If the Company at any time holds or acquires an interest in any electronic chattel paper or any "transferable record," as that term is defined in Section 201 of the federal Electronic Signatures in Global and National Commerce Act, or in §16 of the Uniform Electronic Transactions Act as in effect in any relevant jurisdiction, the Company shall promptly notify the Lender thereof and, at the request of the Lender, shall take such action as the Lender may reasonably request to vest in the Lender control under Uniform Commercial Code §9-105 of such electronic chattel paper or control under Section 201 of the federal Electronic Signatures in Global and National Commerce Act or, as the case may be, §16 of the Uniform Electronic Transactions Act, as so in effect in such jurisdiction, of such transferable record. The Lender agrees with the Company that the Lender will arrange, pursuant to procedures satisfactory to the Lender and so long as such procedures will not result in the Lender's loss of control, for the Company to make alterations to the electronic chattel paper or transferable record permitted under Uniform Commercial Code §9-105 or, as the case may be, Section 201 of the federal Electronic Signatures in Global and National Commerce Act or §16 of the Uniform Electronic Transactions Act for a party in control to make without loss of control, unless an Event of Default has occurred and is continuing or would occur after taking into account any action by the Company with respect to such electronic chattel paper or transferable record.

    4.6.   **Letter-of-credit Rights**. If the Company is at any time a beneficiary under a letter of credit now or hereafter issued in favor of the Company, the Company shall promptly notify the Lender thereof and, at the request and option of the Lender, the Company shall, pursuant to an agreement in form and substance satisfactory to the Lender, either (i) arrange for the issuer and any confirmer of such letter of credit to consent to an assignment to the Lender of the proceeds of any drawing under the letter of credit or (ii) arrange for the Lender to become the transferee beneficiary of the letter of credit, with the Lender agreeing, in each case, that the proceeds of any drawing under the letter to credit are to be applied as provided in the Credit Agreement.

    4.6.   **Commercial Tort Claims**. If the Company shall at any time hold or acquire a commercial tort claim, the Company shall immediately notify the Lender in a writing signed by the Company of the brief details thereof and grant to the Lender in such writing a security interest therein and in the proceeds thereof, all upon the terms of this Agreement, with such writing to be in form and substance satisfactory to the Lender.

    4.8.   **Other Actions as to any and all Collateral**. The Company further agrees to take any other action reasonably requested by the Lender to insure the attachment, perfection and first priority of, and the ability of the Lender to enforce, the Lender's security interest in any and all of the Collateral including, without limitation, (a) executing, delivering and, where appropriate, filing financing statements and amendments relating thereto under the Uniform Commercial Code, to the extent, if any, that the Company's signature thereon is required therefor, (b) causing the Lender's name to be noted as secured party on any certificate of title for a titled good if such notation is a condition to attachment, perfection or priority of, or ability of the Lender to enforce, the Lender's security interest in such Collateral, (c) complying with any provision of any statute, regulation or treaty of the United States as to any Collateral if compliance with such provision is a condition to attachment, perfection or priority of, or ability of the Lender to enforce, the Lender's security interest in such Collateral, (d) obtaining governmental and other third party consents and approvals, including without limitation any consent of any licensor, lessor or other person obligated on Collateral, (e) obtaining waivers from mortgagees and landlords in form and substance satisfactory to the Lender and (f) taking all actions required by any earlier versions of the Uniform Commercial Code or by other law, as applicable in any relevant Uniform Commercial Code jurisdiction, or by other law as applicable in any foreign jurisdiction.

5. Relation to Other Security Documents.

> * * *

6. Representations and Warranties Concerning Company's Legal Status.

> * * *

7. Covenants Concerning Company's Legal Status.

> * * *

8. Representations and Warranties Concerning Collateral, Etc. The Company further represents and warrants to the Lender as follows: (a) the Company is the owner of the Collateral, free from any adverse lien, security interest or other encumbrance, except for the security interest created by this Agreement, (b) none of the Collateral constitutes, or is the proceeds of, "farm products" as defined in §9-102(a)(34) of the Uniform Commercial Code of the State, (c) none of the account debtors or other persons obligated on any of the Collateral is a governmental authority subject to the Federal Assignment of Claims Act or like federal, state or local statute or rule in respect of such Collateral, (d) the Company holds no commercial tort claim except as indicated on the Perfection Certificate, (e) the Company has at all times operated its business in compliance with all applicable provisions of the federal Fair Labor Standards Act, as amended, and with all applicable provisions of federal, state and local statutes and ordinances dealing with the control, shipment, storage or disposal of hazardous materials or substances and (f) all other information set forth on the Perfection Certificate pertaining to the Collateral is accurate and complete.

9. Covenants Concerning Collateral, Etc.. The Company further covenants with the Lender as follows: (a) the Collateral, to the extent not delivered to the Lender hereunder, will be kept at those locations listed on the Perfection Certificate and the Company will not remove the Collateral from such locations, without providing at least 30 days prior written notice to the Lender, (b) except for the security interest herein granted, the Company shall be the owner of the Collateral free from any lien, security interest or other encumbrance, and the Company shall defend the same against all claims and demands of all persons at any time claiming the same or any interests therein adverse to the Lender, (c) the Company shall not pledge, mortgage or create, or suffer to exist a security interest in the Collateral in favor of any person other than the Lender, (d) the Company will keep the

Collateral in good order and repair and will not use the same in violation of law or any policy of insurance thereon, (e) the Company will permit the Lender, or its designee, to inspect the Collateral at any reasonable time, wherever located, (f) the Company will pay promptly when due all taxes, assessments, governmental charges and levies upon the Collateral or incurred in connection with the use or operation of such Collateral or incurred in connection with this Agreement, (g) the Company will continue to operate, its business in compliance with all applicable provisions of the federal Fair Labor Standards Act, as amended, and with all applicable provisions of federal, state and local statutes and ordinances dealing with the control, shipment, storage or disposal of hazardous materials or substances, and (h) the Company will not sell or otherwise dispose, or offer to sell or otherwise dispose, of the Collateral or any interest therein except for (i) sales and leases of inventory in the ordinary course of business and (ii) so long as no Default or Event of Default has occurred and is continuing, use of cash proceeds.

10. Insurance.

10.1. Maintenance of Insurance.

* * *

10.2. Insurance Proceeds.

* * *

10.3. Notice of Cancellation, etc.

* * *

11. Collateral Protection Expenses; Preservation of Collateral.

11.1. Expenses Incurred by Lender. In its discretion, the Lender may discharge taxes and other encumbrances at any time levied or placed on any of the Collateral, make repairs thereto and pay any necessary filing fees. The Company agrees to reimburse the Lender on demand for any and all expenditures so made. The Lender shall have no obligation to the Company to make any such expenditures, nor shall the making thereof relieve the Company of any default.

11.2. Lender's Obligations and Duties. Anything herein to the contrary notwithstanding, the Company shall remain liable under each contract or agreement comprised in the Collateral to be observed or performed by the Company thereunder. The Lender shall not have any obligation or liability under any such contract or agreement by reason of or arising out of this Agreement or the receipt by the Lender of any payment relating to any of the Collateral, nor shall the Lender be obligated in any manner to perform any of the obligations of the Company under or pursuant to any such contract or agreement, to make inquiry as to the nature or sufficiency of any payment received by the Lender in respect of the Collateral or as to the sufficiency of any performance by any party under any such contract or agreement, to present or file any claim, to take any action to enforce any performance or to collect the payment of any amounts which may have been assigned to the Lender or to which the Lender may be entitled at any time or times. The Lender's sole duty with respect to the custody, safe keeping and physical preservation of the Collateral in its possession, under §9-207 of the Uniform Commercial Code of the State or otherwise, shall be to deal with such Collateral in the same manner as the Lender deals with similar property for its own account.

12. Securities and Deposits. The Lender may at any time following and during the continuance of a Default or Event of Default, at its option, transfer to itself or any nominee any securities constituting Collateral, receive any income thereon and hold such income as additional Collateral or apply it to the Obligations. Whether or not any Obligations are due, the Lender may following and during the continuance of a Default or Event of Default demand, sue for, collect, or make any settlement or compromise which it deems desirable with respect to the Collateral. Regardless of the adequacy of Collateral or any other security for the Obligations, any deposits or other sums at any time credited by or due from the Lender to the Company may at any time be applied to or set off against any of the Obligations.

13. Notification to Account Debtors and Other Persons Obligated on Collateral. If a Default or an Event of Default shall have occurred and be continuing, the Company shall, at the request of the Lender, notify account debtors and other persons obligated on any of the Collateral of the security interest of the Lender in any account, chattel paper, general intangible, instrument or other Collateral and that payment thereof is to be made directly to the Lender or to any financial institution designated by the Lender as the Lender's agent therefor, and the Lender may itself, if a Default or an Event of Default shall have occurred and be continuing, without notice to or demand upon the Company, so notify account debtors and other persons obligated on Collateral. After the making of such a request or the giving of any such notification, the Company shall hold any proceeds of collection of accounts, chattel paper, general intangibles, instruments and other Collateral received by the Company as trustee for the Lender without commingling the same with other funds of the Company and shall turn the same over to the Lender in the identical form received, together with any necessary endorsements or assignments. The Lender shall apply the proceeds of collection of accounts, chattel paper, general intangibles, instruments and other Collateral received by the Lender to the Obligations, such proceeds to be immediately credited after final payment in cash or other immediately available funds of the items giving rise to them.

14. Power of Attorney.

14.1. Appointment and Powers of Lender.

* * *

14.2. Ratification by Company.

* * *

14.3. <u>**No Duty on Lender.**</u>

* * *

15. <u>**Remedies.**</u> If an Event of Default shall have occurred and be continuing, the Lender may, without notice to or demand upon the Company, declare this Agreement to be in default, and the Lender shall thereafter have in any jurisdiction in which enforcement hereof is sought, in addition to all other rights and remedies, the rights and remedies of a secured party under the Uniform Commercial Code of the State or of any jurisdiction in which Collateral is located, including, without limitation, the right to take possession of the Collateral, and for that purpose the Lender may, so far as the Company can give authority therefor, enter upon any premises on which the Collateral may be situated and remove the same therefrom. The Lender may in its discretion require the Company to assemble all or any part of the Collateral at such location or locations within the jurisidction(s) of the Company's principal office(s) or at such other locations as the Lender may reasonably designate. Unless the Collateral is perishable or threatens to decline speedily in value or is of a type customarily sold on a recognized market, the Lender shall give to the Company at least ten (10) Business Days prior written notice of the time and place of any public sale of Collateral or of the time after which any private sale or any other intended disposition is to be made. The Company hereby acknowledges that five (5) Business Days prior written notice of such sale or sales shall be reasonable notice. In addition, the Company waives any and all rights that it may have to a judicial hearing in advance of the enforcement of any of the Lender's rights hereunder, including, without limitation, its right following an Event of Default to take immediate possession of the Collateral and to exercise its rights with respect thereto.

16. <u>**Standards for Exercising Remedies.**</u> To the extent that applicable law imposes duties on the Lender to exercise remedies in a commercially reasonable manner, the Company acknowledges and agrees that it is not commercially unreasonable for the Lender (a) to fail to incur expenses reasonably deemed significant by the Lender to prepare Collateral for disposition or otherwise to complete raw material or work in process into finished goods or other finished products for disposition, (b) to fail to obtain third party consents for access to Collateral to be disposed of, or to obtain or, if not required by other law, to fail to obtain governmental or third party consents for the collection or disposition of Collateral to be collected or disposed of, (c) to fail to exercise collection remedies against account debtors or other persons obligated on Collateral or to remove liens or encumbrances on or any adverse claims against Collateral, (d) to exercise collection remedies against account debtors and other persons obligated on Collateral directly or through the use of collection agencies and other collection specialists, (e) to advertise dispositions of Collateral through publications or media of general circulation, whether or not the Collateral is of a specialized nature, (f) to contact other persons, whether or not in the same business as the Company, for expressions of interest in acquiring all or any portion of the Collateral, (g) to hire one or more professional auctioneers to assist in the disposition of Collateral, whether or not the collateral is of a specialized nature, (h) to dispose of Collateral by utilizing Internet sites that provide for the auction of assets of the types included in the Collateral or that have the reasonable capability of doing so, or that match buyers and sellers of assets, (i) to dispose of assets in wholesale rather than retail markets, (j) to disclaim disposition warranties, (k) to purchase insurance or credit enhancements to insure the Lender against risks of loss, collection or disposition of Collateral or to provide to the Lender a guaranteed

return from the collection or disposition of Collateral, or (l) to the extent deemed appropriate by the Lender, to obtain the services of other brokers, investment bankers, consultants and other professionals to assist the Lender in the collection or disposition of any of the Collateral. The Company acknowledges that the purpose of this §16 is to provide non-exhaustive indications of what actions or omissions by the Lender would not be commercially unreasonable in the Lender's exercise of remedies against the Collateral and that other actions or omissions by the Lender shall not be deemed commercially unreasonable solely on account of not being indicated in this §16. Without limitation upon the foregoing, nothing contained in this §16 shall be construed to grant any rights to the Company or to impose any duties on the Lender that would not have been granted or imposed by this Agreement or by applicable law in the absence of this §16.

17. No Waiver by Lender, etc.

* * *

18. Suretyship Waivers by Company.

* * *

19. Marshaling.

* * *

20. Proceeds of Dispositions; Expenses. The Company shall pay to the Lender on demand any and all expenses, including reasonable attorneys' fees and disbursements, incurred or paid by the Lender in protecting, preserving or enforcing the Lender's rights under or in respect of any of the Obligations or any of the Collateral. After deducting all of said expenses, the residue of any proceeds of collection or sale of the Obligations or Collateral shall, to the extent actually received in cash, be applied to the payment of the Obligations in such order or preference as the Lender may determine, proper allowance and provision being made for any Obligations not then due. Upon the final payment and satisfaction in full of all of the Obligations and after making any payments required by Sections 9-608(a)(1)(C) or 9-615(a)(3) of the Uniform Commercial Code of the State, any excess shall be returned to the Company, and the Company shall remain liable for any deficiency in the payment of the Obligations.

21. Overdue Amounts. Until paid, all amounts due and payable by the Company hereunder shall be a debt secured by the Collateral and shall bear, whether before or after judgment, interest at the rate of interest for overdue principal set forth in the Credit Agreement.

22. Governing Law; Consent to Jurisdiction.

* * *

23. Waiver of Jury Trial.

* * *

24. **Miscellaneous.**

* * *

IN WITNESS WHEREOF, intending to be legally bound, the Company has caused this Agreement to be duly executed as of the date first above written.

CARGUYS, INC., a Delaware corporation

By: *Angie Boombox*

Name: Angie Boombox

Title: President

EASTINGHOME CREDIT CORPORATION, a New York corporation

By: *Tabb Collar, III*

Name: Tabb Collar, III

Title: Vice-President

Note the broad range of collateral covered by the granting language in § 2 of the Security Agreement—it covers virtually all types of personal property. Contrast the Revolving Credit Agreement's much narrower definitions of Accounts and Inventory, and its still narrower definitions of Base Accounts and Base Inventory. Under the Borrowing Base formulation, Loans must be supported by the relevant percentages of the Base Accounts (75%) and Base Inventory (60%), but Eastinghome has required Carguys to provide additional collateral beyond those components of the Borrowing Base.

In the terminology used by Kupfer in the foregoing excerpt, the Eastinghome–Carguys facility reflects a **recourse** financing, inasmuch as Carguys is fully liable to repay the Loans, whether or not Eastinghome makes any recovery from the collateral. Moreover, the transaction involves the **indirect collection** of receivables—until a Default or Event of Default has occurred, Carguys is entitled to collect receivables from the various account debtors. See R9–607(a); § 13 of the Security Agreement. In some transactions, a ''lockbox'' or ''cash collateral agreement'' is entered into by the borrower-assignor, a depositary bank, and the lender-assignee. See § 4.2. Account debtors are instructed to send all remittances on receivables to a post office box address controlled by the bank (usually, the post office box is listed as the borrower-assignor's address on its invoices); the receipts are then deposited in a deposit account maintained for this purpose (a **cash collateral account**). In this way, the lender-assignee may gain control over all receipts without the necessity of undertaking an actual **direct collection** from account debtors in is own name.

For present purposes we are interested primarily in the collateral consisting of accounts and inventory (as defined in Revised Article 9; see § 1 of the Security Agreement). Perfection of Eastinghome's security interest in that collateral is straightforward—filing a financing statement in the jurisdiction in which Carguys is located, Delaware. See R9–310; R9–301(1); R9–307(e). (Perfection of Eastinghome's security interest in other types of collateral requires further analysis. See Sections 2, 3, 4, and 6, infra. See also § 4 of the Security Agreement.) To make sure that it has all of the relevant facts necessary for determining the steps required for perfection and priority, Eastinghome requires Carguys to deliver a Perfection Certificate, which contains representations concerning these facts (e.g., the exact corporate name and place of incorporation of Carguys, the mailing address of Carguys, the location of Carguys' chief executive office, the locations of tangible collateral, etc.). Note that during the transition from Former Article 9 to Revised Article 9, Eastinghome is interested in facts related to the applicable law for perfection under Former Article 9 as well as Revised Article 9. The possibility always exists that a financing statement has been filed against Carguys in the filing office designated by F9–103 and F9–401.

(C) Problem Under the Prototype

The following Problem focuses primarily on the business terms of the Prototype and how they relate to both legal issues and Eastinghome's credit analysis.

Problem 9.1.1. (a) Why are the definitions of ''Accounts,'' ''Inventory,'' ''Base Accounts,'' and ''Base Inventory'' in the Revolving Credit Agreement so narrow in comparison with the broad definitions of the terms ''accounts'' and ''inventory'' in R9–102 and in the Security Agreement? See Revolving Credit Agreement §§ 1, 2.1(a); Security Agreement § 1.

(b) Why do you suppose that Eastinghome has insisted on limiting its obligation to make Loans to an amount equal to the *lesser* of the Commitment and the Borrowing Base? See Revolving Credit Agreement § 2.1(a).

(c) If Carguys sells diagnostic equipment on a secured basis, is the right to payment included in the Borrowing Base? See Revolving Credit Agreement § 1. Cf. R9–102(a)(2), (a)(11).

(d) What are the purposes of the conditions precedent listed in § 5 of the Revolving Credit Agreement? What is the significance of the dates on which Carguys makes its representations and warranties? See Revolving Credit Agreement § 4. What is the relationship among the conditions precedent and Carguys' representations and warranties? See Revolving Credit Agreement §§ 4, 5, 6.

(e) What is the relationship among the Events of Default and Carguys' representations and warranties and covenants? See Revolving Credit Agreement §§ 4, 5, 6, 7.

(f) Why does the Revolving Credit Agreement distinguish between a "Default" and an "Event of Default"? See Revolving Credit Agreement §§ 1, 5(b), 7; Security Agreement § 15.

(g) Why does the Revolving Credit Agreement distinguish between payments of principal and payments of interest and other sums? See § 7(a), (b).

(h) Why does the Revolving Credit Agreement distinguish between breach of certain covenants and breach of others? See § 7(c), (d).

(i) Why does Revolving Credit Agreement § 7(e) cover only a representation and warranty that is inaccurate at the time that it is made or deemed made?

(j) Why does the Revolving Credit Agreement distinguish between Events of Default under § 7(h) and (i) and other Events of Default? See § 7(1), (2).

(k) Why is the description of collateral in § 2 of the Security Agreement so long? Wouldn't a list of UCC-defined types of collateral have been sufficient? See R9–108(b)(3).

(*l*) What purpose is served by § 3 of the Security Agreement, given that Carguys' authentication of the security agreement ipso facto authorizes Eastinghome to file a financing statement? See R9–509(b).

(D) SALES OF RECEIVABLES

Problem 9.1.2. In the setting of the Prototype on receivables financing, Carguys approaches a representative of Lax Factor Co., a specialist in the nonrecourse factoring of receivables. (As Kupfer explained, these are transactions in which the "*assignee* assumes the *credit* risk"—i.e., the risk that an account debtor will not pay its debt to the debtor/assignor.) Factor proposes a financing arrangement that would replace the Eastinghome revolving credit facility. Under the proposal, Carguys would sell and Factor would buy, on a nonrecourse basis, accounts generated by Carguys. Factor would pay 85% of the face amount of each account that it buys. The accounts that Factor would be willing to buy are essentially those that would be "Base Accounts" under the Eastinghome facility. Carguys sees certain advantages to the Factor arrangement. Significantly, because of the nonrecourse structure, Carguys would not incur any debt on its balance sheet—the accounts would simply be replaced with cash. Of course, Carguys would be required to warrant to Factor that the accounts are genuine and that none of the account debtors has a defense to payment (i.e., Carguys would retain the "merchandise risk," as Kupfer explained).

Carguys accepted Factor's proposal and satisfied its obligations to Eastinghome, which filed a termination statements for its financing statement. Carguys and Factor entered into a sale agreement under which Factor agreed to buy Carguys' qualifying accounts from time to time up to an aggregate of $25,000,000 face amount at any time outstanding and unpaid. Factor failed to file a financing statement in the appropriate filing office in Delaware.

(a) Lean, a judgment creditor of Carguys', served a **garnishment** summons on three of Carguys' biggest customers. The summons instructs each **garnishee** to inform the court of the amount it owes to Carguys; service of the summons gives rise to a lien in favor of the judgment creditor (here, Lean) in that amount. If a garnishee answers that it is indebted to Carguys, the court will enter judgment in that amount in favor of Lean, and the customer will be obligated to pay Lean instead of Carguys. Prior to the entry of judgment, Factor intervenes, asserting that it is the owner of the accounts, that Carguys retains no interest in them, that the customers owe Carguys nothing, and that Lean is not entitled to payment from the customers. What result? See R9–109(a)(3); R1–201(37) (2d sentence); R9–318; R9–317(a)(2); R9–310(a); Note (1) on Sales of Receivables, infra.

(b) Would the result in part (a) change if, before service of the garnishment summons, Factor had notified Carguys' customers that it had purchased their accounts? If Factor had taken possession of the contracts that gave rise to the accounts (i.e., the contracts pursuant to which Carguys provided repair and maintenance services and sold auto parts and diagnostic equipment)?

(c) Would the result in part (a) change if Carguys had retained purchase-money security interests in the auto parts and diagnostic equipment and sold Factor the secured rights to payment? See R9–102(a)(11); R9–109(a)(3); R1–201(37) (2d sentence).

(d) Assume that instead of obtaining a judicial lien pursuant to a garnishment summons, Lean (i) bought the accounts from Carguys on terms similar to those under which Factor bought them and (ii) filed a financing statement against Carguys covering the accounts in the appropriate filing office in Delaware. Who has the better claim to the accounts? See R9–318(b) & Comment 3; R9–322(a).

Problem 9.1.3. CC Bank issues credit cards to consumers. To raise capital, CC periodically sells its portfolio of credit-card receivables (rights to payment from its credit-card customers). When cardholders use their cards to buy merchandise, CC advances the purchase price to the merchants. The receivables consist in part of the cardholders' obligations to repay those advances, some of which obligations are unsecured and others of which are secured by the merchandise purchased. The receivables also include cardholders' obligations to repay cash advances. Lax Factor agreed to buy the receivables at a discount. What steps, if any, should Factor take to protect its ownership interest against CC's creditors? See R9–102(a)(2), (11); R9–109(a)(3); R1–201(37) (2d sentence); R9–318; R9–317(a)(2); R9–310(a); Note (2) on Sales of Receivables, infra.

Problem 9.1.4. In the setting of the Prototype on financing automobiles, Chapter 7, Section 1, supra, the outstanding principal balance owed by Main Motors to Firstbank under the line of credit is $2,400,000. Unlike the facts of that Prototype, however, assume that the documentation did not include the Demand Note (Form 3.3). To reduce its risk, Firstbank enters into a Participation Agreement with Secondbank, pursuant to which Firstbank sells to Secondbank a 25% undivided interest in the loan for $600,000. In exchange, Secondbank is entitled to receive 25% of all principal and interest payments made by Main under the line of credit. Secondbank also agrees to advance 25% of all future loans made by Firstbank under the line of credit.

(a) What steps, if any, should Secondbank take to protect its ownership interest in the loan against lien creditors of Firstbank? See R9–109(a)(3); R9–102(a)(61), (42); R1–201(37) (2d sentence); R9–318; R9–317(a)(2); R9–310(a), (b)(2); R9–309(3).

(b) The facts are as in part (a), except that Main's obligation to repay the loan is evidenced by the Demand Note, and Secondbank bought a 25% undivided interest in the Demand Note. What steps, if, any, should Secondbank take to protect its ownership interest in the note against lien creditors of Firstbank? See R9–102(a)(65), (47); R9–109(a)(3); R1–201(37) (2d sentence); R9–318; R9–317(a)(2); R9–310(a), (b)(2); R9–309(4). Does the definition of "promissory note" in R9–102(a)(65) include a negotiable note payable to order? What steps should Secondbank take if the note were payable "to Firstbank"? (Do not assume that a security interest having priority over subsequent lien creditors also has priority over subsequent purchasers. See Chapter 1, Section 4, supra; Section 2, infra.)

(c) Both this Problem and the preceding one concern the sale by a bank of its right to repayment of a loan. Can you reconcile the results in this Problem with those in the preceding Problem? See Note (2) on Sales of Receivables, infra.

NOTES ON SALES OF RECEIVABLES

(1) The Broad Scope of Former Article 9: Sales of Accounts and Chattel Paper. Consider the variation on the receivables financing Prototype presented in Problem 9.1.2: Carguys provides goods and services on unsecured credit to a variety of customers. Carguys needs cash to continue to operate. Rather than wait for payment, Carguys approaches Factor, who agrees to buy Carguys' rights under its contracts with its customers. Inasmuch as Factor has become the owner of the accounts (rights to payment), one might jump to the conclusion that Article 9 is irrelevant to the transaction. In doing so, one would be making a serious mistake.

As we have seen, most questions as to the applicability of Article 9 are dominated by the concept of "security interest." We also have seen that although a "security interest" often secures an obligation, the framers of the UCC concluded that other transactions had features that made it unwise to limit the application of Article 9 to transfers of "an interest . . . which secures payment or performance of an obligation." R1–201(37). Thus, "security interest" includes, and Article 9 applies to, consignments. See Chapter 8, Section 1(B), supra.

The term also includes "any interest of a buyer of accounts, chattel paper, a payment intangible, or a promissory note in a transaction that is subject to Article 9." R1–201(37). Article 9 applies broadly to "a *sale* of accounts, chattel paper, payment intangibles, or promissory notes." R9–109(a)(3). But, as we shall see below in Note (3), the sweep of the provision bringing "a sale" of rights to payment (receivables) within Article 9 is slightly narrowed by a set of exclusions from Article 9, see R9–109(d)(4)–(7), as well as by a set of exemptions from the filing requirement. See R9–310(b)(2) and R9–309(2)–(5). (The sharply different treatment of property other than receivables is illustrated by the specific provision in R1–201(37) (3rd sentence) that the property interest of a buyer of *goods* "is not a 'security interest'.")

Revised Article 9 is not the first statute on secured transactions to include outright sales of rights to payment. For most purposes, Former Article 9 abandoned the distinction between an assignment of accounts or chattel paper for collateral purposes and an outright sale.[2] Why? According to Comment 2 to F9–102, "[c]ommercial financing on the basis of accounts and chattel paper is often so conducted that the distinction between a security transfer and a sale is blurred, and a sale of such property is therefore covered by [Article 9] whether intended for security or not[.]"

As Kupfer's description indicates, accounts are used as a source of current capital through two primary types of arrangements. (1) One arrangement is a loan, with repayment secured by the assignment of accounts. This transaction may be expressed as a sale of the account (at a discount), with recourse by the "buyer" against the "seller" to the extent that any obligor (account debtor) fails to pay. (2) A second arrangement provides for the sale of the accounts without a right of recourse; however, even in a "non-recourse" sale (sometimes called **factoring**), the assignor is responsible if an obligor (account debtor) has a claim for breach of warranty or for some other reason returns the goods for credit. Between these two prototypical arrangements lies a range of transactions, tailored to suit the appetite of the parties for accepting (or sharing) the credit risk—the risk that the account debtor will be financially unable to pay the entire amount of the account in a timely manner.

When goods are sold on *secured* credit and the resulting *chattel paper* is sold, as in the case of the automobile financing Prototype in Chapter 7, the parties must agree to allocate not only the credit risk but also the risks attendant to enforcing the security interest that the seller (assignor of the chattel paper) has retained in the goods and assigned to the financer. For an example of some of the ways in which this risk may be allocated, see Form 3.5, supra.

Suppose the drafters of Article 9 had divided the world of accounts and chattel paper financing in two: (1) "recourse" arrangements that would be treated like security interests and would be subject to Article 9 and (2)

---

2. The distinction may affect the assignee's remedies against the assignor. See F9–502(2); F9–504(2); R9–601(g); R9–607(c); R9–615(d); Chapter 12, Section 5, infra.

"non-recourse" arrangements that would be excluded from the Article. A sharp eye would be needed to distinguish between the two arrangements; a fair amount of time and money would be expended on classifying ambiguous arrangements after the fact. The number of ambiguous arrangements might increase, since parties planning these transactions would have incentives to camouflage the substance in order to pull themselves in or out of Article 9.

Indeed, non-UCC law sometimes provides these incentives, adding to the confusion. Even where the transaction in substance clearly is a loan, the lender may wish to make the transaction look like a sale: The lender's return for the loan may exceed the statutory limit for "interest." Usury statutes do not, of course, regulate the *price* for *sales* of accounts. And such a "sale" at a discount coupled with a "warranty" by the "seller" that the account is "good" and will be paid at maturity might conceivably lead a sympathetic (or dull) judge to conclude that the transaction really was a sale and not a usurious loan.

Against this background, it is less surprising that not only Former Article 9 but even the pre-UCC statutes on the assignment of accounts covered not only assignments for security but also outright sales. See 1 Gilmore, Security § 8.7.

(2) Crafting the Even Broader Scope of Revised Article 9: Sales of Payment Intangibles and Promissory Notes. Former Article 9 applied to sales of certain types of receivables—accounts and chattel paper. As defined in F9–106, "accounts" included rights to payments only "for goods sold or leased or for services rendered." Not all rights to payment are accounts or chattel paper as defined under Former Article 9; some are instruments, others are general intangibles. Like accounts and chattel paper, instruments and general intangibles have been the subject of both secured financings and outright sales. For example, to increase its liquid assets (and for regulatory accounting purposes, the details of which are beyond the scope of this discussion), a bank may wish to utilize its portfolio of **credit-card receivables**—obligations of its cardholders to pay for credit they received through the use of the card. See Problem 9.1.3. The reason for including outright sales of payment streams in a law governing secured transactions applies equally to virtually all rights to payment, regardless of the nature of the transaction under which the right arises. However, if these credit-card receivables were "accounts" under Former Article 9, then the Article would have applied regardless of whether the receivables were sold or were used to secure a loan. On the other hand, if the receivables were general intangibles, then Former Article 9 would have applied to the financing only if the receivables secured an obligation.

The exclusion of sales of general intangibles from Former Article 9 gave rise to several problems. The most obvious is that exclusion from Former Article 9 excused assignees from compliance with the public notice (filing) provisions of the Article. See F9–302; Note (1) on Public Notice of Transfers of Receivables, Section 1(E), infra.

The excluded transactions were governed by non-UCC law, typically the common law dealing with the assignment of choses in action. This law may be both hard to find and unclear. (Some of these transactions would have been governed by pre-UCC statutes dealing with assignments of accounts receivable; however, those statutes were repealed in the course of enacting the UCC. See UCC 10–102.) This non-UCC law may include the doctrine of Benedict v. Ratner, 268 U.S. 353, 45 S.Ct. 566, 69 L.Ed. 991 (1925), which held that the grant of a security interest in accounts receivable was fraudulent where the assignor retained unfettered dominion over the proceeds, and which F9–205 repealed insofar as it might have applied to Article 9 transactions (security interests in all kinds of collateral and sales of accounts and chattel paper). For discussions of *Benedict*, see Chapter 7, Section 3(A), supra; and Chapter 10, Section 3(A), infra.

Moreover, as Note (1), supra, suggests, determining whether a transaction should be characterized as a true sale or as a secured transaction often is difficult. In making this determination, courts have used a number of factors, including the existence and nature of recourse against the assignor. According to one writer, the cases addressing the dichotomy "are not easily harmonized, and different readers can argue as to which factors are relevant and which are entitled to the greater weight." S. Schwarcz, Structured Finance 31 (2d ed. 1993). As a result of this uncertainty, prudent parties proceeded on alternative assumptions, thereby further complicating transactions and increasing costs. In a similar vein, classifying certain types of property as accounts, chattel paper, general intangibles, or instruments may be difficult. (Recall Problem 3.3.21, concerning a construction contract.)

The drafters of Revised Article 9 set out to solve these problems. One easy fix—adding sales of general intangibles to the scope of Article 9— would have been disastrous. Many general intangibles (e.g., a franchisee's rights under a franchise agreement) do not consist primarily of rights to payment; sales of these types of property typically are not financing transactions. Accordingly, Revised Article 9 distinguishes "payment intangibles"—i.e., general intangibles "under which the account debtor's principal obligation is a monetary obligation"—from other general intangibles. R9–102(a)(61). Revised Article 9 applies to sales of payment intangibles, but not to sales of other general intangibles. See R9–109(a)(3).

During the drafting process the idea of bringing payment intangibles into Revised Article 9 proved to be popular with those departments of banks and other financial institutions that handle sales of credit-card receivables and other financing transactions. Whether an institution is on the selling or buying side of a given transaction, this change would enable the transaction to proceed with greater certainty, less risk, and less cost. However, other departments of some of the same financial institutions feared that bringing sales of payment intangibles into Revised Article 9 would wreak havoc in the market for **loan participations** and adamantly opposed revising Article 9 along those lines. A loan participation is created when the originator of a loan (the original lender) sells an undivided interest in the loan (and any security for the loan) to a third party, usually another financial institution. See Problem 9.1.4. Banks and other institutional lenders enter into participation agreements with regularity. Often they do so to limit their risk. By selling an interest in certain of its loans, an originator can reduce the amount of credit outstanding to a particular borrower or group of related borrowers, industry, or market sector. The sale of a participation interest may have another advantage: it moves an asset (the right to payment of the loan) off the originating bank's balance sheet and thereby reduces the amount of capital that the originator is required to set aside. (The sale gives rise to this accounting treatment even if, as typically is the case, the participation agreement provides that the originator-assignor retains the exclusive power to enforce the borrower's obligation and that the participant has no direct contractual relationship with the borrower.) Buyers and sellers argued that applying the perfection provisions of Revised Article 9 to sales of loan participations would impose unnecessary delay and costs upon this well functioning, high velocity market.

The Drafting Committee considered and rejected a variety of approaches for distinguishing between sales of loan participations, which would remain outside the scope of Revised Article 9, and sales of other receivables, which would be subject to Revised Article 9. Ultimately the drafters realized that the concern of participants in the loan-participation markets was less with the abstract question of inclusion or exclusion from Revised Article 9 than with the practical impediments that might arise from conditioning perfection on the filing of a financing statement. The elegant solution to this problem was to provide that sales of loan participations are perfected automatically upon attachment. See R9–309(3). To accomplish this result, the Drafting Committee still needed to distinguish sales of loan participations, which were perfected automatically, from sales of other rights to payment, which require some act to perfect. It did so not by defining "loan participation" (a task that proved futile) but rather by defining as an "account" nearly every type of payment stream the Drafting Committee could think of, other than payment streams represented by chattel paper or instruments. Treating all these rights to payment as accounts had the effect of imposing a filing requirement for both outright sales and assignments that secure obligations. It also had the effect of leaving in the residual category of "payment intangibles" the right to repayment of a loan (other than credit-card cash advances, which are accounts, and loans evidenced by chattel paper or an instrument).

Having extended the scope of Revised Article 9 to include sales of accounts (as broadly defined), chattel paper, and payment intangibles, the Drafting Committee decided to extend Revised Article 9 to sales of promissory notes. See R9–109(a)(3). Like sales of payment intangibles, and for the same reason (so as not to interfere with the loan-participation market, inasmuch as many loans in which participations are sold are evidenced by notes), sales of promissory notes are perfected upon attachment. See R9–309(3). For a discussion of whether the exemption of sales of payment intangibles and promissory notes from Article 9's filing requirement offends the Article's public-notice policy, see Note (2) on Public Notice of Transfers of Receivables, Section 1(E), infra.

(3) Narrowing the Scope Through Exclusions. From the outset, the UCC's drafters recognized that the inclusion of all sales of accounts and chattel paper would go too far, in that it would include transactions that, "by their nature, have nothing to do with commercial financing transactions." F9–104(f), Comment 6. Former Article 9 excluded these transactions in accounts and chattel paper; Revised Article 9 contains the same exclusions and extends them to sales of payment intangibles and promissory notes. Excluded transfers include the assignment of a right to payment as part of a sale of the business out of which the receivable arose, the assignment to an assignee who is also obligated to perform under the contract, and the assignment of a single account, payment intangible, or promissory note to an assignee in full or partial satisfaction of a preexisting indebtedness. R9–109(d)(4), (6), and (7). (The term "assignment," used in R9–109(d)(4), (6), and (7), among other provisions, embraces both outright sales of receivables as well as security interests that secure an indebtedness. See R9–102, Comment 26.)

Although these and other exclusions reintroduce the problem of line-drawing that the inclusion of "a sale" eliminates, as a practical matter the problem has not proven to be particularly difficult one under Former Article 9. The amount of litigation on this issue is trivial; it is dwarfed by that concerning the lease/sale distinction and the other ambiguous transactions in goods discussed in Chapter 8, Section 1, supra.

(4) Securitization Transactions: Additional Considerations. Chapter 6, Section 1, supra, provides a thumbnail sketch of secured transactions in a variety of contexts, one of which is "securitization" or "structured finance" transactions. Please review that description of securitization transactions now. The principal issues and concerns in the secured financing of receivables are generally of concern in securitization transactions—i.e., perfection and priority of the SPV's interest in the receivables that it buys from the originator-seller of the receivables. However, in order to ensure that the value of the SPV's interest is unaffected by the originator's financial status, investors in securities issued by the SPV on the strength of the receivables also must have assurances that the purchase by the SPV will be treated as a "true sale" in any bankruptcy proceeding involving the originator. Otherwise, were the purchased receivables to remain property of the originator, and thus property of the originator's bankruptcy estate, the SPV's access to the receivables could be interrupted or delayed. As we shall see, such an interruption or delay could occur even if the SPV's non-ownership security interest in the receivables were perfected. See Chapter 10, Section 1, infra. The investors (through rating agencies assessing the SPV's securities) also seek assurance that any insolvency proceeding of the originator would not be "substantively consolidated" with that of the SPV (i.e., that the debts and assets of the originator would not be combined with those of the SPV as if the two were a single entity).

The necessary assurances on the true sale and substantive consolidation issues (as well as perfection and other important issues) typically are provided by an opinion of counsel. Because the applicable legal standards are general and the outcome depends heavily on the court's judgment in weighing a variety of facts, opinions issued in connection with securitization transactions are extensive, often running in excess of 25 pages. The opinion typically is in the form of a letter addressed to the parties; the letter not only sets forth the opinion itself but also describes the transaction, discusses the applicable law, provides a long list of assumed facts, and applies the law to the facts. Following are examples of the "bottom line" of a substantive consolidation opinion and a true sale opinion of a major law firm:

> *Substantive Consolidation:* Based on the foregoing facts, and subject to the assumptions, qualifications and discussions contained herein and the reasoned analysis of analogous case law (although there is no precedent directly on point), it is our opinion that a United States bankruptcy court, in the event of a case under the Bankruptcy Code involving the Originator as debtor, would not disregard the separate corporate existence of the Buyer so as to consolidate the Buyer's assets and liabilities with those of the Originator.

> *True Sale:* Based on the foregoing facts, and subject to the qualifications and discussion contained herein and the reasoned analysis of analogous case law (although there is no precedent directly on point), it is our opinion that, a court, under the Bankruptcy Code or similar state insolvency law, would hold that the assignment of the Receivables from the Originator to the Buyer pursuant to the Transfer Agreement (even if the purchase price for such Receivables is funded through proceeds of a capital contribution by the Originator) constitutes a true sale, and therefore such Receivables would not constitute property of the estate of the Originator under Section 541(a) of the Bankruptcy Code.

Each of the preceding is followed immediately by the following sentence:

> Our opinion is subject to the further qualifications that (i) the assumptions set forth herein are and continue to be true in all material respects, (ii) there are no additional facts that would materially affect the validity of the assumptions and conclusions set forth herein or upon which this opinion is based and (iii) such case is properly presented and argued.

(5) Classification of Receivables During Transition. Changing the classification of certain receivables, discussed above in Note (2), may result in some headaches during the years of transition from Former Article 9 to the revised Article. For example, if the term "account" is used in a security agreement entered into before Revised Article 9 takes effect, will the term be given the expanded meaning after Revised Article 9's effective date? Will "general intangible" be given the narrowed meaning? See R9–703, Comment 3.

The transition rules are designed to minimize these headaches, but they do not eliminate them. For example, suppose that in 1999 SP–1 perfects a security interest in the debtor's existing and after-acquired accounts. In 2000 SP–2 perfects a security interest in the debtor's right to receive license fees under a patent license. Under Former Article 9, SP–2's collateral is a general intangible; under Revised Article 9 it is an account. SP–1 argues that upon Revised Article 9's effective date, it acquired a perfected security interest in the rights under the license and that its security interest is senior to SP–2's. After all, SP–1 filing against "accounts" preceded SP–2's filing against the license fees. Even if SP–1's security agreement is construed to cover the license fees, the transition rules protect SP–2, which held the only security interest in the license fees under Former Article 9. The rules prevent a security interest from losing priority merely because the collateral has been reclassified under Revised Article 9. See R9–709(a) & Comment 1.

Moreover, SP–2's pre-effective-date filing against "general intangibles" remains effective to perfect a security interest in license fees payable after the effective date, notwithstanding that the collateral has been reclassified as an account. See R9–705(c). SP–2 need not amend its pre-effective-date financing statement to take account of the reclassification of its collateral. Indeed, even if SP–2 is extending credit on the strength not only of the fees owing under a particular license but rather on the strength of all the debtor's existing and after-acquired license fees, SP–2's financing statement will be effective to perfect a security interest in fees arising under licenses entered into after Revised Article 9 takes effect. Id.

Although this rule protects the pre-effective-date filer, it may redound to the detriment of a post-effective-date searcher. A financer who wishes to extend credit to the debtor on the strength of license fees and who finds SP–2's financing statement covering "general intangibles" may be tempted to ignore the financing statement; after all, the collateral in question is "accounts." As you have seen, to ignore the financing statement would be foolish; it remains effective as to collateral that was a general intangible before Revised Article 9 took effect. Thus, to advise clients under Revised Article 9, one must know how the collateral was classified under Former Article 9. (Recall that knowledge of the choice-of-law rules of Former Article 9 likewise was essential to advising clients properly under Revised Article 9. See Chapter 7, Section 4, supra.)

(E) PUBLIC NOTICE OF SECURITY INTERESTS IN RECEIVABLES

Problem 9.1.5. You are partner at a law firm (Firm). One of Firm's clients (Client) owes Firm several hundred thousand dollars, most of which is past due. Client has been manufacturing some custom equipment under one of its larger contracts; it expects to pay Firm once its buyer pays for the equipment. Firm is willing to wait (it has little choice), but it wants to be sure that when Client is paid, Firm will be paid. You prepare a security agreement for Client to sign.

(a) From your past representation of Client, you suspect that Client would be reluctant to have a financing statement filed against it. Do you inform client that Client's authentication of the security agreement ipso facto authorizes Firm to file a financing statement covering the collateral? See R9–509(b)(1).

(b) Assume that the security agreement expressly authorizes the filing of a financing statement against the collateral and that Client is reluctant to have a financing statement filed against it. How would you respond to each of the following alternative suggestions?

(i) Client could sell the account to Firm, instead of granting a security interest in it. See R9–109(d)(7).

(ii) Firm does not need to file a financing statement to protect its security interest. See R9–310(a), (b)(2); R9–309(2) & Comment 4; In re Tri–County Materials, Inc., infra; Note (1) on Public Notice of Transfers of Receivables, infra.

(c) Other than taking the security agreement and filing the financing statement, are there any other steps you would advise Firm to take to bolster its position? See R9–406(a); Note (3) on Rights and Obligations of Account Debtors and Persons Obligated on Promissory Notes, Section 1(F), infra.

———

The following case grapples with F9–302(1)(e) and Comment 5. The language that the court finds troublesome ("significant part," "casual or isolated") appears in R9–309(2) and Comment 4.

In re Tri–County Materials, Inc.

United States District Court, C.D.Illinois, 1990.
114 B.R. 160.

■ MIHM, DISTRICT JUDGE.

FACTS

Tri–County Materials, the Debtor below, operated a sand and gravel pit. Ladd Construction Company was a general contractor which had a contract with the State of Illinois to construct a portion of Interstate 39. Ladd and Tri–County entered into a contract according to which Tri–County would supply Ladd with 100,000 tons of sand and gravel at $2.50 per ton. In order to complete its contractual obligations, Tri–County needed certain equipment to process the sand and gravel from the land it leased. As a result, KMB, Inc. leased equipment to Tri–County for that purpose.
. . .

Although initially the agreement between Tri–County and KMB for the lease of the equipment was oral, that agreement was reduced to writing in June of 1988. In the agreement, Tri–County assigned part of its account with Ladd Construction Company to KMB for the purpose of securing the rental charges which Tri–County owed to KMB. Ladd was notified of the assignment and received bi-weekly notification of the amount due to KMB by Tri–County. KMB did not file a Uniform Commercial Code financing statement regarding the assignment.

Tri–County filed a voluntary petition for bankruptcy under Chapter 11 in October of 1988. At that time, Ladd owed Tri–County $43,413.71 for previously supplied material while Tri–County owed KMB $30,484.

The bankruptcy court found that KMB did not have a security interest in the funds due from Ladd because they had failed to perfect that interest as required under Article 9 of the Uniform Commercial Code. . . .

PERFECTION OF SECURITY INTEREST

Tri–County owed KMB $30,484 at the time of filing bankruptcy. KMB claims that, because Tri–County assigned its right to receive payments from Ladd to the extent that it owed money to KMB, it had a security interest in the money owed to Tri–County.

Ill.Rev.Stat. ch. 26, § 9–302 provides as follows:

(1) a financing statement must be filed to perfect all security interests except the following: . . . (e) an assignment of accounts which does not alone or in conjunction with other assignments to the same assignee transfer a significant part of the outstanding accounts of the assignor.

KMB takes the position that it is entitled to rely on § 9–302(1)(e) because it is not regularly engaged in accounts receivable financing, thus making this a casual and isolated transaction, and because the amount which Tri–County owed to KMB, when compared to the $250,000 which Tri–County was entitled to receive from Ladd was a mere 12%, thus making it an insignificant transfer. Appellant argues that because KMB fails to meet either test it did not have a perfected security interest in the Ladd account.

The burden of proving the applicability of § 9–302(1)(e) rests on the party asserting the exception. See, Consolidated Film Industries v. United States, 547 F.2d 533 (10th Cir.1977). Although the Code does not define "significant part," case law has developed two tests.

The first test is referred to as the percentage test. This test focuses on the size of the assignment in relation to the size of outstanding accounts. In re B. Hollis Knight Co., 605 F.2d 397 (8th Cir.1979); Standard Lumber Company v. Chamber Frames, Inc., 317 F.Supp. 837 (E.D.Ark.1970).

The second test is the "casual or isolated" test. This test is suggested by the language of Comment 5 to UCC § 9–302 which states that:

The purpose of the subsection (e)(1) exemptions is to save from ex post facto invalidation casual or isolated assignments: some accounts receivable statutes have been so broadly drafted that all assignments, whatever their character or purpose, fall within their filing provisions. Under such statute many assignments which no one would think of filing may be subject to invalidation. The subsection (1)(e) exemptions go to that type of assignment. Any person who regularly takes assignments of any debtor's accounts should file.

The totality of circumstances surrounding the transaction determines whether an assignment was casual or isolated. If the transaction was not part of a regular course of commercial financing then under this test filing is not required. The rationale appears to be the reasonableness of requiring a secured creditor to file if assignment of debtor's accounts is a regular part of business and the corresponding unreasonableness of a filing requirement for casual or isolated transactions.

There is no authoritative determination of whether both tests must be met in order to claim the exemption or whether either by itself is sufficient. The bankruptcy court agreed with the *Hollis Knight* court which held that both tests must be met. This Court agrees with that assessment. The statutory language specifically requires that the assignment be an insignificant part of the outstanding account. Thus, at the very least, this test must be met in every instance. A showing of a casual or isolated assignment of a significant part of outstanding accounts would not be entitled to the exemption given this clear statutory requirement. On the other hand, given the comments to the UCC regarding the purpose of this exemption, in a case involving the transfer of an insignificant part of outstanding accounts to a creditor whose regular business is financing, such accounts should not fall within this exemption. Thus it is a logical result of the language and purpose of this section to require that both tests be met.

Under the UCC, an account is "any right to payment for goods sold or leased or for services rendered which is not evidenced by an instrument or chattel paper, whether or not it has been earned by performance." Ill.Rev. Stat. ch. 26, § 9–106.[*]

The Debtor's bankruptcy schedules indicate that Tri–County had ten accounts at the time of the Chapter 11 filing, of which the largest by far was the Ladd contract for $250,000. The assignment to KMB permitted KMB to:

> "request that the Ladd Construction Company ... make any and all payments to [Tri–County] by including on said check payment the name of [KMB] who shall have said check negotiated and endorsed by [Tri–County] and said check shall be deposited in [KMB's] account with [Tri–County's] endorsement, at which time [KMB] shall issue a check to [Tri–County] for the difference between the amount of the check issued and the rental payment owed to [KMB]."

Equipment Rental Agreement p. 5.

It is thus clear that the assignment was not of the entire Ladd account but only of that portion of the account necessary to cover the balance due

---

* [As noted above, Revised Article 9 expands the definition of "account" to include rights to payment arising under many other circumstances. See R9–102(a)(2); Note (2) on Sales of Receivables, Section 1(D), supra.]

to KMB. At the time the parties entered into the Agreement, the total rental amount was estimated at $30,000; the actual figure turned out to be $30,484. The ratio of the amount assigned to the total account, even assuming that the Ladd contract was the *only* account, is approximately 12%.

Although there is no bright line marking the division between significant and insignificant, the 12% figure is surely on the "insignificant" side. See, Standard Lumber Co. v. Chamber Frames, Inc., 317 F.Supp. 837 (D.C.Ark.1970) (16% insignificant). Thus, the first test, contrary to what the bankruptcy court found, has been satisfied. The bankruptcy court based its finding on the assumption that Tri–County had assigned the entire Ladd account to KMB, an assumption that is not supported by the record.

The record also shows without contradiction that KMB was not in the business of accepting contract assignments, nor had either party to the assignment engaged in such a transaction at other times. The bankruptcy court found that despite the "isolated" nature of this assignment, it was "a classic secured transaction," Op. p. 9, and thus failed to fall within the "casual and isolated" exception to the filing requirement.

This Court agrees with that assessment. This is not the type of "casual" transaction in which reasonable parties would fail to see the importance of filing. Rather, it was evidenced by a formal, written agreement between two corporations; notice of the agreement was sent to Ladd, and other conduct engaged in by KMB indicates the degree of formality attached to it. This is the type of transaction for which the UCC requires filing in order to perfect.

Because KMB failed to perfect its security interest, this Court affirms the bankruptcy court's ruling.

CONCLUSION

As stated above, this Court AFFIRMS the bankruptcy court in its finding that . . . KMB did not have a perfected security interest in the Ladd account.

NOTES ON PUBLIC NOTICE OF TRANSFERS OF RECEIVABLES

(1) Construing R9–309(2). As the *Tri–County Materials* case indicates, courts have disagreed over the meaning of F9–302(1)(e), which exempted certain transfers of accounts from the general rule that filing is necessary to perfect a security interest. The range of opinions is even broader than *Tri–County Materials* suggests. See, e.g., Park Avenue Bank v. Bassford, 232 Ga. 216, 205 S.E.2d 861 (1974) (dollar amount of assigned accounts "significant" without regard to percentage); Architectural Woods, Inc. v. Washington, 88 Wn.2d 406, 562 P.2d 248 (1977) (en banc) (applying only "casual and isolated" test).

One way to evaluate the proper scope of the exemption is to determine which types of transfers do not implicate the need for public notice. This, in turn leads one to examine the reason or reasons underlying the general rule. Note (3) on Perfection by Filing, Chapter 7, Section 3, supra, explores a number of these reasons. Please review it now. Do the reasons justifying a filing requirement for security interests in tangible collateral apply equally to secured parties (including buyers, see R9–102(a)(72)(D)) whose collateral consists of intangible property, such as accounts? If so, does any of these reasons support an exemption for a transfer of accounts having insubstantial value? Insubstantial value relative to the assignor's total accounts? Does any of these reasons support an exemption for "casual or isolated assignments"? Assignments as to which "no one would think of filing"? R9–309, Comment 4. Assignments as to which only professionals would think of filing?

Do you suppose the drafters of Revised Article 9 were familiar with the problem of statutory construction raised in *Tri–County Materials* and elsewhere? If so, how do you explain the fact that the drafters did absolutely nothing to solve it? See R9–309(2) & Comment 4. Will the problem be more or less likely to arise under Revised Article 9 than it did under Former Article 9? Consider, in this regard, that the exception in R9–309(2) applies to assignments of payment intangibles as well as to assignments of accounts and that the definition of "account" has itself been expanded.

(2) "Automatic" Perfection of Sales of Payment Intangibles and Promissory Notes. We have seen that, largely in response to the concerns of participants in the loan-participation market, the sale of payment intangibles and promissory notes is perfected upon attachment, without the need for an additional public-notice step. See R9–309(3), (4) (discussed in Note (2) on Sales of Receivables, Section 1(D), supra). Does this approach undermine the integrity of the filing system and the need for public notice? Arguably not. Every potential buyer of a loan participation from a bank knows that the bank sells participations. The filing of a financing statement covering "general intangibles" or "loan" gives no information. Even a financing statement that describes a particular loan is unlikely to give sufficient information to justify the delay that might result if sales of participations routinely were preceded by a search of the files against the seller. Under Former Article 9, a prospective buyer of a loan participation had no way to insure that it was buying something that had not been sold before. Participants took this risk and were forced to rely on the honesty of the seller (typically the originating bank that made the loan to the borrower) to minimize it.

Revised Article 9's automatic-perfection rule applicable to sales of payment intangibles does not exacerbate the situation. Moreover, by expanding the category of accounts to include many rights to payment other than those for goods sold or leased or services rendered, *Revised Article 9 actually increases the sale transactions in which filing is required as a condition of perfection.* In some cases, doubt may arise concerning whether the collateral is a payment intangible or an account or, if the collateral is a payment intangible, whether the transaction a sale or an assignment that secures an obligation. The parties most likely to engage in the assignment of rights to payment are likely to be sophisticated and to file in doubtful cases. By doing so, for very little cost they can protect against the possibility that the collateral is an account or that the transaction is the assignment of a payment intangible to secure an obligation.

(F) COLLECTION OF RECEIVABLES

Problem 9.1.6. Assume the facts in Problem 9.1.2, supra, in which Carguys sold its accounts to Factor. (Ignore the facts in paragraphs (a)-(d), dealing with Lean.) Assume also that Factor perfected its security interest by filing and that the agreement between Factor and Carguys gives Factor the right to notify Carguys's customers to make payment directly to Factor.

(a) Two weeks after its account is sold to Factor, Customer #1 pays Carguys in full. Is Factor out of luck? See R9–406(a); Note (3) on Rights and Obligations of Account Debtors and Persons Obligated on Promissory Notes, infra.

(b) Would the result in part (a) change if, prior to paying Carguys, Customer #1 received a letter from Factor stating as follows: "You are hereby advised that all amounts owing from yourself to Carguys, Inc., have been sold to the undersigned. Kindly remit all future payments to the undersigned at the address shown on the letterhead."?

(c) Would the result in part (a) change if the letter described in part (b) did not contain the second sentence? Compare Vacura v. Haar's Equipment, Inc., 364 N.W.2d 387 (Minn.1985) (notification of assignment will not cut off account debtor's right to pay assignor unless it contains explicit direction that payment is to be made to assignee) with First National Bank of Rio Arriba v. Mountain States Telephone & Telegraph Co., 91 N.M. 126, 571 P.2d 118 (1977) (unconditional language of assignment, which was accepted in writing by account debtor, was notice that payment was to be made to assignee). Courts often have read F9–318(3), the predecessor to R9–406(a), strictly, to protect account debtors from having to pay twice.

(d) Customer #2 received the letter described in part (b) but refuses to pay Factor, citing a provision of its contract with Carguys stating that "this contract is not assignable." Is Factor out of luck? See R9–406(d).

(e) Would the result in part (d) change if Carguys had retained a purchase-money security interest in the diagnostic equipment purchased by Customer #2 and had sold Factor the secured rights to payment? See R9–406(d).

(f) Customer #3 received the letter described in part (b) but refuses to pay Factor, claiming that it doesn't believe Carguys has stooped so low as to "hock its receivables." What, if anything, can Factor do? See R9–406(c). What can Customer #3 do if it remains dubious?

(g) Customer #4 received the letter from Factor. In response it informed Factor that, two weeks before it received the letter, the equipment it bought from Carguys malfunctioned. A manufacturing defect caused sparks to fly from the equipment; these sparks set off a fire causing damage to Customer's repair facility, which damage required Customer to close the facility for three days. Accordingly, Customer #4 not only refuses to pay for the equipment (which does not operate) but also seeks compensation from Factor for property damage and loss of profits.

(i) Is Customer obligated to pay for the equipment? See R9–404(a); Note (4) on Rights and Obligations of Account Debtors and Persons Obligated on Promissory Notes, infra.

(ii) Is Customer entitled to compensation from Factor for its loss? See R9–404(b); Note (4) on Rights and Obligations of Account Debtors and Persons Obligated on Promissory Notes, infra.

(h) Would the result in part (g) change if Customer #4 had paid in full for the equipment that malfunctioned and the account that Factor was assigned was for the sale of a different item of equipment? See R9–404(a).

(i) Would the result in part (h) change if the equipment malfunctioned three days *after* Customer #4 received the letter? See R9–404(a); UCC 2–725 (regarding when a cause of action for breach of warranty accrues). Would it make any difference in part (h) if both items of equipment were the subject of a single contract between Carguys and Customer? If there was a master agreement containing general terms, supplemented by separate agreements containing the specifications for each item of equipment?

NOTES ON RIGHTS AND OBLIGATIONS OF ACCOUNT DEBTORS AND PERSONS OBLIGATED ON PROMISSORY NOTES

(1) "Account Debtor"; Person Obligated on a Promissory Note. The value of a receivable as collateral depends upon the likelihood that the person obligated to pay actually will perform its obligation in full, in a timely manner. The Notes that follow address matters that go to the heart of a receivable's value: the rights and obligations of persons who are obligated to pay. Before turning to those matters, a few words about terminology: Not every person obligated to pay a receivable is an "account debtor." Rather the term is limited to "a person obligated on an account, chattel paper, or general intangible." R9–102(a)(3). Thus it excludes persons obligated on a promissory note or other instrument. In one respect, the definition of "account debtor" distinguishes between negotiable and nonnegotiable promissory notes: It excludes "persons obligated to pay a negotiable instrument, even if the instrument constitutes part of chattel paper," but includes persons obligated to pay a nonnegotiable note that constitutes part of chattel paper. Id. Try to keep these distinctions in mind as you study the following Notes.

(2) Secured Party's Right to Notify Obligated Persons. As the excerpt from Kupfer, supra, suggests, some receivables financing is done on a notification basis, i.e., the obligated persons are notified to remit payment directly to the assignee (secured party). Not surprisingly, Article 9 provides that such an agreement is effective against the debtor. See R9–607(a)(1).

When receivables financing is done on a non-notification basis, upon the debtor's (assignor's) default the secured party is entitled to require obligated persons to make payment to the secured party, regardless of whether the debtor has not agreed to the procedure. See id.

Chapter 12, Section 5, infra, discusses the duties of a secured party and rights of a debtor with respect to the secured party's collection of receivables. The Notes that follow address the rights and obligations of an account debtor or other obligated person.

(3) The Obligated Person's Problem: Whom to Pay? Whereas R9–607(a) governs the secured party's *right*, as against the debtor, to notify a person obligated on a receivable, it does not govern the *obligation* of the person receiving the notification.

Account debtors. When the receivable is an account, chattel paper, or payment intangible, and the secured party is entitled to notify the account debtor, R9–406 sets forth the circumstances under which the account debtor must pay the secured party, who may be a stranger to the transaction, rather than the assignor (debtor), with whom the account debtor has dealt. Knowing the proper party to pay is (or should be) a major concern for the account debtor. If an account debtor pays the wrong party, the account debtor does not discharge its obligation on the contract and will have to pay again—this time to the proper party. (Although the mistaken account debtor will be entitled to recover its payment from a party who is not entitled to it, see Restatement of Restitution § 17 (1937), the account debtor would prefer not to litigate the issue, particularly against a person who wrongfully kept funds to which it was not entitled.) R9–406(a) contains what sometimes is referred to as the "notification" rule: An account debtor becomes obligated to pay an assignee upon receipt of a notification "that the amount due or to become due has been assigned and that payment is to be made to the assignee." R9–406(a). Subsections (b) and (c) help protect the account debtor from having to pay twice.

The account debtor on a contract may wish to avoid entirely the risk of paying the wrong party by simply making the contract non-assignable, or by conditioning assignment on its advance consent. However, R9–406(d)(1) generally makes provisions of this kind, which are not terribly common, "ineffective." An "ineffective" prohibition on assignment will not prevent the assignment from taking effect; that is, the prohibition will not prevent a security interest from attaching to the receivable. The account debtor and assignor might be tempted to circumvent this rule by agreeing that the assignor's violation of the prohibition on assignment constitutes a default under the contract, excusing the account debtor from its contractual obligations. Were this agreement to be given effect, the value of the receivable as collateral would be substantially impaired. Does Article 9 give effect to this agreement? See R9–406(d)(2).

R9–406(d) is one of several UCC rules promoting the free alienability of rights to payment and other (primarily intangible) property. These rules, which appear in R9–406 through R9–409, enable a debtor to create (and, in some cases, a secured party to enforce) a security interest in certain property that otherwise is non-assignable, either by operation of law or by contract. Cf. R9–401(b) (debtor's rights in collateral may be transferred notwithstanding a prohibition in the security agreement). The rules apply to accounts, chattel paper, promissory notes, payment intangibles, letter-of-credit rights, rights under leases of personal property, and the lessor's residual interest in leased goods. The assignability of property not covered by R9–406 through R9–409 is governed by law other than Article 9. See R9–401(a).

The rules in R9–406 through R9–409 are very complex and must be read with unusual care. The complexity is the direct consequence of the diversity of intangible property and the drafters' decision not to interfere with existing transaction patterns. For example, the borrower of a large sum may seek the lender's agreement not to assign, or sell participation interests in, the loan. The borrower may be motivated by a concern that, if a dispute arises or the loan goes into default, the assignee, who usually is a stranger, will be less accommodating than the originator, with whom the borrower typically has a pre-existing relationship. Even if the originator is unwilling to restrict its ability to assign the loan, the originator may have reason to agree with the borrower that the borrower need not make payment to an assignee: An originator may be concerned that an assignee (participant) will establish its own business relationship with the originator's customer. For this reason, among others, participation agreements typically provide that the originator–assignor retains the exclusive power to enforce the borrower's obligation and that the participant has no direct contractual relationship with the borrower.

Article 9 balances the policy of free alienability of rights to payment with respect for these practices in the loan and loan-participation market. When a payment intangible has been *sold* and the seller and account debtor so agree (and the agreement is enforceable under law other than Article 9), even an account debtor who has received a notification under R9–406(a) may discharge its obligation by paying the seller-assignor. See R9–406(b)(2). To the same end, R9–406(d), which renders ineffective a contractual restriction on assignment of a payment intangible, does not apply to sales of payment intangibles. See R9–406(e). R9–408 applies instead. Like R9–406(d), which applies to security interests that secure an obligation, R9–408(a) overrides a contractual restriction on the sale of a payment intangible. But whereas R9–406(d) overrides contractual restrictions for all purposes, including for purposes of enforcement against the account debtor (here, the borrower), R9–408 is much more solicitous of the bargain between the lender and borrower. When a payment intangible is sold and law other than Article 9 would give effect to the contractual restriction on assignment but Article 9 does not, then the buyer's security interest in the payment intangible may not be enforced against the borrower. See R9–408(d). Under these circumstances, the borrower may ignore the assignment (sale) and render performance to the lender with whom it dealt.

Persons Obligated on a Promissory Note. We have seen that R9–406(a) provides that whether an account debtor has received a notification determines whether the account debtor must pay the assignor-debtor or assignee-secured party. But R9–406(a) applies only to account debtors; it does not apply to persons obligated on a promissory note or other instrument. What law does apply? If the promissory note is negotiable, then UCC Article 3 determines whom the maker (or other person obligated on the instrument) must pay to discharge its obligation: "[A]n instrument is paid to the extent payment is made . . . to a person entitled to enforce the instrument." UCC 3–602(a). A person normally must be in possession of an instrument to qualify as a person entitled to enforce. See UCC 3–301. If the promissory note is not negotiable, then law other than the UCC determines whom a person obligated on the instrument must pay to discharge its obligation.

Like an account debtor, the maker of a nonnegotiable promissory note may wish to avoid entirely the risk of paying the wrong party by making the note non-assignable, or by conditioning assignment on its advance consent. Article 9 deals with provisions of this kind, which are very unusual,[3] in the same way it deals with restrictions on the assignment of payment intangibles: They are ineffective to prevent a security interest (whether securing an obligation or arising from a sale) from attaching to the promissory note, and they are ineffective to cause the assignor's violation of the prohibition to constitute a default under the note, excusing the maker (or other obligated person) from its obligation to pay. See R9–406(d), (e); R9–408(a), (b). However, when a promissory note is sold and law other than Article 9 would give effect to the contractual restriction on assignment but Article 9 does not, then the buyer's security interest in the promissory note may not be enforced against the maker. See R9–408(d). Under these circumstances, the maker may ignore the assignment (sale) and render performance to the lender with whom it dealt.

(4) The Secured Party's Problem: Claims and Defenses of the Obligated Person.

Account debtors. As we explored to some extent in Chapter 1, Section 4, R9–404(a) generally reflects the *nemo dat* principle. The assignee (secured party) generally takes its interest in the account subject to defenses of the account debtor. If, for example, the account debtor has a defense to payment, it may assert the defense against the assignee. By notifying the account debtor of the assignment, the assignee may deprive the account debtor of certain defenses that may arise in the future. See R9–404(a)(2). And, as we also saw in Chapter 1, Section 4, an assignee may take free of nearly all defenses if the account debtor agrees. See R9–403(b). (Of course, the account debtor retains its rights against the assignor.)

Suppose an account debtor makes payments to the assignee and then discovers that the goods are worth only half what the account debtor has paid for them. The account debtor seeks to recover the overpayment from the assignee. Had the account debtor known of the defense before payment,

---

3. Negotiable notes containing a restriction on assignment are rare as hen's teeth. Do you understand why?

it could have asserted a defense to the assignee's demand for payment. Do the legal positions of the account debtor and assignee change simply because the account debtor discovers the goods are defective after it has paid for them?

Yes, according to R9–404(b). Although R9–404(a) provides that an assignee takes subject to an account debtor's "claims" as well as "defenses," "the claim of an account debtor against an assignor may be asserted against an assignee under subsection (a) only to reduce the amount the account debtor owes." R9–404(b). What explains this result, which comports with the pre-UCC common law? See Restatement of Restitution § 14(2) (1937) ("An assignee of a non-negotiable chose in action who, having paid value therefor, has received payment from the obligor is under no duty to make restitution although the obligor had a defense thereto, if the transferee made no misrepresentation and did not have notice of the defense.").

The First Circuit had occasion to address some of these issues under Former Article 9 in Michelin Tires (Canada) Ltd. v. First National Bank of Boston, 666 F.2d 673 (1st Cir.1981). Michelin entered into a contract for the design and installation of a carbon black handling and storage system, which was to form part of a Michelin tire factory in Nova Scotia. Michelin agreed to pay the contractor, JCC, periodic progress payments. JCC granted a security interest in its rights under the contract to FNB. FNB notified Michelin of the assignment, and Michelin paid FNB a total of $724,197.60. Thereafter, Michelin discovered that JCC had submitted fictitious invoices and fraudulent sworn statements showing that JCC had paid its subcontractors. JCC filed a bankruptcy petition, and Michelin sued to recover the payments from FNB.

The majority found that Michelin was not entitled to recover under principles of restitution and that F9–318(1), despite providing that an assignee takes subject to "claims," did not create affirmative rights of recovery against an assignee who did not actively participate in the fraudulent transactions. (Former Article 9 contained no analogue to R9–404(b), which expressly limits an account debtor's rights of recovery.) The court found this result to be consistent with sound policy:

> While it is our judgment that analysis of the statutory language, taken in context, indicates that no affirmative right was contemplated and further that those cases that have permitted such a right are factually inapposite, we also believe it would be unwise to permit such suits as a matter of policy. [A]llowing affirmative suits would "make every Banker, who has taken an assignment of accounts for security purposes, a deep pocket surety for every bankrupt contractor in the state to whom it had loaned money."

> We are unwilling to impose such an obligation on the banks of the Commonwealth without some indication that this represents a considered policy choice. By making the bank a surety, not only will accounts receivable financing be discouraged, but transaction costs will undoubtedly increase for everyone. The case at hand provides a good example.

In order to protect themselves, FNB would essentially be forced to undertake the precautionary measures that Michelin attempted to use, independent observation by an intermediary and sworn certifications by the assignor. FNB would have to supervise every construction site where its funds were involved to ensure performance and payment. We simply do not believe that the banks are best suited to monitor contract compliance. The party most interested in adequate performance would be the other contracting party, not the financier. Given this natural interest, it seems likely to us that while the banks will be given additional burdens of supervision, there would be no corresponding reduction in vigilance by the contracting parties, thus creating two inspections where there was formerly one. Costs for everyone thus increase, without any discernible benefit. It is also difficult to predict the full impact a contrary decision would have on the availability of accounts receivable financing in general.

Our holding, of course, is not that § 9–318 *prohibits* claims against the assignee. We hold merely that § 9–318 concerns only the preservation of defenses to the assignee's claims and, as such, is wholly inapposite in an affirmative suit against an assignee.

666 F.2d at 679–80.

In dissent, Judge Bownes concluded that under F9–318(1)(a), "an assignee's rights to retain payments made to it under an assignment are subject to, or are exposed to, affirmative actions brought by the account debtor to recover payments mistakenly made."

This interpretation of section 9–318(1)(a), that the account debtor has rights of action against the assignee, is the fairest way to reconcile the rights of account debtors and secured creditors, particularly where, as here, credit is advanced through a line of credit. This case boils down to the question of whether the secured creditor or the account debtor should bear the cost of not finding out that JCC falsely claimed that it had paid its subcontractors. The secured creditor is in a better position than the account debtor to determine whether the assignor/borrower is complying with the terms of the contract in which the creditor has an interest. The reason is that the secured creditor can employ an effective sanction without having to initiate litigation and without risking any loss itself to ensure compliance; it can threaten to cut off credit unless it is satisfied with the borrower's performance. The other party, the account debtor, has no similar sanction. If he is not satisfied, he must litigate and bear the expense of litigation and the sure delay in completion of the contract. The creditor/assignee is not deterred from enforcing compliance by such costs. Obviously, either the secured creditor or the account debtor can make inquiries regarding compliance with the contract, but at some point both will have to rely on the representations of others, which creates opportunities for fraud, as occurred here. The secured creditor is accustomed to looking over the borrower's shoulder on an ongoing basis and can check compliance. By virtue of his control over credit, the creditor can ensure compliance with the contract. The account debtor can only investigate and if it holds up payments, it puts the contract in jeopardy.

666 F.2d at 684–85.

Which view do you find more persuasive? Had JCC negligently constructed the facility, do you suppose Judge Bownes would have permitted Michelin to recover compensatory damages from FNB? See F9–317, which is substantially identical to R9–402 (mere existence of a security interest does not impose contract or tort liability upon the secured party for the debtor's acts or omissions).

Persons Obligated on a Promissory Note. We have seen that the right to enforce the obligation of a person to pay an instrument is subject to most claims and defenses. See UCC 3–305(a); Chapter 1, Section 4, supra. However, a person who makes a negotiable instrument waives most claims and defenses as against a holder in due course. See UCC 3–305(b); Chapter 1, Section 4, supra. (Recall that a person cannot be a holder in due course of a note bearing the legend required by Federal Trade Commission Rule 433, 16 C.F.R. art 433. See UCC 3–104(d).) On the question whether the maker of a negotiable promissory note may obtain affirmative recovery from an assignee, UCC Article 3 yields a result consistent with *Michelin Tires*, supra, and R9–404(b): "[T]he claim of the obligor may be asserted against a transferee of the instrument only to reduce the amount owing on the instrument at the time the action is brought." UCC 3–305(a)(3). The claims and defenses available to the maker of a non-negotiable promissory note (other than one that is part of chattel paper) is governed by non-UCC law.

(5) Consumer Account Debtors. The account-debtor rules in R9–403 through 9–406 are subject to non-Article 9 law that establishes a different rule for an account debtor who is an individual and who incurred the obligation primarily for personal, family, or household purposes. See, e.g., R9–403(e); R9–404(c); R9–406(h). This non-Article 9 law includes not only federal law (which would preempt in any event) but also state statutes, judicial decisions, and administrative rules and regulations.

As we saw in Chapter 1, Section 4, Federal Trade Commission Rule 433, 16 C.F.R. art. 433 makes it an "unfair and deceptive trade practice" for the seller of goods to fail to incorporate in a contract of sale to a consumer a legend that will preserve the buyer's defenses against a financing agency to which the contract is assigned. In addition, if the seller receives the proceeds from a direct loan made to the buyer by a financing agency to which the seller "refers consumers" or with whom the seller "is affiliated . . . by common control, contract, or business arrangement," the loan contract must include a similar legend. 16 C.F.R. 433.1(d); 433.2. In both cases the legend must state also that the buyer's recovery against an assignee with respect to claims and defenses against the seller may not exceed amounts paid by the buyer under the contract. See 16 C.F.R. 433.2. We also saw in Chapter 1 that a substantial body of case law holds that FTC regulations do not ipso facto modify private rights. Thus, when a contract or note fails to include the required legend, the buyer may be unable to assert defenses against an assignee if other law, such as the UCC, so provides. Revised Article 9 changes this result: Under R9–403(d) an assignee of such a contract takes subject to the consumer account debtor's claims and defenses to the same extent as it would have if the writing had contained the required notice. Similarly, a consumer account debtor has the same right to an affirmative recovery from an assignee of such a contract as the consumer would have had against the assignee had the record contained the required notice. See R9–404(d).

SECTION 2.   PURCHASERS OF CHATTEL PAPER, INSTRUMENTS, AND DOCUMENTS

Introductory Note. Earlier in these materials we considered the rights of purchasers (including Article 9 secured parties) who obtain the status of a holder in due course of a negotiable instrument or a holder to whom a negotiable document of title has been duly negotiated. See Chapter 1, Sections 4 and 5, supra. As we saw, HDC's and HTWANDOTHBDN's take free of competing claims to negotiable instruments and negotiable documents. See UCC 3–306; UCC 7–502(1). Protected purchasers of investment securities acquire similar rights. See UCC 8–303.

R9–331 provides expressly that the rules of Articles 3, 7, and 8, which allow certain purchasers to cut off earlier-in-time claims to negotiable instruments, documents of title, and investment securities, override any rule of Article 9 that otherwise would have given priority to an earlier-in-time security interest. R9–331 merely refers and defers to other UCC Articles for applicable priority rules. Article 9 also provides supplementary priority rules that favor certain ordinary course purchasers of chattel paper and instruments. See R9–330. The following Problems and Notes consider the roles of R9–330 and R9–331 in the Article 9 priority scheme.

Problem 9.2.1. A metals dealer ("Dealer") had a surplus stock of chromium, a valuable metal, in its own warehouse. Dealer needed additional working capital. On June 1 Dealer borrowed $50,000 from Firstbank. At the same time, Dealer signed a security agreement covering the chromium and a proper financing statement; Firstbank immediately filed the financing statement in the proper office.

On July 1 Dealer delivered the chromium to Warehouse. Warehouse issued and delivered to Dealer a warehouse receipt calling for the delivery of the chromium to the order of Dealer.

On July 2 Dealer borrowed $50,000 from Secondbank. Dealer signed a security agreement covering the chromium and the warehouse receipt. Dealer indorsed and delivered the warehouse receipt to Secondbank. Secondbank did not search the UCC filing records and knew nothing about Firstbank's earlier security interest in the same chromium.

(a) Is each bank's security interest in the chromium a perfected security interest? See R9–310(a); UCC 7–104; R9–312(c), (a); R9–313(a).

(b) Which bank has the senior security interest? On what basis? See R9–312(c); R9–331; UCC 7–501; UCC 7–502; UCC 7–503.

(c) What could the junior party have done differently to ensure its seniority?

(d) What are the policy justifications for the ranking of priorities in this case?

Problem 9.2.2. In the setting of the Prototype on receivables financing, Section 1(B), supra, Carguys created an "all-assets" security interest in favor of Eastinghome. Eastinghome perfected its security interest by filing. Carguys is the payee of a negotiable promissory note, payable "to the order of Carguys, Inc.," in the face amount of $25,000. The note becomes due and payable on May 15, 2003. Section 4.1 of the Security Agreement (Form 9.2) requires Carguys to deliver the note to Eastinghome. Nevertheless, faced with a "cash flow problem," on January 10, 2002, Carguys delivers the note to Redemption Bank to secure a loan for $18,000. Redemption Bank did not search the UCC filing records before making the purchase.

(a) Assume Carguys indorsed the note "to Redemption Bank" before delivering it. Does each lender hold a perfected security interest? See R9–308(a); R9–102(a)(47); R9–203(b); R9–312(a); R9–313(a). Who has the better claim to the note, Eastinghome or Redemption Bank? See R9–322(a), (f); R9–331; UCC 3–306; UCC 3–302(a), (b); UCC 3–204(a); UCC 3–205(a); UCC 1–201(20); Note (1) on Purchasers of Instruments, infra. What could the losing party have done to protect itself?

(b) Assume Carguys did not indorse the note before delivering it to Redemption Bank. Who has the better claim to the note, Eastinghome or Redemption Bank? See R9–322(a), (f); R9–330(d) & Comment 7; R9–102(a)(43); UCC 3–306; UCC 3–102(b); Note (1) on Purchasers of Instruments, infra. What could the losing party have done to protect itself?

(c) What result in parts (a) and (b) if the note were payable "to Carguys, Inc."? See R9–102(a)(47); UCC 3–104(a).

Problem 9.2.3. In need of more money to lend to its young, professional clientele, Yuppie Finance Co. approached Firstbank. In a written agreement, Firstbank agreed to purchase at a discount, and Yuppie agreed to sell, Yuppie's entire portfolio of loans. The loans are evidenced by notes payable "to Yuppie Finance Co." To avoid administrative costs, Firstbank permitted Yuppie to retain possession of the sold notes and collect them on Firstbank's behalf as they came due. Firstbank also did not file a financing statement.

(a) Is Firstbank's interest in the notes subject to defeat by a lien creditor of Yuppie's? See R9–317(a)(2); R9–310(b)(2); R9–309(4).

(b) Shortly after the sale, in violation of its agreement with Firstbank, Yuppie purported to sell one of Firstbank's notes to Secondbank, which took possession of the note upon paying for it. Which bank has the better claim to the note? See R9–109(a)(3); R9–102(a)(65); R9–309(a)(4); R9–318;

R9–203(b)(2); R9–322(a), (g); R9–330(d); Note (1) on Purchasers of Instruments, infra. What could the losing bank have done to protect itself?

Problem 9.2.4. Dalrymple borrowed $100,000 from Secondbank on an unsecured basis. After suffering financial reversals, Dalrymple defaulted on the obligation to repay. As part of an effort to restructure its debts out of court, Dalrymple offers to bring interest current, make a $20,000 reduction in principal, and secure the $80,000 balance with one of its major assets, a $1,400,000 promissory note payable to Dalrymple's order. Firstbank holds a possessory security interest in the note to secure a claim of $750,000. Secondbank is content to take a junior security interest but wishes to insure that its security interest is perfected and its ability to turn the note into cash is protected.

Advise Secondbank. In particular, consider:

(i) How should Secondbank perfect its security interest while the note is held by Firstbank? See R9–312(a); R9–313(a), (c), (d), (f).

(ii) What will happen to the note when Dalrymple satisfies the debt to Firstbank?

(iii) How will Secondbank be able to enforce its security interest if Dalrymple defaults on the secured obligation? See R9–607(a), (e); R9–609; UCC 3–412; UCC 3–301; R9–610; R9–313(g).

(iv) Would it be necessary or helpful to obtain Firstbank's assistance in effectuating the transaction? Why might Firstbank be willing to cooperate? What concerns might it have? What might be done to alleviate those concerns?

NOTES ON PURCHASERS OF INSTRUMENTS

(1) Conflicting Priorities in Instruments under Article 9. Under Former Article 9, as under the common law, long-term perfection of a security interest in a note could be achieved only by the secured party's taking possession of the collateral. (Short-term perfection could be achieved under circumstances similar to those set forth in R9–315 and R9–312, which derive from similar provisions of Former Article 9.) Revised Article 9 makes a dramatic break from the past by permitting perfection in instruments, even negotiable instruments, to be achieved by filing a financing statement. It does so largely to enable transactions to proceed when the costs of the secured party's taking possession of large numbers of notes would be prohibitive. See R9–312, Comment 2.

Under existing practices, those who buy or lend against a note typically take possession. The drafters of Revised Article 9 did not wish to upset these practices. If the note is negotiable is negotiated to the secured party under circumstances such that the secured party becomes a holder in due course ("HDC"), then the secured party will take free of all claims to the instrument, including competing security interests. See R9–331(a); UCC 3–306. A purchaser who acquires a negotiable instrument with knowledge of an earlier security interest cannot be an HDC and, consequently, would not be entitled to priority under R9–331. See UCC 3–302; UCC 3–306; R9–331. Similarly, a purchaser who acquires a nonnegotiable instrument cannot become an HDC. Under R9–330(d), however, the purchaser may obtain priority over the earlier security interest notwithstanding the purchaser's knowledge. See R9–330, Comment 7.

In fact, R9–330(d) provides strong protection for most purchasers of notes who take possession. Compare the requirements for priority under R9–330(d) with those in UCC 3–302(a) for achieving HDC status and its attendant freedom from all claims to the instrument. In particular, compare the value and scienter requirements. With respect to the former, recall that the definition of "value" in Article 3 is narrower than the definition generally applicable under the UCC. Compare UCC 3–303(a) with UCC 1–201(44). The concept, in R9–330(d), of "without knowledge that the purchase violates the rights of the secured party" derives from the analogous concept in the definition of "buyer in ordinary course of business" in R1–201(9).

What accounts for the generous treatment R9–330(d) affords to non-HDC's? Why does R9–330(d) protect certain persons who take an instrument with actual knowledge of a conflicting claim to it? In considering these questions, compare the scope of protection that R9–330(d) affords with that of UCC 3–306.

Unlike Former Article 9, Revised Article 9 governs the outright sale of certain instruments—specifically, "promissory notes" (as defined in R9–102(a)(65)). See Section 1(D), supra. As with accounts and chattel paper, the buyer of promissory notes holds a security interest. See R1–201(37). But unlike the case of accounts or chattel paper, the security interest arising from a sale of promissory notes is automatically perfected upon attachment. See R9–309(a)(4). The sale of property normally divests the seller of any interest in whatever the buyer bought. As we saw above in Section 1(D), however, if a buyer (B–1) of accounts or chattel paper fails to perfect its security interest, the seller retains the *power*, even if not the right, to resell the accounts or chattel paper to a third person (B–2) who can acquire good title to them. See R9–318(b) & Comment 3; R9–322(a). However, if B–1 perfects its security interest before the sale to B–2, then B–2 acquires no interest in the sold accounts or chattel paper. See R9–318(a).

Problem 9.2.3 concerns double-dealing by the seller of a promissory note. Because the sale to Firstbank was perfected (automatically), Yuppie retained no interest in the sold notes. See R9–318(a). Firstbank owned them free and clear of any interest that Yuppie had held. How, then, can Secondbank's security interest attach? R9–203(b)(2) gives the answer: Although Yuppie retained no legal or equitable interest in the sold note, it did enjoy "the power to transfer rights in the collateral to a secured party." The fact that R9–330(d) enables qualifying purchasers of instruments to take priority over earlier-perfected security interests necessarily means that the sellers of the instruments have power to transfer rights in the notes to the purchasers.

(2) "Transferable Records" under UETA. As we have just seen, an instrument differs from an account and payment intangible in that a second-in-time purchaser can achieve priority over an earlier-perfected security interest by taking possession of the paper under R9–330(d) or, if the instrument is negotiable, by becoming an HDC under UCC 3–302. Businesses increasingly are using electronic, rather than paper, records to evidence transactions. Although electronic notes are uncommon today, they may well become more common in the future. Should those who finance this kind of intangible collateral have the opportunity to achieve non-temporal priority (i.e., priority not based on priority in the time) analogous to that afforded by R9–330 and R9–331 to purchasers of traditional notes?

The drafters of Revised Article 9 answered this question in the negative. A purchaser of a note cannot qualify for non-temporal priority under R9–330 or take free of claims under R9–331 and UCC 3–306 without taking possession. See UCC 1–201(20) (defining "holder"). An electronic note by its very nature is not susceptible of being possessed. Thus, financers of electronic notes (other than notes that are part of electronic chattel paper) are governed by the first-to-file-or-perfect rule, like those who finance other non-paper-based receivables (accounts and payment intangibles). The drafters of UETA disagreed with this result. As we saw in Chapter 1, Section 4, supra, "control" of a transferable record under UETA is the analogue to possession of a paper-based instrument: A person who takes control of a transferable record, like a person who takes possession of a tangible note, may qualify for priority over earlier-perfected security interests under R9–330[1] and, if the requirements of UCC 3–302(a) are satisfied, take free of competing security interests and other claims as a holder in due course. See UETA 16(d); UCC 3–306; R9–331(a). (Likewise, a person who has control of an electronic document of title may qualify for priority under R9–331(a) if the requirements of UCC 7–501 for becoming a HTWANDOTHBDN are met.)

Recall that not every electronic note is a "transferable record." An electronic note can qualify as a transferable record only if the issuer agrees that it is to be considered a transferable record. See UETA 16(a)(2). Moreover, to meet the definition, an electronic record must be such that it would be a note under UCC Article 3 if it were in writing. See UETA 16(a)(1). Checks (even though negotiable) do not qualify; nor do nonnegotiable notes. (Nonnegotiable electronic notes that are part of chattel paper are discussed in Note (4) on Purchasers of Chattel Paper, infra.)

How should a transferable record be classified for purposes of attachment and perfection under Article 9? By definition a transferable record is not a writing. It would seem to follow that a transferable record cannot be an "instrument." See R9–102(a)(47). Rather, a transferable record would appear to be an account, payment intangible, or part of electronic chattel paper. If this analysis is correct, then (depending on how Article 9 classifies

---

1. At least we hope this will be the case. UETA 16(d) invites each legislature to insert a reference to its own enactment of "Section 3–302(a), 7–501, or 9–308" of the UCC. The last is the predecessor to R9–330.

a particular transferable record) even if a secured party has control of the transferable record, its security interest may be unperfected. See UETA 3(b)(2) (making UETA inapplicable to the extent a transaction is governed by Article 9) & Comment 6. Is this a sensible result?

Problem 9.2.5. In the setting of the automobile financing Prototype (Chapter 7, Section 1, supra), Firstbank has a perfected (by filing) security interest in all of the existing and/after-acquired inventory of Main Motors. As in the Prototype, (i) the security interest secures purchase-money advances made to enable Main to acquire its automobile inventory, and (ii) Main sold an automobile to Lee Abel, who signed the Instalment Sale Contract ("ISC") (Form 3.6) granting Main a security interest in the automobile to secure payment of the balance of its price and related charges. However, unlike the Prototype, the Dealer Inventory Security Agreement (Form 3.2) signed by Main Motors covered only "inventory" (i.e., it did not contain subparagraphs 5(b), (c), and (d) of Form 3.2 in the Prototype).

Instead of assigning the ISC to Firstbank, Main assigned the ISC to a third party, Secondbank, which paid Main $18,380 and took possession of the ISC without having conducted a search of the UCC filing records and without knowledge of Firstbank's security interest. Firstbank gave no additional value in connection with the ISC.

(a) What type of collateral is the ISC? See R9–102(a)(2), (11), (47), (61).

(b) Main enters bankruptcy six months after the assignment to Secondbank. As we shall see in Chapter 10, infra, security interests that are unperfected when the debtor enters bankruptcy can be avoided (nullified). Will Firstbank's security interest in the ISC be avoided in Main's bankruptcy? See BC 544(a); R9–317(a)(2); R9–315(c), (d); R9–310(a); R9–312(a); R9–301(1); R9–501(a). Is Secondbank's security interest avoidable? See BC 544(a); R1–201(37) (2d sentence); R9–109(a)(3); R9–317(a)(2); R9–310(a), (b)(6); R9–313(a).

(c) In the Prototype, Firstbank (Main Motors' assignee) perfected its security interest in Abel's Chevrolet by a notation on the certificate of title. See R9–311(a), (b); Form 3.8, supra. Would Firstbank's failure to perfect a security interest in the car affect your answers to part (b)? Would it have any other potential consequences for Firstbank or Secondbank?

(d) Who has priority in the ISC if Firstbank's security agreement does not mention collateral like the ISC? See R9–330; PEB Commentary No. 8 (discussing the predecessor to R9–330).

(e) Would the answer to part (d) be different if:

(i) Firstbank's security agreement explicitly covers such collateral (as in Form 3.2, ¶ 5(b), supra)?

(ii) Before taking the assignment, Secondbank searches the public records and discovers Firstbank's financing statement, which covers "inventory, accounts and chattel paper"?

(iii) Secondbank knows that Firstbank is financing Main's inventory? See UCC 1–201(25) (definition of "knowledge"); R9–102(a)(43).

(iv) Secondbank knows that Firstbank is financing Main's inventory and that Main is obligated to turn over all chattel paper to Firstbank? See UCC 1–201(25) (definition of "knowledge"); R9–102(a)(43).

(v) Secondbank has a first priority purchase-money security interest in the particular automobile sold by Main to Abel; Secondbank pays Main $18,380 for the ISC, $15,000 of which is applied toward Main's debt for the loan that Secondbank previously made to enable Main to acquire that automobile and $3,380 of which is credited to Main's checking account? See R9–324(b); R9–330(a), (b); R9–102(a)(57); R9–330(e).

(vi) Secondbank has a first priority purchase-money security interest in the particular automobile sold by Main to Abel and claims the ISC under an after-acquired property clause in its security agreement without advancing any additional funds against it? See R9–324(b); R9–330(a), (b); R9–102(a)(57); R9–330(e).

NOTES ON PURCHASERS OF CHATTEL PAPER

(1) Classification of Chattel Paper as a Separate Type of Collateral. Under Former Article 9, the categories of "account," "instrument," and "general intangible" were sufficiently broad to include all kinds of rights to payment that are taken as collateral. Nevertheless, the drafters created yet another, separate type of collateral, "chattel paper." See F9–105(1)(b) (definition of "chattel paper"). Why? The short answer may be that, at the time Former Article 9 was drafted, written payment obligations that were secured by (or represented leases of) specific goods received special treatment by professional financers. Unlike unsecured accounts or general intangibles, which may not be evidenced by a writing, chattel paper frequently was (and still is) physically delivered to the purchaser. To accommodate those financing patterns in which the dealer (debtor) retained possession of the paper, the drafters thought it best that filing, as well as possession, be a permissible means of perfection. See F9–304(1) & Comment 1; F9–305. (Compare the treatment of instruments that are not part of chattel paper, as to which the filing of a financing statement was of no consequence under Former Article 9.) Finally, the drafters saw the need for special treatment to sort out priorities in certain situations on a basis other than the generally applicable first-to-file-or-perfect rule of F9–312(5). See F9–308.

For the same reasons, Revised Article 9 classifies chattel paper separately from other rights to payment. See R9–102(a)(11) (definition of "chattel paper"). Perfection may be achieved by filing a financing statement or taking possession of the chattel paper. See R9–312(a); R9–313(a); Problem 3.3.22. And as discussed more fully in Note (3) below, Revised Article 9 provides a special rule that affords priority under certain circumstances to a person who is not the first to file or perfect. See R9–330. Revised Article 9 also expands the definition of chattel paper to accommodate transactions dealing with both specific goods and software closely associated with the goods. See R9–102(a)(11). It thereby expands the class of transactions eligible for the special priority rule.

(2) The Setting: Circumstances Leading to Purchase of Chattel Paper by a Person Other Than the Inventory Financer. Consider the setting of the automobile financing Prototype in Chapter 7, Section 1, supra. Firstbank has financed the purchase of automobile inventory delivered to Main Motors. Firstbank's perfected security interest will extend to all proceeds of the automobile inventory, such as the chattel paper (the Instalment Sale Contract, Form 3.6, supra) generated by the sale to Lee Abel. See R9–315(a)(2), (c). In this setting, the parties often establish a course of business dealing (sometimes expressed in writing, but often resting on oral understanding) under which the inventory financer (e.g., Firstbank) purchases the chattel paper and shares with the dealer (e.g., Main Motors) part of the handsome return from the buyers' finance charges.

In many cases an inventory financer's security agreement prohibits the debtor from giving a security interest in any of the collateral (including chattel paper and other proceeds) to another lender. See Form 3.2, ¶ ¶ 11(c) and (d), supra. Nevertheless, debtors such as Main Motors sometimes may stray from this arrangement and assign chattel paper to another purchaser. What would lead Main Motors to do this? One possibility is that the other financer (Secondbank) offers Main a larger share of the finance charges to be paid by Lee Abel and the other account debtors. Although the assignment of Abel's Instalment Sale Contract to Secondbank violates Firstbank's security agreement, Firstbank probably would not be seriously concerned—as long as Main uses the funds received from Secondbank to repay the inventory loan made by Firstbank.

A second possibility is that Main Motors faces a financial crisis. Rent or payroll obligations must be met, but Main Motors is short of cash and its credit is exhausted; Main may face an immediate shutdown and bankruptcy unless it can get some extra cash to "tide it over." If Main assigns chattel paper to Firstbank, all or most what Main receives will be credited against Main's inventory loan debt to Firstbank, as in the Prototype. See Chapter 7, Section 1(G), supra. Assignments to Secondbank during this perceived emergency, however, produce *cash*. Main, of course, may hope that Firstbank does not check on which cars are on hand at Main's lot and discover that Main is "out of trust." Main well may believe that it soon can raise enough cash from other sources to meet its obligations to Firstbank.

It is impossible to know what portion of the deviations from arrangements to turn over the chattel paper to inventory financers spring from such financial crises. Certainly that factor seems to be present in the cases that lead to litigation. When a debtor receives a better deal from another financer and uses the cash to repay the inventory financer, the latter may be disappointed at losing the return on the chattel paper. The inventory financer may even refuse to deal further with the debtor. But that development is not likely to lead to litigation.

Bear in mind these two settings while considering the priority rules discussed in Note (3), which follows.

(3) Conflicting Priorities in Chattel Paper: Inventory Financers Claiming Chattel Paper as Proceeds versus Subsequent Purchasers of the Chattel Paper.

R9–330 provides strong protection for a purchaser who gives new value and takes possession of chattel paper in good faith and in the ordinary course of its business. Subsection (b) gives the purchaser seniority over an earlier-in-time, perfected security interest in chattel paper if the purchaser acts "without knowledge that the purchase violates the rights of the secured party." R9–330(b). (This standard applies also to purchasers of instruments who seek special priority. See R9–330(d); Note (1) on Purchasers of Instruments, supra.) Recall that "knowledge" means "actual knowledge." UCC 1–201(25). R9–330(f) contains a rule that imputes knowledge for purposes of subsection (b): if chattel paper indicates that it has been assigned to an identified secured party other than the purchaser, a purchaser of the chattel paper ipso facto has knowledge that the purchase violates the rights of the secured party. This rule reflects the common, longstanding practice whereby chattel paper financers who wish to preserve the priority of their interest in chattel paper place a "legend" on the paper to indicate that it has been assigned. See R9–330, Comment 5.[2]

What if a purchaser *did* know, at the time it gave value and took possession of the chattel paper, "that the purchase violates the rights of a secured party"? Or, what if the purchaser's knowledge is a disputed issue of fact? Subsection (a) of R9–330 may give the purchaser yet another card to play. Notwithstanding the existence or assertion of knowledge, the purchaser can achieve priority over a competing security interest "which is claimed merely as proceeds of inventory subject to a security interest" if "the chattel paper does not indicate that it has been assigned to an identified assignee other than the purchaser." R9–330(a).

The requirements for achieving priority as a purchaser of chattel paper under R9–330(a) or (b) are different from and more stringent than the analogous requirements in R9–330(d) for a purchaser of an instrument. A purchaser of an instrument need not take possession "in the ordinary course of the purchaser's business," nor need the purchaser give "new value"; for instruments, any value, even old value, will do. These differences reflect the perception that, unlike the purchase of notes, the financing of chattel paper is practiced only by specialized, professional financial institutions.

---

2. The presence of a legend on an instrument likewise will prevent a subsequent purchaser from acquiring priority over an earlier perfected security interest. See R9–330(d), (f). However, perhaps because Former Article 9 did not contemplate long-term perfection of a security interest in an instrument without the secured party's taking possession, the practice of placing a "legend" on instruments has not developed.

Some of the issues involved in the application of R9–330 to purchases of chattel paper are considered in the remainder of this Note.

When Is a Security Interest "Claimed Merely as Proceeds"? As the Comments to R9–330 explain:

> Like former 9–308, this section does not elaborate upon the phrase "merely as proceeds." For an elaboration, see PEB Commentary No. 8.

Please study Issue I of Commentary No. 8 now. If, under the facts of the automobile financing Prototype, Main Motors had sold the car to Lee Abel without consulting Firstbank, Firstbank's security interest in the Abel's chattel paper would appear to be one "claimed merely as proceeds." According to that Commentary, the fact that the security agreement covers chattel paper as original collateral (see Form 3.2, ¶ 5(b)) would not, alone, be sufficient to make the transaction more than a mere proceeds claim. However, in the actual Prototype transaction Firstbank did more; it made a specific advance of funds to Main Motors against the chattel paper. According to PEB Commentary No. 8, even less direct reliance on the chattel paper would permit an inventory lender to claim a security interest that is not a mere proceeds claim. (Because Firstbank itself was the inventory financer in the Prototype, the assignment of the chattel paper to Firstbank did not implicate the priority contest envisioned by R9–330.)

What Constitutes "Knowledge That the Purchase Violates the Rights of the Secured Party"? As mentioned above, one who purchases chattel paper or an instrument bearing an indication that the paper is subject to a security interest "has knowledge that the purchase violates the rights of the Secured Party" for purposes of the priority rules in R9–330(b) and (d). R9–330(f). Suppose that the purchaser knows of a security interest in the assignor's inventory and also knows of the legal rule that a security interest continues in proceeds (R9–315(a)(2)). Would the purchaser have the requisite knowledge to disqualify it from priority under R9–330 (b) or (d)? We seriously doubt it. Knowledge that the paper or instrument generally is subject to a security interest is a far cry from knowledge that the purchase violates the rights of the holder of that interest. Recall that questions of this kind do not arise in the normal priority contest between secured parties under the first-to-file-or-perfect rule of R9–322(a), under which knowledge is not material. See Note (1) on the Role of Knowledge in Priority Contests, Chapter 7, Section 6(A), supra. However, you also may recall that even though knowledge may be irrelevant to the application of the first-to-file-or-perfect rule, entering into a transaction with knowledge that it is *wrongful*—i.e., with knowledge that the taking of an interest in another party's collateral violates its agreement with the debtor—may give rise to adverse consequences: In appropriate cases the court may invoke one of several extra-UCC bases for rearranging priorities or may impose tort liability on the wrongdoer. See Note (5) on the Role of Knowledge in Priority Contests, Chapter 7, Section 6(A), supra; UCC 1–103.

Consider the position of a purchaser who qualifies for priority over the inventory financer under R9–330(a) or (b), notwithstanding the purchaser's knowledge that the chattel paper is subject to a security interest. Is the purchaser's position impregnable? Is there any ground for an assault by the inventory financer whose collateral gave rise to the chattel paper? It might be interesting to know whether second-in-time purchasers typically would consult with the inventory financer in this situation, notwithstanding that these purchasers appear to enjoy priority under R9–330. Is there an easy way for the purchaser to ensure that the cash will get to the inventory financer? (What about a check made payable jointly to the assignor and the inventory financer?) If consultation or joint payment were normal (or normal decent) practice, is there any basis for an attack by the inventory financer if the purchaser fails to follow that practice? Is there so little substance for such an argument by the inventory financer that you would advise the purchaser to purchase the paper without taking such steps? What would the purchaser gain if it follows your advice to purchase without consultation or joint payment? What would the purchaser lose if you are wrong?

To qualify under R9–330(a) or (b) the purchaser must act "in good faith." In the setting of the preceding paragraph, is there an argument that even in the absence of disqualifying "guilty" knowledge, a purchaser who fails to consult the inventory financer or fails to undertake a UCC filing search acts in bad faith? Comment 6 to R9–330 suggests a negative answer: "[A] purchaser of chattel paper under this section is not required as a matter of good faith to make a search in order to determine the existence of prior security interests."

Taking Possession: Multiple Signed Counterparts; Master Agreements and Schedules. Suppose that in the automobile financing Prototype transaction Lee Abel signed three identical counterparts of the Instalment Sale Contract and Main Motors received only two of them (Abel keeping the third). Main then delivered only one of the counterparts to Secondbank, which did not file, and Main retained the other counterpart. Is Secondbank's security interest perfected? Has Secondbank "take[n] possession" for purposes of R9–330? In order to take possession for purposes of R9–330 (and R9–313), must a purchaser take possession of *all* signed originals of the writings comprising chattel paper?

These problems are compounded when parties to a chattel paper transaction enter into a **master agreement** (typical in the equipment leasing field) that contains general terms and conditions (inspections, maintenance and repairs, risk of loss, default, and the like) but makes no mention of any specific goods. The master agreement typically contemplates that the parties will enter into separate **schedules** from time to time. The schedules incorporate the terms of the master agreement and supplement the master agreement by specifying the goods that are to be leased or sold, the amount and timing of payments, and the like. What writing or writings comprise the chattel paper?

The court was forced to confront all of these questions in In re Funding Systems Asset Management Corp., 111 B.R. 500 (Bkrtcy.W.D.Pa. 1990). Although the court stated that chattel paper was comprised of both a master agreement and its schedules, it held that, under F9–305, perfection of a security interest could be achieved only by taking possession of a *signed original* of a *schedule*. "It was not the practice in the industry to require one seeking financing for the purchase of computer equipment identified in an equipment schedule to deliver the original master lease along with the equipment schedule." Another court has reached the same result on the perfection question. See In re ICS Cybernetics, Inc., 123 B.R. 467 (Bkrtcy.N.D.N.Y.1989) (master agreement did not constitute monetary obligation or lease of specific goods; intent of parties, as evidenced by language in documents, indicated that equipment schedule alone constituted chattel paper), affirmed without opinion 123 B.R. 480 (N.D.N.Y.1990).

Where multiple counterparts of signed original schedules were involved, however, the *Funding Systems Asset Management* court determined that the security interests were *un*perfected when the debtor retained possession of a signed original of a schedule, even though the secured party also had possession of such an original.

> What really mattered in determining whether or not [Secured Party] had perfected its security interests in all of the other challenged leases was whether or not Debtor possessed an original of the equipment schedules for that particular challenged lease. If Debtor possessed an original equipment schedule, then [Secured Party] had not perfected its security interest by virtue of its possession of the chattel paper which it retained. If, on the other hand, Debtor did not possess an original equipment schedule, then [Secured Party] had perfected its security interest by possession.

111 B.R. at 519. Presumably the court would have taken the same approach if the issue had arisen under F9–308.

There are good reasons why more than one party may wish to have an original, signed copy of writings comprising chattel paper (although in practice one *never* sees more than one signed promissory note, even if the note is non-negotiable). Does Revised Article 9 explain which of the originals the secured party must possess to perfect its security interest? Does it explain whether the master agreement, the schedules, or both constitute the chattel paper? If not, would you rely on *Funding Systems Asset Management*, even though it was decided under Former Article 9?

Suppose that you are charged with drafting documentation that will (i) avoid the problems just described; (ii) allow Abel, Main Motors, and Secondbank each to retain a signed original; and (iii) permit Secondbank to acquire a perfected security interest with priority under R9–330. What would you write? Would each counterpart be identical? See R9–330, Comment 4. See also the legend "ORIGINAL TO BANK" on the reverse side of the Instalment Sale Contract, Form 3.6, supra.

(4) Electronic Chattel Paper. As we have seen, UETA 16 enables a second-in-time purchaser of an electronic negotiable note ("transferable record") to achieve priority over an earlier-perfected security interest by taking control of the collateral. See Note (2) on Purchasers of Instruments, supra. Revised Article 9 affords a similar possibility with respect to "electronic chattel paper"—the oxymoron with which the drafters named the electronic equivalent of chattel paper. See R9–102(a)(31) (defining "electronic chattel paper"). (Revised Article 9 refers to paper chattel paper as "tangible chattel paper," which it defines in R9–102(a)(78).)

Electronic installment sale contracts and electronic leases are uncommon. Nevertheless, the drafters of Revised Article 9 sought to minimize the differences in the legal consequences that otherwise would result from the parties' choice of the medium used for chattel paper. To that end Revised Article 9 introduced a new concept: "control" of electronic chattel paper. See R9–105.[3] "Control" of electronic chattel paper serves the same functions as possession of tangible chattel paper. A person who takes control of electronic chattel paper, like a person who takes possession of tangible chattel paper, may qualify for priority over earlier-perfected security interests under R9–330; control also can serve as a substitute for an authenticated security agreement and as a method of perfecting a security interest. See R9–203(b); R9–313(a); R9–314(a). The definition of "control" is flexible, to accommodate future developments in the business practices surrounding electronic chattel paper.

Why should Article 9 treat electronic chattel paper differently from other rights to payment that are evidenced by electronic, rather than paper, records (e.g., accounts)? Why should a secured party who holds a perfected-by-filing security interest in electronic chattel paper be faced with the risk of having its security interest subordinated to a subsequent purchaser who has control? One explanation may be that, by enabling a later-in-time purchaser of chattel paper to take priority, the non-temporal priority rules in R9–330 may make it more likely that dealers will find purchasers for their paper; the increased number of potential purchasers, in turn, probably increases the ability of dealers to offer purchase-money credit to buyers and lessees of goods.

As we have seen, the control provisions of UETA do not apply an electronic record unless the issuer expressly agrees that the record is to be considered a "transferable record." See UETA 16(a)(2). For this reason, a note issued in paper form cannot be converted into a transferable record; the issuer would not be the issuer of an electronic record. See id., Comment 2. In contrast, nothing in Article 9 prevents the conversion of tangible chattel paper into electronic chattel paper. Rather, the Comments expressly contemplate this possibility. See R9–102, Comment 5.b.

(5) Lease Chattel Paper. The foregoing focuses for the most part on chattel paper consisting of a record evidencing a payment obligation secured by specific goods. Yet the definition of "chattel paper" in R9–102(a)(11) also includes *leases* of specific goods. One kind of recurring problem associated with assignments of personal property lease chattel

---

3. R9–105 is the source of the "control" concept of both UETA and the federal E–SIGN act. The means for obtaining "control" of electronic chattel paper and transferable records are completely different from, and should not be confused with, the means for obtaining "control" of investment property or a deposit account. (Control of investment property and deposit accounts is discussed in Sections 3 and 4, infra.)

paper—the problem associated with the practice of using master leases supplemented by schedules—is discussed above Note (3). A more detailed consideration of issues relating to lease chattel paper appears in Chapter 11, Section 2, infra.

(6) Realty Paper. "Chattel paper" is limited to records relating to specific chattels (goods). A record or records evidencing a monetary obligation and a security interest in real property, e.g., a promissory note and mortgage, may serve as collateral under Article 9; however, the records would not be chattel paper. For a discussion of security interests in mortgage notes and similar obligations, see Chapter 11, Section 4(B), infra. Article 9 does not apply to a security interest in a lease of real property. See R9–109(d)(11), discussed in Chapter 8, Section 4, supra.

R9–330(a) and (b) address priority conflicts between a chattel paper purchaser and an inventory financer as to the *chattel paper*. Priority conflicts also may arise between these two parties as to the *goods* that are the subject of the chattel paper. The following Problem raises a priority conflict of this kind. R9–330(c)(2) resolves the conflict, and Comments 9, 10, and 11 explain the operation of that subsection.

Problem 9.2.6. In the setting of the Prototype, Main Motors sold Abel's chattel paper to Secondbank. Under R9–330, Secondbank achieved priority over Firstbank's security interest in the chattel paper (whether as proceeds or as original collateral). Having perfected by possession, Secondbank did not file a financing statement against the chattel paper. Abel's new Chevrolet is a true "lemon." Abel revoked acceptance of the car, returned it to Main's lot, and walked away.[4]

(a) Does Firstbank have a security interest in the Chevrolet? If so, is the security interest perfected? See R9–315(a)(2); R9–102(a)(64); R9–330, Comments 9 & 10.

(b) Does Secondbank have a security interest in the Chevrolet? See R9–315(a)(2); R9–102(a)(64); R9–330, Comments 9 & 10.

(c) Which security interest is senior? See R9–330(c) & Comments 9 & 10.

SECTION 3. SECURITY INTERESTS IN INVESTMENT PROPERTY

Introductory Note. In this Section we consider security interests in stocks, bonds, and similar property. Our focus will be on financing at the "retail" level; we will not address the special rules that apply when the debtor is a broker or other securities intermediary.

---

4. Recall that in a consumer transaction the assignment of chattel paper must be *subject to* the buyer's defenses. See the dis- cussion of the FTC's "holder in due course" rule in Section 1(F) and Chapter 1, Section 4, supra.

The law governing security interests in investment property is particularly complex (even by Article 9 standards). Part of the complexity derives from the fact that investment property can be held in two different ways: directly, as where the debtor is the holder of a security (stock) certificate registered in the debtor's name, and indirectly, through a broker or other securities intermediary. (The patterns of holding investment property are described in greater detail in Notes (1) and (2) on Security Interests in Investment Property, infra.) Where investment property is held through a broker, enforcement of a security interest is likely to implicate the broker; a secured party who relies on collateral of this kind would be remiss in failing to take into consideration not only the rules governing attachment, perfection, and priority but also the rules governing the broker's obligations with respect to the collateral. (We have seen related issues with respect to receivables. See Notes (3) and (4) on Rights and Obligations of Account Debtors and Persons Obligated on Promissory Notes, Section 1(F), supra.) Finally, part of the complexity derives from the drafters' desire to afford flexibility to secured parties. A secured transaction in investment property—particularly investment property that is held through an intermediary—gives rise to a relatively large variety of risks; the governing law permits a secured party to decide which risks to protect against and which risks to accept. (Here, again, we have seen related issues. See Problem 3.3.19, supra.)

Problem 9.3.1. Drahman is the owner of 1,000 shares of General Motors common stock. The stock certificates, in registered form (see UCC 8–102(a)(13)), are in Drahman's safe deposit box. On July 1 Drahman borrowed $10,000 from Lender and signed a security agreement granting Lender a security interest in "all my General Motors common stock." On July 15 Lean, one of Drahman's judgment creditors, acquired an execution lien on the stock (see UCC 8–112).

(a) Who has the superior claim to the stock? See R9–317(a)(2); R9–102(a)(49); UCC 8–102(a)(15), (a)(4), (a)(16); R9–312(e); R9–102(a)(57); Note (3) on Security Interests in Investment Property, infra.

(b) What result if the execution lien arose on August 1?

(c) What steps could Lender have taken to prevail in part (b)? See R9–312(a); R9–313(a); R8–301(a); R9–314(a); R9–106(a); R8–106(b); UCC 8–102(a)(11); Security Agreement § 4.3 (Form 9.2, supra). If more than one method of perfection is available, which method would you recommend? Include in your analysis the following considerations:

(i) the cost of perfection.

(ii) the risk of existing and future competing claims (including security interests and claims of future buyers). See R9–328(1), (5); UCC 8–302; UCC 8–303; UCC 8–304(d); Note (3) on Perfection by Possession, Chapter 7, Section 3(B), supra; Note (4) on Security Interests in Investment Property, infra.

(iii) the possibility that Drahman may default on the loan. See R9–609; R9–610; UCC 8–401(a)(2), (a)(3); UCC 8–304(d); UCC 8–307 &

Comment 1; Note (3) on Perfection by Possession, Chapter 7, Section 3(B), supra.

(iv) the possibility that General Motors might declare a dividend. See R9–102(a)(64)(B); R9–315(c), (d); Problem 3.5.6, supra.

Problem 9.3.2. A stock certificate covering 50,000 shares of General Motors common stock was issued to and is registered in the name of the Depository Trust Company (actually, in the name of "Cede & Co.," DTC's nominee); the certificate is located in DTC's vault in New York City. DTC's books show that it is holding 7,000 of these shares for Broker and the remaining 43,000 shares for other brokers and banks who are participants in DTC. Broker's records show that it is "holding" 1,000 shares for Drabco, Inc., a Kentucky corporation, and 6,000 for other customers of Broker.

On May 1 Drabco borrowed $10,000 from Lender and signed a written security agreement describing the collateral as "1,000 shares of General Motors common stock in my account with Broker." At the time, Drabco's account contained only 1,000 shares. The loan was used to acquire business equipment. The same day Lender filed a proper financing statement covering the collateral. On June 1 Lean acquired a judicial lien on everything in the account.

(a) What UCC-defined type of collateral does the security agreement cover? See UCC 8–102(a)(17) & Comment 17; UCC 8–501; UCC 8–102(a)(9) & Comment 9, (a)(15), (a)(4); R9–102(a)(49); Note (2) on Security Interests in Investment Property, infra.

(b) As between Lender and Lean, who has the superior claim to the stock? See R9–317(a)(2); R9–310(a); R9–312(a). Which state's law governs this priority dispute? See R9–305.

(c) In which office should the financing statement have been filed? See R9–305(c)(1).

(d) What result in part (b) if the financing statement covered "securities"? (Assume that the filing was authorized.) See R9–317(a)(2); R9–310(a); R9–504; R9–108.

(e) What result in part (b) if the security agreement and financing statement covered "all securities accounts now or hereafter owned by me" and Drabco's account contained 1,000 shares of General Motors and 500 shares of AT & T on June 1? See R9–203(b), (h); R9–308(f); R9–108. What result if the borrower were Drabco's president, D.D. Drabek, who created the security interest to secure a loan that was used to buy home furniture? See R9–108(e); R9–102(a)(26).

(f) Drabco, in violation of the security agreement, instructed Broker on May 5 to sell 600 shares of the General Motors stock. Broker dutifully followed Drabco's instructions and sold the shares through the stock exchange. Is Broker liable to Lender for having sold Lender's collateral? See UCC 8–507; UCC 8–102(a)(8); UCC 8–107(a); UCC 8–102(a)(7); UCC 8–107(b). What could Lender have done to protect itself? See Security Agreement § 4.3 (Form 9.2, supra).

(g) Drabco defaulted, and Lender instructed Broker to transfer 1,000 shares of General Motors common stock from Drabco's securities account to Lender's. What should Broker do? See UCC 8–507; UCC 8–107(a), (b). What could Lender have done to protect itself?

(h) Assume Lender did not file a financing statement. Instead, on May 1 Lender sent a copy of the signed security agreement by overnight courier to Broker. The following day Broker signed an acknowledgment indicating that it had received the envelope. As between Lender and Lean, who has the superior claim to the stock? See R9–317(a)(2); R9–310(a); R9–312(a); R9–310(b)(8); R9–314(a); R9–106(a); R8–106; R9–313(a), (c).

(i) Assume Lender filed a proper financing statement on May 1. On June 5 Drabco borrowed $5,000 from Broker under the "margin loan" provisions of Drabco's account agreement. Under that agreement, Drabco agreed that Broker would have a security interest in "all securities now or hereafter in my account with you" to secure any **margin loans**. Broker did not file a financing statement. Six months later, Lean acquired an execution lien on the securities account. As between Broker and Lean, who has the superior claim to the securities account? As between Broker and Lender? See R9–317(a)(2); R9–310(a), (b)(8); R9–314(a); R8–106(e); UCC 8–102(a)(7), (a)(14).

(j) The facts are as in part (i), except that on May 1 Broker agreed with Drabco and Lender that Broker would comply with Lender's instructions concerning the account without further consent of Drabco. As between Broker and Lender, who has the superior claim to the securities account? See R8–106; R9–328. What should the holder of the subordinate security interest have done to achieve priority? See R9–339.

NOTES ON SECURITY INTERESTS IN INVESTMENT PROPERTY

(1) How Securities Are Held and Transferred. The rules governing the creation and perfection of security interests in stocks, bonds, and other investment property reflect the ways in which investment property is held and transferred. Traditionally, securities such as stocks and bonds were transferred by physically delivering the paper certificates that represented the equity or debt. The centralization of trading into markets, such as the New York Stock Exchange, facilitated this method of transfer. By the late 1960's, however, the volume and speed of transactions in the securities markets reached proportions that posed a crisis for the customary processes of transfer. This "paperwork crunch" generated important proposals to provide a legal framework for transactions in "certificateless" shares. These proposals and a supporting study were embodied in a Report issued on September 15, 1975, by the Committee on Stock Certificates of the ABA Section on Corporation, Banking and Business Law. The Report proposed amendments to the Model Business Corporation Act and also set forth proposed revisions of portions of the UCC—principally in Article 8 and related sections of Article 9.

The Report provided a thorough, 60–page analysis of then-current practices for transfer of certificates and of then-current problems that called for legislative solution. The Report identified the central problem as follows:

> In an era when electronic communication was unknown and buyers and sellers traded stock interests in face-to-face confrontations under a buttonwood tree, the physical delivery of a piece of paper from seller to buyer was a far quicker and safer means of transfer than the alternative—the seller's instruction to the corporation to make a transfer in its records and the corporation's subsequent acknowledgment to the buyer that the transfer had been made. Indeed, if the seller demanded contemporaneous consideration, perhaps only a journey by both parties to the corporation's office could have satisfied his objective.

> In today's securities markets, however, the world has been turned inside-out. In the typical market transaction, the buyer and seller are unknown to each other and may be geographically separated by thousands of miles. On the other hand, the marvels of electronic communication make it possible to transmit instructions and acknowledge their receipt in a matter of minutes. The physical delivery of a piece of paper has become the time-consuming unsafe process, passing, as it must, through the hands of intermediaries and spanning, as it might, an entire continent. Thus, the negotiable stock certificate, an instrument almost indispensable in the environment in which it grew, has become a serious impediment to the very transaction it was designed to promote.

> Notwithstanding the fact that the principal reason for its creation has ceased to exist, the negotiable stock certificate has become so firmly entrenched that an elaborate legal and operational structure has been built on its foundation. The relationships between buyers and sellers, donors and donees, corporations and their shareholders, fiduciaries and beneficiaries, taxing authorities and taxpayers have been delineated on the basic premise that a particular stock certificate uniquely represents every stock interest. The location of that certificate, the information noted thereon, in whose custody it reposes are all important and frequently crucial facts. As will be noted, these facts, in the current environment, often have little bearing on the solution of problems they were originally intended to resolve. In an environment without certificates, these facts will not exist and alternative solutions will have to be provided.

Report, ABA Stock Certificate Committee 2–3 (1975).

To address this situation, the scope of Article 8 was extended in 1977 to include securities that are not represented by a certificate, or "uncertificated" securities. The securities markets, however, could not wait for a legislative solution and developed a practical one. As a result, the "environment without certificates" that the ABA Committee envisioned in its 1975 report never appeared. Instead, stock certificates and bonds often are issued in the name of, and held in a warehouse by, a central depository. Each depository maintains records showing the person on whose behalf it holds each of the securities in its possession. In most cases, the depository holds for other institutional participants in the securities markets, such as stockbrokers and banks. Each of these persons, in turn, maintains records showing the person on whose behalf it "holds" each of securities.

Consider the "simple" case in which the debtor maintains a securities account with Broker A (a "securities intermediary," see UCC 8–102(a)(14)) and wishes to use the securities in the account as collateral for a loan from the bank. The bank will be unlikely to take possession of securities themselves, because they are not likely to be in Broker A's possession. Rather, the securities are likely to in the possession of a depository (a special kind of securities intermediary called a "clearing corporation," see UCC 8–102(a)(5)), and registered in the name of the depository (or its nominee) on the books of the issuer. The depository's books may show Broker B as the owner. Records maintained by Broker B (another "securities intermediary"), in turn, show Broker A as owner, and Broker A's records show the debtor as owner. In other words, the depository is holding for Broker B, which is "holding" for Broker A, which is "holding" for the debtor. The situation becomes even more complex when one takes into account the fact that this chain is likely to be different for each type of security, or even for different quantities of the same issue of stock. Not only might different depositories and securities intermediaries be involved, but some of the securities intermediaries might be in possession of some of the securities.

Despite the fact that, in many markets, ownership of securities was transferred without moving security certificates from hand to hand, the 1977 amendments to Former Article 8 reflected the importance traditionally attached to possession of security certificates. The amendments treated the tiers of relationships among the securities intermediaries and their customers as a series of bailments and sub-bailments. Applying the statutory rules to actual practices in the securities markets was awkward at best and uncertain and impractical at worst. For example, the proper method for taking and perfecting of a security interest in securities "in" a securities account whose contents are likely to change was not nearly so clear as both debtors and secured parties would have liked. The difficulties were compounded when the securities account, as often is the case, contained cash balances as well as financial instruments (e.g., **bankers' acceptances**[1]) that may not have been "securities" and therefore could not have been perfected by the methods available with respect to property covered by the 1977 version of Article 8. The uncertain application of the 1977 amendments was thought to have contributed to the severity of the

---

1. A bankers' acceptance begins as a negotiable time draft drawn on a bank (something like a check that the bank is instructed to pay at a specified time in the future). When the bank accepts the draft, the bank becomes obligated to pay it when it becomes due. See UCC 3–409; UCC 3–413. There is a market for these bank obligations.

"market break" of October, 1987,[2] which led to worldwide efforts to insure that the legal regime was adequate to support the ever-increasing volume of trades. One outgrowth of these efforts was the promulgation of Revised UCC Article 8 in 1994.

(2) The Structure of Revised UCC Article 8; Securities; Security Entitlements. The structure of Revised Article 8 reflects the two prevailing patterns of holding and transferring securities and other investment property. Although Part 1 of Revised Article 8 contains rules applicable to each pattern, each of the other parts of the Article applies only to one. Each pattern has not only its own rules but also its own terminology.

Parts 2, 3, and 4 of Revised Article 8 reflect the traditional pattern of securities holding, in which the owner of the security has a direct relationship with the issuer. In the case of a "certificated security," i.e., one that is represented by a certificate, the person usually is specified on the security itself. See UCC 8–102(a)(4) (defining "certificated security"). For example, in Problem 9.3.1, Drahman holds a certificated security and has a direct relationship with General Motors; General Motors' records show Drahman as the stockholder. Likewise, in Problem 9.3.2, DTC holds a certificated security and has a direct relationship with GM. In the case of an "uncertificated security," the person having the direct relationship with the issuer is shown as the registered owner in the records of the issuer, but no certificate is issued to represent the stock. See UCC 8–102(a)(18) (defining "uncertificated security").

The interest of a person who holds investment property indirectly, through an intermediary, is treated differently from the interest of one who holds directly. Consider the facts of Problem 9.3.2. Drabco is the owner of the General Motors stock; as the owner, Drabco enjoys the right to vote for the board of directors and the right to receive any dividends that General Motors may declare. Yet Drabco has only an indirect relationship with the issuer, General Motors. Drabco holds through a securities intermediary, Broker, which in turn holds through its own securities intermediary, DTC. Part 5 of Article 8 applies to the relationship between Drabco and Broker and the relationship between Broker and DTC. The rights that Drabco enjoys against Broker and that Broker enjoys against DTC with respect to the GM stock are called a "security entitlement," and Drabco and Broker are "entitlement holders." See UCC 8–102(a)(18) (defining "security entitlement"); UCC 8–102(a)(7) (defining "entitlement holder"). The General Motors stock itself is a "financial asset." See UCC 8–102(a)(9).

Unlike Broker and Drabco, DTC has a direct relationship with General Motors; it is the stockholder of record. For this reason, DTC's interest in the General Motors stock is classified as a "security," see UCC 8–102(a)(15), and *not* a security entitlement. The interest of DTC in the General Motors stock is a "certificated security," because the stock is

---

2. On October 19, 1987, the Dow Jones Industrial Average closed down 22.6% for the day and 36.7% from its closing high less than two months earlier. The number of shares traded was nearly double the previous record, which had been set the preceding week.

represented by a certificate. See R8–102(a)(4). If DTC's interest were registered on General Motors' books but no certificate had been issued, DTC would "hold" an uncertificated security. Whether DTC holds a certificated or uncertificated security does not affect the characterization of Broker's or Drabco's interest in the General Motors stock; in either case, each has a security entitlement, not a security.

(3) Creation and Perfection of a Security Interest in Investment Property. The rules governing the transfer of interests (including security interests) in investment property turn on the distinction between transfers by persons who hold directly (i.e., transfers of a security, whether certificated and uncertificated) and transfers by persons who hold indirectly (i.e., transfers of a security entitlement). The failure to understand the distinction and the terminology used to draw it is likely to lead to confusion and error.

Revised Article 9 adopts the terminology that appears in Revised Article 8 and adds the generic term, "investment property." This term includes securities (both certificated and uncertificated) and security entitlements, as well as securities accounts, commodity contracts, and commodity accounts. See R9–102(a)(49). To a limited extent, Revised Article 9 protects secured parties who use the wrong terminology. For example, because a security entitlement may be described by describing the underlying financial asset, "all debtor's securities" adequately describes all debtor's security entitlements with respect to securities. See R9–108(d)(2). Moreover, Revised Article 9 facilitates taking a security interest in all security entitlements carried in a securities account by eliminating any need to describe each particular security entitlement and by providing that perfection as to the securities account automatically perfects as to each security entitlement carried in the account. See R9–203(h) (attachment); R9–308(f) (perfection).

Revised Article 9 provides two principal methods for perfecting a security interest in investment property—filing and control.[3] See R9–312(a); R9–314(a). As one might suspect, the meaning of "control" differs depending on whether the collateral is a certificated security, an uncertificated security, or a security entitlement. See R9–104(a); R8–106. In addition, a security interest in a certificated security may be perfected by taking delivery. See R9–313(a); R8–301(a). In the case of a certificated security, "delivery" occurs when the secured party acquires possession of the security certificate. R8–301(a)(1).

As with respect to instruments and chattel paper, not all methods of perfection with respect to investment property are equal. Although perfection by any method will achieve priority over a subsequent judicial lien creditor, perfection by control affords priority over more different types of competing claims than does perfection by filing. See R9–317(a)(2) (compet-

---

3. A security interest in investment property may be perfected automatically under limited circumstances. See R9–309(b)(9)– (11). Temporary perfection may be available with respect to certificated securities. See R9–312(e), (g).

ing lien creditor); R9–328 (competing secured parties). Of particular importance for our purposes is that a security interest perfected by control has priority over a security interest perfected by filing. See R9–328(1). Perfection by control affords other benefits, as well. See R8–106, Comment 7 (control carries with it "the ability to have the securities sold or transferred without further action by the transferor").

"Control" has a specialized meaning when applied to investment property; in determining the rights of a secured party having control, one must not resort to the vernacular meaning of the term. In particular, do not assume that a secured party's control of a securities entitlement ipso facto prevents the securities intermediary (e.g., broker) from obeying entitlement orders (orders with respect to the transfer or redemption of a financial asset in a securities account) originated by the debtor. A securities intermediary is obligated to obey entitlement orders issued by the entitlement holder. UCC 8–107(b)(1), (a)(3). The securities intermediary's agreement that it will comply with entitlement orders originated by the secured party without further consent by the debtor (entitlement holder) gives the secured party control. R8–106(d)(2). However, if the debtor remains the entitlement holder, the secured party's control is not inconsistent with the debtor's retention of the right to trade the security entitlements. A secured party who satisfies the requirements for control has control, even if the entitlement holder retains the right to make substitutions for the security entitlement, to originate entitlement orders to the securities intermediary, or otherwise to deal with the security entitlement. See R8–106(f).

Also, the fact that the secured party has control, and thus "the *ability* to have the securities sold or transferred without further action by the transferor," R8–106, Comment 7 (emphasis added), does not necessarily mean that the secured party has the *right*, as against the debtor, to issue entitlement orders. The circumstances under which a secured party enjoys the right to issue entitlement orders is determined by the agreement of the debtor and secured party. See, e.g., Security Agreement § 4.3, Section 1(B), supra.

Just as not all methods of perfection are equal, so not all forms of control are equal. If a security interest in a security entitlement is granted by the entitlement holder to the entitlement holder's own securities intermediary, the securities intermediary automatically has control the security entitlement. See UCC 8–106(e). Such a security interest has priority over all conflicting security interests, regardless of when or by what method they were perfected. See R9–328(3). What justifies affording this nontemporal priority to securities intermediaries? The credit extended by a securities intermediary typically is a **margin loan**, i.e., a loan typically used to acquire the collateral (security entitlement). For this reason, a priority analogous to purchase-money priority may be appropriate.

(4) Good–Faith Purchase of Securities and Security Entitlements. The preceding Note and Note (3) on Perfection by Possession, Chapter 7, Section 3(B), supra, suggest some reasons why a secured party may not be indifferent to the method by which its security interest in a security is perfected: certain methods of perfection (e.g., control) afford greater priority than do other methods (e.g., delivery or filing); certain methods (control and delivery) facilitate enforcement of the security interest. The doctrine of good-faith purchase, as applied to securities, may afford another reason to prefer control as a method of perfection. A secured party who qualifies as a "protected purchaser" of a security not only acquires the rights in the security that the debtor had or had power to transfer but also acquires its interest in the security free of any adverse claim. See UCC 8–303(b). The concept of "protected purchaser" is analogous to those of "holder in due course" in UCC Article 3 and "holder to whom a negotiable document of title has been duly negotiated" in UCC Article 7. See generally Chapter 1, Sections 4 and 5, supra. Observe, however, that a protected purchaser need not be a "holder." Indeed, one can be a protected purchaser of an uncertificated security. See UCC 8–303(a). Observe also that the phrase "good faith" does not appear with reference to protected purchasers. See UCC 8–303(a) & Comment 4. Although one cannot be a "protected purchaser" of a security entitlement, a purchaser for value of a security entitlement typically takes free of adverse claims. See UCC 8–502; UCC 8–510(a).

(5) Federal Book–Entry Securities. For many years United States Treasury securities have been "book-entry" (i.e., uncertificated) securities. Proposals for revisions to the federal regulations governing Treasury securities in the late 1980's attracted intense interest and substantial criticism. Indeed, the debates over the appropriate legal structure for the transfer of Treasury securities (including transfers of security interests) was the principal catalyst that gave rise to the project leading to the 1994 revisions of UCC Article 8. Representatives of the Department of the Treasury participated in and closely observed the Article 8 revision process. It is not surprising, then, that the Department effectively adopted Revised Article 8 for Treasury securities. See 31 C.F.R. pt. 357. To summarize briefly, Treasury and other federal agency book-entry securities are transferred in an indirect system in which the Federal Reserve Banks maintain books on behalf of the federal government, as issuer. Participating banks, in turn, claim securities through their accounts with a Federal Reserve Bank, and other intermediaries (e.g., broker-dealers), in turn, have accounts with participating banks. At the bottom of this "tiered" system are the ultimate entitlement holders (i.e., the beneficial owners of the securities), who have accounts with either participating banks or other intermediaries.

The following excerpt provides an overview of the method by which the Treasury Department has deferred to Revised Article 8 for federal securities.

At the federal level, the Department of the Treasury promulgated the final TRADES [i.e., Treasury/Reserve Automated Debt Entry System] regulations, which became effective on January 1, 1997. Substantially identical regulations were adopted by federal agencies responsible for the various government sponsored enterprises (GSEs) that issue securities maintained on the Federal Reserve Bank (FRB) Book–Entry System. The GSE regulations also became effective in January 1997.

The TRADES and GSE regulations apply federal substantive law to the rights and obligations of the United States or the issuing GSE and, subject to some exceptions, the rights and obligations of the FRBs. The regulations, however, defer to state law with respect to the remaining aspects of transactions between the FRBs and their participants [the participants generally are federally insured banks] and for all aspects of transactions on the books of lower-tier intermediaries [i.e., intermediaries that are not participants in the FRB system]. Thus, the rights and obligations of parties who hold federal book-entry securities through broker-dealers, custodian banks, clearing corporations, or other securities intermediaries (other than the FRBs) will be governed by state law.

Wittie, Review of Recent Developments in U.C.C. Article 8 and Investment Securities, 52 Bus. Law. 1575, 1576 (1997).

SECTION 4.   SECURITY INTERESTS IN DEPOSIT ACCOUNTS

Introductory Note. This Section deals with security interests in checking, savings, and other deposit accounts. A deposit account is much like a securities account: each involves a claim against a regulated financial intermediary. It should come as no surprise that the rules governing security interests in deposit accounts are similar to those we explored in the preceding Section on investment property; in fact, the investment property rules were the source of the deposit account rules. The two sets of rules are not identical, however. When working through the following materials, please pay special attention to the differences. Can they be explained by differences between the two types of collateral? If not, what explains them?

Problem 9.4.1. Kinkco, Inc., maintains a checking account at Firstbank. To secure a $50,000 loan, Kinkco granted to Firstbank a security interest in all Kinkco's bank accounts, existing and after-acquired.

(a) What should Firstbank do to perfect its security interest? See R9–102(a)(29); R9–310(a); R9–312(b); R9–314(a); R9–104; Note (3) on Security Interests in Deposit Accounts, infra.

(b) Would your advice in part (a) differ if the checking account belonged to Kinkco's president, Davies, who used the loan to buy home furniture? See 9–109(d)(13); 9–102(a)(26).

Problem 9.4.2. Secondbank would like to make a relatively small loan ($50,000) to Kinkco, Inc. Secondbank is unwilling to make the loan without taking a security interest in Kinkco's bank account at Firstbank.

(a) How can Secondbank perfect its security interest? See R9–102(a)(29); R9–310(a); R9–312(b); R9–314(a); R9–104; R9–102(b); UCC 4–

104(a)(5); Note (3) on Security Interests in Deposit Accounts, infra; Security Agreement § 4.2 (Form 9.2, supra);

(b) If there is more than one option for perfection, which do you recommend? Include in your analysis the following considerations:

(i) the risk that Firstbank might be uncooperative. See R9–342.

(ii) the cost.

(iii) the risk that Kinkco might create other security interests in the bank account. See R9–327; R9–339.

(iv) the risk that Kinkco might draw checks on the account to pay other creditors. See UCC 4–401; R9–341; R9–332(b).

(v) Secondbank's ability to enforce its security interest. See R9–607(a)(4), (a)(5).

Problem 9.4.3. In the setting of the Prototype receivables financing transaction in Section 1(B), supra, Eastinghome obtained a security interest in Carguys' existing and after-arising accounts and filed a financing statement in the Delaware filing office. Thereafter, Carguys opened a deposit account with a branch of Firstbank in Los Angeles, near Carguys' corporate headquarters. The account agreement between Carguys and Firstbank provided that the deposit account secures all existing and future indebtedness of Carguys to Firstbank. As Carguys received payments from its account debtors, it deposited the payments into the deposit account at Firstbank. No other funds were deposited into the deposit account. In September Carguys borrowed $50,000 from Firstbank. A few months later Carguys defaults on its obligations to Eastinghome and Firstbank.

(a) Which state's law governs perfection and priority of the security interests? See R9–304.

(b) Which security interest in the deposit account is senior, Eastinghome's or Firstbank's? See R9–315(c), (d); R9–322(a)(1), (b)(1), (f)(1); R9–327. What could the holder of the junior security interest have done to protect itself? See Security Agreement § 4.2 (Form 9.2, supra).

NOTES ON SECURITY INTERESTS IN DEPOSIT ACCOUNTS

(1) Background. Security interests in checking, savings, and other deposit accounts give rise to special practical problems and policy issues. Comment 7 to F9–104 observed that "[r]ights under ... deposit accounts, are often put up as collateral." Nevertheless, security interests in deposit accounts were excluded from Former Article 9, except insofar as they constituted proceeds of other collateral. See F9–104(g), (l); Chapter 7, Section 5, supra (discussing proceeds). As a consequence, Former Article 9 required a lender who took a consensual lien on (or "pledge" of) the debtor's bank account to consult non-UCC law to determine whether its lien attached and was protected against the competing claims of third parties. This non-UCC law may be both hard to find and unclear. In particular, it may include vaguely articulated requirements with respect to the secured party's dominion over the deposit account. Non–UCC law also regulated the enforcement of these liens.

One might question whether the exclusion of security interests in deposit accounts from Former Article 9 was justified, especially given the UCC's goals of simplifying, clarifying, and modernizing the law governing commercial transactions and of making uniform the law among the various jurisdictions. See UCC 1–102(2)(a), (c). Comment 7 to F9–104 explained that "[s]uch transactions are often quite special, do not fit easily under a general commercial statute and are adequately covered by existing law." Do you find that explanation persuasive? Others have not. See, e.g., Harris, Non–Negotiable Certificates of Deposit: An Article 9 Problem, 29 UCLA L. Rev. 330, 358–61 (1981); Phillips, Flawed Perfection: From Possession to Filing under Article 9 (pt. 1), 59 B.U.L. Rev. 1, 47–48 (1979).

(2) Policy Issues. The Article 9 Study Committee recommended that Revised Article 9 include deposit accounts as original collateral. See Permanent Editorial Board, Report of the Article 9 Study Committee, Recommendation 7.C., at 68 (Dec. 1, 1992). This recommendation proved to be one of the most controversial aspects of the Study Committee's Report.

From the outset of the drafting process that followed the publication of the Study Committee's Report, it was clear that a substantial minority of the Drafting Committee, including some members associated with the secured financing industry, had reservations about including deposit accounts as original collateral. Some thought the common law was adequate to deal with "blocked" accounts, to which the debtor is denied access, and they opposed making "transactional" accounts, which debtors use to pay their bills, easy to use as collateral. They argued that if a debtor enjoys unfettered access to the funds, then when the time comes to enforce its security interest, the secured party is likely to find that the deposit account has been depleted and the collateral is worthless. The Drafting Committee disagreed over whether, given this risk, lenders actually would extend additional credit in reliance on a deposit account to which the debtor had access.

The Drafting Committee also disagreed over whether obtaining a perfected security interest in all deposit accounts of a debtor would become the routine result in the vast run of secured transactions. It disagreed over the appropriate priority rule for resolving a conflict between a security interest in a deposit account as original collateral and a security interest in the deposit account claimed as proceeds of inventory, accounts, or other original collateral; it disagreed over the appropriate priority rule for resolving a conflict between a security interest in a deposit account and the bank's right of setoff; and it disagreed over whether the benefits of including deposit accounts as original collateral justified the many special provisions required to accomplish the task. The Federal Reserve Bank of New York expressed concern that security interests in deposit accounts would impede the free flow of funds through the payment system. Consumer-advocacy groups feared that individuals would inadvertently or unwisely encumber their bank accounts.

(3) Deposit Accounts under Revised Article 9. Ultimately, the Drafting Committee settled on an approach that appears to have satisfied (grudgingly, perhaps) all concerned. The basic principles of the approach are straightforward.

Free Flow of Funds. First, Revised Article 9 deals directly with the concern of the New York Fed by providing that transferees of funds from a deposit account take free of a security interest in the deposit account, even if they actually know of the security interest and even if they give no value. See R9–332(b). The only exception is for a transferee who acts in collusion with the debtor in violating the rights of the secured party. (We have seen this rule before, in Problem 3.5.8. It applies as well to security interests in money. See R9–332(a).)

Consumer deposit accounts. Other than encountering some difficulties articulating the appropriate standard for the exception, the Drafting Committee had little difficulty settling on the "free-flow-of-funds" rule of R9–332(b). The Drafting Committee had greater difficulty deciding what to do about consumer deposit accounts. Representatives of banks that extend consumer credit argued for including consumer deposit accounts as original collateral. They claimed that the applicable common-law requirements for an effective "pledge" of a deposit account were uncertain and costly to implement. Representatives of consumer-advocacy groups did not dispute this claim. Rather, they objected to eliminating the uncertainty and cost, lest the use of deposit accounts as original collateral become more widespread. Ultimately, the Drafting Committee agreed to exclude from Revised Article 9 assignments of deposit accounts in consumer transactions. See R9–109(d)(13). Is this rule a craven response to political pressure, or is the rule supported by a discernable policy? In answering this question, consider whether and the extent to which transactions with consumer debtors differ from those with business debtors, including sole proprietorships and "mom and pop" enterprises.

Perfection by Control. The third basic principle is that a security interest in a deposit account as *original* collateral may be perfected *only* by "control"; it may not be perfected by filing a financing statement. See R9–312(b)(1); R9–314(a). (A security interest in a deposit account that is *proceeds* of most other types of other collateral may be perfected by filing against the original collateral. See R9–315(c), (d)(2).) "Control" of a deposit account is defined in much the same way as "control" of a security entitlement. One option is to use a three-party control agreement: A secured party has control of a deposit account if the debtor, secured party, and bank with which the deposit account is maintained agree in an authenticated record that the bank will comply with instructions originated by the secured party directing disposition of the funds in the deposit account without further consent by the debtor. See R9–104(a)(2). Alternatively, a secured party has control if the secured party becomes the bank's customer with respect to the deposit account. See R9–104(a)(3). If the secured party is the bank with which the deposit account is maintained, the secured party automatically has control. See R9–104(a)(1).

A secured party having control of a deposit account normally has the power (even if not always the right) to appropriate the funds on deposit. For some participants in the drafting process, control served as a proxy for the secured party's having relied on the deposit account as collateral when deciding whether and to what extent to extend credit to the debtor. Perhaps more accurately, lack of control served as a proxy for lack of reliance. A secured party who does not even take the steps necessary to enable itself to reach the funds on the debtor's default is unlikely to rely on the deposit account as original collateral in any meaningful way. Its unperfected security interest is junior to the rights of the debtor's judicial lien creditors and trustee in bankruptcy.

Revised Article 9's control-only perfection rule is in part a response to those who argued that it should not be "too easy" to take a deposit account as original collateral. For third parties, the rule actually makes it more difficult to perfect a security interest in a deposit account as original collateral than under the nonuniform versions of Former Article 9 in force in some jurisdictions. See, e.g., Cal. Com. Code § 9302(1)(g) (perfection is achieved by giving written notice of the security interest to the bank at which the deposit account is maintained). On the other hand, the bank with which a deposit account is maintained obtains control by virtue of nothing more than its status. See R9–104(a)(1). Does the control-as-proxy-for reliance argument apply to such a bank? Does the status-based method for obtaining control (and thus perfection) conflict with Revised Article 9's general insistence on giving public notice as a condition to achieving priority? Even if not, should something more than an oral security agreement (and the giving of value) be required as a condition to the bank's obtaining a perfected security interest?

Priority. Like the provisions defining "control," the rules governing priority of security interests in deposit accounts are analogous, but not identical, to those governing security entitlements. See R9–327. In particular, the bank with which the deposit account is maintained enjoys priority over a third party who enters into a control agreement with respect to the deposit account. See R9–327(3). As indicated in Note (3) on Security Interests in Investment Property, supra, the credit extended by a broker or other securities intermediary typically is a margin loan used to acquire the collateral (security entitlement). For this reason, a priority analogous to purchase-money priority may be appropriate. Banks, on the other hand, do not typically extend credit that enables the borrower to acquire the funds in a deposit account. The proceeds of a loan may be disbursed by crediting the debtor's deposit account, but typically a loan is made with the intention that the debtor spend the funds, not keep them in the deposit account. Is there another reason why the bank's security interest should take priority?

With respect to security entitlements, we have seen that a third party who wishes to achieve priority over the security interest of the securities intermediary must induce the securities intermediary to enter into a subordination agreement. See R9–328(3); Problem 9.3.2, supra. In contrast, a secured party who has control by virtue of having becoming the bank's customer with respect to a deposit account obtains priority over the bank. See R9–327(4). Can you explain this difference?

Enforcement. Because control of a deposit account gives a secured party the ability to direct the disposition of funds in the deposit account without further consent by the debtor, enforcement of a perfected-by-control security interest in a deposit account should be easy. If the secured party is the bank with which the deposit account is maintained, after default the bank may apply the balance of the deposit account to the obligation secured by the deposit account. See R9–607(a)(4). A third-party secured party with control under R9–104(a)(2) or (3) may instruct the bank to pay the balance of the deposit account to or for the benefit of the secured party. R9–607(a)(5). Article 9 does not specifically address the enforcement rights of a secured party whose security interest in a deposit account is perfected by filing or unperfected. (Either of these situations might arise with respect to a deposit account that constitutes proceeds of other collateral.) As a general matter, after default, a secured party "may notify [a] person obligated on collateral to make payment . . . to or for the benefit of the secured party" and "may enforce the obligations of [a] person obligated on collateral and exercise the rights of the debtor with respect to the [person's] obligation . . . to make payment or otherwise render performance to the debtor." R9–607(a)(1), (3). But R9–607(e) makes clear that R9–607 "does not determine whether [a] bank[] or other person obligated on collateral owes a duty to a secured party." R9–607(e). Thus, unless non-UCC law otherwise provides (which it generally does not), a secured party who lacks control of a deposit account must resort to judicial process to obtain the funds on deposit.

Recoupment and Setoff. A bank may have a right of recoupment or setoff under the common law, as a matter of contract, or under a (non-UCC) statute. This right, when available, permits the bank to offset amounts it owes its customer (the depositor) on the deposit account against amounts that the debtor owes the bank. If the depositor creates a security interest in a deposit account, however, an obvious question arises as to the relationship between the security interest in the deposit account and the bank's right of setoff against the same deposit account. R9–340 addresses this relationship. Under R9–340(a), the bank "may exercise any right of recoupment or set-off against a secured party that holds a security interest in the deposit account." An exception is made in R9–340(c), however; if the secured party has perfected its security interest by itself becoming the bank's customer on the deposit account (see R9–104(a)(3)), then the bank may not effectively exercise setoff "based on a claim against the debtor."

A bank that holds a security interest in its debtor's (i.e., the bank's customer's) deposit account assumes an intriguing combination of roles–it is at once the assignee of the deposit account and the obligor on the deposit account. This situation also raises obvious questions about the relationship between the bank's right of setoff and its status as a secured party. R9–340(b) provides that Revised Article 9 "does not affect a right of recoupment of set-off of the secured party as to a deposit account maintained with the secured party." Thus, Revised Article 9 generally leaves the bank's recoupment or setoff rights unimpaired. On the other hand, the secured party must look elsewhere for its right of recoupment or setoff, inasmuch as Revised Article 9 does not create any such right. See R9–340, Official Comment 2.

Chapter 11, Section 5(C), addresses in more detail the relationship between security interests under Revised Article 9 and rights of recoupment and setoff.

(4) Classifying the Collateral. The line between a deposit account and a securities account, as to which an entitlement holder enjoys a security entitlement, is not always clear. The distinction can be important. For example, if a secured party has filed a financing statement against "debtor's account No. 12345, maintained with ABC Bank," the filing would be sufficient to perfect a security interest if the account is a securities account but would be ineffective if the account is a deposit account. See R9–312(a) (security interest in investment property may be perfected by filing); (b)(1) (security interest in deposit account may be perfected *only* by control).

As to the conceptual distinctions between deposit accounts and securities accounts, consider the following excerpt from the Prefatory Note to Revised Article 8:

> An ordinary bank deposit account would not fall within the definition of "security" in Section 8–102(a)(15), so the rules of Parts 2, 3, and 4 of Article 8 do not apply to deposit accounts. Nor would the relationship between a bank and its depositors be governed by the rules of Part 5 of Article 8. The Part 5 rules apply to "security entitlements." .... A person has a security entitlement governed by Part 5 only if the relationship in question falls within the definition of "securities account." The definition of securities account in Section 8–501(a) excludes deposit accounts from the Part 5 rules of Article 8. One of the basic elements of the relationship between a securities intermediary and an entitlement holder is that the securities intermediary has the duty to hold exactly the quantity of securities that it carries for the account of its customers. See Section 8–504. The assets that a securities intermediary holds for its entitlement holder are not assets that the securities intermediary can use in its own proprietary business. See Section 8–503. A deposit account is an entirely different arrangement. A bank is not required to hold in its vaults or in deposit accounts with other banks a sum of money equal to the claims of all of its depositors. Banks are permitted to use depositors' funds in their ordinary lending business; indeed, that is a primary function of banks. A deposit account, unlike a securities account, is simply a debtor-creditor relationship. Thus a bank or other financial institution maintaining deposit accounts is not covered by Part 5 of Article 8.
>
> Today, it is common for brokers to maintain securities accounts for their customers which include arrangements for the customers to hold liquid "cash" assets in the form of money market mutual fund shares. Insofar as the broker is holding money market mutual fund

shares for its customer, the customer has a security entitlement to the money market mutual fund shares. It is also common for brokers to offer their customers an arrangement in which the customer has access to those liquid assets via a deposit account with a bank, whereby shares of the money market fund are redeemed to cover checks drawn on the account. Article 8 applies only to the securities account; the linked bank account remains an account covered by other law. Thus the rights and duties of the customer and the bank are governed not by Article 8, but by the relevant payment system law, such as Article 4 or Article 4A.

SECTION 5. NON-TEMPORAL PRIORITY IN PROCEEDS

INTRODUCTORY NOTE

Former Article 9 dealt with priorities in proceeds in substantially the same way that it dealt with priorities in original collateral. Under F9–312(6), for purposes of the first-to-file-or-perfect priority rule of F9–312(5), the date of filing or perfection for original collateral also was the date of filing or perfection for proceeds of the collateral. With one major exception—proceeds of collateral subject to a purchase-money security interest under F9–312(3) or (4)—the former Article otherwise was silent on the priority of security interests in proceeds. (A minor exception was F9–306(5), which dealt with returned and repossessed goods in the context of accounts and chattel paper financing.) The effect of this silence, however, was to make applicable the first-to-file-or-perfect rule.

We have seen that Revised Article 9 contains several non-temporal priority rules—*i.e.*, rules that award priority on a basis other than priority in time. The include priority rules for security interests in deposit accounts (R9–327), investment property (R9–328), chattel paper and instruments (R9–330), and collateral subject to special priority rules under UCC Articles 3, 7, and 8 (R9–331). During the drafting process, some people expressed concern that a secured party who enjoys non-temporal priority in original collateral would not enjoy priority in proceeds. Indeed, R9–322(a) and (b) indicate that, in the absence of a contrary provision, the first-to-file-or-perfect rule, not the relevant non-temporal priority rule, would apply to proceeds. Moreover, inasmuch as filing is not a permissible method of perfection for certain types collateral covered by these non-temporal rules, the time of perfection would control priority. Because perfection is conditioned upon attachment, which is conditioned in turn upon the debtor's having rights in the collateral, perfection in proceeds of those types of collateral would not occur until (and thus priority under the first-to-file-or-perfect rule of R9–322(a)(1) would date from when) the proceeds came into being as such. See R9–203(b)(2); R9–308(a).

In addition to concerns about the inapplicability of the non-temporal rules to proceeds, the prospect of fully extending the reach of the temporal priority rules to proceeds also generated concerns. For example, assume that on June 1 *SP–1* perfects its security interest in a debtor's deposit account by control, on July 1 *SP–2* perfects its security interest in the debtor's inventory by filing, and on August 1 *SP–1* files a financing statement covering inventory. The debtor then uses cash from the deposit account to purchase new inventory. Under the first-to-file-or-perfect rule, *SP–1*'s security interest would have priority over that of *SP–2*, even though *SP–2* filed first and a search failed to turn up *SP–1*'s filing (which had not yet been made). This effect arguably would undermine the filing system.

The statutory solution is an enormously complex and opaque set of priority rules found in subsections (c), (d), and (e) of R9–322. The upshot is generally to extend the non-temporal priority to most proceeds, see R9–322(c), but to apply a new first-to-file (*not* first-to-file-*or-perfect*) priority rule to proceeds consisting of the types of collateral for which filing is the typical means of perfection. See R9–322(d), (e).

The Problems below illustrate the complexities of the rules governing non-temporal priorities in proceeds. While you are solving them, keep in mind that authors who are more devious (or who have more fertile imaginations) could have come up with even more challenging exercises.

Only time and experience will reveal whether the benefits of the new rules on proceeds priorities outweigh the costs of complexity. If the rules were implicated only in the unusual case, the complexity might not be cause for concern. However, one must confront and understand this scheme to reach the conclusion that the first-to-file secured party claiming inventory or equipment will also have priority in after-acquired inventory or equipment purchased with cash proceeds of an encumbered deposit account—a scenario that may become very typical.

Problem 9.5.1. *SP–1* perfected its security interest in *D*'s investment property by filing. Thereafter, *SP–2* perfected its security interest in *D*'s 1000 shares of General Motors common stock by taking control of the certificated security (see R9–314; R9–106; R8–106; Problem 9.3.2, supra) and by filing against investment property. *D* received a dividend check for $430.00 on account of the stock and deposited the check into a deposit account. Both the check and deposit account constitute cash proceeds. See R9–102(a)(9). Assuming the $430.00 remains identifiable, who has the senior claim to it? See R9–315(c), (d); R9–328(1); R9–322(a)–(e) & Comments 7–9.

Problem 9.5.2. *SP–1* perfected its security interest in *D*'s deposit account (Deposit Account No. 1) by control. See R9–314; R9–104; Problems 9.4.1 and 9.4.2, supra. Thereafter, *SP–2* perfected a security interest in *D*'s inventory by filing. Before filing, *SP–2* conducted a search against *D* in the appropriate filing office and found no conflicting filings. *D* then used funds from Deposit Account No. 1 to buy new inventory. *SP–1* can trace its security interest from Deposit Account No. 1 to the new inventory, as identifiable proceeds of the deposit account. *SP–2* has a security interest in the new inventory as original collateral under the after-acquired property clause of its security agreement.

(a) Which security interest has priority in the new inventory?

(b) *D* sells the new inventory and deposits the buyer's check in Deposit Account No. 2. Assuming the funds remain identifiable as proceeds of the new inventory, which security interest has priority in them? Do you need additional facts to answer this Problem? See R9–315(c), (d); R9–327(1); R9–322(a)–(e) & Comments 7–9.

Problem 9.5.3. *SP*–1 perfected its security interest in *D*'s deposit account by control. Thereafter, *SP*–2 perfected a security interest in *D*'s inventory by filing. Before filing, *SP*–2 conducted a search against *D* in the appropriate filing office and found no conflicting filings. (These facts also appear in Problem 9.5.2.) *SP*–1 then perfected its security interest in *D*'s inventory by filing a financing statement. *D* then used funds from the deposit account to buy new inventory. As in Problem 9.5.2, *SP*–1 can trace its security interest from the deposit account to the new inventory, as identifiable proceeds of the deposit account, and *SP*–2 has a security interest in the new inventory as original collateral under the after-acquired property clause of its security agreement. Unlike Problem 9.5.2, however, *SP*–1 also has a perfected security interest in the new inventory as original collateral. Which security interest has priority in the new inventory? See R9–322(a)–(e) & Comment 9, Example 12.

SECTION 6.   FINANCING OTHER INTANGIBLES

Intangibles other than those that we have encountered thus far (primarily accounts, chattel paper, deposit accounts, instruments (including promissory notes), investment property, and payment intangibles) also may be the subject of secured financing. Important examples are intellectual property consisting of interests in copyrights, patents, and trademarks, each of which is subject to regulation under a federal statute. In addition, the new Uniform Computer Information Transactions Act (1999) ("UCITA") promises to fill significant gaps in applicable state law, although it generally defers to Revised Article 9 as to secured transactions. Treatment of the financing of intellectual property, including the extent to which federal law may supersede provisions of the UCC, generally is beyond the scope of this book's coverage. However, this section identifies some provisions of Revised Article 9 that affect the financing of intellectual property and other intangibles.

We have seen already that software—computer programs—imbedded in goods (e.g., the software that runs the computer regulating the fuel system on an automobile) is treated as part of the goods under R9–102(a)(44). See Problem 3.2.6, supra. We also saw that software associated with specific goods in a transaction may, along with the goods, support chattel paper. See R9–102(a)(11). See Note (1) on Purchasers of Chattel Paper, supra. Software (and many other types of intellectual property) typically is **licensed** by a **licensor**—the owner of the software (or a licensee that has the power to relicense the property)—to a **licensee**, the person who is authorized to use the software. The licensor's right to payment under the license arrangement is an "account." R9–102(a)(2). Revised Article 9 also deals with the licensing of intellectual property in three additional contexts.

Licensee in Ordinary Course of Business. R9–321(b) provides that a licensee in ordinary course of business of a general intangible under a nonexclusive license takes free of a security interest in the general intangible. The term "licensee in ordinary course of business" is defined in R9–312(a). The rule contained in subsection (b) is, of course, analogous to the protection afforded to a buyer in ordinary course of business under R9–320(a) and to a lessee in ordinary course of business in R9–321(c). A typical example of the operation of subsection (b) would be the purchase at retail of word processing software. The purchaser (licensee) would take free of a security interest created by the licensor in the underlying intellectual property. The license is **nonexclusive** because licensor is free to enter into similar licenses with other licensees covering the same software.

Waiver of Defenses Agreement. Because F9–206 explicitly permitted waivers of defenses only in transactions relating to goods (sales and leases), it left open the question of how a licensee may effectively waive its defenses under a license as against its licensor's assignee. R9–403 fills this gap; it validates waivers by any account debtor that complies with its terms.

Restrictions on Assignability. Revised Article 9 goes quite far to facilitate the ability of a licensee of intellectual property to obtain financing secured by its rights under a license. R9–408 permits the creation and perfection of security interests in health-care-insurance receivables, promissory notes, or general intangibles notwithstanding otherwise effective contractual or legal restrictions on transfer. It renders these restrictions ineffective along with any provisions that would give rise to a default based on a violation of the restrictions. R9–408(a), (c). By covering all general intangibles, the scope of R9–408 is much broader than licenses of intellectual property; subsections (a) and (c) refer to: " ... a general intangible, including a contract, permit, license, or franchise." Note that R9–408 applies only to sales of promissory notes and payment intangibles (a type of general intangible). It does not apply to security interests in promissory notes or payment intangibles that secure obligations; those security interests are governed by R9–406(f). As state law, R9–408 cannot, of course, override any contrary federal law. See R9–408, Official Comment 9.

Having facilitated the creation and perfection of certain security interests, R9–408 balances this treatment with considerable protection for the other parties to the collateral that it affects (e.g., account debtors on general intangibles). Subsection (d) limits the ability of a secured party to enforce the collateral against the other party and provides several other protections; please review subsection (d) now. These limitations sharply distinguish R9–408 from R9–406(f); the latter renders legal restrictions "ineffective" in the case of collateral to which it applies. Why do you suppose the limitations in R9–408 were thought necessary? See R9–408, Official Comment 6.

CHAPTER 10

SECURITY INTERESTS (INCLUDING THE "FLOATING LIEN") IN BANKRUPTCY

This Chapter discusses the rights of a secured party when the debtor enters bankruptcy. Although the debtor's insolvency is not a statutory prerequisite to the commencement of a bankruptcy case, the vast proportion of debtors who enter bankruptcy are insolvent. Unsecured creditors are likely to receive much less than the amount of their claims. Thus, bankruptcy is a time when a security interest may be of particular value.

SECTION 1.   OVERVIEW OF BANKRUPTCY

The Bankruptcy Process. As discussed above in Chapter 1, Section 1, the nonbankruptcy law of creditors' rights is a race of diligence: every creditor for itself. Bankruptcy substitutes a collective debt-collection procedure for individual collection activity. The filing of a bankruptcy petition puts an immediate halt to the race. See BC 362(a) (discussed infra). Instead, all creditors must satisfy their claims only through the bankruptcy.

The filing of a bankruptcy petition creates an estate. The property of the estate generally includes "all legal or equitable interests of the debtor in property as of the commencement of the case." BC 541.

Some bankruptcy cases are commenced for the purpose of liquidating the property of the estate and distributing the proceeds to creditors. In these cases, which are filed under Chapter 7 of the Bankruptcy Code, a trustee is appointed to "collect and reduce to money the property of the estate for which such trustee serves, and close the estate as expeditiously as is compatible with the best interests of the parties in interest." BC 704(1). The bankruptcy court may authorize the trustee to operate the debtor's business, but only for a limited period and only if the operation is in the best interests of the estate and consistent with the orderly liquidation of the estate. See BC 721.

Cases filed under Chapter 11 (reorganization) contemplate that the debtor will continue to operate its business as debtor-in-possession ("DIP"). A trustee is not appointed in Chapter 11 cases, except in the relatively unusual circumstances set forth in BC 1104. Instead, the debtor-in-possession enjoys most of the rights and powers, and is charged with performing most of the functions and duties, of the trustee. See BC 1107; BC 1108; BC 1106(a). While the DIP operates the business, Chapter 11 affords creditors and the debtor (or, if the debtor is a corporation, its shareholders) the opportunity to determine what should be done with the assets so as to maximize the return. Should some or all of the assets be sold? Used to continue one or more lines of the prebankruptcy business? Used to enter into a new line of business?[1]

Where corporate debtors are concerned, the principal purposes of bankruptcy are to maximize the value of the corporation and to allocate the value among various claimants. Substituting a collective remedy (bankruptcy) for individual remedies promotes the former purpose. Nonbankruptcy law subjects businesses to piecemeal dissolution: each creditor is free to levy upon and sell whatever assets it chooses. In contrast, bankruptcy enables the assets to be sold together. The sale of a business as a package is likely to yield more than individual sales of each of the assets; a buyer typically will be willing to pay an additional amount to reflect the cost savings in gathering together the different assets needed to operate the business. A business whose assets not only are maintained intact but also are up and running is likely to command an even larger ("going-concern") premium. Moreover, sales conducted to enforce judicial liens are distress sales. The seller (the sheriff) must sell quickly and so is in no position to hold out for a higher price. In contrast, bankruptcy liquidation puts the seller (the trustee, who represents the creditors) in a somewhat better bargaining position by affording the trustee a little more time.

Bankruptcy not only affects the size of the corporate pie but also its distribution. Allocating the value of the corporation requires both a determination of who is entitled to share and a ranking of the entitlements relative to one another. Potential claimants include not only the prebankruptcy creditors but also the postbankruptcy creditors and the shareholders. In a Chapter 7 case, the distribution is fixed by statute. See BC 726. The statute generally (but not always) respects the nonbankruptcy ranking of various claims. Thus, holders of secured claims ordinarily will be entitled to the value of their collateral, see BC 725; holders of unsecured claims may share in the collateral's value only to the extent it exceeds the secured debt. Unsecured creditors are entitled to be paid in full before shareholders receive any distribution. See BC 726(a).

Chapter 11 permits the interested parties to fix the distribution in a "plan." See generally BC 1123 (contents of plan). A Chapter 11 plan divides creditors and holders of equity interests into classes and sets forth

---

1. Chapters 13 (available only to individual debtors with "regular income") and 12 (available only to debtors who are "family farmer[s] with regular annual income") are similar to Chapter 11 in that the debtor remains in possession of the property of the estate and undertakes to pay prebankruptcy debts pursuant to a court-approved plan. But unlike in Chapter 11 cases, creditors in Chapters 12 and 13 cases do not vote on proposed plans. A trustee is appointed in every Chapter 12 and Chapter 13 case; however, the trustee's primary obligation is to serve as a disbursement agent for payments made pursuant to the plan.

what (if anything) the members of each class will receive and when (if ever) they will receive it. See BC 1123(a). Most plans are **compositions** and **extensions**; that is, they provide (i) that the cash or other property (e.g., stock in the reorganized debtor) that creditors receive for their claims will be worth less than 100 cents on the dollar and (ii) that creditors will receive payment over time. The terms of any particular plan typically reflect extensive negotiations by representatives of shareholders and various creditor groups. Most claimants are afforded the opportunity to vote on the plan. Before their acceptances or rejections may be solicited, the court must approve a disclosure statement or summary of the plan as providing information sufficient to enable the voters to make an informed judgment about the plan. See BC 1125. Chapter 11 contains a number of protections for holders of claims in classes that reject the plan and for dissenting members of classes that approve the plan. See, e.g., BC 1129(a)(7), (a)(8); BC 1129(b).

Even when the debtor is an individual, bankruptcy may serve as a collective creditors' remedy. More often than not, however, there are few unencumbered assets available for distribution. For most individual debtors, bankruptcy affords a unique opportunity to begin financial life anew. This **fresh start** consists of three components. First, the individual debtor may keep certain prebankruptcy assets (**exempt** property) free of prepetition claims. See BC 522. Second, to the extent that the debtor's current, nonexempt assets do not suffice to pay prebankruptcy debts, the debts are **discharged**; that is, they no longer may be collected as personal liabilities of the debtor. The discharge has the effect of freeing the debtor's human capital (future earning potential) from the reach of prepetition creditors. See BC 727; BC 524; see also BC 541(a)(6) (property of the estate does not include earnings from services performed by individual debtors after commencement of bankruptcy case).[2] Third, employers and governmental units are prohibited from discriminating against the debtor *solely* because the debtor was insolvent, was in bankruptcy, or received a discharge. See BC 525. Moreover, BC 525(c) prohibits this type of discrimination in student loan programs, but it lacks the "solely" limitation.

What Will the Secured Party Recover From the Bankruptcy? As a first approximation, it is fair to say that bankruptcy respects the value of nonbankruptcy property rights, including security interests. Thus, a secured party is entitled to receive from the bankruptcy its collateral or the value of its collateral up to the amount of its claim. See BC 506(b); BC 724; BC 1129(a)(7). As we explain below, the secured party may be compelled to wait quite some time before receiving this value; however, even with a substantial delay, a creditor usually is much better off to receive the value of its collateral than it would be if it were unsecured. Holders of general unsecured claims share pro rata in whatever unencumbered assets remain after payment of secured claims, expenses of administering the bankruptcy

---

2. In contrast, Chapter 13 contemplates that the debtor will use future income to pay prebankruptcy claims. Chapter 13's discharge provisions are more generous to debtors than those applicable in a Chapter 7; for some debtors this can be a significant advantage.

case, and unsecured claims entitled to priority of payment (priority claims include those for unpaid prebankruptcy wages and taxes). See generally BC 726(a); BC 507(a).

The following Problems demonstrate the desirability of having a security interest in bankruptcy.

Problem 10.1.1. Debtor files a petition under Chapter 7 and has two assets: (i) a piece of equipment worth $100,000, subject to a perfected security interest securing an $80,000 debt to Seller; and (ii) real property worth $500,000, subject to a recorded mortgage securing a $400,000 debt to Bank. In addition, Debtor owes $300,000 to other (unsecured) creditors. How will the assets be distributed? (The effect of Seller's having perfected its security interest is discussed infra, Section 2(A).)

Problem 10.1.2. What result in Problem 10.1.1 if Debtor had purchased the equipment from Seller on an unsecured basis?

Problem 10.1.3. What result in Problem 10.1.1 if the equipment is worth only $70,000 at the time Debtor enters bankruptcy? Note that BC 506(a) would divide Seller's $80,000 claim into two parts: Seller would have a secured claim in the amount of the value of its collateral ($70,000); the balance of its claim ($10,000) would be an unsecured claim.

The Automatic Stay. Bankruptcy cases can be complex and time-consuming. Even the relatively simple consumer bankruptcy can take several months: The debtor's assets must be gathered together, the claims against the debtor must be assessed, and the value of the assets must be distributed among the claimants. Chapter 11 cases typically take much longer. Months, even years, may elapse before a plan is proposed. Approval of the disclosure statement, solicitation of acceptances and rejections, and the confirmation hearing extend the process even further.

To effect the orderly administration of the bankruptcy estate, creditors must be prevented from continuing the nonbankruptcy race to the assets while the bankruptcy case is proceeding. If creditors were free to ignore the pendency of the bankruptcy case, then much of the value of a collective proceeding would be lost: creditors would incur duplicative costs of collection, and assets might be sold piecemeal at distress prices.

Under BC 362(a), the filing of a bankruptcy petition "operates as a stay, applicable to all entities," of all collection activity with respect to prebankruptcy claims. The following Problems address the scope of the automatic stay as it applies to secured parties. Note that any acts taken in violation of the automatic stay are void, and that parties who deliberately violate the stay may be held in contempt of court and fined.

Problem 10.1.4. Debtor is in the printing business. On November 1, Seller sold Debtor a press and retained a security interest in the press to secure its price. Debtor filed a Chapter 11 petition on November 25. Seller has yet to file a financing statement to perfect its security interest. May Seller do so? See BC 362(a)(4); BC 541(a) (defining property of the estate). The consequences of having a security interest that is unperfected at the time the debtor enters bankruptcy are discussed infra, Section 2(A).

Problem 10.1.5. Assume that, in Problem 10.1.4, Seller filed a financing statement on November 5. May Seller repossess the press? See BC 362(a)(3), (a)(5).

Problem 10.1.6. May Debtor continue to use the press if Seller cannot repossess it? See BC 363(c); BC 1108.

Problem 10.1.7. Seller is concerned that the case may last several years, and that the press will decline substantially in value during that time, whether because of depreciation caused by normal wear and tear, obsolescence resulting from technological improvements in presses, or unanticipated damage resulting from misuse or natural calamity. For these reasons, Seller would like to repossess the press and sell it now, rather than wait for a future distribution from the bankruptcy. What can Seller do? See BC 363(e); BC 362(d); BC 362(g); BC 361; Note on Relief from the Automatic Stay, infra.

NOTE ON RELIEF FROM THE AUTOMATIC STAY

BC 362(d) sets forth two circumstances under which the bankruptcy court "shall grant relief from the stay." Under subsection (d)(2), the court shall grant relief from the stay if the debtor "does not have an equity in [the] property" and the property is "not necessary to an effective reorganization." As used in BC 362(d)(2)(A), the debtor's "equity" is calculated by deducting from the value of the collateral the amount of debt that it secures. (When the property secures more than one debt, the cases tend to calculate the debtor's "equity" by deducting the aggregate amount of the secured obligations from the value of the collateral). See, e.g., Stewart v. Gurley, 745 F.2d 1194 (9th Cir.1984); In re Royal Palm Square Associates, 124 B.R. 129 (Bkrtcy.M.D.Fla.1991). Accordingly, if Seller can prove that the press is worth $80,000 and secures a debt of $100,000, the first element of BC 362(d)(2) would be met. The court must grant relief from the stay unless the trustee (or DIP) proves that the property is "necessary to an effective reorganization." See BC 362(d)(2), (g)(2). According to a widely-cited dictum from the Supreme Court,

> [w]hat this requires is not merely a showing that if there is conceivably to be an effective reorganization, this property will be needed for it; but that the property is essential for an effective reorganization *that is in prospect.* This means . . . that there must be "a reasonable possibility of a successful reorganization within a reasonable time."

United Savings Association v. Timbers of Inwood Forest Associates, Ltd., 484 U.S. 365, 375–76, 108 S.Ct. 626, 633, 98 L.Ed.2d 740, 751 (1988) (emphasis in original). Thus, the trustee will not succeed merely by proving that *if* Debtor is to continue in the printing business, continued use of the press would be essential.

The court also is required to lift the stay "for cause, including lack of adequate protection of an interest in property of [a] party in interest." BC 362(d)(1). BC 361 explains the term "adequate protection." To protect against an anticipated decline in the value of the press resulting from continued use by Debtor, the trustee might provide monthly payments to Seller in the amount of the anticipated decline. See BC 361(1). To protect against the risk of obsolescence, the trustee might secure Seller's claim with a lien on other property of the estate. See BC 361(2). Where there is a risk of destruction, the trustee might insure the collateral against loss. See BC 361(3).

But even if the trustee (or DIP) provides the described protection, Seller may be less than content. Seller has bargained for the right, upon Debtor's default, to repossess the collateral, sell it, and apply the proceeds toward its claim against Debtor. See R9–609; R9–610; R9–615. Were the automatic stay not in place, Seller would receive the value of its collateral in a matter of weeks. Even if the trustee insures the press, makes periodic payments, and grants a supplemental lien, Seller will be worse off. Rather than have a certain $80,000 in the very near term, Seller has only part payment now and a promise of the balance when a distribution is made. Even if the promise is kept, Seller will receive the vast proportion of its claim in the future, perhaps years from now. Had the automatic stay been lifted, Seller would receive the money in a matter of weeks; by investing the money, Seller would have considerably more than $80,000 in a few years.

Consider the following statutory argument. Adequate protection of an interest of an entity in property (here, Seller's security interest) may be provided by "granting such other relief . . . as will result in the realization by such entity [Seller] of the indubitable equivalent of such entity's interest in such property." BC 361(3). Receipt of periodic cash payments and a secured promise to pay the balance at an indefinite time in the future is not the "indubitable equivalent" of receiving $80,000 today. If payment is to be deferred, Seller should be entitled to recover an amount equal to $80,000 plus interest on that amount, in order to put Seller in the same position it would have been in had the stay not been in effect. To support the argument, Seller might cite the legislative history of BC 361, which contains the statement that "[s]ecured creditors should not be deprived of the benefit of their bargain." H.R. Rep. No. 595, 95th Cong., 1st Sess. 339 (1977), reprinted in 1978 U.S.C.C.A.N. 5963, 6295; S. Rep. No. 989, 95th Cong., 2d Sess. 53 (1978), reprinted in 1978 U.S.C.C.A.N. 5787, 5839. The benefit of Seller's bargain is to turn the collateral into cash promptly upon Debtor's default.

The Supreme Court considered and unanimously rejected this argument in United Savings Association v. Timbers of Inwood Forest Associates, Ltd., 484 U.S. 365, 108 S.Ct. 626, 98 L.Ed.2d 740 (1988). The Court concluded that the "interest in property" that BC 362(d)(1) protects does not include a secured party's right to foreclose on the collateral. Thus the "value of such entity's interest" in BC 361 means the dollar value of the collateral and not the present value of the secured party's right to use the collateral as a means to satisfy its claim. Accordingly, as long as the trustee takes appropriate steps to protect Seller's ultimate recovery of $80,000, Seller has received "adequate protection" for its security interest and is not entitled to relief from the stay on that ground.

In *Timbers*, the Supreme Court distinguished the undersecured creditor, whose collateral is worth less than its claim, from the oversecured creditor, whose collateral is worth more. In holding that undersecured creditors are not entitled to recover interest as part of the adequate protection required by BC 362, the Court relied in part on BC 502(b)(2) and 506(b). Under the former section, interest that is unmatured at the time of the filing of the petition is not part of the creditor's allowed secured claim; i.e., it ordinarily will not be paid from the bankruptcy. Under BC 506(b), to the extent that a claim is secured by collateral having a value in excess of the claim (i.e., to the extent that the secured creditor is oversecured), "there shall be allowed to the holder of such claim, interest on such claim, and any reasonable fees, costs, or charges provided for under the agreement under which such claim arose." In other words, postpetition interest continues to accrue on oversecured claims. However, interest accruing postpetition becomes part of the allowed secured claim; nothing in the Bankruptcy Code requires that interest be paid as it accrues.

As you might expect from reading the foregoing, secured parties have incentives not to become enmeshed in a bankruptcy case. If they are undersecured, they ultimately will recover the value of their collateral but will lose the value of having received it promptly. Oversecured creditors will be entitled to recover accrued postpetition interest to the extent that the value of the collateral is large enough to cover it, but the rate at which interest accrues may be less than the rate to which the parties have agreed.[3] And even oversecured creditors must wait until the time of distribution before actually recovering interest that accrues postpetition.

Problem 10.1.8. Assume that, in Problem 10.1.5, Seller repossessed the press on November 10 (prior to bankruptcy) and scheduled a sale for December 10.

(a) May Seller conduct the sale? See BC 362(a)(5).

(b) Debtor's trustee demands that Seller return the press so that Debtor can use it during the bankruptcy case. Must Seller do so? See BC 542(a); BC 363(c); BC 541(a)(1); United States v. Whiting Pools, Inc. 462 U.S. 198, 103 S.Ct. 2309, 76 L.Ed.2d 515 (1983) (turnover order was properly issued against IRS, which had seized property subject to federal tax lien before commencement of Chapter 11 case).

(c) Suppose Seller is concerned that, if Debtor uses the press, the value of its collateral will decline? See BC 363(e).

SECTION 2. THE BANKRUPTCY TRUSTEE'S AVOIDING POWERS

Introductory Note. Generally speaking, the holder of a security interest will receive a secured claim in bankruptcy. As we discussed above,

---

3. The courts generally agree that the contract rate is the appropriate rate at which interest accrues under BC 506(b); however, when the contract contains two rates, the higher of which comes into effect upon the debtor's default, courts often consider the equities of the case in determining whether the higher rate applies under BC 506(b).

the holder of a secured claim is entitled to the value of its collateral (up to the amount of its claim) from the bankruptcy estate. However, not all security interests are valid in bankruptcy. The Bankruptcy Code affords the trustee (or DIP) the power to avoid (i.e., undo) certain otherwise valid prebankruptcy transfers, including transfers of security interests. This Section discusses the **avoiding powers** as they apply to security interests.

For the most part, BC 544–548 define the scope of the avoiding powers. BC 550 sets forth the consequence of avoidance: "to the extent that a transfer is avoided under [one of the enumerated sections of the Bankruptcy Code], the trustee may recover, for the benefit of the estate, the property transferred, or, if the court so orders, the value of such property." In other words, if the trustee succeeds in avoiding the transfer of a security interest, the trustee may recover the property transferred (i.e., the security interest) for the benefit of the estate. Any interest in property that the trustee recovers under BC 550 becomes property of the estate, see BC 541(a)(3), and is preserved automatically for the benefit of the estate. See BC 551. As a practical matter, this means that the avoided security interest no longer encumbers the collateral, and that whatever portion of the collateral it previously encumbered becomes available for distribution to creditors generally. Among those creditors will be the (former) secured party.

(A) UNPERFECTED SECURITY INTERESTS: THE STRONG ARM OF THE TRUSTEE

Problem 10.2.1. Debtor files a petition under Chapter 7 and has two assets: (i) a piece of equipment worth $100,000, subject to an unperfected security interest securing an $80,000 debt to Seller; and (ii) real property worth $500,000, subject to a recorded mortgage securing a $400,000 debt to Bank. In addition, Debtor owes $300,000 to other (unsecured) creditors. How will the assets be distributed? See R9–203(b); BC 541(a)(1); BC 544(a)(1); R9–317(a)(2); R9–310(a); BC 541(a)(3); Notes on Bankruptcy Code Section 544(a), infra. (This Problem is identical to Problem 10.1.1, supra, except that Seller's security interest is unperfected.)

Problem 10.2.2. On June 1 Devon bought a set of living-room furniture from Cellar Department Store and executed a security agreement, covering the furniture, to secure payment of the price. Cellar did not file a financing statement. On July 1 Devon went into bankruptcy. What are the rights of Cellar and the trustee? See R9–309(1).

Problem 10.2.3. On June 1 Dramco purchased pharmaceutical equipment from Supplier. Supplier, who retained a security interest to secure payment of the price, filed a financing statement on June 9. In the interim, on June 7, Dramco filed a bankruptcy petition.

(a) What are the rights of Supplier and the trustee? See BC 544(a)(1); BC 546(b); R9–317(e).

(b) Did Supplier violate the automatic stay? See BC 362(b)(3).

NOTES ON BANKRUPTCY CODE SECTION 544(a)

(1) The Operation of BC 544(a). The assets that will be available for distribution in the bankruptcy case are referred to as "property of the estate." Under BC 541(a)(1), property of the estate includes "all legal or equitable interests of the debtor in property as of the commencement of the case." When the bankruptcy case in Problem 10.2.1 was commenced, Debtor was the owner of the equipment, but its ownership interest was encumbered by Seller's security interest. As you know, Seller's failure to file or otherwise "perfect" its security interest does not impair Seller's rights to the collateral against Debtor. See R9–203(b). Hence, at first blush, it would appear that the property of Debtor's estate would not include Seller's unperfected security interest, which would be effective in bankruptcy.

The bad news for Seller is BC 544(a). This section sometimes is called the "strong-arm" clause because of the formidable powers it confers on the bankruptcy trustee. BC 544(a)(1) affords to the trustee, as of the commencement of the case, the rights and powers of a creditor that extends credit to the debtor at the time of the commencement of the case, and that obtains, at that time and with respect to that credit, a judicial lien on all property on which a creditor on a simple contract could have obtained a judicial lien, whether or not such a creditor exists. In other words, BC 544(a)(1) asks us to *imagine* that a specified type of creditor has obtained a "judicial lien" on the property; it affords to the trustee the rights of that *hypothetical* lien creditor.

What is a "judicial lien"? Happily, the Bankruptcy Code gives us a definition that is short and relatively clear. The long list of definitions in BC 101 includes paragraph (36): "'judicial lien' means lien obtained by judgment, levy, sequestration, or other legal or equitable process or proceeding." For personal property, the most significant illustration is a "lien obtained by . . . levy," e.g., seizure of the property by a sheriff under a writ of execution. Thus, if an imaginary levy, on an imaginary judgment of unlimited amount, would have established a lien in favor of an imaginary creditor, the rights and powers that the lien would have afforded to the imaginary creditor are taken over by the very real trustee in bankruptcy.

What are those rights and powers? Under a broad reading of the Commerce Clause of the Constitution, Congress might have established unified national rules on the relative rights of lien creditors and holders of security interests. However, Congress has not done so: the basic rules must be derived from state law. You are familiar with the applicable state law; it is R9–317(a)(2), in the form enacted by the relevant state. Under R9–317(a)(2), at the "commencement of the [bankruptcy] case"—i.e., the filing of the bankruptcy petition—would a judgment creditor of Debtor who obtained an execution lien on the equipment have acquired rights superior to Seller's unperfected security interest? If so, then the trustee likewise will do so and render Seller unsecured.

(2) The Policy Behind BC 544(a). Why does the Bankruptcy Code invalidate certain otherwise valid security interests in bankruptcy? Consider the following explanations:

BC 544(a)(1) Mirrors the Nonbankruptcy Result. Outside of bankruptcy, who would have been entitled to the value of Debtor's equipment? Although Seller retained a security interest effective against Debtor, Seller was not guaranteed "first dibs" on the equipment. Any creditor or group of creditors that acquired a judicial lien on the equipment before Seller perfected its security interest would have taken priority over Seller. In the nonbankruptcy race to this asset, Seller was leading, but had not yet won when bankruptcy occurred. When the ultimate nonbankruptcy outcome has yet to be determined, BC 544 has the effect of creating a "tie": Seller and the competing, unsecured creditors share equally in the value of the equipment. For a fuller explication of this argument, see T. Jackson, The Logic and Limits of Bankruptcy Law 70–75 (1986).

A variation on this argument is as follows: Traditionally, upon the commencement of a bankruptcy proceeding at the behest of creditors (i.e., an **involuntary bankruptcy**), a trustee took possession of the debtor's assets; the creditors represented by the trustee thereby acquired a lien on the debtor's property. Although most bankruptcy petitions now are filed by debtors rather than creditors (i.e., most bankruptcies are **voluntary**), the result should be the same: a judicial officer has taken control over the debtor's property and the creditors (or their representative) thereby should acquire a lien. Like any other lien that arises through the judicial process or through the exercise of a collective creditors' remedy, the lien that arises on bankruptcy should take priority over an unperfected security interest. See R9–317(a)(2); R9–102(a)(52).

BC 544(a)(1) Reflects a Bankruptcy Policy Against Secret Liens. Although phrased in general terms, the primary use of the strong-arm power historically has been the avoidance of unperfected security interests and other secret liens. As a normative matter, one might argue that bankruptcy distribution *should* mirror nonbankruptcy distribution; however, as a descriptive matter, BC 544(a) changes the distribution. Bankruptcy calls off the race to the assets. When the bankruptcy petition is filed, the secured party has an enforceable interest in the collateral; unsecured creditors do not. The secured party has won the race. BC 544(a) deprives the secured party of its victory because it has come at the expense of unsecured creditors, who may have been prejudiced by the secret lien. See McCoid, Bankruptcy, the Avoiding Powers, and Unperfected Security Interests, 59 Am. Bankr. L.J. 175 (1985).

(B) The Trustee's Power to Avoid Preferences

NOTE ON PREFERENCE LAW

Under nonbankruptcy law, each creditor is entitled to take all legal steps to be paid. If the debtor's assets do not suffice to pay all creditors, some creditors will succeed in obtaining payment; others will remain unpaid. The amount a particular creditor receives is likely to depend upon the leverage it enjoys. A trade creditor may threaten to withhold future supplies or services unless it is paid for past credit extensions. A secured creditor may threaten to repossess collateral unless it is paid. Collecting one's claims through persuasion or through the judicial process is perfectly appropriate conduct under nonbankruptcy law. Using unencumbered assets to pay some creditors rather than others typically does not violate any nonbankruptcy principle.

Consider the following scenario: Debtor is hopelessly insolvent, having incurred substantial trade debt as well as bank debt. Debtor has one remaining asset of value—a checking account containing $27,128.50. Debtor withdraws $25,000 and gives it to C, a favored creditor, in satisfaction of C's $25,000 claim. Although other, unpaid creditors may be chagrined to discover that C has beaten them to the assets, this fact alone is insufficient to enable them to cry "foul"; the other creditors ordinarily will have no right to deprive C of its payment.

Bankruptcy calls off the nonbankruptcy race to the assets. After bankruptcy has begun, payment of one creditor's claim at the expense of another creditor would violate the bankruptcy principle of pro rata distribution. Add to the foregoing scenario the additional fact that, immediately after paying $25,000 to C, Debtor files a bankruptcy petition. As before, C is overwhelmed with joy. Because Debtor preferred to pay C (for whatever reason or mix of reasons), C has been made whole. The other, unpaid creditors are not merely chagrined; they are outraged. Why, they ask, should C be paid in full when they receive a pittance? Had bankruptcy been filed 24 hours earlier, C would be sharing equally with them.

Preference law addresses prebankruptcy transfers that have the result of affording a particular creditor more than its pro rata share. BC 547 enables the bankruptcy trustee to avoid certain of these preferential transfers. Under BC 550, "the trustee may recover, for the benefit of the estate, the property transferred, or, if the court so orders, the value of [the] property." In the example, unless C has a defense to the preference action, see BC 547(c) (discussed infra), C would be required to return the property to the estate. C's claim would be restored, and C would share pro rata with other holders of unsecured claims. See BC 502(h).

Traditional preference jurisprudence suggests that preference law is designed to promote equality of distribution among unsecured creditors: "the preference provisions facilitate the prime bankruptcy policy of equality of distribution among creditors of the debtor." H.R. Rep. No. 595, 95th Cong., 1st Sess. 177–78 (1977), reprinted in 1978 U.S.C.C.A.N. 5963, 6138. Without preference law, unsecured creditors would share pro rata in whatever property the debtor has when it enters bankruptcy. The pro rata shares would be based upon the actual size of the claims at the time of the commencement of the bankruptcy case. Avoiding preferential transfers puts the preferred creditor in the same position as the other creditors, who have not been preferred; all will share pro rata in the debtor's bankruptcy estate, which is enhanced by the preference recovery. Preference law thereby blunts the advantage that certain creditors otherwise would enjoy. It prevents some creditors from retaining payments and other transfers of property that otherwise would have been more widely shared.

Some argue that preference law ought to (and, at least to some extent, actually does) do more than protect the bankruptcy rule of pro rata sharing. They assert that preference law should deter creditors from obtaining payment whenever the debtor is approaching bankruptcy. In their view, preference law should be (and largely is) directed to "opt-out behavior"—acts by which creditors seek to remove themselves from an impending collective proceeding (bankruptcy) by "gun-jumping" and, in doing so, reduce the value of the property that is available for all creditors. See, e.g., T. Jackson, The Logic and Limits of Bankruptcy Law 123–138 (1986); Baird, Avoiding Powers Under the Bankruptcy Code, in The Williamsburg Conference on Bankruptcy 305 (1988).

The injurious effects of taking a preference are clearest when the creditor removes real property or goods prior to bankruptcy. Loss, for example, of a printer's presses may diminish the value of the printer's business by an amount greater than the value of the presses themselves. A complete printing business worth, say, $1,000,000 may be worth only $500,000 without the presses, even though the presses would fetch only $250,000 if sold separately. When a preferred creditor receives cash, however, the detrimental effects on the value of the assets available for distribution to creditors are considerably smaller.

As we shall see, preference law in fact does not distinguish among events (including payments) on the basis of their detrimental effect on the total return to creditors. Indeed, the repossession and sale of collateral—an event that is likely to be particularly destructive to the going concern value of the debtor's business—often will not constitute a preference. In contrast, the delayed filing of a financing statement—an event whose principal consequence is distributional—often will result in the secured party losing its collateral and becoming unsecured in bankruptcy.

BC 547(b) describes those prebankruptcy transfers that the trustee may avoid as preferences. Subsection (c) excepts from avoidance certain otherwise preferential transfers. The following Problems address "eve of bankruptcy" transfers.

Problem 10.2.4. On June 1 Debtor borrowed $12,000 from Firstbank and repaid the debt when due on September 1. On October 1 Debtor filed a bankruptcy petition. May the trustee recover the payment from Firstbank? See BC 547(b). (For now, do not worry about the exceptions in subsection (c).)

Problem 10.2.5. What result in the immediately preceding Problem if on September 1, instead of paying Firstbank, Debtor granted Firstbank a perfected security interest in a piece of equipment worth in excess of $12,000? Has there been a prebankruptcy "transfer" to Firstbank? See BC 101(54).

To answer the foregoing Problems, one must read BC 547 carefully. Has there been a "transfer of an interest of the debtor in property"? Is each of the other elements of BC 547(b) met? Observe that many of the terms used in BC 547(b) are defined in BC 101, among them "transfer," "debt," "creditor," and "insolvent." BC 547(g) imposes upon the trustee the burden of proving each element of BC 547(b). BC 547(f) gives the trustee a bit of help: For purposes of BC 547, the debtor is presumed to have been insolvent on and during the 90 days immediately preceding the filing of the bankruptcy petition.[1]

The most difficult element of BC 547(b) to comprehend is subsection (b)(5). This complex language is designed to capture only those transfers that have a preferential effect, i.e., that enable a creditor to receive more than its pro rata share of the property of the estate. BC 547(b)(5) requires one to compare (a) what the creditor would receive if (i) the transfer is allowed to stand and (ii) the creditor receives a distribution on any remaining claim in the bankruptcy, with (b) what the creditor would have received in a Chapter 7 case if the transfer had not been made.

Recall that Chapter 7 of the Bankruptcy Code provides for liquidation of the debtor's property and pro rata distribution of the proceeds to holders of unsecured claims. Suppose that, had the payment to Firstbank not been made, liquidation would have given general creditors (including Firstbank) 50 cents on the dollar. The prebankruptcy transfer in Problem 10.2.4 enabled Firstbank to receive more than 50 cents on the dollar. Thus the requirement of subsection (b)(5) is satisfied. Would the same be true for the transfer of the security interest in Problem 10.2.5? How much would Firstbank receive if the transfer is not avoided? How much would Firstbank have received without the transfer in a Chapter 7 case? (Remember that holders of unavoided secured claims are entitled to receive the value of their collateral; general unsecured claims share pro rata in the unencumbered assets.)

Problem 10.2.6. On August 1 Debtor borrowed $12,000 from Firstbank and secured the loan with a piece of equipment worth in excess of that amount. Firstbank filed a financing statement covering the equipment shortly before the security agreement was signed. On October 1 Debtor filed a bankruptcy petition. May the trustee avoid the transfer of the security interest? Was there a transfer on account of an antecedent debt? See also BC 547(c)(1). What difference, if any, would it make if Firstbank took the security interest with knowledge that Debtor was insolvent?

Problem 10.2.7. What result in the immediately preceding Problem if Debtor repaid the debt when due on September 1? Did the payment enable

---

1. Under Federal Rule of Evidence 301, "a presumption imposes on the party against whom it is directed [in Problems 10.2.4 and 10.2.5, Firstbank] the burden of going forward with evidence to rebut or meet the presumption, but does not shift to such party the burden of proof in the sense of the risk of nonpersuasion, which remains throughout the trial upon the party on whom it was originally cast [in Problems 10.2.4 and 10.2.5, the trustee]." Nevertheless, the debtor's solvency is an issue in preference litigation only infrequently.

Firstbank to receive more than it would have received had the payment not been made and Firstbank received a Chapter 7 distribution? See BC 547(b)(5); BC 547(c)(1); BC 547(a)(2); Note (1) on Prepetition Payments to Secured Parties, infra.

Problem 10.2.8. To alleviate Debtor's "cash flow" problem, Firstbank made a 90–day unsecured loan in the amount of $12,000 to Debtor on June 1. Debtor made no payment until September 20, when Debtor paid First-bank only $8,000. The balance remained unpaid on October 1, when Debtor filed a bankruptcy petition. May the trustee recover the $8,000 payment?

Problem 10.2.9. On June 1 Debtor borrowed $12,000 from Firstbank and secured the loan with a piece of equipment worth only $7,000. Firstbank filed a financing statement covering the equipment shortly before the security agreement was signed. Debtor repaid the entire debt when due on August 1. On October 1 Debtor filed a bankruptcy petition. May the trustee recover the payment from Firstbank? See Note (1) on Prepetition Payments to Secured Parties, infra.

Problem 10.2.10. What result in the immediately preceding Problem if Debtor repaid only $5,000 when the debt was due? For purposes of BC 547(b) does it matter whether the $5,000 payment is applied to the $5,000 unsecured portion of Firstbank's claim or to the $7,000 secured portion? See BC 547(b)(2); BC 547(c)(1); BC 547(a)(2); Note (1) on Prepetition Payments to Secured Parties, infra.

Problem 10.2.11. On June 1 Firstbank made a one-year, unsecured installment loan in the amount of $12,000 to Debtor. Debtor was obligated to repay $1,000 in principal plus accrued interest on the first day of each month. Debtor made timely payments in July, August, and September. Debtor filed a bankruptcy petition on October 1. May the trustee recover the three payments? See BC 547(c)(2); Note (2) on Prepetition Payments to Secured Parties, infra.

NOTES ON PREPETITION PAYMENTS TO SECURED PARTIES

(1) Allocating Payments Between the Secured and Unsecured Portions of Claims. BC 547 does not permit the trustee to avoid every prepetition payment to creditors. Rather, the trustee may avoid and recover only those payments that have the effect of enabling the creditor to receive more than it would have received in a Chapter 7 case had the transfer not been made. See BC 547(b)(5).

Whether a prepetition transfer will meet the test in BC 547(b)(5) may depend on whether, and the extent to which, the creditor's claim is secured. Payments to unsecured creditors almost invariably meet the test and are potentially preferential. An unsecured creditor who is permitted to keep a prepetition transfer receives 100 cents on the dollar for each dollar paid. Unless the creditor would have received 100 cents on the dollar in a Chapter 7 distribution (i.e., unless the bankruptcy debtor is solvent), the creditor always will do better by having received payment of even a portion of its claim prepetition.

On the other hand, perfected secured creditors are entitled to receive the value of their collateral from the bankruptcy estate. Theoretically, then, the claim of a fully-secured creditor (i.e., one whose claim is less than or equal to the value of its collateral) will be paid in full from the bankruptcy. Accordingly, it appears that prepetition payments to fully-secured creditors do not enable them to receive more than they would have received had no payment been made and had they received a Chapter 7 distribution. BC 547(c)(1) is consistent with this approach: to the extent that a fully-secured creditor is paid, the creditor has given "new value" to the debtor; i.e., the value of its collateral is freed up for application to the payment of unsecured claims.[2]

What about a payment to a creditor who, but for the payment, would have held two claims—one secured and one unsecured? This is the case presented by Problems 10.2.9 and 10.2.10. Problem 10.2.9 is the easier of the two. Did the payment meet the test in BC 547(b)(5)? Even if so, didn't Firstbank give "new value" in exchange for the payment?

Problem 10.2.10 is a bit trickier. *In theory*, whether the $5,000 payment is treated as a payment of the secured portion of the claim or the unsecured portion should make no difference; the amount of Firstbank's secured claim can be adjusted to make sure that it receives no more than it would have received in a Chapter 7 case had the transfer not been made. Thus, the payment could be treated as if it were a payment on account of the secured portion of the claim. If so, the payment would be unavoidable; Firstbank would retain the payment and hold a $7,000 bankruptcy claim secured by $2,000 in collateral. Alternatively, the payment could be treated as if it were on account of the unsecured portion of the claim. If so, then the payment would be avoidable; after recovery, Firstbank would hold a $12,000 claim secured by $7,000 of collateral.

As you might have realized, the theory and the practice diverge. Neither Firstbank nor the trustee can be expected to be indifferent about whether Firstbank must return the $5,000 prepetition payment, even though under either scenario Firstbank ultimately would receive $7,000 plus a distribution on a $5,000 unsecured claim. "Ultimately"—there's the rub! To fully appreciate the import of the word, see Note on Relief from the Automatic Stay, Section 1, supra. Given the Supreme Court's decision in *Timbers of Inwood Forest* (discussed in the Note on Relief, supra), Firstbank would be likely to choose to keep the $5,000 prepetition payment so that the funds can generate income while the bankruptcy case is pending. Conversely, the trustee probably would choose to treat the payment as a

---

2. There is, however, a line of cases holding that for purposes of BC 547(b)(5) the collateral should be valued as of the date of the filing of the bankruptcy petition. Thus, if payments are made to a secured party whose collateral is declining in value, the payments may be preferential even though the value of the collateral exceeded the debt at the time the payments were made. See, e.g., In re Paris Industries Corp., 130 B.R. 1 (Bkrtcy. D.Me.1991).

preference, so that the estate could recover the funds and enjoy the use of $5,000 interest-free. (Recall from Section 1, supra, that postpetition interest on unsecured claims is not allowable.)

The reported preference cases generally treat prebankruptcy payments on partially secured claims as having been applied first to the unsecured portion. This approach, which treats Firstbank as having received payment of its $5,000 unsecured claim on August 1, is consistent with the position Firstbank probably would have taken had bankruptcy not been filed. (Suppose that, after paying Firstbank $5,000, Debtor had not entered bankruptcy. Instead, Firstbank repossessed the collateral and sold it for $7,000. Would Firstbank have applied only $2,000 to the debt and remitted the balance to Debtor or a junior lienor?) Under these cases, the payment to Firstbank in Problem 10.2.10 would be avoidable: Firstbank would be compelled to return $5,000 to the estate in exchange for a correspondingly larger secured claim.

(2) "Ordinary Course" Payments. BC 547(c)(2) contains an exception for certain "ordinary course" payments. As originally enacted, the exception shielded only those payments that were made within 45 days after the debt was incurred. The 1984 amendments to the Bankruptcy Code eliminated the 45–day limitation.

As originally written, the exception was of little use to secured parties; secured debts typically are outstanding for more than 45 days. Since the elimination of the 45–day limitation, secured parties who received timely payments on **term loans** and **revolvers** have argued that these payments qualify for BC 547(c)(2) even though they otherwise would be preferential. Some reported decisions took the view that the exception applies only to payments of trade debt and other current expenses, not to payment of longer-term debt. See, e.g., In re CHG International, Inc., 897 F.2d 1479 (9th Cir.1990) (timely interest payments on term loans held not to qualify for BC 547(c)(2)). But in Union Bank v. Wolas, 502 U.S. 151, 112 S.Ct. 527, 116 L.Ed.2d 514 (1991), the Supreme Court held that "payments on long-term debt, as well as payments on short-term debt, may qualify for the ordinary course of business exception." Unfortunately, the Court gave absolutely no guidance on the more difficult issues raised by BC 547(c)(2): What does it mean for a debt to be "incurred by the debtor in the ordinary course of business"? What are the characteristics of a payment "made in the ordinary course of business" and "according to ordinary business terms"?

(3) Payments on Revolving Credit Facilities. Assume the following, rather typical scenario: Bank agrees to make available to Debtor up to $1 million of credit under an unsecured, revolving **line of credit**. During the 90 days prior to bankruptcy, Debtor makes fifteen borrowings of $100,000 each and makes eleven payments of $100,000 each. Debtor's trustee seeks to recover $1,100,000 from Bank under BC 547(b). Bank is outraged, arguing that it never would have made all the advances unless Debtor had made the repayments; indeed, it took great care to insure that no more than $1 million was outstanding at any given time. Moreover, even though Bank has received $1,100,000 during the preference period, Bank has in effect replenished the bankruptcy estate by $1,500,000; accordingly, Bank argues that it should have no liability whatsoever under BC 547.

BC 547(c)(4) affords some relief to Bank under these circumstances, but sometimes not as much relief as Bank would wish. Under that section, the trustee may not avoid a transfer to the extent that, *after* the transfer, the creditor gave "new value" to or for the benefit of the debtor. Thus, to the extent that Bank can show that, after any one or more of the eleven payments, Bank extended additional credit to Debtor, Bank can use that additional credit to nullify the preference. It is as if Bank returned the preference to the estate. Bank may not, however, aggregate the new value and offset it against the aggregate amount of preferential payments. As in comedy, so with preferences: timing is everything!

————

Problem 10.2.12. On January 2 Creditor loaned $10,000 to Debtor. On that date, to secure the loan, Debtor executed a security agreement granting Creditor a security interest in a bulldozer that Debtor had previously purchased. Creditor did not file a financing statement until September 1. On September 2, Debtor filed a petition in bankruptcy. The trustee seeks to avoid the transfer of the security interest as a preference. What result? See BC 547(b); BC 547(e)(2); BC 547(e)(1); R9–317(a)(2); R9–201; R9–203(b); Notes on Delayed Perfection, infra.

NOTES ON DELAYED PERFECTION

(1) The Application of BC 547 to Delayed Perfection. Problem 10.2.12 poses this question: *When* did Debtor transfer an interest in property to Creditor? Clearly, Debtor transferred a property interest to Creditor that was fully effective as between these two parties on January 2. See R9–203(b). If the date of transfer is January 2 for purposes of BC 547(b), then the transfer cannot be avoided for two reasons: the transfer was made for a concurrent, rather than for an "antecedent," debt, and the transfer was made more than 90 days before the filing of the bankruptcy petition. On the other hand, if we deem that the transfer was not made until the financing statement was filed on September 1, then the "antecedent debt" requirement is satisfied and the remaining elements for avoidance probably can be established with ease.

BC 547(e) provides the way to date the transfer. The structure of subsection (e), unhappily, forces us to start with paragraph (2) and then back-track to paragraph (1). Paragraph (2) tells us that "a transfer is *made* . . . (B) at the time such transfer is *perfected*." (The exception in paragraph (2)(A) will be considered later.)

Having learned that the time when the transfer is "perfected" is the key, we move back to paragraph (1)(B), where we learn that a transfer of personal property is perfected "when a creditor on a simple contract cannot acquire a judicial lien that is superior to the interest of the transferee." We explored the meaning of "judicial lien" above in connection with the "strong-arm" clause, BC 544(a). For present purposes we may assume that the quoted language of BC 547(e)(1)(B) refers, inter alia, to the execution lien obtained by the holder of an ordinary contract claim.

Thus, instead of giving us the *answer*, the preference rules of BC 547 provide us with a hypothetical *question*. (In this regard, BC 547 is like the "strong-arm" clause of BC 544(a), discussed in Section 2(A) above.) In the setting of Problem 10.2.12, the question is this: *Suppose* a judgment creditor of Debtor had acquired a judicial lien on the bulldozer during the period leading up to September 1—the date on which Creditor filed the financing statement: Would this lien have been (in the language of BC 547(e)(1)(B)) "superior to the interest of the transferee" of the security interest? (Don't despair—we're almost home!)

Where can we find the answer to this hypothetical question that the Bankruptcy Code has thrown at us? Not in the Bankruptcy Code or in any other federal law! As in dealing with the strong-arm clause we must look to state law—more precisely, to the UCC as enacted in the relevant jurisdiction. Prior to the filing on September 1, could a creditor with a judicial lien have trumped the security interest? R9–317(a)(2) and R9–310(a) provide a clear answer.

Those who have followed the trail this far should be able to answer these questions: (1) In Problem 10.2.12, when was the transfer of the security interest made? (2) Can the trustee avoid the transfer? (If you have any doubts about how to answer these questions, keep going through the steps outlined above until the system is perfectly clear. You will soon need to use this system in solving problems that are much more difficult than Problem 10.2.12. As you probably now realize, Problem 10.2.12 was a sitting duck.)

(2) The Policy Behind Applying BC 547 to Delayed Perfection. On what basis might one argue in support of the result that the transfer occurred upon the filing of the financing statement and not earlier, when the transfer took effect between the debtor and the secured party? Some have argued that delayed perfection is a "false preference"—that preference law has been used to address indirectly an entirely different problem: that of secret liens that operate to the prejudice of unsecured creditors. See, e.g., R. Jordan, W. Warren & D. Bussel, Bankruptcy 432 (5th ed. 1999) ("There is no true preference ... because the transfer of the security interest ... was not on account of an antecedent debt. Rather, the problem of delayed perfection is the evil of the secret lien."). Of course, this argument assumes that bankruptcy law expresses a policy against secret liens that is more stringent than the anti-secret-lien policies of Article 9 and other state laws.

Others have argued that delayed perfection, at least in some cases, implicates the "anti-last-minute-grab" policy that they believe underlies preference law. As we have seen, a security interest that is unperfected at the time a bankruptcy petition is filed ordinarily will be avoidable by the bankruptcy trustee. A secured party who believes bankruptcy is imminent may review the loan files and discover that the security interest is unperfected. (Perhaps no financing statement ever was filed; perhaps the financing statement contained errors than made it ineffective; perhaps an effective financing statement became ineffective because the debtor's name or the location of the debtor changed). By perfecting before bankruptcy, an unperfected secured party improves its position relative to other creditors. Had no filing occurred, the secured party might have been rendered unsecured through the trustee's exercise of the strong-arm clause. By filing, the secured party immunizes the security interest from attack under BC 544(a). Is this not precisely the kind of opt-out behavior that preference law addresses? See Jackson, The Logic and Limits of Bankruptcy Law 138–46 (1986).

In assessing the explanations for using preference law to avoid security interests whose perfection has been delayed, one should consider the fact that the principal effect of delayed perfection is likely to be distributional. Delayed perfection is unlikely to affect the total value of the debtor's business; rather, it affects how the value of the business will be distributed among the creditors.

In working the following Problems, don't lose sight of the requirements of BC 547(b). In particular, be sure you can identify when the transfer was made and when the debt was incurred. You should also consider whether the outcome that the statute appears to compel is consistent with the policies that underlie preference law.

Problem 10.2.13. What result in Problem 10.2.12 if Creditor filed the financing statement on May 9? Would the result change if Debtor was a wholly-owned subsidiary of Creditor? See BC 547(b)(4); BC 101(31); BC 101(2).

Problem 10.2.14. What result in Problem 10.2.12 if Creditor filed the financing statement on January 9 and Debtor filed for bankruptcy on March 1? See BC 547(e)(2)(A). What is the reason for this refinement? Consider the technical attacks that might be made on security arrangements when there is a gap of one day (or one hour) between the loan and the filing.

Problem 10.2.15. What result in the immediately preceding Problem if Creditor mailed the financing statement to the filing office on January 5, but the financing statement did not arrive there until January 13? See BC 547(e)(2)(B); R9–516(a). Can Creditor prevail under BC 547(c)(1)? The cases construing BC 547(c)(1) are divided. One line of cases limits the application of BC 547(c)(1) to security interests perfected within 10 days after attachment. The other treats contemporaneity as a flexible concept that requires a case-by-case inquiry into all relevant circumstances, e.g., the length of and reason for the delay, the nature of the transaction, the intentions of the parties, and the possible risk of fraud.

Problem 10.2.16. What result in Problem 10.2.12 if Creditor filed the financing statement on January 9 but bankruptcy fell on January 8? Note that, as in the other Problems in this set, Debtor owned the bulldozer before getting the loan from Creditor. Don't forget that the trustee is not confined to a preference attack but also enjoys the rights and powers of a judicial lien creditor under BC 544.

A quick glance at BC 546(b) may suggest that this provision gives effect to the postbankruptcy filing. Note, however, that BC 546(b) gives effect to such filing only when state law "permits perfection of an interest in property to be effective against an entity that acquires rights in such property *before* the date of such perfection." Does state law under the UCC protect a non-purchase-money security interest from a levy that occurs before perfection? See R9–317(a)(2).

What does the answer to this Problem suggest concerning the advisability of relying on the 10–day period in BC 547(e)(2)(A)?

Problem 10.2.17. Would the result in the immediately preceding Problem change if Creditor financed Debtor's purchase of a bulldozer that was delivered to Debtor on January 2? Recall Problem 10.2.3 above. What is the relationship between the answer to Problem 10.2.3 and the powers of the trustee in bankruptcy? See BC 544(a); R9–317(e); BC 546(b); BC 362(b)(3).

Problem 10.2.18. On June 1 Bank made a $100,000 term loan to Debtor. The loan was secured by "all Debtor's existing and after-acquired equipment." On June 1 Debtor owned equipment worth $90,000. Bank "prefiled" a financing statement on May 28. On July 1 Debtor purchased and took delivery of an additional piece of equipment worth $12,000. Debtor files a bankruptcy petition on August 1. The trustee seeks to avoid Bank's security interest in all the equipment. What result? See BC 547(e)(2)(A); BC 547(e)(3).

Problem 10.2.19. What result in the immediately preceding Problem if Bank and Debtor agreed that Debtor would use $12,000 of the loan proceeds to acquire an additional piece of equipment, and the proceeds were so used? See BC 547(c)(3).

Problem 10.2.20. On June 1 Creditor loaned $10,000 to Debtor and Debtor delivered to Creditor negotiable bonds in Company *A* worth $10,000. On September 1, at a time when Creditor knew Debtor to be insolvent, Creditor delivered the bonds in Company *A* to Debtor in exchange for bonds of the same value in Company *B*. The bonds of both companies continue to sell at par. On September 2 Debtor went into bankruptcy.

(a) May the trustee avoid the transfer of the Company *B* bonds as a preference? See BC 547(a)(2) & (c)(1).

(b) What difference, if any, would it make if on June 1 Debtor delivered bonds of Company *A* worth only $6,000, and on September 1 Debtor exchanged these bonds for bonds of Company *B* worth $10,000?

What result if on September 1, instead of the exchange, Debtor delivered additional bonds in Company A worth $4,000?

(c) Would it make any practical difference if the bonds of Company A delivered on June 1 were worth $15,000 and these bonds were exchanged on September 1 for bonds in Company B worth $20,000? See BC 547(b)(5).

Problem 10.2.21. On June 1 C loaned $100,000 to D and at the same time, to secure the loan, D delivered to C stock in Company X worth $50,000. In July Company X announced the development of a new product; by the middle of August the stock had increased in value by 50 percent. On August 30 D entered bankruptcy. The trustee argues that C received a $25,000 preference. Do you agree? Was there more than one "transfer of an interest of the debtor in property"? If so, when did each transfer occur?

It is generally assumed that increases in the value of collateral shortly before bankruptcy do not constitute "transfers" giving rise to a voidable preferences. Is the conclusion that the "transfer" of the stock occurred on June 1 consistent with policies underlying the bankruptcy rules governing preferences? Does it violate the "anti-last-minute-grab" policy? Does it violate the "equality of distribution" policy? The latter arguably is directed toward recapturing transfers of the debtor's property that diminish the assets available for distribution to unsecured creditors. When, as in this Problem, the increase in the value of collateral is due to market forces, is the bankruptcy estate diminished within the preference period? See BC 101(5); BC 547(b)(5). As we shall see in Section 3 below, the answer is less clear-cut when the increase in value results from labor or other inputs supplied by the debtor.

SECTION 3.   REPLENISHMENT AND ADDITIONS; THE "FLOATING LIEN"

(A) THE "FLOATING LIEN" UNDER THE UNIFORM COMMERCIAL CODE

NOTES ON THE DEVELOPMENT OF THE LAW GOVERNING THE "FLOATING LIEN"

(1) Security Interests in After–Acquired Property. In this Section we meet problems presented by the transitory character of some types of collateral. Before addressing the bankruptcy treatment of security interests in these types of collateral, we take a closer look at the nonbankruptcy treatment.

A merchant may think of inventory as a fairly constant unit. Inventory at the beginning of the year is compared with inventory at the end without regard to whether any of the items is the same. But, from another point of view, there is a fairly constant process of exhaustion and replenishment, as inventory flows in through a merchant's stockroom and out over the counter or through the shipping room. Consider a hardware store: Each day there may be hundreds of sales (large and small) that convert inventory into cash or accounts. Situations of this kind arise in a wide range of retail, wholesale, and manufacturing settings. Accounts receivable go through a similar cycle: Each time a debtor contracts to sell goods or provide services, a new account is generated; upon payment the account disappears.

Attempts to finance the flow of inventory and accounts have generated serious and important legal problems, both within and outside of bankruptcy. Underlying the legal doctrines are conflicting values: the utility of added operating capital versus the desire to hold assets in reserve for last-ditch financing and to meet the claims of unsecured creditors.

For better or for worse, Article 9 has eliminated most of the nonbankruptcy legal problems for those who take a "floating lien" on inventory and accounts. But life was not always so easy for inventory or accounts financers. As the following excerpt suggests, until the adoption of the UCC, secured parties found it difficult (and sometimes impossible) to maintain an effective security interest in collateral that was subject to a constant process of exhaustion and replenishment.

At common law property to be created or acquired in the future could not be transferred or encumbered prior to the creation or acquisition of the property. Illustrative of the constant striving to make future assets available for present purposes was the attempt of common-law lawyers to add to the conveyances of the day the words: "Quae quovismodo in futurum habere potero." But, as Littleton says, these words were "void in law." The reasoning upon which the rule was based was simple—"A man cannot grant or charge that which he hath not." This infallible bit of syllogistic logic received its first breakdown in the famous case of Grantham v. Hawley, [K.B.1616] the parent of the fictitious doctrine of "potential existence." Briefly stated, this principle permits the sale or encumbrance of future personal property having a so-called potential existence arising from the fact that the processes of creation have already begun, with the limitation that the basic substance which yields the increment must be owned by the vendor or mortgagor. Typical examples would be crops already planted upon land of the vendor, or wool to be grown upon sheep owned by the mortgagor. As stated by the court: "A parson may grant all the tithewool that he shall have in ... a year; yet perhaps he shall have none; but a man cannot grant all the wool, that shall grow upon his sheep that he shall buy hereafter; for there he hath it neither actually nor potentially." The doctrine rests, of course, upon the fiction that a man may own something that is not yet in existence but which in the normal course of events will come into being; thereby the rule that "a man cannot grant or charge that which he has not" is left inviolate. The refusal of the court to recognize the fictional quality of its rule prevented the satisfaction of more than a very small portion of the need for which the rule itself had been evolved. Grantham v. Hawley left us with little more than we had before; but it was the first step toward the solution of a problem, vexing even today—the problem of how to utilize future property for present credit.

The civil law had a simple device—a "mortgage on an estate to come." Therefore, it is not surprising that one of our greatest students of the civil law, Justice Joseph Story, should have been the first on the bench to establish the precedent in Anglo–American law that future property may be presently charged. The case is, of course, Mitchell v. Winslow [1843]. Cutlery manufacturers, in order to bolster their business, borrowed money, and as security therefor executed a deed of trust conveying the manufacturing plant "together with all tools and machinery . . . which we may at any time purchase for four years from this date, and also all the stock which we may manufacture or purchase during said four years." The instrument was recorded and upon default the mortgagee took possession of some after-acquired tools. The mortgagor went into bankruptcy and thereupon perplexing questions arose. Did the trust instrument create a lien upon the after-acquired property? If it did, was such a lien good against creditors? The bankruptcy judge certified these two questions to Circuit Judge Story, and Story answered in the affirmative, stating that although it was true that future property could not be presently charged at common law, nevertheless equity would enforce the agreement. He pointed out that equity precedents existed, if authority was necessary, in the analogous cases of contracts to assign future claims and expectancies. His conclusion is the most frequently quoted passage in the field.

> "It seems to me a clear result of all of the authorities, that wherever the parties, by their contract, intended to create a positive lien or charge, either upon real or upon personal property, whether then owned by the assignor or contractor, or not, or if personal property, whether it is then in esse or not, it attaches in equity as a lien or charge upon the particular property, as soon as the assignor or contractor acquires a title thereto, against the latter, and all persons asserting a claim thereto, under him, either voluntarily, or with notice, or in bankruptcy."

Mitchell v. Winslow was paralleled about twenty years later [1862] by the celebrated English case of Holroyd v. Marshall, decided by the House of Lords. Here, a deed of trust covering the machinery in a mill and containing the provision that "all machinery, implements, and things which, during the continuance of this security, shall be . . . placed in or about the said mill . . . shall . . . be subject to the trusts . . .," was executed and recorded. Subsequently, a creditor of the mortgagor levied on after-acquired property. The mortgagor then defaulted and possession of the property was taken by the mortgagees in disregard of the creditor's levy. The House of Lords upheld the claim of the mortgagees on the ground that "immediately on the new machinery and effects being fixed or placed in the mill, they became subject to the operation of the contract, and passed in equity to the mortgagees. . . ."

With such excellent precedents on the books it would have appeared that the problem was solved and that after-acquired property could be mortgaged and that recording of the mortgaging instrument would constitute notice to would-be purchasers and creditors. Yet, three years after Story's excellent decision the Massachusetts Supreme Judicial Court held [1845] that a recorded mortgage on after-acquired property (stock of goods) was not effective against creditors. The action was at law and left open the possibility that the result might be otherwise in equity. But then came Moody v. Wright [Mass.1847]. Here, the owner of a tanning business executed a purchase-money mortgage which included an after-acquired property clause. The mortgage was recorded. Subsequently an assignee for benefit of creditors was appointed under a state "insolvent law" and the mortgagee contested his right to the after-acquired property. The court held that the assignee prevailed on the ground that nothing had been done by either the mortgagor or the mortgagee to perfect the lien attempted to be created by the after-acquired property clause.

A cursory examination of the cases from a doctrinaire standpoint without consideration of the varying economic factors involved would reveal that some jurisdictions follow Story's Equity rule, others accept the Massachusetts doctrine, a few follow both, and still others have set up independent principles.

Cohen & Gerber, The After–Acquired Property Clause, 87 U.Pa.L.Rev. 635, 635–38 (1939).

Notwithstanding "[t]he widespread nineteenth century prejudice against the floating charge," "[i]n almost every state it was possible before the Code for the borrower to give a lien on everything he held or would have. ... Article [9], in expressly validating the floating charge, merely recognizes an existing state of things." F9–204, Comment 2. Former Article 9 replaced the different rules described in the foregoing excerpt with a uniform legal regime that expressly validates the "floating lien." Comment 2 to F9–204 explained that Former Article 9 "decisively rejects" the "inarticulate premise" underlying pre-UCC hostility to the floating lien—that "a commercial borrower should not be allowed to encumber all his assets present and future, and that for the protection not only of the borrower but of his other creditors a cushion of free assets should be preserved"—"not on the ground that it was wrong in policy but on the ground that it was not effective." Like Former Article 9, R9–204(a) provides explicitly that "a security agreement may create or provide for a security interest in after-acquired collateral." The filing of a single financing statement covering "inventory and accounts" is sufficient to perfect a security interest in inventory and accounts that the debtor acquires after the filing. "There is no need to refer to after-acquired property ... in a financing statement." R9–204, Comment 7. See Chapter 7, Section 3(A), supra.

(2) The Privilege to Dissipate Proceeds; Benedict v. Ratner.
When a lender takes a security interest in inventory and accounts that are

subject to rapid turnover and liquidation into cash, what is the borrower to do with the proceeds? When relatively few sales of expensive items are involved (e.g., automobiles and grand pianos), it would be feasible for the borrower to bring the proceeds to the lender and obtain fresh loans when new inventory is needed. But when individual transactions are small and numerous, both borrower and lender may prefer to cut short the paperwork involved in numerous repayments and fresh loans and allow the debtor to collect the proceeds and use them to run the business, replenish its stock of inventory, and generate new accounts.

Prior to Article 9, the arrangement just described was in grave danger. The operative rule was associated with Justice Brandeis and his opinion in the famous case of Benedict v. Ratner, 268 U.S. 353, 45 S.Ct. 566, 69 L.Ed. 991 (1925). The Hub Carpet Company, doing business in New York, obtained loans from Ratner and assigned to Ratner all its accounts, present and future. Under the arrangement (unless Ratner demanded otherwise) Hub Carpet "was not required to apply any of the collections to the repayment of Ratner's loan. It was not required to replace accounts collected by other collateral of equal value. . . . It was at liberty to use the proceeds of all accounts collected as it might see fit." Hub Carpet went into bankruptcy, and Benedict, the trustee, challenged the validity of Ratner's security interest in all the accounts—including accounts that had not yet been paid by Hub's customers, and for which Ratner was, of course, now demanding direct payment.

The Supreme Court unanimously held that the attempted assignment was void as to all the accounts—including those in which no payment had been made to the debtor, Hub Carpet. Justice Brandeis's opinion, heavily documented by citations of New York authority, stated:

> Under the law of New York a transfer of property as security which reserves to the transferor the right to dispose of the same, or to apply the proceeds thereof, for his own uses is, as to creditors, fraudulent in law and void. . . .

> [The rule rests] upon a lack of ownership because of dominion reserved. It does not raise a presumption of fraud. It imputes fraud conclusively because of the reservation of dominion inconsistent with the effective disposition of title and creation of a lien.

268 U.S. at 360–63, 45 S.Ct. at 568–69, 69 L.Ed. at 997–99.

Although the Supreme Court, in a bankruptcy setting, stated that it was applying the law of New York, the "doctrine of Benedict v. Ratner" was, with a few exceptions, followed in other states. 1 Gilmore, Security §§ 8.2–8.6, at 253–74. A substantial body of case law developed over how much "policing" by the lender of the debtor's accounting for proceeds was necessary to avoid the conclusion that the creditor lacked a property interest in the collateral that was effective against judicial liens obtained by competing creditors.

One of Article 9's steps toward facilitating the "floating lien" was a frontal attack on the doctrine of Benedict v. Ratner. F9–205 provided: "A security interest is not invalid or fraudulent against creditors by reason of liberty in the debtor ... to use, commingle or dispose of proceeds, or by reason of the failure of the secured party to require the debtor to account for proceeds or replace collateral." Since the opinion in Benedict v. Ratner purported to apply state law, the revision of state law by F9–205 (and R9–205) should be effective to change the result.

For second thoughts about the UCC's validation of the floating lien and its rejection of the rule of Benedict v. Ratner, see Gilmore, The Good Faith Purchase Idea and the Uniform Commercial Code: Confessions of a Repentant Draftsman, 15 Ga.L.Rev. 605, 621–27 (1981).

(B) AFTER-ACQUIRED COLLATERAL AND VOIDABLE PREFERENCES

NOTES ON THE "FLOATING LIEN" IN BANKRUPTCY

(1) The Problem. Outside of bankruptcy, a security interest in incoming collateral covered by an appropriate security agreement and financing statement will be senior to a judicial lien acquired by the debtor's other creditors. R9–201(a); R9–317(a)(2); Chapter 7, Section 3(A), supra. Does this mean that new collateral acquired shortly before bankruptcy will be immune from attack as a preference under BC 547?

In the floating lien, the loan is made, the security agreement is signed, and a financing statement is filed at the beginning of the arrangement. When bankruptcy falls, the debtor may hold little or none of the original collateral. The trustee's attack will center on collateral that the debtor acquired within the 90 days before bankruptcy: *When* was this collateral transferred to the creditor? If the transfer occurred only when the debtor acquired the collateral, then the trustee can assert that the new collateral was transferred to the creditor for an "antecedent debt." If so, the trustee is well on the way to proving a voidable preference under BC 547(b).

BC 547 contains special provisions that address potential preference attacks on floating liens. One of those provisions, BC 547(c)(5), is quite complicated and may be understood more easily in its historical context.

(2) The Historical Background of BC 547(c)(5). BC 547(c)(5) derives from a proposal put forward in a report of a committee of the National Bankruptcy Conference[1] known as the "Gilmore Committee." National Bankruptcy Conference, Report of the Committee on Coordination of the Bankruptcy Act and the Uniform Commercial Code (1970) ("Gilmore Committee Report"), reprinted in H.R. Rep. No. 595, 95th Cong., 1st Sess. 204 (1977), reprinted in 1978 U.S.C.C.A.N. 5963, 6164. The report explains:

> In 1966 it appeared that security interests in personal property under Article 9 of the Uniform Commercial Code were in serious

---

1. The National Bankruptcy Conference is a nonprofit, unincorporated organization devoted to the improvement of bankruptcy law. Its members include bankruptcy judges, law professors, and practicing attorneys who specialize in bankruptcy and creditors' rights law.

jeopardy in bankruptcy proceedings. At the time when the revision of [Bankruptcy Act] § 60 which was enacted in 1950 was being prepared, the drafting of Article 9 was in its early stages. The § 60 revision, of necessity, was written in what we may call pre-Code language; it reflected the pre-Code structure of personal property security law.... If the structure of security law had remained as it was, the compromise represented by the 1950 revision of § 60 would have worked perfectly well. With the general enactment of the Code, including Article 9, the situation was radically altered. Arguably, Article 9 contained little or nothing that was revolutionary, or even novel, as a matter of substance. The Article 9 terminology, on the other hand, represented a sharp break with the past. The difficulty of making the two statutes (§ 60 and Article 9) mesh or track with each other was immediately apparent. During the 1950's and continuing into the 1960's a quantitatively impressive amount of literature was devoted to the problem in the law reviews, specialized journals, and treatises. A considerable part of this literature seemed dedicated to the proposition that almost any Article 9 security interest could be turned into a voidable preference under § 60. The Article 9 security interest in after-acquired property (including inventory and receivables) was thought to be particularly vulnerable.... This literature, it is true, was, to start with, merely literature; there were no cases. Nevertheless, the holders of Article 9 security interests became understandably concerned about their fate.

1978 U.S.C.C.A.N. at 6167.

In the late 1960's two circuit court opinions addressing the avoidability of security interests in after-acquired property gave comfort to secured lenders. The Ninth Circuit proclaimed the most sweeping theory for protecting the floating lien in DuBay v. Williams, 417 F.2d 1277 (9th Cir. 1969). The *DuBay* opinion reached its result in two steps. The first step invoked the strong protection that Article 9 gives security arrangements that include a claim of after-acquired property. Under F9–301(1)(b), once the secured party filed a financing statement, the lien acquired by any creditor that levies on any property that might thereafter be acquired by the debtor would be junior to the perfected security interest. The second step integrated this rule of state law with section 60(a)(2) of the Bankruptcy Act, which governed the time when transfers shall be "deemed" to be made:

> a transfer of property ... shall be deemed to have been made or suffered at the time when it became so far perfected that no subsequent lien upon such property obtainable by legal or equitable proceedings on a simple contract could become superior to the rights of the transferee.

As the Ninth Circuit applied the "levying-creditor" test, incoming property would be "deemed" to have been transferred to the debtor when it became immune from levy—the date of filing—even though at that time the debtor had no interest in the property; indeed, at the time of filing the property may not even have been in existence. (An admirer of "Man of La Mancha" has referred to this as the "impossible deem"; and Professor Countryman roundly condemned this approach as "The Abracadabra, or the Transfer Occurred before it Occurred, Theory." Countryman, Code Security Interests in Bankruptcy, 75 Com. L.J. 269, 277 (1970).) The sweeping theory of the *DuBay* case was as comforting to secured lenders as it was disturbing to others, for it set no controls over enlarging the protection given to the holder of the floating lien (at the expense of suppliers and other unsecured creditors) when the debtor purchased additional property shortly before bankruptcy.

During the same year, the Seventh Circuit applied preference law to a floating lien on accounts. In Grain Merchants of Indiana, Inc. v. Union Bank & Savings Co., 408 F.2d 209 (7th Cir.1969), cert. denied 396 U.S. 827, 90 S.Ct. 75, 24 L.Ed.2d 78 (1969), the court used three alternative theories to immunize the floating lien from preference attack. First, using an analysis similar to that of the Ninth Circuit in *DuBay*, the court found that accounts that were generated during the preference period had been transferred to the secured party a year before bankruptcy, when the financing statement was filed.

Second, the court suggested that one ought to consider all accounts, existing and future, as a single entity that was given as collateral at the outset of the transaction, in a contemporaneous exchange for the loan. It quoted Professor Hogan with favor:

> The secured creditor's interest is in the stream of accounts flowing through the debtor's business, not in any specific accounts. As with the Heraclitean river, although the accounts in the stream constantly change, we can say it is the same stream.

Hogan, Games Lawyers Play with the Bankruptcy Preference Challenge to Accounts and Inventory Financing, 53 Cornell L. Rev. 553, 560 (1968). Although the "entity theory" was inconsistent with F9–203(1) (R9–203(b)), the court observed that a contrary result—one that would immunize only those accounts that were taken in exchange for a new loan—would jeopardize the flexible methods of financing that UCC 9–205 made possible by abrogating the requirement that a secured party must maintain dominion over collateral in order to protect its security interest.

The court's third theory was grounded in the long-standing "substitution of collateral" doctrine: a prebankruptcy transfer of collateral is not preferential when the collateral is taken in exchange for a release of other collateral. (Problem 10.2.20, supra, examines this doctrine.) Unlike other courts that had applied the doctrine, the Seventh Circuit found that "the newly arising accounts receivable may be considered as having been taken in exchange for the release of rights in earlier accounts and for a present consideration," without inquiring into either the timing of the supposed exchange (i.e., whether the release was substantially contemporaneous with or subsequent to the transfer of new collateral) or the relative value of the two items of collateral (i.e., whether the released collateral was worth at least as much as the new collateral). Rather, the court found that because the secured party no longer was required to assume dominion over individual accounts, "it is no longer appropriate to apply strict timing or value rules so long as at all relevant times the total pool of collateral, as here, exceeded the total debt."

The alternative grounds set forth in *Grain Merchants* were encouraging to lenders contemplating a floating lien but left nagging doubts as to the precise circumstances for protection. And, of course, one could not have safely predicted the approach of other federal courts. Nevertheless, as the Gilmore Committee reported, as of 1970:

> [T]he secured creditor bar (if there is such a thing) [was] basking happily in the warm glow of Judge Hufstedler's opinion in *DuBay* and, we may assume, [had] lost any interest it may once have had in reform of the Bankruptcy Act.
>
> What may be called the politics of the project of revising § 60 have thus come full circle during the past few years [ending in 1970]. What started out as a rescue mission for secured creditors may end up as a rescue mission for unsecured creditors.

1978 U.S.C.C.A.N. at 6168.

(3) The Bankruptcy Code and the Floating Lien. Drawing on the work of the Gilmore Committee, the drafters of the Bankruptcy Code addressed directly the problems raised by the floating lien, including the problem of determining the time when a transfer of a security interest in after-acquired property occurs. Section 547(e)(3) states that, for purposes of determining whether a transfer of a debtor's interest constitutes a preference, "a transfer is not made until the debtor has acquired rights in the property transferred." The avowed purpose of this provision was to over-rule *DuBay* and *Grain Merchants*. S. Rep. No. 989, 95th Cong., 2d Sess. 89 (1978), reprinted in 1978 U.S.C.C.A.N. 5787, 5875. Certainly, this language leaves no room for either the "Heraclitean river" or "Abracadabra" ("impossible deem") approach.

The rule of BC 547(e)(3) is far from the end of the story. To meet the practical difficulties of maintaining security interests in inventory and receivables, the Bankruptcy Code provides an important exception from the general preference rules of 547(b). That exception is BC 547(c)(5).

Please look at BC 547(c)(5) now. As you can see, the subsection is somewhat forbidding. Its language is easier to understand if one starts with a general idea of what the drafters were trying to accomplish. Their central idea was that the floating lien should be subject to attack only to the extent that the acquisition of additional collateral in the aggregate resulted in an improvement in the secured creditor's position during the 90–day period preceding bankruptcy. More specifically, BC 547(c)(5) focuses on whether the aggregate of preferential transfers of security interests caused a reduction in the secured party's unsecured claim (what the statute calls the "amount by which the debt secured by such security interest exceeded the value of all security interests for such debt"). BC 547(c)(5) does not take into account day-to-day fluctuations in collateral levels; rather, one measures the actual unsecured claim as of the date of the bankruptcy petition and compares it to the secured party's unsecured position at the start of the preference period.[2]

The language of BC 547(c)(5) is difficult to penetrate. The following Problems are designed to facilitate your understanding.

Problem 10.3.1. Debtor filed a Chapter 11 petition on March 31, 2002. At that time, Debtor owed $70,000 to Creditor. This debt was secured by a security interest in all Debtor's existing and after-acquired inventory, then valued at $75,000.

At the end of 2001, Debtor's inventory had a value of $75,000 and secured a debt of $70,000. During the first quarter of 2002, Debtor's entire inventory turned over completely; that is, all the inventory that Debtor held at the start of the year was sold.

(a) How much, if any, of the security interest in the $75,000 of new inventory constitutes a preference under BC 547(b)?

(b) How much, if any, of the security interest in the $75,000 of new inventory can the trustee avoid? See BC 547(c)(5). On the ninetieth day prior to bankruptcy, what was the "amount by which the debt ... *exceeded* the ... security interest[ ] ..."? Did subsequent transfers "cause[ ] a reduction" in that figure? Does the result surprise you?

Problem 10.3.2. Debtor filed a Chapter 11 petition on March 31, 2002. At that time, Debtor owed $70,000 to Creditor. This debt was secured by a security interest in all Debtor's existing and after-acquired inventory. At the end of 2001, Debtor's inventory had a value of $55,000 and secured a debt of $70,000. During the first quarter of 2002, Debtor's entire inventory turned over completely. As of the time of the petition, Debtor's inventory is worth $60,000.

(a) How much, if any, of the security interest in the $60,000 in new inventory can the trustee avoid?

(b) What result in part (a) if Creditor was owed $65,000 at the time of the filing of the petition? Of what relevance, if any, are the facts surrounding the reduction in the amount of the debt? Suppose the $5,000 payment came from unencumbered funds? Suppose it represented proceeds from the sale of inventory? Would it make any difference if the payment was one of a series of monthly payments required under the terms of the credit agreement? See Notes on Prepetition Payments to Secured Parties, supra.

Problem 10.3.3. Debtor filed a Chapter 11 petition on March 31, 2002. At that time, Debtor owed $70,000 to Creditor. This debt was secured by a security interest in all Debtor's existing and after-acquired inventory. At the end of 2001, Debtor's inventory had a value of $55,000 and secured a debt of $70,000. During the first quarter of 2002, Debtor was unable to sell

---

2. In some cases, the secured party may not yet have extended any value to the debtor as of the start of the preference period. If so, then the secured party's actual unsecured claim as of the petition date must be compared to the secured party's unsecured position on the date on which new value was first given under the security agreement. See BC 547(c)(5)(B).

any inventory, but because of market shifts the inventory was worth $60,000 at the time of the filing of the petition.

(a) How much, if any, of the security interest in the $60,000 in inventory can the trustee avoid? In what way, if any, does this Problem differ from Problem 10.3.2? Does this Problem implicate BC 547(c)(5)? If so, to what extent did "*transfers* to the transferee cause[ ] a reduction" in the unsecured portion of Creditor's claim?

(b) Would the result in part (a) change if, the day before bankruptcy, Debtor acquired some additional inventory worth $2,000?

Problem 10.3.4. Surf Advertising has a contract with Calvert Distillers, under which Calvert agreed to pay Surf $1,000 each month for two years, during which time Surf agreed to maintain certain advertising signs. Abrams made a loan to Surf and took a perfected security interest in Surf's rights under the unperformed contract with Calvert. During the 90 days prior to Surf's bankruptcy, Surf collected $3,000 from Calvert and paid those amounts to Abrams.

Did Abrams receive an avoidable preference? See BC 547(b); Rockmore v. Lehman, infra. Precisely what "transfer" would the trustee seek to avoid? How would the trustee distinguish this situation from that presented in Problem 10.3.3?

Rockmore v. Lehman[*]

United States Court of Appeals, Second Circuit, 1942.
129 F.2d 892, cert. denied 317 U.S. 700, 63 S.Ct. 525, 87 L.Ed. 559 (1943).

[Proceedings were instituted for the reorganization of the Surf Advertising Corporation under Chapter X of the Bankruptcy Act. Abrams had advanced sums to Surf; in exchange, Surf assigned to Abrams Surf's rights to payment, still to be earned, under an existing contract to maintain advertising signs for Calvert Distillers Corporation. In an earlier opinion (here reversed on rehearing) the Court of Appeals had held that payment to Abrams of funds earned under these contracts constituted a preference.]

Augustus N. Hand, Circuit Judge. . . . In each of the cases before us, advances were made upon contracts whereby Surf in the first case and Fiegel Advertising Company in the second case were to furnish and maintain advertising signs for Calvert in return for which Calvert bound itself to pay fixed sums over a period of years for the furnishing and maintenance of the signs. The advances were not made upon a mere agreement to assign rights which might arise in the future and did not exist at the time contracts were made, but upon assignments of definite contractual obligations.

We are convinced that the New York Court of Appeals has differentiated assignments of existing contracts by way of pledge from agreements to assign rights that have not yet come into being, even as interests contin-

---

* [Decided under the then-current version of the Bankruptcy Act of 1898.]

gent upon counter-performance. The most recent decision is Kniffin v. State, 283 N.Y. 317, 28 N.E.2d 853, where a building contractor assigned his contract with the State of New York to a subcontractor as security for a pre-existing indebtedness, and then became bankrupt. The State made payments under the contract to the assignor, but the assignee was allowed to recover the amount of its claim in spite of the fact that the assignment embraced moneys "to become due" under the contract.

We cannot agree with appellant's contention that Section 60, sub. a, of the present Bankruptcy Act, 11 U.S.C.A. § 96, sub. a, affects our decision, and that there would be an unlawful preference as to any sums paid or payable after knowledge of insolvency. On the contrary we hold that the date of the assignments governed the imposition of the liens on any sums due from Calvert. This is because the contracts, and not the moneys accruing under them, were the subjects of the assignments. Section 60, sub. a, provides that: "a transfer shall be deemed to have been made at the time when it became so far perfected that no bona-fide purchaser from the debtor and no creditor could thereafter have acquired any rights in the property so transferred superior to the rights of the transferee therein." It has long been the New York law that such an assignment is good against a bona fide purchaser, even though the bona fide purchaser is the first to give notice to the obligor. The same thing is true of an execution creditor or a trustee in bankruptcy. . . .

[The opinion also concluded that New York Lien Law § 230 did not require filing of the assignment.]

It follows from the foregoing that our former decision in this matter was erroneous and that the decision of the court below in both cases should have been affirmed.

Orders affirmed.

Problem 10.3.5. Suppose that, in order to perform the Calvert contract in Problem 10.3.4, Surf was required to hire Employee and purchase from Seller a piece of additional equipment. Surf's trustee makes the following argument: payments to Employee and Seller had the effect of exchanging Surf's unencumbered property for an increase in the value of Abrams's collateral, the Calvert account. Even if these payments were not transfers *to* a creditor (Abrams), they were transfers *for the benefit of a creditor* (Abrams) and thus potentially preferential under BC 547(b). See BC 547(b)(1). If the trustee can prove the other elements of BC 547(b), then BC 550(a)(1) enables the trustee to recover the property transferred (or its value) from "the entity for whose benefit such transfer was made." Thus, argues the trustee, Abrams is liable for payments made to Employee and Seller.

(a) Are you persuaded by the trustee's argument? As to the ability of the trustee to recover transfers that create preferences indirectly, see Note on Dean v. Davis, *infra*.

(b) Suppose Employee and Seller provided their services and goods to Surf on open credit and remained unpaid at the time of bankruptcy. Would the trustee's argument be stronger or weaker?

Problem 10.3.6. On June 1 Crystal Credit loaned $100,000 to the Dream Spinning Co. At the same time Dream granted Crystal a perfected security interest in bales of cotton then worth $60,000. The security interest also extended to after-acquired cotton and yarn. During June, July and August Dream processed this cotton into yarn. As a result of the processing, the yarn was worth $100,000 by August 30, when Dream went into bankruptcy. Can the trustee avoid Crystal's interest as a preference to the extent of the increase in value during the 90 days before bankruptcy? When did the "transfer" of the security interest in the yarn occur? See Note on "Prejudice of Other Creditors," infra.

NOTE ON "PREJUDICE OF OTHER CREDITORS"

At stake in Problems 10.3.4, 10.3.5, and 10.3.6 is nothing less than the continuing vitality of the leading case of Rockmore v. Lehman, supra. That decision rejected a trustee's attack on the secured party's receipt of amounts the debtor earned under a contract that had been assigned to the secured party, even though the debtor had earned those amounts by work performed shortly before bankruptcy.

Grappling with these Problems requires a bit of legislative history. As you know, the two-point test embodied in BC 547(c)(5) emerged from the work of the Gilmore Committee. The Gilmore Committee Report put a case where raw materials worth $10,000 are converted into finished products worth $20,000; the Gilmore Committee stated that under its proposal the $10,000 increase in value was not protected and would go to the trustee. It observed: "If the final holding in *Rockmore v. Lehman* [citation omitted] suggests the contrary conclusion, that holding is here overruled." 1978 U.S.C.C.A.N. at 6177–78.

This feature of the Gilmore Committee's recommendations encountered criticism. Professor Homer Kripke argued that any increase in the value of collateral due, e.g., to harvesting crops, completing work in progress, and sales of inventory, should redound to the benefit of the secured party "so long as it is not at the expense of other parties interested in the estate." H.R. Doc. No. 137, 93d Cong., 1st Sess. pt. 1, at 210 (1973) (quoting a letter from Professor Kripke to the Gilmore Committee). To implement this policy, Professor Kripke mentioned the formula used in Meinhard, Greeff & Co. v. Edens, 189 F.2d 792 (4th Cir.1951), which gave the secured creditor the entire value of the finished goods, less the costs expended in finishing them.

In response to this conflict in views, the provision that became BC 547(c)(5) was amended by inserting the qualifying phrase "and to the prejudice of other creditors holding unsecured claims." Does the meaning of this phrase become clear in the light of the legislative history? In Problem 10.3.6, what facts would show that Crystal's improvement in position resulted from "transfers to the transferee ... to the prejudice of other creditors holding unsecured claims"?

Could this provision jeopardize construction loans, crop loans, and other types of complex financing in which the secured party gives value before the debtor does the work that creates value in the collateral? Can (and should) the Bankruptcy Code be interpreted to avoid such dangers?

One interpretation that would give some comfort to secured parties would be to focus on the requirement that the improvement in position results from "transfers" that otherwise would be avoidable under BC 547(b). The line between an increase in the value of a given item of collateral (which does not constitute a "transfer") and an exchange of one item of collateral for another (which does) may be difficult to discern. Consider, for example, an account receivable. What happens when the debtor earns a right to payment by performing its contractual obligation? Like Rockmore v. Lehman, both BC 547(a)(3) and R9–102(a)(2) suggest that although the right to payment has increased in value, it is the same item of collateral. But under the pre–1972 version of F9–106, only earned rights to payment were accounts; unearned rights to payment were a different type of collateral, "contract rights." Should nonbankruptcy law's characterization of the collateral determine whether a preference has occurred?

NOTE ON *DEAN V. DAVIS*

A favorite aphorism of many first-year law students is "One cannot do indirectly what one cannot do directly." In Dean v. Davis, 242 U.S. 438, 37 S.Ct. 130, 61 L.Ed. 419 (1917), the Supreme Court applied this principle to preference law under the Bankruptcy Act of 1898. Fearing that Bank would have him arrested for fraud, Debtor borrowed $1,600 from his father-in-law, Dean, and secured the debt with a mortgage on substantially all his property. Shortly thereafter an involuntary bankruptcy petition was filed against Debtor. The trustee sought to set aside the mortgage and was successful. The district court held the mortgage constituted a fraudulent conveyance; the court of appeals held it also was a voidable preference.

In affirming the district court, the Supreme Court (Brandeis, J.) rejected the preference attack as follows:

> The mortgage was not voidable as a preference under § 60b. Preference implies paying or securing a preexisting debt of the person preferred. The mortgage was given to secure Dean for a substantially contemporary advance. *The bank, not Dean, was preferred.* The use of Dean's money to accomplish this purpose could not convert the transaction into a preferring of Dean, although he knew of the debtor's insolvency. Mere circuity of arrangement will not save a transfer which effects a preference from being invalid as such. But a transfer to a third person is invalid under this section as a preference, only where that person was acting on behalf of the creditor....

242 U.S. at 443, 37 S.Ct. at 131 (emphasis added).

Inasmuch as the trustee did not proceed against Bank, the court's observation that the Bank was preferred is dictum. The recodification of preference law in the Bankruptcy Code is consistent with the notion that an otherwise nonpreferential transfer to one person may result in a preference to a creditor who received the benefit of the transfer. Thus, BC 547(b)(1) refers to transfers "to *or for the benefit of* a creditor" and BC 550(a)(1) permits recovery of an avoided transfer from "the initial transferee of such transfer *or the entity for whose benefit the transfer was made.*"

A number of reported cases are consistent with this aspect of Dean v. Davis. See, e.g., In re Air Conditioning, Inc. of Stuart, 845 F.2d 293 (11th Cir.1988), cert. denied 488 U.S. 993, 109 S.Ct. 557, 102 L.Ed.2d 584 (1988) (grant of security interest to issuer of letter of credit held preferential to beneficiary); In re Compton Corp., 831 F.2d 586 (5th Cir.1987) (same), rehearing granted per curiam 835 F.2d 584 (1988) (explaining what facts are to be considered on remand). A particularly interesting case is In re Prescott, 805 F.2d 719 (7th Cir.1986). In *Prescott,* transfers were made during the preference period to a partially secured senior creditor. Because the transfers had the effect of increasing the collateral available to a junior secured creditor (i.e., converting part of the unsecured portion of the claim into a secured claim), the court held that the transfers preferred the junior creditor.

Two other aspects of Dean v. Davis are also important. Although the dictum that *Bank was* preferred seems to have survived the enactment of the Bankruptcy Code, a highly controversial holding by the Seventh Circuit casts doubt on the continuing validity of the holding, that *Dean was not* preferred. In re V.N. Deprizio Construction Co., 874 F.2d 1186 (7th Cir.1989). *Deprizio* was followed by a few other courts of appeals, but some lower courts were unpersuaded. The implications of the *Deprizio* case are beyond the scope of this book. Many pages of commentary have been devoted to them and to the issue of statutory construction that the case addressed. In 1994 Congress added subsection (c) to BC 550. This subsection changes the result under the facts of *Deprizio*; however, the logic of the case may survive in other contexts. See In re Williams, 234 B.R. 801 (Bkrtcy.D.Ore. 1999) (enactment of BC 550(c) did not completely overrule the *Deprizio* line of cases; security interest avoided as preference).

Also beyond the scope of this book is whether Dean v. Davis continues as a part of the fraudulent conveyance law applicable in bankruptcy.

NOTE ON VALUATION OF COLLATERAL

As should be apparent by now, most of the issues we have discussed in this Chapter implicate issues of valuing the collateral. For example, one cannot work the two-point test of BC 547(c)(5) without valuing the collateral at each of the two points. Nor can one determine whether the debtor has any "equity" in the collateral for purposes of BC 362(d)(2) unless one knows the collateral's value.

Depending on the circumstances, appraisers apply different standards of valuation to any given piece of property. Among the most common are going-concern value (what the property is worth as part of an ongoing business; this standard requires that the total value of the business be allocated among its various assets), fair market value (what the property would yield at a sale by a willing seller to a willing buyer), and forced-sale (or quick liquidation) value (what would the property yield at an immediate sale by a seller who was compelled to sell).

The Bankruptcy Code does not define the applicable standard. Under BC 506(a), the value of a security interest in property "shall be determined in light of the purpose of the valuation and of the proposed disposition or use of such property, and in conjunction with any hearing on such disposition or use or on a plan affecting such creditor's interest." The legislative history suggests that courts will have to determine value on a case-by-case basis and that a valuation at one time for one purpose (e.g., adequate protection) would not be binding at a later time for another purpose (e.g., distribution). See S. Rep. No. 989, 95th Cong., 2d Sess. 68 (1978), reprinted in 1987 U.S.C.C.A.N. 5787, 5854; H.R. Rep. No. 595, 95th Cong., 1st Sess. 356 (1977), reprinted in 1978 U.S.C.C.A.N. 5963, 6312.

In 1997 the Supreme Court considered the applicable standard for valuing collateral. Associates Commercial Corp. v. Rash, 520 U.S. 953, 117 S.Ct. 1879, 138 L.Ed.2d 148 (1997). In *Rash*, the Chapter 13 debtors proposed to retain the collateral (a truck) for use in a freight-hauling business. Their Chapter 13 plan proposed to "cram down" the secured party by paying the present value of the collateral in 58 monthly installments. The debtors argued that the standard for valuing the collateral should be foreclosure value, i.e., the amount the secured party would have received at a foreclosure disposition under Article 9. The Court rejected this argument and held that a replacement-value standard applied: "the value of property retained because the debtor has exercised the § 1325(a)(5)(B) 'cram down' option is the cost the debtor would incur to obtain a like asset for the same 'proposed ... use.' " Elsewhere in the opinion, the Court referred to replacement value as "the price a willing buyer in the debtor's trade, business, or situation would pay a willing seller to obtain property of like age and condition." The valuation standard may well be different when the collateral is sold as part of a liquidation and not retained for use by the debtor.

Detailed discussion of valuation issues is best left to the Bankruptcy course.

Problem 10.3.7. On June 1, 2002, Castle Finance loaned $100,000 to Diggins Construction Company; Diggins executed an agreement granting Castle a security interest in "all of the construction equipment including bulldozers and other machinery, that Diggins now owns or may hereafter acquire." At the time of the agreement Diggins owned five bulldozers each worth $20,000. On June 9, Castle filed a financing statement, signed by Diggins, that referred to the collateral as "construction equipment."

On July 1, with Castle's approval, Diggins traded one of the bulldozers for a cement mixer that also was worth $20,000. On July 15 the construction business was slack, so Diggins sold two of its remaining four bulldozers for $40,000 and used these funds to pay workers and social security taxes. Castle was not informed of these sales. On August 1, Diggins received a $20,000 down payment from a new construction job and used this money to purchase a new $20,000 bulldozer.

On September 1 several creditors of Diggins threw Diggins into bankruptcy. Which assets of Diggins may Castle Finance claim against opposition by the trustee in bankruptcy? See Eisenberg, Bankruptcy Law in Perspective, 28 UCLA L. Rev. 953, 961–62 & n. 27 (1981) (discussing how BC 547(c)(5) distinguishes equipment from inventory and receivables).

NOTE ON PROCEEDS ARISING AFTER BANKRUPTCY

The filing of a bankruptcy petition does not necessarily coincide with the cessation of the debtor's business. Indeed, the debtor-in-possession may continue to operate the business in Chapter 11 unless the court orders otherwise. BC 1108. See also BC 721 (bankruptcy court may authorize Chapter 7 trustee to operate debtor's business).

In the course of operating the business, the DIP may acquire property that would be covered by an after-acquired property clause in a prepetition security agreement. Although the transfer of a security interest in property acquired postpetition ordinarily would not be avoidable under BC 547—the transfer would not have occurred *before* the date of the filing of the petition, see BC 547(b)(4)—a postpetition transfer of this kind might have the same effect as a voidable preference: the acquisition of additional collateral might improve the position of a secured creditor at the expense of other creditors.

BC 552 addresses this concern. The general rule, set forth in BC 552(a), is that property acquired by the bankruptcy estate after the commencement of the case is not subject to a security interest resulting from a prebankruptcy security agreement. In other words, BC 552(a) generally renders after-acquired property clauses ineffective as to property acquired after the commencement of a bankruptcy case.

Obviously, this rule is overbroad. It invalidates security interests not only in additional collateral but also in substitute collateral (e.g., an account that results from the postpetition sale of inventory collateral acquired by the debtor before bankruptcy). Subsection (b)(1) cuts back on the general rule when a prepetition security agreement "extends to property of the debtor acquired before the commencement of the case and to proceeds, product, offspring, or profits of such property." In that event, the security interest extends to such proceeds, etc., acquired by the estate after the commencement of the bankruptcy case to the extent provided by the security agreement and by applicable nonbankruptcy law. In other words, the filing of the bankruptcy petition does not invalidate a prepetition security agreement insofar as the secured party claims proceeds of prepetition collateral that the debtor acquires postpetition.

BC 552(b)(1) uses two important terms that the Bankruptcy Code leaves undefined: "extends to" and "proceeds." As discussed in Chapter 7, Section 5, supra, Article 9 gives every secured party a security interest in "proceeds" (as defined in R9–102(a)(64)), even if the security agreement does not provide for one. See R9–203(f), R9–315(a)(2). The legislative history makes clear that a security agreement that is silent nevertheless "extends to" proceeds, as the term is used in BC 552(b)(1). See H.R.Rep. No. 595, 95th Cong., 1st Sess. 377 (1977), reprinted in 1978 U.S.C.C.A.N. 5963, 6333.

What constitutes "proceeds" within the meaning of BC 552(b)? In In re Bumper Sales, Inc., 907 F.2d 1430 (4th Cir.1990), the secured party claimed a security interest in inventory acquired by the debtor-in-possession during the bankruptcy case. The parties stipulated that the postpetition inventory was produced entirely with the proceeds of prepetition inventory. The Fourth Circuit held that "the UCC's definition and treatment of proceeds applies to Section 552 of the Bankruptcy Code" and covers "second generation proceeds" that are traceable to the prepetition collateral (e.g., inventory acquired with the proceeds of accounts generated postpetition from the sale of prepetition inventory).

The legislative history suggests that the term "proceeds" in BC 552 may encompass even more than the same term encompasses under the UCC. "The term 'proceeds' is not limited to the technical definition of that term in the U.C.C., but covers any property into which property subject to the security interest is converted." H.R.Rep. No. 595, 95th Cong., 1st Sess. 377 (1977). However, the Fourth Circuit "believe[s] that Section 552(b)'s express reference to 'nonbankruptcy law' should take priority over a vague and isolated piece of legislative history. We also note that the judicial creation of a definition for 'proceeds,' broader post-petition than pre-petition, would produce arbitrary and potentially inequitable results."

The definition of "proceeds" in R9–102(a)(64) is somewhat broader than the definition of the term in Former Article 9, which was in effect when BC 552 was enacted. If a court follows the approach of the Fourth Circuit, will the meaning of "proceeds" in BC 552(b)(1) change to reflect changes in the Article 9 definition?

BC 552(b) contains an important exception to the protection it affords to proceeds arising postpetition: the court may cut back on the security interest "based on the equities of the case." According to the legislative history, in the course of considering the equities, "the court may evaluate any expenditures by the estate relating to proceeds and any related improvement in position of the secured party." 124 Cong.Rec. 32400 (1978) (statement of Rep. Edwards); 124 Cong.Rec. 34000 (1978) (statement of Sen. DeConcini). See, e.g., In re Kain, 86 B.R. 506 (Bkrtcy.W.D.Mich.1988) (proceeds of sale postpetition offspring of prepetition livestock collateral "should be reduced by reasonable postpetition expenses validly and demonstrably paid or incurred by the Debtors to raise, preserve, enhance or market the livestock.") You should realize that the problem addressed by the exception to BC 552(b) also arises under BC 547(c)(5). (The former deals with postpetition activity; the latter, prepetition.)

SECTION 4. EFFECT OF BUYER'S BANKRUPTCY ON SELLER'S RIGHT TO RECLAIM GOODS

(1) Introductory Note. In Chapter 1, Sections 2 and 3, supra, we discussed the right of a seller to reclaim goods delivered to a buyer. You may recall that the UCC contemplates two different rights to reclaim. The credit seller's right to reclaim goods arises when the seller discovers that the buyer has received goods on credit while insolvent. See UCC 2–702(2). The cash seller's right to reclaim goods arises when payment was due and demanded, but not received, upon delivery of the goods. See UCC 2–507(2).

Sellers commonly seek to exercise rights of reclamation when the buyer has entered bankruptcy. The buyer's entry into bankruptcy is the event most likely to cause the credit seller to "discover[ ] that the buyer has received goods on credit while insolvent." UCC 2–702(2). The cash seller may have delivered goods in exchange for a check that subsequently was dishonored, perhaps because the bank on which it was drawn had learned of the buyer's bankruptcy. See UCC 2–511(3) (payment by check is conditional and is defeated, as between the parties, by dishonor); BC 542(b), (c) (requiring those who owe debts to bankruptcy debtor and who have actual notice or knowledge of bankruptcy case to make payment to bankruptcy trustee).

(2) Reclamation Based on Buyer's Insolvency (UCC 2–702). Under the old Bankruptcy Act, attempts by sellers who had delivered goods on credit to reclaim the goods from the estate of a bankrupt buyer were subject to serious objections by the trustee. The trustee would argue that the right to reclaim under UCC 2–702 when "the seller discovers that the buyer has received goods on credit while insolvent" was inconsistent with various provisions of the Bankruptcy Act, particularly section 67c(1)(A), which invalidated as against a trustee "every statutory lien which first becomes effective upon the insolvency of the debtor."

As we saw in Sections 1 and 2, supra, in bankruptcy, the difference between recognizing an *in rem* remedy against specific goods and an *in personam* claim for damages against the bankruptcy estate is crucial. Successful reclamation is likely to make the seller whole (or close to it), even though it precludes the seller from asserting a damage claim against the estate. See UCC 2–702(3). In contrast, when a trustee avoids a seller's reclamation rights, the goods remain in the estate, and their value ordinarily will be distributed to unsecured creditors pro rata according to the size of their claims.

Suppose, for example, that UCC 2–702 affords Seller the right to reclaim $25,000 of goods delivered to Buyer before bankruptcy. If reclamation is successful, Seller will recover the goods, which Seller ordinarily can resell for about $25,000. But if the trustee can avoid the reclamation right, Seller would receive instead an unsecured claim against the estate. As the holder of an unsecured claim, Seller would share with all the other unsecured creditors in the proceeds of the sale of the goods. If, for example, unsecured creditors receive only ten percent of their claims, Seller would receive only $2,500. Although the balance of Seller's claim against Buyer ($22,500) would remain unpaid, Seller almost never will be entitled to recover any of this amount. To the extent a debt is not paid through the bankruptcy, it normally is discharged and cannot be collected as a personal liability of the debtor. See BC 727; BC 1141; BC 524. For this reason, neither sellers nor trustees are indifferent between the exercise of reclamation rights and the assertion of a claim for damages.

Unlike its predecessor statute, the current Bankruptcy Code directly addresses sellers' reclamation rights. Although the Bankruptcy Code retains strong provisions for avoiding state statutory liens that first "become[ ] effective against the debtor ... when the debtor becomes insolvent," BC 545(1)(D), it also includes a provision limiting the trustee's attack on reclamations under UCC 2–702. This provision is BC 546(c). Please read it now.

Observe that, unlike UCC 2–702(2), BC 546(c)(2) gives the bankruptcy court the option to deny reclamation and instead grant the reclaiming seller a lien on property of the estate or a priority administrative claim. From the seller's perspective, reclamation is preferable to either a lien or an administrative claim. Recall that, generally speaking, holders of liens are entitled to receive their collateral or its value from the bankruptcy estate, but they run the risk that, by the time of distribution, the collateral will have diminished in value and no other assets will be available to satisfy the claims. To guard against this risk, secured claims may receive "adequate protection" under BC 361. See Section 1, supra. In some cases, however, the court-approved protection may prove inadequate and the secured party will receive an administrative claim of the highest priority. See BC 507(b). Administrative claims, including also the trustee's fees and expenses and other costs of maintaining and preserving the estate, are paid from unencumbered assets ahead of general unsecured claims. See BC 507(a)(1). However, bankruptcy estates have been known to be or become **administratively insolvent**. Of course, when the buyer is in bankruptcy, either a lien or an administrative claim is preferable to an general unsecured claim for the price of goods sold.

(3) Fraud, "Rubber" Checks, and the Bankruptcy Code. Important questions remain notwithstanding (or perhaps because of) the enactment of BC 546(c). The section is silent with respect to the exercise of a number of the reclamation rights that nonbankruptcy law provides. For example, the credit seller's demand may be sufficient for purposes of UCC 2–702(2) but not in conformity with BC 546(c)(1). That is, the seller might give an oral demand or, having received a written misrepresentation of solvency, might make demand more than ten days after delivery of the goods to the buyer. Or the seller may not have delivered the goods to the buyer on credit, but rather in exchange for a "rubber" check that "bounced." And a seller may have the right to recover goods obtained through active fraud unrelated to the buyer's solvency. See generally Chapter 1, Section 2, supra.

Does BC 546(c) provide the exclusive remedy for a seller attempting to reclaim goods from a bankruptcy trustee? In other words, does the inclusion of BC 546(c) mean that reclaiming sellers who do not fall within its scope automatically lose their reclamation rights in bankruptcy? Or does the section afford a safe harbor for certain reclamation rights and leave to the trustee the burden of proving the avoidability of other reclamation rights under other sections of the Bankruptcy Code, such as 544, 545, and 547? The following case addresses these questions.

In re Contract Interiors, Inc.

United States Bankruptcy Court, Eastern District of Michigan, 1981.
14 B.R. 670.

■ GEORGE BRODY, BANKRUPTCY JUDGE.

This controversy involves the construction to be given to section 546(c) of the Bankruptcy Code, 11 U.S.C.A. § 546(c) (1979).

On December 24, 1980, B. Berger & Co. (the "plaintiff") shipped certain decorative goods to Contract Interiors, Inc. On February 6, 1981, Contract Interiors filed a petition for relief under chapter 11 of the Bankruptcy Code. The plaintiff made demand in writing for the return of the goods on February 20, 1981. When the defendant (the "debtor") failed to honor this request, the plaintiff instituted this action contending that it was induced to ship the goods in reliance upon a false financial statement submitted by the debtor and, therefore, it was entitled to reclaim them either by virtue of section 2–702 of the Uniform Commercial Code, M.S.A. § 19.2702 [M.C.L.A. § 440.2702], or based upon a theory of common-law fraud.

The parties agree that whether the plaintiff may prevail depends, at least initially, upon the construction to be given to section 546(c) of the Code.

"§ 546. *Limitations on avoiding powers*

.   .   .

(c) The rights and powers of the trustee under sections 544(a), 545, 547, and 549 of this title are subject to any statutory right or common-law right of a seller, in the ordinary course of such seller's business, of goods to the debtor to reclaim such goods if the debtor has received such goods while insolvent, but—

(1) such a seller may not reclaim any such goods unless such seller demands in writing reclamation of such goods before ten days after receipt of such goods by the debtor;

(2) the court may deny reclamation to a seller with such a right of reclamation that has made such a demand only if court—

(A) grants the claim of such a seller priority as an administrative expense; or

(B) secured such claim by a lien."

Based upon section 546(c), the debtor argues that a seller may reclaim the goods he was induced to sell by fraudulent representation only if the seller complies with the requirements set forth in section 546(c) and, since the plaintiff did not make a written demand within ten days of the receipt of the goods by the debtor no right to reclaim exists.

Counsel for the plaintiff, however, maintains that section 546 deals with the limitation of the trustee's avoiding powers and, therefore, subsection (c) of section 546 should be construed to mean that it merely prevents the trustee from relying upon sections 544(a), 546, 547 and 549 to defeat any statutory or common-law right of the seller to reclaim the goods sold in the ordinary course of business if the seller complies with the conditions set forth in section 546(c); but that a seller may still rely upon any statutory or common-law right that he may have to reclaim goods he has sold to a debtor even though he does not comply with the conditions set forth in section 546(c), but if a seller does so, the trustee may employ all of his avoiding powers to resist the seller's claim. In support of this construction of section 546(c), plaintiff relies on a law review article by Mann & Phillips analyzing section 546(c), entitled "Section 546(c) of the Bankruptcy Code: An Imperfect Resolution of the Conflict Between the Reclaiming Seller and the Bankruptcy Trustee," 54 Am.Bankr.L.J. 239 (1980). In that article, the writers concede that section 546(c) may be construed to mean that it is the "exclusive and conclusive bankruptcy provision governing [a seller] reclamation rights," and that the failure to comply with section 546(c) precludes any recovery by the seller. The writers then state:

"Although this interpretation of section 546(c) cannot be dismissed peremptorily, it is unpersuasive for a number of reasons. First, section 546(c) does not expressly state the effect of a failure to comply with its requirements; nor does it directly state that consideration of the listed Reform Act sections is precluded in cases where the seller fails so to comply. Second, the only legislative history specifically addressing this point suggests that section 546(c) should not prevent the non-complying seller from contesting the trustee under other bankruptcy provisions. Third, the basic idea that seller reclamation rights outside of section 546(c)'s coverage are therefore ineffective in bankruptcy leads to entirely ludicrous results if extended to any degree. For example, this reasoning could deny the recovery to sellers exercising a right of stoppage in transit or even asserting a perfected Article 9 security interest. Finally, the view severely undermines any coherent reading of the Bankruptcy Reform Act as a whole, for it would dictate that the trustee's right to invalidate certain statutory liens or to assume the status of an ideal lien creditor is no longer dependent upon whether the reclamation right falls within the purview of these bankruptcy provisions but now is solely determined by the parameters of section 546(c)."

Based upon this analysis, the writers suggest that

"... it is preferable to treat section 546(c) as providing the seller with a 'non-exclusive safe harbor' against a trustee proceeding under the Reform Act sections it lists. Thus, sellers complying with section 546(c) would be immune from attack under the listed sections, while those who did not comply would be free to defend themselves against the trustee on the merits as defined by the Reform Act section used by the trustee."

A brief discussion of the background leading to the adoption of section 546(c) may be of aid in resolving this controversy. The common law recognized the right of a defrauded seller to rescind the contract of sale and to reclaim the goods sold. State law, however, differed as to what fact had to be established to give rise to this remedy. ... To the extent that the state law recognized the remedy of reclamation on a given set of facts, the remedy was available as against a trustee in bankruptcy. For whatever reason, the lack of state law uniformity did not cause any significant difficulties when the debtor filed a petition in bankruptcy.

The American Law Institute and the National Conference of Commissioners on Uniform State Laws proposed the first Official Draft of the Uniform Commercial Code in 1952. The Uniform Commercial Code was first adopted in Pennsylvania in 1954 and has since been adopted by every state except Louisiana. The Uniform Commercial Code became effective in Michigan in 1964. P.A. 174 (1962). Section 2–702(2) of the Uniform Commercial Code (14 M.S.A. § 19.2702 [M.C.L.A. § 440.2702]) provides:

"Sec. 2–702. *Seller's Remedies on Discovery of Buyer's Insolvency.*

(1) Where the seller discovers the buyer to be insolvent he may refuse delivery except for cash including payment for all goods theretofore delivered and stop delivery under this Article (Section 2–705).

(2) Where the seller discovers that the buyer has received goods on credit while insolvent he may reclaim the goods upon demand made within ten days after the receipt, but if misrepresentation of solvency has been made to the particular seller in writing within three months before delivery the ten day limitation does not apply. Except as provided in this subsection the seller may not base a right to reclaim goods on the buyer's fraudulent or innocent misrepresentation of solvency or of intent to pay."

With the adoption of section 2–702 of the Uniform Commercial Code, relative stability was displaced by confusion and uncertainty. Attempts by sellers to reclaim goods from bankrupt estates was resisted by debtors in possession and trustees on various grounds. The areas of conflict have been summarized as follows:

> "Trustees claimed that the right of reclamation was a statutory lien triggered by the debtor's insolvency and voidable by former section 67c(1)(A); that it was a priority in conflict with former section 64; or that it was subordinate to the rights of a judicial lien creditor under former section 70c." 4 Collier on Bankr. ¶ 546.04 (15th ed. 1980), at 546-9.

This conflict "produced a body of case law notable for its intricacy, its profession of doctrinal approaches, and its general incoherence." Mann & Phillips, supra, at 239.

Section 546(c) was adopted in an attempt to resolve the problems created by section 2-702(2). The legislative history states that the purpose of section 546(c) is "to recognize, in part, the validity of section 2-702 of the Uniform Commercial Code which has generated much litigation, confusion, and divergent decisions in different circuits." H.R.Rep. No. 95-595, 95th Cong., 1st Sess. 372 (1977); S.Rep. No. 95-989, 95th Cong., 2d Sess. 87 (1978), U.S.Code Cong. & Admin.News 1978, pp. 5787, 5873, 6328. Section 2-702(2) permits a seller to reclaim goods if the buyer received the goods while insolvent if the seller made a demand for the goods within ten days after the receipt of the goods by the buyer. If the buyer induced the seller to ship goods based upon a written misrepresentation of solvency and the goods were shipped within three months of such misrepresentation, the ten-day limitation does not apply. The legislative history accompanying section 546(c), when read in conjunction with section 546(c), makes it clear that the drafters intended to retain only that part of the section 2-702 which permits reclamation if demand was made for the return of the goods within ten days after receipt and to make this right to reclaim exclusive in order to put an end to the disruptive litigation engendered by section 2-702(2).[3] The purpose set forth in the legislative history can be given effect only if it is held that section 546(c) provides the exclusive remedy for a reclaiming seller.

The Mann & Phillips article, supra, relied upon by the plaintiff is a scholarly and comprehensive analysis of section 546(c). However, the arguments marshalled by them to support the contention that section 546(c) should not be given exclusive effect, are not persuasive.

Admittedly, section 546(c) does not expressly state the effect of a failure to comply with its requirements, nor does it directly state that section 546(c) is an exclusive remedy for a seller who seeks to reclaim

---

3. This is actually the solution that was suggested by Weintraub & Edelman: "Seller's Right to Reclaim Property Under Section 2.702(2) of the Code Under the Bankruptcy Act: Fact or Fantasy," 32 Bus.Law 1165 (1977). This recommendation was based, in part, on the view that so limiting the right of seller to reclaim goods would eliminate costly, time-consuming litigation, enhance the likelihood of successful reorganization, and give relief in those cases in which there is an 'overwhelming aura of fraud' cases in which sellers were induced to deliver goods to a debtor on the eve of bankruptcy." Henson, "Reclamation Rights of a Seller Under § 2.702," 22 N.Y.L.F. 41, 49 (1975).

property. The mere failure to state the effect of noncompliance with section 546(c) does not, of itself, support the conclusion that section 546(c) is non-exclusive. Mann & Phillips' assertion that the only legislative history which addresses the exclusivity issue supports a "safe harbor" interpretation is based on a letter written to the Minority Counsel of the Committee on Improvement in the Judicial Machinery, United States Senate, by Professor Minahan of the University of Vermont Law School. The letter was written when the Senate was considering section 4–407, an earlier version of section 546(c)—a version essentially similar to that of section 546(c).[4] In the letter, Professor Minahan stated that the proposed section 4–407 should not be construed to provide the exclusive remedy for a defrauded seller but that whether a seller could reclaim property, if he did not comply with section 4–407,

"... should be left to the courts to decide in light of the particular circumstances of the case. Here the courts have discretion, absent notification within the ten-day period, to declare that the particular reclamation is a statutory lien or that it conflicts with the federal priorities. Section 4–407 merely gives a minimum of ten days worth of protection. Beyond the ten day period, the courts could go either way." Mann & Phillips, supra, at 265 n. 181.

Professor Minahan was not directly involved in the drafting of the Code. "[R]emarks other than by persons responsible for the preparation or the drafting of bill are entitled to little weight." Ernst & Ernst v. Hochfelder, 425 U.S. 185, 203 n. 24, 96 S.Ct. 1375, 1386 n. 24, 47 L.Ed.2d 668 (1976). The only pertinent legislative history that sheds light on the interpretation to be given to section 546(c) is that which accompanies section 546(c) and which, as previously stated, indicates that section 546(c) is to be given exclusive effect.

Mann & Phillips also maintain that if section 546(c) is held to be the exclusive remedy governing a seller's right to reclamation, it "could deny recovery to a seller exercising a right of stoppage in transit or asserting a perfected Article 9 security interest." A realistic reading of section 546(c) reveals that such fears are unjustified. A seller's right to stop goods in transit is governed by section 2–705 of the Uniform Commercial Code. This

---

4. The proposed section 4–407 provided as follows:

"Sec. 4–407. *Right of Reclaiming Seller.*—A seller's right under state law to recover property sold upon subsequent discovery that buyer received the property while insolvent or at a time when buyer had ceased to pay his debts in the ordinary course of business or had an inability to pay his debts as they became due shall not be defeated upon the commencement of a case under this Act by or against the buyer as debtor because of anything contained in section 4–405 or 4–406 provided:

(1) debtor received the property on credit or payment by draft which was subsequently dishonored; and

(2) within ten days of debtor's written receipt of property seller made a written demand of debtor that property be returned; and

(3) at the time of debtor's receipt of the property seller had no actual knowledge of the contemplation of the filing of a petition under this Act by or against the debtor."

right continues until the buyer has either actually or constructively received the goods. § 2–705(2). It is only when the debtor either has actual or constructive possession that a seller is compelled to rely on section 546(c). There is nothing in section 546(c) that remotely indicates that it deprives a seller of any remedy that he may have had under the Bankruptcy Act by virtue of section 2.705 Nor does section 546(c) impact on the right of a seller who has a valid security interest in goods received by a debtor. If a seller has a valid security interest, he has no need to rely upon section 546(c). Section 546(c) does not invalidate any such interest.

Finally, the authors contend that if section 546(c) means that a seller can reclaim goods only if he complies with the conditions set forth in section 546(c), it leads to "the absurd conclusion that the seller's recovery rights included by section 546(c) *are not* statutory liens or rights subordinate to a lien creditor so long as the seller complies with the section's procedural requirements, but *would* be so designated if the seller fails to comply." Inquiry as to whether a seller's right to reclaim is a statutory lien or a priority or a preference is no longer pertinent. It is no longer necessary to characterize the seller's right. A seller has a remedy if he complies with the condition set forth in section 546(c); he does not have a remedy if he does not so comply. This is the result that the drafters of the Code intended.

It is evident from the tenor of their comments that Mann & Phillips' basic concern is that to hold that section 546(c) provides more than a "safe harbor" is ill-advised. The court recognizes that to give exclusive effect to section 546(c) permits a debtor, who either actively or passively defrauds a seller of goods in the ordinary course of business, to insulate such fraudulent transactions unless the seller complies with the conditions therein.[7] The court also recognizes that to limit the right of a defrauded seller to recover property only if he complies with the conditions set forth in section 546(c), for all practical purposes, makes the right meaningless. The event that generally triggers demand for reclamation is the filing of a petition in bankruptcy. Unless the filing of the petition is preceded by extensive publicity, a seller will ordinarily not be able to comply with the conditions set forth in section 546(c). A court, however, does not have the power to legislate; it must merely accept what the legislature has written. It is "not at liberty to revise while professing to construe." Sun Printing and Publishing Assoc. v. Remington Paper and Power Co., 235 N.Y. 338, 346, 139 N.E. 470 (1923).[8]

For the foregoing reasons, the complaint is dismissed.

---

7. Not only is a defrauded seller unable to exercise the right of reclamation unless he complies with the conditions set forth in § 546(c), but he is also precluded—if the debtor is a corporation—from bringing an action to except his debt from discharge. § 1141.

8. It should be noted that the limitation of a defrauded seller to recover property applies only to sales which have been made in the ordinary course of business. The right of a seller to reclaim property based upon allegations of fraud is not limited by § 546(c) if the transaction is not in the ordinary course of business.

An appropriate order to be submitted.

NOTE ON *CONTRACT INTERIORS*

The opinion in *Contract Interiors* observed that permitting a defrauded seller to reclaim only if the seller has given written notice within ten days after delivery "for all practical purposes, makes the right meaningless," but that a court "must merely accept what the legislature has written." An amendment in 1994 extended to 20 days the time within which a demand might be made, if the ten-day period expires after the commencement of the bankruptcy case. Nevertheless, this approach calls for a close look at the language of BC 546(c).

Does BC 546(c) say that a defrauded seller may reclaim goods only if the seller has given a timely written notice? Or does the section say that the trustee's right to avoid transfers of property under BC 544(a), 545, 547, and 549 does *not* apply if the required notice has been given? The question is important, for under the latter reading one must first determine whether the trustee *has* the right to avoid the property interest of a defrauded seller under the sections of the Bankruptcy Code cited in BC 546(c).[1] If the answer to this inquiry is "no," then BC 546(c) becomes irrelevant. Most of the reported decisions have read BC 546(c) to be the exclusive mode of reclamation once the debtor has entered bankruptcy.

Matters become even more complex if the goods that are the subject of a reclamation right also are encumbered by a security interest. See Chapter 11, Section 3, infra.

---

1. For example, UCC 2–702(3) was amended in 1966 to delete the words "or lien creditor," thereby suggesting that the credit seller's reclamation right would prevail over a judicial lien creditor. In states that have adopted this amendment, the reclamation right would not be avoidable under BC 544(a).

COMPETING CLAIMS TO COLLATERAL: OTHER PRIORITY RULES

SECTION 1. CHANGES IN BUSINESS STRUCTURE

Introductory Note. X Corp merges into Y Corp; Y Corp survives and X Corp ceases to exist. As is typical, X Corp and Y Corp each has granted security interests: Each has a **working capital** lender, whose loan is secured with a **blanket lien** on all assets; other creditors hold purchase-money security interests in specific equipment and inventory. What are the consequences of the merger for the secured parties?

Quite probably, the merger constitutes a default under the security agreements. If so, lawyers for X Corp and Y Corp are likely to have obtained consent to the merger from the secured parties. In the course of doing so, the various creditors of X Corp and Y Corp probably determined their rights (including the priority of their security interests) by contract. See R9–339 (permitting subordination by agreement). If not, the parties will resort to Article 9 to resolve their differences.

Some changes in business structure are less likely to be lawyered—or, if lawyered, less likely to be well-lawyered—than are mergers of large corporations. For example, a sole proprietor or partnership whose inventory is subject to a security interest might incorporate the business (i.e., transfer the proprietor's business assets to a newly formed corporation) without taking into account the secured lender and the terms of the security agreement. Similarly, the shareholders of a closely-held corporation might "reincorporate" in another state (i.e., transfer the closely-held corporation's business assets to a corporation newly formed in the other state) without giving a thought to the secured party's rights. In either case, the original secured party's claim to a security interest in property of the new corporation may come into conflict with a judicial lien or security interest claimed by another creditor of the corporation.

Resolution of the issues raised by changes in business structure has proven difficult for the courts under Former Article 9, whose provisions apparently were not drafted with these issues in mind. In contrast, Revised Article 9 includes several provisions expressly addressing changes in business structure. This Section explores those provisions.

958

Problem 11.1.1. Oldcorp is a California corporation in the manufacturing business. *SP*–1 has a security interest in Oldcorp's existing and after-acquired inventory and equipment, all of which is located in Downey, California. *SP*–1 filed a proper financing statement against Oldcorp in 2004. On March 1, 2005, Oldcorp sells a used drill press to Buyer, a California corporation.

(a) Does *SP*–1's security interest in the drill press survive the sale? If so, does the security interest remain perfected? See R9–315(a)(1); R9–507(a).

(b) If *SP*–1's security interest survives the sale and remains perfected, for how long does *SP*–1's financing statement remain effective against the drill press? See R9–515(a).

(c) Can *SP*–1 maintain the perfected status of its security interest in the drill press indefinitely? If so, how? See R9–515(c), (d); R9–509(c).

Problem 11.1.2. The facts are as in the immediately preceding Problem. In 2003 *SP*–2 acquired a security interest in Buyer's existing and after-acquired equipment and filed a proper financing statement covering the equipment.

(a) Is *SP*–1's security interest in the drill press senior or junior to *SP*–2's security interest? See R9–325 & Comment 3; R9–322(a); Note on "Double Debtor" Problems, infra. What could the losing party have done to prevent this result?

(b) Would the result in part (a) change if *SP*–2 financed Buyer's acquisition of the equipment from Oldcorp and filed a financing statement covering the equipment three days after Buyer took delivery? If so, how? What could the losing party have done to avoid the loss?

Problem 11.1.3. Would the answer to any of the questions in Problems 11.1.1 and 11.1.2, supra, change if Buyer is a Nevada corporation? If so, how? See R9–316(a), (b); R9–301; R9–307; R9–325; R9–322(a)(2); Note (2) on Authorized and Unauthorized Dispositions, Chapter 7, Section 6(B), supra.

NOTE ON "DOUBLE DEBTOR" PROBLEMS

Problem 11.1.2, supra, invites you to consider the appropriate solution for what has become known as the "double debtor" problem: the priority contest that arises when (i) a person acquires collateral subject to a security interest created by another and (ii) the person creates a security interest in the same collateral in favor of another secured party.

Consider how the "normal" priority rules would resolve the competing claims in the scenario presented by Problem 11.1.2: Buyer acquires goods subject to a perfected security interest. Once Buyer obtains "rights in the collateral," *SP*–2's security interest attaches. In both parts (a) and (b), the "normal" rules would award priority to *SP*–2: In Problem 11.1.2(a), *SP*–2 was the first to file under R9–322(a)(1); in Problem 11.1.2(b), *SP*–2's purchase-money security interest qualifies for priority under R9–324(a). Do the "normal" rules yield the correct results in these cases, which concern security interests created by more than one debtor? Addressing the issue under Former Article 9, one commentator argued "no" in the following passage:

The first-to-file-or-perfect rule ... is a variation of the "first in time, first in right" rule that pervades property law. The latter rule is a specific application of the basic principle of conveyancing: one cannot convey better title than he has. Once the debtor encumbers his interest in the goods with a security interest, any person whose interest derives from the debtor will take subject to the encumbrance. Thus, under a strict first-in-time rule, the first party to take a security interest in collateral would have priority over later secured parties. [The first-to-file-or-perfect rule] modifies the [first-in-time] rule to cure the ostensible ownership problem.... For the first security interest to be effective against a subsequent secured party, the first creditor must publicize his interest, usually by filing. Among the penalties for failure to publicize is the loss of priority to subsequent creditors who may be disadvantaged by the absence of publicity.

Comment 1 to section 1–102 explains that "the proper construction of the [Code] requires that its interpretation and application be limited to its reason." In the case under consideration—[the buyer] acquires goods subject to *SP1*'s perfected security interest, *SP2*'s security interest attaches automatically to the after-acquired [property], and *SP2* has filed before *SP1*—the reason for [the first-to-file-or-perfect rule] is inapplicable. Prior to the contract of sale between the buyer and the seller, the buyer had no rights in the [property]. Accordingly, *SP2* had no interest in the goods and could not possibly have been disadvantaged by a secret security interest in favor of *SP1*. *SP1* publicized its interest by filing before *SP2*'s interest attached, and *SP2* could have discovered the encumbrance by checking the files. Having failed to discover *SP1*'s security interest, *SP2* should take subject to it. Conversely, having appropriately cured the ostensible ownership problem before *SP2* could have relied to its detriment on the seller's apparently unencumbered ownership, *SP1* should not suffer a penalty when its debtor, without authorization, later sells the collateral.... If one does not impose the penalty of [the first-to-file-or-perfect rule], one must apply the ordinary rule of section 2–403(1), under which the purchaser (*SP2*) acquires no greater rights than his transferor (the buyer) had or had power to convey; that is, *SP2* takes his security interest subject to those encumbrances that are effective against the buyer, including *SP1*'s security interest.

Comment 5 to section 9–312 suggests a second justification for the first-to-file rule: "the necessity of protecting the filing system—that is, of allowing the secured party who has first filed to make subsequent advances without each time having, as a condition of protection, to check for filing later than his." [Compare R9–322, Comment 4.] In the usual case, concerning only one debtor, the consequences of removing the search burden from the first to file and placing it on the second to file are not clearly undesirable. A potential creditor can check the filings, discover the first secured party's filing, and conduct himself accordingly. Ordinarily he will take second priority, but he can acquire first priority by taking a purchase money security interest and notifying the first secured party of that fact.

When two debtors are involved ... the consequences of applying [the first-to-file-or-perfect rule] are clearly undesirable. When *SP1* takes a security interest in the seller's [property], it will not discover *SP2*'s security interest because it has no reason to investigate the title of goods owned by persons other than its debtor. If [the first-to-file-or-perfect rule] were applied to the case under consideration, then *SP1* may be completely unable to protect itself; whereas if *SP1* were afforded priority, then *SP2* would be able to discover that the [property] was encumbered and would refuse to make an advance against it. The Code generally affords the ... lender considerable protection against third party claims to the collateral and so minimizes the need for a[ ] ... lender to investigate the source of his collateral. Nevertheless, a[ ] ... lender may become aware that his debtor has acquired [property subject to a security interest]. Placing the risk of loss on *SP2*, who can prevent the loss by refusing to lend, rather than on *SP1*, who may be unable to prevent it, seems reasonable. Thus, [in this context], I would read Article 9 to grant priority to *SP1* regardless of when each secured party filed.

Harris, The Interaction of Articles 6 and 9 of the Uniform Commercial Code: A Study in Conveyancing, Priorities, and Code Interpretation, 39 Vand.L.Rev. 179, 222–25 (1986).

Professor Harris argued that the buyer's purchase-money secured party likewise should not enjoy priority over a perfected security interest that encumbered the collateral before its debtor (the buyer) acquired rights in it:

The reason for the purchase-money priority is to aid a debtor in obtaining credit, without adversely affecting the interests of the original secured party. In a two-debtor case, *SP2* does not need a special priority rule as an incentive to finance the ... purchase. If the buyer were to purchase unencumbered [goods], instead of goods subject to a security interest, *SP2* would be able easily to acquire a first-priority security interest. In that case, *SP2* should be willing to extend credit to the buyer for the acquisition of [collateral], even without a purchase-money priority over *SP1*. When there are two debtors, *SP2*'s need for the special priority arises not because the Code's ordinary priority rules favor the first to file, but because *SP2*'s debtor chooses to acquire encumbered goods. Moreover, in a two-debtor case, one cannot justify giving *SP2* priority on the ground that but for *SP2*'s enabling loan, *SP1* would not acquire any rights in the collateral. On the contrary, the award of priority to *SP2* would come at the expense of *SP1* and often would have the effect of depriving *SP1* of its collateral altogether. The buyer took subject to *SP1*'s security interest; *SP2*'s rights derive from the buyer; *SP2* can discover *SP1*'s perfected interest. In the absence of a good reason to prefer *SP2* at *SP1*'s expense, section 9–312(3) should not be read to apply to cases ... that concern two debtors. Instead, the basic conveyancing principle—the transferee acquires no greater title than his transferor has—should apply.

39 Vand. L. Rev. at 229–30.

Revised Article 9 follows this approach in a new rule designed to deal with the "double-debtor" problem: When each security interest is created by a different debtor, R9–325 protects *SP–1* both as against the holder of an earlier-filed non-PMSI and as against the holder of a PMSI that otherwise would qualify for purchase-money priority. Observe that *SP–1* does not get the benefit of this protection under all circumstances. Assume that, unlike in the Problems and the examples discussed by Professor Harris in the preceding excerpts, *SP–1*'s security interest is *un*perfected but the buyer's interest is *junior* to that of *SP–1* because the buyer has *knowledge* of *SP–1*'s interest. See R9–317(b). In that case, Professor Harris's reasoning would work to give *SP–2* priority. Even if the buyer and *SP–2* had been careful to search against *SP–1*'s debtor, they could not have discovered *SP–1*'s interest in a search of the public records. Does Revised Article 9 adopt this reasoning? See R9–325(a)(2) & Comment 4.

The "double debtor" issues raised in Problems 11.1.1 and 11.1.2 involved the transfer of collateral to a person who thereby becomes the debtor. Because Oldcorp and Buyer both were located in California, however, the law governing perfection and priority did not change; California law governed at all times. Problem 11.1.3 is different, in that Buyer is located in Nevada. R9–316 deals with the circumstances under which a security interest perfected under the law of one jurisdiction continues to be perfected following a change in the governing law. We saw in Chapter 7, Section 4, supra, that R9–316(a)(3) provides for continued perfection for up to "one year after a transfer of collateral to a person that thereby becomes the debtor and is located in another jurisdiction." If the security interest is (re)perfected under the law of the new jurisdiction before the one-year period expires, then the security interest remains perfected thereafter. If it is not, then it not only becomes unperfected, but it is deemed never to have been perfected as against a purchaser of the collateral. See R9–316(b). (Observe that R9–316(a) only constitutes the perfection of security interests; perfection requires attachment). See R9–308(a). Thus R9–316(a) does not apply to security interests that attaches after a change in governing law. To see how this limitation be significant, see R9–316, Comment 2, Example 5; Problem 11.1.7, infra.

———

The following Problems address several variations on a theme: Before the transaction in question, a secured party held a security interest in the debtor's inventory; after the transaction, the debtor's business was being operated by a third party who acquired the collateral. Does Article 9 afford identical treatment to each of these transactions? If not, do the differences among the transactions justify any differences in treatment?

Problem 11.1.4. *SP*–1 has a security interest in all Oldcorp's existing and after-acquired inventory and equipment. *SP*–1 filed a proper financing statement against Oldcorp in 2004. Without *SP*–1's knowledge and in violation of the security agreement, Oldcorp sold all its assets, including its inventory and equipment to Buyer, a competitor, whereupon Oldcorp promptly liquidated. Buyer continued to conduct Oldcorp's business. Both Oldcorp and Buyer are Maryland corporations.

(a) Is Buyer liable for Oldcorp's debts? What, if any additional information do you need to answer this question? See Note (1) on Changes in Business Structure, infra.

(b) Does *SP*–1 retain a perfected security interest in the assets sold to Buyer? Assume alternatively that Buyer is and is not liable for Oldcorp's debts. See R9–315(a); R9–507(a); Problem 11.1.1, supra.

(c) Assume that *SP*–1's security interest survived the sale. In 2003 *SP*–2 acquired a security interest in Buyer's existing and after-acquired equipment and inventory and filed a proper financing statement. Is *SP*–1's security interest senior or junior to *SP*–2's security interest? See R9–325; R9–322(a); Note on "Double Debtor" Problems, supra; Problem 11.1.2(a), supra. What could the holder of the junior security interest have done to prevent this result?

(d) During the year following the purchase from Oldcorp, Buyer acquired additional inventory.

(i) Does *SP*–1 have a security interest in the additional inventory? (What, if any, additional facts do you need to answer this question?) See R9–203(b), (d), (e); R9–102(a)(56), (60); Note (1) on Changes in Business Structure, infra. If so, is the security interest perfected? See R9–508; Note (2) on Changes in Business Structure, infra.

(ii) Who has a better claim to this inventory, *SP*–1 or *SP*–2? See R9–326(a) & Comment 2; Note (3) on Changes in Business Structure, infra. What could the holder of the junior security interest have done to prevent this result?

Problem 11.1.5. Jack and Diane owned and operated a grocery store near their home in Brooklyn, New York. Home Bank provided inventory financing to the business. It properly perfected its security interest by filing. Jack and Diane decided to incorporate the business. On May 15, J/D Grocery, Inc., was chartered by the State of New York. In exchange for their stock, Jack and Diane contributed all their business assets. J/D assumed all the business debts. The business continued to operate as before. One year later, J/D, Jack, and Diane filed Chapter 7 petitions. You represent the trustee. What arguments can you make to reduce the size of Home Bank's security interest in bankruptcy? To what extent do the arguments depend on when J/D acquired the inventory? What could Home

Bank have done to avoid any loss? See R9–315(a); R9–203(d), (e); R9–508; R9–506(c), (d); R9–509(b); Notes on Changes in Business Structure, infra.

Problem 11.1.6. *SP*–1 has a perfected security interest in Oldcorp's existing and after-acquired inventory and equipment. *SP*–1 filed a proper financing statement against Oldcorp in 2004. Without *SP*–1's knowledge and in violation of the loan agreement, Oldcorp merged into Newcorp. Immediately upon the merger, the surviving corporation (Newcorp) changed its name to Oldcorp. Newcorp continued Oldcorp's business, acquiring more inventory in the ordinary course of business. Ten months after the merger, Newcorp filed a Chapter 11 petition.

Both Oldcorp and Newcorp are incorporated under the law of the same state. That state has adopted the Revised Model Business Corporation Act, which provides that, as a consequence of the merger, "the surviving corporation has all liabilities of each corporation party to the merger." Rev. M.B.C.A. § 11.06(a)(3).

(a) You represent the debtor in possession. What arguments can you make to reduce the size of *SP*–1's security interest in bankruptcy? See R9–315(a); R9–507; R9–203(d), (e); R9–508; R9–506(c), (d). To what extent do the arguments depend on when Newcorp acquired the inventory? What could *SP*–1 have done to avoid any loss?

(b) *Before* the merger, *Newcorp* granted *SP*–2 a security interest in its existing and after-acquired inventory to secure a line of credit. *SP*–2 perfected its security interest by filing a financing statement *before* the merger (but *after SP*–1 filed its financing statement). The financing statement named Newcorp as debtor. Which security interest, *SP*–1's or *SP*–2's, has priority in the surviving corporation's inventory? See R9–315(a); R9–507; R9–325; R9–326; R9–508; R9–322(a). Does it matter when the surviving corporation acquired the inventory? What could the losing party have done to avoid any loss?

(c) Shortly *after* the merger the surviving corporation granted Finance Company a security interest in its existing and after-acquired inventory to secure a line of credit. Finance Company immediately perfected its security interest by filing a financing statement naming the surviving corporation as debtor. Which security interest, *SP*–1's or Finance Company's, has priority? Does it matter when the surviving corporation acquired the inventory? What could the losing party have done to avoid any loss?

Problem 11.1.7. *SP*–1 has a perfected security interest in Oldcorp's existing and after-acquired inventory and equipment. *SP*–1 filed a proper financing statement against Oldcorp in 2004. Without *SP*–1's knowledge and in violation of the loan agreement, the shareholders of Oldcorp (a New York corporation) "reincorporated" Oldcorp in Delaware. That is, they established a new Delaware corporation (Newcorp) and caused Oldcorp to merge into Newcorp. Upon the merger, Oldcorp ceased to exist. Newcorp continued Oldcorp's business, acquiring more inventory in the ordinary course of business. Ten months after the merger, Newcorp filed a Chapter 11 petition. Applicable non-UCC law follows the Revised Model Business

Corporation Act, which provides that, as a consequence of the merger, "the surviving corporation has all liabilities of each corporation party to the merger." Rev. M.B.C.A. § 11.06(a)(3).

(a) You represent the debtor in possession. What arguments can you make to reduce the size of *SP*–1's security interest in bankruptcy? See R9–315; R9–507; R9–203; R9–316(a), (b); R9–301; R9–307. To what extent do the arguments depend on when Newcorp acquired the inventory? What could *SP*–1 have done to avoid any loss? See R9–509(c); BC 362(b)(3).

(b) Would the fact that, immediately upon the merger, the surviving corporation (Newcorp) changed its name to Oldcorp, affect your answer to part (a)? If so, how? What could *SP*–1 have done to avoid any loss?

NOTES ON CHANGES IN BUSINESS STRUCTURE

(1) Determining Whether a Third Party Is Bound by the Debtor's Security Agreement. Problems 11.1.4 through 11.1.7, supra, concern transactions in which one legal entity (the "new debtor") acquires collateral from, and takes over the business of, another legal entity (the "original debtor"). We already have examined the law governing security interests in collateral that a debtor sells or otherwise *transfers*. See Note on "Double Debtor" Problems, supra; Chapter 7, Section 6(B), supra. The same principles apply to that aspect of Problems 11.1.4 through 11.1.7. Our focus here is on property that the *new debtor acquires* from sources *other than the original debtor*.

If the new debtor enters into a security agreement in favor of the old debtor's secured party (*SP*–1), then *SP*–1's security interest will attach to the collateral described in the agreement. But suppose the new debtor does not enter into such a security agreement. Is the security agreement entered into by the original debtor sufficient to bind the new debtor?

Nothing in all of Former Article 9 delineated the circumstances under which a third party becomes bound as debtor by a security agreement entered into by another person. Courts addressing this issue under Former Article 9 used a variety of statutory and common-law theories and reached a variety of results. Some courts have not been reluctant to bind a new debtor to a security agreement signed by the original debtor, particularly when the two debtors are related. In protecting the original debtor's secured party, a number of courts seem to have been oblivious altogether to the attachment problem; others seem to have misread F9–402(7); still others have relied on poorly articulated "alter ego" notions.[1] Many of those courts appear to share the Ninth Circuit's concern that a debtor should not "be able to evade the obligations of a validly executed security agreement

---

1. The "alter ego" doctrine has been developed in a sizeable body of case law unrelated to Article 9: When a person who controls a corporation causes the corporation to commit a fraud or other wrong, a court may find the corporation to be the "alter ego" or "instrumentality" of the controlling person; if so, the court will "pierce the corporate veil," thereby imposing liability for corporate debts on the controlling person. See generally R. Clark, Corporate Law § 2.4 (1986).

by the simple expedient of an alteration in its business structure." In re West Coast Food Sales, Inc., 637 F.2d 707 (9th Cir.1981). On the other hand, is a secured party who fails to discover that its debtor has gone out business—or no longer even exists—worthy of protection?

Revised Article 9 addresses this issue directly: R9–203(d) sets out the circumstances under which a third party becomes bound as debtor by a security agreement; R9–203(e) explains the consequences of the new debtor's having become bound. Observe that one may need to look to non-UCC law to determine whether a person becomes a new debtor. The answer may turn on whether the person becomes obligated for the debtor's obligations. A person who acquires another person's assets—even all the assets—generally does not ipso facto become obligated for the other person's obligations. However, there are exceptions to the general principle, and the scope of the exceptions may vary from state to state. Is the resulting nonuniformity in results, attributable to the diversity of existing non-UCC law on the point, inconsistent with the need for uniformity in secured transactions?

(2) Effectiveness of a Financing Statement Naming the Original Debtor With Respect to Collateral Acquired by the New Debtor. Assume now that a new debtor becomes bound by the security agreement of the original debtor under R9–203(d). Under what circumstances, if any, is the financing statement filed against the original debtor effective to perfect a security interest in property acquired by the new debtor?

As with the attachment question, discussed in the preceding Note, Former Article 9 did not provide a clear answer, and the case law construing F9–402(7) reveals a variety of judicial views on the subject. Here, again Revised Article 9 addresses the issue directly. R9–508 treats a transaction in which a new debtor becomes bound by the original debtor's security agreement in much the same way as R9–507(c) treats a change in the debtor's name: As a general matter, a financing statement is not rendered ineffective unless the difference between the two names renders the financing statement seriously misleading; if the financing statement becomes seriously misleading, then the financing statement is effective only with respect to collateral acquired more than four months after the new debtor's becoming bound (or the debtor's name changes), unless the secured party files an initial financing statement against the new debtor (or an amendment reflecting the debtor's new name). See R9–508; R9–507(c); Note on Post–Filing Changes, Chapter 7, Section 3(A), supra. No special authorization is needed for the filing of an initial financing statement (or amendment) under these circumstances. See R9–509(b), (d).

Consider the following argument: Ordinarily, a financing statement is ineffective against a debtor who did not authorize it to be filed. See R9–510(a); R9–509(a). Application of this principle would mean that a security interest in property acquired by the new debtor would be unperfected until the secured party files an otherwise effective financing statement whose filing is authorized by the new debtor.

This approach would result in distinctions between functionally similar transactions. For example, a financing statement would remain effective against a debtor into which a sister corporation is merged and which thereafter takes on the sister's name; however, it would become ineffective against a debtor that merges into a surviving sister corporation. Does the difference between these two transactions justify distinguishing between them? In answering this question, keep in mind that this distinction would not be unique to Article 9; many existing loan agreements contain covenants drawing the same distinction (e.g., permitting only those mergers in which the debtor is the surviving corporation).

The foregoing approach has the virtue of being relatively clear cut: If the legal entity that was the original debtor survives but with a new name (a determination that one makes for a variety of other purposes), then R9–507(c) would apply, as it does to simple name changes. If the legal entity does not survive, or if the legal entity survives but another legal entity becomes bound by the security agreement, then the case would be treated like Article 9 treats any other debtor.[2]

Notwithstanding its simplicity and relative ease of application, the forgoing approach may yield results that some find objectionable. We have mentioned the concern that some courts have expressed for secured parties whose debtors engage in corporate or similar restructurings without the secured parties' knowledge or consent. Changes in business structure may occur under circumstances such that even a diligent secured party would not discover them and so would be unaware of the need to refile against the new debtor to maintain the perfected status of its security interest in after-acquired property. The force of this argument becomes particularly strong when applied to individual debtors who incorporate their businesses into new debtors and large partnerships that become new debtors several times a year because a partner dies, retires, or otherwise leaves the partnership.

One response to this objection would be to have the status of a security interest—perfected or unperfected—turn on whether the secured party knew about the new debtor. Would a scienter-based rule of this kind be just? Would it be workable?

The approach that Revised Article 9 actually adopts—i.e., that a financing statement remains effective with respect to collateral acquired by the new debtor within four months after it becomes bound by the original debtor's security agreement—likewise is not without its problems. First, whenever the original debtor remains in existence, a single financing statement would be effective to perfect a security interest both in property acquired by the original debtor and in property acquired by the new debtor. Second, as discussed in the following Note, this approach has required the promulgation of a special priority rule.

---

2. Note that, although the rule may be clear, its application may present difficulties in some cases, particularly when corporate managers have not respected corporate forms.

(3) Priority of Competing Security Interests in Collateral Acquired by a New Debtor. Now consider this scenario: A new debtor (Newcorp) becomes bound by the original debtor's (Oldcorp's) security agreement in favor of its secured party (*SP*–1), and the financing statement filed against the original debtor remains effective to perfect a security interest in collateral in which the new debtor has or acquires rights. The new debtor has granted a security interest in the collateral to a competing secured party (*SP*–2), which has perfected its security interest by filing.

Who should have priority? As to collateral acquired by Newcorp subject to a security interest created by Oldcorp, we have seen that the basic conveyancing principle (*nemo dat*) and the rationale behind the Article 9 filing system support the award of priority to *SP*–1, regardless of which secured party was the first to file or perfect its security interest. See R9–325; Note on "Double Debtor" Problems, supra. Does it follow that *SP*–1 should enjoy first priority as to all other property acquired by Newcorp?

To the contrary, a strong case can be made for awarding priority to *SP*–2. *SP*–2 gave value and took its security interest at a time when *SP*–1 had no filing against *SP*–2's debtor, Newcorp. Even if subsequent events somehow cause *SP*–1's financing statement, naming Oldcorp, to become effective against Newcorp, should *SP*–1's priority date from the time its financing statement became effective against Oldcorp? This result would prevent *SP*–2 from relying on the fact that, when it filed against Newcorp, no other financing statements were of record. What justifies creating this uncertainty for *SP*–2? Would it not be more appropriate to give priority to *SP*–2, and thereby impose upon *SP*–1 the risk that its debtor might merge into another entity and cease to exist?

This strong case persuaded the drafters. R9–326(a) subordinates a security interest in collateral of a new debtor if the security interest is perfected *solely* under R9–508. As Comment 2 explains, R9–326(a) subordinates a security interest that is perfected solely by a financing statement filed against the original debtor that continues to be effective against the new debtor under Section 9–508.

As discussed above in Note (2), an alternative approach to perfection would require the original debtor's secured party (*SP*–1) to file against the new debtor in order to perfect against the new debtor's after-acquired collateral. Under this approach, the priority of the original debtor's secured party would date from the filing against the new debtor. If the new debtor has another secured party, that secured party's priority would date from its filing. R9–322 contains appropriate rules to resolve the relative priorities, inasmuch as both security interests were created in the first instance by the same debtor (the new debtor). There would be no "double debtor" problem, and there would be no need for a special priority rule. Another desirable feature of this approach would be that priorities would date from readily ascertainable events (the filing of financing statements) and not from a difficult to discover, secret event (a new debtor's becoming bound by another debtor's security agreement). Would this approach have been preferable to the one adopted by the drafters?

(4) Commingling of Transferred Goods. In Problem 11.1.6, supra, Newcorp acquired collateral subject to a security interest created by Oldcorp in favor of *SP*–1. Suppose the inventory acquired from Oldcorp was fungible and became "commingled goods," i.e., it was so commingled with Newcorp's other inventory that its identity was lost in the mass? See R9–336(a) (defining "commingled goods"). *SP*–1's security interest would attach to the mass and would be perfected. See R9–336(c), (d). If, as in Problem 11.1.6(b), *SP*–2 held a perfected security interest in Newcorp's existing and after-acquired inventory, then *SP*–1 and *SP*–2 each would hold a perfected security interest in the mass, and the security interests would rank equally in proportion to the value of the collateral at the time it became commingled goods. See R9–336(f)(2).

SECTION 2.   LEASE CHATTEL PAPER

Introductory Note. For the most part, our consideration of chattel paper in Chapter 9, Section 2, supra, addressed chattel paper consisting of a record of a payment obligation secured by specific goods. However, the definition of "chattel paper" in R9–102(a)(11) also includes *leases* of specific goods. This Section deals with issues that spring from the inherent differences between leases and security interests. The following Problem and Note illustrate some special considerations for chattel paper financers that arise only with lease chattel paper.

Problem 11.2.1. Your client, Clearinghouse Credit Corp., is negotiating the terms of a prospective financing transaction with TV Shack Leasing Co. TV Shack is in the business of leasing small-to medium-priced electronic equipment and appliances to consumers and small businesses.

TV Shack proposes to sell (on a "non-recourse" basis) a pool of leases and the related goods to Clearinghouse for a price of approximately $25,000,000. Some of the leases contain purchase options. The parties contemplate that, after the sale, TV Shack would serve as a **servicing agent** for Clearinghouse; i.e., TV Shack would continue to collect the rentals and would remit them to Clearinghouse.

TV Shack's standard practice is to have three counterparts of each lease agreement signed by TV Shack and the lessee: the lessee gets one copy, TV Shack's local office gets another, and TV Shack's regional office gets the third. These local and regional offices are located in 35 states.

Clearinghouse has asked you to advise it concerning the structure of the transaction and the precautions that should be taken to protect its interests against claims of TV Shack's creditors and the creditors of the lessees. You have been warned by Clearinghouse that any attempt to require physical delivery of the leases would be met with stiff objection (on cost and administrative grounds) by TV Shack and probably would cause the deal to "crater."

What advice do you give? In particular:

(a) How will you recommend that the interest of Clearinghouse in the leases be perfected? What are Clearinghouse's risks if it leaves TV Shack in possession of the leases? See R9–102(a)(11); R9–109(a)(3); R9–312(a); R9–313(a), (c); R9–330; Notes on Purchasers of Chattel Paper, Chapter 9, Section 2, supra; Note on *Leasing Consultants* and Lease Chattel Paper, infra. How could those risks be reduced while still structuring the transaction within the parameters set by your client?

(b) What body of law governs Clearinghouse's purchase of TV Shack's "ownership" or "residual" interest in the leased goods? See Note on *Leasing Consultants* and Lease Chattel Paper, infra. How will you recommend that Clearinghouse perfect its interest in the residuals?

(c) Would your answer to part (b) be different if the transaction were structured as a loan to TV Shack secured by the leases and the residual interests?

NOTE ON *LEASING CONSULTANTS* AND LEASE CHATTEL PAPER

By definition, both security interest chattel paper (such as Lee Abel's Instalment Sale Contract (Form 3.6) in the Prototype on financing automobiles) and lease chattel paper embody two related property rights. See R9–102(a)(11). One is the receivable—the right to be paid by the account debtor (i.e., the obligor). R9–102(a)(11) refers to this as a "monetary obligation." The other is the right, upon default or under agreed circumstances, to apply the value of the specific goods involved (or the value of the lessee's leasehold interest in the goods) toward satisfaction of the monetary obligation.[1] A secured party enjoys this right under Article 9. See R9–610; Chapter 12, Section 2, infra. And the remedies provisions of UCC Article 2A as well as the terms of many leases provide that, after a lessee's default, the lessor may dispose of the leased goods and credit a portion of the proceeds received against the lessee's obligation to pay damages. See UCC 2A–523 to–532 (lessor's remedies on lessee's default).

We saw in Chapter 8, Section 1(A), supra, that an essential attribute of a lease of goods is the existence of a meaningful residual (sometimes called a "reversion") for the lessor. Article 2A refers to this property interest as the "lessor's residual interest," which "means the lessor's interest in the goods after expiration, termination, or cancellation of the lease contract." UCC 2A–103(1)(q). Depending on the terms of the lease, the lessor's residual interest may be quite valuable; by definition it never is trivial.

In contrast, an Article 9 secured party does not enjoy a residual interest. Rather, in a secured transaction covering goods, the debtor is entitled to any collateral value remaining after the secured obligation is satisfied. See R9–615(d) (discussed in Chapter 12, Section 2, infra). Stated

---

1. Recall that the definition of "chattel paper" in R9–102(a)(11) covers records evidencing interests in software associated with specific goods in addition to interests in the goods. This Section focuses solely on the interests in goods, however, because it is the nature of the interests in goods that distinguishes lease chattel paper from other chattel paper.

otherwise, the only interest in goods that the assignor of security interest chattel paper has to assign is the assignor's *security interest* in the goods. And that security interest is embodied in the chattel paper.

In *In re Leasing Consultants*, 486 F.2d 367 (2d Cir.1973), which was decided under the pre–1972 version of the UCC, the court had occasion to consider whether a lessor's residual interest, like a secured party's security interest, is embodied in the chattel paper. In *Leasing Consultants*, the Bank held a perfected security interest in Leasing's chattel paper, which included several leases of equipment to Plastimetrix. The dispute centered around which interests of the debtor (Leasing) were encompassed by the chattel paper. To the extent that a property interest of Leasing was embodied in the chattel paper, the Bank held a perfected security interest in that property interest. To the extent that a property interest was not so embodied and the Bank had not perfected separately as to it, Leasing's bankruptcy trustee could use its "strong-arm power" to avoid the Bank's unperfected security interest. Cf. BC 544(a); Chapter 10; Section 2(A), supra.

In *Leasing Consultants* the Bank argued that, by perfecting a security interest in the chattel paper, the Bank had perfected a security interest in the lessor's residual interest. The court concluded that the residual interest constitutes collateral—goods—that is distinct from the chattel paper. Any security interest in the residual thus must be analyzed separately to determine whether it is perfected. Because a "lease" that in fact is a secured transaction (e.g., the secured sale of goods from the debtor (Leasing) to a buyer (Plastimetrix)) does not leave the "lessor" with any residual interest, the court remanded the case for a determination whether the leases at issue in *Leasing Consultants* were true leases or disguised sales.[2]

Both the reasoning and the result of *Leasing Consultants* have become a part of the accepted wisdom among those who finance lease chattel paper. Those financers not only take and perfect a security interest in the leases (chattel paper) but also normally take and perfect a security interest in the leased goods ("inventory," under R9–102(a)(48)).[3] This practice is likely to continue; Comment 11 to R9–330 cites *Leasing Consultants* with approval.

One final concern affecting financers of lease chattel paper should be mentioned. The lessor's residual interest in goods that are leased to others

---

2. The leases provided that, following the lessee's default, all net proceeds of a disposition of the goods would be applied to unpaid rentals; provisions of this kind are strong indications that the leases are not true leases but, instead, create security interests. See Note (4) on Distinguishing Leases from Secured Transactions, Chapter 8, Section 1(A), supra. In addition, the Bank contended that there was no reversionary interest in the goods; if correct, this would be another indication that the chattel paper may not have consisted of true leases.

3. Under Revised Article 9, a single filing covering both inventory and chattel paper will perfect against both types of collateral. See R9–301(1). In contrast, the choice-of-law provisions of Former Article 9 may have required the filing against chattel paper to be in a different jurisdiction from the filing against inventory. See F9–103. In *Leasing Consultants*, the Bank's filed financing statement covered chattel paper but was not filed in the proper jurisdiction for inventory.

is classified as "inventory." See R9–102(48). Even if the prospective purchaser of the lease chattel paper is satisfied that it will receive priority in the *paper* under R9–330, it still must be concerned with the existence of an earlier-filed inventory financer who might enjoy priority as to the *residual*. In many leasing transactions the lender to the lessor will obtain a PMSI in the goods to be leased and, upon consummation of the lease, a security interest in the lease chattel paper. However, to take advantage of the inventory PMSI priority, the lender must search the UCC filings and then comply with the notification requirements of R9–324(b). See Chapter 7, Section 6(A)(II), supra.

SECTION 3. "FLOATING LIEN" VERSUS RECLAIMING SELLER

In Chapter 1, Section 3, supra, we considered the rights of a reclaiming cash seller and a reclaiming credit seller as against third parties—lien creditors of, buyers from, and secured creditors of the buyer. Now that we have seen the reach of a "floating lien" under Article 9, it is useful to revisit the priority contest between a reclaiming seller and a buyer's secured creditor claiming the sold goods as after-acquired collateral.

Problem 11.3.1. On June 1 Seller and Buyer tentatively agreed on a sale to Buyer of a load of cotton; the price was $4,000. Buyer then said, "I hope you can give me a week to pay." Seller replied, "I'm afraid I'll have to have your check within three days after delivery, with the understanding that you won't dispose of the cotton until the check clears." Buyer agreed. Buyer took delivery on June 2 and sent Seller the check on June 5. On June 10, Seller received word that the check had "bounced." On June 12, Seller brought a replevin action to recover the cotton.

Under these facts, Seller (a credit seller) will be entitled to reclaim the goods if it discovers that Buyer received the goods while "insolvent." UCC 2–702; UCC 1–201(23).[1] You may assume that Buyer was insolvent on June 2.

Now suppose that before the transaction between Buyer and Seller took place, Buyer, a cotton dealer, had granted a security interest to Lender in all of Buyer's existing and after-acquired cotton inventory. Lender has intervened in Buyer's replevin action, claiming that its security interest is senior to the reclamation rights of Seller. Lender's security interest secures loans that remain unpaid.

What result? See UCC 2–702; UCC 2–403; House of Stainless, Inc. v. Marshall & Ilsley Bank, infra; Note on the Reclaiming Seller versus the "Floating Lien" Financer, infra.

---

1. In Problem 1.3.5, supra., we saw that a cash seller who delivers goods in exchange for a check that "bounces" also may be entitled to reclaim the goods. See UCC 2–507; UCC 2–511.

House of Stainless, Inc. v. Marshall & Ilsley Bank

Supreme Court of Wisconsin, 1977.
75 Wis.2d 264, 249 N.W.2d 561.

FACTS

Plaintiff-respondent The House of Stainless Steel, Inc. (Stainless) commenced this action against defendant-appellant Marshall & Ilsley Bank (M & I) in regard to certain goods delivered by Stainless to Alkar Engineering Corporation, Lodi, Wisconsin. Stainless alleged priority of claim over these goods against M & I pursuant to sec. 402.702(2), Stats.

On November 1, 1971, Alkar Engineering entered into a general revolving loan and security agreement with M & I, the latter lending money to Alkar and taking back a security interest in " ... all Debtor's Inventory, documents evidencing Inventory, ... whether now owned or hereafter acquired, and all proceeds or products of any of them." (This security agreement was properly perfected by the timely filing of financing statements.)

In January, 1973, Stainless shipped certain stainless steel goods to Alkar on open account with an invoice value of $36,130.66. Subsequently Stainless discovered that Alkar had received such goods on credit while insolvent, and demanded in writing the return of said goods from Alkar. (This demand was within ten days of receipt of the goods pursuant to sec. 402.702(2), Stats. On January 17, 1973, notice of this demand was given to M & I.) On January 31, 1973, M & I sold the goods claimed by Stainless to DEC International, Inc.

On July 3, 1973, Stainless commenced this action for conversion against M & I. M & I interposed the following affirmative defenses: (1) That M & I had a perfected security interest in the goods superior to that of Stainless; and (2) that Stainless should not be permitted to maintain this action because it is transacting business in Wisconsin without a certificate of authority as required by sec. 180.847(1), Stats.[*]

Both parties moved for summary judgment, each filing supporting affidavits. The motion of plaintiff Stainless was granted and judgment was entered in its favor in the amount of $36,130.66, plus interest and costs (total $39,954.71). Defendant Marshall & Ilsley Bank appeals from this judgment and the denial by the trial court of the M & I motion for summary judgment.

■ ROBERT W. HANSEN, JUSTICE.

[The court found that Stainless was not required to secure a certificate of authority and was entitled to bring this action in Wisconsin.]

PRIORITIES AMONG CREDITORS.

M & I claims priority over Stainless via a perfected security interest in the after-acquired property of Alkar. Under its loan and security agreement

---

* [Discussion of the second issue is omitted.]

dated November 1, 1971, and the financing statements properly filed and recorded in connection therewith, M & I did have a security interest in all of Alkar's inventory, then owned or thereafter acquired. There is no dispute as to the validity of this perfected security interest.

M & I claims priority for its claim under sec. 409.312, Stats., which determines priority among conflicting interests in the same collateral.

Stainless, as a supplier of goods on credit, claims priority for its claim under sec. 402.702(2), Stats., providing for seller's remedies on discovery of buyer's insolvency. This statute provides a right to reclaim upon demand made within ten days after receipt of the goods. It is undisputed that Stainless delivered goods to Alkar and within ten days sought reclamation of said goods.

However, Stainless did not secure possession or repossession of the goods sold and shipped to Alkar. The right to reclaim on discovery of insolvency is subject to an exception where the rights of "a buyer in ordinary course or other good faith purchaser" are involved. Thus, while possessing only voidable title to the goods transferred, Alkar here could transfer title to a good faith purchaser. The trial court here held M & I not to be a "good faith purchaser" drawing a distinction between "goods" and "future goods" and treating differently the M & I interest under its security agreement as to then-held and after-acquired property of Alkar. The issue as to applicability of the exemption to M & I as a "good faith purchaser" is one of law, to be resolved by this court.

Thus, Stainless' only basis of priority is sec. 402.702, Stats. The second question of law raised on this appeal is whether M & I is a "good faith purchaser" and thus within the exception to the right of reclamation granted by sec. 402.702, Stats. What cases there are dealing with this narrow question appear to agree with the affirmative answer sought by M & I on this appeal.

In re Hayward Woolen Co. [3 U.C.C. Rep. Serv. 1107 (Bkrtcy.D.Mass. 1967)] dealt with the opposing claims of a reclaiming seller on credit and a secured party under provisions identical with those in our Wisconsin law. There, wool goods were delivered to a bankrupt buyer and rights to reclaim these goods were asserted by the sellers, otherwise unsecured, and their assignees. The opposing claimant held a perfected security interest in the after-acquired wool inventory of the bankrupt buyer.

The court in *Hayward* reasoned as follows: Seller's right to reclaim on the ground of buyer's insolvency is subject to the rights of a good faith purchaser under U.C.C. 2–702(3). U.C.C. sec. 2–403(1) provides "a person with voidable title has power to transfer a good title to a good faith purchaser for value." Hayward, the insolvent buyer, is a party having a voidable title. Textile, the party with a security interest in after-acquired collateral, qualifies as a purchaser under U.C.C. sec. 1–201(32, 33). Textile's preexisting claim constitutes value under U.C.C. sec. 1–201(44)(b).

The *Hayward* court referred to the opinion of two commentators who have expressed the opinion that the seller's right of reclamation is inferior to a perfected security interest in the goods arising under an after-acquired property clause.[21]

The court held, therefore, "that Textile, as the holder of a security interest in the debtor's after-acquired inventory, acquired title to the goods remaining in Hayward's possession, as a good faith purchaser for value, and that Textile's rights to such goods are superior to those of the reclamation petitioners. It follows that the reclamation petitions must be denied."

Analyzing the result reached in *Hayward*, one commentator concluded that " . . . it is hard to quarrel with the decision as an application of statutory provisions."[23] Stainless argues the 1969 amendment deleting "lien creditor" as one subject to the rights of reclamation mandates a contrary conclusion. But we do not find that amendment as intending or resulting in a changed definition of good faith purchaser under sec. 402.702, Stats. In part because uniform codes ought be interpreted uniformly, we follow *Hayward* and the decisions in other jurisdictions to hold that M & I here was a "good faith purchaser" and exempted by sec. 402.702(3) from the Stainless right of reclamation under that statute.

It follows that the trial court order granting the Stainless motion for summary judgment must be reversed and set aside. It likewise follows that the trial court order denying the M & I motion for summary judgment must be set aside. Judgment is reversed and cause remanded with directions to the trial court to grant summary judgment in favor of the appellant, Marshall & Ilsley Bank, and against the respondent, The House of Stainless Steel, Inc.

Order and judgment reversed, and cause remanded for further proceedings consistent with this opinion. Costs are awarded to appellant.

NOTE ON THE RECLAIMING SELLER VERSUS THE "FLOATING LIEN" FINANCER

In Chapter 1, Section 3(B), supra, we saw that the second sentence of UCC 2–403(1) distinguishes between a "good faith purchaser for value," who takes good title from a person with voidable title, and a "lien creditor," who does not. We examined in some detail whether the position

---

21. See: Hogan, The Marriage of Sales to Chattel Security in the UCC: Massachusetts Variety, 38 BU L.Rev. 571, 580, 581; Note, Selected Priority Problems in Secured Financing under the UCC, 68 Yale L.J. 751, 758.

23. Skilton, Security Interest in After–Acquired Property Under the Uniform Commercial Code, 1974 Wis.L.R. 925, 946, commenting further on *Hayward*: "Fireside equities may seem to favor the seller over the secured party who did not give new value in latching on to the after-acquired property.

The secured party with the after-acquired property clause may seem to get a windfall at the expense of the sellers, who provided the property. But it is hard to quarrel with the decision as an application of statutory provisions. . . .

"The case illustrates the 'voidable title' area. Title passes to buyer, but seller has a right to rescind the title, until a bona fide purchaser for value intervenes—that is the general restitutionary rule. Section 2–702 merely tinkers with it."

of a secured party whose debtor has voidable title to goods more closely resembles that of a prototypical good faith purchaser (i.e., buyer) or that of a lien creditor. We also examined the role of reliance in resolving competing claims to goods acquired by wrongdoers. See Notes on Reliance and Nonreliance Parties, Chapter 1, Section 3(B), supra. We now return to these inquiries in the context of the "floating lien."

As you know, unless an inventory financer takes a security interest in future inventory (and accounts), its collateral base will erode and the loan may become less and less secured. Sometimes a lender agrees to make recurring advances as the debtor continues to acquire inventory and generate accounts; sometimes not. In the former case, the secured party with a floating lien acts more like a buyer, giving value in exchange for an interest in particular property; in the latter, less so. But even when after-acquired property secures an antecedent debt, the secured party usually bargains for a security interest in the after-acquired property at the time it extends the credit. In this respect it is unlike a judicial lien creditor, who extends unsecured credit and acquires its lien only in conjunction with judicial collection procedures.

Most courts have subordinated reclamation claims of sellers based on fraud or UCC 2–702 to claims of creditors under after-acquired property clauses in security agreements. As in *House of Stainless*, the courts generally treat secured creditors as "good faith purchasers for value" (UCC 2–403) under literal applications of the definitions of "purchase" (UCC 1–201(32)) and "value" (UCC 1–201(44)(d)), without inquiring whether the secured creditor gave value subsequent to or in exchange for the property that the seller delivered to the buyer. However, critics of the prevailing view have argued that a secured party with a floating lien should be entitled to good-faith-purchase protection only to the extent it extends credit against particular items of inventory or particular accounts.

Most courts have reached the same result with regard to cash sellers, although the route to the result is somewhat more circuitous. Unlike UCC 2–702, which creates a reclamation right for credit sellers and provides explicitly that the right to reclaim is "subject to the rights of a ... good faith purchaser under this Article (Section 2–403)," UCC 2–507 does not even explicitly provide for reclamation, let alone purport to address priorities. Moreover, unlike a misrepresentation of solvency, which was considered a fraud at common law and gave rise to "voidable title," failure to abide by an agreement to pay for goods upon delivery was sometimes treated as theft, giving the buyer "void title." In protecting the secured party against a reclaiming cash seller, courts have looked to UCC 2–507, Comment 3. That Comment suggests that 2–507(2) addresses the cash seller's rights only as against the buyer, not against third parties who may be protected under "the bona fide purchase sections of this Article." Among those sections, clause (b) of UCC 2–403(1) supports the view that, at least when the cash seller took a "rubber check" upon delivery, the voidable title rule applies to cash sales. See also clause (d) (applying the voidable title rule to buyers who procure delivery through fraud punishable as larcenous under the criminal law).

One may wonder whether the committees and councils that prepared and reviewed the UCC faced the problem that since has been exposed by cases like *House of Stainless*. One also may wonder whether the UCC's provisions on "after-acquired property," "purchase," and "value" were focused on saving "floating lien" financing from the threat of invalidity under state law and in bankruptcy, rather than on claims to specific goods obtained by fraud or other wrongdoing by the debtor. Regardless, the drafters of Revised Article 9 took no steps to undo these consequences of the validation of the floating lien. If anything, the sponsors of the UCC approved the prevailing view by making explicit that an Article 9 secured party is a "purchaser." See R1–201(32).

The inaction of the sponsors in 1998 contrasts with the sponsors' earlier solicitude toward reclamation rights, as reflected in a 1966 amendment to UCC 2–702(3). Prior thereto, the credit seller's reclamation right was "subject to the rights of a buyer in ordinary course or other good faith purchaser *or lien creditor* under this Article (Section 2–403)." In a paragraph that was deleted in 1966, Comment 3 to UCC 2–702 indicated that the rights of lien creditors may have priority over reclaiming sellers under non-UCC law, which, according to UCC 1–103, may supplement the UCC's rules. The Comment referred to In re Kravitz, 278 F.2d 820 (3d Cir.1960), in which the court held that the debtor's bankruptcy trustee defeated the seller's rights under UCC 2–702 because under the pre-UCC law of Pennsylvania, the right of reclamation would have been subordinate to the rights of a lien creditor who extended credit to the debtor after the debtor received the goods. In proposing the deletion of the words "or lien creditor" from UCC 2–702(2), the PEB noted that "[t]he result in Pennsylvania is to make the right of reclamation granted by this section almost entirely illusory. In most states the pre-UCC law was otherwise, and the right of reclamation seems to be fully effective." Report No. 3 of the Permanent Editorial Board for the Uniform Commercial Code 3 (1967).[2]

Is the Article 9 secured party with a floating lien more or less sympathetic than the lien creditor? Than the buyer's bankruptcy trustee? See Chapter 10, Section 4, supra.

In Chapter 10, Section 4, we discussed the circumstances under which a right of reclamation may be enforced in bankruptcy. What result if the goods that are the subject of a reclamation right also are encumbered by a perfected security interest? The case law reflects a variety of approaches. There is authority to support the view that the mere presence of the senior

---

2. It may seem odd that the drafters sought to protect the reclaiming seller's priority over a lien creditor by *deleting* three words ("or lien creditor") from UCC 2–702(3) rather than by providing that the reclamation right is superior. The PEB appears to have chosen its drafting technique with care:

"Six states have resolved the problem by deleting the words 'or lien creditor' from this section, and there seems to be no other practicable route to uniformity among the states." Report No. 3 of the Permanent Editorial board for the Uniform Commercial Code 3 (1967).

claim extinguishes the reclamation right; there is contrary authority to the effect that the reclaiming seller is entitled to an administrative claim or replacement lien in an amount equal to the full value of the goods sought to be reclaimed. However, the majority provide the reclaiming seller only with the amount that it would have received outside of bankruptcy. Thus, to the extent the goods (or their proceeds) are used to satisfy the senior claim of the secured party, the reclaiming seller would not be entitled to reclaim them or otherwise recover their value through an administrative claim or replacement lien. As is the case outside of bankruptcy, the reclamation right has value only when the reclaiming seller's goods or traceable proceeds from those goods exceeds the value of the superior claimant's claim.

SECTION 4.   REAL PROPERTY-RELATED COLLATERAL: FIXTURES AND RECEIVABLES

(A) FIXTURES

NOTES ON SECURITY INTERESTS IN FIXTURES

(1) "Fixtures" in Article 9. Elevators, furnaces, kitchen stoves, refrigerators, air conditioners, "mobile" homes, printing presses, power lathes—these examples only suggest the wide range of goods that, when placed for use on land or in a building, generate problems associated with the concept of a "fixture."

"Fixtures" problems are interesting and challenging. A principal reason is that "fixtures" lie on the border between two legal worlds—real property and personalty. The following example sets the stage for consideration of the conflicting interests that are at stake: Dealer sells furnaces and retains purchase–money security interests to secure the purchase price. The furnaces are installed in homes, office buildings, and manufacturing plants. Upon installation the furnaces become part of the related real property: if the real property is sold, the furnace passes to the vendee under the deed; if the real property is subjected to a mortgage, the furnace becomes subject to that encumbrance.

Consider, first, what happens to Dealer's Article 9 security interest once the goods become real property. Article 9, for all its breadth, does not take over the field of mortgages.[1] Recall that Article 9 generally does not apply to "the creation or transfer of an interest in or lien on real property, including a lease or rents thereunder." R9–109(d)(11). Notwithstanding the general inapplicability of Article 9 to real property, Article 9 does apply "to the extent that provision is made for ... fixtures in Section 9–334." Id.

---

1. The chattel mortgage having become an Article 9 security interest decades ago, we use the term "mortgage" to refer to a consensual lien on real property. See R9– 102(a)(55) (" 'Mortgage' means a consensual interest in real property, including fixtures, which secures payment or performance of an obligation.").

An unforgettable classroom definition, still resonant with the frightening roar of Professor E. H. ("Bull") Warren, laid it down that a fixture is "realty, with a chattel past, and a hope of chattel future."[2] Article 9 contains its own definition, not unlike that of Professor Warren's: " 'Fixtures' means goods that have become so related to particular real property that an interest in them arises under real property law." R9–102(a)(41). In other words, fixtures are realty with a chattel past. In addition, no Article 9 security interest exists in ordinary building materials incorporated into an improvement on land. See R9–334(a). That is, even if realty with no hope of a chattel future (such as the concrete that forms the foundation of a building) might be a fixture, one cannot have an Article 9 security interest in it.

An Article 9 security interest may be created in goods that become fixtures or may continue in goods that become fixtures. See R9–334(a). Accordingly, Dealer's Article 9 security interest remains in the furnaces, even after they are installed.

(2) Fixtures in Real Property Law: Affixation and the "Institutional" Approach. It may not have escaped your attention that reference to Article 9 alone is insufficient to enable one to determine whether particular goods have become fixtures. Rather, the definition of "fixtures" in R9–102(a)(41) in effect poses a question that only applicable real property law can answer: have the goods "become so related to particular real property that an interest in them arises under real property law"?

The factors that work the change from personalty to realty are elusive; they vary from context to context, and from state to state. Writers, both judicial and academic, often discuss the issue in terms of whether a chattel has been "affixed" to the realty. This suggests that "affixing" is a physical process, accomplished with nails or bolts. "Affixation," however, is a conclusory word: the physical tie-in is relevant, but not decisive. In some states, production machinery in a factory provides a dramatic example.

Some courts (those in Pennsylvania and New Jersey are examples) have gone far to treat readily removable factory machinery as "fixtures." In an 1841 Pennsylvania case a judgment creditor levied on steel rollers for a rolling mill; the rollers were not attached to the mill but were available for use when needed. The mortgagee successfully attacked this levy. Chief Justice Gibson proclaimed: "Whether fast or loose . . . all the machinery of a manufactory . . . without which it would not be a manufactory at all, must pass for a part of the freehold . . ." At stake was the factory's going-concern value that would be destroyed by dismemberment. In Gibson's graphic prose, "a cotton-spinner . . . whose capital is chiefly invested in loose machinery, might be suddenly broken up in the midst of a thriving business, by suffering a creditor to gut his mill of every thing which happened not to be spiked or riveted to the walls, and sell its bowels not only separately but piecemeal. A creditor might as well be allowed to sell

---

2. Students of "the Bull" have no doubt that he was the model for the fictional Professor Kingsfield. See E. H. Warren, Spartan Education 20–28 (1942).

the works of a clock, wheel by wheel." Voorhis v. Freeman, 2 Watts & Serg. 116 (1841). A century later, this view was applied to a security interest retained by the seller who provided new machinery for a candy factory; although the machinery could be removed with little or no damage to the physical structure, the seller could not enforce this security interest as against the mortgagee. The case was governed by a provision of the Uniform Conditional Sales Act that had been designed to strengthen purchase-money security in equipment that could be removed "without material injury to the freehold." But, the Pennsylvania court stubbornly insisted, physical injury was not the test; removal of the machinery would seriously injure "the operating plant." Central Lithograph Co. v. Eatmor Chocolate Co., 316 Pa. 300, 175 A. 697 (1934).

The "institutional" doctrine has not been followed in most states. However, an element of that approach may explain some widely-accepted and traditional "fixture" rules. For example, although the doors of a house can be readily removed, they are considered, as a matter of course, to be part of the realty; this legal conclusion must reflect the part they play in the use of the house as a dwelling.

The dichotomy between realty and personalty is drawn in many other settings; for example: the right of a tenant to remove, say, a stove or an air conditioner that the tenant has added to leased property; property taxes; recovery of possession upon a debtor's default. This dichotomy is used for many different purposes. The reason underlying the distinction, of course, may affect where the line is drawn. For example, the question whether a tenant forfeits to the landlord assets that the tenant has brought to the property is quite different from the question whether a sale of Blackacre includes removable things (like a kitchen stove) that usually "go with" the land. Unsophisticated handling of the realty-personalty distinction is common, and flirts with disaster.

(3) The Trouble With Fixtures: Source of the Problems. The conclusion that, in the example in Note (1), supra, Dealer retained an Article 9 security interest in furnaces that had been installed in buildings, provides little comfort. As we have seen, an unperfected security interest is subordinate to most competing claims to the collateral. See, e.g., R9–317(a)(2); BC 544(a)(1). Transfers of interests in realty and personalty typically are governed by very different legal rules. Transfers of real property, whether by deed, trust deed, or mortgage, must be recorded in separate registers for real property; usually the document submitted for recording must be notarized and include a description of the real property that, even in simple cases, may be long and complex and call for the aid of a local real property lawyer. Financing statements for security interests in personal property subject to Article 9 need not comply with these formalities; they will be filed in a different registry—and almost always in a different office.

Will Dealer's filing of a financing statement in the personal property records operate to perfect its security interest once the goods have become real property? If the building is subject to a mortgage, will Dealer's security interest be entitled to priority? If the owner sells the building, will Dealer's security interest survive the sale? These are the kinds of questions that the following materials address.

Problem 11.4.1. Dowel Manufacturing Company, a Delaware corporation, owns and operates a large factory in Rantoul, Illinois. Production depends on a wide variety of machinery—power shafts built into the walls; heavy stamping presses held in place by their own weight; power lathes bolted to the floor; machinery on wheels. In 1995, when Dowel built the factory it obtained a $3,000,000 loan from Firstbank; payments were to be amortized over a period of twenty years. To secure the loan, Dowell executed and delivered to Firstbank a mortgage covering the land and buildings that comprise the factory, with the usual clauses bringing within the mortgage all "appurtenances and fixtures," then owned or thereafter acquired. Firstbank properly recorded the mortgage.

In 2002 Dowel Manufacturing obtained a loan from Secondbank; the borrowed funds were used to purchase a wide range of factory equipment: a stamping press built into the walls of the building, power lathes bolted to the floor, robotic electric carts that carry materials from one machine to another. Dowel executed and delivered to Secondbank a security agreement covering this equipment. Before the equipment arrived, Secondbank filed a "fixture filing" in the local office where mortgages are recorded. See R9–102(a)(40); R9–301(3)(A); R9–502(b), (a); R9–501(a)(1)(B). Dowel now is in default to Firstbank and Secondbank and has filed a petition under the Bankruptcy Code.

(a) Is Secondbank's security interest effective against the trustee in bankruptcy? See BC 544(a)(1); R9–317(a)(2); R9–310(a); R9–102(a)(41); R9–501(a); R9–334(e)(3); Note on Perfection by Fixture Filings and Non–Fixture Filings, infra. Will the answer be the same (i) in the few states that follow the "institutional" approach, outlined above; and (ii) in states that reject that approach? In some of these states did Secondbank file in the wrong place? See Note on Perfection by Fixture Filings and Non–Fixture Filings, infra.

(b) Is Secondbank's security interest in the new equipment senior to any interest that Firstbank may claim? See R9–334(c), (d). Which state's law governs this priority dispute? See R9–301(3)(C).

(c) Suppose that in July 2001 Dowel granted a security interest in all its equipment, existing and after-acquired, to Lender, who properly perfected by filing in the Office of the Delaware Secretary of State.

(i) Which state's law governs the relative priority of Secondbank's security interest in the new equipment and Lender's?

(ii) Is Secondbank's security interest in the new equipment senior to Lender's? Does R9–334 resolve this priority dispute? Does R9–322? Does R9–324?

(d) If you had acted as counsel for Secondbank at the time its loan was made, would you have advised it to take any additional precautions?

Problem 11.4.2. Firstbank is considering making a 20–year loan to a manufacturing company like Dowel; the loan would be secured by a first mortgage covering plant and equipment. Firstbank asks you (i) to evaluate the threat (if any) to its security posed by R9–334, (ii) to consider what provisions should be included in the mortgage to minimize any problem you find, and (iii) to suggest operating procedures in the administration of the loan which might be useful to deal with the problem.

What is your advice?

Problem 11.4.3. In 1997 Dripps Faucet Company obtained from Firstbank a 20–year loan, secured by a mortgage covering the land, building, and appurtenances that comprise one of Dripps' two factories in the state. Firstbank promptly recorded the mortgage. In June 2002 Dripps purchased and paid cash for a new steam boiler and a power lathe; the power lathe is held to the concrete floor by large bolts. Applicable state law treats the steam boiler, but not the lathe, as having become part of the real property.

In September 2002 Dripps borrowed $100,000 from Secondbank and executed to Secondbank a security agreement covering the boiler and the lathe. Secondbank immediately filed a financing statement, in proper form, in the Office of the Secretary of State. See R9–501(a). Thereafter Dripps defaulted on its obligations to Firstbank and Secondbank and filed a petition under the Bankruptcy Code.

(a) As among the trustee in bankruptcy, Firstbank, and Secondbank, what are the relative priorities as to the steam boiler? See R9–334(c), (e)(3); Note on Perfection by Fixture Filings and Non–Fixture Filings, infra.

(b) What are the relative priorities as to the power lathe? Cf. R9–334(e)(2).

(c) Would the results in parts (a) and (b) change if, instead of filing with the Secretary of State, Secondbank had made a fixture filing in the office where mortgages are recorded?

Problem 11.4.4. Darned Mills Co. obtained from Firstbank a 20–year loan, secured by a mortgage covering the land, building, and appurtenances that comprise Darned's sock factory. Firstbank promptly recorded the mortgage. In June 2002 Darned purchased and paid cash for a new furnace for the factory. Under applicable state law the furnace is considered a "fixture."

In September 2002 Darned borrowed $100,000 from Secondbank and executed to Secondbank a security agreement covering the furnace. Secondbank immediately made a fixture filing, in proper form, in the office where mortgages are recorded. In December 2002 Firstbank assigned to Thirdbank all of Firstbank's interest in the note evidencing the Darned loan together with its interest in the mortgage securing the Darned note. Thirdbank took possession of the note and recorded the assignment in the local real property records. Thereafter, following a Darned default to Firstbank and Secondbank, Darned filed a petition under the Bankruptcy Code.

As among the trustee in bankruptcy, Secondbank, and Thirdbank, what are the relative priorities as to the Darned furnace? See R9–334(e)(1) & Comment 6.

NOTE ON PERFECTION BY FIXTURE FILINGS AND NON–FIXTURE FILINGS

The rules of R9–334 dealing with the priority of Article 9 security interests as against interests obtained through real property law lie at the heart of that section. (As among Article 9 secured parties claiming fixtures, priority would seem to be governed by R9–322 and the other provisions generally applicable to competing Article 9 security interests.) For some purposes—and in particular for PMSI's under R9–334(d)—an Article 9 secured party must file a fixture filing in order to achieve priority. See R9–334(d), (e)(1). But the priority rules of R9–334(e)(2) (certain "readily removable" goods) and (e)(3) ("lien on the real property obtained by legal or equitable proceedings"—e.g., an execution lien) turn on perfection "by any method permitted by this article."

A close reading of R9–501(a)(1) reveals that the treatment of fixtures differs from the treatment afforded other real property-related collateral. In the case of timber, minerals, and certain minerals-related accounts, the proper place to file is in the real property records. The failure to file in those records means that a security interest is unperfected. However, a filing covering fixtures need be filed in those records only if it is to be "filed as a fixture filing." R9–501(a)(1). (As explained below, a financing statement filed as a "fixture filing" must provide additional information.) One may infer from this distinction that filing in the "regular" place of filing designated by R9–501(a)(2) (e.g., the Office of the Secretary of State) is adequate to *perfect* a security interest in fixtures.[3] But no inference is needed to reach this conclusion; R9–501(a)(2) expressly applies in "a case in which the collateral is goods that are or are to become fixtures and the financing statement is not filed as a fixture filing." R9–501(a)(2). A filing in the "regular" filing office is among the "method[s] permitted by this article" to which R9–334(e)(2) and (3) refer.

In addition to being filed in a different filing office, a financing statement filed as a "fixture filing" must provide more information than an "ordinary" financing statement. See R9–102(a)(40); R9–502(a), (b). Please

---

3. Under BC 544(a)(3) the "strong arm" of the bankruptcy trustee has the strength of a bona fide purchaser of real property instead of the weaker muscle of a hypothetical lien creditor available in the case of personal property. See BC 544(a)(1) (discussed in Chapter 10, Section 2(A), supra). The priority over a creditor with "a lien on the real property obtained by legal or equitable proceedings," given by R9–

334(e)(3), would be chimerical indeed if the security interest remained vulnerable to a trustee in bankruptcy. However, the trustee's bona fide purchaser powers under BC 544(a)(3) extend only to "real property, *other than fixtures*," BC 544(a)(3), leaving fixtures to the treatment afforded property other than real property. See BC 544(a)(1). See also BC 547(e)(1) (treating fixtures like personalty for preference purposes).

review the additional requirements in R9–502(b). Can you explain why they are required?

Although both a non-fixture filing and a fixture filing can perfect a security interest in fixtures, a fixture filing *is not effective* to perfect a security interest in *non-fixtures*. In view of the difficulty of characterizing property as a fixture or non-fixture in many jurisdictions, it is not surprising that secured parties often file both a fixture filing and non-fixture filing as a precaution. The non-fixture filing may have two other advantages: it could eliminate any need to show that the goods "are to become fixtures" in the event that a competing interest in them arises before they are affixed to land, see R9–501(a)(1)(B), and it could provide continued perfection should fixture collateral subsequently become unaffixed.

Not every secured party appreciates the subtleties in the law governing fixtures and makes both a fixture and non-fixture filing. A secured party may file in the UCC filing office, not realizing that the collateral is a fixture and that the security interest, while perfected, will be subordinate to many types of competing claims to the real property. See R9–334(d), (e)(1). Likewise, having relied on the erroneous assumption that the collateral is a fixture and made a fixture filing, a secured party may be disappointed to learn that the collateral is not a fixture and the security interest is unperfected. Eliminating the concept of "fixture filing" would eliminate these complications: A filing in the UCC filing office would be sufficient to perfect as to both fixtures and non-fixtures; it would afford the same priority as does a fixture filing under R9–334. Under this approach, a potential mortgagee who is concerned about a possible senior interest in fixtures would search not only the real property records but also the UCC records. If potential mortgagees routinely will conduct two searches in any event (because the possibility for subordination under R9–334(e)(2) is perceived to be sufficiently great or because mortgagees are concerned about junior, as well as senior, security interests), then the elimination of fixture filings would achieve the benefit of simplicity without imposing additional costs in most transactions. This thinking led the New Jersey Law Revision Commission to recommended the elimination of fixture filings. See New Jersey Law Revision Commission, [untitled report on Revised Article 9] 4 http://www.lawrev.state.nj.us/rpts/ucc9.pdf (visited August 30, 2000) ("[l]enders worried about prior security interests in debtor's fixtures must check both the land records and the [UCC filing] office. 'Fixture filings' are an unnecessary and confusing legal creation that does not spare lenders the expense of checking the central office records."). Should Revised Article 9 have eliminated fixture filings? (Consider, in this regard, that filing in the real property records is the exclusive method of perfection for minerals and related accounts as well as timber to be cut. See R9–501(a)(1)(A).)

Problem 11.4.5. On June 1 Realty and Builder made a contract for Builder to erect a $10,000,000 apartment building on Realty's lot. Realty was to make progress payments to Builder at defined stages of the construction. Realty made an arrangement with Firstbank to lend Realty the sums needed for the progress payments, and executed to Firstbank a mortgage covering its lot, any structures to be erected thereon, and any appurtenances thereto. Firstbank promptly recorded the mortgage.

The construction contract with Builder did not include installation of (a) the elevator; (b) stoves, refrigerators, dishwashers, and carpeting in the apartments; or (c) office furniture, computers, and other business equipment in the management office of the apartment building. Realty contracted directly with various appliance and furniture dealers for the delivery and installation of these items. Realty arranged for loans from Secondbank to pay the suppliers for these items. Realty executed and delivered to Secondbank a security agreement covering these items. The items were added when construction of the apartment building was nearly complete. Before the items were delivered, Secondbank filed a financing statement covering "equipment" in the Office of Secretary of State and made a "fixture filing" in the local office for the recording of mortgages. See UCC R9–102(a)(40); R9–502(b), (a); R9–501(a)(1)(B).

(a) Realty is in default to Secondbank. Secondbank has instituted proceedings to recover and remove the items ((a), (b), and (c), above) covered by its security agreement. Firstbank has intervened and asserted that it has a senior security interest. What result? See R9–334(d), (h), (e), (f); Note on Purchase–Money Security Interests in New Equipment and the Construction Mortgage, infra.

(b) If you had acted as counsel for Secondbank at the time its loan was made, would you have advised it to take any additional precautions?

NOTE ON PURCHASE–MONEY SECURITY INTERESTS IN NEW EQUIPMENT AND THE CONSTRUCTION MORTGAGE

Proponents of purchase-money security interests argue for priority on the ground that this priority makes it possible for a debtor to acquire new assets. During the review of Article 9 that led to the 1972 amendments, lenders engaged in financing the erection of new buildings pointed out that the construction loan, extended through a series of progress payments, provided a stream of new value during the construction process. They urged that their claim to priority as to the structure should not be subordinated to purchase-money security interests of unpredictable and uncontrollable scope. In the words of one of the drafters, "A construction mortgagee who thought he was getting a lien on an operable apartment house has a right to be surprised to learn that his debtor has financed the elevators through another channel." Coogan, The New UCC Article 9, 86 Harv.L.Rev. 477, 498 (1973). R9–334(h) reflects this point of view, as did its predecessor, F9–313.

(B) REAL PROPERTY-RELATED RECEIVABLES

Introduction. Real property transactions can spawn an enormous variety of rights to payment. Attempts to use real property-related receivables as collateral frequently give rise to some difficult problems under both Article 9 and applicable real property law. The general nonuniformity of real property law among the states exacerbates the difficulties. A full explication of the problems and issues would require in-depth treatment of real property recording systems and priority rules—a task beyond the scope of this book. The following materials nevertheless endeavor to scratch the surface, at least as it pertains to the relationship between Article 9 and real property law. We consider, here, three common types of real property-related receivables: promissory notes secured by mortgages or deeds of trust, rights to payment under installment land sale contracts, and rights to payment of rentals under leases of real property.

Problem 11.4.6. Gold Neckchain, Inc. (GNI), is a real property development concern. Needing additional cash for some front-burner, be-hind-schedule, over-budget, under-funded, in-trouble, and out-of-luck projects, GNI has approached your client, Firstbank, for additional financing in the amount of $2.5 million. GNI proposes to secure the loan with three receivables: (i) a promissory note secured by a duly recorded first mortgage on a choice piece of beachfront property, (ii) the remaining payments under a duly recorded installment land sale contract owed to GNI by the buyer of a tract of undeveloped land that GNI sold several years ago, and (iii) the remaining rental payments owed to GNI under a written and duly recorded lease of a warehouse (GNI also has offered to Firstbank a first mortgage on the leased real property).

Firstbank is satisfied with the aggregate amount of the streams of payments included in the proposed collateral, with the creditworthiness of the three obligors, and with the value of the real property interests involved. Because of some concerns about GNI's financial condition, however, Firstbank's credit policy committee is willing to proceed only if you can give "ironclad assurance that if GNI 'bites the dust' Firstbank will have a first priority security interest in the payment streams."

(a) Can you give that assurance to Firstbank? What steps would you take to ensure both perfection and priority with respect to each type of receivable? See R9–109(b) & Comment 7; R9–109(a)(1), (d)(11); R9–203(g); R9–308(e); Notes on Real Property–Related Receivables, infra.

(b) Are these steps sufficient to assure first priority in the payment streams if any of the three obligors goes "belly up"?

NOTES ON REAL PROPERTY–RELATED RECEIVABLES

(1) Notes Secured by Mortgages—"Realty Paper." Notwith-standing the fact that it applies to fixtures, as a general matter Article 9 is inapplicable to "the creation or transfer of an interest in or lien on real property." R9–109(d)(11). Thus, if the owner of Blackacre borrows money and secures the debt with the real property, the rights of the owner-mortgagor (debtor) and the mortgagee (creditor) are determined entirely by non-UCC law.

Suppose, as sometimes is the case, a mortgagee becomes a debtor—it uses its interest in the note and mortgage to secure a loan. R9–109(b) leaves little doubt that Article 9 applies to a security interest in the note (a R9–102(a)(47) "instrument"), even though it is secured by real property collateral: "The application of this article to a security interest in a secured obligation is not affected by the fact that the obligation is itself secured by a transaction or interest to which this article does not apply."

Suppose a mortgagee grants a security interest in the mortgage. The secured party (Lender) takes possession of the note but does not record an assignment (for collateral purposes) of the mortgage in the real property records. Although R9–109(b) seems straightforward enough, it is silent as to the relationship between a security interest in a secured note and the mortgage that secures the note.

Lender's primary concern is likely to be its priority over competing creditors of mortgagee. The prevailing common law view is that a mortgage is incident to any note it secures; rights in the mortgage follow ownership of the note. See, e.g., Carpenter v. Longan, 83 U.S. (16 Wall.) 271, 21 L.Ed. 313 (1872) ("An assignment of the note carries the mortgage with it, while an assignment of the latter alone is a nullity"); Epstein, Security Transfers by Secured Parties, 4 Ga. L. Rev. 527 (1970). We have seen that Article 9 adopts this principle with regard to security interests in notes secured by personalty (i.e., with regard to security interests in chattel paper): Attachment and perfection of a security interest in chattel paper is effective to create and perfect an enforceable security interest in the assignor's security interest in specific goods. See Chapter 9, Section 2, supra. The same result obtains with respect to what one might call "realty paper": Attachment of a security interest in the mortgage note or other secured obligation is also attachment of a security interest in the mortgage; perfection of the security interest in the obligation is also perfection of the security interest in the mortgage. See R9–203(g) (attachment); R9–308(e) (perfection).

The wisdom of this approach becomes apparent when one considers the consequences that may arise when the mortgage does not follow the note, i.e., when the mortgage is considered an interest in real property, separate from the note it secures. (This approach is reflected in the non-UCC law of some jurisdictions.) Under this approach, because Lender failed to record its interest in the real property records, Lender's priority in the note would not ensure its priority in the mortgage; rather, a competing creditor of the mortgagee (or the mortgagee's bankruptcy trustee) may have priority in the mortgage.

As a practical matter, what happens if Lender enjoys priority in the note but loses its interest in the mortgage by virtue of the bankruptcy trustee's power to avoid unrecorded transfers (BC 544(a))?[4] Can Lender reach only collections from the maker of the note (the owner-mortgagor)

---

4. If the mortgage is considered an interest in real property, then the trustee has the rights and powers of a bona fide purchaser of the mortgage and not merely those of a judicial lien creditor. Compare BC 544(a)(3) with BC 544(a)(1). See note 2, supra.

that are unrelated to the mortgage? Can a trustee who has avoided the assignment of the mortgage foreclose as against the defaulting mortgagor?

The flip side of this scenario appeared in In re Maryville Savings & Loan Corp., 743 F.2d 413 (6th Cir.1984), clarified on reconsideration 760 F.2d 119 (1985). In *Maryville Savings* the secured party *had recorded an assignment* of the mortgages (actually, deeds of trust) but *failed to take possession of the notes*. The court, relying in part on the pre–1966 version of F9–102, Comment 4, explained its holding as follows:

> [W]e conclude that article nine applies to the plaintiff's security interest but only in the promissory notes themselves. Since plaintiff did not take possession of the notes, plaintiff's security interest in the notes was not perfected. See Tenn.Code Ann. § 47–9–304(1). On the other hand, we conclude that article nine does not apply to plaintiff's security interest in the deeds of trust. While defendant argues in his reply brief that plaintiff's security interest in the deeds of trust was not perfected even if article nine were held not to apply, he admits that he did not raise that issue below; plaintiff's security interest in the deeds of trust is therefore deemed to be a perfected interest.

743 F.2d at 416–17. What is the ultimate effect of having a perfected security interest in a mortgage and an unperfected security interest in the note that it secures? Wouldn't all collections received from enforcing the mortgage also be collections on the note? On reconsideration, the court attempted to clarify its opinion. Inasmuch as the security interest in non-foreclosure collections on the notes was unperfected, the trustee was entitled to them. As to funds that might be realized on foreclosure, "the result might be to the contrary."

R9–203(g) and R9–308(e) are intended to overrule cases like *Maryville Savings*, make clear that Article 9 and not real property law governs perfection of a security interest in both a mortgage obligation and the mortgage securing it, and prevent splitting the mortgage from the obligation it secures. R9–109, Comment 7 explains:

> It ... follows from [R9–109(b)] that an attempt to obtain or perfect a security interest in a secured obligation by complying with non-Article 9 law, as by an assignment of record of a real-property mortgage, would be ineffective. Finally, it is implicit from [R9–109(b)] that one cannot obtain a security interest in a lien, such as a mortgage on real property, that is not also coupled with an equally effective security interest in the secured obligation. This Article rejects cases such as In re *Maryville Savings & Loan Corp.*.....

Of course, perfection is not a secured party's only concern. Consider again the case of Lender, who has a security interest in a mortgage note, takes possession of the note, but fails to record an assignment (for collateral purposes) of the mortgage. If the mortgage defaults, Lender may wish to enforce the mortgage by forcing a sale of the real property. Local real property law may limit the enforcement of the mortgage to the mortgagee of record. But recording can be expensive. When a transaction involves hundreds or thousands of mortgage-secured notes, as a securitization often does, see Chapter 6, Section 1(B), the cost of recording assignments may be prohibitive. To reduce the cost under these circumstances, secured parties sometimes obtain assignments at the outset of the transaction but record them on an "as needed" basis, i.e., only when necessary to enforce the mortgage.

A secured party who neglects to obtain an assignment of mortgage in recordable form at the outset of a transaction may find that the mortgagee-debtor is unwilling to provide one later, particularly if the mortgagee has defaulted on its obligation to the assignee. If local law permits the mortgage to be enforced nonjudicially, R9–607(b) enables the secured party to become the mortgagee of record by recording in the applicable real property records the security agreement and an affidavit certifying that a default has occurred.

The failure to record an assignment of mortgage may have other consequences. Suppose the mortgagor (the owner of the real property and the maker of the secured note) sells the real property to a bona fide purchaser. Suppose also that, prior to the purchase, the mortgagee wrongfully executed and delivered a *release* of the assigned mortgage: Would the bona fide purchaser cut off Lender's rights? Yes, according to the Restatement. See Restatement (Third) of Property (Mortgages) § 5.4, Comment *b* (1997) (good faith purchaser for value "is entitled to rely on the record"). That scenario—protection against the assignor's wrongful (or mistaken) release of the mortgage—illustrates another reason why an assignee would prefer to have the assignment recorded.[5]

(2) Installment Land Sale Contracts. The principle that the collateral follows the secured obligation applies to **installment land contracts**. The most straightforward form of installment land sale contract (sometimes called a "**contract for deed**") is like a conditional sale agreement covering personal property. The seller agrees to sell, the buyer agrees to buy, and the seller agrees to convey title by delivering a deed to the real property when the buyer has made all of the required installment payments. Buyers typically insist that the installment land sale contracts be recorded in the real property records in order to protect their interests against bona fide purchasers from the seller and against the seller's trustee in bankruptcy.

These contracts are functionally equivalent to mortgages, and in many jurisdictions they are treated like mortgages for many purposes (such as protection for the buyer-debtor's equity of redemption upon a default). Unlike a mortgage secured by a note, however, there is unlikely to be an "instrument" in which a security interest could be perfected by possession. See R9–102(a)(47); R9–313(a). Rather, the rights to payment under install-

---

5. The same risks exist with respect to assignments of Article 9 security interests, of course. But noting the assignment of a financing statement in the public record makes the assignee the "secured party of record," who has the power to amend the financing statement, e.g., by releasing collateral or by continuing or terminating the effectiveness of the financing statement. See R9–514; R9–511; R9–510(a); R9–509(d)(1).

ment land sale contracts are "accounts"; they are "right[s] to payment of a monetary obligation, whether or not earned by performance, . . . for property that has been or is to be sold." R9–102(a)(2).

Under Revised Article 9, attachment of a security interest in the obligation under the contract (an account) is attachment of a security interest in the real property securing the obligation. See R9–203(g). Perfection of a security interest in the account perfects a security interest in the real property securing the obligation. See R9–308(e). Revised Article 9 rejects cases holding that recording an assignment of the contract in the real property records is necessary and sufficient to protect the assignee against competing claims. See R9–109, Comment 7.

(3) Real Property Leases and Rents. Reading R9–109(d)(11), standing alone, you may be hard put to see how Article 9 possibly could apply to a transaction in which a lessor assigns its rights to a rental stream under a lease of real property. Article 9 "does not apply . . . to the creation or transfer of an interest in or lien on real property, *including a lease or rents thereunder.*" R9–109(d)(11). The potential for mischief arises, however, because under the law of some states a lessor's interest in a lease is considered *personal property* for some purposes. Does R9–109(d)(11) exclude only leases that are treated as interests in real property under non-UCC real property law? Or, does it also exclude leases and rents that would be considered personal property under non-UCC law? This ambiguity aside, the overwhelming weight of authority is to the effect that an assignment of a lessor's interest under a lease of real property is not covered by Article 9. (Of course, this authority construes Former Article 9, which contains the exclusion now found in R9–109(d)(11). See, e.g., In re Dorsey, 155 B.R. 263 (Bkrtcy.D.Me.1993).)

The most serious problems relating to assignments of leases as security arise under applicable real property law and under the Bankruptcy Code; and these problems are largely outside the scope of this book. To generalize, a security assignment of a lease typically is not "choate" (good as against third-party claims) until the assignee has actually or constructively taken "possession" of the rents or the underlying real property, such as by the appointment of a receiver or (in some states) by collecting rentals directly from the tenant. This doctrine often leaves the assignee vulnerable to a trustee in bankruptcy under BC 544(a), thereby precluding the assignee from claiming the benefits of postpetition "rents" under BC 552(b). See Note on Proceeds Arising After Bankruptcy, Chapter 10, Section 3, supra.

(4) Mortgage Warehouse Lending; "Transferable Records." Mortgage lenders (**originators**) lend such substantial sums to their customers (buyers of real property) that they typically must borrow funds as they need them. The loans that banks and other financial institutions extend to originators typically are secured by the notes and mortgages. Because banks and other **warehouse lenders** obtain much of their funds from short-term deposits, they usually are content to make short-term mortgage warehouse loans. Towards this end, they enter into arrangements that permit the originator-borrower to sell the note in the secondary mortgage market, provided that the purchaser remit the proceeds of the sale to the warehouse lender.

The transfer of notes historically has been accomplished by delivering the note to the purchaser. A purchaser of a note has strong incentives to take possession of it. See UCC 3–203(b), (a); R9–330; R9–331; UCC 3–306; Chapter 1, Section 4, supra; Chapter 9, Section 2, supra. The administrative costs of transferring the paper and keeping it safe are not trivial; and despite their value, notes are lost with surprising frequency. See, e.g., Dennis Joslin Co. v. Robinson Broadcasting Corp., 977 F.Supp. 491 (D.D.C. 1997) (action on lost note with principal amount in excess of $550,000). We have seen that section 16 of the UETA affords to a person having control of an electronic note ("transferable record") many of the same benefits afforded to the holder of a negotiable instrument, including eligibility for obtaining the rights of a holder in due course. See Chapter 1, Section 4, supra; Chapter 9, Section 2, supra. Even in states in which UETA has not been enacted, a person in control of an electronic mortgage note may obtain these benefits. See E–SIGN § 201. Section 201 of E–SIGN generally tracks section 16 of UETA. However, it applies only to an electronic record that "relates to a loan secured by real property." Id. § 201(a)(1)(C).

Problem 11.4.7. The Dexters borrowed $200,000 from First Mortgage Lenders (FML) for the purchase of their new home. The debt is evidenced by a note secured by a mortgage on the home. FML borrowed the funds from Bank Two, in whose favor FML granted a security interest in the Dexters' note and mortgage. After the closing of the mortgage loan, FML indorsed the note in blank and forwarded the signed note and mortgage to Bank Two.

A past agreement between FML and Bank Two provides that FML will attempt to sell the note in the secondary mortgage market and use the sale proceeds to repay its obligation to Bank Two. To accomplish this result, Bank Two sent the original note and mortgage to the Mortgage Buyers Association ("MBA") for its consideration. The documents were accompanied by a **bailee letter** in which Bank Two informed MBA of its security interest, stated that the note and mortgage were to be held by MBA as a bailee for Bank Two, directed MBA to return the note and mortgage to Bank Two if MBA decided not to purchase them or to remit to Bank Two the proceeds of any sale, and agreed that its security interest terminates upon Bank Two's receipt of the proceeds.

(a) MBA holds the note and mortgage for 30 days without paying for it. Is Bank Two's security interest in the note perfected? See R9–312(g); R9–313(a), (g), (h).

(b) MBA purchases the note and mortgage but pays the proceeds to another creditor at FML's direction. What remedy for Bank Two? Assume alternatively that the mortgage note is negotiable and nonnegotiable. See R9–102(a)(47); R9–406(a); R9–102(a)(3); R9–609; R9–330(d); R9–331; UCC 3–306; UCC 3–302; R9–315(a); R9–332.

(c) Would you advise Bank Two to insist that FML use electronic notes that qualify as transferable records under UETA and E–SIGN?

SECTION 5. NONCONSENSUAL LIENS

(A) LANDLORD'S LIENS

Introductory Note. Household furnishings and other consumer goods sold on a secured instalment basis often will be kept in a rented apartment or home; industrial and farm equipment and growing crops also may be located in rented premises. Because a debtor in financial difficulty is likely to be delinquent in the payment of rent, the holder of a security interest must cope with the threat of a lien in favor of the landlord.

The landlord's powers stem from the ancient common-law remedy of distress. At common law, and still in some states, distress for rent is an interesting example of a self-help remedy with echoes of the powers of the feudal lord; for this remedy traditionally was effected, without legal process, by the landlord's seizure of goods on the premises.

Are state rules permitting seizure without a hearing subject to attacks based on constitutional guaranties of due process? Compare Hall v. Garson, 430 F.2d 430 (5th Cir.1970) (self-help enforcement of statutory landlord's lien implicated state action and the due process clause of Fourteenth Amendment) with Anastasia v. Cosmopolitan National Bank, 527 F.2d 150 (7th Cir.1975) (no violation of due process because creation and enforcement of innkeeper's lien did not constitute state action). There is good reason to believe that the Supreme Court would consider the "state action" component of a due process violation to be missing in the case of common-law or statutory landlord's liens. See Flagg Bros. v. Brooks, 436 U.S. 149, 98 S.Ct. 1729, 56 L.Ed.2d 185 (1978) (no state action is involved in enforcement of UCC 7–210 warehouseman's lien). The due process issue is considered in more detail in Chapter 12, Section 1, infra. At this point we are concerned with the substantive rules, still honored in many states, that expose a tenant's goods to distraint by the landlord, even if those goods are subject to an Article 9 security interest.

It is clear enough that Article 9 does not apply to a statutory or common-law landlord's lien, other than a statutory "agricultural lien." See R9–109(d)(1); R9–102(a)(5) (defining "agricultural lien"); Section 5(B), infra (discussing agricultural liens). But that exclusion says nothing about the priority contest between a landlord and an Article 9 secured party. Some states have enacted statutes that give priority to the secured party when, for example, a security interest is perfected before the goods are brought to the rented premises or the secured party affords advance notice to the landlord. In the absence of such a statute, however, one must ask whether security interests remain subject to the threat of senior landlord's liens after adoption of the UCC. And where the pre-UCC law protected only certain "types" of security interests from the landlord (e.g., conditional sales), what is the result under the UCC's unified approach to "security interests"? Each of these issues is encountered in the following case. Although the case was decided under Former Article 9, it remains relevant. Revised Article 9 contains statutory provisions that are similar to those that the court construes; in particular, R9–109(d)(1) and (d)(2) follow F9–104(b) and (c), and R9–333 (discussed in Section 5(B), infra) derives from F9–310.

Universal C.I.T. Credit Corp. v. Congressional Motors, Inc.[*]

Court of Appeals of Maryland, 1967.
246 Md. 380, 228 A.2d 463.

■ HAMMOND, CHIEF JUDGE. At issue is the priority between a landlord's lien on automobiles of his tenant, a dealer, in the leased premises and the lien of a lender who had advanced the dealer the purchase price of the automobiles and prior to the levy under the warrant of distraint had perfected a security interest in them under the Uniform Commercial Code to cover his advances.

Congressional Motors, Inc. had leased premises in Montgomery County to Peter Palmer, Ltd., an automobile dealer. In early December 1965 Palmer owed rent to Congressional which directed the sheriff to levy upon seven automobiles owned by Palmer and located on the leased premises. The sheriff, having learned that Universal C.I.T. Credit Corporation was claiming a lien for its advances to Palmer superior to that of the landlord, refused to sell the automobiles as directed by Congressional, which then sought mandamus to compel the sale. Universal intervened, asserting its claimed prior lien. Judge Pugh ruled that the landlord had priority and ordered the sale of the automobiles.

The priority between the landlord's lien and Universal's lien must be determined by the state of the law in December 1965 when the levy under the distraint warrant was made. If the levy had been made on or after January 1, 1966, Universal's security interest would have been explicitly preferred to the landlord's lien under § 16 of Ch. 915 of the Laws of 1965, effective January 1 (Code, Art. 53, § 16), which completely revised and formalized the law of distress.

Universal, the lender, asserts, as it did below, that the provisions of the Uniform Commercial Code are applicable and controlling. In considering the contention we must examine the law of distress as it existed before 1966, including the extent to which it exempted property on the demised premises subject to security devices and the effect the passage of the Code had on the preexisting law.

Before 1966 distress was a mixture of rules of the common law (many stemming from feudal times), implementing and supplementing Maryland legislation, and long-standing practice.

_____

* [The court's citations are to the applicable pre–1972 version of the UCC.]

In 1964 the Committee on Laws of the Maryland State Bar Association said in reporting on the bill which later became Ch. 915 of the Laws of 1965:

> "The present distraint law in Maryland is archaic in that a landlord's remedy of distress is exercised without supervision by any court in spite of the substantial rights, and important interests, of tenants and landlords which are involved. The sheriff or constable now acts merely as an agent of the landlord. No court record is made with respect to a distress proceeding including the levy and sale of goods on the leased premises."

Despite its somewhat amorphous structure, the Maryland law of distress prior to 1966 had definitely established rules and principles. A landlord had a "quasi-lien" for unpaid rent on the goods of his tenant subject to distress, even before the levy under the distraint warrant. Rhynhart, Law of Landlord and Tenant, 20 Md.L.Rev. 1, 36 ... In Calvert Bldg. & Const. Co. v. Winakur, 154 Md. 519, 531, 141 A. 355, 359, Judge Parke, speaking for the Court said:

> "But a *quasi* lien in the sense used in Thomson v. Baltimore, etc., Co., supra, and the other cases cited, means nothing more than the potential right of a landlord to subject to distress the goods and chattels on the demised premises for the rent in arrears."

The cases have held that the quasi lien of the landlord becomes a lien either upon levy ... or upon assertion of the right, under the Statute of 8 Anne, Ch. 14, § 1, to be paid up to one year's rent in arrears by another creditor levying execution or attachment.... Rhynhart, op. cit., says (p. 36):

> "This quasi-lien may be converted to a lien, even without a distress under the Statute of 8 Anne, Ch. 14, and if the landlord's claim for rent is properly established it will take precedence over the debt on which an attachment issues and he is entitled to be first paid out of the proceeds of the property condemned."

In bankruptcy the landlord had a prior lien on the proceeds of sale of the bankrupt's asset sold by the trustee if the landlord had levied distress before the tenant's adjudication as a bankrupt, ... and the lien acquired by such a levy within four months of a bankruptcy petition was not voidable as it was regarded as one secured other than through legal proceedings. In re Potee Brick Co. of Baltimore City, 179 F. 525, 530 (Rose, J., D.Md., 1910).

The landlord could distrain on any goods and chattels on the premises whether owned by the tenant or owned by another or subject to liens in favor of another, except as such goods were exempted by law.... The rule that the goods of a stranger were liable equally with those of the tenant had its origin in feudal times. This ancient privilege was regarded as an inseparable incident of the seigniory and as a remedy which was confined to the land out of which the rent issued. The tenant owed the rent but the remedy was enforced against the land as if it were the debtor.

Goods and chattels of strangers which at the times here pertinent were exempt from distress and liens which were then superior to the landlord's lien were set out in detail in § 18 of Art. 53, as it read in 1965. That section after exempting from distress a number of specified articles not the property of the tenant provided that, except in Prince George's County, if the landlord should distrain on any non-exempt goods or chattels covered by "a conditional contract of sale defined in § 66 of Article 21 or mortgaged by the tenant by a purchase money chattel mortgage under the terms of §§ 41 to 51, inclusive, of Article 21," he should either release such property from the distraint or pay the balance due "under such conditional contract of sale or mortgage."

Universal's lien was not a conditional contract of sale as defined in § 66 of Art. 21 of the Code as it read before its express repeal by the Uniform Commercial Code because title to the liened automobiles was never in Universal, the lender, nor was that lien a purchase money chattel mortgage within the terms of §§ 41–51 of Art. 21 and the contemplation of § 18 because the money it secured was not due from Palmer, the vendee, to the vendor of the automobiles for or on account of the purchase price, but was money advanced by a third person to provide the purchase price. The purchase money chattel mortgage exempted by § 18 was such a mortgage as it was defined by Maryland law prior to the enactment of the Uniform Commercial Code, § 9–107. Thus under Maryland law as it existed before the enactment of the Uniform Commercial Code, the landlord's lien would have had priority over Universal's perfected interest since Universal did not have an interest of the types specifically excepted from distraint by § 18 of Art. 53.

We turn to whether the Uniform Commercial Code repealed § 18 of Art. 53 of the Code and enacted its own rules as to priority between a landlord's lien and a perfected Code security interest or amended that section to do this. It did not do either in terms. The lender explicitly concedes, as it must, that there was no complete repeal of § 18 of Art. 53 by virtue of Code ... § 10–103, declaring that "all laws and parts of laws inconsistent with this article are hereby repealed." It really argues only that the Commercial Code impliedly amended § 18 of Art. 53 so as to add ... chattels covered by security "financing statements" to [chattels exempted from distress] under conditional contracts of sale and purchase money chattel mortgages. We think Universal's concession is correct but that its contention of implied amendment is not....

The matter of whether the Commercial Code impliedly amended § 18 of Art. 53 requires consideration of the purposes of that Code and the provisions enacted to accomplish those purposes.

The basic plan of Art. 95B [the Code] is to deal with the normal and ordinary aspects of a commercial transaction from start to finish by means of nine subtitles, eight of which are devoted to a specific phase or facet of commercial activity.

Subtitle 1 provides the general rules of construction and definitions applicable to all of the other subtitles. Section 1–103 ... provides that "unless displaced by the particular provisions of this article, the principles of law and equity including the law merchant ... shall supplement its provisions." ...

Section 9–102(2) says:

> "This subtitle applies to security interests created by contract including pledge, assignment, chattel mortgage, chattel trust, trust deed, factor's lien, equipment trust, conditional sale, trust receipt, other lien or title retention contract and lease or consignment intended as security. *This subtitle does not apply to statutory liens except as provided in § 9–310.*" (Emphasis supplied.)

The official comment states that the purpose of § 9–102 is to bring all consensual security interests in personal property, with exceptions specified in §§ 9–103 and 9–104, under subtitle 9....

Section 9–310 gives those who furnish services or materials to goods subject to a security interest a prior lien over a perfected security interest, with specified exceptions. Section 9–312 defines priority among conflicting security interests in the same collateral, and §§ 9–401–406 and 9–501–507, respectively, establish the mechanics and effects of filing and procedures upon default.

The purposes and provisions of the Uniform Commercial Code lead us to believe that it did not impliedly amend § 18 of Art. 53 by exempting from distress security interests not previously exempted. We find persuasive indications to support that view. Bell v. State, 236 Md. 356, 365–367, 204 A.2d 54, recognized the theory of implied amendment as applicable in Maryland and delineated its controlling rules. An implied amendment is an act which does not state that it is amendatory but which in substance alters, modifies or adds to a prior act. Like repeals by implication, amendments by implication are not favored and will not be found unless there is a manifest repugnancy or irreconcilable conflict between the prior and the later act. If the two statutes can stand and be read together, there is no amendment of the first by the second, and the Code and § 18 of Art. 53 can be read together.

As we have noted subtitle 9 of the Commercial Code applies to all consensual security interests that are not specifically excluded by §§ 9–103 and 9–104, as § 9–102 makes plain. Section 9–104 lists a number of the "transactions excluded from subtitle" 9. The operative words here pertinent are:

> "This subtitle does not apply ... (b) to a landlord's lien; or (c) to a lien given by statute or other rule of law for services or materials except as provided in § 9–310 on priority of such liens."

It appears that a landlord's lien and an artisan's lien were excluded from the applicability of subtitle 9 because they are nonconsensual. Comment 1 to § 9–102 says that " ... the principal test whether a transaction comes under this Subtitle is: Is the transaction intended to have effect as security? For example, Section 9–104 excludes certain transactions where the security interest (such as an artisan's lien) arises under statute or common law by reason of status and not by consent of the parties." 2 Hawkland, A Transactional Guide to the Uniform Commercial Code, § 2.2201, p. 569, states:

> "The policy of Article 9 is to bring within its scope all transactions that are intended to create security interests in personal property or fixtures, and this policy, therefore, excludes real estate security, such as mortgages and landlord's liens, as well as personal property transactions that are not consensual in nature. Thus, artisan's liens generally are excluded from Article 9 because they are created not by agreement but by operation of positive law. Positive law creating nonconsensual liens often reflects local considerations and value judgments, and the draftsmen of the Code decided not to interfere with it."

We conclude that the flat and unqualified exclusion of landlord's liens from the application of the subtitle left the law on such liens as it was. The exclusion was not limited to ruling landlord's liens out as a Code security interest or to freeing them from procedural requirements applicable to such security interests; it provided in effect that no part, including rules as to priorities, of subtitle 9 controlled or governed them. This left their status and priority vis-a-vis those of security interests to the existing law. This was the view taken by the District Court for the Eastern District of Pennsylvania, In re Einhorn Bros., Inc., D.C., 171 F.Supp. 655, 660, and the Court of Appeals for the Third Circuit, which affirmed under the same name in 272 F.2d 434, 440–441. On the point here involved, the federal courts, in applying the law of Pennsylvania which adopted the Uniform Commercial Code in 1958 and which had a body of law on distress essentially the same as that of Maryland, held that as the Commercial Code in terms did not apply to a landlord's lien it did not deprive a landlord of the priority his perfected rent claim had under Pennsylvania law and therefore a landlord's lien continued to be superior to those consensual liens to which it was superior before the Code. See also 2 Anderson Uniform Commercial Code, § 9–104:3, pp. 480–481, and Schwartz, Pennsylvania Chattel Security and the Uniform Commercial Code, 98 U. of Pa. L.Rev. 530, 540–541, where the author in discussing whether a landlord's distraint for rent would take precedence over a Code security interest, pointed out that it had been held that the Pennsylvania exemption-from-distress statute did not exempt chattel mortgages, and suggested: "Should this decision be followed, form might retain importance even under the Commercial Code. To avoid such an unfortunate result, it is suggested that the exemption statutes be revised to protect any security interest in the designated types of collateral." Maryland as we have seen, did by Ch. 915 of the Laws of 1965, just what was suggested.

We think the intention to completely exclude a landlord's lien from every part of subtitle 9 is emphasized by the provision of § 9–104(c), immediately following that as to landlord's liens, which gives artisan's liens priority over perfected security interests as in § 9–310 provided. The comment to § 9–310 makes plain that the reason for giving priority expressly to artisan's liens is that "there was generally no specific statutory rule as to priority between security devices and liens for services or materials" since many decisions made the priority turn on whether the secured party did or did not have "title." A major Code purpose was to do away with differences and distinctions based on form (although allowing the retention of differences for other purposes, such as between the parties or for purposes of taxation) and the express rule of priority of § 9–310 accomplished this.

The lender argues that the landlord's lien which the Commercial Code excludes from the ambit of subtitle 9 must be a statutory lien. . . .

As has been noted, the landlord in Maryland had a lien by operation of law when the levy was made under the warrant of distraint. We conclude that this lien was "a landlord's lien" as that term is used in § 9–104(b) of the Commercial Code, and therefore is excluded from the operation of subtitle 9. . . . Liens of landlords arising by operation of law meet the test of being nonconsensual. . . .

Order affirmed, with costs.

NOTE ON THE PRIORITY OF LANDLORD'S LIENS

Most courts have concluded, as in *Congressional Motors*, that the priority contest between a landlord's lien and a security interest must be resolved by looking to law outside of Article 9. But see Peterson v. Ziegler, 39 Ill.App.3d 379, 350 N.E.2d 356 (5th Dist.1976) (landlord's lien arises only upon levy for rent; holder of landlord's lien was a "lien creditor" and, under F9–301(1)(b), lien was subordinate to earlier perfected security interest). The Illinois Appellate Courts for three other districts have disagreed with the *Peterson* case's holding that Article 9 resolves the priority issue under Illinois law. See First State Bank of Maple Park v. De Kalb Bank, 175 Ill.App.3d 812, 125 Ill.Dec. 386, 530 N.E.2d 544 (2d Dist.1988).

The opinion in the *Congressional Motors* case noted that the dominance of the landlord's lien was reduced by Maryland legislation effective in 1966. How can one best evaluate the relative merits of claims to priority by landlords and secured creditors? Is the landlord's claim as strong as that of the service providers who repair or improve property subject to a security interest? See R9–333 and Section 5(B), infra. Is the claim of either the landlord or the service provider comparable to that of the PMSI, which enjoys priority under R9–324?

Why not determine priority by applying the *nemo dat* principle? See Chapter 1, Section 3(A), supra. Or would it be preferable to apply *nemo dat* as modified by the law's general distaste for "secret liens"? In many states, a landlord's lien arises only upon seizure of the goods but its priority relates back to the date of the lease. Should the unrecorded landlord's lien be subordinate to a security interest that is perfected before levy, or does recordation of the landlord's ownership of the real property suffice to give sufficient public notice of its potential lien?

To secure their obligation to pay rent, tenants sometimes grant a consensual security interest in personal property located on rented premises. Does this create a "landlord's lien," excluded under R9–109(d)(1)? Consider the following Problem.

Problem 11.5.1. A lease of store facilities from Landlord to Tenant, a furniture retailer, provided: "To secure the payment of all rent due and to become due hereunder, Tenant hereby grants to Landlord a lien on all property, chattels or merchandise that Tenant may place on the leased premises." The lease was recorded in the real property records but not elsewhere. One year after Landlord and Tenant entered into the lease, Tenant obtained a line of credit from Bank, secured by all of Tenant's existing and after-acquired inventory. Bank properly perfected by filing. Under the law of the state, landlords have no right to distrain for rent.

Subsequently, Elsie, a judgment creditor of Tenant, levied on Tenant's inventory. Does Landlord have a lien on Tenant's inventory that is senior to Elsie's execution lien? Is Landlord's lien senior to Bank's security interest? See R9–109(d)(1) & Comment 10; R9–109(a)(1); Butters v. Jackson, 917 P.2d 87 (Utah Ct.App.), cert. denied 925 P.2d 963 (Utah 1996) (lien created by contract is separate and distinct from lessor's statutory lien and is a security interest under Former Article 9); Bank of North America v. Kruger, 551 S.W.2d 63 (Tex.Civ.App.1977) (exclusion provided by F9–104(b) applies only to statutory liens, not to contractual liens, of landlord, the latter being subject to Article 9).

(B) LIENS IN FAVOR OF PROVIDERS OF GOODS AND SERVICES; AGRICULTURAL LIENS

The general exclusion of statutory and common-law liens from the scope of Article 9 is subject to two exceptions, each of which is discussed in this Part of the materials. First, R9–333 governs the priority of liens, other than agricultural liens, given by statute or other rule of law for services or materials. See R9–109(d)(2). (These liens sometimes are referred to as "artisan's liens"; R9–333 refers to them as "possessory liens.") Second, Article 9 applies to statutory "agricultural liens." See R9–109(a)(2).

We turn first to artisan's liens. The following case, Gulf Coast State Bank v. Nelms, grapples with F9–310, the predecessor to R9–333.

Gulf Coast State Bank v. Nelms[*]

Supreme Court of Texas, 1975.
525 S.W.2d 866.

■ GREENHILL, CHIEF JUSTICE.

The bank has a perfected security interest in an automobile, and a mechanic later performs substantial repairs on the car. Neither the bank nor the mechanic has been paid. The sole question presented is whether an artisan, claiming a lien on an automobile in his possession under Articles 5503 and 5506, is entitled to priority over a prior secured party who has perfected his security interest on the vehicle's certificate of title. We hold that under the Texas Business and Commerce Code the mechanic's lien is entitled to priority.

On April 29, 1971, Elmo Nelms purchased a 1971 Chevrolet from the Beaumont Motor Company. As part of the purchase price, Nelms signed an installment contract and security agreement, which was assigned to our petitioner, Gulf Coast State Bank. It had the security interest properly noted on the car's certificate of title. The car was later damaged and Nelms took it to a body shop owned by M.R. Buchanan who agreed to make repairs for $1,160.63. Nelms failed to pay the debt for the repairs or to reclaim his car when the repairs were completed. The car payments were in arrears; so Gulf Coast State Bank sought possession of the car from Buchanan. Upon Buchanan's refusal to release the car, Gulf Coast State Bank brought suit against Nelms and Buchanan for judgment on the installment contract and foreclosure of the security interest. Buchanan asserted a cross-action against Nelms and the bank seeking to recover the value of the repairs and storage charges. Both parties sought a declaration that their respective liens were superior. Nelms has evidenced no interest in the matter.

After a trial before the court, judgment was entered for both the bank and Buchanan against Nelms for the respective amounts owed. The judgment also declared the bank's lien to be superior to Buchanan's and ordered the car sold and the proceeds of the sale applied to the amounts due the bank and Buchanan, in the order of their determined priority. The Court of Civil Appeals reversed. It held that Buchanan's lien was superior to the security interest of Gulf Coast State Bank and that the trial court erred in determining that the bank's lien was entitled to priority. 516 S.W.2d 421. We affirm the judgment of the Court of Civil Appeals.

Prior to the adoption of the Certificate of Title Act in 1939, the holder of a recorded chattel mortgage was entitled to priority over a mechanic's lien. Commercial Credit Co. v. Brown, 284 S.W. 911 (Tex.Com.App.1926). The Certificate of Title Act, Acts 1939, 46th Leg., p. 602, ch. 4, provided in part:

* [The court's citations are to the applicable pre–1972 version of the UCC.]

Sec. 43. All liens on motor vehicles shall take priority according to the order of time the same are recorded on the receipt or certificate of title of all such recordings to be made by the Department.

Sec. 46. Only liens noted on a receipt or certificate of title shall be valid as against creditors of the mortgagor in so far as concerns the motor vehicle.

After passage of this Act, a lien noted on the certificate of title was held to be superior to a mechanic's lien by virtue of the above Sections.... However, these sections were repealed by Acts 1971, 62nd Leg., p. 896, ch. 123, effective May 10, 1971.

With its effective date in 1966, the Texas Business and Commerce Code preserved the certificate of title system for *perfecting* security interests in motor vehicles except for vehicles held as inventory. Tex.Bus. & Comm. Code § 9.302(c) & (d), V.T.C.A.; Ruud, Amendment of the Texas Certificate of Title Act to conform it to the Uniform Commercial Code, 33 Tex.B.J. 968 (1970). The subject of *priority* of mechanic's and artisan's liens is specifically covered by the Texas Business and Commerce Code in § 9.310, which provides:

When a person in the ordinary course of his business furnishes services or materials with respect to goods subject to a security interest, a lien upon goods in the possession of such person given by statute or rule of law for such materials or services takes priority over a perfected security interest unless the lien is statutory and the statute expressly provides otherwise.

The intent of § 9.310 is to give a lien arising from work enhancing or preserving the value of property priority over a prior perfected security interest, except in jurisdictions where the mechanic's lien statutes *expressly* declare the lien to be subordinate. Tex.Bus. & Comm.Code Ann. § 9.310, comments 1 & 2; Manufacturers Acceptance Corporation v. Gibson, 220 Tenn. 654, 422 S.W.2d 435 (1967); e.g., 2 G. Gilmore, Security Interests in Personal Property § 33.5 (1965).

This section establishes priority for the artisan " ... unless the lien is statutory and the statute expressly provides otherwise." From this alone it would seem that one need go only to the lien statute and determine if it provides that the artisan shall not have priority. The comments to § 9.310 support this view. Comment 2 provides that " ... [s]ome of the *statutes creating such liens* expressly make the lien subordinate...." However, where a state has adopted a certificate of title act, some courts have decided it to be necessary to go beyond the lien statutes. They have brought in the title laws.... Commonwealth Loan Co. v. Berry, 2 Ohio St.2d 169, 31 Ohio Op.2d 321, 207 N.E.2d 545 (1965). The Court of Civil Appeals, in the case at bar, has based its decision, in part, on the repeal of Sections 43–46 of the Certificate of Title Act, holding that the Act no longer provides that the perfected security interest be given priority. The practice of referring to a certificate of title act to determine priorities has drawn criticism. Murphey, Cars, Creditors, and The Code: The Diverse Interpretations of Section 9–

310, 1970 Wash.U.L.Q. 135, 139; Note, Security Interests in Motor Vehicles under the UCC: A New Chassis for Certificate of Title Legislation, 70 Yale L.J. 995, 1013 (1961). The Editor's Note at 2 UCC Reporter 750 criticized the Commonwealth Loan Co. v. Berry, supra, decision for referring to the Certificate of Title Act by stating:

> The effect of the court's decision is to write an additional exception into § 9.310 ... "or unless some other statute expressly provides otherwise." It does this by holding that since [the Certificate of Title Act] makes a security agreement conveying a security interest in an automobile valid against other lienholders if proper notation has been made on the certificate of title, it prevails over the contrary but more general language of § 9.310.

We agree with this rationale, and we hold that § 9.310 requires that we refer to Articles 5503 and 5506 which are the statutes *creating* the mechanic's and artisan's lien, to determine whether they "expressly provide otherwise." See generally Ruud, The Texas Legislative History of the Uniform Commercial Code, 44 Texas L.Rev. 597, 621 (1966); Note, The Automobile Mechanic and The UCC, 21 Baylor L.Rev. 512 (1969).

Article 5506 provides:

> Nothing in this title shall be construed or considered as in any manner impairing or affecting the right of parties to create liens by special contract or agreement, nor shall it in any manner affect or impair other liens arising at common law or in equity, or by any statute of this State, or any other lien not treated of under this title.

There is no question as to the power of the Legislature to give a statutory lien priority over an existing lien where its object is to secure a charge necessary for the preservation of property. Texas Bank & Trust v. Smith, 108 Tex. 265, 192 S.W. 533 (1917). Although Article 5506 has been interpreted as preserving "the general rule of sanctity of contract" that subsequently acquired liens are inferior to prior existing liens (Commercial Credit Co. v. Brown, supra), to hold that the phrase, "nor shall it in any manner affect or impair other liens," expressly provides that artisan's and mechanic's liens are inferior, would defeat the clear intent of § 9.310. The comments to this section provide, in part:

> If the statute creating the lien is silent, even though it has been construed by decision to make the lien subordinate to the security interest, this Section provides a rule of interpretation that the lien should take priority over the security interest. Tex.Bus. & Comm.Code Ann. § 9.310, comment 2.

In First National Bank at Dallas v. Whirlpool Corporation, 517 S.W.2d 262 (Tex.1974), this Court was met with the contention that the portion of Article 5459, "provided, any lien ... on the land or improvement at the time of the inception of the lien ... shall not be affected thereby," gave a prior recorded deed of trust priority over a mechanic's and materialman's lien. In disagreeing with this contention, we wrote:

Petitioners' argument is that Whirlpool's preference lien would adversely "affect" the bank's prior lien. We cannot agree with petitioners' contention.

The effect of the bank's interpretation ... would attribute to the legislature an intent to nullify the preference which it had just given in clear and unambiguous terms to mechanic's and materialman's liens.

The rationale of *Whirlpool* is equally applicable to the case at bar, and we hold that Articles 5503 & 5506 do not "expressly provide" that an artisan's or mechanic's lien is subordinate to a prior perfected security interest. Therefore, by the express terms of § 9.310, Buchanan's possessory mechanic's lien is entitled to priority over Gulf Coast State Bank's security interest.

The Court of Civil Appeals correctly reversed the judgment of the trial court and remanded the cause to that court. The judgment of the Court of Civil Appeals is affirmed.

[Dissenting opinion omitted.]

Problem 11.5.2. In January, 2002, Barnett purchased a 1997 Plymouth under an installment sales contract; the contract provided that Seller would retain title until Barnett's payment in full thereunder (a "conditional sale"). Seller immediately assigned the contract to Finance Corporation, which perfected its security interest in the car the following day by having its interest noted on the certificate of title in accordance with the applicable certificate of title act. In September, 2002, when Barnett still owed $2,200 on the car, Barnett took the car to Champa, a mechanic. Champa tore down the engine and replaced the crankshaft, for which Barnett was charged $1,000. Finance had no knowledge of these repairs. Barnett could not pay, and Champa claimed the statutory right to hold (and sell) the car to secure payment of the bill for repairs. In December, 2002, the car was sold at a public auction for $2,800.

Who is entitled to the proceeds? See UCC 9–333; Note (2) on Non–UCC Liens for Suppliers of Materials and Services, infra.

NOTES ON NON–UCC LIENS FOR SUPPLIERS OF MATERIALS AND SERVICES

(1) R9–333 and Non–UCC Lien Law. Under F9–310 an artisan's lien was senior to a perfected security interest "unless the lien is statutory and the statute expressly provides otherwise." The *Nelms* case, supra, addresses two issues arising from the quoted phrase: Which statute is "the statute," and when does a statute "expressly provide[] otherwise"?

In holding that the reference to "the statute" in F9–310 is a reference to the statute that *creates* the statutory lien, the court in *Nelms* rejected the holding of Commonwealth Loan Co. v. Berry, 2 Ohio St.2d 169, 207

N.E.2d 545 (1965). The latter case held that a common-law garageman's lien was subordinate to a security interest that was perfected by notation upon the certificate of title covering the collateral. In its brief opinion, the court relied on section 4505.13 of the Ohio Revised Code, "the specific statute which deals with motor vehicle liens and which states that a lien noted upon the certificate shall be valid against other liens."

How would *Nelms* and *Berry* be decided under R9–333?

(2) Does Article 9 Affect Whether a Non–UCC Lien Attaches? Problem 11.5.2, supra, which concerns a conditional sale of an automobile, is based on Champa v. Consolidated Finance Corp., 231 Ind. 580, 110 N.E.2d 289 (1953). The principal opinion in the *Champa* case concluded that Champa, the mechanic, was not entitled to the benefit of a statutory mechanic's lien because the repair work was not authorized by the "owner." The court held that a conditional vendee (buyer) in a conditional sale is not an "owner" for purposes of that statute. Would the court decide the case differently today, given the unified approach to security interests under Article 9?

Indeed, would R9–202 compel the court to decide the case differently? That section provides that "the provisions of this article with regard to rights and obligations apply whether title to collateral is in the secured party or the debtor." According to Comment 2:

> The rights and duties of parties to a secured transaction and affected third parties are provided in this Article without reference to the location of "title" to the collateral. For example, the characteristics of a security interest that secures the purchase price of goods are the same whether the secured party appears to have retained title or the debtor appears to have obtained title and then conveyed title or a lien to the secured party.

R9–202, Comment 2. On the other hand, Comment 3.b. indicates that "Article [9] does not determine which line of interpretation (e.g., title theory or lien theory, retained title or conveyed title) should be followed in cases in which the applicability of another rule of law depends upon who has title." R9–202, Comment 3.b. The Comment gives two examples of such rules of law: those imposing taxes on the legal "owner" of goods and those requiring shareholder consent for a corporation "giving" a security interest but not for a corporation acquiring property "subject to" a security interest. Is the statutory mechanic's lien a rule of law of this kind? Would the Indiana legislature have amended the mechanic's lien statute when enacting the UCC if someone had thought about this issue of "ownership"?

Consider, in this regard, the *Congressional Motors* case in Section 5(A), supra. The court concluded that the security interest was not a "conditional sale" or a "purchase money chattel mortgage" qualifying for preferred treatment under the Maryland landlord's lien statute. Should the court have looked to F9–202 (which is substantially the same as R9–202)? Although F9–202 made title irrelevant with respect to "[e]ach provision of this Article," landlord's liens are wholly excluded from Article 9. See F9–

104(b); R9–109(d)(1). Moreover, inasmuch as it favors both purchase-money chattel mortgagees and conditional sellers, the Maryland statute seems to be directed to the character of a transaction—a purchase-money transaction in favor of a seller—and not the location of "title."

The principal opinion in *Champa* also concluded that Champa did not qualify for any of the exceptions to the general rule in Indiana that artisans' claims are inferior to those of conditional vendors. In particular, the finance company did not know that the repairs were to be made, and the repairs were not of a real benefit to the finance company (although the car's engine had thrown a rod and the crankshaft was bent!).

The court reached a similar result in Associates Financial Services v. O'Dell, 491 Pa. 1, 417 A.2d 604 (1980). Reasoning that common-law possessory liens for improvement to personal property are based on actual or implied consent of the "owner," the court held that the absence of the secured party's consent to the improvement was fatal to the establishment of a lien. Although the court considered the secured party to be an "owner" for this purpose, it did not do so on the formalistic basis employed by the *Champa* court. Rather, it considered the secured party to have a significant property interest warranting "ownership" treatment for purposes of consent. Having found that the common-law lien never attached, the court did not reach the priority contest addressed by F9–310. Can the decision be squared with the letter of F9–310 or R9–333? With the policy and spirit of F9–310 or R9–333?

(3) Priority Rules When R9–333 Does Not Apply. In many circumstances the priority rule of R9–333 will not apply. One important circumstance is mentioned prominently in that section—"unless the lien is created by a statute that expressly provides otherwise." When that proviso applies, of course, the governing priority rule is clear. But what if the priority given to a qualifying lien by R9–333 does not apply because the lien is not a "possessory lien" as defined in R9–333(a). Suppose, for example, that the lien remains effective under non-UCC law even if the claimant loses possession of the goods. Does R9–333 create a negative implication that the lien then would be *junior* to the security interest? A negative answer seems appropriate. Remember that R9–109(d)(2) makes Article 9 generally inapplicable to liens "for services or materials," with the exception of agricultural liens and the priority rule of R9–333. When R9–333 does not apply, then one must consult other law.

What priority rules apply when the non-UCC lien is not one "for services or materials" (a state tax lien, for example)? It is clear enough that such a nonconsensual, statutory lien would not be an Article 9 security interest. See R9–109(a). Does Article 9 nevertheless determine priority when the non-UCC lien conflicts with an Article 9 security interest? Arguably, R9–201 provides a controlling priority rule—i.e., the security interest is always senior except as otherwise provided in the UCC. Is it likely that the drafters intended R9–201 to have such a broad sweep? (The caption to the section reads "General Effectiveness of Security Agreement." Section captions are part of the Code. See UCC 1–109.) Is it more likely that the drafters intended to "interfere" with non-UCC lien priorities only in the limited context of R9–333?

Problem 11.5.3. Doobie grows corn on the family farm. Canopy sells seed to Doobie on unsecured credit. A state statute gives those who sell seed to farmers a lien on all crops grown from the seed. Doobie planted the seed, grew the corn, harvested the crop, and stored the corn in a silo.

(a) Elsie, a judgment creditor of Doobie's, causes the sheriff to levy on the corn. Which lien, Canopy's statutory lien or Elsie's execution lien, is senior? See R9–109(a)(2); R9–102(a)(5), (34), (35); R9–317(a)(2); R9–310(a); R9–501(a); Note (2) on Agricultural Liens and Production–Money Security Interests, infra. Could the holder of the junior lien have achieved priority? If so, how?

(b) The preceding year, Doobie had obtained from Farmers Bank a line of credit, secured by Doobie's existing and after-acquired crops. Farmers Bank properly perfected by filing. Is Canopy's lien on the crops senior or junior to Bank's security interest? Could the holder of the junior claim have achieved priority? If so, how? See R9–322(a), (g); Revised Article 9, Appendix II; Note (3) on Agricultural Liens and Production–Money Security Interests, infra.

NOTES ON AGRICULTURAL LIENS AND PRODUCTION–MONEY SECURITY INTERESTS

(1) The Problem. Statutory liens seem to be the rule, not the exception, in the agricultural industry. Consider the following excerpt:

> [U]nlike security interests under Article 9 of the U.C.C., where uniformity between the states is quite extensive, agricultural statutory liens are noted for their lack of uniformity. Uniformity is lacking in two respects: as between states, and within a state.
>
> First, each state has its own unique set of agricultural liens that reflects each state's own agricultural history. Many of these liens, on their face, reflect an agricultural history and past agricultural needs that seem quaint and old-fashioned, or possibly even anachronistic and detrimental when compared to today's agricultural realities. Just to hear the names of such agricultural liens makes one recall the times in which these agricultural liens arose: thresher's liens, horseshoer's liens, livery stable liens, moss gatherer's lien. Yet these liens cannot be easily dismissed as outmoded and unneeded. Naming other agricultural liens immediately makes their modern relevance clear: landlord's liens, seed supplier liens, fertilizer supplier liens, veterinarian's liens. . . .
>
> Second, each state adopted its various agricultural liens at different times and under different pressures. As a state adopted an agricultural lien, no common pattern or organized approach was followed. Hence, within a particular state, agricultural liens may have different requirements as to how and when the lien is created, how and whether the lien is perfected through public notice, how and within what period

of time the lien is enforced, or what priority the lien has vis-à-vis the claim of other creditors—whether they be other lienholders claiming the same crop, livestock, or farm equipment under a different agricultural lien or secured parties claiming a security interest.

Turner, Barnes, Kershen, Noble & Schumm, Agricultural Liens and the U.C.C.: A Report on Present Status and Proposals for Change, 44 Okla. L.Rev. 9, 12 (1991).

(2) The Solution. Revised Article 9 resolves many of the problems described in the preceding Note by expanding the scope of the Article to cover those statutory liens on farm products that fall within the definition of "agricultural lien." See R9–102(a)(5) (defining "agricultural lien"); R9–109(a)(2). Although an agricultural lien is not a security interest, the affected farm products are "collateral," the owner of the collateral is a "debtor," and the holder of the agricultural lien is a "secured party." See R9–102(a)(12), (a)(28), (a)(72). An agricultural lien is created by statute; no security agreement is required. An agricultural lien is perfected by filing a financing statement in the Article 9 filing office. See R9–310(a); R9–501(a). An unperfected agricultural lien is subordinate to the rights of a person who becomes a lien creditor before the agricultural lien is perfected. See R9–317(a)(2). Priority between competing, perfected agricultural liens or between a perfected agricultural lien and a competing, perfected security interest is determined by the first-to-file-or-perfect rule of R9–322(a). However, a perfected agricultural lien has priority over a competing security interest or agricultural lien if the statute creating the agricultural lien so provides. See R9–322(g). The enforcement provisions of Article 9 generally apply to enforcement of agricultural liens. See R9–601(a).

In short, Revised Article 9 affords a clear, easy, and uniform way for a holder of any one of the many, diverse agricultural liens to obtain priority over the debtor's judicial lien creditors and bankruptcy trustee, to ascertain the agricultural lien's priority as against conflicting security interests and agricultural liens in the same collateral, and to enforce the agricultural lien. At the same time, by subjecting agricultural liens to Article 9's filing requirements, Revised Article 9 enables potential secured lenders to ascertain with ease and at low cost, by searching the Article 9 filing records, whether farm products previously have been encumbered with an agricultural lien. This statutory approach proved so popular that some people questioned why it should be limited to agricultural liens on farm products. They urged the Drafting Committee to extend the perfection and priority provisions of Revised Article 9 to cover all nonpossessory statutory liens on all kinds of collateral. The potential advantages of such an expansion of Article 9's scope are evident. Why do you suppose the Drafting Committee declined to proceed along these lines?

(3) Production–Money Priority. Suppliers often provide new value (e.g., seed or fertilizer) that is used in the production of the crops. Some have argued that any security interest or agricultural lien on the crops in favor of the supplier should be afforded a special, PMSI-like priority over a competing security interest in the crops. As with both PMSI's and "possessory liens" under R9–333, a claimant who files second would achieve priority nevertheless, on the theory that without the latecomer's new value, there would be no collateral as such.

F9–312(2) was intended to afford special priority to those who provide secured credit that enables a debtor to produce crops. However, it generally has been regarded as unworkable. Despite years of work, the Drafting Committee was unable to forge a consensus among themselves or among the interested groups on whether the section should be revised or removed from Article 9 entirely. Ultimately the Drafting Committee decided to present "model provisions" for a production-money security interest ("PrMSI") priority. These provisions are found in Appendix II to Revised Article 9. Only a few states have chosen to enact them. A quick look reveals that they track very closely the provisions governing purchase-money security interests in inventory. Observe also that the PrMSI provisions apply only to security interests; they do not afford a special priority to agricultural liens. See R9–324A. If a secured party holds both an agricultural lien and an Article 9 production-money security interest in the same collateral, the priority rules applicable to agricultural liens govern. See R9–324A(e). If the priority rules applicable to PrMSI's would be more favorable, the secured party can waive its agricultural lien. See R9–324A, Comment 4.

(C) RIGHTS OF SETOFF

Problem 11.5.4. In the Prototype receivables financing transaction in Chapter 9, Section 1(B), supra, Eastinghome Credit Corporation has a perfected security interest in the inventory and accounts of Carguys. Section 13 of the Security Agreement (Form 5.2) reflects the fact that both Eastinghome and Carguys prefer that Carguys' customers remain ignorant of the transaction unless Carguys defaults. (Do you understand why?)

Assume that the Security Agreement requires Carguys to deposit all collections from its account debtors into a segregated, proceeds-only deposit account maintained with Firstbank. (As a finance company, Eastinghome is prohibited from taking the deposits itself.) On October 15, this account had a balance of $162,309, all of which constituted Eastinghome's proceeds.

Carguys owed Firstbank $50,000 on an unsecured loan on which Carguys defaulted. On October 15, Secondbank set off against the deposit account; that is, it applied $50,000 of the deposit account balance to the unpaid loan, leaving a balance of $112,309 in the deposit account and an unpaid balance of $0 on the loan.

Carguys defaults on its obligations to Eastinghome at a time when its debt under the Revolving Credit Agreement is in excess of $2,000,000. Eastinghome demands $162,309 from Firstbank, arguing that Firstbank misappropriated its collateral—the deposit account. What result? See R9–109(d)(10); R9–340; R9–341; Notes (1)–(3) on the Conflict Between Security Interests and Setoff Rights, infra. What could the losing party have done to avoid the loss?

Problem 11.5.5. Drekko borrowed $50,000 from Banco Coolio and agreed to secure the loan with a $50,000 negotiable certificate of deposit issued by Issuer "to the order of Drekko." See UCC 3–104(j) (definition of "certificate of deposit"). Drekko indorsed the certificate in blank and delivered it to Banco Coolio.

Drekko defaulted on its obligations to Banco Coolio. When Banco Coolio makes demand upon Issuer, see R9–607(a)(1), Issuer refuses to pay, asserting that its obligation under the certificate has been set off against an unpaid debt owed by Drekko.

(a) Does Issuer prevail against Banco Coolio? See R9–109(d)(10); R9–201; UCC 3–102; UCC 3–412; UCC 3–301; UCC 3–302; UCC 3–305; Note (4) on the Conflict Between Security Interests and Setoff Rights, infra; Problem 1.4.4, supra; Note (2) on Defenses to Payment Obligations, Chapter 1, Section 4, supra.

(b) Would the result in part (a) change if Banco Coolio took delivery of the certificate without obtaining Drekko's indorsement? See UCC 1–201(20); UCC 3–412; UCC 3–301; UCC 3–203; UCC 3–305.

(c) Would the result in part (a) change if Banco Coolio took a security interest in the certificate without obtaining delivery? See R9–312(a), (e); UCC 3–412; UCC 3–301; R9–607(a), (e).

(d) Would the result in part (a) or (b) change if Issuer refused to pay because Drekko had purchased the certificate with a check that "bounced"? See UCC 3–305 & Comment 3.

(e) Would the result in part (a) change if the certificate ran "to Drekko"? See UCC 3–104 & Comment 2; Restatement (Second) of Contracts § 336(1) ("the assignee acquires a right against the obligor only to the extent that the obligor is under a duty to the assignor; and if the right of the assignor would be ... unenforceable against [the assignor] if no assignment had been made, the right of the assignee is subject to the infirmity").

NOTES ON THE CONFLICT BETWEEN SECURITY INTERESTS AND SETOFF RIGHTS

(1) How the Conflict Often Arises. When each of two persons owes the other a money debt, each normally has the right to offset (subtract) the amount of one debt from the other and pay (or recover) only the difference. Although this right of setoff may arise in a variety of contexts, setoffs frequently are exercised by banks and other depositary institutions against funds on deposit. When these funds are encumbered by a security interest, a conflict arises between the bank and the secured party.

Problem 11.5.4, supra, presents a common fact pattern, one reflected in Universal C.I.T. Credit Corp. v. Farmers Bank, Chapter 7, Section 5, supra: The debtor disposes of collateral and deposits the proceeds in a deposit account maintained with the bank. The debtor defaults on an obligation to the bank, which attempts to satisfy its claim by setting off against the account. The secured party argues that the bank may not set off against an account in which the secured party claims a security interest. The facts of Problem 11.5.4 suggest that the secured party held a security interest in the deposit account as proceeds. See R9–315(a)(2); R9–102(a)(64) (defining "proceeds"); Chapter 7, Section 5, supra.

Our discussion of *Farmers Bank* concerned the circumstances under which proceeds deposited in a deposit account maintain their identifiability (and hence remain subject to a security interest) notwithstanding that they have been commingled with non-proceeds. We saw that courts generally permit a secured party to establish a security interest in commingled funds by using the "lowest intermediate balance" tracing rule. See Note on Tracing and Commingled Cash Proceeds, Chapter 7, Section 5, supra.

We turn now to another issue raised in *Farmers Bank*: Under what circumstances, if any, is the bank precluded from effectively setting off against a deposit account because the secured party holds a security interest in the account?

(2) Resolution of the Conflict. A number of courts have been called upon to apply Former Article 9 to the resolution of the conflict described in the preceding Note. They have taken a variety of approaches. Despite the apparently absolute terms of F9–104(i) (Article 9 "does not apply ... to any right of set-off"), most courts have resolved the conflict by applying Former Article 9. Relying on a passage in Grant Gilmore's treatise, these courts have read the exclusion in F9–104(i) to mean only that a right of setoff is not an Article 9 security interest and that, therefore, the attachment and perfection provisions of Article 9 are irrelevant to setoffs. Having decided to apply Former Article 9, the courts generally have ruled in favor of the secured party, usually under F9–201 (R9–201(a)). Some courts have held that Former Article 9's exclusion of setoff rights is complete. In their view Former Article 9 did not govern the conflict between a security interest and a setoff right; they applied non-UCC law instead. Under the prevailing common-law rule, if the bank can be charged with knowledge of the interest of a third party in a deposit account, or notice of facts sufficient to put it on inquiry that such an interest exists, then the bank may not apply the deposit account to satisfy a debt owed by the depositor.[1] Perhaps not surprisingly, courts applying the common-law rule often have concluded that the bank was charged with notice of the security interest and that the secured party has priority.

---

1. This "legal" rule is to be distinguished from the "equitable" rule that a few states follow: The bank may not set off against a deposit account subject to a security interest, even if the bank lacks knowledge of the security interest, unless the bank can show that its equities are superior to those of the secured party. See, e.g., Commercial Discount Corp. v. Milwaukee Western Bank, 61 Wis.2d 671, 214 N.W.2d 33 (1974). Among the "equities" that may be relevant are whether the secured party permitted the debtor to deposit proceeds into a general bank account instead of requiring the debtor to deposit them into a special account and whether the bank acted in reliance on the appearance that the funds were unencumbered (e.g., by deferring collection on the debtor's obligation to the bank).

Revised Article 9 eliminates any doubt about whether Article 9 resolves the conflict between a security interest and a bank's right of setoff. Although the revised Article generally is inapplicable to a right of setoff, R9–340 applies with respect to the effectiveness of a right of setoff against a deposit account. See R9–109(d)(10). R9–340 expressly resolves the conflict between a security interest in a deposit account and the bank's right of setoff—but in a manner that rejects the prevailing case law under Former Article 9: Under R9–340 the bank may exercise its right of setoff against a secured party who holds a security interest in the deposit account. See R9–340(a). However, if the secured party has control under R9–104(a)(3) (i.e., if the secured party is the bank's customer with respect to the deposit account), then any setoff against a debt owed to the bank by the debtor (as opposed to a debt owed to the bank by the secured party) is ineffective against the secured party. See R9–340(c).

What accounts for this dramatic rejection of the decided cases? A bank may hold both a security interest in, and a right of setoff against, the same deposit account. See R9–340(b). The rules governing setoff yield the same results as would obtain if the bank with which a deposit account is maintained asserted a security interest in the deposit account. Specifically, a security interest held by the bank with which the deposit account is maintained has priority over a conflicting security interest. See R9–327(3). However, a secured party who has control under R9–104(a)(3) has priority even against the bank with which the deposit account is maintained. See R9–327(4). This parallelism is not coincidental. What consequences would follow from a legal regime in which, say, a bank's security interest was senior to a competing security interest but its setoff right was junior (or vice versa)? (Consider, in this regard, the fact that enforcement of the security interest is accomplished in the same way as exercise of the setoff right, by applying the balance of the deposit account to the obligation secured by the deposit account. See R9–607(a)(4).) Of course, the mere acknowledgment that the rules should be parallel does not dictate the substance of the rule. The decision to conform the setoff rules in R9–340 to the priority rules in R9–327 is sensible only if one is persuaded that the priority rules are appropriate. Are they? See Note (3) on Security Interests in Deposit Accounts, Chapter 9, Section 4, supra.

If one were to undertake a resolution of the conflict between a security interest and a right of setoff from first principles, which rule should one adopt? One might construct a simple argument that favors the secured party: Every debtor has a bank account; it is a necessity of doing business. A bank into which proceeds are deposited (or that subsequently takes a security interest in a deposit account) should enjoy no greater rights than any other third party who deals with collateral. On the other hand, one might argue for the bank: The secured party should enjoy no greater rights than any other third party claiming an interest in another person's bank account. Any secured party concerned about the risk of setoff should take appropriate steps to protect the proceeds of its collateral by monitoring the debtor's behavior.

Alternatively, one might rely on the basic conveyancing principle (*nemo dat*), discussed in Chapter 1, Section 3, to resolve the conflict. The rights in collateral to which a security interest attaches generally extend no further than the debtor's rights. See Note (1) on Attachment, Chapter 7, Section 2, supra. It follows that a secured party who claims a receivable as collateral generally does not acquire rights against an account debtor that are better than the those of the debtor. The deposit account is nothing more than the debtor's unsecured claim against the bank. Since there is no question that the bank is entitled to set off against the deposit account as between the bank and the debtor, on what conceptual basis can the secured party acquire its interest free of the bank's right of setoff? There is no "property" to which the secured party can lay claim. The issue is simply whether the bank must pay the secured party, the debtor's assignee, even though the bank is not obliged to pay the debtor. Are you persuaded by the foregoing analysis?

(3) The Right of Recoupment. R9–340 addresses the bank's right of recoupment as well as its right of setoff. The two rights are quite similar; the exercise of each involves the offset of mutual claims. The principal difference is that recoupment concerns claims that arise from the same transaction, whereas setoff concerns claims that arise from different transactions. We have seen an example of recoupment in Chapter 1, Section 4, supra: If goods are delivered to and accepted by the buyer but do not conform to the contract of sale, the buyer has the right to deduct from its obligation for the price (UCC 2–709) its damages for breach of warranty (UCC 2–714). See UCC 2–717. With respect to a deposit account, the bank's claim in recoupment is unlikely to be substantial. It consists primarily of the right to payment for fees related to the deposit account.

(4) The Conflict in Another Setting. Problem 11.5.5, supra, poses the conflict between a security interest and a setoff right in another setting: The secured party has a security interest in a certificate of deposit; the issuer of the certificate of deposit seeks to set off against its obligation under the certificate.

The general exclusion of setoff rights from Article 9 would appear to leave the resolution of the priority contest to other law. See R9–109(d)(10). If the certificate is negotiable, then UCC Article 3 would seem to govern the rights of the parties. See UCC 3–102(a). Thus, resolution of the conflict would turn on whether the issuer enjoyed the right to assert against the secured party the particular defense or claim in recoupment. This, in turn, might depend on whether the secured party had the rights of a holder in due course. See UCC 3–305(a), (b).

If, however, the certificate is not negotiable and thus outside the scope of Article 3, what law applies? Should a court apply UCC 3–305 by analogy? Should it apply R9–404 in appropriate cases?[2] Should it look to the common

---

2. R9–404(a) applies only when there is an "account debtor," i.e., a person obligated on an account, chattel paper, or a general intangible. See R9–102(a)(3) (defining "account debtor"). A number of cases have held that non-negotiable certificates of deposit are

law of contracts, which is similar to R9–404? Or, should the court follow cases construing the exclusion in F9–104(i), read the exclusion in R9–109(d)(10) narrowly (as if it means only that a right of setoff is not an Article 9 security interest), and automatically award priority to the secured party under R9–201(a)?

Interestingly, whereas the reported cases have tended to hold for the secured party when the dispute arises over proceeds in a deposit account, they have tended to award priority to the setting-off issuer in cases concerning a certificate of deposit. One might expect the same divergence were the courts to resolve the conflicts by applying the *nemo dat* principle.

(D) FEDERAL TAX LIENS

Introductory Note. A debtor who defaults on obligations to the secured party is likely also to be indebted to others. We already have considered the competing claims of a variety of private creditors holding consensual, judicial, common-law, and statutory liens. We turn now to a special creditor—the United States government.

Although the government may become a creditor under a variety of circumstances, its most prominent role is that of tax collector: "[I]n this world nothing is certain but death and taxes."[3] Debtors in financial difficulty may be tempted to "borrow" from the government by wrongfully manipulating the tax system. Examples of this misconduct include understating tax liability and failing to remit sums withheld from workers for income and social security taxes. The accumulated liability to the government may be substantial; indeed, it may exceed the debtor's total assets.

In establishing the rights of the United States as a creditor for unpaid taxes, Congress has given the government a particularly strong set of entitlements. These are set forth in Chapter 64 (Collection) of the Internal Revenue Code (IRC). Of particular importance to secured parties is subchapter C, concerning the government's lien for taxes. 26 U.S.C. §§ 6321–27.[4]

"instruments." See, e.g., General Elec. Co. v. M & C Mfg., Inc., 283 Ark. 110, 671 S.W.2d 189 (1984).

3. "Our constitution is in actual operation; everything appears to promise that it will last; but in this world nothing is certain but death and taxes." From Benjamin Franklin's letter to M. Leroy (1789), quoted in Bartlett, Familiar Quotations 348 (15th & 125th anniv. ed. 1980).

4. The priority provisions of the Federal Tax Lien Act apply to liens for unpaid liabilities to the Pension Benefit Guaranty Corporation. See 29 U.S.C. § 1368(c)(1).

Generally, in the absence of a specific federal statute, the UCC as enacted by the appropriate jurisdiction applies to the government's rights as an extender of consensual credit. See Chapter 8, Section 4, supra. One federal statute of particular importance purports to grant priority in payment to *all* claims (whether secured or unsecured) of the federal government when, inter alia, a debtor is insolvent. 31 U.S.C. § 3713(a) (commonly known as R.S. 3466). Where this statute conflicts with the Federal Tax Lien Act, the latter governs. See United States v. Estate of Romani, 523 U.S. 517, 118 S.Ct. 1478, 140 L.Ed.2d 710 (1998). As a result of an amendment made when the Bankruptcy Reform Act was enacted in 1978, 31 U.S.C. § 3713(a) does not apply when the taxpayer is a debtor under the Bankruptcy Code.

The federal tax lien is pervasive. IRC § 6321, which creates the lien, provides as follows:

> If any person liable to pay any tax neglects or refuses to pay the same after demand, the amount (including any interest, additional amount, addition to tax, or assessable penalty, together with any costs that may accrue in addition thereto) shall be a lien in favor of the United States *upon all property and rights to property, whether real or personal,* belonging to such person.

This lien arises "at the time the assessment is made." IRC § 6322. The assessment is an administrative act—a letter from the Internal Revenue Service to the taxpayer. Upon the occurrence of this private event, the government obtains a secret lien on *all* the taxpayer's property.

During the early part of this century, the consequences of the tax lien for third persons were unpredictable and disastrous. In 1928, however, Congress afforded statutory protection to any "mortgagee, purchaser, or judgment creditor" against any tax lien as to which the government had not filed a notice in a designated public office. This appears to be a more generous concession than it turned out to be. Although the statute specifically protected a "mortgagee" from unfiled tax liens, courts construing the statute held that a recorded mortgage nevertheless was subordinate to the tax lien if the mortgage was "inchoate"—a mysterious concept of indefinite and elastic scope that, at the very least, threatened security interests based on an after-acquired property clause or a contractual provision contemplating future advances.

The threat of the federal tax lien was profoundly disturbing to the commercial community. The American Bar Association set up a Special Committee on Federal Liens; years of drafting and persuasion led to the enactment in 1966 of important amendments to the law governing the federal tax lien. A member of and draftsman for the Committee, William T. Plumb, Jr., reported on the results of their labor.

Plumb, Legislative Revision of the Federal Tax Lien

22 Bus. Law. 271, 271–76 (1967).

> *"Now is the winter of our discontent*
> *Made glorious summer by this sun . . . ."*

... [W]e have known 16 winters of growing discontent since the Supreme Court began the parade of decisions which expanded the priority of federal tax liens and eroded the protections on which the business and banking community rely for their security. The American Bar Association worked for many of those years to bring about an accommodation between the legitimate necessities of revenue collection and the practicalities of modern credit transactions. Now at last those efforts have borne fruit in the enactment of the first comprehensive revision of the law of federal tax liens in over half a century. Truly, the summer sun is shining!

What is this federal tax lien? It is a powerful collection tool, which serves the dual function of putting pressure on delinquent taxpayers to discharge their liabilities and of preserving the government's priority as against other claimants to their property. It attaches to "all property and rights to property, whether real or personal, belonging to" the taxpayer, including after-acquired property. It is a secret lien which arises automatically as of the moment a tax is assessed, if the taxpayer fails to make payment on demand. Originally, the secret lien prevailed even over a later bona fide purchaser; but for many years the law has protected mortgagees, pledgees, purchasers and judgment creditors against the tax lien unless notice thereof was filed in the office designated by state law. Other creditors were unprotected, not merely against pre-existing secret tax liens but also against those which arose *after* the other creditors had obtained statutory liens which were valid against everyone else.

The Supreme Court paid lip-service to the view that "the first in time is the first in right," but nullified that principle by prescribing that, in order to be "first in time," the competing lien must first have become "choate." That word (which, like "couth" and "ruly" and "sheveled," was not in most dictionaries until the Supreme Court gave it respectability) was not truly an antonym for "inchoate," but had its own peculiar meaning. A lien might be complete and perfected for every purpose of state law, and hence not "inchoate" as we understand that term. Yet it would also not be "choate," by federal tax standards, unless the identity of the lienor, the property subject to the lien, and the amount payable were fixed beyond possibility of change or dispute. Except for certain liens for state and local taxes and some possessory liens, it appeared that no statutory lien could qualify until the lienor's claim had been reduced to judgment. Furthermore, even mortgages and other contractual security, despite their specially favored position under the federal statute, were vulnerable to subsequently arising federal tax liens to the extent that the security embraced after-acquired property or involved disbursements later to be made.

Now at last the government has recognized that the "choateness" doctrine was inequitable and that it created risks and deterrents to business transactions generally which far outweighed the relatively few extra dollars of tax that might be collected in distress situations. Although the doctrine has not been wholly eliminated, the great bulk of business transactions have been freed from its effect by the adoption of express relief provisions. In the interest of equity, those provisions were, in general, made immediately and retroactively effective.

Secured Financing

Definition of "security interest"—The new law substitutes the term "holder of a security interest" for the terms "mortgagee" and "pledgee," among the classes which are protected from unfiled federal tax liens. This was a technical change, but a necessary one, because the government had argued that assignments of contracts and accounts receivable, and other forms of modern commercial financing, did not fit the conventional concept of either a mortgage or a pledge. "Security interest" is broadly defined [IRC 6323(a) & (h)(1)] as "any interest in property acquired by contract for the purpose of securing payment or performance of an obligation or indemnifying against loss or liability." Although the term is borrowed from the Commercial Code, the definition clearly embraces real estate mortgages and deeds of trust as well as all forms of commercial security.

Future advances and after-acquired property—The most serious deficiency of the former law, as it affected secured lenders, was that they could not safely make additional advances under an existing financing arrangement, or permit the substitution of security, without again searching for federal tax liens—a practical impossibility in many commercial finance situations. The new law deals with those problems by prescribing strict general rules and then carving out liberal exceptions to meet meritorious situations.

It is stated as a general rule [IRC 6323(h)(1)] that a security interest "exists" only "to the extent that, at such time [of filing a federal tax lien], the holder *has parted* with money or money's worth," and only if the property is "in existence"—no doubt meaning "owned by the taxpayer"—at such time. Therefore, unless one of the exceptions is applicable, the holder of an open-end real estate mortgage, for example, would be protected in making subsequent loans, without searching for intervening federal tax liens. And after-acquired property clauses in general mortgages and equipment trusts, even when they secure existing debts, would be ineffective, as against intervening federal tax liens, to give the lenders priority in the debtors' subsequent acquisitions.

All the exceptions to that general rule are subject to two conditions precedent. A written security agreement, which covers the subsequent advances or acquisitions, must have been entered into before notice of the federal tax lien was filed. And the security interest must be protected under local law (by recording, filing, taking possession, giving notice to the account debtor, or whatever such law requires) against a judgment lien arising, as of the time of tax lien filing, out of an unsecured obligation.

One of the exceptions is of general application. Any lender who meets the foregoing conditions is protected [IRC 6323(d)] with respect to disbursements made within *45 days after* a tax lien is filed, unless he sooner obtains *actual* (not merely constructive) notice or knowledge of such filing. This general exception, however, does not permit the addition or substitution of any property which was not owned by the borrower at the time the federal tax lien was filed. Its principal usefulness will be in making a new search for intervening federal tax liens unnecessary when there is a short delay between the perfecting of the security interest and the full disbursement of the loan. One such instance would arise in the case of an issue of mortgage bonds, which technically involves the making of optional advances by each original purchaser, at a date later than the search of the title and the execution of the mortgage.

Commercial financing—The first of several exceptions designed to meet special situations relates to loans on "commercial financing security," which is defined as inventory, accounts receivable, real estate mortgages, and "paper of a kind ordinarily arising in commercial transactions." Such security must have been acquired by the *borrower* in the ordinary course of his trade or business, and the loan must have been made in the course of the *lender's* trade or business. The lender need not be in the business of lending money, however; a business loan to a supplier or customer would qualify.

The exception for commercial financing is really a special case of the general exception last discussed, in that, . . . loans (or purchases) made as much as 45 days after the filing of a tax lien are protected, in the absence of actual notice or knowledge thereof. The added feature is that, when "commercial financing security" is involved, the protection is not confined to property owned by the borrower when the tax lien was filed, but may embrace property "acquired" by him within 45 days thereafter. This latter 45–day period is not cut short by earlier knowledge of the lien.

Some interesting questions may arise concerning when property is "acquired" for this purpose. Suppose the borrower assigns to the lender the expected proceeds of an executory contract, which is still not fully performed when the 45 days expire. Under earlier decisions, such expected proceeds were regarded as after-acquired property, and a security assignment thereof was deemed "inchoate" as against an intervening federal tax lien. However, the specific mention of "contract rights," as defined in the Commercial Code, among the items which qualify as "commercial financing security," suggests that the expected proceeds of an existing executory contract will now be considered as property already "acquired," since "contract rights" by definition are rights "not yet earned by performance." Similarly, the reference to "chattel paper," which under the Commercial Code embraces leases of tangible personal property, suggests that a security interest in the future rents from such a lease would be deemed to involve existing and not after-acquired property of the borrower.

The effect of the two 45–day rules is that a commercial lender or factor, having found no tax liens on file when he perfected his security interest, can now protect himself by making new searches for such liens at 45–day intervals, rather than before every advance. If he learns of a filed tax lien, and desires full priority, he must *immediately* cease new advances or purchases, and he must terminate the substitution of collateral 45 days from the date the tax lien was filed. . . .

A lender financing a manufacturing contract may not find it economically feasible to cut off his loans upon discovery of a tax lien, since he may be left with unfinished goods or the proceeds (if any) payable under an uncompleted contract as the only source of repayment of advances already made. The lender may then be able to work out an agreement with the tax collector, whereby the tax liens would be subordinated to the further loans necessary to complete the contract. Since completion would, in such circumstances, afford the only hope of recovery for the tax collector as well as for the lender, such a subordination agreement should be obtainable.... If it is not, and the lender nevertheless feels he must continue, he may rely on a decision under prior law which viewed a manufacturing loan as analogous to a purchase money mortgage, and held that nothing but the *residue* of the contract proceeds, after satisfying the lender, ever became property "belonging to" the debtor, to which a pre-existing federal tax lien could attach. Nothing in the new law seems to detract from that principle.

Mr. Plumb's discussion was concerned primarily with IRC 6323(c) and (d). These sections are as important as they are difficult. Read them carefully as you work the following problems.

Problem 11.5.6. One of your clients, Lender, is considering whether to establish a secured **line of credit** in favor of Borcorp, a Delaware corporation engaged in the manufacture of automobile parts. Borcorp's manufacturing plants and warehouses are in Michigan, and its corporate offices are in California. You wish to make sure that the potential collateral is not encumbered by a federal tax lien. How would you find out whether the government holds a tax lien in any property of Borcorp? See IRC § 6323(f). Would the fact that, prior to 1999, Borcorp's corporate offices were located in Illinois affect your answer? See IRC § 6323(g).

Problem 11.5.7. Lender agreed to extend to Borcorp a line of credit, which Borcorp secured with its existing and after-acquired equipment, inventory, and accounts. Under the terms of the written loan and security agreement, all advances were discretionary on Lender's part. Proper financing statements were filed in California, Delaware, and Michigan on June 1. On June 10 Lender advanced $50,000 to Borcorp. The IRS previously had assessed Borcorp for $20,000 in unpaid taxes; however, it did not file a notice of tax lien until July 1.

(a) Who has priority in the $60,000 of inventory on hand on June 10? On June 30? See IRC § 6323(a); IRC § 6323(h)(1). Does your answer change if the issue is litigated in December? See IRC § 6323(a) (tax "lien ... shall not be valid as against any ... holder of a security interest ... until notice thereof ... has been filed.")

(b) What result in part (a) if Lender had failed to file a financing statement in Michigan?

(c) What result in part (a) if Lender had failed to file a financing statement in Delaware?

(d) What result in part (a) if Borcorp had signed the security agreement on July 2?

(e) What result in part (a) if Lender did not make an advance until July 2?

(f) What result in part (a) if the tax lien filing occurred on May 29?

Problem 11.5.8. Under the facts of Problem 11.5.7, Borcorp acquires raw materials and manufactures them into completed goods in the ordinary course of business.

(a) Who has priority in the raw materials acquired during the week of July 5? See IRC § 6323(c). Observe that the applicable rule of law, found in IRC § 6323(c)(1), contains several defined terms, including "security interest," "qualified property," and "commercial transactions financing agreement." The last two are defined in IRC § 6323(c)(2). The definition of "qualified property" itself contains another defined term, "commercial financing security," which is defined in IRC § 6323(c)(2)(C).

(b) What result in part (a) if Lender had seen the tax lien filing on July 2? Does the notice provision of IRC § 6323(c)(2)(A) apply?

(c) Who has priority in the raw materials acquired during the last week of August?

(d) Would it make any difference in part (c) if Lender could show that Borcorp paid for the raw materials with a check drawn on its account at Firstbank and that the account contained only the proceeds of completed goods that were sold before August 10? Treasury Regulation § 301.6323(c)–1(d) (1976) provides as follows:

> Identifiable proceeds, which arise from the collection or disposition of qualified property by the taxpayer, are considered to be acquired at the time such qualified property is acquired if the secured party has a continuously perfected security interest in the proceeds under local law. The term "proceeds" includes whatever is received when collateral is sold, exchanged, or collected. For purposes of this paragraph, the term "identifiable proceeds" does not include money, checks and the like which have been commingled with other cash proceeds. Property acquired by the taxpayer after the 45th day following tax lien filing, by the expenditure of proceeds, is not qualified property.

(e) Who has priority in the completed goods manufactured in September? Would it make any difference if Lender could show that these goods were manufactured from raw materials acquired in July? Consider the approach of the Tenth Circuit in Donald v. Madison Industries, Inc., 483 F.2d 837, 844–45 (10th Cir.1973):

> While we find it evident from the face of the statute that property not yet owned or "acquired" by the debtor-taxpayer by the 45th day after the tax lien filing, such as purchases of new raw materials or new equipment, would not be subject to the creditor's priority, we find it equally clear that where property owned by the debtor within the 45–day period subsequently undergoes transformations in character and

form, such as the evolution of raw materials into final products and eventually into cash proceeds, as occurred herein, the creditor does not lose his security interest in the value of that property which was owned on the 45th day. Implicit in this conclusion, however, is the fact that the creditor would have no rights to the "value-added" to the product after the 45th day by the addition of either labor or *parts subsequently acquired.*

Thus, the crucial fact which should have been determined in this case was an analysis of what portion of the finished products' value was attributable to the inclusion of property which was owned by the taxpayer before the 46th day after the tax lien filing. [The burden of proof on this issue is on the taxpayer.]

Problem 11.5.9. Under the facts of Problem 11.5.7, supra, Borcorp entered into a requirements contract with General Motors two months before the transaction with Lender. See UCC 2–306(1). The contract requires Borcorp to make deliveries of specified parts to GM upon 48 hours' notice; it requires GM to pay for the parts 30 days after delivery. On September 15 Borcorp receives notice of GM's need for parts; Borcorp makes a timely delivery.

Who has priority in Borcorp's right to payment from GM? Does it matter when the parts were manufactured? See IRC 6323(c); J.D. Court, Inc. v. United States, infra. See also Texas Oil & Gas Corp. v. United States, 466 F.2d 1040 (5th Cir.1972), cert. denied 410 U.S. 929, 93 S.Ct. 1367, 35 L.Ed.2d 591 (1973) (accounts receivable were not "acquired" by taxpayer until it performed the work). But see Pine Builders, Inc. v. United States, 413 F.Supp. 77 (E.D.Va.1976) (where taxpayer's right to receive weekly payments for services rendered arose under single contract and was subject to condition precedent, right to payment was "in existence" for purposes of IRC § 6323(h)(1) whether or not taxpayer had earned right to payment by performance). Cf. In re Ralls & Associates, Inc., 114 B.R. 744 (Bkrtcy.W.D.Okl.1990) (granting IRS priority over secured party in accounts *invoiced* more than 45 days after tax lien filing).

Texas Oil & Gas, supra, was decided under the pre–1972 version of Article 9, which distinguished between a "contract right," which was not yet earned by performance, and an "account," which was earned. The Supreme Court has held that state law determines whether, and the extent to which, a taxpayer has property or rights to property to which a federal tax lien can attach. See Aquilino v. United States, 363 U.S. 509, 80 S.Ct. 1277, 4 L.Ed.2d 1365 (1960). Should the fact that the definition of "account" in Article 9 was amended to include a right to payment for goods sold, "whether or not [the right has been] earned by performance," change the outcome? R9–102(a)(2). Does state law determine the meaning of "accounts receivable" in IRC § 6323(c)(2)(C)(ii)? Under the Treasury Regulations, a security interest in an account receivable is in existence "when, and to the extent, a right of payment is earned by performance." Treas. Reg. § 301.6323(h)–1(a)(1) (1976).

We have examined the issues posed by this Problem and the preceding one in another context, that of preference law. See Chapter 10, Section 3, supra. Is there any reason why the analysis should differ depending on the context?

Problem 11.5.10. Under the facts of Problem 11.5.7, supra, Lender advanced an additional $30,000 to Borcorp on July 15.

(a) On July 30 Borcorp's inventory is worth $60,000. Who has priority in the inventory? See IRC § 6323(d); R9–323(b).

(b) What result in part (a) if Lender had seen the tax lien filing on July 2? As to the meaning of "actual notice or knowledge," see IRC § 6323(i), which derives from UCC 1–201(27).

(c) What result in part (a) if Lender made the advance during the last week in August?

(d) Would the result in part (c) change if, in the credit agreement, Lender had undertaken to make advances upon Borcorp's demand, provided Borcorp met certain specified conditions precedent? See IRC § 6323(d); IRC § 6323(c)(1), (4).

Problem 11.5.11. Cuspid, a dentist, owes $25,000 in back taxes to the IRS. On May 1 the IRS filed a proper notice of tax lien. On October 15 Cuspid took delivery of a new X–Ray machine from Manufacturer, who retained a security interest in the machine. Manufacturer had filed a proper financing statement on October 10.

(a) Who has priority? Was the security interest "in existence" before the tax lien filing? See IRC § 6323(a); IRC § 6323(h)(1). The Treasury Regulations are silent concerning the priority of purchase-money security interests. Should a court be moved by the following passage from the legislative history:

> Although the so-called purchase money mortgages are not specifically referred to under present law, it has generally been held that these interests are protected whenever they arise. This is based upon the concept that the taxpayer has acquired property or a right to property only to the extent that the value of the whole property or right exceeds the amount of the purchase money mortgage. This concept is not affected by the bill.

S.Rep. No. 1708, 89th Cong., 2d Sess. 4 (1966), reprinted in 1966 U.S.C.C.A.N. 3722, 3725.

(b) What result in part (a) if Manufacturer filed on October 20? On November 15? See IRC § 6323(h)(1); R9–323(b). Is the foregoing excerpt of any assistance to Manufacturer?

(c) What result in part (a) if, instead of obtaining financing from Manufacturer, Cuspid borrowed the funds from Bank, which paid Manufacturer the purchase price directly? Is the foregoing excerpt of any assistance to Bank?

J.D. Court, Inc. v. United States

United States Court of Appeals, Seventh Circuit, 1983. 712 F.2d 258.
Cert. denied 466 U.S. 927, 104 S.Ct. 1708, 80 L.Ed.2d 182 (1984).

■ COFFEY, CIRCUIT JUDGE.

This appeal involves a determination of the respective priority between a federal tax lien on a taxpayer's accounts receivable and a private individual's security interest in the same accounts receivable. The district court granted summary judgment in favor of the government finding that the federal tax lien was entitled to priority in all of the taxpayer's accounts receivable arising more than 45 days after the Internal Revenue Service first filed notice of its tax lien. We affirm.

I.

On June 20, 1977, the Director of the Illinois Department of Public Aid certified the taxpayer, Eventide Homes, Inc., to participate in the Title XIX Medicaid Program as a skilled and intermediate nursing care facility. Eventide Homes' initial certification for participation in the Medicaid Program was effective from March 1977 through March 1978, and was later extended through 1980. Under the certification agreement between Eventide Homes and the Illinois Department of Public Aid, Eventide Homes was under no obligation to provide medical and health care services to public aid recipients of the State of Illinois, but if they decided to provide such care, the Department agreed to reimburse Eventide Homes.

On May 10, 1979, Eventide Homes gave a $75,000 promissory note for value to Mervin Beil and executed a security agreement granting Beil a security interest in the taxpayer's "accounts receivable, and all goods, equipment, fixtures or inventory now or hereafter existing" to secure payment of the promissory note. Beil perfected his security interest ... by filing a financing statement with the Illinois Secretary of State's office on May 17, 1979. Beil later sold his security interest in Eventide Homes' accounts to the plaintiff J.D. Court. The assignment of that security interest was recorded with the Illinois Secretary of State on December 21, 1979.

During 1979 and 1980, the taxpayer Eventide Homes provided medical and health care services to Illinois public aid recipients entitling Eventide Homes to receive approximately $33,000 from the Illinois Department of Public Aid. Of this amount, $907.38 was for services rendered to Illinois public aid recipients by Eventide Homes prior to December 1, 1979, with the remainder representing amounts due for the services rendered after December 1, 1979.

Because of Eventide Homes' failure to pay its federal income taxes, the Internal Revenue Service assessed delinquent taxes against Eventide Homes and imposed a federal tax lien on Eventide Homes' property sometime prior to September 1979. On September 17, 1979, the Internal Revenue Service filed in the Kankakee County, Illinois Recorder's Office the first of four notices of tax liens against Eventide Homes' property, in the amount of $3,802.00. The three other notices of tax liens against Eventide Homes were filed in the Kankakee Recorder's Office on the following dates and for the following amounts: (1) October 10, 1979 for $11,084; (2) October 16, 1979 for $10,484; and (3) January 30, 1980 for $43,555.

On January 23, 1980, the Internal Revenue Service levied on the funds then due and owing to Eventide Homes from the Illinois Department of Public Aid for services rendered to public aid recipients. Approximately two weeks later, on February 15, 1980, Eventide Homes (the taxpayer) was placed in receivership. The plaintiff J.D. Court filed this action to enjoin the government from levying on the funds of the Illinois Department of Public Aid owed to Eventide Homes alleging that it is entitled to priority to all of the levied funds by virtue of its position as assignee of the security interest in Eventide Homes' "accounts receivable." The levied funds are presently being held in escrow pending resolution of this lawsuit.

In its summary judgment order, the trial court found that the plaintiff J.D. Court's security interest took priority in the taxpayer's accounts receivable which came into existence within forty-five days of the IRS's first filing of a notice of tax lien. The court further determined that the government had priority in the accounts receivable that came into existence after the forty-five days had expired from the filing of the first tax lien pursuant to 26 U.S.C. § 6323(c). The plaintiff J.D. Court appeals from the decision of the district court.

II.

Since one of the parties in this case is the United States holding a lien for unpaid taxes, federal law governs the priority of the conflicting liens on Eventide Homes' accounts receivable. Specifically, the Federal Tax Lien Act of 1966, 26 U.S.C. §§ 6321–6326 sets forth the rights of private creditors with respect to a federal tax lien.

The Tax Lien Act follows the general rule that a "lien first in time is first in right." In general, a federal tax lien arises (i.e., "attaches") "at the time the [tax] assessment is made," 26 U.S.C. § 6322, and therefore a tax lien normally takes priority over other liens arising subsequent to assessment of the delinquent tax. Section 6323(a) of the Act creates an exception to § 6322's rule that a federal tax lien generally attaches at the time the delinquent tax is assessed; under § 6323(a), when the "holder of a security interest" also claims an interest in property subject to a federal tax lien, the federal tax lien is deemed to have attached when the IRS files a notice of tax lien, rather than when the delinquent tax was first assessed. Thus, the holder of a security interest in a taxpayer's property will prevail against a government tax lien on the same property if the security interest "attaches" and is perfected before the government files its notice of tax lien, see Coogan, The Effect of the Federal Tax Lien Act of 1966 Upon Security Interests Created Under the Uniform Commercial Code, 81 Harv. L.Rev. 1369 (1968).

Therefore, to determine the priority between a federal tax lien and a security interest in the same property, it is necessary to determine (1) when the federal tax lien "attaches"; and (2) when the state law security interest "attaches." As we have noted above, § 6323(a) provides that a federal tax lien "attaches" in these circumstances when the notice of tax lien is filed in the appropriate place. However, the Act fails to expressly state when the competing state law security interest is deemed to have "attached." In answering this question, courts have long relied on the judicially created "choateness doctrine." Under the "choateness doctrine," where a security interest arising under state law (such as the plaintiff's) comes into conflict with a federal tax lien, the state law security interest "attaches" only when it becomes "choate." A state law security interest is deemed to be "choate" when all three of the following elements are satisfied: "the identity of the lienor, the property subject to the lien, and the amount of the lien are established." If this three-part "choateness" test is satisfied at the time the IRS files its notice of tax lien, *or within 45 days thereafter,* the state law security interest takes priority over the competing tax lien. 26 U.S.C. § 6323(c).

In the instant case, the district court applied the foregoing rules, including the "choateness doctrine," to determine the respective rights of the plaintiff and the United States in Eventide Homes' accounts receivable. The court found that the plaintiff's security interest in the Eventide Homes' accounts receivable did not satisfy the three-part "choateness" test until the property subject to the security interest (i.e., the accounts receivable) actually came into existence—namely, at the moment in time when the Illinois Department of Public Aid became indebted to Eventide Homes for the provision of health and medical services to Illinois public aid recipients. Applying this reasoning, the district court determined that the plaintiff's security interest was "choate" only with regard to the $907.38 of accounts receivable coming into existence within 45 days of the government's filing its first notice of tax lien and thus was only entitled to priority over the competing tax lien to that extent. The court further found that the IRS's tax liens were entitled to priority with regard to any accounts receivable coming into existence thereafter, totalling $31,965.34, since the plaintiff's security interest in those accounts receivable did not become "choate" until more than 45 days after the government filed notice of its tax liens.

In this appeal, the plaintiff first challenges the district court's reliance on the "choateness doctrine." The plaintiff states that the "choateness doctrine" was developed by the federal courts prior to enactment of the Tax Lien Act of 1966 and that the "choateness doctrine" is solely a tax lien concept not embodied in the Uniform Commercial Code. Since the Tax Lien Act was intended to "conform the lien provisions of the internal revenue laws to concepts developed in [the] Uniform Commercial Code," H.R.Rep. No. 1884, 89th Cong., 2d Sess., 35 (1966), the plaintiff concludes that the "choateness doctrine" was abrogated by the Tax Lien Act of 1966.

We disagree with the plaintiff's contention that the Tax Lien Act of 1966 abrogated the "choateness doctrine" since this court, as recently as 1979, recognized the continued viability of the "choateness doctrine" under the Tax Lien Act of 1966. In Sgro v. United States, 609 F.2d 1259 (7th Cir.1979) this court held that a government tax lien took priority over a state law security interest in a taxpayer's accounts receivable, and discussed the "choateness doctrine" as follows:

> "Notwithstanding the attachment of a tax lien upon assessment, [§ 6323(a)] provides that ... holders of security interests, ... will prevail if their interest attaches before the Government files appropriate notice. *Attachment occurs at the moment the interest becomes choate,* which is a question of federal law.... If 'the identity of the lienor, the property subject to the lien, and the amount of the lien are established' before the Government files notice, those falling within the statutory class will prevail over a prior tax lien."

* * *

> "[A] common way to secure a line of credit is to use one's accounts receivable as collateral. Such a loan may be secured by the outstanding balances in the debtor's accounts receivable at the time the loan is made and by further balances as they become due.... Since a subsequently arising balance is not in existence at the time the loan is made, *the resulting lien remains inchoate until the underlying debt becomes due.* ... [T]he resulting lien remains unprotected by [§ 6323(a)] until it becomes choate and *therefore would be subject to a tax lien filed in the interim.*"

... [I]n determining priority between state law liens and federal tax liens under the Tax Lien Act of 1966, the "choateness doctrine" is recognized in this circuit as a valid legal principle, not abrogated by the Tax Lien Act.

Our conclusion that the "choateness doctrine" has continued validity under the Tax Lien Act is buttressed by the Supreme Court's opinion in United States v. Kimbell Foods, Inc., 440 U.S. 715, 99 S.Ct. 1448, 59 L.Ed.2d 711 (1979). In *Kimbell Foods,* the Court held that the "choateness doctrine" did not apply in determining priority between the government's *contractual* liens arising from federal loan programs and private liens. Although the holding of *Kimbell Foods* does not directly affect our resolution of this case, the Court emphasized the critical distinction between a *contractual* lien arising from a government loan program and a government *tax* lien:

> "That collection of taxes is vital to the functioning, indeed existence, of government cannot be denied.... Congress recognized as much over 100 years ago when it authorized creation of federal tax liens.... *The importance of securing adequate revenues to discharge national obligations justifies the extraordinary priority accorded federal tax liens through the choateness and first-in-time doctrines.*"

Id. at 734, 99 S.Ct. at 1461 (emphasis added) (citations omitted).

We conclude that the "choateness doctrine" is a valid legal principle in determining the priority between the government's tax lien in Eventide Homes' accounts receivable and the plaintiff's security interest in the same accounts receivable. Having reached this conclusion, we consider only briefly the plaintiff's additional arguments. The plaintiff argues that its security interest in Eventide Homes' accounts receivable was in fact "choate" prior to September 17, 1979 when the government filed its first notice of tax lien. However, as we indicated in *Sgro,* a security interest in accounts receivable does not become "choate" until the accounts receivable actually come into existence, that is, at the time the services giving rise to the accounts receivable are performed. . . .

. . . The judgment of the district court is AFFIRMED.

SECTION 6.   IS SECURED CREDIT EFFICIENT?

Introduction. Over the past two decades, several legal scholars have debated whether the institution of secured credit is "efficient" (as that term is used by economists). Now that we have studied many of the effects of secured credit under current law—in particular, the priority rules and the favored treatment afforded to secured claims in bankruptcy—we can consider these effects in the context of this debate.

The question whether security interests are efficient is a positive, not a normative, inquiry. However, the literature reflects strong undercurrents of a normative debate as well. In particular, whether a legal regime that respects—indeed, fosters—secured transactions should be retained if it is found to be inefficient clearly is a normative question. And that question lies at (or just below) the surface in much of the commentary. (Not surprisingly, some of the participants demonstrate a normative preference for economically efficient legal rules.)

In concluding his important article on the security interest debate, Professor Paul Shupack wrote:

> This Article has shown that there is a social gain from secured transactions, which must be set off against their social cost. Secured transactions have an economic function other than to act as conduits for the transfer of wealth from ignorant and involuntary creditors to shrewd debtors and creditors. Knowing whether that economic function outweighs the social harm that secured transactions can cause requires information, not only about the economy at large, but also about legal rules that have the effect of constraining secured creditors from taking full advantage of their capacity to use these normatively suspect transactions for their own benefit.

> Solving the puzzle of secured transactions from the initial perspective of a perfect market does not tell us much about secured transactions. Identifying efficiency gains within the abstract model does not guarantee that those efficiency gains, though present in every secured transaction, are in reality the motivation for every secured transaction.

This inability to move from the model to reality means that the explanation of how secured transactions are, and might be, efficient has little to say about the social structures built around secured transactions. Showing that secured transactions *can* be efficient justifies only that they *might* exist. The forms in which they exist depend upon a series of empirical claims, into which the model can give little insight. Solving the puzzle of secured transactions, therefore, offers surprisingly little help in answering the important public policy questions surrounding their creation and use in the real world.

Shupack, Solving the Puzzle of Secured Transactions, 41 Rutgers L. Rev. 1067, 1124 (1989).

The following excerpts from Dean Robert E. Scott's article illustrate much of the flavor and substance of the debate, in particular during the years following Professor Shupack's article.

Scott, The Truth About Secured Financing
82 Cornell L. Rev.1436, 1437, 1447–50, 1451,1453–61 (1997).

The debate over the social value of secured credit (and the appropriate priority for secured claims in bankruptcy) is entering its nineteenth year. Yet the continuing publication of succeeding generations of articles exploring the topic have yielded precious little in the way of an emerging scholarly consensus about the nature and function of secured credit. Put simply, we still do not have a theory of finance that explains why firms sometimes (but not always) issue secured debt rather than unsecured debt or equity. Moreover (and perhaps because of the lack of any plausible general theory), we lack any persuasive empirical data to predict whether, in any particular case, a later security-financed project will generate sufficient returns to offset any reduction in the value (i.e., the bankruptcy share) of prior unsecured claims.

* * *

II

WHAT WE DO (AND DO NOT) KNOW ABOUT SECURED DEBT

* * * The debate [concerning the social value of secured credit] persists with relatively small increments of progress largely because participants are asking fundamentally different questions. It is not that either side is wrong; rather it is that both sides are guilty of incomplete analyses. In truth, we cannot solve the puzzle of secured credit until we have both a coherent theory of finance that explains the welfare benefits of security and a database (derived from observation) that describes the patterns of security that actually exist in the world. Only then can we evaluate the regulatory regime of Article 9 and the Bankruptcy Code in order to make normative recommendations to policymakers. * * *

A.   The Search for a Theory of Secured Finance

* * * The question at the core of the secured financing puzzle is not whether a given security-financed project is efficient for a firm to pursue. The answer to that question is quite clear: security-financed projects are efficient when the reduction in the expected bankruptcy share of prior creditors is less than the expected returns to the firm from the financed project. This question, however, is tangential to the security debate. Rather, the fundamental theoretical question requires a comparison between project financing with security and project financing without security. Thus the core question remains: why and when does the *method of financing* increase the net revenues from any positive value project the firm elects to pursue?

1.   A Promising Beginning: Using Leverage to Respond to the Problem of Risk Alteration

* * * Virtually all the explanations for the efficiencies of secured financing focus on the ways in which secured credit can better control agency costs within the firm by reducing conflicts of interest between the debtor's managers (representing the residual equity claimants) and the firm's debt holders. Four main types of conflict (commonly designated as "debtor misbehavior") have been identified. Of these, the twin problems of overinvestment (or risk alteration) and underinvestment are the most promising candidates for explaining the welfare benefits of secured financing.

The risk alteration conflict has the most general application. Debt is, in many cases, an optimal means of financing new projects that add value to the firm. However, debt carries as well the potential conflict of risk alteration: there is an incentive for the firm's managers, who represent residual equity interests, to engage in higher-risk projects than they would if they bore the full share of the down-side risk of project failure. If the project succeeds, the equity interests capture all the gains, but if the project fails, the losses are shared with the debtholders. The debt cushion, in other words, can lead to excessively risky investments.

* * * [I]f one method of financing offers the parties a superior mechanism for ameliorating the risk alteration problem, it is in the interests of all to select the cost minimizing alternative. There are plausible reasons, supported by some substantial empirical data, to believe that secured financing is superior to other financing alternatives in reducing the costs of risk alteration by permitting the debtor credibly to commit not to pursue inferior higher-risk projects. The empirical data suggests that the comparative advantage of security derives principally for the singular advantages of leverage. By taking a security interest in specific assets of the debtor, the secured creditor enjoys rights of foreclosure upon default that can inflict substantial costs on the debtor's business. The leverage of secured financing

reduces the enforcement costs of loan covenants that forbid the debtor from incurring additional debt without permission.

Precisely how does security function to reduce the costs of financial contracts? The contractual relationship between debtor and creditor is a relational contract in which one party performs a service for another. A key goal in the regulation of such agency relationships is to encourage the agent to serve its principal's interests as well as its own. Several characteristics of agency relationships contribute to the risk of self-interested actions. In contrast to performance under a simple contingent contract, the agent's [debtor's] performance is complex and not readily reducible to specific obligations. Satisfactory performance demands considerable decisionmaking discretion, and monitoring the quality of the agent's performance may be difficult. The objective for the parties in structuring the optimal financial contract is, first, to encourage the debtor to take the creditor's interests properly into account in making decisions, and second, to facilitate detection of its failure to do so.

The means used to achieve the desired goals are usefully grouped into two broad categories. Monitoring arrangements allow the creditor to supervise the debtor's actions so as to detect and sanction conduct, such as risk alteration, in pursuit of selfish ends. Bonding arrangements, on the other hand, align the interest of the debtor with that of the creditor through self-limiting constraints that serve a precommitment function. Although they constrain the debtor's behavior, bonding arrangements will be desired equally by both debtors and creditors, to the extent that they substitute for even more costly monitoring efforts. Thus, a debtor is motivated to accept the imposition of foreclosure sanctions upon default, thereby providing assurance to a creditor that the debtor will not act contrary to the creditor's ends. In sum, the unique features of security function as a highly effective bonding mechanism to ensure faithful compliance with the terms of the financial contract. By offering its assets as a hostage, the debtor invites the sanction of foreclosure should it breach the terms of the agreement.

* * *

Thus, security solves a contracting problem for the parties by allowing them to "design verifiability" in the contract. Although the financer cannot verify that a subsequent investment is inefficient, it can observe such action. The ability to foreclose on the collateral once an inefficient investment decision is observed precludes the necessity of verifying that action to a court. In an important sense, the contract becomes self-enforcing.

* * *

2. Using Leverage to Reduce Underinvestment Conflicts

The risk alteration conflict is ubiquitous and occurs in all debt contracts. There is a final conflict that is peculiar to exclusive financing arrangements, and for which secured financing offers similar advantages over financing alternatives. The problem of underinvestment occurs when a debtor, having recouped a portion of its investment in a joint venture with a creditor, siphons off its resources to other projects from which it will reap more of the gain. The debtor will act in this manner even if further effort in the joint venture would enhance the firm's net worth. Once again, the leverage offered by a security interest in the debtor's assets gives a secured creditor the ability credibly to threaten sanctions if it discovers that the debtor is undertaking inadequate efforts to fully develop the financed project.

A wrap-around security interest (or "floating lien") offers several advantages to the creditor and debtor seeking to cement an exclusive financing relationship. The leverage of security has the effect of giving the creditor an economic hostage to ensure the debtor's faithful performance of the financed project. If the debtor defaults on any of the covenants in the financial contract, the creditor retains the power to foreclose and take operational control of the assets. The debtor agrees to this arrangement because there are significant costs to the creditor in exercising the power of foreclosure that deter frivolous or bad faith actions by the creditor. The effectiveness of the debtor's bond encourages the creditor, in turn, to provide financial management and counseling to enhance the general business prospects for the debtor. The creditor cannot provide these valuable services as cheaply unless it can structure the relationship so as to capture the returns from its efforts. Secured financing ensures that the debtor will heed the creditor's financial advice. Once again, however, the benefits of leverage are not cost-free. Debtors must submit to substantial administrative supervision that imposes significant burdens on the firms' decisionmaking processes.

Justifying secured financing as a uniquely effective means of controlling the conflicts of interest generated by risk alteration and underinvestment seems quite promising as a normative theory of finance. The theory claims that secured debt is able to reduce agency costs for firms financing positive value projects and thus returns benefits to the firm that other financing alternatives could not capture. The theory recognizes, however, that the leverage benefits of security carry offsetting costs. Thus, it does not predict that secured credit would be ubiquitous. Rather, it predicts that parties to financial contracts will choose this method of financing in those contexts where the expected benefits from leverage exceed the costs. To the extent, then, that the net returns inform value from this method of financing are greater than those obtainable from other methods of financing the project, and exceed any reduction in the bankruptcy share of unsecured creditors, secured credit is Kaldor–Hicks efficient.

3. *Testing the Theory of Leverage Against the Rules of Article 9*

The first test of any theory of secured financing requires that the theory be roughly congruent with the priority scheme that is institutionalized in Article 9. As Hideki Kanda and Saul Levmore have shown, we can rationalize many of the priority rules of Article 9 as attempts to balance the advantages and disadvantages of using security to ameliorate the agency costs of risk alteration. Specifically, we can understand the first-in-time priority granted to perfected secured creditors over prior-in-time unsecured creditors, and the superpriority granted to both subsequent purchase money security interests and subsequent purchasers of chattel paper over prior-in-time perfected secured creditors, as means of metering subsequent new money financing.

The first-in-time priority granted to secured claims by the terms of Article 9 can be explained as a cost-effective mechanism for preventing risk alterations that would disadvantage prior creditors. * * *

Nevertheless, the first-in-time rule is something of a blunt instrument. Using security as a hostage may control the debtor's incentives, but it also sets in motion a parallel set of conflicts involving the creditor's incentives. Fully protected by the hostage of security, creditors are motivated to be excessively cautious in refusing to permit subsequent financing that would enhance total returns to the firm. Thus, the first-in-time rule must be tempered with a scheme of superpriorities that offer the debtor an escape hatch to guard against creditor myopia. Hence, purchase money security interests and subsequent purchasers of chattel paper are granted priority over prior-in-time secured creditors as a means of balancing the effects of using assets as hostages. As Kanda and Levmore suggest, therefore, one can explain the prominent contours of the priority system in Article 9 largely as a crude, but effective, compromise between the advantages and disadvantages of new money financing.

The Kanda and Levmore explanation leaves one salient feature of Article 9 unexplained: the institutionalization of the floating lien. Here, the underinvestment problem is a useful supplement. Some classes of debtors (the current estimate is twenty-six percent of secured claims) choose to enter into exclusive financing relationships with creditors. For certain classes of debtors, these long term relationships offer singular advantages in terms of providing financial counseling and general business guidance. For those firms that find exclusive financing optimal, the problem of underinvestment is peculiarly salient. Once the debtor and creditor enter into these kinds of joint ventures, the financing creditor is properly concerned about a further conflict: the motivation that the debtor may have to pursue other projects through which it can capture a greater share of the returns. The unique priority Article 9 grants to the floating lien general creditor in all the debtor's present and future assets appears to be a sensible method of using the same hostage device to solve the underinvestment problem that exclusive financing arrangements generate. In a world without secured credit, these arrangements might proceed only at greater cost, and some parties would not pursue otherwise beneficial exclusive financing arrangements.

For certain debtors, then, the blanket priority Article 9 gives to the floating lien secured creditor invites the creditor to become a joint venturer in the business opportunity. Thereafter, the creditor has an incentive to provide financial counseling and management advice to the debtor firm and, just as importantly, has the leverage to ensure that firm acts on the advice. These benefits accrue to all parties with claims against the firm to the extent that they enhance the returns from financed projects.

In sum, it is fair to conclude that a regime that privileges secured credit *may* enhance social welfare and that the scheme of priorities institutionalized in Article 9 is roughly congruent with plausible explanations of the comparative advantages of secured financing over other financing alternatives.

B.   Theory v. Practice: Explaining Observed Patterns of Secured Debt

The central problem with this (and any other) theory of secured financing is the inconsistency between the predictions of the theory and observations of the actual patterns of secured financing that exist in the world. The leverage theory would predict that secured credit, although not ubiquitous (because it entails substantial costs), would nonetheless be observed in all segments of the credit market. This is because the agency problems upon which the theory rests are common to firms of all types, large and small, stable and volatile. Here, however, the empirical evidence casts substantial doubt on the efficacy of any agency cost explanation to explain fully the puzzle of secured debt. In a recent study of over one million business loans, Allen Berger and Gregory Udell concluded that the issuance of secured debt positively correlates to both the riskiness of the project and the financial volatility of the debtor. This study confirms the evidence from field studies that secured debt remains, to this day, a method of financing that dominates second-class markets as the "poor man's" means of obtaining credit. Although security is observed in large and small firms, the single most salient correlation is the relative absence of secured credit from the balance sheets of most financially sound companies.

Why should that be? Ron Mann's field study suggests that, for many debtors, the substantial administrative costs of submitting to creditor monitoring and supervision outweigh the efficiency benefits of leverage. Most debtors and creditors see these costs as sufficiently high such that the decision to grant security can be justified only when the efficiency benefits of leverage work in combination with the ability of the creditor to use that same leverage to improve its probability of repayment vis-a-vis other creditors. The leverage the secured creditor can use to reduce the conflicts stemming from risk alteration is also available to increase the probability of repayment of the secured creditor's debt.

Let me hasten to note that neither Mann nor his subjects seem to recognize the powerful theoretical implications of this data. Indeed, Mann seems to believe that his work provides some support for the grant of full priority to secured creditors in bankruptcy. But, if these field observations accurately reflect the justifications for issuing secured debt, they clearly imply that the efficiency benefits of security are generally insufficient to justify the substantial administrative costs occasioned by loss of control and flexibility in decisionmaking. Only when those social benefits combine with a private benefit—the reduction in the issuing creditor's risk of nonpayment—will a secured loan be cost-justified.

A moment's reflection reveals the problem: this private benefit is redistributional. The only way that a creditor can increase the probability of repayment out of a fixed pool of assets is by insuring that its debt will be preferred over others. The risk of nonpayment arises when the total amount of creditors' claims exceeds the value of the debtor's assets. Thus, any increase that leverage can generate in the probability of repayment of a secured creditor produces a corresponding reduction in the probability of repayment of other creditors' claims.

Even though secured debt is perceived as carrying the singular benefit of increasing the probability of repayment, financing parties understand it as an extremely crude device. Because providing assets as hostages imposes corresponding risks of creditor misbehavior, Mann reports that creditors and debtors are reluctant to use security except where significant reductions in nonpayment risks supplement its efficiency advantages. In other words, when the ex ante risk of nonpayment is significant, the redistributional benefits derived from leverage offer the additional advantages that justify the costs of using secured financing. Mann's analysis thus provides a coherent account for the persistent pattern of secured debt issued primarily by firms with unproven track records or firms that are financially volatile. For financially stable firms, secured debt remains unattractive presumably because the risk of nonpayment is trivial and the efficiency benefits of security are inadequate, standing alone, to justify the substantial costs.

C. Market Imperfections that Support the Redistributional
     Story: The Nonadjustment Phenomenon

It is dangerous, of course, to draw too many conclusions from observations by market participants. Perceptions by debtors and creditors that secured credit is cost-justified only when the redistributional benefits of leverage are substantial may not reflect the underlying economic reality. Thus, the related question recurs: if the market for credit is competitive, would not increases in the costs of extending credit experienced by unsecured creditors, whom secured debt disadvantages, be reflected in higher interest charges, and thus, in the debtor's total interest bill? Many have long recognized that nonconsensual creditors—such as warranty claimants and tort claimants—can recover only fixed-rate interest charges form debtors and would not be able to adjust to the presence of secured debt. But surely, this relatively small group of creditors cannot drive the institution of secured finance?

Lucian Bebchuk and Jesse Fried have offered the most promising explanation for why debtors do not internalize the redistributional effects of secured credit. Bebchuk and Fried explain the long term persistence of important classes of consensual creditors as "non-adjusting" creditors. They rely essentially on a transaction-costs argument to explain why prior-in-time consensual unsecured creditors (even those with large claims) and all consensual creditors with small claims would not rationally adjust to the increased risk occasioned by a particular debtor's decision to issue secured debt. If the cost of designing and enforcing adjustable rate provisions is too high, a rational creditor will assign an average value to the heightened risk of nonpayment, a value that is not sensitive to the lending patterns of the particular debtor. Any one of the classes of creditors Bebchuk and Fried identify may be insufficiently large to account for the redistributional effects of security. However, in combination, the presence of large numbers of creditors who either cannot or do not rationally choose to adjust to the increased risk of secured debt offers a strong market-based explanation for why debtors may systematically fail to internalize the redistributional costs of security.

Bebchuk and Fried emphasize the efficiency implications of nonadjustment. It may well be that nonadjusting consensual creditors who are repeat players are fully compensated for the increased risks of doing business in competition with secured debt. Nevertheless, the redistributional costs of security are independent of any fairness arguments that might be advanced in favor of involuntary or single-play participants in credit markets. The negative externalities that nonadjustment generates will skew the debtor's incentives in important respects. To the extent that debtors and secured creditors do not internalize the costs of secured credit, the debtor's investment decisions are skewed. Debtors will issue more secured debt than would be issued in a world where the contracting parties appreciated all the costs and benefits. This inefficiency leads to underutilization of other financing alternatives that might better enhance the returns from financing positive-value projects.

D. The "Discontinuity Assumption": Secured Debt as the Only Method of Financing Positive–Value Projects

Several commentators have mounted a strong defense of secured credit that posits a class of debtors with positive value financing projects that is unable to secure financing except by issuing secured debt. In other words, the claim goes, there is a discontinuity in the financing alternatives that are typically available to solvent debtors with positive-value projects. This claim was advanced some years ago by Homer Kripke and subsequently by Charles Mooney and Steve Harris. Most recently, Steven Schwarcz has argued that solvent debtors who confront a "liquidity crisis" are often unable to finance their projects or to fully realize the benefits from existing projects without new money that debtors can obtain on the market only by issuing secured debt. Schwarcz, along with Kripke and Harris and Mooney, support this "discontinuity assumption" by reference to experience and to (unsystematic) field studies.

The discontinuity assumption is the linchpin of the argument for preserving full priority for secured credit. From the assumption that for many debtors new money financing can be obtained only by offering security, it follows that the security-financed project that offers a greater return to the firm than any corresponding reduction in bankruptcy share to unsecured creditors is Kaldor–Hicks efficient. Indeed, the efficiency problem of nonadjusting creditors largely disappears. Because using security to finance these projects is efficient, it follows that the misinvestment and precaution concerns Bebchuk and Fried raise are nonexistent. A redistributional issue remains, of course, but even there one can advance the argument that most nonadjusting creditors are fully compensated in the enhanced returns from projects that creditors could not pursue but for security. Thus, given the assumption, the burden of proof on the empirical question should shift to those who wish to constrain the choices market actors would otherwise select. The normative implication follows: secured claims that facilitate positive value projects should be accorded full priority in bankruptcy.

But, of course, nothing is as easy as it seems. The discontinuity assumption is not a theoretical claim about the efficiency of secured debt. Rather, it is an empirical claim that, given a world with secured credit, and given the reasons why debtors and creditors choose to finance new money with security, whatever those reasons happen to be, some positive-value projects can be financed only with security. This is not to say that, in a world without secured credit (or a world that granted reduced priority to secured claims), unsecured debt or equity would not finance these positive-value projects. Nor does it suggest that all (or even most) of the security-financed projects currently undertaken are efficient. Indeed, it is perfectly consistent with the discontinuity assumption, and with the evidence from field studies of existing patterns of secured financing, to assert that these liquidity-crisis projects demand security primarily for its redistributional effects rather than its efficiencies. The most plausible reason why solvent, high-risk debtors can issue only secured debt is that the leverage security provides can substantially reduce the risk of nonpayment for the secured creditor. It is unlikely, after all, that new money secured financing of viable, high-risk debtors is primarily aimed at controlling risk alteration or underinvestment conflicts.

Thus, the discontinuity assumption merely begs the question. Even if true, it tells us what we already know from observation: secured credit is issued for a number of complex reasons that all center on the unique advantage of leverage to the secured creditor. To some extent, that leverage seems to be a singularly useful means of reducing conflicts of interest inherent in financial contracting relationships. These benefits are efficiency enhancing. To some degree, however, that leverage also appears to be a singularly useful means of enhancing the creditor's probability of repayment relative to other creditors. If, as seems plausible, some (or many) of these other creditors do not adjust to this reduction in bankruptcy share, there is a redistributional benefit to the creditor that the debtor does not fully internalize in assessing its total interest bill. This, then, would lead to some inefficient uses of security (as well as raise problems of distributional fairness). The question, in short, is simple: What are the relative values of these two offsetting effects? At this point we do not have a clue.

———

In a 1994 article, Professors Harris and Mooney raised fundamental questions about the utility and ground rules of the security interest debate. Consider the following:

The securing of debt is similar to a vast array of other voluntary transactions in which a debtor may dispose of its property. This Section compares two other transactions—the payment of debt and the sale of assets—to secured loans. As we shall see, payments and asset sales are like secured loans in that they may impose costs on unsecured creditors that exceed any attendant benefits. But, also like secured loans, these other transactions may redound to the net benefit of unsecured creditors. Many of the questions about secured transactions that the contributors to the Efficiency Literature and the adherents to Sympathetic Legal Studies have raised also might be raised with respect to payments and asset sales. Curiously, they have not been.

Consider the payment by a solvent debtor (. . . "D") of a debt owed to an unsecured creditor ("UC–1"), leaving another unsecured creditor ("UC–2") unpaid. Immediately after the payment (at T_0), holding other factors constant, UC–2's expected recovery actually will increase upon D's payment to UC–1 at T_0. This outcome merely recognizes that the incurrence of the debt to UC–1 itself exposed existing creditors (here, UC–2) to a risk of a lower distribution in the event of future insolvency; payment to UC–1 simply puts matters where they were just prior to UC–1's extension of credit. The same result would occur if, instead of paying UC–1, D secured UC–1's claim with collateral that did not decline in value or declined proportionately less than the unencumbered assets; that is, UC–2 would be better off if D secured UC–1's claim than if it did not.

Just as a debtor's receipt of new credit may work to the *advantage* of the debtor's existing creditors by reducing the risk of default, so D's loss of the use of the assets transferred to UC–1 may *disadvantage* UC–2 by increasing the risk of default. Securing, rather than paying, UC–1 would leave the assets available for D's use and would seem to be likely to increase the risk of default to a lesser extent than payment would (or perhaps not at all). Just as one needs additional information to determine whether UC–2 is better off if D pays UC–1 at $T|SUB-SCRIPT\text{\OE}0|*SUBSCRIPT\text{\OE}$ rather than leave UC–1 unpaid, so one cannot determine whether UC–2 is better off if D secures UC–1's claim rather than pay it. Both determinations turn on facts that cannot be known in the abstract, including the extent to which any given transaction affects the risk of default and (in the case where D gives security) the extent to which UC–1's collateral declines in value relative to D's unencumbered assets.

Another useful means of considering how a payment to one unsecured creditor affects other unsecured creditors is to examine the consequences of D's decision to pay UC–1 *instead of* paying UC–2. By virtue of that decision, UC–1 received 100% of its claim at T_0, leaving UC–2 to receive only a fraction of its claim in liquidation at T_1. (A similar, but less pronounced, effect would result from D's decision to give security to SP for a new loan instead of paying or securing an existing creditor.) The law does, of course, respect payments by solvent debtors to their creditors even in the absence of pro rata payments to other creditors. As far as we know, no one has suggested that fraudulent transfer law should reach so far as to invalidate such payments.

Payment of an antecedent debt by an *insolvent* debtor is another matter. Any payment at T_0 clearly reduces the pool of assets available to the remaining unsecured creditors at that time and, if we hold constant the probability of default, thereby transfers wealth to the preferred creditor from the non-preferred creditors. Giving security for an antecedent debt has the same effect. At T_1 the remaining unsecured creditors will receive less than they would have received had the preferential transfer not been made. Both transactions are potentially vulnerable as preferences under Bankruptcy Code § 547, which generally does not distinguish between payments and transfers as security. But, because the grant of a security interest does not necessarily deplete the assets available for use by the debtor, a preferential transfer of security may well have a less deleterious effect on the expected recovery of other creditors than would a preferential payment.

The foregoing suggests that, from the perspective of UC–2, the consequences of D's making a payment to UC–1 are indeterminate. The expected value of UC–2's recovery might increase; it might decrease. The same would be true if D were to secure its debt to UC–1: One cannot ascertain the implications of the transaction for UC–2 *a priori*.

Now consider the consequences to existing creditors (UC–1 and UC–2) of D's selling an asset. Whether the expected return to creditors will increase or decrease depends on whether D makes more productive use of the cash received or of the asset sold. The grant of security for a new loan is quite similar to the sale of property; in both cases, D receives cash and parts with an asset. Of course, there are differences between a cash sale at T_0, on one hand, and giving security to SP for a new loan at T_0, on the other. One such difference arises from the possibility that at T_1 the unpaid and now undersecured SP may assert a deficiency claim that competes with the claims of UC–1 and UC–2 against a now insolvent D. Holding everything else constant, the secured transaction with SP reduces the expected return of the other creditors. In contrast, the cash seller to D is out of the picture at T_1 and does not hold a competing claim in an insolvency proceeding.

But, once again, the distributive effects in insolvency are only part of the story. In the cash sale D would lose the use of the asset sold, whereas in the secured loan D normally retains the use and possession of the collateral as well as the proceeds of the loan. D's retention of the use, possession, and control of collateral has value—value that would not be available if a buyer carries the collateral away. This additional value typically is reflected in the difference between the amount of the secured loan (which is the measure of the secured creditor's property interest in the collateral) and the (presumably greater) value of the collateral. Thus, unlike a seller, a debtor who grants a security interest enjoys more than the value represented by the cash it receives in the transaction. The debtor's retention of the additional value represented by the continued right to use, possess, and control the collateral may reduce the risk of default, perhaps enough to offset the reduction in the expected recovery of creditors' claims that otherwise would occur.

Cash payments, purchases, and sales, like secured loans, can result in wealth transfers from the unsecured creditors of a buyer or seller and can expose the unsecured creditors to additional risk, although these transactions do not necessarily do so. Thus, one cannot develop a plausible hypothesis for questioning the utility or equity of security interests on distributional grounds involving transfers of wealth, such as the reduction of the pool of assets remaining for unsecured creditors or the present value of remaining unsecured claims, unless one also questions, on similar grounds, other transactions such as payments, sales, and purchases. Consequently, one cannot view the creation of effective security interests with suspicion on those grounds unless one also questions the general effectiveness of these transactions.

Harris & Mooney, A Property–Based Theory of Security Interests: Taking Debtors' Choices Seriously, 80 Va. L. Rev. 2021, 2037–41 (1994).

NOTE ON THE EFFICIENCY DEBATE AND A PROPOSAL FOR RADICAL CHANGE

In Chapter 6, Section 1, supra, we observed:

[F]actors such as disparities in bargaining power and information, profit margins of sellers of goods and providers of services on unsecured credit, the relative size and duration of credit extensions, the costs of creating secured financings, disparities among creditors in their ability to monitor the debtor's financial activities and use of collateral, and market competition all serve to explain current financing patterns, ... which involve a mix of secured and unsecured credit.

... A positive explanation of why debtors sometimes give and creditors sometimes take secured credit under current law does not provide a normative justification for the advantages the current legal regime affords to secured claims.

Given what Professor Shupack calls the "transactional efficiency" of current law that facilitates the creation of effective security interests, is it difficult to understand why debtors sometimes give security in order to obtain credit and sometimes do not? Remember that the question whether there is an efficiency (or other) "normative" justification for our system of secured transactions underlies and drives the efficiency debate. That question is quite different from the question of why security is in fact given under the current regime. (Some of the participants in the debate have failed, at times, to keep this distinction in mind.) Professor Shupack systematically relaxed the economists' "perfect market" assumptions until he discovered examples of secured transactions that were "Kaldor–Hicks efficient"—i.e., the gains of the winners exceed in the aggregate the losses of the losers. Do examples of efficient secured lending under current rules necessarily mean that those rules should be retained intact?

Dean Scott concluded that "we do not have a clue" as to how to balance the "offsetting effects" of a legal regime (like Article 9) that facilitates secured credit. Scott, 82 Cornell L.Rev. at 1461. Assuming that he is correct, what lessons should lawmakers glean from the debate over security? In concluding his article, Dean Scott criticized the *process* employed by "private legislatures," such as The American Law Institute and the National Conference of Commissioners on Uniform State Laws (co-sponsors of the UCC). He argued that "admirably clear, bright-line rules so distinctively present in Article 9 ... [are] strong evidence that a dominant interest group has influenced the process." Id. at 1463. In contrast, Dean Scott hails the benefits of "log-rolling" and hearings before state legislators to afford lawmakers better information, and he laments the "poor quality of information the voters in the private legislature possess." Id. at 1464. Does it seem likely to you that the members of 50 state legislatures would possess a better quality of information about secured credit than that presented to The American Law Institute and the National Conference of Commissioners on Uniform State Laws during the process of drafting and revising Article 9? As a thought experiment, consider whether a typical state legislator would be likely to grasp the analysis of secured financing presented in Dean Scott's article.

One might consider searching for any efficiency gains in moving from current law to a world that would not honor consensual security interests in personal property. Consider how that world would look. Would judicial liens be retained? Presumably *sales* and *exchanges* of property would be allowed. But would a sale for cash and a lease-back of equipment be honored (perhaps with a public notice requirement)? Would abolishing security interests put too much strain on already fuzzy lines between secured transactions and other kinds of dispositions of interests in property? Does this exercise suggest that respecting secured transactions can be seen as merely one genre of a more general principle of respect for the alienability of property? In thinking about how and where one might draw the line, consider the spectrum from a discrete sale of specifically identified receivables to a security interest in virtually all of a debtor's existing and after-acquired personal property securing all existing and future obligations to a secured party.

Do you find the indeterminacy of Shupack's, Scott's, and Harris & Mooney's conclusions unsatisfying? Assuming, as Professor Shupack concludes, that there can be no "general theory" of secured credit that consistently predicts behavior, does that mean that the participants in the debate have wasted their time (and ours)?

In an earlier article, Dean Scott recognized that "[i]t is unlikely that a single explanation can rationalize all of these various forms of security." Scott, A Relational Theory of Secured Financing, 86 Colum.L.Rev. 901, 912 (1986). However, theoretical explorations of legal institutions can accomplish much even if no general theory emerges. For example, the efficiency debate has served to identify areas in need of further empirical research and those where empirical research (even if "necessary") would be largely impossible. It has served to heighten sensitivities to the relationship between finance theory and the legal rules that regulate security interests and priorities in bankruptcy. And it has underscored the enormous variety of transactions (secured and unsecured) that are affected by Article 9.

Professor Alan Schwartz seems to have been the most frequent participant in the earlier years of the efficiency debate. In one offering, he stepped beyond consideration of secured credit as we know it. Although he remained puzzled about why security is given under the current regime, he nonetheless recommended that the decisionmakers consider making radical changes to the structure of the Article 9 priority scheme. Schwartz, A Theory of Loan Priorities, 18 J. Legal Stud. 209, 247 (1989). Professor Schwartz acknowledged that "[t]ractability is not the same thing as moral acceptability," but he concluded that his proposal's "central results serve the most affected parties better in some cases, and as well in others, as existing law does, without contradicting the equality norm in obviously unacceptable fashion. There is a prima facie case for amending current law to realize such results." Id. at 260. In suggesting consideration of an actual change in current law, Professor Schwartz set himself apart from most other participants in the academic literature. Consider Professor Schwartz's "prima facie case."

In his article Professor Schwartz makes three claims. First, he claims that the statutory priority scheme should mirror the priorities that would be reflected in a contract between a borrower and its "initial financer." (He defines "initial financer" as "the first creditor that made a substantial loan that would be outstanding for a nontrivial time period"—i.e., *not* a typical unsecured trade creditor who is supposed to be paid within 30 to 45 days.) Second, if borrowers and initial financers would agree to confer a first priority on the initial financer's claim, then Professor Schwartz argues that this should be the legal priority rule even if the initial financers are unsecured and even if they give no public notice of their claim. Third, he claims (and endeavors to demonstrate with an economic model) that "the optimal priority contract—the typical acceptable priority proposal—actually would rank the initial financer first, whether it is secured or not." Id. at 211.

Professor Schwartz's priority scheme would rank the creditors of an insolvent debtor as follows:

> 1. Secured purchase money lenders, if any exist, but only to the extent permitted in the loan contract between the debtor and initial financer. Later credit sellers should not be presumed to be secured but must actually take purchase-money security interests. This is because the parties to initial loan contracts would not subordinate the financer to all later sellers.

> 2. Financers in the order in which they appear, whether secured or not. This status should be a consequence of the enactment of the modified ... [first in time] rule as the legal priority scheme and thus should obtain unless the parties contract out.

> 3. Nonpurchase-money creditors who are not financers but who take security in particular assets rank ahead of later creditors with respect to these assets.

> 4. Trade and other small creditors take pro rata with each other and with any financers that appeared after these creditors' claims arose. The costs of ranking in order of appearance the numerous creditors of an insolvent debtor would probably exceed any gains. Consistent with this view, there is no evidence that actual trade and other creditors contract for particular priority positions (apart from the creditors who take purchase-money security interests).

Id. at 248. Professor Schwartz also would abolish the priority for chattel paper purchasers under F9–308 (R9–330) as well as the PMSI priority for inventory under F9–312(3) (R9–324(b)). Id. at 250–54. (The article never mentions real property. One wonders if the initial financers in Professor Schwartz's world would have claims senior to those of a first mortgagee of real property.)

Note that Professor Schwartz's system creates a de facto "secret lien" in favor of earlier-in-time financers. He dismisses the Article 9 filing system as unnecessary for providing information and ranking priorities, because a private information system—debtor disclosure—is cheaper; "good debtors" will be motivated to give an accurate account of their debts. Of course, bad debtors would have the opposite motivation, but Professor Schwartz reasons that creditors will simply refuse credit until prospective debtors prove the negative—i.e., that there are no earlier-in-time financers. Moreover, he argues, collateral does not seem to be all that important to secured lenders anyway and secured lenders make the same credit investigations as do unsecured creditors. Id. at 222. However, he concludes that the filing system should be retained to protect *buyers* from earlier-in-time security interests and he also would allow buyers to take ahead of earlier-in-time financers. Id. at 223.

In some ways Professor Schwartz's proposal is reminiscent of a proposal that the "public files should be scrapped," which was made by the original Reporters who drafted Article 9. 1 Gilmore, Security § 15.1, at 464. Professor Gilmore wrote of this proposal:

> The key to the proposal was the imposition of a duty on a secured party to use due diligence to see that his debtor's financial statements made full disclosure of the security interest;.... The details of the proposal were never reduced to statutory language since the Reporters were unable to convince anyone of the soundness of their position, and the proposal was shortly abandoned.

Id. Professor Schwartz seems to have expanded the idea underlying the earlier proposal and dispensed with the need for a security agreement as well.

If, as Professor Schwartz believes, initial financers typically extract loan agreement covenants that restrict borrowers' rights to incur later indebtedness, and if borrowers in fact typically comply with those covenants, why adopt a new scheme? Why worry about the "optimal priority contract" when the *actual* priority contract typically controls? Professor Schwartz has ventured a partial answer to these questions (which must be answered if his proposals are not to become unglued) in a footnote:

> If a later lender is aware of the earlier contract restrictions, the lender may be liable for inducing breach of contract if it lends. Few such tort suits against later lenders are brought, apparently because knowledge of restrictive loan covenants is a necessary but not sufficient condition for tort liability; the later lender also must *induce* the breach rather than lend to a debtor that had already decided to breach. Most debtors that approach later lenders have already made the breach decision. Accordingly, this article assumes that the threat of tort liability does not discourage later lenders from dealing with debtors that are violating loan covenants.

Id. at 210 n. 5.

Professor Schwartz provides no support for his assumptions about the behavior of lenders and borrowers and about the law of tortious interference with contractual relations. Perhaps the reason that few suits against subsequent lenders are brought is that few later lenders in their right minds would dream of walking into the trap that Professor Schwartz has hypothesized. Almost invariably the default in the first lender's agreement would give it a right to accelerate its debt. And that default (or the acceleration) would almost invariably constitute a default under the later lender's new loan agreement. What lenders knowingly would lend into a situation like that?

Consider, also, the applicable legal liability rules. Professor Schwartz's assertion that the later lender would have nothing to fear of tort liability if the debtor had "already made the breach decision" is questionable. See Restatement (Second) of Torts § 766, comment *h* ("The rule stated in this Section applies to any intentional causation whether by inducement or otherwise. The essential thing is the intent to cause the result."), comment *j* ("The rule applies . . . to an interference that is incidental to the actor's independent purpose and desire but known to him to be a necessary consequence of his action.") (1977).

How does Professor Schwartz's "prima facie case" fare when tested against the background of fact and law?

CHAPTER 12

DEFAULT; ENFORCEMENT OF SECURITY INTERESTS

Introductory Note. The preceding Chapters focused primarily on the acquisition and perfection of security interests and the priority of competing claims to the collateral. For the most part, these issues become moot if the debtor pays the secured obligation.[1] Secured credit typically is extended with the expectation that the debtor *will* pay and that the secured party will not need to recover its claim from the collateral. A creditor's need to enforce its security interest typically is an indication that the credit transaction has failed.

Of course, transactions do fail and secured parties do find the need to turn their collateral into cash. This Chapter examines the rights and duties of a secured party who enforces a security interest. Section 1 deals with the scope of the secured party's right to take possession of collateral when the debtor is in default. Section 2 considers the right of a secured party to dispose of (e.g., sell) collateral and to apply the proceeds to the secured obligation. It also covers the effect of a secured party's noncompliance with its duties under Article 9. Section 3 addresses the implications of enforcement for certain third parties—secondary obligors (such as guarantors of the secured obligation), holders of competing security interests and other liens, and transferees from a secured party who disposes of collateral after default. Section 4, which deals with "redemption," examines the scope of the debtor's right to satisfy the secured obligation and recover the collateral before the secured party disposes of it. Section 5 then considers the enforcement of security interests in accounts and other rights to payment through "collections" from the account debtors or other enforcement of collateral. Finally, Section 6 deals with a secured party's acceptance of collateral in satisfaction of all or a portion of the secured obligation, sometimes called "strict foreclosure."

The term "foreclosure" is commonly used to refer to the process by which security interests are enforced against collateral, although the word appears only once in the text of Revised Article 9. Under pre-UCC personal property security law (as well as current real property law), the term "foreclosure" embraces the process by which the debtor's right to "redeem" the encumbered property is "foreclosed." R9–623 provides for the

---

1. Even if the debtor pays the secured obligation, questions of perfection and priority may be implicated if the debtor enters bankruptcy within the preference period. See BC 547; Chapter 10, Section 2, supra.

debtor's right to redeem collateral by paying in full the secured obligation at any time before the secured party has collected, disposed of, entered into a contract for the disposition of, or accepted collateral. Consistent with common parlance, these materials sometimes refer to "foreclosure," "foreclosure sale," and the like.

Most of the issues we have considered thus far involve three parties— the debtor, the secured party, and the holder of a competing claim to the collateral. Although the enforcement of a security interest sometimes affects the rights of third parties, more often only the debtor and secured party are involved. Questions of perfection and priority often are irrelevant; Part 6 of Revised Article 9 (the 9–600's) takes center stage. And, as we shall see, important legislation intended to protect consumers often supplements and modifies the rules of the UCC.

As you work through the materials in this Chapter, you would do well to keep in mind what is at stake. A security interest, you will recall, is a limited "interest in . . . *property*." R1–201(37). Unless the security interest has been perfected by possession or the debtor agrees otherwise, the secured party's right to exercise any dominion over collateral is contingent on the debtor's default. When the secured party does exercise dominion, it may do so only for the limited purpose of obtaining payment of the secured obligation. Indeed, the secured party's property interest is limited to the amount of the secured obligation (except in the cases of outright sales of accounts, chattel paper, payment intangibles, or promissory notes). These limitations on the interest that the secured party enjoys should not be overemphasized. Immediately upon the debtor's default, creditors who hold security interests can look to specific property to satisfy their claims; unsecured creditors cannot.

The debtor, too, holds a property interest, one that typically includes the right to possess, use, and otherwise exercise dominion over the collateral. The debtor also takes the risks and enjoys the benefits of changes in collateral value. Thus, enforcement implicates a delicate interplay of interests: Curtailing the secured party's dominion over the collateral can impair the security on which the transaction depends; taking the dominion over collateral away from the debtor can impair personal and economic well-being.

Perhaps for this reason, Part 6 of Revised Article 9 departs from the UCC's general emphasis on freedom of contract. See UCC 1–102(3) (the effect of UCC provisions generally may be varied by agreement). Part 6 contains a number of rules that cannot be waived or varied, even by sophisticated debtors who are represented by counsel. See R9–602. As you study these rules, you should consider whether the departures from freedom-of-contract principles are justified.

This Chapter focuses primarily on the rights and remedies of debtors and secured parties under Part 6 of Revised Article 9. Part 5 of Former Article 9 was an important and frequently litigated area of legal regulation. Although there is every reason to believe that this will continue to be so under Part 6, we have some optimism that the clarity offered by the revisions may reduce litigation. Keep in mind, however, that there is a large body of other, non-Article 9 law that features prominently in the relationship between creditors and debtors. Two aspects of this other law are particularly noteworthy. First, during the last twenty to twenty-five years a rapidly growing body of law, generally dubbed **lender liability**, has emerged. The courts have been developing myriad theories of liability, ranging from claims based on common-law fraud and duress to claims based on securities regulation statutes and claims based on the failure to observe duties of good faith and fair dealing.

Second, a secured creditor who engages in inequitable conduct in the course of enforcing its security interest runs the risk that its claim will be subordinated to claims of other creditors in bankruptcy. See BC 510(c). The doctrine of **equitable subordination** has developed through the case law since it appeared in 1939. The prevailing approach is that a creditor's claim will be equitably subordinated if the creditor has engaged in fraud or other inequitable conduct that resulted in an unfair advantage to the creditor or in harm to other creditors, provided that subordination would not be contrary to the principles of bankruptcy law. There are cases suggesting that secured creditors who act in accordance with their security agreements—albeit aggressively—are unlikely to have their claims subordinated.

As you work your way through the following materials, do not forget that much law other than the UCC regulates a creditor's behavior, as just noted. Before proceeding to the following Problems, cases and Notes, you may find it useful to peruse the brief overview of Revised Article 9, Part 6, found in Chapter 6, Section 2, supra. Finally, please bear in mind that when a debtor enters bankruptcy *the rules change* (even if equitable subordination is not at issue). In particular, recall the broad sweep of the automatic stay under BC 362 and the bankruptcy trustee's turnover powers under BC 542, discussed in Chapter 10, Section 1, supra.

NOTE ON RIGHTS AND DUTIES AFTER DEFAULT

R9–601 explains generally the rights and remedies of the secured party and the debtor. Subsections (a) and (d) make clear that the secured party may proceed without judicial process under Article 9, may exercise the rights and remedies agreed by the parties, and may enforce the security interest by any judicial procedure. Although the secured party's rights and remedies are cumulative under R9–601(c), they are not entirely independent from one another. For example, R9–601(e) and (f) explain the interplay between enforcement by judicial process and the secured party's rights under Article 9.

The rights and remedies of the debtor and secured party arise "after default." R9–601(a), (d). The UCC neither defines the term nor explains the concept of "default." In common parlance, the primary meaning of the term is "to fail to perform a task or fulfill an obligation." We have seen in Chapter 8 that a security interest is "an interest in personal property or fixtures which secures payment or performance of an obligation." R1–

201(37). As to these security interests, a failure to perform a secured obligation clearly would constitute a default. Indeed, the most common default is the debtor's failure to make a required payment on a secured obligation when it becomes due. Most security agreements specify several other events of default as well. See Form 3.2, ¶ 12, and Form 3.6, ¶ 3.b.5, supra. As we shall see in Section 4, infra, determining whether a payment or other default has occurred sometimes can be difficult.

We have seen that some security interests do not secure an obligation: "[A]ny interest of a consignor and a buyer of accounts, chattel paper, a payment intangible, or a promissory note in a transaction that is subject to Article 9" is a security interest. R1–201(37). Consignments and contracts to sell receivables typically create obligations on the part of the debtor (consignee or seller), but these obligations are not secured by the consigned goods or the sold receivables. The remedial provisions of Part 6 are not designed to address a default in these obligations. Accordingly, with one exception (discussed in Section 5, infra), Part 6 of Article 9 "imposes no duties upon a secured party that is a consignor or is a buyer of accounts, chattel paper, payment intangibles, or promissory notes." R9–601(g).

SECTION 1. TAKING POSSESSION OF COLLATERAL AFTER DEFAULT

(A) IN GENERAL

THEY'RE THE NIGHT STALKERS
On the prowl, silent and fast: Repo Men

By Edward Power

Inquirer Staff Writer

You are now entering Repo Reality:

Somewhere out on the dark side streets, or tucked away in the fringe neighborhoods of Philadelphia, there was a gold 1988 Hyundai Excel, parked by the curbside pretty as a trophy.

Two months ago, the car's owner had walked onto a dealer's lot and then signed a loan agreement with a Philadelphia bank. The value of the contract: $13,124.14.

Sixty days after driving away, the new owner had yet to make his first payment of $218.59 per month. "Never even got out of the gate," as Dick Harris put it.[*]

That was when Harris, 58, and Jim Carden Jr., 25, got involved. They are repo men.

---

* [Mr. Harris, who is quoted in this article, is not related to any of the authors of this book.]

So there, motoring along the 1400 block of Fanshawe Street in Northeast Philadelphia, at 12:20 a.m. Friday, Carden and Harris let their eyes roam the taillights and license plates.

"You develop a feel, almost smell it," Harris said of the hunt for such cars.

"A sixth sense," Carden agreed, nodding.

And then Carden's sixth sense kicked like a turbocharger. There was the gold Excel, three cars ahead, a loan officer's dream.

"We've got to break into it and move it back so we can tow it," Harris said as Carden got out a long silver wire with a hook on one end. The street was dark, but suddenly a single porch light flicked on.

The two men ignored it. Within 30 seconds, Carden had the door open and was silently rolling the Hyundai back, just enough so he could get the tow boom from his truck under the fender.

Less than four minutes after spotting the car, Carden gunned the tow truck's engine, and he and Harris were rolling again.

"That's the name of that tune," Harris said, and on into the Philadelphia night he and Carden went, looking for more of the repossessions they call "deals."

Cruising the streets a little earlier, Harris had remarked on the reason he and Carden spend their nights fending off crack dealers, narrowly escaping irate car owners and looking for a prize $50,000 BMW owned by a drug dealer who is wanted by the police for stealing the car, not to mention executing his enemies.

"We're adrenalin freaks," Harris said smiling.

Inside the North Philadelphia warehouse where his repossession business is based, Jim Carden Sr., president of East Coast Recovery Inc., was readying the crews to go out one night last week; among them was his son, Jim.

. . .

"Because I'm a repossessor there's a stigma attached to me," Carden [Sr.] said. "It's difficult when you've always had acceptance and now you're looked at as a dirt bag or something."

"Picture yourself walking up somebody's driveway at 3 o'clock in the morning," the younger Carden said of the perils of the repo business.

"And King Kong comes out of the house," Harris added.

Find it. Hook it up. Hit the gas.

Repo man.

The Philadelphia Inquirer, Nov. 20, 1988, at 1–B, 3–B.

Problem 12.1.1. In the setting of the Prototype on automobile financing, Chapter 7, Section 1, supra, Lee Abel purchased a new Chevrolet and signed the Instalment Sale Contract. See Form 3.6, supra. As in the Prototype, Main Motors assigned the contract to Firstbank.

Abel made five monthly payments from August through December. Just after Christmas, Abel was laid off work and was unable to continue the payments. Two weeks after Abel missed the January 24 payment, an employee of Firstbank phoned to remind Abel that the payment was overdue. Firstbank wrote and phoned Abel several more times in February, and on February 20 Firstbank wrote to Abel stating that unless prompt payment was forthcoming, Firstbank would be required to repossess the car. Abel was still unable to find the money for the payments.

Abel kept the car at home, parked in the street. At around 11:00 P.M. on February 25, Abel saw a car stop in front of the house. Two people got out and approached Abel's car, inserted a key in the lock, and opened the door. Abel said to a friend who was visiting at the time: "Someone's messing around with my car. Call the police." Abel then rushed out the door. Before Abel got outside the two people had entered the Chevrolet and closed and locked the car doors. Abel ran up to the car and shouted: "Get out of my car." One of the people said: "Sorry, but we're repossessing the car for Firstbank." The other started the engine and they drove off with the car.

Before the car reached the corner, a patrol car arrived in response to a radio message that relayed the call from Abel's friend. Abel pointed to the departing Chevrolet; the patrol car caught up with the Chevrolet and stopped the car. The driver and passenger in the Chevrolet identified themselves as employees of a repossession firm retained by Firstbank, and showed the officers a copy of the Instalment Sales Contract and a copy of the February 20 letter to Abel giving notice that the payment was overdue. The officers then allowed the repo team to proceed with the Chevrolet.

(a) Abel sues Firstbank for conversion, for compensation for loss of the use of the car, and for punitive damages. What result? See R9–609; R9–625(b) & Comment 3, UCC 1–106; R9–625(c)(2); Stone Machinery Co. v. Kessler, infra; Williams v. Ford Motor Credit Co., infra; Wade v. Ford Motor Credit Co., infra; Notes on Wrongful Repossession, infra.

(b) Suppose that Abel jumped into another car and gave chase, leading to traffic violations. What result? See Jordan v. Citizens & Southern National Bank, 278 S.C. 449, 298 S.E.2d 213 (1982) (high speed chase involving traffic violations following repossession was not a breach of the peace in the repossession; conduct at a distance from the place of repossession (plaintiff's home) was not "conduct at or near and/or incident to the seizure of the property"); Wallace v. Chrysler Credit Corp., 743 F.Supp. 1228, 1233 (W.D.Va.1990) (threatening to throw daughter and plaintiff in jail after repossession of property was not "incident to" the seizure of the property; "[o]nce a creditor has gained sufficient dominion over his collateral, objection by the debtor will be of no avail.").

(c) Now suppose that Abel rushed outside, confronted the repo team *before* they entered the car, and demanded that they leave the car where it was. Without responding, the repo team jumped in the Chevrolet and drove it away. What result?

(d) Suppose, instead, that, while still inside, Abel noticed that the repo team was armed with shotguns. Abel, being no fool, remained inside, did not confront the repo team, and watched as they drove away the Chevrolet. (You may assume that their possession of the shotguns was legal under applicable law.) What result? Is this scenario or the one presented in part (c) above more likely to result in actual violence?

(e) Suppose that the police had arrived before the repo team entered the car. Would their presence alone have affected the outcome? See *Stone Machinery*, infra.

Problem 12.1.2. Misako Inaba bought a food freezer from Cellar Department Store pursuant to an installment sales contract that gave Cellar a security interest in the freezer. After making eight monthly payments, Inaba missed the next two installments. Cellar's employees phoned and sent written notices to Inaba; these messages warned Inaba that, unless payments were made, Cellar would be required to repossess the freezer. Inaba failed to pay. One afternoon two people knocked on Inaba's door. When Inaba opened the door, one of them said, "We've come to repossess the freezer," and then walked in. Inaba responded, "I think that's a terrible thing to do. I'll pay you as soon as I can." The other replied, "I'm awfully sorry, but we have our orders." Inaba spoke further, with considerable feeling, of the personal and family hardship of losing the freezer. But they picked up the freezer and carried it away.

Inaba sued Cellar for wrongful repossession. What result from the courts that decided the *Stone Machinery*, *Williams*, and *Wade* cases, infra?

NOTE ON SELF–HELP REPOSSESSION UNDER FORMER AND REVISED ARTICLE 9

Both Former and Revised Article 9 entitle a secured party to take possession of collateral following a "default" (as noted above, "default" is an undefined term left to the agreement of the parties). See F9–503; R9–609. Although F9–503 has given rise to a large number of reported cases, it remains essentially unchanged in R9–609. The case law under F9–503 has been generally consistent as to certain issues relating to taking possession of collateral. For example, the cases generally have held a secured party liable for the wrongful acts of an independent contractor who takes possession of collateral on the secured party's behalf. Should Revised Article 9 have codified the results of the cases, addressed the issues in the comments, or been silent altogether? In general, Revised Article 9 treats these issues in the comments (see R9–609, Comment 3) or is silent.

One of the most controversial and frequently litigated issues that arose under F9–503 was the meaning of that section's significant limitation on a secured party's right to take possession of collateral through nonjudicial self-help: A secured party may take possession nonjudicially only "without breach of the peace." F9–503. R9–609 contains the same limitation. Comment 3 to R–9–609 states that the section follows F9–503 in that it "does not define or explain the conduct that will constitute a breach of the peace, leaving that matter for continuing development by the courts." The drafters resisted appeals to provide more explicit statutory guidance. See, e.g. Braucher, The Repo Code: A Study of Adjustment to Uncertainty in Commercial Law, 75 Wash. U. L.Q. 549 (1997) (hereinafter, "Braucher, Repo Code").

Professor Braucher argues that "breach of the peace" is a vague and unpredictable standard. Id. at 566–91. In consumer transactions, in particular, she believes that the lack of certainty based on case-by-case determinations provides inadequate deterrence. Id. at 614–15. In her article (published while Revised Article 9 was being drafted and debated), she urged the drafters to codify "a number of common types of repossession practices that are breaches of the peace," explaining that this approach "would likely lead to compliance by most repossessors." Id. at 615. As noted above, however, the drafters declined to adopt this suggestion; R9–609 retains the general "breach of the peace" standard. As you read the following cases dealing with F9–503 and the related Problems and Notes, consider the relative merits of the broad standard retained by R9–609 and a more specific listing of "common types of.... breaches of the peace" urged by Professor Braucher.

Stone Machinery Co. v. Kessler

Court of Appeals of Washington, 1 Wash.App. 750, 463 P.2d 651 (1970).
Review denied 77 Wn.2d 962 (1970).

■ Evans, Chief Judge. Plaintiff Stone Machinery brought this action in Asotin County to repossess a D–9 Caterpillar Tractor which plaintiff had sold to defendant Frank Kessler under conditional sales contract. Service of process was not made on the defendant but plaintiff located the tractor in Oregon and repossessed it. The defendant then filed an answer and cross-complaint in the Asotin County replevin action, alleging that the plaintiff wrongfully and maliciously repossessed the tractor, and sought compensatory and punitive damages under Oregon law. Trial was to the court without a jury and the court awarded defendant compensatory damages in the sum of $18,586.20, and punitive damages in the sum of $12,000 on defendant's cross-complaint.

The operative facts are not in serious dispute. Defendant Kessler purchased, by conditional sales contract, a used D–9 Caterpillar Tractor from the plaintiff Stone Machinery, for the sum of $23,500. The unpaid balance of $17,500 was to be paid in monthly installments, with skip payments.[*] The defendant's payment record was erratic and several payments were made late. However, payments of $3600 on March 29, 1966,

---

* [A "skip payment" arrangement allows the debtor to skip a certain number of payments each year; these arrangements are seen most often in transactions involving debtors in seasonal lines of business, such as agriculture and construction.]

and $1800 on July 18, 1966, put the contract payments on a current basis. The payment due on August 10, 1966 was not made and, on September 7, 1966, plaintiff's credit manager, Richard Kazanis, went to the defendant's ranch in Garfield, Washington, and demanded payment of the balance due on the contract or immediate possession of the tractor. At this time defendant had made payments on the purchase price totaling $17,200, including the trade-in. The defendant was unable to make full payment, or any payment at that time, and informed Mr. Kazanis that he would not relinquish possession of the tractor to him at that time, or at any time in the future, in the absence of proper judicial proceedings showing his right to repossess, and that "someone would get hurt" if an attempt was made to repossess without "proper papers." At that time the defendant informed Mr. Kazanis that he, the defendant, expected to be awarded a contract by the U.S. Bureau of Fisheries to do some work with the D-9 at their installation on the Grande Ronde River near Troy, Oregon, and that he would then be able to pay on the tractor.

On September 13, 1966, the plaintiff instituted this action in Asotin County, Washington, but the sheriff was unable to locate the tractor in that county. Thereafter, the plaintiff instituted another action in Garfield County, but the sheriff was unable to locate the tractor in that county. The evidence indicates that on September 24 Kessler took the tractor to Oregon to work the Bureau of Fisheries job.

On September 27, 1966, Mr. Kazanis, by use of an airplane, located the tractor on the Grande Ronde River, west of Troy, Wallowa County, Oregon. He then contacted the sheriff of Wallowa County and requested him to accompany them in the repossession of the tractor to prevent any violence by the defendant. The sheriff agreed to meet with Mr. Kazanis at Troy, Oregon, and on September 27, 1966, Mr. Kazanis in his private car, plaintiff's mechanic in a company pickup, and the plaintiff's truck driver in the company lo-boy truck, left Walla Walla, and the following morning met the Wallowa County Sheriff at Troy, where the sheriff was shown a copy of the conditional sales contract. The sheriff confirmed previous legal advice plaintiff had received that the plaintiff had the right to repossess the tractor (although not by the use of force) and thereupon the sheriff, in his official sheriff's car, followed by Mr. Kazanis in his private car, the mechanic in the pickup, and the truck driver in the lo-boy, proceeded to the scene where the defendant was operating the D-9 tractor in the Grande Ronde River approximately 7 miles west of Troy, pursuant to contract with the U.S. Bureau of Fisheries.

Upon arriving at the scene the sheriff, accompanied by Mr. Kazanis, walked to the edge of the river and motioned the defendant, who was working with the tractor in the river, to bring the tractor to shore. The sheriff was in uniform and wearing his badge and sidearms. The sheriff informed the defendant that the plaintiff Stone Machinery had a right to repossess the tractor, and stated, "We come to pick up the tractor." The defendant asked the sheriff if he had proper papers to take the tractor and the sheriff replied, "No." The defendant Kessler protested and objected to the taking of the tractor but offered no physical resistance because, as he testified, "he didn't think he had to disregard an order of the sheriff." The plaintiff's employee then loaded the tractor on the lo-boy and left for Walla Walla, Washington.

Within a few days the tractor was sold to a road contractor at Milton–Freewater, Oregon, for the sum of $7447.80 cash, on an "as is" basis. The sale price represented the balance due on the contract, plus the plaintiff's charges for repossession.

Plaintiff's first assignments of error are directed to the following findings of the trial court:

XII

That the plaintiffs actions in repossessing the defendant's tractor on September 28, 1966, and the actions of the Wallowa County Sheriff, in aid of the plaintiffs, amounted to constructive force, intimidation and oppression, constituting a breach of the peace and conversion of defendant's tractor.

XIV

That the plaintiffs failed to show just cause or excuse for the wrongful act of repossession of the defendant's tractor on September 28, 1966.

XV

That the wrongful act of repossession, done intentionally on September 28, 1966, was malicious and was so wanton and reckless as to show disregard for the rights of the defendant Frank Kessler.

Retaking possession of a chattel by a conditional seller, upon the default of the buyer, is governed by O.R.S. 79.5030 (U.C.C. 9–503):

Secured party's right to take possession after default. Unless otherwise agreed a secured party has on default the right to take possession of the collateral. In taking possession a secured party may proceed without judicial process *if this can be done without breach of the peace* or may proceed by action. * * *

(Italics ours.)

Defendant Kessler was admittedly in default for nonpayment of the August and September contract installments. By the terms of the above statute Stone Machinery had the right to take possession of the tractor without judicial process, but only if this could be done without a breach of the peace. The question is whether the method by which they proceeded constituted a breach of the peace.

No Oregon cases have been cited which define the term "breach of peace" so we must look to other authority. In 1 Restatement of Torts 2d, § 116 (1965), the term is defined as follows:

A breach of the peace is a public offense done by violence, or one causing or likely to cause an immediate disturbance of public order.

In the case of McKee v. State, 75 Okl.Cr. 390, 132 P.2d 173, breach of peace is defined (headnote 9, 132 P.2d 173), as follows:

> To constitute a "breach of the peace" it is not necessary that the peace be actually broken, and if what is done is unjustifiable and unlawful, tending with sufficient directness to break the peace, no more is required, nor is actual personal violence an essential element of the offense. * * *

In the instant case it was the sheriff who said that he had no legal papers but that "we come over to pick up this tractor." Whereupon, the defendant Kessler stated, "I told him I was resisting this; there was an action started and I wanted to have a few days to get money together to pay them off." At this point defendant Kessler had a right to obstruct, by all lawful and reasonable means, any attempt by plaintiff to forcibly repossess the tractor. Had the defendant offered any physical resistance, there existed upon both the sheriff and plaintiff's agents a duty to retreat. However, confronted by the sheriff, who announced his intention to participate in the repossession, it was not necessary for Kessler to either threaten violence or offer physical resistance. As stated by the court in Roberts v. Speck, 169 Wash. 613, at 616, 14 P.2d 33 at 34 (1932), citing from Jones on Chattel Mortgages (4th ed.), § 705:

> "The mortgagee becomes a trespasser by going upon the premises of the mortgagor, accompanied by a deputy sheriff who has no legal process, but claims to act *colore officii*, and taking possession without the active resistance of the mortgagor. To obtain possession under such a show and pretence of authority is to trifle with the obedience of citizens to the law and its officers."

Acts done by an officer which are of such a nature that the office gives him no authority to do them are "*colore officii*." See 7A Words & Phrases Perm.Ed. at 296.

In Burgin v. Universal Credit Co., supra, the conditional seller retook possession from the buyer, after default in payments, and in order to do so secured the presence of a police officer, without legal papers. The only act of the officer was to order the buyer to release the brakes and drive the car to the curb. The court said:

> "Because a party to a contract violates his contract, and refuses to do what he agreed to do, is no reason why the other party to the contract should compel the performance of the contract by force. The adoption of such a rule would lead to a breach of the peace, and it is never the policy of the law to encourage a breach of the peace. The right to an enforcement of this part of the contract must, in the absence of a consent on the part of the mortgagor, be enforced by due process of law, the same as any other contract."

In the case of Firebaugh v. Gunther, 106 Okl. 131, 233 P. 460 (1925), the defendant secured the services of a deputy sheriff to take possession of the property. The deputy sheriff, not having legal papers, stated "he was going to take the property and did not want to make any trouble." It was held that his conduct constituted intimidation amounting to force.

In the instant case, when the sheriff of Wallowa County, having no authority to do so, told the defendant Kessler, "We come over to pick up this tractor," he was acting *colore officii* and became a participant in the repossession, regardless of the fact that he did not physically take part in the retaking. Plaintiff contends that its sole purpose in having the sheriff present was to prevent anticipated violence. The effect, however, was to prevent the defendant Kessler from exercising his right to resist by all lawful and reasonable means a nonjudicial take-over. To put the stamp of approval upon this method of repossession would be to completely circumvent the purpose and intent of the statute.

We hold there is substantial evidence to support the trial court's finding that the unauthorized actions of the sheriff in aid of the plaintiff amounted to constructive force, intimidation and oppression constituting a breach of the peace and conversion of the defendant's tractor.

Plaintiff's final assignment of error relates to the trial court's award of punitive damages. The Oregon law regarding punitive damages has recently been set forth in the case of Douglas v. Humble Oil & Refining Co., 445 P.2d 590 (Or.1968):

> As a general rule, punitive damages will be allowed only when the proof supports a finding that the defendant acted with improper motives or with willful, wanton, or reckless disregard for the rights of others. * * *

> We held recently that it is only in those instances where the violation of societal interests is sufficiently great and of a kind that sanctions would tend to prevent that the use of punitive damages is proper. "Regardless of the nomenclature by which a violation of these obligations is described (grossly negligent, willful, wanton, malicious, etc.), it is apparent that this court has decided that it is proper to use the sanction of punitive damages where there has been a particularly aggravated disregard * * * "of the rights of the victim. Noe v. Kaiser Foundation Hospitals, Or., 435 P.2d 306 (1967).

Defendant Kessler was in default of his contract and had announced his intention to resist any attempted nonjudicial repossession. The words used in announcing his intention, namely, "someone would get hurt," were of such a nature as to justify the presence of a sheriff during any attempt at peaceable repossession although, as we have already held, this did not justify participation by the sheriff in the process of repossession. However, the fact that the sheriff did undertake to act *colore officii* in the repossession was not, under the circumstances, sufficient to support a finding that the plaintiff thereby displayed a particularly aggravated disregard for the rights of Kessler, within the meaning of Douglas v. Humble Oil & Refining Co., supra.

Judgment for compensatory damages is affirmed. Judgment for punitive damages is reversed.

Williams v. Ford Motor Credit Co.

United States Court of Appeals, Eighth Circuit, 1982.
674 F.2d 717.

■ BENSON, CHIEF JUDGE.

In this diversity action brought by Cathy A. Williams to recover damages for conversion arising out of an alleged wrongful repossession of an automobile, Williams appeals from a judgment notwithstanding the verdict entered on motion of defendant Ford Motor Credit Company (FMCC). In the same case, FMCC appeals a directed verdict in favor of third party defendant S & S Recovery, Inc. (S & S) on FMCC's third party claim for indemnification. We affirm the judgment n.o.v. FMCC's appeal is thereby rendered moot.

In July, 1975, David Williams, husband of plaintiff Cathy Williams, purchased a Ford Mustang from an Oklahoma Ford dealer. Although David Williams executed the sales contract, security agreement, and loan papers, title to the car was in the name of both David and Cathy Williams. The car was financed through the Ford dealer, who in turn assigned the paper to FMCC. Cathy and David Williams were divorced in 1977. The divorce court granted Cathy title to the automobile and required David to continue to make payments to FMCC for eighteen months. David defaulted on the payments and signed a voluntary repossession authorization for FMCC. Cathy Williams was informed of the delinquency and responded that she was trying to get her former husband David to make the payments. There is no evidence of any agreement between her and FMCC. Pursuant to an agreement with FMCC, S & S was directed to repossess the automobile.

On December 1, 1977, at approximately 4:30 a.m., Cathy Williams was awakened by a noise outside her house trailer in Van Buren, Arkansas. She saw that a wrecker truck with two men in it had hooked up to the Ford Mustang and started to tow it away. She went outside and hollered at them. The truck stopped. She then told them that the car was hers and asked them what they were doing. One of the men, later identified as Don Sappington, president of S & S Recovery, Inc., informed her that he was repossessing the vehicle on behalf of FMCC. Williams explained that she had been attempting to bring the past due payments up to date and informed Sappington that the car contained personal items which did not even belong to her. Sappington got out of the truck, retrieved the items from the car, and handed them to her. Without further complaint from Williams, Sappington returned to the truck and drove off, car in tow. At trial, Williams testified that Sappington was polite throughout their encounter and did not make any threats toward her or do anything which caused her to fear any physical harm. The automobile had been parked in an unenclosed driveway which plaintiff shared with a neighbor. The neighbor was awakened by the wrecker backing into the driveway, but did not come out. After the wrecker drove off, Williams returned to her house trailer and called the police, reporting her car as stolen. Later, Williams commenced this action.

The case was tried to a jury which awarded her $5,000.00 in damages. FMCC moved for judgment notwithstanding the verdict, but the district court, on Williams' motion, ordered a nonsuit without prejudice to refile in state court. On FMCC's appeal, this court reversed and remanded with directions to the district court to rule on the motion for judgment notwithstanding the verdict. The district court entered judgment notwithstanding the verdict for FMCC, and this appeal followed.

Article 9 of the Uniform Commercial Code (UCC), which Arkansas has adopted and codified as Ark.Stat.Ann. § 85–9–503 (Supp.1981), provides in pertinent part:

> Unless otherwise agreed, a secured party has on default the right to take possession of the collateral. In taking possession, a secured party may proceed without judicial process if this can be done without breach of the peace. . . . [4]

In Ford Motor Credit Co. v. Herring, 27 U.C.C.Rep. 1448, 267 Ark. 201, 589 S.W.2d 584, 586 (1979), which involved an alleged conversion arising out of a repossession, the Supreme Court of Arkansas cited Section 85–9–503 and referred to its previous holdings as follows:

> In pre-code cases, we have sustained a finding of conversion only where force, or threats of force, or risk of invoking violence, accompanied the repossession.

The thrust of Williams' argument on appeal is that the repossession was accomplished by the risk of invoking violence. The district judge who presided at the trial commented on her theory in his memorandum opinion:

> Mrs. Williams herself admitted that the men who repossessed her automobile were very polite and complied with her requests. The evidence does not reveal that they performed any act which was oppressive, threatening or tended to cause physical violence. Unlike the situation presented in Manhattan Credit Co. v. Brewer, supra, it was not shown that Mrs. Williams would have been forced to resort to physical violence to stop the men from leaving with her automobile.

In the pre-Code case Manhattan Credit Co. v. Brewer, 232 Ark. 976, 341 S.W.2d 765 (1961), the court held that a breach of peace occurred when the debtor and her husband confronted the creditor's agent during the act of repossession and clearly objected to the repossession, 341 S.W.2d at 767–68. In *Manhattan*, the court examined holdings of earlier cases in which repossessions were deemed to have been accomplished without any breach

---

4. It is generally considered that the objectives of this section are (1) to benefit creditors in permitting them to realize collateral without having to resort to judicial process; (2) to benefit debtors in general by making credit available at lower costs; and (3) to support a public policy discouraging extrajudicial acts by citizens when those acts are fraught with the likelihood of resulting violence.

of the peace, id. In particular, the Supreme Court of Arkansas discussed the case of Rutledge v. Universal C.I.T. Credit Corp., 218 Ark. 510, 237 S.W.2d 469 (1951). In *Rutledge*, the court found no breach of the peace when the repossessor acquired keys to the automobile, confronted the debtor and his wife, informed them he was going to take the car, and immediately proceeded to do so. As the *Rutledge* court explained and the *Manhattan* court reiterated, a breach of the peace did not occur when the "Appellant [debtor-possessor] did not give his permission but he did not object."

We have read the transcript of the trial. There is no material dispute in the evidence, and the district court has correctly summarized it. Cathy Williams did not raise an objection to the taking, and the repossession was accomplished without any incident which might tend to provoke violence.

Appellees deserve something less than commendation for the taking during the night time sleeping hours, but it is clear that viewing the facts in the light most favorable to Williams, the taking was a legal repossession under the laws of the State of Arkansas. The evidence does not support the verdict of the jury. FMCC is entitled to judgment notwithstanding the verdict.

The judgment notwithstanding the verdict is affirmed.

■ HEANEY, CIRCUIT JUDGE, dissenting.

The only issue is whether the repossession of appellant's automobile constituted a breach of the peace by creating a "risk of invoking violence." See Ford Motor Credit Co. v. Herring, 267 Ark. 201, 589 S.W.2d 584, 586 (1979). The trial jury found that it did and awarded $5,000 for conversion. Because that determination was in my view a reasonable one, I dissent from the Court's decision to overturn it.

Cathy Williams was a single parent living with her two small children in a trailer home in Van Buren, Arkansas. On December 1, 1977, at approximately 4:30 a.m., she was awakened by noises in her driveway. She went into the night to investigate and discovered a wrecker and its crew in the process of towing away her car. According to the trial court, "she ran outside to stop them ... but she made no *strenuous* protests to their actions." (Emphasis added.) In fact, the wrecker crew stepped between her and the car when she sought to retrieve personal items from inside it, although the men retrieved some of the items for her. The commotion created by the incident awakened neighbors in the vicinity.

Facing the wrecker crew in the dead of night, Cathy Williams did everything she could to stop them, short of introducing physical force to meet the presence of the crew. The confrontation did not result in violence only because Ms. Williams did not take such steps and was otherwise powerless to stop the crew.

The controlling law is the UCC, which authorizes self-help repossession only when such is done "without breach of the peace * * *." Ark.Stat.Ann. § 85-9-503 (Supp.1981). The majority recognizes that one important policy consideration underlying this restriction is to discourage "extrajudicial acts by citizens when those acts are fraught with the likelihood of resulting violence." Despite this, the majority holds that no reasonable jury could find that the confrontation in Cathy Williams' driveway at 4:30 a.m. created a risk of violence. I cannot agree. At a minimum, the largely undisputed facts created a jury question. The jury found a breach of the peace and this Court has no sound, much less compelling, reason to overturn that determination.

Indeed, I would think that sound application of the self-help limitation might require a directed verdict in favor of Ms. Williams, but certainly not against her. If a "night raid" is conducted without detection and confrontation, then, of course, there could be no breach of the peace. But where the invasion is detected and a confrontation ensues, the repossessor should be under a duty to retreat and turn to judicial process. The alternative which the majority embraces is to allow a repossessor to proceed following confrontation unless and until violence results in fact. Such a rule invites tragic consequences which the law should seek to prevent, not to encourage. I would reverse the trial court and reinstate the jury's verdict.

Wade v. Ford Motor Credit Co.

Court of Appeals of Kansas, 1983.
8 Kan.App.2d 737, 668 P.2d 183.

■ SWINEHART, JUDGE:

This is an appeal by defendant Ford Motor Credit Company (Ford) from a judgment against it and in favor of plaintiff Norma J. Wade, awarding her damages for conversion, loss of credit reputation, punitive damages and attorney fees in an action arising out of Ford's alleged breach of the peace in the repossession of Wade's car.

Wade entered into an automobile retail installment contract on August 9, 1979, for the purchase of a 1979 Ford Thunderbird automobile. The contract was assigned to Ford which advanced $6,967.75 to enable her to purchase the car. Pursuant to the terms of the contract, Ford had a security interest in the car which had been fully perfected. Wade contracted to pay Ford forty-eight equal monthly installments of $194.52 commencing September 8, 1979. Wade was late with these payments right from the start. The following illustrates her payment record:

Payment Due:	Payment Made:
September 8, 1979	September 17, 1979
October 8, 1979	October 23, 1979
November 8, 1979	January 18, 1980
December 8, 1979	February 14, 1980
January 8, 1980	March 4, 1980

No other payments were made.

On December 6, 1979, Ford mailed Wade a notice of her default and of her right to cure the default. The notice was mailed to Wade pursuant to

K.S.A. 16a–5–110 and 16a–1–201(6), and was sent by certified mail to the address listed in Ford's records from the information provided by Wade. [Kansas had adopted legislation based on the Uniform Consumer Credit Code (U3C); the section-numbers of the Kansas legislation conform to those of the U3C, quoted infra.] It was returned to Ford several days later marked "Return to sender, moved, left no address." Wade had moved and not notified Ford of a new address. K.S.A. 16a–1–201(6) provides:

> "For the purposes of K.S.A. 16a–1–101 through 16a–9–102, and amendments thereto, the residence of a consumer is the address given by the consumer as the consumer's residence in any writing signed by the consumer in connection with a credit transaction. Until the consumer notifies the creditor of a new or different address, the given address is presumed to be unchanged."

The trial court found that Ford had complied with the statutory notice requirements precedent to repossession. That finding stands since Wade has not appealed from it.

Collection efforts continued after the mailing of the above notice. After communication with Wade, a payment was received and promises of additional payments were made. With the account still in arrears, Ford assigned it on February 4, 1980, to the Kansas Recovery Bureau, a subsidiary of Denver Recovery Bureau, as independent contractors to repossess the car.

On or about February 10, 1980, in the early afternoon, David Philhower, an employee of Kansas Recovery Bureau, located the car in the driveway of Wade's residence. He had a key for the car, so he unlocked the door, got in and started it. Philhower then noticed an apparent discrepancy between the serial number of the car and that listed in his papers. He shut the engine off, got out and locked the car door. At that time Wade appeared at the door of her house. Philhower told her that he had been sent there by Ford to repossess the car, and she replied that he was not going to take it because she had made the payments on it. She invited him in the house to prove her claim, but was unable to locate the cancelled checks and receipts for the payments made. Philhower told her of the serial number discrepancy, and stated that he was not going to take the car until he confirmed the number, and advised her to contact Ford to straighten out the problem.

Wade then told him that if he came back to get the car that she had a gun in the house, which she had obtained because of several burglaries in the area, and she would not hesitate to use it. She then called a representative of Ford and stated she had a gun and that if she caught anyone on her property again trying to take her car, that "I would leave him laying right where I saw him."

Ford then received two more payments, the last being received March 4, 1980. On March 5, 1980, Ford reassigned the account to Kansas Recovery Bureau for repossession. In the early morning hours of March 10, 1980, at around 2:00 a.m., Philhower made another attempt to repossess the car from the driveway of Wade's residence. This time he was successful.

Wade heard a car "burning rubber" at around 2:00 a.m., looked out the window, and discovered her car missing. There was no confrontation between Wade and Philhower, since Wade was not even aware of the fact her car was being repossessed until after Philhower had safely left the area in the car. Upon calling the police, Wade was informed that her car had been repossessed. Philhower had informed the police just prior to the repossession that he was going to recover the car in case they received reports of a prowler.

Wade subsequently brought an action against Ford for wrongful repossession, conversion and loss of credit, and sought both actual and punitive damages, along with attorney fees. Ford filed a counterclaim for breach of contract, seeking the deficiency of $2,953.44 remaining after the car was sold at public auction.

After a trial to the court, the trial court found Ford had breached the peace in repossessing the car and found in favor of Wade. The trial court also found for Ford on its counterclaim. Wade was awarded damages and attorney fees.

Ford appeals, raising the following two issues: (1) Did the trial court err in finding that Ford breached the peace on March 10, 1980, when it repossessed Wade's car? (2) Did the trial court err in assessing damages against Ford?

Defendant Ford contends that the trial court erred in finding that Ford breached the peace on March 10, 1980, when its agent repossessed Wade's car. The issue presented can be stated as follows: Does the repossession of a car, when there is no contact or confrontation between the repossessor and the debtor at the time and place of repossession, constitute a breach of the peace when there has been a prior threat of deadly violence if repossession is attempted? This particular set of facts has not been addressed by the courts before.

The trial court found that Ford had breached the peace in repossessing Wade's car. In its findings and conclusions made at the conclusion of the trial, the trial court emphasized Wade's lack of consent to the repossession and stated: "It's this Court's view that the Legislature, when it permitted self-help repossession, it was meant to cover amicable situations where there was no dispute as there apparently was in this particular case." At the hearing on defendant's motion to alter the judgment, the trial court stated:

> "[I]n no way did she consent at no time did she consent to the peaceful recovery of the security, namely, one automobile that she kept and maintained on her private property, namely, that of her residence. The plaintiff, having threatened Mr. Philhower, the recovery agent, with bodily harm through the use of a lethal weapon known as a revolver, having informed Mr. Philhower never to enter her property again, otherwise she would shoot him. So, that being the last communication between Philhower and the plaintiff, at a later date when it was a month or so later, I don't recall since this hearing was seven months

ago, Mr. Philhower, after that initial confrontation at 2:00 o'clock in the morning, 1:00 in the morning, quietly entered this private property, in effect, in this Court's opinion, taking the law in its own hands, come what may.

"Now, fortunately, no harm resulted from his entry on this private property. He was willing to assume that risk and that danger, knowing full-well that had he awakened the plaintiff, violence could very well have occurred and ensued. He knowingly and willfully brought that situation about in our community.

"I am reminded in some ways of the old frontier Wichita, Kansas in where firearms were used as a settlement of personal differences. Fortunately, the law and the courts have supplemented that mode or method of settling private differences.

"We have in this state the replevin action, which provides for an orderly process for the recovery of personal property held under a security for a debt and under oath, the parties are privileged to come into the court and expose through the witnesses and their evidence to the court, their claims such as in this case, the defendant claimed that the plaintiff was past due on her note involving the automobile involved here. Then, likewise, in that same hearing, the plaintiff in a replevin action would have had the right and the privilege to be heard by a judge or a jury to determine and make the finding as to whether or not she was in fact delinquent and in violation of her promise to pay thus providing for her being relieved of the security of the automobile in this case.

. . .

"These facts violate every principle of civilized procedures that is understood as to why we have the courts and why we have the law to avoid confrontations between parties to avoid dangers to life, limb, and property. It's an orderly process that we seek to serve in this case.

"The Court is very grateful that no violence did ensue, result from the ultimate repossession of the car by Mr. Philhower, but nevertheless, is of the view that such action as came out in this court, done by Mr. Philhower was a breach of the peace.

"The Court is convinced that the purpose of permitting creditors to obtain a peaceful repossession, recovery of their securities such as an automobile in this case, would apply to instances where the recovery is freely done without threats of violence with consent of the parties and in view of the facts, this Court feels that the threat of firearms that this was a breach of the peace and will affirm the decision made in October, 1981, after hearing the evidence. The motion of the defendant is denied."

It appears that the trial court put a great deal of emphasis on Wade's lack of consent and the great potential for violence involved in the second repossession attempt.

K.S.A. 16a–5–112 [U3C 5.112] provides:

"Upon default by a consumer, unless the consumer voluntarily surrenders possession of the collateral to the creditor, the creditor may take possession of the collateral without judicial process only if possession can be taken without entry into a dwelling and without the use of force or other breach of the peace."

K.S.A. 84–9–503 provides in part:

"Unless otherwise agreed a secured party has on default the right to take possession of the collateral. In taking possession a secured party may proceed without judicial process if this can be done without breach of the peace or may proceed by action."

The statutes do not define the term "breach of the peace." The courts are left with that job. There are few Kansas cases doing so, but numerous cases from other jurisdictions. The leading Kansas case is Benschoter v. First National Bank of Lawrence, 218 Kan. 144, 542 P.2d 1042 (1975), where the court found that the self-help repossession provisions of K.S.A. 84–9–503 do not violate constitutional due process. The court also held:

"A creditor may repossess collateral without judicial process if this can be done without breach of the peace. Standing alone, stealth, in the sense of a debtor's lack of knowledge of the creditor's repossession, does not constitute a breach of the peace." Syl. ¶ 2.

. . .

An extensive search of the cases in other jurisdictions does not reveal a case on point which involved an initial confrontation with a threat of future violence, an intervening period of time with communication between the parties, and a subsequent successful repossession without incident.

In Morris v. First Natl. Bank & Trust Co., 21 Ohio St.2d 25, 254 N.E.2d 683 (1970), the court considered a case involving a self-help repossession statute similar to Kansas'. The facts included a confrontation at the time of repossession. The court noted:

"While we leave the question of conversion to be determined in future proceedings below, we are constrained to hold that when appellee's agents were physically confronted by appellant's representative, disregarded his request to desist their efforts at repossession and refused to depart from the private premises upon which the collateral was kept, they committed a breach of the peace within the meaning of Section 1309.46, Revised Code, lost the protective application of that section, and thereafter stood as would any other person who unlawfully refuses to depart from the land of another." p. 30, 254 N.E.2d 683.

. . .

In Census Federal Credit Union v. Wann, Ind.App., 403 N.E.2d 348 (1980), the court also considered self-help repossession under U.C.C. 9–503 and what constitutes breach of the peace. There the creditor made demand on the debtor for possession of the secured car. The debtor refused to give possession of it to the creditor. Unlike the present case, there were no threats of future violence. Thereafter, the creditor, through its agents and without benefit of any judicial process, took possession of the car at approximately 12:30 a.m. by taking it from the parking lot of the apartment building where the debtor lived. During this second, successful, repossession attempt, no contact whatever was had by the creditor's agents with the debtor or any other person in the immediate control of the car. The court provided the following discussion on breach of the peace:

"In Deavers v. Standridge, (1978) 144 Ga.App. 673, 242 S.E.2d 331, the court held that blocking the movement of the defaulting debtor's automobile after his oral protest to the secured party's repossession attempt was a breach of the peace.

"Cases in other jurisdictions have held that absence of consent of the defaulting party to repossession is immaterial to the right of a secured party to repossess without judicial process. This, of course, is a necessary result, for contrary to the argument of plaintiff, Ind.Code 26–1–9–503, by its very existence, *presupposes that the defaulting party did not consent*. Should the defaulting party consent, no statutory authority would be required for a secured party to repossess, with or without judicial process. To hold otherwise would emasculate that statute."

We find it is clear from a survey of the cases dealing with self-help repossession that the consent of the debtor to the repossession is not required. K.S.A. 16a–5–112 even presupposes the lack of consent: "Upon default by a consumer, unless the consumer *voluntarily surrenders* possession...." (Emphasis supplied.) The trial court's emphasis on the lack of consent by Wade in the present case and its view that "the Legislature, when it permitted self-help repossession ... meant to cover amicable situations where there was no dispute...." are not found in case law. Repossession, without the consent of the debtor, absent more, does not constitute a breach of the peace by the creditor.

The trial court also emphasized the potential for violence brought on by Wade's threats made during the first repossession attempt. A breach of the peace may be caused by an act likely to produce violence. The facts presented in this case do not, however, rise to that level. A period of one month elapsed between the repossession attempts. During that period, Wade and Ford were in communication and two payments were made. We find the potential for violence was substantially reduced by the passage of this time. Moreover, the actual repossession was effected without incident. The time of the repossession was such that in all likelihood no confrontation would materialize. In fact, Wade was totally unaware of the repossession until after Philhower had successfully left the premises with the car. We therefore find that as a matter of law there was no breach of the peace in the repossession of Wade's car.

The trial court's judgment finding a breach of the peace is reversed, and the case is remanded for a modification of the award of damages in accordance with this opinion.

Wade's motion for attorney fees on appeal is denied.

Reversed and remanded with directions.

NOTES ON WRONGFUL REPOSSESSION

(1) Measure of Damages for Wrongful Repossession. In the *Stone Machinery* case the court concluded that only "compensatory damages" would be awarded. How does one compute such damages for repossession by a secured party who (as in *Stone Machinery*) had a legal right to obtain possession by the use of appropriate procedures? (The *Stone Machinery* opinion does not explain how the trial court computed the "compensatory damages" of $18,586.20.) If damages are based on the interruption of the debtor's use of the collateral, should the relevant period of interruption be limited to the time that would have been required to repossess by judicial proceedings? In the *Stone Machinery* case, would it have been wrong for a judge to defer repossession of the tractor until Kessler, the debtor, could complete his current job—at least if Kessler would assign to the plaintiff the sums to become payable under the contract? Even if that approach would be sensible, how could a judge overcome the fact that F9–503 conferred upon Stone Machinery the unequivocal right to possession?

In *Stone Machinery* the court upheld the debtor's judgment for conversion. According to the Restatement (Second) of Torts, "[c]onversion is an intentional exercise of dominion or control over a chattel which so seriously interferes with the right of another to control it that the actor may justly be required to pay the other the full value of the chattel." Restatement (Second) of Torts § 222 A(1) (1965). Consider also Comment *c* to that section:

> The importance of the distinction between trespass to chattels and conversion ... lies in the measure of damages. In trespass the plaintiff may recover for the diminished value of his chattel because of any damage to it, *or for the damage to his interest in its possession or use.* Usually, although not necessarily, such damages are less than the full value of the chattel itself. In conversion the measure of damages is the full value of the chattel, at the time and place of the tort. [Emphasis added.]

Is there any plausible justification for the debtor, who is in default, to recover the full value of the collateral from the secured party? Perhaps, but only if the secured party is entitled to setoff the secured debt against the debtor's recovery. If a worthwhile compensatory measure of damages cannot be found (e.g., where the wrongful possession did not interrupt profitable use of the equipment), should further thought be given to the assessment of punitive damages?

Now consider *Stone Machinery* from another perspective. It was undisputed that Kessler, the debtor, was in default. It follows that, as between Kessler and Stone Machinery, the latter was entitled to possession under

F9–503. Notwithstanding that Kessler was not (and did not claim to be) entitled to possession, Kessler refused to deliver the tractor to Stone Machinery and even made a threat of physical injury if a non-judicial repossession were to be attempted. Does it seem anomalous that it is Kessler, and not Stone Machinery, that is entitled to a judgment for conversion?

Section 272 of the Restatement (Second) of Torts provides that "[o]ne who is entitled to immediate possession of a chattel is not liable to another for dispossessing him of it." Relying in large part on Section 272 and the related comments, Professor Braucher has argued persuasively that a secured party's breach of the peace in connection with taking possession following default is *not* a conversion. See Braucher, Repo Code, supra, 74 Wash. U. L.Q. at 604–06. (Of course, if the secured party is not entitled to possession, e.g., because no default has occurred, then Section 272 would not apply.) Professor Braucher asserts, however, that even the measure of damages for conversion (i.e., the entire value of the collateral) with an offset for the unpaid secured debt provides an inadequate recovery for the non–converting secured party's breach of the peace:

> With breaches of the peace, the object of the remedy is not so much compensation of the debtor as putting a stop to a socially offensive practice, with the debtor's enforcement action serving the function of a private attorney general. In short, deterrence is the most important function of a breach-of-the-peace remedy, so the proper inquiry is what remedy will deter repossessors from offensive self-help.

Braucher, Repo Code, supra, 74 Wash. U. L.Q. at 613. Instead, she advocates the debtor's recovery of the *fair market value of the collateral plus a cancellation of the secured debt!* Id. at 613–14. Would that approach be consistent with the UCC's general approach of awarding compensatory, but not punitive, damages? See R9–625(b), imposing liability for "any loss caused by a failure to comply with this article." See also UCC 1–106(1) (remedies are to be compensatory except as "specifically provided in this Act or by other rule of law"). And should the same measure of damages apply in cases of a breach of the peace by a secured party who is entitled to possession as in cases in which the secured party is not entitled to possession but takes possession nevertheless? Of course, if breach of the peace constitutes an independent tort (e.g., assault), nothing in Article 9 would restrict the debtor from obtaining an independent recovery in tort (assuming no double recovery). See R9–625, Comment 3 (second paragraph).

(2) What is a Breach of the Peace? Procedural Aspects of the Breach–of–the–Peace Exception to Self–Help. Perhaps the results of cases like *Stone Machinery* can be understood best by viewing the breach of peace exception to self-help repossession as *procedural* in nature. The secured party is entitled to possession if, in fact, the debtor is in default. But the debtor can prevent self-help, and force the secured party to recover the collateral through judicial proceedings, *if* the debtor is able to control the circumstances so that self-help would constitute a breach of the peace.

As illustrated by the *Williams* and *Wade* cases, sometimes the debtor may find it difficult to challenge a successfully completed, self-help repossession on the basis that the secured party breached the peace.

Might this procedural conceptualization also explain why courts generally treat unauthorized involvement by law enforcement officials (*"colore officii"*) as a breach of the peace? It seems highly unlikely that the involvement of a peace officer will result in an actual breach of the peace. But the appearance of authority that the officer conveys is likely to deprive the debtor of the opportunity to protest and to insist on a judicial recovery. This conceptualization also is consistent with finding a breach of the peace when the secured party proceeds to take possession in the face of a contemporaneous objection by the debtor. Should the test for a breach of the peace focus on circumstances in which the *risk* of violence (i.e., an *actual* breach of the peace) is likely? This reasoning might explain cases in which a breach of the peace was based on circumstances such as breaking and entering the premises on which collateral is located (especially the debtor's residence), trickery, and the debtor's interruption of a repossession coupled with an objection.

(3) Replevin, Due Process, and State Action. The traditional requirements for obtaining a writ of replevin (a procedure for recovering possession of personal property) were an *ex parte* application by the plaintiff, accompanied by an affidavit affirming the plaintiff's right to possession and a bond to assure compensation for the defendant if seizure under the writ was unjustified. The Supreme Court invalidated these procedures in Fuentes v. Shevin, 407 U.S. 67, 92 S.Ct. 1983, 32 L.Ed.2d 556 (1972). See also North Georgia Finishing, Inc. v. Di–Chem, 419 U.S. 601, 95 S.Ct. 719, 42 L.Ed.2d 751 (1975) (holding invalid the *ex parte* garnishment of an industrial corporation's bank account).[1]

Fuentes concerned the seizure of property by sheriffs who had acted pursuant to state legislative authority. The Supreme Court held that this procedure violated the following provision of the Fourteenth Amendment: "[N]or shall *any State* deprive any person of life, liberty, or property without due process of law." Does the *Fuentes* doctrine apply to *self-help* repossession of collateral by a private person? Does the *state* violate the Due Process Clause when, as in F9–503 and R9–609, it authorizes repossession by the creditor?

The *Fuentes* decision led to widespread litigation challenging the constitutionality of self-help repossession by Article 9 secured parties. Several Courts of Appeals rejected Due Process attacks on self-help repossession. The prevailing view (in brief) has been that, although F9–503 permitted (just as R9–609 permits) self-help in some circumstances, the creditor's action is based on the creditor's property right rather than on the "state action" contemplated by the Fourteenth Amendment. Consider, for

---

1.   State procedural rules generally have been revised to require judicial supervision of replevin actions. These rules generally provide an opportunity for the defendant to be heard before seizure of property unless a court finds that emergency action is justified, in which case a hearing is held immediately after seizure.

example, the effects of a state's *repeal* of F9–503 or R9–609. Nothing would seem to impair the effectiveness of a *contractual* right to self-help repossession. The prevailing view received support in the 1978 decision of the Supreme Court that a warehouse's sale of goods for unpaid storage fees, although permitted by UCC 7–210, was not "state action" in violation of the Due Process Clause. Flagg Brothers v. Brooks, 436 U.S. 149, 98 S.Ct. 1729, 56 L.Ed.2d 185 (1978) (Justices Stevens, White, and Marshall dissented). See Brest, State Action and Liberal Theory: A Casenote on Flagg Brothers v. Brooks, 130 U.Pa.L.Rev. 1296, 1330 (1982) ("The [state action] doctrine has seldom been used to shelter citizens from coercive federal or judicial power. More often, it has been employed to protect the autonomy of business enterprises against the claims of consumers, minorities, and other relatively powerless citizens.").

Unlike the typical self-help repossession, the participation of a sheriff *colore officii*, as in the *Stone Machinery* case, clearly seems to implicate state action. Does a debtor affected by that kind of state action have a *federal* claim against the secured party based on a violation of the debtor's constitutional rights? Cf. Lugar v. Edmondson Oil Co., 457 U.S. 922, 102 S.Ct. 2744, 73 L.Ed.2d 482 (1982) (a private creditor can be liable for use of unconstitutional state procedures as a "state actor" under 42 U.S.C. § 1983).[2] In Wyatt v. Cole, 504 U.S. 158, 112 S.Ct. 1827, 118 L.Ed.2d 504 (1992), the Court held that qualified *immunity from suit* is not available for private defendants faced with Section 1983 liability for having invoked a state replevin, garnishment or attachment statute that is declared unconstitutional. However, the court did not "foreclose the possibility that private defendants faced with § 1983 liability under *Lugar* ... could be entitled to an affirmative defense based on good faith and/or probable cause or that § 1983 suits against private, rather than governmental, parties could require plaintiffs to carry additional burdens." On remand, the Fifth Circuit accepted *Lugar*'s invitation and held that private defendants may be held liable for damages under Section 1983 only if they knew or should have known that the statute upon which they relied was unconstitutional. Wyatt v. Cole, 994 F.2d 1113 (5th Cir.1993). It might interest you to learn that, in *Wyatt,* the attorney who assisted his client in filing a replevin action was sued along with the client.

(B)   CONSUMER PROTECTION LEGISLATION

Problem 12.1.3. In the setting of the Prototype on automobile financing, Lee Abel purchased a new Chevrolet and signed the Instalment Sale Contract. See Form 3.6, supra. As in the Prototype, Main Motors assigned

---

2. 42 U.S.C. § 1983 provides in relevant part as follows:

Every person who, under color of any statute ... of any State ... subjects, or causes to be subjected, any citizen of the United States or any other person within the jurisdiction thereof to the deprivation of any rights, privileges, or immunities secured by the Constitution and laws, shall be liable to the party injured in an action at law, suit in equity, or other proper proceeding for redress.

the contract to Firstbank. Paragraph 1.b. (on the reverse side) of the contract provides, in part:

"You agree not to remove the vehicle from the U.S. or Canada, or to sell, rent, lease, or transfer any interest in the vehicle or this contract without our written permission."

Paragraph 3.b. (on the reverse side) of the contract provides, in part:

"If you break your promises (default), we may demand that you pay all you owe on this contract at once. Default means:

    1.   You do not pay any payment on time;

    2.   You start a proceeding in bankruptcy or one is started against you or your property; or

    3.   You break any agreements in this contract."

The monthly payments were due on the 24th of the month; Abel made the first seven payments (through February 24). On March 10 Abel was in desperate need of cash, took the Chevrolet to a used car dealer in another city, and offered it for sale. Dealer's manager asked to see the certificate of title; Abel said that the certificate was at home and that Dealer could have it as soon as Dealer bought the car. (In fact, Firstbank held the certificate, as in the Prototype, Chapter 7, Section 1, supra.) The manager indicated the price that Dealer would be willing to pay, but added that there could be no deal without a clean certificate of title. Abel agreed to bring in the car and certificate the next day in order to close the deal.

Dealer's manager took note of the number of the car's license and, as soon as Abel left, Dealer phoned the Bureau of Motor Vehicles to inquire about ownership and liens. Later that afternoon the Bureau reported by telephone that their records showed that Firstbank held a security interest in the Chevrolet. Dealer phoned Firstbank to inquire if the lien had been discharged. That night, employees of Firstbank found the Chevrolet parked at the curb three blocks from Abel's residence and towed it away.

(a) Abel sued Firstbank for compensatory and punitive damages. Does the Instalment Sale Contract authorize the repossession? If not, is Firstbank aided by UCC 1–208? Does UCC 2–609 apply to the seller's *assignee* of a security interest, such as Firstbank? If so, are its provisions adequate for the current situation?

(b) Suppose that Abel (promising to bring in the certificate of title the next day) actually sold the Chevrolet to the out-of-town dealer on March 10. That clearly would be a default under the terms of the Instalment Sales Contract, and R9–609 would permit repossession. The state has enacted the Uniform Consumer Credit Code (1974) (U3C). In this case, Firstbank has not given Abel the notice specified in U3C 5.110. Does the U3C bar repossession? See Notes (2) and (3) on Legislation Limiting Self–Help Repossession Against Consumers, infra. (Note (2) sets forth U3C 5.109(2), 5.110(1), and 5.111(1).)

(c) Now suppose that Abel failed to make the payments due on December, January, and February 24. The U3C remains applicable. Does the U3C bar repossession? If the court concludes that the repossession was improper under U3C, what judgment should be entered?

(d) On the morning after Firstbank's repossession of the Chevrolet (March 11), Firstbank concluded that its repossession was inconsistent with the provisions of the U3C. What can Firstbank do to extricate itself with a minimum of difficulty and liability?

NOTES ON LEGISLATION LIMITING SELF–HELP REPOSSESSION AGAINST CONSUMERS

(1) Article 9. As you know, the UCC contains only a few provisions that apply only to consumer transactions. A few of these concern enforcement of security interests. See, e.g., R9–620(e) (discussed in Section 6, infra); R9–625(c)(2) (discussed in Section 2, infra). Article 9 contains no special rules regulating repossession of collateral from consumers, despite the widespread belief that these repossessions may have particularly disruptive and destructive effects. In the face of Article 9's silence, regulation has come from other sources.

(2) The Uniform Consumer Credit Code. One of the UCC's sponsors, the National Conference of Commissioners on Uniform State Laws, has dealt with repossession in another of its products, the Uniform Consumer Credit Code. As initially promulgated in 1968, the U3C did not significantly restrict repossession. Experience with the 1968 version and pressure from consumer groups (including the National Consumer Law Center) led to the promulgation in 1974 of a second version that strengthens the rights of debtors.

Neither version of the U3C has been widely adopted. However, the U3C has been an influential model for states enacting legislation dealing with consumer credit.

Provisions of the U3C that relate to default and repossession follow.

UNIFORM CONSUMER CREDIT CODE (1974)

Section 5.109 [Default]

An agreement of the parties to a consumer credit transaction with respect to default on the part of the consumer is enforceable only to the extent that:

(1) the consumer fails to make a payment as required by agreement; or

(2) the prospect of payment, performance, or realization of collateral is significantly impaired; the burden of establishing the prospect of significant impairment is on the creditor.

Section 5.110 [Notice of Consumer's Right to Cure]

(1) With respect to a consumer credit transaction, after a consumer has been in default for ten days for failure to make a required payment and has not voluntarily surrendered possession of goods that

are collateral, a creditor may give the consumer the notice described in this section. A creditor gives notice to the consumer under this section when he delivers the notice to the consumer or mails the notice to him at his residence (subsection (6) of Section 1.201).

(2) Except as provided in subsection (3), the notice shall be in writing and conspicuously state: the name, address, and telephone number of the creditor to whom payment is to be made, a brief identification of the credit transaction, the consumer's right to cure the default, and the amount of payment and date by which payment must be made to cure the default. A notice in substantially the following form complies with this subsection:

(name, address, and telephone number of creditor)

(account number, if any)

(brief identification of credit transaction)

_____ is the LAST DAY FOR PAYMENT   _____ is the
(date)   (amount)

AMOUNT NOW DUE

You are late in making your payment(s). If you pay the AMOUNT NOW DUE (above) by the LAST DAY FOR PAYMENT (above), you may continue with the contract as though you were not late. If you do not pay by that date, we may exercise our rights under the law.

If you are late again in making your payments, we may exercise our rights without sending you another notice like this one. If you have questions, write or telephone the creditor promptly.

(3) If the consumer credit transaction is an insurance premium loan, the notice shall conform to the requirements of subsection (2) and a notice in substantially the form specified in that subsection complies with this subsection, except for the following:

(a) in lieu of a brief identification of the credit transaction, the notice shall identify the transaction as an insurance premium loan and each insurance policy or contract that may be cancelled;

(b) in lieu of the statement in the form of notice specified in subsection (2) that the creditor may exercise his rights under the law, the statement that each policy or contract identified in the notice may be cancelled; and

(c) the last paragraph of the form of notice specified in subsection (2) shall be omitted.

Section 5.111 [Cure of Default]

(1) With respect to a consumer credit transaction, except as provided in subsection (2), after a default consisting only of the consumer's failure to make a required payment, a creditor, because of that default, may neither accelerate maturity of the unpaid balance of the

obligation, nor take possession of or otherwise enforce a security interest in goods that are collateral until 20 days after a notice of the consumer's right to cure (Section 5.110) is given, nor, with respect to an insurance premium loan, give notice of cancellation as provided in subsection (4) until 13 days after a notice of the consumer's right to cure (Section 5.110) is given. Until expiration of the minimum applicable period after the notice is given, the consumer may cure all defaults consisting of a failure to make the required payment by tendering the amount of all unpaid sums due at the time of the tender, without acceleration, plus any unpaid delinquency or deferral charges. Cure restores the consumer to his rights under the agreement as though the defaults had not occurred.

(2) With respect to defaults on the same obligation other than an insurance premium loan and subject to subsection (1), after a creditor has once given a notice of consumer's right to cure (Section 5.110), this section gives the consumer no right to cure and imposes no limitation on the creditor's right to proceed against the consumer or goods that are collateral. For the purpose of this section, in open-end credit, the obligation is the unpaid balance of the account and there is no right to cure and no limitation on the creditor's rights with respect to a default that occurs within 12 months after an earlier default as to which a creditor has given a notice of consumer's right to cure (Section 5.110).

(3) This section and the provisions on waiver, agreements to forego rights, and settlement of claims (Section 1.107) do not prohibit a consumer from voluntarily surrendering possession of goods which are collateral and the creditor from thereafter accelerating maturity of the obligation and enforcing the obligation and his security interest in the goods at any time after default.

[Subsection (4), dealing with insurance premium loans, is omitted.]

Section 5.112 [Creditor's Right to Take Possession After Default]

Upon default by a consumer with respect to a consumer credit transaction, unless the consumer voluntarily surrenders possession of the collateral to the creditor, the creditor may take possession of the collateral without judicial process only if possession can be taken without entry into a dwelling and without the use of force or other breach of the peace.

(3) Consequences of Violating the U3C's Default and Repossession Rules. What are the consequences of a creditor's noncompliance with the foregoing provisions of the U3C? A court may have some difficulty in finding the answer. U3C 5.201(1) lists 22 provisions of the U3C and states that if any of these provisions is violated the consumer may "recover actual damages and also a right in an action other than a class action, to recover from the person violating this Act a penalty in an amount determined by the court not less than $100 nor more than $1,000." The list of the 22 duties for which the U3C imposes a penalty does *not* include U3C 5.109–5.112.

Do U3C 5.109–5.112 specify legal consequences of failing to comply with the requirements set forth in these provisions? See U3C 5.111(1). Should one conclude that the *only* legal consequences of these provisions are those that are specified therein? U3C 1.103, in language closely comparable to UCC 1–103, states that "the principles of law and equity" and the UCC supplement the provisions of the U3C, unless displaced by its "particular provisions."

It should be noted that U3C 5.201, after a series of limited remedial provisions (including the listing in subsection (1) of the 22 provisions mentioned above), ends with the following subsection that seems to be of general applicability:

> (8) In an action in which it is found that a creditor has violated this Act, the court shall award to the consumer the costs of the action and to his attorneys their reasonable fees. In determining attorney's fees, the amount of the recovery on behalf of the consumer is not controlling.

(4) Other Approaches to the Problem. The Model Consumer Credit Act (1973) (MCCA), drafted by the National Consumer Law Center, gives short shrift to self-help repossession. Under Section 7.202 of the MCCA:

> No person shall take possession of collateral by other than legal process pursuant to this Part, notwithstanding any provision of law or term of a writing.

Wisconsin has taken a less extreme, but still restrictive, approach. Under the Wisconsin Consumer Act a secured creditor may repossess only after obtaining a court determination that the creditor is entitled to the collateral; following such a determination the creditor may repossess by self-help, provided there is no breach of the peace. Wis. Stat. Ann. §§ 425.203–.206. The effect of this Act, as evidenced by field studies, is analyzed in Whitford and Laufer, The Impact of Denying Self–Help Repossession of Automobiles: A Case Study of the Wisconsin Consumer Act, 1975 Wis.L.Rev. 607. The authors conclude that fears that the Act would cripple consumer finance are largely unfounded. While the cost of repossessions rose significantly and the volume of repossessions dropped, the principal impact on credit seemed to be confined to requiring larger down payments in the sale of used cars. Id. at 654.

SECTION 2.   DISPOSITIONS OF COLLATERAL; DEFICIENCY AND SURPLUS; CONSEQUENCES OF NONCOMPLIANCE

Introductory Note. Taking possession of collateral following a debtor's default only begins the process of enforcing a security interest in collateral. A secured party in possession of tangible collateral following a default typically wishes to sell the collateral and then to apply the net proceeds of the sale to the secured obligation. If the proceeds are insufficient to satisfy the secured obligation, the secured party may wish to pursue the debtor to collect the remaining, unsecured portion of the debt (the "deficiency"). If a disposition yields proceeds sufficient to satisfy the secured obligation, the secured party will pay over any excess funds (the "surplus") to the debtor (or, in some circumstances, to junior claimants).

R9–610 through R9–618 regulate dispositions of collateral after default. These sections deal with the actual disposition of the collateral (R9–610), notification of a disposition (R9–611 through R9–614), application of the proceeds of a disposition (R9–615), calculation and explanation of a surplus or a deficiency claim (R9–615 and R9–616), the rights that a disposition transfers to a transferee of the collateral (R9–617), and certain rights and duties of secondary obligors (R9–618).

When a secured party opts to "sell, lease, license, or otherwise dispose of ... collateral" under R9–610, "[e]very aspect of ... [the] disposition, including the method, manner, time, place, and other terms, must be commercially reasonable." R9–610(a), (b). In addition, subject to narrow exceptions, a secured party is required to give a debtor, a secondary obligor (such as a guarantor), and certain other persons "a reasonable authenticated notification of disposition." R9–611. This Section of the book deals with the strict, albeit (with a few exceptions) general, standards for dispositions of collateral after default. The requirements provided by Revised Article 9 generally follow those imposed by F9–504. In some cases, however, the text of and comments to Part 6 of Revised Article 9 provide more detail than did F9–504; the additional detail often reflects an effort to clarify issues that arose under the former provision.

This Section of the book also considers how the secured party's failure to comply with Part 6 when disposing of collateral affects the rights of the secured party and the debtor. See R9–625 through R9–627. Although these provisions replace F9–507, they provide considerably more detail and include more instances of special treatment for consumer transactions than did their predecessor. The two cases that follow the Problems deal with noncompliance with Part 5 of Former Article 9. As explained in Note 7, infra, they remain relevant to consumer transactions under Part 6 of Revised Article 9. They also provide background for understanding the approach taken to noncompliance in Revised Article 9.

Before continuing on to the Problems, cases, and Notes that follow, please read carefully R9–610 through R9–618 and R9–625 through R9–627.

Problem 12.2.1. Schmelli Services, Inc., is an Arkansas-based personnel agency that provides temporary office employees to businesses. It has offices in twenty-four cities in several eastern and southeastern states. Schmelli owes your client, Atlanta Industrial Bank (AIB), approximately $4,500,000 under a **line of credit** facility, secured by a perfected, first priority security interest in Schmelli's accounts receivable and a first priority real property mortgage on Schmelli's home office building (located in Little Rock, Arkansas). The security agreement covering the accounts provides that the collateral secures not only Schmelli's $6,000,000 note executed pursuant to the line of credit facility, but also "all other obligations of Borrower to Bank now existing or hereafter incurred, whether (i) contingent or noncontingent, (ii) liquidated or unliquidated, (iii) disputed or undisputed, (iv) contemplated or uncontemplated, or (v) of the same or different type as the indebtedness evidenced by the Note."

Schmelli also owes AIB about $2,500,000, secured by a perfected, first priority security interest in a Learjet Model 35A–596. (Schmelli's flamboyant CEO, Telli Schmelli, uses the Learjet to fly from city to city while making monthly visits to each office.) There are about 1,500 hours on the airframe and engines, and Schmelli has maintained the aircraft in accordance with applicable Federal Aviation Administration regulations. The security agreement covering the Learjet provides that it secures the purchase-money loan (originally, $3,300,000) and also other obligations, using language identical to that in the line of credit security agreement, quoted above. Each security agreement provides that it is "governed by the law of the State of Georgia."

Schmelli is in default under both the line of credit facility and the aircraft loan. AIB has not yet "pulled the plug" on Schmelli; it continues to make discretionary advances against Schmelli's accounts receivable. However, yesterday a repo team retained by AIB peacefully took possession of the Learjet at the Pine Bluff, Arkansas, airport. AIB stored the aircraft with an aircraft dealer located at that airport.

The loan officer assigned to Schmelli wants to "turn the Learjet into cash as soon as possible." The officer, who has little experience with repossessions and enforcement, has asked you for advice on how to proceed.

For purposes of this Problem, assume that Revised Article 9 took effect in Georgia shortly before Schmelli defaulted and that Arkansas has yet to enact Revised Article 9.

(a) Which state's law governs a disposition of the Learjet by AIB? See UCC 1–105; R9–301; Note (11) on Commercially Reasonable Dispositions and Reasonable Notification, infra. Will you recommend that AIB remove the Learjet from Arkansas before disposing of it? Compare R9–626 (which codifies a "rebuttable presumption" approach similar to the approach adopted in Emmons v. Burkett, infra) with First State Bank of Morrilton v. Hallett, infra; Note (6) on Commercially Reasonable Dispositions and Reasonable Notification, infra.

(b) If Georgia law governs, may AIB choose to enforce its security interest under Georgia's version of *Former* Article 9? (Recall that the security interest was created under Former Article 9.) See R9–702.

(c) Do you recommend a "public" or "private" disposition of the aircraft? What considerations bear on what approach to take? See Notes on Commercially Reasonable Dispositions and Reasonable Notification, infra. You may assume that Georgia law applies. Will your recommendation be affected by whether AIB expects to sell the aircraft to a third person or expects (at least in the first instance) to buy the aircraft itself? See R9–610 & Comment 7; R9–626(a)(5); R9–615(f); Note (2) on Commercially Reasonable Dispositions and Reasonable Notification, infra. Consider also that a secured party who buys at its own disposition normally pays itself for the collateral by "bidding in" its claim against the debtor, i.e., by giving the debtor credit against the obligation secured by the collateral.

(d) After settling on a general approach, what specific steps will you recommend? Assume, alternatively, that (i) Schmelli is very cooperative, being grateful for the continued financing, and (ii) shortly after the repossession AIB cut off Schmelli's financing, and now Schmelli and AIB are "not on speaking terms." (Telli Schmelli's ride in a crowded bus from Pine Bluff to Little Rock following the "surprise" repossession did not help matters!) You may continue to assume that Georgia law applies. You might begin your analysis with R9–610(b) and R9–611(b).

(e) Would you change any of your recommendations under part (c) or (d) if Arkansas law were applicable? Would you consider taking any additional steps? See F9–501(1),(5)(R9–601(a), (f)); F9–507(2) (R9–627(c)); Note (1) on Commercially Reasonable Dispositions and Reasonable Notification, infra.

(f) Would your answers in part (e) be different if Schmelli were hopelessly insolvent, leaving no chance for AIB to recover any deficiency? If there were no other collateral (i.e., the accounts and real property)?

(g) What provisions might the security agreement have included that would have made your advice, at the disposition stage, more definite and easier to give? See R9–603; Note (5) on Commercially Reasonable Dispositions and Reasonable Notification, infra.

(h) Suppose that, three weeks after the repossession, while en route from Pine Bluff to Atlanta, the Learjet crashed and was destroyed. The loan officer has just told you that the insurer under Schmelli's policy (AIB is the loss payee on the policy) has denied AIB's claim for loss because the policy does not cover loss or damage incurred when the Learjet is flown by anyone other than an agent or employee of Schmelli. Are there any *additional* steps that you *wish* you had recommended in part (c) above? See R9–603; R9–207(a) & (b)(2); Note (12) on Commercially Reasonable Dispositions and Reasonable Notification, infra.

(i) Assume that the Learjet did not crash. AIB disposed of the Learjet at a public sale to an unrelated third person for $1,500,000 (net of expenses and attorney's fees) and sued Schmelli for a deficiency of $1,000,000. Schmelli's answer to the complaint asserted that AIB is not entitled to a recovery because (i) the notification of the sale failed to state that Schmelli is entitled to an accounting of the unpaid indebtedness, and (ii) a public disposition of a Learjet is not commercially reasonable. There is no doubt that the notification was as asserted. (The inexperienced loan officer prepared the notification based on a form that AIB had used under Former Article 9.) You think it is highly likely that Schmelli can establish the second assertion, as well, based on advice from several potential expert witnesses that (i) expensive aircraft are almost never sold at auctions and (ii) in a private, retail sale the Learjet would have brought between

$2,500,000 and $3,000,000. What options are available to AIB? Which option would you recommend? Assume Georgia law applies. See R9–615(d); R9–626(a); R9–613(1)(D), (2); R9–610(b); R9–627(a).

Problem 12.2.2. In the setting of the Prototype on automobile financing, Lee Abel purchased a new Chevrolet and signed the Instalment Sales Contract (Form 3.6, supra). As in the Prototype, Main Motors assigned the contract to Firstbank. Abel failed to make several payments required by the contract. After Firstbank properly repossessed the Chevrolet, Main paid Firstbank all amounts due under Abel's contract and received an assignment of the contract from Firstbank. See the Assignment and Repurchase Agreement (Form 3.5, supra). By virtue of its payment, Main acquired Firstbank's rights and duties as a secured party. See R9–618. Main sold the Chevrolet to a retail customer in a commercially reasonable manner. However, Main inadvertently neglected to notify Abel before the sale.

Immediately after the sale, Main sues Abel in Philadelphia for $4,450.75, representing the unpaid time balance ($10,396.25) plus costs of repossession and sale ($400.00), less finance charge rebate ($1,345.50) and proceeds of the foreclosure sale ($5,000.00).

(a) What result? Assume that the Pennsylvania Supreme Court had applied the "rebuttable presumption" rule to both consumer and non-consumer transactions under Former Article 9. See R9–611(b), (c); R9–616; R9–625; R9–626; Form 3.6, supra; Notes (6), (7), and (9) on Commercially Reasonable Dispositions and Reasonable Notification, infra.

(b) What result in part (a) if the Pennsylvania Supreme Court had applied the "absolute bar" rule to both consumer and non-consumer transactions under Former Article 9?

(c) What result in part (a) if Main had notified Abel before the sale? See R9–616; R9–625; R9–628.

Emmons v. Burkett

Supreme Court of Georgia, 1987.
256 Ga. 855, 353 S.E.2d 908.

■ BELL, JUSTICE.

We granted certiorari in this case to determine whether the Court of Appeals correctly concluded that the appellee creditor, who had sold a small portion of the debtor's collateral without the notice required by OCGA § 11–9–504(3), was not barred from obtaining an in personam judgment against or selling the other collateral of the debtor. Emmons v. Burkett, 179 Ga.App. 838(1) (348 S.E.2d 323) (1986).

The facts of this case are well-stated in the Court of Appeals' opinion, see Emmons v. Burkett, supra, 179 Ga.App. at 838–840, and will be reiterated here only when necessary to a discussion of the issues presented.

1. In Gurwitch v. Luxurest Furniture Mfg. Co., 233 Ga. 934 (214 S.E.2d 373) (1975), this court adopted the rule that, if a creditor sells

collateral of a debtor without the notice required by OCGA § 11–9–504(3), the creditor is barred from proceeding to obtain a personal judgment against the debtor to recover the difference between the amount obtained from the sale of the collateral and the amount the court determines is due on the note. In Reeves v. Habersham Bank, 254 Ga. 615(2) (331 S.E.2d 589) (1985), this court was presented with the question whether the Gurwitch rule barring a deficiency recovery should be applied to cases in which a creditor attempted to recover a deficiency against the collateral of a guarantor. We answered this question in the affirmative, and have reiterated that answer in United States v. Kennedy, 256 Ga. 345 (348 S.E.2d 636) (1986).

In the instant case, relying on Gurwitch, Reeves, and Kennedy, Emmons, the debtor, argues that Burkett, the creditor, should be barred from proceeding against his remaining collateral or from obtaining a personal judgment against him, to satisfy the deficiency remaining on his note following the sale of the collateral.

The Court of Appeals concluded that, because Burkett filed a suit for recovery on the note before selling the collateral in question,[1] this was not a deficiency action and the effect of Burkett's noncompliance with OCGA § 11–9–504(3) was not the same as if he had first sold the collateral and then sued to recover a deficiency. We disagree with this conclusion.

We do so because we see no reason to distinguish between a situation where the creditor first sues on the note and then sells collateral, and a situation where the creditor first proceeds against collateral and then sues on the note. In both situations, the creditor must obtain a judgment on the note and must attempt to recover the deficiency between the amount obtained on the sale of the collateral and the amount determined to be due on the note.

Moreover, the fact that a creditor may have proceeded to judgment on a note before selling collateral without notice does not in any manner satisfy the ultimate purposes of OCGA § 11–9–504(3), which are to enable the debtor to exercise his right of redemption under OCGA § 11–9–506, if he or she so chooses, and, if not, to minimize any possible deficiencies remaining after the sale. Reeves, supra, 254 Ga. at 619; Kennedy, supra, 256 Ga. at 347. As is readily apparent, the debtor has the same interest in the disposition of the collateral whether the creditor first obtains a judgment on the note and then sells the collateral or first sells the collateral and then obtains a judgment on the note. Since OCGA § 11–9–504(3) is designed to protect the debtor, the effect of the creditor's noncompliance with that code section should be the same in either instance, and we now so hold.

2. Having determined that the effect of a creditor's noncompliance with the notice provision of OCGA § 11–9–504(3) should be the same

---

1. When we refer to the sale of collateral in this opinion, we refer to a sale carried out pursuant to the creditor's rights under the security agreement and the UCC, and not to a sale carried out by judicial process following a judgment on the note.

whether the creditor first obtains a judgment on the note or first sells the collateral, we must now examine the effect of the creditor's noncompliance.

As previously noted, in Gurwitch v. Luxurest Furniture Mfg. Co., supra, 233 Ga. 934, 214 S.E.2d 373, this court adopted the "absolute-bar" rule, holding that the failure of the creditor to comply with the notice requirements of OCGA § 11–9–504(3) when selling collateral operates as an absolute bar to the recovery of a deficiency. This rule has been followed since its inception without reanalysis of its merits. See, for example, Reeves v. Habersham Bank, supra, 254 Ga. 615, 331 S.E.2d 589, and United States v. Kennedy, supra, 256 Ga. 345, 348 S.E.2d 636, in which the primary issues involved the application of the rule rather than the wisdom of it. We are now convinced, however, that the harshness of the absolute-bar rule of Gurwitch should be reevaluated.

An alternative rule which we find merits our consideration has been termed the "rebuttable-presumption" rule. In fact, in Farmers Bank v. Hubbard, 247 Ga. 431, 276 S.E.2d 622 (1981), we carved out an exception to the absolute-bar rule of Gurwitch, and adopted the rebuttable-presumption rule for cases in which the only issue is whether, concerning the commercial reasonableness of the sale, see OCGA § 11–9–504(3), the sale price of the collateral was adequate.

Under the rebuttable-presumption rule, if a creditor fails to give notice or conducts an unreasonable sale, the presumption is raised that the value of the collateral is equal to the indebtedness. To overcome this presumption, the creditor must present evidence of the fair and reasonable value of the collateral and the evidence must show that such value was less than the debt. If the creditor rebuts the presumption, he may maintain an action against the debtor or guarantor for any deficiency. Any loss suffered by the debtor as a consequence of the failure to give notice or to conduct a commercially reasonable sale is recoverable under § 11–9–507 and may be set off against the deficiency. For example, if a creditor has conducted a commercially unreasonable sale, the debtor may suffer a loss, in that he will not receive as much of a credit from the sale of the collateral as he should have. In such an instance, the debtor is entitled to be awarded an additional credit equalling the difference between the fair market value of the collateral and the amount for which the collateral was sold.

In examining the merits of the absolute-bar rule of Gurwitch and of the rebuttable-presumption rule outlined above, we conclude that the fairer rule and the rule most consistent with the intent of the Uniform Commercial Code is the rebuttable-presumption rule. First, we note that OCGA § 11–9–504(2) expressly states that the creditor has a right to recover any deficiency from the debtor. Significantly, the code provisions concerning a debtor's default nowhere provide that a lack of notice bars a deficiency judgment or that proper notice is a condition precedent to the bringing of a deficiency action. Moreover, OCGA § 11–9–507 explicitly provides a remedy for a creditor's noncompliance with the requirements of OCGA § 11–9–504(3). Under § 11–9–507(1), "[i]f the [creditor's] disposition has occurred the debtor or any person entitled to notification or whose security interest has been made known to the secured party prior to the disposition has a right to recover from the secured party any loss caused by a failure to comply with the provisions of this part." OCGA § 11–9–507 does not provide that a failure to comply with § 11–9–504 bars the creditor from bringing an action to recover any deficiency. Based on the foregoing we conclude that the code provisions themselves do not require the imposition of an absolute-bar rule.

In addition, and most importantly, we find that the absolute-bar rule is contrary to the intent of the Uniform Commercial Code. OCGA § 11–1–106 expressly prohibits penal damages, and provides that the remedies provided by the UCC should be liberally administered so that the aggrieved party "may be put in as good a position as if the other party had fully performed." Yet, by absolutely barring a deficiency action, even if the debtor has suffered no damage from a lack of notice or a commercially unreasonable sale, the debtor receives a windfall and the creditor is arbitrarily penalized. This is so despite the fact that it is the debtor's default on his obligation which necessitated the sale of the collateral.

We conclude that the rebuttable-presumption rule, by placing the burden on the creditor to show the propriety of the sale and making him liable under § 11–9–507 for any injury to the debtor, provides an adequate deterrent to an improper sale on the part of a creditor, and adequately protects the debtor's interest, without arbitrarily penalizing the creditor. This is consistent with the conclusion reached in many, if not most, jurisdictions which have considered the question. We therefore now adopt the rebuttable-presumption rule, both for situations in which the creditor fails to give notice of a sale, and for situations in which the creditor fails to conduct a commercially reasonable sale.

3. Because of our adoption of the rebuttable-presumption rule, this case must be remanded for further consideration consistent with this rule. In this regard, we note that, pursuant to Reeves v. Habersham Bank, supra, 254 Ga. 615, 331 S.E.2d 589, and United States v. Kennedy, the rebuttable-presumption rule should be applied to this creditor's efforts to collect a deficiency either from the debtor's collateral or by way of a personal judgment.

All the Justices concur, except SMITH, J., who dissents.

First State Bank of Morrilton v. Hallett

Supreme Court of Arkansas, 1987.
291 Ark. 37, 722 S.W.2d 555.

■ HOLT, CHIEF JUSTICE.

The appellant, First State Bank (FSB), concedes it failed to give the appellee, Edith Hallett, proper notice before it sold her collateral which it repossessed when she defaulted on a promissory note. FSB nevertheless sought a deficiency judgment against Hallett for the balance owed on the note. The trial court granted Hallett's motion for summary judgment, dismissing the FSB claim. The issue on appeal is whether the failure of FSB as a secured party, to give proper notice to debtor Hallett of the time and place of the sale of repossessed collateral, as required by Ark. Stat. Ann. § 85–9–504(3) (Supp. 1985), absolutely bars FSB's right to a deficiency judgment. We hold that it does and affirm the trial court. . . .

Hallett gave FSB a promissory note in the amount of $11,342.90, secured in part by a security interest in a 1983 pickup truck. Hallett defaulted. FSB repossessed the truck and sold it without written notice to Hallett of the sale date. A deficiency of $4,057.40 remained on the note. The trial court granted Hallett's motion for summary judgment because FSB had not complied with § 85–9–504(3)'s guidelines for the disposition of repossessed collateral. That section states in pertinent part:

> Unless collateral is perishable or threatens to decline speedily in value or is of a type customarily sold on a recognized market, reasonable notification of the time and place of any public sale or reasonable notification of the time after which any private sale or other intended disposition is to be made shall be sent by the secured party to the debtor, if he has not signed after default a statement renouncing or modifying his right to notification of sale.

The trial court's ruling complies with our most recent decision, Rhodes v. Oaklawn Bank, 279 Ark. 51, 648 S.W.2d 470 (1983). In Rhodes, we reversed a deficiency judgment in favor of the secured party, and held:

> When a creditor repossesses chattels and sells them without sending the debtor notice as to the time and date of sale, or as to a date after which the collateral will be sold, he is not entitled to a deficiency judgment, unless the debtor has specifically waived his rights to such notice.

FSB does not attempt to distinguish Rhodes, but rather argues that it should be overruled in favor of an earlier line of cases which took a different approach to this issue. Those cases did not bar a deficiency judgment altogether, but instead "indulg[ed] the presumption in the first instance that the collateral was worth at least the amount of the debt, thereby shifting to the creditor the burden of proving the amount that should reasonably have been obtained through a sale conducted according to law." Norton v. Nat'l Bank of Commerce, 240 Ark. 143, 398 S.W.2d 538 (1966). We think Rhodes represents the right approach and, although it did not expressly overrule these cases, its effect was to change our law.

Creditors are given the right to a deficiency judgment by Ark. Stat. Ann. § 85–9–502(2) (Supp. 1985): "If the security agreement secures an indebtedness, the secured party must account to the debtor for any surplus, and unless otherwise agreed, the debtor is liable for any deficiency." As stated, § 85–9–504(3) requires the creditor to send reasonable notification to the debtor before he disposes of this type of collateral. If the creditor does not dispose of the collateral in accordance with the code provisions, Ark. Stat. Ann. § 85–9–507 (Supp. 1985) gives the debtor "a right to recover from the secured party any loss caused by a failure to comply with the provisions of this Part [§§ 85-9-501—507]."

There is a split of authority nationwide on the correlation of these provisions of the code. A group of cases follows the position that § 85-9-507 gives the debtor a defense to a deficiency judgment when the creditor has failed to give proper notice, and that the deficiency judgment is reduced by the damages the debtor can prove. Our previous cases, as represented by Norton, supra, followed this approach with the presumption in favor of the debtor that the collateral and the debt were equal and the burden placed on the creditor to prove a deficiency. The apparent majority position, however, with which we concur, is that § 85-9-507 is not applicable to the creditor's action to recover a deficiency judgment, but is separate affirmative action by the debtor to recover damages. The creditor's right to a deficiency judgment is not merely subject to whether the debtor has a right to damages under § 85-9-507, but instead depends on whether he has complied with the statutory requirements concerning disposition and notice.

This view was explained in Atlas Thrift Co. v. Horan, 27 Cal.App. 3d 999, 104 Cal.Rptr. 315 (1972), quoting Leasco Data Processing Equip. Corp. v. Atlas Shirt Co., 66 Misc.2d 1089, 323 N.Y.S.2d 13 (1971):

"The plaintiff's contention that a secured creditor's right to a deficiency judgment under the described circumstances is limited only by the remedies set forth in 9-507 seems to me a tenuous one indeed, apart from the fact that no such effect was ever accorded the corresponding section in the Uniform Conditional Sales Act....

"Preliminarily, it may be noted that Section 9-507 makes no direct allusion to the circumstances under which a right to a deficiency judgment may arise.

"More significant is the special nature of the language used: 'the debtor or any person entitled to notification ... has a right to recover from the secured party any loss caused by a failure to comply with the provisions of this Part.' If this were intended to authorize a defense to action for a deficiency judgment, it is hard to envisage language less apt to that purpose. The words used plainly contemplate an affirmative action to recover for a loss that has already been sustained—not a defense to an action for a deficiency. The distinction between an affirmative action and a defense is a familiar one, phrases that articulate the different concepts are familiar in the law, and it is unlikely that the experienced authors of the [Uniform Commercial Code] intended by the above language to provide a limited defense to an action for a deficiency judgment based on a sale that had violated the simple and flexible statutory procedure.

"It seems far more probable that this latter section has nothing whatever to do with defenses to an action for a deficiency, since it was never contemplated that a secured party could recover such a judgment after violating the statutory command as to notice."

The Horan court concluded: "The rule and requirement are simple. If the secured creditor wishes a deficiency judgment he must obey the law. If he does not obey the law, he may not have his deficiency judgment."

When the code provisions have delineated the guidelines and procedures governing statutorily created liability, then those requirements must be consistently adhered to when that liability is determined. Here, FSB failed to comply with the code's procedures for disposition of collateral, and is therefore not entitled to a deficiency judgment under the code.

Affirmed.

■ HAYS, NEWBERN, and GLAZE, JJ., dissent.

■ GLAZE, JUSTICE, dissenting. The majority court decision overrules Norton v. National Bank of Commerce, 240 Ark. 143, 398 S.W.2d 538 (1966) and its progeny as those cases have interpreted and applied Arkansas's Uniform Commercial Code §§ 85–9–504 and 9–507 during the past twenty years. Because I believe the rule established in Norton to be a fair one and the one adopted in this cause to be punitive, I am obliged to dissent.

Unlike the court's holding here, the Norton court rejected the debtor's contention that the bank's failure to give him notice of the intended sale completely discharged his obligation. Instead, that court, Justice George Rose Smith writing, held that, because the bank disposed of the debtor's car without notice, the just solution is:

> to indulge the presumption in the first instance that the collateral was worth at least the amount of the debt, thereby shifting to the creditor the burden of proving the amount that should reasonably have been obtained through a sale conducted according to law.

Id. at 150, 398 S.W.2d 538.

As one can readily see, our court in Norton wrestled with the same situation as presented in the instant case, and it derived a most workable and equitable solution which was designed to treat both debtors and creditors fairly. Frankly, I am unaware of any serious problems or criticisms that have arisen in the application of the Norton rule, especially that would demand or warrant this court's changing the "rules-of-the-game" at this late date. The rule this court adopts today is a drastic and punitive one, and no public policy argument has been offered to support it.

Finally, I note the majority court seems to premise its holding, in part, on the California case of Atlas Thrift Co. v. Horan, 27 Cal.App. 3d 999, 104 Cal.Rptr. 315 (1972) which, in turn, quotes from Leasco Data Processing Equip. Corp. v. Atlas Shirt Co., 66 Misc.2d 1089, 323 N.Y.S.2d 13 (1971). While California may have adopted the same "no notice-no deficiency" rule now embraced by this court, the New York courts have since overruled the Atlas Shirt Co. case, thereby rejecting that punitive rule. The New York courts, I might add, have adopted Arkansas's rule as set out in Norton. See Leasco Computer v. Sheridan Industries, 82 Misc.2d 897, 371 N.Y.S.2d 531 (1975) and Security Trust Co. of Rochester v. Thomas, 59 A.D.2d 242, 399

N.Y.S.2d 511 (1977) (citing Universal C.I.T. Credit Co. v. Rone, 248 Ark. 665, 453 S.W.2d 37 (1970)).

I would reverse.

■ HAYS and NEWBERN, JJ., join in this dissent.

NOTES ON COMMERCIALLY REASONABLE DISPOSITIONS AND REASONABLE NOTIFICATION

(1) What Is a "Commercially Reasonable" Disposition? A secured party who is enforcing a security interest faces considerable uncertainty as to whether a proposed disposition will be "commercially reasonable," as required by R9–610(b) (and F9–504(3)). How will a court or a jury view the circumstances in an after-the-fact examination? The serious consequences (and potentially disastrous consequences in a consumer transaction) of failing to dispose of collateral in a commercially reasonable manner underscore the importance of taking the proper approach. See Notes (6) and (7), infra (discussing the consequences of noncompliance with R9–610).

It should be apparent that predicting what is "commercially reasonable" in a given context is an enormously subjective enterprise. What is "reasonable" leaves much to the imagination. A review of the case law and commentary often can leave a student or lawyer confused and uncertain about a given, specific set of facts. Might a more principled approach emerge from examining the *purpose* or *function* of the commercial reasonableness requirement?

Consider the following proposition: A commercially reasonable disposition is one in which all aspects of the disposition are reasonably calculated to bring a reasonable and fair price for the collateral. Although R9–627(a) seems to instruct that the failure to sell for the highest possible price does not ipso facto render the disposition commercially unreasonable, it is clear enough that whether procedures followed in a disposition are commercially reasonable is a function of the price that those procedures could be expected to produce. (It is the price, of course, that will determine whether a debtor remains liable for a deficiency or entitled to a surplus under R9–615.) Comment 10 to R9–610 and Comment 2 to R9–627 explain in identical words the relationship between the price for which collateral is disposed and the secured party's satisfaction of the commercial reasonableness requirement: "While not itself sufficient to establish a violation of this Part, a low price suggests that a court should scrutinize carefully all aspects of a disposition to ensure that each aspect was commercially reasonable." These comments reject the result in cases holding that a *really* low price is ipso facto sufficient to spell commercial unreasonableness under Former Article 9. See F9–504(3) ("terms" must be commercially reasonable). Note (2), infra, discusses the background of this comment, as well as Revised Article 9's special treatment of certain low-price dispositions.

The commercial reasonableness of a disposition normally is a question of fact for the trier of fact. See, e.g., Dischner v. United Bank Alaska, 725 P.2d 488 (Alaska 1986). A secured party seeking a deficiency judgment bears the burden of proof as to compliance with Part 6, including the commercial reasonableness of a disposition and the reasonableness of a notification, once compliance is placed in issue. R9–626(a)(1); Note (3), infra (discussing notification requirements). Case law under F–9–504 was to the same effect. In a very real sense, however, the trial preparation begins during the process of disposing of collateral and before any challenge to commercial reasonableness has surfaced. Whether the proposed disposition involves unique or very expensive collateral (as in Problem 12.2.1, supra) or a routine disposition of an automobile (as in Problem 12.2.2, supra), secured creditors would do well to proceed on the assumption that the disposition will be challenged. Unless the case for commercial reasonableness is made and documented at the time of the disposition, an attack on the commercial reasonableness (or, indeed, any aspect of compliance with Part 6)—which could be asserted years in the future—may be difficult to withstand.

A secured party who desires enhanced certainty of compliance can obtain court approval (or certain other approvals) of the terms of a disposition, in which case the disposition "is commercially reasonable." R9–627(c). R9–627(b) offers useful guidance on what constitutes a commercially reasonable disposition, but hardly provides a sharply delineated "safe harbor." A secured party also could obtain a judgment on the secured debt, levy execution on the collateral, and have the collateral sold at a sheriff's sale, thereby obviating the need to comply with Part 6's notice and commercial reasonableness requirements. See R9–601(f). Either route, however, is likely to be more expensive and time-consuming than non-judicial enforcement.

A secured party also may achieve a high level of comfort if the debtor is cooperative. Absent circumstances suggesting coercion or unfair advantage, a debtor's post-default agreement that particular procedures will constitute a commercially reasonable disposition can do much to reduce the risk of a contrary assertion by the debtor down the road. Even if the debtor is not cooperative, a secured party sometimes will be well-advised to communicate the proposed disposition procedures to the debtor; the debtor's failure to object or to make a reasonable counter-proposal may weigh heavily in favor of the secured party in a later dispute concerning commercial reasonableness.

The requirement of a commercially reasonable disposition must be applied in a wide variety of circumstances. Smith v. Daniels, 634 S.W.2d 276 (Tenn.App.1982), provides useful guidance as to factors to consider. Among specific factors, such as adequate advertising and display, the court emphasized the relevance of customary commercial practices for selling a particular type of asset (the collateral, there, was amusement equipment). What will do for thoroughbred horses may not do for a Learjet aircraft and vice versa. Other factors considered by the courts have included (i) the circumstances under which the sale was conducted (e.g., collateral was not present, sale held during a snowstorm); (ii) appropriateness of the method of sale (i.e., either private or public); (iii) adequacy of the advertising; (iv) preparation of collateral prior to the sale; (v) passage of time between repossession and sale; and (vi) whether the collateral was sold as a unit or individually.

Some lenders and their counsel may develop substantial expertise concerning market practices for certain collateral—automobiles being a good example. But in many situations neither the staff of a secured creditor nor its lawyer will have sufficient expertise, and it will be necessary to retain or consult with experts. Nevertheless, the creditor and the lawyer responsible for conducting a commercially reasonable disposition must know the right kinds of questions to ask the experts.

(2) Low–Price Dispositions to Secured Party, Person Related to Secured Party, or Secondary Obligor. During the drafting process for Revised Article 9, a controversy arose over whether the "price" received for collateral in a disposition following default was an "aspect" or "term" of the disposition that must be "commercially reasonable" under R9–610(b). (The same issue had long been debated under F9–504(3).) Some argued that under the "plain meaning" of F9–504(3) and R–9–610(b) it was indisputable that the price was an "aspect" or "term"–indeed, probably the most important "aspect" or "term" imaginable. Others took the position that, properly read (together with R9–627(a) and F9–507(2) (first sentence)), R9–610(b) (and F9–504(3)) imposed only *procedural* requirements of reasonableness. Under that reading, if all of the steps taken were reasonable, the secured party could not be second-guessed by an attack on the price alone (although the price certainly would be relevant to an evaluation of the procedural reasonableness, as explained in Note (1), supra).

Eventually, a compromise emerged to deal with a specific class of dispositions that are procedurally commercially reasonable but nevertheless produce a very low price. The compromise is reflected in R9–615(f). That provision applies only if the transferee in the disposition is "the secured party, a person related to the secured party, or a secondary obligor." R9–615(f)(1). (Note that the terms "secured party," "person related to the secured party," and "secondary obligor" are defined in R9–102(a).) Why were procedurally conforming dispositions to those persons thought to be suspect? Comment 6 to R9–615 explains that in these cases the secured party may lack the incentive to maximize the proceeds of the disposition (i.e., the price). A disposition to the secured party itself or to a person related to the secured party are obvious examples of self-dealing. In the case of a disposition to a secondary obligor, the secured party may lack incentive because it is counting on being paid in full by the guarantor–it is indifferent as to how much derives from the collateral. And the less the guarantor pays for the collateral the larger will be *its* deficiency claim against the debtor. (More about secondary obligors follows in Section 3, infra).

R9–615(f) contains another condition to its application:

> (2) the amount of proceeds of the disposition is significantly below the range of proceeds that a complying disposition to a person other than the secured party, a person related to the secured party, or a secondary obligor would have brought.

In other words, subsection (f) applies when the proceeds are very low when compared to the proceeds that would have been received in a disposition to an unrelated third party. When subsection (f) applies, then, the surplus or deficiency is calculated not on the (very low) actual proceeds received but on the proceeds that *would have* been received in a complying disposition to an unrelated third party.

We suspect that it is unlikely that any trier of fact could feel confident about a determination of the highly speculative and hypothetical amount of proceeds that R9–615(f) mandates that it determine. On the other hand, the compromise does permit a trier of fact to reduce the otherwise applicable deficiency (or increase the otherwise applicable surplus) when the proceeds are very low. That possibility pleased those who had advocated that price should be an "aspect" or a "term" of a disposition. But the compromise provision also accommodates a reduction of the deficiency (or increase in surplus) without the necessity of determining that the disposition itself did not comply with Part 6 (e.g., was not made in a commercially reasonable manner). That result pleased those who had advocated that price should not be an "aspect" or "term." Indeed, the fact that subsection (f) contemplates a commercially reasonable disposition that yields a very low price supports the inference that, at least under Revised Article 9 if not also under Former Article 9, the price for which collateral is disposed is not an "aspect" or "term" of the disposition. See R9–610, Comment 10; R9–627, Comment 2.

(3) "Reasonable Authenticated Notification of Disposition." R9–611(b) provides that, with certain exceptions, a secured party undertaking a disposition of collateral under R9–610 shall send "a reasonable authenticated notification" to the "persons specified in subsection (c)." Subsection (d) excepts from the notification requirement collateral that "is perishable or threatens to decline speedily in value or is of a type customarily sold on a recognized market."

To Whom Must a Notification be Sent? Why Require Notification? The secured party must send the notification required by R9–611(b) to the persons specified in R9–611(c): the debtor, any secondary obligor, and, in the case of collateral other than consumer goods, certain persons who may have competing claims to the collateral involved. This last category of competing claimants includes persons from whom the secured party has received an authenticated notification of a claim and, subject to somewhat complex timing rules, persons who have security interests in the collateral perfected by filing. The timing complexity, found in R9–611(a), the definition of "notification date," and R9–611(c)(3)(B) and (e), is designed to protect the enforcing secured party from long delays in receiving a report from a filing office as to financing statements filed against the debtor covering the collateral. See 9–611, Comment 4.

Why require that reasonable notification of a proposed disposition be given to these particular classes of persons? The short answer is that they all may have a stake in whether the secured party complies with Part 6 in connection with the disposition. (One exception may be competing claimants who have an interest *senior* to that of the enforcing secured party, but we shall hold that issue for Section 3, infra.) The debtor and junior claimants would prefer to see the secured party recover the maximum value from the collateral. They wish to enhance their chances of picking up any excess over the enforcing secured party's claim. The notification requirement is a procedural safeguard intended to aid the debtor and competing claimants in protecting their own interests.

How does a reasonable notification assist a notified person in protecting its interests? A person may wish to attend a public sale in order to observe, first-hand, the procedures that are followed. Knowing the time of a public sale and the time after which a private sale may take place (the contents of a reasonable notification are discussed below in this Note) also may permit a debtor to arrange for a third-party buyer who otherwise would not have been attracted to the collateral. Moreover, the act of disposition (or contracting for a disposition) cuts off the debtor's right to pay the secured obligation in full and thereby "redeem" the collateral. See R9–623. Reasonable notification informs the debtor of the earliest date on which redemption rights could be lost. (Redemption is considered in Section 4, infra.) Moreover, particularly with respect to intangible collateral that has not been repossessed, the notification may alert the debtor to the need for a bankruptcy filing to stay the disposition. See BC 362(a) (discussed in Chapter 10, Section 1, supra). And it may induce a subordinate claimant to explore the possibility of an involuntary bankruptcy filing against the debtor so as to preserve the value of the collateral.

The exceptions to the notification requirement found in R9–611(d) reflect the situation in which the benefits of notification are outweighed by other risks (i.e., that the collateral will quickly perish or decline in value) or in which the protection afforded by a notification is not necessary (disposition on recognized market).

Timeliness of Notification of Disposition. Implicit in R9–611(b) is the idea that to be "reasonable" a notification must be sent within a reasonable time in advance of the date of the disposition. The question of timeliness is addressed more directly in R9–612(a). See R9–612, Comment 2 ("A notification that is sent so near to the disposition date that a notified person could not be expected to act or take account of the notification would be unreasonable.") How much time between giving a notification and a disposition is sufficient? Case law under F9–504(3) indicated that the secured party should feel reasonably safe in giving 10 days' notice. But this question of fact may turn on considerations such as the type, value, and location of the collateral; the knowledge and sophistication of the debtor; and general market conditions. Moreover, it should be answered in the context of the underlying purposes of the notification requirement, discussed above. The new 10–day "safe harbor" provided by R9–612(b) for non-consumer transactions offers the prospect of greater certainty under Revised Article 9. However, questions as to whether a notification was *sent* in a reasonable manner will remain. See R9–612, Comment 3.

Contents of a "Reasonable Authenticated Notification"; Authentication Requirement. The contents of a notification of disposition are specified in R9–613(1) for transactions other than a consumer-goods transaction and in R9–614(1) for a consumer-goods transaction. Each also contains a "safe-harbor" form of notification. In addition to information that serves to identify the relevant transaction, the most important requirements are found in R9–613(1)(C) ("the method of intended disposition") and (1)(E) ("the *time and place* of a *public sale* or the *time after which* any *other disposition* is to be made") (emphasis added). The information required by R9–613(1) is incorporated by reference in R9–614(1); the latter provision also requires additional information thought to be particularly important in consumer-goods transactions. Note also the "plain English" formulation of the form of notification found in R9–614(3).

Relying on the requirement in F9–504(3) that a notification be "sent" and the definition of "send" in UCC 1–201(38), some cases applying Former Article 9 held oral notifications to be ineffective. Others upheld oral notification, especially when it was clear that the debtor had actual knowledge of all information that a written notification would have contained. Revised Article 9, as well, requires the Secured Party to "send" (now defined for Article 9 purposes in R9–102(a)(74)) the notification of disposition. R9–611(b). And it resolves the issue against the effectiveness of an oral notification by requiring the secured party to "send ... a reasonable *authenticated* notification." R9–611(b) (emphasis added); see R9–102(a)(7) (defining "authenticate"), (69) (defining "record").

Send versus Receive; "Second Try." As just noted, R9–611(b) does not require that a person to be notified actually *receive* a notice; it provides only that the secured party "send ... a reasonable authenticated notification." Consider a secured party who sends a notification to a debtor's last known address, only to have the letter returned by the Postal Service: "Addressee unknown." Can the secured party comfortably proceed with a disposition? Must the secured party undertake at least "reasonable efforts" to locate the debtor's current address, taking into account whatever information is readily available to the secured party (e.g., telephone book, knowledge of the debtor's place of employment, etc.)? Some courts concluded under F9–504(3) that the secured party may need to "keep trying," at least for awhile. Comment 6 to R9–611 observes that Revised Article 9 "leaves to judicial resolution, based upon the facts of each case," whether a "second try" may be necessary in order to effect a reasonable notification.

Confusion: Notification of Disposition versus Advertisement of Collateral. Courts sometimes have confused notification of disposition under F9–504(3), which is carried forward in R9–611, with the advertising that may be a necessary component of a commercially reasonable disposition. (We believe it likely that some courts may have been confused by confused briefs filed by confused lawyers who relied upon confused opinions by other confused courts!) Although an inadequate notification to the debtor could bear on the issue of commercial reasonableness, that relationship normally is quite attenuated. The notification requirement is separate and independent from the commercially reasonable disposition requirement. The requirement of commercial reasonableness encourages secured parties to dispose of collateral in a manner that is likely to bring a good price. As explained above, the notification requirement is a procedural safeguard intended to aid the debtor and other interested persons in protecting their own interests.

(4) Application of Proceeds of Disposition; Right to Surplus or Obligation for Deficiency. An enforcing secured party's duties with respect to application of proceeds are found in R9–615(a) and (c). Subsection (a) substantially follows its predecessor, F9–504(1). Subsection (c) deals with noncash proceeds and is explained in R9–615, Comment 3. Section 3(B), infra, deals in more detail with the application of proceeds to junior interests. A debtor's right to any surplus and an obligor's obligation for a deficiency following application of the proceeds of a disposition are established by R9–615(d). Under subsection (e), however, these surplus and deficiency rules do not apply when the underlying transaction was a sale of accounts, chattel paper, payment intangibles, or promissory notes. Both subsections generally follow F9–504(2).

A secured party is required to send a written explanation of its calculation of a surplus or deficiency to a debtor in a consumer-goods transaction or to a consumer obligor in the circumstances described in R9–616. That provision is new; it had no predecessor under Former Article 9. Can you think of a reason why a secured party would object to the requirement? Can you think of a reason why the requirement should be limited to consumer-goods transactions?

(5) Pre-and Post–Default Debtor Waivers; Agreed Standards of Compliance. When the duties that a legal rule imposes are uncertain, the parties to a transaction may wish to eliminate the uncertainty through contract. For example, a secured party might seek the debtor's agreement that the secured party need not notify the debtor of a proposed disposition and need not dispose of the collateral in a commercially reasonable manner. Notwithstanding that the UCC generally promotes freedom of contract, see UCC 1–102(3), Article 9 provides that the parties may not waive or vary the most significant rights or duties that it imposes. See R9–602, which specifies the non-waivable rights and duties; please review these rights and duties now. For some narrow exceptions that permit certain post-default waivers, see R9–624.

Subject to limitations of its scope, Article 9 permits a debtor to encumber *all* its assets simply by signing a single piece of paper; yet the statute prohibits the debtor from agreeing as part of the same transaction to waive the right, for example, to notification of a disposition upon default. What explains Article 9's solicitude for debtors? Professor Gilmore's treatise gives one the impression that the original drafters of the UCC did not examine this issue anew.

> Since the beginnings of mortgage law, *it has never been questioned* that the mortgagor's equity is entitled to absolute protection and cannot be frittered away. No agreement, we have long been told, will be allowed to "clog the equity of redemption." And not even the most drastic of pledge agreements has ever purported to free the pledgee from his inescapable duties of accounting to the pledgor for the value of the pledged property and of remitting any surplus. *Article 9, therefore, merely reflects history* when it provides that the debtor's rights and the secured party's correlative duties following default "may not be waived or varied."

2 Gilmore, Security § 44.4, at 1228–29 (emphasis added). The drafters of Revised Article 9 did not reexamine this hoary principle. Should they have?

Although R9–602 is hostile to waivers, R9–603(a) provides that "the parties may determine by agreement standards measuring the fulfillment of the rights of a debtor or obligor and the duties of a secured party under a rule stated in R9–602 if the standards are not manifestly unreasonable." Security agreements that contain standards concerning the timeliness of notifications of disposition appear to be widely used, based on the reported cases. R9–603(a) follows closely F9–501(3).

Agreed standards concerning what constitutes a commercially reasonable disposition seem to be comparatively rare. One explanation for this phenomenon may be the widespread use of standard printed forms that normally are intended to cover many types of collateral. And in large business financings involving highly negotiated documentation, perhaps the anticipated result of a default is bankruptcy, not repossession; negotiating elaborate standards may not be considered worthwhile. On the other hand, might there be many kinds of repetitive transactions in which agreed standards may be advisable (e.g., secured financings of automobiles, trucks, farm equipment, horses)? Consider the types of standards that might be utilized (e.g., agreements as to the names and locations of publications where advertisements should be placed; the number of issues or days or weeks of advertising; whether the sale is to be public or private; specified auctioneer; maximum amount of sale-preparation expenses).

(6) Effects of Noncompliance Under Former Article 9: Three Approaches. What result if a secured party fails to dispose of collateral in a commercially reasonable manner under R9–610(b)? What result if it fails to send reasonable notification under R9–611? Or what result if it otherwise fails to comply with Part 6 of Revised Article 9 in enforcing its security interest? (We have already considered in Section 1 the question of damages when a secured party creates a breach of the peace in using self help to take possession of collateral under R9–609.) Revised Article 9 deals with the effects of noncompliance in Subpart 2 of Part 6, R9–625 through R9–628. Before turning to the substance of those rules, however, it is important to have some background on the approaches taken by the courts to noncompliance under Former Article 9, and in particular under F9–504 and F9–507.

Reported decisions reflect three sharply conflicting approaches to whether, and, if so, how a secured party's noncompliance with the foreclosure procedures prescribed by R9–504 affects the right to a deficiency.

Subsection (1) of F9–507 provided that the debtor "has a right to recover from the secured party any loss caused by a failure to comply with the provisions of this Part." R9–625(b) is to a similar effect concerning noncompliance with Revised Article 9 as a whole. One might understand F9–507 to have limited the debtor's remedy for noncompliance to the assertion of a cause of action: If the noncomplying secured party does not claim a deficiency, then the debtor would be entitled to an affirmative recovery; if the secured party does claim a deficiency, then the debtor would be entitled to set off its damages for noncompliance against the deficiency claim. (The third sentence of R9–507(1) afforded the debtor a minimum recovery for noncompliance when the collateral is consumer goods. R9–625(c) is similar. See Note (9), infra.)

Some courts adopted this reading of R9–507(1), which is known as the "offset" rule. Indeed, the plain meaning of the statutory text of Former Part 5 does not seem to support any other reading. Nonetheless, most courts adopted either the "rebuttable presumption" rule, as did Emmons v. Burkett, supra, or the "absolute bar" or "loss of deficiency" rule, which the court in First State Bank of Morrilton v. Hallett, supra, approved. As those opinions indicate, a substantial body of authority developed in support of each point of view. However, we doubt the accuracy of the Arkansas Supreme Court's statement in *First State Bank* that the absolute bar rule is the "apparent majority position." See Lloyd, The Absolute Bar Rule in UCC Foreclosure Sales: A Prescription for Waste, 40 UCLA L. Rev. 695 (1993) (indicating that 26 jurisdictions have adopted the rebuttable presumption rule, 11 the absolute bar rule, and 3 the offset rule).[2]

In any event, as the project to revise Article 9 began in 1993, the battle lines were drawn. And, as described in Note (7) below, the "battle" continued throughout the revision process.

Application of the Absolute Bar Rule: Impact on Other Collateral; Partial Dispositions. Consider the following scenario: Debtor gives Lender a security interest in collateral worth $10,000 to secure a loan of $100,000. On Debtor's default, Lender sells the collateral in a commercially unreason-

---

2. In a more recent case, the Supreme court of Arkansas cited *First State Bank* with approval for the proposition that "[w]hile a creditor is given the right to a deficiency judgment under ... [F9–504(2)], the creditor's right to such judgment depends on whether he has complied with the statutory requirements concerning disposition and notice." Mercantile Bank v. B & H Associated, Inc., 330 Ark. 315, 319, 954 S.W.2d 226, 229 (1997). However, the court then cited White & Summers and two cases predating *First State Bank* for the proposition that the rebuttable presumption rule applies when the noncompliance consists of a commercially unreasonable disposition. Id. (Recall that the noncompliance involved in *First State Bank* was the failure to give notification of the disposition.)

able manner or without reasonable notification to Debtor. Application of the absolute bar rule would prohibit Lender from recovering the balance of the debt, even if Debtor were solvent and able to pay.

Are you persuaded by the opinion in *First State Bank* that this result is desirable? As the foregoing scenario suggests, the rule is blatantly penal: any correlation between the harm done a debtor by the secured party's noncompliance and the sanction imposed on the secured party is entirely fortuitous. Why should a secured party's noncompliance put a debtor in a better position than would have been the case had the secured party complied? Indeed, UCC 1–106(1) makes clear that the UCC disapproves of such results.

The absolute bar rule has other potentially penal aspects. For example, under the facts set forth above, assume that Lender sold (again, employing defective procedures) only one item of collateral, worth $5,000; another item, also worth $5,000, remains unsold. Logically, having stripped Lender of its right to recover a deficiency (i.e., the remaining balance of the debt), the absolute bar rule would deprive Lender of any further right to recover on the remaining item. At least one court, however, permitted a secured party to recover on an *in rem* claim against the remaining collateral in this context.[3] Other secured parties have not been so fortunate, even when the remaining collateral was real property.

Arguably, the absolute bar rule has a proper domain in certain contexts, such as PMSI's in consumer goods, where some equivalence between the secured debt and the collateral might be expected. Distinguishing among various contexts would require legislative action, of course.

Even acknowledging that the absolute bar rule is penal and that UCC remedies generally are compensatory, is there a case to be made for adopting the rule? Consider this argument: Noncompliance with Article 9 is difficult to discover and prove, and in many cases the damages likely to be recovered (or offset against a deficiency) are not sufficiently large to justify the cost of litigation. As a result, secured parties who fail to comply with the remedial provisions of Article 9 often suffer no adverse consequences. By increasing the stakes, the absolute bar rule increases the likelihood that a noncomplying secured party will be held to task. Moreover, when viewed in the aggregate, it is not penal. Many secured parties are repeat players. The loss of deficiency in the few cases that are litigated is a rough substitute for the many smaller deficiencies that would have been lost had every case of noncompliance found its way into the judicial system. Do you find this argument persuasive? Does it have more bite in consumer or consumer-goods transactions than in commercial cases?

Significance of the Nature of Noncompliance: Unreasonable Notification or Commercially Unreasonable Disposition. Several of the early cases that adopted the absolute bar rule involved defective notification, not commercially unreasonable dispositions. There is some judicial support for applying the absolute bar rule to the failure to give the required notifica-

---

3. The same result would obtain if the secured debt were discharged in bankruptcy.

tion while applying the rebuttable presumption rule to noncompliance consisting of the failure to dispose of collateral in a commercially reasonable manner. There also is some authority for the converse: applying the rebuttable presumption rule to cases of improper (or missing) notification and the absolute bar rule to commercially unreasonable dispositions. Do you see any reason to treat noncompliance consisting of defective notification differently from that consisting of a commercially unreasonable disposition? The *Emmons* court makes it clear that the rebuttable presumption rule applies in the case of either defect. Although less explicit, the court's broad language in *First State Bank* indicates that it would apply the absolute bar rule in either case.

Application of the Rebuttable Presumption Rule. As noted by the court in the *Emmons* case, "[u]nder the rebuttable-presumption rule, if a creditor fails to give notice or conducts an unreasonable sale, a presumption is raised that the value of the collateral is equal to the indebtedness." However, compliance with Former Part 5 would not necessarily have resulted in the recovery of the "value" of collateral. See F9–507(2) (1st sentence); accord R9–627(a). Perhaps a better, more precise formulation of the rule would have been to create a rebuttable presumption that compliance with Former Part 5 would have yielded an amount sufficient to satisfy the secured debt. Stated otherwise, the noncomplying secured party would have the burden of proving the amount that would have been recovered had the secured party complied with Former Part 5, and the secured party's deficiency recovery would have been limited to the difference between that amount and the amount of the secured debt. As discussed in the following Note, this is essentially the formulation adopted by R9–626(a).

(7) Effect of Secured Party's Noncompliance Under Revised Article 9. The preceding Note explains the problem of divergent case law concerning the consequences of noncompliance under Former Article 9's enforcement provisions. In the previous edition of this book we predicted that "a statutory solution will emerge, whether in a revised Article 9 or in state-by-state nonuniform amendments." Our prediction proved only partially correct. For non-consumer transactions, R9–626(a) contains a detailed, statutory rebuttable presumption rule. For consumer transactions, however, Revised Article 9 is less forthcoming. It "leave[s] to the court the determination of the proper rules in consumer transactions." R9–626(b).

Statutory "Rebuttable Presumption" Test. The version of the rebuttable presumption rule codified in R9–626(a) for non-consumer transactions is straightforward, but nonetheless worth a close reading along with the comments. Unlike some of the formulations in the case law, the statutory rule does not presume the *value* of the collateral to be equal to the secured obligation; instead, it focuses on the amount that would have been realized in a complying disposition (or other enforcement). See R9–626(a)(3)(B), (4), and Comment 3. Consider also R9–625(d) and Comment 3, which address and prevent the possibility of a debtor's obtaining double recovery or overcompensation.

The Statutory "Silent Treatment" for Noncompliance in Consumer Transactions. As mentioned above, in consumer transactions Revised Article 9 invites the court to fashion the rule governing the consequences of noncompliance with the Article. See R9–626(b). You may find it odd for the legislature to prescribe statutory duties, such as the duty to conduct a commercially reasonable disposition of collateral, and yet leave to the courts the legal rules governing the consequences of noncompliance with those duties. How did this unusual state of affairs come about?

The consequence of noncompliance with Article 9's enforcement provisions was a matter upon which the advocates for consumer-credit providers and the advocates for consumer debtors and obligors sharply disagreed.[4] Recognizing that this disagreement would be likely to be reflected in debates before the state legislatures, the Drafting Committee decided that Revised Article 9 should offer statutory alternatives. Under a draft approved relatively late in the revision process, each legislature would have been invited to choose between (i) application of the rebuttable presumption rule (in substantially the form of R9–626(a)) to all transactions and (ii) application of the absolute bar rule to consumer transactions and the rebuttable presumption rule to other transactions. The draft version of the absolute bar rule was tempered by providing that a secured party who is barred from a deficiency nonetheless could seek a recovery from remaining *collateral*. The statutory alternatives were accompanied by a variety of other consumer-protection provisions. Considering that neither set of advocates was entirely satisfied by this approach to the effect of noncompliance (or by the consumer-protection provisions taken as a whole), the Drafting Committee realized that it probably had the balance about right. It was content with its centrist approach.

Long and intense discussions among consumer and creditor representatives followed. With few exceptions, neither the members of the Drafting Committee nor the Reporters participated in these discussions. Eventually, as part of a "compromise" on a variety of consumer issues, and over the objections of the Reporters, representatives of firms that provide consumer credit and representatives of consumer-advocacy groups settled upon language similar to that of R9–626(b). The Drafting Committee and then the UCC's sponsors approved. Assuming that nonuniformity on this issue is inevitable, what reasons might there be for favoring judicial, as opposed to legislative, rulemaking in this context? Does anything other than political expediency justify the adoption of different rules for determining the consequences of noncompliance in commercial and consumer transactions? See Note (6), supra.

How will counsel for enforcing creditors and defaulting consumers be likely to respond to the "neutrality" of R–626(b)? Consider the Reporters'

---

4. These advocates included representatives of the American Financial Services Association (a national trade organization of consumer finance companies), the finance companies of the "big three" domestic automobile manufacturers, the California Bankers Association, Consumers Union, and the National Consumer Law Center, as well as a few law professors and legal services lawyers.

Comments to the March 10, 1998, draft of Revised Article 9 (the first draft to incorporate the "consumer compromise"). Note that what became R9–625 and R9–626 were denominated 9–624 and 9–625 in that draft.

Reporters' Comments

Changes from Prior Draft:

A. This draft deletes Alternative A of Section 9–625, which contemplated that a legislature might choose to adopt the absolute bar rule statutorily. Instead, Section 9–625 now codifies the rebuttable presumption rule for non-consumer-goods transactions. Except as to actual damages recoverable under Section 9–624(b), however, the draft is silent as to whether a secured party's noncompliance in a consumer-goods transaction affects a deficiency claim and, if so, the nature of the effect. Thus, if a jurisdiction is to adopt an absolute bar rule, it must do so judicially.

How the courts construe revised Article 9 will determine whether the status of consumer-goods transactions ultimately remains unchanged from that under former Article 9. Unlike this draft, former Article 9 contained no hint that deficiencies in consumer-and non-consumer transactions should receive differing treatment. This draft can be read to indicate that rebuttable presumption treatment should not (and certainly that it might not) be appropriate for consumer-goods transactions. Moreover, counsel for debtors in jurisdictions that have adopted the "actual damages" rule based on a straightforward reading of former Section 9–507 (in lieu or either absolute bar or rebuttable presumption) will be compelled to argue for absolute bar under revised Article 9. Courts may be loathe to embrace a rule that is *less* favorable for consumers (actual damages) than the rule applicable in non-consumer-goods transactions (rebuttable presumption). On the other hand, counsel for creditors in absolute-bar jurisdictions can be expected to argue that the legislative approval of the rebuttable presumption rule for non-consumer-goods transactions signals rejection of the absolute bar rule for all transactions, on the ground that all the policy reasons supporting the rebuttable presumption rule apply with equal force to consumer-goods transactions. Thus, the approach taken in the draft may lead to extensive litigation and relitigation under revised Article 9, even in jurisdictions where the law already had been settled under former Article 9. On the other hand, the Official Comments will indicate that the silence in this section with respect to consumer-goods transactions leaves courts free to continue to apply established law. See Comment y, below. If followed, this comment would leave the law where it was under former Article 9.

B. Alternative A of Section 9–625 also was intended to rationalize and clarify the law even in jurisdictions that may already have opted judicially for the absolute bar rule. For example, it dealt with the effect of noncompliance when other collateral securing the deficiency remains following a disposition. Section 9–625(c) also clarifies the application of the rebuttable presumption rule. Because subsection (c) does not apply to consumer-goods transactions, however, the benefits of the clarifications (e.g., allocation of the burden of proof) may be unavailable in those transactions. A court might be reluctant to apply the statutory rule embodied in Section 9–625 to consumer-goods transactions by analogy, inasmuch as it does not apply to those transactions by its terms. However, the Official Comments could attempt to negate any inferences that might otherwise be drawn from silence.

Subsequently, what is now R9–626(b), the "no-inference" or "neutrality" provision was put in the draft. Do you think it will have the intended effects?

Revised Article 9 distinguishes between consumer and non-consumer transactions in other aspects of enforcement. These provisions are listed in R9–101, Comment 4.j., items (v) through (ix).

Nonuniform Statutory Treatment. Not every state legislature has been content to leave the consequences of noncompliance with Revised Article 9 in consumer transactions to the judiciary. For example, California's enactment of Revised Article 9 rejects outright the "consumer compromise" with respect to R9–626. Instead, it adopts a nonuniform R9–626(b) that embraces for consumer transactions a version of the absolute bar rule along the lines of that found in California's nonuniform version of F9–504. See Cal. Com. Code § 9626(b) (effective July 1, 2001); Cal. Com. Code § 9504(2). Under California R9–626(b), a debtor or secondary obligor is not liable for a deficiency unless, inter alia, notification was given in accordance with R9–611 and the disposition or other enforcement was conducted in good faith and in a commercially reasonable manner. A secured party who loses a deficiency under R9–626(b) or R9–615(f) (dealing with "low price" dispositions to the secured party or a related person) remains liable for any damages and also loses the benefits of any remaining collateral securing the deficiency: The secured party may not retain a security interest in any other collateral; and, if the secured party subsequently disposes of collateral that had secured the deficiency, the debtor may recover from the secured party the proceeds of the disposition.

Other states have not been so solicitous of defaulting consumer debtors. For example, several states apply the rebuttable presumption rule of R9–626(a) to all transactions, including consumer transactions. These states include Illinois, Indiana, Maryland, Nebraska, South Dakota, Tennessee, Virginia, and Washington.

(8) Restrictions on Deficiency Recoveries in Consumer Transactions. The preceding Note describes the California approach to the liability of consumers for a deficiency. Massachusetts has taken a different tack. In consumer credit transactions involving $2,000 or less that are secured by "a non-possessory security interest in consumer goods," the debtor is entirely excused from any deficiency liability once the secured party takes or accepts possession. In consumer credit transactions involving $2,000 or more (at the time of default), the deficiency is calculated by deducting from the outstanding secured obligation the "fair market value" of the collateral, *not* by deducting the net sale proceeds as provided by R9–504(2). Mass. Ann. Laws ch. 255B, § 20B(d) & (e). (If the debt is *exactly* $2,000, *both* rules seem to apply!)

The Massachusetts legislation reflects an approach to deficiencies in consumer transactions that is a throwback to pre-UCC rules and that has gained some support nationally. In the classical conditional sale (in which "title" did not pass to the buyer until the buyer paid the purchase price in full), the conditional seller was required to elect between alternative remedies when the buyer defaulted: The seller could (i) repossess the goods sold *or* (ii) sue for the price (i.e., the remaining balance due). If the seller repossessed the goods, it had no further claim against the buyer. A claim for a "deficiency" was an attribute of a "mortgage" and not permitted in the setting of a conditional sale. See Gilmore, Security §§ 3.2, 43.1.

Before the UCC, most experts on the law of conditional sales concluded that the election doctrine was awkward and harsh; it was generally assumed that the Uniform Conditional Sales Act made a significant contribution to the law by permitting the seller, on repossession, to establish a deficiency (usually by a public sale) for which the buyer would be liable. See Uniform Conditional Sales Act § 22 (1918) (superseded).

With that background, one can appreciate the sensation of *deja vu* in encountering the election doctrine in the 1974 version of U3C 5.103, set out at the end of this Note. The 1968 version similarly restricted deficiency judgments with respect to consumer credit sales of goods or services. Although neither version of the U3C has been widely adopted, several states have adopted election-of-remedies statutes modeled, to a greater or lesser extent, on U3C 5.103.

Would Lee Abel, in the Prototype transaction, and most other buyers of automobiles have protection from deficiency judgments under the U3C? What types of transactions and what buyers typically would receive protection under U3C 5.103? Would this provision provide some assistance when goods prove to be shoddy? Does it afford sufficient protection to the secured party when the goods are abused?

The denial of deficiency claims when the creditor repossesses has been characterized as self-defeating. Apart from cars, most consumer goods have little resale value; a creditor could avoid losing a claim for deficiency by not repossessing and pressing for collection of the debt. Perhaps the only consequence of this reform "is to leave the poor with the dissatisfaction of his merchandise." See Kripke, Gesture and Reality in Consumer Credit Reform, 44 N.Y.U.L.Rev. 1, 32–34 (1969). Professor Kripke suggests that a logical extension of the thinking behind the denial of deficiency judgments is a proposal to limit the creditor's recourse to the *collateral*. But such proposals to restrict the creditor's remedies, he suggested, could result in withdrawal of credit from the poorest credit risks, or in raising of the price level of merchandise "thus taxing the poor who struggle through their payment requirements with an added cost absorbing the losses of others who do not pay."

UNIFORM CONSUMER CREDIT CODE (1974)

Section 5.103   [Restrictions on Deficiency Judgments]

(1) This section applies to a deficiency on a consumer credit sale of goods or services and on a consumer loan in which the lender is subject to claims and defenses arising from sales and leases (Section 3.405). A consumer is not liable for a deficiency unless the creditor has disposed of the goods in good faith and in a commercially reasonable manner.

(2) If the seller repossesses or voluntarily accepts surrender of goods that were the subject of the sale and in which he has a security interest, the consumer is not personally liable to the seller for the unpaid balance of the debt arising from the sale of a commercial unit of goods of which the cash sale price was $1,750 or less, and the seller is not obligated to resell the collateral unless the consumer has paid 60 per cent or more of the cash price and has not signed after default a statement renouncing his rights in the collateral.

(3) If the seller repossesses or voluntarily accepts surrender of goods that were not the subject of the sale but in which he has a security interest to secure a debt arising from a sale of goods or services or a combined sale of goods and services[*] and the cash price of the sale was $1,750 or less, the consumer is not personally liable to the seller for the unpaid balance of the debt arising from the sale, and the seller's duty to dispose of the collateral is governed by the provisions on disposition of collateral (Part 5 of [Former] Article 9 [i.e., Part 6 of Revised Article 9]) of the Uniform Commercial Code.

(4) If the lender takes possession or voluntarily accepts surrender of goods in which he has a purchase money security interest to secure a debt arising from a consumer loan in which the lender is subject to claims and defenses arising from sales and leases (Section 3.405) and the net proceeds of the loan paid to or for the benefit of the consumer were $1,750 or less, the consumer is not personally liable to the lender for the unpaid balance of the debt arising from that loan and the lender's duty to dispose of the collateral is governed by the provisions on disposition of collateral (Part 5 of Article 9) of the Uniform Commercial Code.

(5) For the purpose of determining the unpaid balance of consolidated debts or debts pursuant to open-end credit, the allocation of payments to a debt shall be determined in the same manner as provided for determining the amount of debt secured by various security interests (Section 3.303).

(6) The consumer may be held liable in damages to the creditor if the consumer has wrongfully damaged the collateral or if, after default

---

* [This provision would come into play only infrequently under current law, given the FTC's restrictions on nonpossessory, non-PMSI's. See 16 C.F.R. 444.2(a)(4) (it is an unfair practice for lenders or retail installment sellers to obtain from consumers nonpossessory security interests, other than PMSI's, in household goods).]

and demand, the consumer has wrongfully failed to make the collateral available to the creditor.

(7) If the creditor elects to bring an action against the consumer for a debt arising from a consumer credit sale of goods or services or from a consumer loan in which the lender is subject to claims and defenses arising from sales and leases (Section 3.405), when under this section he would not be entitled to a deficiency judgment if he took possession of the collateral, and obtains judgment:

(a) he may not take possession of the collateral, and

(b) the collateral is not subject to levy or sale on execution or similar proceedings pursuant to the judgment.

(8) The amounts of $1,750 in subsections (2), (3) and (4) are subject to change pursuant to the provisions on adjustment of dollar amounts (Section 1.106).

(9) The Consumer Debtor's "Minimum Recovery." An injury caused by a secured party's noncompliance with Part 6 of Revised Article 9 normally is limited by the monetary value of the collateral. Inasmuch as the value of most consumer goods is small and the cost of litigation often is high, one might expect that consumers often would be unwilling or unable to avail themselves of the remedy of damages under R9–625(b). Perhaps for this reason, R9–625(c)(2) (which closely follows F9–507(1)) affords what Comment 4 calls a "minimum recovery" as follows:

> if the collateral is consumer goods, a person that was a debtor or a secondary obligor at the time a secured party failed to comply with this part may recover for that failure in any event an amount not less than the credit service charge plus ten per cent of the principal amount of the obligation or the time-price differential plus 10 per cent of the cash price.

Observe that, like the absolute bar rule, this remedy for noncompliance in the case of consumer goods need not bear any relationship to the injury resulting from the secured party's misconduct. Indeed, there may have been no injury at all. Isn't the "minimum recovery" more property called a "civil penalty"? At least one case has construed F9–507(1) to impose upon a noncomplying secured party *two* penalties—loss of deficiency and an adverse judgment. Does Revised Article 9 contemplate such a result? See UCC 1–106(1); R9–625(c) & Comment 3 ("the statute is silent as to whether a double recovery or other over-compensation is possible in a consumer transaction.").

(10) Consumer Advocacy. In discussing the special provisions for consumers in Part 6 we have referred to "advocates for consumer borrowers" and "consumer advocacy groups." Keep in mind, however, that in the context of default and remedies these advocates were speaking on behalf of consumers who *default* (presumably, a distinct minority of consumer debtors and obligors). Is it possible (probable?) that legal rules protecting and benefiting defaulting consumers do not necessarily benefit consumers generally? To the extent that "consumer-protection" provisions reduce the net recoveries of creditors, who bears the ultimate cost of those reductions? Do you suppose that the creditors' profit margins will decline correspondingly? Or, will the costs instead be passed on to other, non-defaulting consumers (e.g., in the form of increased finance charges)? Will the two groups, consumers and creditors, share the costs? (The vigor with which the advocates for consumer-credit providers fought against many of the consumer-protection provisions proposed for inclusion in Revised Article 9 suggests that they thought at least some of the costs would have come to rest with creditors.)

It may not be possible to answer these questions in the abstract; the answers may turn on facts such as the characteristics of the particular credit market and the size of the costs imposed by the particular consumer-protection provisions. For example, recall the reported effects of the Wisconsin Consumer Act, which permits repossession collateral only after the secured party obtains a court determination that the creditor is entitled to the collateral: While the cost of repossessions rose significantly and the volume of repossessions dropped, the principal impact on credit seemed to be confined to requiring larger down payments in the sale of used cars. Whitford and Laufer, The Impact of Denying Self–Help Repossession of Automobiles: A Case Study of the Wisconsin Consumer Act, 1975 Wis. L.Rev. 607, 654. In his study of real property mortgagor-protection laws, Professor Schill concluded:

> In this Article I argue that the accepted wisdom regarding mortgagor protection laws requires substantial revision. I find, contrary to the results of other empirical studies, that it is unlikely that mortgagor protection laws substantially increase the costs of home credit. This empirical finding is consistent with the theory that when viewed from an ex ante perspective, mortgagor protections may promote, rather than impede, economic efficiency by functioning as a form of insurance against the adverse effects of default and foreclosure. Government intervention in mortgage markets to mandate protection, in the form of deficiency judgment prohibitions, statutory rights of redemption, or a compulsory mortgage foreclosure insurance program, may be necessary to correct market failures attributable to imperfect information.

Schill, An Economic Analysis of Mortgagor Protection Laws, 77 Va. L. Rev. 489, 537–38 (1991).

Assume that statutory consumer-protection requirements impose costs on every consumer borrower, and that the requirements actually benefit only a very small proportion of consumer borrowers. Does it necessarily follow that the requirements are a bad idea? Or, can they be justified as a form of mandatory insurance against the risk of default? (I.e., were the "consumer advocacy groups" advocating not for every consumer who *does* default but rather for every consumer who *may* default?) Can statutorily-imposed mandatory insurance of this kind be justified only if all consumer borrowers would willingly pay for it? Most consumer borrowers?

(11) Applicable Law. It seems to be settled that an effective agreement as to the applicable law, under UCC 1–105(1), will be controlling for purposes of enforcement under Article 9. See, e.g., Bancorp Leasing & Financial Corp. v. Burhoop, 749 F.2d 36, 39 U.C.C. Rep. Serv. 1426 (9th Cir.1984) (unpublished) (parties' choice of Colorado law, which follows rebuttable presumption rule for defective notification of disposition, controlled in California forum, notwithstanding California's adherence to absolute bar rule); Jones v. First National Bank of Pulaski, 505 So.2d 352 (Ala.1987) (parties' choice of Tennessee law controlled, in Alabama forum, as to adequacy of notification of disposition). As each state's approach to noncompliance in consumer transactions becomes clear, the parties in consumer transactions may wish to avail themselves of the opportunity to opt in or out of the absolute bar rule or rebuttable presumption rule (or other judicially created or statutory rule), particularly when a transaction is likely to bear a reasonable relation to more than one state. Note that consumer transactions may be subject to special legal restrictions on the selection of applicable law, thereby affording less flexibility than UCC 1–105 permits.

(12) Rights and Duties of Secured Parties Under R9–207. When we considered perfection of security interests by possession we noted the rights and duties of secured parties under R9–207. See Note (4) on Perfection by Possession, Chapter 7, Section 3(B), supra. The most significant duty, of course, is the requirement to use "reasonable care in the custody and preservation of collateral" when it is in the secured party's possession. R9–207(a). R9–207 also applies when a secured party has taken possession after a debtor's default. R9–601(b).

SECTION 3.   RIGHTS OF THIRD–PARTY CLAIMANTS

Introduction. Sections 1 and 2 of this Chapter dealt with the enforcement rights of the secured party and the duties it owes to the debtor. This Section deals with the rights of certain third parties when a secured party enforces a security interest in collateral. Part (A) considers the rights of secondary obligors for secured obligations, such as guarantors of payment; Part (B) addresses competing secured parties and other lienholders, both senior and junior to the enforcing secured party, and the position of a transferee of collateral at a disposition conducted under R9–610.

(A) SECONDARY OBLIGORS (INCLUDING GUARANTORS)

Introductory Note: The Elements of Suretyship. Secured lenders and sellers frequently bargain for (perhaps more accurately, insist on) a third-party **guaranty of payment**. Under a guaranty, a third party (the "guarantor") undertakes to pay an obligation of the debtor (the borrower or buyer). If the debtor defaults in payment of the obligation, then the guarantor must step up and pay it (or an agreed portion thereof). Most guaranties provide that the guarantor "unconditionally guarantees the punctual payment when due" of the debtor's obligations; they normally do not condition liability on the debtor's default. In practice, however, a guarantor usually will not be prepared to pay the guaranteed obligation unless it is informed that the debtor has failed to pay. Guaranties are given in transactions that span the spectrum of secured and unsecured credit. Examples abound: Large corporations guaranty payment of debts incurred by their subsidiaries; parents guaranty payment by young daughters and sons who do not have an established credit rating; principal shareholders of closely-held corporations guaranty the corporate borrowings.

A guaranty of payment is governed by the law of **suretyship.** There are many other kinds of suretyship contracts. A common example is the **performance bond**, under which an insurance company or other surety company agrees to complete the performance of a construction contract if the contractor fails to perform as agreed. Before focusing specifically on the guaranty of payment in the context of secured credit, the chief area of concern here, it will be useful to have a nodding acquaintance with the elements of suretyship law.

Although the obligation of a third party who acts as a surety is not "collateral" (R9–102(a)(12)) subject to a "security interest" (R1–201(37)), the obligation nevertheless was classified within the general category of "security" by the Restatement of Security: "Suretyship is included in the general field of Security because the obligation of a surety is an additional assurance to the one entitled to the performance of an act that the act will be performed." Restatement of Security, Scope Note to Division II (1941). Division II of that Restatement has been superseded by the Restatement (Third) Suretyship and Guaranty ("Restatement"), promulgated in 1996 by the American Law Institute. The discussion that follows is based primarily on the Restatement.

What Is "Suretyship"? Fortunately, we need not attempt here a hair-splitting analysis of a of "surety" or "suretyship"; the materials here are in the mainstream, and far from the penumbra, of suretyship law. The Restatement § 1(1) provides a satisfactory working definition:

> (1) This Restatement applies ... and a secondary obligor has suretyship status whenever:

>> (a) pursuant to contract (the "secondary obligation"), an obligee has recourse against a person (the "secondary obligor") or that person's property with respect to the obligation (the "underlying obligation") of another person (the "principal obligor"); and

>> (b) to the extent that the underlying obligation or the secondary obligation is performed the obligee is not entitled to performance of the other obligation; and

>> (c) as between the principal obligor and the secondary obligor, it is the principal obligor who ought to perform the underlying obligation or bear the cost of performance.

(The Restatement uses generic terms such as "secondary obligor" and "secondary obligation" because considerable (and unnecessary) confusion surrounds the exact meaning of "guaranty," "guarantor," and "surety." If there is any sense in attempting to dispel this confusion, the task is best left for another time and place.)

Take a simple example. Suppose that *P* wishes to borrow $5,000 from *O*. To induce *O* to make the loan, *P* has *S* join with *P* in promising to repay. As further security, *P* pledges $30,000 worth of corporate bonds to *O*. Both *P* and *S* are under an obligation to *O*; *O* is entitled to but one performance; and as between *P* and *S*, *P* rather than *S* should perform. This relationship clearly fits the Restatement conception of suretyship. *P* is the *principal obligor, S* is the *secondary obligor,* and *O* is the *obligee.* If *S* engages in the business of executing surety contracts for a premium determined by a computation of risks spread over a large number of transactions, *S* typically is subject to state law regulation as an insurance company. Such a secondary obligor may not be discharged from liability as readily as an uncompensated or gratuitous surety.

O's rights against *P* are governed basically by contract law: Absent a contract defense (e.g., *O*'s fraud upon *P*; *P*'s infancy), *O* will have the right to enforce the obligation against *P*.

The Obligee's Rights Against the Secondary Obligor. In the alternative, *O* may proceed against *S*, the secondary obligor. If *P* defaults, generally *O* need not attempt to collect from *P* before enforcing *S*'s liability; nor need *O* look first to the corporate bonds. Immediate recourse against *S* upon *P*'s default was one of the advantages that *O* expected from *S*'s suretyship contract. Even if *O*'s lack of diligence in pursuing *P* causes loss, *S* is not discharged.[1] In a number of states this rule is subject to an exception under which *O*'s failure to sue *P* at *S*'s request discharges *S*.[2] (Compare the

---

1. See Restatement § 50(1). It is, of course, possible for the surety to limit its engagement to a guaranty of *collection* of the principal's obligation. Such a **guarantor of collection** is, by the nature of the undertaking, discharged to the extent of any loss caused by the creditor's lack of diligence in proceeding against the principal. See Restatement § 50(2). Understandably, guaranties of collection are rare in the credit markets. The Restatement also recognizes exceptions to the rule preserving the obligee's right to recover from the secondary obligor, e.g., when the rule is overridden by statute or agreement of the parties and when the Obligee allows the statute of limitations to lapse on the underlying obligation. See Restatement § 50(1).

2. The exception was laid down in Pain v. Packard, 13 Johns. (N.Y. Sup. Ct.) 174 (1816). In that case the secondary obligor, when sued by the obligee, pleaded that he had requested the obligee to proceed immediately to collect from the principal obligor; that the obligee had not done so; and that

although the principal obligor could have then been compelled to pay, he later became insolvent and absconded. The court held that his plea stated a good defense; since the defendant was known to be a secondary obligor, the obligee, was "bound to use due diligence against the principal [obligor] in order to exonerate the surety." A number of other states have adopted some form of the rule in Pain v. Packard, in most instances by statute. It was rejected by the Restatement of Security § 130 and by the great majority of courts that have faced the issue without statutory guidance. It also was rejected by the Restatement:

> Since the secondary obligor may seek enforcement of the principal obligor's duty of performance (§ 21) even if the obligee has not sought enforcement of the underlying obligation, the obligee's inaction generally affords no equitable basis for a claim of discharge by the secondary obligor.

engagement of an accommodation party on a negotiable instrument under UCC 3–414(b), (e); UCC 3–415(a), (b); UCC 3–419.)

S, who is subject to an action by *O* should *P* default, has in turn three major remedies against *P*: exoneration, subrogation, and reimbursement. *S*'s right of **exoneration** is an equitable one. Basically it allows *S*, upon *P*'s default, to compel *P* in a suit in equity to pay *O*. Restatement § 21(2) and comment *i*. It is reasoned that without this remedy *S* might undergo considerable hardship in raising the money to pay *O*, even though *S* could afterwards recover over from *P*. However, secondary obligors rarely assert the right to exoneration, probably because most principal obligors who *do not* pay probably *cannot* pay. Moreover, the right to exoneration against *P* does not give *S* any right to delay paying *O*. Thus, the secondary obligor usually will pay the creditor and then attempt to recover from the principal under the right to subrogation or reimbursement.

When *S* pays in full *P*'s debt to *O*, *S* is subrogated to the rights of *O*. See Restatement §§ 27–28. **Subrogation** may be viewed as equitable assignment. *S* would therefore succeed, as by assignment, to *O*'s rights (as holder of the secured debt and as pledgee of the corporate bonds) against *P* and to the priority of *O*'s security interest as against third parties. Since the right is an equitable one, it is subject to equitable limitations.[4] An important qualification is that if the debt has not been paid *in full*, the surety ordinarily has no right of subrogation. Thus in the usual case if *S* should pay *O* only $40,000, leaving a balance of $10,000 due, *S* would not thereby be entitled to any part of *O*'s security interest in the bonds. This is to insure that the benefits of *P*'s collateral are applied first to the satisfaction of *P*'s debt to *O*.

A surety that pays any part of the principal obligor's debt is, however, entitled to **reimbursement** (sometimes called **indemnification**) of the amount paid. See Restatement §§ 22–23. So, even though *S* paid only $40,000 of the $50,000 debt to *P*, *S* is entitled to reimbursement to that extent. Because *S* became bound as surety at the request of *P*, *S*'s right to reimbursement can be spelled out from *P*'s implied request to *S* to pay the debt at maturity and from *P*'s implied promise to reimburse *S* for any such payment. (Well-drafted suretyship contracts explicitly provide for a right to reimbursement.) Of course, the right to reimbursement is only a right *in personam* against *P* and may be, for this reason, less satisfactory to *S* than subrogation, particularly if *S* must compete with other creditors of *P*.

The Secondary Obligor's Defenses. Exoneration, subrogation and reimbursement, then, are the three principal remedies of *S* against *P*. An elementary understanding of them is necessary to answer the next question: In what circumstances will an agreement between *O* and *P* to *modify* *P*'s obligation to *O* operate to *discharge S* from its obligation as surety?[5]

Restatement § 50, comment *a*. Pain v. Packard was overruled by statute in New York in 1968. See N.Y. Gen. Oblig. Law § 15–701.

4. This is particularly true where the secondary obligor attempts to enforce a right that the obligee would have had against a third party.

5. This discussion of discharge of a surety is premised upon the assumption that the obligee has knowledge of the suretyship relationship of *S*. See Restatement § 32.

Suppose that *O* and *P* were to modify their original agreement so as to increase the interest rate from eight to nine per cent. Under traditional doctrine supported by much case law, *S* would be discharged. The modification has increased the burden on *P* and made it more likely that *P* will default. However, should the modification decrease the interest rate from eight to seven per cent, it is difficult to justify discharge of *S* because *S* is not prejudiced. Nevertheless, there is authority for the proposition that since a suretyship contract is *strictissimi juris,* the secondary obligor will be discharged whether the modification increases or decreases the burden of the principal's performance! Under the Restatement, however, the secondary obligor's obligation is discharged only to the extent that the modification imposes "fundamentally different" risks on the secondary obligor or causes the secondary obligor loss. Restatement § 41(b).

Consider two other common types of modification—*O*'s release of *P* and *O*'s extension of the time for *P* to perform. It is hardly surprising that under traditional doctrine release of *P* generally discharges *S*. However, *O* could easily preserve *S*'s liability. To accomplish this result, *O* could merely reserve its rights against *S* at the time of *P*'s release. One might question the fairness of this rule to *P*, who would be "released" but may not realize that it remains liable to *S* (via reimbursement or subrogation) for the full amount of the obligation. One might also question its fairness to *S*. *S* may not realize that *P* was released and instead assume that *P* had paid the underlying obligation. Had *S* been informed, *S* might have taken prompt action to protect its rights against *P*.

The Restatement takes an approach towards suretyship defenses that differs somewhat from the traditional doctrine. *O*'s release of *P*'s obligation to pay money is a type of "impairment of recourse" under the Restatement. See Restatement § 37(3)(a). Although in general the release would discharge *S*, the Restatement, like traditional doctrine, permits *O* to preserve *S*'s liability. The Restatement replaces the "reservation of rights" doctrine with the doctrine of "preservation of the secondary obligor's recourse." Like its predecessor, the preservation-of-recourse doctrine enables *O* to release *P* while affecting no change in *P*'s liability to *S*. See Restatement § 39(b). A release or extension effects a preservation of recourse if the *express terms* of the release or extension provide that (i) *O* retains the right to seek performance from *S* and (ii) *S*'s rights to recourse against *P* continue as though the release or extension had not been granted. Restatement § 38(1).

Unlike a reservation of rights, a preservation of recourse does not necessarily prevent *S* from being discharged. Even if *S*'s recourse has been preserved, *S* will be discharged to the extent that the release or extension would otherwise cause *S* a loss. Restatement § 39(c). The comments to the Restatement suggest that *O* can prevent the release or extension from causing a loss to *S* by informing *S* promptly of the release or extension and the fact that recourse has been preserved. Restatement § 38, comment *b*.

Nevertheless, the comments indicate that even when S has been informed, "loss can still occur." Id. For example, the release may induce behavior on P's part that lessens P's ability to perform. In many cases, however, S will not suffer a loss because it would be unlikely that S could have had any recovery against an impecunious P. Restatement § 39, comment f.

A binding agreement between O and P extending the time for P's performance is another type of "impairment of recourse" under the Restatement. Restatement § 37(3)(b). That impairment, as with a release of P's payment obligation, will discharge S to the extent that the extension causes a loss, even if O has preserved the secondary obligor's recourse. Restatement § 40(a), (b). If O has preserved S's recourse against P, then S may avoid any prejudicial effect of the extension by paying at the original maturity and proceeding against P in spite of the extension. Restatement § 40(c).

Finally, a third type of impairment of recourse under the Restatement occurs if O "impair[s] the value of an interest in collateral securing the underlying obligation," as by releasing the security interest in the bonds that O holds to secure P's debt. Restatement § 37(d). This impairment discharges S "to the extent that such impairment would otherwise increase the difference between the maximum amount recoverable by the secondary obligor pursuant to its subrogation rights ... and the value of the secondary obligor's interest in the collateral." Restatement § 42(1). Thus, if O should release the security interest in the $30,000 worth of bonds, S would be discharged to the extent of $30,000. O's failure to perfect the security interest also could constitute an impairment of collateral if a buyer or other conflicting claimant were to prevent S from receiving the benefit of the collateral.

UCC 3–605 deals explicitly with issues of discharge of a secondary obligor who is an "accommodation party" to a negotiable instrument, i.e., who "signs the instrument for the purpose of incurring liability on the instrument without being a direct beneficiary of the value given for the instrument." UCC 3–419(a). (The "co-maker" of a negotiable note is an "accommodation party.") Extensions of time, other material modifications of terms, and impairment of collateral will discharge an accommodation party only to the extent that the accommodation party suffers loss thereby. UCC 3–605(c), (d), (f), & (g). Moreover, an accommodation party is not discharged if it gives consent to the event or conduct involved or waives in advance its suretyship defenses. UCC 3–605(i). These UCC Article 3 provisions rarely come into play when the obligee is in the business of extending credit. Even if the obligation is evidenced by a negotiable note (which is uncommon), such obligees customarily obtain a separate guaranty.

Waiver of Suretyship Defenses; Consent by Secondary Obligor. Both Restatement § 48 and its predecessor, Restatement, Security, give effect to a secondary obligor's consent to acts that otherwise would discharge the secondary obligor and to a secondary obligor's waiver of its suretyship defenses. Indeed, these consents and waivers almost universally are contained in guaranties of payment that feature in financing transactions. On the other hand, good practice often dictates that a careful lender will request express and explicit consent from guarantor before pursuing a course of action that, absent effective consent or waiver, would cause a discharge (e.g., release of collateral). The relationship between the generally applicable ability of a secondary obligor to waive its suretyship defenses and the non-waivable rights and duties under R9–602 is addressed in Note (2), infra.

Secondary Obligor vs. Secured Party: A Brief Excursus. One additional aspect of the relationship between suretyship law and Article 9 should be mentioned. Assume that a principal debtor (*P*) has a contract to build a building for the owner of land (*O*). As is customary, *P* obtains a performance bond, under which a third-party secondary obligor (*S*) undertakes to complete the building if *P* should default in its performance. In addition, a secured party, *SP*, has a security interest in *P*'s accounts, including *P*'s right to payment from *O*. Following *P*'s default and *S*'s completion of the contract, both *S* and *SP* claim the remaining amounts owing by *O* to *P*. The source of *S*'s claim is the law of suretyship: Having completed the contract, *S* is subrogated to *P*'s rights against *O*, which include the right to be paid for a completed building. *S*'s claim may include the right to funds earned by *P*'s pre-default performance but withheld by *O* pursuant to the contract. This right is premised on the notion that *S* is subrogated to *O*'s rights.

Although *SP* has perfected its security interest by filing, *S* has not filed. Whose claim is senior? The law has become well-settled since the leading case of National Shawmut Bank v. New Amsterdam Casualty Co., 411 F.2d 843 (1st Cir.1969). *S* wins. *S*'s rights do not derive from a consensual security interest under Article 9, but instead are born of suretyship law. Accordingly, the priority rules of Article 9 are inapplicable.

As we have seen, F9–201 has been construed to award priority to a security interest over a conflicting non-Article 9 interest (the right of setoff). See Chapter 11, Section 5(C), supra. What accounts for the near unanimity of judicial opinion in favor of sureties? An intuitive approach might be to ask, what would the value of *SP*'s collateral have been had *S* not performed? Is it fair to pay *S* for the value its performance created? Alternatively, one might (but courts generally have not) rank the competing claims by reference to F9–318(1). The secured party ordinarily takes its rights subject to "all the terms of the contract between the account debtor [*O*] and assignor [*P*] and any defense or claim arising therefrom." Accord R9–404(a)(1). Wouldn't *P*'s breach have given *O* a defense to payment, or at least a partial setoff? *S*, having performed the contract, simply steps into *O*'s shoes as against *SP*. One can reach the same result by subrogating *S*, who rendered performance to *O*, to *O*'s rights against *P* (including the right to retain amounts unpaid under the construction contract).

Problem 12.3.1. Under the facts of Problem 12.2.1, supra, suppose that Telli Schmelli, the CEO, had executed in favor of the bank (AIB) an absolute, unconditional guaranty of payment, whereby Telli, individually, guaranteed to AIB the punctual payment when due of all existing and future indebtedness of Schmelli Services, Inc., to AIB. The guaranty thus covers the outstanding indebtedness on the line of credit facility as well as the Learjet indebtedness. Under the terms of the guaranty Telli waived all possible suretyship defenses and all rights (including rights to notice) relating to any collateral.

You are counsel for both Schmelli Services and Telli. The Learjet has been sold by AIB for an amount that left a substantial deficiency on the Learjet debt. AIB has accelerated the line of credit indebtedness and is in the process of collecting the accounts receivable, but Telli expects a deficiency on that loan as well.

Prior to selling the Learjet AIB sent a notification of private sale (by certified mail, return receipt requested) addressed to:

Schmelli Services, Inc.

1000½ E. Markham

Little Rock, Arkansas 72206

Attention: Telli Schmelli, Pres. & CEO

When the envelope containing the notice was delivered to Schmelli's headquarters, Telli's private secretary, Melli Vanelli, signed for it. Telli saw the notice the next day, while reading the mail, and immediately faxed a copy to you.

AIB has sued Telli on the personal guaranty of payment for an amount equal to the outstanding balance on all Schmelli corporate debt. Assume that the Learjet security agreement was governed by the law of a jurisdiction that has adopted Revised Article 9. What defenses, if any, will you raise? What is the likelihood of success? See R9–611(b); R9–102(a)(71); R9–102(a)(74); R9–602(7); R9–624; R9–626(a); Notes on Rights of Guarantors of Secured Obligations, infra.

NOTES ON RIGHTS OF GUARANTORS OF SECURED OBLIGATIONS

(1) Guarantors of Secured Obligations Under Former Article 9. there was considerable litigation under Former Article 9 as to whether a guarantor was a "debtor" who would be entitled to notification of a disposition of collateral under F9–504(3) and to whom various duties, e.g., to dispose of collateral in a commercially reasonable manner, would run. The vast majority of the cases were decided in favor of the guarantor. Most of these cases recognized that a disposition may affect the size of the deficiency claim against the guarantor in much the same way as it affects the size of the claim against the principal obligor.

A substantial number of reported cases also addressed whether a guarantor who is entitled to notice under R9–504(3) nevertheless may make an effective pre-default waiver of the right to receive notice. These cases were fairly evenly divided between those enforcing the waiver and those refusing to do so. In these cases the non-waivability of rights and duties under F–9–501 (generally followed by R9–602) came into direct conflict with suretyship law, which permits a secondary obligor to waive suretyship defenses, including impairment of collateral, as discussed in the Introductory Note, supra.

(2) Guarantors of Secured Obligations Under Revised Article 9. Revised Article 9 resolves the issues discussed above in Note (1), i.e., whether a guarantor is an Article 9 "debtor" and the efficacy of a guarantor's waivers of Article 9 rights. Under F9–105(1)(d), the meaning of "debtor"–owner of the collateral, person who owes the secured obligation, or both–depended upon the context in which the term appeared. In contrast, R9–102 distinguishes between a "debtor," who has an interest in the collateral, and an "obligor," who owes payment of the secured obligation. In many transactions, one person is both a debtor and an obligor. This would be the case, for example, as to the Prototype automobile financing transactions in Chapter 7, Section 1, supra: Main Motors is both debtor and obligor in the inventory financing transaction with Firstbank, and Lee Abel is both debtor and obligor in the Chevrolet transaction. A guarantor of the secured obligation is a "secondary obligor." That term also includes a "hypothecator," referred to below in Note (3).

Even when a secondary obligor is not a debtor, the secondary obligor is entitled to notification of a disposition. See R9–611(b), (c). In addition a secondary obligor who suffers loss as a result of the secured party's noncompliance with Article 9, e.g., from the secured party's failure to dispose of the collateral in a commercially reasonable manner, may obtain the benefit of the rebuttable presumption rule of R9–626(a) or, in a consumer transaction, any deficiency-reducing rule the court may impose.

Having given rights to guarantors and other secondary obligors, Revised Article 9 restricts a secondary obligor's ability to waive those rights. See R9–602; R9–624. In other contexts, guarantors and other secondary obligors enjoy the virtually unrestricted ability to waive their rights. See, e.g., Restatement § 48. What policy supports restricting a guarantor's ability to waive rights under Revised Article 9? Suppose that a secured party fails to comply with Part 6 and the noncompliance reduces its recovery from the collateral. Is a guarantor's liability for the resulting deficiency affected in the same way as that of the principal obligor?

(3) Security Interests in One Debtor's Collateral Securing Obligations of Another Debtor. There are means other than giving a guaranty by which a third party can lend support to an obligation of another. Sometimes a third party **(hypothecator)** will give a security interest in property that it owns to support another's obligation. For example, Telli's stock might be used to secure Schmelli Services' debt. Under these circumstances the hypothecator (Telli) is an obligor. See R9–102(a)(59)(ii). Because Telli's obligation is secondary (as between Schmelli and Telli, Schmelli should pay the debt to AIB), Telli is a "secondary obligor," regardless of whether Telli also guaranties the obligation. In addition, with respect to the stock, Telli is a "debtor." See R9–

102(a)(28)(A). However, inasmuch as Telli has no interest in the corporate Learjet and accounts, Telli is not a "debtor" with respect to that collateral. See R9–102, Comment 2.a.

Suppose, in the example, AIB enforces its security interest in all the collateral (including Telli's stock) and remains unpaid in part. Is Telli, an obligor, liable for a deficiency? R9–615(d)(2) says plainly that "the obligor is liable for any deficiency." But what is the deficiency? The answer depends on Telli's obligation, which is governed by Telli's agreement with AIB. If, for example, Telli hypothecated the stock but did not undertake personally to pay (i.e., did not guarantee) the corporate debt, there would be no deficiency with respect to Telli's obligation once AIB disposes of the stock; under these circumstances, Telli would not be become liable for any deficiency. On the other hand, if Telli guaranteed Schmelli's debt, then Telli would be liable for any deficiency with respect to that obligation.

Similar care must be taken in determining who is entitled to a surplus. If the surplus arises from the disposition of Telli's stock, then Telli, as the debtor with respect to that collateral (and not as obligor), would be entitled to the surplus. See R9–615(d)(1). Any surplus arising from the disposition of corporate assets would, of course, go to Schmelli, the debtor with respect to that collateral. Does this create undesirable incentives for Schmelli and Telli to compete in persuading AIB which collateral to look to first?

(B) Competing Secured Parties and Lienholders; Transferees of Collateral in Dispositions Under R9–610

We now leave (for a brief time) the paradigm of enforcement of security interests against obligors on secured indebtedness and owners of the collateral. The Problems and Notes in this part consider some of the difficulties and questions that can arise when collateral is subject to multiple security interests and other liens and one or more of the claimants seeks to enforce a security interest. Most of the issues that have arisen over the duties that are or should be imposed upon an enforcing secured party in favor of a competing claimant concern (a) whether and under what circumstances the foreclosing secured party should be required to afford notice of a foreclosure sale to a competing claimant and (b) the appropriate allocation of the proceeds of the sale.

Problem 12.3.2. Under the facts of Problem 12.2.1, supra, suppose that AIB's security agreement covering accounts also covers all equipment at any time owned by Schmelli Services. Suppose also that Revised Article 9 is in effect in Arkansas at all relevant times and that AIB has perfected its security interest by filing in Arkansas, Schmelli's state of incorporation.

You now represent Tuleight Co., one of Schmelli's trade creditors. Several months ago Tuleight's president was pressing Schmelli's treasurer for payment of past due invoices. To "buy some time," the treasurer offered Tuleight a security interest in all of Schmelli's office equipment located in Arkansas (where Tuleight's sole office is located). Tuleight agreed. To "save time and money," Tuleight did not consult you or any other lawyer. Tuleight's president bought a form security agreement and financing statement at a stationery store, completed the documents (properly, as luck would have it), obtained Schmelli's execution of the security agreement, and filed the financing statement in the Arkansas filing office. Also as luck would have it, Tuleight's president did not think to search the filings and was (and remains) ignorant of AIB's earlier filing and senior security interest.

Tuleight now asks for your advice about how to take possession of and sell the equipment. The outstanding balance that Schmelli owes Tuleight is $50,000.

(a) If Tuleight can recover possession of the equipment, to whom should Tuleight give notification of a disposition? Will you request a search of the UCC filing office in Arkansas? See R9–611; Note (1) on Duties Owed by an Enforcing Secured Party to a Competing Secured Party or Lienholder and Rights of Transferees, infra.

(b) Assume, for the time being, that AIB has *no other collateral* for the Schmelli debt (i.e., assume that AIB already has liquidated the accounts, the equipment in other states, and the Learjet, and that a deficiency remains unpaid). Under which, if any, of the following scenarios will Tuleight be liable to AIB? See R9–625(b), (c); Note (3) on Duties Owed by an Enforcing Secured Party to a Competing Secured Party or Lienholder and Rights of Transferees, infra.

(i) Tuleight takes possession of the equipment. See R9–609 & Comment 5.

(ii) After Tuleight takes possession, AIB demands that Tuleight deliver the equipment to AIB and Tuleight refuses. Does it matter whether AIB's loan is in default?

(iii) After Tuleight takes possession, Tuleight sells the equipment. Does it matter whether the buyer at the sale disappears with the equipment? See R9–610 & Comment 5.

(iv) Tuleight sells the equipment at a public sale following two days' advertising in a local "throw-away" newspaper.

(v) Tuleight sells the equipment at a commercially reasonable sale for $30,000 and keeps the money. Does it matter whether Tuleight gave reasonable notification of the disposition to AIB? See R9–615; R9–611 & Comment 4.

(vi) Tuleight sells the equipment at a commercially reasonable sale for $90,000, keeps $55,000 (including $5,000 costs of sale), and gives $35,000 to Schmelli.

Problem 12.3.3. How would the existence of the other collateral for the AIB debt affect any of the results in Problem 12.3.2(b)? See Note (4) on Duties Owed by an Enforcing Secured Party to a Competing Secured Party or Lienholder and Rights of Transferees, infra.

Problem 12.3.4. Under the facts of Problem 12.3.2, assume that Schmelli Services enters bankruptcy.

(a) If AIB wishes to satisfy its claim first from the Arkansas equipment, can Tuleight compel AIB to satisfy its claim first from the other collateral instead? See Note (4) on Duties Owed by an Enforcing Secured Party to a Competing Secured Party or Lienholder and Rights of Transferees, infra.

(b) If AIB wishes to satisfy its claim first from the other collateral, can the bankruptcy trustee compel AIB to satisfy its claim first from the Arkansas equipment instead?

Problem 12.3.5. Assume the facts of Problem 12.3.2. Assume also that Schmelli Services did not enter bankruptcy. You now represent Bonzo Co. Bonzo has reached tentative agreement with Tuleight to buy, in a private sale, various office equipment that Tuleight has repossessed from Schmelli. What steps do you take to protect Bonzo? See R9–617; R9–610(d)—(f) & Comment 5; UCC 2–312(1), (2); Note (3) on Duties Owed by an Enforcing Secured Party to a Competing Secured Party or Lienholder and Rights of Transferees, infra. What, if any, special provisions will you insist on in the sale agreement?

NOTES ON DUTIES OWED BY AN ENFORCING SECURED PARTY TO A COMPETING SECURED PARTY OR LIENHOLDER AND RIGHTS OF TRANSFEREES

(1) Duties of Senior Secured Parties to Junior Claimants: Notification Requirements. We have seen that R9–610(b) requires an enforcing secured party to send "a reasonable authenticated notification of disposition." R9–610(c) specifies the parties to be notified; they include "the debtor," "any secondary obligor," and certain other persons claiming an interest in the collateral, as specified in subsection (c)(3). Please read carefully R9–611(a) (defining "notification date"), (c)(3), and (e).

Prior to the 1972 amendments to Article 9, F9–504(3) required the foreclosing secured party to send reasonable notification of the sale "except in the case of consumer goods to any other person who has a security interest in the collateral and who has duly filed a financing statement indexed in the name of the debtor in this state or who is known by the secured party to have a security interest in the collateral." To comply with the pre–1972 text, a foreclosing secured party not only had to search the UCC filings for financing statements showing a competing security interest but also had to review its own records to discover whether some communication, perhaps informal, had given the secured party knowledge of another security interest. In the view of the Article 9 Review Committee, "[t]hese burdens of searching the record and of checking the secured party's files were greater than the circumstances called for because as a practical matter there would seldom be a junior secured party who really had an interest needing protection in the case of a foreclosure sale." Review Committee for Article 9, Final Report, R9–504, Reasons for 1972 Change. Accordingly, F9–504(3) was revised to require a secured party to send notice of a foreclosure sale only to those secured parties "from whom the secured party has received ... written notice of a claim of an interest in the collateral." A secured party who wished to receive notice of another secured party's disposition had to do more than simply file a financing statement.

Reflecting the view that "[m]any problems arising from dispositions of collateral encumbered by multiple security interests can be ameliorated or solved by informing all secured parties of an intended disposition and affording them the opportunity to work with one another," Revised Article 9 expands the duty of a foreclosing secured party to notify competing secured parties of an intended disposition. R9–611, Comment 4. In some cases, the burden may be greater than that imposed by the pre–1972 text of F9–504(3), quoted above and in R9–611, Comment 1. Observe that requiring the enforcing secured party to give notice to others of record could delay the sale by the amount of time necessary to search the public record and determine whether other secured parties are on file. In an ideal world, this delay would be trivial; in the real world it may not be. Concerns about the potential for delay gave rise to R9–611(e): If a secured party requests a search of the appropriate filing office between 20 and 30 days before the notification date, it need only give notice to the secured parties or other lienholders of record uncovered by that search. And if no response to the search request is received before the notification date, the secured party has complied with the notification requirement contained in R9–611(c)(3)(B).

(2) Duties of Senior Secured Parties to Junior Claimants: Allocation of Proceeds. Revised Article 9 gives greater guidance than its predecessor (F9–504(1)) concerning the duties of a senior secured party with respect to proceeds of a disposition. See R9–615. After payment of (i) the reasonable expenses of the disposition and (ii) any reasonable attorney's fees and legal expenses incurred by the secured party (to the extent provided for in the agreement and not prohibited by law), the proceeds are to be applied first to the satisfaction of the indebtedness secured by the security interest under which the disposition is made and, if any proceeds remain, then to "the satisfaction of obligations secured by any subordinate security interest or other lien the collateral." R9–615(a)(3)(A). But the secured party must apply the proceeds to obligations secured by a subordinate interest only if the secured party has received an "authenticated demand for proceeds before distribution of the proceeds is completed." Id.[6] This rule has the effect of requiring a junior secured party who wishes to share in the proceeds of a senior's foreclosure sale to make written demand upon the senior.

Suppose that a junior secured party makes demand and receives payment from a senior under circumstances giving rise to an objection by

---

6. Part 6 does not apply to the enforcement of a consignor's security interest. See R9–601(g). However, when a non-consignor secured party enforces its security interest, special distribution rules apply to the proceeds of collateral that is the subject of a consignment. These rules take account of the fact that the consignor is the owner of the collateral. See R9–615(a)(3)(B), (4), (d)(1), and Comment 2 (second paragraph).

the debtor. For example, the debtor may claim that the junior's purported security interest is invalid (perhaps the security agreement contains a defective collateral description) or that the junior's loan is not yet due. Would the *senior* face liability to the debtor for having complied with the statute in good faith? Presumably not. Any recovery from the *junior* to which the debtor may be entitled would be governed by the law of restitution.

Now suppose that three secured parties (in order of priority, *SP*–1, *SP*–2, and *SP*–3) claim a security interest in the same collateral. Assume further that *SP*–3 gives to *SP*–1 (the enforcing secured party) an authenticated demand, *SP*–2 does not, and *SP*–1 is deemed to have complied with its notification duty in respect of *SP*–2 because it received no response to its search request before the notification date. See R9–611(e). When *SP*–3 receives payment under R9–615(a)(3)(A) but *SP*–2 does not, what rights, if any, does *SP*–2 have against *SP*–1 or *SP*–3? Once again, *SP*–1 should face no liability, and any recovery against *SP*–3 by *SP*–2 should be governed by the law of restitution.

Can one derive these results readily from Article 9? If not, should the statute have been amended to reflect these results explicitly? The Drafting Committee decided early in the drafting process that it would not be wise to undertake a statutory resolution of every possible problem that might arise in connection with junior interests. However, assuming that in most cases the enforcing secured party *will* receive a response to its search request and *will*, in turn, send notification to all junior interests of record, who *will* make authenticated demands for proceeds, there should be many fewer instances of an application of proceeds to a junior interest (here, *SP*–3) before payment to a more senior interest (here, *SP*–2). The view of the Drafting Committee was that if interested parties know about each other the problems generally will be resolved.

Observe that under R9–615(a)(3) the secured party is required to apply proceeds to the obligations securing a "subordinate security interest or other lien." Under F9–504(1)(c) that obligation extended only to the holder of a "subordinate security interest." The revision clarifies and rationalizes the rights of lienholders other than Article 9 secured parties. (Professor Gilmore thought that the benefits conferred on a non-enforcing "secured party" under F9–504(3) (as well as under UCC 9–505) (retention in satisfaction of indebtedness, discussed in Section 6, *infra*) and F9–506 (redemption, discussed in Section 4, *infra*)) did extend to a non-Article 9 lienor, blaming the more narrow statutory grant on "drafting inadvertence." 2 Gilmore, Security § 44.2, at 1217–18, § 44.3, at 1225, § 44.6, at 1240; cf. F9–504(4) (a disposition under F9–504 "discharges the security interest under which it is made and any security interest *or lien* subordinate thereto.").

Finally, R9–615(c) provides a framework for dealing with the application of noncash proceeds of a foreclosure disposition, such the buyer's promissory note. Comment 3 to that section provides an overview and an example.

(3) Dispositions of Collateral by Junior Secured Parties Pursuant to R9–610. The notice provisions of F9–504(3), if not the entire section, appear to have been written with sales by a senior secured party in mind. See Review Committee for Article 9, Final Report, R9–504 Reasons for 1972 Change. Although they were not entirely problem-free (the major issue was the appropriateness of the notice requirement, considered in Note (1), supra), the rules seem to have worked reasonably well in that context. Except for the adjustments to the notification rules in R9–611 and the rules for application of proceeds in R9–615 (see Notes (1) and (2), supra), R9–610 and the accompanying provisions dealing with the disposition of collateral also generally contemplate the paradigm in which the enforcing party will have the senior interest.

Article 9 clearly contemplates the existence of multiple security interests in collateral. R9–401(b) explicitly recognizes a debtor's ability to create junior interests (as did F9–311), although creation of a competing security interest (even if junior) may cause a default as to a senior. By its terms, Part 6 of Article 9 applies to all security interests, regardless of priority. Unlike the enforcement of security interests by seniors, however, questions abound concerning foreclosure sales conducted by juniors. For the most part, these questions are addressed, if at all, in the comments to Revised Article 9. See, in particular, R9–610, Comment 5.

Junior's Right to Take Possession of and Dispose of Collateral. Inasmuch as Article 9 recognizes junior security interests in collateral, it would be odd indeed if the Article did not permit a junior secured party to enforce its security interest by taking possession of and disposing of collateral. There is nothing in Article 9 to suggest that the holder of a junior security interest does not have the right to enforce its security interest. See R9–609 and Comment 5; R9–610 and Comment 5.

Senior's Right to Take Possession From Junior. What are the rights of a senior secured party when a junior has taken possession of collateral after default? In most cases the debtor also will be in default as to the senior security interest, even if the debtor has not missed a payment on the senior secured obligation. Credit agreements often provide that the creation of a junior lien, the debtor's default under a junior secured obligation (a **cross-default**), and a junior's taking possession of collateral each constitutes a default. Is it a reasonable implication from a senior's senior status that its right to possession after default is superior to that of a junior? For an affirmative answer, see R9–609, Comment 5.

Senior's Right to Control the Junior's Proposed Disposition. Assuming a senior secured party rightfully takes possession of collateral from a junior secured party, may the senior pick up where the junior left off? For example, may the senior avail itself of any advertisements concerning the proposed disposition and any notifications sent by the junior to the debtor and other secured parties? Or must the senior start the process all over again? On the other hand, is the senior necessarily *entitled* to begin anew? Perhaps the senior is concerned that the junior's planned procedures would not be commercially reasonable. But, could the debtor later argue successfully that the delay caused by the senior's starting all over again rendered the senior's (otherwise commercially reasonable) disposition commercially unreasonable? Neither the text of Revised Article 9 nor the comments undertake to provide specific answers to these questions.

Senior's Right to Notification From Junior. In specifying the class of secured parties entitled to notification of a disposition, R9–611(c) does not distinguish between junior and senior creditors. Do you find it anomalous to require juniors to notify seniors of a disposition? If the notification is intended to afford parties an opportunity to protect their interests, arguably the senior does not need notification. Unlike a security interest that is junior to the interest being enforced, the senior's interest will not be cut off by the disposition. R9–617(a)(3). Nevertheless, the disposition in fact may affect the senior adversely. In some cases, the senior may be unable to locate the collateral after sale and so in effect will have become unsecured. Even if the senior can locate the collateral, the senior will have incurred the costs of searching for it as well as the costs of repossessing it from the buyer, who may be less cooperative than the debtor would have been. (A buyer who did not take account of the senior's security interest when calculating the price is likely to be particularly ornery.) Moreover, when the senior has a security interest in all the assets of a debtor's business, the proceeds the senior will receive from the resale of a single item of collateral upon repossession from a buyer are likely to be less than the allocable portion of proceeds that the senior would have received upon a foreclosure sale of all the assets of the debtor's business.

Senior's Right to Recover Collateral From Transferee at Junior's Sale. Even if the senior has the right to control a disposition, in any given case it might not do so. Assume that the junior proceeds with its disposition of the collateral (because, for example, neither the junior nor the senior secured party is aware of the other's interest). One of the few issues, in this context, on which Article 9 does speak with clarity is the rights of a transferee in a disposition under R9–610. As already mentioned, the transferee cuts off only "the security interest under which it is made and any security interest or lien *subordinate thereto.*" R9–617(a)(3). (F9–504(4) was to the same effect.) If the senior did not authorize the disposition and if its security interest is perfected, the senior's security interest would continue notwithstanding the junior's disposition; the senior would be entitled to take possession of the collateral from the junior's transferee. See R9–315(a)(1); R9–317(b); Chapter 7, Section 6(B), supra.

What can a buyer do to protect itself against claims of a senior? As with any sale out of the ordinary course of business, the prudent buyer must undertake UCC searches and investigate the seller's source of title. However, there was an additional risk for a transferee in a disposition under F9–504. Many non-ordinary course buyers fear little for hidden conflicting interests because they are satisfied with the creditworthiness of their seller and the seller's warranty of title. In a foreclosure sale under Former Article 9, it was likely that seller made no warranty of title. See UCC 2–312, Comment 5 (pre-Revised Article 9). In a disposition under R9–

610, however, the contract for disposition of collateral includes the otherwise applicable warranties "which by operation of law accompany a voluntary disposition of property of the kind subject to the contract." R9–610(d). Comment 5 to UCC 2–312 has been conformed to this approach in connection with the promulgation of Revised Article 9. This change is consistent with the overarching goal of encouraging all interested persons to find out about the others. Unless the enforcing secured party disclaims its warranties, the transferee will have the benefit of that secured party's warranty obligations. A disclaimer of warranties by an enforcing secured party should alert the prospective transferee to undertake appropriate due diligence.

Rights to Proceeds Received Upon Junior's Disposition; Liability of Junior to Senior. Suppose that a junior secured party takes possession of collateral and sells it to a buyer pursuant to R9–610. The buyer then flees with the collateral and cannot be found. The senior secured party then sues the junior, asserting that the junior converted the collateral by (alternatively) (i) taking possession of it in the first place, (ii) selling it, or (iii) failing to turn over the proceeds to the senior. What result?

Under Former Article 9, one case (citing F9–503) held that a junior in a similar situation acted properly and within its rights in taking possession of the collateral. The court implicitly came to the same conclusion about the junior's right to dispose of the collateral. However, the court went on to hold that "once [the junior] achieved repossession, . . . the junior secured party . . . had an obligation to turn proceeds of the sale of the collateral over to . . . the senior secured party. Failure to so act is a conversion." Consolidated Equipment Sales, Inc. v. First State Bank & Trust Co., 627 P.2d 432, 438 (Okl.1981). If *Consolidated Equipment* were correct, how could a junior *ever* effectively enforce its security interest? Would it be forced to wait for the senior's disposition and hope for a distribution under R9–504(1)(c)? For a cogent argument that the result in *Consolidated Equipment* is wrong, based in part on the negative implication of the provision for subordinate security interests in F9–504(1), see Hillman, McDonnell & Nickles, Common Law ¶ 25.02[4], at 25–68 to 25–79. Oddly, one case reached a result similar to that in *Consolidated Equipment* while citing and relying substantially on Hillman, McDonnell & Nickles. Stotts v. Johnson, 302 Ark. 439, 791 S.W.2d 351 (1990). After presenting their argument that the junior should be entitled to retain the proceeds of its disposition, the three authors balanced their presentation with several policy arguments that favored the senior. It was this discussion, taken out of context, on which the *Stotts* court relied. See also PEB Commentary No. 7 (secured party with a junior security interest in receivables who collects cash proceeds may achieve a senior security interest in the cash proceeds either as a holder in due course of a negotiable instrument or under analogous rules applicable to currency).

Revised Article 9 addresses explicitly and ameliorates the plight of the enforcing junior secured party in this context. The junior secured party can retain cash proceeds without the duty to apply them to the senior's obligation or to account to or pay the senior, so long as the junior acts "in good faith and without knowledge that the receipt [of the proceeds] violates the rights of the holder of the" senior interest. R9–615(g).

A Different Approach. Several commentators who addressed these issues under Former Article 9 recommended a different approach to protecting an enforcing junior and its transferee from claims of a senior secured party: If a notified senior fails to act by taking over the junior's disposition, the junior should be entitled to sell the collateral free of the senior interest. See Byrne, Murphy, & Vukowich, Junior Creditors' Realization on Debtors' Equity Under U.C.C. Section 9–311: An Appraisal and a Proposal, 77 Geo. L.J. 1905 (1989). See also Wechsler, Rights and Remedies of the Secured Party After an Unauthorized Transfer of Collateral: A Proposal for Balancing Competing Claims in Repossession, Resale, Proceeds, and Conversion Cases, 32 Buff.L.Rev. 373 (1983) (arguing for a similar result). Is this approach preferable to the one adopted by Revised Article 9?

(4) Determining Who Is Senior: Herein of Marshaling. In Problem 12.3.3, supra, both AIB and Tuleight held security interests in the Arkansas equipment. AIB's security interest was senior. AIB held a security interest in other collateral as well. Is AIB entitled to look to the Arkansas equipment, thereby leaving Tuleight with no collateral? Tuleight's counsel will, no doubt, invoke the doctrine of "marshaling of assets."

As explained by the Supreme Court, " '[t]he equitable doctrine of marshalling rests upon the principle that a creditor having two funds to satisfy his debt, may not by his application of them to his demand, defeat another creditor, who may resort to only one of the funds.' " Meyer v. United States, 375 U.S. 233, 236, 84 S.Ct. 318, 321, 11 L.Ed.2d 293, 297 (1963), quoting Sowell v. Federal Reserve Bank, 268 U.S. 449, 456–57, 45 S.Ct. 528, 530–31, 69 L.Ed. 1041, 1049 (1925). The purpose of the doctrine is "to prevent the arbitrary action of a senior lienor from destroying the rights of a junior lienor or a creditor having less security." Id. at 237, 84 S.Ct. at 321, 11 L.Ed.2d at 297. Because it is an equitable doctrine, marshaling is applied only when it can be equitably fashioned as to all of the parties having an interest in the property. In order to successfully invoke marshaling, there must be two creditors of a common debtor and two separate assets or funds of that debtor. In addition, one of the creditors must have a lien on only one of the funds and the other a lien on both of the funds. Tuleight's situation presents a classic case for marshaling. And case law supports the availability of marshaling where an Article 9 security interest is involved. Comment 5 to R9–610 approves of the foregoing analysis. (Indeed, if you notice the similarity between that comment and the foregoing, keep in mind that the foregoing passage appeared in the previous edition of this book, years before we wrote the Official Comments.) See also R9–401, Comment 6, (suggesting, in a somewhat different factual setting, that marshaling "may be appropriate").

Now assume that all the collateral is sold in Schmelli's bankruptcy and that the proceeds of the other collateral is sufficient to repay AIB in full. Which would be fairer to Tuleight: to pay AIB's claim, in part, from the proceeds of the Arkansas equipment and give Tuleight nothing, or to pay Tuleight's claim from the proceeds of the Arkansas equipment and pay AIB from the proceeds of the other collateral? Which approach would be fairer to AIB?

A number of cases have raised questions concerning the applicability of marshaling to secured claims in bankruptcy. Under the guise of marshaling, efforts have been made to require a secured party to seek recovery from sources other than the bankruptcy estate (e.g., from secured or unsecured guaranties). The cases are conflicting. Compare In re Jack Green's Fashions for Men—Big & Tall, Inc., 597 F.2d 130 (8th Cir.1979) (upholding marshaling order that compelled secured party to look first to secured guaranties instead of collateral owned by debtor) with In re Computer Room, Inc., 24 B.R. 732 (Bkrtcy.N.D.Ala.1982) (rejecting *Jack Green* and declining to require secured creditor to look first to guarantor). In other cases, the bankruptcy trustee has attempted, with mixed success, to impose what may be called "reverse marshaling," i.e., to require a senior to look *first* to collateral in which a junior *has* a security interest, so as to reduce the size of secured claims against the bankruptcy estate. Compare In re Center Wholesale, Inc., 759 F.2d 1440 (9th Cir.1985) (denying junior secured party's request for marshaling order because the order would prejudice rights of trustee in bankruptcy, as hypothetical lien creditor under BC 544(a)(1), leaving less property in estate for general creditors) with *Computer Room*, supra (applying marshaling doctrine, senior secured creditor was required to look first to collateral not claimed by junior secured creditor).

SECTION 4.   REDEMPTION

Introductory Note. R9–623 gives "[a] debtor, any secondary obligor, or any other secured party or lienholder" a right to redeem collateral by "tender[ing] ... fulfillment of all obligations secured by the collateral" together with related expenses incurred by the secured party. R9–623(a) and (b).

> If the entire balance of a secured obligation has been accelerated, it would be necessary to tender the entire balance. A tender of fulfillment obviously means more than a new promise to perform an existing promise. It requires payment in full of all monetary obligations then due and performance in full of all other obligations then matured. If unmatured secured obligations remain, the security interest continues to secure them (i.e., as if there had been no default).

R9–623, Comment 2. R9–623 follows closely F9–506, except that the latter did not expressly extend redemption rights to secondary obligors or non-secured party lienholders. (However, some courts treated guarantors as "debtors." See Section 3(A), supra.) The *Williams* and *Dunn* cases, infra, dealing with F9–506, remain relevant under R9–623. The right of redemption must be exercised before the secured party has collected on collateral (R9–607), disposed of collateral or entered into a contract for disposition (R9–610), or accepted the collateral in full or partial satisfaction of the secured obligations (R9–622). Upon the occurrence of one of these events, the debtor's "equity of redemption" is *foreclosed*. Although R9–602(11) generally prohibits waiver of redemption rights before default, R9–624(c) explicitly permits waiver by agreement "entered into and authenticated after default."

Redemption is an ancient common law right. Professor Gilmore saw the right of redemption preserved by F9–506 as a "ghostly remnant of the seventeenth century right":

> Three centuries ago ... the equity courts deduced the post-default right to redeem out of the mortgagor's pre-default equity.... To our ancestors the principal thing must have seemed to be not so much the fair resolution of a debtor-creditor relationship as it was the maintenance of stability in land tenure. Whatever could be done to keep the land in the ownership of the mortgagor and his family was a good thing.

2 Gilmore, Security § 44.2, at 1216. As described by Mr. Clark, the right to redeem gives "the debtor one last opportunity to recover the collateral. The debtor may desire to scrape the redemption money together—perhaps through a refinancing—because it fears that the collateral will not be sold for a good price, or because there is sentimental attachment irrespective of price." Clark, Secured Transactions ¶ 4.11, at 4–304. It appears that debtors infrequently exercise the right of redemption—probably because defaulting debtors typically cannot, to repeat Mr. Clark's words, "scrape the redemption money together."

Problem 12.4.1. In the setting of the Prototype on automobile financing, Lee Abel purchased a new Chevrolet and signed the Instalment Sale Contract (Form 3.6, supra). As in the Prototype, Main Motors assigned the contract to Firstbank.

Abel made five monthly payments from August through December. Just after Christmas, Abel was laid off work and was unable to continue the payments. Two weeks after Abel missed the January 24 payment, an employee of Firstbank phoned to remind Abel that the payment was overdue. Firstbank wrote and phoned Abel several more times in February, and on February 20 Firstbank wrote to Abel stating that unless prompt payment was forthcoming, Firstbank would be required to repossess the car. Abel was still unable to find the money for the payments. On the night of February 25 the repo team repossessed the Chevrolet. (These are the facts of Problem 12.1.1, supra, omitting the details of the repossession.)

On February 27 Firstbank sent Abel a Notice of Repossession (Form 3.9, supra). On March 2 Abel met with one of Firstbank's loan officers and offered to pay the January and February payments ($461.79 for each month) plus the default charges specified in the agreement (including the costs of repossession and storage). The loan officer pointed to provisions in paragraph 3.b. on the reverse of the Instalment Sales Contract that provide for acceleration of payments; the officer explained that the Chevrolet would be returned to Abel only on payment of the full unpaid balance and other charges specified in the Notice of Repossession.

Abel has sued Firstbank for recovery of the Chevrolet and for damages. The only applicable legislation is the UCC. What result? See R9–623; Williams v. Ford Motor Credit Co., infra; Dunn v. General Equities of Iowa, Ltd., infra; Notes on Acceleration and Redemption of Collateral, infra.

Problem 12.4.2. The facts are the same as in the preceding Problem, except that the U3C is in force. See U3C 5.111(1) (quoted in Section 1, supra). What result?

Williams v. Ford Motor Credit Co.[*]

Supreme Court of Alabama, 1983.
435 So.2d 66.

■ MADDOX, JUSTICE.

Although several issues are presented for review, the issue which is dispositive of this appeal involves the question of whether a security agreement can be modified either orally or by waiver if the security agreement requires that all modifications be in writing. The directed verdict of the trial court is affirmed.

On November 1, 1976, Curtis Williams, plaintiff-appellant, entered into a contract to purchase a 1974 Oldsmobile from Joe Meyers Ford in Houston, Texas. The contract was financed through Ford Motor Credit Company (FMCC), the defendant-appellee. Thirty payments of $136.40 were to be made, commencing December 7, 1976, with subsequent payments to be made on the like day of each month thereafter.

The payment which was due on February 7, 1977, was not timely made, but on March 4, 1977, Mrs. Williams mailed two money orders to FMCC, one in the amount of $151.40 to include payment, plus late charges, for February, and another in the sum of $136.40 to be applied on the March 7, 1977, payment. On March 5, 1977, the vehicle was repossessed.

Mr. James Osbourn testified on behalf of FMCC that the two payments in question were received by FMCC on March 7, 1977, which was Monday after the unit was repossessed on Saturday. The deposition testimony of Samuel Wright, who was employed by the Houston West Branch of FMCC, indicated that as Customer Account Supervisor, he had custody and control of Williams's file. On March 4, 1977, Wright initiated action to repossess the car and accelerated the contract balance by means of a mailgram. He did so, he stated, after reviewing Williams's account and ascertaining that Williams was located in Mobile, and seeing that Williams was past due and

---

* [The court's citations are to the applicable pre–1972 version of the UCC.]

that default in the March payment was imminent. FMCC had tried to contact Williams by phone, but his telephone was not in service. Williams stated that he had moved from Houston to Mobile on about the 11th or 12th of February, 1977, but he did not notify FMCC of his change in address. An independent contractor was employed by FMCC to repossess the vehicle.

By affidavit and by deposition, Mrs. Williams stated that she made a long distance telephone call to FMCC on or about March 3 or 4. She stated that the substance of the call was that a representative of FMCC told her if the Williamses sent in two payments plus the $15.00 late charge, there would be no problem with the account. FMCC's motion in limine to suppress this evidence was granted over objection. The trial court sustained objection to Mrs. Williams's testifying that she made the call to FMCC.

After repossessing the automobile, FMCC, by letter dated March 11, 1977, sent Williams a notice of private sale. This notice informed Williams he had 10 days in which to redeem the automobile. It also stated that Williams would be liable for any deficiencies. Williams's attorney, on March 7, 1977, contacted FMCC by telephone and demanded return of the automobile because of the two payments submitted. FMCC denied that any employee of FMCC ever received a letter confirming the call.

Williams commenced this action against FMCC and other named defendants who were later dismissed from the case. The complaint, as amended, contained five counts seeking damages for the wrongful detention and conversion of a vehicle and the two money orders, and for fraud and misrepresentation. Williams sought $50,000 in damages under each of the first four counts, and $1,000,000 under the fifth count.

At the close of the plaintiff's evidence, FMCC submitted a written motion for directed verdict. After lengthy argument, this motion was later granted as to counts 3, 4, and 5. At the close of all the evidence, FMCC filed a further motion for directed verdict, which was granted as to the remaining two counts in the complaint. Williams's motion for J.N.O.V. or in the alternative a new trial was denied. This appeal followed.

We think our decision in Hale v. Ford Motor Credit Co., 374 So.2d 849 (Ala.1979), in which this Court delineated the rights and obligations of the parties under the terms of a security agreement containing both a non-waiver acceleration clause and a non-modification clause, is controlling here. In *Hale*, supra, this Court ruled that the secured party is not required to give notice to the debtor prior to repossession, even though past-due payments have been accepted on previous occasions. Further, this Court concluded that a security agreement is effective according to the terms expressed in the agreement and that the inadvertence of the debtor in failing to make timely payments cannot raise an estoppel against the contractual interest of the creditor under the express terms of the security agreement, when there has been no written modification as required by the terms of the agreement.

Assuming, *arguendo*, that Mrs. Williams's telephone conversation on March 3 or 4, 1977, was admissible to show that the contract between the Williamses and FMCC had been modified to extend the time for payment, that testimony would not change the outcome of this case since the security agreement expressly provided that any modification of its terms must be in writing. Likewise, the acceptance of the late payment could not, without a writing evidencing the modification, operate as a waiver of default. Thus, we need not decide whether the trial court erred by granting the motion in limine as to Mrs. Williams's testimony concerning the telephone call.

Mr. Wright testified that he exercised FMCC's right to accelerate the contract on March 4, 1977, by mailgram, because the appellant was in default on his February 7, 1977, payment. Paragraph 19 of the security agreement provides in pertinent part:

"Time is of the essence of this contract. In event [sic] Buyer defaults in any payment ... Seller shall have the right to declare all amounts due or to become due hereunder to be immediately due and payable and Seller shall have the right to repossess the property wherever the same may be found with free right of entry, and to recondition and sell the same at public or private sale. Seller shall have the right to retain all payments made prior to repossession and Buyer shall remain liable for any deficiency. Buyer agrees to pay ... expenses incurred by Seller in effecting collection, repossession or resale hereunder. Seller's remedies hereunder are in addition to any given by law and may be enforced successively and concurrently. Waiver by Seller of any default shall not be deemed waiver of any other default."

The evidence shows that FMCC received on March 7, 1977, subsequent to the acceleration and repossession, two money orders which, acceleration and repossession aside, would have made the appellant's account current through March 1977; however, in repossessing the automobile, FMCC incurred expenses of $323.50, which it was also entitled to recover.

We agree with FMCC that under the terms of the security agreement, its right to repossess the vehicle due to the default of the appellant existed independently of any right to accelerate the indebtedness due to that default. Consequently, the acceptance by FMCC of the late payment for February and the timely payment for March did not nullify the acceleration nor the remainder of the indebtedness; rather the payments received on March 7 must be considered as payments on the full indebtedness due on the appellant's account immediately after repossession on March 5. Had the appellant paid the entire contract balance, plus expenses incurred by FMCC in retaking the collateral, he would have been entitled to redeem the vehicle. The facts indicate, however, that the appellant did not redeem the automobile.

In a directed verdict case, such as the one here, the function of this Court is to view the evidence most favorably to the non-moving party; and if, by any interpretation, the evidence can support any inference supportive of a conclusion in favor of the non-moving party, we must reverse. After a review of the record, we conclude that there was no factual dispute requiring the trial court to submit the case to the jury; therefore, the trial court did not err in granting the directed verdict.

Affirmed.

Dunn v. General Equities of Iowa, Ltd.[*]

Supreme Court of Iowa, 1982.
319 N.W.2d 515.

■ McCORMICK, JUDGE.

The question here is whether the trial court erred in holding that the payees of two promissory notes waived their right to invoke acceleration clauses by accepting late payments on several prior occasions. We must decide if acceleration clauses can be waived by a previous course of dealing between the parties and, if so, whether the finding of waiver in this case is supported by substantial evidence. Because we give affirmative answers to each of these issues, we affirm the trial court.

Plaintiffs W.A. and Lola Dunn are payees on separate notes executed by defendant General Equities of Iowa, Inc., on March 31, 1974. The notes are identical except for the payees' names. Each provides for payment of $121,170 with seven percent annual interest. They are payable over a period of ten years, with annual installments due on or before March 31 of each year starting in 1975. Delinquent installments draw interest of nine percent. The acceleration clauses provide: "Upon default in payment of any interest, or any installment of principal, the whole amount then unpaid shall become due and payable forthwith, at the option of the holder without notice."

The parties agree that the 1979 payments were not made until April 10, 1979. Plaintiffs returned defendant's single check for both 1979 installments and demanded payment of the entire unpaid balance, with interest, in accordance with the acceleration clause. Defendant refused payment, and this suit resulted.

The determinative issue at trial was whether defendant established its defense that plaintiffs had waived their right to invoke the acceleration clause by accepting late payments in the past. The case was tried to the court at law, and the court found for defendant on the basis of its defense. This appeal followed.

I. *Waiver by course of dealing.* This court has not previously decided whether the right to enforce an acceleration clause can be waived by a course of dealing of accepting late payments on prior occasions. The issue is not affected by statute and therefore must be decided under common law principles.

The court has long held that acceleration clauses are subject to principles governing contracts generally:

* [The court's citations are to the applicable pre–1972 version of the UCC.]

Stipulations such as are found in these notes and in the mortgage under consideration are not regarded in the nature of a penalty or forfeiture, and, for that reason, viewed with disfavor by the courts, but as agreements for bringing the notes to an earlier maturity than expressed on their face, and are to be construed and the intention of the parties ascertained by the same rules as other contracts.

Swearingen v. Lahner and Platt, 93 Iowa 147, 151, 61 N.W. 431, 433 (1894).

Contract rights, of course, can be waived, and an option to accelerate a debt is one such waivable right. Acceleration provisions are not self-executing, and "the holder of an instrument ... must take some positive action to exercise his option to declare payments due under an acceleration clause. ..." Weinrich v. Hawley, 236 Iowa 652, 656, 19 N.W.2d 665, 667 (1945). A failure to exercise the option or an acceptance of late payment will establish waiver:

The notes did not become absolutely due on default in payment of the interest installment. Appellee had the right or "option" to so consider them, and to proceed at once to bring suit upon them, but was under no obligation so to do. It could waive the default and permit the notes to run without payment of any interest until they fell due on July 5, 1912, and the statute of limitations would not begin to run against the principal debt before that date. If, the interest installment being past due, its payment was tendered or offered by the defendant, and plaintiff received and accepted the same as interest, or if, knowing that defendant paid it, understanding that it was being received in satisfaction of the past-due interest, it will be held to have waived the default, and can not thereafter make it a ground for declaring the whole debt due.

Farmers' & Merchants' Bank v. Daiker, 153 Iowa 484, 487, 133 N.W. 705, 705–06 (1911).

Moreover, this court has recognized that one way to prove waiver of contract provisions is "by evidence of a general course of dealing between the parties." Livingston v. Stevens, 122 Iowa 62, 69, 94 N.W. 925, 927 (1903). The court has held, for example, that a prior "course of dealing," as defined in the Uniform Commercial Code, "may overcome express terms in [a] security agreement and translate into an authorization for sale free of lien." Citizens Savings Bank v. Sac City State Bank, 315 N.W.2d 20, 26 (Iowa 1982). As defined in the UCC, "course of dealing" means "a sequence of previous conduct between the parties to a particular transaction which is fairly to be regarded as establishing a common basis of understanding for interpreting their expressions and other conduct." § 554.1205(1), The Code. This definition is similar to the definition of course of dealing in Restatement (Second) of Contracts § 223 (1979):

(1) A course of dealing is a sequence of previous conduct between the parties to an agreement which is fairly to be regarded as establish-

ing a common basis of understanding for interpreting their expressions and other conduct.

(2) Unless otherwise agreed, a course of dealing between the parties gives meaning to or supplements or qualifies their agreement.

It is obvious, therefore, that waiving an acceleration option on prior occasions may constitute a course of dealing sufficient to establish waiver of the right to exercise the option on a subsequent occasion. This court has previously applied the rule in the context of real estate contract forfeitures:

> There is another reason why we think it should be held that appellees could make payment at the time the tender was made. The entire record shows a course of dealings between the buyer and the seller wherein the seller accepted payments made on dates other than those fixed by the contract. In so doing, we hold that the seller waived [its claim that payments could be made only at the time fixed in the contract].

Westercamp v. Smith, 239 Iowa 705, 717, 31 N.W.2d 347, 353 (1948). Because the rule is applicable to contract rights generally, the forfeiture context is not of controlling significance. Consequently we hold that the holder of an installment note who has engaged in a course of dealing of accepting late payments waives the right to accelerate the obligation upon a subsequent late payment unless the holder has notified the obligor that future late payments will not be accepted.

Other courts that have considered the issue have reached a similar conclusion.

The right to withdraw a waiver of time for performance upon reasonable notice to the other party has been recognized previously by this court.

The trial court was correct in holding that acceleration options in installment notes can be waived by a course of dealing of accepting late payments.

II. *Sufficiency of evidence.* Because the case was tried to the court at law, the court's findings of fact have the force of a jury's special verdict. They are binding on us if supported by substantial evidence. When reasonable minds could differ, a waiver issue is for the trier of fact.

The evidence here showed that plaintiff accepted late payments on at least three of the four prior occasions. The 1975 payments were made by a single check dated April 1, 1975. The 1976 payments were made in two installments, one on April 13 and the other on June 16 of that year. Although letters from plaintiffs following the partial payments in April demanded payment of the installment balance with interest, they did not invoke the acceleration clause or demand timely payment of future installments. The 1977 payments were made on April 11, 1977, and the 1978 payments were made by a check dated March 31, 1978.

This evidence provides a substantial basis for the trial court to find a course of dealing demonstrating waiver of timely payment of the 1979 installments. An issue of fact was presented. Therefore the trial court's finding of waiver has sufficient evidentiary support.

Affirmed.

NOTES ON ACCELERATION AND REDEMPTION OF COLLATERAL

(1) **The Value of the Right of Redemption.** One often hears of, or reads references to, the great value attributed to a debtor's right of redemption. As a practical matter, however, debtors infrequently are in a position to pay in full the secured obligation. Although the court in the *Williams* case observed that "[h]ad the appellant paid the entire contract balance, plus expenses incurred by FMCC in retaking the collateral, he would have been entitled to redeem the vehicle[,]" neither that case nor the *Dunn* case directly involved an issue of redemption under F9–506. As the *Dunn* case illustrates, however, a debtor may have better luck by arguing that no default occurred or that the default was cured.

(2) **Acceleration, Reinstatement, and Cure.** The UCC does not regulate generally the powerful right of acceleration. For the most part it leaves to the parties' agreement both acceleration and the issue of curing defaults. It does contain limitations on the use of "at will" or "insecurity" acceleration clauses, however. UCC 1–208 limits the effectiveness of these provisions to situations where the accelerating party "in good faith believes that the prospect of payment or performance is impaired." Moreover, do not infer that the absence of specific regulation in the UCC is the end of the matter. See, e.g., Urdang v. Muse, 114 N.J.Super. 372, 276 A.2d 397 (Essex County Ct.1971) (secured party's refusal to return repossessed car to debtor upon debtor's credible offer to pay $900, when total amount of delinquent installment payments was $266.39 and expenses of repossession were $52.77, was a breach of secured party's duty of good faith under UCC 1–203; equitable solution was to deny secured party's deficiency and leave parties as they were).

A debtor's right to cure a default prior to acceleration, a creditor's right to accelerate, and a debtor's right to reinstatement following acceleration are matters of considerable regulation in the case of consumer credit transactions. See, e.g., U3C 5.110; U3C 5.111 (quoted in Section 1, supra). Other statutes in effect in numerous states also provide a grace period following a default and a right to cure. In some states consumer debtors enjoy a right to "reinstate" the secured debt and obtain possession of collateral after repossession and acceleration. Reinstatement rights typically are conditioned upon the debtor's not only curing past defaults but also paying any required fees or charges and expenses of repossession.

(3) **Who Is Entitled to Redeem Collateral?** As noted in the Introductory Note, supra, F9–506 conferred the right to redeem collateral on the "debtor" and "any ... secured party." R9–623(a) now explicitly extends that right to "any secondary obligor." The right of redemption also extends to "any ... lienholder." The latter extension addresses what Professor

Gilmore considered a "drafting inadvertence." 2 Gilmore, Security § 44.2, at 1217–18.

F9–506 apparently did not provide a statutory right of redemption to a *buyer* of collateral subject to a senior security interest. Consider the potential plight of Bonzo Co. in Problem 12.3.5, supra. Assume that Bonzo fails to discover AIB's senior security interest and buys the office equipment from Tuleight for $50,000. Even if Bonzo had a right to redeem the equipment, under F9–506, Bonzo would have been required to pay several million dollars to AIB because the equipment secures all Schmelli's indebtedness to AIB! But, would AIB have any incentive *not* to accept the fair value for the collateral instead? For an argument that a junior buyer should enjoy a statutory right to redeem collateral by paying to the senior secured party the fair market value of the collateral, *not* the entire amount of the secured debt, see Wechsler, Rights and Remedies of the Secured Party After an Unauthorized Transfer of Collateral: A Proposal for Balancing Competing Claims in Repossession, Resale, Proceeds, and Conversion Cases, 32 Buff. L. Rev. 373, 381–84 (1983). To what extent, if any, does Revised Article 9 adopt Professor Wechsler's proposal to afford a redemption right to the buyer of collateral subject to a security interest? See R9–102(a)(28) & Comment 2.a. (2d paragraph).

(4) Is There a Duty to Give Notice of Redemption Rights? F9–506 did not, by its terms, require a secured party to notify the debtor or any other secured party of a right to redeem. Some states afford that protection to consumer debtors by statute other than the UCC. See, e.g., Pennsylvania Motor Vehicle Sales Finance Act, Pa. Stat. Ann., tit. 69 § 623D (Supp. 2000). In consumer-goods transactions, Revised Article 9 requires the notification of disposition to provide "a telephone number from which the amount that must be paid to the secured party to redeem the collateral under Section 9–623 is available." R9–614(1)(C). The statutory "safe-harbor" form of notice includes the following: "You can get the property back at any time before we sell it by paying us the full amount you owe (not just the past due payments), including our expenses. To learn the exact amount you must pay, call us at [*telephone number*]." R9–614(3). Should Article 9 require an enforcing secured party to give notice of redemption rights in all transactions?

What is the consequence of including an incorrect statement of the debtor's right to redeem? Suppose, for example, a debtor is notified that redemption of collateral by payment in full must be made earlier than the time specified in R9–623, or may be made only by payment of a sum greater than that necessary to redeem. In consumer-goods transactions, the consequence depends on whether the secured party uses the statutory form. If the form is used, then the notice will be sufficient notwithstanding the error unless, as appears to be the case in the example, "the error is misleading with respect to rights arising under this article." R9–614(5). If the notice is not in the statutory form, then law other than Article 9 "determines the effect of including information not required" in the notice. R9–614(6). In consumer transactions, the notice need not include the redemption amount, only a telephone number from which the amount can be obtained. Nor need the notice include information concerning the time before which the right must be exercised. See R9–614(1). Accordingly, non-Article 9 law determines the consequence of including an incorrect statement of the debtor's right to redeem.

In other (non-consumer-goods) transactions, there is no requirement even to mention redemption in the notice. R9–613(3) says that "The contents of a notification providing substantially the information specified in paragraph (1) are sufficient, even if the notification includes (A) information not specified by that paragraph; or (B) minor errors that are not seriously misleading." The notification probably would not qualify for the safe harbor in subparagraph (B), inasmuch as the errors appear to be seriously misleading. In addition, a notification containing incorrect information that pertains to important rights relating to the disposition of collateral would not seem to qualify as a "reasonable ... notification" required by 9–611(b).

SECTION 5.   COLLECTIONS FROM AND ENFORCEMENT AGAINST ACCOUNT DEBTORS AND OTHER PERSONS OBLIGATED ON COLLATERAL

Introductory Note. This book examines rights in and concerning receivables in many and varied contexts. For example, Chapter 1, Section 4, supra, introduces the basic principles governing the good faith purchase of rights to payment. Security interests in receivables and related priority contests are considered in several places. See, e.g., Chapter 7, Section 1, supra (Lee Abel's Instalment Sales Contract assigned to Firstbank, in the Prototype transaction); Chapter 7, Section 5, supra (collections of cash proceeds); Chapter 7, Section 6(B)(II), supra (priority contests between buyers of accounts and general intangibles and unperfected security interests); Chapter 9, Section 1(B) (receivables financing Prototype); Chapter 9, Section 1(F), supra (collections of receivables and rights and duties of account debtors); Chapter 9, Section 2, supra (special priority rules for purchasers of chattel paper, instruments, and documents); Chapter 10, Section 3, supra (treatment of "floating lien" on receivables and inventory); Chapter 11, Section 4(B), supra (real property-related receivables); Chapter 11, Section 5(C), supra (account debtors' defenses and rights of setoff).

This Section deals with collections by secured parties from, and enforcement by secured parties against, account debtors and other persons obligated on collateral. As between a debtor and a secured party, the rights and duties of the secured party concerning collections and enforcement are governed by R9–607. (The rights and duties of the account debtor are, of course, the subject of R9–341 and R9–403 through R9–408. See R9–607(e) and Comment 6; Chapter 9, Section 1(F), supra; Chapter 11, Section 5(C), supra.) R9–607(a) entitles a secured party (again, vis-a-vis the debtor) to undertake direct collections from account debtors and other persons obligated on collateral and to enforce collateral against account debtors and other persons obligated on collateral "[i]f so agreed, and in any event after default[.]" The following materials focus primarily on the rights and duties of secured parties who elect to undertake collections or to enforce collateral following a debtor's default. As to the debtor's agreement to the assignee's collections on the collateral before default, recall Mr. Kupfer's discussion of the distinction between "notification" receivables financing, where account debtors are notified and instructed at the inception of the transaction to remit payments to the assignee, and "non-notification" financing, where the debtor is permitted to collect the receivables—at least until a default occurs. See Chapter 9, Section 1(A), supra. See also R9–607, Comments 1 and 4.

Problem 12.5.1. Under the facts of Problem 12.2.1, supra, you now represent AIB once again. AIB has ceased making new advances against Schmelli's accounts and has demanded payment of the $4,500,000 owed on the line of credit facility. The loan officer fears that the lagging economy and Schmelli's more aggressive collection efforts are combining to shrink Schmelli's pool of accounts receivable; the officer has asked you for advice on how to collect Schmelli's accounts as soon as possible.

(a) What alternatives are available? What do you recommend? Would your advice be different if AIB had bought the accounts from Schmelli "outright," on a non-recourse basis? See R9–607(a), (c); R 9–608(b); Notes on Collections by Secured Parties, infra.

(b) After AIB notified Schmelli's account debtors, instructing them to remit all payments directly to AIB, a "funny" thing happened: the account debtors quit paying Schmelli and many of them *also* have not paid AIB. The loan officer has written letters to the delinquent account debtors. What else, if anything, should be done? See R 9–608(b); Note (1) on Collections by Secured Parties, infra.

(c) The loan officer has informed you that Fractured Factors, Inc. (FFI), has made an offer to buy all of Schmelli's accounts—on a non-recourse basis and at a very steep discount. However, considering how long it may take to collect the accounts, and considering the interest charges that continue to run (at the default rate) on Schmelli's loans, the officer thinks that selling to FFI "may be just about the best thing for us and for Schmelli as well." What advice do you give? What steps should be taken? See R9–610; R9–611; Note (4) on Collections by Secured Parties, infra.

(d) One of the largest accounts, about $50,000, is disputed. The account debtor, Gravilumps Corp. (GC), has demanded a credit of $18,000 because of "grossly unqualified personnel" supplied by Schmelli. (One of Schmelli's temps caused GC's computer to "eat" the payroll records.) GC refuses to pay anything until the matter is resolved. Schmelli adamantly denies GC's claims. The loan officer thinks that the matter could be settled by offering a $10,000 credit. What do you recommend? Would you give different advice if the amount involved were $180? $180,000? See Note (1) on Collections by Secured Parties, infra. What, if anything, might have been provided in the security agreement that would make your advice more certain? See R9–602(3); R9–603.

(e) Another of the largest accounts involves a financially troubled customer, Nodough Co. (NC). Last year Schmelli took a negotiable note from NC evidencing NC's two-year installment obligation; NC is current on the note and is willing and able to make this month's payment. Schmelli refuses to deliver the note to AIB. Is AIB entitled to collect the payment from NC? See R9–607(a), (e); UCC 3–412; UCC 3–301; Note (6) on Collections by Secured Parties, infra.

NOTES ON COLLECTIONS BY SECURED PARTIES

(1) Commercially Reasonable Collections and Enforcement; Surplus and Deficiency. A secured party who "undertakes to collect from or enforce and obligation of an account debtor or other person obligated on collateral" generally is required to "proceed in a commercially reasonable manner." R9–607(c). This obligation is imposed only "if the secured party . . . is entitled to charge back uncollected collateral or otherwise to full or limited recourse against the debtor or a secondary obligor." Id. And if the "security interest secures payment or performance of an obligation," the debtor is entitled to any surplus and liable for any deficiency. R9–608(a)(4). (These provisions recognize that a transaction could be a "true" sale but nonetheless impose *some* recourse against the debtor based on the amount recovered by the secured party from the receivable involved. See Note (2), infra. In such a transaction the secured party must act in a commercially reasonable manner.) Most of the factors and issues relating to commercially reasonable dispositions under R9–610(b), considered in Section 2, supra, are equally applicable to the determination of whether a secured party's collections or enforcement efforts are commercially reasonable; the rules also share a common rationale. A secured party's failure to proceed in a commercially reasonable manner exposes the secured party to the same sanctions that can result from conducting a commercially unreasonable disposition. See Note (7) on Commercially Reasonable Dispositions and Reasonable Notification, Section 2, supra.

R9–607(a)(1) and (2) follow closely F9–502(1). However, R9–607(a)(3) provides to the secured party a broader and more general right to "enforce" collateral. It recognizes that much collateral does not consist of a simple right to payment that the secured party could "collect." For example, if the collateral consists of the debtor's rights as a franchisee under a franchise agreement, the secured party might seek an injunction against the franchisor's termination of the agreement. One would hope that F9–502(1) coupled with the debtor's agreement also would have permitted enforcement as well as more straightforward collection of payment rights, but paragraph (a)(3) eliminates any uncertainty. Paragraphs (a)(4) and (5) provide special rules for security interests in deposit accounts that are perfected by control. See Chapter 9, Section 4, supra. Subsection (b) provides a means by which a secured party can become the assignee of record in order to utilize nonjudicial procedures to foreclose a real property mortgage that secures an obligation included in collateral. See Chapter 11, Section 4(A), supra.

The issue of whether collections are commercially reasonable has not been a frequent and major point of litigation, unlike the issue of commercially reasonable dispositions under F9–504(3). Although foreclosure sales typically are out-of-the-ordinary transactions, collections normally are routine, whether undertaken by the debtor or an assignee. When an account debtor or other obligated person fails to pay, however, the reasonableness of the collecting assignee's response may be put to the test.

Note that R9–607 and F502(2) differ in one important respect from their analogues for dispositions of collateral, R9–611 and F9–504(3). There is no requirement in R9–607 or F9–502(2) that notification be given to the debtor or any other interested persons. What justifications are there for the absence of a notification requirement? Is the interest of a debtor in commercially reasonable collections any less than in the case of dispositions? To take the most straightforward and typical example, perhaps the distinction results from the drafters' perception that a debtor is more likely to be able to increase the price that collateral fetches at a disposition (e.g., by finding potential buyers) than to increase the amount that an account debtor pays on a receivable.

Nothing in Article 9 would seem to impose a *duty* on an assignee of a receivable to undertake collection. The obligations in R9–607(c) are triggered only when and if a secured party "undertakes to collect ... or enforce...." If a secured party endeavors to collect one receivable, is it obliged to attempt collection of *all* receivables in which it has a security interest? What actions constitute an undertaking to collect or enforce that triggers R9–607(c)? The statutory language is less than clear on these issues. See DeLay First National Bank & Trust Co. v. Jacobson Appliance Co., 196 Neb. 398, 243 N.W.2d 745 (1976) (secured creditor that took possession of all of debtor's records concerning its accounts, wrote two letters to some account debtors, and then took no further action failed to meet its burden of proof as to commercially reasonable collections under F9–502(2)).

(2) Sale versus Security for Obligation. The contours of R9–607 and R9–608 have been carefully crafted to take account of the scope of Article 9, which includes the sale of accounts, chattel paper, instruments, and payment intangibles. See Chapter 9, Section 1(D), supra. R9–608(b), as did the last sentence of R9–502(2), makes explicit what is implicit in R9–608(a), dealing with application of proceeds (see Note (3), infra)—when there is a *sale* of a receivable the debtor (seller) is neither entitled to any surplus nor (absent agreement to the contrary) liable for a deficiency. With the exception of this provision and the corresponding provision in R9–615(e), Part 6 provides identical treatment for secured transactions consisting of sales of accounts, chattel paper, payment intangibles, and promissory notes, and those where the receivables secure payment or performance of an obligation. Even if the transaction is a sale of receivables covered by Article 9, however, if the secured party has recourse against the debtor or a secondary obligor following the secured party's collection or enforcement efforts, the secured party is obliged to "proceed in a commercially reasonable manner." R9–607(c).

When the right to a surplus or the liability for a deficiency is at stake under R9–608(b), it will be necessary to distinguish a sale of accounts, chattel paper, payment intangibles, or promissory notes from a security interest that secures payment or performance of an obligation. At the extremes the distinction is easy to make. For example, a putative sale pursuant to terms that unconditionally require the assignor to repurchase the receivable upon default of the account debtor, for a price equal to the outstanding balance of the account, is the functional equivalent of a loan and would be treated as such. On the other hand, where the assignee has absolutely no recourse whatsoever against the assignor, regardless of whether the account debtor performs, characterization as an outright sale seems appropriate. Other arrangements may be much less clear.

Unlike its treatment of leases, the definition of "security interest" in R 1–201(37) provides no explicit guidance as to when an assignment of receivables constitutes a "sale." "[T]he cases [dealing with the sale/secured loan dichotomy] are not easily harmonized, and different readers can argue as to which factors are relevant and which are entitled to greater weight." S. Schwarcz, Structured Finance 31 (2d ed. 1993). Mr. Schwarcz identifies the following factors, among others, as relevant: the existence and nature of recourse against the transferor, the extent to which the transferor retains rights (including the right to surplus collections), the nature of the pricing mechanism, and the arrangements for administration and collection.

(3) **Application of Proceeds of Collection or Enforcement.** R9–608(a) contains provisions regulating a secured party's application of proceeds of collection or enforcement. These provisions are analogous to those contained in R9–615(a) through (c) for the proceeds of dispositions of collateral. Curiously, F9–502, unlike F9–504(1), did not address the application of proceeds at all.

(4) **Dispositions of Receivables as an Alternative to Collection.** Is a secured party entitled to sell a receivable in lieu of collection or enforcement under R9–607? The references to accounts, chattel paper, payment intangibles, and promissory notes in R9–615(e) clearly indicate that receivables can be the subject of a disposition under R9–610. (F504(2) was similar.) Of course, the disposition must itself be commercially reasonable, and one could imagine circumstances where the ease and certainty of collection would render unreasonable any disposition for a price less than the full present value of the receivable.

(5) **"Lockbox" Arrangements.** Collection of a debtor's receivables by a secured party following the debtor's default typically, and understandably, reflects poorly on the debtor's continued economic viability. Account debtors who fear that the debtor may be unable to perform future contracts

may be tempted to withhold payments for goods or services that the debtor previously provided. Additionally, the account debtors' uncertainty about whether to pay a notifying secured party and their requests for evidence of the assignment (see R9–406) frequently disrupt and delay the collection of the receivables.

To avoid these problems and to facilitate the secured party's collections following a default, the parties sometimes enter into a **lockbox** arrangement at the inception of a transaction. A typical lockbox arrangement involves a special **cash collateral deposit account** that is under the control of the secured party. The debtor is required to change its billing practices by instructing all account debtors to remit their payments to a particular post office box to which only the depository bank has access. The bank then deposits all receipts into the cash collateral account. The secured party typically agrees that the debtor may make withdrawals from the account, provided that no default has occurred. If a default does occur, collection efforts are facilitated and (unless the debtor wrongfully changes the payment instructions on its bills) the secured party need not disclose the fact of the default to the account debtors.

(6) Collections on Instruments. A secured party's collection and enforcement rights also extend to collections from persons obligated on instruments. See R9–607(a) and (c) (collection and enforcement against "person obligated on collateral"); R9–102(a)(3) (defining "account debtor" so as to exclude a person obligated to pay a negotiable instrument). Because the term "account debtor" includes only those persons obligated on an account, chattel paper, or general intangible, it also excludes a person obligated on a nonnegotiable instrument, unless the instrument in included in chattel paper. See R9–102(a)(3) (defining "account debtor"), (a)(47) (defining "instrument"). However, with certain limited exceptions, a secured party cannot enforce an obligation evidenced by a negotiable instrument governed by UCC Article 3 unless the secured party is in possession of the instrument. See UCC 3–412; UCC 3–301; UCC 3–203; Chapter 1, Section 4, infra. This does not present a problem when the instruments involved are delivered to the secured party at the inception of a financing transaction. When this is not the case, the secured party must rely on the debtor's compliance with covenants to deliver them for the purpose of perfection (R9–313), unless a financing statement has been filed, or the purpose of collection and enforcement in the event of a default. Non–UCC law determines whether possession is required to enforce a nonnegotiable instrument that is not part of chattel paper.

SECTION 6.   ACCEPTANCE OF COLLATERAL IN SATISFACTION OF SECURED OBLIGATIONS: "STRICT FORECLOSURE"

Introductory Note. After a debtor's default a secured party may agree with the debtor and other interested persons to accept collateral in satisfaction of the secured obligations. The procedures for the secured party's acceptance of collateral are set forth in a somewhat intricate statutory framework: R9–620 through R9–622. This remedy is commonly known as "strict foreclosure." It is an alternative to the secured party's disposition of collateral or collection and enforcement of collateral. The conditions for an effective strict foreclosure are specified in R9–620(a) and (b); please review those conditions.

Strict foreclosure can be advantageous to both secured parties and debtors. Section 9–620 "reflects the belief that strict foreclosure should be encouraged and often will produce better results than a disposition for all concerned." R9–620, Comment 2. Through strict foreclosure, a secured party can avoid the time and expense of a disposition under R9–610, can protect itself from later objections by the debtor to the commercial reasonableness of the disposition, and can eliminate the obligation to account to the debtor for any surplus. Because deficiencies arise much more often than surpluses, a debtor also may be advantaged by a strict foreclosure, especially one that satisfies the secured obligations in full.

In the case of collateral that is consumer goods, if an obligor has paid 60% or more of the principal amount of a secured loan or the cash price (i.e., the price of the goods, without taking into account finance charges and other amounts included in the secured obligations), R9–620(e) prohibits strict foreclosure unless the debtor has signed after default a statement modifying or waiving the right to insist upon a disposition. R9–624(b). As explained below in the Notes following the Problem, there are other special provisions that apply in consumer transactions. The Notes also explain the principal ways in which the Revised Article 9 structure for strict foreclosure differs from its predecessor (F9–505).

Problem 12.6.1. You continue to represent AIB under the facts of Problem 12.2.1, supra. As in Problem 12.5.1, supra, AIB has ceased making new advances against Schmelli's accounts and has demanded payment of the $4,500,000 owed on the line of credit facility. So far AIB has not disposed of any of the collateral or collected any of the receivables.

The loan officer met today with Telli Schmelli. Although relationships remain strained, AIB and Schmelli have agreed in principle that the bank will accept ownership of the Learjet in full satisfaction of the $2,500,000 balance on the Learjet loan and in satisfaction of $600,000 of the line of credit debt. Both Schmelli and AIB recognize that the market for corporate aircraft is poor right now. Schmelli believes that it will receive a credit on the debts approximately equal to the fair market value of the Learjet. The loan officer is pleased not to be faced with the hassles and risks of a foreclosure sale.

(a) The loan officer has asked you to "draft the papers as soon as possible." How do you proceed? See R9–620; Notes on Acceptance of Collateral, infra.

(b) Unbeknownst to AIB, in violation of the security agreement, and before AIB demanded payment of the $4,500,000, Schmelli created a junior security interest in the Learjet in favor of Hardluck Bank. Hardluck properly perfected its security interest under federal law by recording immediately with the Federal Aviation Administration. See R9–109(c)(1); R9–311. Two weeks after the papers referred to in part (a) are signed, AIB receives a letter from Hardluck demanding that AIB turn over the Learjet so that Hardluck can enforce its security interest. Advise AIB. (Assume that federal law defers to Article 9 on these issues.) See R9–622; R9–620(a), (c), (d); R9–621.

NOTES ON ACCEPTANCE OF COLLATERAL

(1) **Debtor's Consent to Acceptance.** An obvious, and essential, condition to an effective acceptance is the debtor's consent. R9–620(a)(1). For example, a disposition of the collateral might bring an amount many times the amount of the secured obligation. The debtor is entitled to the difference between the value of the collateral and the amount of the secured obligation. (This amount is often referred to as the **debtor's equity**.) Conditioning the secured party's acceptance of the collateral in satisfaction of the secured obligation enables the debtor to protect its equity. (The requirement of R9–610(b) that a disposition be conducted in a commercially reasonable manner can perform the same equity-protecting function.)

R9–620(c) specifies the elements of an effective consent by the debtor. This subsection contains two alternative methods for consent. First, the debtor may agree to the terms of the acceptance. This straightforward approach contrasts with that of F9–505(2), which worked on the fiction that each acceptance (called a "retention" in F9–505) would be based on a secured party's proposal and a debtor's failure to object. See R9–620, Comment 1. The second alternative in R9–620(c)(2) harks back to the structure of F9–505(2). A secured party who opts for this alternative must send a "proposal" to the debtor. See R9–620(c)(2)(A); R9–102(a)(66) (defining "proposal"). If the secured party does not receive the debtor's authenticated objection within 20 days after sending the proposal, the debtor's consent is effective. R9–620(c)(2)(C). Although R9–620(a) provides that "a secured party may accept collateral in full or partial satisfaction of the obligation it secures," a *proposal* to a debtor will be the basis for an effective consent only if it is for *full* satisfaction of the secured obligations. For a partial satisfaction the debtor's actual agreement is required. Do you see any basis for this limitation?

(2) **Objection to Acceptance by Claimants Other Than the Debtor; Notification Requirements.** The second condition for an effective acceptance is specified in R9–620(a)(2); it is a negative event: the secured party's failure to receive an objection to the acceptance from a specified person within the times provided in R9–620(d). The persons specified include those to whom the secured party is required to send a proposal under R9–621. These are the same persons who are to be given notification of disposition under R9–611. Under R9–621, however, there is no "safe harbor" to protect against filing office delays in responding to

search requests. For an explanation, see R9–621, Comment 2. Any other person who claims a subordinate interest in the collateral also may object and thereby prevent an effective acceptance from occurring. See R9–620, Comment 3 (3d paragraph). A secured party is required to notify a broader class of persons under R9–621 than was the case under F9–505(2). Under the former section, the proposing secured party was required to notify only secured parties from whom the proposing secured party had received notice of a claim to the collateral.

R9–620(d) specifies the time within which an objection must be made in order to be effective. A person to whom a proposal is sent must object within 20 days after the notice was sent to that person. R9–620(d)(1). A person to whom a proposal is required to be sent but is not sent (e.g., because the secured party does not know about that person) also has a right to object; the time for that person to make an effective objection expires within 20 days after the last notification of the proposal was sent pursuant to Section 9–621. If no proposal was sent to anyone, the time expires when the debtor consents to the acceptance under subsection (c). R9–620(d)(2).

(3) Requirement That Collateral Be in Secured Party's Possession. F9–505(2) provided that a secured party must be "in possession" of collateral in order to propose a retention. R9–621 generally eliminates that requirement. (Hence the concept is now called "acceptance" instead of "retention" of collateral.) This change makes clear that strict foreclosure is not limited to tangible collateral, such as goods. Not only can a secured party effect an acceptance of collateral without dispossessing a debtor, strict foreclosure is available for collateral such as accounts and other intangibles that *cannot* be possessed. The possession requirement has been retained for consumer-goods collateral; the goods must not be in the debtor's possession when the debtor consents to the acceptance. R9–621(a)(3).

There was no consensus in the commentary on F9–505(2) as to the reason for the possession requirement. For example, Professor Gilmore speculated that the secured party's possession might be thought to give notice to interested third parties, but he suggested that it would be more effective to require notice by *publication* in order to alert competing parties to a pending strict foreclosure. 2 Gilmore, Security § 44.3, at 1223–24. We suspect that the concerns about debtors in consumer-goods transactions arise from the fact that a debtor's consent can be achieved by sending a proposal followed by no timely objection. There is no requirement that the debtor actually *receive* the proposal. Compare R9–621(a)(1). In the absence of the dispossession requirement for consumer goods, it would be possible for a secured party to become the *owner* of a debtor's consumer goods before the debtor had actual knowledge that an enforcement step was underway. At least when the secured party dispossesses the debtor of the collateral, the debtor normally would realize that an enforcement has begun.

(4) Acceptance in Partial Satisfaction. The commentary and re- ported judicial decisions under Former Article 9 generally agreed that F9– 505(2) did not permit a secured party to propose to retain collateral in *partial* satisfaction of the secured obligations. There was disagreement, however, concerning the effectiveness of post-default agreements by debt- ors to modify, renounce, or waive rights so as to result in a retention in partial satisfaction. Note that the effect of a retention in partial satisfaction would be equivalent to the acquisition by a secured party at a private sale, which (except in limited circumstances) was prohibited by F9–504(3). It seems clear that a debtor could not effectively have waived that prohibition. It follows that permitting retention in partial satisfaction would have enabled the parties to accomplish indirectly what they could not have accomplished directly under R9–504(3).

For non-consumer transactions Revised Article 9 has rendered this disagreement moot. Like Former Article 9, Revised Article 9 generally prohibits a secured party from acquiring collateral at its own disposition. See R9–610(c)(2). However, R9–620(a) explicitly permits acceptance of collateral in partial satisfaction of the secured obligations. The Drafting Committee thought that the benefits of encouraging strict foreclosure over dispositions of collateral outweighed any potential for overreaching. Recall, however, that under R9–620(c)(1) a debtor must actually agree to the terms of a partial satisfaction acceptance; the proposal and objection structure of subsection (c)(2) is available only for full satisfaction acceptances. (Note however, that Revised Article 9 does not make explicit provision for a debtor's waiver of the prohibition on a secured party's acquiring collateral at a private sale. See R9–624, Comment 2.) In consumer transactions, acceptances in partial satisfaction are not permitted. See R9–620(g).

(5) Effect of Acceptance of Collateral. Like a disposition of collat- eral, an acceptance of collateral discharges subordinate security interests and liens and terminates other subordinate interests. See R9–622(a)(3) and (4). Moreover, under R9–622(b) an acceptance discharges these subordinate interests and liens *"even if the secured party fails to comply with this article"* (emphasis added). The upshot of this provision is that the secured party's failure to send a proposal to the persons specified in R9–621 does not render the acceptance ineffective. The acceptance nonetheless will discharge or terminate the lien or interest held by a person to whom the secured party was required to send, but did not send, a proposal. See 9– 620(a)(2) (secured party's failure to receive an objection satisfies the condition for acceptance; actually sending a proposal under R9–621 is not a condition). Of course, the secured party may be liable to a person to whom it fails to send a proposal. See R9–625(b); R9–622, Comment 2 (second paragraph).

Curiously, F9–505(2) was silent as to the effect of a strict foreclosure by a senior secured party on the claims to the same collateral of junior secured parties and other junior lienholders. However, Professor Gilmore nonetheless took the position that strict foreclosure should have the same effect (discharge of junior parties) as a disposition under R9–504(3). See 2 Gilmore, Security § 44.3, at 1225–26.

(6) Acceptance of Collateral Followed by Immediate Sale; Good Faith. Nothing in Revised Article 9 prohibits a secured party from accepting collateral under R9–620 and then selling it immediately. F9–505 likewise contained no such restriction. However, one court held a sale under these circumstances to be impermissible. In Reeves v. Foutz & Tanner, Inc., 94 N.M. 760, 617 P.2d 149 (1980), the secured party proposed to retain jewelry that was worth much more than the secured obligation. After the debtor (an individual) failed to make a timely objection, the secured party placed the jewelry in its inventory and promptly sold it. The court relied in part on F9–505, Statement of Reasons for 1972 Changes in Official Text: "Under subsection (2) of this section the secured party may in lieu of sale give notice to the debtor and certain other persons that he proposes to retain the collateral *in lieu of sale.*" (Emphasis added.) The court also relied on a Federal Trade Commission decision interpreting the cited Statement for the proposition that a waiver of surplus or deficiency rights is appropriate only when the creditor does not contemplate the prompt resale of the repossessed collateral in the ordinary course of business. See *Reeves*, 617 P.2d at 151 (citing and quoting In the Matter of Ford Motor Company, Ford Motor Credit Co., and Francis Ford, Inc., 94 F.T.C. Rep. 564, 3 Trade Reg. Rep. (CCH) 21756, 21767 (1979)). Mr. Clark argued that *Reeves* "puts the court in the position of repealing" F9–505 and, if that is the case, "the decision is obviously wrong." Clark, Secured Transactions ¶ 4.10[1], at 4–279.

Revised Article 9 suggests another approach to a proposal for an acceptance under which there is a substantial difference between the value of the collateral to be accepted and the (much lower) amount of the obligation to be satisfied. See R9–620, Comment 11 (great disparity between value of collateral and obligation to be satisfied may constitute bad faith and render acceptance ineffective); UCC 1–103.

(7) "Constructive" Strict Foreclosure. Under Former Article 9 a number of courts held that a secured party's conduct in retaining possession of collateral without disposition for an unusually long period of time could constitute a retention in satisfaction within the scope of F9–505(2), whether or not the secured party intended to invoke that remedy. These decisions effectively denied the secured party any right to a deficiency judgment. Of course, courts were not likely to find an involuntary strict foreclosure when it was the creditor, instead of the debtor, who advanced the implied election argument.

There also existed a line of decisions under Former Article 9 that refused to find an involuntary strict foreclosure in cases of delay. Revised Article 9 follows these decisions and the recommendations of most commentators. Under R9–620(b)(1), an acceptance is ineffective unless the secured party "consents in an authenticated record or sends a proposal to the debtor." Consequently, "constructive" strict foreclosures cannot occur under the revised Article; instead, a delay in collection or disposition of collateral is a factor relating to whether the secured party acted in a commercially reasonable manner for purposes of R9–607 or R9–610. See R9–620, Comment 5.

INDEX

✝